Cisco WAN Switching Professional Reference

Tracy Thorpe

Cisco Press

Cisco Press
201 West 103rd Street
Indianapolis, IN 46290 USA

Cisco WAN Switching Professional Reference

Tracy Thorpe

Copyright © 2002 Cisco Systems, Inc.

Published by:
Cisco Press
201 West 103rd Street
Indianapolis, IN 46290 USA

All rights reserved. No part of this book may be reproduced or transmitted in any form or by any means, electronic or mechanical, including photocopying, recording, or by any information storage and retrieval system, without written permission from the publisher, except for the inclusion of brief quotations in a review.

Printed in the United States of America 1 2 3 4 5 6 7 8 9 0

Library of Congress Cataloging-in-Publication Number: 2001092015

ISBN: 1-58705-055-2

First Printing March 2002

Warning and Disclaimer

This book is designed to provide information about WAN switching. Every effort has been made to make this book as complete and as accurate as possible, but no warranty or fitness is implied.

The information is provided on an "as is" basis. The author, Cisco Press, and Cisco Systems, Inc. shall have neither liability nor responsibility to any person or entity with respect to any loss or damages arising from the information contained in this book or from the use of the discs or programs that may accompany it.

The opinions expressed in this book belong to the author and are not necessarily those of Cisco Systems, Inc.

Feedback Information

At Cisco Press, our goal is to create in-depth technical books of the highest quality and value. Each book is crafted with care and precision, undergoing rigorous development that involves the unique expertise of members of the professional technical community.

Reader feedback is a natural continuation of this process. If you have any comments regarding how we could improve the quality of this book, or otherwise alter it to better suit your needs, you can contact us through e-mail at feedback@ciscopress.com. Please be sure to include the book title and ISBN in your message.

We greatly appreciate your assistance.

Trademark Acknowledgments

All terms mentioned in this book that are known to be trademarks or service marks have been appropriately capitalized. Cisco Press or Cisco Systems, Inc. cannot attest to the accuracy of this information. Use of a term in this book should not be regarded as affecting the validity of any trademark or service mark.

Publisher	John Wait	
Editor-in-Chief	John Kane	
Executive Editor	Brett Bartow	
Cisco Systems Management	Michael Hakkert	Tom Geitner
	William Warren	
Production Manager	Patrick Kanouse	
Acquisitions Editor	Michelle Stroup	
Development Editor	Howard Jones	
Project Editors	Marc Fowler	
	Sheri Cain	
Copy Editor	Gayle Johnson	
Course Developers	Jim Heddell	Vince Foecke
	Laurina Ferro	Peter Tunney
Technical Editors	Roy Spencer	
	Zoran Vidanovic	
	David Warren	
Team Coordinator	Tammi Ross	
Book Designer	Gina Rexrode	
Cover Designer	Louisa Klucznik	
Production Team	Octal Publishing, Inc.	
Indexer	Tim Wright	

CISCO SYSTEMS

Corporate Headquarters
Cisco Systems, Inc.
170 West Tasman Drive
San Jose, CA 95134-1706
USA
http://www.cisco.com
Tel: 408 526-4000
800 553-NETS (6387)
Fax: 408 526-4100

European Headquarters
Cisco Systems Europe
11 Rue Camille Desmoulins
92782 Issy-les-Moulineaux
Cedex 9
France
http://www-europe.cisco.com
Tel: 33 1 58 04 60 00
Fax: 33 1 58 04 61 00

Americas Headquarters
Cisco Systems, Inc.
170 West Tasman Drive
San Jose, CA 95134-1706
USA
http://www.cisco.com
Tel: 408 526-7660
Fax: 408 527-0883

Asia Pacific Headquarters
Cisco Systems Australia,
Pty., Ltd
Level 17, 99 Walker Street
North Sydney
NSW 2059 Australia
http://www.cisco.com
Tel: +61 2 8448 7100
Fax: +61 2 9957 4350

Cisco Systems has more than 200 offices in the following countries. Addresses, phone numbers, and fax numbers are listed on the Cisco Web site at www.cisco.com/go/offices

Argentina • Australia • Austria • Belgium • Brazil • Bulgaria • Canada • Chile • China • Colombia • Costa Rica • Croatia • Czech Republic • Denmark • Dubai, UAE • Finland • France • Germany • Greece • Hong Kong Hungary • India • Indonesia • Ireland • Israel • Italy • Japan • Korea • Luxembourg • Malaysia • Mexico The Netherlands • New Zealand • Norway • Peru • Philippines • Poland • Portugal • Puerto Rico • Romania Russia • Saudi Arabia • Scotland • Singapore • Slovakia • Slovenia • South Africa • Spain • Sweden Switzerland • Taiwan • Thailand • Turkey • Ukraine • United Kingdom • United States • Venezuela • Vietnam Zimbabwe

Copyright © 2000, Cisco Systems, Inc. All rights reserved. Access Registrar, AccessPath, Are You Ready, ATM Director, Browse with Me, CCDA, CCDE, CCDP, CCIE, CCNA, CCNP, CCSI, CD-PAC, *CiscoLink*, the Cisco NetWorks logo, the Cisco Powered Network logo, Cisco Systems Networking Academy, Fast Step, FireRunner, Follow Me Browsing, FormShare, GigaStack, IGX, Intelligence in the Optical Core, Internet Quotient, IP/VC, iQ Breakthrough, iQ Expertise, iQ FastTrack, iQuick Study, iQ Readiness Scorecard, The iQ Logo, Kernel Proxy, MGX, Natural Network Viewer, Network Registrar, the Networkers logo, *Packet*, PIX, Point and Click Internetworking, Policy Builder, RateMUX, ReyMaster, ReyView, ScriptShare, Secure Script, Shop with Me, SlideCast, SMARTnet, SVX, TrafficDirector, TransPath, VlanDirector, Voice LAN, Wavelength Router, Workgroup Director, and Workgroup Stack are trademarks of Cisco Systems, Inc.; Changing the Way We Work, Live, Play, and Learn, Empowering the Internet Generation, are service marks of Cisco Systems, Inc.; and Aironet, ASIST, BPX, Catalyst, Cisco, the Cisco Certified Internetwork Expert Logo, Cisco IOS, the Cisco IOS logo, Cisco Press, Cisco Systems, Cisco Systems Capital, the Cisco Systems logo, Collision Free, Enterprise/Solver, EtherChannel, EtherSwitch, FastHub, FastLink, FastPAD, IOS, IP/TV, IPX, LightStream, LightSwitch, MICA, NetRanger, Post-Routing, Pre-Routing, Registrar, StrataView Plus, Stratm, SwitchProbe, TeleRouter, are registered trademarks of Cisco Systems, Inc. or its affiliates in the U.S. and certain other countries.

All other brands, names, or trademarks mentioned in this document or Web site are the property of their respective owners. The use of the word partner does not imply a partnership relationship between Cisco and any other company. (0010R)

About the Author

Tracy Thorpe, CCNP-WS #CSC010159543, is a technical writer at Cisco Systems. Previously, she was employed as a technical writer at Sun Microsystems and Covad. She holds a B.S. in telecommunications and applied computing.

About the Technical Reviewers

Roy Spencer is a CCNA for WAN switching and a Certified Cisco Systems Instructor with more than 15 years of experience in the education segment of the networking industry. He has worked as a course developer for Cisco Systems, 3Com Corporation, and Nortel Networks. He has written and taught classes on ATM switch configuration, network management, router configuration, LAN switch configuration, SONET multiplexers, Ethernet, and TCP/IP. He is currently employed as a course developer for a leading SONET optical switch manufacturer.

Zoran Vidanovic, CCNP-WS, is a wireless data network specialist within Telus Mobility Canada. He has six years of experience in voice communications and two years of experience with data communications. He graduated with a B.S. in electrical engineering in 1994. Currently, he is involved in many WAN and LAN projects in IDEN, PCS, and corporate networks.

An independent consultant and trainer, **David Warren** has been in the computer and networking industry since the early 1980s. For the past five years, he has been teaching courses on an array of software and hardware products, both Cisco and beyond. He holds CCNP and CCDP certifications, as well as all the Microsoft certifications and he has passed the CCIE-WAN written exam. David is one of an extremely small group of course trainers who have been training internal Cisco SEs and AMs in the Cisco optical product line, a unique circumstance that has made him instrumental in the growth and planning of the product line.

Dedication

This book is dedicated with love and appreciation to my parents, Karen and Richard Thorpe.

Acknowledgments

A book like this is never written or edited by just one person. Many people made the idea of this book a reality. Most of them went above and beyond the call of duty to help produce a first-rate study and reference guide for Cisco WAN switching professionals.

I would first like to thank my friend Paul R. Miller, who supported and encouraged me (via e-mail) from book conception to the final author review chapter, and who inspired me to continue when I wanted to give up. Without his unwavering support, this book would not exist.

Words are not enough to express my thanks and appreciation to the technical reviewers: Zoran Vidanovic, Roy Spencer, Dave Warren, and Ron Treat. Their sincere interest in the Cisco WAN product line, dedication to quality courseware, and exceptional teaching skills added immeasurable value to this book. And their great senses of humor helped tremendously during review feedback.

I am especially grateful to my manager, Dr. David Trousdale, for valuable advice and direction in the early stages of my work and all the way up to the finished product.

Thanks to Brett Bartow at Cisco Press for providing encouragement and support.

Special thanks to Michelle Stroup, Acquisitions Editor at Cisco Press, for patiently and graciously walking me through my first publishing experience, and for always making herself available to me when I had questions or concerns.

Special thanks also to Howard Jones, Development Editor, for his graceful, professional, and good-natured handling of the hundreds of figures and pages required for this book.

I am grateful to all the contributors who have so generously given their knowledge, time, energy, and advice. My sincere thanks go to the following people for their direct or indirect support: Don Proctor, Vince Foecke, Morgan Littlewood, and Bob Marinconz for providing the stories and perspective I needed to write Chapter 1, "Cisco and WAN Switching." Also, a special thanks to Tom Kelly and Charlie Giancarlo for their contributions to this book.

I would also like to thank Graeme Wood, Sandrella Salins, John Sabasteanski, Joe Stewart, Ripin Checker, Alex Hadden-Boyd, Chris Frost, Barbara Rose, Elizabeth Tinker, Lionel Martin, Joel Straughan, Erick Pong, Rick Rosenblum, David Santen, Kellee Erdman, Tom Geitner, Ian McDonald, Lisa Li, Maggie Men, Shyyunn Lin, Joseph Hingst, Kenneth Bell, Kimberly Bean, Corina Sanders, Tim Ilian, Ray Meadows, and Shawna Darling. Thanks to Greg Kihn for laughs and great classics.

A special thanks to the course developers: Vince Foecke, Laurina Ferro, Peter Tunney, and Jim Heddell.

I must also thank my family and friends, who treated me with far more consideration than I deserved during the many months I obsessively spent weekends and evenings working on this book: Karen and Richard Thorpe; Kim Thorpe; Megan Thorpe; Hilary Alison Collins; Sheridan Rodriguez; Lisa Muhawi; Bridget, Frank, and Tony DiMambro; Ami Sugahara; Barbara Rose; Julie Langtry; and Elizabeth Tinker.

Finally, heartfelt thanks to Professor Robert van Spyke for introducing me to the incredible world of telecommunications.

Contents at a Glance

Part I   **Introduction   3**

Chapter 1   Cisco and WAN Switching   5

Part II   **Multiband Switch and Service Configuration   13**

Chapter 2   IGX Product Overview and System Hardware   15

Chapter 3   IGX Node Administration, Trunks, and Lines   39

Chapter 4   Voice and Data Channels and Connections   101

Chapter 5   Frame Relay Ports and Connections   179

Chapter 6   ATM Ports and Connections and ATM-to-Frame Relay Interworking   235

Chapter 7   Connection Routing, Synchronizing the Network, and Managing Jobs   283

Chapter 8   Troubleshooting   329

Part III   **BPX Switch and Service Configuration   359**

Chapter 9   BPX Product Overview and System Hardware   361

Chapter 10   Accessing the CLI and Initial Configuration of the BPX Switch   411

Chapter 11   Configuring Network Trunks and Access Lines   463

Chapter 12   Configuring SONET APS   501

Chapter 13   Configuring ATM Ports   529

Chapter 14   Configuring ATM Connections and Routing AutoRoute Connections   563

Chapter 15   Synchronizing the Network and Troubleshooting   671

Part IV   **MGX ATM Concentrator Configuration   727**

Chapter 16   MGX Product Overview and System Hardware   729

Chapter 17   The User Interface and MGX Network Configuration   767

Chapter 18   Lines, Feeder Nodes, and SONET APS   795

Chapter 19   Connection Types   851

Chapter 20   Frame Relay Ports and Connections   907

Chapter 21   ATM Ports and Connections   973

Chapter 22   Voice, IP, and ATM MPLS Features   1053

Appendix A   Answers to Review Questions   1147

Index   1231

Table of Contents

Overview   xl

Foreword   xli

Professional Training and Career Development   xliii

Part I Introduction   3

Chapter 1   Cisco and WAN Switching   5

Joining Forces   8

What Lies Ahead   9

Part II Multiband Switch and Service Configuration   13

Chapter 2   IGX Product Overview and System Hardware   15

IGX System Hardware   15
8410 Rack-Mount Chassis   16
8420 Standalone Chassis   17
8430 Standalone Chassis   19
IGX Cards   20
IGX Power Supplies   23

IGX Network, Trunks, and Lines   24

IGX Message Formats   25
FastPacket Format   25
ATM and STI Cell Formats   27

Reliability Features   27
NPM Card Redundancy   28
Y-Cable Redundancy   28
Automatic Fault-Management Features   29
Fault Management   29
Bandwidth Management Features   30

IGX Cellbus   30
Cellbus Lanes   30

Packet Flow   31
Voice Packet Flow   31
Data Packet Flow   32
Frame Relay   33

ATM Connections   34

Frame Relay-to-ATM Interworking   34

Summary   36

Review Questions   36

Chapter 3   IGX Node Administration, Trunks, and Lines   39

IGX Access   39

Control Port   39

Auxiliary Port   40

LAN Port   40

Logging into the Network   40

Command-Line Interface Screen   41

Syntax   43

Privilege Levels and IGX Entry Methods   43

IGX Privilege Levels   43

Direct Entry   43

Menu-Driven   44

IGX Commands   44

help Command   44

dspcds Command   45

dspcd Command   47

dsppwr Command   48

cnfpwd Command   49

dsppwd Command   49

cnfdate and **cnftime** Commands   50

cnftmzn Command   51

cnfterm Command   51

dsptermfunc Command   52

cnfprt Command   53

dspnds Command   54

cnfname Command   55

dsplancnf Command   56

dspnwip Command   57

Trunk Definition and Types   59

Trunk Card Groups Hardware Review   60

Trunk Technologies and Formats   60

ATM Cell Payloads   61

Framed Versus Unframed Trunks   62

Fractional T1, E1, or Y1 Trunks   62

IMA (Inverse Multiplexed ATM) Trunks   63
Transmitting FastPackets or ATM Cells on Unframed Trunks   63
Transmitting FastPackets or ATM Cells on Framed Trunks   63
Trunk Notation   63
Calculating NTM Trunk Capacity   64
Calculating UXM Trunk Capacity   64

IGX Trunks   65
Displaying Trunks   65
Upping a Trunk   66
Adding a Trunk Between Nodes   67
Displaying a Trunk's Configuration   68
Configuring a Trunk   69
Configurable Trunk Parameters   70
Displaying the Network   79
Accessing Remote Nodes in the Network   80
Deleting a Trunk Between Nodes   81
Downing a Trunk   82

Line Definition   83
Line Types   83
Line Card Groups Hardware Review   84
Line Technologies and Formats   84
Multiplexed Versus Unmultiplexed Lines   85
Time-Division Multiplexing Review   85
Line Framing Review   86
Line Notation   86
Displaying Lines   87
Upping a Line   87
Displaying a Line's Configuration   88
Configuring a Line   89
Configurable Line Parameters   90
Downing a Line   97

Summary   97

Review Questions   97

Chapter 4   Voice and Data Channels and Connections   101

Voice Connections   101
Voice Connections and Channels   101

Voice FastPackets   102
Voice Compression Techniques   103
Voice Activity Detection   104

Voice Connection and Channel Commands   105
    Adding a Voice Connection   106
    CVM Voice Connection Types   107
    UVM Voice Connection Types   108
    Configuring Line Pass-Through on a UVM   109
    Displaying Line Pass-Through on a UVM   111
    Adding a Voice Connection   111
    Displaying All Connections   112
    Displaying Detailed Parameters of One Connection   114
    Deleting Connections   115

Voice Connection and Channel Review   115
    PCM Voice Sample Processing   116
    Voice Activity Detection   116
    Configuring Voice Channel Utilization   116
    Adaptive VAD   117
    High-Speed Modem Detection and Fax Detection   118
    Modem/Fax Upgrades   119
    Configuring Gain   121
    Echo in a Voice Circuit   122
    Echo Perception and Echo Cancellation   122
    Displaying Echo Canceller Parameters   123
    Configuring Echo Canceller Parameters   124

Signaling Transport and Processing   125
    Voice Signaling Review   125
    CAS Signaling Review   125
    IGX Voice Signaling Topics   126
    Signaling Bit Transport   126
    Signaling Bit Timing   126
    Voice Channel Dial Types   127

Data Networks   141
    Private Line Replacement   141
    Data Card Groups Hardware Review   142
    Data Connections and Channels   142
    Data Connection Characteristics   143

Data FastPackets   143
    Building Data FastPackets   143
    Data Frame Multiplexing   144
    Data FastPackets with DFM   144
    Adding a Data Connection   144
    Data Connection Types   146
    Partially Filled FastPackets   147

Transporting Control Signal States   148
UVM/CVM Super-Rate Connections   150
CVM DS0A Subrate Connections   151
UVM/CVM Transparent Data Connections   152
Zero Code Suppression Review   152
FastPacket Coding   153
Displaying All Connections   154
Displaying Detailed Parameters of One Connection   154
Deleting Connections   155
Data Channel Commands   156

Data Channels   156
Data Channel Types   157
Configurable Data Channel Characteristics   158
Configuring Data Channel Utilization   162
Serial Data Channel Review   163
DCE and DTE   164
Input Control Signal Transport   164
Configuring Input Control Signal Sampling   165
Specifying Output Control Signals   166
Interface Control Templates Example   167
Displaying Interface Control Templates   167
Configuring Output Control Signals   168
Configuring an ICT   169
Copying Interface Control Templates   170
Data Channel Clocking   171
Isochronous Data Clocking   172
Configuring a Data Channel's Clock Mode   173
Displaying Real-Time Control and Clock Signals   174
Data Channel Configuration Summary Display   175
References   176

Summary   176

Review Questions   176

Chapter 5   Frame Relay Ports and Connections   179
Frame Relay   179
Frame Relay Cards   180
Port Queues   182

Signaling Protocols   184
Signaling Protocol Timers and Counters   184
Asynchronous Update Mode   185
Network-to-Network Interface   186

Frame Relay Port Commands   187
  Configuring Frame Relay Ports   188
  Modifying Frame Relay Ports   190

Frame Relay Connections   207
  Global Addressing   208
  Converting Frame Relay Frames to FastPackets   209
  First or Middle FastPacket Header   209
  Explicit Forward Congestion Notification   210
  Cell Loss Priority   210
  Rate Adjustment   210
  Hop Count   211
  Last FastPacket Header   211

VC Queues   212
  VC Queue Parameters   212
  Standard Versus Cisco Parameters   213
  UFM Leaky Bucket Policing   213

ForeSight in the Network   214
  What Is Congestion?   215
  ForeSight Rate Adjustments   216
  ForeSight and VC Queue Servicing   216

Bit-Oriented Protocol Frame Structures   217
  Frame Forwarding   218
  Frame Relay Channel Statistics   219

Frame Relay Connection Commands   220
  Configuring Frame Relay Connections   220

Summary   233

Review Questions   233

Chapter 6   ATM Ports and Connections and ATM-to-Frame Relay Interworking   235

ATM Ports   235

ATM Port Commands   236
  dspcd Command   236
  dspports Command   237
  dspport Command   238
  upport Command   238
  cnfport Command   239
  dspportq Command   241
  cnfportq Command   242

ATM Connections   243
    Types of ATM Connections   244

Connection Policing   245
    Leaky Bucket Model   246
    Dual Leaky Bucket Model   246
    CBR Traffic Policing   247
    VBR Traffic Policing   248
    ABR Traffic Policing   251
    UBR Traffic Policing   252
    ABR Flow Control   254

VC Queuing for ABR Traffic   254
    Congestion Control Segments   255
    Standard ABR   256
    ABR Implementation on the UXM   259
    ABRSTD Rate Adjustment   259
    ABR ForeSight Rate Adjustments   260
    ABRFST Rate Adjustment   261

ATM Connection Commands   262
    addcon Command   262
    delcon Command   268
    cnfcls Command   269
    dspcls Command   269
    dspcon Command   269
    dspcons Command   269
    cnfcon Command   269
    References   270

Interworking ATM and Frame Relay   270
    Frame Relay Service-Specific Convergence Sublayer   272
    Service Interworking   273
    ATM Encapsulation   276
    Frame Relay Encapsulation   277
    Adding ATM-Frame Relay Connections   278

Summary   279

Review Questions   280

Chapter 7   Connection Routing, Synchronizing the Network, and Managing Jobs   283

Connection Admission Control   283
    Load Model Versus Actual Utilization   284
    Estimating Connection Load   285
    Connection Characteristics   285

Expected Versus Actual Trunk Loading   286
Handling Bursts   288
Statistical Reserve   288

IGX Commands Used to Configure Routes   289

Configuring Routes   290
Types of Routes   290
Reasons for Rerouting   291
Rules for Rerouting   291
dspload Command   292
dsptrkutl Command   294
dsprts Command   296
cnfpref Command   297
cnfrtcost Command   300
cnfcos Command   301
dncon Command   302
upcon Command   303

IGX Commands Used for Network Synchronization   304

Network Synchronization   304
Carrier Network Timing   305
Clock Sources   305
IGX Trunks as Clock Sources   307
Rules for Selecting a Clock Reference   308
dspclksrcs Command   309
dspcurclk Command   310
cnfclksrc Command   311
dspalms Command   313
dsptrks Command   314
clrclkalm Command   314

IGX Commands Used to Manage Jobs   315

Managing Jobs   316
Job Privilege Levels   316
Creating Jobs   316
Planning a Job   317
Job Execution   317
Editing a Job   317
Stopping a Job   318
Creating Job Triggers   318
addjob Command   318
dspjobs Command   319
dspjob Command   320

editjob Command   321

runjob Command   322

stopjob Command   323

deljob Command   323

addjobtrig Command   324

deljobtrig Command   325

Summary   326

Review Questions   326

Chapter 8   Troubleshooting   329

Major and Minor Alarms   329

Locating Alarms   329

Hardware LEDs   330

Alarm Categories   330

Card Alarms   330

Bus Alarms   331

Trunk Alarms   332

Line Alarms   332

Port Alarms   332

Connection Alarms   333

Troubleshooting Commands   333

dspalms Command   334

dsplog Command   335

clrlog Command   336

dsptrkerrs Command   336

cnftrkalm Command   338

clrtrkalm Command   339

dsplnerrs Command   340

dsplnalmcnf Command   341

cnflnalm Command   342

clrlnalm Command   344

resetcd Command   345

addloclp Command   346

addrmtlp Command   347

addextlp Command   348

dellp Command   349

tstcon Command   350

Connection Testing   352

tstcon Command   352

Local Loopback   353

Remote Loopback   354
External Loopback   355
Using the Data Faceplate   356

Summary   356

Review Questions   357

Part III BPX Switch and Service Configuration   359

Chapter 9   BPX Product Overview and System Hardware   361

The BPX Product Family   361

Trunks, Lines, and Connections   362
Trunks   362
Lines   362
Connections   362

BPX Service Types   363
Traffic and QoS Parameters   364

ATM Cell Format and Cell Relay Switching Features   365
ATM Cell Format   365
Cell Relay Switching Features   366

Administrative Access to BPX   367

Reliability Features   368
Y-Cable Redundancy   368
SONET/SDH Automatic Protection Switching   368
Automatic Fault Management   369

BPX Network Features   369
Network Types   369
Sample Cisco WAN Network   370
Service Expansion Shelf   371
BPX Functions   371

BPX System Hardware   372
Chassis   373
Card Groups   374
BPX Card Module Groups   374
BPX Common Core   375
Broadband Network Interface   386

Polling   392
Polling Cycle   392
Polling Cycle Example   393

BPX System Software   394
   Network Operating System   394
   Network and Platform Software   395
   Connection Admission Control   399

Traffic Management   400
   Usage Parameter Control   400
   Frame-Based Traffic Control   401
   Closed-Loop Congestion Avoidance   402
   QoS Management   402

Summary   404

Review Questions   404

Chapter 10   Accessing the CLI and Initial Configuration of the BPX Switch   411

The BPX CLI   411
   Control Port   411
   Auxiliary Port   412
   LAN Port   413
   IP Relay   413
   Summary of CLI Access Methods   413
   CLI Command Syntax   413
   Examples of Command Structure   415
   Command Examples   415
   Command Entry Modes and Privilege Levels   416
   Logging into and Out of the Network   417
   CLI Screen   418
   Keyboard Shortcuts   419
   Using **help** or **?**   420
   Using the **help** *[character string]* or **?** *[character string]* Command   421
   Using the **help [command]** or **? [command]** Command   421
   Using Repeating Commands: . (Dot)   422
   Logging Out of the BPX: **bye**   423

Commands for the Initial Configuration of BPX   423
   adduser Command   425
   cnfpwd Command   426
   dspcds Command   427
   dspcd Command   428
   dsppwr Command   428
   cnfasm Command   429
   cnfname Command   429
   dspnds Command   430
   cnftmzn Command   430

cnfdate Command   430
cnftime Command   430
cnfterm Command   430
cnftermfunc Command   432
window Command   433
dspprtcnf Command   433
cnfprt Command   433
cnflan Command   433
cnfnwip Command   434

Adding New Users and Modifying Passwords   434
How to Add and Display Users and Modify Passwords   435

Displaying and Monitoring System Data   435
How to Display and Monitor System Data   436
Displaying All Cards: **dspcds**   436
Displaying Specific Cards: **dspcd**   438
Displaying Power: **dsppwr**   439
Displaying the Alarm Status Monitor: **dspasm**   439
Configuring the Alarm Status Monitor: **cnfasm**   440

Assigning Node Names   441
Node Names and Node Numbers   441
How to Assign and Verify Node Names   442
Configuring Node Names: **cnfname**   442
Displaying Nodes: **dspnds**   442

Setting the System Time and Date   443
Network-Wide Settings   443
cnftmzn Command   443
cnfdate Command   445
cnftime Command   445
How to Set the Time Zone, Date, and Time   445

Displaying and Configuring Serial Ports   446
Serial Port Communications Parameters   446
Serial Port Functions   446
How to Display and Modify Serial Port Configurations and Functions   447
Displaying Terminal Port Configurations: **dsptermcnf**   448
Configuring Terminal Ports: **cnfterm**   449
Displaying Port Functions: **dsptermfunc**   450
Displaying the Printer Configuration: **dspprtcnf**   451
Configuring Print Modes: **cnfprt**   451

Using an External Device Window   452
How to Display and Use the External Device Window   452
Windowing to External Devices: **window**   453

Configuring Node and Network IP Addresses   453
    BPX IP Addressing Schemes   453
    IP Address Locations   454
    How to Configure IP Addresses   454
    Configuring the LAN Port: **cnflan**   455
    Configuring Network IP: **cnfnwip**   456
    Displaying the Network IP Address: **dspnwip**   457

Summary   457

Review Questions   458

Chapter 11   Configuring Network Trunks and Access Lines   463

What Is a Trunk?   463
    Trunk Definition   463
    BPX Card Modules That Support Trunks   464

What Is a Virtual Trunk?   465
    Virtual Trunk Definition   465
    Physical and Virtual Trunk Differences   466
    BXM Virtual Interface   466
    BPX Support for Virtual Trunks   467

Trunk Resource Partitions   468
    Virtual Switch Interface Controllers   468
    Which Resources Are Partitioned?   469
    Example of Trunk Resource Partitioning   471
    Summary of Enabled Partitions   473

Dynamic Partitioning   473

Activating, Configuring, and Deactivating Network Trunks   474

How to Activate, Configure, and Deactivate Network Trunks   476
    uptrk Command   476
    cnftrk Command   477
    addtrk Command   481
    dsprtks Command   482
    dsptrkcnf Command   483
    deltrk Command   484
    dntrk Command   485
    vt Command   485

Steps Used to Activate, Configure, and Deactivate Network Trunks   486
    Steps Used to Activate and Configure Network Trunks   486
    Deactivating Network Trunks   487

What Is a Line?   487
    BPX Modules Supporting Access Lines   488
    Commands for Access Lines   488

Activating, Configuring, and Deactivating Access Lines   489
    dsplns Command   489
    upln Command   490
    cnfrsrc Command   491
    dsplncnf Command   492
    cnfln Command   493

Steps Used to Activate, Configure, and Deactivate Access Lines   495
    How to Activate and Configure Access Lines   495
    Deactivating Access Lines   496

Summary   496

Review Questions   496

Chapter 12   Configuring SONET APS   501

SONET APS   501
    Basic APS Operation   501
    APS Versions   502
    APS 1:1 Line Redundancy   502
    APS 1+1 Card and Line Redundancy   504
    APS Automatic Operation   505
    APS Manual Operation   505
    K1K2 Control Protocol   506

APS Implementation on BPX   506
    APS 1:1   507
    APS 1+1   508
    APS 1+1 G.783 Annex B   508
    APS Compared to Y-Redundancy   509

Activating and Configuring APS   509
    APS Configuration   510
    APS 1+1 Implementation on BXM   511
    Commands for APS   513

Configuring and Verifying APS Operation   518
    Displaying Cards: **dspcd**   520
    Adding Card Redundancy: **addcdred**   521
    Adding APS Line Pairs: **addapsln**   521

Configuring APS Lines: **cnfapsln**   522
Switching APS Lines: **switchapsln**   522
Command Precedence   523

Summary   524

Review Questions   524

Chapter 13   Configuring ATM Ports   529

What Is an ATM Port?   529
Port Definition   529
Virtual Port Applications   530
Physical and Virtual Port Differences   531
BXM Virtual Interface   532

What Is a Port Queue?   532
Port Queue Definition   532
BXM Port Queues   532
Configurable Thresholds   532

What Is Traffic Shaping?   534
Definition   534
Implementation   534
Virtual Port Traffic Shaping   535

Signaling Protocols   535
LMI/ILMI Overview   535
LMI Signaling Protocol   536
ILMI Signaling Protocol   537

Activating, Configuring, and Deactivating
ATM Ports   538
Commands for ATM Ports   538

Steps for Activating, Configuring, and Deactivating ATM Ports   550

Monitoring and Resolving ATM Port Failures   552
Commands for Monitoring ATM Port Failures   552

Steps for Monitoring and Resolving ATM Port Failures   557

Summary   558

Review Questions   558

Chapter 14 Configuring ATM Connections and Routing AutoRoute Connections   563

  ATM Connections   563
    ATM Connection Definition   563

  ATM Connection Types   565
    Constant Bit Rate   566
    Variable Bit Rate   566
    Available Bit Rate   566
    Unspecified Bit Rate   566

  Traffic Management Overview   567
    The Role of Traffic Management   567
    Traffic Control Mechanisms   567
    Congestion Control Mechanisms   570

  Traffic Policing   572
    Leaky Bucket Model   572
    Dual Leaky Bucket Model   573
    Policing Implementation for Different Service Types   574

  VC Queues   582
    VC Queue Thresholds   583

  Frame-Based Traffic Control   583
    FBTC Implementation on BXM   584

  Standard ABR   587
    ABR Feedback Mechanism   587
    Resource Management Cells   588
    RM Cell Generation   590
    Operation of Standard ABR in BPX   591
    ABR Standard Implementation on BXM   598
    ABR Standard Rate Adjustments   601

  ABR with ForeSight   604
    Comparison of ABR Standard and ABR ForeSight   604
    ABRFST RM Cell   604
    ABRFST Rate Adjustments   605

  ATM-to-Frame Relay Interworking   607
    NIW and SIW Implementation   608
    BPX Interworking Connection Types   608
    NIW Operation   610
    SIW Operation   611

Multicast Services   613
    Adding BME Multicast Connections   613
    Multicast Addressing Conventions   615

Establishing and Configuring ATM Connections   615
    Commands for Establishing and Configuring ATM Connections   616
    How to Establish and Configure ATM Connections   628
    Verifying That BXM Lines and Ports Are Free of Alarms   630

Monitoring ATM Connections   630
    Channel Statistics   630
    Statistics Applications   631
    Testing   632
    Troubleshooting   632
    Multilevel Channel Statistics   632
    Commands for Monitoring ATM Connections   634
    How to Monitor ATM Connections   634
    Verifying the Card Statistics Level   635

Determining Connection Routes   643
    BPX Routing Criteria   644
    AutoRoute Routing   646
    Types of Routes   647
    Reasons for Rerouting   648
    Rules for Rerouting   648
    Optional Routing Schemes   649
    Trunk Bandwidth Allocation   650
    Load Model Versus Actual Utilization   650
    Handling Bursts   650
    Connection Load   652
    Connection Characteristics   652
    Connection Load Uses   653
    Expected Versus Actual Trunk Loading   653
    Commands for Routing Networks   656
    How to Route and Configure Connections   657

Summary   666

Review Questions   666

Chapter 15   Synchronizing the Network and Troubleshooting   671

Network Synchronization   671
    Carrier Network Timing   671
    Clock Sources   672
    BPX Trunks as Clock Sources   673

Rules for Selecting a Clock Reference   673
Synchronization Example   674
Commands for Synchronizing Networks   680
How to Synchronize Networks   680

What Is an Alarm?   687
Node and Network Alarms   687

Monitoring and Resolving BPX Trunk Alarms   690
Statistical and Physical Trunk Errors   690
Commands for BPX Trunk Alarms   691
How to Monitor and Resolve BPX Trunk Alarms   699

Monitoring and Resolving BPX Line Alarms   701
Statistical and Physical Line Errors   701
Commands for BPX Line Alarms   701
How to Monitor and Resolve BPX Line Alarms   704

Locating Alarms   705
Local Alarms   705
Remote Alarms   706
Hardware LEDs   707
Alarm Categories   708
Card Alarms   708
Bus Alarms   709
Connection Alarms   709
Multicast Connection Alarms   710

Monitoring Multicast Connections   711
Connection Testing   712
Testing Connection Integrity   714

Commands for Troubleshooting   716
dspslotalms Command   717
dspsloterrs Command   718
dspslotalmcnf Command   720
addloclp Command   721
addrmtlp Command   721
dellp Command   722
resetcd Command   723

Summary   723

Review Questions   724

Part IV MGX ATM Concentrator Configuration   727

Chapter 16   MGX Product Overview and System Hardware   729

    The MGX Product Family   729
      MGX Feature Comparison   730

    MGX Product Features   730
      MGX User Services   731
      MGX Optional Features   732

    Network Management   732
      CLI   732
      CWM   733
      Customized SNMP Management Tools   734

    MGX Networking   734
      MGX 8850-PXM45/8230 Tiered Network   734
      BPX/MGX 8250 Tiered Network   735
      MGX Standalone Devices   736
      MGX 8850-PXM45 and a BPX/SES PNNI Network   736

    MGX 8850 Processor Cards   737
      The PXM1   737
      PXM1 Back Cards   738
      PXM1 Functions   741

    The SRM Card   741
      SRM Functions   743

    The RPM Card   744
      RPM Functions   744
      Types of RPM   745
      RPM Front and Back Cards   745

    MGX Service Modules   745
      CESM Features   748
      FRSM Features   749
      AUSM Features   750
      VISM Features   750
      Reserved Card Slots   751
      High and Low-Speed Card Modules   751
      Configuring Double-Height Card Slots   753

MGX Required Features and Hardware   754
   Guidelines   754
   Frame Relay Only Example   754
   Multiservice Example   757

Summary   760

Review Questions   760

Chapter 17   The User Interface and MGX Network Configuration   767

Methods for Connecting to the Command-Line Interface   767

MGX Command Syntax   768
   Add Port Command Example   769
   Configure Line Command Example   770
   Help Command   770
   Finding Command Syntax   771
   MGX CLI Error Messages   772

MGX User IDs and Passwords   773
   Commands for Managing User IDs and Passwords   773
   Logging into and out of the MGX CLI   775

Card and Port Resource Partitions   775
   FRSM Example   777

MGX Node Configuration Commands   778
   Display Cards Command   778
   Display Card Command   781
   Display Interface IP Command   782
   Configure Name Command   782
   Display Card Resource Partitions Command   783

Redundancy on the MGX Switch   783
   Service Module Redundancy   783
   1-to-N Redundancy Process   785

MGX Card Redundancy Commands   786
   Add Redundancy Command   786
   Display Redundancy Command   787

Summary   787

Review Questions   788

Chapter 18 Lines, Feeder Nodes, and SONET APS   795

    Lines   795
        PXM1 OC-3c Example   796
        FRSM-8T1 Example   797

    MGX Commands   798
        Display Lines Command   798
        Display Line Command   799
        Add Line Command   800
        Configure Line Command   800
        Display Alarm(s) Commands   802
        Display and Configure ATM Line Commands   804
        Add Port, Configure Port, and Delete Port Commands   805
        Display Ports Command   805
        Display Port Resource Partition Command   806
        Display Trunks Command   806
        Configure Interface as Trunk Command   807

    Commands for Displaying, Adding, and Configuring Lines   807
        The Display Lines Command   807
        The Display DS3 Lines Command   809
        Display DS3 Line Command   810
        The Add Line Command for MGX Service Modules   811
        The Configure Line Command   811

    Commands for Monitoring Line Alarms and Errors   812
        The Display Alarms Command   813
        The Display Alarm Command   814
        The Display Alarm Counter Command   814
        The Configure Bit Error Rate Test Command   815
        The Display BERT Command   817

    How to Add Lines to an MGX Service Module   818

    SRM-3T3 Distribution of T1 Lines   819
        SRM-3T3 Features   819

    T1 Line Distribution Process   820
        Commands for T1 Line Distribution   821

    How to Test T1 and E1 Lines on MGX Service Modules   825
        Bit Error Rate Testing   825
        Procedures for Testing T1 and E1 Lines on MGX Service Modules   826

Feeder Nodes   828

    Types of Feeder and Backbone Nodes   829

    How to Add a Feeder to a BPX Network   830

    How to Add a Feeder to an MGX 8850-PXM45 Network   831

    Setting Up an MGX 8850 Standalone Switch   833

Sonet APS   834

    APS Versions   834

    APS 1+1 Unidirectional Example   836

    Commands for Configuring SONET APS on a PXM1 Line   840

Summary   842

Review Questions   843

Chapter 19   Connection Types   851

Supported VC Types: PVCs, SPVCs, and SVCs   851

    PVC Definition   851

    SPVC Definition   853

    SVC Definition   855

    PVC Example   856

    SPVC Example   858

    SVC Example   859

Connection Types in the Backbone Network   861

    BPX Connection Types   861

    MGX 8850-PXM45 Connection Types   861

    Connection Types for MGX Feeder Connections   862

MGX Connections   863

    Network Connections   863

    Slave and Master Connection Definitions   864

Commands for Adding, Configuring, and Displaying MGX 8850-PXM45 Connections   865

    Add Connection Command   866

    Delete Connection Command   869

    Delete Connections Command   869

    Configure Connection Command   870

    Display Connections Command   870

    Display Connection Command   872

How to Add a Connection in an MGX 8850-PXM45 Network   875

Circuit Emulation Ports   876
   Support of Unstructured and Structured Ports   877
   Unstructured Example   878
   Structured Example   878

Circuit Emulation Connections   879
   Signaling on Connections   879
   Feeder Example   880
   Local Example   881

Circuit Emulation Clocking Modes   881
   Synchronous Clocking   882
   SRTS Clocking   882
   Adaptive Clocking   882

How the CESM Manages Traffic   882
   CESM Egress Queues   882
   Ingress Traffic   883
   Egress Traffic   884

Commands for Adding, Configuring, and Displaying Circuit Emulation Ports   885
   Add Port Command   885
   Display Ports Command   886
   Display Port Command   887

Commands for Adding, Configuring, and Displaying Circuit Emulation
Connections   888
   Add Connection Command   888
   Display Connections Command   889
   Display Connection Command   891
   Configure Connection Command   893

Commands for Verifying Circuit Emulation Connections   894
   Test Connection Command   894
   Test Delay Command   895
   Display Channel Count Command   896

How to Create Circuit Emulation Services in an MGX Network   897

Summary   900

Review Questions   900

Chapter 20   Frame Relay Ports and Connections   907

Frame Relay Ports   907
   Port Types   907
   Serial Frame Relay Ports   908

Narrowband Channelized Frame Relay Ports   908
Narrowband Fractional Frame Relay Ports   909

FRSM Port Queues   910
Low-Speed FRSM Port Queues   910
High-Speed FRSM Port Queues   911

How Traffic Moves Through the FRSM   912
Ingress Frame Relay Traffic for Low-Speed FRSMs   913
Ingress Frame Relay Traffic for High-Speed FRSMs   913
Egress Frame Relay Traffic for Low-Speed FRSMs   914
Egress Frame Relay Traffic for High-Speed FRSMs   914

Commands for Adding, Configuring, and Displaying Frame Relay Ports   914
Display Ports Command   915
Display Port Command   916
Add Port Command   919
Configure Port Command   920
Extended Configure Port Command   920
Configure Port CLLM Command   921

Commands for Monitoring Frame Relay Ports   922
Display Port Counter Command   922

Configuring a Frame Relay Port on an FRSM   925

Frame Relay Connections   926
Connection Types   926
Feeder Example   927
Local Example   928

Interworking   928
Network Interworking   928
Service Interworking   929

Frame Relay Policing   931
Low-Speed FRSM Policing   931
Low-Speed FRSM Example   931
High-Speed FRSM Policing   933
High-Speed FRSM Example   934

ForeSight on Frame Relay Connections   935
Potential Congestion Locations   936
ForeSight Congestion Criteria   937
ForeSight Configurable Characteristics   938
Example of a Congested Network   939
Example of an Uncongested Network   940

ABR for Frame Relay   940
    The RM Cell   941
    When Are RM Cells Sent?   942
    Potential Congestion Locations   942
    ABR Rate Adjustments   942
    Configurable ABR Connection Parameters   943
    Example of a Congested Network   944
    Example of an Uncongested Network   945

VC Queues on the FRSM   946
    Initial Burst Size Definition   947
    Initial Burst Size Example   948

Commands for Adding, Configuring, and Displaying Frame Relay Connections   948
    Add Connection Command   949
    Display Connections Command   950
    Display Connection Command   951
    Configure Channel Policing Command   955
    Configure Channel Excess Information Rate Command   955
    Configure Channel ABR Parameters Command   956
    Configure Channel ForeSight Command   956
    Configure Channel Mapping Command   957
    Configure Channel Ingress and Egress Queue Commands   957

Commands for Verifying Frame Relay Connections   958
    Test Connection Command   958
    Test Delay Command   959
    Display Channel Count Command   959

Creating Frame Relay Connections in an MGX Network   962

Summary   964

Review Questions   964

Chapter 21   ATM Ports and Connections   973

ATM Ports   973
    ATM Port   974
    IMA Port   974

Inverse Multiplexing Over ATM   975

AUSM Port Queues   975
    QBin Characteristics   976
    QBin Configuration Example   976
    Virtual Circuit Queues   977

How Cells Move Though the AUSM   977
    Ingress ATM Traffic   977
    Egress ATM Traffic   978

Commands for Adding, Configuring, and Displaying ATM Ports on the AUSM   979
    Display Ports Command   979
    Display Port Command   980
    Add Port Command   983
    Add IMA Group Command   984
    Configure IMA Group Command   984
    Display Port Queues Command   985
    Display Port Queue Command   986
    Extended Configure Port Queue Command   987
    Display ILMI Command   987
    Configure ILMI Command   989

Commands for Adding, Configuring, and Displaying ATM Ports on the PXM1   989
    Display Ports Command   990
    Add Port Command   990
    Display Port Resource Partition Command   991
    Configure ILMI Command   991
    Display ILMIs Command   992

Commands for Monitoring ATM Ports   993
    Display Port Counter Command   993
    Display ILMI Counter Command   998

How to Configure an ATM Port on the AUSM and PXM1   1000

ATM Connections   1001
    Connection Types   1001
    ATM Feeder Connection   1002
    ATM Local Connection   1002

ATM Class of Service   1002
    ATM Classes of Service   1003

ATM Policing   1004
    Leaky Bucket Model   1004
    Dual Leaky Bucket Model   1004
    Leaky Bucket Characteristics   1005
    Policing Based on Class of Service   1005
    Time-Based Model for PCR and CDVT   1007
    CBR Example   1007
    VBR Example   1008

ForeSight on ATM Connections   1009
    Potential Congestion Locations   1009
    ForeSight Congestion Criteria   1010
    ForeSight Configurable Characteristics   1010

ABR for ATM   1011
    Potential Congestion Locations   1012

VC Queues on the AUSM   1012
    Frame-Based Traffic Control   1012
    Configuration Example   1014
    Queue Characteristics   1014

Commands for Adding, Displaying, and Configuring ATM Connections on the
AUSM   1015
    Add Connection Command   1016
    Display Connections Command   1016
    Display Connection Command   1017
    Configure Channel ForeSight Command   1020
    Configure UPC CBR Command   1021
    Configure UPC VBR Command   1021
    Configure UPC rt-VBR Command   1022
    Configure UPC ABR Command   1022
    Configure UPC UBR Command   1022
    Configure Connection ABR Parameters Command   1022
    Display Connection Standard ABR Command   1023
    Configure Channel Queue Command   1024

Commands for Adding, Displaying, and Configuring ATM Connections on the
PXM1   1024
    Add Connection Command   1025
    Display Connections Command   1025
    Display Connection Command   1026
    Display Channels Command   1027
    Display Channel Command   1028
    Configure UPC CBR Command   1030
    Configure UPC VBR Command   1031
    Configure UPC ABR Command   1031
    Configure UPC UBR Command   1032
    Configure Channel Queue Command   1032

Commands for Verifying ATM Connections   1033
    Display Channel Count Command   1033
    Test Connection Command   1037
    Test Delay Command   1037
    Test Connection Segment Command   1038

How to Create ATM Connections on the AUSM and PXM1   1038
    AUSM Procedure   1038
    PXM1 Procedure   1040

Summary   1042

Review Questions   1042

Chapter 22   Voice, IP, and ATM MPLS Features   1053

VISM Overview   1053

MPLS Overview   1055

RPM Overview   1055

VISM Voice Features   1056
    VISM Release 1.5 Features   1056
    VISM Release 2.0 Features   1058
    VISM Release 2.1 Features   1058

Voice Connections   1059
    Endpoints   1059
    Channel Identifiers   1059
    Feeder Example   1060
    Local Example   1060
    How PCM Samples Are Converted into ATM Cells   1061
    AAL2 Segmentation   1062
    AAL2 Coding   1063

Voice Over AAL2 Network   1064

VoIP Network   1065

Voice Over ATM Services on the VISM   1067

Digital Signal Processors   1070

VISM Clocking   1070
    VISM Clocking Options   1070
    Configuration Procedures   1072

Commands for Adding, Configuring, and Displaying Voice Connections   1073
    Display VISM Parameter Command   1074
    Configure VISM Mode Command   1076
    Add Port Command   1076
    Display Port Command   1076
    Add Resource Partition Command   1077
    Display Resource Partition Command   1077
    Configure Line Signaling Command   1078

Display Line DSP Command   1079
Add Endpoint and Add Endpoints Commands   1079
Display Endpoints Command   1080
Display Endpoint Command   1081
Add Connection Command   1082
Display Connections Command   1082
Display Connection Command   1083
Add CID Command   1085
Display CIDs Command   1086
Display CID Command   1086

Commands for Verifying Voice Connections   1087
Test Connection Command   1087
Test Delay Command   1087
Display Connection Count Command   1088
Display Managed CID Counter Command   1089

Introduction to Multiprotocol Label Switching   1090
ATM MPLS Technical and Business Benefits   1092
Label Switching Advantages   1092

The Problem of Persistent Loops Due to Protocol Conflicts   1094

Cisco WAN Switches with MPLS Support   1095
MPLS Features Supported on the MGX Switch   1096
MPLS Networks Using the MGX Switch   1098

Setting Up MPLS on the MGX Switch   1101
Network Topology   1101

MPLS and Virtual Private Networks Using the Route Processor Module   1103
VPN Requirements   1103
MPLS VPN Features   1104
Supported Platforms   1105
How Do VPNs Work?   1105
VPNs for MPLS   1105
VPN Route-Target Communities and Export and Import Lists   1105
IBGP Distribution of VPN Routing Information   1106
Label Forwarding   1106

RPM Memory Locations   1107

RPM Port Numbering   1107
Definition   1107

Cisco IOS Command-Line Interface   1108
    RPM CLI Access   1108
    CLI Modes   1108
    Entering Commands   1109
    Changing the RPM Configuration   1109

Commands for Configuring the RPM   1111
    Enable Command   1112
    Show Running Configuration and Show Startup Configuration Commands   1112
    Copy Command   1114
    Reload Command   1114
    Configure Terminal Command   1115
    Boot System Command   1115
    Hostname Command   1115
    Enable Password Command   1116
    Line Command   1116
    Password Command   1117
    RPM Resource Partition Command   1117

Commands for Setting Up the RPM ATM Switch Interface   1118
    Show Interface Command   1119
    Interface Command   1120
    Shutdown Command   1120

How to Set Up the RPM   1121

Configuring Subinterfaces   1122
    Subinterface Example   1123

PVCs on the RPM   1124

Commands for Configuring Subinterfaces   1125
    Show Interface Command   1125
    Interface Command   1127
    Shutdown Command   1127
    IP Address Command   1127

Commands for Creating and Displaying PVCs on the RPM   1128
    ATM PVC Command   1128
    Show ATM Virtual Circuit Command   1129
    Map Group Command   1130
    Map List Command   1131
    IP Command   1131
    Show ATM Map Command   1131
    Add Connection Command   1132
    Show Switch Connections Command   1133

Creating Connections on the RPM   1134

Summary   1136

Review Questions   1136

Appendix A   Answers to Review Questions   1147

Index   1231

Overview

Cisco WAN Switching Professional Reference contains switching technologies associated with Cisco's three WAN switching platforms: MGX, BPX, and IGX. The Cisco courses that correspond to these switches are the MACC (MGX), BSSC (BPX) and MSSC (IGX), and are contained in full in this study and reference guide.

When I first became interested in pursuing the recently retired CCNP WAN (Cisco Certified Network Professional WAN Switching) certification, I searched bookshelves and online book stores for information that would help me better prepare for the four required exams. I was amazed to discover that, except for Cisco's instructor lead courses, no published study or reference materials existed for customers and students wanting to learn the Cisco WAN switching technologies at the professional level of expertise. As a result, I was concerned that the cost, time, and travel requirements for the instructor-lead courses would limit their accessibility, and that these technologies should therefore be available in book form as an alternative or supplement to the classroom courses. To my delight, Cisco Systems and Cisco Press agreed to let me put this book together; to my astonishment, it took close to one year to complete.

This three course study and reference guide can be used as a supplementary study guide in combination with other Cisco courses or Cisco Press books (I highly recommend *Cisco WAN Quick Start* by Ronald W. McCarty, Jr.), or as a reference guide for the day-to-day maintenance and operation of your Cisco WAN switch network. You should also find it useful preparation for the WAN switching portion of the *CCIE Communications and Services*, and any other Cisco WAN switching certifications.

Cisco's Web site (www.cisco.com) is the best resource for receiving the latest information concerning Cisco's career certifications.

This book is divided into four parts. Part I includes a foreward by Don Proctor, VP/GM of the Multiservice Switching Business Unit (MSSBU), home of Cisco's WAN switch product line. Part I also includes the history of WAN Switching at Cisco, and an introduction to "Professional Training and Career Development" by Tom Kelly, VP of World Wide Training.

Part II covers the Multiband Switch and Service Configuration (MSSC) course that focuses on the IGX switch technologies and services, including configuration, operation, interworking, and troubleshooting.

Part III covers the BPX Switch and Service Configuration (BSSC) course that focuses on the BPX switch technologies and services, including configuration, operation, interworking and troubleshooting.

Part IV covers the MGX ATM Concentrator Configuration (MACC) course that focuses on the MGX switch technologies and services, including voice, IP and ATM MPLS features, configuration, operation, and troubleshooting.

If you are interested in learning about the Cisco WAN Manager (CWM) and its role in providing fault, configuration, and performance management functionality for IGX, BPX and MGX switches, go to Cisco's Web site at www.cisco.com and select Technical Documents to search for the CWM Installation Guide and CWM User's Guide. These documents provide information for the installation and operation of CWM.

Whether you are purchasing this book to use as a reference or study guide, I hope that you find the information contained herein comprehensive, interesting, and above all, useful.

Foreword

Frame Relay, now 10 years old, has become the most widely deployed data service in the world. ATM is now used as the cornerstone of many telecom carrier services. Technologies such as MPLS are helping telecommunications carriers cope with the demand of building scalable, reliable, and secure solutions for the growing volume of IP traffic generated by today's business applications. From a standing start in the early 1990s, data now accounts for over half of all traffic carried on the world's telecommunications infrastructure. It's hard for anyone not to be awed by the speed with which the WAN switching industry has developed and matured, but my connection to many of these technologies is a personal one.

On March 25th, 1991, the first public Frame Relay service was launched by a tiny telecommunications carrier from Tulsa, Oklahoma called WilTel, which is now a part of WorldCom. WilTel was one of the Williams Companies, a 90-year old energy conglomerate whose main business is transporting natural gas across the country via a network of pipelines. In the mid-eighties Williams got the idea that running fiber-optic cables through decommissioned gas lines around the country could make an interesting side business.

In 1990, WilTel's engineers became interested in Frame Relay as an attractive alternative to the dominant packet technology of the time, X.25. Because WilTel had fiber in the ground, its network did not need X.25's robust—and slow—error-correction capabilities. Frame Relay relies primarily on end stations to perform error-correction, so it is capable of operating much faster than X.25, given a clean transport infrastructure. Later that year, WilTel acquired a few switches from a startup company in California called StrataCom, which had recently implemented the Frame Relay protocol on its family of network switches.

In 1991, I was a network engineer working at another California startup, a software company called Sybase. Sybase was the leading vendor of client/server databases and at that time was experiencing rapid growth; we were opening new offices faster than we could network them. More importantly, using client/server technology meant that our bandwidth needs would grow quickly and become less predictable as databases and applications were deployed in Sybase offices around the world. All of which made us a perfect candidate for Frame Relay services. In 1992, we became WilTel's second Frame Relay customer (the first was Convex Computer, now part of Hewlett-Packard).

The Sybase Frame Relay network was designed over lunch one day with Robert Gourley, WilTel's chief engineer, on a paper tablecloth in Emeryville's Townhouse Bar & Grill (originally a notorious gin mill during the Prohibition). The network's topology was simple—a fully meshed core with smaller sites hubbed into core sites—but was ideally suited for accommodating the onslaught of mostly-IP applications that were causing our old leased line network to come apart at the seams.

Over the next three years, I spent most of my waking hours, and many long nights, working with WilTel's technicians and engineers to build the Sybase Wide Area Network (WAN). In the beginning our progress was slow and tedious. As the number of sites increased, so did the difficulty in keeping up the Frame Relay network. I found out only much later that I was the first network engineer to attempt to connect a Cisco router (at my site) to a StrataCom Frame Relay switch (on WilTel's network). This was all fresh ground; we were moving into new territory where no one had been before. It was predictable that we'd encounter our share of problems as we rolled the new Frame Relay network out.

A week or so after the first handful of Frame Relay sites went live, I began to get complaints about network performance. Even when all sites were accessible, network performance would periodically slow to a crawl. At first I didn't pay a lot of attention to the slow-downs, since getting the network up and stable was clearly the top priority. Then we started losing connectivity to remote sites entirely.

We could sometimes get the network up and running for hours or days, but then would begin to lose connectivity to remote sites—first one site, then three, then five, etc... And just as suddenly the sites would come back up—sometimes hours later. I wrote a simple program that paged me whenever this happened—a decision I lived to regret as time went on! I was stumped. WilTel was stumped. Even Cisco was stumped.

Then I noticed a peculiar pattern to the slow-downs. I could observe the problem by sending IP "ping" packets over the network and measuring the round-trip time. Most of the packets had a round-trip time in the acceptable range—less than 100 ms—but every so often the round-trip times of three or four packets in a row would balloon up to 500, 800, even 1200 ms! Network performance would stabilize only to repeat the same pattern a moment later. By keeping a steady stream of ping packets going, I could see that the problem seemed to appear every 30 seconds, like clockwork. Coincidentally, 30 seconds also happened to be the update interval of the Routing Information Protocol (RIP) we were using for IP traffic on the network.

This led Cisco's engineers to the discovery that our router's buffers were overflowing whenever a RIP update was broadcast—every 30 seconds! Sometimes, this simply made the link slow, but other times it prevented the routing information from reaching the remote site, thus causing the site to become unreachable. Because Frame Relay allows multiple logical connections over a single physical link, the router sent a separate copy of the RIP table for every PVC. Those tables were getting big, and it was more than the router's default queue could handle. To fix this, Cisco's engineers added a feature that let me adjust the buffer size. They also sent me a special build of the IOS. I ran a version of this Cisco IOS called "9.21.Sybase" for over a year. As a result of our discovery, every Cisco router now supports a feature called the Frame Relay Broadcast Queue.

Congratulations on embarking along this journey into the heart of the world's telecom networks. Whether in good times or bad, it's undeniable that this technology will forever change the world in which we live. As you study, learn and use the technologies contained in this book, you too will become part of the amazing history of WAN switching.

Donald R. Proctor
Vice President and General Manager
Multiservice Switching Business Unit
Cisco Systems, Inc.

Professional Training and Career Development

Certification has two different, but related roles in the technology industry. The first is the most traditional and obvious: validating the knowledge level of individuals. This has become increasingly important as the number of technology based jobs have expanded globally, and as these jobs become more challenging and complex.

In the past, employers have been uncertain about whether or not job candidates, and even existing employees, actually knew the technology, or possessed the competency required for the job. Over the years, however, certification testing has proven to be an accurate and reliable means of measuring an individual's understanding of a job function, product or technology, and at the same time has grown into a not-too-small global industry on that basis.

The second and more recent role is in entity certification: when a company is selected or authorized by another company to represent them in a sales, training, or support role. How does one company ensure the skills, knowledge or competence of another? Require the employees to be certified, and you then authorize the entity that employs them.

Both roles provide direct value to the companies and individuals.

Certification for the most part today gives us confidence in the knowledge that people possess. It also offers confidence in the competence of those tested. What can they *do*? Can they do what I am hiring them or promoting them to do?

The certification industry is continually striving to meet the promise of skills based testing through the validation of knowledge. The acquisition of such knowledge can be achieved today through numerous tools that are available to help meet the individualistic learning styles of students, providing a solid and broad base from which to study.

Whether students use study guides, e-learning tools, instructor lead courses, or a combination of methods to increase one's understanding of a job, product or technology, the testing of that knowledge through certification examinations ultimately assists in measuring competencies. By mixing current testing methods with complex scenario testing and simulation skill testing, companies and individuals will have increased confidence that certification is a reliable and complete measure of skill and knowledge.

Cisco WAN Switching Professional Reference has been developed with skills based knowledge and competency in mind, and as a learning resource for individuals and companies interested in increasing their understanding of Cisco WAN Switching products and technologies.

Tom Kelly, VP World Wide Training
Internet Learning Solutions Group
Cisco Systems, Inc.

Introduction

Chapter 1   Cisco and WAN Switching

Cisco and WAN Switching

Cisco has become a leader in the wide-area network (WAN) market that offers diversified next-generation technologies that are designed to meet the needs of a growing and more demanding customer base. How did Cisco achieve this leadership? Interviews with some of Cisco's top engineers and leaders, including Don Proctor, Vice President and General Manager of the Multiservice Switching Business Unit, and Morgan Littlewood, Senior Director within Cisco's Service Provider Line of Business, present an intimate picture of where Cisco has been, where it is today, and where it is going with WAN products and capabilities. This is a story that demonstrates the inner spirit and hard work of Cisco's employees and the determination to provide unprecedented value and opportunity to Cisco's customers.

A company known for its enterprise routers did not appear a likely candidate for investing in WAN switching products, but Cisco could see that customer needs, technology trends, and the customers themselves were rapidly changing. There was a strong emerging demand from larger enterprise customers and service providers for technologies that could seamlessly integrate routing, Frame Relay, ATM, and voice across a single network. Cisco responded to this demand by merging high-performance ATM switches with the intelligence and control of IP routing to develop the next-generation networking infrastructure. Cisco knew that this combined entity would deliver integrated, scalable multiservice network solutions to public carriers and enterprises. Cisco approached this challenge with the same vigor and experienced, forward-thinking strategies that made it the leader of router sales and deployment by first anticipating the need for networks to support multiple services such as cell relay, permanent virtual circuits (PVCs), switched virtual circuits (SVCs), Frame Relay, and local-area network (LAN) interconnectivity.

In 1990, the Frame Relay services market was kick-started by four major players: Cisco, StrataCom, DEC, and Northern Telecom (now Nortel), also known in the industry as "The Gang of Four." Around this time, Cisco developed the first Frame Relay router interface and was interested in the ability of Frame Relay services to lower the cost of bandwidth for enterprise customers. With this interest in mind, Cisco led the development of the key technologies that allowed multiprotocol enterprise networks to leverage Frame Relay services to connect their LANs.

As the market for Frame Relay services grew, Cisco invested in a startup called Cascade that focused on lowering the cost of Frame Relay service delivery. Although Cisco had an equity investment in this company, it would eventually decide that a StrataCom acquisition would be a better fit for the Cisco product line. StrataCom had the highest-quality products and was based in San Jose. Most significantly, StrataCom had developed a full product line of enterprise and carrier switches that could seamlessly connect to Cisco routers. Many carriers and mission-critical enterprise networks, such as large banks, actively embraced this architecture.

Cisco's real entry into the WAN market started with the acquisition of StrataCom, Inc. on July 9, 1996. With this $4 billion acquisition, Cisco entered the ATM WAN switching and telco market and also brought together two of "The Gang of Four." A leading supplier of Asynchronous Transfer Mode (ATM), Frame Relay high-speed WAN switching equipment, and a key customer base, StrataCom and its products added value to Cisco's routing and LAN switching product line by allowing Cisco to leverage its expertise and vision across a broader technology base. The addition of WAN switching technologies facilitated Cisco's ability to provide customers with a superior network infrastructure for integrated data and voice environments, and to become the only vendor to offer end-to-end connectivity across public, private, and hybrid networks. In addition, it resulted in Cisco's first venture into the service provider line of businesses.

StrataCom was founded in January of 1986 as a spin-off of a failed startup called Packet Technologies that was ahead of its time with the implementation of interactive TV. Packet Technologies was made up of two lines of business: cable and interactive communication path development. When venture capital funding dried up, the engineers who had participated in the development of the interactive technologies started their own company and named it StrataCom.

In mid-1986, the Internetwork Packet Exchange (IPX) was the first product released by this new company. All traffic carried through the IPX used a fixed 24-byte packet size (to match the size of a T1 frame) and was given the proprietary name of FastPacket. StrataCom's fast packet technology was ATM-like and anticipated many of the features of the ATM standard. Eventually this resulted in a quick and easy implementation of ATM.

The original IPX was strictly a digital voice switch. This was an industry first and a revolutionary and pioneering concept designed to carry voice over FastPackets. The IPX accepted the voice stream in digital PCM (Pulse Code Modulation) format and then compressed it using Adaptive Differential Pulse Code Modulation (ADPCM) and Voice Activity Detection (VAD). This helped decrease costs to customers compared with traditional 64 K Time Division Multiplexing (TDM). An IPX network was established and maintained by a novel and proprietary connection-oriented routing technology called AutoRoute that was designed to automatically select paths across a complex network.

It was difficult to convince companies to abandon the comfort of TDM and to embrace the revolutionary concept of FastPacket voice transport that the IPX provided. That the IPX could be relied upon to not only transport voice in digits but could also make better use of a company's T-1 line and save the customer money took some convincing, but with some persuasion, May Department Stores became StrataCom's first customer. Eventually, transportation companies including McDonalds trucking service and energy companies became customers as well, helping to build a broad customer base.

In the middle of 1987, the IPX became a 32-slot box and included some new diagnostics. The first major change to the IPX came in 1988, with data interfaces becoming an integral part of the IPX switch. It was no longer a strictly digital voice switch.

Many companies had separate voice and data devices, so the new IPX was an attractive alternative, with both services streamlined into one switch. The new IPX features served as an attempt to consolidate voice and data networks to create a single network. IPX would eventually succeed in becoming the first multiservice technology. But at this point, consolidating voice and data networks was the name of the game.

Another major change to the IPX came in 1989 with the addition of Data Frame Multiplexing (DFM). This new feature improved bandwidth efficiency by eliminating repetitive patterns (such as HDLC flags) within the incoming bit stream.

The IPX was originally designed with the North American standard T-1 (Trunk Level 1, a digital transmission link with a total signaling speed of 1.544 Mbps) for transmissions within the United States and Canada. However, by late 1990, the IPX contained the first international concept, the E-1, which operates outside of the United States and Canada at a total signaling rate of 2.048 Mbps.

The most significant improvement to the IPX came with the incorporation of Frame Relay capabilities. This was a new and emerging protocol, similar to X.25 PVC, but much faster and more efficient. The IPX was the first commercial release of a Frame Relay switch. The new Frame Relay capabilities became the third service (with voice and data) tied into the IPX box and helped get Frame Relay off the ground.

New voice cards, designed with an improved architecture and a greater number of voice ports were also introduced around this time, allowing older and less efficient cards to be phased out.

The next revolutionary change came with the introduction of ForeSight. This feature is a closed-loop relative-rate feedback mechanism designed to dynamically adjust network Frame Relay traffic to help utilize available bandwidth. Rate adjustments take place in supervisory FastPackets to allow for the optimization of bandwidth when network congestion occurs. Customers could use a dynamically adaptive rate-control mechanism to ensure that critical traffic could get through even under a heavy load. This was the only dynamic rate control on a Frame Relay service. It was a major enhancement to the Frame Relay capability, with the focus on maximizing the efficiency of the E-1 or T-1 lines to the switches. This feature allowed very robust connectivity for all the routers on a Frame Relay network.

In the early 1990s, ATM was becoming a reasonably agreed-upon standard, and ATM platforms and interfaces were being created throughout the industry. As a result of this, StrataCom created a new switch called the BPX as the first dedicated ATM switch with T3, E3, and OC-3 interfaces. The BPX was rebranded by Cisco as the Cisco BPX 8600. It has become the most widely deployed ATM switch in the industry, with over 5000 nodes installed in networks throughout the world.

Then the IGX came along. This switch was designed as a replacement to the IPX. Its initial design focus concentrated on increasing the capacity of the old IPX 32 Mbps bus by increasing bus capacity to 1 Gbps. The first IGX had only voice, data, and Frame Relay features, but eventually ATM interfaces were incorporated into the IGX, creating a fully featured box.

A new product, AXIS, was designed to work as an access shelf on the BPX to allow efficient access at T1/E1 and slower speeds. The AXIS shelf supported Frame Relay, ATM, and circuit over an ATM backbone. The first member of the Cisco MGX family, the AXIS shelf was later rebranded as the Cisco MGX 8220.

The BPX originally used some proprietary ATM signaling, but as the ATM standards grew and became solidified over time, the BPX hardware had to be modified to accommodate changes in standards. The BXM card was designed to address this. It included the first carrier implementation of ABR traffic management.

The ultimate fruit of the StrataCom acquisition was the development of Multiprotocol Label Switching (MPLS), which is the industry's preferred method of delivering IP traffic over an ATM network. As IP and ATM come together, the idea is one of "route at the edge and switch at the core." With MPLS, switches are used at the core of the network, where they can utilize intelligent routing instructions, and where fast switching speeds are advantageous.

MPLS grew out of Tag Switching, which is a technique developed by Cisco for high-performance packet forwarding through a router, using labels or "tags" that are assigned to destination networks or hosts. By adding MPLS to the BPX 8600, Cisco created the industry's first WAN switch capable of the full suite of carrier data services. Frame Relay, ATM, and IP could be simultaneously supported on a common infrastructure.

Joining Forces

The bringing together of StrataCom and Cisco has ultimately proven to be a solid and rewarding marriage. However, one of the risks and challenges faced with any acquisition is to smoothly and successfully absorb the new company's staff. Merging an ATM company with an IP company was challenging enough, and Cisco's short six-to-nine-month selling cycles put some initial strain on the StrataCom sales group. Mixing a small workforce with a large workforce, while blending and integrating the two cultures, required determined and experienced leadership. This leadership was eventually put to the test on April 13, 1998 with the meltdown of AT&T's Frame Relay network. This became a galvanizing event in Cisco's history.

AT&T's Frame Relay network consisted of Cisco's WAN switches, which formed the backbone network that carried 30 percent of the financial transaction traffic in the U.S. It was the most mission-critical public network of its time. The 22-hour meltdown happened while AT&T was upgrading the firmware on a BXM card during normal business hours. Ironically, the network's previous stability had enabled AT&T to become one of the first operators to upgrade network software without impacting customer traffic. The April 13 event became a positive turning point for Cisco because it emphasized the critical demand for high-availability data service by businesses. The service demand had grown beyond e-mail and basic Web surfing support, and with this, Cisco realized that availability had to become a core focus of the organization. From this event came many positive things, including the Reliability, Availability, and Serviceability (RAS) blueprint that was developed to help improve RAS networking standards.

Despite this major setback, a strong relationship with AT&T has been key to the ongoing development of the network that Cisco provides for AT&T's Frame Relay customers and the high availability since achieved in this switch network. Combined efforts and compromises on both sides helped develop a network that meets our joint customers' desire for high-availability services. Like a shuttle launch, we have focused on scrutiny of design for high availability and the development of even better tools with the help and cooperation of AT&T. Without question, this teamwork improved high-availability services. In July of 2000, AT&T reported a precedent-setting "five nines" performance on its market-leading Frame Relay network, which has been consistently performing above 99.999 percent reliability.

What Lies Ahead

With a sense of where Cisco has been, and an unprecedented history of product development serving as the basis of where the company is today, the next question to ask is where does Cisco see itself going as it continues to grow, diversify, and meet customer and industry needs for WAN switching products? A strong base of technologies and the brightest engineers in the business will help propel Cisco forward, as it envisions itself improving and building on its existing technologies to best meet the demands of its worldwide customers and breaking away from its competition. Cisco's history of WAN switching and its current position in the market are just the beginning. Cisco believes that tomorrow's worldwide multiservice networks will continue to demand the scalable, superior, and cost-effective solutions that have made its WAN product line a leader in the industry.

Thanks to the hard work of its employees, Cisco has succeeded in creating a diverse line of WAN products and capabilities that include the following:

- **MPLS VPN over ATM**—The MPLS VPN over ATM solution lets an enterprise or Internet service provider (ISP) connect its sites via a public network and enjoy the same security and service levels of high-growth IP Virtual Private Network (VPN) services that are provided by private networks. MPLS is an innovative method for forwarding packets through an existing ATM network with minimal up-front costs and a quick return on investment (ROI). By leveraging a customer's existing Frame Relay or ATM network, the MPLS VPN over ATM offers many business-class services over a common infrastructure that are highly scalable and very easy to manage. They also provide optimal routing and well-defined mechanisms for quality of service (QoS).

- **BPX 8600 series**—The BPX 8600 series is the most widely deployed IP+ATM carrier switch. It uses leading-edge MPLS technology to provide the industry's most cost-effective backbone infrastructure for broadband, IP, and broadband/narrowband service delivery. Cisco's BPX 8600 series lets service providers cost-effectively deliver ATM, Frame Relay, SNA, voice, and circuit emulation services while simultaneously adding emerging services such as voice over IP, IP-based VPNs, managed intranets, and premium Internet services.

- **MGX 8800 series**—The Cisco MGX 8850 wide-area IP+ATM multiservice switch allows the delivery of a complete portfolio of differentiated service offerings while scaling to OC-48C/STM-16 speeds. Its deployment flexibility provides the agility for service providers to be first to market with the services that customers demand and to deploy IP-enabled ATM networks up to OC-48c/STM-16 speeds.

- **Private Network to Network Interface (PNNI) networking**—PNNI capabilities are provided across the BPX and MGX product lines. PNNI is the utilization of a single physical transport infrastructure to simultaneously provide several network services with different characteristics and quality requirements. This multiservice switching product line was designed and developed specifically for robust multiser-vice networking for the service provider market. Multiservice switching products have key networking capabilities, including superior forwarding, control, and management functions that put this product family in a class ahead of the competition.

- **Cisco WAN Manager (CWM)**—CWM is a high-performance element and network management product for service provider networks. Cisco WAN Manager resides at the element and network management layer of the Telecommunications Management Network (TMN) model and integrates with other Cisco applications, such as Cisco Info Center and Cisco Provisioning Center. These provide higher-level applications, such as Service-Level Agreement (SLA) functions, provisioning, fault performance, and accounting management. CWM manages the Cisco BPX Service Expansion Shelf

(SES) and the entire IP+ATM multiservice switch product line. CWM allows network operators to easily monitor usage, quickly provision connections, efficiently detect faults, configure devices, and track network statistics.

- **TransPath**—The Cisco TransPath Multiservice (MS) System is an integrated, cost-effective solution for MPLS, Frame Relay, ATM, packet voice, and circuit emulation services that enable a broad range of carrier applications, including network-based IP VPNs, DSL backhaul, and mobile wireless transport. The Cisco TransPath MS leverages Cisco Multiservice IP+ATM WAN Switches and Ecosystem partnerships to offer service providers a pre-engineered, multiservice, carrier-class WAN solution including products, training, and implementation services. Cisco TransPath MS is designed to offer broadband access providers, mobile wireless providers, and carriers that want to rapidly deploy network-based IP VPNs a fully configurable solution that is cost-effective, highly reliable, and expandable to a range of services and port densities.

PART II

Multiband Switch and Service Configuration

Chapter 2   IGX Product Overview and System Hardware

Chapter 3   IGX Node Administration, Trunks, and Lines

Chapter 4   Voice and Data Channels and Connections

Chapter 5   IGX Frame Relay Ports and Connections

Chapter 6   ATM Ports and Connections and ATM-to-Frame Relay Interworking

Chapter 7   Connection Routing, Synchronizing the Network, and Managing Jobs

Chapter 8   Troubleshooting

This chapter covers the following key topics:

- IGX System Hardware
- IGX Network, Trunks, and Lines
- IGX Message Formats
- Reliability Features
- IGX Cellbus
- Packet Flow

CHAPTER 2

IGX Product Overview and System Hardware

The IGX switch is part of the family of Cisco WAN switching products that can use a wide range of cards to provide a variety of services. The IGX 8400 series wide-area switch is a multiservice node with the flexibility of both narrow and broadband communication. It can interface with Asynchronous Transfer Mode (ATM) services, voice services, serial data services, High-Speed Serial Interface (HSSI) data services, and Frame Relay services.

This chapter examines the IGX switch, IGX card groups and their operation, and general IGX switch features and services.

IGX System Hardware

There are currently three types of IGX chassis: 8410, 8420, and 8430. The primary difference between them is the number of available card slots.

Node and card functionality, bus architecture, throughput, and management are identical among the three node types. Fan and power distribution can vary. Figure 2-1 shows the 8410 switch rack mount front view.

Figure 2-1   *8410 Rack Mount: Front View*

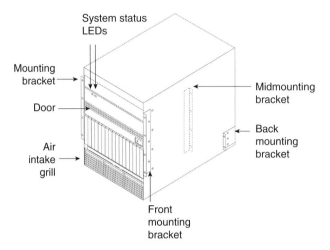

8410 Rack-Mount Chassis

The 8410 rack-mount chassis contains the following components:

- An eight-slot card shelf
- System status LEDs
- A front door with a tool-operated latch
- Air intake grill
- A backplane for plugging in the front and back cards
- A fan tray with four fans
- An exhaust plenum
- Power connections
- An optional AC power tray that holds up to four power supplies

The power supplied at the 8410 switch can be either AC or DC. Fans mounted in a fan tray cool the system. In an 8410 system, the fan tray resides immediately below the card cage. Each fan tray contains four fans. Figure 2-2 shows the 8410 switch rack mount rear view.

The 8410 is also available as a standalone system with cards, cabling, and power supplies installed in the cabinet. Four plastic feet support the 8410 standalone system as its base. No mounting brackets are on the cabinet.

Figure 2-2   *8410 Rack Mount: Rear View*

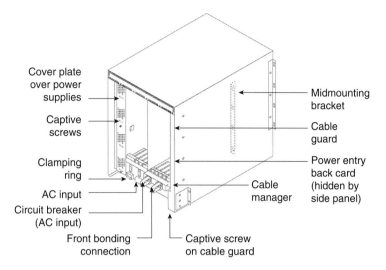

Cover plate
over power
supplies

Captive
screws

Clamping
ring

AC input

Circuit breaker
(AC input)

Front bonding
connection

Captive screw
on cable guard

Cable
manager

Midmounting
bracket

Cable
guard

Power entry
back card
(hidden by
side panel)

The rack-mount 8410 fits in a 19-inch (48.25 cm) rack with a minimum of 17.75 inches between rails. For mounting the chassis in a rack, brackets are attached to the front of the chassis. A pair of mounting brackets is attached at the back of the chassis after it is placed in the rack. Brackets for midrack mounting also come with the kit.

Because of the weight of the 8410 system, Cisco includes two temporary spacer brackets and a temporary-mounting bracket to help with the installation. These pieces are removed after installation. The temporary spacer brackets stabilize the rack, and the temporary-mounting bracket together with the spacer brackets creates a partial shelf onto which the installers can slide the node. These pieces support the system while installers secure the permanent front- and back-mounting brackets to the rack.

8420 Standalone Chassis

Figure 2-3 shows the 8420 Standalone front view.

The 8420 Standalone chassis contains the following components:

- A 16-slot card shelf
- A front door with a tool-operated latch
- A backplane for plugging in the front and back cards
- A main (lower) fan tray with six fans
- An exhaust plenum
- Power connections for the shelf
- An optional AC power tray that holds the power supplies

Figure 2-3   *8420 Standalone: Front View*

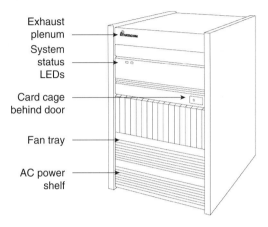

System status LEDs are visible on all IGX nodes with the front door open or closed. These LEDs indicate the current node alarm status, as follows:

- **Green**—No alarm
- **Yellow**—At least one minor alarm and no major alarms
- **Red**—At least one major alarm and possibly some minor alarms

With the front door open, the installed front card modules are visible.

Figure 2-4 shows the 8420 Standalone rear view.

Figure 2-4   *8420 Standalone: Rear View*

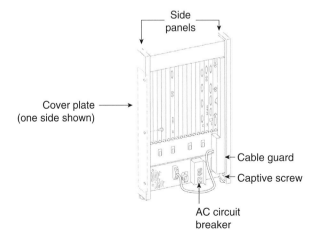

The 8420 Standalone system comes with four wheels at the base of the unit to allow it to be rolled into position. The unit also includes levelers. The 8420 standalone enclosure holds all the system modules, including the following:

- A backplane into which plug front cards, the System Clock Module (SCM), and the Power Entry Back Cards (PE-BCs)
- A fan tray with six fans
- An exhaust plenum
- An optional AC power tray that holds the power supplies

8430 Standalone Chassis

Figure 2-5 shows the 8430 Standalone front view.

Figure 2-5   *8430 Standalone: Front View*

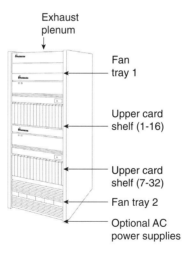

The 8430 Standalone chassis contains the following components:

- Two 16-slot card shelves
- Two front doors with tool-operated latches
- Two backplanes into which plug the front and back cards
- A main (lower) fan tray with six fans
- A booster (upper) fan tray
- An exhaust plenum
- Power connections for each shelf
- An optional AC power tray that holds up to six power supplies

Figure 2-6 shows the 8430 Standalone rear view.

Figure 2-6   *8430 Standalone: Rear View*

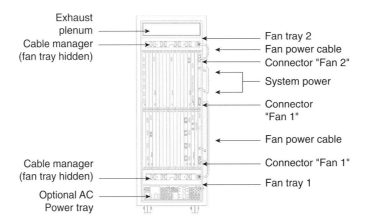

The 8430 Standalone enclosure holds all the system modules, including the following:

- Two backplanes, into which plug front cards, the SCM, and PE-BCs
- A main (lower) fan tray and a booster (upper) fan tray, each with six fans
- An exhaust plenum
- An optional AC power tray that holds up to six power supplies

IGX Cards

Each card slot supports a separate front card and back card. The *front card* contains the programming to support card services such as connection and routing tables and user traffic processing.

The *back card* provides the electrical or optical interface for one or more framed (E1, T1, J1, E3, T3, or OC-3c) or serial (EIA-232, V.35, HSSI, and so on) interfaces.

A front card communicates with its associated back card and with other front cards in the switch. The IGX features a midplane design to allow intercard communication.

IGX cards are organized into the following card groups:

- Processor card group
- Trunk card groups
- Voice card groups

- Data card groups
- Frame Relay card groups
- ATM card group

These groups are discussed in the following sections.

Processor Card Group

The processor card group includes the following front and back cards:

- The Nodal Processor Module (NPM) front card manages the switch and Cellbus, creates connections, and assigns routes. NPM cards are installed in slots 1 and 2.

  — The System Clock Module (SCM) back card offers Ethernet and EIA/TIA-232 connections for switch management and external clock interfaces. One SCM card can support one or two NPM front cards.

- The Alarm Relay Module (ARM) front card and the Alarm Relay Interface (ARI) back card signal alarm states to an external collection device.

Trunk Card Groups

The trunk card groups include the following front and back cards:

- The Network Trunk Module (NTM) front card receives FastPackets over the Cellbus and transports them to another IGX.

  — The NTM back cards support a single E1, T1, or Y1 framed circuit, or a "subrate" (SR) serial interface.

- The Universal Switching Module (UXM) front card acts as an ATM trunk card. The UXM can support up to 310 Mbps throughput.

  — The Universal ATM Interface (UAI) back card supports four or eight E1 or T1, three or six E3 or T3, or two or four OC-3c circuit interfaces.

NOTE   Switch software releases prior to Release 9.3 supported other trunk cards: the BTM and the ALM/B. Neither of these cards is supported in Release 9.3.00 (or later), so they are not included in this book.

Voice Card Groups

The voice card groups include the following front and back cards:

- The Universal Voice Module (UVM) front card receives pulse-code modulated (PCM) voice samples on individual DS-0 channels and converts them to FastPackets. The UVM supports adaptive differential pulse-code modulation (ADPCM), Conjugate Structure Algebraic Code Exited Linear Prediction (CS-ACELP), and low-delay CELP (LDCELP) voice compression.

  — The Universal Voice Interface (UVI) back card supports one or two E1, T1, or J1 framed circuits and one or two pass-through lines.

- The Channelized Voice Module (CVM) front card receives PCM voice samples on individual DS-0 channels and converts them to FastPackets. The CVM supports ADPCM voice compression.

  — The CVM back card supports a single E1, T1, or J1 framed circuit.

Data Card Groups

The data card groups include the following front and back cards:

- The High-Speed Data Module (HDM) front card converts a transparent data bit stream to FastPackets. The HDM has a throughput of up to 1.344 Mbps per interface.

  — The Synchronous Data Interface (SDI) back card supports four EIA-232, V.35, or EIA-449/X.21 serial interfaces.

- The Low-Speed Data Module (LDM) front card converts a transparent data bit stream to FastPackets. The LDM has a throughput of up to 56 Kbps per interface on a four-port LDI or 19.2 Kbps on an eight-port LDI.

- The Low-Speed Data Interface (LDI) back card supports either four or eight EIA-232 serial interfaces.

Frame Relay Card Groups

The Frame Relay card groups include the following front and back cards:

- The Universal Frame Relay Module (UFM) front card converts Frame Relay frames to FastPackets. The UFM has a throughput of 16 Mbps per card. Channelized (UFM-C, or simply UFM) and unchannelized (UFM-U) versions of this card are available.

  — The Universal Frame Relay Interface (UFI) back cards for use with the UFM-C provide eight E1 or T1 (channelized) lines. Either four or eight of the lines can be activated, depending on the UFM front card used.

— The Universal Frame Relay Interface (UFI) back cards for use with the UFM-U provide six interfaces, each of which provides two serial (unchannelized) V.35 or X.21 ports (using a special "splitter" cable). If no splitter cable is used, only one port per interface can be used. Also, a UFI provides four serial (unchannelized) HSSI ports.

- The Frame Relay Module (FRM) front card converts Frame Relay frames to FastPackets. The FRM-2 supports Frame Relay connections to the PCS port concentrator.

  — The Frame Relay Interface (FRI) back card supports one E1 or T1 (channelized) line or four serial (unchannelized) interfaces.

ATM Card Group

The ATM card group includes the UXM front card. Beginning with Release 9.2.20, the UXM supports trunks and lines simultaneously.

- The Universal Switching Module (UXM) front card maps incoming ATM cells to trunk cells. The UXM supports constant bit rate (CBR), non-real-time variable bit rate (NRT-VBR), real-time variable bit rate (RT-VBR), unspecified bit rate (UBR), and available bit rate (ABR) traffic types with a rich set of ATM connection features.

  — The Universal ATM Interface (UAI) back card supports four or eight E1 or T1 lines, three or six E3 or T3 lines, or two or four OC-3c lines.

NOTE Switch software releases prior to Release 9.3 supported another ATM port card group: the ALM/A. This card is not supported in Release 9.3.00 (or later), so it is not included in this book.

IGX Power Supplies

The IGX power supply features, illustrated in Figure 2-7, include -48V DC to all the card modules in the node. They can be installed or removed without disrupting power to the node. All installed power supplies share the total load equally.

AC Power

AC power can be used to power an IGX node. AC power supplies require an AC power tray to hold the supplies. The 8430 and 8420 AC power tray is a separate shelf installed below the node fan assembly that holds up to six power supplies. The 8410 AC power tray is installed vertically next to the card shelf.

Figure 2-7   *IGX Power Supplies*

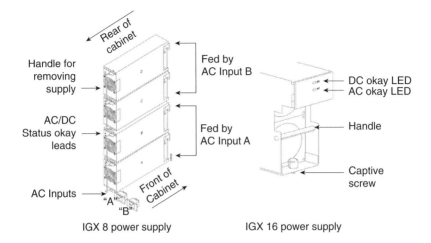

IGX 8 power supply   IGX 16 power supply

The DC output from the AC power tray is plugged into the AC Power Entry Module (PEM) that is installed on the right side of the back card shelf. All necessary PEM internal wiring and installation are done at the factory.

AC input between 180 and 264V is supported.

DC Power

DC power does not require a separate power tray or power supplies. A DC PEM is installed in the node, and the DC input is directly wired to the PEM.

All IGX card groups consist of a front card and a back card. In most cases, the front card runs the necessary firmware to process traffic and perform other functions. Back cards interface with any attached facilities and perform tasks such as line framing and line alarm detection.

IGX Network, Trunks, and Lines

A typical IGX network consists of multiple geographically dispersed nodes and interconnects using high-speed digital trunks. The IGX brings in user traffic on multiplexed access lines or serial interfaces and transports digital voice, transparent data, Frame Relay, and ATM user traffic. The IGX can be integrated with BPX and MGX equipment.

This chapter assigns specific meanings to terms such as *trunk* and *line*. A *trunk* is a circuit connecting IGX switches that form the backbone IGX network. It is typically a framed

Cisco IGX carrier circuit such as E1 or T1. Trunks carry user traffic and control and topology information between IGX switches.

Lines connect user equipment to the IGX. They are framed carrier circuits such as E1 or T1, carrying user traffic and user-to-network signaling where appropriate. User equipment can also connect to the IGX via serial interfaces.

All nodes, trunks, lines, ports, and connections in an IGX network can be managed from any switch using a technique called *virtual terminal (VT)*. (VT is discussed in Chapter 3, "IGX Node Administration, Trunks, and Lines.")

Multiple, simultaneous command-line access allows several operators to look at one or more switches at the same time using direct access methods (control and auxiliary ports), VT sessions, or Telnet sessions.

In an IGX network, network management platforms include terminal or PC with VT100 emulation directly connected or dialing into a control or auxiliary port, a LAN-connected PC or workstation using Telnet, and a UNIX workstation running Cisco WAN Manager network management software.

IGX Message Formats

For voice, data, and Frame Relay, the IGX front card places the traffic in proprietary FastPackets. Both locally-switched and remotely-switched traffic is converted to FastPackets. Figure 2-8 is a simplistic presentation of IGX message format conversion.

UXM cards support both ATM lines and trunks. If the ATM traffic stream originates and terminates at UXM cards, the user cells may be mapped into trunk cells without conversion to FastPackets. However, if the connection is routed through any non-UXM trunk card, the cells must be transported within FastPackets.

FastPacket Format

The 24-byte FastPacket shown in Figure 2-9 is unique to Cisco networks. A fixed-length packet or cell requires less processing to switch. In addition, cells facilitate predictable queuing, which results in low end-to-end delay variation, making them ideal for time-dependent traffic such as voice and synchronous data.

Every FastPacket has at least a 3-byte header. Some FastPackets have a 4- or 5-byte header. All FastPackets contain a 16-bit address field used to identify the connection across each IGX. The address is locally significant and might change as the packet is routed through the network. However, the packet address on each node or trunk is unique to each connection.

Figure 2-8   *IGX Message Formats*

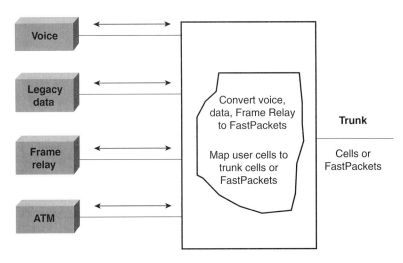

Figure 2-9   *FastPacket Format*

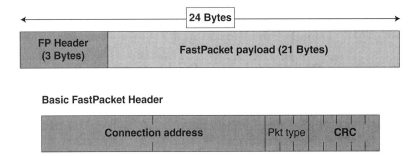

The 3-bit *packet type* identifies one of the following connection types:

- **High priority**—Control and management traffic between IGX processors.
- **Non-time-stamped data**—High-speed transparent data traffic, voice traffic without voice activity detection (VAD), and ATM traffic over FastPacket trunks.
- **Time-stamped data**—Low-speed transparent data traffic.
- **Voice**—Voice traffic with VAD.
- **Bursty data A**—Frame Relay traffic without ForeSight control features.
- **Bursty data B**—Frame Relay traffic with ForeSight control features.

The 5-bit *cyclic redundancy check* (CRC) is calculated on the FastPacket header only and is used to confirm that this information is error-free. Any packet with an error in the header is discarded.

All cards in the Processor card group, the Voice card groups, the Data card groups, and the Frame Relay card groups generate *only* FastPackets.

The various FastPacket types that are identified by the 3-bit FastPacket type field are as follows:

- **000**—Not used
- **001**—Not used
- **010**—Real-time VBR (RT-VBR) (this is the same as the Voice type in earlier releases of the software)
- **011**—Bursty Data B (BdataB)
- **100**—High Priority
- **101**—Bursty Data A (BdataA)
- **110**—Non-Time-Stamped data (NTS)
- **111**—Time-Stamped data (TS)

Some packet types might have additional control information in the fourth or fifth byte, thereby decreasing the payload length.

ATM and STI Cell Formats

ATM-capable trunks may use either standard ATM or special STI cell headers. Chapter 9, "BPX Product Overview and System Hardware," explains the ATM and STI cell formats.

Reliability Features

The IGX supports 1:1 card redundancy for processor, trunk, and service cards. If it is used, one card is active and the second is a hot standby.

The IGX nodes support any trunk topology. No single trunk is typically vital to the network, which allows the network to remain stable even if a trunk fails. However, if *all* trunks to a node fail, the switch becomes unreachable, affecting service and administrative flows.

The network configuration data is distributed to all nodes as network changes occur. Every node has knowledge of network characteristics, including node names, trunk characteristics, trunk bandwidth allocation, node alarm status, network synchronization sources, and user IDs and passwords.

NPM Card Redundancy

The IGX Nodal Processor Modules (NPMs) have redundancy when two processors are installed. One is always active, and the second is a hot standby.

A single System Clock Module (SCM) back card accesses both active and standby NPM cards. The SCM card contains control and auxiliary port EIA/TIA-232 connectors, a LAN port, and external clock interfaces.

Y-Cable Redundancy

Trunk, voice, data, Frame Relay, and ATM cards may be optionally configured for Y-cable redundancy. Active and standby cards used for Y-cable redundancy are illustrated in Figure 2-10.

Figure 2-10 *Y-Cable Redundancy*

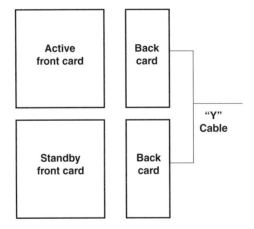

The **addyred** command adds Y-cable redundancy to a front card. Any configuration change or connection added to the active card is automatically communicated to the standby card.

Automatic Fault-Management Features

All the following fault-management features are automatic and do not require operator intervention:

- **Hardware diagnostics**—Background and self-tests are periodically run on the hardware modules.

- **Card and bus switchover**—If redundancy is provided, a standby card or bus takes over in case of failure on the active card or bus.

- **Trunk diagnostics**—Tests whether the node can communicate with the neighbor nodes that send and receive FastPackets. Trunks are point-to-point.

- **Dynamic rerouting**—Performed by the node when a connection fails due to a network outage.

- **Alarm reporting**—Automatically informs all nodes of node or network alarm status and can provide alarm or event information to network management devices (StrataView Plus, command-line interface, or printers).

Fault Management

As connections are added, the local IGX checks the trunk load model for routes to the destination switch, available bandwidth, and queuing resources. If the selected route fails, the IGX automatically attempts to find an alternate route and move the connection to the new route. Figure 2-11 illustrates fault management on the IGX.

Figure 2-11 *Fault Management*

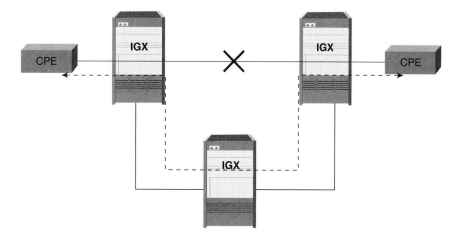

Bandwidth Management Features

IGX bandwidth management features include Voice Activity Detection (VAD), voice compression techniques, and Data Frame Multiplexing (DFM):

- **Voice activity detection (VAD)**—Configurable silence suppression on incoming voice traffic.

- Available voice compression techniques are adaptive differential pulse code modulation (ADPCM), Conjugate Structure Algebraic Code Exited Linear Prediction (CS-ACELP), and low-delay CELP (LDCELP).

- **Data Frame Multiplexing (DFM)**—Repetitive pattern suppression on transparent data up to 128 Kbps.

- Transmission of frames without intervening idle flags for Frame Relay traffic.

- Transport of cells, discarding idle cells for ATM services.

IGX Cellbus

The IGX Cellbus is a time-division multiplexed bus. The NPM allocates Cellbus time slots to front cards based on the card type, interface type and speed, connection rates, and so on. A front card may transmit only during its time slots.

To receive traffic from the bus, all cards monitor *all* bus time slots and compare the FastPacket or cell address field with their RAM-based routing tables. If the address of a packet is listed in the card's routing table, the card retrieves the packet from the bus and processes it.

For example, a UVM card creates FastPackets from an incoming voice stream. These packets are placed on the Cellbus in any of the time slots allocated to that card. The trunk card that forwards the packet to the next switch has the packet address in its own routing table. When the trunk card sees the packet, it pulls it off the bus and puts it in the appropriate traffic queue to be sent across the trunk. When the remote trunk card packet arrives at the remote trunk card, it places the packet on the bus. The process continues in this fashion until the packet reaches the destination card group, where it is disassembled and sent to the end user.

NOTE   NPM processors are not involved with user traffic flow after the connection is routed. Other buses are the timing bus, switch synchronization bus, and power distribution bus.

Cellbus Lanes

The Cellbus is organized into A and B bus structures. The two buses provide active/standby redundant services for each other. Only one bus is active at a time.

Both A and B buses are divided into five lanes: Four 256 Mbps lanes carry traffic, and the fifth lane serves as a standby lane for the other four. Lane 1 carries cells or FastPacket traffic, and lanes 2 through 4 carry ATM cells. All cards other than the UXM transmit and receive FastPackets across lane 1 during their time slots; they cannot use the other lanes. Figure 2-12 illustrates Cellbus operations.

Figure 2-12 *Cellbus Lanes*

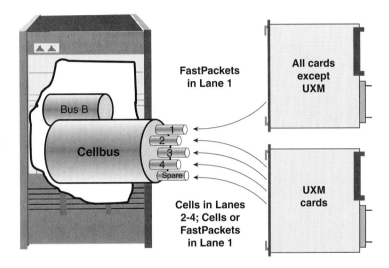

If a UXM card is communicating with another UXM card on the same switch, it can transmit ATM cells in all four lanes during that time slot.

Packet Flow

Packet flow includes voice, data, and Frame Relay traffic, as described in this section.

Voice Packet Flow

As voice traffic is received from the user equipment, the UVM card may remove silent intervals or apply voice compression to the traffic received from the private branch exchange (PBX) or channel bank. NPM cards are shown in Figure 2-13 to demonstrate connection setup. NPM processors are not involved with user traffic.

Figure 2-13 *Voice Packet Flow*

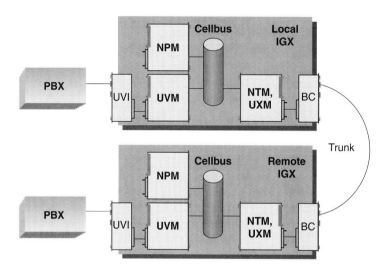

Data Packet Flow

Data packet flow is illustrated in Figure 2-14. For data connections below 128 Kbps, a bandwidth efficiency technique called Data Frame Multiplexing (DFM) can remove repetitive bit patterns.

Figure 2-14 *Data Packet Flow*

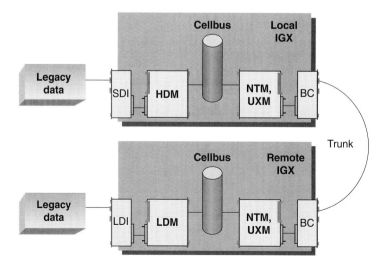

NOTE	The NPM cards are required for connection setup.

Frame Relay

Frame Relay frames are converted to FastPackets to travel over the Cellbus, as illustrated in Figure 2-15. ATM trunks can perform a complex gateway function to remove the FastPacket headers and carry the Frame Relay frames directly on top of ATM Adaptation Layer 5 (AAL5) messages.

Figure 2-15 *Frame Relay Packet Flow*

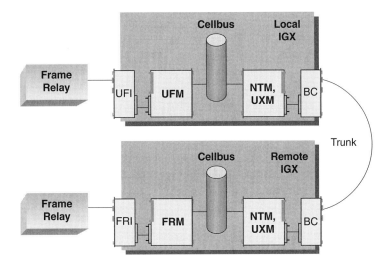

Frame Relay: Two Hops

Figure 2-16 shows a Frame Relay connection routed through an intermediate switch. Each trunk card must check the incoming FastPacket or cell stream, compare the connection address with the trunk card connection table, and forward to the next card.

Figure 2-16 *Frame Relay Flow: Two Hops*

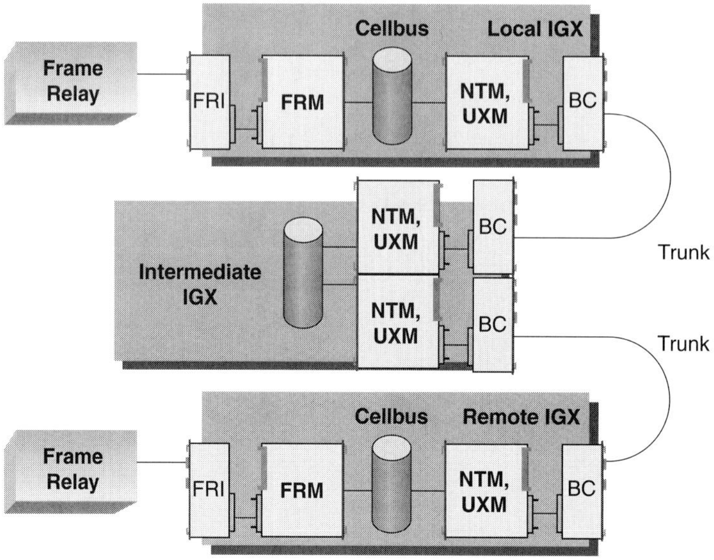

NOTE   NPM cards are required for connection setup.

ATM Connections

ATM connection traffic may travel over FastPacket or cell trunks. For all trunks except UXM trunks, the ATM cell is divided into three FastPackets and carried as a FastPacket stream. Connections between UXM line cards may optionally request *trunk cell routing restrict*. When enabled, the connection must be routed across UXM trunks only. Figure 2-17 illustrates the ATM connection flow.

Frame Relay-to-ATM Interworking

UXM, UFM, and FRM cards support network and service interworking connections between Frame Relay and ATM interfaces, as illustrated in Figure 2-18. Interworking ATM and Frame Relay is described in greater detail in Chapter 6, "ATM Ports and Connections: ATM-to-Frame Relay Interworking."

Figure 2-17 *ATM Connections*

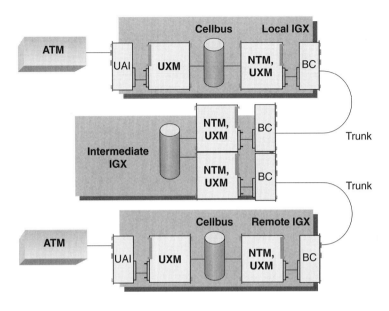

Figure 2-18 *Frame Relay-to-ATM Interworking*

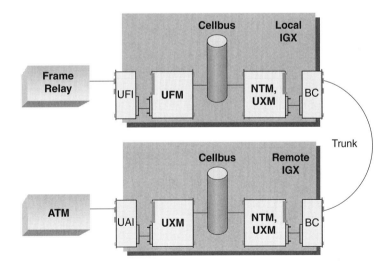

NOTE   NPM cards are required for connection setup.

Summary

This chapter provided an overview of the IGX WAN switch and described its basic capabilities, service types, and features. You were also introduced to the basic FastPacket format and components.

The IGX cards and their functions were presented in detail. You should understand these cards and card groups and be able to describe the transport of traffic on the Cellbus and the traffic flow process in an IGX network.

Review Questions

1   What characteristic of cell or FastPacket traffic results in lower network delay?

2   The IGX supports what kinds of services?

3   The IGX converts incoming voice, data, and Frame Relay user traffic into what?

4   What are circuits between IGX switches called?

5   Which IGX reliability features protect against hardware and network failures?

6   List the five automatic fault-management features of IGX switches.

7   Why is it important to know which node is the "owner" of a connection?

8   The originating end card _____ the incoming data, and the receiving card _____ .

9   The Cellbus is what kind of bus?

This chapter covers the following key topics:

- IGX Access
- Logging into the Network
- Privilege Levels and IGX Entry Methods
- IGX Commands
- Trunk Definition and Types
- ATM Cell Payloads
- IGX Trunks
- Line Definition

CHAPTER 3

IGX Node Administration, Trunks, and Lines

This chapter introduces the command-line interface (CLI) and covers the commands that enable basic node configuration and administration. It introduces the concept of trunks and lines on the Cisco IGX. It also describes the trunk configuration parameters that are available on the various types of trunk cards and line configuration parameters that are available on the various types of lines.

IGX Access

IGX access methods include the control port, auxiliary port, and LAN port, as described in the following paragraphs. After you gain access to the CLI, you have the option of browsing, configuring, and administering the IGX nodes, depending on your established privilege level, as described in the section "Privilege Levels and IGX Entry Methods."

Control Port

The control port is an EIA/TIA-232 DCE interface on the System Clock Module (SCM). Initially, the control port is the only means available to access the node. A dumb terminal or PC running a VT100 emulation program may be used to communicate with the node through this interface.

The control port may also be connected to a modem configured with auto-answer for remote access.

The default settings for the Control Port are 9600 baud, 8 data bits, 1 stop bit, and no parity.

Auxiliary Port

The auxiliary port provides a second EIA/TIA DCE interface for the VT100 terminal, modem, or printer access.

The default settings for the auxiliary port are 9600 baud, 8 data bits, 1 stop bit, and no parity.

LAN Port

The LAN port allows the node to communicate with other devices (PCs, workstations, and so on) across an Ethernet LAN. The LAN port is an Attachment Unit Interface (AUI) for use with an Ethernet LAN. A LAN transceiver must be plugged into this interface.

The initial configuration for this interface is accomplished through the control port using the CLI.

Cisco WAN Manager (CWM) workstations connected to the LAN port may communicate with other IGX, BPX, or MGX nodes through IP Relay.

IP Relay is a method to propagate IP traffic (Telnet, Simple Network Management Protocol [SNMP], TFTP, and so on) across IGX trunks.

Logging into the Network

Logging into the network is a two-step process requiring the entry of both a user ID and a password. The system administrator can provide a user ID and password for the network. Any user can maintain a lower privilege level as soon as he or she is on the network. After a password is assigned, a user can change the password. For security reasons, users should periodically change their passwords. Example 3-1 shows the Enter User ID prompt.

Example 3-1 *Logging into the Network*

```
igx1   TRM   No User   IGX 8420   9.2.20      July 29 1999 07:02 CDT


Enter User ID:
```

Entering a user ID and password gives you access at a particular level of user privilege. User IDs may have up to 12 characters; passwords may have up to 15 characters.

For initial sign-on, enter the user ID and password you have been assigned when prompted. The password does not appear on the screen. Upon correct user ID and password entry, the login is recorded in the event log.

When your login is accepted by the system, the "Next Command" prompt appears. The system is ready for command entry.

The **bye** command ends the current session from the local node. When the local connection ends, the "Enter User ID" prompt appears.

Command-Line Interface Screen

After you log into the switch, you see a command-line interface that prompts you to enter a command, as shown in Figure 3-1.

Figure 3-1   *IGX CLI*

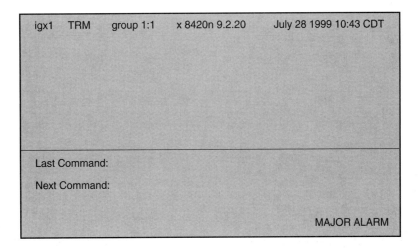

```
igx1    TRM      group 1:1      x 8420n 9.2.20      July 28 1999 10:43 CDT













Last Command:

Next Command:


                                                                    MAJOR ALARM
```

The screen is divided into two sections. The top two-thirds of the screen contains display information. The bottom third is the command area. It provides a command prompt and any system responses associated with entering commands, such as error messages and appropriate parameter values.

After login, the screen provides the following information (clockwise from the upper-left corner):

- Node name
- Access method:
  - TRM—Control or auxiliary port direct access
  - VT—Virtual terminal from another node
  - TN—Telnet from the LAN port or using IP Relay
- User ID and privilege level

- Node type
- System software release
- System date and time
- Local time zone
- Network alarm status
- Next Command—Command line
- Last Command—Previous command

Table 3-1 shows a number of keyboard shortcuts that may be used, depending on the terminal emulation software running on your workstation.

Table 3-1   *Command-Line Interface Shortcuts*

Key Sequence	Action
Ctrl-B	Moves the cursor left one word.
Ctrl-F	Moves the cursor right one word.
Ctrl-L	Moves the cursor right one character.
Ctrl-G	Moves the cursor left one character.
Arrow keys	Moves the cursor in the direction of the arrow.
Ctrl-W	Deletes a character.
character-Delete	Deletes a character.
Ctrl-H	Moves the cursor left one character and deletes that character.
Ctrl-D	Deletes all characters from the cursor to the end of the line.
Ctrl-X	Deletes a line.
Backspace	Moves the cursor left one character and deletes that character.
Ctrl-I	Toggles insert mode (Tab and *character*-Insert do the same).
Ctrl-^	Inserts a line.
*	Leaves the parameter as is and goes to the next field.
Delete	Aborts the command.
Ctrl-M	Carriage return (Return does the same).
Ctrl-S	Stops the data flow from the node to the terminal screen.
Ctrl-Q	Restarts the flow of data to the terminal.
!(...)	The exclamation mark followed by the first character or characters of a command brings that command back to the command line.

Syntax

A command is a single word made up of a combination of abbreviated verbs and nouns. Commands are followed by required and optional parameters. Parameters are separated by spaces.

The **help** command provides the syntax for each command, including the parameters, both required and optional. This book uses angle brackets (< >) to indicate required parameters and square brackets ([ ]) to indicate optional parameters. You do not enter these indicators when issuing the command.

Privilege Levels and IGX Entry Methods

The following sections describe user command privilege levels and IGX CLI entry methods. Entry methods on the IGX include direct entry and menu-driven.

IGX Privilege Levels

Each command falls into a range of command privilege levels. When a user ID is created, it is assigned a privilege level and can issue only commands that are allowed by that level and less-privileged levels.

For example, user levels 1 or 2 may issue the **addcon** command. If you are assigned a user ID that has privilege level 3, you cannot use the **addcon** command.

The following are the command privilege levels above user privilege level 1:

- **StrataCom**—Cisco product engineering personnel
- **Service**—Cisco and partner support personnel
- **SuperUser**—Network administrator

These levels exist above levels 1 to 6 (in order) and can issue all level 1 commands, as well as other commands that are not covered in this book.

Direct Entry

The direct-entry method is most often used for commands that have limited required parameters or when optional parameters are needed. The command is followed on the command line by each parameter value, in order according to syntax, and separated by spaces.

When you type the command only and then press the **Return** or **Enter** key, the system prompts you for the next required parameter. The prompts continue until you have entered appropriate values for all the required parameters. IGX does not prompt you for optional parameters.

Menu-Driven

Pressing the Esc key displays a menu-driven command interface. You can highlight menu choices using the arrow keys and make selections using the **Return** or **Enter** key. When you select a command, the command is issued, and prompts for any required parameters are provided. You can then get a list of all the commands that are available from each individual menu choice. Note that typing **help** or **?** without any other parameters also gives you menus.

In all cases, you must enter appropriate values for all parameters. The system edits and reprompts you for any invalid responses. It does not complete the process until an appropriate value is provided. To abort a command, use the Delete key or an equivalent sequence such as Shift-Delete, depending on your terminal setup.

IGX Commands

The commands discussed in this section are used on the IGX switch.

help Command

After you are logged into the system, you can request information on the commands you want to use with the **help** command. The **help** or **?** command entered without any qualifiers displays the screen shown in Example 3-2. You can use the arrow keys to highlight one of the categories and then select that category by pressing the **Enter** or **Return** key. A list of commands specific to that category is returned. You may use the arrow keys to scroll through the list and select the command you want to use. Note that the Esc key also displays the screen shown in Example 3-2.

Example 3-2   **help** *Command Output*

```
igx1    TRM    group4:1    IGX 8420    9.2.20    July 30 1999 06:50 CDT

All commands fall into one (or more) of the following categories:

Control Terminal
Configuration
Lines
Network
Connections
Cards
Alarms and Failures



This Command: help
Use cursor keys to select category and then hit <RETURN> key
```

Entering **help** or **?** followed by a space and either part of a command or the full command returns information on that command, including the following:

- A short description of the command
- An indication of whether the command can be used in a job
- The command syntax
- Required or optional prompts

You use the **help** command to display command information and syntax.

NOTE   Only commands available to the current user (based on the privilege level) are shown in the help screens.

---

dspcds Command

The **dspcds** command is used to display summary information on all the front and back cards installed on the IGX. For 8430 models, slots 1 through 16 are displayed. Responding **y** to the Continue prompt displays slots 17 through 32. The **dspcds** command output is shown in Example 3-3.

Example 3-3   **dspcds** *Output*

```
igx1              TN      group1:1          IGX 8420   9.2.20    Aug. 26 1999 19:26 G+03
FrontCard
BackCard                  FrontCard  BackCard
    Type Rev Type    Rev   Status   Type Rev  Type
Rev Status
1  NPM   EFP               Active    9  FTM   CKB  FPC-X21 AC  Standby
2  NPM   EFP
Standby   10 NTM    FDH    SR       AH  Active
3  UVM   EFB E1-2   AB     Standby  11  NTM   FDH
E1        AN  Active
4  UVM   EFB E1-2   AB     Standby  12  NTM   FDH   T1      AL  Active
5
HDM   CFF RS449  AV    Active    13  UXM   BAD  T1-IMA  AA  Active
6  UFMU CKA X21    AB
Standby   14 UXM    BAD    E1-IMA   AA  Active
7  UFM   CJA T1D   AB     Standby  15  UXM   BAD
T3        AA  Active
8  UFM   CLA E1D   AB     Standby  16  UXM   BAD  E3      AA  Active

Last Command: dspcds
Next Command:
```

The following information is displayed:

- **Front card type**
- **Card revision**—Three characters indicating the following:

  — Model—The model is associated with the firmware on the card. It can be changed only by Cisco or its partners.

  — Hardware revision

  — Firmware revision—A variation on the model to incorporate feature enhancements. Burning new firmware into the card can change the firmware revision.

- **Back card type**
- **Back card revision**—Model and hardware revision, neither of which can be modified.
- **Status**—Possible card status descriptions are defined in the next section.

Here is the **dspcds** command syntax:

```
dspcds
```

Card Status

Table 3-2 describes possible card states.

Table 3-2   *Card States*

State	Description
Active	Card in use; no failure.
Active-T	Card in use; self-test in progress.
Active-F	Card in use; self-test failed.
Active-F-T	Card in use; minor failures detected; self-test in progress.
Standby	Card idle; no failures.
Standby-T	Card idle; self-test in progress.
Standby-F	Card idle; self-test failure.
Standby-F-T	Card idle; self-test failure; self-test in progress.
Failed	Card failed.
Down	Card downed by user.
Down-T	Card downed; self-test in progress.
Down-F	Card downed; self-test failure.
Down-F-T	Card downed; self-test failure; self-test in progress.

Table 3-2   *Card States (Continued)*

State	Description
Mismatch	Mismatch between front card and back card.
Update	Standby NPM being updated by active processor card.
Locked	Incompatible revision of old software being maintained, if needed.
Dnlding	Downloading new system software from adjacent node or workstation.
Dnldr	Downloading software and configuration from active processor card.
Empty	The expected front card is not present.
Empty reserved for NPM	The expected NPM is not present.
Missing	An active front card has been removed or has failed.
Empty Universal Backplane	Indicates the slot is empty or the front card was recently removed.

dspcd Command

The **dspcd** command screen provides detailed information on a particular card, as shown in Example 3-4.

Example 3-4   **dspcd** *Output*

```
igx1           TN     group1:1       IGX 8420  9.2.20    Aug. 26 1999 19:27 G+03

Detailed Card Display for UXM in slot 13

Status:          Active           (Front Card Supports Virtual Trunks)
Revision:        BAD              (Front Card Supports OAMLpbk & TrfcGen)
Serial Number:   226584           (Front Card Supports SIW, CGW, CellFwd)
Fab Number:      28-2164-02       (Front Card Supports Hot Standby)
Backplane Installed               (Front Card Supports Traffic Shaping)
Backcard Installed                (Front Card Supports IMA Compliance)
Type:            T1-IMA          (Front Card Supports ChanStat Level 1)
Revision:        AA              (Front Card Supports 8000 Channels)
Serial Number: 237369            (Front Card Supports 8191 RCMP Entries)
Ports:           8

Last Command: dspcd 13

Next Command:
```

The information provided depends on the card type and may include the following:

- Front and back card serial numbers
- Card failure type
- Card features
- Port types (DCE/DTE)
- Memory size for network processor cards
- Software revision

Here is the **dspcd** command syntax:

```
dspcd
```

dsppwr Command

The **dsppwr** command screen provides information about environmental measurements that are made by the node, as shown in Example 3-5.

Example 3-5   dsppwr *Output*

```
igx1             TN     group6:1      IGX 8420   9.2.20    Aug. 27 1999 13:24 CDT

Power Supply Status                                    Cabinet Temperature

Monitor Rev AT, Ser # 221487   -  Status: Active           25          77

    AC Supply     Status                        C   60  ¦  ¦  140  F
A   1  Present    OK                            e          ¦  ¦       a
B   1  Present    OK                            n   50  ¦--¦  122  h
C   1  Present    OK                            t          ¦  ¦       r
D   1  Empty                                    i   40  ¦  ¦  104  e
E   1  Empty                                    g          ¦  ¦       n
F   1  Empty                                    r   30  ¦  ¦   86  h
                                                a          ¦  ¦       e
                                                d   20  ¦  ¦   68  i
                                                e       '--'          t


Last Command: dsppwr


Next Command:
```

Environmental measurements for the **dsppwr** command include the following:

- Monitor status, revision, and serial number
- Power supply type

- Power supply status
- Cabinet temperature in degrees centigrade and Fahrenheit
- Temperature alarm threshold

Here is the **dsppwr** command syntax:

```
dsppwr
```

cnfpwd Command

When you enter the **cnfpwd** command, the software prompts you for the current password (Enter current password:). When you enter the correct current password, the program prompts you for the new password (Enter new password:). When you enter the new password, you are prompted to enter the new password again (Retype new password:). At this point, the screen should clear and prompt you for another command. The **cnfpwd** command is shown in Example 3-6.

Example 3-6   cnfpwd *Output*

```
igx1            TRM    group7:1        IGX 8420 9.2.20      July 29 1999 17:41 CDT




Last Command:

Next Command: cnfpwd
```

Here is the **cnfpwd** command syntax:

```
cnfpwd
```

NOTE   To ensure the security of your system, you should change your password on a regular basis.

dsppwd Command

The **dsppwd** command displays the password of the current user ID or any user at a lower privilege level. The password is displayed for only a short time. The **dsppwd** command is shown in Example 3-7.

Example 3-7 dsppwd *Output*

```
igx1          TN     group6:1        IGX 8420  9.2.20    Aug. 27 1999 13:25 CDT



The password for group12 is newuser



This Command: dsppwd group12

This screen will self-destruct in ten seconds
Enter User ID: group12
```

Here is the **dsppwd** command syntax:

> **dsppwd** *<userid>*

cnfdate and cnftime Commands

The **cnfdate** and **cnftime** commands (**cnftime** sets the network-wide time, but only after it was initially set by **cnfdate**) allow the system administrator to modify the date and time of the node (switch) connected to. If the node is part of a network, these changes are propagated network-wide. The **cnfdate** command is shown in Example 3-8.

Example 3-8 cnfdate *Output*

```
igx1            TRM    group7:1       IGX 8420 9.2.20  July 30 1999 08:11 CDT


This Command: cnfdate


Enter Year:
```

You should always set the time zone before setting the time in order to prevent erroneous times from being set.

Here is the **cnfdate** command syntax:

> **cnfdate** *<year> <month> <day> <hour> <minute> <second>*

Here is the **cnftime** command syntax:

> **cnftime** *<hour> <minute> <second>*

cnftmzn Command

The **cnftmzn** command modifies the local time zone for this node only. Enter **?** when prompted to see a list of time zones.

Here is the **cnftmzn** command syntax:

```
cnftmzn <timezone | g+/-hours>
```

cnfterm Command

The **cnfterm** command configures the Control or Auxiliary ports to work with your equipment, as shown in Example 3-9.

Example 3-9 **cnfterm** *Output*

```
igx1            TRM     group7:1        IGX 8420 9.2.20   July 30 1999 08:29 CDT


Control port                          Auxiliary port

Baud Rate:          9600              Baud Rate:          9600

Parity:             None              Parity:             None
Number of Data Bits: 8                Number of Data Bits: 8
Number of Stop Bits: 1                Number of Stop Bits: 1
Output flow control: XON/XOFF         Output flow control: XON/XOFF
Input flow control:  XON/XOFF         Input flow control:  XON/XOFF
CTS flow control:    No               CTS flow control:    Yes
Use DTR signal:      Yes              Use DTR signal:      Yes



This Command: cnfterm

Select Control port (c) or Auxiliary port (a):
```

Here is the **cnfterm** command syntax:

```
cnfterm <a | c> <baud rate> <parity> <data bits> <stop bits>
   <output flow control> <input flow control> <CTS flow control>
   <use DTR signal>
```

Table 3-3 describes the parameters associated with the **cnfterm** command.

Table 3-3 **cnfterm** *Command Parameter Descriptions*

Parameter	Description	Required/Optional
a | c	Auxiliary or Control port	Required
baud rate	Port speed in bits per second	Required

continues

Table 3-3 **cnfterm** *Command Parameter Descriptions (Continued)*

Parameter	Description	Required/Optional
parity	Even, odd, or no parity	Required
data bits	7 or 8 data bits per character	Required
stop bits	Stop bits per character	Required
output flow control	XON, XOFF, or no flow control	Required
input flow control	XON, XOFF, or no flow control	Required
CTS flow control	Asserts CTS in response to a DTE RTS signal	Required
use DTR signal	Allows communication only if the DTE asserts a DTR signal	Required

dsptermfunc Command

The **dsptermfunc** command displays the current functions of the Control and Auxiliary ports, as shown in Example 3-10.

Example 3-10 dsptermfunc *Output*

```
igx1            TRM   group7:1      IGX 8420 9.2.20   July 30 1999 09:51 CDT


Control port                        Auxiliary port

1. VT100/Cisco StrataView            1. Okidata 182 Printer
2. VT100                             2. Okidata 182 Printer with LOG
3. External Device Window            3. VT100
                                     4. Alarm Message Collector
                                     5. External Device Window $$$
                                     6. Autodial Modem



Last Command: dsptermfunc


Next Command:
```

You learned how to connect to the node earlier in this chapter, and you just saw how to use the **cnfterm** command to configure the Control or Auxiliary ports to work with your equipment. The following information is displayed for the Control port:

- Control terminal
- Direct-dial modem
- External EIA/TIA-232 device

The following information is displayed for the Auxiliary port:

- Printer
  - Print screens (**prtscrn**) and other information (**prtrts**, **prttrkerrs**, and so on)
  - With or without a network log
- VT100 emulation for command-line interface
- Alarm message collector
  - Receives ASCII messages from intelligent devices
  - Date- and time-stamps a message and puts in a local and network log
  - Creates a minor alarm
  - May have an auto-answer modem
- External device window
  - Bidirectional communications with intelligent device
  - VT100 emulation
  - Accessed using the **window** command
  - Use the character string (for example, **$$$**) to escape from the external device and return to the IGX command-line interface
- Dial-out modem
  - Dials out when the network alarm status changes
  - Posts the date and time, network name, and alarm status

Three print options are available on the IGX:

- **Local**—Prints to a printer attached to the local auxiliary port.
- **Remote**—Prints to the printer attached to a specified node auxiliary port.
- **None**—No print capability.

cnfprt Command

To configure print modes, use the **cnfprt** command. The command output is shown in Example 3-11.

Example 3-11 cnfprt *Output*

```
igx1       TN     group6:1      IGX 8420  9.2.20    Aug. 27 1999 13:27 CDT




Printing Mode


Remote Printing at igx4
Local Printing
No Printing



Last Command: cnfprt r igx4
```

Here is the **cnfprt** command syntax:

```
cnfprt <mode> [remote node]
```

Table 3-4 describes the parameters associated with the **cnfprt** command.

Table 3-4 **cnfprt** *Command Parameter Descriptions*

Parameter	Description	Required/Optional
mode	Displays the specified printing mode for this switch: **l**—Local **r**—Remote **n**—None	Required
remote node	If remote printing is specified, this is the remote node name for printing.	Optional

dspnds Command

The **dspnds** command displays all the nodes known to the network, including the nodes' name, type, and alarm status, as shown in Example 3-12. For large networks, the **dspnds** command might be better than the **dspnw** command, because it lists (in columns) all the nodes on a single screen. The alarm status fields are the same as those for the **dspnw** command, as described in the section "Displaying the Network."

The nodes are listed in the order of their internal node number, as shown in Example 3-12.

Example 3-12 dspnds *Output*

```
igx1          TN     group6:1      IGX 8420  9.2.20    Aug. 27 1999 13:28 CDT

NodeName Alarm
igx1      MAJOR
igx2      MAJOR
```

Example 3-12 dspnds *Output (Continued)*

```
igx3
igx4
igx5      MAJOR
igx6



Last Command: dspnds



Next Command:
```

If a node is in alarm, its name is highlighted, and the alarm type (UNRCH [for "Unreachable"], MAJOR, or Minor) is displayed.

Here is the **dspnds** command syntax:

dspnds [+n | -p | -d | *domain number*]

Table 3-5 describes the parameters associated with the **dspnds** command.

Table 3-5   **dspnds** *Command Parameter Descriptions*

Parameter	Description	Required/Optional
+n	Displays the node number for each node.	Optional
-p	Displays the controller card type and node type for each node.	Optional
-d	Displays the node type of each node (for example, 8420).	Optional
domain number	Displays only the nodes in the specified domain. Note that this parameter is no longer useful because network domains are no longer supported.	Optional

cnfname Command

The **cnfname** command specifies the name by which a node is known within the network. It can be changed at any time. The new node name is automatically distributed to the other nodes in the network. Duplicate names are not allowed in the same network. The **cnfname** command output is shown in Example 3-13.

Example 3-13 cnfname *Output*

```
igx4           TRM    group7:1      IGX 8420 9.2.20   July 30 1999 10:54 CDT


NodeName           Alarm        Packet Line
igx1               MAJOR
    15-15/igx2                  13-14igx2              12-13/igx4
```

continues

Example 3-13 cnfname *Output (Continued)*

```
igx2                 MAJOR
    15-15/igx1                    14-13/igx1              13-12/igx3
igx3                 MAJOR
    15-15/igx4                    12-13/igx2              13-14/igx4
igx4                 MAJOR
    15-15/igx3                    13-12/igx1              14-13/igx3



Last Command: cnfname igx4

Next Command:
```

Node names are case-sensitive. Thus, Paris and paris are different node names.

Here is the **cnfname** command syntax:

```
cnfname <node name>
```

Table 3-6 describes the parameter associated with the **cnfname** command.

Table 3-6   **cnfname** *Command Parameter Description*

Parameter	Description	Required/Optional
node name	Specifies a new name using the following rules:	Required
	Node names must be from one to eight characters in length	
	Node names must start with a letter	
	Node names may include "_" or "."	

dsplancnf Command

The **dsplancnf** command screen provides information about the LAN interface on the SCM or SCC. Only the first four fields can be configured with the SuperUser **cnflan** command. The **dsplancnf** command output is shown in Example 3-14.

Example 3-14 dsplancnf *Output*

```
igx1        TRM     group7:1    IGX 8420  9.2.20    July 30 1999 10:59 CDT

Active IP Address:             150.200.100.80
IP Subnet Mask:                255.255.255.0
IP Service Port:               5120
Default Gateway IP Address:    None
Maximum LAN Transmit Unit:     1500
Ethernet Address:              00.C0.43.00.78.DC
```

Example 3-14 dsplancnf *Output (Continued)*

```
Type      State
LAN       READY
TCP       UNAVAIL
UDP       READY
Telnet    READY
TFTP      READY
TimeHdlr  READY
SNMP      READY



Last Command: dsplancnf

Next Command:
```

This output has the following fields:

- **Active IP Address**—Specifies the IP address associated with the LAN port.
- **IP Subnet Mask**—Specifies a 32-bit subnet mask associated with the LAN IP address. The default value (in decimal notation) is 255.255.255.0.
- **IP Service Port**—Specifies the node's service port used by TCP. TCP is always indicated as being unavailable.
- **Default Gateway IP Address**—Specifies the IP gateway address, which is used by Cisco WAN Manager.

Here is the **dsplancnf** command syntax:

```
dsplancnf
```

dspnwip Command

The **dspnwip** command screen lists the current IP Relay address of all nodes in the network, as shown in Example 3-15. The IP Relay address can be used to Telnet to a node in-band through the IGX network. It is usually used by the Cisco WAN Manager workstation to manage nodes and collect statistics.

Example 3-15 dspnwip *Output*

```
igx1            TN     group6:1      IGX 8420  9.2.20    Aug. 27 1999 13:30 CDT

Active Network IP Address:           10.10.7.11
Active Network IP Subnet Mask:       255.255.255.0

NodeName    IP Address
igx1        10.10.7.11
igx2        10.10.7.19
igx3        10.10.7.27
```

continues

Example 3-15 dspnwip *Output (Continued)*

```
igx4        10.10.7.35
igx5        10.10.7.43
igx6        10.10.7.51


Last Command: dspnwip


Next Command:
```

More than one IP address can be listed for a node. The first is the node's network IP address. Subsequent addresses are the network IP addresses of feeder nodes attached to that node.

The SuperUser **cnfnwip** command is used to modify the IP Relay address and subnet mask.

Here is the **dspnwip** command syntax:

```
dspnwip
```

Table 3-7 lists additional IGX commands that are described in greater detail later in this chapter.

Table 3-7   *Additional IGX Commands*

Command	Description	Privilege Level
addtrk	Introduces a trunk as a network resource and begins intelligent communication between nodes.	1
cnftrk	Modifies trunk configuration parameters.	1
deltrk	Removes a trunk as a network resource.	1
dntrk	Deactivates trunk hardware.	1 and 2
dsptrk	Displays configuration parameters for a particular trunk. (This is a new command for 9.3.20 and above.)	1 to 6
dsptrkcnf	Same as **dsptrk**.	1 to 6
dsptrks	Displays summary information for all trunks on the node.	1 to 6
uptrk	Activates trunk hardware and physical-layer characteristics.	1
vt	Accesses a remote node via the command-line interface.	1 to 6
cnfln	Modifies line configuration parameters.	1
dnln	Deactivates the line.	1 and 2
dspln	Displays line configuration parameters. (This is a new command for 9.3.20 and above.)	1 to 6
dsplncnf	Same as **dspln**.	1 to 6
dsplns	Displays the status summary for all lines on the node.	1 to 6
upln	Activates the line.	1 and 2

Trunk Definition and Types

In an IGX network, a *trunk* is a digital transport facility that carries user and management traffic between any two nodes (IGX, BPX, or MGX).

A *trunk* may be either a *routing trunk*, which is defined as any trunk between any two routing nodes in a network, or a *feeder trunk*, which is defined as any trunk between a feeder node and a routing node in a network. This chapter focuses exclusively on routing trunks, although most of the information about routing trunks applies equally to feeder trunks.

A *routing trunk* may be one of the following:

- A physical trunk uses a cable or leased-line circuit from a local or long-distance carrier.

- A virtual trunk uses an ATM Virtual Path Connection (VPC) from an ATM service provider.

- An IMA trunk uses T1 or E1 to connect into a single broadband facility, over which ATM cells can then be transmitted. The section "IMA (Inverse Multiplexed ATM) Trunks" contains additional information on IMA trunks.

Figure 3-2 illustrates the different types of trunks.

Figure 3-2 *Trunk Types*

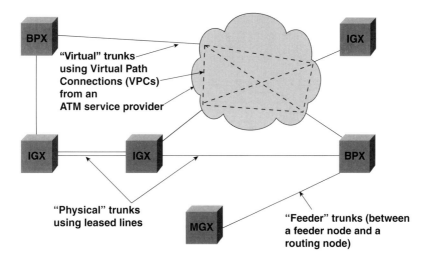

Trunk Card Groups Hardware Review

The NTM card group supports one T1, E1, Y1, or subrate trunk per card group. It also supports feeder trunks, but it does *not* support virtual trunks.

The UXM card group supports multiple T1, E1, T3, E3, or OC3 trunks per card group. It also supports feeder trunks and virtual trunks (up to a maximum of 15 virtual trunks per card group).

Each IGX node supports up to 32 physical or virtual trunks and up to four feeder trunks. Note that you can have up to 223 IGX routing nodes (excluding feeders) in one interconnected network.

Trunk Technologies and Formats

The IGX supports many types of trunks that differ in *technology* (ATM versus FastPacket) and *format* (framed versus unframed), depending on the trunk card group used. Table 3-8 lists the trunk types, technologies, formats, and card types that are used on the IGX switch.

Table 3-8 *Trunk Technologies and Formats*

Trunk Type	Technology	Framed Format	Unframed Format	Hardware
T1	FastPacket	X		NTM
Fractional T1	FastPacket	X		NTM
E1	FastPacket	X	X	NTM
Fractional E1	FastPacket	X		NTM
Y1	FastPacket	X		NTM
Fractional Y1	FastPacket	X		NTM
Subrate	FastPacket		X	NTM
T1	ATM	X		UXM
NxT1	ATM IMA	X		UXM
E1	ATM	X	X	UXM
NxE1	ATM IMA	X	X	UXM
T3	ATM	X	X	UXM
E3	ATM	X		UXM
OC-3c/STM1	ATM	X		UXM

The IGX network supports trunks using the following types of transmission facilities:

- T1 format, used primarily in North America
- Y1 format, used exclusively in Japan

- E1 format, used in most of the rest of the world
- Subrate format (serial V.35, X.21, or EIA/TIA-449/EIA/TIA-442 interface), used in many parts of the world for low-speed circuits
- T3 format, used primarily in North America
- E3 format, used in most of the rest of the world
- OC-3c or STM1 format

ATM Cell Payloads

The IGX uses ATM cells to transport traffic across UXM trunks and across the CellBus between UXM cards within the node. Figure 3-3 illustrates the ATM cell payloads.

Figure 3-3   *ATM Cell Payloads*

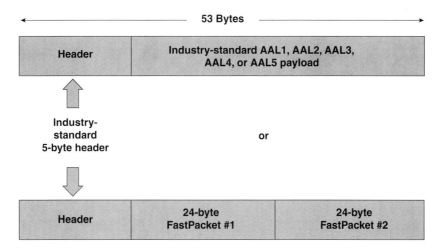

The ATM cells carried across a UXM trunk or on the CellBus between UXM cards in the node may be any of the following:

- Industry-standard ATM cells (using any ATM adaptation layer [AAL]) received from a CPE connected to a UXM port.
- Industry-standard AAL5 ATM cells generated by a UXM card by converting Frame Relay FastPackets (BdataA or BdataB) to ATM cells as per the FRF.5 and FRF.8 standards published by the Frame Relay Forum. (This conversion from FastPackets to AAL5 ATM cells is known in the IGX as the *complex gateway* process.)
- Cells with an industry-standard header but with a payload consisting of either one or two 24-byte FastPackets. (This encapsulation of FastPackets inside ATM cells, performed by a UXM card, is known in the IGX as the *simple gateway* process.)

Framed Versus Unframed Trunks

An *unframed* trunk in the IGX is a trunk that uses a digital facility on which all bit times of the physical transmission medium are available to the IGX to send FastPackets or ATM cells. On such trunks, the entire raw bit rate of the transmission facility can be used.

A *framed* trunk in the IGX is a trunk that uses a digital facility on which some bit times of the physical transmission medium are reserved for, and used to carry, a framing pattern defined by the applicable industry standards. Any bit positions devoted to the framing pattern can not be used by the IGX to transmit FastPackets or ATM cells.

The following types of transmission facilities use either mandatory or optional framing structures:

- T1 (mandatory framing)
- E1 (optional framing)
- Y1 (mandatory framing)
- T3 (optional framing)
- E3 (mandatory framing)
- OC3/STM1 (mandatory framing)

For a review of the different framing structures, refer to the *WAN Quick Start* CD-ROM or Ronald W. McCarty's *Cisco WAN Quick Start*, published by Cisco Press.

Fractional T1, E1, or Y1 Trunks

A fractional trunk is a framed T1, E1, or Y1 circuit on which only a portion of the timeslots are used to carry FastPackets.

NOTE   Only the NTM supports fractional trunks. The UXM does *not* support fractional T1 or E1 trunks.

One possible configuration of a fractional T1 trunk is to use 12 of the possible 24 timeslots. Such a trunk is designated by the IGX software as a T1/12 trunk.

Similarly, a fractional E1 trunk that is configured to use only eight of the possible 31 timeslots (not counting timeslot 0) is designated by the IGX software as an E1/8 trunk.

IMA (Inverse Multiplexed ATM) Trunks

An IMA trunk is one that consists of multiple T1 or E1 circuits that are used by the nodes at each end as a single logical trunk. The UXM supports T1 or E1 IMA trunks, and all circuits of an IMA trunk must terminate on the same UXM at each end of the trunk. An IMA trunk can consist of up to eight circuits, and a UXM can support up to eight IMA groups. (In that trivial case, each IMA trunk consists of only one circuit.) A UXM can support IMA and non-IMA trunks at the same time.

Some trunk bandwidth is used by the UXMs at each end to coordinate the management of the IMA trunk. Approximately 16 kbps is consumed on each circuit for this IMA protocol overhead. Therefore, an IMA trunk consisting of two T1 circuits has slightly less available bandwidth than the aggregate bandwidth of two T1 circuits.

Transmitting FastPackets or ATM Cells on Unframed Trunks

An unframed trunk is a clear-channel, bit-transparent digital transport facility in which every bit position on the trunk is available to carry FastPackets or ATM cells between the nodes at each end of the trunk. Transmission of FastPackets or cells may start at any bit position and continue uninterrupted forever, because there is no predefined structure on an unframed trunk into which the FastPackets or cells must fit.

On an NTM trunk, a 4-byte idle FastPacket is inserted any time there is no user or management FastPacket to send. On a UXM trunk, a 53-byte idle cell is inserted any time there is no user or management cell to send.

The 5-bit CRC in the FastPacket header or the HEC byte in the ATM cell header is used to identify and track the boundaries between adjacent FastPackets or ATM cells. In the ATM world, this technique is known as HEC framing or HEC cell delineation.

Transmitting FastPackets or ATM Cells on Framed Trunks

On a framed trunk, certain bit positions or byte positions can be reserved for framing (always), for signaling (sometimes), and as unused timeslots on a fractional trunk. Any such reserved bit or byte position must be skipped and cannot be used to carry any portion of a FastPacket or an ATM cell.

On framed trunks, FastPackets or cells are placed on the trunk starting at any byte boundary.

Trunk Notation

Each IGX trunk is characterized in the IGX software by its type and its total usable bandwidth.

Because the usable bandwidth on any IGX trunk is stored in the IGX software as an integer multiple of 64 kbps, any trunk can be fully described by its type and by the total usable bandwidth as a multiple of 64 kbps using the following format:

type/n

type is T1, E1, Y1, SR, T3, E3, or OC3, and *n* is the usable bandwidth in units of 64 kbps.

For example:

T1/24 represents a (full) T1 with 24×64 kbps of usable bandwidth.

E1/32 represents an (unframed) E1 with 32×64 kbps of usable bandwidth.

SR/16 represents a subrate trunk with 16×64 kbps of usable bandwidth.

T1/95 represents a T1 IMA trunk (consisting of four T1 circuits) with 95×64 kbps of usable bandwidth. Note that 64 kbps of usable bandwidth has been deducted to account for the IMA protocol overhead.

T3/576 represents a T3 trunk with 576×64 kbps of usable bandwidth.

Calculating NTM Trunk Capacity

Trunk capacity for an NTM trunk is described in FastPackets per second. Each FastPacket is 24 bytes, or 192 bits. Therefore, each 64 kbps of usable bandwidth on an NTM trunk can carry 64000 / 192 = 333.33 FastPackets per second.

For example, an NTM T1/24 can carry

$333.33 \times 24 = 8000$ FastPackets per second

An NTM E1/30 trunk can carry

$333.33 \times 30 = 10000$ FastPackets per second

An NTM SR/16 trunk can carry

$333.33 \times 16 = 5333.33$ FastPackets per second (rounded down to 5333)

NOTE   All trunk capacity calculations are rounded down.

Calculating UXM Trunk Capacity

Trunk capacity for a UXM trunk is described in cells per second. Each ATM cell is 53 bytes, or 424 bits, with a cell payload of 48 bytes and a header containing 5 bytes. Therefore, each 64 kbps of usable bandwidth on a UXM trunk can carry 64000 / 424 = 150.94 cells per second.

For example, a UXM T1/24 trunk can carry

$24 \times 150.94 = 3622$ cells/second

A UXM T1/95 trunk can carry

$95 \times 150.94 = 14339$ cells/second

A UXM E1/32 trunk can carry

$32 \times 150.94 = 4830$ cells/second

A UXM E3/530 trunk can carry

$530 \times 150.94 = 80000$ cells/second

NOTE   All trunk capacity calculations are rounded down.

You have reviewed framing and have learned how trunks are used in an IGX network. You should now be prepared for the following sections, which describe the process of adding trunks to the network.

IGX Trunks

This section describes IGX trunks and presents commands for displaying, upping, and adding trunks in the network.

Displaying Trunks

The **dsptrks** command displays summary information on the status of all active trunks that terminate on this node, as shown in Example 3-16.

Example 3-16 dsptrks *Output*

```
igx1    TRM    group7:1    IGX 8420 9.2.20    July 30 1999 14:36 CDT

TRK      Type     Current Line Alarm Status            Other End
 9.2     E3/530   Major - Loss of Sig (RED)               -
13       T1/24    Clear - OK                           igx1/12
14       E1/32    Clear - OK                           igx3/13
15       T3/576   Clear - OK                           igx3/15
```

continues

Example 3-16 dsptrks *Output (Continued)*

```
Last Command: dsptrks

Next Command:
```

The possible states are as follows:

- **Upped**—An upped trunk is monitored for physical-layer status, but it carries no traffic. An upped trunk has "Current Line Alarm Status" reported but no "Other End" information.

- **Added**—An added trunk is part of the network and can carry traffic. An added trunk reports a destination node name and trunk number in the "Other End" column.

Trunks that are neither upped nor added are not shown on the **dsptrks** screen. Consequently, the **dsptrks** screen is blank initially in a new node.

The TRK column shows the ID by which the trunk is referred to in the IGX software:

- *slot* for a single-trunk card
- *slot.port* for a single trunk on a multitrunk card
- *slot.port(n)* for an IMA trunk, where *port* is the primary line and *n* is the total number of circuits in the IMA group

The Type column shows the trunk type and capacity.

Here is the **dsptrks** command syntax:

```
dsptrks
```

Upping a Trunk

The **uptrk** command activates the hardware and physical characteristics that support the trunk, including sending out the correct framing (if appropriate) and idle FastPackets or cells. After you issue the **uptrk** command, there is no intelligent communication between the two nodes. The **uptrk** command must be issued from both ends of the trunk and then may be configured using the **cnftrk** command. Example 3-17 shows the **uptrk** command output.

Example 3-17 uptrk *Output*

```
igx1           TRM    group6:1        IGX 8420  9.2.20    Aug. 27 1999 13:35 CDT

TRK          Type   Current Line Alarm Status          Other End
10           SR/16  Clear - OK                         igx5/10
11           E1/32  Clear - OK                         igx4/11
12           T1/24  Clear - OK                         igx2/12
15.1         T3/636 Clear - OK                         -
```

Example 3-17 uptrk *Output (Continued)*

```
16.1          E3/530 Clear - OK                              igx2/16.1


Last Command: uptrk 15.1


Next Command:
```

Here is the **uptrk** command syntax:

```
uptrk <trunk ID>
```

Adding a Trunk Between Nodes

The **addtrk** command introduces the trunk as a bandwidth resource in the network. When a trunk is added, network communication begins between the two nodes. Figure 3-4 illustrates the process of adding a trunk.

Figure 3-4   *Adding a Trunk*

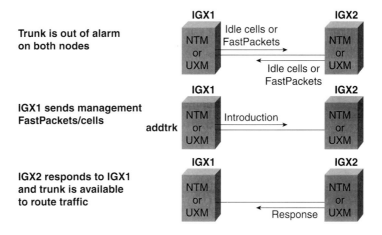

Note that the **uptrk** command must be issued from both ends of the trunk and then may be configured using the **cnftrk** command. The **addcon** command is used to activate a trunk, but not until both ends of the trunk have been enabled with the **uptrk** command.

This activity adds the node to the network if it was not already part of the network. Note the following:

- The trunk must be out of alarm before you issue the **addtrk** command.

- The **addtrk** command needs to be issued from only one side.

- Nodes initially exchange their name, node number, and trunk number.

- Database exchanges follow (topology, user IDs and passwords, network synchronization, and load models).

A trunk cannot be added while any of the following conditions is true:

- Another node is attempting to change the network topology by adding or deleting a trunk.

- Another node is notifying all nodes that it has been renamed.

- An unreachable node exists in the network.

- The node names across the two networks are not unique.

When the **addtrk** command is used to add a new node to a network or to join one network to another network, the user ID and password lists of the two networks are merged.

Displaying a Trunk's Configuration

The **dsptrk** or **dsptrkcnf** command provides detailed configuration information about a trunk, as shown in Example 3-18.

Example 3-18 dsptrkcnf *Output*

```
igx1            TRM    group6:1      IGX 8420  9.2.20   Aug. 28 1999 13:04 CDT

TRK 15.1 Config      T3/636   [96000 cps]  UXM slot:15
Transmit Trunk Rate: 96000  cps        Payload Scramble:    No
Rcv Trunk Rate:      96000  cps        Connection Channels: 256
Pass sync:           Yes               Gateway Channels:    200
Loop clock:          No                Traffic:
Statistical Reserve: 1000   cps        V,TS,NTS,FR,FST,CBR,NRT-VBR,ABR,RT-VBR
Header Type:         NNI               Deroute delay time:  0 seconds
VPI Address:         1                 VC Shaping:          No
Routing Cost:        10
Idle code:           7F hex
Restrict PCC traffic: No
Link type:           Terrestrial
Line framing:        PLCP
Line cable length:   0-225 ft.
HCS Masking:         Yes

Last Command: dsptrkcnf 15.1


Next Command:
```

The parameters used with the **dsptrk** or **dsptrkcnf** command depend on the following:

- The type of trunk (T1, E1, Y1, SR, T3, E3, or OC3)
- Whether it is a physical trunk or virtual trunk
- Whether it is an IMA trunk

See the next section on the **cnftrk** command for descriptions of the parameters that apply to each trunk type.

Here is the **dsptrk** command syntax:

```
dsptrk <trunk ID>
```

Here is the **dsptrkcnf** command syntax:

```
dsptrkcnf <trunk ID>
```

<trunk ID> is of the same format as that used in the **addtrk** command.

Configuring a Trunk

The **cnftrk** command is used to modify trunk parameters. Normally, the **cnftrk** command is used after the **uptrk** command but before the **addtrk** command. The **cnftrk** command output is shown in Example 3-19.

Example 3-19 cnftrk *Output*

```
igx1        TRM     group7:1          IGX 8420 9.2.20    July 30 1999 14:46 CDT

TRK  9.2 Config         E3/530 [80000 cps]   UXM slot: 9
Transmit Trunk Rate:    80000   cps          Payload Scramble:     Yes
Rcv Trunk Rate:         80000   cps          Connection Channels:  256
Pass sync:              Yes                  Gateway Channels:     200
Loop clock:             No                   Valid Traffic Classes:
Statistical Reserve:    1000    cps          V,TS,NTS,FR,FST,CBR,VBR,ABR
Header Type:            NNI                  Deroute delay time: 0 seconds
VPI Address:            1
Routing Cost:           10
Idle code:              F hex
Restrict PCC traffic:   No
Link type:              Terrestrial
Line framing:           HEC
Line cable length:      0-225 ft.
HCS Masking:            Yes


This Command: cnftrk 9.2

Transmit Trunk Rate in cps (80000) :
```

The **cnftrk** command must be entered at both ends.

The parameters used with the **cnftrk** command depend on the following:

- The type of trunk (T1, E1, Y1, SR, T3, E3, or OC3)
- Whether it is a physical trunk or virtual trunk
- Whether it is an IMA trunk

Parameters can fall into the following categories:

- Can always be modified
- Can be modified only when the trunk is upped but not added
- Can be modified only by a SuperUser
- Cannot be modified—informational only

Here is the **cnftrk** command syntax:

```
cnftrk <trunk ID> <parameters for specific trunk type>
```

<trunk ID> is of the same format as that used in the **addtrk** command. *<parameters for specific trunk type>* are as described in the next section.

Configurable Trunk Parameters

Table 3-9 specifies which trunk parameters can be configured on each type of trunk:

- P indicates that the parameter is configurable *only* on a physical trunk of that type.
- V indicates that the parameter is configurable *only* on a virtual trunk of that type.
- VA indicates that the parameter is configurable *only* on a virtual trunk of that type and that *all* virtual trunks that share the same physical interface must have the same setting for that parameter.
- Y indicates that the parameter is configurable for any trunk of that type.
- YA indicates that the parameter is configurable for any supported trunk (physical or virtual) of that type and that *all* virtual trunks that share the same physical interface must have the same setting for that parameter.

Table 3-9 *Configurable Trunk Parameters*

Parameter	Changeable When Added	NTM-T1/Y1	NTM-E1	NTM-SR	UXM-T1	UXM-T1 IMA	UXM-E1	UXM-E1 IMA	UXM-T3	UXM-E3	UXM-OC3
Line DS-0 map	Y	Y	Y				YA	YA			
IMA group member(s)	Y				YA	YA	YA	YA			
Retained links	Y				YA	YA	YA	YA			
Transmit trunk rate	Y (UXM only)				Y	Y	Y	Y	Y	Y	Y
Rcv trunk rate	Y				Y	Y	Y	Y	Y	Y	Y
Subrate interface				Y							
Subrate data rate				Y							
Pass sync	Y	Y	Y	Y	YA	YA	YA	YA	YA	YA	YA
Loop clock	Y	Y	Y	Y	YA	YA	YA	YA	YA	YA	YA
Statistical reserve	Y	Y	Y	Y	Y	Y	Y	Y	Y	Y	Y
Header type					YA	YA	YA	YA	YA	YA	YA
VPI address					Y	Y	Y	Y	Y	Y	Y
Routing cost	Y	Y	Y	Y	Y	Y	Y	Y	Y	Y	Y
Idle code	Y	Y	Y		YA	YA	YA	YA	YA	YA	YA
Restrict PCC traffic	Y	Y	Y	Y	Y	Y	Y	Y	Y	Y	Y
Link type	Y	Y	Y	Y	Y	Y	Y	Y	Y		Y
Line framing			Y		YA	YA			Y		Y
Line coding		Y	Y								
Line CRC			Y				YA	YA			

continues

Table 3-9 *Configurable Trunk Parameters (Continued)*

Parameter	Changeable When Added	NTM-T1/Y1	NTM-E1	NTM-SR	UXM-T1	UXM-T1 IMA	UXM-E1	UXM-E1 IMA	UXM-T3	UXM-E3	UXM-OC3
Line recv impedance			Y								
Line cable type		Y			YA	YA					
Line cable length		Y			YA	YA			YA	YA	
HCS masking					Y	Y	Y	Y	Y	Y	Y
Payload scramble					YA	YA	YA	YA	YA	YA	YA
Gateway channels	Y				Y	Y	Y	Y	Y	Y	Y
Traffic	Y	Y	Y	Y	Y	Y	Y	Y	Y	Y	Y
Virtual trunk type					V	V	V	V	V	V	V
Virtual trunk VPI					V	V	V	V	V	V	V
Frame scramble											Y
IMA protocol option	Y				YA	YA	YA	YA			
IMA max. diff. dly	Y					YA		YA			
IMA clock mode											
Deroute delay time	Y		Y	Y	Y	Y	Y	Y	Y	Y	Y
VC shaping	Y				Y	Y	Y	Y	Y	Y	Y
VPC conns disabled					Y	Y	Y	Y	Y	Y	Y

Line DS-0 Map

This parameter specifies the timeslots to use for a fractional NTM trunk or for a framed E1 UXM trunk.

For the UXM E1 trunk, the choices are 0-31 or 0-15,17-31. For a fractional T1 or E1 NTM trunk, any set of contiguous timeslots (separated by hyphens) and/or individual timeslots (separated by commas) may be specified.

IMA Group Member(s)

This parameter specifies the physical interfaces that constitute an IMA group. This parameter may be used to add members to an IMA group or to delete members (except the first one) from an IMA group.

Retained Links

This parameter specifies the number of T1 or E1 circuits of the IMA group that *must* be available in order for the trunk to remain in service. If members of the IMA group fail such that fewer members than specified by this parameter remain, the entire trunk is removed from service.

Transmit Trunk Rate

This parameter specifies, in cells per second, the trunk's total transmit rate. For a physical trunk, this parameter defaults to the maximum interface rate, but it may be reduced if you like. For a virtual trunk, this parameter defaults to a portion of the interface rate and may be increased (up to the interface rate) or decreased as you like.

Rcv Trunk Rate

This parameter specifies, in increments of 64 kbps (but expressed in cells per second), the trunk's receive rate.

Subrate Interface

This parameter specifies, for an NTM subrate trunk, whether the V.35, RS-449, or X.21 interface is to be used.

Subrate Data Rate

This parameter specifies, for an NTM subrate trunk, the trunk's selected bit rate. The following bit rates are supported:

- 64 kbps
- 128 kbps
- 256 kbps
- 384 kbps
- 512 kbps
- 768 kbps
- 1024 kbps
- 1536 kbps
- 1920 kbps

NOTE   Bit rates below 256 kbps are supported but are not recommended because they require special traffic engineering to ensure data integrity.

Pass Sync

This parameter specifies whether this trunk may be used in the automatic network synchronization clock distribution algorithm. For more details, refer to Chapter 7, "Connection Routing, Synchronizing the Network, and Managing Jobs."

Loop Clock

This parameter specifies whether the transmit clock on this trunk should be derived from the receive clock on the trunk (Loop Clock = Yes) or derived from the node's internal bus frequency (Loop Clock = No).

Statistical Reserve

This parameter specifies, in FastPackets per second or cells per second, the amount of bandwidth on the trunk to be reserved for

- Node-to-node administration traffic
- Statistical variations on the user traffic carried on the trunk

Header Type

This parameter specifies whether the ATM cells on this trunk should use the UNI header format or the NNI header format.

VPI Address

This parameter specifies the VPI to be used for all management cells and user connection cells (other than VPC connections) on this trunk. Any VPC carried on this trunk uses the next available VPI starting at this value.

Routing Cost

This parameter assigns an administrative cost to this trunk. This cost is used only if Cost-Based Connection Routing is used.

Idle Code

This parameter specifies, as a hexadecimal value, the code to be placed

- In unused timeslots of a fractional NTM trunk
- In the payload of idle cells transmitted on a UXM trunk

Restrict PCC Traffic

This parameter specifies whether this trunk should be used to carry network administration traffic between nodes.

This parameter may only be changed by a SuperUser.

If a trunk is designated restricted with this parameter, network administration traffic uses a different trunk if one is available. If no unrestricted trunk is available, this trunk may be used.

Link Type

This parameter specifies whether this trunk is designated as a terrestrial or satellite trunk. Whenever possible, network administration traffic tries to avoid satellite trunks. Also, user connections can be designated to never use satellite trunks.

Line Framing

This parameter allows the selection of

- D4 or ESF framing for T1 trunks
- PLCP or HEC framing for T3 and OC3 trunks

Line Coding

This parameter allows the selection of

- AMI, B8ZS, or ZCS ones-density enforcement for NTM T1 trunks
- AMI, HDB3, or ZCS ones-density enforcement for NTM E1 trunks

Generally, B8ZS or HDB3 should be used, because these algorithms guarantee sufficient ones density without compromising data integrity in any way.

AMI should be avoided, because it does not ensure sufficient ones density.

ZCS should be avoided, because it guarantees sufficient ones density but might introduce uncorrectable bit errors in user information.

For further details on these transmission formats, refer to the *WAN Quick Start* CD-ROM.

Line CRC

This parameter specifies whether the optional CRC-4 algorithm defined for E1 trunks in the ITU-T G.703 standard is enabled or disabled on this trunk.

Line Recv Impedance

This parameter specifies whether the line receive impedance is to be 75 or 120 ohms, balanced or unbalanced.

Line Cable Type

Line cable type is a choice between MAT cable and ABAM cable. You should leave it at the default.

Line Cable Length

The line cable length and line cable type (specified together) determine the circuit's line build-out (LBO) based on the type of cable used and the cable distance to the next active component, usually a CSU. The LBO is specified in feet and defines the signal strength. For example, the shorter the LBO, the lesser the cable strength signal that is sent by the IGX; the longer the LBO, the greater the cable strength signal that is sent by the IGX. The greater-strength signal is the default.

HCS Masking

This parameter specifies whether the 8-bit CRC in the HCS field of the ATM cell header is calculated using a seed value of 0 or a seed value of 0x55 hexadecimal.

A seed value of 0 might result in an ATM cell header that is all 0s. Such a cell header is difficult to identify accurately when using HEC line framing, in which cell delineation is accomplished by searching for valid HCS fields to identify valid ATM cell headers. In such a case, it is better to use a nonzero seed value.

Payload Scramble

This parameter specifies whether ATM cell payloads are scrambled (unscrambled at the far end) to reduce the chance of repeating data patterns, causing clock recovery problems on the trunk.

Gateway Channels

This parameter specifies the maximum number of simple gateway or complex gateway connections that may use this trunk.

Traffic

This parameter specifies which types of connections are allowed to use this trunk.

NTM trunks allow any combination of the following types:

- **V**—Voice
- **TS**—Time-stamped data
- **NTS**—Non-time-stamped data
- **FR**—Frame Relay
- **FST**—Frame Relay connections with ForeSight

UXM trunks allow any of the connection types just mentioned plus any of the following types:

- **CBR**—CBR ATM connections
- **N&RVBR**—Non-real-time VBR and real-time VBR ATM connections
- **ABR**—ABR ATM connections

Virtual Trunk Type

This parameter specifies the type of VP service (CBR, VBR, or ABR) used for this virtual trunk.

Virtual Trunk VPI

This parameter specifies the VPI used for all cells carried on this virtual trunk.

Frame Scramble

Frame scramble is an optional standard for SONET interfaces only. Like cell scrambling, it is vital to have both the BPX and user equipment interfaces set with or without frame scrambling.

IMA Protocol Option

This parameter specifies whether the IMA protocol should be used on a T1 or E1 trunk with only a single circuit. If this is enabled, additional circuits may be added later to increase the size of the IMA trunk.

IMA Max. Diff. Dly

This parameter specifies the maximum difference in end-to-end delay that is allowed between members of an IMA group.

The UXM buffers cells carried on each member of the IMA group such that the total delay (actual delay plus buffer delay) is the same for each member of the IMA group.

IMA Clock Mode

This parameter is a display parameter only. The value CTC stands for Common Transmit Clock. This means that all members of an IMA group *must* use the same clock source.

Deroute Delay Time

This parameter specifies, in seconds, how long the IGX software should wait, following the detection of the failure of this trunk, to start the process of rerouting the connections carried on this trunk.

This parameter can be specified only if the Deroute Delay feature is enabled in the network using parameter 23 of the **cnfsysparm** command.

VC Shaping

This parameter specifies whether egress traffic shaping is to be performed on each individual connection using this trunk.

NOTE	This feature is not currently supported and should *not* be enabled.

VPC Conns Disabled

This parameter specifies whether Virtual Path Connections (VPCs) are allowed to use this trunk.

Displaying the Network

The **dspnw** command displays the network topology in tabular form, as shown in Example 3-20. For a large network, this listing might require multiple screens.

Example 3-20 dspnw *Output*

```
igx1     TRM     group7:1    IGX 8420 9.2.20    July 30 1999 15:23 CDT

NodeName     Alarm              Packet Line
igx1
   15-15/igx2                   13-14/igx2                  12-13/igx4
igx2
   15-15/igx1                   14-13/igx1                  13-12/igx3
igx3
   15-15/igx4                   9.1-9.1/igx4                12-13/igx2
   13-14/igx4
igx4
   15-15/igx3                   9.1-9.1/igx3                13-12/igx1
   14-13/igx3

Last Command: dspnw
Next Command:
```

Nodes are listed in order of their node numbers.

For each node, this command displays the following:

- The node name
- The node's alarm status. Here are the possible alarms statuses:
    - UNRCH—Indicates that the local node can no longer communicate with this remote node. This might be caused by a failure of all trunks to the node, a loss of power, a processor failure without an available redundant processor, and so on.

— MAJOR—Indicates that there is a major (service-affecting) alarm condition at the node.

— Minor—Indicates that there is a minor (not service-affecting) alarm condition at the node.

— <blank>—Indicates that the node is free of alarms.

- A list of all trunks that terminate at the node. Each trunk is represented as the following:

  — The trunk number at the local node

  — A hyphen (-), indicating a terrestrial trunk, or a tilde (~), indicating a satellite trunk

  — The trunk number at the remote node

  — The remote node name

A failed trunk is shown as a flashing hyphen or tilde on the CLI screen.

If the network has more nodes and trunk connections than are currently on the screen, a Continue? prompt appears. Press **Return** to display other nodes or **N** to exit the command.

Here is the **dspnw** command syntax:

```
dspnw [+b | -b] [+z | -z]
```

Table 3-10 lists the parameters for the **dspnw** command.

Table 3-10   **dspnw** *Command Parameter Descriptions*

Parameter	Description
+b	-b	Displays only trunks that support (+b) or don't support (-b) bursty data.
+z	-z	Displays only ZCS trunks (+z) or non-ZCS trunks (-z).

Accessing Remote Nodes in the Network

The **vt** command establishes a virtual terminal session to a remote node, as shown in Example 3-21.

Example 3-21 **vt** *Command*

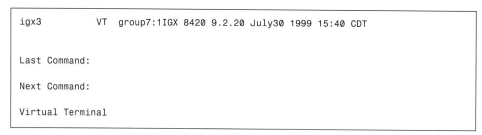

```
igx3          VT  group7:1IGX 8420 9.2.20 July30 1999 15:40 CDT


Last Command:

Next Command:

Virtual Terminal
```

A virtual terminal session has the following properties:

- The **vt** session uses trunks to connect to the remote node. A direct trunk between the nodes is not required as long as a network path exists between the nodes.
- User IDs and passwords are network-wide, so no login is necessary for the **vt** session.
- On the remote node, any command except **vt** can be executed. In other words, **vt** sessions cannot be "chained."
- User access cannot be limited to just one node in a network.
- By default, only one **vt** session may be established per node. With a software license, up to six **vt** sessions may be available.
- The **bye** command terminates a virtual terminal session, and the terminal reverts to local usage. After a default timeout of 4 minutes of inactivity, a **vt** session is automatically ended. This timeout is equivalent to using the **bye** command.

During a **vt** session, the following things happen:

- The remote node name and date flash on the local terminal screen.
- Virtual Terminal appears in the lower-left corner.
- VT appears at the top of the screen.

Here is the **vt** command syntax:

vt *<node name>*

Deleting a Trunk Between Nodes

The **deltrk** command deletes a trunk, as shown in Example 3-22. This removes the trunk from the network topology databases network-wide. The trunk is removed as a communication path between the nodes. Any user connections and network management traffic that are using the trunk are forced to find another path if one is available.

Example 3-22 **deltrk** *Output*

```
igx1     TRM    group7:1 IGX 8420 9.2.20    July 30 1999 14:56 CDT

TRK     Type        Current Line Alarm Status        Other End
 9.1    E3/530      Clear - OK                        igx3/9.1
13      T1/24       Clear - OK                        igx1/12
14      E1/32       Clear - OK                        igx3/13
15      T3/576      Clear - OK                        igx3/15


This Command: deltrk 9.1
```

continues

Example 3-22 deltrk *Output (Continued)*

```
Warning: Connections may be deleted if the network is split
Delete this line (y/n)?

                                                    Minor Alarm
```

Following the **deltrk** command, only framing (where appropriate) and idle FastPackets or cells are carried on the trunk.

Because deleting a trunk removes the communication path between two nodes, using the **deltrk** command might split a network into two separate networks. If **deltrk** splits the network, any connections between the two resulting separate networks are automatically deleted.

Here is the **deltrk** command syntax:

```
deltrk <trunk ID>
```

<trunk ID> is of the same format as that used in the **addtrk** command.

Downing a Trunk

The **dntrk** command deactivates the hardware supporting a trunk, after which it no longer carries framing, idle FastPackets or cells, or traffic of any kind.

Before a trunk can be downed with the **dntrk** command, it must first be removed from the network topology databases with the **deltrk** command. The **dntrk** command output is shown in Example 3-23.

Example 3-23 dntrk *Output*

```
igx1   TRM   group7:1   IGX 8420 9.2.20   July 30 1999 15:01 CDT

TRK      Type       Current Line Alarm Status        Other End
13       T1/24      Clear - OK                        igx1/12
14       E1/32      Clear - OK                        igx3/13
15       T3/576     Clear - OK                        igx3/15


Last Command: dntrk 9.2


Next Command:
```

After a trunk has been downed with the **dntrk** command, it is removed from the **dsptrks** screen entirely.

Here is the **dntrk** command syntax:

```
dntrk <trunk ID>
```

Line Definition

In an IGX network, a *line* is a T1, E1, T3, E3, or OC3/STM1 digital transport facility that carries information between a node and external equipment. Figure 3-5 illustrates a line.

Figure 3-5   *Line Definition*

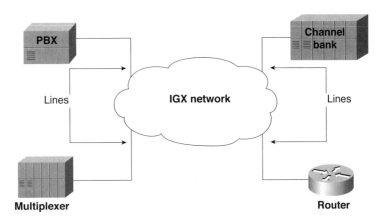

This definition of a line specifically excludes any synchronous data interface, such a V.35, RS232, x.21, and so on.

Typical external equipment that can be connected to an IGX with a line can include any of the following, or others:

- Private branch exchanges (PBXs)
- Channel banks
- Multiplexers
- Routers

Line Types

The IGX supports lines for many different types of services:

- Voice lines, typically used to connect a PBX or central office (CO) to an IGX
- Data lines, typically used to connect a PBX or data/video multiplexer to an IGX
- Frame Relay lines, typically used to connect a router or other Frame Relay access device (FRAD) to an IGX
- ATM lines, typically used to connect a router to an IGX

Line Card Groups Hardware Review

The UVM card group supports one or two T1, E1, or J1 lines that may be used to carry voice and/or data traffic between the IGX and the attached equipment.

The CVM card group supports one T1, E1, or J1 line that may be used to carry voice and/or data traffic between the IGX and the attached equipment.

The UFM-C card group supports four or eight T1 or E1 lines that may be used to carry Frame Relay traffic between the IGX and the attached router or FRAD.

The FRM-31 card group supports one T1 or E1 line that may be used to carry Frame Relay traffic between the IGX and the attached router or FRAD.

The UXM card group supports different lines that may be used to carry ATM traffic between the IGX and the attached router or ATM equipment:

- Four or eight T1 or E1 lines
- Three or six T3 or E3 lines
- Two or four OC-3c/STM1 lines

Line Technologies and Formats

The IGX supports many types of lines that differ depending on the line card group used, as shown in Table 3-11.

Table 3-11 *Line Technologies and Formats*

Service	Line Type	Source	Framed Format	Unframed Format	Hardware
Voice/data	T1	Multiplexed	X		UVM/CVM
Voice/data	E1	Multiplexed	X		UVM/CVM
Voice/data	J1	Multiplexed	X		UVM/CVM
Frame Relay	T1	Multiplexed or unmultiplexed	X		UFM/FRM
Frame Relay	E1	Multiplexed or unmultiplexed	X	X	UFM/FRM
ATM	T1	Unmultiplexed	X		UXM
ATM	T1 IMA	Unmultiplexed	X		UXM
ATM	E1	Unmultiplexed	X	X	UXM
ATM	E1 IMA	Unmultiplexed	X	X	UXM
ATM	T3	Unmultiplexed	X	X	UXM
ATM	E3	Unmultiplexed	X		UXM
ATM	OC-3c/STM1	Unmultiplexed	X	X	UXM

The IGX network supports lines using any of the following types of transmission facilities:

- T1 format, used primarily in North America
- J1 format, used exclusively in Japan
- E1 format, used in most of the rest of the world
- T3 format, used primarily in North America
- E3 format, used in most of the rest of the world
- OC-3c or STM1 format

Multiplexed Versus Unmultiplexed Lines

A *multiplexed* line carries information between the IGX and multiple sources of information using a time-division multiplexing (TDM) line format.

A voice line or a data line is always time-division multiplexed because it carries multiple independent voice or data streams from multiple voice or data sources.

An *unmultiplexed* line carries information between the IGX and a single source of information using an unmultiplexed line format.

An ATM line is always an unmultiplexed line that carries ATM cells between an IGX and a single ATM router or other ATM device. (Any multiplexing of data from multiple data sources is done at the ATM layer, not using a TDM line format.)

A Frame Relay line may be either multiplexed or unmultiplexed as needed.

Time-Division Multiplexing Review

All multiplexed T1, E1, and J1 lines are composed of TDM channels.

Time-division multiplexing (TDM) consists of taking one octet (8 bits) from each of n inputs every 125 microseconds, or 8000 times per second. The n octets are assembled into a frame. For a T1, $n = 24$, and for an E1 and a J1, $n = 31$.

Each input channel always occupies the same position, or time slot, in every frame. This provides 64,000 bits per second (64 kbps) to each time slot.

In some cases, an attached device may be assigned multiple channels to allow that device to transmit $n \times 64$ kbps.

For more details, refer to the *WAN Quick Start* CD-ROM.

Line Framing Review

Framing is required on any multiplexed T1, E1, or J1 line that is to be used to carry multiplexed digital voice, data, or Frame Relay services over the IGX. A review of T1, E1, and J1 framing is provided in the following sections.

An unframed line in the IGX is a line that uses a digital facility on which *all* bit times of the physical transmission medium are available to send user information. On such lines, the entire raw bit rate of the transmission facility may be used. Because there is no framing, no time-division multiplexing is possible on an unframed line. The IGX supports unframed lines for Frame Relay E1 lines and ATM E1, T3, and OC3c/STM1 lines.

T3, E3, and OC3c/STM1 lines, even though they are not time-division multiplexed, support either mandatory or optional framing to comply with industry standards:

- T3 (optional framing)
- E3 (mandatory framing)
- OC3/STM1 (mandatory framing)

Line Notation

Each IGX line is characterized in the IGX software by its type and its number of usable channels (for a multiplexed line) or its total usable bandwidth (for an unmultiplexed line).

Because the usable bandwidth on any IGX line is stored in the IGX software as an integer multiple of 64 kbps, any line can be fully described using the following format:

type/n

where *type* is T1, E1, T3, E3, or OC3 and *n* is the number of channels (for a multiplexed line) or the usable bandwidth in units of 64 kbps.

For example:

T1/24 represents a T1 line with 24 channels (for a multiplexed line) or 24×64 kbps of usable bandwidth (for an unmultiplexed line).

E1/30 represents an E1 line with 30 channels (for a multiplexed line) or 30×64 kbps of usable bandwidth (for an unmultiplexed line).

T3/576 represents a T3 line with 576×64 kbps of usable bandwidth.

E3/150 represents an E3 line with 150×64 kbps of usable bandwidth.

Line capacity for a UXM line (which is unmultiplexed) is described in cells per second. Each ATM cell is 53 bytes, or 424 bits. Therefore, each 64 kbps of usable bandwidth on a UXM line can carry $64,000 / 424 = 150.94$ cells per second.

For example, a UXM E3/530 trunk can carry $150.94 \times 530 = 80,000$ cells per second.

Conversely, a T3 UXM line that is configured for a capacity of 20,000 cells per second is represented in the IGX software as T3/132 because 20,000 / 150.94 = 132.5, which is rounded down to 132.

Displaying Lines

The **dsplns** command displays summary information about the status of all active lines that terminate on this node, as shown in Example 3-24. Lines appear when the **upln** command is issued.

Example 3-24 dsplns *Output*

```
igx3             TN     group8:1      IGX 8420  9.2.20    Sep. 8 1999  13:44 CDT

Line     Type    Current Line Alarm Status
 3.1     T1/24  Clear - OK
 9.1     E3/530 Clear - OK




Last Command: dsplns


Next Command:
```

The Line column shows the ID by which the line is referred to in the IGX software:

- *slot*—A single-line card
- *slot.port*—A single line on a multiline card
- *slot.port(n)*—An IMA line where *port* is the primary line and *n* is the total number of lines in the IMA group

The Type column shows the line type and capacity.

Here is the **dsplns** command syntax:

```
dsplns
```

Upping a Line

The **upln** command activates (ups) a line, as shown in Example 3-25. This command makes the line available for configuring. Initially, the line simply sends out framing (if needed) and idle code or idle cells.

Example 3-25 upln *Output*

```
igx1              TRM    group7:1       IGX 8420 9.2.20 July 30 1999 15:49 CDT

Line      Type     Current Line Alarm Status
11.1      T1/24    Clear - OK


Last Command: upln 11.1


Next Command:
```

Here is the **upln** command syntax:

upln *<line ID>*

<line ID> is in one of the following formats:

- CVM, FRM-31 line (single-line cards)

  <slot>

  Example: **upln 6**

- UVM, UFM-C, and non-IMA UXM line (multiline cards)

  <slot>.<interface>

  Example: **upln 9.4**

- UXM IMA line

  <slot>.<interface list>

<interface list> may be a range of interfaces and/or individual interfaces separated by commas.

Displaying a Line's Configuration

The **dspln** or **dsplncnf** command provides detailed configuration information about a line. The **dsplncnf** command output is shown in Example 3-26.

Example 3-26 dsplncnf *Output*

```
igx1              TN     group6:1       IGX 8420  9.2.20   Aug. 28 1999 13:08 CDT

LN  14.1 Config         E1/30               UXM slot:14
Line DS-0 map:          1-15,17-31
Loop clock:             No
Line coding:            HDB3
Line CRC:               Yes
Line recv impedance:    120 ohm
```

Example 3-26 dsplncnf *Output (Continued)*

```
Idle code:            54 hex
HCS Masking:          Yes
Payload Scramble:     Yes
VC Shaping:           No

Last Command: dsplncnf 14.1

Next Command:
```

The parameters used with the **dspln** or **dsplncnf** command depend on

- The type of line (T1, E1, J1, T3, E3, or OC3)

- Whether it is an IMA trunk

See the information for the **cnfln** command in the next section for a listing of the parameters that apply to each line type and a description of each parameter.

Here is the **dspln** command syntax:

dspln *<line ID>*

Here is the **dsplncnf** command syntax:

dsplncnf *<line ID>*

<line ID> is of the same format as that used in the **upln** command.

Configuring a Line

The **cnfln** command is used to modify line parameters. The line must be activated with the **upln** command before the **cnfln** command can be used. The **cnfln** command output is shown in Example 3-27.

Example 3-27 cnfln *Output*

```
igx3              TN      group8:1       IGX 8420  9.2.20    Sep. 8 1999  13:48 CDT

LN   3.2 Config        T1/24              UVM slot: 3
Loop clock:            No
Line framing:          ESF
Line coding:           B8ZS
Line encoding:         u-LAW
Line T1 signalling:    CCS
Line cable type:       ABAM
Line length:           0-133 ft.
Line 56KBS Bit Pos:    msb
Line pct fast modem:   20
Line cnfg:             External
Line cnf slot.line:    --
```

continues

Example 3-27 **cnfln** *Output (Continued)*

```
Line CAS-Switching:   --
Line SVC-Caching:     Off
Traffic Shaping:      No

Last Command: cnfln 3.2 N ESF B8ZS U CCS 4 msb 20 N


Next Command:
```

The parameters used with the **cnfln** command depend on

- The type of line (T1, E1, J1, T3, E3, or OC3)
- Whether it is an IMA line

Parameters can fall into the following categories:

- Can always be modified
- Can be modified only when no user connection is configured on the line
- Cannot be modified—informational only

Here is the **cnfln** command syntax:

```
cnfln <line ID> <parameters for specific line type>
```

<line ID> is of the same format as that used in the **upln** command. *<parameters for specific line type>* are as described next.

Configurable Line Parameters

Table 3-12 specifies which line parameters can be configured on each type of voice, data, or Frame Relay line.

Table 3-12 *Configurable Line Parameters*

Parameter	Changeable with Connections Added	CVM-T1	CVM-E1/Y1	UVM-T1	UVM-E1/J1	FRM-T1	FRM-E1	UFM-T1	UFM-E1
Line DS-0 map	Y								
IMA group member(s)	Y								
Retained links	Y								
IMA protocol option	Y								
IMA max. diff. dly	Y								

Table 3-12 *Configurable Line Parameters (Continued)*

Parameter	Changeable with Connections Added	CVM-T1	CVM-E1/Y1	UVM-T1	UVM-E1/J1	FRM-T1	FRM-E1	UFM-T1	UFM-E1
IMA clock mode									
Loop clock	Y	Y	Y	Y	Y	Y	Y	Y	Y
Line framing	Y	Y		Y		Y	Y	Y	Y
Line coding	Y	Y	Y	Y	Y				
Line CRC	Y		Y		Y		Y		Y
Line recv impedance	Y		Y		Y		Y		Y
Line E1/J1 signal			Y		Y		Y		Y
Line encoding		Y	Y	Y	Y				
Line T1 signalling	Y	Y		Y					
Line cable type	Y	Y		Y		Y		Y	
Line length	Y	Y		Y		Y		Y	
Line 56KBS bit pos		Y	Y	Y	Y				
Line pct fast modem	Y	Y	Y	Y	Y				
Line cnfg	Y								
Line cnf slot.line	Y								
Line CAS-switching	Y								
Idle code	Y								
HCS masking	Y								
Payload scramble	Y								
Frame scramble	Y								
Line SVC-caching	Y	Y	Y	Y	Y				

Table 3-13 specifies which line parameters can be configured on each type of ATM line.

Table 3-13 *Configurable ATM Line Parameters*

Parameter	Changeable with Connections Added	UXM-T1	UXM-T1 IMA	UXM-E1	UXM-E1 IMA	UXM-T3	UXM-E3	UXM-OC3
Line DS-0 map	Y			Y	Y			
IMA group member(s)	Y	Y	Y	Y	Y			
Retained links	Y		Y		Y			
IMA protocol option	Y	Y	Y	Y	Y			
IMA max. diff. dly	Y		Y		Y			
IMA clock mode								
Loop clock	Y	Y	Y	Y	Y	Y	Y	Y
Line framing	Y	Y	Y					
Line framing						Y		Y
Line coding	Y							
Line CRC	Y			Y	Y			
Line recv impedance	Y							
Line E1/J1 signal								
Line encoding								
Line T1 signalling	Y							
Line cable type	Y							
Line length	Y		Y	Y		Y	Y	
Line 56KBS bit pos								
Line pct fast modem	Y							
Line cnfg	Y							
Line cnf slot.line	Y							
Line CAS-switching	Y							
Idle code	Y	Y	Y	Y	Y	Y	Y	Y
HCS masking	Y	Y	Y	Y	Y	Y	Y	Y
Payload scramble	Y	Y	Y	Y	Y	Y	Y	Y
Frame scramble	Y							Y
Line SVC-caching	Y							

Line DS-0 Map

This parameter specifies the timeslots to use for an E1 ATM line. The choices are 0-31 or 0-15,17-31.

IMA Group Member(s)

This parameter specifies the physical interfaces that constitute an IMA group. This parameter may be used to add members to an IMA group or to delete members (except the first one) from an IMA group.

Retained Links

This parameter specifies the number of T1 or E1 circuits of the IMA group that *must* be available in order for the IMA line to remain in service. If members of the IMA group fail such that fewer members than specified by this parameter remain, the entire line is removed from service.

IMA Protocol Option

This parameter specifies whether the IMA protocol should be used on a T1 or E1 line with only a single circuit. If this is enabled, additional circuits may be added later to increase the size of the IMA line.

IMA Max. Diff. Dly

This parameter specifies the maximum difference in end-to-end delay that is allowed between members of an IMA group.

The UXM buffers cells carried on each member of the IMA group such that the total delay (actual delay plus buffer delay) is the same for each member of the IMA group.

IMA Clock Mode

This parameter is a display parameter only. The value CTC stands for Common Transmit Clock. This means that all members of an IMA group *must* use the same clock source.

Loop Clock

This parameter specifies whether the transmit clock on this line should be derived from the receive clock on the line (Loop Clock = Yes) or derived from the node's internal bus frequency (Loop Clock = No).

Line Framing

This parameter allows the selection of

- D4 or ESF framing for T1 lines
- PLCP or HEC framing for T3 and OC3 lines

Line Coding

This parameter allows the selection of

- AMI, B8ZS, or ZCS ones-density enforcement for CVM and UVM T1 lines
- AMI, HDB3, or ZCS ones-density enforcement for CVM and UVM E1 lines

Generally, B8ZS or HDB3 should be used, because these algorithms guarantee sufficient ones density without compromising data integrity in any way.

AMI should be avoided, because it does not ensure sufficient ones density.

ZCS should be avoided, because it guarantees sufficient ones density but might introduce uncorrectable bit errors in user information.

For further details on these transmission formats, refer to the *WAN Quick Start* CD-ROM.

Line CRC

This parameter specifies whether the optional CRC-4 algorithm defined for E1 lines in the ITU-T G.703 standard is enabled or disabled on this line.

Line Recv Impedance

This parameter specifies whether the line receive impedance is to be 75 or 120 ohms, balanced or unbalanced.

Line E1/J1 Signal

This parameter specifies whether CAS or CCS signalling is used on an E1 voice/data line.

Line Encoding

This parameter specifies whether the Pulse Code Modulation (PCM) encoding of digital voice samples on this line uses the μ-law algorithm (commonly used on T1 lines) or the A-law algorithm (commonly used on E1 and J1 lines).

For further details on these encoding formats, refer to the *WAN Quick Start* CD-ROM.

Line T1 Signalling

This parameter specifies the voice-signaling format used on a T1 voice line. The options are

- CCS
- AB (available with D4 framing only)
- ABCD (available with ESF framing)
- ABAB (available with ESF framing)

For further details on these signaling formats, refer to the *WAN Quick Start* CD-ROM.

Line Cable Type

Line cable type is a choice between MAT cable and ABAM cable. You should leave it at the default.

Line Length

Line length and line cable type (specified together) determine the circuit's line build-out (LBO) based on the type of cable used and the cable distance to the next active component— usually a CSU.

Line 56KBS Bit Pos

This parameter is used whenever a 56 kbps or Nx56 kbps data connection is carried on a CVM or UVM line. Because 56 kbps uses only seven of the eight bits available in a 64 kbps timeslot, this parameter is needed to specify whether the unused bit is the timeslot's least-significant bit (LSB) or most-significant bit (MSB).

Line Pct Fast Modem

This parameter is used to specify what percentage of the voice channels on the line are expected to be carrying fast modem or fax traffic at any time. This parameter ensures that sufficient CellBus bandwidth is available to the card, because fast modem or fax connections generate more FastPackets per second than the otherwise compressed voice connection.

Line Cnfg

This parameter specifies the line configuration.

Line Cnf slot.line

Line Cnf slot.line and Line Cnfg are for display only. They work together for the UVM line pass-through feature.

Line CAS-Switching

This parameter cannot be configured. It was intended for a feature that was planned but has not yet been developed.

Idle Code

This parameter specifies, as a hexadecimal value, the code to be placed in the payload of idle cells transmitted on a UXM line.

HCS Masking

This parameter specifies whether the 8-bit CRC in the HCS field of the ATM cell header is calculated using a seed value of 0 or a seed value of 0x55 hexadecimal.

A seed value of 0 might result in an ATM cell header that is all 0s. Such a cell header is difficult to identify accurately when using HEC line framing, where cell delineation is accomplished by searching for valid HCS fields to identify valid ATM cell headers. In such a case, it is better to use a nonzero seed value.

Payload Scramble

This parameter specifies whether ATM cell payloads are scrambled (and unscrambled at the far end) to reduce the chances of repeating data patterns causing clock recovery problems on the trunk.

Frame Scramble

Frame scramble is an optional standard for SONET interfaces only. Like cell scrambling, it is vital to have both the BPX and user equipment interfaces set with or without frame scrambling.

Line SVC-Caching

This parameter is not supported.

Downing a Line

The **dnln** command deactivates the hardware supporting a line, after which it no longer carries framing or traffic of any kind.

Before a line can be downed with the **dnln** command, all connections and ports must be removed from it, as described in later chapters.

After a line has been downed with the **dnln** command, it is removed from the **dsplns** screen entirely.

Here is the **dnln** command syntax:

```
dnln <line ID>
```

<line ID> is of the same format as that used in the **upln** command.

Summary

This chapter provided an overview of the methods used to log into the network and discussed how to identify the node software revision, card types, card revisions, and status. It described how to monitor environmental characteristics used to activate and display trunks and how to use online help.

This chapter also discussed how to configure the node name, date, time, and time zone, as well as how to display and modify control and auxiliary port configurations and functions.

You should be able to identify the IP address of the node you are viewing, identify, display, and modify trunk configuration parameters, and display and modify node print capabilities. Also, you should be able to identify and list other trunks and nodes in the network and remotely access other nodes.

In addition, you should be able to describe the performance impact of modifying selected trunk configuration parameters; give examples of commands and identify the function of each; and activate, display, and modify line configuration parameters.

Review Questions

1 Commands are a combination of _____ and _____. The < > brackets indicate _____ parameters, and the [ ] brackets indicate _____ parameters.

2 What are the four categories of command privilege levels?

3 Which command would you use to view summary information about the status of all node interfaces?

4 Which command would you use to view a node's environmental conditions?

5 In checking the interfaces' status, you see that one interface displays "Standby-F." This indicates that the card is what?

6 To define the node name, you use the _____ command and specify a name that is _____ characters long.

7 To define the date, you use the _____ command. To define the local time zone, you use the _____ command.

8 Which command would you use to specify the control and auxiliary port configuration parameter?

9 Which command would you use to specify printer characteristics and modes?

10 What are the three printer modes?

11 Which command would you use to discover which trunks exist in the network?

12 To display trunk configuration details, use the _____ or _____ command, and to modify them, use the _____ command.

13 In what order do you use the **dntrk** and **deltrk** commands in order to deactivate a trunk?

14 True or false: The **addcon** command is used to activate a trunk, but not until both ends of the trunk have been enabled with the **uptrk** command.

15 Which command would you use to determine the status of all lines on the node?

16 The _____ command activates a line, and the _____ command modifies a line's configuration parameters.

17 In an IGX network, a _____ is defined as a T1, E1, T3, E3, or OC3c/STM1 digital transport facility, carrying information between the node and an _____.

18 What are the total user channels available on T1, E1, and J1 voice or data lines?

This chapter covers the following key topics:

- Voice Connections
- Voice FastPackets
- Voice Connection and Channel Commands
- Voice Connection and Channel Review
- Signaling Transport and Processing
- Data Networks
- Data FastPackets
- Data Channels

CHAPTER 4

Voice and Data Channels and Connections

An IGX network can provide a voice transport service by providing voice connections that are typically used to interconnect private branch exchanges (PBXs). Each voice connection places incoming digital voice samples into FastPackets. The IGX cards can also compress the voice signals, significantly reducing bandwidth requirements. This chapter covers the IGX commands used to create, display, and delete voice connections and configure voice channels.

An IGX network can also provide a legacy (transparent) data transport service by providing data connections to interconnect a wide variety of data equipment. Each transparent data connection places incoming data bits into FastPackets. The IGX cards may also significantly reduce bandwidth requirements by eliminating repetitive data patterns from the data stream. This chapter covers the IGX commands used to create, display, and delete legacy or transparent data connections and to configure data channels.

Voice Connections

Channelized Voice Module (CVM) and Universal Voice Module (UVM) cards interconnect PBXs using packet voice connections.

As described in Chapter 3, "IGX Node Administration, Trunks, and Lines," a voice line, typically connected to a PBX, is used to carry digital voice samples into a CVM or UVM card group. The line carries n independent voice channels multiplexed on the T1, E1, or J1 line.

Voice Connections and Channels

A voice connection is a point-to-point permanent virtual circuit (PVC) that links two voice channels in an IGX network. Figure 4-1 illustrates voice connections and channels.

Figure 4-1 *Voice Connections and Channels*

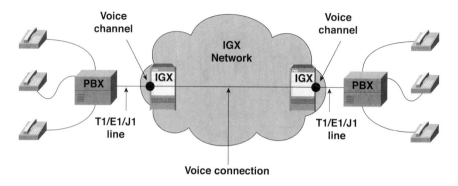

A voice channel is a single timeslot of a voice line on a CVM or UVM card in an IGX.

This chapter describes how to add, configure, display, and delete voice connections and channels. It also details how digital voice samples are transported across the IGX network. Furthermore, it covers the configuration of voice channels and how they work with the particular PBX or other attached CPE.

Before voice connections can be created or configured, and before voice channels can be configured, the voice line supporting the connections and channels must be upped, as described in Chapter 3.

However, voice connections may be added without regard for the channels at each end. Conversely, a voice channel may be configured regardless or whether a voice connection terminates on that channel.

Voice FastPackets

The attached PBX or other device represents analog voice frequencies as digital signals using Pulse Code Modulation (PCM). The PCM algorithm samples the voice source 8000 times per second and represents each sample of the signal using an 8-bit value. Streams of PCM samples from multiple voice sources are multiplexed using time-division multiplexing (TDM). The samples from a particular voice source are placed in a timeslot assigned to that source conversation.

The CVM or UVM cards receive the incoming T1, E1, or J1 frames and build FastPackets containing PCM or compressed voice samples, as shown in Figure 4-2. When a FastPacket is full, it is sent across the network to the destination CVM or UVM card.

Figure 4-2   *Building Voice FastPackets*

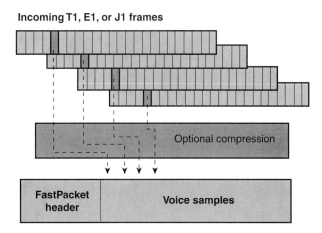

The CVM and UVM cards use Digital Signal Processors (DSPs) to build these voice FastPackets.

Voice Compression Techniques

In addition to creating FastPackets, the DSP can compress the incoming voice samples. Compression schemes can dramatically reduce bandwidth requirements while approaching PCM voice quality. Supported voice compression techniques include PCM, ADPCM, LD-CELP, and CS-ACELP, as described in the following sections.

PCM

In the simplest case, the UVM or CVM can perform no compression at all. In that case, the CVM or UVM simply places the incoming PCM samples into the voice FastPackets. (The UVM or CVM is does not perform the PCM algorithm.)

Each DSP on the CVM or UVM can build FastPackets with PCM samples for two voice connections simultaneously.

ADPCM

Adaptive differential pulse code modulation (ADPCM), described in G.726, encodes only the difference between one PCM-encoded sample and the following sample, not the actual sample values. Because the range of values for the difference between successive samples is much smaller than the actual value of the sample, ADPCM requires fewer bits for encoding.

The CVM and UVM cards support ADPCM connections using 32 kbps (4 bits per sample) and 24 kbps (3 bits per sample). The CVM also supports ADPCM connections using 16 kbps (2 bits per sample).

Each DSP on the CVM or UVM can build FastPackets with ADPCM samples for two voice connections simultaneously.

LD-CELP

Low-Delay Code Excited Linear Prediction (LD-CELP) compression, described in G.728, creates low-bandwidth, low-delay, packet-based traffic for transport across a WAN. LD-CELP is supported on the UVM at a 16 kbps rate.

Each DSP on the UVM can build FastPackets with LD-CELP samples for only one voice connection at a time.

CS-ACELP

Conjugate Structure Algebraic Code Excited Linear Prediction (CS-ACELP) compression, described in G.729, also creates low-bandwidth, low-delay, packet-based traffic for transport across a WAN. CS-ACELP is supported on the UVM at an 8 kbps rate. Each of the CELP algorithms encodes a group or structure of PCM voice samples, allowing predictions on voice signal frequency and power.

Each DSP on the UVM can build FastPackets with G.729 CSA-CELP samples for only one voice connection at a time.

A simplified version of CS-ACELP, described in G.729 Annex A, is also supported on the UVM. This algorithm, commonly known as G.729A, allows each DSP on the UVM to build FastPackets for two voice connections simultaneously.

Voice Activity Detection

Voice Activity Detection (VAD) further reduces bandwidth requirements by suppressing silent periods. VAD can be used with any type of voice connection:

- With VAD, FastPackets are created only when voice is detected.
- Without VAD, FastPackets are created all the time (including when the voice connection is not in use).
- VAD is not dependent on the connection's signaling state (on-hook or off-hook). Instead, VAD works by analyzing the speech power level of the incoming PCM voice samples.

Voice Connection and Channel Commands

Table 4-1 lists the commands that are introduced in this chapter. This list includes commands for configuring, displaying, adding, and deleting voice and data connections.

Table 4-1   *Voice and Data Connection Commands*

Command	Description	Privilege Level
addcon	Adds a connection between two specified channels.	1 and 2
cnflnpass	Configures a UVM line for line pass-through.	1
delcon	Deletes a connection.	1 and 2
dspcon	Displays detailed characteristics of one connection.	1 through 6
dspcons	Displays a summary listing of all connections.	1 through 6

Table 4-2 lists the commands used to display and configure voice and data channels.

Table 4-2   *Voice and Data Channel Commands*

Command	Description	Privilege Level
cnfchadv	Configures a voice channel for adaptive VAD.	1 and 2
cnfchdl	Configures a voice channel's dial type.	1 and 2
cnfchec	Configures a voice channel's echo canceller parameters.	1
cnfchfax	Configures a voice channel for fax detection.	1 and 2
cnfchgn	Configures a voice channel's input and output gain.	1 and 2
cnfchutl	Configures a voice channel's utilization.	1 and 2
cnfcond	Configures or creates a conditioning criteria.	1 through 6
cnfrcvsig	Configures the receive signaling bit mapping for a voice channel.	1 through 6
cnfvchtp	Configures a voice channel's interface type.	1 and 2
cnfxmtcvsig	Configures the transmit signaling bit mapping for a voice channel.	1 through 6
dspchcnf	Displays a voice channel's configuration.	1 through 6
dspchdlcnf	Displays a voice channel's dial type.	1 through 6
dspchec	Displays voice channel's echo canceller configuration.	1 through 6
dspcond	Displays a voice channel conditioning template.	1 through 6
dspconst	Displays the real-time signaling state for many voice channels.	1 through 6
dspsigqual	Displays a voice channel's signaling qualifiers.	1 through 6

Adding a Voice Connection

The **addcon** command adds a voice connection between two UVM cards, two CVM cards, or one UVM and one CVM card.

Here is the **addcon** command syntax:

```
addcon <local channel(s)> <remote node> <remote channel(s)> <type> [route avoid]
```

Table 4-3 describes the **addcon** command parameters.

Table 4-3   addcon *Command Parameters*

Parameter	Description
local channel(s)	Specifies the local channel, or range of channels, to connect. The maximum number of channels allowed is 16. If multiple channels are specified, they must be contiguous.
	CVM—*slot.channel*[-*channel*]
	UVM—*slot.line.channel*[-*channel*]
remote node	Specifies the destination node name.
remote channel(s)	Specifies the remote channel, or range of channels, to connect.
	If multiple channels are specified in the *local channel(s)* parameter, the range of channels need not be specified in the *remote channel(s)* parameter. It is sufficient to specify only the first channel of the range.
	If multiple channels are specified, the number of channels must match the number of channels specified by the *local channel(s)* parameter.
	CVM—*slot.channel*[-*channel*]
	UVM—*slot.line.channel*[-*channel*]
type	Specifies the connection type, as described in Table 4-4.
route avoid	Specifies the type(s) of trunk that the connection is not allowed to use.
	The default is no avoidance. Possible values are as follows:
	*s—Avoid satellite trunks
	*t—Avoid terrestrial trunks
	*z—Avoid zero code suppression (ZCS) trunks
	*s *z—Avoid satellite and ZCS trunks
	*t *z—Avoid terrestrial and ZCS trunks

CVM Voice Connection Types

Table 4-4 shows the voice connection types supported on the CVM card. The codes shown in the Type columns are used to specify the choice of compression and/or VAD when a connection is created with the **addcon** command.

Table 4-4   *CVM Voice Connection Types*

Algorithm	Number of Connections Per DSP	Type	
		Without VAD	With VAD
64 kbps PCM (G.711)	2	P	V
32 kbps ADPCM (G.726)	2	A32	C32
32 kbps ADPCM (G.726)	2	A32D[1]	C32D[1]
24 kbps ADPCM (G.726)	2	A24	C24
16 kbps ADPCM (G.726) Unsuitable for ZCS trunks	2	A16Z[2]	C16Z[2]
16 kbps ADPCM (G.726) Suitable for ZCS trunks	2	A16[3]	C16[3]
64 kbps transparent data	2	T[4]	

In Table 4-4, connection types that are referenced with a 1 use a specialized form of 32 kbps ADPCM compression that can carry both voice traffic and high-speed modem traffic. For all other connection types, if a high-speed modem is detected, the connection is upgraded to 64 kbps by disabling the ADPCM compression for the duration of the modem transmission. In contrast, when a high-speed modem is detected on one of these types of connections, it remains compressed to 32 kbps.

The connection types that are referenced with a 2 use 2-bit samples. Possible samples are 00, 01, 10, and 11. If a long string of 00 samples were included in a FastPacket that is sent across a ZCS trunk, the ZCS algorithm would change every fourth sample from 00 to 01 (to maintain ones density on the trunk), thereby introducing a large error in the ADPCM sample. Thus, these connection types are not allowed to traverse ZCS trunks. However, they may use any other trunk type.

The connection types that are referenced with a 3 are connection types that solve the problem just described by using only the ADPCM samples 01, 10, and 11. Because no 00 sample is allowed, the ZCS algorithm would never change an ADPCM sample. Therefore, these connection types may be carried on ZCS trunks. However, because fewer distinct ADPCM samples are used, there is increased voice distortion on these connections.

The connection type that is referenced with a 4 is technically not a voice connection. Nonetheless, it is included here because this type of connection is used to carry the signaling timeslot on a CCS line.

Because the CVM contains 16 DSPs, and each DSP can support two connections of any type, the CVM can support any combination of connections. This makes it different from the UVM, which is described in the following section.

UVM Voice Connection Types

Table 4-5 shows the voice connection types supported on the UVM card. The codes shown in the Type columns are used to specify the choice of compression and/or VAD when a connection is created with the **addcon** command.

Table 4-5 *CVM Voice Connection Types*

Algorithm	Number of Connections Per DSP	Type	
		Without VAD	With VAD
64 kbps PCM (G.711)	2	P	V
32 kbps ADPCM (G.726)	2	A32	C32
24 kbps ADPCM (G.726)	2	A24	C24
16 kbps LD-CELP (G.728)	1	L16	L16V
8 kbps CS-ACELP (G.729)	1	G729R8	G729R8V
8 kbps CS-ACELP (G.729A)	2	G729AR8	G729AR8V
64 kbps transparent data	2	T[1]	
64 kbps transparent data with HDLC idle flag suppression	1	TD[1]	

The connection types that are referenced with a 1 are technically not voice connections. Nonetheless, they are included here because they are the types of connections used to carry the signaling timeslot on a CCS line.

Each DSP on the UVM connection types described in Table 4-5 supports the following:

- Either one or two of any combination of connection types P, V, A32, C32, A24, C24, and T
- Either one or two of any combination of connection types G729AR8 and G729AR8V
- One L16, L16V, G729R8, or G729R8V connection
- One TD connection
- One Fax Relay connection

Fax Relay is a feature of the UVM that allows a fax transmission (up to a maximum data rate of 9600 baud) to be carried across the network as a 9.6 kbps data connection instead of as a 64 kbps uncompressed voice connection. However, because a Fax Relay connection uses an entire DSP, the Fax Relay feature is supported only with voice connection types that also use an entire DSP. In other words, the Fax Relay feature is supported only with L16, L16V, G729R8, and G729R8V connections. Chapter 5 describes how to enable or disable this feature.

Configuring Line Pass-Through on a UVM

Any combination of connections is possible on the UVM card as long as the configuration does not exceed the capacity of the 16 DSPs on the card. However, as shown in Table 4-5, there are not enough DSPs on the UVM card to process all the possible 24 (for T1) or 31 (for E1/J1) channels when using L16, L16V, G729R8, or G729R8V connections, because each of these connection types uses an entire DSP.

Figure 4-3 illustrates the UVM line pass-through process. If the number and types of connections exceed the UVM's DSP capacity, a second UVM may be configured in pass-through mode to process the extra channels.

Figure 4-3   *UVM Line Pass-Through*

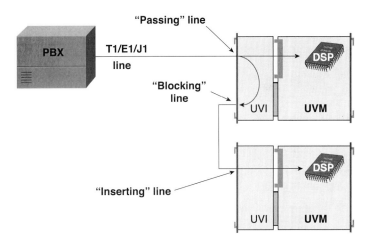

In line pass-through mode, one UVM is cabled to a second UVM. The first UVM passes the unprocessed channels to the second UVM. Example 4-1 shows the **cnflnpass** command output.

The possible line configuration states are designated as follows:

- **Passing**—Connected to the external equipment and configured for pass-through mode.

- **Blocking**—Feeding the unprocessed channels to the second UVM.

- **Inserting**—Receiving the unprocessed channels from the first UVM.

- **External**—Default for a newly upped line. In this state, the line is not participating in a pass-through configuration.

Example 4-1 cnflnpass *Output*

```
Igx4    TN    group8:1    IGX 8420    9.2.20    Sep. 9 1999    16:07 CST

LN3.1 Config    T1/24   UVM slot: 3
Loop clock:    No
Line   framing:    D4
Line   coding:    ZCS
Line   encoding:    u-LAW
Line   T1 signalling:    AB
Line   cable type:    ABAM
Line   length: 0-133 ft.
Line   56KBS Bit Pos:    msb
Line   pct fast modem:    20
Line   cnfg: Passing
Line   cnf slot.line:    4.1
Line   CAS-Switching:--
Line   SVC-Caching:    Off
Traffic Shaping:    No

Last Command: cnflnpass 3.1 4.1

Next Command:
```

Here is the **cnflnpass** command syntax:

    cnflnpass <passing line> <inserting line>

Table 4-6 describes the parameters associated with the **cnflnpass** command.

Table 4-6   cnflnpass *Command Parameters*

Parameter	Descriptions
passing line	In the form *slot.line*. The line passing the unprocessed channels. This *must* be line 1 on the first UVM.
inserting line	In the form *slot.line*. The line receiving the unprocessed channels. This can be either line 1 or line 2 on the second UVM.

The IGX software ensures that a channel that is used on the first UVM (processing the "passing" line) cannot also be used on the second UVM (processing the "inserting" line).

Displaying Line Pass-Through on a UVM

The **dspln** or **dsplncnf** command indicates the state of line pass-through. Example 4-2 shows the **dsplncnf** command output.

Example 4-2   **dsplncnf** *Output*

```
Igx4   TN  group8:1   IGX 8420  9. 9.2.20 Sep. 9 1999 16:08 CST


LN      4.1 Config       T1/24              UVM slot: 4
Loop  clock:          No
Line    framing:        D4
Line    coding:         ZCS
Line    encoding:       u-LAW
Line    T1 signalling: AB
Line    cable type:     ABAM
Line    length:         0-133 ft.
Line    56KBS Bit Pos: msb
Line    pct fast modem: 20
Line    cnfg:           Inserting
Line    cnf slot.line:    3.1
Line    CAS-Switching:
Line    SVC-Caching: Off
Traffic Shaping:        No


Last Command: dsplncnf 4.1


Next Command:
```

The Line cnfg: parameter shows whether the line is External, Passing, Blocking, or Inserting, as defined previously. If the displayed line is Passing, the Line cnf slot.line parameter shows the number of the corresponding Inserting line. If the displayed line is Inserting, the Line cnf slot.line parameter shows the number of the corresponding Passing line. If the displayed line is External or Blocking, the Line cnf slot.line parameter shows nothing.

Adding a Voice Connection

With an understanding of the various voice connection types, their DSP limitations, and the work-arounds, it is now possible to complete the task of adding voice connections. Example 4-3 shows the **addcon** command.

Here is the **addcon** command syntax:

```
addcon <local channel(s)> <remote node> <remote channel(s)> <type> [route avoid]
```

The **addcon** command parameters were explained in Table 4-3.

Example 4-3 addcon *Output*

```
igx1  TN  group1:1  IGX 8420 9.2.20  Jun. 30 1999  10:49 CDT
Local Remote Remote
Channel NodeName Channel State Type Compress Code COS
3.1.1    igx4    7.1.10  Ok  g729r8v  VAD/CSACELP  2
3.1.2    igx4    7.1.1   Ok  a32      ADPCM        2
3.1.3-5  igx4    7.1.2-4 Ok  v        VAD          2

This Command: addcon 3.1.1 igx4 7.1.10 g729r8v
Next Command:
```

Displaying All Connections

The **dspcons** command displays summary information for all connections that terminate on this node, as shown in Example 4-4.

Example 4-4 dspcons *Output*

```
igx1 TN  group1:1  IGX 8420  9.2.20  Jun. 30 1999  10:50  CDT
Local  Remote  Remote
Channel NodeName  Channel State Type  Compress  Code  COS
3.1.1   igx4     7.1.10  Ok  g729r8v VAD/CSACELP   2
3.1.2   igx4     7.1.1   Ok  a32     ADPCM         2
3.1.3-5 igx4     7.1.2-4 Ok  v       VAD           2

This Command: dspcons
Next Command:
```

Here is the **dspcons** command syntax:

dspcons [*start channel*] [*node name*] [*filter*]

The **dspcons** command parameters are described in Table 4-7.

Table 4-7 dspcons *Command Parameters*

Parameter	Descriptions
start channel	If specified, this parameter causes only connections with a local channel number equal to or greater than this to be displayed. This parameter is most useful in nodes that have a large number of connections.
node name	If specified, this parameter causes only connections to this node to be displayed. This parameter is most useful in nodes that have a large number of connections.

Table 4-7   **dspcons** *Command Parameters (Continued)*

Parameter	Descriptions
filter	If specified, this parameter causes only connections of a certain type or status to be displayed.
	Many filters are available. Here are those that are relevant to displaying voice connections:
	-v—Displays only voice connections.
	–fail—Displays only failed connections.
	Other filters are described in other chapters.

Each line of the **dspcons** display shows summary information about one connection or a range of contiguous connections if all connections in the range have the same values in the other fields. The fields displayed are listed in Table 4-8.

Table 4-8   **dspcons** *Command Field Descriptions*

Fields	Description
Local Channel	The local channel number(s) of the connection(s) on this line.
Remote NodeName	The name of the destination node for the connection(s) on this line.
Remote Channel	The channel number(s), at the remote node, of the connection(s) on this line.
State	**Ok**—The connection is available for use.
	Failed—The connection is unavailable for use. See the **dspcon** command for possible reasons for the failure.
	Other possible connection states are described in later chapters.
Type	Connection type.
Compression	Compression methods currently in use (VAD, ADPCM, CS-ACELP, or LD-CELP).
Code	Applies only to data connections.
COS	Class of Service.

Displaying Detailed Parameters of One Connection

The **dspcon** command displays detailed information for one connection, as shown in Example 4-5.

Example 4-5 **dspcon** *Output*

```
igx1  group1:1   IGX 8420   9.2.20   Jun. 30 1999  08:51 CDT
Conn:  3.1.5    igx3   3.1.5            v
Status:OK

Owner: LOCAL  Restriction: NONE  COS: 2 Compression: VAD

Path:  igx1      12--   13igx4
Pref:   Not Configured


igx1   UVM:   OK        igx3    UVM:   OK
       Line  3.1 : OK   OFFHK   Line  3.1 : OK

This Command: dspcon  3.1.5
```

Here is the **dspcon** command syntax:

dspcon *<channel>*

channel specifies the channel number of the connection to be displayed.

The information about this connection from the **dspcons** screen is repeated near the top of this screen. This includes the local channel, remote node name, remote channel, connection type, connection status, and CoS.

Additional details provided are as follows:

- **Owner**—Determines which end issued the **addcon** command. If local, the connection was added from this node; if remote, the connection was added from the remote node.

- **Restriction**—Based on the route avoid parameter. Specifies any trunk type that the connection cannot use.

- **Path**—The route (the series of nodes and trunks) currently used by the connection.

- **Preferred route**—A user-configured preferred route. Connection routing is discussed in detail in Chapter 7, "Connection Routing, Synchronizing the Network, and Managing Jobs."

- **Endpoint status**—The status of the card group and line supporting the channels at each end of the connection.

- **On-hook or off-hook status**—The local channel state for the connection based on the channel type (described in Chapter 5, "Frame Relay Ports and Connections").

Deleting Connections

The **delcon** command removes one or more connections from the network. A connection may be deleted from either end of the connection.

The **delcon** command screen is essentially the same as the **dspcons** screen. Example 4-6 shows the **delcon** command output.

Example 4-6 **delcon** *Output*

```
igx1   TN   group1:1   IGX 8420   9.2.20   Jun. 30 1999   10:49   CDT
Local     Remote     Remote
Channel NodeName   Channel  State  Type  Compress    Code COS
3.1.1     igx4     7.1.10     Ok    g729r8v VAD/CSACELP   2
3.1.2     igx4     7.1.1      Ok    a32     ADPCM         2
3.1.3-5   igx4     7.1.2-4    Ok    v       VAD           2
3.1.24    igx3     6.1.10     Failed        td            2


This Command: delcon   3.1.1
Delete these connections (y/n)?
```

Here is the **delcon** command syntax:

delcon *<local channel(s)>*

local channel(s) is the local channel number(s) of the connection(s) to be deleted.

Voice Connection and Channel Review

As described earlier in this chapter, a *voice connection* is a point-to-point permanent virtual circuit (PVC) that links two voice channels in an IGX network.

A *voice channel* can be a timeslot of a T1, E1, or J1 line on a CVM or UVM card. Each voice channel carries a 64 kbps stream of PCM-encoded voice (or voice-frequency modulated data), typically from a PBX. Voice channels are endpoints of voice connections.

This section describes how to configure voice channels to provide the necessary interface to the PBX.

NOTE   In general, a voice channel can be configured regardless of whether a voice connection terminates on that channel.

Each voice channel in an IGX can support a variety of options. For the purposes of this chapter, the configurable characteristics are grouped into two categories: PCM voice sample processing and signaling transport and processing.

PCM Voice Sample Processing

Each voice channel in an IGX may support a variety of PCM voice sample processing options.

Voice Activity Detection

Voice Activity Detection (VAD) is a silence suppression algorithm available on the UVM and CVM.

VAD suppresses the transmission of FastPackets on a voice channel any time the channel is found to be silent based on an analysis of the average power of the incoming PCM voice samples.

NOTE   VAD does not consider a voice channel's signaling state to distinguish silence from speech. This allows VAD to operate on voice channels that use any type of voice signaling, including Common Channel Signaling (CCS).

Configuring Voice Channel Utilization

On any voice channel that is using VAD, it is likely that the voice channel will generate far fewer FastPackets per second than the channel would generate if VAD were not in use. Therefore, VAD allows the IGX software to reserve less trunk bandwidth for such a connection than would otherwise be necessary. The **cnfchutl** command is shown in Example 4-7.

Example 4-7   **cnfchutl** *Output*

```
igx1            TRM    group6:1        IGX 8420   9.2.20    Aug. 28 1999 13:37 CDT


            %   Adaptive          Gain (dB)  Dial   Interface        OnHk       Cond
Channels  Util Voice      Fax    In   Out    Type   Type         A  B  C  D Crit
3.1.1      32  Enabled  Enabled   0    0    Inband  Unconfig     ?  ?  -  - a
3.1.2-4    32  Enabled  Disabled -6    2    Pulse   Unconfig     ?  ?  -  - a
3.1.5-15   60  Enabled  Disabled -6    2    Pulse   Unconfig     ?  ?  -  - a
3.1.17-31  60  Enabled  Disabled  0    0    Inband  Unconfig     ?  ?  -  - a
3.2.1-31   60  Enabled  Disabled  0    0    Inband  Unconfig     ?  ?  -  - a


Last Command: cnfchutl 3.1.1-4 32


Next Command:
```

The **cnfchutl** command specifies, as a percentage, the expected *average* utilization rate for a voice channel. (There is no way for the IGX software to guess what percentage of the total possible FastPacket rate is really needed for a voice channel, because that is determined by the speaker's voice characteristics and the dynamics of each conversation.) The percent utilization is multiplied by the channel's full FastPacket rate (assuming that VAD finds *no* silence) to determine the trunk bandwidth reserved for the connection.

The percent utilization for a voice channel may be configured to any value from 0% to 100% (60% is the default). The configured percent utilization is ignored if VAD is not used on the channel.

Here is the **cnfchutl** command syntax:

```
cnfchutl <channel(s)> <% utilization>
```

Table 4-9 describes the parameters associated with the **cnfchutl** command.

Table 4-9   **cnfchutl** *Command Parameters*

Parameter	Description
channel(s)	Specifies the voice channel(s) to be configured in this format:
	CVM—*slot.timeslot[-timeslot]*
	UVM—*slot.line.timeslot[-timeslot]*
% utilization	Specifies the expected utilization, in the range 0 to 100 percent. The default value for voice channels is 60 percent.

Adaptive VAD

The Adaptive VAD feature, also known as Adaptive Voice, is an old feature that is now obsolete and is no longer supported. Unfortunately, the commands relating to this feature have not yet been removed from the IGX software.

The Adaptive VAD feature allowed any connection configured to use VAD to automatically disable VAD whenever sufficient trunk bandwidth was available and to re-enable VAD whenever trunk bandwidth was needed (as a result of new connections being added or a trunk failure, for example).

In order for the feature to operate, it was necessary for the feature to be

- Enabled on the channel at each end of the connection. (By default, it is enabled on all voice channels.)
- Enabled on the node at each end of the connection. (By default, it is not enabled on the node.) Because this feature is not supported, it should never be enabled on the node. If it were enabled, unpredictable results might occur.

Configuring Adaptive Voice

The **cnfchadv** command, as shown in Example 4-8, enables or disables the Adaptive VAD feature on one or more voice channels. If this feature is globally disabled on the node, this command has no practical effect.

Example 4-8   cnfchadv *Output*

```
igx4              TN    group8:1        IGX 8420  9.2.20     Sep. 9 1999  12:39 CST

               %   Adaptive          Gain (dB)  Dial   Interface        OnHk      Cond
Channels    Util  Voice     Fax     In   Out   Type   Type         A  B  C  D Crit
3.1.1        50   Disabled    -      0    -2   User   4W E&M       0  X  -  -  a
3.1.2        55   Enabled     -     -3     0   User   4W E&M       0  X  -  -  a
3.1.3        90   Enabled     -      0     0   Pulse  Unconfig     ?  ?  -  -  a
3.1.4        55   Enabled     -     -6     6   Inband 4W E&M       0  X  -  -  a
3.1.5        55   Enabled     -      0     0   Pulse  4W E&M       0  X  -  -  a
3.1.6-12     55   Enabled     -      0     0   Inband Unconfig     ?  ?  -  -  a
3.1.13-15    90   Enabled     -      0     0   Inband Unconfig     ?  ?  -  -  a
3.1.16-17    90   Enabled     -      0     0   Inband Unconfig     ?  ?  -  -  a
3.1.18-23    90   Enabled     -      0     0   Inband Unconfig     ?  ?  -  -  a
3.1.24       90   Disabled    -     -6     3   Inband Unconfig     ?  ?  -  -  a
3.2.1        90   Enabled     -      2     2   Pulse  4W E&M       0  X  -  -  a
3.2.2-11     90   Enabled     -      0     0   Inband Unconfig     ?  ?  -  -  a
3.2.12       90   Enabled     -      0     0   Pulse  Unconfig     ?  ?  -  -  a

Last Command: cnfchadv 3.1.1 d


Next Command:
```

NOTE   Because this feature is no longer supported, this command should not be used. It is included here only to give you a full understanding of the display screens shown in this chapter.

Here is the **cnfchadv** command syntax:

```
cnfchadv <channel(s)> <e | d>
```

channel(s) is the channel or range of channels to be configured.

e | d enables or disables Adaptive VAD.

High-Speed Modem Detection and Fax Detection

As described in the preceding sections, many types of voice connections are available to carry voice traffic across an IGX network. Many of these connections types include one or more types of compression.

Naturally, it is possible that such connections might, at times, carry traffic that originates in a high-speed modem or fax machine. Unfortunately, most compression algorithms cannot adequately transmit high-speed modem or fax transmissions.

Consequently, the IGX monitors every voice channel in use (in other words, any channel that has a connection terminating on it) to detect the characteristic signals from high-speed modems of fax machines. Depending on the card type (UVM or CVM), the connection type, and various parameters, various actions may be taken to provide an error-free transmission path for the duration of the modem or fax transmission.

Modem/Fax Upgrades

There are several considerations when doing a fax or modem upgrade. The following sections describe the 64 kbps upgrade, the Fax Relay feature, Fax Relay configuration, and channel gain and configuration.

64 kbps Upgrade

By default, all connection types on all voice cards are upgraded to 64 kbps uncompressed PCM connections whenever a high-speed modem or fax signal is detected at the voice channel at either end.

Fax Relay

Fax Relay is a feature supported on a UVM card that is running Model D firmware or later.

Fax Relay is supported on G3 fax transmissions up to a maximum speed of 9600 bps.

The Fax Relay feature allows the voice-frequency modulated fax data to be demodulated to a native data stream and transported across the IGX network as transparent data. At the far-end UVM, the data is remodulated for delivery to the destination fax machine. Naturally, this feature represents very significant bandwidth savings compared to a conventional 64 kbps PCM upgrade.

Fax Relay is available only on voice channels that have the Fax Relay feature enabled (discussed next) and that terminate one of the following voice connection types:

- L16
- L16V
- G729R8
- G729R8V

Configuring Fax Relay

The **cnfchfax** command, as shown in Example 4-9, enables or disables the Fax Relay feature on a UVM voice channel.

Example 4-9 **cnfchfax** *Output*

```
igx1            TN    group6:1        IGX 8420  9.2.20    Aug. 28 1999 13:38 CDT


              %   Adaptive          Gain (dB)  Dial   Interface        OnHk      Cond
Channels  Util Voice      Fax      In  Out  Type   Type         A  B  C  D Crit
3.1.1       32  Enabled  Enabled    0   0   Inband Unconfig     ?  ?  -  -  a
3.1.2-3     32  Enabled  Disabled  -6   2   Pulse  Unconfig     ?  ?  -  -  a
3.1.4       32  Enabled  Enabled   -6   2   Pulse  Unconfig     ?  ?  -  -  a
3.1.5-15    40  Enabled  Disabled  -6   2   Pulse  Unconfig     ?  ?  -  -  a
3.1.17-31   40  Enabled  Disabled   0   0   Inband Unconfig     ?  ?  -  -  a
3.2.1-31    40  Enabled  Disabled   0   0   Inband Unconfig     ?  ?  -  -  a


Last Command: cnfchfax 3.1.4 e


Next Command:
```

NOTE   Enabling Fax Relay on a UVM voice channel precludes the use of the conventional 64 kbps PCM upgrade when a high-speed modem or fax signal is detected. Therefore, you must be careful to enable this feature only on voice channels that are used to terminate L16, L16V, G729R8, and G729R8V connection types.

Here is the **cnfchfax** command syntax:

cnfchfax `<channel(s)> <e | d>`

e | d enables or disables Fax Relay.

Channel Gain Considerations

In a telephone network (whether public or private), the core of the network typically consists of digital switches (such a PBXs) and digital transmission facilities. Frequently, the subscriber loops at the edge of the network are analog and carry voice frequency speech signals over copper transmission facilities.

The digital portion of a telephone network carries voice signals with no loss (or gain) and extremely low levels of signal distortion. Unfortunately, loss is unavoidable on the analog portions of the network as a result of the resistance on the copper circuits.

Adding Gain in a Telephone Network

To maintain sufficient end-to-end speech volume on a voice connection, a network must implement a level loss plan to compensate for any losses that might occur.

If it is necessary to add gain to a voice circuit, it is always best to add gain in the analog portion of the overall circuit. This is done to avoid amplifying any quantization distortion caused by the analog-to-digital conversion algorithm.

Unfortunately, it is often difficult to know exactly how much gain is needed on a voice circuit. It is also quite difficult to actually adjust the gain on a circuit.

To aid in the task of making small gain adjustments in a voice circuit for troubleshooting purposes, the IGX network provides the ability to add between –8 dB (decibels) and +6 dB of gain on a per-channel basis. However, whenever possible, any final gain adjustment should be done at the channel bank or PBX rather than within the IGX network to minimize the distortion introduced.

Configuring Gain

The **cnfchgn** command, as shown in Example 4-10, configures the amount of gain inserted by the IGX for a given channel or range of channels. The input gain is inserted at the receive side of a CVM or UVM and is applied before the signal is packetized by the card. The output gain is inserted at the transmit side of a CVM or UVM and is applied after the card has depacketized the signal.

Example 4-10 cnfchgn *Output*

```
igx1            TN     group6:1        IGX 8420  9.2.20    Aug. 28 1999 13:39 CDT


            %  Adaptive          Gain (dB)  Dial   Interface      OnHk      Cond
Channels  Util Voice      Fax    In  Out    Type   Type       A  B  C  D Crit
3.1.1       32 Enabled  Enabled   4   -3    Inband Unconfig    ?  ?  -  -  a
3.1.2-3     32 Enabled  Disabled -6    2    Pulse  Unconfig    ?  ?  -  -  a
3.1.4       32 Enabled  Enabled  -6    2    Pulse  Unconfig    ?  ?  -  -  a
3.1.5-15    40 Enabled  Disabled -6    2    Pulse  Unconfig    ?  ?  -  -  a
3.1.17-31   40 Enabled  Disabled  0    0    Inband
3.2.1-31    40 Enabled  Disabled  0    0    Inband Unconfig    ?  ?  -  -  a


Last Command: cnfchgn 3.1.1 4 -3


Next Command:
```

Here is the **cnfchgn** command syntax:

```
cnfchgn <channel(s)> <input gain> <output gain>
```

Table 4-10 describes the parameters associated with the **cnfchgn** command.

Table 4-10 cnfchgn *Command Parameters*

Parameter	Description
channel(s)	Specifies the channel or range of channels to be configured.
input gain	Specifies the input gain, in decibels, to be added to the channel. The range is –8 dB to +6 dB.
output gain	Specifies the output gain, in decibels, to be added to the channel. The range is –8 dB to +6 dB.

Echo in a Voice Circuit

Echo is caused in a voice circuit by an impedance mismatch on the two-wire side of a four-wire-to-two-wire converter hybrid circuit used in many places in the analog portions of a voice circuit.

The echo's amplitude is described as the Echo Return Loss (ERL), measured in dB. The ERL is a function of the severity of the impedance mismatch on the two-wire side of the hybrid.

Echo Perception and Echo Cancellation

Echo perception is illustrated in Figure 4-4 by showing acceptable and unacceptable echo ranges against echo return loss and echo path delay.

Figure 4-4 *Echo Perception*

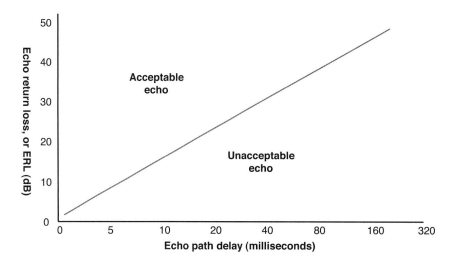

The subjective severity of the perceived echo heard by a telephone user is a function of how much energy is reflected to the talker and the time delay between the original signal and the reflection. The figure illustrates the generally accepted boundary between acceptable and unacceptable echo.

An IGX network adds approximately 30 to 70 milliseconds of delay to a voice circuit. The increased delay is primarily due to VAD, packetizing, and queuing. Figure 4-4 suggests that, for this delay, the echo must be reduced by 20 to 30 dB in order for the perceived echo to be tolerable. If nothing were done, the echo would be unacceptable.

The CVM and UVM provide integrated echo cancellers. An echo canceller is a digital signal processor that continuously monitors the digitized speech in the transmit, or egress, direction and compares it to the digitized speech in the receive, or ingress, direction. It detects echo in the ingress speech path and eliminates it digitally. Therefore, the ERL can be increased by 30 to 50 dB. This results in an acceptable perceived echo.

Echo cancellers have a tone detection feature for fax or fast modems. If a 2100 Hz tone is detected, echo canceling is disabled until the signal power in the connection has fallen, indicating the end of the call. This feature should normally be enabled.

Displaying Echo Canceller Parameters

The **dspchec** command, as shown in Example 4-11, displays the echo canceller parameters for a channel or range of channels.

Example 4-11 dspchec *Output*

```
igx4              TN     group8:1          IGX 8420   9.2.20    Sep. 9 1999   16:18 CST


              Echo     Echo Return  Tone      Conver-  Non-Linear Voice Bkgrnd
  Channels    Cancel   Loss(.1 dBs) Disabler  gence    Processing Tmplt Filter
  3.1.1       Disabled      -       Enabled     -      Enabled      -   Enabled
  3.1.2       Enabled       -       Enabled     -      Enabled      -   Enabled
  3.1.3-24    Disabled      -       Enabled     -      Enabled      -   Enabled
  3.2.1-24    Disabled      -       Enabled     -      Enabled      -   Enabled


  Last Command: dspchec 3.1.1


  Next Command:
```

The CVM and UVM echo cancellers support slightly different parameters. Unavailable parameters appear on the screen as a dash.

Here is the **dspchec** command syntax:

```
dspchec <start channel>
```

start channel specifies the first channels for which the echo canceller parameters are to be displayed. All higher-numbered voice channels on the same card are also displayed.

Configuring Echo Canceller Parameters

The **cnfchec** command, as shown in Example 4-12, configures the echo canceller parameters associated with a voice channel. The CVM and UVM have slightly different parameters. Unavailable parameters appear on the screen as a dash and cannot be configured.

Example 4-12 **cnfchec** *Output*

```
igx4          TN    group8:1        IGX 8420  9.2.20    Sep. 9 1999  16:19 CST


           Echo     Echo Return  Tone     Conver-  Non-Linear Voice Bkgrnd
Channels   Cancel   Loss(.1 dBs) Disabler gence    Processing Tmplt Filter
3.1.1      Enabled     -         Enabled     -     Enabled      -    Disabled
3.1.2      Enabled     -         Enabled     -     Enabled      -    Enabled
3.1.3-24   Disabled    -         Enabled     -     Enabled      -    Enabled
3.2.1-24   Disabled    -         Enabled     -     Enabled      -    Enabled




Last Command: cnfchec 3.1.1 e e e d


Next Command:
```

The most important use of this command is to enable the echo canceller for each voice channel.

Here is the **cnfchec** command syntax:

```
cnfchec <channel(s)> <echo canceller> <minimum echo return loss> <tone disabler>
   <convergence> <non-linear processing> <background filter>
```

The parameters for the **cnfchec** command are described in Table 4-11.

Table 4-11 **cnfchec** *Command Parameters*

Parameter	Description
channel(s)	Specifies the channel or range of channels to be configured.
echo canceller	CVM and UVM. Enables (e) or disables (d) the echo canceller.
minimum echo return loss	CVM only. Sets the minimum required echo return loss to be interpreted as echo. Possible values are high (h) and low (l).

Table 4-11   **cnfchec** *Command Parameters (Continued)*

Parameter	Description
tone disabler	CVM and UVM. Enables (e) or disables (d) the elimination of echo cancellation when a high-speed modem or fax tone is detected.
convergence	CVM only. Enables (e) or disables (d) convergence. Except for test purposes, the normal state of convergence is enabled.
non-linear processing	CVM and UVM. Enables (e) or disables (d) nonlinear processing, which is the elimination of any low-level residual signal after echo has been cancelled.
background filter	UVM only. Enables (e) or disables (d) the background filter.

Signaling Transport and Processing

This section describes signaling transport and processing using CAS signaling, IGX voice signaling, and signaling bit transport and timing. Voice channels and connection types are discussed, along with voice channel conditioning criteria, connection states, voice dial types, and signaling bit conversion.

Voice Signaling Review

As described in Chapter 3, any IGX voice line can be configured for either

- Channel Associated Signaling (CAS), wherein a small number of signaling bits are allocated to each voice channel and are carried in preallocated bit positions on the line
- Common Channel Signaling (CCS), wherein a full 64 kbps timeslot on the line is devoted to carrying signaling information between the attached end devices in a format or protocol known to those devices

Because CCS protocols are carried transparently across an IGX network, they are not considered in this chapter. This chapter addresses only the transport and processing of signaling bits used in CAS environments.

CAS Signaling Review

In the T1 CAS format, the least-significant bit of every timeslot in every sixth frame is used to carry a signaling bit instead of carrying the voice bit that would normally be placed there. In T1 D4 framing (in which one superframe consists of 12 consecutive frames), signaling bit A is in frame 6, and signaling bit B is in frame 12. In T1 ESF framing (where one superframe consists of 24 consecutive frames), frame 18 carries signaling bit C (or another A bit), and frame 24 carries signaling bit D (or another B bit).

In the E1 CAS format, timeslot 16 is used to carry 4 signaling bits (A, B, C, and D bits) for each of the other 30 voice channels.

In the J1 format, the signaling information for the other 31 channels is included in timeslot 0. Only one signaling bit is defined for each channel. Timeslot 16 is not used to carry signaling.

NOTE   For more details on the T1, E1, and J1 CAS formats, refer to *Cisco WAN Quick Start* by Ronald W. McCarty.

IGX Voice Signaling Topics

Each voice channel in an IGX may support a variety of signaling bit processing options, such as transparent transport of signaling bits from end to end across the network. The IGX can monitor the signaling bits on each voice channel and interpret them to determine whether a channel is in use. This information can be displayed and/or gathered for statistical or troubleshooting purposes.

The IGX can also be programmed to provide a wide variety of signaling bit activity to inform an attached PBX of the failure of a voice connection through the network. Furthermore, the IGX can apply certain signaling bit conversions to allow compatibility between certain dissimilar signaling protocols.

Signaling Bit Transport

By default, the IGX voice cards carry all voice channel signaling bits transparently across a voice connection. As will be discussed later in this chapter, it is possible to modify this transparent transport behavior. In either case, the mechanism used to transport signaling bits is the same.

Signaling bits received from the attached device (usually a PBX) are monitored for changes once every 500 microseconds. Any detected change triggers the creation of a time-stamped data FastPacket used to carry the signaling bit change to the far end of the voice connection. Note that the signaling bits are extracted from the appropriate bit positions on the T1, E1, or J1 line and are transported in FastPackets separate from the actual voice samples.

Signaling Bit Timing

In some cases, the timing between signaling bit transitions is not terribly critical to the attached PBXs. This is typically true when the signaling bits are used only to convey off-hook (start of call) and on-hook (end of call) transitions, as shown in Figure 4-5. In such cases, the actual dialed digits are typically carried as Dual Tone Multifrequency (DTMF) tones in-band in the circuit's voice path. This is frequently called tone dialing or in-band dialing. In this case, there are few signaling bit transitions.

Figure 4-5   *Signaling Bit Timing*

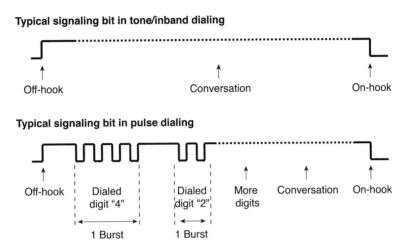

Dialing protocols, such as tone dialing or in-band dialing, typically require that the relative timing between successive signaling bit transitions be preserved within a range of tens or hundreds of milliseconds.

In other cases, the timing between signaling bit transitions is critical to the attached PBXs. This is particularly true when the signaling bits are used to convey dialed digits between PBXs. This is frequently called *pulse dialing*. In this case, there are many signaling bit transitions with carefully regulated timing between them. Such dialing protocols typically require that the relative timing between successive signaling bit transitions be preserved within a range of just a few milliseconds.

To carefully preserve the timing between successive signaling bit transitions, the CVM and UVM cards group signaling bit transitions into bursts. A burst includes any number of transitions in which the maximum time between two consecutive transitions is a parameter called the *signaling delay*.

Voice Channel Dial Types

The signaling bit timing on a voice channel is defined as follows:

- Signaling delay is the maximum time between two consecutive transitions.

- Minimum wink is the minimum time allowed between the last signaling bit transition of one burst and the first signaling bit transition of the next burst.

- Playout delay is a null-timing buffer delay used to eliminate any jitter caused by slight variations in queuing delays experienced by successive signaling FastPackets as they travel through the network.

Each of these three parameters can be configured on a per-channel basis. However, in most networks, these parameters are the same for all voice channels. If a differentiation is needed, it is typically only a small difference between channels that use pulse dialing compared to channels that use in-band dialing.

Therefore, the IGX software defines a *pulse* dialing template and an *in-band* dialing template, each with values for each of the three parameters just mentioned. It is then simply a matter of specifying whether a particular voice channel should use the in-band template or the pulse template. By default, all voice channels use the in-band template.

If needed, a channel may be programmed to use nonstandard values for the three parameters using *user*-defined values for these parameters. This capability, however, is almost never necessary.

Configuring a Voice Channel Dial Type

The **cnfchdl** command, as shown in Example 4-13, configures the dial type for a channel or range of channels. The dial type may be in-band, pulse, or user-configured.

Example 4-13 cnfchdl *Output*

```
igx1            TRM    group6:1        IGX 8420   9.2.20    Aug. 28 1999 13:37 CDT


             %   Adaptive          Gain (dB)  Dial   Interface        OnHk      Cond
Channels   Util Voice      Fax    In  Out    Type   Type        A  B  C  D Crit
3.1.1       32  Enabled  Enabled   0   0     Inband  Unconfig    ?  ?  -  -  a
3.1.2-4     32  Enabled  Disabled -6   2     Inband  Unconfig    ?  ?  -  -  a
3.1.5-15    60  Enabled  Disabled  0   0     Pulse   Unconfig    ?  ?  -  -  a
3.1.17-31   60  Enabled  Disabled  0   0     Inband  Unconfig    ?  ?  -  -  a
3.2.1-31    60  Enabled  Disabled  0   0     Inband  Unconfig    ?  ?  -  -  a


Last Command: cnfchdl 3.1.5-15 p

Next Command:
```

By default, the in-band and pulse signaling bit timing parameter templates are identical. Therefore, the **cnfchdl** command usually has no effect whatsoever. The default timing parameters work for either pulse or DTMF dialing protocols.

Here is the **cnfchdl** command syntax:

```
cnfchdl <channel(s)> <dial type> <signaling delay> <minimum wink> <playout delay>
```

The parameters associated with the **cnfchdl** command are described in Table 4-12.

Table 4-12 cnfchdl *Command Parameters*

Parameter	Description
channel(s)	Specifies the channel or range of channels to be configured.
dial type	Specifies the dial type to assign: **I**—In-band **p**—Pulse **u**—User-configured If **u** is selected, the following parameters are also required.
signaling delay	The user-configured signaling delay. The range is 30 to 96 milliseconds.
minimum wink	The user-configured minimum wink. The range is 120 to 300 milliseconds.
playout delay	The user-configured playout delay. The range is 100 to 200 milliseconds.

Displaying Voice Channel Signaling Timing Parameters

The **dspchdlcnf** command, as shown in Example 4-14, displays the selected dial type and the signaling bit timing parameters for a channel or range of channels.

Example 4-14 **dspchdlcnf** *Output*

```
igx4            TN    Service        IGX 8420  9.2.20    Sep. 9 1999  10:52 CST


Channels        Type  Sig Delay  Min Wink  IntDigit Time  Playout Delay
3.1             User      31       121          -             100
3.2             User      30       120          -             200
3.3             Pulse     96       140          -             200
3.4             Inband    96       140          -             200
3.5             Pulse     96       140          -             200
3.6-24          Inband    96       140          -             200


Last Command: dspchdlcnf 3.1


Next Command:
```

Here is the **dspchdlcnf** command syntax:

```
dspchdlcnf <start channel>
```

start channel specifies the first channel for which the dial type and signaling bit timing parameters are to be displayed. All higher-numbered voice channels on the same card are also displayed.

Signaling Bit Monitoring and Interpretation

The IGX makes no direct use of the signaling bit information. (The only feature that uses the signaling bit information is the courtesy down feature.)

Nonetheless, the IGX does monitor the signaling bits on each CAS channel, primarily for display and statistical purposes. For example, the **dspcon** command, described in Chapter 3, shows whether the voice channel at each end of a voice connection is on-hook or off-hook.

Naturally, this ability to determine a voice channel's on-hook/off-hook state requires that the IGX be told how to interpret the signaling bits on each voice channel, because many CAS signaling protocols are in use in the telecommunications industry.

Voice Channel Type

The voice channel type defines the signaling states that represent a voice channel's on-hook condition. When all signaling bits match the defined condition, the channel is interpreted as being on-hook. Whenever one or more bits differ from the defined condition, the channel is interpreted as being off-hook. Consequently, in the default state (with the voice channel type unconfigured), all voice channels are assumed to be off-hook.

Configuring a Voice Channel Type

The **cnfvchtp** command, as shown in Example 4-15, defines the signaling type for a channel or range of channels. In most cases, all channels on a line use the same signaling type. The signaling type defines the channel's on-hook signaling bit states and the conditioning criteria.

Example 4-15 cnfvchtp *Output*

```
Paris            TN    YourID:1        IGX 8410  9.3.24   Aug. 15 2001 15:55 PDT

No Intf. Type     OnHk        Cond       No  Intf. Type    OnHk         Cond
 1  User Config                          13  RPT           0  X  -  -   a
 2  Unconfig       ?  ?  -  -   a         14  SDPO          0  X  -  -   a
 3  No Sig         ?  ?  ?  ?   a         15  DX            0  X  -  -   a
 4  Force Sig      ?  ?  -  -   a         16  ETO           ?  ?  -  -   e
 5  2W E&M         0  X  -  -   a         17  PLAR          ?  ?  -  -   d
 6  4W E&M         0  X  -  -   a         18  PLR           0  X  -  -   a
 7  FXO            1  1  -  -   b         19  RD            ?  ?  -  -   a
```

Example 4-15 cnfvchtp *Output (Continued)*

```
 8  FXS G/S      0  1  -  -  c        20  R1 (SOCOTEL)  0  -  -  -  e
 9  FXS L/S      0  X  -  -  d        21  SSDC5A        1  1  0  1  f
10  DPO          0  X  -  -  a        22  R2 (backward) 1  1  -  -  e
11  DPT          0  X  -  -  a        23  R2 (forward)  1  0  -  -  d
12  RPO          0  X  -  -  a



This Command: cnfvchtp 3.1.1


Enter Interface Type:
```

A user-configured voice channel interface can also be defined using type 1 of the **cnfvchtp** command, as described in Table 4-13. In that case, the on-hook condition for each signaling bit must be specified, as well as the conditioning template (defined later).

Here is the **cnfvchtp** command syntax:

```
cnfvchtp <channel(s)> <interface type> [on-hook A] [on-hook B] [on-hook C]
    [on-hook D] [conditioning template]
```

Table 4-13   **cnfvchtp** *Command Parameters*

Parameter	Description
channel(s)	Specifies the channel or range of channels to be configured.
interface type	Specifies the number of the interface type to assign to the channel(s). If type 1 (user-configured) is selected, the following parameters are also required.
on-hook A	A-bit value for the on-hook state. The possible values are **1**—High **0**—Low **X**—Don't care **?**—Don't know **—**—Not used
on-hook B	B-bit value for the on-hook state. See *on-hook A* for possible values.
on-hook C	C-bit value for the on-hook state. See *on-hook A* for possible values.
on-hook D	D-bit value for the on-hook state. See *on-hook A* for possible values.
conditioning template	The conditioning template ID for user-configured channel types.

After you select the desired voice channel type (see Example 4-15), the screen in Example 4-16 is displayed to show the results of the channel type selection.

Example 4-16 cnfvchtp *Output*

```
igx4            TN     group8:1        IGX 8420   9.2.20    Sep. 9 1999   12:39 CST

                %   Adaptive           Gain (dB)  Dial    Interface        OnHk      Cond
Channels   Util Voice       Fax      In   Out   Type    Type        A  B  C  D Crit
3.1.1      50   Disabled    -        0    -2    User    4W E&M      0  X  -  -  a
3.1.2      55   Enabled     -        -3   0     User    4W E&M      0  X  -  -  a
3.1.3      90   Enabled     -        0    0     Pulse   Unconfig    ?  ?  -  -  a
3.1.4      55   Enabled     -        -6   6     Inband  4W E&M      0  X  -  -  a
3.1.5      55   Enabled     -        0    0     Pulse   4W E&M      0  X  -  -  a
3.1.6-12   55   Enabled     -        0    0     Inband  Unconfig    ?  ?  -  -  a
3.1.13-15  90   Enabled     -        0    0     Inband  Unconfig    ?  ?  -  -  a
3.1.16-17  90   Enabled     -        0    0     Inband  Unconfig    ?  ?  -  -  a
3.1.18-23  90   Enabled     -        0    0     Inband  Unconfig    ?  ?  -  -  a
3.1.24     90   Disabled    -        -6   3     Inband  Unconfig    ?  ?  -  -  a
3.2.1      90   Enabled     -        2    2     Pulse   4W E&M      0  X  -  -  a
3.2.2-11   90   Enabled     -        0    0     Inband  Unconfig    ?  ?  -  -  a
3.2.12     90   Enabled     -        0    0     Pulse   Unconfig    ?  ?  -  -  a

Last Command: cnfvchtp 3.2.1 6


Next Command:
```

Displaying Connection States

After you define a channel's signaling type using the **cnfvchtp** command, the IGX software can monitor the channel to determine whether it is on-hook or off-hook. This information is visible on the **dspcon** screen, as described in the previous chapter. The **dspconst** command, as shown in Example 4-17, displays the current state of all voice channels that have a terminated connection on one or all of the node's UVM/CVM lines.

Example 4-17 dspconst *Output*

```
igx1    TN    group1:1    IGX 8420     9.2.20    Jun. 30 1999    10:53    CDT
Connection status display

+ offhook, - onhook, m slow modem, M fast modem, F Fax
          1 1 1 1 1 1 1 1 1 1 2 2 2 2 2 2 2 2 2 2 3 3
Line   1 2 3 4 5 6 7 8 9 0 1 2 3 4 5 6 7 8 9 0 1 2 3 4 5 6 7 8 9 0 1

3.1                 -  +                     +  -  +              +
3.2
4.1     -  +  +  -  -  +  +  +  +  +  -  -  -  +  F  +
```

Example 4-17 dspconst *Output (Continued)*

```
4.2


This Command: dspconst

Hit DEL key to quit:
```

While the display is on the screen, the status is automatically updated (until the **Delete** key is pressed) at the rate of 1 second for each line being displayed. For example, if one line is displayed, the update frequency is once every second. If three lines are displayed, the update frequency is once every three seconds.

The following connection states are displayed as follows:

Symbol	Description
+	Off-hook
–	On-hook
m	Slow modem
M	Fast modem
F	Fax
Blank	Channel not connected

Here is the **dspconst** command syntax:

```
dspconst [line]
```

line specifies the line for the channel state display. If no line is specified, all upped lines (up to a maximum of eight) are displayed.

Voice Channel Conditioning

As described earlier, the IGX normally transports voice channel signaling bits transparently (by default) across the network.

Whenever a failure in the network causes a voice connection to fail, both the flow of voice FastPackets and the flow of signaling FastPackets are interrupted. When this occurs, the voice card at each end of the failed connection must generate a replacement for both the missing PCM samples and the missing signaling bits.

These replacement PCM samples and the A, B, C, and D signaling bits are specified in the *conditioning template* assigned to each voice channel.

Pre-established conditioning templates are associated with the various voice channel types specified in the **cnfvchtp** command. It is also possible to create a custom-made conditioning template with the **cnfcond** command, as described in a moment.

In general, a voice channel's conditioning template is designed to do the following things, in order:

1 It generates an on-hook signaling state toward the PBX to force it to disconnect any call that might have been using the failed connection.

2 After approximately two seconds, it generates an off-hook signaling state toward the PBX to prevent it from assigning any new call to the failed connection.

3 It remains in the off-hook state as long as the connection remains failed.

Displaying a Voice Channel Conditioning Template

The **dspcond** command, as shown in Example 4-18, displays an existing voice channel conditioning template's signaling bit states and data bit pattern used for the channel when the associated connection fails.

Example 4-18 dspcond *Output*

```
igx4            TN     group8:1      IGX 8420  9.2.20    Sep. 9 1999  16:11 CST

Conditioning criterion a:

  Data Pattern
  01010100 - E1
  01111111 - T1


  Signalling Pattern
  A            0(40)/1
  B            1
  C            1
  D            1


Last Command: dspcond a

Next Command:
```

Data Pattern defines the bit pattern used in the failed channel on the line toward the end-user equipment. The Signalling Pattern list defines the signaling bit states and transitions for the failed channel.

Each conditioning template is identified by a one- or two-character alphanumeric identifier. The a through f templates are predefined for use with the standard signaling protocols seen in the **cnfvchtp** command.

Here is the **dspcond** command syntax:

```
dspcond <conditioning template identifier>
```

conditioning template identifier specifies the identifier of the conditioning template to be displayed.

Configuring a Voice Channel Conditioning Template

If no existing conditioning template meets a channel's needs, a custom-made conditioning template can be created using the **cnfcond** command, as shown in Example 4-19. Doing so specifies the data bit pattern and the signaling bit states to be transmitted to the attached PBX whenever the connection using the channel fails.

Example 4-19 cnfcond *Output*

```
igx4              TN     group8:1      IGX 8420  9.2.20    Sep. 9 1999  16:13 CST

Conditioning criterion zz:

  Data Pattern
  01010111 - E1/T1



  Signalling Pattern
  A            1(10)/0(10)/1
  B            0(5)/1
  C            0
  D            1


Last Command: cnfcond zz 01010111 1(10)/0(10)/1 0(5)/1 0 1

Next Command:
```

A conditioning template is typically intended to program the signaling bits to generate a two-second on-hook condition followed by an indefinite off-hook condition. The data bit pattern is usually unimportant.

A one-character or two-character alphanumeric ID is used to uniquely identify a conditioning template. The a through f templates are predefined and cannot be modified.

Each of the A, B, C, and D signaling bits is specified independently and may be held permanently high or low or programmed to transition between the high and low states up to five times.

If a signaling bit is programmed to transition one or more times, the duration of each high or low state must be specified in multiples of 50 milliseconds.

For example, if signaling bit B is programmed as 1(40)/0(20)/1, whenever the connection fails, the B signaling bit

- Is set to 1 for 2 seconds (40 × 50 milliseconds = 2 seconds)
- Is set to 0 for 1 second (20 × 50 milliseconds = 1 second)
- Returns to 1 for the duration of the failure

Each bit can be defined to have a maximum of five states.

Here is the **cnfcond** command syntax:

```
cnfcond <conditioning template identifier> <data bit pattern> <A-bit state>
    <B-bit state> <C-bit state> <D-bit state>
```

Table 4-14 describes the parameters for the **cnfcond** command.

Table 4-14   **cnfcond** *Command Parameters*

Parameter	Description
conditioning template identifier	Specifies the conditioning template to create or modify. The identifier can be any one- or two-character alphanumeric code.
data bit pattern	Specifies an 8-bit binary value to use in the event that a connection terminating on a channel using this template fails.
A-bit state *B-bit state* *C-bit state* *D-bit state*	The signaling state or sequence to be transmitted for each bit in the event that a connection terminating on a channel using this template fails. Each bit is expressed as a 1 (high) or 0 (low), followed by a number in parentheses to indicate how long the state remains on the channel. The duration is expressed in 50-millisecond intervals. The final state has no duration specified. For example: 1(40)/0(20)/1 A maximum of five states may be specified for each bit.

Signaling Bit Conversions

As illustrated in Figure 4-6, and as described earlier, the IGX, by default, transports signaling bits transparently across a voice connection.

However, it is also possible to configure the voice channels at each end of a voice connection to perform certain limited conversions on the signaling bits as they are received from the attached PBX (using the **cnfrcvsig** command) and/or before they are transmitted to the attached PBX (using the **cnfxmtsig** command).

Figure 4-6   *Signaling Bit Conversions*

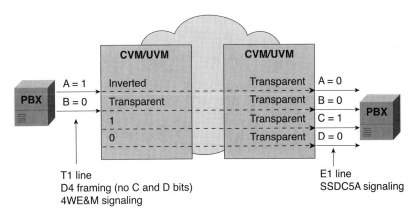

This capability is intended primarily to

- Allow interoperation between signaling protocols that would otherwise be incompatible.

- Set signaling bits to a known state when a connection is created between two channels that support a different number of signaling bits. Recall that J1 lines support only one signaling bit, T1 lines support either 2 or 4 signaling bits, and E1 lines support 4 signaling bits.

Each signaling bit can be configured as one of the following:

- **Transparent**—The bit is passed without changes.

- **Inverted**—The bit is inverted (1 becomes 0 and 0 becomes 1).

- **1**—The bit is set permanently to 1.

- **0**—The bit is set permanently to 0.

Configuring Receive Signaling Bit Conversions

The **cnfrcvsig** command, as shown in Example 4-20, configures a voice channel's receive signaling bit conversions. These bit conversions are applied after the signaling bits are extracted from the line and before they are placed in the signaling FastPackets to be transported across the network.

Example 4-20 cnfrcvsig *Output*

```
igx4            TN    group8:1        IGX 8420  9.2.20    Sep. 9 1999  16:16 CST

                              Signalling Qualifiers
From 3.1.1  TXAbit  TXBbit  TXCbit  TXDbit  RXAbit RXBbit RXCbit RXDbit
3.1.1         T       T       T       T       0      1      T      I
3.1.2-24      T       T       T       T       T      T      T      T
3.2.1-24      T       T       T       T       T      T      T      T


Last Command: cnfrcvsig 3.1.1 0 1 T i

Next Command:
```

Each signaling bit can be configured as one of the following:

- **t or T**—The bit is passed without change.
- **i or I**—The bit is inverted.
- **0**—The bit is forced low.
- **1**—The bit is forced high.

Here is the **cnfrcvsig** command syntax:

cnfrcvsig <*channel(s)*> <*A*> <*B*> <*C*> <*D*>

Table 4-15 describes the parameters for the **cnfrcvsig** command.

Table 4-15 cnfrcvsig *Command Parameters*

Parameter	Description
channel(s)	Specifies the channel or range of channels to be configured.
A	Specifies the conversion applied to the A-bit: **t or T**—Bit is passed transparently **i or I**—Bit is inverted **1**—Always 1 **0**—Always 0
B	Specifies the conversion applied to the B-bit. See *A* for possible values.
C	Specifies the conversion applied to the C-bit. See *A* for possible values.
D	Specifies the conversion applied to the D-bit. See *A* for possible values.

Configuring Transmit Signaling Bit Conversions

The **cnfxmtsig** command, as shown in Example 4-21, configures the transmit signaling bit conversions for a voice channel. These bit conversions are applied after the signaling bits are removed from the signaling FastPackets used to transport them across the network and before they are placed in the appropriate bit positions on the line to the attached PBX.

Example 4-21 cnfxmtsig *Output*

```
igx4            TN     group8:1        IGX 8420  9.2.20     Sep. 9 1999  16:18 CST


                              Signalling Qualifiers
From 3.1.1   TXAbit  TXBbit  TXCbit  TXDbit  RXAbit RXBbit RXCbit RXDbit
3.1.1        T       T       T       T       0      1      T      I
3.1.2-4      T       T       T       T       T      T      T      T
3.1.5        I       T       0       1       T      T      T      T
3.1.6-24     T       T       T       T       T      T      T      T
3.2.1-24     T       T       T       T       T      T      T      T



Last Command: cnfxmtsig 3.1.5 i t 0 1

Next Command:
```

Each signaling bit can be configured as one of the following:

- **t or T**—The bit is passed without change.
- **i or I**—The bit is inverted.
- **0**—The bit is forced low.
- **1**—The bit is forced high.

Here is the **cnfxmtsig** command syntax:

```
cnfxmtsig <channel(s)> <A> <B> <C> <D>
```

Table 4-16 describes the parameters for the **cnfxmtsig** command.

Table 4-16   **cnfxmtsig** *Command Parameters*

Parameter	Description
channel(s)	Specifies the channel or range of channels to be configured.
A	Specifies the conversion applied to the A-bit:
	t or T—Bit is passed transparently
	i or I—Bit is inverted
	1—Always 1
	0—Always 0
B	Specifies the conversion applied to the B-bit. See *A* for possible values.
C	Specifies the conversion applied to the C-bit. See *A* for possible values.
D	Specifies the conversion applied to the D-bit. See *A* for possible values.

Displaying Signaling Bit Conversions

The **dspsigqual** command, as shown in Example 4-22, displays signaling bit conversion configuration information for some or all channels on a voice card.

Example 4-22 dspsigqual *Output*

```
igx4            TN    group8:1          IGX 8420  9.2.20    Sep. 9 1999  16:15 CST

                                  Signalling Qualifiers
From 3.1.1  TXAbit  TXBbit  TXCbit  TXDbit  RXAbit RXBbit RXCbit RXDbit
3.1.1        T       I       1       0       I      1      T      0
3.1.2-4      T       T       T       T       T      T      T      T
3.1.5        T       T       T       T       I      1      T      0
3.1.6        T       I       1       0       T      T      T      T
3.1.7-24     T       T       T       T       T      T      T      T
3.2.1        T       I       1       0       I      1      T      0
3.2.2-24     T       T       T       T       T      T      T      T



Last Command: dspsigqual 3.1.1

Next Command:
```

The screen shown is the same as the one shown with the **cnfrcvsig** and **cnfxmtsig** commands.

The transmit direction refers to the signaling bits being sent from the network to the local end-user device (usually a PBX). The receive direction is from the user device toward the network.

Here is the **dspsigqual** command syntax:

```
dspsigqual <start channel>
```

start channel specifies the first channel for which the signaling bit conversions are to be displayed. All higher-numbered voice channels on the same card are also displayed.

Voice Channel Configuration Summary Display

The **dspchcnf** command, as shown in Example 4-23, displays configuration details for voice channels on UVM and CVM cards.

Example 4-23 dspchcnf *Output*

```
igx1            TN    group6:1          IGX 8420  9.2.20    Aug. 28 1999 13:36 CDT

           %   Adaptive            Gain (dB)  Dial    Interface        OnHk      Cond
Channels  Util Voice      Fax      In  Out    Type    Type         A  B  C  D Crit
3.1.1      60  Enabled  Enabled    0    0     Inband  Unconfig     ?  ?  -  -  a
3.1.2-15   40  Enabled  Disabled  -6    2     Pulse   Unconfig     ?  ?  -  -  a
```

Example 4-23 dspchcnf *Output (Continued)*

```
3.1.17-31  40  Enabled  Disabled  0   0   Inband  Unconfig   ? ? - - a
3.2.1-31   40  Enabled  Disabled  0   0   Inband  Unconfig   ? ? - - a


Last Command: dspchcnf 3.1.1

Next Command:
```

The screen in Example 4-23 is the same screen as that for the **cnfchutl, cnfchadv, cnfchfax, cnfchgn, cnfchdl,** and **cnfvchtp** commands. This command displays the appropriate configuration information, starting with the specified channel.

> **dspchcnf** *<start channel>*

start channel specifies the first channel for which the configuration summary is to be displayed. All higher-numbered voice channels on the same card are also displayed.

Data Networks

Typically, legacy data networks use private lines to connect host computers, minicomputers, front-end processors (FEPs), cluster controllers, and so on. Data networks support a wide range of data communications architectures and protocols, including the following:

- **Bisync**—Binary Synchronous Protocol
- **DDCMP**—Digital Data Communications Message Protocol
- **HDLC**—High-Level Data Link Control
- **LAP-B**—Link Access Procedure–Balanced
- **PPP**—Point-to-Point Protocol
- **SDLC**—Synchronous Data Link Control
- **SNA**—Systems Network Architecture

In addition, legacy data networks may use private lines to carry any type of proprietary, or nonstandard, protocol dreamed up by manufacturers over many decades.

Private Line Replacement

An IGX network can provide an attractive alternative to a private line to carry legacy data traffic transparently. In many cases, the IGX offers more efficient bandwidth usage than traditional private lines, because data traffic is routed across the IGX trunks along with voice, Frame Relay, and ATM traffic. IGX data cards can directly connect to customer data equipment, modems, or CSUs/DSUs.

Data Card Groups Hardware Review

As described in Chapter 2, "IGX Product Overview and System Hardware," the HDM and LDM card groups are the primary card groups used for legacy data transport. However, as discussed earlier, the UVM and CVM card groups can also be used to carry data on T1, E1, and J1 lines.

Data Connections and Channels

Figure 4-7 illustrates data connections and data channels.

Figure 4-7 *Data Connections and Channels*

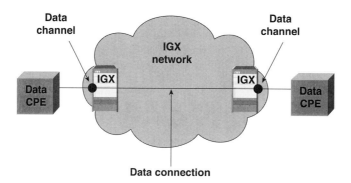

A *data connection* is a point-to-point permanent virtual circuit (PVC) that links two data channels in an IGX network.

A *data channel* may be

- Provided by one of the ports on an HDM or LDM card
- One timeslot or multiple contiguous timeslots of a line on a CVM or UVM card

This chapter describes how to add, configure, display, and delete data connections and how to configure data channels. This includes a variety of topics, detailing how digital data is transported transparently across the IGX network.

Before data connections on a UVM or CVM can be created or configured, and before data channels can be configured, the line supporting the connections and channels must be upped, as described in Chapter 3. This is not the case for data connections on an HDM or LDM card. Data connections on HDM or LDM cards can be added, and their channels configured, at any time.

In either case, data connections can be added without regard for the channels at each end. Conversely, a data channel can be configured regardless or whether a data connection terminates on that channel.

Data Connection Characteristics

An IGX data connection is said to be *transparent*. This means that the exact sequence of data bits received from the attached CPE at one end of the connection is delivered to the attached CPE at the other end of the data connection.

As a result of a data connection's transparency, it is *protocol-independent*. Because the IGX is concerned only about delivering the received sequence of bits across the network, it does not need to look for, or pay attention to, the structure of the data pattern within the bit stream. In particular, the IGX does not recognize any difference between data frames and idle patterns in framed or packetized data streams. Consequently, the IGX can transparently carry any standard or nonstandard data protocol.

IGX data connections are *synchronous*. This means that the data bits are exchanged between the IGX and the attached CPE at an explicitly defined bit rate that is provided by explicit clock pins on an HDM or LDM port or that is derived from the line rate of the T1, E1, or J1 line carrying the data channel.

Connections between asynchronous devices can be supported, but only by oversampling— that is, by using a data rate that is at least four or five times the nominal bit rate.

Data FastPackets

There are two types of data FastPackets:

- **Non-time-stamped (NTS) data FastPackets**—Used for all data connections above 128 kbps and some slower-speed connections.
- **Time-stamped (TS) data FastPackets**—Used for low-speed data connections (below 128 kbps) and some data connections between 64 and 128 kbps.

As FastPackets travel across the network, each FastPacket might experience slightly different queuing delays, resulting in slightly different end-to-end delays across the network. To ensure end-to-end data transparency, it is necessary to eliminate any delay variation between successive FastPackets in a data connection. The time stamp in a time-stamped data FastPacket is used to record the queuing delay experienced by that FastPacket. That time stamp is used to ensure that FastPackets on the same connection experience the same end-to-end delays.

A slightly different technique is used for high-speed data connections to eliminate delay variations in order to ensure data transparency.

Building Data FastPackets

Because the data traffic entering the network is transparent (protocol-independent), the IGX treats incoming data as a simple bit stream. In particular, FastPackets are created without regard to byte boundaries, because the IGX has no knowledge of the data protocol or format. When the payload portion is full, the FastPacket is complete and is sent across the network to its destination.

Data Frame Multiplexing

Data Frame Multiplexing (DFM) is a Repetitive Pattern Suppression (RPS) algorithm. It improves bandwidth efficiency by eliminating repetitive patterns within the incoming bit stream.

DFM is used automatically on any connection that meets all the following conditions:

- The connection must terminate on an HDM or LDM card at each end.

- The connection's data rate must be 128 kbps or less.

- The data connection may not use interleaved control signal updates (explained later in this chapter).

- DFM must be enabled on the channel at each end of the connection. (By default, it is enabled on all data channels.) See the "Data Channels" section for details on how to enable or disable DFM for an individual channel.

- DFM must be enabled on the node at each end of the connection. (By default, it is not enabled on the node. DFM is a separately licensed feature that must be enabled using a special password. This is usually done by the Cisco TAC.)

When in use, DFM causes a FastPacket to be suppressed if

- All data bits in the FastPacket repeat the same pattern of 7 bits, 8 bits, or 16 bits. See the "Data Channels" section for details on how to specify the DFM pattern length for an individual channel.

- At least one copy of the repetitive pattern was present at the end of the previous FastPacket sent.

- At least one of the previous 15 FastPackets was sent.

Data FastPackets with DFM

DFM can be used on connections that use either non-time-stamped or time-stamped data FastPackets.

If DFM is enabled on a data connection, each FastPacket is assigned a sequence number, including FastPackets that are suppressed.

The destination data card detects when one or more FastPackets are suppressed by examining the sequence number in each FastPacket received. The destination data card recreates the missing FastPackets by repeating the pattern at the end of the last FastPacket received.

Adding a Data Connection

The **addcon** command adds a data connection between HDM, LDM, UVM, and CVM cards.

Here is the **addcon** command syntax:

```
addcon <local channel(s)> <remote node> <remote channel(s)> <type> [coding]
    [route avoid]
```

Table 4-17 describes the parameters for the **addcon** command.

Table 4-17   **addcon** *Command Parameters*

Parameter	Description
local channel(s)	Specifies the local channel, or range of channels, to connect. If multiple channels are specified, they must be contiguous.
	HDM/LDM—*slot.port*[*-port*]
	CVM—*slot.channel*[*-channel*]
	UVM—*slot.line.channel*[*-channel*]
remote node	Specifies the destination node name.
remote channel(s)	Specifies the remote channel, or range of channels, to connect.
	If multiple channels are specified in the *local channel(s)* parameter, the range of channels need not be specified in the *remote channel(s)* parameter. It is sufficient to specify only the first channel of the range.
	If multiple channels are specified, the number of channels must match the number of channels specified by the *local channel(s)* parameter.
	HDM/LDM—*slot.port*[*-port*]
	CVM—*slot.channel*[*-channel*]
	UVM—*slot.line.channel*[*-channel*]
type	Specifies the connection type, as described in the next section.
coding	Specifies the connection coding, as described in the section "FastPacket Coding." Options are
	7/8
	8/8
	8/8i
	7/8e
route avoid	Specifies the type(s) of trunk(s) that the connection is not allowed to use. The default is no avoidance. The possible values are
	*s—Avoid satellite trunks
	*t—Avoid terrestrial trunks
	*z—Avoid ZCS trunks
	*s *z—Avoid satellite and ZCS trunks
	*t *z—Avoid terrestrial and ZCS trunks

Data Connection Types

Table 4-18 shows the data connection types supported on each type of data card in the IGX. The codes shown in the Type columns are used to specify the bit rate (in kbps) and other features when a connection is created with the **addcon** command. The other features are described further on the following pages.

Table 4-18 *Data Connection Types*

Type				HDM	Four-Port LDM	Eight-Port LDM	UVM	CVM
2.4	4.8	9.6		Yes	Yes	Yes		Yes[1]
56				Yes	Yes			Yes[1]
1.2	6.4	12.8	19.2	Yes	Yes	Yes		
1.8	7.2	14.4						
3.2	8	16						
3.6	12	16.8						
24	32	48		Yes	Yes			
28.8	38.4							
57.6	115.2	256	768	Yes				
64	128	288	772					
72	144	336	896					
76.8	168	384	1024					
84	192	448	1152					
96	224	512	1344					
112	230.4	672						
1.2f	12.8f	57.6f	192f	Yes				
1.8f	14.4f	64f	224f					
2.4f	16f	72f	230.4f					
3.2f	16.8f	76.8f	256f					
3.6f	19.2f	84f	288f					
4.8f	24f	96f	336f					
6.4f	28.8f	112f	384f					
7.2f	32f	115.2f	448f					
8f	38.4f	128f	512f					
9.6f	48f	144f						
12f	56f	168f						

Table 4-18 *Data Connection Types (Continued)*

Type				HDM	Four-Port LDM	Eight-Port LDM	UVM	CVM
1.2f/2	2.4f/2	3.6f/5	6.4f/5	Yes				
1.8f/2	3.2f/5	3.6f/2	7.2f/5					
2.4f/5	3.2f/2	4.8f/5						
3.2/4	6.4/4	8/10	14.4/10	Yes	Yes	Yes		
3.6/4	7.2/10	12/10						
6.4/10	7.2/4	12.8/10						
2.4/4	4.8/10	4.8/4	9.6/10	Yes	Yes	Yes		Yes[1]
2.4/4t	4.8/10t	4.8/4t	9.6/10t					Yes[1]
2.4t	4.8t	9.6t	56t					Yes[1]
1x56				Yes	Yes		Yes	Yes
2x56	5x56	1x64	5x64	Yes			Yes	Yes
3x56	6x56	2x64	6x64					
4x56	7x56	3x64	7x64					
	8x56	4x64	8x64					
T							Yes	Yes
TD							Yes	

[1] These connection types are supported *only* on the CVM Model A.

Partially Filled FastPackets

For low-speed data connections, completely filling the FastPacket payload with 160 data bits introduces delay that might be unacceptable to certain data applications. Therefore, the IGX provides the option of reducing that delay by limiting the amount of data in the FastPacket. This is done by providing connection types that specify a smaller number of bytes (2, 4, 5, or 10) as part of the connection type. When that number of data bytes has been received and placed in the FastPacket, padding is added to fill the rest of the FastPacket, and the FastPacket is sent.

For example, the following **addcon** command creates a 4.8 kbps data connection with 4 bytes of user data per FastPacket:

```
addcon 5.1 igx4 6.2 4.8/4
```

Naturally, a connection that uses partially-filled FastPackets generates more FastPackets per second than a connection of the same bit rate that uses full FastPackets.

Transporting Control Signal States

Figure 4-8 illustrates the transporting control signal states on the IGX switch.

Figure 4-8   *Transporting Control Signal States*

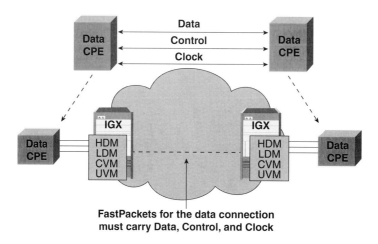

**FastPackets for the data connection
must carry Data, Control, and Clock**

When two data devices are directly connected over a serial synchronous interface, the cable between them carries

- Data pins
- Control signal pins
- Clock pins

Naturally, when the same two data devices are connected through an IGX network, it is important that the IGX network be able to emulate a direct cable by providing the means to transport the necessary data, control signal, and clock information across the network.

Here is how the various mechanisms used in the IGX network transport control signal states across the network:

The IGX network has three methods that may be used to carry control signal states across a data connection:

- Normal control signal transport
- Interleaved (or fast) control signal transport
- Partially interleaved (or embedded) control signal transport

See Chapter 5 for more details about which control signals are supported on each interface type and how those control signals can be manipulated.

Normal Control Signal Transport

In the normal control signal transport mechanism, shown in Figure 4-9, a separate stream of FastPackets, known as supervisory FastPackets, carries control signal status updates. These supervisory FastPackets are the same type (NTS or TS) as those of the corresponding data FastPackets.

Figure 4-9   *Normal Control Signal Transport*

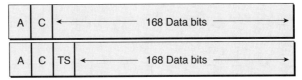

For each connection, the supervisory FastPackets may carry updates for up to 12 control signals, because 12 is the maximum number of ingress or egress control signals defined by the appropriate standards for any of the serial interfaces supported on the IGX.

These same supervisory FastPackets are also used to carry data clock information between the connection endpoints.

Interleaved ("Fast") Control Signal Transport

Interleaved control signal transport carries user data and control signal updates interleaved byte-by-byte in the same stream of FastPackets.

Updates for seven control signals are included in every alternate byte of the FastPacket payload. (The remaining bit in each byte is set to 1 to maintain necessary ones density.) The remaining control signals are updated in normal supervisory FastPackets.

This format is used by any connection that has an f in its type. For example:

- 19.2f is a 19.2 kbps data connection with interleaved control signal updates.
- 7.2f/5 is a 7.2 kbps data connection with interleaved control signal updates and partially filled FastPackets.

Naturally, a connection that uses interleaved control signal updates generates more FastPackets per second than a connection of the same bit rate but that uses only normal control signal updates.

Partially Interleaved Control Signal Transport

Partially interleaved control signal transport carries a single control signal update bit in the least-significant bit position of every data byte in the FastPacket.

NOTE	In many places in the IGX software documentation, this feature is called Embedded EIA.

By default, the clear to send (CTS) or request to send (RTS) control signal (whichever is an input from the attached CPE) is carried in this format. However, any other control signal can be selected using the **cnfleadmon** command.

The remaining control signals are updated in normal supervisory FastPackets.

You select this format by specifying 7/8e for the optional Coding parameter of the **addcon** command.

Naturally, a connection that uses partially interleaved control signal updates generates slightly more FastPackets per second than a connection of the same bit rate that uses only normal control signal updates.

NOTE	This feature is available only on connections using 8-bit Data Frame Multiplexing (DFM, described later) with a maximum data rate of 19.2 kbps that terminate in different nodes on LDM cards where *no* other connections are above 19.2 kbps.

Because the data bits and control bit in a byte might be all zeroes, the format does not guarantee a minimum ones density and therefore cannot be routed across ZCS trunks. The IGX software automatically applies the ***z** route avoid parameter to these connections.

UVM/CVM Super-Rate Connections

A *super-rate* data connection is defined by its type. It can have one of these forms:

- Nx56, where $1 \leq n \leq 8$
- Nx64, where $1 \leq n \leq 8$

At least one end of a super-rate data connection must terminate on a UVM or CVM card. The other end may terminate on an HDM or LDM card.

In a super-rate connection, *n* contiguous timeslots on the UVM or CVM line are bundled to form a single logical channel.

When both ends of a super-rate connection terminate on CVM or UVM lines, timeslot alignment is maintained across the connection. For example, in the super-rate connection created with the following **addcon** command (between UVM cards):

```
addcon 12.1.1-4 igx2 5.1.17-20 4x64
```

Data is transferred between endpoint timeslots as follows:

> 12.1.1 <--> 5.1.17
> 12.1.2 <--> 5.1.18
> 12.1.3 <--> 5.1.19
> 12.1.4 <--> 5.1.20

CVM DS0A Subrate Connections

A CVM Model A card supports the DS0A data framing format for carrying low-speed data inside a single timeslot on a T1 line. Only the following DS0A data rates are supported:

- 2.4 kbps
- 4.8 kbps
- 9.6 kbps
- 56 kbps

DS0A data connections can be one of two types, depending on the card types at each end of the connection, as shown in Table 4-19.

Table 4-19 *Subrate Connection Types*

	Types		Description
Interpretive	2.4	2.4/4	An interpretive DS0A data connection terminates on a CVM card at one end and an HDM or LDM card at the other end. It is called interpretive because control signal status is mapped between the HDM/LDM control signal pins and the DS0A control signal bits.
	4.8	4.8/10	
	9.6	4.8/4	
	56	9.6/10	
Transparent	2.4t	2.4/4t	A transparent DS0A data connection terminates on CVM cards at both ends. It is called transparent because the DS0A control signal status bits are not extracted from the DS0A framing format. Instead, they are carried transparently across the connection.
	4.8t	4.8/10t	
	9.6t	4.8/4t	
	56t	9.6/10t	

UVM/CVM Transparent Data Connections

This section describes the two types of transparent data connections that are supported on CVM and UVM cards.

T Connections

A *T connection* provides a transparent clear-channel 64 kbps connection between CVM and/or UVM cards. These connections are typically used to transport CCS signaling D channels between UVM or CVM lines configured for CCS voice signaling.

TD Connections

A *TD connection*, supported only on the UVM, provides a transparent data connection with D-channel compression. The D-channel compression feature assumes that the data carried on the connection is in HDLC format. In that case, only the actual data frames are placed in FastPackets and sent across the network. The HDLC idle flags are suppressed from the data stream.

Naturally, the effective bandwidth of a TD connection may be anywhere from 0 kbps to 64 kbps, depending on the amount of HDLC traffic being sent.

Zero Code Suppression Review

Zero Code Suppression (ZCS) is an old technique (before B8ZS, B3ZS, and HDB3 came into widespread use) to enforce the necessary ones density on T1 and E1 lines and trunks.

The ZCS algorithm works by simply replacing any 00000000 byte in the data stream with 00000001, thereby introducing an uncorrectable bit error.

These bit errors were generally considered acceptable on voice FastPackets because the substitutions were likely to be infrequent and would cause only minor distortion of the voice signal, whether compressed or not.

On data FastPackets, however, such bit errors are clearly unacceptable.

Therefore, it was necessary to design a technique to ensure that a data FastPacket carried across a ZCS trunk could *never* contain a byte of all zeroes. If data FastPackets are certain to maintain the necessary ones density, the ZCS algorithm will never make any byte substitutions.

FastPacket Coding

The coding choices are 7/8, 7/8e, 8/8, and 8/8i:

- 7/8 coding guarantees at least a single 1 bit for every 8 bits by inserting a 1 in the last bit position of each payload byte. 7/8 is the default coding for most, but not all, data connection types. Both of the following **addcon** commands create a 128 kbps data connection with 7/8 encoding:

  addcon 5.1 igx4 6.2 128 7/8

  addcon 5.1 igx4 6.2 128

- 7/8 embedded (7/8e) coding is designed to allow for high speed updates for a single control lead.

- 8/8 coding uses all eight bit positions of each payload byte to carry data bits. Because 8/8 coding does not guarantee ones density, use the optional ***z** route avoid option on the **addcon** command to avoid ZCS trunks. Routing across ZCS trunks may result in data corruption. The following **addcon** command creates a connection with the optional ***z** route avoid option:

  addcon 5.3 igx4 6.1 19.2 8/8 *z

- 8/8 inverted (8/8i) coding is designed for HDLC/SDLC-based data protocols. These protocols ensure a minimum density of 0 bits by inserting a 0 bit after any five consecutive 1 bits. 8/8i coding maintains ones density by simply inverting all data bits (0 to 1 and 1 to 0). The resulting FastPackets may be routed, without corruption, across ZCS trunks. The receiving data card restores the original value of the data bits. The following **addcon** command creates a connection with 8/8 inverted coding:

  addcon 5.3 igx4 6.1 19.2 8/8i

Now that you understand the various data connection types and the optional parameters, you can complete the task of adding data connections using the **addcon** command, as shown in Example 4-24.

Example 4-24 **addcon** *Output*

```
igx3                group8:1       IGX 8420  9.2.20    July 8 1999  08:45 CST

Local          Remote       Remote
Channel        NodeName     Channel        State  Type       Compress  Code COS
3.1.1          igx3         3.1.1          Ok     v
3.1.5          igx1         3.1.5          Ok     c32        VAD/ADPCM       2
3.1.22         igx1         3.1.20         Ok     c32        VAD/ADPCM       2
6.3            igx4         7.3            Ok     19.2       DFM       7/8  0


Last Command: addcon 6.3 igx4 7.3 19.2


Next Command:
```

Displaying All Connections

The **dspcons** command, as shown in Example 4-25, displays summary information for all connections that terminate on this node.

Example 4-25 **dspcons** *Output*

```
igx3                 group8:1       IGX 8420  9.2.20    July 8 1999  08:45 CST

Local           Remote      Remote
Channel         NodeName    Channel            State  Type    Compress    Code COS
3.1.1           igx3        3.1.1              Ok     v
3.1.5           igx1        3.1.5              Ok     c32     VAD/ADPCM        2
3.1.22          igx1        3.1.20             Ok     c32     VAD/ADPCM        2
6.3             igx4        7.3                Ok     19.2    DFM         7/8  0
5.1             igx4        6.1                Ok     256                 7/8  0


Last Command: dspcons

Next Command:
```

Here is the **dspcons** command syntax:

> **dspcons** [*start channel*] [*node name*] [*filter*]

Each line of the **dspcons** display shows summary information about one connection or a range of contiguous connections if all connections in the range have the same values in the other fields. Refer to Tables 4-7 and 4-8 for parameter and summary descriptions.

Displaying Detailed Parameters of One Connection

The **dspcon** command displays detailed information for one connection, as shown in Example 4-26.

Example 4-26 **dspcon** *Output*

```
igx3                 group8:1       IGX 8420  9.2.20    July 8 1999  08:45 CST

Conn:  6.3              igx4       7.3              19.2 7/8
                                                          Status:OK


Owner: REMOTE  Restriction: NONE  COS: 0 Compression: NONE

Path:   igx3      15--  15igx4
Pref:   Not Configured

igx3       LDM:  OK                     igx4       LDM:  OK
           LDI:  OK                                 LDI:  OK
           Clock: OK                                Clock: OK
```

Example 4-26 dspcon *Output (Continued)*

```
Last Command: dspcon 6.3

Next Command:
```

Here is the **dspcon** command syntax:

dspcon *<channel>*

channel specifies the channel number of the connection to be displayed.

The information about this connection from the **dspcons** screen is repeated near the top of this screen. This includes the local channel, remote node name, remote channel, connection type, connection status, and COS.

Additional details are as follows:

- **Owner**—Determines which end issued the **addcon** command. If local, the connection was added from this node; if remote, the connection was added from the remote node.

- **Restriction**—Based on the **route avoid** parameter. Specifies any trunk type that the connection cannot use.

- **Path**—The route (the series of nodes and trunks) currently used by the connection.

- **Preferred route**—A user-configured preferred route. Connection routing is discussed in detail in Chapter 7.

- **Endpoint hardware and clock status**—The status of the card group and the data clock at each end of the connection. A clock failure means that the incoming clock is at least 2 percent above the configured connection data rate. A low clock rate does not cause a failure.

Deleting Connections

The **delcon** command, as shown in Example 4-27, removes one or more connections from the network. A connection can be deleted from either end of the connection.

Example 4-27 delcon *Output*

```
igx3               group8:1      IGX 8420  9.2.20    July 8 1999  08:45 CST

Local         Remote      Remote
Channel       NodeName    Channel         State  Type     Compress   Code COS
3.1.1         igx3        3.1.1           Ok     v
3.1.5         igx1        3.1.5           Ok     c32      VAD/ADPCM        2
3.1.22        igx1        3.1.20          Ok     c32      VAD/ADPCM        2
5.1           igx4        6.1             Ok     256                 7/8   0
```

continues

Example 4-27 **delcon** *Output (Continued)*

```
Last Command: delcon 6.3

Next Command:
```

The **delcon** command screen is essentially the same as the **dspcons** screen.

Here is the **delcon** command syntax:

delcon *<local channel(s)>*

local channel(s) is the local channel number(s) of the connection(s) to be deleted.

Data Channel Commands

Table 4-20 lists data channel commands that have not yet been introduced in this chapter.

Table 4-20 *Additional Commands*

Command	Description	Privilege Level
cnfchdfm	Defines the Data Frame Multiplexing (DFM) bit pattern length and enables or disables DFM on the channel.	1 and 2
cnfcheia	Defines the maximum EIA control lead transmission rate for a data channel.	1 and 2
cnfchutl	Defines the percent utilization for the data channel.	1 and 2
cnfdch	Enables or disables Idle Code Suppression (ICS) on the channel.	1 and 2
cnfdclk	Defines the clock mode for a data channel.	1 and 2
cnfict	Changes a control lead interface control template for a data channel.	1 and 2
cpyict	Copies all interface control templates from one data channel to another on the same IGX switch.	1 and 2
dspbob	Displays the real-time state of a data channel's data, control, and clock signals.	1 through 6
dspchcnf	Displays data channel (interface) characteristics.	1 through 6
dspict	Displays a control lead interface control template for a data channel.	1 through 6

Data Channels

As mentioned earlier in this chapter, a data connection is a point-to-point permanent virtual circuit (PVC) that links two data channels in an IGX network.

A data channel can be

- Provided by one of the ports on an HDM or LDM card
- One timeslot or multiple contiguous timeslots of a line on a CVM or UVM card

This chapter describes how to configure data channels. But first, a discussion of data channel types and configurable data channel characteristics is presented.

NOTE   In general, a data channel can be configured regardless of whether a data connection terminates on that channel. Some exceptions to this rule are noted in this chapter.

Data Channel Types

Depending on the card type that supports it, a data channel in the IGX can be one of a variety of types, as described in the following sections.

EIA/TIA-232 Data Channels

EIA/TIA-232 (formerly known as RS-232-D) is an EIA standard that describes the physical and electrical requirements for a low-speed, synchronous, unbalanced serial data interface operating at data rates at or below 56 kbps. (Notwithstanding the speed limitation defined in the standard, the HDM allows data connections at much higher speeds using this channel type.)

Only the HDM supports a fully standard EIA/TIA-232 interface. The LDM supports a subset of the full EIA/TIA-232 standard. The LDM supports all the data, control signal, and clock pins used by the vast majority of data equipment in use in the industry.

V.35 Data Channels

V.35 is an International Telecommunication Union Telecommunication Standardization Sector (ITU-T) standard that describes the physical and electrical requirements for a synchronous, balanced, or unbalanced serial data interface. Although the original V.35 standard described interface speeds up to 48 kbps, this type of interface is commonly used in the industry at speeds up to 2 Mbps.

Only the HDM supports V.35 interfaces.

EIA/TIA-449 Data Channels

EIA/TIA-449 (formerly known as RS-449) is an EIA standard that describes the physical requirements for a 37-pin, high-speed serial data interface. RS-422 and RS-423 describe the electrical characteristics of the balanced and unbalanced data, clock, and control signals.

Only the HDM supports EIA/TIA-449 interfaces.

X.21 Data Channels

X.21 is an ITU-T standard that describes the physical and electrical requirements for a 15-pin, high-speed, synchronous, balanced data interface at rates up to approximately 2 Mbps. Unlike EIA/TIA-232, EIA/TIA-449, and V.35, X.21 manages the interface using the Control and Indication control leads in combination with special signals on the Transmit Data and Receive Data leads.

Only the HDM supports X.21 interfaces using special converter cables with the EIA/TIA-449 back card.

Super-Rate (Nx56 or Nx64) Data Channels on T1, E1, or J1 Lines

As previously described, up to eight contiguous timeslots of a T1, E1, or J1 line on a UVM or CVM can be used as a super-rate data channel.

Subrate DS0A Data Channels on T1 Lines

As previously described, a CVM Model A supports DS0A data channels in timeslots of a T1 line on a CVM.

Transparent Data Channels on T1, E1, or J1 Lines

As previously described, individual timeslots of a T1, E1, or J1 line on a UVM or CVM may be configured as a transparent data channel.

Configurable Data Channel Characteristics

Each data channel in an IGX can support a variety of options. Certain data channels can support Data Frame Multiplexing (DFM) compression or Idle Code Suppression (ICS) techniques. DFM is a repetitive pattern-suppression algorithm available on the HDM and LDM cards. ICS is a repetitive pattern-suppression algorithm available on the UVM and CVM cards.

In addition to these compression techniques, the HDM and LDM cards support a wide variety of features for the monitoring, transport, and manipulation of data channel control signals, and a variety of data channel clocking options, as described later in this chapter.

Data Frame Multiplexing

As just mentioned, DFM is a Repetitive Pattern Suppression (RPS) algorithm. It improves bandwidth efficiency by eliminating repetitive patterns within the incoming bit stream.

DFM is used automatically on any connection that meets all the following conditions:

- The connection must terminate on an HDM or LDM card at each end.
- The connection's data rate must be 128 kbps or less.
- The data connection can not use interleaved control signal updates.
- DFM must be enabled on the channel at each end of the connection. (By default, it is enabled on all data channels.)
- DFM must be enabled on the node at each end of the connection. (By default, it is not enabled on the node.)

When in use, DFM causes a FastPacket to be suppressed if

- All data bits in the FastPacket are repetitions of the same pattern of 7 bits, 8 bits, or 16 bits
- At least one copy of the repetitive pattern was present at the end of the previous FastPacket sent
- At least one of the previous 15 FastPackets was sent

Configuring Data Frame Multiplexing

The **cnfchdfm** command, as shown in Example 4-28, enables or disables DFM for one or more data channels and sets the DFM pattern length.

Example 4-28 **cnfchdfm** *Output*

```
igx3          TN     group8:1        IGX 8420    9.2.20   July 8 1999  08:07 CDT


             Maximum EIA     %      DFM Pattern     DFM
Channels     Update Rate    Util      Length       Status
5.1             10          99         16         Enabled
5.2              5          50          8         Enabled
5.3             10          75          8         Enabled
5.4             10          50          8         Enabled



Last Command: cnfchdfm 5.1 16 e

Next Command:
```

By default, DFM is enabled for all data channels that have a pattern length of 8 bits. If DFM is not enabled on the node, the **cnfchdfm** command has no effect on the channel(s) being configured.

Both HDM and LDM data cards support DFM.

To function properly, DFM must be enabled for the channels at both ends of a connection. The IGX software does not enforce this requirement.

Here is the **cnfchdfm** command syntax:

```
cnfchdfm <channel(s)> <7 | 8 | 16> [e | d]
```

Table 4-21 describes the parameters for the **cnfchdfm** command.

Table 4-21 **cnfchdfm** *Command Parameters*

Parameter	Description
channel(s)	Specifies the data channel(s) in the format *slot.port* or *slot.port-port*.
7	8	16	Specifies the pattern length in bits for the DFM algorithm. The default is 8 bits.
e	d	Enables or disables DFM.

Idle Code Suppression

Figure 4-10 illustrates the ICS algorithm and shows how it is enabled on an Nx64 super-rate data channel.

Figure 4-10 *Idle Code Suppression*

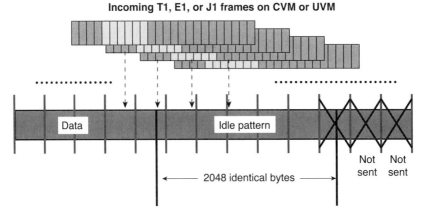

Incoming T1, E1, or J1 frames on CVM or UVM

Data

Idle pattern

Not sent   Not sent

2048 identical bytes

Supported on UVM and CVM Nx64 super-rate data channels

The ICS algorithm is supported on Nx64 data channels on the UVM and CVM. The ICS algorithm is enabled on an Nx64 super-rate data channel if the following conditions are met:

- ICS must be enabled on the channel using the **cnfdch** command. By default, ICS is not enabled on any channel.

- The channel must be used in an Nx64 super-rate data connection that terminates on a UVM or CVM card at the other end.

The ICS algorithm is specifically designed to allow bandwidth savings on an Nx64 super-rate data connection that is used to carry video traffic from a device that conforms to the H.221 video codec frame protocol.

In the H.221 protocol, an Nx64 video channel is defined as being idle any time the data in the relevant timeslots of 256 consecutive T1, E1, or J1 frames is the same. For an Nx64 data channel, that corresponds to Nx256 consecutive identical bytes. For the largest supported super-rate data channel (N = 8), that equates to 2048 consecutive identical bytes.

Consequently, the UVM or CVM stops generating FastPackets on an Nx64 super-rate data channel as soon as 2048 consecutive identical bytes are detected (regardless of the value of N used in the Nx64 connection). The UVM or CVM starts generating FastPackets again as soon as a different byte is detected.

Configuring Idle Code Suppression

The **cnfdch** command, as shown in Example 4-29, enables or disables ICS for a super-rate data channel. By default, ICS is not enabled.

Example 4-29 cnfdch *Output*

```
Paris            TN     YourID:1        IGX 8410  9.3.24    Aug. 2 2001  16:19 PDT

                 Maximum EIA    %      DFM Pattern    DFM      Idle Code
Channels         Update Rate   Util     Length      Status     Suppr
3.1.5-8             -           -         -            -       Enabled
3.1.9-20            -           -         -            -       Disabled




Last Command: cnfdch 3.1.5 e

Warning: Channel(s) is in use.  Be sure to reconfigure other end(s).
Next Command:
```

Both UVM and CVM data cards support ICS.

Although it would not typically be used this way, ICS can be enabled at only one end of an Nx64 data connection.

Here is the **cnfdch** command syntax:

```
cnfdch <channel(s)> <e | d>
```

Table 4-22 describes the parameters for the **cnfdch** command.

Table 4-22 cnfdch *Command Parameters*

Parameter	Description
channel(s)	Specifies the data channel(s) on which ICS is to be enabled or disabled:
	CVM—*slot.timeslot*[*-timeslot*]
	UVM—*slot.line.timeslot*[*-timeslot*]
	You need to provide only the starting timeslot of the super-rate data channel.
e	d	Enables or disables ICS.

Configuring Data Channel Utilization

On any data channel that is using DFM, it is likely that the data channel will generate far fewer FastPackets per second than it would generate if DFM were not in use. Therefore, DFM allows the IGX software to reserve less trunk bandwidth for such a connection than would otherwise be necessary.

The **cnfchutl** command, as shown in Example 4-30, specifies, as a percentage, a data channel's expected *average* utilization rate. (There is no way for the IGX software to guess what percentage of the total possible FastPacket rate is really needed for a data channel, because that is determined by the actual data stream delivered to the IGX from the attached equipment.) The percent utilization is multiplied by the channel's full FastPacket rate (assuming that DFM finds no repetitive patterns to suppress) to determine how much trunk bandwidth is reserved for the connection.

Example 4-30 cnfchutl *Output*

```
igx3            TN    group8:1        IGX 8420    9.2.20    July 8 1999  08:07 CDT

            Maximum EIA    %      DFM Pattern    DFM
Channels    Update Rate   Util      Length      Status
5.1             2          35        16        Enabled
5.2-4           2         100         8        Enabled


Last Command: cnfchutl 5.1 35

Next Command:
```

The percent utilization for a data channel may be configured to any value from 0% to 100% (the default). The configured channel utilization is ignored if DFM is not used on the channel.

The percent utilization cannot be configured for a super-rate data channel on a CVM or UVM, whether ICS is in use or not. This ensures that enough trunk bandwidth is available whenever a video session is active on the UVM or CVM.

Here is the **cnfchutl** command syntax:

```
cnfchutl <channel(s)> <% utilization>
```

Table 4-23 describes the parameters for the **cnfchutl** command.

Table 4-23   **cnfchutl** *Command Parameters*

Parameter	Description
channel(s)	Specifies the data channel(s) in the format *slot.port*[-*port*].
% utilization	Specifies the expected utilization in the range 0 to 100 percent. The default value for data channels is 100 percent.

Serial Data Channel Review

In the IGX, a serial port is defined as any port that uses any of the following interface standards:

- EIA/TIA-232
- EIA/TIA-449
- ITU-T V.35
- ITU-T X.21

NOTE   Strictly speaking, all other IGX interfaces (T1, E1, J1, Y1, T3, E3, and OC3) are also serial interfaces. Nonetheless, this book uses the term *serial* to refer exclusively to the interface standards just described.

As described previously, the HDM and LDM cards provide serial synchronous data interfaces. Also as described previously, a serial synchronous data interface between any two data devices (or between a data device and an IGX serial data port) consists of

- Data exchange pins
- Control signal exchange pins
- Data timing (clock) pins

Previous sections and chapters have provided details on the processing of data bits received and transmitted on an IGX data port's data exchange pins. The following sections describe control signal and clock signal processing on serial data ports.

DCE and DTE

Each of the serial data interface standards supported on the IGX defines one or more pins on a multipin interface to carry data, control signals, and clock signals in each direction on the multipin interface. Each interface standard defines the signal exchange between a Data Terminal Equipment (DTE) device and a Data Communication Equipment (DCE) device. Each interface standard defines the following:

- Which pins carry the data signal(s) from the DTE to the DCE
- Which pins carry the data signal(s) from the DCE to the DTE
- Which pins carry the control signal(s) from the DTE to the DCE
- Which pins carry the control signal(s) from the DCE to the DTE
- Which pins carry the clock signal(s) from the DTE to the DCE
- Which pins carry the clock signal(s) from the DCE to the DTE

In conformance with the interface standards, each IGX serial data port may be configured as either a DCE or a DTE to allow direct connection to any DTE or DCE data equipment.

DCE/DTE Selection on IGX Serial Data Ports

An HDM data port is configured as a DCE or a DTE depending on the position of a daughter board installed on the SDI back card. The SDI must be removed from its slot to change a port from DCE to DTE or vice versa.

An LDM data port is configured as a DCE or DTE depending on the adapter cable connected to the port. A port may be changed from DCE to DTE or vice versa simply by changing the adapter cable.

Input Control Signal Transport

Control signals can be used by data devices for many different reasons and in many different ways. Sometimes they are used for flow control between end devices. Sometimes, they are used to notify the other device of alarm conditions or status changes. Sometimes, they are not used at all.

Because it is impossible for the IGX to know the intended use of the control signals by any attached data device, the IGX monitors the input control signals (from the attached devices) and sends periodic samples of the control signals to the data port at the other end of the connection using one of the methods described earlier in this chapter.

Configuring Input Control Signal Sampling

The HDM and LDM cards monitor the incoming control signals for changes by polling, or sampling, the incoming control signals at a fixed, configurable frequency. By default, the incoming control signals are sampled every 500 milliseconds, or twice every second.

The **cnfcheia** command, as shown in Example 4-31, sets the control lead sampling rate, in samples per second, on a data channel. It can be set to any value from 0 (no sampling) to 20 samples per second.

Example 4-31 **cnfcheia** *Output*

```
igx3            TN    group8:1       IGX 8420   9.2.20   July 8 1999  08:07 CDT

              Maximum EIA    %     DFM Pattern    DFM
  Channels    Update Rate   Util      Length     Status
  5.1             2          35        16         Enabled
  5.2            10         100         8         Enabled
  5.3-4           2         100         8         Enabled



Last Command: cnfcheia 5.2 10

Next Command:
```

Each time the control signals are sampled, a supervisory FastPacket is sent across the connection if one or more signals have changed since the previous sample. However, a minimum of one supervisory FastPacket per second is sent if the update rate is greater than 0 (1 through 20). Note that multiple changes occurring within one sampling interval might not be detected.

For a 1344 kbps data connection, the sampling rate is fixed at 0 (in other words, no control signal updates are supported).

Here is the **cnfcheia** command syntax:

```
cnfcheia <channel(s)> <sampling rate>
```

Table 4-24 describes the **cnfchutl** command parameters.

Table 4-24   **cnfchutl** *Command Parameters*

Parameter	Description
channel(s)	Specifies the data channel(s) in the format *slot.port*[*-port*].
sampling rate	Specifies the control signal sampling rate in samples per second, from 0 to 20.

Specifying Output Control Signals

Figure 4-11 illustrates output control signals.

Figure 4-11 *Output Control Signals*

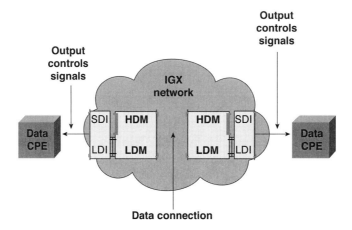

Output control signals (from the IGX serial data port to the attached device) can be configured using interface control templates. An *interface control template* (ICT) is a set of control signal state definitions that specifies the state of every possible output control signal on a serial data port. There are five interface control templates for each channel:

- **Active (a)**—Used whenever the connection status is OK.

- **Conditioned (c)**—Used whenever the connection status is Failed or Down.

- **Looped (l)**—Used whenever there is a software-configured loopback anywhere on the connection.

- **Near (n)**—Used whenever the connection has a near-end external modem loopback test in progress.

- **Far (f)**—Used whenever the connection has a far-end external modem loopback test in progress.

The existence of multiple ICTs on an IGX data port allows the port to present a different appearance to the attached device, depending on the state of the connection through the network. For example, the *active* ICT might be configured to set DSR high whenever the connection is OK, and the *conditioned* ICT might be configured to set DSR low whenever the connection is Failed or Down.

Interface Control Templates Example

Figure 4-12 illustrates interface control templates.

Figure 4-12 *Interface Control Templates*

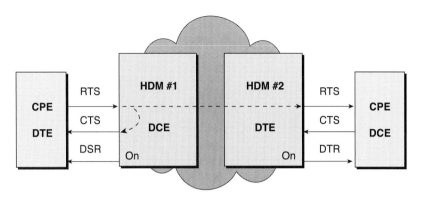

Figure 4-12 shows a possible use of active interface control templates on two HDM data channels. Table 4-25 lists the HDM #1 and HDM #2 signals and states.

Table 4-25 *HDM #1 and HDM #2 Signals and States*

HDM #1 (DCE)		HDM #2 (DTE)	
Signal	**State**	**Signal**	**State**
CTS	Follows the local RTS signal	RTS	Follows the remote RTS (the control signal state passed across the network in supervisory FastPackets)
DSR	Always ON	DTR	Always ON

Displaying Interface Control Templates

The **dspict** command, as shown in Example 4-32, is used to display any of the five interface control templates for a data channel.

Example 4-32 dspict *Output*

```
igx3           TN    group8:1      IGX 8420    9.2.20    July 8 1999  08:25 CDT

Data Channel:      5.1
Interface:         RS232D    DCE
Clocking:          Normal
```

continues

Example 4-32 dspict *Output (Continued)*

```
              Interface Control Template for Connection while ACTIVE

    Lead    Output Value                   Lead    Output Value
    TST     OFF                            RI      ON
    DSR     ON                             CTS     ON
    SRxD    OFF                            DCD     ON
    SCTS    OFF                            SDCD    OFF



    Last Command: dspict 5.1 a

    Next Command:
```

NOTE By default, every output control signal in every interface control template is either ON or OFF. This means that the control signal updates carried in supervisory, interleaved, or embedded FastPackets from the opposite end of the connection are not delivered to the attached device.

Here is the **dspict** command syntax:

dspict *<channel> <template>*

Table 4-26 describes the **dspict** command parameters.

Table 4-26   **dspict** *Command Parameters*

Parameter	Description
channel	Specifies the data channel in the format *slot.port*.
template	Specifies the template to display:
	a—Active
	c—Conditioned (connection failed or downed)
	l—Looped (local or remote loopback)
	n—Near-end external loopback
	f—Far-end external loopback

Configuring Output Control Signals

Using the **cnfict** command, each control signal in each ICT may be configured to

- Be always ON
- Be always OFF

- Follow a local control signal—that is, another control signal (either input or output) on the same data port

- Follow a "remote" control signal—that is, an input control signal from the other end of the data connection

NOTE   It is only by configuring one or more control signals to follow a remote control signal that the control signal updates received in supervisory, interleaved, or embedded FastPackets are used.

Configuring an ICT

The **cnfict** command, shown in Example 4-33, specifies an individual control signal in an individual ICT of an individual data port. The control signals that can be configured depend on the type of port (V.35, X.21, and so on) and whether the port is configured as a DCE or a DTE.

Example 4-33 cnfict *Output*

```
igx3            TN     group8:1       IGX 8420    9.2.20    July 8 1999  08:27 CDT

Data Channel:      5.1
Interface:         RS232D    DCE
Clocking:          Normal

              Interface Control Template for Connection while ACTIVE

Lead     Output Value              Lead      Output Value
TST      OFF                       RI        Remote RI
DSR      Local DTR                 CTS       Local RTS delay 10 msec
SRxD     OFF                       DCD       ON
SCTS     ON                        SDCD      OFF



Last Command: cnfict 5.1 a cts local rts 10

Next Command:
```

Control signals being configured can be described using the standard control signal nomenclature for EIA/TIA-232, EIA/TIA-449, or ITU-T-V.35. However, the signal names displayed on the **cnfict** or **dspict** screens are always those corresponding to the true interface type.

Here is the **cnfict** command syntax:

```
cnfict <channel> <template> <output control signal> <state | source>
   [followed control signal] [delay]
```

Table 4-27 describes the command parameters for the **cnfict** command.

Table 4-27 **cnfict** *Command Parameters*

Parameter	Description
channel	Specifies the data channel in the format *slot.port*.
template	Specifies the template to change. Valid templates are active (a), conditioned (c), looped (l), near (n), and far (f).
output control signal	The output control signal to configure.
*state	source*	Sets the specified control signal to always on or always off, or specifies that it should follow another local or remote control signal. Allowed values are on, off, l, local, r, and remote.
followed control signal	If local or remote is specified, this is the local or remote control signal to be followed.
delay	If CTS is following local RTS, this is the time from the OFF to ON transition in milliseconds. There is no delay for an ON to OFF transition.

Copying Interface Control Templates

Because the **cnfict** command, shown in Example 4-34, configures only one control signal in one ICT on one data channel, it can require many commands to configure all necessary control signals in all ICTs for a given data channel.

Example 4-34 **cnfict** *Output*

```
igx3            TN    group8:1     IGX 8420    9.2.20    July 8 1999  08:28 CDT

Data Channel:      5.3
Interface:         RS232D    DCE
Clocking:          Normal


          Interface Control Template for Connection while ACTIVE

 Lead    Output Value                    Lead     Output Value
 TST     OFF                             RI       Remote RI
 DSR     ON                     CTS      Local RTS delay 10 msec
 SRxD    OFF                             DCD      ON
 SCTS    ON                              SDCD     OFF



Last Command: cpyict 5.1 5.3

Next Command:
```

To save time in a situation in which many data channels must be configured with identical or similar ICTs, the **cpyict** command is available to copy the current settings of all interface control templates associated with a given channel to a destination channel. After you copy the templates, you can edit them using the **cnfict** command. The source and destination channel need not have similar DTE or DCE configurations.

Here is the **cpyict** command syntax:

```
cpyict <source channel> <destination channel>
```

Table 4-28 describes the command parameters for the **cpyict** command.

Table 4-28 **cpyict** *Command Parameters*

Parameter	Description
source channel	Specifies the source data channel from which the ICTs are copied, in the format *slot.port*.
destination channel	Specifies the destination data channel to which the ICTs are copied, in the format *slot.port*.

Data Channel Clocking

On a synchronous data interface between a DCE and a DTE, data is exchanged (on the transmit data [TxD] and receive data [RxD] pins) at bit rates that are determined by explicit clock signals.

In most synchronous data interface standards, two separate clock signals are used—one for the transmit data and one for the receive data.

NOTE   X.21 is an exception to this rule. The X.21 standard defines a single clock signal, generated by the DCE, that is used for both transmit data and receive data.

In all cases, the DCE provides the clock (RxC) used for the receive data (from the DCE to the DTE).

The clock signal for the transmit data may be provided by the DCE (transmit clock, or TxC), or it may be provided by the DTE (external transmit clock, or XTC, sometimes also called terminal timing, or TT).

NOTE   Data channel clocking is not the same as IGX network synchronization and clocking. Please refer to Chapter 7 for more information on network synchronization.

Data Channel Clocking Modes

HDM cards support synchronous clocking using normal, looped, or split clock modes. The LDM supports a limited number of clock modes, as described in this section.

Normal Clock Mode

In normal clock mode, the DCE provides both the transmit clock (TxC) and the receive clock (RxC).

An HDM port, whether it is a DCE or a DTE, supports normal clock mode.

An LDM port that is a DCE supports only normal clock mode.

Looped Clock Mode

In looped clock mode, the DCE provides the receive clock (RxC), and the DTE provides the transmit clock (XTC/TT). In this mode, the IGX data port requires that the attached device (whether it is a DCE or a DTE) provide a clock that is frequency-locked to the clock provided by the IGX data port.

An HDM port, whether it is a DCE or a DTE, supports looped clock mode.

An LDM port that is a DTE supports only looped clock mode.

Split Clock Mode

In split clock mode, the DCE provides the receive clock (RxC), and the DTE provides the transmit clock (XTC/TT). In this mode, the two clocks cannot be frequency-locked.

An HDM port, whether it is a DCE or a DTE, supports split clock mode.

An LDM port does not support split clock mode.

Isochronous Data Clocking

To ensure end-to-end bit transparency, it is critical that all clock signals that control the flow of data bits in a particular direction be the same. That is accomplished by ensuring that there is one master clock in each direction of the circuit and that all other clock signals are frequency-locked to the master.

The master clocks for data bit timing in each direction can be provided either by the IGX network (with the attached device at each end frequency-locked to the IGX-provided clock) or by the attached devices at either end of the connection.

If an attached device is providing a master clock, the IGX data port must measure the clock provided by the attached device and inform the data port at the far end of the data connection of the measured frequency. The data port at the far end must then generate an equal clock frequency to clock out the data bits to the attached device.

This mechanism used to measure and propagate an externally-provided clock is called *isochronous clocking*. Isochronous clocking

- Is supported only on the HDM.
- Allows only one measured clock to be propagated in each direction.
- Uses supervisory FastPackets (20 per second) to carry clock measurements.
- Can only provide guaranteed error-free transmission for data rates up to 112 kbps. Data rates above 112kbps might work error-free, but this cannot be guaranteed.

Configuring a Data Channel's Clock Mode

The **cnfdclk** command, as shown in Example 4-35, configures the clock mode for an HDM data channel to be normal, split, or looped. No options are available for an LDM data port.

Example 4-35 **cnfdclk** *Output*

```
igx3            TN     group8:1      IGX 8420    9.2.20    July 8 1999  08:30 CDT

Data Channel:      5.2
Interface:         RS232D    DTE
Clocking:          Looped

             Interface Control Template for Connection while ACTIVE

Lead     Output Value                   Lead     Output Value
LL       Remote RI                      DTR      Local DTR
RTS      Local RTS                      STxD     OFF
RL       OFF                            SRTS     ON



Last Command: cnfdclk 5.2 l

Next Command:
```

Here is the **cnfdclk** command syntax:

```
cnfdclk <channel> <n | s | l>
```

Table 4-29 describes the command parameters for the **cnfdclk** command.

Table 4-29 **cnfdclk** *Command Parameters*

Parameter	Description
channel	Specifies the data channel to be configured. Formatted as *slot.port*.
n | s | l	Specifies the channel's clocking type:
	n—Normal
	s—Split
	l—Looped

Displaying Real-Time Control and Clock Signals

The **dspbob** command displays a data channel's current data, control, and clock signal states, as shown in Example 4-36. The signals are divided into inputs (on the left) and outputs (on the right).

Example 4-36 dspbob *Output*

```
igx3                    group8:1      IGX 8420  9.2.20    July 8 1999   08:45 CST

Port:           5.3
Interface:      RS232D    DCE
Clocking:       Normal        (19198 Baud)

        Inputs from User Equipment              Outputs to User Equipment
   Lead  Pin  State   Lead  Pin  State     Lead  Pin  State   Lead  Pin  State
   TxD    2   Idle     SF   23   Off       RxD    3   Idle     RxC   17   Active
   RTS    4   Off      XTC  24   Unused    CTS    5   Off      RI    22   Off
   ***   11   Off                          DSR    6   Off      TST   25   Off
   STxD  14   Off                          DCD    8   On
   LL    18   Off                          SDCD  12   Off
   SRTS  19   Off                          SCTS  13   On
   DTR   20   Off                          TxC   15   Active
   RL    21   Off                          SRxD  16   Off

This Command: dspbob 5.3

Hit DEL key to quit:
```

The display is real-time and is updated every five seconds (by default) or at an optional user-specified interval. The display refreshes at the designated interval until you press the **Delete** key or until a node-specific timeout timer has expired (after 3 minutes by default).

NOTE	This command can be used only when a data connection terminates on the data channel to be displayed.

Here is the **dspbob** command syntax:

```
dspbob <channel> [update interval]
```

Table 4-30 describes the command parameters for the **dspbob** command.

Table 4-30 dspbob *Command Parameters*

Parameter	Description
channel	Specifies the data channel whose input and output signals are to be displayed, in the form *slot.port*.
update interval	Specifies the time, in seconds, between updates of the breakout box display. The range is from 1 to 60 seconds. If no interval is specified, the display is updated at 5-second intervals.

Data Channel Configuration Summary Display

The **dspchcnf** command, as shown in Example 4-37, displays configuration details for data channels on HDM and LDM cards.

Example 4-37 dspchcnf *Output*

```
igx3            TN      group8:1        IGX 8420    9.2.20    July 8 1999  08:00 CDT

                Maximum EIA     %       DFM Pattern     DFM
Channels        Update Rate     Util    Length          Status
5.1                 2           100         7           Disabled
5.2                10           100         8           Enabled
5.3                 2            35         8           Enabled
5.4                 2           100        16           Enabled



Last Command: dspchcnf 5.1

Next Command:
```

This is the same screen seen previously in this chapter with the **cnfchdfm**, **cnfchutl**, and **cnfcheia** commands. This command displays the appropriate configuration information, starting with the specified channel:

Here is the **dspchcnf** command syntax:

```
dspchcnf <starting channel>
```

starting channel specifies the starting channel in the format *slot.port*.

References

Table 4-31 lists the sources that are referenced in this chapter.

Table 4-31   *Standards and References*

Reference	Organization	Title
G.711	ITU-T	Pulse Code Modulation (PCM)
G.726	ITU-T	Adaptive Differential Pulse Code Modulation (ADPCM)
G.728	ITU-T	Low-Delay Code-Excited Linear Prediction (LD-CELP)
G.729	ITU-T	Conjugate-Structure Algebraic Code-Excited Linear Prediction (CS-ACELP)

Summary

This chapter provided an overview of voice FastPacket construction and discussed how to create compressed and uncompressed voice connections. You learned how to display voice connection parameters and delete voice connections.

You should be able to describe and configure voice channel voice-processing options including bandwidth savings due to Voice Activity Detection (VAD), Adaptive VAD, Fax Relay, gain adjustment, and echo cancellation.

You saw how to configure voice channel signaling options including signaling transport, signal monitoring, signaling conversions, and channel conditioning.

You should be able to create data connections and display their characteristics and describe the different types of data connections supported. You should also be able to describe data FastPacket construction and configure data channel control signal and data channel clocking options.

Review Questions

1 What is a point-to-point PVC that provides service for user devices in an IGX network?

2 What is the silence-suppression technique supported on CVM and UVM cards?

3 Which command creates a new connection in the network?

4 Which command checks all the connections on a node?

5 What is the endpoint of a voice connection?

6 The item that defines the on-hook condition and conditioning template is the _____, which is defined using the _____ command.

7 What command would you use to view the configuration of a range of voice channels on a single line?

8 What two commands would you use to modify receive and transmit signaling?

9 Which command displays a channel's echo canceller configuration?

10 What is the algorithm used to minimize the transmission of repetitive data patterns in the incoming data stream?

11 Which command eliminates a connection?

12 What command would you use to configure the control signal sampling rate?

13 What command would you use to configure channel bandwidth allocation?

14 Which command modifies an interface control template?

15 What command would you use to modify a data channel's clock mode?

16 What command would you use to view the current settings of an interface control template?

This chapter covers the following key topics:

- Frame Relay
- Signaling Protocols
- Frame Relay Port Commands
- Frame Relay Connections
- VC Queues
- ForeSight in the Network
- Bit-Oriented Protocol Frame Structures
- Frame Relay Connection Commands

CHAPTER 5

Frame Relay Ports and Connections

This chapter introduces Frame Relay services on the IGX and covers channelized and unchannelized Frame Relay ports, their parameters, and pertinent port statistics. It also presents Frame Relay connection characteristics as seen by the user and the network and examines ForeSight flow control and its effect on virtual circuit queue service rates.

Frame Relay

Frame Relay is a connection-oriented, statistical multiplexing, Layer 2 WAN switching technology designed to transport variable-length data messages. Routers, front-end processors (FEPs), and other customer premises equipment (CPE) are typically connected to Frame Relay networks.

As a popular, efficient data transport service, Frame Relay is commonly used for high-performance data communication for high-speed, frame-oriented bursty data applications. Typically, these are LAN-based applications that use a private or public Frame Relay WAN service.

Frame Relay is derived from more traditional frame-oriented data services such as X.25. Unlike X.25, however, Frame Relay services generally rely on the low error rates of high-speed data-carrying facilities available today, such as T1/E1, T3/E3, and higher-speed fiber-based technologies. As a result of the increased reliability of the available facilities, Frame Relay has been greatly simplified, compared to X.25, by the elimination of most of the overhead that is required in X.25 to recover from transmission facility errors.

The Frame Relay standards simply provide the definition of a data network *interface standard*. As such, these standards merely define how data must be formatted for submission to a Frame Relay service network for transmission. In particular, the Frame Relay standards do not specify how the Frame Relay network must deliver the data from one point to another. The implementation details are left to the manufacturers of the Frame Relay service network equipment.

A Frame Relay access device (FRAD) is equipment that is responsible for adapting data into Frame Relay frames. A router, switch, multiplexer, or concentrator can be a FRAD. Many of the figures in this chapter show routers as FRADs, but remember that many different devices can fulfill that role in a network.

For a more complete review of Frame Relay, refer to *Cisco WAN Quick Start* by Ronald McCarty, Jr.

Frame Relay Cards

The Frame Relay Module (FRM) front card supports one to four data ports and, in single-port mode, operates at up to 2.048 Mbps.

The Universal Frame Relay Module (UFM) supports up to 16 Mbps throughput for the card, with multiple serial interfaces or lines supported on the back card. Figure 5-1 shows the UFM and FRM front and back cards.

Figure 5-1 *Frame Relay Cards*

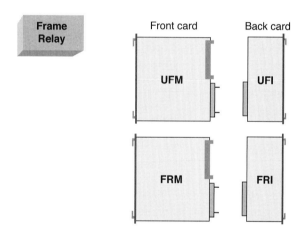

Table 5-1 lists the UFM and FRM front and back card features.

Table 5-1 *UFM and FRM Front and Back Cards*

Front Card	Back Card
FRM Model D (unchannelized)	FRI-V.35
	FRI-X.21
FRM Model E or Model J (channelized)	FRI-T1
	FRI-E1

Table 5-1   *UFM and FRM Front and Back Cards (Continued)*

Front Card	Back Card
UFM-4C and UFM-8C (channelized)	UFI-8 T1-DB15
	UFI-8 E1-DB15
	UFI-8 E1-BNC
UFM-U (unchannelized)	UFI-12 V.35
	UFI-12 X.21
	UFI-4 HSSI

Frame Relay Ports

As illustrated in Figure 5-2, a Frame Relay port is the serial interface between the network and a single Frame Relay device.

Figure 5-2   *Frame Relay Ports*

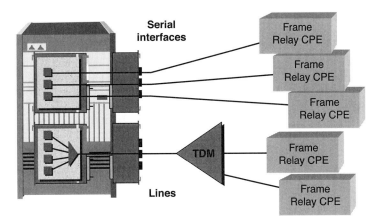

Two types of Frame Relay ports are supported on the UFM and FRM cards:

- **Physical**—Frame Relay ports on UFM-U/FRM Model D cards (V.35 or X.21 interfaces)

- **Logical**—Frame Relay ports on channelized UFM-C/FRM cards (T1 or E1 interfaces) created using the **addport** command

The IGX Frame Relay ports are actually located at the edge of the Cisco network, where their port connections link to the Frame Relay CPE devices.

After they are configured, both types of ports function in the same way.

Frame Relay Frames

The Frame Relay frame payload and header are illustrated in Figure 5-3.

Figure 5-3   *Frame Relay Frame*

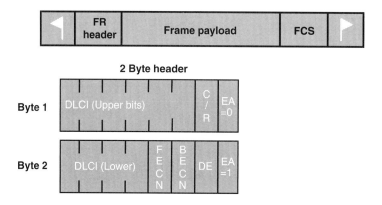

The following fields in the Frame Relay header are associated with Frame Relay port parameters:

- Data-link connection identifier (DLCI)
- Command/response (C/R)—not used in Frame Relay
- Extended address (EA)
- Forward explicit congestion notification (FECN)
- Backward explicit congestion notification (BECN)
- Discard eligibility (DE)

All frames are separated by flags (hexadecimal 7E) to mark the beginning and end of the frame. The FRAD is responsible for ensuring that the flag is not contained inside the data portion of the frame.

The maximum supported Frame Relay frame size is 4510 bytes.

Port Queues

Port queues are shared queues in the egress direction (toward the CPE). The port queue provides traffic management from multiple virtual circuits terminating on a single physical interface. The port queue is shared by all frames of any permanent virtual circuit (PVC) terminating at that port, as illustrated in Figure 5-4. In contrast, incoming frames pass through *virtual circuit* (VC) queues. VC queues are discussed in more detail later in this chapter.

Figure 5-4 *Egress Port Queue*

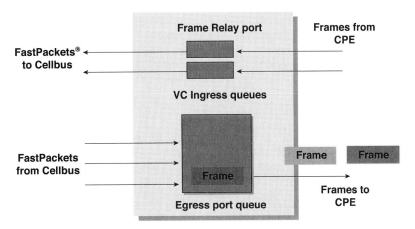

Port queue characteristics or parameters are set using the cnfport command. They include the following:

- **Port queue depth**—Determines the total number of bytes that are buffered by this port.
- **DE threshold**—Determines whether DE frames are dropped.
- **ECN threshold**—Determines whether frames are marked with FECN or BECN congestion notification.

Figure 5-5 illustrates these parameters.

Figure 5-5 *Port Queue Parameters*

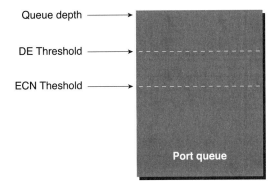

Signaling Protocols

Periodically, a Frame Relay CPE requests the network's status. This signaling can be a simple confirmation of the other device's existence, or more detailed information, such as the DLCIs, the bandwidth, and the state of all PVCs. This signaling occurs between the following:

- The user equipment and a Frame Relay port across the User-to-Network Interface (UNI)

- Frame Relay ports in the network across the Network-to-Network Interface (NNI)

UNI signaling consists of status enquiries from the user and status responses from the network. Figure 5-6 illustrates the signaling protocol process.

Figure 5-6 *Signaling Protocols*

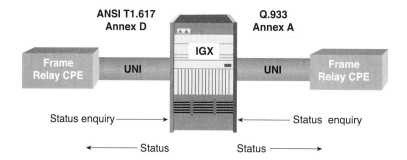

Each user-network interface is configured and managed independently. Note that the two UNIs shown in Figure 5-6 use different signaling protocols.

Each Frame Relay port can be configured for Cisco StrataCom Local Management Interface (LMI): DLCI 1023 and UNI; the ITU Q.933, Annex A: DLCI 0, and UNI or NNI; and the ANSI T1.617, Annex D: DLCI 0, and UNI or NNI signaling protocols. Each of these three signaling protocols uses the same basic handshake mechanism consisting of a sequence of status enquiry frames and status response frames. For signaling to work across the UNI, the user device and switch port must use the same signaling protocol.

Signaling Protocol Timers and Counters

Figure 5-7 illustrates the signaling protocol timers and counters process.

Figure 5-7 *Signaling Protocol Timers and Counters*

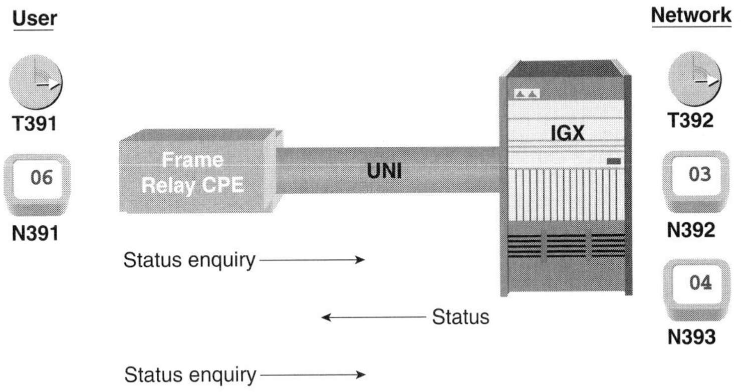

Here are the parameters associated with signaling protocol timers and counters:

- **T391**—Link integrity timer. The T391 parameter defines, in seconds, how often a status enquiry is sent to the network.

- **N391**—Full status poll. The N391 parameter defines how often to send a full status enquiry. The N391 parameter is in cycles, a single cycle being the T391 timer value.

- **T392**—Polling verification timer. The T392 parameter defines how often a status enquiry is expected from the user. If this timer expires and an enquiry has not been received, a timeout occurs. The parameters N392 and N393 define the thresholds for announcing alarms based on the timeouts.

- **N393**—Error threshold. The N393 parameter defines how many missed status enquiries from the user generate an alarm.

- **N393**—Monitored events count. The N392 parameter defines the window for determining an alarm. In general, if N392 enquiries are not received out of N393 expected enquiries, the port announces an alarm. Provided that the error threshold is not met, the port remains out of alarm.

Asynchronous Update Mode

Normal UNI signaling is based on polls (status enquiries) from the user device. PVC status is reported only on *full* status messages.

This introduces two potential problems: a delay before the user discovers the PVC status, and *no* status reporting for some PVCs when large numbers of PVCs are configured for a port.

Asynchronous update mode addresses both problems. If asynchronous update mode is enabled, the switch sends unsolicited status messages when a PVC changes state.

Network-to-Network Interface

At an NNI, a Frame Relay port can generate status enquiries to the other network and independently receives status enquiries. In this way, the signaling between networks mirrors each other, as illustrated in Figure 5-8.

Figure 5-8   *NNI Interface*

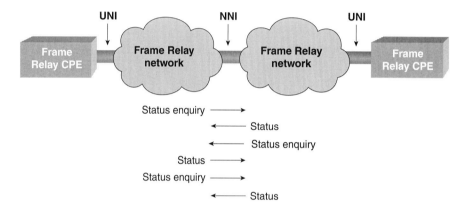

The bidirectional signaling protocol used on the NNI simply consists of two independent unidirectional signaling protocols, one initiated from each network.

The NNI bidirectional protocol is defined in the following:

- CCITT standard Q.933, Annex A
- ANSI standard T1.618, Annex D

Note that the original Local Management Interface (LMI) does not support NNI.

Frame Relay Port Commands

Frame Relay port statistics commands provide cumulative counts of user traffic and signaling traffic flowing between the port and the attached FRAD or network, as well as between the port and the rest of the IGX network. Table 5-2 describes the port commands and their privilege levels that are introduced in this chapter.

Table 5-2   *IGX Commands for Configuring Frame Relay Ports*

Command	Description	Privilege Level
dspln	Displays line configuration parameters.	1 through 6
dsplns	Displays the status summary of all lines on the node.	1 through 6
addport	Creates a logical Frame Relay port from a T1 or E1 line by defining the port's timeslot allocation.	1 and 2
clrportstats	Clears port statistics for one or all ports on the node.	1 through 5
cnfmode	Selects a card mode for a UFM-U back card.	1 and 2
cnfport	Modifies configuration parameters, including queuing and signaling protocols, on a Frame Relay port.	1 and 2
delport	Removes a logical Frame Relay port.	1 and 2
dnport	Deactivates a Frame Relay port from service.	1 and 2
dspmode	Displays the mode of the UFM-U back card.	1 through 6

continues

Table 5-2 *IGX Commands for Configuring Frame Relay Ports (Continued)*

Command	Description	Privilege Level
dspmodes	Displays the ports that are active with each mode of an unchannelized UFM.	1 through 6
dspport	Displays status and configuration information on one port, all ports on a card, or all ports on the node.	1 through 6
dspportstats	Displays historical and real-time Frame Relay or ATM statistics.	1 through 6

Configuring Frame Relay Ports

This section describes the steps and commands used to activate Frame Relay ports.

dsplns Command

To activate a Frame Relay port, begin by using the **dsplns** (or **dspln**) command to verify line configuration. The **dsplns** command output, shown in Example 5-1, displays basic configuration and status information for all the lines on the node. The information includes the line number, the type of line, the number of configured DS-0 channels, and the alarm status.

Example 5-1 **dsplns** *Output*

```
igx3        TN    group8:1       IGX 8420    9.2.20    Aug. 2 1999  18:46 CDT


Line      Type   Current Line Alarm Status
 3.1      T1/24  Clear - OK
 9.1      E3/530 Clear - OK
 9.2      E3/530 Clear - OK
11.1      T1/24  Clear - OK
11.2      T1/24  Clear - OK
11.3      T1/24  Major - Out of Frm (RED)
11.4      T1/24  Clear - OK
16        T3/3   Major - Loss of Sig (RED)                 (UNI)
```

addport Command

The **addport** command creates a logical Frame Relay port on a channelized FRM or UFM card set. Only T1 and E1 lines carry channelized Frame Relay traffic. This step is necessary only if you have a channelized port.

Here is the **addport** command syntax for FRM:

```
addport <slot>.<channel [-channel]> [56 | 64]
```

Here is the **addport** command syntax for UFM:

```
addport <slot>.<port> <line>.<channel [-channel]> [56 | 64]
```

Table 5-3 describes the required and optional parameters for the **addport** command.

Table 5-3   **addport** *Command Syntax*

Parameter	Description	Required/Optional
slot	The slot number of the FRM or UFM.	Required
port	The number (in the range 1 to 250) assigned to a UFM port.	Required
line	The line number of the UFM interface: 1 to 4 for four-line cards 1 to 8 for eight-line cards	Required
channel	The number of the port's first timeslot.	Required
-channel	The number of the last timeslot of a port that uses more than one timeslot. Timeslots must be contiguous.	Optional
56 | 64	Specifies the rate (56 kbps or 64 kbps) of a single-timeslot logical port. If no rate is entered, the default is 64 kbps.	Optional

For example:

addport 11.26 1.1-6 creates logical port 11.26, consisting of timeslots 1 through 6 on line 1.

addport 6.250 2.1 56 creates logical port 6.250, consisting of timeslot 2 on line 1. The port rate is specified as 56 kbps.

addport 9.1-12 creates logical port 9.1, consisting of timeslots 1 through 12.

In Example 5-2, port 11.1 is created. Port 11.1 is associated with slot 11, line 1, channels 1 through 6.

Example 5-2   **addport** *Output for a Multichannel Port*

```
igx3            TN     group8:1  IGX 8420  9.2.20   Aug. 2 1999  18:47 CDT

Port configuration for UFM 11

Port  Line   Chan    Speed    Interface         State      Protocol
1     1      1-6     384 Kbps T1D               INACTIVE   None


Last Command: addport 11.1 1.1-6


Next Command:
```

In Example 5-3, port 11.250 is associated with slot 11, line 1, channel 10. Port 11.250 operates at 56 kbps.

Example 5-3   **addport** *Output for a Single-Channel Port*

```
igx3            TN     group8:1    IGX 8420  9.2.20   Aug. 2 1999  18:48 CDT

Port configuration for UFM 11

From  Line   Chan    Speed    Interface         State      Protocol
250   1      10       56 Kbps T1D               INACTIVE   None


Last Command: addport 11.250 1.10 56


Next Command:
```

Modifying Frame Relay Ports

This section describes the steps and commands used to configure Frame Relay ports.

cnfport Command

The **cnfport** command applies to any Frame Relay port. It configures the port queue and signaling parameters.

Here is the **cnfport** command syntax for the UFM-C, UFM-U, and FRM Frame Relay ports.

UFM-C, T1/E1 ports:

```
cnfport <slot.port> <port-queue-depth> <ecn-queue-threshold>
  <de-threshold> <signaling-protocol> <protocol-parameters>
```

UFM-U unchannelized ports:

```
cnfport <slot.port> <port-type> <port-queue-depth>
  <ecn-queue-threshold> <de-threshold> <signaling-protocol>
  <protocol-parameters>
```

FRM, T1/E1 ports:

```
cnfport <slot.port> <port-queue-depth>
  <ecn-queue-threshold> <de-threshold> <signaling-protocol>
  <protocol-parameters>
```

FRM, all other ports:

```
cnfport <slot.port> <speed> <port-queue-depth>
  <clocking> <de-threshold> <min-flags-bet-frames> <ECN-q-threshold>
  <port-ID> <signaling-protocol> <protocol-parameters>
```

Table 5-5, shown in a moment, lists the **cnfport** parameters, which also apply to the **dspport** command.

Example 5-4 shows the configuration for port 10.1. Note the slight differences when configuring ports on different card types.

Example 5-4 **cnfport** *Output*

```
igx3           TN      group8:1        IGX 8420  9.2.20    Aug. 2 1999  18:51 CDT

Port:       10.1                [INACTIVE]
Interface:  X21     DCE                    Configured Clock:     512 Kbps
Clocking:   Normal                         Measured Rx Clock:      0 Kbps

Port ID                       0     Min Flags / Frames        1
Port Queue Depth          65535     OAM Pkt Threshold         3 pkts
ECN Queue Threshold       50000     T391 Link Intg Timer     10 sec
DE Threshold               92 %     N391 Full Status Poll     6 cyl
Signalling Protocol  Annex A UNI    EFCI Mapping Enabled    Yes
Asynchronous Status         Yes     CLLM Enabled/Tx Timer   No/  0 msec
T392 Polling Verif Timer     15     IDE to DE Mapping       Yes
N392 Error Threshold          3     Interface Control Template
N393 Monitored Events Count   4       Lead    I
Communicate Priority         No      State   ON
Upper/Lower RNR Thresh  75%/ 25%

Last Command: cnfport 10.1 DCE 512 NORMAL 0 65535 50000 92 a N Y 15 3 4 3 Y N Y 1
Next Command:
```

Serial interfaces control lead states using an active control temple. X.21 ports use a fixed, active control template. In contrast, although V.35 ports use an active control template, you can set the signals that are active to on or off. Frame Relay ports cannot use other control templates. Example 5-5 shows the **cnfport** command output for a T-1.

Example 5-5   cnfport *Output for T-1*

```
 igx3            TN    group8:1        IGX 8420   9.2.20    Aug. 2 1999   18:53 CDT

 Port:      11.1                  [INACTIVE]
 Interface:  T1D                              Configured Clock:    384 Kbps
 Clocking:   None                             Measured Rx Clock: None

 Port ID                     -        Min Flags / Frames        1
 Port Queue Depth          65535      OAM Pkt Threshold         3 pkts
 ECN Queue Threshold       50000      T391 Link Intg Timer     10 sec
 DE Threshold              95 %       N391 Full Status Poll     6 cyl
 Signalling Protocol   Annex D UNI    EFCI Mapping Enabled      No
 Asynchronous Status       Yes        CLLM Enabled/Tx Timer   No/  0 msec
 T392 Polling Verif Timer   15        IDE to DE Mapping         Yes
 N392 Error Threshold        3        Channel Speed            64
 N393 Monitored Events Count 4        Line Number               1
 Communicate Priority      No         Channel Range            1-6
 Upper/Lower RNR Thresh  75%/ 25%

 Last Command: cnfport 11.1 65535 50000 95 d y y 15 3 4 3 10 6 N N Y 1

 Next Command:
```

During port configuration, a prompt for each parameter appears. To keep the current value of the parameter, press the **Return** key without entering any characters. When a parameter cannot be configured for an application, it appears shaded or with dashed lines. You can mix the data rate for each of the ports if the total for all ports does not exceed the maximum composite data rate that the card set supports.

upport Command

The **upport** command activates a physical or logical port on a Frame Relay card, as shown in Example 5-6. If the port has not been configured through the **cnfport** command, a set of default configuration values apply.

Example 5-6   upport *Output*

```
 igx3            TN    group8:1        IGX 8420   9.2.20    Aug. 2 1999   18:54 CDT

 Port:      11.1                  [ACTIVE  ]
 Interface:  T1D                              Configured Clock:    384 Kbps
 Clocking:   None                             Measured Rx Clock: None
```

Example 5-6 **upport** *Output (Continued)*

```
Port ID                     -      Min Flags / Frames        1
Port Queue Depth         65535     OAM Pkt Threshold         3 pkts
ECN Queue Threshold      50000     T391 Link Intg Timer     10 sec
DE Threshold                95 %   N391 Full Status Poll     6 cyl
Signalling Protocol  Annex D UNI   EFCI Mapping Enabled      No
Asynchronous Status        Yes     CLLM Enabled/Tx Timer  No/ 0 msec
T392 Polling Verif Timer    15     IDE to DE Mapping        Yes
N392 Error Threshold         3     Channel Speed            64
N393 Monitored Events Count  4     Line Number               1
Communicate Priority        No     Channel Range           1-6
Upper/Lower RNR Thresh  75%/ 25%


Last Command: upport 11.1


Next Command:
```

With a port concentrator shelf (PCS), upping the first port causes the FRM card to begin communicating with the four PCS modules and to download code to them if necessary.

Here is the **upport** command syntax:

upport <*slot.port*>

Table 5-4 describes the required parameter for the **upport** command.

Table 5-4   **upport** *Command Syntax*

Parameter	Description	Required/Optional
slot.port	Slot and port of the port to be upped. The port number can range from:	Required
	1 to 250 on a UFM-C	
	1 to 12 on a UFM-U with a UFI-12V.35 or UFI-12 X.21	
	1 to 4 on a UFM-U with a UFI-4 HSSI	
	1 to 4 on an FRM Model D	
	1 to 31 on an FRM Model E	

dspport and **cnfport** Command Parameters

You configure Frame Relay port parameters using the **cnfport** command. After they are configured, you can display the results using the **dspport** command. Table 5-5 lists the possible fields that might be seen.

Table 5-5 *Output Fields for* **dspport** *and* **cnfport**

Field	Description
slot.port	Specifies the logical port on the FRM or UFM-U in the format *slot.port*. For a T1/E1 line on an FRM port, this is a logical number. For a UFM-C, the range for a port is 1 to 250.
Port type	For a UFM-U, this specifies whether a port on the UFM-U is DCE or DTE. The prompt appears if the system detects a UFM-U. The default is DCE. For an FRM, port type is display-only, because jumper blocks on the back cards set the mode.
slot.port.line	Specifies the UFM-C slot, port, and line number, where port can be 1 to 250 and *line* can be 1 to 8. Note that the maximum number of T1/E1 lines per node is 32. For example, this maximum could be spread over four UFM-8C card sets that utilize all eight lines on each back card.
Speed	Specifies a port clock speed in kbps for a 2 Mbps UFM or FRM. The configured speed appears under the Configured Clock heading. The actual clock rate appears under the Measured Rx Clock heading. Note that this option does not apply to T1/E1 lines, because these line types use 64 or 56 kbps timeslots. Here is the range of speeds, according to the number of active ports: One port (selected speeds, 56 to 2048 kbps) Two ports (selected speeds, 56 to 1024 kbps) Three ports (selected speeds, 56 to 672 kbps) Four ports (selected speeds, 56 to 512 kbps)
Clocking	Specifies the port's clock type for HSSI, V.35, and X.21 lines. The clock is either normal or looped. Note that the clock and data direction in DCE mode is the opposite of the direction for DTE mode. Here are the possible clock combinations: FRM or UFM-U port is DCE with normal clocking (HSSI, V.35, X.21) FRM or UFM-U port is DCE with looped clocking (V.35 only) FRM or UFM-U port is DTE with normal clocking (HSSI, V.35, X.21) FRM or UFM-U port is DTE with looped clocking (V.35 only)
Port ID	Specifies the DLCI associated with the port (0 to 1024) {with 0 as the default}. A node uses this number when you add bundled connections. Otherwise, the port ID can be used as a network destination number in global addressing. The port ID does not apply to T1, E1, or PCS ports.
Port queue depth	Specifies the maximum bytes in the transmit queue at the UFM or FRM port. The range is 0 to 65,535 bytes. The default is 65,535 bytes.
ECN queue threshold	Specifies the threshold at which the system begins to generate explicit congestion notification (BECN and FECN bits) for the port. The range is 0 to 65,535 bytes. The default is 65,535 bytes.

Table 5-5 *Output Fields for* **dspport** *and* **cnfport** *(Continued)*

Field	Description
DE threshold	Specifies the port queue depth above which the system discards frames with a set discard eligibility (DE) bit. The range is 0 to 100 percent. The default is 100 percent. A threshold of 100 percent disables DE for the port, because a queue cannot contain more than 100 percent of its capacity.
Signaling protocol	Selects the signaling protocol. The first time you execute **cnfport** on a port, the command-line interface displays the following options for this parameter: none, Strata LMI, a (for Annex A), and d (for Annex D). If you enter a or d, the subsequent prompt asks if the interface is NNI.
	For any Frame Relay card set that has a maximum frame length of 4510 bytes, the use and type of a signaling protocol result in a limit on the possible number of connections per port. The maximum numbers of connections per port for each protocol are as follows:
	Annex A: 899
	Annex D: 899
	StrataLMI: 562
	Neither **addcon** nor **cnfport** prevents you from adding more than the maximum number of connections on a port. (For example, you might use **cnfport** to specify an LMI when too many connections for that particular LMI already exist.)
	If the number of connections is exceeded for a particular signaling protocol, the full status messages that result are discarded, and timeouts occur on the port. A port failure results and also subsequently leads to A-bit failures in other segments of the connection path.
Asynchronous status	Specifies whether the node should send unsolicited update messages when they appear or wait for the user device to poll. Enter y (yes) or n (no).
Polling verify timer	Specifies a Link Integrity Verification Timer heartbeat (keepalive) period. The range is 5 to 30. The default is 15. Set the timer to 5 seconds more than the setting in the user equipment.
Error threshold	Specifies the number of failures in the monitored events that cause the keepalive process to report an alarm. The theoretical range is 0 to 255. The valid range is 1 to 10. A threshold of 0 reverts to 1. A threshold greater than 10 reverts to 10.

continues

Table 5-5 *Output Fields for* **dspport** *and* **cnfport** *(Continued)*

Field	Description
Monitored events count	Specifies the number of monitored events for the keepalive process. It has a theoretical range of 0 to 255 and a valid range of 1 to 10. A port communication-fail condition is cleared after this number of successful polling cycles. A value of 0 reverts to 1, and a value of more than 10 reverts to 10.
Communicate priority	Specifies whether the system should communicate the priority of the connections to the user device on the port. Enter y (yes) or n (no). (The priority is either High or Low.)
Upper/lower RNR	Specifies the receiver not ready (RNR) thresholds. The upper threshold is the percentage of buffer fill required to generate RNR signaling for this port. The lower RNR threshold is the percentage of buffer fill to clear RNR signaling. The default for the upper RNR threshold is 75 percent. The default for the lower RNR threshold is 25 percent.
Min. flags/frame	Specifies the minimum number of flags between frames when the direction of transmission is from the node to the user equipment. The range is 1 to 255. The default is 1.
OAM FastPacket Threshold	Specifies how many OAM FastPackets must arrive from a remote NNI port before the local port threshold generates A-bit = 0 in the signaling protocol message to the locally attached device. The range for this parameter is 0 to 15 packets. The default is 3 packets. A 0 disables this function. The OAM FastPacket threshold setting applies to UNI and NNI ports.
	On any Frame Relay port (UNI or NNI) using a signaling protocol, the UFM or FRM provides a status message to the attached equipment in response to a status enquiry message or as an asynchronous update. These status messages contain details about every PVC configured on the port. In particular, the PVC Active bit (the A-bit) represents whether a PVC is active (A-bit = 1) or out of service (A-bit = 0). If the other end of the PVC connection is on a UNI port, here are the only conditions that can cause the local Frame Relay card to send an A-bit = 0:
	The PVC is down (intentionally taken out of service).
	The PVC is failed for any reason (such as a hardware failure, trunk failure with no ability to reroute, and so on).
	If the other end of the PVC terminates on an NNI port, one additional condition can cause the local UFM or FRM to send an A-bit = 0 to the local device: If the remote NNI port on the card receives an A-bit = 0 from the remote network over the remote NNI, the local card can propagate an A-bit = 0 out the local port. The remote card notifies the local card that the A-bit = 0 comes from the remote network by transmitting OAM FastPackets. The remote card sends one OAM FastPacket every 5 seconds for as long as the A-bit coming from the remote network is 0.

Table 5-5   *Output Fields for* **dspport** *and* **cnfport** *(Continued)*

Field	Description
Link Integrity Timer (T391)	Specifies the interval after which the system sends a status enquiry message across the NNI port. The range for the interval is 5 to 30 seconds. The default is 10 seconds. Both networks do not need to have the same T391 value. The card should receive a status message for every status enquiry message it transmits. If the Frame Relay card receives either no responses or invalid responses, a port communication failure results (and causes a minor alarm).
N392 Error Threshold	Specifies the number of bad or undelivered responses to status enquiry messages that can occur before the system records a port communication failure. The range is 1 to 10. The default is 3.
N393 Monitored Events Count	Specifies the number of status enquiry messages in a period wherein the system waits for responses to the enquiries. The range is 1 to 10. The default is 4. See the description of the Link Integrity Timer parameter for sample usage.
Full Status Polling Cycle (N391)	Specifies the interval at which the system sends the full status report request for all PVCs across the NNI port. The range is 1 to 255 polling cycles. The default is 6 cycles. The full status reports the status of all the connections across the NNI.
Card Type	Specifies the card type when you enter the **cnfport** command in a job. This parameter is not available except when you specify **cnfport** in a job by using the **addjob** command.
	During the job specification, you enter the card type just after *slot.port* during the command specification phase of **addjob**. Valid card types are V.35, X.21, port, and line, where line indicates a T1 or E1 line.
CLLM status /x Timer	Specifies an interval for the system to send CLLM congestion messages across the NNI. The range is 40 to 350 milliseconds (ms). The default is 100.
IDE to DE Mapping	Specifies whether the destination system should map the internal DE bit (IDE) status in the FastPacket or ATM cell to the Frame Relay DE bit at the destination. Enter y (yes) or n (no). If you specify the nonstandard case of CIR = 0 with either **addcon** or **cnffrcls**, you must first enable IDE-to-DE mapping.
Channel Range	Displays the DS-0s for the T1 or E1 logical port. The value can be 1 or a contiguous combination in the range 1 to 24 for T1, or 1 to 31 for E1. For example, 7 to 12 indicates six DS-0s for the port, starting with DS-0 7. Before you use this command, specify the valid channel range with the **addport** command.
Channel Speed	Displays the bandwidth available to a logical port. The speed is 64 kbps times the number of DS-0s you specify with the Channel Range parameter.

dspports Command

The **dspports** command output provides summary or detailed information about Frame
Relay ports, depending on the parameters provided. Without any parameters, the command
shows all ports on the IGX node, as shown in Example 5-7.

Example 5-7   dspports *Output*

```
igx3              TN     group8:1          IGX 8420  9.2.20     Aug. 2 1999  18:55 CDT

 Port States
Port     ID    State     Port    ID    State
9.1            ACTIVE    10.11   0     INACTIVE
9.2            INACTIVE  10.12   0     INACTIVE
10.1     0     FAILED    11.1    0     FAILED
10.2     0     INACTIVE  11.250  0     ACTIVE
10.3     2     INACTIVE
10.4     0     INACTIVE
10.5     3     INACTIVE
10.6     6     INACTIVE
10.7     0     INACTIVE
10.8     0     INACTIVE
10.9     0     INACTIVE
10.10    0     INACTIVE



Last Command: dspports

Next Command:
```

The **dspports** command output information includes the following:

- Port number

- **Port ID**—An optional configurable value used with bundled Frame Relay
  connections on FRM cards.

- **State**—The port's current status. Includes the following:

  — **ACTIVE**—The port has been upped and is free of alarms.

  — **INACTIVE**—The port has not been upped.

  — **FAILED**—The port has a failure condition, either a signaling protocol
     failure (any ports) or a line failure (logical ports only).

dspport Command

The **dspport** command, when used with a slot number, provides information on the ports on a particular card module.

Example 5-8   **dspport** *Output*

```
igx3            TN     group8:1        IGX 8420  9.2.20    Aug. 2 1999  18:56 CDT

Port configuration for UFM 11

Port  Line  Chan    Speed    Interface         State       Protocol
1     1     1-6     384 Kbps T1D               FAILED      Annex D UNI
250   1     10       56 Kbps T1D               ACTIVE      None



Last Command: dspport 11


Next Command:
```

The following information is provided when using the dspport command:

- Port number
- Port ID (serial interfaces only)
- **Channels (channelized interfaces only)**—The channels or timeslots used by this logical Frame Relay port
- **Speed**—The configured port speed
- **Interface**—The type of interface, including serial or channelized line type (V.35 or X.21, T1 or E1, and HSSI on the UFM) and serial interface type (DTE or DCE)
- State
- **Protocol**—The configured signaling protocol (Strata LMI, Annex A, Annex D, or none)

The **dspport** command, when used with a port number, provides detailed configuration information for a port, as shown in Example 5-9.

Example 5-9   **dspport** *Output*

```
igx3            TN     group8:1        IGX 8420  9.2.20    Aug. 2 1999  18:56 CDT

Port:       11.250              [ACTIVE  ]
Interface:  T1D                          Configured Clock:    56 Kbps
Clocking:   None                         Measured Rx Clock: None
```

continues

Example 5-9 **dspport** *Output (Continued)*

```
Port ID                    -      Min Flags / Frames        1
Port Queue Depth        65535     OAM Pkt Threshold         3 pkts
ECN Queue Threshold     65535     T391 Link Intg Timer     10 sec
DE Threshold             100 %    N391 Full Status Poll     6 cyl
Signalling Protocol      None     EFCI Mapping Enabled      No
Asynchronous Status        No     CLLM Enabled/Tx Timer  No/  0 msec
T392 Polling Verif Timer   15     IDE to DE Mapping        Yes
N392 Error Threshold        3     Channel Speed            56
N393 Monitored Events Count 4     Line Number               1
Communicate Priority       No     Channel Range            10
Upper/Lower RNR Thresh  75%/ 25%


Last Command: dspport 11.250


Next Command:
```

Here is the dspport command syntax:

dspport [*slot* | *port*]

slot | *port* displays all ports on a specific slot or detailed information about a specific port.
The default is all ports.

dspmode Command

The **dspmode** command displays the mode of a UFM-U back card, as shown in Example 5-10.
It also includes the card's current mode, a bit map of the ports that can be used in this mode
(Available Ports), and a bitmap of the ports that are currently activated. The UFM-U back
cards are UFI-12 V.35, UFI-12 X.21, and UFI-4 HSSI. A card mode is a combination of
maximum port speeds and specific port numbers.

Example 5-10 dspmode *Output*

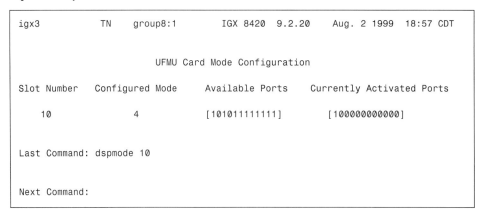

```
igx3          TN    group8:1        IGX 8420  9.2.20    Aug. 2 1999  18:57 CDT


                        UFMU Card Mode Configuration

Slot Number    Configured Mode     Available Ports    Currently Activated Ports

    10                4            [101011111111]       [100000000000]


Last Command: dspmode 10


Next Command:
```

Here is the **dspmode** command syntax:

```
dspmode <slot>
```

slot specifies the slot of the UFM-U card set.

dspmodes Command

The **dspmodes** command displays the ports that are active with each mode of an unchannelized UFM. The mode applies only to a UFM-U back card, as shown in Example 5-11. The UFM-U back cards are UFI-12 V.35, UFI-12 X.21, and UFI-4 HSSI. A card mode is a combination of maximum port speeds and specific port numbers.

Example 5-11 **dspmodes** *Output*

```
igx3              TN    group8:1         IGX 8420  9.2.20    Aug. 2 1999  18:57 CDT


                    UFMU MODES AND PORT AVAILABILITY BITMAP

Mode[ 1]:111111111111   Mode[ 2]:101010101010   Mode[ 3]:100010001000
Mode[ 4]:101011111111   Mode[ 5]:100011111111   Mode[ 6]:101010101111
Mode[ 7]:100010101111   Mode[ 8]:100010001111   Mode[ 9]:100010101010
Mode[10]:100010001010   Mode[11]:111110101111   Mode[12]:111111111010
Mode[13]:111110001111   Mode[14]:111111111000   Mode[15]:101011111010
Mode[16]:111110101010   Mode[17]:101010001111   Mode[18]:101011111000
Mode[19]:111110101000   Mode[20]:111110001010   Mode[21]:100011111010
Mode[22]:100011111000   Mode[23]:111110001000   Mode[24]:101010001010
Mode[25]:101010101000   Mode[26]:100010101000   Mode[27]:101010001000


Last Command: dspmodes


Next Command:
```

cnfmode Command

The **cnfmode** command selects a mode of the card for a UFM-U back card, as shown in Example 5-12. A card's mode is a combination of maximum port speeds and specific port numbers. The **cnfmode** command lets you select one of 27 modes for either a UFI-12 V.35 back card or a UFI-12 X.21 back card. For a UFI-4 HSSI back card, three modes are available. Note that you specify an individual port's actual speed using **cnfport**.

Example 5-12 cnfmode *Output*

```
igx3            TN    group8:1        IGX 8420  9.2.20    Aug. 2 1999  18:58 CDT



                    UFMU MODES AND PORT AVAILABILITY BITMAP

Mode[ 1]:111111111111    Mode[ 2]:101010101010    Mode[ 3]:100010001000
Mode[ 4]:101011111111    Mode[ 5]:100011111111    Mode[ 6]:101010101111
Mode[ 7]:100010101111    Mode[ 8]:100010001111    Mode[ 9]:100010101010
Mode[10]:100010001010    Mode[11]:111110101111    Mode[12]:111111111010
Mode[13]:111110001111    Mode[14]:111111111000    Mode[15]:101011111010
Mode[16]:111110101010    Mode[17]:101010001111    Mode[18]:101011111000
Mode[19]:111110101000    Mode[20]:111110001010    Mode[21]:100011111010
Mode[22]:100011111000    Mode[23]:111110001000    Mode[24]:101010001010
Mode[25]:101010101000    Mode[26]:100010101000    Mode[27]:101010001000



This Command: cnfmode 10



Enter The New UFMU Mode [4]: 2
```

Here is the **cnfmode** command syntax:

cnfmode *<slot> <mode>*

Table 5-6 describes the required parameters for the **cnfmode** command.

Table 5-6   **cnfmode** *Command Syntax*

Parameter	Description	Required/Optional
slot	Specifies the slot of the UFM-U card set.	Required
mode	Specifies the mode of the UFM-U card set. The range for V.35 and X.21 ports is 1 to 27. The range for HSSI ports is 1 to 3. You might need to delete connections and down one or more ports before you execute cnfmode.	Required

dnport Command

The **dnport** command, shown in Example 5-13, deactivates (downs) the specified Frame Relay port. Before deactivating a port, you must delete all connections on the port (see the **delcon** description).

Example 5-13 dnport *Command*

```
igx3            TN    group8:1        IGX 8420  9.2.20    Aug. 2 1999  19:00 CDT

Port:        10.1              [INACTIVE]
Interface:   X21     DCE                  Configured Clock:    512 Kbps
```

Example 5-13 dnport *Command (Continued)*

```
Clocking:    Normal                        Measured Rx Clock:    0 Kbps

Port ID                      0     Min Flags / Frames       1
Port Queue Depth         65535     OAM Pkt Threshold        3 pkts
ECN Queue Threshold      50000     T391 Link Intg Timer     10 sec
DE Threshold              92 %     N391 Full Status Poll    6 cyl
Signalling Protocol   Annex A UNI  EFCI Mapping Enabled     Yes
Asynchronous Status        Yes     CLLM Enabled/Tx Timer    No/0 msec
T392 Polling Verif Timer    15     IDE to DE Mapping        Yes
N392 Error Threshold         3     Interface Control Template
N393 Monitored Events Count  4       Lead    I
Communicate Priority        No       State   ON
Upper/Lower RNR Thresh  75%/ 25%


Last Command: dnport 10.1


Next Command:
```

Here is the **dnport** command syntax:

dnport `<slot.port>`

slot.port is the slot and port to be downed.

The information in this description applies only to Frame Relay ports using a T1 or E1 line.

delport Command

The **delport** command, shown in Example 5-14, deletes logical ports on FRM or UFM-C cards and unassigns associated timeslots. The deleted timeslots are available to assign to new logical ports (with the **addport** command). The port display (normally visible by using the **dspport** command) appears, regardless of successful port deletion. The screen displays the defined port numbers for the specified line. Before deleting a Frame Relay port, you must down the port.

Example 5-14 delport *Command*

```
igx3            TN      group8:1        IGX 8420  9.2.20    Aug. 2 1999  19:01 CDT

Port configuration for UFM 11

Port   Line   Chan    Speed      Interface          State        Protocol
250    1      10      56 Kbps    T1D                ACTIVE       None


Last Command: delport 11.1


Next Command:
```

Here is the **delport** command syntax:

```
delport <slot.port>
```

slot.port is the slot and port to be deleted.

dspportstats Command

The **dspportstats** command, shown in Example 5-15, displays a summary of port statistics for a Frame Relay port. Statistics include the data byte count in the transmit and receive directions, and error counts associated with the port.

Example 5-15 dspportstats *Command*

```
igx2            VT     group8:1        IGX 8420  9.2.20    Aug. 2 1999   19:25 CDT

Port Statistics for 11.2        Cleared: Aug. 2 1999   19:21
Port Speed: 1536 kbps    Collection Time: 0 day(s) 00:03:32      Corrupted: NO
Sig Protocol: Annex D UNI
                        Bytes        Average (kbps)     Util (%)          Frames
From Port:                336            0                0                  21
To Port:                  336            0                0                  21
LMI Receive Protocol Stats LMI Transmit Protocol Stats  CLLM (ForeSight) Stats
Status Enq Rcvd         21 Status Enq Xmit     --       Frames Rcvd       --
Status Xmt              21 Status Rcd          --       Bytes Rcvd        --
Asynch Xmit              0 Asynch Rcvd         --       Frames Xmt        --
Seq # Mismatches         0 Seq # Mismatches    --       Bytes Xmt         --
Timeouts                 0 Timeouts            --       CLLM Failures     --
Invalid Frames           0
Elmi Ver Req             0 Elmi Ver Rsp         0
Elmi QOS Req             0 Elmi QOS Rsp         0

This Command: dspportstats 11.2 5

Next page? (+/-/DEL key to quit)
```

Corrupted statistics result from channel/port loopbacks or port tests. A No in the Corrupted field at the top right of the screen output in Example 5-15 indicates that loopback or port tests have not occurred since the statistics were last cleared. The statistics for UNI ports (connections to user devices) are displayed on one screen.

Here is the **dspportstats** command syntax:

```
dspportstats <slot.port> [interval]
```

Table 5-7 describes the required and optional parameters for the **dspportstats** command.

Table 5-7 **dspportstats** *Command Syntax*

Parameter	Description	Required/Optional
slot.port	The slot and port of the physical port.	Required
interval	The refresh interval for data, from 1 to 60 seconds. The default interval is 1 second.	Optional

The first screen of the **dspportstats** command output displays the fields listed in Table 5-8.

Table 5-8 *Output Fields for the* **dspportstats** *Command*

UNI and NNI Fields	Description
Cleared	Last time the **clrportstats** command was issued.
Collection Time	Amount of time since a **clrportstats** or **upport** command.
Port speed	Configured port speed.
Corrupted	Indicates that loopback or port tests have or have not occurred since the statistics were last cleared. Received from/transmitted to ports.
Bytes	Traffic received/transmitted in bytes.
Average (kbps)	Average rate of traffic received/transmitted in kbps.
Utilization (%)	Traffic received/transmitted as a percentage of port speed.
Frames	Traffic received/transmitted in frames.
Invalid CRCs	Received frame dropped due to CRC failure.
Invalid Alignment	Received frame dropped with non-byte-aligned payload.
Invalid Frame Length	Received frame dropped less than 5 bytes or greater than 4510 bytes in length.
Invalid Frame Format	Received frame dropped with incorrect EA bits.
Unknown DLCIs	Received frame dropped with invalid or unknown DLCI.
Last Unknown DLCI	DLCI of last dropped "unknown DLCI" frame.
Average Transmit Port Queue	Current port queue depth in bytes.
FECN Frames	Frames transmitted with the FECN bit set.
FECN Frames Ratio	Percentage of total frames transmitted with the FECN bit set.
BECN Frames	Frames transmitted with the BECN bit set.
BECN Frames Ratio	Percentage of total frames transmitted with the BECN bit set.
Resource Overflow	Pooled card buffer overflow.
DE Frames Dropped	Transmit DE frames dropped because the queue threshold was met.

NNI ports require two screens to display all the parameters. The first screen is the same as that described previously for UNI ports. The second screen appears when you respond with a y for yes to the Continue? prompt. The second screen compares receive LMI statistics with transmit LMI statistics. The LMI receive statistics are repeated from the middle column of the first screen and are displayed again for easy comparison.

The second screen of the **dspportstats** command output displays the fields listed in Table 5-9.

Table 5-9   *Additional Output Fields for the* **dspportstats** *Command*

NNI Field	Description
Status Enquiries Received	Status enquiries received.
Status Transmitted	Status messages transmitted.
Asynch Updates Transmitted	Asynchronous updates transmitted.
Sequence Number Mismatches	Enquiries received with skipped or repeated sequence numbers.
Timeouts	Expected enquiries not received based on T392.
Invalid Requests	Invalid or unrecognizable received enquiry.
Signaling Protocol	Configured signaling protocol for the port.
Status Enquiries Transmitted	Status enquiries transmitted.
Asynchronous Updates Received	Asynchronous updates received.
Sequence Number Mismatches	Status messages received with skipped or repeated sequence numbers.
Timeouts	Number of enquiries without received responses.
CLLM Frames Received	CLLM update frames received.
CLLM Bytes Received	CLLM update bytes received.
CLLM Frames Transmitted	CLLM update frames transmitted.
CLLM Bytes Transmitted	CLLM update bytes transmitted.
Status Received	Status messages received.
CLLM Failures	No CLLM update received in the last second.

clrportstats Command

The **clrportstats** command, shown in Example 5-16, clears the statistics for any Frame Relay or ATM port. The data byte count in the transmit and receive directions and error counts associated with the port are also cleared. Statistical accumulation then resumes for that port.

Example 5-16 clrportstats *Command*

```
igx2          VT    group8:1        IGX 8420  9.2.20    Aug. 2 1999  19:26 CDT

Port Statistics for 11.2       Cleared: Aug. 2 1999  19:26           Snapshot
Port Speed: 1536 kbps   Collection Time: 0 day(s) 00:00:00     Corrupted: NO
Sig Protocol: Annex D UNI
                        Bytes      Average (kbps)     Util (%)          Frames
From Port:                  0          0                 0                  0
To Port:                    0          0                 0                  0
Frame Errors              LMI Receive Protocol Stats   Misc Statistics
Invalid CRC             0   Status Enq Rcvd        0   Avg Tx Port Q          0
Invalid Alignment       0   Status Xmit            0   FECN Frames            0
Invalid Frm Length      0   Asynch Xmit            0      Ratio (%)           0
Invalid Frm Format      0   Seq # Mismatches       0   BECN Frames            0
Unknown DLCIs           0   Timeouts               0      Ratio (%)           0
Last Unknown DLCI       0   Invalid Req            0   Rsrc Overflow          0
                                                        DE Frms Dropd          0


Last Command: clrportstats 11.2

Next Command:
```

Statistics collecting takes place once every minute, so **clrportstats** might not clear statistics that are less than one minute old.

Here is the **clrportstats** command syntax:

```
clrportstats <slot.port | *>
```

slot.port is the slot and port of the physical port. An asterisk (*) specifies all physical ports.

Frame Relay Connections

Frame Relay carries data over permanent virtual circuits (PVCs). A Frame Relay PVC is a point-to-point connection that terminates at Frame Relay Module (FRM) or Universal Frame Relay Module (UFM) Frame Relay ports, as illustrated in Figure 5-9.

Each PVC is identified by a unique data-link connection identifier (DLCI) at the port. Multiple connections may terminate on a single port and are differentiated by their assigned DLCIs.

- DLCIs are locally significant.
- DLCIs from 16 to 1007 are available for user services. DLCIs 0 to 15 and 1008 to 1023 are reserved for signaling protocols or other management functions.
- DLCIs must be unique on a given port.

Figure 5-9 *Frame Relay Connections*

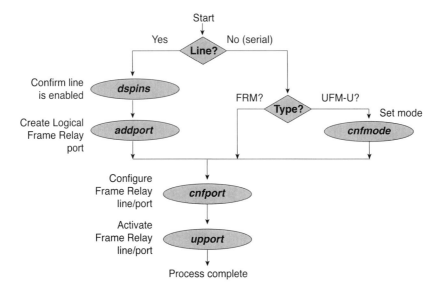

Global Addressing

Figure 5-10 illustrates the concept of global addressing. The key points of global addressing are that it is optional and that the network is unaware of the addressing scheme.

Figure 5-10 *Global Addressing*

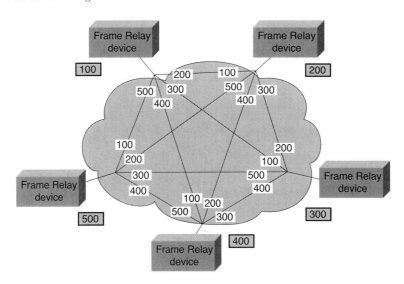

Converting Frame Relay Frames to FastPackets

To reduce possible delays, packets are created when the first part of the frame arrives at the FRM/UFM port. Packets are identified as start, middle, or end-of-frame, as illustrated in Figure 5-11. Sequence numbers are not needed, because the packets are created and are then queued in order throughout the network.

Figure 5-11 *Converting to FastPackets*

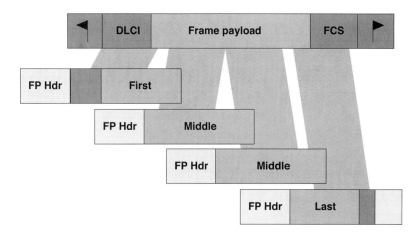

As the frame arrives, the FRM/UFM calculates the cyclic redundancy check (CRC) to compare it with the CRC at the end of the frame. If the values do not match, the portion of the frame that is not packetized is abandoned. The other packets, already sent to the network, are dropped at the destination FRM/UFM.

The original DLCI and CRC are sent intact within the packets and are verified by the destination FRM/UFM upon reassembly. As soon as the frame is complete, the DLCI (and other header changes, such as FECN, BECN, and DE) and the resulting CRC are modified.

First or Middle FastPacket Header

The relative position of the packet is identified so that the destination FRM/UFM can distinguish one frame from the next, as illustrated in Figure 5-12.

Figure 5-12 *First or Middle FastPacket Header*

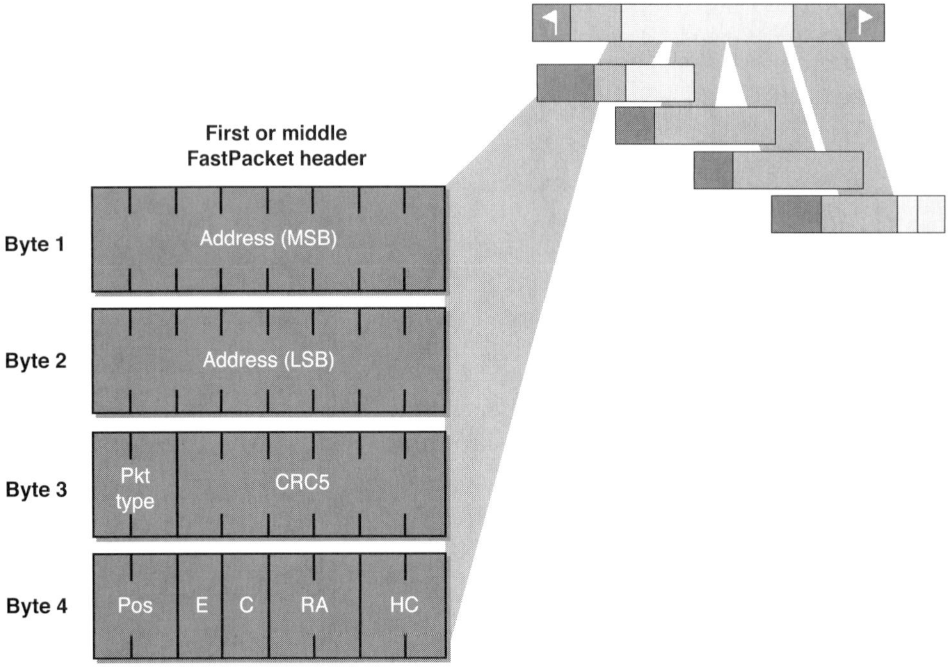

Explicit Forward Congestion Notification

The EFCN bit is marked on intermediate trunks to detect congestion within the network. The destination FRM/UFM uses this information to determine appropriate ForeSight Rate Adjustment (RA) bits.

Cell Loss Priority

The cell loss priority (CLP) bit is set if the incoming frame exceeds the committed information rate (CIR) set for the connection. Trunk queue thresholds determine whether the packet is dropped within the network.

Rate Adjustment

The RA bits are set by the destination FRM/UFM. The RA bits are determined based on network congestion (EFCN) and control the ForeSight process.

Hop Count

The hop count (HC) is used for queue servicing on the trunks in the network.

Last FastPacket Header

The last FastPacket header, illustrated in Figure 5-13, carries other fields that are not included in the first or middle FastPacket header. These fields are detailed in the following sections.

Figure 5-13 *Last FastPacket Header*

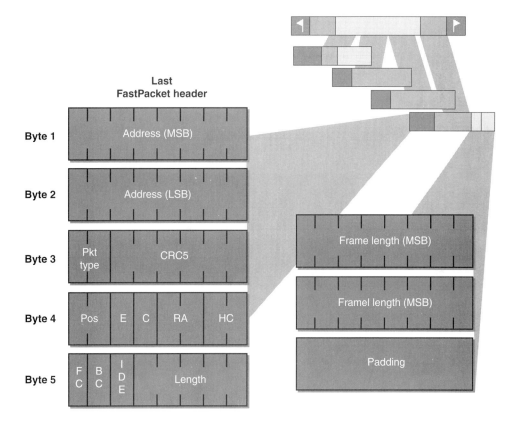

Forward and Backward Congestion

The forward congestion (FC) and backward congestion (BC) bits are marked due to ingress PVC queue congestion. They are mapped into the FECN and BECN bits on egress.

Internal Discard-Eligible

The internal discard-eligible (IDE) bit is set as a result of the original incoming frame's exceeding the CIR. The IDE bit can be mapped to the Frame Relay frame's DE bit at the egress to the network. If the incoming frame already has its DE bit set, the IDE bit is not set.

Length

The length (octet 5) indicates how many bytes of data are in the last FastPacket.

At the end of the last frame length FastPacket, another length field indicates the total length of the original Frame Relay frame.

VC Queues

The key points to keep in mind about Virtual Circuit (VC) queues, illustrated in Figure 5-14, are that they are in the ingress direction (from the CPE toward the CellBus) and that the VC queue provides traffic shaping. VC queues are defined by the class specified during the **addcon** command and can be modified using the **cnfcon** command.

Figure 5-14 *VC Queues*

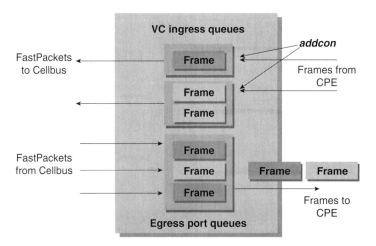

VC Queue Parameters

Figure 5-15 illustrates the VC queue parameters. Configurable characteristics include queue depth, Explicit Congestion Notification (ECN) threshold, and DE thresholds that are set for all VCs of the associated port using the **cnfport** command.

Figure 5-15 *VC Queue Parameters*

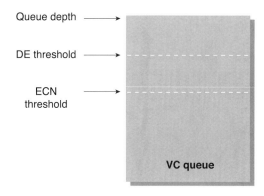

Queue depth ──────►

DE threshold ──────►

ECN
threshold ──────►

VC queue

Standard Versus Cisco Parameters

Frame Relay connections are described using both standards-based and proprietary Cisco parameters. For example, Frame Relay standards describe the CIR, Committed Burst size (Bc), and Excess Burst size (Be), as illustrated in Figure 5-16.

Figure 5-16 *Standard Versus Cisco Parameters*

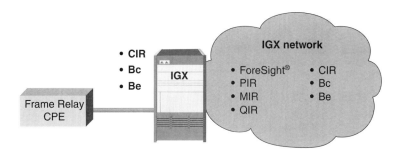

IGX networks manage Frame Relay traffic using standards-based or ForeSight parameters. ForeSight parameters include the Peak Information Rate (PIR), Quiescent Information Rate (QIR), and Minimum Information Rate (MIR).

UFM Leaky Bucket Policing

The *leaky bucket* model performs policing on ingress for UFM Frame Relay connections, as illustrated in Figure 5-17. The UFM policing function measures the ingress traffic and decides whether to queue or discard it based on a leaky bucket algorithm.

Figure 5-17 *UFM Leaky Bucket Policing*

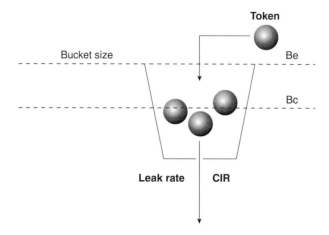

The leaky bucket model has four basic components:

- **Token**—Arrives into the bucket at a rate defined by the incoming traffic. For UFM Frame Relay traffic, each bit is represented in the leaky bucket model as a single token. The rate at which the tokens fill the bucket is variable. A token can be represented by a bit or a byte, as long as the chosen unit of information is used consistently throughout the leaky bucket model.

- **Leak rate**—Determines the average acceptable token rate to maintain compliance. If the tokens arrive at approximately the same rate or less than the leak rate, the bucket never fills up. If the tokens arrive at a rate greater than the leak rate, they eventually become noncompliant.

- **Compliance threshold**—Any frame that arrives when the contents of the bucket exceed the first threshold (Bc) is in excess of CIR and is tagged as noncompliant by setting the CLP bit in the corresponding FastPackets.

- **Bucket size**—As soon as the bucket reaches its full capacity, newly arriving tokens and the corresponding data are dropped.

ForeSight in the Network

The ForeSight algorithm is a closed-loop relative-rate feedback mechanism designed to adjust network Frame Relay traffic to utilize available bandwidth, as illustrated in Figure 5-18.

Figure 5-18 *ForeSight in the Network*

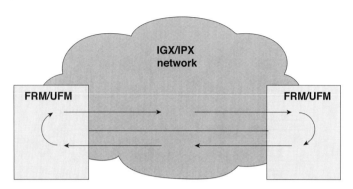

The ForeSight feature is enabled when the connection is created using the **addcon** command.

In Figure 5-18, the straight arrows indicate data flow. The curved arrows in the FRM/UFM boxes indicate control bits (EFCN and RA). Key points are as follows:

- As congestion occurs within the network, trunk cards set the EFCN bit.
- The destination card makes a congestion state decision and passes the results to the source card through the RA bits.
- The source FRM/UFM controls the VC queue service rate based on received RA bits.
- Rate adjustment takes place in supervisory FastPackets.

What Is Congestion?

Congestion is measured on egress trunk and port queues. BdataB queues are used for Frame Relay with ForeSight enabled. BdataA queues are used for Frame Relay with ForeSight disabled. Figure 5-19 illustrates BdataB trunk queues.

Each queue has a threshold for determining congestion:

- **ECN threshold on port queue**—**cnfport** command
- **EFCN threshold on trunks**—SuperUser command (the default value is approximately 30 packets of queue depth)

Figure 5-19 *What Is Congestion?*

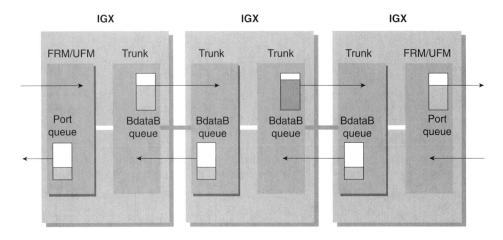

ForeSight Rate Adjustments

Table 5-10 shows the three levels of congestion recognized by ForeSight.

Table 5-10 *ForeSight Rate Adjustments*

Congestion Type	Definition	RA Message	New Rate
Congested	At least half of the packets/cells have the congestion bit set (EFCN on packets, EFCI on cells), or the egress port queue has exceeded the ECN threshold.	Rate down	Current × .87
Severely congested	At least half of the packets/cells have the congestion bit set, or the egress port queue is full and one or more fast packets are missing.	Rate fast down	Current × .5
Not congested	Less than half of the packets/cells have the congestion bit set, and the egress port queue is below the ECN threshold.	Rate up	Current + (.1 × MIR)

ForeSight and VC Queue Servicing

Figure 5-20 shows ForeSight adjusting the VC queue service rate based on congestion states in the network.

Figure 5-20 *ForeSight Adjustments*

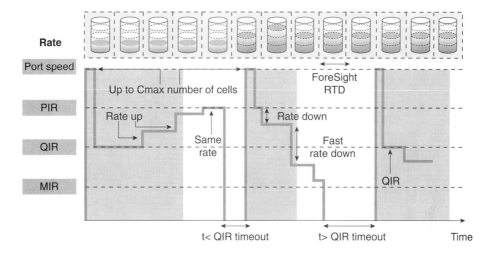

Here are the ForeSight and VC queue servicing features shown in Figure 5-20:

- **Credit maximum**—Cmax
- **Minimum Information Rate**—MIR
- **Peak Information Rate**—PIR
- **Quiescent Information Rate**—QIR
- **ForeSight Round Trip Delay**—FST RTD
- Rate Up
- Rate Down
- Fast Rate Down

Bit-Oriented Protocol Frame Structures

Frame forwarding is a means of connecting non-Frame Relay data devices to a Frame Relay interface to take advantage of the processing capabilities of the FRM/UFM. BOP frame structures, including Frame Relay, High-Level Data Link Control (HDLC), Synchronous Data Link Control (SDLC), and X.25, are illustrated in Figure 5-21.

Figure 5-21 *BOP Frame Structures*

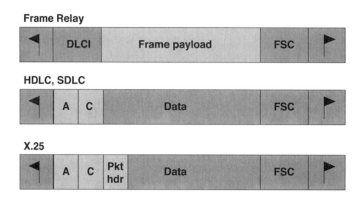

The non-Frame Relay devices must communicate using a bit-oriented protocol (BOP) such as HDLC, SDLC, or X.25.

A frame-forwarding frame has a structure similar to a Frame Relay frame and contains the following elements:

- 7E flag and idle code
- 3 to 4510 bytes in length
- 16-bit CRC at end of frame

Frame Forwarding

The frame forwarding concept is illustrated in Figure 5-22.

The frame forwarding key points are as follows:

- Frame forwarding is point-to-point on a per-port basis.
- No DLCI is specified.
- All FRM/UFM features are available.
- An idle code between frames is not transmitted.
- ForeSight when enabled.
- Defined with the **addcon** command by specifying * for the DLCI.

Figure 5-22 *Frame Forwarding*

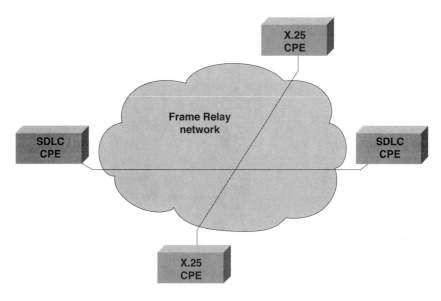

Frame Relay Channel Statistics

The Frame Relay channel statistics process is illustrated in Figure 5-23.

Figure 5-23 *Frame Relay Channel Statistics*

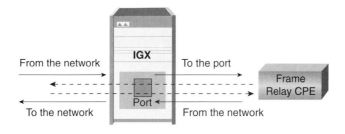

The **dspchstats** command displays a live view of channel operation, including the bandwidth currently used, frames discarded, and congestion states. The **dspchstats** command is essentially a filtered view of the **dspportstats** command.

Another valuable command is **tstdelay**. It measures the end-to-end delay in milliseconds for an ATM or Frame Relay connection. (This is a disruptive command and that it corrupts statistics.)

Frame Relay Connection Commands

Table 5-11 describes the Frame Relay connection commands and their privilege levels that are introduced in this chapter.

Table 5-11 *IGX Commands for Configuring Frame Relay Connections*

Command	Description	Privilege Level
addcon	Adds a Frame Relay PVC to the network.	1 and 2
clrchstats	Clears the statistics for one or all Frame Relay connections.	1 through 5
cnfchpri	Configures a Frame Relay connection as a high- or low-priority PVC.	1 and 2
cnfcls	Modifies the parameters associated with a Frame Relay or ATM class.	1 and 2
cnfcon	Modifies the parameters associated with a Frame Relay or ATM connection.	1 and 2
dspchstats	Displays live statistics for a specific Frame Relay connection.	1 through 5
dspcls	Displays all Frame Relay and ATM classes in the network.	1 and 2
tstdelay	Measures the end-to-end delay for a Frame Relay or ATM connection.	1 through 5

Configuring Frame Relay Connections

This section describes the steps and commands used to add, configure, and delete Frame Relay connections.

dspcls Command

For each Frame Relay connection you add, you must specify a Frame Relay class. A Frame Relay class is a set of parameters that specify a connection's bandwidth and congestion-prevention characteristics. The **dspcls** command displays a system-wide Frame Relay or ATM connection class, as shown in Example 5-17.

Example 5-17 dspcls *Output*

```
igx3           TN     group8:1        IGX 8420  9.2.20    Aug. 2 1999  19:28 CDT

                         Frame Relay Connection Classes

 #     MIR         CIR     VC Q Depth     PIR      Cmax     ECN QThresh
 1   128/128     256/256   65535/65535  1024/1024  15/20    65535/65535
    QIR:   384/384   FST: y % Util: 100/100 Description: "Oliverclass1"
 2    16/16       12/16    65535/65535     */*      100/10   65535/65535
    QIR:    16/16   FST: y % Util: 100/100 Description: "*"
```

Example 5-17 dspcls *Output (Continued)*

```
3     32/32        32/32      65535/65535      */*      10/10    65535/65535
   QIR:     32/32    FST: n % Util: 100/100 Description: "Default 32"
4     56/56        56/56      65535/65535      */*      10/10    65535/65535
   QIR:     56/56    FST: n % Util: 100/100 Description: "Default 56"
5     64/64        64/64      65535/65535      */*      10/10    65535/65535
   QIR:     64/64    FST: n % Util: 100/100 Description: "Default 64"


This Command: dspcls fr

Continue?
```

Ten classes are available for each category.

Here is the dspcls command syntax:

```
dspcls <atm | fr>
```

atm | fr: enter atm to display the ATM connection classes or fr to display the Frame Relay classes.

cnfcls Command

The **cnfcls** command modifies a network-wide Frame Relay or ATM connection class. Ten classes are available for each category. A Frame Relay or ATM class is relevant only at the time you add a connection with **addcon**.

All the **cnfcls** parameters are optional. They can be entered as follows:

- **Local value/remote value**—Modifies the values in both directions.
- **Value**—Modifies the local-to-remote value only.
- ***/remote value**—Modifies the remote-to-local value only.
- *****—A placeholder if subsequent parameter values are to be changed. Leaves current values unchanged or sets the PIR to the port speed.

Here is the **cnfcls** command syntax:

```
cnfcls <atm | fr> <class-number> [parameters in order shown on screen]
```

Table 5-12 describes the required and optional parameters for the **cnfcls** command.

Table 5-12 cnfcls *Command Syntax*

Parameter	Description	Required/Optional
atm	fr	Enter atm to display the ATM connection classes or fr to display the Frame Relay classes.	Required
class-number	The class number in the range 1 to 10.	Required
parameters	ATM or Frame Relay connection parameters.	Optional

Connection Class Parameters

Table 5-13 describes the parameters and ranges of the **cnfcls** command.

Table 5-13   **cnfcls** *Command Parameters*

Parameter	Definition and Range
MIR/MIR	The connection's minimum information rate. The range for MIR is 2.4 kbps to 2048 kbps.
CIR/CIR	The committed information rate is the rate that defines compliance. Any data in excess of the CIR may be tagged (CLP = 1) or discarded. The range for CIR is 2.4 kbps to 2048 kbps. CIR = 0 is valid only if the connection terminates at both ends on either a UFM or FRM. Before you can specify CIR = 0 with either **addcon** or **cnfcls**, you must enable IDE-to-DE mapping with **cnfport**. If you do not first enable IDE-to-DE mapping, the range for CIR is 2.4 kbps to 2048 kbps. Additionally, the CIR = 0 specification is necessary at only one end of the connection.
VC_Q/VC_Q	VC maximum queue depth. Specify the VC_Q in bytes within the range 1 to 65535.
PIR/PIR	The peak information rate for the PVC. The PIR range is 2.4 to 2048 kbps. You can also specify the value * to cause the PIR to default to the port speed.
Cmax/Cmax	Cmax is the maximum number of credits that the connection can accrue. Cmax is in the range 1 to 255 packets per second (pps).
ECN threshold	The level above which ingress frames have the FECN bit set and egress frames have BECN set. The range for the ECN threshold is 1 to 65535 bytes. The default is 65535, which effectively disables congestion notification.
QIR/QIR	The quiescent information rate for the connection, which is the initial transmit rate after a period of inactivity. The values are specified in kbps and must be in the range MIR $\leq$ PIR. In addition, you can specify the value 0 to default to the MIR. QIR has meaning for ForeSight connections only.
FST	Enables or disables ForeSight for a connection. Valid entries are y (use ForeSight) or n (do not use ForeSight). If the ForeSight status changes, the network reroutes the connection.
%util	The percentage transmit and receive utilization settings for the Frame Relay class. This value is specified as a percentage in the range 0 percent to 100 percent.
description	Any text string of up to 25 characters, terminated by pressing **Return**. This description entry is available to users so that they can provide a descriptive identifier for the class.

The **cnfcls** command, shown in Example 5-18, configures a network-wide Frame Relay connection class.

Example 5-18 cnfcls *Output*

```
igx3           TN    group8:1        IGX 8420  9.2.20    Aug. 2 1999  19:33 CDT

                        Frame Relay Connection Classes

 #    MIR          CIR      VC Q Depth     PIR      Cmax     ECN QThresh
 1   128/128     128/128   65000/65000   1200/1024  100/100   50000/65535
   QIR:   384/384   FST: y % Util: 100/100 Description: "New class"
 2    16/16       12/16     65535/65535    */*      100/10    65535/65535
   QIR:    16/16   FST: y % Util: 100/100 Description: "*"
 3    32/32       32/32     65535/65535    */*       10/10    65535/65535
   QIR:    32/32   FST: n % Util: 100/100 Description: "Default 32"
 4    56/56       56/56     65535/65535    */*       10/10    65535/65535
   QIR:    56/56   FST: n % Util: 100/100 Description: "Default 56"
 5    64/64       64/64     65535/65535    */*       10/10    65535/65535
   QIR:    64/64   FST: n % Util: 100/100 Description: "Default 64"


Last Command: cnfcls fr 1 128/128 128/128 65000/65000 1200/* 100/100 50000 384 y
100 New class

Next Command:
```

The following are characteristics of the **cnfcls** command:

- Network-wide classes should be configured only when all nodes can be reached.
- Changing a class does not affect any existing connections. An altered Frame Relay class affects only connections that are added using the changed class.
- The **cnfcls 1 * * * * * * * y** command string configures Frame Relay class 1 to operate with ForeSight. The list of * parameters leaves those parameters unchanged, and y enables ForeSight. Because the utilization and description parameters are not entered, any existing values for these parameters remain in effect.
- Ten ATM classes are available network-wide.
- The **cnfcls** command is used to modify a class.
- The connection classes can be changed without affecting existing connections.
- Connections can be changed without affecting the class.

Table 5-14 describes the parameters of the **cnfcls** command.

Table 5-14 cnfcls *Command Parameters*

Parameter	Description	Required/Optional
local-channel	Identified as *slot.port.DLCI*. Frame-forwarding connections use the format *slot.port.**.	Required
remote-node	Destination switch name.	Required
remote-channel	Identified as *slot.port.DLCI*. Frame-forwarding connections use the format *slot.port.**.	Required
connection-type	If one endpoint is an ATM card, the type of service interworking desired.	Optional
frame-relay-class	Frame Relay connection class 1 to 10.	Required
connection-parameters	Optional modifications of connection class parameters for this connection only.	Optional
avoid	Restricts the connection from routing over satellite (*s), terrestrial (*t), or ZCS (*z) trunks. Same as voice and data connections.	Optional

addcon Command

The **addcon** command, shown in Example 5-19, adds a Frame Relay connection to the network. After you add a connection, the system automatically routes the connection. The node on which you execute **addcon** is the owner of the connection. The concept of ownership is important because you specify preferred routing information at the node that owns the connection. Before the connection is actually added, the system displays the parameters you have specified and a prompt for confirmation.

Example 5-19 addcon *Output*

```
igx3            TN    group8:1      IGX 8420  9.2.20   Aug. 2 1999  19:35 CDT

Local           Remote      Remote
Channel         NodeName    Channel       State  Type     Compress   Code COS
10.1.100        igx2        11.2.200      Ok     fst                       0




Last Command: addcon 10.1.100 igx2 11.2.200 1

Warning: Peak bandwidth > port speed
Next Command:
```

For cards with Y-cable redundancy specified, you can add connections only to primary cards.

The **addcon 9.1.100 igx3 11.1.200 4** command creates DLCI 100 on port 9.1 and connects it to DLCI 200 on igx3, port 11.1 using Frame Relay class 4.

The **addcon 9.2.37 igx3 8.1.10.301 5** *z command creates DLCI 37 on port 9.2 and connects it to ATM VPI 10, VCI 301 on igx3, port 8.1 using Frame Relay class 5 and avoiding ZCS trunks.

The **addcon 10.2.* igx4 12.5.* 9** command creates a frame-forwarding connection on port 10.2 and connects it to igx4, port 5 using Frame Relay class 9.

When you add a Frame Relay connection with the **addcon** command, a prompt appears, requesting a Frame Relay class. At this prompt, you can do one of the following:

- Enter the number of a Frame Relay class. The range is 1 to 10.

- Override one or more parameters in a connection class by entering the class number without pressing the **Return** key, and then continue the line by entering either a new value or an asterisk (*) for each parameter. Separate each item with a space and no comma.

cnfcon Command

The **cnfcon** command, shown in Example 5-20, configures individual connection parameters. Because you normally specify bandwidth parameters through the Frame Relay class, **cnfcon** is used when you must customize the parameters for a single connection.

Example 5-20 cnfcon *Output*

```
igx3          TN      group8:1       IGX 8420  9.2.20    Aug. 2 1999  19:37 CDT

Conn:  10.1.100           igx2        11.2.200             fst       Status:OK
   MIR        CIR      VC Q Depth      PIR     Cmax   ECN QThresh     QIR
   96/128    128/128   65000/65000   1200/1024  50/100 50000/50000   384/384

Owner: LOCAL  Restriction: NONE  COS: 0                 FST: y  % Util: 100/100
Pri: L  FST-RTD: 40 msec  Test-RTD: 0 msec
Path:   igx3       12--  13igx2
Pref:   Not Configured


igx3      UFMU:   OK                    igx2     UFM:   OK
          UFI:    Port Comm Fail                 Line 11.2 : OK


Last Command: cnfcon 10.1.100 96/128 * * */* 50 50000/50000

Warning: Peak bandwidth > port speed
Next Command:
```

Here is the cnfcon command syntax:

```
cnfcon <connection> [parameters in order shown on screen]
```

Table 5-15 describes the parameters of the **cnfcon** command.

Table 5-15   **cnfcon** *Command Parameters*

Parameter	Description	Required/Optional
connection	Frame Relay connection in the format *slot.port.DLCI* or *slot.port.**.	Required
parameters	Enter parameter values in the order shown on the screen. Enter an asterisk (*) to retain the current value.	Optional

Be sure the MIR you specify is appropriate. If the MIR is too high, bandwidth is wasted. If it is too low, the connection might drop data. The statistics reports are the best source of information to help you determine the appropriate MIR.

If the PIR is too low, frames are dropped. If it is too high, bandwidth might be wasted unless ForeSight is enabled.

The Cmax, VC Q, and ECN Q values should be changed only when tuning data is available to support the determination of appropriate values. These values affect system buffering resources.

If the connection type has ForeSight enabled, the result of the last test round-trip delay command (Test RTD) is displayed. This is not the current RTD, but the result of the last user-specified test. High or low connection priority is displayed for all Frame Relay connections.

The node checks the bandwidth parameters to promote efficient use of network bandwidth. The following messages reflect the checks on bandwidth usage:

- **Error**—Min cannot exceed peak
- **Warning**—Min exceeds this port's speed
- **Warning**—Sum of mins exceeds port's speed
- **Warning**—Peak exceeds this port's speed

Warning messages are informational and do not indicate that the command failed to execute. Error messages indicate that the command did not complete successful execution.

dspcons Command

The **dspcons** command screen is shown in Example 5-21.

Example 5-21 dspcons *Output*

```
igx3            TN     group8:1        IGX 8420  9.2.20    Aug. 2 1999  19:40 CDT

Local           Remote      Remote
Channel         NodeName    Channel         State  Type    Compress    Code COS
10.1.100        igx2        11.2.200        Ok     fst                      0
11.1.300        igx2        11.1.176        Ok     fst                      0
11.250.23       igx4        10.1.102        Ok     fr                       0




Last Command: dspcons


Next Command:
```

The **dspcons** command screen, shown in Example 5-21, displays the following summary status information for connections that terminate on this node:

- Local channel
- Remote node
- Remote channel
- **State**—OK, failed, or down
- **Type**—Frame Relay (fr) or ForeSight (fst) (ATM to FR, or interworking)
- **Compression**—Applies to voice and data connections only
- **Code**—Applies to data connections only
- **COS**—Class of service; relevant to connection management and rerouting delay

dspcon Command

The **dspcon** command screen, shown in Example 5-22, provides detailed information on a given connection.

Example 5-22 dspcon *Output*

```
igx3            TN     group8:1        IGX 8420  9.2.20    Aug. 2 1999  19:41 CDT

Conn:  11.250.23          igx4          10.1.102          fr        Status:OK
   MIR         CIR        VC Q Depth     PIR       Cmax    ECN QThresh    QIR
   32/32       32/32      65535/65535    56/256    10/10   65535/65535    32/32
```

continues

Example 5-22 dspcon *Output (Continued)*

```
Owner: LOCAL  Restriction: NONE  COS: 0              FST: n  % Util: 100/100
Pri: L  Test-RTD: 0 msec
Path:   igx3       13-- 14igx4
Pref:   Not Configured


igx3      UFM:  OK                        igx4    UFMU:  OK
               Line 11.1 : Port Comm Fail          UFI:   OK


Last Command: dspcon 11.250.23


Next Command:
```

Information provided (in addition to **dspcons** information) includes the following:

- **Parameters defined during the addcon command**—MIR, CIR, VC Queue Depth, PIR, Cmax, ECN queue threshold, QIR, ForeSight, and % utilization
- **Priority**—The connection's configured priority, either high or low
- **ForeSight RTD**—The current ForeSight rate adjustment interval, determined with test packets sent periodically
- **Test RTD**—The most recent result of the **tstdelay** command

Here is the **dspcon** command syntax:

> **dspcon** *<connection>*

connection is the Frame Relay connection identifier, including the slot, port, and DLCI.

cnfchpri Command

The **cnfchpri** command, shown in Example 5-23, sets the channel priority for a Frame Relay connection. This feature permits some Frame Relay connections to receive a higher priority within a port queue than other Frame Relay traffic on a per-connection basis. You must configure the priority on both ends of the connection.

Example 5-23 cnfchpri *Output*

```
igx3            TN    group8:1       IGX 8420  9.1.12    Aug.  2 1999  19:42 CDT

Conn:  11.250.23       igx4      10.1.102         fr      Status:OK
   MIR       CIR     VC Q Depth     PIR     Cmax   ECN QThresh    QIR
   32/32    32/32   65535/65535    56/256  10/10  65535/65535    32/32

Owner: LOCAL  Restriction: NONE  COS: 0              FST: n  % Util: 100/100
Pri: H  Test-RTD: 0 msec
```

Example 5-23 cnfchpri *Output (Continued)*

```
Path:    igx3        13--   14igx4
Pref:    Not Configured


igx3       UFM:   OK                    igx4      UFMU:  OK
           Line 11.1 : Port Comm Fail             UFI:   OK


Last Command: cnfchpri 11.250.23 h


Next Command:
```

You can configure Frame Relay ports to communicate the priority to a router.

Here is the **cnfchpri** command syntax:

```
cnfchpri <connection> <h | l>
```

Table 5-16 describes the parameters of the **cnfchpri** command.

Table 5-16 cnfchpri *Command Parameters*

Parameter	Description	Required/Optional
connection	The Frame Relay connection identifier, including the slot, port, and DLCI.	Required
h | l	Set to high (h) or low (l) priority. The default priority is low.	Required

delcon Command

The **delcon** command, shown in Example 5-24, removes connections from the network. As soon as this command is issued, the connection is highlighted in the screen display. A delcon *xx.x y/n* prompt appears to confirm the deletion.

Example 5-24 delcon *Output*

```
igx3           TN     group8:1      IGX 8420   9.2.20    Aug. 2 1999  19:43 CDT

Local          Remote      Remote
Channel        NodeName    Channel        State  Type   Compress   Code COS
10.1.100       igx2        11.2.200       Ok     fst                     0
11.1.300       igx2        11.1.176       Ok     fst                     0


Last Command: delcon 11.250.23


Next Command:
```

Connections can be deleted from the node at either end of the connection. Do not delete a connection when the node at the other end of the connection is unreachable, because the unreachable node will not recognize the deletion. It is especially important not to delete a connection to an unreachable node and then connect that channel to another node.

Here is the **delcon** command syntax:

```
delcon <connection>
```

dspchstats Command

The **dspchstats** command presents a statistical view of connection activity, as shown in Example 5-25.

Example 5-25 dspchstats *Output*

```
igx3            TN     group8:1        IGX 8420  9.2.20    Aug. 2 1999  19:46 CDT

Channel Statistics: 10.1.100      Cleared: Aug. 2 1999  19:35    (/)
MIR: 96/128 kbps          Collection Time: 0 day(s) 00:01:22      Corrupted: NO
                    Frames   Avg Size Avg     Util          Packets      Avg
                             (bytes)  (fps)   (%)                        (pps)
From Port:               0        0       0     0
To Network:              0        0       0     0              0           0
Discarded:               0        0       0     0
From Network:            0        0       0     0              0           0
To Port:                 0        0       0     0
Discarded:               0        0       0     0              0           0
             ECN Stats:  Avg Rx VC Q:            0     ForeSight RTD     40
Min-Pk bytes rcvd: --     FECN Frames:           0     FECN Ratio (%)     0
Minutes Congested: --     BECN Frames:           0     BECN Ratio (%)     0
Frames rcvd in excess of CIR:      0  Bytes rcvd in excess of CIR:       0
Frames xmtd in excess of CIR:      0  Bytes xmtd in excess of CIR:       0

This Command: dspchstats 10.1.100 5

Hit DEL key to quit:
```

The statistics fields were described with the **dspportstats** command.

Here is the **dspchstats** command syntax:

```
dspchstats <connection> [interval]
```

Table 5-17 describes the parameters of the **dspchstats** command.

Table 5-17   dspchstats *Command Parameters*

Parameter	Description	Required/Optional
connection	The Frame Relay connection identifier, including the slot, port, and DLCI.	Required
interval	The screen refresh interval, in seconds. The default is 5 seconds.	Optional

clrchstats Command

The **clrchstats** command, shown in Example 5-26, clears the gathered statistics for either a specific channel or all channels. When you enter a specific channel number, a display of the current channel statistics appears.

Example 5-26 clrchstats *Output*

```
igx3            TN    group8:1        IGX 8420  9.2.20    Aug. 2 1999  19:55 CDT

Channel Statistics: 11.1.300     Cleared: Aug. 2 1999  19:55         Snapshot
MIR: 16/16 kbps          Collection Time: 0 day(s) 00:00:00     Corrupted: NO
                  Frames   Avg Size Avg    Util          Packets      Avg
                           (bytes)  (fps)  (%)                        (pps)
From Port:          0          0      0     0
To Network:         0          0      0     0              0           0
Discarded:          0          0      0     0
From Network:       0          0      0     0              0           0
To Port:            0          0      0     0
Discarded:          0          0      0     0              0           0
              ECN Stats:  Avg Rx VC Q:            0    ForeSight RTD     40
Min-Pk bytes rcvd: --      FECN Frames:           0    FECN Ratio (%)     0
Minutes Congested: --      BECN Frames:           0    BECN Ratio (%)     0
Frames rcvd in excess of CIR:    0  Bytes rcvd in excess of CIR:        0
Frames xmtd in excess of CIR:    0  Bytes xmtd in excess of CIR:        0

Last Command: clrchstats 11.1.300

Next Command:
```

The display prompts you to confirm the choice for clearing. If you enter * (all channels) for the channel specification, the display prompts you to confirm the decision to clear all channel statistics.

Here is the **clrchstats** command syntax:

```
clrchstats <connection | *>
```

connection is the Frame Relay connection identifier, including the slot, port, and DLCI. The * indicates all connections on this switch.

tstdelay Command

The **tstdelay** command, shown in Example 5-27, puts the remote end of a Frame Relay or ATM connection into a loopback state, asks the Frame Relay or ATM card to generate a test packet, calculates the round-trip delay (RTD), and displays the round-trip delay. This delay includes the service card and trunk queuing and processing delays throughout the network. The measured delay using **tstdelay** differs from the ForeSight RTD, which uses a high-priority packet and does not include processing and queuing delays.

Example 5-27 **tstdelay** *Output*

```
igx4            TN     group8:1        IGX 8420  9.2.20    Aug. 3 1999  14:51 CDT

Conn:  9.1.30.31        igx3       9.1.30.41        abrfst    Status:OK
   PCR(0+1)     % Util    MCR        CDVT(0+1)   FBTC  FST  VSVD  FCES
   1000/1000    5/5      50/50      250000/250000  y    y    -    n

Owner: LOCAL  Restriction: NONE  COS: 0 Pri: L  Test-RTD: 3 msec  Max Cost: 100
Path:   igx4      14--  13igx3
Pref:   Not Configured

igx4     UXM:   OK              igx3     UXM:   OK
         Line  9.1 : OK                  Line  9.1 : OK
         OAM Cell RX: Clear              NNI:   OK
         NNI:   OK

Last Command: tstdelay 9.1.30.31

Round trip delay is 3 msec.
Next Command:
```

This test interrupts transmission on the connection during the test. Test results appear at the bottom of the screen (the display might include a timeout message, as shown here).

Here is the **tstdelay** command syntax:

tstdelay *<connection>* *[repeat-count]* *[ForeSight RTD (y/n)]*

Table 5-18 describes the parameters of the **tstdelay** command.

Table 5-18 **tstdelay** *Command Parameters*

Parameter	Description	Required/Optional
connection	Specifies the ATM or Frame Relay connection to be tested.	Required
repeat-count	Specifies the number of times to repeat the test, in the range 1 to 50. If you do not specify a count, the test runs once.	Optional
ForeSight RTD (y/n)	Specifies that the ForeSight RTD is included and applies to ATM connections only.	Optional

Summary

This chapter showed you how to contrast channelized and unchannelized Frame Relay interfaces and how to create Frame Relay ports on channelized interfaces. Given CPE requirements, you should be able to modify Frame Relay characteristics and analyze Frame Relay port activity.

Displaying, modifying, and creating Frame Relay connections and classes was discussed, and standards-based and Cisco ForeSight Frame Relay parameters were contrasted. You should be able to identify the impact of connection parameters, including ForeSight parameters.

You should be able to analyze Frame Relay connection activity, including connection statistics, and add and modify Frame Relay connections using connection classes. You should also be able to create logical Frame Relay ports from lines, activate and modify Frame Relay ports, and analyze Frame Relay port statistics.

Review Questions

1   What is the interface between the network and a single external Frame Relay device?

2   List the steps to activate a Frame Relay port on a UFM-C card.

3   To verify line configuration, use the _____ command, and to check an individual port, use the _____ command.

4   Which command would you use to modify port parameters?

5   Which command would you use to create a logical Frame Relay port?

6   List the command and parameters used to display the Port, ID, Speed, Interface, State, and Protocol fields in the display.

7   While displaying port statistics, some ports might have corrupt statistics. What might be the cause?

8   When a frame is received with a CRC error, is the CRC regenerated correctly before the frame is passed on?

9   When clearing port statistics, some statistics cannot be cleared. Why?

10   What is a point-to-point VC that provides transport services for an attached user device in an IGX network?

11   What is ForeSight?

12   Which commands modify and display connection parameters?

13   Which commands modify and display the ten Frame Relay classes?

14   Which command would you use to specify high- or low-priority connections?

This chapter covers the following key topics:

- ATM Ports
- ATM Port Commands
- ATM Connections
- Connection Policing
- VC Queuing for ABR Traffic
- ATM Connection Commands
- Interworking ATM and Frame Relay

CHAPTER 6

ATM Ports and Connections and ATM-to-Frame Relay Interworking

This chapter describes ATM ports on the IGX and ATM-to-Frame Relay Interworking. The ATM service card is the Universal Switching Module (UXM) card that supports both lines and trunks. This chapter also describes ATM connections on the IGX, and covers the capabilities of the UXM card for ATM connections, connection policing, and connection statistics.

The method used for transporting Frame Relay over ATM and converting Frame Relay frames to native ATM cell streams is described. This chapter also compares the encapsulation techniques for ATM and Frame Relay and discusses methods for interworking between them.

ATM Ports

A *port* is the interface between the network and a single ATM device. ATM connections terminate on UXM ATM ports. Multiple connections may terminate on a single port. They are differentiated by their assigned VPI and VCI, as described later in this chapter.

With the UXM card, the line and port must be activated and configured separately. One port is available per line.

Here is a general list of UXM characteristics:

- An aggregate throughput of 310 Mbps
- ATM Forum UNI v3.0 and v3.1 headers
- Constant bit rate (CBR), real-time variable bit rate (rt-VBR), nonreal-time variable bit rate (nrt-VBR), available bit rate (ABR), and unspecified bit rate (UBR) connection types are supported for ATM
- Interworking between Frame Relay and ATM endpoints
- Ingress policing
- Up to 4000 connections per card at an aggregate rate of up to DS-3
- Optional Y-cable redundancy
- Support for port and connection statistics

ATM Port Commands

Table 6-1 introduces new commands for this section and reintroduces others that were discussed in previous chapters.

Table 6-1 *ATM Port Commands*

Command	Description	Privilege Levels
dspcd	Displays summary information on all the front and back cards installed on the IGX.	1 through 6
dspports	Displays summary information about ATM ports.	1 through 6
dspport	Displays status and configuration information on one port, all ports on a card, or all ports on the node.	1 through 6
upport	Activates a physical or logical port.	1 and 2
cnfport	Modifies configuration parameters, including queuing and signaling protocols, on an ATM port.	1 and 2
dspportq	Displays port queue characteristics.	1 through 6
cnfportq	Modifies port queue characteristics.	1 and 2

dspcd Command

The **dspcd** command, shown in Example 6-1, displays a card's status, revision, and serial number. If a back card is present, its type, revision, and serial number appear. The displayed information can vary with different card types.

Example 6-1 **dspcd** *Output*

```
igx4     TRM    group7:1        IGX 8420  9.1.12    Aug. 2 1999  16:54 CDT

Detailed Card Display for UXM in slot 9

Status:            Active          (Front Card Supports SIW)
Revision:          AAD             (Front Card Supports Cell Forwarding)
Serial Number:     239098          (Front Card with GW installed)
Fab Number:        28-2164-02      (# of trunks that can be upped = 3)
Backplane Installed                (Front Card Supports Hot Standby)
Backcard Installed
  Type:            E3
  Revision:        AA
  Serial Number:   241724
  Ports:           3

Last Command: dspcd 9

Next Command:
```

The notation "Front Card Supports SIW" means that service interworking (SIW) is implemented either on ingress or on a gateway between networks to translate between ATM and Frame Relay services. SIW is discussed in a later section of this chapter.

dspports Command

The **dspports** command, shown in Example 6-2, displays ATM port characteristics.

Example 6-2 **dspports** *Output*

```
igx4            TN     group8:1       IGX 8420  9.2.20    Sep. 10 1999 09:10 CST

Port configuration for ATM 9

Port   Chan       Speed     Interface     State      Protocol    Type
1      1       80000 (cps)  E3            INACTIVE   NONE        UNI
2      2       80000 (cps)  E3            ACTIVE     ILMI        NNI
3      3       80000 (cps)  E3            INACTIVE   NONE        UNI


Last Command: dspports 9


Next Command:
```

Example 6-2 shows **dspports** with a card slot specified. The following information is displayed:

- **Port**—The port number
- **Channel**—The channel number
- **Speed**—The port speed, in cells per second
- **Interface**—The interface or line type
- **State**—The port's state
- **Protocol**—The configured signaling protocol—Local Management Interface (LMI), Interim Local Management Interface (ILMI), or none
- **Type**—The cell header type—either UNI (User-Network Interface) or Network Node Interface (NNI)

dspport Command

The **dspport** command, shown in Example 6-3, displays detailed port characteristics.

Example 6-3 **dspport** *Output*

```
igx4            TRM   group7:1      IGX 8420  9.2.20    Aug. 2 1999  17:51 CDT

Port:   9.1     [INACTIVE]
Interface:      E3                  CAC Override:     Enabled
Type:           UNI                 %Util Use:        Disabled
Speed:          80000 (cps)
SIG Queue Depth: 640


Protocol:       NONE



Last Command: dspport 9.1



Next Command:
```

Port characteristics include the following:

- **Interface**—Physical port and line interface.
- **CAC Override**—Connection admission control (CAC) limits the total of all connections to the port capacity. If CAC override is enabled, the port might be overbooked.
- **Type**—Cell header type—either UNI or NNI.
- **%Util Use**—Enable or disable the use of percent utilization on connections when determining queue service rates and oversubscription warnings.
- **Speed**—The port speed based on the line type and configuration.
- **SIG Queue Depth**—The queue depth, in cells, used to signal traffic on the port.
- **Protocol**—The signaling protocol—NONE, LMI, or ILMI. When either LMI or ILMI is selected, additional protocol-specific parameters are displayed.

upport Command

The **upport** command activates a physical or logical port for ATM or Frame Relay, as described in Chapter 5, "Frame Relay Ports and Connections."

cnfport Command

Before the line can be used as a resource for adding connections to the network, you must use the **upport** command to activate the port. Then it can be configured using the **cnfport** command, as shown in Example 6-4, to agree with the equipment at the other end of the line.

Example 6-4 **cnfport** *Output*

```
igx4          TRM   group7:1      IGX 8420  9.2.20    Aug. 2 1999  17:38 CDT


Port:     9.1   [INACTIVE]
Interface:        E3            CAC Override:    Enabled
Type:             UNI           %Util Use:       Disabled
Speed:            80000 (cps)
SIG Queue Depth:  640


Protocol:         NONE



This Command: cnfport 9.1



NNI Cell Header Format? [N]:
```

A signaling protocol is used to exchange PVC status and configuration information across the UNI or NNI.

Two signaling protocols are defined for ATM interfaces—LMI and ILMI. Neither is required for an ATM port to transmit and receive data, but some user equipment might depend on the signaling protocol to maintain an active interface. ILMI signaling is defined using the **cnfport** command, as shown in Example 6-5.

Example 6-5 **cnfport** *Output for ILMI Signaling*

```
igx4          TN    group8:1      IGX 8420  9.2.20    Sep. 10 1999 09:11 CST

Port:     9.2   [INACTIVE]
Interface:        E3            CAC Override:    Enabled
Type:             NNI           %Util Use:       Enabled
Speed:            80000 (cps)
SIG Queue Depth:  640

Protocol:         ILMI
  VPI.VCI:                      0.16
  ILMI Polling Enabled          N
  Trap Enabled                  Y
  T491 Polling Interval         30
```

continues

Example 6-5   **cnfport** *Output for ILMI Signaling (Continued)*

```
    N491 Error Threshold              3
    N492 Event Threshold              4


Last Command: cnfport 9.2 y i 0 16 N y 30 3 4 y N
```

If you select a signaling protocol, you are prompted for several additional parameters.

Signaling Display Fields

ILMI fields are described in Table 6-2.

Table 6-2   *ILMI Field Descriptions*

ILMI Field	Description
VPI.VCI	The VPI and VCI reserved for the ILMI protocol messages. The VPI/VCI defaults to 0.16.
ILMI Polling Enabled	Enables or disables periodic status polls.
Trap Enabled	Enables or disables unsolicited event or alarm transmission.
T491 Polling Interval	The time period, in seconds, between status polls sent by the port if polling is enabled.
N491 Error Threshold	If N491 messages out of N492 messages do not receive a response from the attached device, a "Port Communication Failure" alarm is declared.
N492 Event Threshold	The number of attempted messages, in conjunction with the N491 threshold that determines an alarm condition.

LMI fields are described in Table 6-3.

Table 6-3   *LMI Field Descriptions*

LMI Field	Description
VPI.VCI	The VPI and VCI reserved for the LMI protocol messages. The VPI/VCI defaults to 0.31.
LMI Polling Enabled	Enables or disables periodic status inquiries.
T393 Status Enquiry Timer	The timeout period, in seconds, for expected responses to be received from the attached device as a result of the port's sending a status inquiry. If the timer expires, the port attempts to transmit another inquiry.

Table 6-3   *LMI Field Descriptions (Continued)*

LMI Field	Description
T394 Update Status Timer	The timeout period, in seconds, for expected responses to be received from the attached device as a result of the port's sending an update status message. If the timer expires, the port attempts to transmit another update status message.
T396 Polling Timer	The time, in seconds, between status inquiries sent by the port if polling is enabled.
N394 Max Status Enquiry Retry	The maximum number of status inquiry retries sent by the port before a "Port Communications Failure" alarm is declared.
N395 Max Update Status Retry	The maximum number of update status retries sent by the port before a "Port Communications Failure" alarm is declared.

dspportq Command

There are four egress queues for each port, for CBR, nrt-VBR, rt-VBR, and ABR types of traffic. The **dspportq** command, shown in Example 6-6, displays the queue depth and thresholds for each queue. The CLP high threshold is the point at which the system throws away cells that have a CLP of 1. The CLP low threshold is the point at which the system stops discarding cells that have a CLP of 1 after the discard process has started. UBR connections are not mentioned here because they are variable-rate connections without a guaranteed service rate, and if there is congestion or no available bandwidth, a UBR connection is not given bandwidth in the network.

Example 6-6   dspportq *Output*

```
igx1            TN      group6:1        IGX 8420  9.2.20    Aug. 28 1999 12:24 CDT


Port:        16.2    [ACTIVE  ]
Interface:           E3
Type:                UNI
Speed:               80000 (cps)


CBR Queue Depth:               600    rt-VBR Queue Depth:               5000
CBR Queue CLP High Threshold: 80%     rt-VBR Queue CLP High Threshold:   80%
CBR Queue CLP Low Threshold:  60%     rt-VBR Queue CLP Low Threshold:    60%
CBR Queue EFCI Threshold:     60%     rt-VBR Queue EFCI Threshold:       60%
nrt-VBR Queue Depth:          5000    ABR Queue Depth:                 20000
nrt-VBR Queue CLP High Threshold: 80% ABR Queue CLP High Threshold:      80%
nrt-VBR Queue CLP Low Threshold:  60% ABR Queue CLP Low Threshold:       60%
nrt-VBR Queue EFCI Threshold: 60%     ABR Queue EFCI Threshold:          20%



Last Command: dspportq 16.2



Next Command:
```

The EFCI threshold is the level reached in the queue when the EFCI bit is set to 1 to indicate congestion. All these queues can be configured by using the **cnfportq** command.

cnfportq Command

The **cnfportq** command, shown in Example 6-7, modifies the queue depth and thresholds for each port queue.

Example 6-7 **cnfportq** *Output*

```
igx1            TN     group6:1        IGX 8420  9.2.20    Aug. 28 1999 12:24 CDT

Port:      16.2    [ACTIVE   ]
Interface:         E3
Type:              UNI
Speed:             80000 (cps)

CBR Queue Depth:                700    rt-VBR Queue Depth:              5000
CBR Queue CLP High Threshold: 90%      rt-VBR Queue CLP High Threshold:  80%
CBR Queue CLP Low Threshold:  70%      rt-VBR Queue CLP Low Threshold:   60%
CBR Queue EFCI Threshold:     60%      rt-VBR Queue EFCI Threshold:      60%
nrt-VBR Queue Depth:            5000   ABR Queue Depth:                 25000
nrt-VBR Queue CLP High Threshold: 80% ABR Queue CLP High Threshold:     95%
nrt-VBR Queue CLP Low Threshold:  60% ABR Queue CLP Low Threshold:      80%
nrt-VBR Queue EFCI Threshold: 60%      ABR Queue EFCI Threshold:         30%




Last Command: cnfportq 16.2 700 90 70 60 * * * * * * * * 25000 95 80 30


Next Command:
```

The queue depth is described in cells, and the thresholds indicate some percentage (%) of queue depth.

The syntax for the **cnfportq** command and different types of traffic are as follows:

```
cnfportq <port> <CBR-queue-depth> <CBR-CLP-High>
  <CBR-CLP-Low> <CBR-EFCI-threshold>
  <NRT-VBR-queue-depth> <NRT-VBR-CLP-High>
  <NRT-VBR-CLP-Low> <NRT-VBR-EFCI-threshold>
  <RT-VBR-queue-depth> <RT-VBR-CLP-High>
  <RT-VBR-CLP-Low> <RT-VBR-EFCI-threshold>
  <ABR-queue-depth> <ABR-CLP-High>
  <ABR-CLP-Low> <ABR-EFCI-threshold>
```

ATM Connections

An *ATM connection* is a point-to-point virtual circuit that provides transport service for attached user devices through an IGX network, as illustrated in Figure 6-1. ATM connections terminate on UXM ATM ports. Multiple connections may terminate on a single port and are differentiated by their assigned VPI and VCI.

Figure 6-1   *ATM Connection Definition*

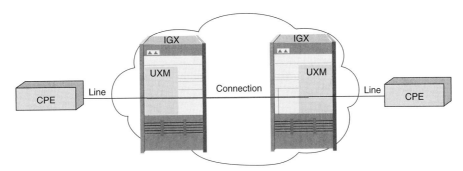

ATM connections on the IGX are supported between UXM cards or a UXM and the older ALM/A.

In addition, the UXM can terminate an ATM connection with BPX ASI or BXM cards or the MGX AUSM card.

When a VPI and VCI are assigned to a connection, the following requirements must be met:

- VPI/VCIs are locally significant.
- VPI/VCIs must be unique on a given port.
- The VPI and VCI cannot both be set to 0.
- The combinations VPI 0 and VCI 0 to 31 are reserved and should not be used.
- MPLS uses VCI 32.
- VPI and VCI ranges depend on the cell header type.
- Some systems might restrict VPI and VCI values.

You should have a basic understanding of the functions of an ATM network. If you do not, refer to *Cisco WAN Quick Start* by Ronald W. McCarty for more information.

Types of ATM Connections

The following types of ATM connections are supported on the UXM card. Remember that the IGX network is responsible for transport and management of user traffic but has no knowledge of the cell payload or the end-user application. It is up to you, as the administrator, to define the connection type appropriately.

Constant Bit Rate

Constant bit rate (CBR) traffic is used for time-dependent constant-rate traffic, such as uncompressed voice, video, or synchronous data. Few allowances are made to accommodate burstiness on CBR connections. Most often, CBR connections carry cells that were created using ATM adaptation layer 1 (AAL1).

Variable Bit Rate

Variable bit rate (VBR) traffic is used for bursty traffic that might have some time dependency such as compressed voice, video, or synchronous data. Traffic is permitted to burst within set limitations. There are two types of VBR traffic—nonreal-time VBR (nrt-VBR) and real-time VBR (rt-VBR). nrt-VBR is suitable for applications that can tolerate delays, but rt-VBR is not.

Available Bit Rate

Available bit rate (ABR) traffic is a variation on VBR commonly used for LAN/WAN services such as router traffic. ABR adds the ability to adjust the connection data rates to accommodate for congestion and bandwidth availability in the network. There are two types of ABR connections—those defined by a standard and those that utilize the ForeSight feature. Both types of ABR connections are typically used to support AAL5 ATM cells:

- **Standard ABR**—The UXM card module supports standard ABR connections as defined by the ATM Forum's Traffic Management 4.0 (TM 4.0) recommendation.
- **ABR with ForeSight**—The UXM also supports ABR based on ForeSight. Similar to standard ABR, the ForeSight feature is used to dynamically manage variable-rate traffic based on the availability of network resources.

Unspecified Bit Rate

Unspecified bit rate (UBR) connections are variable-rate connections without a guaranteed service rate. If there is congestion or no available bandwidth, a UBR connection is not given bandwidth in the network. UBR connections are used for variable-rate applications that are tolerant of zero-transmission periods such as batch-processed e-mail or LAN emulation services.

Connection Policing

All ATM connections, depending on policing type, are subject to policing as the cells enter the network. *Policing* is the process of monitoring ingress traffic to determine compliance with the traffic contract and controlling how traffic is handled as soon as it is inside the network. Each connection's *traffic contract* includes characteristics such as burst sizes and data rates. The end-user device is responsible for meeting the defined policing requirements. Otherwise, cells are declared *noncompliant* and can be dropped by the network.

The *leaky bucket* model, shown in Figure 6-2, defines policing for ATM connections. It is important to remember that the leaky bucket is not a queue structure, but a way to describe how the network monitors and controls incoming user cells.

Figure 6-2 *Leaky Bucket Model*

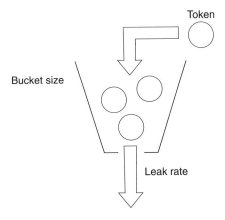

NOTE   The leaky bucket model is also described for the BPX switch in Chapter 14, "Configuring ATM Connections and Routing AutoRoute Connections," and for the MGX switch in Chapter 20, "Frame Relay Ports and Connections." Although these models are similar for the BPX and IGX switches, there are differences on the MGX switch, as described in Chapter 20.

It is easiest to think of the model as a test done on the traffic to answer two questions:

- Should the cell be allowed into the network?
- If so, should it be given a normal or low priority (set the CLP bit to 1)?

Leaky Bucket Model

The leaky bucket model has three components:

- **Token**—Arrives in the bucket at a rate defined by the incoming traffic. For ATM traffic, each cell is represented in the leaky bucket model as a single token. The rate at which the tokens fill the bucket is variable. The actual user cell does *not* go into the bucket.

- **Bucket size**—Determines how many tokens can be held before the bucket is full. As soon as the bucket has reached its capacity, any new tokens represent cells that are noncompliant. Noncompliant cells may be dropped or tagged with a 1 in the CLP field, depending on the situation.

- **Leak rate**—Determines the average acceptable token rate to maintain compliance. If the tokens arrive at approximately the same rate as the leak rate, the bucket never fills up. If the tokens arrive at a rate greater than the leak rate, they eventually become noncompliant. If the tokens arrive at a rate less than the leak rate, the bucket is always empty.

Dual Leaky Bucket Model

Many connections use a dual leaky bucket model for policing, as illustrated in Figure 6-3. A dual leaky bucket is made up of two different leaky bucket models, each with its own configurable characteristics

Figure 6-3   *Dual Leaky Bucket Model*

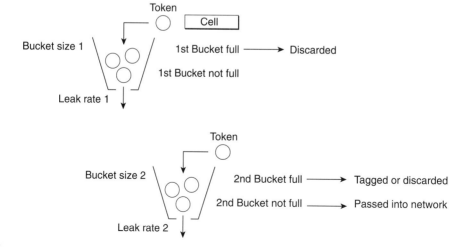

In general, the first leaky bucket is set to discard any noncompliant cells, which means that all incoming traffic must meet the requirements of the first leaky bucket to be accepted by the network. If a cell is dropped at the first leaky bucket, it does not get checked by the second leaky bucket.

The second leaky bucket can be disabled, dropped on noncompliance, or tagged with CLP on noncompliance. The behavior of the second bucket is dependent on the configured policing type, as shown in Table 6-4.

Table 6-4   *The Second Leaky Bucket*

Type	Cells Tested in First Bucket	If Noncompliant in First Bucket	Cells Tested in Second Bucket	If Noncompliant in Second Bucket	Connection Types
1	All	Discard	CLP = 0 or 1	Discard	ABR, nrt-VBR, rt-VBR
2	All	Discard	CLP = 0 only	Discard	ABR, nrt-VBR, rt-VBR
3	All	Discard	CLP = 0 only	Tag with CLP	ABR, nrt-VBR, rt-VBR, UBR
4	All	Discard	None	—	CBR, ABR, nrt-VBR, rt-VBR, UBR
5	None	—	None	—	CBR, nrt-VBR, rt-VBR, ABR

CBR Traffic Policing

CBR Traffic Policing is illustrated in Figure 6-4. CBR connections typically use policing type 4, in which traffic is policed using a single leaky bucket that discards all noncompliant cells. Another option is to use policing type 5, which disables all policing and results in all cells being accepted into the network.

The nature of CBR traffic implies that cells arrive at a constant rate. In other words, the intercell time is expected to be constant. However, demanding that cells arrive exactly as expected is unreasonable, because there might be traffic from many different sources on one physical line.

Figure 6-4 *CBR Traffic Policing*

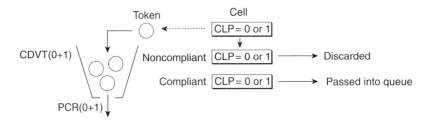

Two values determine compliance for CBR cells. The peak cell rate (PCR) value defines the bucket leak rate, and the cell delay variation tolerance (CDVT) value determines the bucket size. Cells are expected to arrive, on average, at the PCR. However, if they exceed the PCR, they are limited to a variation tolerance defined by the CDVT:

- **Size of first bucket**—CDVT(0+1) for cells with CLP = 0 or CLP = 1, in microseconds
- **Leak rate of first bucket**—PCR(0+1) for cells with CLP = 0 or CLP = 1, in cells per second

VBR Traffic Policing

VBR connections typically use policing types 1, 2, or 3, all of which use a dual leaky bucket model. These types are called VBR.1, VBR.2, and VBR.3.

VBR.1

VBR traffic with policing type 1 is implemented using two leaky bucket models, both of which discard noncompliant cells (see Figure 6-5).

The first leaky bucket functions like CBR traffic, using the PCR(0+1) and CDVT(0+1) values to limit the flow of cells into the network. The bucket ensures that the network does not receive cells in excess of the peak rate allowed for a given PVC. All noncompliant cells are discarded at the first leaky bucket. Compliant cells go on to be checked by the second leaky bucket.

The second leaky bucket uses the maximum burst size (MBS) and the sustainable cell rate (SCR). The second leaky bucket maintains an average cell rate of SCR while still allowing some burstiness up to the PCR. The MBS is the number of cells that will be compliant on the second leaky bucket if the cells are arriving at a rate of PCR(0+1). All noncompliant cells on the second leaky bucket are discarded.

Figure 6-5   *VBR.1 Traffic Policing*

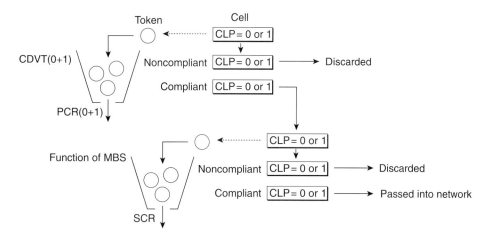

In summary, VBR policing parameters include the following:

- **Size of the first bucket**—CDVT(0+1) for cells with CLP = 0 or CLP = 1, in microseconds

- **Leak rate of the first bucket**—PCR(0+1) for cells with CLP = 0 or CLP = 1, in cells per second

- **Size of the second bucket**—Based on the MBS, in cells

- **Leak rate of the second bucket**—SCR, in cells per second

VBR.2

VBR traffic configured with policing type 2 uses a dual leaky bucket model, with both buckets discarding noncompliant cells (see Figure 6-6). Unlike VBR.1, VBR.2 checks only cells with CLP set to 0 on the second leaky bucket. As a result, cells tagged with CLP = 1 have an advantage on ingress over cells with CLP = 0. In all other ways, VBR.1 and VBR.2 are identical.

VBR.3

The most commonly used VBR policing type, VBR.3, also uses a dual leaky bucket model, as shown in Figure 6-7. The first bucket checks all cells and discards any that are noncompliant. The second bucket polices cells with CLP = 0 only and tags any noncompliant cells with CLP = 1. Cells already tagged with CLP = 1 are not checked on the second leaky bucket because they cannot be tagged again. VBR.3 is similar to VBR.2, except that cells are tagged, not dropped on the second leaky bucket.

Figure 6-6 *VBR.2 Traffic Policing*

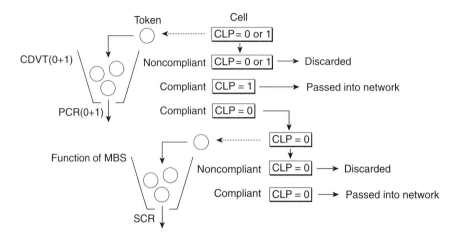

Figure 6-7 *VBR.3 Traffic Policing*

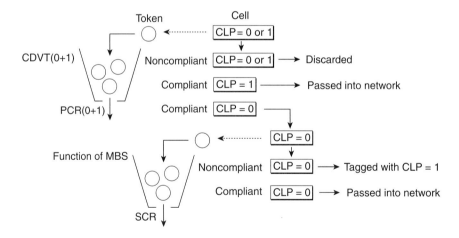

VBR Policing Results

The results of VBR policing can be summarized as shown in Figure 6-8. This figure shows the cell rates over time and how they are treated by the network for a VBR.3 connection if the cell arrival rate is greater than the configured PCR.

Figure 6-8 *VBR Policing Results When ABR Is Greater Than PCR*

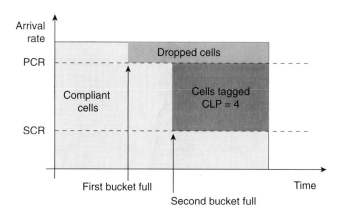

Figure 6-9 shows the results of policing a VBR.3 connection when the arrival rate is less than the configured PCR. Notice that no cells are dropped in this example because the first leaky bucket never fills up at a rate less than the PCR.

Figure 6-9 *VBR Policing Results When ABR Is Less Than PCR*

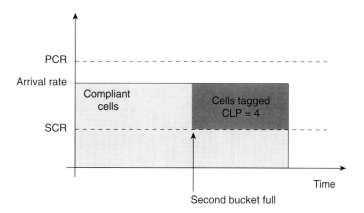

ABR Traffic Policing

ABR connections, both standard and with the ForeSight feature, are policed in exactly the same fashion as VBR connections based on the policing type selected for the connection. Figure 6-10 shows the policing model for an ABR connection using policing type 3. Notice that the cells, unlike those on a VBR connection, are put into a virtual circuit (VC) queue after being subjected to admission control. The VC queue is used to shape ABR traffic based on network availability.

Figure 6-10 *ABR Traffic Policing*

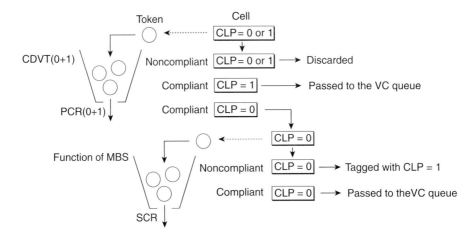

UBR Traffic Policing

UBR connections are policed using a single or dual leaky bucket, either with or without CLP tagging enabled. A UBR connection with CLP tagging enabled uses a second leaky bucket, as shown in Figure 6-11.

Figure 6-11 *UBR with CLP Tagging*

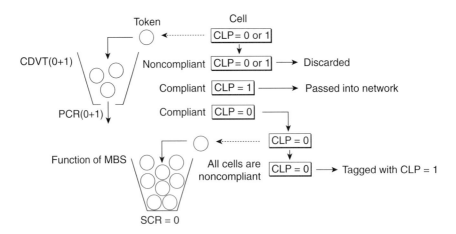

If a UBR connection is configured with CLP tagging enabled, it is policed like a VBR.3 connection with an SCR of 0 cells per second. As a result, all cells are tagged with CLP = 1 on the second leaky bucket, giving them a low priority in the network.

A UBR connection with CLP tagging disabled does not use the second leaky bucket, as shown in Figure 6-12. Similar to CBR connections, only the first leaky bucket is used for policing, and all noncompliant cells are dropped.

Figure 6-12 *UBR Without CLP Tagging*

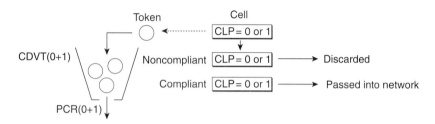

Frame-Based Traffic Control

Frame-based traffic control (FBTC) is a mechanism that lets an ATM device discard part or all of an AAL5 frame based on predefined criteria. FBTC can be enabled or disabled on all VBR, ABR, and UBR connections.

In general, if part of a frame is discarded, the rest of the frame has no value to the destination device and should also be discarded. Because the destination device depends on the last cell from a frame to delineate between frames, in most cases, this cell is not dropped and is sent to its final destination.

Within the cell header, the third bit of the PTI field identifies the location of that cell within the original frame. If the bit is a 0, the cell is either the beginning or continuation of a frame. If the bit is a 1, the cell marks the end of the frame.

The UXM supports the following implementations of FBTC:

- **Partial packet discard (PPD)**—If a cell must be discarded due to congestion, PPD ensures that subsequent cells of the frame, except for the last (marked in the PTI field), are also discarded. PPD is implemented on UXM trunk cards and line cards at the egress queues.

- **Early packet discard (EPD)**—If congestion occurs at the beginning of a frame, the entire frame, including the last cell, is discarded. EPD is implemented on UXM trunk cards and line cards at the egress queues. The EPD threshold is numerically the same value as the configured CLP low threshold on a UXM port queue.

- **Frame-based generic cell rate algorithm (FGCRA)**—The UXM card, on ingress, implements PPD as the result of discarded cells due to policing.

ABR Flow Control

ABR is a closed-loop flow-control mechanism that reacts to network congestion states, as illustrated in Figure 6-13. The UXM card supports standards-based or ForeSight-based ABR.

Figure 6-13   *Available Bit Rate*

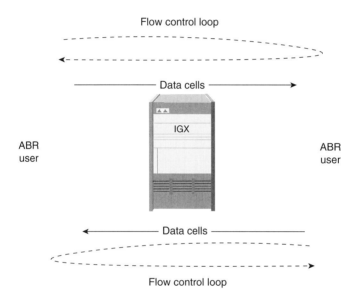

Each ABR device must examine the congestion indicator in the resource management (RM) cell payload or the explicit forward congestion indication bit. If congestion exists, the user must reduce the current cell rate in that direction.

VC Queuing for ABR Traffic

For each ABR connection, an ingress VC queue buffers the cells after they are policed, as illustrated in Figure 6-14.

Figure 6-14 *VC Queuing for ABR Traffic*

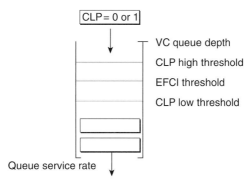

The purpose of the VC queue is to shape the traffic as it enters the network. The congestion measurement and rate notification information determine the rate at which the VC queue is serviced.

The VC queue has the following characteristics:

- **VQ queue depth**—The size of the VC queue, in cells, up to 64,000. When the VC queue reaches its configured depth, all arriving cells are discarded.

- **CLP high threshold**—Determines when to start dropping CLP tagged (CLP 1) cells. When the VC queue reaches the CLP high threshold, all arriving cells with CLP 1 are dropped. Any cells already in the queue, regardless of the CLP bit, are not dropped. The CLP high threshold is configured as a percentage of the VC queue depth.

- **CLP low threshold**—Determines when to stop dropping CLP tagged cells. After the VC queue reaches the CLP high threshold, CLP tagged cells continue to be dropped until the queue has been emptied to the level determined by the CLP low threshold. The CLP low threshold is configured as a percentage of the VC queue depth.

- **EFCI threshold**—Determines congestion marking. When the VC queue reaches the EFCI threshold, all arriving cells into the VC queue have their EFCI bit set to 1 to notify other nodes or ABR users of congestion. The EFCI threshold is configured as a percentage of the VC queue depth.

Congestion Control Segments

A *segment* is a portion of a connection that can be managed separately from other segments. At each end of a segment are a virtual source (VS) and a virtual destination (VD). The VS and VD might not be the actual endpoints of the connection, but they are considered endpoints of the congestion control segment. In the simplest case, an ATM connection has one segment between the PVC terminating devices and, therefore, a VS and VD at each end. In the second case, the connection is viewed as three segments—two outside the IGX network at either end, and one inside the IGX network (see Figure 6-15).

Figure 6-15 *Congestion Control Segments*

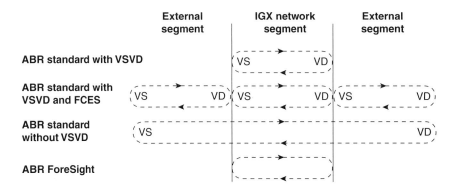

It is possible to have many segments within a single PVC, especially when other networks, public or private, are involved with transporting traffic end-to-end.

The following characteristics can be set for an ABR connection:

- Connection type

    — **ABRFST**—An ABRFST connection uses ForeSight control bits to report congestion control information.

    — **ABRSTD**—Standard ABR uses RM control cells to report congestion control information.

- **Virtual source/virtual destination (VS/VD)**—When a standard ABR connection is defined with VS/VD, the connection's terminating UXM ports become virtual sources and destinations. If VS/VD is not enabled, the IGX network is simply part of a larger connection segment in which the VS and VD are external to the network. VS/VD can be enabled only on ABR standard connections.

- **Flow control external segments (FCES)**—In a multisegment environment, the IGX service node can view the external segment as having another VS and VD. If this is the case, congestion control messaging occurs toward the end-user equipment as well as within the IGX network.

Standard ABR

Standard ABR uses an RM cell to measure and report network conditions to determine the virtual circuit queue service rate, as illustrated in Figure 6-16. Periodically, the source sends an RM cell in the data stream to the destination. Along the way, the IGX network might alter bits in the RM cell to report network conditions and availability. The destination, when it receives the RM cell, turns it around and sends it back to the source.

Figure 6-16 *RM Cell Format*

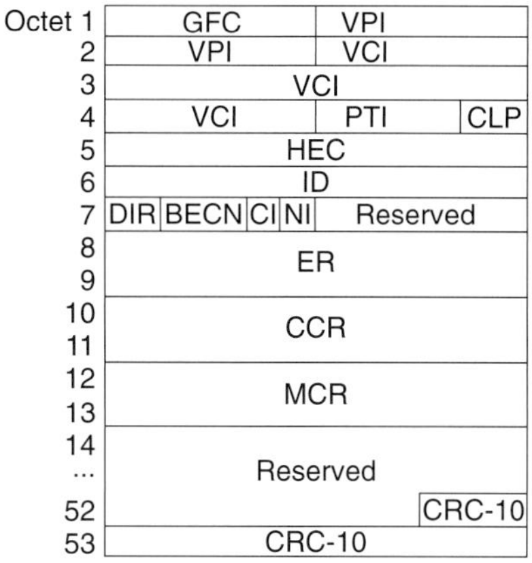

```
Octet 1 |   GFC    |     VPI     |
      2 |   VPI    |     VCI     |
      3 |         VCI            |
      4 |   VCI    | PTI   | CLP |
      5 |         HEC           |
      6 |          ID           |
      7 |DIR|BECN|CI|NI| Reserved |
      8 |                        |
      9 |          ER            |
     10 |                        |
     11 |         CCR            |
     12 |                        |
     13 |         MCR            |
     14 |                        |
     ... |       Reserved        |
     52 |              |CRC-10    |
     53 |         CRC-10         |
```

The source, when it receives the RM cell, is required to adjust the queue service rate accordingly.

The fields in the RM cell are as follows:

- **Generic flow control (GFC)**—Always set to 0000.

- **VPI**—The same VPI that the connection uses.

- **VCI**—If the connection is a virtual channel connection, the VCI is the same as the connection uses. If the connection is a virtual path connection, the VCI is 6.

- **Payload type identifier (PTI)**—Always set to 110 for RM cells.

- **CLP**—Set to 0 for in-rate RM cells and set to 1 for out-of-rate RM cells.

- **Header error control (HEC)**—An 8-bit cyclic redundancy check (CRC) on the cell header only.

- **Protocol identifier (ID)**—Set to hexadecimal 1 for a standard ATM RM cell and set to hexadecimal FF for an STI supervisory cell.

- **Direction (DIR)**—Determines the direction of the cell—either from source to destination (set to 1) or destination to source (set to 0).

- **Backward explicit congestion notification (BECN)**—Determines whether the cell is a switch-generated backward congestion cell (set to 1) or not (set to 0). A BECN RM cell is generated by a network element and is used to notify the source of congestion. A BECN cell must have either the congestion indicator (CI) or no increase (NI) set to 1.

- **Congestion indicator (CI)**—The network sets the CI bit to 1 if the RM cell experiences congestion.

- **No increase (NI)**—The NI bit is set to 1 by a network element that cannot allow the connection to increase in rate.

- **Explicit rate (ER)**—In most cases, the RM cell reports whether a connection can increase or decrease its rate. A network element might define an ER to tell the source to use a particular rate.

- **Current cell rate (CCR)**—Placed in the RM cell by the source, the CCR is the rate currently being used for the connection.

- **Minimum Cell Rate (MCR)**—Placed in the RM cell by the source, the MCR is the configured minimum allowable rate for the connection.

- **CRC-10**—A 10-bit error detection field on the entire cell.

- **Reserved**—Some bits might be defined but are not implemented or are reserved for future use.

The virtual source sends RM cells based on several parameters, some of which are configurable per connection:

- **Number per RM (NRM)**—The NRM value determines the maximum number of cells a source can send for each forward RM cell. In other words, an RM cell must be sent for every NRM-1 data cell. The NRM is configured per PVC.

- **Time RM (TRM)**—The maximum time between RM cells is defined by the TRM, which can be configured per connection.

- **Fixed round-trip time (FRTT)**—The amount of time it takes for an RM cell to travel through the network from the source to the destination and back again. The FRTT is configurable per connection.

- **Transient buffer exposure (TBE)**—The number of cells that can initially be sent by the source before it must wait for a BRM cell from the network. The TBE is configurable per PVC.

- **Tagged cell rate (TCR)**—The rate at which the source can send out-of-rate RM cells. Out-of-rate RM cells are cells that exceed the allowed cell rate (ACR). They are always tagged with a CLP of 1. The TCR cannot be configured and is set to 10 cells per second.

ABR Implementation on the UXM

The source UXM line card is the card that receives ATM user traffic from the line. It is responsible for the following:

- **Virtual circuit queue**—Buffers incoming data for traffic shaping. The VC queue receives Backward RM (BRM) cells from the network and adjusts the VC queue service rate based on congestion information. If FCES is enabled and the VC queue has exceeded the CLP high threshold, No Increase (NI) in the RM cell from the external segment is set to 1, and ER = ACR – (ACR/16). If FCES is enabled and the VC queue is less than the CLP low threshold, ER = ACR + (ACR/16).

- Turns RM cells back toward the external segment if FCES is enabled.

As a result of measuring and reporting congestion utilizing RM and BRM cells, the source UXM card must adjust the VC queue service rate accordingly.

ABRSTD Rate Adjustment

As BRM cells are received by the source device, the VC queue service rate is adjusted accordingly, as illustrated in Figure 6-17.

Figure 6-17 *ABRSTD Rate Adjustment*

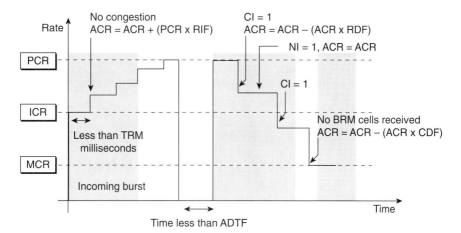

The following parameters apply to the ABRSTD rate adjustment:

- **PCR**—The maximum rate at which the source can generate traffic into the network.

- **CRM**—Cutoff RM is the maximum number of RM cells that can be sent before a BRM returns. CRM is not a user-configurable parameter. It is calculated by the system using CRM = (TBE/NRM).

- **MCR**—The minimum rate at which the source can generate traffic into the network.

- **Initial cell rate (ICR)**—The rate at which the source transmits traffic after an idle period defined by the allowed-cell-rate decreased time factor (ADTF).

- **ADTF**—The time between RM cells before the source rate returns to the ICR.

- **TRM**—The maximum time between RM cells.

- **Rate Increase Factor (RIF)**—A percentage that determines the rate increase when there is no congestion.

- **Rate Decrease Factor (RDF)**—A percentage that determines the rate decrease when there is congestion.

- **Cutoff Decrease Factor (CDF)**—A percentage that determines the rate decrease when BRM cells are not being received from the network.

- **Allowed Cell Rate (ACR)**—The current rate in cells per second at which a source is allowed to send.

ABR ForeSight Rate Adjustments

ABR ForeSight connections use ForeSight FFCI and CC bits to adjust the VC queue service rate. Table 6-5 lists the conditions necessary for the ForeSight feature to declare a congested, severely congested, or not congested condition.

Table 6-5   *ABR ForeSight Conditions and States*

Conditions	Congestion Control State
Last sampled data cell, FFCI = 1	Congestion
VC queue > EFCN threshold	Congestion
Last sampled data cell, FFCI = 1, and VC queue > queue depth	Severe congestion
Last sampled data cell, FFCI = 0, and VC queue < EFCN threshold	No congestion

Table 6-6 describes the adjustments made by the source card depending on the CC message received.

Table 6-6 *ForeSight Congestion Control and Results*

Congestion Control	Result
Congestion	New ACR = ACR × RDF
Severe congestion	New ACR = ACR × CDF
No congestion	New ACR = ACR + RIF

ABRFST Rate Adjustment

As congestion control information is received by the source device, the VC queue service rate is adjusted accordingly, as illustrated in Figure 6-18.

Figure 6-18 *ABRFST Rate Adjustment*

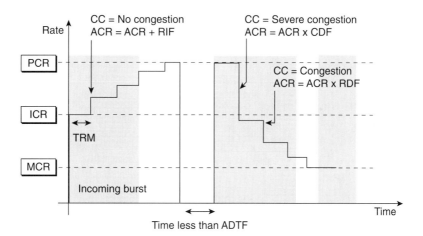

The following parameters apply to the ABRFST rate adjustment:

- **PCR**—The maximum rate at which the source can generate traffic into the network.
- **ICR**—The rate at which the source transmits traffic after an idle period defined by the ADTF.
- **MCR**—The minimum rate at which the source can generate traffic into the network.
- **ADTF**—The idle timeout period before the source rate returns to the ICR.
- **TRM**—The maximum time between RM cells.

- **RIF**—A percentage that determines the rate increase when there is no congestion.
- **RDF**—A percentage that determines the rate decrease when there is congestion.
- **CDF**—A percentage that determines the rate decrease when BRM cells are not being received from the network.

ATM Connection Commands

Table 6-7 introduces new commands for this section and reintroduces others that were discussed in previous chapters.

Table 6-7 *ATM Connection Commands*

Command	Description	Privilege Levels
addcon	Creates a connection across the IGX network by specifying all connection parameters.	1 and 2
delcon	Removes the specified connection from the network.	1 and 2
cnfcls	Modifies the parameters associated with a Frame Relay or ATM class.	1 and 2
dspcls	Displays all Frame Relay and ATM classes in the network.	1 and 2
dspcon	Displays the specified node connection.	1 through 6
dspcons	Displays all node connections.	1 through 6
cnfcon	Modifies the connection parameters.	1 and 2

addcon Command

Example 6-8 shows the **addcon** command used to add CBR connections.

Example 6-8 **addcon** *Output*

```
igx1           TN      group1:1         IGX 8420  9.2.20    Sep. 13 1999 11:40 CDT

 From           Remote        Remote
 9.1.5.100      NodeName      Channel        State  Type    Compress   Code COS
 9.1.5.100      igx4          9.1.5.101      Ok     cbr                      0



 Last Command: addcon 9.1.5.100 igx4 9.1.5.101 cbr 5000/3000 * * * Y


 Next Command:
```

Here is the general **addcon** command syntax:

```
addcon <local-channel> <remote-node> <remote-channel> <connection-class-or-type>
  [connection-parameters] [route-avoid]
```

The **addcon** command for an ATM connection differs quite a bit from an **addcon** used for a Frame Relay connection, because the connection class is not a required parameter.

Table 6-8 describes the parameters used with the **addcon** command.

Table 6-8 addcon *Command Parameter Descriptions*

Parameter	Description
local-channel	The local channel is identified as *<slot.port.VPI.VCI>* for a VC switched connection and as *<slot.port.VPI.*>* for VP switched connections.
remote-node	The name of the destination node.
remote-channel	The local channel is identified as *<slot.port.VPI.VCI>* for a VC switched connection and as *<slot.port.VPI.*>* for VP switched connections.
connection-class	The ATM connection class, numbered 1 to 10. The class defines many of the parameters associated with the connection. You can list the classes using the **dspcls** command.
connection-type	The type of connection to be added: CBR, nrt-VBR, rt-VBR, ABRSTD, ABRFST, or UBR.
connection-parameters	If a connection type is used instead of a connection class, each appropriate connection parameter must be entered during the **addcon** command. Most of the connection-specific parameters can be entered as a single number that applies the same value to the local and remote sides. To apply different values to each end, enter the local value followed by a slash, and then the remote value—for example, 10/50. Detailed descriptions of all connection-specific parameters are provided next.
route-avoid	Restricts the connection from routing over certain types of trunks.

Here is the **addcon** command syntax:

```
addcon <local-channel> <remote-node> <remote-channel> cbr <PCR(0+1)>
  <percent-utilization> <CDVT(0+1)> <policing-type> [route-avoid]
```

Table 6-9 describes the parameters used with the **addcon** command for CBR.

Table 6-9 **addcon** *Command Parameter Descriptions for CBR*

addcon CBR Parameters	Description
PCR(0+1)	The PCR is the maximum rate for all cells (CLP = 0 and 1) on the connection in cells per second.
percent-utilization	The percent utilization is used when determining the necessary bandwidth for a connection. CBR connections require PCR × *percent-utilization* cells per second of bandwidth on a trunk in order to route through the network.
CDVT(0+1)	The CDVT for all cells (CLP = 0 and 1) is used to police the connection. CDVT is defined in the range 1 to 250,000 microseconds.
policing-type	The policing type for a CBR connection can be either 4 or 5. Type 4 uses a single leaky bucket and discards all noncompliant cells. Type 5 disables all policing functions.

Example 6-9 shows the **addcon** command used to add VBR connections.

Example 6-9 **addcon** *Output*

```
igx1            TN    group1:1       IGX 8420  9.2.20     Sep. 13 1999 11:43 CDT

From            Remote      Remote
9.1.10.200      NodeName    Channel        State  Type       Compress    Code COS
9.1.10.200      igx3        9.2.27.333     Ok     nrt-vbr                      0




Last Command: addcon 9.1.10.200 igx3 9.2.27.333 nrt-vbr 10000 30 50000 e 3000 50 * y

Next Command:
```

Here is the **addcon** command syntax:

```
addcon <local-channel> <remote-node> <remote-channel> nrt-vbr <PCR(0+1)>
   <percent-utilization> <CDVT(0+1)> <FBTC> <SCR> <MBS> <policing-type> [route-avoid]
```

The **addcon** parameters that are specific to nrt-VBR and rt-VBR connections are listed in Table 6-10.

Table 6-10   addcon *Command Parameter Descriptions for VBR*

addcon VBR Parameters	Description
FBTC	Enables or disables frame-based traffic control.
SCR	The average rate of cells that will be compliant on the second leaky bucket. The SCR must be equal to or less than the PCR. It is defined in cells per second.
MBS	Defines the number of cells that are compliant on the second leaky bucket if the cells are arriving at the PCR. The MBS is defined as a number of cells.
policing-type	The policing type for a VBR connection. Can be set to 1, 2, 3, 4, or 5.

Example 6-10 shows the **addcon** command used to add ABRFST connections.

Example 6-10 addcon *Output*

```
igx1            TN    group1:1      IGX 8420  9.2.20     Sep. 13 1999 11:48 CDT

From            Remote      Remote
9.1.15.450      NodeName    Channel         State  Type      Compress    Code COS
9.1.15.450      igx2        9.2.100.3000    Ok     abrfst                     0




Last Command: addcon 9.1.15.450 igx2 9.2.100.3000 abrfst 10000 * 1000 * * * d 30
00 500 * * 90 60 50 3000 * * 200 90 n

Next Command:
```

Here is the **addcon** command syntax:

```
addcon <local-channel> <remote-node> <remote-channel> abrfst <PCR(0+1)>
   <percent-utilization> <MCR> <CDVT(0+1)> <FBTC> <FCES> <default-parameters>
   <SCR> <MBS> <policing-type> <VC-queue-depth> <CLP-high> <CLP-low> <EFCI> <ICR>
   <ADTF> <Trm> <RIF> <RDF> [route-avoid]
```

The **addcon** parameters that are specific to ABRFST connections are listed in Table 6-11.

Table 6-11   addcon *Command Parameter Descriptions for ABRFST*

Parameter	Description
MCR	The MCR used by the ForeSight algorithm. The MCR must be equal to or less than the PCR.
FCES	Determines whether a congestion control loop is used outside the IGX network. For ForeSight connections, this should be disabled.
default-parameters	If this is enabled, defaults are used for all subsequent ABRFST connection parameters, and the command is complete. If it is disabled, subsequent parameters must be entered for the connection.
policing-type	The policing type for an ABRFST connection can be set to 1, 2, 3, 4, or 5.
VC-queue-depth	The size of the ingress VC queue used for traffic shaping. The VC queue depth is configured in cells. It can be the same or different at each end of the connection.
CLP-high	The high threshold on the VC queue for determining when to discard CLP tagged cells. *CLP-high* is configured as a percentage of the VC queue depth.
CLP-low	The low threshold on the VC queue for determining when to stop discarding CLP tagged cells. *CLP-low* is configured as a percentage of the VC queue depth and must be less than the *CLP-high* threshold.
EFCI	The EFCI threshold determines when to start marking the EFCI congestion bit on incoming cells. The EFCI threshold is configured as a percentage of the VC queue depth.
ICR	The starting queue service rate after an idle period. The ICR must be less than or equal to the PCR and greater than or equal to the MCR.
ADTF	Defines the idle time necessary to return the queue service rate to the ICR. The ADTF is defined in milliseconds.
Trm	The time between RM cells. For ForeSight connections, the TRM determines the time period between CC messages from the destination to the source. The TRM is entered in milliseconds.
RIF	Determines how much to increase the queue service rate if the connection is not congested.
RDF	Determines how much to decrease the queue service rate if the connection is congested.

Example 6-11 shows the **addcon** command used to add ABRSTD connections.

Example 6-11 addcon *Output*

```
igx3            TN    group1:1        IGX 8420  9.2.20    Sep. 13 1999 11:54 CDT

From            Remote      Remote
9.1.30.1000     NodeName    Channel         State  Type     Compress    Code COS
9.1.30.1000     igx4        9.1.30.1500     Ok     abrstd                     0




Last Command: addcon 9.1.30.1000 igx4 9.1.30.1500 abrstd 5000 * 500 * e e d d 30
00 500 * 15000 90 70 50 1500 * * * 17 35 * 50000 n

Next Command:
```

Here is the **addcon** command syntax:

```
addcon <local-channel> <remote-node> <remote-channel> abrstd <PCR(0+1)>
    <percent-utilization> <MCR> <CDVT(0+1)> <FBTC> <VSVD> <FCES>
    <default-parameters> <SCR> <MBS> <policing-type> <VC-queue-depth>
    <CLP-high> <CLP-low> <EFCI> <ICR> <ADTF> <Trm> <RIF> <RDF> <Nrm>
    <FRTT> <TBE> [route-avoid]
```

The **addcon** parameters that are specific to ABRSTD connections are listed in Table 6-12.

Table 6-12   addcon *Command Parameter Descriptions for ABRSTD*

Parameter	Description
VSVD	Enables or disables VS/VD. If this is enabled, the UXM line card is a VS/VD. If this is disabled, the UXM line card is considered an intermediate hop, and the VS and VD are external to the IGX network. When VS/VD is disabled, all subsequent parameters are invalid, and the command is complete.
RIF	Determines how much to increase the queue service rate if the connection is not congested.
RDF	Determines how much to decrease the queue service rate if the connection is congested.
Nrm	The maximum number of data cells between RM cells.
FRTT	The sum of the fixed and propagation delays through the BPX network.
TBE	Determines the number of cells that can be sent by the source before the first RM cell returns from the destination.

Example 6-12 shows the **addcon** command used to add UBR connections.

Example 6-12 addcon *Output*

```
igx1            TN    group1:1        IGX 8420  9.2.20    Sep. 13 1999 11:50 CDT

From            Remote      Remote
9.1.20.500      NodeName    Channel        State  Type     Compress    Code COS
9.1.20.500      igx4        9.1.20.500     Ok     ubr                       0




Last Command: addcon 9.1.20.500 igx4 9.1.20.500 ubr 10000 5 * e e n


Next Command:
```

Here is the **addcon** command syntax:

> **addcon** *<local-channel>* *<remote-node>* *<remote-channel>* ubr *<PCR(0+1)>*
>   *<percent-utilization>* *<CDVT(0+1)>* *<FBTC>* *<CLP-setting>*

The **addcon** parameters that are specific to UBR connections are listed in Table 6-13.

Table 6-13   addcon *Command Parameter Descriptions for UBR*

Parameter	Description
percent-utilization	The percent utilization for UBR connections is often set very low. The default value is 1 percent.
CLP-setting	Enables or disables CLP tagging during the UBR policing process. If this is disabled, the second leaky bucket is disabled, and no cells are tagged by the UXM with a CLP of 1. If it is enabled, the second leaky bucket is defined with an SCR of 0 cells per second, and all cells are tagged.

delcon Command

As described in Chapter 5, the **delcon** command removes connections from the network. After the command is issued, the connection is highlighted in the screen display. A "delcon xx.x y/n" prompt appears to confirm the deletion.

Connections can be deleted from the node at either end of the connection. Do not delete a connection when the node at the other end of the connection is unreachable, because the unreachable node will not recognize the deletion. It is especially important not to delete a connection to an unreachable node and then connect that channel to another node.

Here is the **delcon** command syntax:

> **delcon** *<connection>*

cnfcls Command

The **cnfcls** command, described in Chapter 5, modifies a network-wide Frame Relay or ATM connection class. Ten classes are available for each category. A Frame Relay or ATM class is relevant only at the time you add a connection with **addcon**.

Here is the **cnfcls** command syntax:

```
cnfcls <atm | fr> <class-number> [parameters in order shown on screen]
```

dspcls Command

The **dspcls** command, described in Chapter 5, displays the configuration of an ATM or Frame Relay connection class. You can use a connection class as a template when you add a new ATM connection.

Here is the **dspcls** command syntax:

```
dspcls <atm | fr>
```

With the *atm | fr* parameter, enter **atm** to display the ATM connection classes or **fr** to display the Frame Relay classes.

dspcon Command

The **dspcon** command, described in Chapter 5, provides detailed information on a given connection.

Here is the **dspcon** command syntax:

```
dspcon <connection>
```

connection is the ATM or Frame Relay connection identifier.

dspcons Command

The **dspcons** command, described in Chapter 5, displays the summary status information for connections terminating on a node.

Here is the **dspcons** command syntax:

```
dspcons
```

cnfcon Command

The **cnfcon** command, described in Chapter 5, modifies the parameters associated with a Frame Relay or ATM connection.

Here is the **cnfcon** command syntax:

```
cnfcon <connection>
```

References

Table 6-14 lists standards and organizations associated with protocols and standards mentioned in this book.

Table 6-14 *ISO, IETF, and Frame Relay Forum References*

Reference	Organization	Title
FRF 3.1	Frame Relay Forum	Multiprotocol Encapsulation over Frame Relay Implementation Agreement
FRF 5	Frame Relay Forum	Frame Relay/ATM PVC Network Interworking Implementation Agreement
FRF 8	Frame Relay Forum	Frame Relay/ATM PVC Service Interworking Implementation Agreement
RFC 1483	IETF	Multiprotocol Encapsulation over ATM Adaptation Layer 5
RFC 1490	IETF	Multiprotocol Interconnect over Frame Relay
TR 9577	ISO	Protocol Identification in the Network Layer

Interworking ATM and Frame Relay

To better understand the ATM and Frame Relay interworking concepts presented in this section, this section offers a review of network and service interworking.

Network interworking (NIW) carries traffic between Frame Relay users over an ATM network; *service interworking (SIW)* carries Frame Relay traffic between Frame Relay and ATM users.

The encapsulation of FastPackets inside ATM cells, with an industry-standard header and a payload consisting of either one or two 24-byte FastPackets, is known in the IGX as the *simple gateway* process.

Frame Relay frames are converted to FastPackets to travel over the Cellbus. ATM trunks may perform a *complex gateway* function to remove the FastPacket headers and carry the Frame Relay frames directly on top of ATM Adaptation Layer 5 (AAL5) messages.

ATM-Frame Relay connections carry traffic between devices supporting different message structures and capabilities. Although both ATM and Frame Relay support virtual connections, ATM also supports substantially different queuing schemes and bandwidth. An interworking function must translate ATM and Frame Relay characteristics. The interworking ATM and Frame Relay function is illustrated in Figure 6-19.

Figure 6-19 *Interworking ATM and Frame Relay*

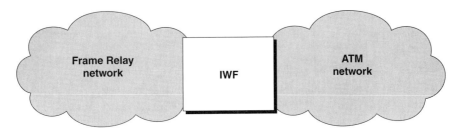

IWF—Interworking Function

The conversion between ATM and Frame Relay occurs on the ingress UXM, UFM, or FRM front card or on complex gateway trunk cards.

In addition, ATM-Frame Relay connections might terminate on a BPX ASI or BXM card or an MGX AUSM or FRSM card. BPX operation is covered in Part III of this book; MGX operation is covered in Part IV.

Figure 6-20 illustrates several elements of interworking ATM and Frame Relay, including common part convergence sublayer (CPCS), Frame Relay service-specific convergence sublayer (FR-SSCS), Interworking Unit (IWU), Link Access Procedure Frame Relay (LAP-FR), and segmentation and reassembly (SAR) sublayer.

Figure 6-20 *Interworking ATM and Frame Relay Elements*

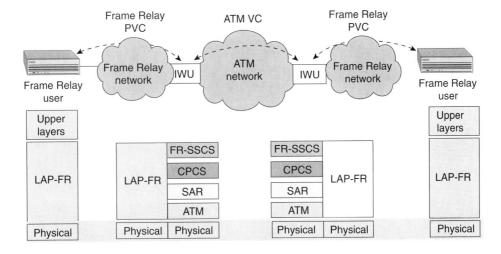

ATM networks can serve as a backbone for Frame Relay traffic or can connect ATM and Frame Relay users. Frame Relay traffic is converted to ATM (and vice versa) by a function called the IWU. The interworking function is performed by IGX trunk or service front cards. Messages are converted from Frame Relay to ATM formats via network or service interworking.

Network interworking carries traffic between Frame Relay users over an ATM network. The data link connection identifier (DLCI) and other Frame Relay information is preserved inside AAL5 frames and is then segmented into cell payloads. Refer to Chapter 14, "Configuring ATM Connections and Routing AutoRoute Connections," for an illustration of network interworking.

Frame Relay Service-Specific Convergence Sublayer

Network interworking relies on the FR-SSCS to carry Frame Relay (DLCI) information inside AAL5 frames, as shown in Figure 6-21. This function is performed for all Frame Relay connections on complex gateway (ATM) trunk cards.

Figure 6-21 *Service-Specific Convergence Sublayer*

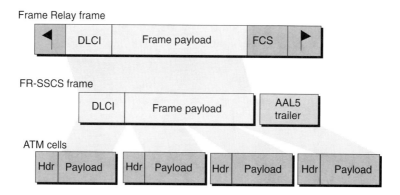

You can also set up ATM-Frame Relay network interworking connections using the **addcon** command.

- An FR-SSCS message is the same as a Frame Relay frame without the flags and frame check sequence (FCS).

- The FR-SSCS message is placed inside an AAL5 frame.

- The AAL5 frame is segmented into cell payloads. If necessary, the last cell payload in the message is padded to 48 bytes.

Service Interworking

Service interworking (SIW), illustrated in Figure 6-22, carries Frame Relay traffic between Frame Relay and ATM users. The DLCI and other Frame Relay information is removed and converted to the equivalent ATM function.

Figure 6-22 *Service Interworking*

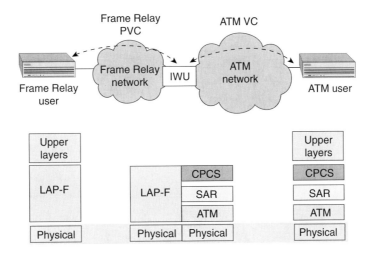

In addition, the multiprotocol encapsulation header inside the data portion of the frame may be translated to the ATM encapsulation header format. The service interworking function is performed by IGX service front cards.

Transparent and Translational Service Interworking

For SIW transparent connections, illustrated in Figure 6-23, the IGX front cards *convert* Frame Relay header information to ATM and vice versa. The DLCI is mapped to a virtual path identifier/virtual channel identifier (VPI/VCI) combination, the discard eligible (DE) bit is mapped to ATM's cell loss priority (CLP) bit, and the forward explicit congestion notification (FECN) bit is mapped to the Explicit Forward Congestion Indication (EFCI) bit.

Service interworking translational connections perform the same conversions but also convert the Frame Relay encapsulation header to the corresponding ATM format.

Figure 6-23 *Service Interworking for Transparent Connections*

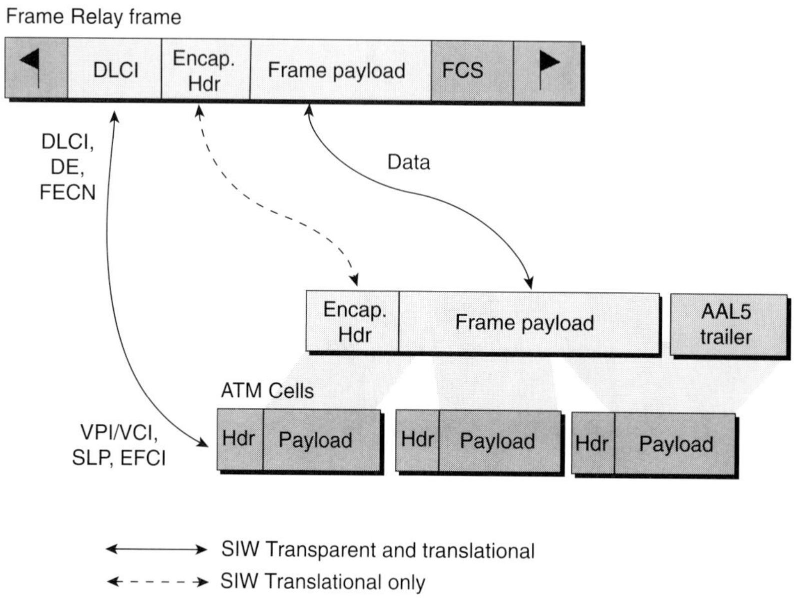

Frame Relay frame

| ◀ | DLCI | Encap. Hdr | Frame payload | FCS | ▶ |

DLCI, DE, FECN

Data

| Encap. Hdr | Frame payload | AAL5 trailer |

ATM Cells

VPI/VCI, SLP, EFCI

| Hdr | Payload | | Hdr | Payload | | Hdr | Payload |

◀──────▶ SIW Transparent and translational

◀ - - - - ▶ SIW Translational only

Gateway to ATM Connections

The IGX BTM, ALM/B, and UXM cards must perform a simple or complex gateway function between FastPacket and ATM networks.

A simple gateway packs two FastPackets into one ATM cell payload for transport across a trunk, as shown in Figure 6-24.

Figure 6-24 *Simple Gateway-to-ATM Connections*

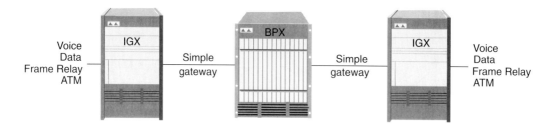

Voice
Data
Frame Relay
ATM

IGX

Simple gateway

BPX

Simple gateway

IGX

Voice
Data
Frame Relay
ATM

A simple gateway is used when FastPacket traffic originates on one IGX routing node and terminates on another. To transport the traffic as quickly as possible, two complete FastPackets from the same connection are placed in the payload of an ATM cell and are forwarded across the network. It takes two FastPackets to build a simple gateway cell.

A complex gateway connection is used when Frame Relay traffic originating on an IGX node terminates on an IGX feeder or MGX shelf, as illustrated in Figure 6-25. The FastPacket header must be removed, and only the packet payload is placed in the ATM cell payload.

Figure 6-25 *Complex Gateway*

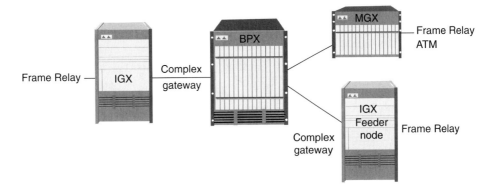

The resulting ATM cells are identical to those created using AAL5 on the MGX FRSM.

Complex gateway connections provide network interworking services for any Frame Relay connections traveling over ATM trunks.

The complex gateway on the BTM, UXM, or ALM/B trunk card is responsible for translating Frame Relay FastPackets into standard AAL5-segmented ATM cells, as illustrated in Figure 6-26. This translation is accomplished by removing the payload from the FastPacket and encapsulating multiple FastPacket payloads into an AAL5 frame.

NOTE   It is not necessary to receive all FastPackets from a frame before beginning the translation to ATM cells.

Figure 6-26 *Complex Gateway Frame-to-Cell Conversion*

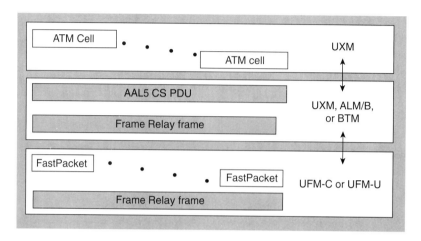

ATM Encapsulation

RFC 1483, "Multiprotocol Encapsulation over AAL5," describes ATM data transport using multiple virtual connections or multiprotocol encapsulation. In either case, messages are placed in AAL5 protocol data units and are then segmented into cells. The concept of ATM encapsulation is illustrated in Figure 6-27.

Figure 6-27 *ATM Encapsulation*

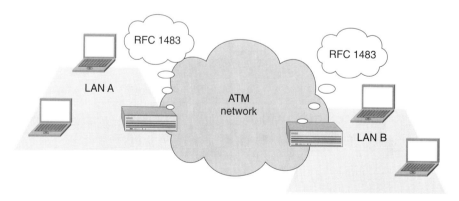

RFC 1483 defines the following encapsulation techniques for ATM:

- Logical Link Control/Subnetwork Access Protocol (LLC/SNAP) encapsulation headers identify routed protocols with the appropriate 2-byte Ethertype values. RFC 1483 extends traditional LLC/SNAP operation to identify bridged LAN protocols using special bridged LAN protocol identifiers. LLC/SNAP is the default encapsulation technique for ATM.

- Logical Link Control/International Standards Organization (LLC/ISO) encapsulation headers identify ISO protocols using a 1-byte Network Layer Protocol Identifier (NLPID). The ISO Network Layer Protocol Identifiers are listed in the ISO TR 9577 standard.

- Q.2931 code points extend LLC/ISO encapsulation by adding Layer 2 and 3 connection-oriented protocol identifiers, as listed in the Q.2931 standard.

- X.25 packets are encapsulated using a special service access point followed by a 2-byte 802.2 LLC Type 2 (connection-oriented) Information Control field. The encapsulating device terminates the LLC conversation, intercepting supervisory messages and requesting retransmissions as necessary.

Frame Relay Encapsulation

FRF 3.1, "Multiprotocol Encapsulation over Frame Relay Implementation Agreement," and RFC 1490, "Multiprotocol Interconnect over Frame Relay," describe encapsulation techniques for Frame Relay. FRF 3.1 does not support multiple virtual connections. The concept of Frame Relay encapsulation is illustrated in Figure 6-28.

Figure 6-28 *Frame Relay Encapsulation*

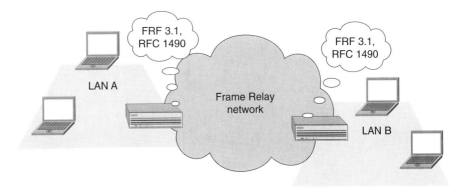

FRF 3.1 defines the following encapsulation techniques for Frame Relay:

- Direct NLPID encapsulation headers identify ISO protocols as listed in the ISO TR 9577 standard. Direct NLPID is the default encapsulation technique for Frame Relay.

- SNAP encapsulation headers identify routed or bridged LAN protocols that do not have an ISO TR 9577 NLPID value.

- Connection-oriented protocols are encapsulated by adding Layer 2 and 3 connection-oriented protocol identifiers, as listed in the Q.933 standard.

- X.25 packets are directly encapsulated into the Frame Relay user data field.

Adding ATM-Frame Relay Connections

The connection types described in Table 6-15 are used when adding ATM-Frame Relay connections. These connection types are described with and without ForeSight.

Table 6-15 *Adding ATM-Frame Relay Connections*

Connection	Connection Type with ForeSight	Connection Type Without ForeSight
NIW	atfr	atfrfst
SIW transparent	atft	atftfst
SIW translational	atfx	atfxfst

NOTE NIW connection types are implied for connections added from the Frame Relay side. Use these connection types for NIW connections added from the ATM side.

Network Interworking

For network interworking, the **addcon** command syntax looks like this:

```
addcon <local-channel> <remote-node> <remote-channel>
  <frcon class | atfr | atfrfst> [atm-parameters]
```

Service Interworking

For service interworking translational and transparent, the **addcon** command syntax looks like this:

```
addcon <local-channel> <remote-node> <remote-channel> <SIW-type>
  <frcon-class | atm-parameters>
```

SIW translational:

```
addcon <local-channel> <remote-node> <remote-channel> <atfx | atfxfst>
    <frcon-class | atm-parameters>
```

SIW transparent:

```
addcon <local-channel> <remote-node> <remote-channel> <atfx | atftfst>
    <frcon-class | atm-parameters>
```

Table 6-16 lists the parameters associated with the **addcon** command for service interworking.

Table 6-16   *Service Interworking* **addcon** *Parameters*

Parameter	Description and Syntax	Required/Optional
local-channel	*slot.port.dlci* (UFM and FRM cards)	Required
	slot.port.vpi.vci (UXM cards)	
remote-node	Destination node name	Required
remote-channel	*slot.port.dlci* (UFM and FRM cards)	Required
	slot.port.vpi.vci (UXM cards)	
SIW-type	SIW translational: atfx (without ForeSight) or atfxfst (with ForeSight)	Required
	SIW transparent: atft (without ForeSight) or atftfst (with ForeSight)	
frcon-class	Frame Relay connection class number 1 to 10 if the connection is added from the Frame Relay side	Required
ATM-parameters	ATM connection parameters if the connection is added from the ATM side	Required

Summary

This chapter showed you how to activate and configure ATM lines and ports, configure port queues, and display port statistics. Given CPE requirements, you should be able to modify ATM line and port characteristics, including ILMI, and analyze ATM port and connection activity.

Displaying, modifying, and creating ATM connections on UXM cards was discussed, along with ATM parameters for CBR, VBR, ABR, and UBR connections. You should be able to describe ATM traffic policing and resource management cell structure and operation.

You should also be able to describe Frame Relay transport over ATM and contrast network and service interworking between ATM and Frame Relay networks. Also, you should be able to compare the encapsulation alternative for ATM and Frame Relay and create and modify ATM-to-Frame Relay connections.

Review Questions

1 Which command lists all ATM and Frame Relay ports?

2 Which command displays port details?

3 Which command activates an ATM port?

4 List the port queues available on a UXM port.

5 Which command modifies ATM port queues?

6 UXM supports which ATM connection types?

7 What three things locally identify an ATM connection associated with a UXM card?

8 Which command establishes an ATM connection between two lines in the network?

9 Which command displays ATM connections?

10 Which command sets the ABR VC queue depth?

11 Which command modifies the percent utilization of the connection bandwidth?

12 What does standards-based ABR use to carry flow control information?

13 Which feature allows an IGX to insert RM cells into a user's traffic stream?

14 True or false: The rate increase factor and rate decrease factor must be the same size.

This chapter covers the following key topics:

- Connection Admission Control
- IGX Commands Used to Configure Routes
- Configuring Routes
- IGX Commands Used for Network Synchronization
- Network Synchronization
- IGX Commands Used to Manage Jobs
- Managing Jobs

Connection Routing, Synchronizing the Network, and Managing Jobs

Efficient use of the IGX network depends on overbooking trunks. This chapter explores the trunk load model and its role in connection bandwidth allocation. It also looks at automatic connection routing and assigning specific routes for connection.

IGX switches must be synchronized to a common network clock to avoid data loss (slips). This chapter describes how to select potential clock sources and discover which clock source is used by the network.

Jobs are user-defined "batch files" or scripts of IGX commands that allow switch administrators to automate simple repetitive actions. This chapter describes how to create, edit, and execute jobs.

Connection Admission Control

As new connections are requested, the IGX checks local and network resources before adding the connection, as illustrated in Figure 7-1. If network resources are not available to meet bandwidth and quality of service (QoS) requirements, the connection is marked "failed."

This Connection Admission Control (CAC) process relies on a database of trunk resources called the *trunk load model*. The load model describes the *expected* amount of traffic on network trunks. The expected traffic is based on the connection rates specified with the **addcon** command and the configured connection percent utilization, not the actual measured traffic rates.

As each connection is routed, the switches allocate bandwidth in the trunk load model to control overbooking. The allocated bandwidth determines how many connections can route over the trunk and how the trunk queues should be serviced. However, the load model has no impact on connection behavior *after* the connection is added. The load model is strictly used to route new connections based on predicted requirements. The **dspload** command displays the current state of the load model.

Figure 7-1 *Connection Admission Control*

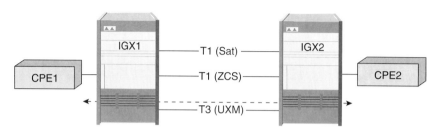

Load Model Versus Actual Utilization

Trunk usage is based on the trunk's instantaneous traffic flow. Because many connections are bursty in nature, they do not always have packets or cells to send. As a result, multiple connections might share the same bandwidth. Bandwidth is offered to traffic as it arrives. Figure 7-2 illustrates the load model versus actual usage.

Figure 7-2 *Load Model Versus Actual Usage*

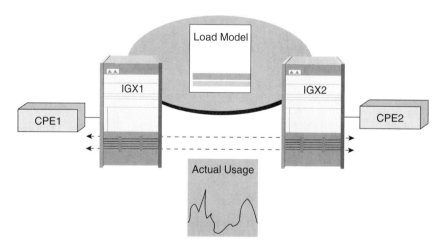

To prevent any type of traffic from taking over the entire trunk bandwidth, the traffic is controlled based on the load model. Packets of a particular type (Voice, TS Data, BDataA, and so on) are serviced from their OptiClass queues based on the expected load. For example, if a large burst of Frame Relay traffic occurs, the voice traffic is still given its allocated portion of the trunk. OptiClass uses a weighted-queue implementation to ensure that each type of traffic has fair access to trunk bandwidth. The weights are dynamic, based on configured connections.

Estimating Connection Load

When you calculate loads in a network, the load allocated to a connection is as follows:

channel utilization × full load for the connection type

For example, with a channel utilization of 50 percent and a full load of 480 packets per second (pps), the load allocated to a connection is

0.50×480 pps $= 240$ pps

The system adds bandwidth to allow for signaling, control leads, and so on. The percent utilization is ignored for a voice channel without voice activity detection (VAD) or a data channel without data frame multiplexing (DFM).

If you use the **cnfchutl** command to increase a connection's utilization, the system verifies that the additional bandwidth is available on the connection's current route. If the bandwidth is unavailable, the system attempts to reroute the connection. If no other route is found, the connection fails.

If you use the **cnfchutl** command to decrease a connection's utilization, the system makes the bandwidth available in the load model to other connections that require a route.

Connection Characteristics

Table 7-1 shows the traffic type, criteria, and bandwidth requirements associated with connection characteristics.

Table 7-1   *Connection Characteristics*

Traffic Type	Criteria	Comments	Bandwidth Requirements
Voice	Voice connection type and VAD	Channel percent utilization is applied if VAD is used.	Without VAD: rate is based on connection type. With VAD: rate × channel percent utilization
Data	Data rate, coding, fast EIA, partially filled packets, DFM	IGX adds overhead to meet coding and other connection requirements. Channel percent utilization is applied if DFM is used.	Without DFM: Data rate / number of data bits per packet. With DFM: data rate / number of data bits per packet × percent utilization

continues

Table 7-1 *Connection Characteristics (Continued)*

Traffic Type	Criteria	Comments	Bandwidth Requirements
Frame Relay	MIR, percent utilization	Traffic studies of Frame Relay connections should be used to determine optimum utilization settings.	MIR × percent utilization
ATM	PCR, MCR, percent utilization	Adjust percent utilization for VBR, ABR, and UBR traffic.	PCR × percent utilization for CBR, VBR, and UBR MCR × percent utilization for ABR

Expected Versus Actual Trunk Loading

Figures 7-3 through 7-5 illustrate the concept of expected versus actual trunk loading.

The load model (expected) in Figure 7-3 shows one connection allocated; the utilization (actual) shows one bursty connection activity (VAD, DFM, Frame Relay, VBR). Both are compared against the other's trunk capacities.

Figure 7-3 *Expected Versus Actual Trunk Loading, Part I*

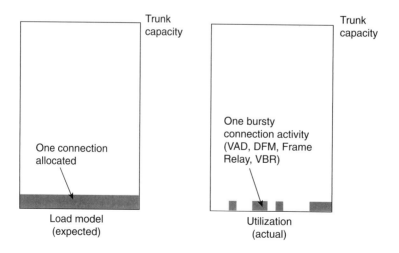

The load model (expected) in Figure 7-4 shows three connections allocated, with the utilization (actual) showing three bursty connection activities. The expected load and actual utilization continue to be compared against each other's trunk capacities.

Figure 7-4   *Expected Versus Actual Trunk Loading, Part 2*

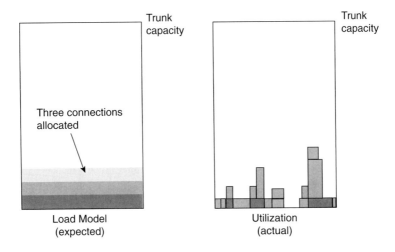

The load model (expected) in Figure 7-5 shows that the sum of all connection bandwidth is equal to the trunk capacity in a fully loaded trunk. Therefore, the trunk cannot route any additional connections. The utilization (actual) shows a white area within the trunk capacity to illustrate wasted bandwidth.

Figure 7-5   *Expected Versus Actual Trunk Loading, Part 3*

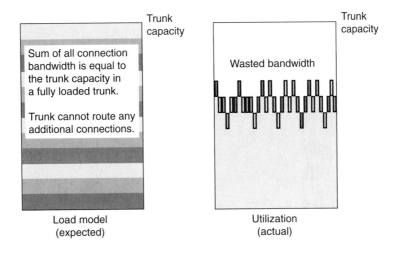

Handling Bursts

What happens if several connections burst beyond their predicted bandwidth? Frame Relay connections are allocated bandwidth based on the *minimum* information rate (MIR). What happens to the connection's cells or FastPackets when it sends at the *peak* information rate (PIR)? You must reserve bandwidth, called the statistical reserve, to accommodate bursting. Figure 7-6 shows what happens when bursts are not accommodated.

Figure 7-6   *Handling Bursts*

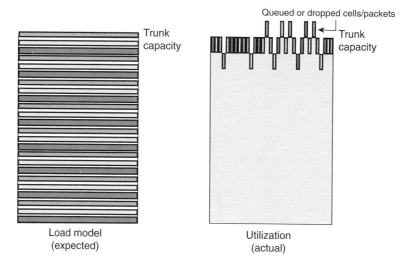

In Figure 7-6, the load model (expected) and utilization (actual) are compared against each other's trunk capacities. The actual utilization shows the rate of queued or dropped cells or packets. A statistical reserve reduces the possibility of dropped packets due to short-term bursts of traffic.

Statistical Reserve

The *statistical reserve*, shown in Figure 7-7, is a portion of bandwidth that cannot be allocated in the load model. The statistical reserve is designed to accommodate statistical variations in the traffic but is not assigned to any specific connection.

The size of the statistical reserve is set with the **cnftrk** command.

The statistical reserve carries the following traffic:

* IGX control traffic

* User traffic bursts

* Resources to allow time for the ForeSight feature to respond to trunk congestion with a low probability of cell loss

Figure 7-7   *Statistical Reserve*

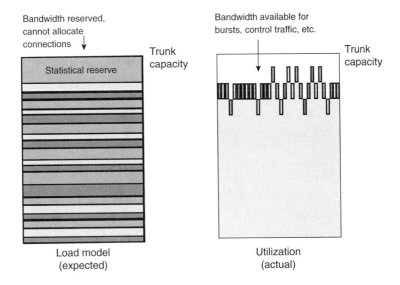

Load model
(expected)

Utilization
(actual)

IGX Commands Used to Configure Routes

Table 7-2 lists the IGX commands that are used to configure routes. IGX route criteria is explained after the table, with output screens showing how these commands are used to configure routes in the network.

Table 7-2   *IGX Commands Used to Configure Routes*

Command	Description	Privilege Level
dspload	Displays the trunk load model for a switch or trunk.	1 to 6
dsptrkutl	Displays a trunk's actual usage.	1 to 6
dsprts	Displays the trunk routing for all connections terminating on a switch.	1 to 6
cnfpref	Configures a preferred route for a connection.	1 and 2
cnfrtcost	Sets a maximum route cost for a connection.	1 and 2
cnfcos	Assigns a class of service to a connection.	1 and 2
dncon	Suspends connection operation and removes the connection from a route.	1 and 2
upcon	Routes a downed connection and restores operation.	1 and 2

Configuring Routes

IGX connection route criteria includes the following:

1 Connection route avoidance

2 Bandwidth availability, including trunk connection IDs and trunk cost (if used)

3 Hop count

4 Avoiding bandwidth bottlenecks

5 Lowest-numbered trunk

The first two criteria, route avoidance and bandwidth requirements, are based on connection characteristics described with the **addcon** command. The other criteria are based on the current load in the load model. Trunk characteristics are controlled by the **cnftrk** command.

Types of Routes

Several types of routes are available on the IGX, including Network-Assigned, Preferred, and Directed.

Network-Assigned Route

When the connection is added, the owning IGX node calculates and assigns the route. The connection remains on this initial route until a new route is selected, the route fails, or the connection is taken out of service.

Preferred Route

A preferred or operator-specified route is configured using the **cnfpref** command. After it is configured, the switch attempts to keep the connection on that preferred route. If the preferred route fails and the connection is rerouted, it returns to the preferred route when the route recovers.

Directed Route

A directed route is a preferred route that does not reroute under any circumstance. If the preferred route is unavailable, the connection fails.

Reasons for Rerouting

There are several reasons for rerouting traffic in a network:

- The current route failed.
- A preferred route is configured.
- A defined preferred route is restored.
- A connection is downed and then upped.

When a trunk fails, all connections utilizing that trunk must find new routes through the network. When a trunk failure is detected, the connection status indicates the following in succession:

1 The connection has been derouted.

2 Looking for a route. The owning switch checks the trunk load model and attempts to reroute the connection.

If the reroute attempt is unsuccessful, the connection goes into a failed status.

When a preferred route is configured using the **cnfpref** command, the connection owner checks to see whether the route is available. If the preferred route is available, the connection is rerouted. If, for any reason, a connection is not using its preferred route (due to a trunk failure, no bandwidth, and so on), and the preferred route becomes available, it reroutes.

When connections are downed using the **dncon** command, they are removed from the current route and remain idle until they are upped using the **upcon** command. When the connection is upped, the node must determine the best available route. The **dncon** command can affect either a single connection or an entire class.

Rules for Rerouting

The class of service (CoS) is how long, in seconds (0 to 15), a connection must wait after a trunk failure before the owning switch attempts to find a new route. In this way, connections may be given an advantage by being assigned a low CoS. The CoS is modified using the **cnfcos** command.

The CoS does not guarantee routing order. Within a class, higher-bandwidth connections are routed before lower-bandwidth connections to increase the probability of rerouting the connection.

As soon as a connection route is determined, the switch checks for other connections that terminate on the same destination node. Multiple connections are then routed simultaneously to speed up the reroute process.

All the connections of one CoS are rerouted before the IGX attempts to reroute the next CoS.

dspload Command

The **dspload** command, shown in Example 7-1, displays the allocated and available transmit and receive bandwidth for each trunk at the specified switch. The transmit direction is from the specified node to the node at the other end of the trunk. Failed trunks appear in dim reverse video on the screen.

Example 7-1   dspload *Output*

```
igx1              TN     group8:1        IGX 8420  9.2.20    July 19 1999 16:18 CDT

Trunk loads for node 'igx1'

        Units     Used              Available        Reserved       Con ID
TRK     Xmt  Rcv  Xmt      Rcv      Xmt      Rcv      Xmt    Rcv     Used  Avail
9.1     Cell Cell    500      550   78500    78450    1000   1000       1   255
9.2     Cell Cell      0        0   79000    79000    1000   1000       0  1000
12      Pkt  Pkt    6992     6685     408     1215     600    100       5   208
13      Pkt  Pkt    7286     7286    2780     2780     600    600       2   211
15      Pkt  Pkt   75000    75000  116000   116000    1000   1000       1  1770




Last Command: dspload


Next Command:
```

The **dspload** command displays the following summary information:

- Trunk number
- **Transmit and receive units**—FastPackets or cells
- **Transmit and receive used**—Bandwidth allocated to connections
- **Transmit and receive available**—Bandwidth available to route additional connections
- **Transmit and receive reserved**—Statistical reserve

Here is the **dspload** command syntax:

```
dspload [node-name] [trunk-id]
```

Table 7-3 describes the command parameters for the **dspload** command.

Table 7-3   dspload *Command Parameters and Descriptions*

Parameter	Description	Required/Optional
node-name	Displays the load model for a specific switch. If a node is not specified, the display shows loading on the local node.	Optional
trunk-id	Displays the load model for a specific trunk.	Optional

Example 7-2 shows the **dspload** command with a trunk id. The **dspload** command output contains load characteristics for that trunk.

Example 7-2 dspload *Output*

```
igx1          TN    group6:1        IGX 8420  9.2.20    Aug. 28 1999 13:27 CDT

Configured Trunk Loading:  TRK  igx1 16.1--16.1 igx2
 Load Type           Xmt-c   Rcv-c
 NTS                   262     262  Conid In Use           7
 TS                      0       0  Conid Available      249
 Voice                  28      28  Total Capacity       256
 BData A               334     228
 BData B                 0       0  Trunk cost: 10
 CBR                 10000   10000  Trunk type is Terrestrial
 nrt-VBR               700     500  Trunk supports cell routing
 rt-VBR                  0       0  Trunk does not use ZCS
 ABR                  5000    2000  Trunk end supports all gateway types
 Total In Use        16324   13018  Gateway conns:    4/196
 Reserved             1000    1000  Traffic: V TS NTS FR FST CBR NRT-VBR ABR
 Available           62676   65982           RT-VBR
 Total Capacity      80000   80000  VPC conids:       0/4096

Last Command: dspload 16.1


Next Command:
```

The **dspload** command with a trunk ID lists the following detailed load characteristics for that trunk:

- Local and remote node names and trunk IDs
- Non-time-stamped (NTS) allocated traffic
- Time-stamped (TS) allocated traffic
- Voice allocated traffic
- Frame Relay without ForeSight traffic (BDataA) allocated traffic
- Frame Relay with ForeSight traffic (BDataB) allocated traffic
- Constant bit rate (CBR) allocated traffic
- Real-time and nonreal-time variable bit rate (VBR) allocated traffic
- Available bit rate (ABR) allocated traffic
- Total FastPackets or cells in use
- Available FastPackets or cells
- Statistical reserve

- Total capacity
- Connection identifiers in use, available and total capacity
- Miscellaneous trunk characteristics

dsptrkutl Command

The **dsptrkutl** command displays real-time trunk usage statistics for a specified trunk, as shown in Example 7-3. Unlike some of the other statistics screens, the **dsptrkutl** command display screen does not provide any historical information.

Example 7-3 **dsptrkutl** *Output*

```
igx4            TN    group8:1       IGX 8420  9.2.20    July 30 1999 13:19 CDT

TRK 9.1 Utilization Display

Elapsed time (seconds)        21.3      Terminated Connection Statistics
Total cells transmitted       20264       Voice terminated         16
Overall cell rate (cells/sec) 947         Data terminated          2
Overall utilization           2%          Frame Relay terminated   0
Peak interval utilization     2%          Num voice OffHook        16
Last interval (seconds)       5.0         ATM terminated           0
Interval cells generated      4790      Connection    Modem Modem VAD
Interval cell rate (cells/sec) 948      Type    Num   On    V.25  Enabled
Interval utilization          2%          c      0     0     0     0
                                          a      0     0     0     -
Terminated Connections        18          v      0     0     0     0
Via Connections               0           p/t    0     0     0     -
                                          l      16    0     0     16

This Command: dsptrkutl 9.1 5


Hit DEL key to quit:
```

The trunk must be upped and added before you use this command.

Comparing the load model and utilization for a particular trunk can provide insight into bandwidth efficiency and network capacity requirements.

Here is the **dsptrkutl** command syntax:

```
dsptrkutl <trunk id> [interval]
```

Table 7-4 describes the command parameters for the **dsptrkutl** command.

Table 7-4   **dsptrkutl** *Command Parameters and Descriptions*

Parameter	Description	Required/Optional
trunk id	Displays a trunk's current bandwidth usage.	Required
interval	Time, in seconds, between screen updates. If no value is specified, the command defaults to 5 seconds.	Optional

The **dsptrkutl** command displays the parameters and statistics described in Table 7-5.

Table 7-5   **dsptrkutl** *Command Parameter and Statistics Descriptions*

Parameter/Statistic	Description
Elapsed time (seconds)	Elapsed time, in seconds, since the command was started.
Total packets transmitted	Number of cells/packets transmitted during the elapsed time.
Overall packet rate	Number of cells/packets transmitted per second during the elapsed time.
Overall utilization	Bandwidth used. Expressed as a percentage of the available bandwidth during the elapsed time: $100 \times$ (Total Packets Transmitted / Elapsed Time $\times$ bandwidth in packets per second).
Peak interval utilization	Bandwidth used. Expressed as a percentage of the available bandwidth during the *peak* interval: $100 \times$ (Total Packets Transmitted / Peak Interval $\times$ bandwidth in packets per second).
Last interval (seconds)	Elapsed time, in seconds, for the last screen update interval.
Interval packets generated	Number of packets transmitted during the last interval.
Interval packet rate (pkts/sec)	Number of packets transmitted per second during the last interval.
Interval utilization	The used bandwidth expressed as a percentage of the available bandwidth during the last interval. The derivation of interval utilization is as follows: $100 \times$ (Interval Packets Transmitted) / (Last Interval $\times$ bandwidth in packets per second).
Total Connections	Total number of connections routed over the trunk.
Terminated Connections	Number of connections routed over the trunk that terminates at this node.
Via Connections	Number of connections routed over the trunks that do not terminate at this node.

The **dsptrkutl** command displays the terminated connection statistics described in Table 7-6.

Table 7-6   *Terminated Connection Descriptions for the* **dsptrkutl** *Command*

Terminated Connection Statistic	Description
Voice terminated	Number of voice connections terminated at this node that are routed over this trunk.
Data terminated	Number of data connections terminated at this node that are routed over this trunk.
Frame Relay terminated	Number of Frame Relay connections terminated at this node that are routed over this trunk.
Num voice off-hook	Number of voice connections off-hook that are terminated at this node and routed over this trunk.
Connection Type	Voice connection types: c, a, v, p, or t.
Connection Num	Number of terminated voice connections of each type: c, a, v, p, and t.
Modem On	Number of terminated connections with a modem detected.
Modem V.25	Number of terminated connections with a V.25 modem detected.
VAD Enabled	Number of terminated connections with VAD enabled.

dsprts Command

The **dsprts** (display routes) command shows the current routing information for all connections on a switch, as shown in Example 7-4. The display shows the trunk numbers and names of all switches in the path. A blinking trunk indicates a failed circuit. A tilde (~) indicates a satellite trunk.

Example 7-4   **dsprts** *Output*

```
igx1            TN     group8:1         IGX 8420   9.2.20    July 21 1999 17:55 CDT

Conn    Route
3.1.1-6
        igx1       15--   15igx2
Pref:   Not Configured
5.1
        igx1       12--   13igx4    15--   15igx3
Pref:   Not Configured
16.10.100
        igx1       12--   13igx4
Pref:   Not Configured

```

Example 7-4 dsprts *Output (Continued)*

```
Last Command: dsprts


Next Command:
```

The **dsprts** screen also appears as the result of the **cnfpref** command.

Here is the **dsprts** command syntax:

> **dsprts** [*start-channel*] [*node-name*]

Table 7-7 describes the **dsprts** command parameters.

Table 7-7   dsprts *Command Parameters and Descriptions*

Parameter	Description	Required/Optional
start-channel	Specifies the starting channel with which to begin the display. If you do not specify a starting channel, the display begins with the first connected channel.	Optional
node-name	Displays only connections from the local switch to the specified node. All connections are displayed if the node name is omitted.	Optional

cnfpref Command

The **cnfpref** command specifies the preferred route for a connection, connection group, or range of connections, as shown in Example 7-5. Enter **cnfpref** at the owning node of the connection.

Example 7-5 cnfpref *Output*

```
igx1              TN     group8:1        IGX 8420   9.2.20    July 21 1999 18:03 CDT

From 5.1           Route
5.1
        igx1      12--   13igx4      15--   15igx3
Pref:...igx1      12--   13igx4      15--   15igx3
16.10.100
        igx1      12--   13igx4
Pref:   Not Configured


Last Command: cnfpref 5.1


Next Command:
```

The preferred route for a connection is used when possible. If the preferred route is different from the existing route, the connection automatically moves to the preferred route whenever network conditions allow (for example, when trunks are out of alarm and sufficient bandwidth exists).

In Example 7-6, the current route for connection 5.1 is selected as a directed (required) route. Note the "(D)" in the preferred routing field for 5.1.

Example 7-6 **cnfpref** *Output*

```
igx1            TN    group8:1        IGX 8420  9.2.20    July 21 1999 18:03 CDT

From 5.1            Route
5.1
        igx1      12--  13igx4    15--  15igx3
Pref:(D)igx1      12--  13igx4    15--  15igx3
16.10.100
        igx1      12--  13igx4
Pref:   Not Configured



Last Command: cnfpref 5.1 + d



Next Command:
```

Here is the **cnfpref** command syntax:

> **cnfpref** `<channel | * > <+ | - | route>` [d]

Table 7-8 describes the **cnfpref** command parameters.

Table 7-8   **cnfpref** *Command Parameters and Descriptions*

Parameter	Description	Required/Optional
channel | *	Specifies the channel or range of channels for preferred route configuration. * specifies all locally owned connections.	Required
+ | - | *route*	+ makes the current route the preferred route.	Required
	- removes the current route as the preferred route.	
	route designates a specific preferred route through the network in the format *trunk/node*.	
d	Specifies directed routing. If the preferred route is unavailable, the connection fails.	Optional

In Example 7-7, a preferred route between igx1 and igx2 is configured for connection 3.1.1.

Example 7-7 **cnfpref** *Output*

```
igx1            TN     group8:1        IGX 8420  9.2.20    July 21 1999 17:59 CDT

Conn    Route
3.1.1
        igx1      13--  14igx2
Pref:   igx1      13--  14igx2
3.1.2-6
        igx1      15--  15igx2
Pref:   Not Configured
5.1
        igx1      12--  13igx4     15--  15igx3
Pref:   Not Configured
16.10.100
        igx1      12--  13igx4
Pref:   Not Configured




Last Command: cnfpref 3.1.1 14/igx2


Next Command:
```

The **cnfpref** command specifies 14/igx2. Trunk 14 is the interface on igx2, *not* igx1. For longer routes, specify multiple trunk/node pairs.

If route costing is enabled, the route cost is calculated by adding the costs for all trunks in the trunk route.

Individual trunk costs are set using the **cnftrk** command, but note that the route cost information is displayed by **dsprts**, as shown in Example 7-8.

Example 7-8 **dsprts** *Output*

```
igx4            TN     group8:1        IGX 8420  9.2.20    Sep. 9 1999  08:22 CST

Conn    Route
3.1.4-6             (Cost = 20)
        igx4      14--  13igx3
Pref:   Not Configured
9.1.10.100          (Cost = 20)
        igx4      14--  13igx3
Pref:   Not Configured

```

continues

Example 7-8 **dsprts** *Output (Continued)*

```
Last Command: dsprts


Next Command:
```

cnfrtcost Command

The **cnfrtcost** command, shown in Example 7-9, sets the maximum route cost for a connection.

Example 7-9 **cnfrtcost** *Output*

```
igx4            TN    group8:1        IGX 8420  9.2.20    Sep. 9 1999   08:23 CST

Conn:  9.1.10.100       igx3        9.1.100.32000     cbr       Status:OK
   PCR(0+1)      % Util    CDVT(0+1)      Policing
   2000/2000    100/100   15000/15000     4/4

Owner: LOCAL  Restriction: NONE  COS: 0 Pri: L  Test-RTD: 0 msec  Max Cost: 10
Path:   igx4       14-- 13igx3
Pref:   Not Configured


igx4      UXM:   OK                    igx3     UXM:   OK
          Line  9.1 : OK                        Line  9.1 : OK
          OAM Cell RX: Clear                    NNI:   OK
          NNI:   OK

Last Command: cnfrtcost 9.1.10.100 10


Next Command:
```

The maximum route cost is not enforced until the connection is rerouted. If all available routes exceed the configured maximum route cost, the connection is failed.

Also, if you have configured a preferred route, and you then configure a route cost that is lower than the configured preferred route, the preferred route is removed.

Here is the **cnfrtcost** command syntax:

cnfrtcost *<con id> <cost>*

Table 7-9 describes the **cnfrtcost** command parameters.

Table 7-9   **cnfrtcost** *Command Parameters and Descriptions*

Parameter	Description	Required/Optional
con id	Specifies the connection ID.	Required
cost	The maximum route cost. The cost values range from 1 to 500.	Required

cnfcos Command

The **cnfcos** command, shown in Example 7-10, determines the priority for rerouting a connection.

Example 7-10 cnfcos *Output*

```
igx1            TN     group8:1       IGX 8420  9.2.20    July 21 1999 18:04 CDT

Local          Remote        Remote
Channel        NodeName      Channel            State  Type    Compress    Code COS
3.1.1-6        igx2          3.1.1-6            Ok     t                        0
5.1            igx3          5.1                Ok     64                  7/8  0
16.10.100      igx4          16.11.100          Ok     vbr                      10



Last Command: cnfcos 16.10.100 10


Next Command:
```

You determine the priority by specifying a 0 to 15-second delay before the network reroutes one or more failed connections. The CoS applies to the following:

- A single connection
- A range of connections
- A connection group

The CoS is the delay in seconds before the network reroutes a connection in the event of a trunk failure.

Here is the **cnfcos** command syntax:

```
cnfcos <channel> <CoS>
```

Table 7-10 describes the **cnfcos** command parameters.

Table 7-10   **cnfcos** *Command Parameters and Descriptions*

Parameter	Description	Required/Optional
channel	Specifies the channel to configure.	Required
CoS	Delay in seconds before rerouting starts for this connection. CoS may range from 0 to 15 seconds.	Required

dncon Command

The **dncon** command, shown in Example 7-11, deactivates a connection, a group of connections, or all connections within a CoS or CoS range. When a connection is downed, the system removes it from the route and releases its bandwidth in the trunk load model.

Example 7-11 dncon *Output*

```
igx1            TN    group8:1      IGX 8420  9.2.20    July 21 1999 18:00 CDT

Local           Remote    Remote
Channel         NodeName  Channel        State  Type   Compress    Code COS
3.1.1           igx2      3.1.1          Down   t                       0
3.1.2-6         igx2      3.1.2-6        Ok     t                       0
5.1             igx3      5.1            Ok     64                 7/8  0
16.10.100       igx4      16.11.100      Ok     vbr                     0



Last Command: dncon 3.1.1 i


Next Command:
```

Voice connections can be downed immediately or with courtesy. With courtesy downing, the system waits until the connection is on-hook before downing it. Courtesy downing is possible only if the on-hook status has been configured with the **cnfvchtp** command.

The State column in the **dspcons** screen has the following values:

- **Ok**—Routed
- **Down**—Downed
- **Ok(Dn)**—Voice connections that have been courtesy downed are waiting for on-hook
- **Failed**—Not routed, but trying

Here is the **dncon** command syntax:

```
dncon <channel(s) | cos> [cos-range] [c | i]
```

Table 7-11 describes the **dncon** command parameters.

Table 7-11   **dncon** *Command Parameters and Descriptions*

Parameter	Description	Required/Optional
channel(s) | cos	The channel(s) to deactivate. Alternatively, you can specify cos followed by a CoS number to deactivate all connections within that CoS.	Required
cos-range	The CoS number or range to deactivate.	Optional
c | i	Immediately down (i) or courtesy down (c) off-hook voice connections. The default is immediate.	Optional

upcon Command

The **upcon** command, shown in Example 7-12, ups (activates) a downed connection, a group of connections, or all connections within a CoS or CoS range.

Example 7-12 upcon *Output*

```
igx1             TN     group8:1      IGX 8420   9.2.20     July 21 1999 18:01 CDT

Local            Remote      Remote
Channel          NodeName    Channel          State  Type     Compress    Code COS
3.1.1-6          igx2        3.1.1-6          Ok     t                         0
5.1              igx3        5.1              Ok     64                   7/8  0
16.10.100        igx4        16.11.100        Ok     vbr                       0



Last Command: upcon 3.1.1


Next Command:
```

When a connection is upped, the system tries to route. If the connection cannot immediately be routed, the connection is marked failed and generates a major alarm.

Here is the **upcon** command syntax:

```
upcon <channel(s) | cos> [cos-range]
```

Table 7-12 describes the **upcon** command parameters.

Table 7-12   **upcon** *Command Parameters and Descriptions*

Parameter	Description	Required/Optional
channel(s)	cos	The channel or range of channels to activate. Alternatively, you may specify cos followed by a CoS number to activate all connections within that CoS.	Required
cos-range	The CoS number or range to activate.	Optional

IGX Commands Used for Network Synchronization

Table 7-13 lists the IGX commands that are used for network synchronization. Network timing and clock sources are explained after the table, with output screens showing how these commands are used to synchronize the network.

Table 7-13   *IGX Commands Used for Network Synchronization*

Command	Description	Privilege Level
dspclksrcs	Displays all configured network clock sources.	1 to 6
dspcurclk	Displays the clock source used by the switch.	1 to 6
cnfclksrc	Adds or removes a network clock source.	1 and 2
dspalms	Displays a count of alarm conditions by category on this switch and a total count of remote switch alarms.	1 to 6
dsptrks	Lists trunks and their alarm states.	1 to 6
clrclkalm	Clears a bad clock source or bad clock path alarm.	1 and 2

Network Synchronization

The IGX network operates as a synchronous network, as illustrated in Figure 7-8. This means that IGX switches select a single master clock source and propagate that clock frequency to every other switch via trunks. Possible clock sources include internal oscillators, external clock interfaces on the System Clock Module (SCM) back card, lines, and trunks. Framed interfaces such as T1 and E1 are used as clock sources rather than serial interfaces.

Because time-division multiplexing (TDM) circuits must be synchronized, carrier facilities are typically good clock sources.

Figure 7-8   *Network Synchronization*

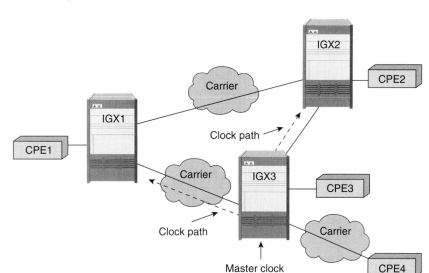

Carrier Network Timing

Carrier central offices use a clocking hierarchy called the Building Integrated Timing Supply (BITS), in which each carrier device can trace its clock source back to a Stratum 1 or Stratum 2 clock. Clocks are described in terms of their stability, or their ability to maintain framing consistency without slips for a defined interval. The highest level, a Stratum 1 clock, might be a Cesium atomic clock employing direct control from Coordinated Universal Time (UTC) frequency and time services, such as Global Positioning System (GPS) navigational systems. The Stratum clock levels in a carrier network are shown in Figure 7-9.

A Stratum 1 clock provides timing for lower-stability clocks such as Stratum 2 clocks. Stratum 2 clocks provide timing for other Stratum 2, Stratum 3, and Stratum 4 clocks. The BPX has a Stratum 3 clock, and the IGX has a Stratum 4 clock.

Clock Sources

An IGX switch can derive timing from a clock attached to one of the external clock interfaces on the SCM card, an internal oscillator, a framed line, or a framed trunk, as illustrated in Figure 7-10.

Figure 7-9 *Carrier Network Timing*

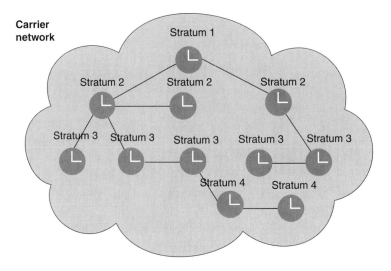

Figure 7-10 *Clock Sources*

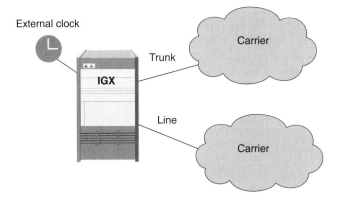

The following key points apply to external clock sources, line sources, and trunk sources when you use any of them to derive timing:

- External clock source
    - Attaches to SCM
    - EIA/TIA-422 square wave at 1.544 kHz or 2048 kHz
- Line
    - Can be a T1, E1, T3, E3, or J1 access line

- Trunk
  - — T1, E1, T3, E3, or Y1 network trunk
  - — Trunk must be configured for "pass sync" = no

IGX Trunks as Clock Sources

Trunks that "pass sync" are not allowed to be clock sources. Use the **cnftrk** command to change this option. If a trunk does not pass sync, it may be configured as a clock source. A trunk passes synchronization if the clock information transmitted from one end arrives as the identical clock at the other end. Normal T1 or E1 trunks pass sync. Pass sync yes and no are illustrated in Figure 7-11.

Figure 7-11 *IGX Trunks as Clock Sources*

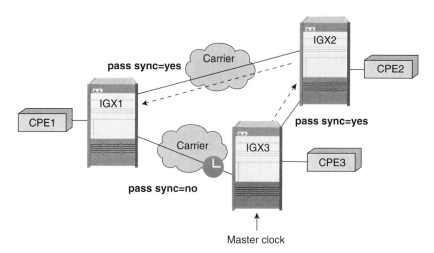

Trunks that do not normally pass clock (sync) include the following:

- Satellite trunks
- Subrate trunks
- Fractional trunks
- Virtual trunks

Ask your carrier how a T1/E1 circuit is timed before selecting that circuit as either a clock source or clock path.

Rules for Selecting a Clock Reference

The clocking scheme ensures that all nodes in the network automatically synchronize to the nearest, most stable clock available. After you specify a clock source using the **cnfclksrc** command, the location and type of the network clock source go out to all nodes in the network. This synchronization remains in effect despite line failures, power outages, controller card switchovers, line repairs, and all other network topology changes.

Rules for selecting a clock reference include always choosing primary over secondary and secondary over tertiary clock sources. If you are choosing between equal clock sources, the following rules apply:

- Least number of hops away
- From the lowest node number
- External
- Line—lowest line number first
- Trunk—lowest trunk number first
- Choosing the path to the clock source:
    — Least number of hops away
    — Via lowest node number
- Default or fallback clock source
- Internal clock from the highest node number
- Same routing rules as for configured clock sources

Clock sources in an IGX network are defined as primary, secondary, or tertiary sources. Any type of clock source can be configured as any of the three levels. This hierarchy is based on clock source stability. Each network node's clock is based on the most stable clock source. A continuous clock test compares the frequency of the node clock source to a reference on the control card. If it detects a clock source outside preset frequency limits, the controller declares the source defective and selects another source. If multiple, equal clock sources are available, each node chooses the closest one (measured in the number of hops). The **dspclksrcs** command displays all clock sources in a network.

Clock sources can be changed manually or automatically by a node. If no primary, secondary, or tertiary clock sources are defined or working in a network, the internal oscillator of the highest node number is automatically selected as the active network clock source. Whenever a clock source changes, the node ensures that the clock path remains hierarchical.

- In an IGX network, a clock source functions as a source for the entire network.
- To avoid unnecessary clock disruptions, configure all primary clock sources for the network first.

- A line must be upped and not in alarm before you configure it as a network clock source.
- Defining a trunk as a clock source is incompatible with defining it as passing clock. Before you define a trunk as a clock source, use the **cnftrk** command to specify that the trunk does not pass synchronization.
- Carrier limitations may restrict clocking options. Possible restrictions include the following:
  — Trunks and lines must be clocked by the IGX nodes.
  — Trunks and lines cannot be clocked by the IGX nodes ("loop" the clock).
  — Multiple carrier facilities in a single IGX network.

The following sections show commands used to synchronize the network.

dspclksrcs Command

The **dspclksrcs** command, shown in Example 7-13, lists all potential network clock sources and their levels (primary, secondary, or tertiary).

Example 7-13 dspclksrcs *Output*

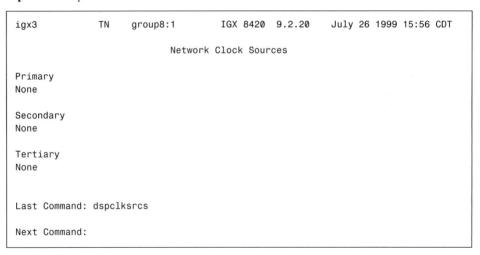

```
igx3            TN      group8:1        IGX 8420   9.2.20    July 26 1999 15:56 CDT

                                Network Clock Sources

Primary
None

Secondary
None

Tertiary
None


Last Command: dspclksrcs

Next Command:
```

As you can see, the **dspclksrcs** command returns a screen empty of information because, in this case, there are no *potential* network clock sources.

dspcurclk Command

The display for unreachable or failed clock sources flashes on and off. Clock sources are defined using the **clkclksrc** command. The **dspcurclk** command displays the *current* network clock source.

The **dspcurclk** command screen, shown in Example 7-14, shows the current clock reference for the node and the path to the clock reference.

Example 7-14 **dspcurclk** *Output*

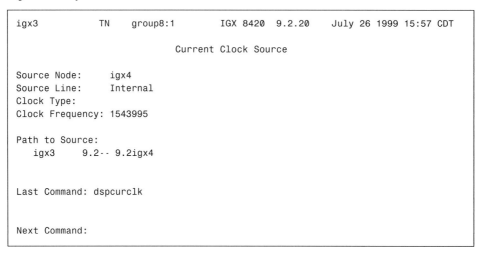

```
igx3            TN    group8:1        IGX 8420  9.2.20    July 26 1999 15:57 CDT

                              Current Clock Source

Source Node:     igx4
Source Line:     Internal
Clock Type:
Clock Frequency: 1543995

Path to Source:
   igx3     9.2-- 9.2igx4


Last Command: dspcurclk


Next Command:
```

Table 7-14 describes the fields found in the output display for the **dspcurclk** command.

Table 7-14 **dspcurclk** *Command Fields and Descriptions*

Field	Description
Source Node	The IGX switch where the clock source originates.
Source Line	The type of line used as the clock source and its back slot and interface number (for example, CLN 15, TRK 9.1, External 1, or Internal).
Clock Type	The clock type configured for the source clock (primary, secondary, or tertiary). If the source clock is an internal oscillator, no clock type is given.
Clock Frequency	The received clock frequency, as measured by the local NPM.
Path to Source	The trunk path from the current node to the clock source. This path to the source includes all intermediate nodes and trunks.

cnfclksrc Command

The **cnfclksrc** command, shown in Example 7-15, specifies a network-wide clock source. The clocking scheme ensures that all nodes in the network automatically synchronize to the nearest, most stable clock available.

Example 7-15 *cnfclksrc Output*

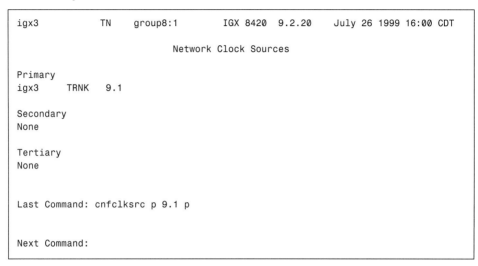

```
igx3           TN     group8:1        IGX 8420  9.2.20     July 26 1999 16:00 CDT

                            Network Clock Sources

Primary
igx3       TRNK   9.1

Secondary
None

Tertiary
None


Last Command: cnfclksrc p 9.1 p


Next Command:
```

After you specify a clock source, the location and type of the network clock source go out to all nodes in the network. To remove a clock source, enter **r** as the source type.

Here is the **cnfclksrc** command syntax:

```
cnfclksrc <line-type> <line-number> <source-type> [frequency]
```

Table 7-15 describes the **cnfclksrc** command parameters.

Table 7-15 *cnfclksrc Command Parameters and Descriptions*

Parameter	Description	Required/Optional
line-type	Specifies the type of line as circuit line (c), external clock interface (e), or packet line (p) for trunks.	Required
line-number	Clock source formatted as *slot* or *slot.interface*. For external clock sources, enter 1 or 2 to identify the external clock interface on the SCM.	Required
source-type	Identifies the clock source as primary (p), secondary (s), or tertiary (t). Enter **r** to remove the clock source.	Required
frequency	Specifies the clock source frequency for an external clock only. Enter **1** for 1.544 MHz or **2** for 2.048 MHz.	Optional

You might define multiple primary, secondary, and tertiary clock sources, as shown in Example 7-16. The network regards all primary clocks as equal in the network clocking hierarchy, all secondary clocks as equal, and all tertiary clocks as equal. If multiple, equal clock sources are available, the node synchronizes to the closest source (the fewest hops away). If none of the clock sources is available, the network synchronizes to the internal oscillator of the node with the highest node number in the network.

Example 7-16 cnfclksrc *Output*

```
igx3            TN    group8:1       IGX 8420  9.2.20    July 26 1999 16:00 CDT

                             Network Clock Sources

Primary
igx3     EXT-1 1.544 MHz  igx3      TRNK   9.1

Secondary
None

Tertiary
None


Last Command: cnfclksrc e 1 p 1


Next Command:
```

Example 7-17, the **dspcurclk** output, shows igx3, trunk 9.1 as the current clock source.

Example 7-17 dspcurclk *Output*

```
igx1            VT    group8:1       IGX 8420  9.2.20    July 26 1999 16:18 CDT

                             Current Clock Source

Source Node:     igx3
Source Line:     TRNK  9.1
Clock Type:      Primary
Clock Frequency: 1543978

Path to Source:
   igx1    13--14igx2    13--12igx3


Last Command: dspcurclk


Next Command:

Virtual Terminal
```

Because trunk 9.1 on igx3 is the clock source, it cannot pass clock (sync) to igx1, as shown in Example 7-17. Instead, other trunks are used to distribute clock.

dspalms Command

The **dspalms** command, shown in Example 7-18, displays counts of local alarms by category, and a total count of remote alarms.

Example 7-18 dspalms *Output*

```
igx4           TN    group8:1        IGX 8420  9.2.20    July 26 1999 16:02 CDT

Alarm summary   (Configured alarm slots: None)
Connections Failed:       None                EXT-1 Bad clock source
TRK Alarms:               None
Circuit Line Alarms:      None
Physical Line Alarms:     None
Cards Failed:             None
Missing Cards:            None
Remote Node Alarms:       1 Minor

Interface Shelf Alarms:   None


FastPAD/Access Dev Alms:  None

Last Command: dspalms

Next Command:
MINOR ALARM
```

External clock interface 1 was activated by the **cnfclksrc** command in Example 7-16. In Example 7-18, no clocking circuit is actually connected to that interface, and a minor alarm is generated. Example 7-19 shows the **cnfclksrc** command used to remove external clock interface 1.

Example 7-19 cnfclksrc *Output*

```
igx4           TN    group8:1        IGX 8420  9.2.20    July 26 1999 16:04 CDT

                        Network Clock Sources

Primary
igx3    EXT-1 1.544 MHz  igx3    TRNK   9.1

Secondary
None
```

continues

Example 7-19 cnfclksrc *Output (Continued)*

```
Tertiary
None



Last Command: cnfclksrc e 1 r



Next Command:
```

dsptrks Command

The **dsptrks** command lists trunks and their alarm states, as shown in Example 7-20. Note that trunk 9.1 displays a bad clock source alarm. This does not imply that trunk 9.1 has any difficulty passing user traffic, but the clock frequency on the circuit has wandered enough to generate an alarm.

Example 7-20 dsptrks *Output*

```
igx3            TN    group8:1      IGX 8420  9.2.20    July 26 1999 16:15 CDT

TRK     Type    Current Line Alarm Status              Other End
 9.1    E3/530  Minor - Bad clock source               igx4/9.1
 9.2    E3/530  Clear - OK                             igx4/9.2
 9.3    E3/530  Clear - OK                             igx4/9.3
12      T1/24   Clear - OK                             igx2/13
13      E1/32   Clear - OK                             igx4/14


Last Command: dsptrks



Next Command:
```

clrclkalm Command

The **clrclkalm** command, shown in Example 7-21, clears a clock alarm state for a specific clock source. This example removes the alarm shown in Example 7-21. (Clock alarms do not clear automatically.)

Example 7-21 clrclkalm *Output*

```
igx3            VT    group8:1      IGX 8420  9.2.20    July 26 1999 16:15 CDT

TRK     Type    Current Line Alarm Status              Other End
 9.1    E3/530  Clear - OK                             igx4/9.1
 9.2    E3/530  Clear - OK                             igx4/9.2
 9.3    E3/530  Clear - OK                             igx4/9.3
```

Example 7-21 clrclkalm *Output (Continued)*

```
12        T1/24  Clear - OK                        igx2/13
13        E1/32  Clear - OK                        igx4/14


Last Command: clrclkalm t 9.1


Next Command:
```

Here is the **clrclkalm** command syntax:

```
clrclkalm <line-type> <line-number>
```

Table 7-16 describes the **clrclkalm** command parameters.

Table 7-16   clrclkalm *Command Parameters and Descriptions*

Parameter	Description	Required/Optional
line-type	Specifies the type of line as circuit line (c), external clock interface (e), or trunk (t).	Required
line-number	Specifies the line number formatted as *slot* or *slot.interface.*	Required

IGX Commands Used to Manage Jobs

Table 7-17 lists the IGX commands that are used to manage jobs. Job functions are explained after the table, with output screens showing how these commands are used to manage jobs in a network.

Table 7-17   *IGX Commands Used to Manage Jobs*

Command	Description	Privilege Level
addjob	Creates a new job on the local IGX.	1 to 6
dspjobs	Displays all jobs and their execution states on the local IGX.	1 to 6
dspjob	Displays a job's lines and execution state.	1 to 6
editjob	Modifies a job.	1 to 6
runjob	Executes a job.	1 to 6
stopjob	Stops all currently executing and waiting jobs.	1 to 6
deljob	Deletes a job.	1 to 6
addjobtrig	Indicates that a job should execute based on a state change (trigger).	1 to 6
deljobtrig	Deletes a specific job trigger.	1 to 6

Managing Jobs

A job is a user-specified "batch file" or script containing IGX commands. Although jobs are local to an IGX, a job might contain commands of network-wide impact. Jobs are created using the **addjob** command and are removed using the **deljob** command.

You can create up to 20 jobs on each IGX. The IGX assigns a consecutive number from 1 to 20 when the job is created. Jobs are executed, changed, and deleted based on their job number. You may view all or specific jobs using the **dspjobs** or **dspjob** commands.

Job Privilege Levels

Each job is associated with a privilege level based on the administrative privilege level in use when the job was created. The job privilege level limits the contents of a job and its operation as follows:

- **Job contents**—Only commands that are available at your privilege level can be in your job specification. For example, a level 3 user cannot include the **addtrk** command in a job, because **addtrk** requires a level 1 privilege. In addition, some commands cannot be placed in a job. For example, display commands such as **dspcons** cannot be executed as part of a job.

- **Job operation**—You must have a privilege level equal to or higher than the job level to run, edit, stop, or delete that job. Job privilege levels are displayed by the **dspjob** and **dspjobs** commands. A job may execute another job using the **runjob** command. The nested job must be an equal or lower privilege level and must not invoke (run) the calling job.

Creating Jobs

The **addjob** command creates a new job on the IGX. The IGX assigns the job number, but you can input a brief job description to identify the job. After you enter the **addjob** command, the IGX builds a working template, assigns a job number, and prompts you for the following fields:

- **Description (optional)**—The description can contain up to 16 characters of text, including spaces.

- **Execution time (optional)**—The execution time indicates the first (or only) time to automatically run the job. If you specify an execution time, the first (unprompted) parameter is four digits, indicating the year. The system then prompts you for the month, day, hour (24-hour clock), minute, and second (optional).

- **Interval (optional)**—The interval indicates how often the job should automatically run after the date and time specified for the execution time. This prompt appears only if you have specified an execution time. The first interval prompt is for units, in days, hours, and minutes. The system then prompts you for a number of these units.

- **Commands (required)**—The IGX prompts you for each command to input into the job. After each command and its parameters, the system prompts you for an action to take if a failure occurs.

NOTE   The system does not check the validity of the commands as it does for "live" execution. For example, if you enter **dncd 20** on a 16-slot IGX, the system detects the error during job creation. In contrast, if **dncd 13** points to a valid card slot with a missing card, the system does not detect the error during job creation.

Planning a Job

Before you create a job, you must plan it. This includes deciding which commands you will use and selecting the privilege level, execution time, interval, and job contents. Keep in mind that, after you issue the **addjob** command, you will be prompted for parameters, and that the system assigns and increments job numbers up to a maximum of 20 jobs per IGX.

Job Execution

Three techniques are available for executing jobs: an automatic execution time, **runjob**, and response to a trigger condition.

- Automatic execution times are set inside a job using the **addjob** and **editjob** commands.

- Jobs can be manually forced to execute using the **runjob** command. The **runjob** command overrides a job's execution time and immediately executes the job.

- One or more triggers can be associated with a job using the **addjobtrig** command. Essentially, triggers tell the job to execute when a state change occurs, typically a trunk or line failing or being restored.

Editing a Job

The **editjob** command modifies the job description, execution time, interval, and contents.

The following is a list of actions you can take with **editjob**:

- To change an item in the job template, enter or type over the existing information on the command line and press **Enter**.

- Use your keyboard to change information on the command line. To keep an item's value, press **Enter** at the prompt.

- To add a new command between existing commands in a job, hold down the **Ctrl** key while you press the ^ key. A new, highlighted line appears above the command. Enter the new command after the Enter Cmd: prompt and press **Enter**.

- To add a new command to the end of a job, press **Enter** after the last command in the job template.

- To delete a command from a job, either backspace over the command when it appears on the command line and press **Enter**, or press **Ctrl-X**.

- To end the editing session, press **Enter** when prompted for a new command, or press the **Delete** key.

When commands are added to or deleted from a job, the system renumbers them. To test an edited job, run it with the **runjob** command.

Stopping a Job

The **stopjob** command stops all executing or waiting commands. When the **stopjob** command is issued, the template for the current job appears on the screen, along with the prompt "Stop this and all currently executing jobs (y/n)?"

CAUTION   Because stopping a job can leave a task partially completed, use **stopjob** with caution.

Creating Job Triggers

A trigger executes a job if a trunk, line, or HDM/LDM port changes state. Here are some important questions to ask:

- Which trunk or line should be monitored?

- Should the job execute when the trunk, line, or port fails, or when it is repaired?

- How many triggers are needed? Using multiple **addjobtrig** commands, up to four triggers can be associated with a job.

addjob Command

As previously described, the **addjob** command creates a new job. The system does not check command validity with respect to the network's current state, or for relationships to other commands in the job. To ensure that it works as expected, try running the job with the **runjob** command, described in the section, "runjob Command." The temporary display of the Enter Cmd: prompt at the bottom of the screen indicates that you can enter the next command for the job. To exit **addjob**, press **Enter** without entering a command.

Here is the **addjob** command syntax:

```
addjob[description] [execution-time] [interval] <command> <failure-reaction>
```

Table 7-18 describes the **addjob** command parameters.

Table 7-18   addjob *Command Parameters and Descriptions*

Parameter	Description	Required/Optional
description	0 to 16 characters of text description.	Optional
execution-time	Specifies the start day and time for execution.	Optional
interval	If the execution time is specified, the interval in days, hours, or minutes for subsequent execution.	Optional
command	Command to include in the job. The number of commands in a job is limited only by available memory.	Required
failure-reaction	Desired reaction to the failure of a command. Each command must have a failure reaction in the format <c | a | rc | ra> <*number of repetitions*>, where:	Required
	c—Continue running the job.	
	a—Abort the job.	
	rc—Retry the command for the specified number of times and then continue running the job even if the command fails.	
	ra—Retry the command for the specified number of times, and abort the job if the command always fails.	

dspjobs Command

The **dspjobs** command displays the summary and execution status for all current jobs, as shown in Example 7-22.

Example 7-22 dspjobs *Output*

```
igx1            TN      group8:1        IGX 8420   9.2.20    July 19 1999 16:15 CDT

Job   Description       Next Execution     Status    Interval    Access Group
1     Add trunk         08/19/99 16:30:00  Idle      1 days      SuperUser
      Trigger 1 -  PLN    12        REPAIR
2     Delete con                           Idle                  Group 1
```

continues

Example 7-22 **dspjobs** *Output (Continued)*

```
Last Command: dspjobs


Next Command:
```

The **dspjobs** command displays the following information on each job:

- Job number
- Job description
- Next execution date and time
- Execution interval between jobs
- Status of jobs
- Interval between performance
- Access group—The privilege level required to run or display the job

To see details on an individual job, use the **dspjob** command.

dspjob Command

The **dspjob** command displays the summary and execution status for a specific job, as shown in Example 7-23.

Example 7-23 **dspjob** *Output*

```
igx1            TN    group8:1        IGX 8420  9.2.20    July 19 1999 16:17 CDT

                                  Job 2    Delete con
Last Execution Results: None                    Status: Locked
Next Execution Time:                            Interval:

 1: delcon 5.1
   - Failure Reaction: Abort                       Exec. Results: None


This Command: dspjob 2
```

The **dspjob** command displays the following information for the specified job:

- Job number and description
- Next execution date and time

- Status
- The time interval between successive executions of the job
- The results of the last execution of the job

This command requires the same or higher privilege level as that held by the person who created the job.

Here is the **dspjob** command syntax:

```
dspjob <job-number>
```

job-number specifies the number of the job to display (1 to 20).

editjob Command

When you enter the **editjob 2** command, the template for job 2 appears on the screen, as shown in Example 7-24.

Example 7-24 editjob *Output*

```
igx4            TN      group8:1      IGX 8420  9.2.20    July 30 1999 13:03 CDT


                             Job 2   PM Traffic
Last Execution Results: None                    Status: Idle
Next Execution Time: 07/30/99 17:00:00          Interval: 1 days

  1: dncon cos 10 i
    - Failure Reaction: Continue                Exec. Results: None
  2: upcon cost 11
    - Failure Reaction: Abort                   Exec. Results: None



Last Command: editjob 2


Next Command:
```

The system displays the existing job description, which you can change or keep. To keep it, press **Enter**. The system then displays the execution time. You can change the execution time and interval by inputting new values. You can insert new commands, delete commands, and change commands by overtyping. See the earlier section, "Editing a Job" for specific edit actions.

To exit, press **Enter** when prompted for a new command.

Here is the **editjob** command syntax:

```
editjob <job-number>
```

job-number specifies the number of the job to edit.

runjob Command

The **runjob** command runs a job regardless of its execution time. The **runjob** command does not change a job's assigned execution time. Example 7-25 shows the **runjob** command output.

Example 7-25 **runjob** *Output*

```
igx4            TN    group8:1        IGX 8420  9.2.20    July 30 1999 13:05 CDT


                                Job 2    PM Traffic
Last Execution Results: None                    Status: Idle
Next Execution Time: 07/30/99 17:00:00          Interval: 1 days

 1: dncon cos 10 i
   - Failure Reaction: Continue                    Exec. Results: None
 2: upcon cost 11
   - Failure Reaction: Abort                       Exec. Results: None


This Command: runjob 1


Run this job (y/n)?
```

When you enter **runjob**, the system displays the job contents and prompts you with "Run this job (y/n)?" Enter **y** to start the job or **n** to exit **runjob**. Four seconds pass before a job begins running after you enter **y**. Pressing any key briefly suspends a job, and four seconds of no keyboard activity must pass before the job resumes. While a job is running, the system highlights the current command and updates command results.

You can include the **runjob** command in a job, forcing one job to run another. The only limitation is that a job cannot cause itself to run. For example, job 1 cannot include the **runjob 1** command. Also, job 1 cannot include the **runjob 2** command if job 2 contains the **runjob 1** command.

Here is the **runjob** command syntax:

```
runjob <job-number>
```

job-number specifies the number of the job to execute.

stopjob Command

The **stopjob** command stops all running and all waiting jobs, as shown in Example 7-26.

Example 7-26 stopjob *Output*

```
igx4            TN     group8:1      IGX 8420  9.2.20    July 30 1999 13:07 CDT


This Command: stopjob


Stop all running and waiting jobs (y/n)? y
```

When you enter the **stopjob** command, the system prompts you with "Stop all running and waiting jobs (y/n)?" Enter **y** to stop running jobs and prevent all waiting jobs from beginning, or enter **n** to exit **stopjob**. Because the **stopjob** command can leave a task partially executed, use **stopjob** with caution. You must have at least the same or higher privilege level as the creator of the jobs you want to stop.

deljob Command

The **deljob** command deletes a job, as shown in Example 7-27. To delete a job, you must have a privilege level at least as high as the job itself.

Example 7-27 deljob *Output*

```
igx1            TN     group8:1      IGX 8420  9.2.20    July 19 1999 16:17 CDT

                              Job 2    Delete con
Last Execution Results: None                 Status: Locked
Next Execution Time:                         Interval:

 1: delcon 5.1
   - Failure Reaction: Abort                     Exec. Results: None


This Command: deljob 2


Delete this job (y/n)?
```

A job that is currently running cannot be deleted. If necessary, use **stopjob** to stop the job so that you can delete it.

Here is the **deljob** command syntax:

```
deljob <job-number>
```

job-number specifies the number of the job to delete.

addjobtrig Command

The **addjobtrig** command configures a job to run if a failure or repair occurs on a circuit line or trunk. A line acquires a failed status when an alarm condition is invoked. A repair of a line occurs when the alarms on the line are removed. Jobs can be triggered upon either a failure or repair of a line.

The **addjobtrig** command, shown in Example 7-28, also configures a job to allocate or release bandwidth from other connections. This bandwidth decision depends on whether the EIA lead status is up or down.

- The template on the screen prompts you for the slot number of the line on which an alarm triggers the job.

- The prompt asks you to specify whether the trigger should occur on the failure (f) or repair (r) of a line.

- The prompt asks you to specify whether the trigger occurs on an up or down condition for the EIA lead status.

  — The up condition indicates that the system should allocate bandwidth from other connections to enable data transfer.

The down condition indicates that the system should release bandwidth to other connections because the connection does not require the bandwidth for data transfer. The applicable cards are HDM and LDM.

Example 7-28 **addjobtrig** *Output*

```
 igx1            TN     SuperUser       IGX 8420  9.2.20    July 19 1999 16:07 CDT

 Job   Description              Next Execution     Status     Interval    Access Group
 1     Add trunk                08/19/99 16:30:00  Idle       1 day         SuperUser
       Trigger 1 -  PLN          12        REPAIR


 Last Command: addjobtrig 1 t 12 r

 Next Command:
```

Here is the **addjobtrig** command syntax:

```
addjobtrig <job-number> <line-type> <line-specifier> <fail | repair> [up | down]
```

Table 7-19 describes the **addjobtrig** command parameters.

Table 7-19   **addjobtrig** *Command Parameters and Descriptions*

Parameter	Description	Required/Optional
job-number	Specifies the number of the job to trigger.	Required
line-type	Specifies the type of line: p or t indicates a trunk (TRK). l or c indicates a line (LN). d indicates a DS-3 line.	Required
line-specifier	Specifies the slot number or slot interface for TRK and LN.	Required
fail | repair	Specifies whether the trigger occurs on the failure or repair of the line or trunk. To enable triggering on leads other than RTS, use the **cnfict** command.	Required
up | down	Specifies the trigger's EIA lead state. The state is either up or down. These states apply to HDM, LDM, and LDP cards.	Optional

NOTE   For HDM or LDM data cards, the trigger defaults to the transitions of RTS (regardless of whether the port is DCE or DTE), where fail equals the transition of RTS from on to off and repair equals the transition of RTS from off to on.

deljobtrig Command

The **deljobtrig** command deletes a job trigger one trigger at a time, as shown in Example 7-29.

Example 7-29 deljobtrig *Output*

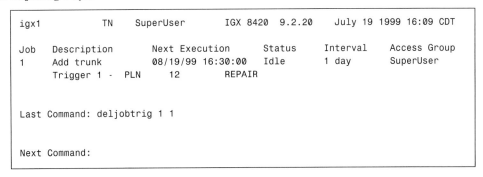

```
igx1              TN    SuperUser      IGX 8420  9.2.20    July 19 1999 16:09 CDT


Job   Description        Next Execution    Status    Interval    Access Group
1     Add trunk          08/19/99 16:30:00  Idle     1 day       SuperUser
      Trigger 1 -  PLN    12          REPAIR



Last Command: deljobtrig 1 1



Next Command:
```

If a job is deleted by the **deljob** command, all associated job triggers are deleted.

Here is the **deljobtrig** command syntax:

```
deljobtrig <job-number> <trigger-number>
```

Table 7-20 describes the **deljobtrig** command parameters.

Table 7-20 **deljobtrig** *Command Parameters and Descriptions*

Parameter	Description	Required/Optional
job-number	Specifies the job's number.	Required
trigger-number	Specifies the trigger number to delete.	Required

Summary

This chapter described the role of the trunk load model in connection admission control and connection routing and compared and contrasted the trunk load model and actual trunk utilization. It also explained how to display trunk utilization statistics and connection routes and how to select preferred connection routes.

This chapter also explained how to configure and display network clock sources and how to monitor and resolve clock alarms. You were shown how to predict and identify node clock references and how to create, edit, and execute jobs.

Review Questions

1 How is **dspload** information different from **dsptrkutl** information?

2 What is the purpose of the statistical reserve?

3 Which command specifies a certain route for a connection?

4 True or false: The **dsprts** command shows all terminating or through connections on this node.

5 Connections in CoS Class 10 have a ——————— connection rerouting priority than connections in CoS Class 1.

6 What are the three IGX network clock source levels?

7 By default, which trunks pass clock?

8 Which command would you use to view clock sources in the network?

9 To avoid unnecessary clock disruptions, configure the ——————— clock source for the network first.

10 What are the clock line types?

11 Which command would you use to delete the clock alarm on circuit line 7.1?

12 True or false: Using a specific job number as part of the **stopjob** command causes only that job to be stopped.

13 The **deljobtrig** command deletes how many job trigger(s) at a time?

This chapter covers the following key topics:

- Major and Minor Alarms
- Alarm Categories
- Troubleshooting Commands
- Connection Testing

CHAPTER 8

Troubleshooting

This chapter covers troubleshooting through identifying possible alarm conditions. It explains the steps needed to isolate and resolve alarms. It describes both major and minor alarms and defines alarm categories in an IGX network. It also examines the commands required to set up connection loopback tests.

Major and Minor Alarms

Major alarms are service-affecting conditions such as failed trunks or lines. *Minor alarms* indicate degraded performance or potential problems and do not necessarily affect service.

Major alarms always affect traffic because they often result in failed connections. It is important to remember that a failed connection is always the result of a major alarm, such as a failed trunk, line, or card.

Minor alarms do not result in failed connections and, therefore, do not necessarily affect traffic. However, a degraded trunk or line might create problems on a connection (usually from the end user's perspective), such as retransmissions or low throughput.

Locating Alarms

The **dspalms** command is typically the first command used in troubleshooting the IGX node because it lists alarm counts by category for the local switch. Remote-switch alarms are counted but not identified.

The **dspalms** command identifies the alarm category. For a historical view, the switch log file indicates when the alarm occurred and which resource entered an alarm state. The **dsplog** command displays the log file. The **clrlog** command clears the log file.

The **dspnw** command displays switch names, alarm state, and connecting trunks for the network. For trunks, a ~ indicates a satellite line, and a flashing entry indicates a failed trunk. A blinking node name indicates that the switch is executing a software download.

The **dspnds** command displays the name, type, and alarm status of all nodes. The **dspnw** and **dspnds** commands only indicate the general alarm state of a remote node. You must **vt** to the remote node to get specific alarm information.

Hardware LEDs

Hardware alarm states are triggered by card failures, fan or power supply failures, or bus errors. The IGX features LEDs on the cards to indicate card or line state.

Alarm Categories

As indicated by the **dspalms** command, alarms fall into the following general categories:

- Card
- Bus
- Trunk
- Line
- Port
- Connection

Each of these categories is discussed in detail in the following sections. Most of the commands that are presented in this section (that have not been introduced in previous chapters) are also described in detail in the section, "Troubleshooting Commands."

Card Alarms

Card information and alarm states are indicated with the **dspcds** and **dspcd** commands. The **dspcds** command displays the cards in a shelf, front and back, with their type, revision, and status. For front and back card sets, the status field applies to the cards as a set. A letter T opposite a card indicates that it is running a self-test. A letter F indicates that it has failed a test. If lines or connections have been configured for a slot, but no suitable card is present, the display lists the missing cards at the top of the screen. If a card was previously installed, empty slots are identified as "reserved."

For an IGX 8430, the screen initially displays only the upper shelf with a Continue? prompt. Enter **y** at the prompt to display the cards in the lower shelf. The command **dspcds** followed by the letter L (for lower shelf) displays the card status for just the lower shelf.

The **resetcd** command resets the hardware and software for a specified card. A hardware reset is equivalent to physically removing and reinserting the front card of a card group and causes the card's logic to be reset. The **resetcd** command should not be run against an active NPM card because it will take the node down and cause node reboot temporarily.

The **switchcc** command switches the active processor (control) card to standby state and the standby processor to active state.

Switching NPM Cards

The **switchcc** command switches the standby NPM processor card to active and the active card to standby. If a standby processor is unavailable, the command is not executed. If a standby processor is available but is not ready to go active, you are prompted to confirm or abort the operation. The **switchcc** command should cause little or no interruption of service.

Executing **switchcc** has the following effects:

- Control is transferred to the standby controller card.

- Any job currently running is aborted.

- The user is logged off.

- The new standby processor reverts to a download mode indicated by the flashing FAIL lamp. The system software image stored in ROM is downloaded to RAM in the event that the system software was corrupted.

- After these transitions are complete, the configuration database is downloaded from the newly active controller card to complete the download. This process takes a number of minutes, so this controller card is unavailable for standby operation until the download process is completed.

WARNING   Do not perform **switchcc** if the processor cards contain different software levels, such as 9.1.12 and 9.2.01! The **dsprevs** command displays the software revision level on each processor card in the network.

Bus Alarms

The IGX features a redundant bus structure known as the A and B buses. Only one bus actively carries traffic at a time. The **dspbuses** command indicates the active and standby bus, and the **cnfbus** command switches the indicated bus to the active state or toggles the bus states.

The **diagbus** command can be used to diagnose bus problems. However, you can use the **diagbus** command only if indicated by the **dspbuses** command, because **diagbus** will disrupt service.

Trunk Alarms

In order to verify any existing trunk alarms, begin by using the **dsptrks** command to display errors on one or all trunks on the switch and to list basic trunk information and alarm states for all trunks on a node. This command applies to both physical and virtual trunks. For disabled trunks, the trunk numbers appear in dim reverse video on the screen.

Next, to display trunk errors, use the **dsptrkerrs** command. You see a summary of historical statistical errors that have occurred on one or all trunks on the node, including Out of Frame, Loss of Signal, and Packets Dropped.

The **clrtrkerrs** command clears statistical error counts for trunks, and the **cnftrkalm** command enables or disables trunk alarm reporting. When trunks are upped and added to the network, alarm reporting is automatically enabled. Disabling alarms might be useful, for example, for trunks that are connected to the node but are not yet in service.

The **clrtrkalm** command clears statistical alarms associated with either a physical or virtual trunk. Because statistical alarms have associated integration times, they can keep a major or minor alarm active for some time after the condition has been resolved.

Line Alarms

In order to verify any existing line alarms, begin by using the **dsplns** command to display basic line information and alarm states for all lines on a node.

Next, the **dsplnerrs** command provides a summary of historical statistical errors that have occurred on one or all lines on the node, including Out of Frame, Loss of Signal, and Packets Dropped.

The **clrlnerrs** command clears statistical error counts for lines, and the **cnflnalm** command sets the trunk and line alarm values and thresholds for statistical failures. The **dsplnalmcnf** command displays alarm configuration by alarm type.

Port Alarms

In order to verify any existing port alarms, begin by using the **dspports** command to display basic port information and alarm states for all Frame Relay and ATM ports on a node.

Next, the **dspportstats** command provides a live view of port activity, including user traffic, Local Management Interface (LMI) or Interim Local Management Interface (ILMI) signaling traffic, error conditions, and congestion states.

The **dspbob** command displays the EIA control lead states for a data serial interface. You must add a connection to the interface before activating **dspbob**.

Connection Alarms

In order to verify any existing connection alarms, begin by using the **dspcons** command to list all connections that terminate at the node. The display includes the connection state, loopback state, and test state if present.

The **dspcon** command displays detailed information for a specific connection, and the **dsprts** command displays routing information for all connections terminating at the node.

Troubleshooting Commands

Table 8-1 lists the commands introduced in this chapter that are used to troubleshoot the network.

Table 8-1   *IGX Troubleshooting Commands*

Command	Description	Privilege Level
addextlp	Adds an external loop.	1 to 2
addloclp	Adds a loop at the local port or channel.	1 to 2
addrmtlp	Adds a loop at the remote channel.	1 to 2
clrlnalm	Clears a minor statistical alarm from a line.	1 to 5
clrlnerrs	Clears error statistics for all lines on the switch.	1 to 5
clrlog	Clears the entries from the alarm and event log.	1 to 5
clrtrkalm	Clears a minor statistical alarm from a trunk.	1 to 5
clrtrkerrs	Clears error statistics for all trunks on the switch.	1 to 5
cnflnalm	Modifies line or trunk major and minor alarm thresholds for statistical alarms.	1 to 5
cnftrkalm	Configures alarm reporting for a trunk.	1 to 5
dellp	Removes any type of loop.	1 to 2
dspalms	Displays the alarm summary for this switch.	1 to 6
dsplnalmcnf	Displays the line or trunk major and minor alarms.	1 to 6
dsplnerrs	Displays the errors on one or all lines on the switch.	1 to 6
dsplog	Displays the alarm and event log for this switch.	1 to 6
dsptrkerrs	Displays errors on one or all trunks on the switch.	1 to 6
resetcd	Performs either a "failure" or "hardware" reset on a card to clear a failure condition.	1 to 3

continues

Table 8-1 *IGX Troubleshooting Commands (Continued)*

Command	Description	Privilege Level
switchcc	Switches the standby NPM to active and the active NPM to standby.	1 to 3
tstcon	Tests a connection from end to end using test packets generated by the IGX/IPX.	1 to 2

dspalms Command

The **dspalms** command, shown in Example 8-1, is typically the first command used in troubleshooting the IGX node because it displays all alarm conditions throughout the local IGX.

Example 8-1 **dspalms** *Output*

```
igx4            TN     group8:1        IGX 8420  9.2.20    July 30 1999 13:23 CDT

Alarm summary    (Configured alarm slots: None)
Connections Failed:       1
TRK Alarms:               1 Major
Circuit Line Alarms:      None
Physical Line Alarms:     None
Cards Failed:             None
Missing Cards:            2
Remote Node Alarms:       3 Majors
                                          Too many invalid login attempts


Interface Shelf Alarms:   None

FastPAD/Access Dev Alms:  None       Cable Mismatch Condition

Last Command: dspalms

Next Command:
```

This alarm summary includes the following:

- The number of failed connections on the node
- The number of major and minor line alarms on the node
- The number of major and minor trunk alarms on the node
- The number of failed and missing cards on the node
- The number of alarms on other nodes in the network
- The power supply and power monitor failures on the node

- Bus failures (either Failed or Needs Diagnostics)
- Frame Relay port communication failed (OAM packet threshold exceeded)
- Frame Relay NNI A-bit alarms (connections with A bits = 0)

dsplog Command

The **dsplog** command screen provides a local node event and alarm log, as shown in Example 8-2. Events affecting the node are displayed in chronological order, with the most recent events at the top of the log.

Example 8-2 dsplog *Output*

```
igx4            TN    group8:1        IGX 8420  9.2.20    July 30 1999 13:24 CDT

Most recent log entries (most recent at top)
Class   Description                                    Date      Time
Major   TRK 15 Front Card Missing                      07/30/99  13:19:02
Major   ALM 15 Down - No backup available              07/30/99  13:19:02
Info    Clock switch to TRK 13 of igx3 via TRK 9.1     07/30/99  13:18:09
Clear   TRK 9.1 OK                                     07/30/99  13:16:15
Clear   TRK 9.1 Activated                              07/30/99  13:16:15
Clear   PHYSLN 9.1 OK                                  07/30/99  13:16:15
Clear   PHYSLN 9.1 Activated                           07/30/99  13:16:15
Info    UXM 9 Activated                                07/30/99  13:16:15
Clear   LN 9.3 Deactivated                             07/30/99  13:12:50
Info    UXM 9 Freed                                    07/30/99  13:12:50
Clear   LN 9.2 Deactivated                             07/30/99  13:12:47
Clear   LN 9.1 Deactivated                             07/30/99  13:12:43
Info    Port 9.3 Deactivated                           07/30/99  13:12:38


This Command: dsplog

Continue?
```

Events from the FastPAD are integrated into the log. The log includes the following information:

- Event class—Major alarms, minor alarms, information, and events clearing alarms
- Event description
- Date
- Time

clrlog Command

The log can hold up to 500 messages before the oldest events are overwritten. A more complete event log can be found on Cisco WAN Manager or on a network printer with logging enabled. The **clrlog** command clears the event log. When the log is cleared, one entry remains—Info Log Cleared. Before the event log is cleared, you are prompted to confirm the clearing activity.

dsptrkerrs Command

The **dsptrkerrs** command screen provides a summary of historical statistical errors that have occurred on all trunks on the node, as shown in Example 8-3.

Example 8-3 **dsptrkerrs** *Output*

```
igx4            TN     group8:1        IGX 8420  9.2.20    July 30 1999 13:25 CDT

Total Statistical Errors

                                                     Tx Pkts
         Code    Rx Pkts Out of  Loss of Frame   CRC /Cells  Packet Packet
  PLN    Errors  Dropped Frames  Signal  BitErrs Errors Dropped Errors Oofs
   9.1   -       -       -       -       -       -       0       -      -
   13    0       -       0       0       0       0       0       0      0
   14    -       -       0       0       0       0       0       2      2
   15    0       0       2       1       -       0       0       0      -




Last Command: dsptrkerrs


Next Command:
```

Table 8-2 lists the **dsptrkerrs** command error counts.

Table 8-2 **dsptrkerrs** *Error Counts*

Type	Description
Code Errors	Bipolar violations (BPVs) or coded mark inversion (CMI) line-code violations.
Rx Packets Dropped	BTM only.
Out of Frames	Statistical out-of-frames; short duration.
Loss of Signal	Statistical loss-of-signal; short duration.
Frame Bit Errors	Error in the framing bit.
CRC Errors	Optional frame cyclic redundancy check (CRC) did not match the trunk card's calculated CRC. This is applicable only to trunks with CRC checking enabled.

Table 8-2 **dsptrkerrs** *Error Counts (Continued)*

Type	Description
Tx Packets Dropped	Packets were dropped due to egress trunk queue overflow or packet expiration.
Packet Errors	FastPacket header CRC did not match the trunk card's calculated CRC. This is performed on receive packets only.
Packet Out of Frames	Unable to delineate packets on the trunk. This is usually due to multiple packet errors.

Here is the **dsptrkerrs** command syntax:

```
dsptrkerrs [trunk]
```

trunk displays statistical error counts for the specified trunk. If no trunk is specified, a summary of errors for all trunks is displayed.

The **dsptrkerrs** command, when used with an optional trunk number parameter, provides detailed error statistics for a selected trunk, as shown in Example 8-4.

Example 8-4 **dsptrkerrs** *Output*

```
igx4            TN     group8:1       IGX 8420  9.2.20    July 30 1999 13:26 CDT


TRK 15          Status:Major - Front Card Missing        Clrd:07/28/99 14:55:43
Statistical Alarm Count ETS    Status    Integrated Alarm  Count ETS    Status
Out of Frms            1     1            Comm Fails            0     -
Loss of Sig            1     1            Loss of Sig (RED)     1     -
Tx Voice Pkt Drp       0     0            AIS         (BLUE)    0     -
Tx TS Pkt Drp          0     0            Out of Frms (RED)     0     -
Tx Non-TS Pkt Drp      0     0            Rmt OOF     (YEL)     1     -
Tx CC Pkt Drp          0     0
Tx BData A Pkt Drp     0     0
Tx BData B Pkt Drp     0     0
Packet Err             0     0
Line Code Errs         0     0
P-bit Parity Errs      0     0
C-bit Parity Errs      0     0
                                         Last failure time: 07/30/99 13:19:02


This Command: dsptrkerrs 15


Continue?
```

Error counts are provided for each type of error, as well as an "errored ten seconds" (ETS). The ETS field indicates the errors that occurred during the 10-second period. The ETS activity provides a means to determine how the errors were distributed over time. For example, if 2000 packet errors occurred in one 10-second period (ETS = 1), you can assume that the errors were part of a single burst or hit on the trunk. However, if the 2000 packet errors occurred in 500 different 10-second periods (ETS = 500), you can assume that the errors were spread over a longer period of time and should be monitored.

Error counts that indicate an ETS might cause major or minor alarms if they exceed the configured alarm thresholds. Alarm thresholds are displayed using the **dsplnalmcnf** command and can be modified using the **cnflnalm** command.

Error counts that do not indicate an ETS are considered physical errors. In other words, the trunk experienced an error that caused the trunk to fail and traffic to be rerouted. These physical errors always generate major alarms.

Some types of errors, such as out of frame and loss of signal, appear twice—as statistical and physical errors. Statistical errors occur for a short duration; physical errors that result in trunk failure occur for a longer period of time.

cnftrkalm Command

The **cnftrkalm** command enables or disables trunk alarm reporting, as shown in Example 8-5. When trunks are upped and added to the network, alarm reporting is automatically enabled.

Example 8-5 **cnftrkalm** *Output*

```
igx4              TN     group8:1        IGX 8420  9.2.20    July 30 1999 13:27 CDT


Last Command: cnftrkalm 15 d


Next Command:
```

The **cnftrkalm** command lets you disable alarms on a trunk. Disabling alarms might be useful for trunks that are connected to the node but are not yet in service.

Example 8-5 disables alarm reporting on trunk 15. After you use this command to disable the alarms, the only indication that alarms have been disabled is the display on the **dspalms** screen while a trunk alarm exists. The **dspalms** screen displays the word "disabled" after "PLN Alarms." Remember to enable alarms after the cause of the trunk failure has been corrected.

Here is the **cnftrkalm** command syntax:

```
cnftrkalm <trunk> <e | d>
```

Table 8-3 lists the **cnftrkalm** command parameters.

Table 8-3 **cnftrkalm** *Parameter Descriptions*

Parameter	Description	Required/Optional
trunk	Identifies the trunk to configure.	Required
e	d	Enables (e) or disables (d) trunk alarm reporting.	Required

clrtrkalm Command

The **clrtrkalm** command clears statistical alarms associated with either a physical or virtual trunk, as shown in Example 8-6. Because the statistical alarms associated with a trunk have associated integration times, they can keep a major or minor alarm active for some time after the condition is resolved. The **clrtrkalm** command allows these alarms to be cleared and any new alarms to be quickly identified.

Example 8-6 **clrtrkalm** *Output*

```
igx3           TN     group1:1        IGX 8420  9.2.20    Sep. 13 1999 11:56 CDT

                             Line Alarm Configuration

                     Minor                              Major

   Violation    Rate    Alarm Time  Clear        Rate    Alarm Time  Clear
   1) Bpv       10E-7   10 min      3 min        10E-3   30 sec      10 sec
   2) Fs        .01%    10 min      3 min        .1%     30 sec      10 sec
   3) Oof       .0001%  10 min      3 min        .01%    30 sec      10 sec
   4) Los       .0001%  10 min      3 min        .01%    30 sec      10 sec
   5) Fer       .01%    10 min      3 min        .1%     200 sec     10 sec
   6) CRC       .01%    10 min      3 min        .1%     200 sec     10 sec
   7) Oom       .001%   10 min      3 min        .1%     30 sec      10 sec
   8) Ais16     .0001%  10 min      3 min        .01%    30 sec      10 sec


This Command: clrtrkalm 15 3


Next Command:
```

The **clrtrkalm** command can only clear alarms caused by the collection of statistical data. Alarms caused by a network failure cannot be cleared. For example, an alarm caused by a collection of bipolar errors can be cleared, but an alarm caused by a card failure cannot.

Here is the **clrtrkalm** command syntax:

```
clrtrkalm <trunk> <failure-type>
```

Table 8-4 lists the **clrtrkalm** command parameters.

Table 8-4 **clrtrkalm** *Parameter Descriptions*

Parameter	Description	Required/Optional
trunk	Identifies the trunk to configure in the format *slot* or *slot.port*. Virtual trunks are identified by *slot.port*.	Required
failure-type	Specifies the type of alarm to clear.	Required

dsplnerrs Command

The **dsplnerrs** command screen provides a summary of historical statistical errors that have occurred on all lines on the node, as shown in Example 8-7.

Example 8-7 **dsplnerrs** *Output*

```
igx4              TN    group8:1        IGX 8420  9.2.20    July 30 1999 13:29 CDT

Total Statistical Errors

          Code   Frame   Out of  Loss of Frame    CRC     Out of
CLN       Errors Slips   Frames  Signal  BitErrs  Errors  MFrames AIS-16
 3.1          0      0       0       0       -        0       -      -
 3.2          0      0       0       0       -        0       -      -
 4.1          0      0       0       0       -        0       -      -
 4.2          0      0       0       0       -        0       -      -
11.1          0      -       0       0       -        0       -      -
11.2          0      -       0       0       -        0       -      -
11.4          0      -       0       0       -        0       -      -
16         9818      -       2       1       -      349       -      -


Last Command: dsplnerrs

Next Command:
```

Table 8-5 lists the error counts for the **dsplnerrs** command.

Table 8-5 **dsplnerrs** *Command Types and Definitions*

Type	Definition
Code Errors	Bipolar violations (BPVs) or CMI line-code violations.
Frame Slips	Frames that are discarded in order to resynchronize the time-division multiplexing (TDM) line.
Out of Frames	Statistical out of frames; short duration.
Loss of Signal	Statistical loss of signal; short duration.

Table 8-5   **dsplnerrs** *Command Types and Definitions (Continued)*

Type	Definition
Frame Bit Errors	Error in the framing bit.
CRC Errors	Optional frame CRC did not match the line card's calculated CRC. This is applicable only to lines that have CRC checking enabled.
Out of Multiframe	For E1 only. Loss of multiframe due to timeslot 16 errors.
AIS 16	For E1 only. The Alarm Indicator Signal (Blue alarm) bit in time slot 16 was set by the remote device.

Here is the **dsplnerrs** command syntax:

```
dsplnerrs [line]
```

line displays statistical error counts for the specified line. If no line is specified, a summary of errors for all lines is displayed.

dsplnalmcnf Command

The **dsplnalmcnf** command displays alarm configuration by alarm type, as shown in Example 8-8.

Example 8-8   **dsplnalmcnf** *Output*

```
igx4            TN      group8:1          IGX 8420  9.2.20     July 30 1999 13:30 CDT

                                 Line Alarm Configuration

                         Minor                                   Major

   Violation   Rate     Alarm Time  Clear        Rate    Alarm Time  Clear
   1) Bpv      10E-7    10 min      3 min        10E-3    30 sec      10 sec
   2) Fs         .01%   10 min      3 min          .1%   30 sec      10 sec
   3) Oof      .0001%   10 min      3 min          .01%  30 sec      10 sec
   4) Los      .0001%   10 min      3 min          .01%  30 sec      10 sec
   5) Fer        .01%   10 min      3 min          .1%   200 sec     10 sec
   6) CRC        .01%   10 min      3 min          .1%   200 sec     10 sec
   7) Oom       .001%   10 min      3 min          .1%   30 sec      10 sec
   8) Ais16    .0001%   10 min      3 min          .01%  30 sec      10 sec

This Command: dsplnalmcnf

Continue?
```

Table 8-6 lists major and minor alarm type violation fields.

Table 8-6 *Major and Minor Alarms*

Major	Minor
Alarm threshold	Alarm threshold
Alarm time	Alarm time
Alarm clear time	Alarm clear time

These parameters are set using the **cnflnalm** command. Four display screens result from issuing the **dsplnalmcnf** command. Example 8-8 shows the first screen only.

cnflnalm Command

The **cnflnalm** command sets both trunk and line alarm values for statistical failures, as shown in Example 8-9. Statistical alarms are declared by the switch software when cards supporting these trunks or lines report too many errors.

Example 8-9 **cnflnalm** *Output*

```
igx4            TN     group8:1        IGX 8420  9.2.20    July 30 1999 13:32 CDT

                              Line Alarm Configuration

                     Minor                              Major

     Violation    Rate    Alarm Time   Clear       Rate   Alarm Time   Clear
     9) Pkoof      .01%   10 min       3 min        .1%   200 sec      10 sec
     10) Pkterr    .01%   10 min       3 min        .1%   125 sec      10 sec
     11) Badclk    .001%  10 min       4 min        1%     50 sec      10 sec
     12) Vpd         2%    5 min       3 min        5%     60 sec      10 sec
     13) Tsdp      .01%    5 min       3 min        .1%    60 sec      10 sec
     14) Ntsdp     .01%    5 min       3 min        .1%    60 sec      10 sec
     15) Pccpd     .001%   5 min       3 min        .1%    60 sec      10 sec
     16) Bdapd     .001%   5 min       3 min        .1%    60 sec      10 sec

Last Command: cnflnalm 11 1 4 10 4

Next Command:
```

The switch declares an alarm if the detected error rate equals the **cnflnalm** parameter error rate for the period of time designated by the alarm time parameter. Error rates that exceed the specified error rate cause an alarm in a proportionately shorter period of time. An alarm is cleared when the error rate remains below the rate specified for a period of time designated by the clear time.

Example 8-9 shows setting Alarm Type 11, the minor alarm time clearing threshold, to 4 minutes. In this example, the **cnflnalm** command is followed by the violation type (11), the alarm class (1 for minor, 2 for major), the current rate (the default of 0.001 percent, or value 4), the value for an alarm time of 10 minutes, and the alarm clear time of 4 minutes.

Here is the **cnflnalm** command syntax:

```
cnflnalm <failure-type> <alarm-class> <rate> <alarm-time> <clear-time>
```

Table 8-7 lists the **cnflnalm** command parameters.

Table 8-7   **cnflnalm** *Parameter Descriptions*

Parameter	Description	Required/Optional
failure-type	Specifies the type of alarm to configure.	Required
alarm-class	1 = minor alarm, 2 = major alarm.	Required
rate	The rate at which the error must occur before an alarm is declared. The default error rates are indicated.	Required
alarm-time	The time that a condition must exceed the *rate* threshold before an alarm is declared. For minor alarms, the alarm time has a range of 3 to 10 minutes. For major alarms, the alarm time has a range of 10 to 250 seconds.	Required
clear-time	The time before the alarm is cleared. For minor alarms, the clear time has a range of 3 to 10 minutes. For major alarms, the clear time has a range of 10 to 250 seconds.	Required
error-rate-options	The error rate entry follows the table values shown in Table 8-8.	Required

Table 8-8 lists alarm classes and error rates.

Table 8-8   *Alarm Error Rates*

Alarm Option	Class	Error Rate 1	2	3	4	5
A	Minor	1%	.1%	.01%	.001%	.0001%
	Major	1%	.1%	.01%		
B	Minor	10E to 4	10E to 5	10E to 6	10E to 7	10E to 8
	Major	10E to 2	10E to 3	10E to 4	10E to 5	10E to 6

clrlnalm Command

The **clrlnalm** command clears the alarms associated with a line, as shown in Example 8-10. Because the statistical alarms associated with a line have associated integration times, they can keep a major or minor alarm active for some time after the cause has been rectified. This command allows these alarms to be cleared, allowing any new alarms to be quickly identified.

Example 8-10 clrlnalm *Output*

```
igx3          TN    group1:1        IGX 8420  9.2.20    Sep. 13 1999 12:00 CDT

                           Line Alarm Configuration

                     Minor                            Major

     Violation   Rate    Alarm Time  Clear      Rate    Alarm Time  Clear
     1) Bpv      10E-7   10 min      3 min      10E-3   30 sec      10 sec
     2) Fs       .01%    10 min      3 min      .1%     30 sec      10 sec
     3) Oof      .0001%  10 min      3 min      .01%    30 sec      10 sec
     4) Los      .0001%  10 min      3 min      .01%    30 sec      10 sec
     5) Fer      .01%    10 min      3 min      .1%     200 sec     10 sec
     6) CRC      .01%    10 min      3 min      .1%     200 sec     10 sec
     7) Oom      .001%   10 min      3 min      .1%     30 sec      10 sec
     8) Ais16    .0001%  10 min      3 min      .01%    30 sec      10 sec


 Last Command: clrlnalm 9.1 4


 Next Command:
```

The **clrlnalm** command can clear only alarms caused by the collection of statistical data. Alarms caused by a network failure cannot be cleared. For example, an alarm caused by a collection of bipolar errors can be cleared, but an alarm caused by a card failure cannot.

The **clrlnalm 14 2** command string clears the minor alarm caused by frame slips on line 14. The 2 indicates frame slips.

Here is the **clrlnalm** command syntax:

```
clrlnalm <line> <failure-type>
```

Table 8-9 lists the **clrlnalm** command parameters.

Table 8-9   **clrlnalm** *Parameter Descriptions*

Parameter	Description	Required/Optional
line	Specifies the line for which to clear the alarm.	Required
failure-type	Specifies the type of alarm to clear. See **cnflnalm** for a list of failure types.	Required

resetcd Command

The **resetcd** command resets the hardware and software for a specified card, as shown in Example 8-11. A hardware reset is equivalent to physically removing and reinserting the front card of a card group and causes the card's logic to be reset. When you reset the hardware of an active card other than a controller card (NPM or BCC), a standby card takes over if one is available. A failure reset clears the card failures associated with the specified slot. If a slot contains a card set, both the front and back cards are reset.

Example 8-11 resetcd *Output*

```
igx4            TN      group8:1      IGX 8420  9.2.20    July 30 1999 13:34 CDT



    FrontCard  BackCard                  FrontCard  BackCard
    Type  Rev  Type    Rev  Status       Type  Rev  Type    Rev  Status
 1  NPM   BWR              Active      9  UXM   AAD  E3      AA   Active
 2  NPM   EBR              Upgraded   10  UFMU  ADE  X21     AB   Active
 3  UVM   ADA  T1-2   AB   Active     11  UFM   AFL  T1D     AB   Active
 4  UVM   ADA  T1-2   AB   Active     12  NTM   FDH  SR      AH   Standby
 5  Empty universal backplane         13  NTM   FDH  T1      AL   Active
 6  HDM   CFF  RS232D BW   Active      14  NTM   FDH  E1      AN   Active
 7  LDM   CKB  232-4  AL   Active      15  ALM   BEH  UAI-T3  AB   Active
 8  Empty universal backplane         16  ALM   AEE  UAI-T3  AB   Active


Last Command: resetcd 6 f

Next Command:
```

Do not use **resetcd** on an *active* NPM processor card, because a temporary interruption of all traffic will occur while the card is rebooting. (Resetting a controller card does not destroy configuration information.) Where a redundant NPM is available, the **switchcc** command is used to switch the active controller card to standby and the standby controller card to active. If a standby card is available, resetting an active card (except for an NPM or BCC) does not cause a system failure. Hardware (H) or background test (F) resetting of an active card that is not in standby does disrupt service until the self-test finishes.

Here is the **resetcd** command syntax:

```
resetcd <slot> <h | f>
```

Table 8-10 lists the **resetcd** command parameters.

Table 8-10   **resetcd** *Parameter Descriptions*

Parameter	Description	Required/Optional
slot	Specifies the card to be reset based on the slot location.	Required
h | f	Indicates a hardware (h) reset or test failure (f) reset.	Required

addloclp Command

Example 8-12 shows the **addloclp** command output, which places types of channels in local loopback mode. The types of channels are described after the output.

Example 8-12 addloclp *Output*

```
igx4             TN    group8:1      IGX 8420  9.2.20    July 30 1999 13:35 CDT

 From            Remote     Remote
 6.1             NodeName   Channel            State  Type    Compress   Code COS
 6.1             )igx3      5.2                Ok     9.6f               7/8  0
 7.1             igx3       5.1                Ok     24                 7/8  0
 7.3             igx1       6.3                Ok     24                 7/8  0
 10.1.*          igx1       11.7.*             Ok     fr                      0
 11.1.187        igx1       16.1.87            Ok     atft                    8
 11.240.99       igx1       11.240.99          Ok     fr                      0
 11.240.107      igx1       16.1.107           Ok     atfx                    0
 16.1.90         igx3       16.1.90            Failed cbr                     0
 16.1.97         igx1       16.1.97            Ok     vbr                     0
 16.20.200       igx1       16.30.200          Ok     vbr                     0

Last Command: addloclp 6.1

Next Command:
```

The **addloclp** command places the following types of channels in local loopback mode:

- **Voice**—For voice connections, **addloclp** creates a signal path from a channel or group of channels on an incoming line and then back out to the line.

- **Data**—For data connections, **addloclp** creates a signal path from the incoming data port or set of ports back to these same port(s) through the local CVM, HDM, or LDM.

- Frame Relay port

- **Frame Relay connection**—In Frame Relay connection loopback mode (DLCI is included in the command), all packets from the far end of the connection are dropped. The far-end system software is informed of the loopback. In port loopback mode (the port is specified without a DLCI), all packets for this port are dropped, and each opposite end is informed of the loopback mode. The format *slot.port* is used in port mode to loop just the port. The data is looped directly in the FRI back card, so no data reaches the Cellbus. The format *slot.port.DLCI* is used in connection mode to loop a specific connection. These slight differences in command formats can affect many connections in port loopback mode.

- ATM connection

- Access device port

Use the **dspcons** command to learn which connections are looped back. A flashing close parenthesis ( )) or open parenthesis (( ) is used in the connections display to indicate a loopback. The direction and location of the parenthesis depends on whether the loopback is local or remote and which end of the connection was used to establish the loopback.

Here is the **addloclp** command syntax:

```
addloclp <connection | port>
```

connection | port specifies the connection or port to be looped.

addrmtlp Command

The **addrmtlp** command places channels in remote loopback mode. Its output is shown in Example 8-13.

Example 8-13 **addrmtlp** *Output*

```
igx4            TN     group8:1        IGX 8420  9.2.20    July 30 1999 13:38 CDT

 Local          Remote     Remote
 Channel        NodeName   Channel         State  Type    Compress    Code COS
 3.1.1-4        igx3      )3.1.1-4         Down   116v    VAD/LDCELP       2
 3.1.5-16       igx3       3.1.5-16        Down   116v    VAD/LDCELP       2
 6.1           )igx3       5.2             Ok     9.6f                7/8  0
 F7.1           igx3       5.1             Ok     24                  7/8  0
 7.3            igx1       6.3             Ok     24                  7/8  0
 10.1.*         igx1       11.7.*          Ok     fr                       0
 11.1.187       igx1       16.1.87         Ok     atft                     8
 11.240.99      igx1       11.240.99       Ok     fr                       0
 11.240.107     igx1       16.1.107        Ok     atfx                     0
 16.1.90        igx3       16.1.90         Failed cbr                      0
 16.1.97        igx1       16.1.97         Ok     vbr                      0
 16.20.200      igx1       16.30.200       Ok     vbr                      0

Last Command: addrmtlp 3.1.1-4

Next Command:
```

The **addrmtlp** command places the following types of channels in remote loopback mode:

- **Voice**—For voice connections, **addrmtlp** loops the information stream from the designated channel or group of channels on an incoming line across the network and loops it back to the line by way of the remote CVM. External test equipment can then test the integrity of the path at the T1 DS-0 level.

- **Data**—For data connections, **addrmtlp** transfers the information stream from the designated channels through the network and loops it back to the data port(s) through a remote HDM or LDM. External test equipment can then test the path's integrity.

- Frame Relay port
- **Frame Relay connection**—For remote loopback of Frame Relay connections. In remote loopback mode, if the transmit minimum bandwidth exceeds the receive minimum bandwidth, loopback data might be dropped. For this reason, the connection speeds are checked, and the user receives the following message if there is a problem:

  Warning---Receiver's BW < Originator's BW-Data may be dropped.

- ATM connection

Remote loopbacks are established with the **addrmtlp** command. Both local and remote loopbacks are removed using the **dellp** command. Loopbacks for data channels can also be initiated by pressing a button on the front of the associated data card.

Here is the **addrmtlp** command syntax:

addrmtlp *<connection | port>*

connection | port specifies the connection or port to be looped.

addextlp Command

The **addextlp** places channels in external loopback mode. The **addextlp** command output is shown in Example 8-14.

Example 8-14 **addextlp** *Output*

```
igx4          TN    group8:1        IGX 8420  9.2.20    July 30 1999 13:36 CDT

 From          Remote      Remote
 7.1           NodeName    Channel          State  Type    Compress   Code COS
 F7.1          igx3        5.1              Ok     24                  7/8  0
 7.3           igx1        6.3              Ok     24                  7/8  0
 10.1.*        igx1        11.7.*           Ok     fr                       0
 11.1.187      igx1        16.1.87          Ok     atft                     8
 11.240.99     igx1        11.240.99        Ok     fr                       0
 11.240.107    igx1        16.1.107         Ok     atfx                     0
 16.1.90       igx3        16.1.90          Failed cbr                      0
 16.1.97       igx1        16.1.97          Ok     vbr                      0
 16.20.200     igx1        16.30.200        Ok     vbr                      0

 Last Command: addextlp 7.1 f

 Next Command:
```

Here is the **addextlp** command syntax:

addextlp *<channel>* *<n | f>*

Table 8-11 lists the **addextlp** command parameters.

Table 8-11   **addextlp** *Parameter Descriptions*

Parameter	Description	Required/Optional
channel	Loops the external device attached to the specified channel.	Required
n | f	Specifies whether the loopback is near (n) or far (f).	Required

dellp Command

The **dellp** command, shown in Example 8-15, deletes an external, local, remote, or local-remote loopback from the designated channel, set of channels, or port.

Example 8-15 **dellp** *Output*

```
igx4            TN    group8:1     IGX 8420  9.2.20    July 30 1999 13:40 CDT

Local           Remote      Remote
Channel         NodeName    Channel         State  Type    Compress    Code COS
3.1.1-16         igx3        3.1.1-16        Down   116v    VAD/LDCELP       2
6.1             )igx3        5.2             Ok     9.6f                7/8  0
F7.1             igx3        5.1             Ok     24                  7/8  0
7.3              igx1        6.3             Ok     24                  7/8  0
10.1.*           igx1        11.7.*          Ok     fr                       0
11.1.187         igx1        16.1.87         Ok     atft                     8
11.240.99        igx1        11.240.99       Ok     fr                       0
11.240.107       igx1        16.1.10.107     Ok     atfx                     0
16.1.1.90        igx3        16.1.1.90       Failed cbr                      0
16.1.2.97        igx1        16.1.100.999    Ok     vbr                      0
16.2.20.200      igx1        16.3.30.201     Ok     vbr                      0

Last Command: dellp 3.1.2-4

Next Command:
```

After the loopback is deleted, any conditioning applied during the loopback process is removed, and service is restored. A local loop can be deleted only from the node that added it. However, a remote loop can be deleted from the node at either end of the connection. Local-remote loopbacks are added with the **addlocrmtlp** command. With local-remote loopbacks, execution of **dellp** is mandatory after testing is complete. Otherwise, continuity errors will follow.

Here is the **dellp** command syntax:

```
dellp <channel>
```

channel removes the loopback from the specified channel.

tstcon Command

The **tstcon** command displays the connections screen, highlights the channel selected for testing, and prompts you to confirm the test. Table 8-12 lists some **tstcon** command examples.

Table 8-12   **tstcon** *Command Examples*

Command	Description
tstcon *	Tests all connections.
tstcon * f	Tests all Frame Relay connections.
tstcon * v x	Tests all voice connections and aborts on the first failure.
tstcon 1.3	Tests the connection on channel 1.3.
tstcon 4.2.200	Tests the connection on channel 4.2.200.
tstcon 1.13-16	Tests the connections on channels 1.13 through 16.
tstcon 3.21-24 x	Tests the connections on channels 3.21 through 24 and aborts on the first failure.
tstcon 3.11-20 v	Tests voice connections only on channels 3.11 through 20.
tstcon 3.11-20 v x	Tests voice connections only on channels 3.11 through 20 and aborts on the first failure.
tstcon 3.21-22 v 5	Tests voice connections only on channels 3.21 through 22 and repeats the test five times.
tstcon 3.14-15 d x 5	Tests data connections on channels 3.14 through 15, repeats the test five times, and aborts on failure.

The **tstcon** output is shown in Example 8-16. A T after the local channel being tested indicates that the test is currently running on that channel. When the first test is complete, a message appears that indicates the results of the test. As each test is completed, the T moves to the next channel to be tested, and the message is updated to include the cumulative results of the tests. When the test is completed for all the specified connections, the T disappears, and the message indicates the total number of tests and the cumulative results of the tests.

Example 8-16 **tstcon** *Output*

```
igx4            TN     group8:1        IGX 8420  9.2.20    July 30 1999 13:43 CDT

Local           Remote        Remote
Channel         NodeName      Channel          State  Type     Compress   Code COS
3.1.1           igx3          (3.1.1           Down   l16v     VAD/LDCELP      2
3.1.2-16        igx3          3.1.2-16         Down   l16v     VAD/LDCELP      2
6.1             igx3          5.2              Ok     9.6f                7/8  0
7.1             igx3          5.1              Ok     24                  7/8  0
7.3             igx1          6.3              Ok     24                  7/8  0
10.1.*          igx1          11.7.*           Ok     fr                       0
```

Example 8-16 *tstcon Output (Continued)*

```
11.1.187       igx1      16.1.87      Ok     atft                8
11.240.99      Tigx1     11.240.99    Ok     fr                  0
11.240.107     igx1      16.1.107     Ok     atfx                0
16.1.90        igx3      16.1.90      Failed cbr                 0
16.1.97        igx1      16.1.97      Ok     vbr                 0
16.20.200      igx1      16.30.200    Ok     vbr                 0

This Command: tstcon * f 4

Tests: Completed = 9, Aborted = 1, Failed = 4, Connections Repaired = 0
Hit DEL key to quit:
```

Although **tstcon** is intrusive, connection service is affected for only a few seconds. If multiple connections are specified, only one channel at a time is tested to minimize the disruption. Because service is disrupted for only a short time, no conditioning is applied during the test. Repaired connections indicate that a test failed previously but that the current test has succeeded.

Here is the **tstcon** command syntax:

tstcon <channel | *> [v | d | f] [x] [repeat-count]

Table 8-13 lists the **tstcon** command parameters.

Table 8-13   *tstcon Parameter Descriptions*

Parameter	Description	Required/Optional
channel | *	Tests the specified channel or all channels (*).	Required
v | d | f	Tests only voice (v), data (d), or Frame Relay (f) connections.	Optional
x	If a test fails, aborts the **tstcon** command.	Optional
repeat-count	Repeats the test the specified number of times. The default is 1.	Optional

The **dspcons** screen provides current loopback and testing information on the connections on the local node. Possible states are shown in Table 8-14.

Table 8-14   *Loopback Testing Information*

Loopback Type	Added By	Symbol	dspcons Display
Local connection loop	Local IGX	)	To the left of the remote node name
Remote connection loop	Local IGX	)	To the right of the remote node name
Local connection loop	Remote IGX	(	To the right of the remote node name

continues

Table 8-14 *Loopback Testing Information (Continued)*

Loopback Type	Added By	Symbol	dspcons Display
Remote connection loop or local remote loop	Remote IGX	(	To the left of the remote node name
Frame Relay local port loop	Local IGX	]	To the left of the remote node name
Frame Relay local port loop	Remote IGX	[	To the right of the remote node name
Connection in test	---	T	To the right of the local channel

Connection Testing

This section describes how connections can be tested via the **tstcon** command for local, remote, or external loopback tests. The loopback commands only create a loopback *condition,* so external test equipment is required to generate a test pattern. In contrast, the IGX generates the test patterns for the **tstcon** command. This section also describes how HDM and LDM data cards can add and delete local and remote loops using the buttons on the faceplate of the card modules.

The following types of loopbacks are available on the IGX:

- **Local loopback**—Tests continuity up to the local interface. A local loop can be added to any connection or Frame Relay port.

- **Remote loopback**—Tests continuity through the network on a given connection from the local to the remote interface. Remote loops can be added to any connection that terminates on a remote node.

- **Local-remote loopback**—Tests continuity through the network on a given connection from the remote to the local interface. The local-remote connection loop is identical to the remote connection loop but is added from the other end of the connection. Remote loops can be added to any connection that terminates on a remote IGX or MGX.

- **External loopbacks**—Tests continuity through the network on a given connection from the local interface to the remote user. The external user equipment is looped and must return the test pattern.

tstcon Command

The **tstcon** command tests the integrity of a connection by inserting IGX-generated test data. Although **tstcon** is intrusive, connection service is affected for only a few seconds. Because service is disrupted for only a short time, no conditioning is normally applied during the test, as follows:

- If a failure is detected, the fault is isolated to a specific IGX node and card. If a standby card is available, it automatically goes into service. During fault isolation, conditioning is applied to both ends of the connection.

- A connection can be repaired if the network can detect and resolve a problem.
- Repairing can include clearing buffers, switching to a redundant card, and so on.
- Loopbacks and external test equipment provide more complete testing capabilities.

The **tstcon** command reports the following results:

- **Completed**—The total number of tests that were run.
- **Aborted**—The number of tests that did not run because of loopbacks or missing or failed hardware.
- **Failures**—The number of tests that failed.
- **Repaired**—A connection that failed a previous test and has passed the current test.

Local Loopback

Local loopback tests front and back card pairs by looping incoming traffic back out for a Frame Relay port, a voice channel, or a data interface, as illustrated in Figure 8-1.

Figure 8-1 *Local Loopback*

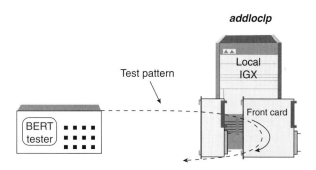

You must use external test equipment such as a Bit Error Rate Tester (BERT) to generate the test pattern and analyze the traffic for errors. Local loopback checks the traffic path from the electrical interface at the port through the card set to the Cellbus in both directions of transmission.

WARNING   Because this is a disruptive test, you must notify your network administrator before performing it.

To perform a local loopback, follow these steps:

Step 1 Disconnect the data cable connection to the card to be tested, and connect the test equipment in its place.

Step 2 Set up an internal loopback on the Frame Relay port or connection to be tested using the **addloclp** command.

Step 3 Turn on the test equipment, make sure it indicates circuit continuity, and observe the indicated error rate.

Step 4 If any unexpected errors are detected, replace the back card and retest. If the errors remain after retesting, replace the front card and retest. Cisco strongly recommends downing a card (use the **dncd** command) before removing it.

Step 5 When the test is complete, disconnect the test equipment and reconnect the data cable. Release the local loopback using the **dellp** command. Repeat at the node at the other end of the connection if necessary.

Step 6 While testing, use the **dspcons** command to see which connections are looped back. A flashing right parenthesis [ )] or left parenthesis [( ] indicates a loopback.

A local loopback can exist simultaneously at both ends of a connection. However, a local loopback and a remote loopback cannot coexist on a connection. Prior to executing a loopback, the IGX node performs signal and code conditioning to remove the connection from service. The loopback remains in place until it is removed by the **dellp** command.

Remote Loopback

The **addrmtlp** command transmits an information stream over a voice or data channel across the network and loops it back to the local transmitting interface by way of the remote front card, as illustrated in Figure 8-2. External test equipment is used to generate and analyze a test pattern.

Prior to executing remote loopback on a voice channel, the remote IGX node signals using the A, B, C, and D signaling bits at the remote end to remove the connection from service. The loopback remains in place until it is removed by the **dellp** command. You cannot establish a remote loopback on a connection that is already looped back, either locally or remotely.

WARNING Because this is a disruptive test, notify your network administrator before performing it.

Figure 8-2   *Remote Loopback*

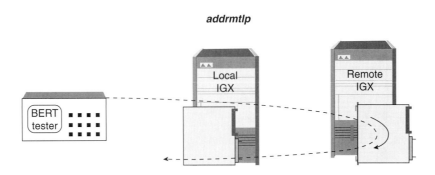

addrmtlp

External Loopback

The **addextlp** command places an external device connected to an HDM or LDM card in loopback mode, as shown in Figure 8-3.

Figure 8-3   *External Loopback*

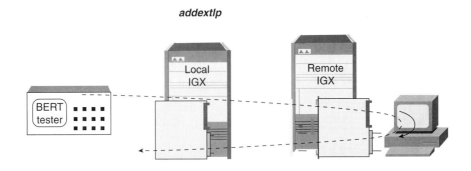

addextlp

A near (or near-side) loopback causes the NEAR EIA interface control template to be applied. A far (or far-side) loopback causes the FAR EIA interface control template to be applied to the data port. The loopback remains in place until it is removed by the **dellp** command.

The near side is defined as the point where signal injection occurs. The far side is the side where the signal is looped back.

WARNING Because this is a disruptive test, notify your network administrator before performing it.

Using the Data Faceplate

The HDM and LDM data cards can add and delete local and remote loops using the buttons on the faceplate of the card modules, as illustrated in Figure 8-4.

Figure 8-4 *Using the Data Faceplate*

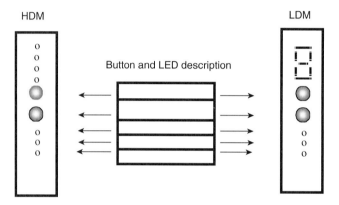

WARNING Local-remote loops cannot be added from the faceplate. They can, however, be removed using the buttons on the faceplate. Because this is a disruptive test, notify your network administrator before performing it.

Summary

This chapter explained how to locate and display network alarms and how to troubleshoot trunk, line, port, and connection alarms and errors. It also showed you how to set up connection loopbacks to test ports and connections. This chapter also discussed the methods used to monitor and resolve card failures, and how to specify types and locations of network alarms.

Review Questions

1. Contrast the effects of major and minor alarms.

2. Which two commands display the alarm status of all nodes in the network?

3. Which command displays a history of alarms and when they occurred?

4. Which command would you use to clear accumulated statistics on trunks?

5. Which command sets line and trunk alarm thresholds for statistical alarms?

6. When you test connections, what are the possible results?

7. If an external device supports loopback, the loopback is configured using which command?

8. When loopback testing is complete, you should use which command to delete the loop?

9. Which command indicates that a connection is looped?

10. How will you know when the testing of connections is finished?

PART  III

BPX Switch and Service Configuration

Chapter 9   BPX Product Overview and System Hardware

Chapter 10   Accessing the CLI and Initial Configuration of the BPX Switch

Chapter 11   Configuring Network Trunks and Access Lines

Chapter 12   Configuring SONET APS

Chapter 13   Configuring ATM Ports

Chapter 14   Configuring ATM Connections and Routing AutoRoute Connections

Chapter 15   Synchronizing the Network and Troubleshooting

This chapter covers the following key topics:

- The BPX Product Family
- Trunks, Lines, and Connections
- BPX Service Types
- ATM Cell Format and Cell Relay Switching Features
- Administrative Access to BPX
- Reliability Features
- BPX Network Features
- BPX System Hardware
- Polling
- BPX System Software
- Traffic Management

CHAPTER 9

BPX Product Overview and System Hardware

This chapter presents the Cisco BPX switch, which is part of a family of Cisco WAN switching products. This chapter also provides a high-level introduction to the Cisco WAN switching family, including general switch features.

Trunks, lines, and connections are defined for the BPX switch, and basic ATM cell characteristics are presented, including UNI, NNI, and STI cell header types and the five types of ATM services.

Tiered and flat network topologies are discussed, along with methods for accessing the BPX switch. The Service Expansion Shelf (SES), BPX hardware reliability features, and BPX switch functionality and components, including BPX card modules and the polling process, are also described.

The BPX Product Family

The Cisco BPX is part of a family of Cisco WAN switching products. The Cisco WAN switching family consists of IGX, BPX, and MGX equipment.

The BPX is a high-speed, high-capacity ATM switch that sends and receives ATM cells through the network. All traffic entering the BPX node is already in cell format. The BPX node does not segment and reassemble (SAR) other data formats into cells. This is done by either a feeder shelf (MGX 8220/8230/8250/8850) or by other external access devices.

The ATM cell is the only data structure that is used in a BPX network. There are three different cell types, as discussed in the section, "ATM Cell Format and Cell Relay Switching Features."

The BPX switch products were previously offered under different names:

- Any switch in the BPX switch family is called a BPX 8650 broadband switch. It was previously called the Cisco BPX 8620 broadband switch.

- The Cisco BPX 8620 broadband switch was formerly called the BPX Service Node switch.
- The Cisco BPX 8650 broadband switch can be used as a Label Switch Controller (LSC). This was formerly called a Tag Switch Controller.

Trunks, Lines, and Connections

This section assigns specific meanings to terms such as trunk, line, and connection, and describes how they are used and defined for the BPX switch.

Trunks

- A trunk is a circuit that connects Cisco WAN switches.
- Trunks are typically framed carrier circuits, such as T3, E3, OC3, or OC12.
- Trunks form the backbone network.
- Trunks carry user traffic and control and topology information between switches.
- Trunks support Statistical Reserve for a variety of traffic types.

Lines

- Lines connect user equipment to the switch.
- Lines are framed or unframed carrier circuits, such as T3, E3, OC3, or OC12.
- Lines carry user traffic and user-to-network signaling where appropriate.

Connections

A *connection* is a permanent virtual circuit (PVC), soft permanent virtual circuit (SPVC), or switched virtual circuit (SVC) in a network that originates on one Asynchronous Transfer Mode (ATM) port and terminates on another.

Each connection carries end-user data through the BPX network.

In the BPX node, a connection is defined as an ATM or ATM-Frame Relay (ATM-FR) connection. Note that ATM-FR is ATM traffic with Frame Relay in the payload.

BPX Service Types

Each connection is defined as a particular service type, along with traffic policing and management characteristics.

NOTE

The ATM Forum refers to BPX service types as Traffic Management version 4.0.

The BPX service types are as follows:

- **Constant bit rate (CBR)**—Carries constant-rate traffic with a fixed timing relationship. CBR is typically for circuit emulation supporting uncompressed voice and video-conferencing communications.

- **Variable bit rate (VBR)**—There are two types of VBR service: one that requires a fixed timing relationship (real-time VBR) and one that does not (nonreal-time VBR):

  — **Real time VBR (rt-VBR)**—Used for connections that carry VBR traffic in which there is a fixed timing relationship between samples—for example, for such applications as variable bit rate video or voice compression.

  — **Nonreal-time VBR (nrt-VBR)**—Used for connections that carry VBR traffic in which there is no timing relationship between data samples but a guarantee of QoS (on bandwidth or latency) is still required. This class is used for Frame Relay (FR) interworking, in which the CIR of the FR connection is mapped into a bandwidth guarantee within the ATM network.

- **Available bit rate (ABR)**—Supports variable-rate data transmission and does not preserve any timing relationships between source and destination. The network provides a best-effort service above a specified Minimum Cell Rate (MCR). A feedback control within the network is used to increase bandwidth when no congestion is present and to decrease bandwidth when congestion is present. This best effort maximizes the use of the network. ABR is designed to map to existing LAN protocols that opportunistically use as much bandwidth as is available from the network, but it can either back off or be buffered in the presence of congestion.

- **Unspecified bit rate (UBR)**—This type is best characterized as a free-for-all, with no QoS guarantees at all. UBR is a good match for the bursty, unpredictable traffic from LAN protocols served by ATM routers. UBR does not offer any service guarantees. The user is free to send any amount of data up to a specified maximum, while the network makes no guarantees at all on the cell loss rate, delay, or delay variation that might occur. UBR does not have any flow-control mechanisms.

- **ATM-Frame Relay**—The BPX node recognizes ATM cells only and is unaware of the payload carried inside a cell. Other Cisco WAN switching products (such as MGX feeders and switches and the IGX switch) often support Frame Relay services. To interwork between the different interfaces on the various products, the BPX node supports several ATM-Frame Relay services. It is important to note that the BPX node does not convert ATM traffic to Frame Relay traffic, but simply transports the ATM cells as required to and from the other products.

Traffic and QoS Parameters

Table 9-1 lists the traffic descriptors and QoS parameters that define how the network switches treat each service type.

Table 9-1   *Traffic and QoS Parameters*

Service Category	Typical Application	Traffic and QoS Parameters			
		Cell Rate	Cell Delay	Cell Loss	Feedback
CBR	Uncompressed voice	X	X		
rt-VBR	Compressed voice	X	X	X	
nrt-VBR	LAN traffic	X	X	X	
ABR	Frame Relay	X		X	X
UBR	File transfer	X			

The traffic and QoS parameters in Table 9-1 are defined as follows:

- **Cell rate**—Defines the connection's cell transmission rate. Depending on the service type, the cell rate is defined in terms of the Peak Cell Rate (PCR) and Cell Delay Variation Tolerance (CDVT). For some service types, additional traffic parameters are the Sustained Cell Rate (SCR) and the Maximum Burst Size (MBS) or the Minimum Cell Rate (MCR).

- **Cell delay guarantee**—Defines the maximum Cell Transfer Delay (CTD) and Cell Delay Variation (CDV). Specific values for CTD and CDV depend on the ATM service type for the connection and other network characteristics that exist at the time the connection is established.

- **Cell loss guarantee**—Defines the maximum Cell Loss Ratio (CLR) as a percentage of total cells transmitted on the connection.

- **Feedback**—For the ABR service type only, an additional traffic parameter attribute provides for feedback of congestion control information on a per-connection basis.

  — ForeSight is a proprietary Cisco traffic management algorithm and a prestandard version of ABR. The Foresight feature is described in more detail in the section, "Closed-Loop Congestion Avoidance."

ATM Cell Format and Cell Relay Switching Features

The BPX node is an ATM switch that sends and receives ATM cells through the network. All traffic entering the BPX node is already in cell format. The BPX node does not segment and reassemble (SAR) other data formats into cells, because this is done by either a feeder shelf (MGX 8220/8230/8250/8850) or by other external access devices.

ATM Cell Format

The ATM cell is the only data structure that is used in a BPX network. There are three different cell types—User-Network Interface (UNI), Network Node Interface (NNI), and StrataCom Trunk Interface (STI)—each of which fits the general format described in Figure 9-1.

Figure 9-1   *ATM Cell Format*

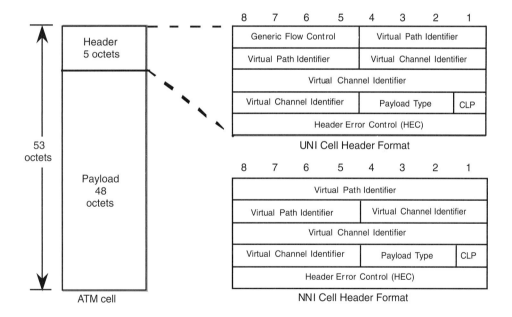

The ATM cell has a fixed-size data structure of 53 bytes (424 bits). The cell always has a 5-byte header containing a 4-byte address and control field and an HEC field (an 8-bit cyclic redundancy check [CRC] calculated on the header only). The payload portion of the cell is 48 bytes (384 bits) and might contain user traffic, as well as control and management information.

The three different cell types are defined as follows:

- **UNI**—Specifies the protocols and procedures between user equipment and (in this case) an ATM network. UNI cell headers contain the following fields: Generic Flow Control (GFC), Virtual Path Identifier (VPI), Virtual Channel Identifier (VCI), Payload Type Identifier (PTI), Cell Loss Priority (CLP), and Header Error Control (HEC).

- **NNI**—The interface between two public network pieces of equipment. NNI is also a protocol that governs (in this case) how ATM switches establish connections and how ATM signaling requests are routed through an ATM network. NNI cell headers contain the following fields: Virtual Path Identifier (VPI), Virtual Channel Identifier (VCI), Payload Type Identifier (PTI), Cell Loss Priority (CLP), and Header Error Control (HEC).

- **STI cell**—Some trunk cards support a proprietary cell structure called STI cells, as shown in Figure 9-2. STI cell headers contain the following fields: Header Control Field (HCF), Virtual Path Identifier (VPI), Virtual Channel Identifier (VCI), Payload Class, Congestion Control (CC), ForeSight Forward Congestion Indication (F), Supervisory Bit (S), Payload Type Identifier (PTI), Cell Loss Priority (CLP), and Header Check Sum (HCS).

Figure 9-2 *STI Cell Format*

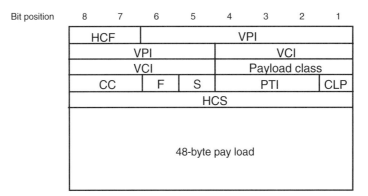

NOTE   The BNI and ASI trunk and line cards that support STI are near End of Life (EOL).

Cell Relay Switching Features

Many advantages exist to using cell-based switching across the WAN. Because of their fixed size, cells do not require any additional processing to determine necessary buffer allocation. In addition, the time delay to service the cell within a queue or buffer is predictable—which makes cell switching an ideal solution for time-dependent traffic.

Another feature of cell switching is that the hardware modules (trunk and interface cards) can facilitate traffic flow without the need for constant interaction with a central processor. In general, as soon as a connection is established in the network, the central processor has little to do with traffic propagation.

Between nodes, trunks provide the bandwidth to carry cells across the network. Often, traffic in the network is bursty and might not need bandwidth all the time. To take advantage of this, the cells are given bandwidth as needed on the trunks, utilizing the full resources in the network. If one connection is not transmitting, another can "borrow" the bandwidth to achieve a higher throughput. To prevent possible data loss, bandwidth is allocated based on the minimum requirements of each connection as traffic is routed across the network.

Because of the network's ability to dynamically allocate bandwidth, cells are queued by traffic type to prevent unlike traffic from competing for bandwidth. As a result, a constant-rate time-sensitive connection carrying voice traffic cannot be overwhelmed by LAN traffic that is more variable and less time-sensitive.

Administrative Access to BPX

Several different devices can manage the BPX network, including a PC, a dumb terminal, and Cisco WAN Manager (CWM). Configuration is done primarily from the command-line interface (CLI) regardless of the platform and method used to access the network.

BPX network management provides the following control features:

- Network—including all nodes, trunks, lines, ports, and connections—can be managed from any switch using a *virtual terminal*.

- Multiple, simultaneous, command-line access allows several operators to look at one node at the same time:

    — Direct-access methods (control and auxiliary ports)

    — Virtual terminal (VT) sessions

    — Telnet sessions

- Network management platforms:

    — Terminal or PC with VT100 emulation directly connected or dialing into a control or auxiliary port to access the CLI

    — PC or workstation on a LAN using Telnet to access the CLI

    — UNIX or NetView workstation running CWM network management software

Reliability Features

As an ATM core switch, the BPX switch is designed to provide carrier-class reliability. A number of system hardware and software features that are included for enhanced reliability are described in this section.

Details on card and bus redundancy are provided in later chapters.

Y-Cable Redundancy

BPX cards can optionally be configured for Y-cable redundancy. Any configuration change or connection added to the active card is automatically communicated to the standby card.

SONET/SDH Automatic Protection Switching

Broadband Switch Module (BXM) cards with optical interfaces support industry-standard Automatic Protection Switching (APS). Depending on the type of APS, either line and card redundancy (with APS 1+1) or line redundancy only (APS 1:1) is provided. Details of APS operation on the BPX switch are provided in later chapters, but Figure 9-3 illustrates the basic functionality of SONET/SDH APS with APS 1+1 and APS 1:1.

Figure 9-3 *SONET/SDH APS*

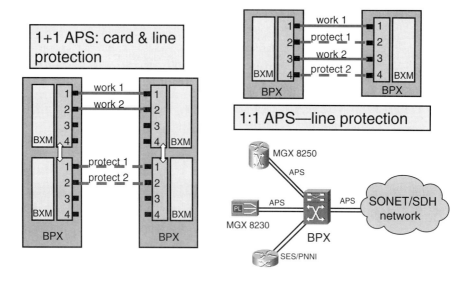

In addition to the BPX switch, other Cisco products, such as the MGX 8230, 8250, and 8850, switches support one or more versions of APS.

Automatic Fault Management

As connections are added, the local BPX switch checks the trunk load model for routes to the destination switch, available bandwidth, and queuing resources. If the selected route fails, the BPX switch automatically tries to locate an alternative route and moves the connection to the new route.

All the following fault management features are automatic and do not require operator intervention:

- **Hardware diagnostics**—Background tests and self-tests are periodically run on the hardware modules.
- **Card and bus switchover**—If redundancy is provided, a standby card or bus takes over if the active card or bus fails.
- **Trunk diagnostics**—Tests the node's ability to communicate (send and receive cells) with the neighbor nodes.
- **Dynamic rerouting**—Performed by the node when a connection fails due to network outages.
- **Alarm reporting**—Automatically informs all nodes of node or network alarm status and provides alarm or event information to network management devices (CWM, CLI, or printers).

BPX Network Features

The BPX node is designed to accept user traffic and propagate it through the network on broadband facilities. These facilities include T3 (45 Mbps), E3 (34 Mbps), OC-3c/STM-1 (both at 155 Mbps), and OC-12c/STM-4 (both at 622 Mbps).

The BPX node is standards-compliant on all standards-based features such as ingress traffic policing and Operation, Administration, and Maintenance (OAM) cell support. Standard UNI and NNI cells are transmitted and received on all interface cards attached to customer premises equipment (CPE) or on other vendor switches and access devices.

The BPX node supports peer-to-peer networking and transports end-user, management, and control traffic across broadband trunks to and from Cisco multiservice IGX and MGX switches.

Network Types

Cisco network topologies include flat and tiered networks.

Flat networks consist of nodes attached to each other using trunks. All nodes perform routing, are aware of each other, and fully communicate with one another.

Tiered networks consist of routing nodes and interface shelves (feeder nodes).

Routing nodes behave like nodes in a flat network. Interface shelves are single-trunk devices and do not have contact with other network nodes.

A BPX node is always a routing node. Other Cisco switches (such as the IGX and MGX 8850) can be configured as either routing nodes or interface shelves.

Sample Cisco WAN Network

The BPX node is a versatile, scalable ATM switch. It can exist in a network that has only BPX switches or in conjunction with a variety of other network devices, as shown in Figure 9-4.

Figure 9-4   *Sample Cisco WAN Network*

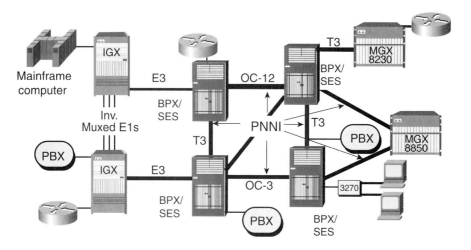

The simple network shown in Figure 9-4 includes the following elements:

- Multiple, geographically dispersed BPX nodes.

- Collocated or geographically dispersed IGX nodes—The IGX node is a multiservice FastPacket switch that supports voice, synchronous data, Frame Relay, and ATM traffic. The IGX switch in Figure 9-4 is a routing node. The IGX nodes can be configured as feeder shelves in a tiered network. With UXM cards, the IGX switch can also be an ATM switch.

- Collocated MGX 8220, 8230, and 8250 edge devices—The MGX shelf is an ATM interface shelf that works with the BPX node to provide high-density multiprotocol narrowband interfaces. The MGX shelf can support Frame Relay, narrowband ATM (T1 and E1), circuit emulation, and ATM inverse multiplexing services. All interface processing and ATM adaptation, segmentation, and reassembly are done by the MGX shelf.

- Broadband trunks between BPX nodes and between BPX nodes and IGX nodes or MGX shelves

- Remote or collocated ATM devices attached to BPX nodes

- Remote or collocated Frame Relay devices attached to the IGX nodes and MGX shelves

- BPX switches with SES Controllers as Private Network-to-Network Interface (PNNI) peers with MGX 8850-PXM45 switches

Service Expansion Shelf

The Service Expansion Shelf (SES) is an optional component that can be connected directly to the BPX switch to provide PNNI signaling and routing for the establishment of ATM SVCs and SPVCs over a BPX WAN. The SES can be used in several WAN switching applications and is not limited to functioning only as a BPX SES PNNI Controller.

Every BPX switch that deploys PNNI signaling and routing is collocated and attached to a BPX SES PNNI Controller. The BPX SES PNNI Controller uses Cisco's Virtual Switch Interface (VSI) protocol to control the BPX switch for its networking application.

The BPX SES PNNI Controller is a seven-slot chassis that contains two Processor Switch Modules (PXMs) that run the PNNI and SVC software. One of the PXMs serves as the active processor, and the other serves as the standby. The PNNI Controller is mounted directly atop the BPX switch and is cabled to it through either the OC-3 ATM interface or the DS3 interfaces.

You can build mixed PNNI networks of BPX switches (with SES Controllers) and MGX8850-PXM45 platforms with connection management interoperability.

For further information about PNNI and the SES, refer to the *Cisco SES PNNI Controller Software Configuration Guide*.

BPX Functions

The following list details the relationship of the BPX switch with other system elements. If the BPX switch is used as the core element in the system, it can perform the following functions:

- Provide the foundation for the multiservice network, allowing service providers to increase revenue from today's services while adding new products and services to support plans for future growth.

- Perform high-throughput, high-reliability ATM switching, with support for trunk and line rates ranging from E3/T3 through OC-12c/STM-4.

- Support multiple MGX/IGX feeder shelves (up to 16) per BPX switch. The feeder shelves effectively provide high-density multiplexing capability into the hub BPX ATM switch, supporting a range of user facilities:

    — Narrowband ATM services—1.5 Mbps (T1) through 16 Mbps ($8 \times$ E1 IMA)

    — Frame services—56 kbps, fractional T1/E1, T1/E1, through 45 Mbps DS3 and 51Mbps HSSI, Frame Relay, frame forwarding for legacy frame protocols

    — Circuit emulation services

    — Channelized E1 and T1 circuit emulation services $N \times$ DS0

    — Clear channel services for E1 and T1—These services support many types of traffic, including IP (Internet, intranet, extranet applications), SNA (financial applications), wireless traffic (data and voice), voice and fax traffic, video, and more.

- Enable oversubscription of the network in order to exploit the statistical nature of ATM networking. Each BPX node supports this oversubscription capability for densities up to 24×622 Mbps (OC-12c/STM-4) and 96×155 Mbps (OC-3c/STM-1).

- The advanced traffic management features of the BPX switch, including closed-loop congestion avoidance, enable effective use of the backbone network facility.

- Using the BPX switch as a base, you can add additional services. For example, you can implement Multiprotocol Label Switching (MPLS) in the existing environment by upgrading the BPX with a Label Switch Controller (LSC). Adding an LSC enables the introduction of new services, such as managed IP services or IP VPNs.

- You can enable PNNI capabilities by adding a SES to the BPX nodes. With the SES/PNNI Controller, SVC and SPVC capability are available in the network. The BPX switch fully supports the coexistence in the same network of standards-based PNNI SVCs and SPVCs and MPLS LVCs with the AutoRoute PVCs.

NOTE   To configure SVC or SPVC connections in a BPX switch, you must enable the switch with a PNNI.

BPX System Hardware

This section discusses the BPX system hardware, including the BPX switch chassis, main system components, and BPX card module groups. It also compares card functions, capabilities, limitations, and features.

Chassis

The BPX switch is housed in a rack-mountable 15-slot chassis. The BPX switch has a nominal peak throughput of 19.2 Gbps using a crosspoint matrix switch that interconnects all cards in the chassis.

Card modules are of two basic types: common core cards and service modules. Three slots in the chassis are reserved for common core cards, housing one or two Broadband Controller Cards (BCCs) and one Alarm/Status Monitor (ASM). The remaining 12 slots are available for the service modules, such as the Broadband Multicast Engine (BME) cards.

BXM cards can function in both line and trunk mode. They support a range of broadband interfaces, ranging from E3 to OC-12c/STM-4.

Chassis Subsystems

Figure 9-5 shows a cutaway view of the BPX chassis. It shows the main subsystems for power, cooling, card modules, and the backplane.

Figure 9-5   *BPX Chassis Subsystems*

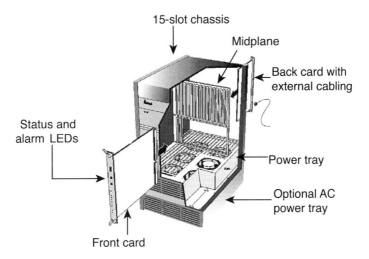

The BPX backplane has connectors on the front and back to attach the front and back card modules. The backplane supports several bus systems. It allows the cards to communicate with each other and the active processor card.

Each BPX node has a fan assembly that is used to cool the chassis. Three fans on the back of the chassis draw air through a vent in the front of the chassis, through the card modules, and out the back of the cabinet. Fans are field-replaceable with independent power connectors.

The BPX node can be powered from either an AC or DC source. One or two power supplies can be used to power the node, depending on the need for redundancy. The DC power supplies are mounted directly into the chassis; the AC power supplies require a separate power distribution shelf to be mounted below the chassis.

Card Groups

A front and back card pair creates a card group. Each card group performs a specific function on the BPX node.

The front card has the intelligence to perform the functions of the card group. On each front card, LEDs are used to notify local personnel of the current card conditions. A detailed description of each card's LEDs can be found in the *BPX 8600 Series Installation and Configuration Guide* on your Cisco Documentation CD. Card status can be viewed from software.

The back card is typically concerned with physical-layer functions and interfacing with the attached customer equipment or carrier trunk equipment.

BPX Card Module Groups

Figure 9-6 shows a high-level block diagram of the BPX card groups. The cards are referred to using a three-letter abbreviation, such as BCC for the Broadband Controller Card. Each card group is discussed in detail in this chapter.

Figure 9-6 *BPX Card Module Groups*

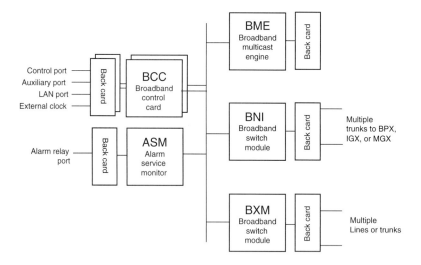

BPX Common Core

The BPX switch common core card group includes the following:

- BCCs
- ASM

BCC

The BCC, shown in Figure 9-7, is the central processor for the BPX node. It stores system software and all configuration information. The BCC also contains the crosspoint switch—the heart of BPX cell switching. The BCC also communicates with other nodes in the network and network management platforms, such as the Cisco WAN Manager system.

Figure 9-7   *BCC Block Diagram*

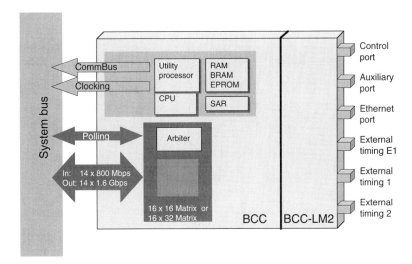

Most BPX switches have redundant BCCs installed in card slots 7 and 8. One BCC is always active; the other is a hot standby. All information, including statistics, event logs, and configurations, is passed between the two BCCs so that they are up-to-date. The BPX switch can run on a single BCC, but if it fails, the node fails.

BCC Models

Figure 9-8 shows several models of the BCC, which vary in functionality and capability. BCC cards need to be identical in type and memory configuration. The following BCC models are supported:

- BCC-4V and BCC-4V/B
- BCC-3-32M
- BCC-3-64M

Figure 9-8 *BCCs*

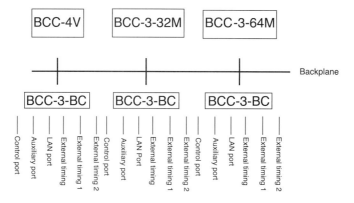

NOTE   The only BCC card that can be ordered is the BCC-4V/B.

BCC Back Cards

Each broadband controller front card requires a corresponding back card. The ports on the BCC back card are as follows:

- **Control port**—A 25-pin EIA/TIA-232 DCE port that is used to attach a VT100 terminal or a PC running terminal emulation for CLI access.
- **Auxiliary port**—A 25-pin EIA/TIA-232 DCE port that can be configured as a secondary CLI port, a network event log printer, or other functions.
- **LAN port**—A 15-pin 802.3 LAN AUI (attachment unit interface, requiring an external transceiver) port for network management using CWM and Telnet access for other LAN devices to the CLI.

- **External clock ports**—Used to bring in a synchronization signal from an external clock source. The BCC-LM2 has a 75-ohm BNC connector and primary and backup redundant DB-15 interfaces. The BNC interface is for an E1 clock source only. The DB15 connector(s) can be connected to an E1 or T1 clock source.

BCC-3-BC for BCC-4V Only   The BCC-3-BC for the BCC-4V card module only includes the following features:

- **External clock**—A 75-ohm BNC connection for clock input. An E1 source with 75-ohm impedance typically uses this connector.

- **External clock**—A DB15 connector for a primary and optional redundant external source of system clock. A T1 source with 100-ohm impedance or an E1 source with 100/120-ohm impedance typically uses this connector.

- **External clock**—A second DB15 connector for a primary and optional redundant external source of system clock.

BCC15-BC for BCC-32 Only   The BCC-15-BC for the BCC-32 card module only includes the following features:

- **Transfer timing**—A DB15 connector that sends out the BPX service's clock signal (8 kHz) to an external device.

- **External clock**—A 75-ohm BNC connection for clock input. An E1 source with 75-ohm impedance typically uses this connector.

- **External clock**—A DB15 connector for a primary and optional redundant external source of system clock. A T1 source with 100-ohm impedance or an E1 source with 100/120-ohm impedance typically uses this connector.

BCC Functions

The main functions of the BCC are as follows:

- **Central processor**—The BCC runs the system software for controlling, configuring, diagnosing, and monitoring the BPX switch.

- **Software and configuration storage**—System software and the configuration database are stored on the BCC. Dynamic RAM (DRAM) stores a working copy of the system software. Flash electronically erasable programmable read-only memory (EEPROM) stores a nonvolatile copy of the system software. Flash memory also stores new system software during an upgrade. A nonvolatile copy of the configuration database, statistics, and event logs is stored in BRAM (battery RAM).

- **Crosspoint switch**—Moves traffic from one card module to another. The arbiter polls each card (except the ASM) in the switch to determine whether there are cells to send and where they need to go. The crosspoint switch matrix operates at 800 Mbps per serial link or up to 1600 Mbps (BCC-4V). This path is reconfigured to create paths from transmitting cards to receiving cards every 687.5 nanoseconds (ns). The BCC-4 has a 16×32 switch; all the other BCC modules have a 16×16 switch. The switch size determines how many cells can be passed through the node at any one time. With the BPX switch equipped with two BCCs, cell switching is completely redundant in that there are two arbiters, two crosspoint switches, two completely independent data buses, and two independent polling buses. Only 14 cards have switch fabric access, so the usable fabric ports are 14×14 or 14×28.

- **Intranodal communication**—The BCC communicates with other nodes in the network to exchange database and status information. Data between nodes is a proprietary protocol encapsulated in ATM cells.

- **Network management devices**—Devices such as a CWM workstation, PC, or dumb terminal communicate directly with the BCC. When you log into a BPX node to access the CLI, you are communicating with the BCC.

- **Node and network synchronization**—This synchronization is controlled by the BCC. The BCC monitors and distributes synchronization signals to the other cards in the BPX node. The BCC also has a built-in Stratum 3 oscillator that can be used as a network clock source.

- **Hitless rebuild**—Enables a software restart without initiating a disruptive system rebuild. This feature is transparent to customer traffic and does not disrupt service. The BCC returns to normal operation in a minimum amount of time and maintains all existing user connections.

19.2 Gbps Operation with BCC-4V Components   To operate the BPX switch at up to 19.2 Gbps peak throughput, the following core components are required:

- 19.2 Gbps backplane

- BCC-4V or later controller cards

- One or more BXM cards

- Release 8.4.00 or later BPX switch software

- Backplane NOVRAM that is programmed to identify the backplane as a 19.2 Gbps backplane

ASM

The ASM measures the local environmental conditions and reports local and network alarms using LEDs and an external alarm relay, as shown in Figure 9-9. The ASM is always installed in card slot 15. If slot 15 is not used for the ASM, it cannot be used for any other card.

The LEDs report local alarm conditions on the BPX switch. The external alarm relay provides multiple dry-contact relay switch points that can be attached to audible and visual alarm notification devices to report local and remote network alarms.

Figure 9-9   *Alarm/Status Monitor*

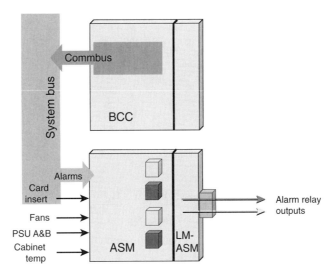

The ASM and LM-ASM back card are noncritical cards used to monitor the node's operation. They are not directly involved in system operation. Therefore, there is no provision or requirement for card redundancy or switch fabric access.

ASM Functions

The ASM performs the following functions:

- **Measures cabinet temperature**—It measures the BPX cabinet temperature and reports it to the system software. If the temperature exceeds a configurable threshold, a minor alarm is declared on the node.

- **Monitors fan speeds**—It monitors the speed of each of the three fans. If a fan speed drops below a configurable RPM threshold, a minor alarm is declared.

- **Monitors power supply voltages**—It monitors the status of the –48V supply to the switch on each of the two power buses, A and B. If the measured voltage is outside a configurable threshold, a minor alarm is declared.

- **Reports local alarms with LEDs**—Two LEDs (one for major alarms and one for minor alarms) are on the front of the ASM card. These LEDs report active local BPX switch alarms.

- **Reports local and remote alarms with an external alarm connector**—The external alarm connector is a 15-pin interface that can attach to audible or visual alarm notification devices such as bells, sirens, or lights. The ASM either opens or closes relays when node or network alarms occur to set off the attached notification device.

Broadband Switch Module

The Broadband Switch Module (BXM) card provides T3/E3, OC3/STM-1, and OC12/STM-4 interfaces. It supports both lines and trunks in any combination on a single card.

As a trunk interface, the BXM can support broadband trunks to the following equipment:

- BPX node with a BXM card
- MGX concentrator with a T3, E3, or OC-3/STM-1 trunk card
- MGX 8850 edge switch with a T3, E3, OC3/STM-1, or OC12/STM-4 Processor Switch Module (PXM) card
- The MGX 8250
- IGX node with a UXM card

A line on a BXM card can terminate on any of the following devices:

- ATM router, such as a Cisco 4500 or Cisco 7000
- ATM switch, such as the Cisco LightStream 1010
- ATM access device, such as the Cisco 3810
- Any device that transmits ATM UNI or NNI cells at T3, E3, OC-3/STM-1, or OC-12/STM-4 rates

BXM Functions

The BXM performs the following functions:

- **Supports lines and trunks**—Interfaces can be activated as a trunk or line on an individual basis.
- **Transmits and receives standard UNI or NNI cells**—In either line or trunk interfaces, the BXM transmits and receives standard ATM cells. The BXM uses proprietary StrataCom Trunk Interface (STI) cells on the system bus to be compatible with the BNI cards.
- **Performs standard ABR and the ForeSight feature**—The BXM supports prestandard ForeSight ABR connections as well as standard ABR connections with or without Virtual Source/Virtual Destination (VS/VD) capability.
- **Polices ingress traffic (line only)**—In line mode, the BXM polices incoming user traffic as defined by the ATM Forum.
- **Services egress QBins**—It separates traffic types into egress class of service (CoS) buffers (QBins).
- **Supports LMI or ILMI signaling protocols (line only)**—In line mode, the BXM provides LMI or ILMI signaling protocols.

- **Performs physical-layer functions**—It checks the HEC field, performs line and cell framing, extracts timing, and detects line alarms.
- **Provides card redundancy**—Industry-standard SONET/SDH APS is supported for BXM modules that have fiber-optic interfaces.

BXM Standard Models Comparison

Table 9-2 compares the BXM standard models against the number of ports, number of connections, line bit rate, line cell rate, and ingress and egress queuing for each BXM card.

NOTE   The BXM uses the same back card for eight or 12 ports and for the T3 or E3 line format.

On some BXM cards, you can increase the number of connections and decrease the number of supported statistics. Because channel statistics level 0 is no longer supported on some models, the ability to configure for 32,000 connections is curtailed.

Four BXM models with fiber-optic interfaces are supported:

- BXM-155-4 with a single-mode fiber (SMF), single-mode fiber long reach (SMFLR), or multimode fiber (MMF) interface
- BXM-155-8 with an SMF, SMFLR, or MMF interface
- BXM-622 with an SMF, SMFLR, or single-mode fiber extra long reach (SMFXLR) interface
- BXM-622-2 with an SMF, SMFLR, or SMFXLR interface

Note the following:

- The number of connections depends on the card configuration and exceeds the current per-node maximums.
- A Redundant Frame Assembly and an associated pair of special back cards are required for APS 1+1 redundancy on BXM cards with fiber-optic interfaces. Any card with an aggregate line rate greater than 622 Mbps exceeds the backplane's 800 Mbps service rate. Special design considerations should be made. For MFJ firmware and above, channel statistics level 0 is no longer supported for the following models: BXM-155-4, BXM-155-8, BXM-622, BXM-622-2, BXM-T3-12, BXM-T3-8, BXM-E3-8, and BXM-E3-12. However, it is still supported for the other models (BXM-155-8DX, BXM-155-8D, BXM-155-4DX, BXM-155-4D, BXM-622-2DX, BXM-622-2D, BXM-622-DX, BXM-T3-12EX, BXM-T3-12E, BXM-T3-8E, BXM-E3-12EX, BXM-E3-12E, and BXM-E3-8E). Therefore, the ability to configure these legacy BXM cards for 32,000 connections will be curtailed.

Table 9-2 *BXM Standard Models*

	Number of ports	Number of connections	Line bit rate (in Mbps)	Line cell rate (in cells per second)	Ingress/egress queuing (times 1000 calls)
BXM-T3-8	8	16,000 or 32,000	44.736	96,000	100/130
BXM-T3-12	12	16,000 or 32,000	44.736	96,000	100/230
BXM-E3-8	8	16,000 or 32,000	34.368	80,000	100/130
BXM-E3-12	12	16,000 or 32,000	34.368	80,000	100/230
BXM-155-4	4	16,000	155.52	353,208	100/230
BXM-155-8	8	16,000	155.52	353,208	230/230
BXM-622	1	16,000 or 32,000	622.08	1,412,830	100/230
BXM-622-2	2	16,000	622.08	1,412,830	230/230

BXM Enhanced Models Comparison

Enhanced BXM cards (identified by the word "enhanced" on the cards) improve the standard BXM cards by delivering even more cost-effective ATM switching and traffic management. For example, the enhanced cards offer greater cell storage and connections and increased cell and processor memory. They also support up to 12 ATM interfaces per card at speeds from T3/E3 to OC-12/STM-4. Table 9-3 compares the BXM enhanced models.

Table 9-3 *BXM Enhanced Models*

Model Number	Physical I/F	Ports Per Card	Ingress Cell Buffers	Egress Cell Buffers	Connections Per Card
BXM-155-8DX	OC-3c/STM1	8	512 K	512 K	64 K
BXM-155-8D	OC-3c/STM1	8	256 K	256 K	16 K
BXM-155-4DX	OC-3c/STM1	4	256 K	256 K	64 K
BXM-155-4D	OC-3c/STM1	4	128 K	256 K	16 K
BXM-622-2DX	OC-12c/STM4	2	512 K	512 K	64 K
BXM-622-2D	OC-12c/STM4	2	256 K	256 K	16 K

Table 9-3 *BXM Enhanced Models (Continued)*

Model Number	Physical I/F	Ports Per Card	Ingress Cell Buffers	Egress Cell Buffers	Connections Per Card
BXM-622-DX	OC-12c/STM4	1	256 K	256 K	64 K
BXM-E3-12EX	E3	12	256 K	512 K	64 K
BXM-E3-12E	E3	12	128 K	256 K	32 K
BXM-E3-8E	E3	8	128 K	128 K	32 K
BXM-T3-12EX	T3	12	256 K	512 K	64 K
BXM-T3-12E	T3	12	128 K	256 K	32 K
BXM-T3-8E	T3	8	128 K	128 K	32 K

BXM Block Diagram

Figure 9-10 shows the major functional blocks of the BXM module. (Note that this is a generic figure that covers all the BXM's variants. There are differences between the T3/E3 and fiber-optic cards, particularly in how the physical interfaces are supported.)

Figure 9-10 *BXM Block Diagram*

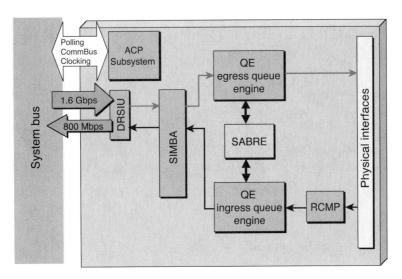

The following information summarizes the major functional blocks of the BXM module shown in Figure 9-10:

- **Administration and Control Processor (ACP)**—Performs the overall administration for the card, including configuration and status monitoring. The ACP communicates with all the other functional modules and with the BCC via the system bus.

- **Dual Receiver Serial Interface Unit (DRSIU)**—Interfaces between the serial system bus interface (crosspoint paths) and the 50 MHz 16-bit bus of the SIMBA subsystem.

- **Serial Interface and Multicast Buffer ASIC (SIMBA)**—Communicates with the arbiter for the crosspoint switch polling algorithm and for cell replication for multicast support.

- **Ingress and Egress Queuing Engines (QE)**—Maintain all queues on the card and operate the service algorithm for the QBins and the VI egress queues. Perform explicit rate (ER) stamping for ABR connections. Maintain connection and port statistics.

- **Scheduling and ABR Engine (SABRE)**—Operates with the QE subsystem for implementation of ATM Forum standard Traffic Management 4.0 ABR Virtual Source/Virtual Destination (VS/VD). Maintains VC queues for ABR connections. Controls the flow of Resource Management (RM) cells for ABR.

- **Routing Control, Monitoring, and Policing (RCMP)**—Identifies the LCN from the VPI/VCI for incoming cells. Polices connections using the dual leaky-bucket Generic Cell Rate Algorithm. Handles OAM cell flows for performance monitoring. Maintains alarm status for each connection.

Broadband Multicast Engine

The Broadband Multicast Engine (BME) supports multicast connections on the BPX switch. A connection originating from a BXM card terminates on the BME and is then multicast from the BME to multiple terminating BXM cards. The BME does not interface to any end-user equipment. The BME uses a two-port OC-12 back card.

Multicasting of point-to-multipoint services meets the demands of virtual circuit replication of data (Frame Relay and ATM). The following are examples of functions that benefit from multicasting:

- Retail point-of-sale updates
- Router topology updates
- Desktop multimedia
- Videoconferencing/distribution (IP multicast video networks to desktop)
- Remote learning
- Medical imaging

BME standards are

- UNI 3.1 Multicast Server
- UNI 4.0 Leaf-Initiated Joins and related standards

Multicasting point-to-multipoint connections benefits include

- Decreased delay in receiving data
- Near-simultaneous reception of data by all leaves

BME Features

The BME hardware has the following features:

- **Two-port single-mode fiber 622 Mbps interface**—The BME back card has two 622 Mbps single-mode fiber-optic interfaces.
- **OC-12 or STM-4 line option**—The BME lines are configurable for either OC-12 or STM-4 line framing.
- **BXM hardware similarity**—The BME hardware is based on the hardware technology used on the BXM card module.
- **Hot standby redundancy**—The BME can support a hot standby. No Y-cable is required. However, the **cnfyred** command must be issued to establish the primary and secondary card modules.
- **Hardwire loop required**—For the BME multicasting service to function correctly, a hardwire (cable) loop must be installed between the two ports. The transmit side of port 1 must attach to the receive side of port 2, and vice versa.

BME Capabilities and Limitations

The BME has the following capabilities and limitations:

- It supports up to 8064 connections per card and up to 4032 connections per port. The connections may be roots, leaves, or a combination.
- It supports up to 1000 multicast groups per card. A multicast group consists of one root connection and multiple leaf connections.
- It supports CBR, VBR, UBR, and ATM-Frame Relay (ATM-FR) connections. The BME supports all non-ABR/ForeSight connection types.
- The BME can be installed only in configurations that have BCC-4 and all BXM cards.

Broadband Network Interface

The Broadband Network Interface (BNI) card provides two or three network trunks between the BPX switch and any of the following devices:

- Another BPX switch with a BNI trunk card
- Cisco MGX 8220 interface shelf with a T3, E3, or OC-3c/STM-1 BNM trunk card
- Cisco IGX multiservice cell relay switch with a T3, E3 BTM, or ALM/B trunk card

There are three types of BNI models:

- BNI-T3
- BNI-E3
- BNI-155E (enhanced) with single-mode, single-mode long reach, or multimode fiber interface

NOTE   **Important!** Software support for BNI cards depends on the release version. Support will be discontinued in July 2002.

BNI Model Comparison

Table 9-4 compares the three BNI models.

Table 9-4   *BNI Models*

	BNI-T3	BNI-E3	BNI-155E
Number of physical trunks	3	3	2
Number of virtual trunks	32	32	11
Trunk bit rate (in Mbps)	44.736	34.368	155.52
Trunk cell rate (in cells per second)	96,000	80,000	353,208
Trunk egress queuing capacity (cells)	24,000	24,000	36,000
Number of connections per physical trunk	1771	1771	15,867 (3837 maximum virtual trunks)

BNI Functions

The BNI performs the following functions:

- **Transmits and receives STI cells**—The BNI card transmits cells to and receives cells from the attached trunk. The BNI card does not support the standard UNI and NNI cell types.

- **Services egress queues**—Cells sent from other cards in the BPX switch and through the crosspoint switch to the BNI are buffered before exiting the trunk. Physical trunks queue cells by traffic type in OptiClass QBins. Virtual trunks queue cells per trunk. The BNI determines the cell sequence based on the defined queue service algorithm for each traffic type.

- **Checks HCS on cells**—When cells arrive from the attached trunk, the BNI card calculates the Header Check Sum (HCS) and compares it to the 8-bit cyclic redundancy check (CRC) in the cell header. If the HCS is incorrect, the cell is dropped.

- **Provides line and cell framing**—The BNI card generates line framing appropriate for the attached facility (T3, E3, OC-3c, or STM-1). Cell delineation and cell extraction are also performed by the BNI card.

- **Extracts timing, if required**—If the trunk is a configured clock source or if the current network clock source is accessible across the trunk, the BNI card extracts the timing signal from the trunk and passes it to the BCC.

- **Monitors trunks for alarms and errors**—The BNI card detects and reports all physical-layer alarms, such as loss of signal (red alarm) and remote loss of signal (yellow alarm).

Card Placement in the Chassis

Figure 9-11 shows how common core cards and service modules are placed in the system chassis.

There are 15 vertical slots in the front and rear of the BPX enclosure for card modules. Follow these guidelines when installing cards in the BPX switch:

- Use slot 7 for the BCC front card and the BCC-BC back card.

- If the node includes redundant BCCs, use slot 8 for the standby BCC and its back card. If there is a single BCC, leave slot 8 empty.

- Use slot 15 for the ASM front card. If you are using the LM-ASC back card, install it in back slot 15. If you are not using an ASM, leave both front and back slots 15 empty. If you are using only an ASM front card, leave the back slot empty.

- Use slots 1 through 6 and 9 through 14 for network interface and service interface cards. If APS 1+1 is supported, the two BXMs must be in adjacent slots because they use a special paired back card set.

- Cover any unused slots with blank faceplates to ensure proper cooling airflow.

Figure 9-11 *Card Placement*

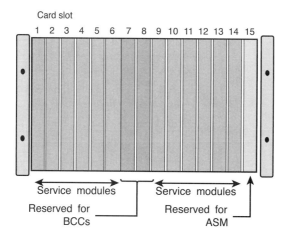

System Bus Structure

All communications devices share a common path. The BPX backplane is essential to the BPX switch. It carries control and user traffic between card modules. Figure 9-12 shows the BPX switch system bus structure and the overall system architecture and indicates how the controller and BXM service modules communicate via the backplane system bus.

Figure 9-12 *System Bus Structure*

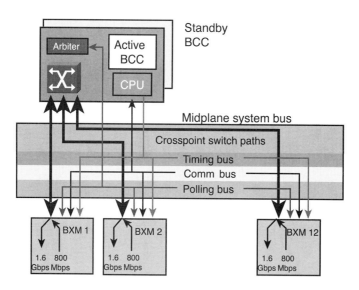

The BPX backplane supports either 9.6 Gbps or up to 19.2 Gbps operation. The 19.2 Gbps backplane can be physically identified by the card slot fuses on the bottom rear of the backplane. All BPX modules are interconnected by the BPX backplane, which is located between the front card slots and the back card slots.

Although the ATM data paths between the switching fabric and the interface modules are individual data connections, there are also several system bus paths for controlling the operation of the BPX switch. The backplane, in addition to the 15 card connectors, contains these signal paths:

- **ATM crosspoint switch paths**—Individual paths carry ATM cells between all service modules and the crosspoint switch, which is on the BCC card in slot 7 or 8. The crosspoint switch creates multiple temporary connections between cards transmitting cells and cards receiving cells. Each crosspoint switch path is serial and is serviced at 800 Mbps (inward) or 1.6 Gbps (outward to BCC).

- **Arbiter polling bus**—Carries the crosspoint switch polling signals. The arbiter polls each card in the BPX node (except the ASM) to determine which pair of cards can transmit a cell on the next cycle.

- **Communications bus**—Carries internal communications between the processor card and the other card modules. Status information, statistics, and configuration details are exchanged across the communications bus. The communications bus does not carry user data.

- **Timing bus**—Carries timing signals between the processor card and the other card modules. These signals are used by the cards to clock the lines and trunks that they support.

The backplane also includes the following, which are not shown in Figure 9-12:

- **Control bus**—Provides a signal to the cards in the node that defines which processor card is active, either A (slot 7) or B (slot 8)

- **Power bus**—Provides –48 VDC to all cards in the BPX node

Crosspoint Switch

The heart of the BPX node is the crosspoint switch on the BCC processor card module. Two different crosspoint switches are supported. All processor cards except the BCC-4 support a 16×16 switch. (The BCC-4 card module supports a 16×32 switch.) The 16×16 crosspoint switch uses 14 input and 14 output paths; the 16×32 crosspoint switch uses 14 input and 28 output paths.

The crosspoint switch creates temporary paths among the card modules installed in the BPX node. All cards that can send and receive cells (BXM, BCC, and BNI) have access to the crosspoint switch. BXM cards can receive two cells at a time (provided that the 16×32

crosspoint switch is available); all other cards can receive one cell at a time. The ASM in slot 15 does not have a path to the crosspoint switch.

Figure 9-13 shows the main elements of the crosspoint switch. The arbiter determines switch paths between cards that must transmit cells to other cards. Each BXM card has an 800 Mbps interface in the ingress direction, giving the BPX a full-duplex switching throughput of 9.6 Gbps. With the BCC-4, each BXM can receive two cells simultaneously, representing 1.6 Gbps in the egress direction, for 19.2 Gbps of peak throughput.

Figure 9-13 *Crosspoint Switch*

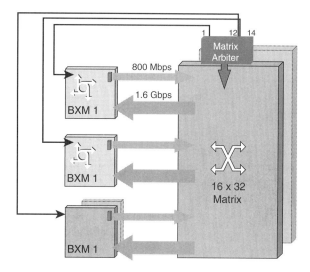

The reason for an 800 Mbps path is due to the fact that 64-byte Bframes carry 53-byte cells to and from the fabric. At 622 Mbps, 64-byte Bframes require 800 Mbps. The additional overhead protects the cell header and payload.

On the BPX switch, there is usually a redundant pair of BCC cards, with a switch fabric on each card. One of the BCC cards is used as a hot standby, meaning that the data loss is close to zero on user connections if a BCC encounters a software or hardware failure.

Arbiter

The central arbiter, also on the BCC, controls the configuration and access to the crosspoint switch. Up to 14 unique paths may be created at any time in the crosspoint switch.

Figure 9-14 shows the paths and buses on the backplane that are used by the BCC and other card modules to exchange cells across the crosspoint switch.

Figure 9-14 *Arbiter*

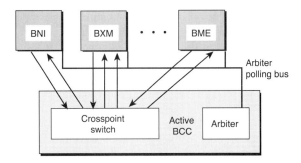

The following describes how the central arbiter functions on the BCC and other card modules:

- Each card module has one transmit path to the crosspoint switch.
- The BNI and BME have one receive path from the crosspoint switch.
- The BXM has two receive paths from the crosspoint switch (provided that the appropriate BCC and backplane are installed in the node).
- The arbiter controls the polling bus to all the card modules.

Commbus

The commbus, shown in Figure 9-15, is the internal communications bus for the BPX switch. It connects every BXM card to the active BCC. All commbus communications are initiated by the BCC master. The BXMs are commbus slaves and never initiate a commbus message exchange. Also, BXM cards do not communicate with each other through the commbus.

Figure 9-15 *Commbus*

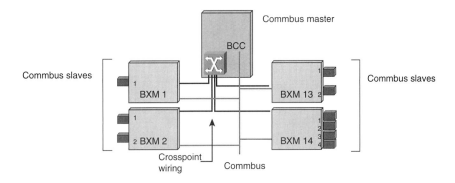

The commbus uses a command-response protocol in which the BCC sends commands to the service modules, and the modules acknowledge or supply the requested information. The commbus is used for all configuration and monitoring operations on service modules except for non-AutoRoute (VSI) connections.

Polling

The arbiter polls all active cards in the BPX node every 687.5 nanoseconds (ns) to determine which crosspoint switch paths need to be created. If too many cards request the same destination card, the arbiter must decide which paths to create during the cycle, and the other cards must wait until subsequent cycles to transmit their cells.

It is possible for a single card to transmit and receive cells at the same time. The arbiter is responsible for determining which paths are created in order to prevent collisions across the switch matrix. A collision is the result of transmit and receive cells using the same path simultaneously. The arbiter determines transmission paths to help avoid collisions.

Polling Cycle

Table 9-5 shows the arbiter polling cycle to demonstrate how the arbiter requests calls from the card modules.

Table 9-5 *Arbiter Polling Cycle*

Slot Number Polled

Polling Cycle	1	2	3	4	5	6	7	8	9	10	11	12	13	14
	2	3	4	5	6	7	8	9	10	11	12	13	14	1
	3	4	5	6	7	8	9	10	11	12	13	14	15	2
	4	5	6	7	8	9	10	11	12	13	14	1	2	3
	5	6	7	8	9	10	11	12	13	14	1	2	3	4
	6	7	8	9	10	11	12	13	14	1	2	3	4	5
	7	8	9	10	11	12	13	14	1	2	3	4	5	6
	8	9	10	11	12	13	14	1	2	3	4	5	6	7
	9	10	11	12	13	14	1	2	3	4	5	6	7	8
	10	11	12	13	14	1	2	3	4	5	6	7	8	9
	11	12	13	14	1	2	3	4	5	6	7	8	9	10
	12	13	14	1	2	3	4	5	6	7	8	9	10	11
	13	14	1	2	3	4	5	6	7	8	9	10	11	12
	14	1	2	3	4	5	6	7	8	9	10	11	12	13

The first card (and the second card if the destination is a BXM card) in the polling cycle to request a specific output is granted access to the switch. Cards transmitting to other cards are also granted access to the switch. During the following polling interval (687.5 ns), any card that was granted access to the switch sends out one cell. The arbiter rotates the first card in each polling cycle to ensure fairness.

Polling Cycle Example

Figure 9-16 shows an example of three arbiter polling cycles. In each cycle, a card requests a destination card, and either the arbiter grants the card access to the crosspoint switch or the card must wait and request the same destination card during the next poll.

Figure 9-16 *Polling Cycle Example*

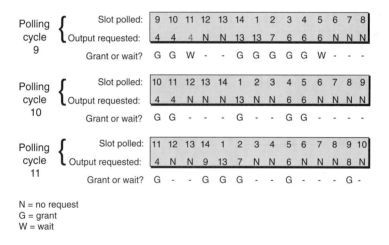

Figure 9-16 shows polling cycles 9, 10, and 11. In polling cycle 9, cards 9, 10, and 11 are all requesting access to destination card 4. Only cards 9 and 10 are granted access to the crosspoint switch.

In polling cycle 10, card 1 is still requesting card 4. This is the same cell that was ready for switching in polling cycle 9.

BPX System Software

This section describes the BPX operating system, network and platform software, multiple controllers, AutoRoute, PNNI, Multiprotocol Label Switching, and Connection Admission Control.

Network Operating System

Many of the features of the BPX operating system software are designed to enhance reliability and availability:

- **Protection against network failure**—The network can remain stable and operational even if a single node fails. However, some topologies, such as a star configuration, might create a single point of failure.

- Any topology is supported, including star, ring, and full mesh.

- **Distributed network database**—The network database is distributed to all nodes as network changes occur. Every node knows the network characteristics, including, but not limited to, node names, trunk characteristics, trunk bandwidth allocation, node alarm status, network synchronization sources, and user IDs and passwords.

- **Trunk diagnostics**—The system continually tests the node's ability to communicate (send and receive cells) with all neighbor nodes.

- **Dynamic rerouting**—Performed by the node when a connection fails due to trunk outages.

- **Alarm reporting**—The system automatically informs all nodes of node and network alarm status and can provide alarm and event information to network management devices (CWM, CLI, or printers).

- **Card and bus switchover**—If redundancy is available, a standby card or bus takes over if the active card or bus fails.

- **Hardware diagnostics**—Background tests and self-tests are periodically run on the hardware modules.

- **Hitless rebuild**—Enables redundant BCC controller modules to perform a system software restart without disrupting user service.

- **Release interoperability**—Lets the network operate with some nodes running an earlier software release. In this case, system software features and capabilities revert to the level supported by the earliest release present in the network.

- **Choice of management platforms with multiple access**—Management access to the network is possible via a variety of different methods, providing both primary and backup systems.

Network and Platform Software

This section provides a high-level overview of some of the networking software that extends the capabilities of the BPX switch.

Multiple Controllers

The Virtual Switch Interface (VSI) is the enabling technology that provides application flexibility and software modularity by allowing multiple, diverse services to operate independently on the same platform, as illustrated in Figure 9-17. VSI allows independent overlay networks to coexist on a common ATM infrastructure. Examples of such networks include the traditional AutoRoute, PNNI, and MPLS. The design of VSI ensures that the control plane for each network is completely separate and that system resources are appropriately shared between the different applications.

Figure 9-17 *Virtual Switch Interface*

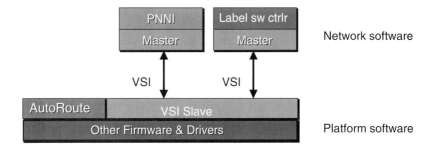

AutoRoute

AutoRoute is the current default connection routing protocol that is embedded in the BPX system software. When a connection is first added to the network or in the event of network trunk failure, the initiating node automatically determines the best available path through the network for the connection. Figure 9-18 summarizes the operation of AutoRoute in routing a new PVC connection.

To initiate a new connection, the network administrator defines the connection endpoints and the service characteristics required. The AutoRoute process in the switch where the connection originates (the connection "owner") uses the network database in its controller module to determine whether a viable route exists and, if multiple routes are possible, which one is the best according to a set of predefined system rules. As soon as a route is selected, the connection owner collaborates with the other switches that are on the connection route to place the connection in the network. Different connections with the same source and destination often take different routes.

Figure 9-18 *AutoRoute*

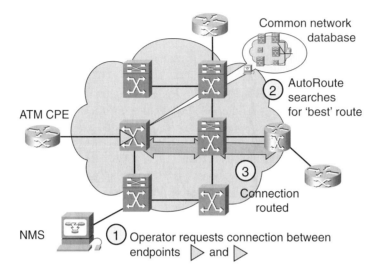

AutoRoute networks are self-healing: If a trunk or node fails, connections are automatically rerouted.

Private Network-to-Network Interface

Private Network-to-Network Interface (PNNI) is an industry-standard routing protocol for ATM networks. Whereas the Cisco-proprietary AutoRoute protocol is intended for PVCs, PNNI can route both SVCs and SPVCs. (Cisco considers AutoRoute connections to be PVCs, but the rest of the industry considers them to be SPVCs.) The PNNI 1.0 standards define both a routing and signaling protocol. The routing protocol is based on dynamic link-state routing similar to OSPF. The PNNI 1.0 signaling protocol is based on ATM Forum UNI 4.0.

A BPX switch becomes PNNI-enabled through the use of the SES PNNI Controller. The SES PNNI Controller uses the VSI protocol to manage and control PNNI signaling and routing across the BPX network.

Figure 9-19 illustrates the basic process of establishing an SVC.

The process is initiated by the ATM CPE that uses ATM Forum UNI signaling to ask the switch network to set up an ATM SVC.

Each PNNI-enabled switch maintains the PNNI topological database, including the QoS level supported by each trunk. The PNNI routing process searches for a path that meets the QoS characteristics requested as part of the setup request.

Figure 9-19 *PNNI*

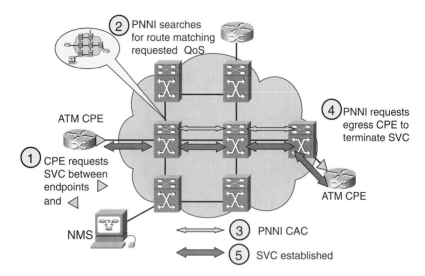

The PNNI software in the ingress switch then initiates the Connection Admission Control (CAC) process. CAC verifies that all switches in the selected path can accommodate the SVC at the requested QoS level. If CAC fails, the search continues until all possible paths have been exhausted.

Assuming that a suitable path is found, the egress PNNI-enabled switch system uses UNI signaling to ask the destination ATM CPE to set up the SVC termination. After that, the SVC is established and is available for user traffic.

Multiprotocol Label Switching

Multiprotocol Label Switching (MPLS) is a standards-based solution for mapping IP services onto an ATM backbone. MPLS is a direct derivative of Cisco's proprietary Tag Switching protocol. It is a widely supported method of speeding up IP-based data communication over ATM networks.

Although it is of value to many enterprise networks, MPLS is primarily intended for service providers. In the past, it was common to find service providers maintaining separate networks offering a variety of value-added services. For example, a TDM network supported Systems Network Architecture (SNA) services, an ATM network supported ATM and Frame Relay services, and an IP network supported Internet services. Managed IP VPN services were often handcrafted for customers, which required manually linking multiple TDM channels and Frame Relay PVCs across a WAN.

MPLS seeks to replace these costly and inefficient overlay infrastructures by creating a single IP+ATM infrastructure that minimizes operating costs and bandwidth usage by efficiently integrating multiple traffic types, such as IP, ATM, Frame Relay, LAN, voice, and circuit emulation.

The MPLS switch controller is a 7200 Series router.

Figures 9-20 and 9-21 provide a high-level overview of how MPLS operates.

Figure 9-20 *MPLS Process*

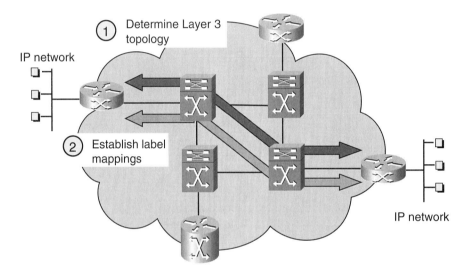

Figure 9-21 *MPLS Process, Continued*

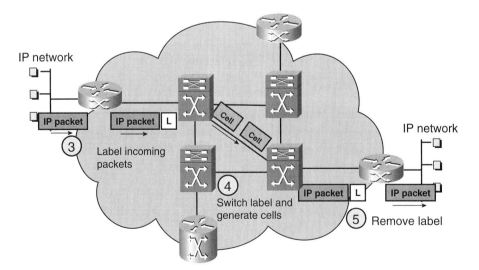

The BPX8650 is the BPX plus a 7200 Series router acting as an LSC.

The initial step is for IP routing protocols (such as OSPF or IS-IS) to establish routing tables identifying paths between every MPLS-capable switch and router on the edge of the network. In this example, the four BPX switches in the network core are not considered to be MPLS edge devices.

Following the IP discovery phase, the MPLS Label Distribution Protocol (LDP) assigns sets of labels that identify the interfaces linking every pair of adjacent MPLS systems in the network, this time including the core switches. Each MPLS switch then has a table mapping the assigned labels and its physical ingress and egress ports.

The ingress Edge Label Switch Router (ELSR) receives the incoming IP packets, performs any Layer 3 services, such as QoS buffering or traffic shaping, and attaches the label associated with the appropriate interface.

In the examples shown in Figures 9-20 and 9-21, the labeled packet arrives at a core LSR that segments the packet into ATM cells and attaches a new label before transmitting the cells out of the correct interface to the next core switch. Notice that the Layer 3 header is still present in the ATM cell payload but is not used for routing within the ATM network. All intermediate core LSRs perform label lookup and swapping.

As shown in Figure 9-21, the egress core reassembles the Layer 3 packet, which is forwarded to the egress ELSR. Finally, the ELSR removes the label and delivers the original IP packet to the destination IP network.

MPLS is discussed in greater detail in Chapter 22, "Voice, IP, and ATM MPLS Features."

Connection Admission Control

Connection Admission Control (CAC) is the task undertaken by the network at the time of connection setup (or during a subsequent configuration change) to determine whether the connection can be accepted into the network. This determination is based on the available bandwidth and Quality of Service requirements of the existing connections. CAC is applied on ports and trunks in the network, as shown in Figure 9-22.

The BPX implements a CAC scheme, which varies according to the requested service type. For example, the CLR required for a CBR connection is more stringent than that required for a VBR connection. So the QoS guarantee means that more system resources are needed to support a CBR connection.

Figure 9-22 *CAC*

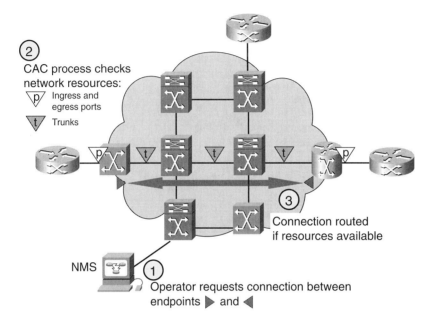

Traffic Management

Congestion control is a critical issue in ATM WANs. Without mechanisms that implement congestion avoidance, fair resource sharing, and firewalling, ATM WANs cannot deliver the CLR required by user data applications such as TCP/IP.

Usage Parameter Control

Usage Parameter Control (UPC) is simply a policing function at the network ingress that verifies that the user cells entering the network comply with the agreed-upon traffic contract. It is important to note that this policing function merely checks on traffic contract compliance and forwards compliant cells into the network regardless of the internal network congestion state.

Depending on the service type and the policing function defined for the connection, non-compliant cells may be dropped immediately or tagged for eventual discard later in the network. Tagged cells have the CLP set to 1 in the cell header. Figure 9-23 shows cell discard resulting from policing and congestion.

Figure 9-23 *UPC Cell Discard*

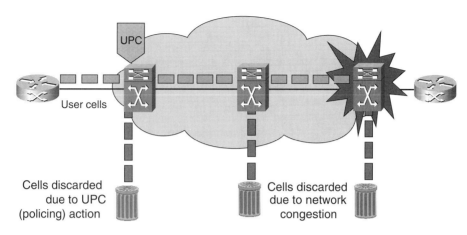

Frame-Based Traffic Control

Selective cell discard as just described has some serious disadvantages in that dropping data cells as a means of congestion control is likely to lead to even more congestion.

Frame-Based Traffic Control (FBTC) is intended as a more sophisticated and effective discard mechanism. As soon as cells are dropped, the frame discard mechanism attempts to minimize the effect by dropping a complete frame. The frame is the higher-level data unit. For example, an Ethernet frame can require up to 32 ATM cells to transport across the network.

Two standard mechanisms exist for frame discard: Partial Packet Discard (PPD) and Early Packet Discard (EPD). PPD and EPD work best in the network ingress. On trunks, where thousands of different connections are handled in common queues, it is more difficult to identify and extract a sequence of cells required to drop a frame within the network.

When the ATM network needs to drop cells, the ATM WAN congestion avoidance and higher-layer protocols do not complement each other well. While the network tries to alleviate the congestion by dropping cells, the higher-layer protocol running on the end system immediately resends the frame, causing even more load. As a result, congestion avoidance within the WAN is the key. PPD and EPD are not the best solution because they are reactive. In other words, they address the problem after it happens rather than before it occurs.

Closed-Loop Congestion Avoidance

For effective utilization of the network, cell and frame discard within the network should be avoided. The BPX switch provides this capability by implementing either of the following closed-loop congestion-avoidance schemes:

- ForeSight is a proprietary Cisco traffic-management algorithm and a prestandard version of ABR. With ForeSight, the UPC still monitors traffic contract compliance, but designated supervisory cells flow across the network and monitor the usage of critical network resources (such as the trunk queues). Periodically, a feedback cell is sent back to the ingress point, indicating the network congestion state. Thus, the ingress point is accurately informed of the network load situation and can either raise or lower the connection's effective information rate.

- BXM cards also support the ATM Forum Traffic Management 4.0 standards, which define the ABR Standard service. The ABR Standard incorporates many of the innovations of ForeSight, along with some important additional new capabilities.

In both schemes, large per-VC buffers at the network ingress buffer cells for the initial burst or for congestion situations, thus safeguarding the application from the effects of cell loss for a relatively long time.

QoS Management

QoS management of the BPX embraces several mechanisms to fulfill the QoS requirements of different applications. We have already reviewed how UPC and ABR provide an architectural framework for implementing advanced traffic management feedback loops for congestion control.

The remainder of this section explains how ingress and egress mechanisms are implemented on the BPX switch for QoS management.

VC Queues

The BPX switch is designed with very large ingress queues specifically for ABR traffic. Each user connection (VC) is assigned its own queue that provides traffic firewalling. Therefore, if one user consistently transmits in excess of the contracted rate, the other users are protected from the effects of unintentional or malicious noncompliance.

The queues allow the system to accommodate large bursts of incoming frames and to buffer incoming data during times of network congestion.

Each queue is controlled by a per-VC rate scheduler that "meters" the flow of cells into networks according to congestion feedback messages received from the ATM network. The cell admission rate is adjusted down if a congestion indication is received and may be adjusted up if no congestion is present.

CoS Buffers

BPX switches have dedicated queues and queuing algorithms for the different subclasses of service defined in the network. This lets the network provide performance guarantees for different types of traffic.

The BXM modules in a BPX switch implement multiple CoS buffers at the card egress interface. Each of up to 32 Virtual Interfaces (VIs) on the BXM contains 16 CoS buffers that are dedicated to specific service types such as CBR, VBR, and ABR.

Specialized queue servicing algorithms for each CoS buffer ensure optimal distribution of available bandwidth and guarantee desired levels of service.

BPX Queuing Architecture

Figure 9-24 summarizes the queuing architecture for the BPX switch with BXM modules.

Figure 9-24   *BPX Queuing Architecture*

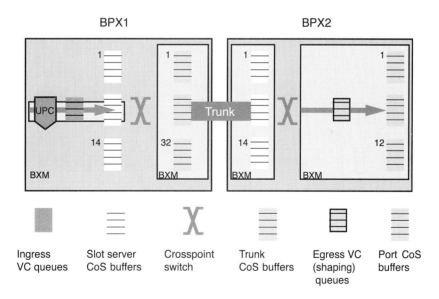

User cells enter the BPX switch on the left side and are normally policed by the UPC function. Cells then enter VC queues prior to being queued in the CoS buffers or QBins. Each slot server QBin, in common with the other CoS buffers shown in the figure, has separate queues for 16 traffic types. Each slot server QBin buffers traffic destined for one of the other 14 cards (BXM or BCC) in the BPX switch.

After the crosspoint switch, cells that are to cross the network to a remote BPX are placed in a trunk QBin. Each BXM card supports 32 VIs, each of which can be a single physical or virtual trunk.

At the destination BPX switch, cells are again buffered in a slot server QBin before being switched to the egress port on the egress BXM. If connection traffic shaping has been enabled on the port, cells for all connections are buffered in egress per-VC queues that operate in a manner similar to ingress queues.

Summary

This chapter provided an overview of the BPX switch and other Cisco WAN switching products. Trunks, lines, and connections were defined, and basic ATM cell characteristics were presented, including UNI, NNI, and STI cell header types. The five types of ATM services were also discussed.

Tiered and flat network topologies were discussed, and methods for accessing the BPX switch were described. Hardware reliability features and the purpose SES were detailed. The basic functions of the BPX switch and hardware components were also covered.

The BPX card modules and their functions were presented, and the BPX polling process was explained. You should be able to determine what hardware and software are necessary to support basic applications and be able to identify all the BPX card modules.

Review Questions

1 What is a BPX node?

A. ATM switch

B. ATM access device

C. Multiprotocol access device

D. Multiprotocol packet switch

2 Which of the following functions does the BPX node perform?

A. Switches ATM cells

B. Can be a feeder node in a tiered network

C. Segments and reassembles Frame Relay frames

D. Supports CBR, VBR, ABR, and UBR ATM traffic

E. Communicates with a CWM network management station

F. Can provide PNNI signaling and routing

G. Performs MPLS switching

3 Match the service type with its definition.

1. _____ CBR   A. Variable-rate traffic without a service guarantee

2. _____ rt-VBR   B. Bursty traffic with low delay sensitivity

3. _____ ABR   C. Time-dependent variable-rate traffic—compressed voice, data, and video

4. _____ nrt-VBR   D. Variable-rate traffic with congestion avoidance—router LAN-WAN traffic

5. _____ UBR   E. Time-dependent constant-rate traffic—uncompressed voice, data, and video

4 Which one of the following fault management functions does the BPX node *not* perform?

A. Bus switchover

B. Card module self-tests

C. N:1 card module redundancy

D. Dynamic connection rerouting

E. Automatic alarm reporting to CWM stations

5 Of the following elements, which three are part of the BPX switch?

A. Fan assembly

B. AC power shelf

C. Crosspoint switch

D. 32-card slot chassis

E. Multishelf bus cable

F. Standalone cabinet with front and back doors

6 Which card slots are reserved for the BCCs and the ASM?

A. 1, 2, and 3

B. 7, 8, and 11

C. 7, 8, and 15

D. 1, 2, and 15

7 Of the following devices, which two use a BXM card to attach to a BPX switch?

A. Cisco 7000 router

B. Cisco LightStream 1010 ATM switch

C. MGX shelf with a BXM trunk card

D. IGX switch with a BTM or ALM/B trunk card

E. BPX switch with a BXM trunk card

8 Mark the following statements as true or false.

A. _____ BPX nodes support up to 15 service modules.

B. _____ The maximum number of trunks on a single BXM card is 12.

C. _____ Slots 7, 8, and 15 are reserved for core controller cards.

D. _____ APS 1:1 provides card and line redundancy.

E. _____ APS 1+1 provides card and line redundancy.

9 The BME back card connects to which of the following?

A. Another BME with a 622 Mbps back card

B. BXM with a 622 Mbps back card

C. Itself

D. None of the above

10 Which of the following are features of the BPX system software?

A. Support for routing and feeder nodes

B. Connection admission control for PVCs, SVCs, and SPVCs

C. Automatic routing and rerouting of trunks following a node failure

D. IP routing with MPLS

E. VSI master capability

F. Automatic bus switchover

11 Mark the following statements as true or false.

A. _____ PPD, EPD, and CAC are examples of FBTC.

B. _____ All cells entering the network are subject to policing.

C. _____ QBins service up to 16 different traffic types.

D. _____ ForeSight and ABR Standard both cause cell discard in trunk queues.

12 Which of the following are functions of the ASM?

A. Monitors DC power voltage thresholds

B. Senses the presence of other cards in the chassis

C. Generates a major alarm in the event of a fan failure

D. Transmits alarm messages to an external device

E. Notifies the network administrator if the cabinet temperature exceeds the configured threshold

13 How many crosspoints are used in the BCC-4 crosspoint switch matrix?

A. 256

B. 392

C. 196

D. 512

14 When does the BBC-4 arbiter permit two cells to be transmitted to a single card?

A. Only when source and destination cards are all BXMs

B. Whenever two cards ask to transmit to the same BXM card

C. When two cards ask to transmit to the same BXM during the same polling cycle

D. If a card received a Wait command during the previous cycle

15 Which of the following are functions of the BXM?

A. Ingress policing for ABR connections

B. Signaling protocols on UNI interfaces

C. Generation of RM cells for ABR VS/VD

D. CAC for new PVCs and SVCs

E. Trunk interface to any Cisco WAN switch trunk card

16 Which of the following BXM card modules support APS?

A. BXM-155-8

B. BXM-622-1

C. BXM-622-2

D. BXM-E3-12

E. BXM-155-4

F. All of the above

17 What is the major difference between the BCC-4 and the other BCC card modules?

A. The BCC-4 is less expensive.

B. The BCC-4 has a faster polling cycle.

C. The BCC-4 has a 16×32 crosspoint switch.

D. The BCC-4 is needed to support the system software.

E. The BCC-4 allows all cards to transmit and receive two cells simultaneously.

18 Mark the following statements as true or false.

A. _____ You must use a BCC-4 if you have BXM cards.

B. _____ Up to 32 cells can be switched at the same time.

C. _____ Only the BXM card can receive two cells at a time.

D. _____ The crosspoint switch can support 14 input paths and 28 output paths.

E. _____ The arbiter polls each active card module once every 200 microseconds.

F. _____ Up to three cards can transmit cells to the same destination card simultaneously.

19 Mark the following statements as true or false.

A. _____ PNNI uses distance-vector routing.

B. _____ PNNI is based on newly developed protocols and standards.

C. _____ PNNI uses link-state routing.

D. _____ PNNI is based on existing protocols and standards.

20 Which of the following is not specified by the PNNI standard?

A. Network topology

B. UNI cell format

C. Network routing

D. All of the above

This chapter covers the following key topics:

- The BPX CLI
- Commands for the Initial Configuration of BPX
- Adding New Users and Modifying Passwords
- Displaying and Monitoring System Data
- Assigning Node Names
- Setting the System Time and Date
- Displaying and Configuring Serial Ports
- Using an External Device Window
- Configuring Node and Network IP Addresses

CHAPTER 10

Accessing the CLI and Initial Configuration of the BPX Switch

This chapter teaches you how to access the BPX command-line interface (CLI) to perform basic functions, such as logging in and out and displaying online help. It also introduces you to the BPX switch command structure.

After you have accessed the CLI, you have the option to browse, configure, and administer the BPX nodes, depending on your user ID privilege. In this chapter, you learn how to perform the initial BPX configuration that prepares the node for later introduction into a network. You define the local characteristics of the node, such as the node name, time zone, port configurations, and printing mode.

The BPX CLI

The BPX switch can be accessed by using the CLI or the Cisco WAN Manager (CWM) workstation. This section describes the four methods of accessing the CLI on the BPX switch: control port, auxiliary port, LAN port, and IP Relay. The CWM workstation is described in Part V of this book.

Control Port

Initially, for a newly installed BPX switch, the control port is the only method available to access a node. You must first access the node and perform some additional software configuration before the other methods can be used.

The control port is an EIA/TIA-232 (RS-232) DCE interface on the BCC back card. A dumb terminal or PC running a VT100 terminal emulation program can be used to communicate with this interface. The control port can also be connected to a modem configured with auto-answer for remote access.

By default, the control port is configured with the following characteristics:

- 9600 bps
- 8 data bits
- 1 stop bit
- No parity
- XON/XOFF flow control

NOTE   The control port on the BCC is a DB-25 female connector. Because the control port is DCE, a null modem cable is normally needed for a remote connection via a modem.

Auxiliary Port

The auxiliary port provides a second VT100 terminal access port. If the auxiliary port is used, auto-answer modems are often connected to provide remote dial-in access to the node. The auxiliary port is also an EIA/TIA-232 DCE interface, and the default parameters are the same as for the Control port.

The auxiliary port is used for several purposes, including the following:

- Printer
    — Prints screens (**prtscrn**) and other information (using **prtrts** and **prttrkerrs**)
    — A network event log printer
- VT100 terminal emulation for the CLI
- Alarm message collector
    — Receives ASCII messages from an intelligent device
    — Stamps messages with the date and time and puts them in a local and network log
    — Creates a minor alarm
    — May have an auto-answer modem
- External device window
    — Bidirectional communication with an intelligent device
    — VT100 terminal emulation
    — Access using the **window** command

- Dial-out modem
  - Dials out when the network alarm status changes
  - Posts the date and time, network name, and alarm status

LAN Port

The LAN port allows the node to communicate with other devices (such as PCs and work-stations) out-of-band across a LAN. The LAN port is a 15-pin attachment unit interface (AUI) for use with an Ethernet LAN. It requires an external LAN transceiver. The initial configuration for this interface is accomplished through the Control port using the CLI.

IP Relay

IP Relay is a method to propagate IP traffic (Telnet, Simple Network Management Protocol [SNMP], and Trivial File Transfer Protocol [TFTP]) in-band across trunks in the network. The originating workstation, such as the CWM station, communicates with the network through the LAN port of one or more gateway nodes.

Summary of CLI Access Methods

Table 10-1 summarizes the four CLI access methods—Control port, Auxiliary port, LAN port, and IP Relay—and their associated physical interfaces, default states, and device support.

Table 10-1   *CLI Access Methods*

Access Method	Physical Interface	Default State	Device Support
Control port	DB-25, DCE, female	Active	VT100
Auxiliary port	DB-25, DCE, female	Active	VT100
LAN port	DB-15 AUI	Inactive (unconfigured)	PC or workstation
IP Relay	Not applicable	Inactive (unconfigured)	PC or workstation

CLI Command Syntax

This section introduces the CLI command syntax used on the BPX switch. You learn how CLI commands are structured and how to differentiate between different types of command parameters.

You can use the CLI to monitor and configure the BPX switches, including network, node, trunk, line, port, and connection characteristics. The CLI is an alternative to the graphical user interface (GUI) provided on the CWM station.

All commands consist of a single word made up of a combination of abbreviated verbs and nouns. Commands can be followed by a combination of required and optional parameters. Commands can have both types of parameters, only one type, or no parameters at all. A command's syntax looks like this:

```
command <required parameter> ... [optional parameter]
```

NOTE   In this book, required parameters are enclosed in angle brackets (< >), and optional parameters are enclosed in square brackets ([ ]). The brackets differentiate between the two types of parameters and should not be entered on the command line. Note that the **help** command provides the syntax for each command, including the required and optional parameters.

The following example of the **addcon** command, used here to add a connection in a BPX network, shows how CLI commands are structured and how you can identify the different types of command parameters:

```
addcon <local-channel> <remote-node> <remote-channel> <connection-class | type>
    [connection-parameters] [route-avoid]
```

The syntax in this example includes required and optional parameters, as indicated by the angle brackets and square brackets.

The following three examples show a variety of values for the required and optional parameters presented in the **addcon** command and how they are entered into the system:

```
addcon 5.1.20.45 Node 6.2.24.44 5
addcon 5.1.20.46 Node 6.2.24.45 cbr 1000...
addcon 5.1.20.47 Node 6.2.24.46 9 *s
```

These parameters and additional examples of the **addcon** command are described in detail in Chapter 14, "Configuring ATM Connections and Routing AutoRoute Connections."

Figure 10-1 illustrates the CLI syntax.

Figure 10-1 *CLI Syntax*

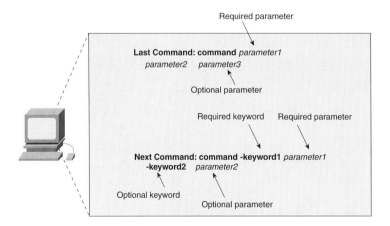

Examples of Command Structure

Typically, commands begin with an abbreviated verb and are followed by abbreviated nouns. Here are some of the most commonly used verbs:

display	dsp
configure	cnf
up	up
down	dn
add	add
delete	del
clear	clr
print	prt

Here are some of the most commonly used nouns:

trunk	trk
line	ln
port	port
connection	con
card	cd
statistics	stats

Many verb and noun combinations are used throughout this book. Remember the verbs and nouns most often used in the BPX CLI.

Command Examples

Most commands follow the conventions described in this chapter. However, there are always exceptions. Keep in mind that the **help** command is useful for finding a command's exact spelling.

Some commands, such as **dspcd**, are altered with the addition of an s (representing the plural) at the end of the command. For example, the **dspcd** command displays a particular card in the node, and the **dspcds** command displays all cards in the node.

Other examples include **dspcon/dspcons** and **dspport/dspports**. These commands are described in Chapter 14.

Some commands use multiple nouns or verbs, such as **dspchstats** and **dspatmcls**. These commands are also described in Chapter 14.

Command Entry Modes and Privilege Levels

Commands can be entered in the CLI in any of the following ways:

- **Menu-driven**—The **Esc** key displays a menu-driven command interface. You can highlight menu choices using the arrow keys and then make selections by pressing the **Return** or **Enter** key. When you select a command, it is issued, and you are prompted to enter any required parameters.

- **Prompted**—When you enter only the command on the command line (and then press the **Return** or **Enter** key), the system prompts you for the next required parameter. The prompts continue until you have entered appropriate values for all the required parameters. The system does not prompt you for optional parameters.

- **Direct entry**—The direct entry method is often used for commands with limited required parameters or when optional parameters are needed. Follow the command on the command line with each parameter value, in order according to syntax, and separated by spaces.

In all cases, you must enter appropriate values for all parameters. The system rejects any invalid entries and does not complete the process until you provide an appropriate value. To abort a command, use the **Delete** key (or an equivalent, such as **Shift-Backspace**).

Command Privilege Levels

Each command falls into a range of privilege levels. When a user ID is created, it is assigned a privilege level and can issue only commands allowed by that level and less-privileged levels.

Nine privilege levels exist. On the BPX switch, level 6 is the lowest privilege level, and Cisco is the highest.

- Levels 1 through 6
- **Cisco**—Cisco product engineering personnel
- **Service**—Cisco and partner support personnel
- **SuperUser**—Network administrator (referred to as level 0)

For example, user levels 1 and 2 can issue the **addcon** command. If you have been assigned a user ID of level 3, you would be unable to enter this command. The levels SuperUser, Service, and Cisco can issue level 1 commands, as well as many others not covered in this book.

Logging into and Out of the Network

This section describes the procedure for logging into the BPX for the first time. You learn how to log in, how to interpret the CLI screen display, how to use the online help, how to repeat commands, and how to log out.

Login Requirements

To log into the BPX switch and use the CLI, you must do the following:

- A terminal or PC with a terminal emulator must be physically connected to either the control port or the auxiliary port on the BPX switch you want to access.

- The terminal or PC must be configured with communications parameters (such as baud rate) that match the serial port you are using.

- You should be familiar with the basic CLI syntax.

- You must know the user ID and password for SuperUser access.

Logging into the BPX

Follow these steps to log into the BPX switch for the first time:

Step 1 Connect your terminal or PC to the control or auxiliary port on the BPX switch. If your terminal display is blank or garbled, recheck your physical connection and/or communications parameters.

Step 2 At the User ID prompt, enter the user ID for SuperUser (or higher) access. This displays the password prompt. There is no user other than SuperUser (or higher) until you create a new user using the **adduser** command.

Step 3 At the Password prompt, enter the password. For a new user, the password defaults to newuser. Ensure that you type the password correctly because it is case-sensitive. For first-time access, using the newuser password displays the following prompt: "You are using the default password, please change it." You should see the BPX CLI screen.

After you connect your terminal or PC to the control or auxiliary port on the BPX switch, logging into the network is a two-step process, requiring the entry of both a user ID and a password. The system administrator can provide a user ID and password for the network. Any user can maintain a lower privilege level as soon as he or she is on the network. After a password has been assigned, a user can change only his or her password. For security reasons, users should periodically change their passwords.

User IDs can have up to 12 characters. Passwords can have up to 15 characters.

CLI Screen

After you log into the switch, you see the screen shown in Figure 10-2, prompting you to enter a command. The screen is divided into two sections. The top two-thirds of the screen contains display information. The bottom third is the command area. It provides a command prompt and any system responses associated with entering commands, such as error messages and appropriate parameter values.

Figure 10-2 *CLI Screen*

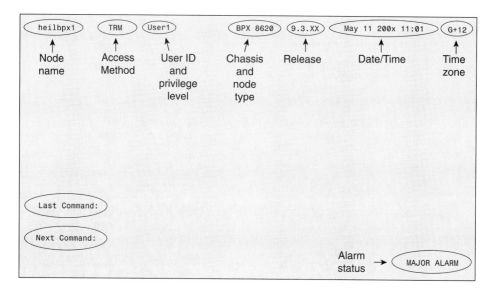

After login, the screen provides the following information (clockwise from the upper-left corner):

- Node name
- Access method
    - **TRM**—Control or auxiliary port direct access
    - **VT**—Virtual terminal from another node
    - **TN**—Telnet from the LAN port or using IP Relay
    - **CW**—Cisco WAN Manager
- User ID and privilege level
- **Chassis and node type**—BPX 8620
- System software release
- System date and time

- **Local time zone**—U.S. time zones, GMT, or an offset of GMT
- **Network alarm status**—Major, minor, or none
- **Next command**—Command line available for a new command
- Last command entered

Keyboard Shortcuts

Keyboard shortcuts make it easier to move the cursor along the command line of the BPX terminal window to delete, modify, or add characters as needed. Table 10-2 shows several keyboard shortcuts that you can use, depending on the terminal emulation software running on your workstation.

Table 10-2   *Keyboard Shortcuts*

Key Sequence	Action
Ctrl-B	Moves the cursor one word to the left.
Ctrl-F	Moves the cursor one word to the right.
Ctrl-L	Moves the cursor one character to the left.
Ctrl-G	Moves the cursor one character to the right.
Arrow keys	Moves the cursor in the direction of the arrow.
Ctrl-W	Deletes a character.
character-**Delete**	Deletes a character.
Ctrl-H	Moves the cursor one character to the left and deletes that character.
Ctrl-D	Deletes all characters from the cursor through the end of the line.
Ctrl-X	Deletes a line.
Backspace	Moves the cursor one character to the left and deletes that character.
Ctrl-I	Toggles insert mode (**Tab** and *character*-**Insert** do the same).
Ctrl-^	Inserts a line.
*	Leaves the parameter as is and advances the cursor to the next field.
Delete	Aborts the command.
Ctrl-M	Carriage return (**Return** does the same).
Ctrl-S	Stops the data flow from the node to the terminal screen.
Ctrl-Q	Restarts the flow of data to the terminal.
!(...)	The exclamation mark followed by the first character or characters of a command bring that command back to the command line.

Using help or ?

Now that you have logged into the system, you can enter the **help** command to request information on commands. To use help, follow these steps:

Step 1 At the Next Command prompt, enter **help** or **?** (question mark). This displays the list of command categories (menus) for which help is available.

Step 2 Press **Return** (or **Enter**) until a command category is highlighted, and then press **Return** again. This displays all the commands in that category that are available for your access privilege level.

Step 3 Highlight one of the commands and press **Return**. This displays the command syntax and other information.

NOTE   The **help** command is not a tutorial and does not provide information about the use of a command or the meaning of any parameters.

Example 10-1 shows the output for the **help** command or **?**.

Example 10-1 **help** *Command*

```
hei1bpx1        TRM    User1          BPX 8620  9.3.XX     May  11 200X 11:11 G+12

All commands fall into one (or more) of the following categories:

Control Terminal
Configuration
Lines
Network
Connections
Cards
Alarms and Failures
Diagnostics
Debug




This Command: help


Use cursor keys to select category and then hit <RETURN> key:
```

Using the help [character string] or ? [character string] Command

You can enter a character string as an optional parameter with the **help** command to list commands that contain that character string. Use the optional character string to search for a specific command, especially if you have forgotten how to spell it.

To display this type of help, do the following:

At the Next Command prompt, enter **help** followed by a character string. For now, enter **help cd**. This displays a list of commands in which the string **cd** appears. Note that commands available for your privilege level are the only ones that are displayed.

Example 10-2 shows the output for the **help** [*string*] or **?** [*string*] command.

Example 10-2 help *[string] or* **?** *[string] Command*

```
hei1bpx1       TRM    User1           BPX 8620  9.3.XX    May  11 200X 11:21 G+12


Commands that contain the string "cd"

addcdred        - Add Card Redundancy
clrcderrs       - Clear Detailed Card Failure Information
cnfcdaps        - Configures a card for APS
cnfcdparm       - Configure Card Parameter Values
cnfcdstats      - Configure Slot Statistics Collection
cnfbkcd         - Configure CC/BNI/ASI/BXM BKCD BRAM Parameters
delcdred        - Delete Card Redundancy
dncd            - Down Card
dspcd           - Display Card
dspcderrs       - Display Detailed Card Failure Information
dspcdred        - Display Card Redundancy
dspcds          - Display Cards
dspcdstatcnf    - Display Statistics Enabled For A Card


This Command: help cd

Use cursor keys to select command, then hit <RETURN> key for detailed help:
```

NOTE   To refresh the last screen display, enter **redscrn**. To clear the screen of all display information (except the initial display parameters), enter **clrscrn**.

Using the help [command] or ? [command] Command

If you enter a character string that is a complete command, the help screen for that command is displayed. The same screen also appears if you select a command using the menu shown in the help screen.

To display this type of help, do the following:

At the Next Command prompt, enter **help** followed by the command for which you want help. For now, enter **help dspcd**. (You could also enter **? dspcd**.) This displays the syntax and other information for the command **dspcd**.

Example 10-3 shows the output for the **help** [*command*] or **?** [*command*] command.

Example 10-3 **help** [*command*] or **?** [*command*] Command

```
hei1bpx1        TRM    User1          BPX 8620  9.3.XX    May  11 200X 11:25 G+12

dspcd               - Display Card
Cannot be included in Jobs.
Usage: dspcd <slot number>


Last Command: help dspcd

Next Command:
```

The **help** screen for a particular command provides the following information:

- **Command description**—The command's unabbreviated definition.

- **Availability in jobs**—A job is a predefined script that is stored locally on the BPX node. In the job, a series of commands and failure responses (if a command does not succeed) are listed in steps that are to be performed by the node at a particular time, when a specified event occurs, or when the job is run manually. Some commands, especially display commands, cannot be included in a job.

- **Required and optional parameters**—The required and optional parameters are listed in order following the command. For complex commands with many different possible required and optional parameters, only the common parameters are listed.

Using Repeating Commands: . (Dot)

Use the **.** (dot, period, full stop, or decimal) key to list the previous 12 commands that were issued. Example 10-4 shows the results of the **.** command.

Example 10-4 *Repeating Commands*

```
hei1bpx1        TRM    User1          BPX 8620  9.3.XX    May  11 200X 11:30 G+12

Command history

12: help
11: help cd
10: help dspcd
```

Example 10-4 *Repeating Commands (Continued)*

```
9: dspcds
8: cnfterm c 38400 none 8 1 x x no no
7: dsppwd StrataCom Bob 3
6: dspcds
5: dspnds
4: dspcds
3: dptrk
2: dsptrk
1: cnfterm c


Last Command: cnfterm c


Next Command:
```

To repeat a command, enter that command's index number on the command line. The index number indicates how many back commands will be repeated. For example, enter **1** (or press **Ctrl-A**) for the last command, or enter **2** to view the second to the last command.

When you enter a command index number, the command and its parameters are automatically entered on the command line. You can change the command line before issuing the command. Edit the command line in one of the following ways:

- **Arrow keys**—Move the cursor to the left or right on the command line without changing the existing text.
- **Backspace key**—Moves the cursor to the left and deletes the characters as it moves.
- **Tab key**—Toggles between insert and overwrite mode.

Logging Out of the BPX: bye

Use the **bye** command to log out of the BPX node. You can also use the **Ctrl-]** (right bracket) key combination to drop a Telnet session.

Commands for the Initial Configuration of BPX

The node configuration commands shown in Table 10-3 are used for the initial configuration of the BPX switch. The table describes the commands and the privilege level necessary to issue each.

Table 10-3 *Commands for Initial BPX Configuration*

Command	Description	Privilege Level
adduser	Add user. Defines a new user ID and its associated privilege level.	5
dspusers	Display user. Displays all the users at or below your privilege level.	5
dsppwd	Display password. Displays the current user password or the password of a lower privilege level user ID.	6
cnfpwd	Configure user password. Changes the current user password to a new one.	6
dspcds	Display cards. Displays summary information on all cards in the node.	6
dspcd	Display card. Displays details on a particular card in the node.	6
dsppwr	Display power. Displays environmental measurements for the node, including the power supply status and cabinet temperature.	6
dspasm	Display alarm service monitor. Displays environmental measurements for the node, including the power supply status and cabinet temperature.	6
cnfasm	Configure alarm service monitor. Configures the environmental alarm thresholds.	1
cnfname	Configure node name. Modifies the node name for this node.	1
dspnds	Display nodes. Displays all nodes in the network.	6
cnftmzn	Configure time zone. Modifies the local time zone for this node.	1
cnfdate	Configure date. Configures the date and time for the network.	1
cnftime	Configure time. Modifies the time for the network.	1
dsptermcnf	Display terminal port configuration. Displays the control and auxiliary port interface configuration, including baud rate, data bits, and flow control.	6
cnfterm	Configure terminal port. Configures the control and auxiliary port interface configuration, including baud rate, data bits, and flow control.	6
dsptermfunc	Display terminal port functions. Displays the configuration for the control port and auxiliary port at a node.	6
cnftermfunc	Configure terminal port functions. Modifies the function of the control and auxiliary ports.	0
dspprtcnf	Display print configuration. Displays the current print mode.	6
cnfprt	Configure print mode. Modifies the current print mode.	6

Table 10-3   *Commands for Initial BPX Configuration (Continued)*

Command	Description	Privilege Level
window	Window to external device. Provides an interface to an external EIA/TIA-232 device via the control or auxiliary ports.	4
cnflan	Configure LAN port. Modifies the LAN IP address and subnet mask for LAN access to the node.	0
dsplancnf	Display LAN configuration. Displays the LAN and default gateway IP addresses and the subnet mask for LAN access to the node.	5
cnfnwip	Configure network IP. Modifies the node's IP Relay address.	0
dspnwip	Display network IP. Displays the IP Relay addresses of all nodes in the network.	6

adduser Command

The **adduser** command adds a new user to the network. A user can add new users who have a lower privilege level than his or her own. Therefore, a user at privilege level 6 can not add new users.

User IDs and passwords become a shared network resource as soon as nodes are joined into a single network.

Here is the **adduser** command syntax:

```
adduser <user id> <privilege level>
```

Example 10-5 shows the screen display for the **adduser** command.

Example 10-5 adduser *Command*

```
hei1bpx1        TRM    Teacher:1        BPX 8620   9.3.xx    May  17 200X 12:30 G+12

Cisco
Service
SuperUser
group1       1
group2       1
group3       1
group4       1
group5       1
group6       1
Teacher      1
newuser1     1

```

continues

Example 10-5 adduser *Command (Continued)*

```
Last Command: adduser newuser1 1

Next Command:
```

Refer to the upcoming section, "How to Add and Display Users and Modify Passwords" for further details on the **adduser** command.

Related commands are **deluser** and **dspusers**. The **dspusers** command displays users. The privilege levels in the display are restricted to those of the current user and any privilege levels below the current user. The **deluser** command deletes a user.

cnfpwd Command

The **cnfpwd** command changes the password associated with a user ID. To change a password, you must log into the node using the user ID whose password you want to change. Passwords are case-sensitive and must have 6 to 15 characters.

Here is the **cnfpwd** command syntax:

```
cnfpwd <old password> <new password>
```

To change the password given to you by your system administrator, or to change your present password, follow these steps:

Step 1 Enter the **cnfpwd** command. The system prompts for your current password.

Step 2 Enter your current password. The system prompts you for a new password.

Step 3 Enter a new password. Passwords must have 6 to 15 characters. The system prompts you to confirm the new password by typing it again. To ensure your system's security, change your password on a regular basis.

NOTE   Do not enter old and new passwords on the initial command line with **cnfpwd**. The system prompts you for each in turn.

Refer to the upcoming section, "How to Add and Display Users and Modify Passwords" for further details on the **cnfpwd** command.

A related command is **dsppwd**. The **dsppwd** command displays the password of the current user ID or any user at a lower privilege level if you enter that user ID. The password is displayed for only 10 seconds.

dspcds Command

The **dspcds** command displays the cards in a shelf, front and back, with their type, revision, and status. For front and back card sets, the status field applies to the cards as a set. A T opposite a card indicates that it is running a self-test or a background test. An F opposite a card indicates that it has failed a test.

If lines or connections have been configured for a slot, but no suitable card is present, the display lists the missing cards at the top of the screen.

If a special backplane is installed, or if a card was previously installed, empty slots are identified as *reserved*.

For a two-shelf node, the screen initially displays only the upper shelf with a Continue? prompt. Typing **y** at the prompt displays the cards in the lower shelf.

Here is the **dspcds** command syntax:

```
dspcds
```

A related command is **dspcd**.

Table 10-4 lists possible card status descriptions found when using the **dspcds** command.

Table 10-4   *Card Status Descriptions*

Status	Description
Active	Card in use; no failures.
Active-T	Card in use; background test in progress.
Active-F	Card in use; background test failed.
Active-F-T	Card in use; minor failures detected; background test in progress.
Standby	Card idle; no failures.
Standby-T	Card idle; background test in progress.
Standby-F	Card idle; background test failed.
Standby-F-T	Card idle; background test failed; background test in progress.
Failed	Card failed.
Down	Card downed by user.
Down-T	Card downed; background test in progress.

continues

Table 10-4 *Card Status Descriptions (Continued)*

Status	Description
Down-F	Card downed; background test failed.
Down-F-T	Card downed; background test failed; background test in progress.
Mismatch	Mismatch between front card and back card. A mismatch also occurs if an active card is removed and an unlike card replaces it.
Update	Standby processor card is being updated by active processor card.
Locked	Incompatible revision of old software is being maintained in case it is needed.
Dnlding	Downloading new system software from adjacent node or workstation.
Dnldr	Downloading software and configuration from active processor card.
Empty	The expected front card is not present.
Missing	An active card has been removed or has failed.
Empty Universal Backplane	Indicates that the slot is empty or the front card was recently removed.

dspcd Command

The **dspcd** command displays a card's status, revision, and serial number. If a back card is present, its type, revision, and serial number appear. The displayed information varies with different card types.

Here is the **dspcd** command syntax:

```
dspcd <slot>
```

A related command is **dspcds**.

dsppwr Command

The **dsppwr** command displays the current status of the power supply monitor, the current power supply configuration (which may consist of one or two power supplies, depending on node requirements), and the current cabinet temperature.

Here is the **dsppwr** command syntax:

```
dsppwr
```

A related command is **dspasm**.

cnfasm Command

The **cnfasm** command enables the configuration of power, cooling, and environmental parameters monitored by the BPX Alarm and Status Monitor (ASM) card in slot 15.

Here is the **cnfasm** command syntax:

```
cnfasm <parameter index> <value>
```

A related command is **dspasm**.

Configurable parameter options for the **cnfasm** command are described in Table 10-5.

Table 10-5   *Configurable Parameters for the **cnfasm** Command*

Parameter Index	Parameter	Description
1	Cabinet temperature threshold	Alarm notification threshold in degrees centigrade (Celsius). This threshold determines the temperature that will generate a minor alarm on the BPX node.
2, 3	Power A and B deviation	Number of volts above or below -48 V at which to declare an alarm.
4	Polling interval	Frequency of ASM measurements.
5	Fan threshold	Minimum fan RPM before declaring an alarm.
8	Cabinet temperature	Enables or disables cabinet temperature alarms. If you disable the temperature alarm, the ASM still measures the temperature but does not declare an alarm when it exceeds the configured threshold.
9, 10	Power A and B voltage	Enables or disables power supply voltage alarms.
11, 12, 13	Fan 1, 2, and 3 RPM	Enables or disables fan RPM alarms.
15, 16	Power supply unit A and B failure	Enables or disables power supply failure alarms (failure latch).
17, 18	Power supply unit A and B removal	Enables or disables power supply removal alarms.

cnfname Command

The **cnfname** command specifies the name by which a node is known within the network. It can be changed at any time. The new node name is automatically distributed to the other nodes in the network. Node names are case-sensitive and must be unique within the network. The node name is from one to eight characters in length and must begin with a letter.

Here is the **cnfname** command syntax:

```
cnfname [node name]
```

The **cnfname** command is described in greater detail in the section, "Configuring Node Names."

dspnds Command

The **dspnds** command displays the name, type, and alarm status of all nodes within the network of the node executing the command. If a node is in alarm, its name is highlighted and the alarm type (major/minor) is displayed.

Here is the **dspnds** command syntax:

```
dspnds [+n] [-p]
```

+*n* includes the node numbers.

-*p* includes the type of controller card in the node (always BCC for a BPX switch).

A related command is **dspnw**.

The **dspnds** command is described in greater detail in the section, "Displaying Nodes."

cnftmzn Command

The **cnftmzn** command is used to configure the time zone for the node. It is described in the section, "Setting the System Time and Date."

cnfdate Command

The **cnfdate** command is used to set the date and time for the entire network. It is described in the section, "Setting the System Time and Date."

cnftime Command

The **cnftime** command is used if you need to set only the time. It is described in the section, "Setting the System Time and Date."

cnfterm Command

The **cnfterm** command configures data transmission parameters for the control and auxiliary ports. The IGX and BPX nodes support two EIA/TIA-232 serial ports on the upper bus expansion card. The top port is called the control terminal port. The lower port is called the auxiliary port (AUX). Parameters can vary according to the equipment that is connected to the port. The control port can connect to a control terminal, a direct-dial modem, or an external EIA/TIA-232 device. The auxiliary port can connect to either a printer or an external EIA/TIA-232 device.

After you set a port's data transmission parameters, use the SuperUser command **cnftermfunc** to specify the equipment attached to the port, such as VT100, printer, window, and so on. The configuration parameters must match the equipment that is physically attached to the port.

Here is the **cnfterm** command syntax:

```
cnfterm <a | c> <baud> <parity> <data bits> <stop bits> <out flow cntl>
    <in flow cntl> <cts flow cntl> <use dtr>
```

A related command is **dsptermcnf**. The "Displaying Terminal Port Configurations" section describes the **dsptermcnf** command in greater detail.

Configurable parameter options for the **cnfterm** command are described in Table 10-6:

Table 10-6   *Configurable Parameters for the **cnfterm** Command*

Parameter	Description
*a	c*	Specifies whether the command is to operate on the auxiliary (a) or control (c) port.
baud	The bit rate of the data between the port and the attached device. Choices are 1200, 2400, 4800, 9600, 19200, and 38400.
parity	The parity of the asynchronous characters sent between the port and the attached device. Choices are odd, even, and none.
data bits	The number of data bits in the asynchronous characters sent between the port and the attached device. Choices are 7 and 8.
stop bits	The number of stop bits in the asynchronous characters sent between the port and the attached device. Choices are 1 and none.
out flow cntl	The flow control mechanism used by the port in the output direction. Choices are XON/XOFF and none.
in flow cntl	The flow control mechanism used by the port in the input direction. Choices include XON/XOFF and none.
cts flow cntl	Enables or disables CTS flow control. For terminals and modems, CTS flow control is usually disabled. Printers often use CTS flow control.
use dtr	Enables or disables DTR detection to determine whether a session should be terminated. If DTR is disabled, a CLI session remains active even if communication between the node and the attached terminal is broken.

cnftermfunc Command

The **cnftermfunc** command configures the port functions for the control and auxiliary ports. If either port is configured as an external device window, you can use the **window** command to begin a session with the external device.

If the auxiliary port is configured as an autodial modem, designate a network ID and a phone number. Configuring the auxiliary port for an autodial modem causes the modem to dial the specified number when a change in alarm status happens anywhere in the network.

If the call is directed to the Cisco Technical Assistance Center (TAC), the alarm is logged under the specified network ID.

NOTE   You must have SuperUser access to use the **cnftermfunc** command.

Here is the **cnftermfunc** command syntax:

```
cnftermfunc <a | c> <index> [escape string | network ID and dial string]
```

A related command is **dsptermfunc**.

Configurable parameter options for the **cnftermfunc** command are described in Table 10-7.

Table 10-7   *Configurable Parameters for the* **cnftermfunc** *Command*

Parameter	Description
a | c	Defines whether the command is to operate on the auxiliary (a) or control (c) port.
index	Control port:
	1—VT100/Cisco WAN Manager
	2—VT100
	3—External device window
	Auxiliary port:
	1—Okidata 184 printer
	2—Okidata 184 printer with LOG
	3—VT100
	4—Alarm Message Collector
	5—External device window
	6—Autodial modem
escape string	Specifies a string of one to eight characters used to terminate a session with an external device. This parameter is valid only for external device window interfaces. The default escape string is quit.

Table 10-7 *Configurable Parameters for the* **cnftermfunc** *Command (Continued)*

Parameter	Description
network ID	Specifies a string of 1 to 12 characters that may be used to identify the network during an autodial connection. This parameter is valid only for autodial modem interfaces.
dial string	Specifies the telephone number to be dialed when the network is reporting alarm status changes via the autodial modem. This parameter is valid only for autodial modem interfaces. The phone number can be up to 16 characters long and normally consists of digits and commas only. A comma is used to indicate that the autodial modem should pause two seconds before continuing to dial. For example, the number 9,4083700736 would cause the modem to dial a 9, pause two seconds, then dial the remaining digits.

window Command

The "Windowing to External Devices" section describes the **window** command.

dspprtcnf Command

The "Displaying the Printer Configuration" section describes the **dspprtcnf** command.

cnfprt Command

The "Configuring Print Modes" section describes the **cnfprt** command.

cnflan Command

The **cnflan** command configures the LAN port parameters for the Ethernet port on the BCC back card. Refer back to the "LAN Port" section for a reminder of the purposes of LAN ports.

NOTE   You must have SuperUser access to use the **cnflan** command.

Here is the **cnflan** command syntax:

```
cnflan <IP address> <subnet mask> <TCP service port> <default gateway>
```

A related command is **dsplancnf**.

Configurable parameter options for the **cnflan** command are described in Table 10-8.

Table 10-8 *Configurable Parameters for the* **cnflan** *Command*

Parameter	Description
IP address	IP address assigned to the LAN port on the processor back card.
subnet mask	32-bit mask for the active IP address. The default is 255.255.255.0.
TCP service port	Required for TCP, and always coded to 5120 as required by the CWM management station.
default gateway	The address to which management traffic is directed in the event that the WAN Manager management station is not located on the same LAN segment as the node LAN port. The default gateway is usually the address of a router interface to which the node should direct management traffic.

cnfnwip Command

The **cnfnwip** command configures the address and subnet mask for the Network IP (or IP Relay) used by CWM (or any IP traffic destined to traverse Cisco WAN trunks) to communicate in-band with network nodes. These addresses are normally private. A user with a properly configured static route can also use this to Telnet in-band.

NOTE   You must have SuperUser access to use the **cnfnwip** command.

Here is the **cnfnwip** command syntax:

```
cnfnwip <IP address> <subnet mask>
```

A related command is **dspnwip**.

Configurable parameter options for the **cnfnwip** command are described in Table 10-9.

Table 10-9 *Configurable Parameters for the* **cnfnwip** *Command*

Parameter	Description
IP address	IP address assigned for IP Relay.
subnet mask	32-bit mask for the network IP address. The default is 255.255.255.0.

Adding New Users and Modifying Passwords

In this section, you learn how to add a new system user, how to display passwords, and how to change passwords for yourself and other users.

How to Add and Display Users and Modify Passwords

Follow these steps to add a new network user and to display users currently recognized by your node:

Step 1 At the Next Command prompt, enter **adduser** *<username>*, where *username* is a string from one to eight characters. This ensures that the username is unique and then adds it to the switch database. If this is successful, the switch displays the list of users, including the newly added user.

Step 2 Enter **dspusers**. This displays all the users at or below your privilege level.

Step 3 Enter **dsppwd SuperUser**. If you are not logged in at the SuperUser level or above, an error message is displayed.

Step 4 Enter **dsppwd** *<username>*, where *username* is your current username. This displays your current password for about 10 seconds and then clears the screen. You can also display the password of a user at a lower privilege level.

Step 5 Enter **cnfpwd** *<username>*, where *username* is your current username. You are prompted for a new password.

Step 6 Enter your new password. You are prompted to repeat the new password.

Step 7 Enter your new password again. The Next Command prompt is displayed.

Step 8 Enter **bye**. This terminates your CLI session and returns you to the login prompt.

Displaying and Monitoring System Data

In this section, you learn how to do the following:

- Display the current installed card inventory in a BPX node
- Determine the operational status of each card
- Determine the software and firmware release levels
- Monitor node environmental conditions such as chassis temperature
- Modify certain alarm thresholds associated with environmental faults

How to Display and Monitor System Data

Follow these steps to verify which cards are installed in your BPX node and see the hardware and firmware release levels that are associated with each card:

Step 1   At the Next Command prompt, enter **dspcds**. The output for this command is shown in the section, "Displaying All Cards." It displays all the cards currently installed in your BPX switch.

Step 2   Enter **dspcd** <*slot*>. The output for this command is shown in the section, "Displaying Specific Cards." It displays detailed information about the card identified by the slot number.

Step 3   Enter **dsppwr**. The output for this command is shown in the section, "Displaying Power." It displays information on fan and power supply status and current cabinet internal temperature.

Step 4   Enter **dspasm** and note the current actual cabinet temperature measurement. The output for this command is shown in the section, "Displaying Alarm Status Monitor." This displays the same information as the **dsppwr** command, with additional details on polling performed by the Alarm Status Monitor (ASM) card.

The following example shows you how to test and see the results of environmental changes within the BPX. Enter the **cnfasm** command to temporarily modify the cabinet temperature alarm threshold. The output for this command is shown in the section, "Configuring Alarm Status Monitor." Enter **cnfasm** <*n*>, where *n* is an integer representing a temperature that is about 5 degrees Celsius less than the current actual temperature as shown by the **dspasm** command. This displays the new cabinet temperature threshold. It also displays the words "Minor Alarm" in the lower-right corner.

Enter the **cnfasm** command to return the cabinet temperature threshold to its original setting. This resets the threshold setting, and the minor alarm disappears.

Displaying All Cards: dspcds

Example 10-6 shows the screen display for the **dspcds** command.

Example 10-6 dspcds *Command*

```
hei1bpx1        TRM    Teacher:1        BPX 8620   9.3.XX    May  11 200X 12:47 G+12


     FrontCard   BackCard                   FrontCard   BackCard
     Type   Rev  Type  Rev   Status         Type   Rev  Type  Rev   Status
  1  BNI-T3 CJL  T3-3  BE    Standby      9  Empty
  2  BXM-T3 FDH  TE3-12BA    Active      10  Empty
```

Example 10-6 **dspcds** *Command (Continued)*

```
 3  BXM-155 FDH  MM-8  BB    Standby    11 Empty
 4  BXM-155 FEH  SM-4  BB    Active      12 Empty
 5  Empty                                 13 Empty
 6  Empty                                 14 Empty
 7  BCC-3   DSM  LM-2  AC    Active      15 ASM      ACC  LMASM AC    Active
 8  BCC-3   DSM  LM-2  AC    Standby


Last Command: dspcds


Next Command:
```

The **dspcds** command provides summary information on the status of all the cards in the BPX node. Cards are automatically detected by the node and need not be installed or defined in the software. Use the **dspcds** command to display the types of cards installed in your BPX node and their statuses.

The **dspcds** command provides the following information:

- Card type
- **Card revision**—Three characters indicating the following:
    - **Model**—The card's feature set. The model is associated with the firmware on the card and can only be changed by Cisco or its partners. The model is represented by the first character.
    - **Hardware revision**—The hardware revision is represented by the second character.
    - **Firmware revision**—A variation on the model to incorporate minor feature enhancements. The firmware revision can be changed by burning new firmware into the card. The firmware revision is represented by the third character.
- Back card type
- **Back card revision**—Model and hardware revision, neither of which can be modified.
- Card status

Displaying Specific Cards: dspcd

Example 10-7 shows the screen display for the **dspcd** command.

Example 10-7 dspcd *Command*

```
hei1bpx1        TRM    Teacher:1        BPX 8620   9.3.XX     May  11 200X 12:54 G+12

Detailed Card Display for BXM-155 in slot 4
Status:         Active
Revision:       FEH                  Backcard Installed
Serial Number:  781007                 Type:        LM-BXM
Top Asm Number: 28215802               Revision:    BB
Queue Size:     228300                 Serial Number: 824593
Support: 4 Pts, OC3, FST, VcShp        Supp: 4 Pts,OC3,SMF,RedSlot:NO
Supp: VT,ChStLv 1,VSI(Lv 3,ITSM)
Support: APS(FW,ChHlv)
Support: LMIv 1,ILMIv 1,NbrDisc
Support: OAMLp, TrfcGen
#Ch:8128,PG[1]:4064,PG[2]:4064
PG[1]:1,2,PG[2]:3,4,
#Sched_Ch:16384



Last Command: dspcd 4


Next Command:
```

The **dspcd** command provides detailed information on a card module. Use this command to display additional information about a card, including failure information.

The information provided (in addition to what is shown in the **dspcds** screen) depends on the card type and might include the following:

- Front and back card serial numbers
- Card failure type
- Card features
    - Number of ports supported
    - Features supported, such as ForeSight[r]
    - Number of connections supported
    - Buffer size
- Memory size
- Software revision

Displaying Power: dsppwr

Example 10-8 shows the screen display for the **dsppwr** command.

Example 10-8 dsppwr *Command*

```
hei1bpx1       TRM   Teacher:1      BPX 8620  9.3.XX   May  11 200X 12:55 G+12

         Power Status                              Cabinet Temperature

ASM Status: Active                                    21        69

Power voltage A/B:     49 / 49 V                  C  60  ¦ ¦  140  F
                                                  e           a
PSU  Ins Type Rev SerNum Failure                  n  50  ¦--¦  122  h
  A   Y  240V  0A ja1024  None                    t           r
  B   Y  240V  0A ja1025  None                    i  40  ¦ ¦  104  e
                                                  g           n
          Fan Status                              r  30  ¦ ¦   86  h
                                                  a           e
     FAN   1    2    3                            d  20  ¦ ¦   68  i
          3240 3300 3240 RPM                      e  '--'       t


Last Command: dsppwr


Next Command:
```

The **dsppwr** command provides information about environmental measurements made by the node, including the following:

- Current status of the ASM card
- Fan speeds
- **Power supply type and status**—AC power supply type and status fields are displayed only if AC supplies are installed.
- Actual cabinet temperature in both centigrade (Celsius) and Fahrenheit
- **Temperature alarm threshold**—The line across the thermometer

Displaying the Alarm Status Monitor: dspasm

Example 10-9 shows the screen display for the **dspasm** command.

Example 10-9 dspasm *Command*

```
hei1bpx1       TRM   Teacher:1      BPX 8620  9.3.XX   May  11 200X 12:56 G+12

ASM Status:            Active         ASM Alarms
```

continues

Example 10-9 dspasm *Command (Continued)*

```
Statistics count:        111903           None
Statistics timeouts:     0
Cabinet temperature:     21 C
Power voltage A/B:       49 / 49 V

PSU   Ins Type Rev SerNum Failure
 A     Y   240V  0A ja1024  None
 B     Y   240V  0A ja1025  None


FAN    1    2    3
      3240 3300 3240 RPM



Last Command: dspasm


Next Command:
```

The **dspasm** command provides information similar to that displayed with the **dsppwr** command. In addition to the information from the **dsppwr** command, the **dspasm** command also provides the following:

- **Statistics count**—Successful polls. The ASM card periodically makes environmental measurements based on the configured polling interval. The polling interval can be changed using the **cnfasm** command.

- **Statistics timeouts**—Unsuccessful polls.

Configuring the Alarm Status Monitor: cnfasm

Example 10-10 shows the screen display for the **cnfasm** command.

Example 10-10 cnfasm *Command*

```
hei1bpx1      TRM   Teacher:1       BPX 8620  9.3.XX    May  11 200X 12:57 G+12

[1] Cabinet temp threshold:       50 C  [4] Polling interval (msec):     10000
[2] Power A deviation:      6 V (49.1)  [5] Fan threshold (RPM):          2000
[3] Power B deviation:      6 V (48.5)



                     ALM                                          ALM
[6]   ACO button       -              [14] BPX 8600 card slot   -
[7]   History button   -              [15] PSU A failure        Y
[8]   Cabinet temp     Y              [16] PSU A removed        Y
[9]   Power A volt      Y              [17] PSU B failure        Y
[10] Power B volt      N              [18] PSU B removed        Y
[11] Fan 1 RPM         Y
```

Example 10-10 **cnfasm** *Command (Continued)*

```
[12] Fan 2 RPM      Y
[13] Fan 3 RPM      Y


Last Command: cnfasm 10 n


Next Command:
```

The **cnfasm** command enables the configuration of power, cooling, and environmental parameters monitored by the ASM card. Use this command to set ASM alarm thresholds and to enable or disable alarm notification.

Assigning Node Names

This section describes the procedure for assigning the name to a BPX switch.

Node Names and Node Numbers

Each node in the network is identified with a unique node name and node number. Before introducing a node into a network, ensure the following:

- Node numbers must be unique within the network:
  - All nodes default to number 1 prior to installation configuration.
  - Numbers may be negotiated automatically between the nodes when a single node is introduced into an existing network.
  - To configure a node number, use the Service-level **rnmnd** (renumber node) command. Note, however, that allowing the node to negotiate its node number is preferred over setting it with the **rnnmd** command.
- Node names must be unique within the network:
  - Node names must be one to eight characters in length and are case-sensitive.
  - Node names must start with a letter, and they may include hyphens, underscores, or periods. Note that no spaces are allowed in node names.
  - Node names are configured using the **cnfname** command.

How to Assign and Verify Node Names

Follow these steps to assign the node name for a BPX switch:

Step 1 Enter **cnfname** *<name>*, where *name* is the unique name for this switch. This displays the new node name in the upper-left corner of the screen.

Step 2 Enter **dspnds** [+*n*], where *n* is the node number. This displays a list of all nodes in the network that have the associated node number.

Configuring Node Names: cnfname

Example 10-11 shows the screen display for the **cnfname** command.

Example 10-11 **cnfname** *Command*

```
SantRosa        TRM    Cisco         BPX 8620  9.3.XX    May  11 200X 12:39 G+12

NodeName                  Alarm
2.1-2.1/hei3bpx1
hei2bpx1                  MAJOR
2.1-2.2/SantRosa
hei3bpx1                  MAJOR
2.1-2.1/SantRosa



Last Command: cnfname SantRosa

Next Command:
```

The **cnfname** command specifies the name by which a node is known within the network. It can be changed at any time. The new node name is automatically distributed to the other nodes in the network. Node names are case-sensitive and must be unique within the network.

In this example, the name has been changed to SantRosa from the factory default NodeName. The upper-left corner of the screen shows the new name.

Displaying Nodes: dspnds

Example 10-12 shows the screen display for the **dspnds** command with the optional +n parameter. In this example, two other nodes are in the network.

Example 10-12 **dspnds** *Command*

```
hei1bpx1        TRM    Teacher:1     BPX 8620  9.3.XX    May  11 200X 13:40 G+12

NodeName Alarm
hei1bpx1 MAJOR
```

Example 10-12 *dspnds Command (Continued)*

```
hei2bpx1 MAJOR
hei3bpx1 MAJOR


Last Command: dspnds +n

Next Command:
```

The **dspnds** command displays the name, type, and alarm status of all nodes within the network of the node executing the command. If a node is in alarm, its name is highlighted, and the alarm type (major or minor) is displayed.

Initially, you should see only one node in the network (the local node). An optional parameter, +n, provides the node number. The node numbers are typically preassigned by the network designers to ensure unique values.

Setting the System Time and Date

In this section, you learn how to set the local time zone and the system date and time.

Network-Wide Settings

All BPX nodes in the network use a common time and date setting. As soon as you change the time or date on one node, the change is broadcast to all other nodes in the network.

Although all nodes share a common time and date setting, the setting might display differently if nodes are configured with different local time zone settings. For example, a node in London set for GMT would display the date and time as March 10, 2001 02:31, and a node in San Jose, California, set for PST on the same network would display March 9, 2001 18:31.

cnftmzn Command

The **cnftmzn** command configures the time zone for the node. Configuring the time zone for a node ensures that the node's time is correct for the local area regardless of the node at which the network date and time are set.

Here is the **cnftmzn** command syntax:

```
cnftmzn <time zone | gmt offset>
```

Related commands are **cnfdate** and **cnftime**.

Configurable parameter options for the **cnftmzn** command are described in Table 10-10.

Table 10-10 *Configurable Parameters for the **cnftmzn** Command*

Parameter	Description
time zone	Specifies one of the predefined system time zones:
	gmt (or g)—Greenwich Mean Time
	cst (or c)—Central Standard Time
	est (or e)—Eastern Standard Time
	mst (or m)—Mountain Standard Time
	pst (or p)—Pacific Standard Time
	yst (or y)—Yukon Standard Time
	cdt—Central Daylight Saving Time
	edt—Eastern Daylight Saving Time
	md—Mountain Daylight Saving Time
	pdt—Pacific Daylight Saving Time
	ydt—Yukon Daylight Saving Time
gmt offset	Specifies an offset from GMT in hours. The range is $g + 12$ to $g - 12$. For example, Singapore is g+8.

The **cnftmzn** command ensures that the node's time is correct for the local area regardless of the node at which the network date and time are subsequently set. As soon as it is configured, the time zone for the node is saved in battery-backup memory. After a power failure, a node's date and time are restored if at least one other node in the network has the current time and date.

The time zone can be set using an abbreviation such as g or gmt for Greenwich Mean Time or pst for Pacific Standard Time, or by specifying an offset from GMT, such as $g - 8$ for 8 hours behind GMT.

As soon as the local time zone has been set for all nodes as necessary, the **cnfdate** command (described in the next section) sets the date and time for the entire network. This command has network-wide implications: Setting a new date or time on one node causes all the other nodes to reset their clocks. The time is set using the 24-hour clock. The node broadcasts the specified date and time to every node in the network. Setting the time also affects the time stamp that is used by the CWM management station for statistics.

A related command, **cnftime**, can be used to set the time if, for example, only a closer resynchronization to the second is needed.

cnfdate Command

The **cnfdate** command sets the date and time for the entire network. The node broadcasts the specified date and time to every node in the network. The time displayed at each node is consistent with the time zone where the node resides. For the first-time configuration of the date and time in a network, **cnfdate** requires all the parameters except *second*. The default for *second* is 0. If a date and time already exist in the network, the defaults are the existing values at the moment you enter the **cnfdate** command.

Here is the **cnfdate** command syntax:

```
cnfdate <year> <month> <day> <hour> <minute> [second]
```

A related command is **cnftime**.

cnftime Command

The **cnftime** command is used if you need to set only the time. As mentioned a moment ago, this command can be used to set the time if, for example, only a closer resynchronization to the second is needed.

Each BPX node shows the local date, time, and time zone in the upper-right corner of the CLI screen. The time zone for each BPX node can be different, based on the node's physical location. The date and time are consistent throughout the network but are displayed in the local time zone for each BPX node. The local date and time are used in the BPX node event and alarm log and with statistics display screens. Both the **cnfdate** and **cnftime** commands alter the network date and time. Note that you should set the time zone on each node before you set the date and time.

How to Set the Time Zone, Date, and Time

Follow these steps to set the local time zone and to set the system (network) date and time:

Step 1 At the Next Command prompt, enter **cnftmzn** without any parameters. This displays the options for the required parameter to specify the local time zone.

Step 2 Enter the time zone parameter, as required. This displays the configured time zone setting for this node in the upper-right corner.

Step 3 Enter **cnfdate**. You are prompted for the year.

Step 4 Enter the year as four digits, such as 2001. You are prompted for the month.

Step 5 Enter the month as two digits, 01, 02, ..., 12. You are prompted for the day.

Step 6 Enter the day as two digits, 01, 02, ..., 31. You are prompted for the hour.

Step 7 Enter the hour as two digits, 00, 01, ... 23. You are prompted for the minutes.

Step 8 Enter the minutes as two digits, 00, 01, ... 59. You are prompted for the seconds.

Step 9 Enter the seconds as two digits, 00, 01, ... 59. This displays a warning message that changing the date or time will affect the statistics time stamps.

Step 10 Press **Return** or **Enter**. This displays the new date and time setting.

Displaying and Configuring Serial Ports

In this section, you can learn how to display and modify the communications parameters and functional characteristics of the two serial ports (control and auxiliary) on the BCC back card of the BPX switch.

Serial Port Communications Parameters

The control and auxiliary ports are EIA/TIA-232 serial ports that can be configured separately to match the communications parameters (baud rate, parity, and so on) used by the attached external equipment.

Serial Port Functions

Table 10-11 summarizes the different functions that can be assigned to the control and auxiliary ports. Notice that only one function can be configured per port, although the control and auxiliary port functions might be different (and usually are).

Table 10-11 *Serial Port Functions*

Port Function	Description	Control Port	Auxiliary Port
Printer	Prints screens (**prtscrn**) and other information (**prtrts**, **prttrkerrs**, and so on). With or without a network event log.	No	Yes
VT100 emulation	VT100 emulation for the CLI.	Yes	Yes

Table 10-11 *Serial Port Functions (Continued)*

Port Function	Description	Control Port	Auxiliary Port
Alarm message collector	Receives ASCII messages from an intelligent device.	No	Yes
	Stamps a message with the date and time and puts in a local and network log.		
	Creates a minor alarm.		
	Might have an auto-answer modem.		
External device window	Bidirectional communications with an intelligent device.	Yes	Yes
	VT100 emulation.		
	Access using the **window** command.		
Dial-out modem	Dials out when the network alarm status changes.	No	Yes
	Posts the date and time, network name, and alarm status.		

How to Display and Modify Serial Port Configurations and Functions

Follow these steps to verify and modify the current configuration and assigned function for the control and auxiliary ports:

Step 1 At the Next Command prompt, enter **dsptermcnf.** This displays the current configuration (communications parameters) of the control and auxiliary ports.

Step 2 Enter **cnfterm**. You are prompted for the port to be configured.

Step 3 Enter **c** for control or **a** for auxiliary. You are prompted in turn for each of the configurable parameters.

Step 4 Enter the new parameters as required. You are prompted to confirm the changes. After you do, you see the modified configuration.

Step 5 Enter **dsptermfunc.** This displays in highlighted text the currently assigned functions for the control and auxiliary ports.

Step 6 Enter **cnftermfunc c** or **cnftermfunc a** to modify the control or auxiliary ports, respectively. You are prompted for the index of the desired function. The index is the line number on the display. For example, the index is 5 for the external device window on the auxiliary port.

Step 7   Enter the index. One of the following things happens: If you select
External Device Window, you are prompted to enter an escape string. If
you select **Dial-out Modem**, you are prompted to enter a network name
and dial string. Otherwise, you are prompted to confirm the change.

Step 8   Verify that the auxiliary port is configured as a printer port. If not, enter
cnftermfunc a 1 or **cnftermfunc a 2**. Depending on the index you select
(1 or 2), this displays the new port configuration as Printer or Printer with
LOG.

Step 9   Enter **cnfterm a**. You are prompted in turn for each of the configurable
parameters for the auxiliary port.

Step 10   Enter the communications parameters as required for the printer. This
displays the new auxiliary port configuration.

Step 11   Enter **dspprtcnf**. This displays in highlighted text the currently assigned
print mode, which should be None.

Step 12   Enter **cnfprt r**. You are prompted for the name of a remote node. If this
is the only node in the network, the command fails.

Step 13   Enter **cnfprt l**. This displays in highlighted text the currently assigned
print mode, which should be Local.

Displaying Terminal Port Configurations: dsptermcnf

Example 10-13 shows the screen display for the **dsptermcnf** command.

Example 10-13 dsptermcnf *Command*

```
hei1bpx1        TRM    Teacher:1        BPX 8620   9.3.XX     May   11 200X 13:01 G+12


Control port                              Auxiliary port

Baud Rate:              9600              Baud Rate:             9600

Parity:                None              Parity:                None
Number of Data Bits: 8                   Number of Data Bits: 8
Number of Stop Bits: 1                   Number of Stop Bits: 1
Output flow control: XON/XOFF            Output flow control: XON/XOFF
Input flow control:    XON/XOFF          Input flow control:    XON/XOFF
CTS flow control:      No                CTS flow control:      Yes
Use DTR signal:        Yes               Use DTR signal:        No
```

Example 10-13 dsptermcnf *Command (Continued)*

```
Last Command: dsptermcnf


Next Command:
```

The **dsptermcnf** command shows the configuration of the control and auxiliary ports. The configuration parameters define the interfaces' transmission characteristics.

Configuring Terminal Ports: cnfterm

Example 10-14 shows the screen display for the **cnfterm** command.

Example 10-14 cnfterm *Command*

```
hei1bpx1          TRM    Teacher:1        BPX 8620  9.3.XX    May  11 200X 13:05 G+12


Control port                             Auxiliary port

Baud Rate:          9600                 Baud Rate:          9600

Parity:             None                 Parity:             None
Number of Data Bits: 8                   Number of Data Bits: 8
Number of Stop Bits: 1                   Number of Stop Bits: 1
Output flow control: XON/XOFF            Output flow control: XON/XOFF
Input flow control:  XON/XOFF            Input flow control:  XON/XOFF
CTS flow control:    No                  CTS flow control:    Yes
Use DTR signal:      Yes                 Use DTR signal:      No




This Command: cnfterm


Select Control port (c) or Auxiliary port (a):
```

The **cnfterm** command allows you to configure the terminal ports. The configuration parameters define the interfaces' transmission characteristics.

Displaying Port Functions: dsptermfunc

Example 10-15 shows the screen display for the **dsptermfunc** command.

Example 10-15 dsptermfunc *Command*

```
hei1bpx1        TRM    Teacher:1      BPX 8620  9.3.XX    May  11 200X 12:59 G+12


Control port                          Auxiliary port

1. VT100/Cisco StrataView             1. Okidata 182 Printer
2. VT100                              2. Okidata 182 Printer with LOG
3. External Device Window             3. VT100
                                      4. Alarm Message Collector
                                      5. External Device Window  $$$
                                      6. Autodial Modem



Last Command: dsptermfunc


Next Command:
```

The **dsptermfunc** command displays the currently configured functions of the control and auxiliary ports.

The following information is displayed for the control port:

- Control terminal
- Direct-dial modem
- External EIA/TIA-232 device

Additional configuration information includes the following:

- **External device window**—An escape string is defined and is used to return to the CLI when you are windowed out to another device.
- **AutoDial modem**—A network identifier and number to dial are defined when you choose the AutoDial modem option.

To configure the port configuration, you use the **cnftermfunc** command.

Displaying the Printer Configuration: dspprtcnf

Example 10-16 shows the screen display for the **dspprtcnf** command.

Example 10-16 dspprtcnf *Command*

```
hei1bpx1        TRM    Teacher:1        BPX 8620  9.3.XX    May  11 200X 13:13 G+12


Printing Mode

Remote Printing
Local Printing
No Printing


Last Command: dspprtcnf


Next Command:
```

The **dspprtcnf** command displays the node's printing configuration. The three printing modes—remote, local, and no—are listed, and the currently selected mode is highlighted.

If remote printing is selected, the node name where the remote printer is located also appears. Remote mode indicates that the destination of any output resulting from a print command (such as **prtrts** or **prttrkerrs**) will be printed at the listed remote node.

Local mode indicates that any print commands issued on this node print on the local printer.

No printing mode indicates that the log for the node does not print.

In the case where the auxiliary port is configured for log printing, the attached printer prints messages from the network log, which is an expanded version of the system log kept on each node. Each log printer configured in the network prints a record of the same network log entries.

Configuring Print Modes: cnfprt

Example 10-17 shows the screen display for the **cnfprt** command.

Example 10-17 cnfprt *Command*

```
hei1bpx1        TRM    Teacher:1        BPX 8620  9.3.XX    May  11 200X 13:22 G+12


Printing Mode
Remote Printing
```

continues

Example 10-17 **cnfprt** *Command (Continued)*

```
Local Printing
No Printing


This Command: cnfprt r hei1bpx1

Enter nodename:
```

The BPX node can support a printer on its auxiliary port. Because it is unlikely that a network will have a printer attached to every node, you can designate a remote printer for some of the BPX nodes. The **cnfprt** command configures the printing function. Three print options are available on the node:

- **Local**—The output of a print command is sent to the local auxiliary port.
- **Remote**—The output of a print command is sent to a remote node's auxiliary port. You must specify the remote node name.
- **None**—No printing is supported for the node.

In the case where the auxiliary port is configured for log printing, the attached printer prints messages from the network log, which is an expanded version of the system log kept on each node. Each log printer configured in the network prints a record of the same network log entries.

The **cnfprt** and **cnftermfunc** commands interact. If the auxiliary port on the node is configured for anything other than a printer (with or without the network log), the local printing configuration automatically changes to no printing. Printing is not possible because the auxiliary port is being used for another purpose.

Using an External Device Window

In this section, you learn how to use the external device window to communicate with an external device connected to the control or auxiliary port.

How to Display and Use the External Device Window

Follow these steps to display and use the external device window:

Step 1   Verify that the auxiliary port is configured for the external device window. If it isn't, enter **cnftermfunc a 5** *<string>*, where *string* is an escape sequence, such as $$$. This displays the new port configuration as an external device window, with the configured escape sequence.

Step 2   Verify that the external device is connected to the auxiliary port using an appropriate serial cable.

Step 3   At the Next Command prompt, enter **window a**, where **a** signifies the auxiliary port. This displays the command-line prompt for the attached external device. It might be necessary to press **Return** or **Enter** to activate the command-line interpreter. If there is no response, or if the response is garbled, check the communications parameters for the serial ports.

Step 4   At the external device command prompt, display the current device configuration. For a Cisco router, enter the **show run** command. This displays the current configuration for the attached router.

Step 5   To return to the BPX CLI, you must enter the window escape sequence, **$$$**.

Windowing to External Devices: window

An external device with an EIA/TIA-232 serial port such as a router can be connected to the control or auxiliary port. If the BPX port is configured for the window function, you can initiate communication with the router—for example, to check or modify the router configuration.

To begin a session, enter the **window** command and specify the control or auxiliary port. The control terminal screen subsequently clears, after which characters entered at the control terminal go to the external device and vice versa.

To return to the BPX CLI, you must enter the window escape sequence, **$$$**.

The **window** command can be executed over a virtual terminal connection, which makes it possible to control all external devices from a single point in the network. Virtual terminal (vt) is discussed later in this book.

Configuring Node and Network IP Addresses

In this section, you learn how to configure IP addresses that have been defined for the BPX node LAN port and for the network IP Relay.

BPX IP Addressing Schemes

The BPX node can be configured with up to three different IP addresses:

- LAN port IP address
- Default gateway IP address
- IP Relay (Network IP) address

The LAN interface on the BCC back card is used to attach the node to a LAN for management purposes. Both the CWM workstation and other devices on the LAN can communicate with the nodes using, for example, Telnet, SNMP, or TFTP. Each node that is attached to a LAN must have a unique IP address.

NOTE   Not all nodes in the network need to be attached to a LAN for network management access.

If the node is not connected to the same LAN segment as the WAN Manager management station, a default gateway IP address must be configured. The default gateway is usually the address of a router interface to which the node directs network management traffic.

The IP Relay address is required by CWM for node management and statistics collection. If CWM is not implemented, the IP Relay address need not be configured, although it can be used to Telnet to a node in-band through the network trunks.

NOTE   The IP Relay address, if configured, must be on a separate subnet than that of the LAN port IP address.

IP Address Locations

Figure 10-3 shows where each of these IP addresses is used. The LAN port need only be enabled on nodes where external management access is required, and that an IP Relay address is needed for every node with which CWM will communicate or Telnet in-band to.

How to Configure IP Addresses

Follow these steps to verify the IP addresses on your node. Note that you must have SuperUser access privilege to modify any of the addresses.

Step 1   At the Next Command prompt, enter **cnflan**. As prompted, enter the LAN port IP address and subnet mask and optionally the TCP service port and the default gateway IP address. This requires you to confirm the entry. You then see the new configuration for the BPX LAN port.

Step 2   Enter **cnfnwip**. As prompted, enter the network IP address and subnet mask. This requires you to confirm the entry. You then see the new configuration for the switch's IP Relay address.

Step 3   Enter **dspnwip**. This displays the IP Relay addresses of all nodes in the network.

Figure 10-3 *IP Address Locations*

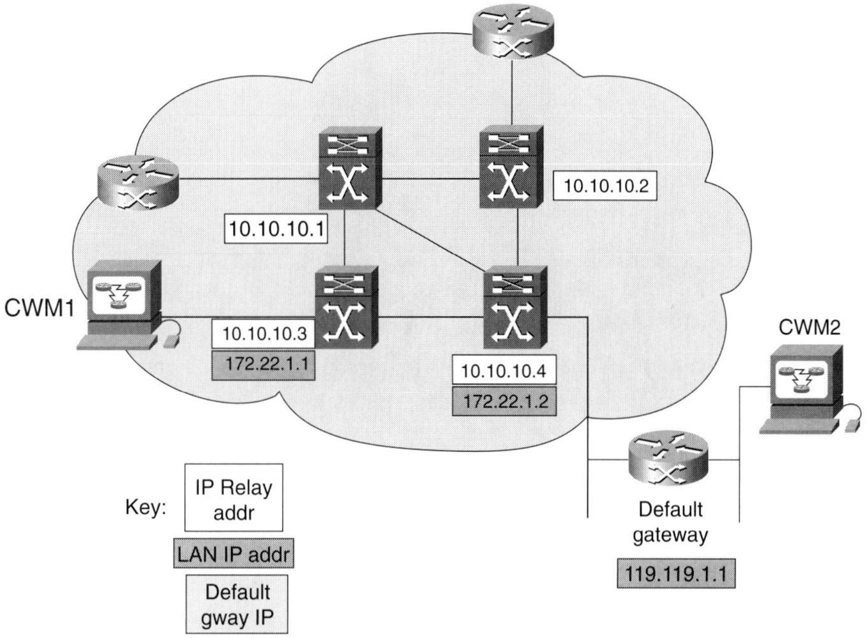

Configuring the LAN Port: cnflan

Example 10-18 shows the screen display for the SuperUser **cnflan** command. The **cnflan** command configures the LAN port parameters for the Ethernet port on the BCC back card.

Example 10-18 **cnflan** *Command*

```
SantRosa      TN     SuperUser      BPX 8620  9.3.XX    Apr. 10 200X 18:09 PST

Active IP Address:                  172.30.241.11
IP Subnet Mask:                     255.255.255.128
IP Service Port:                    5120
Default Gateway IP Address:         172.30.241.1
Maximum LAN Transmit Unit:          1500
Ethernet Address:                   00.C0.43.00.90.66


Type      State
LAN       READY
TCP       UNAVAIL
UDP       READY
Telnet    READY
```

continues

Example 10-18 *cnflan Command (Continued)*

```
TFTP      READY
TimeHdlr  READY
SNMP      READY


Last Command: cnflan 172.30.241.11 255.255.255.128 5120 172.30.241.1


Next Command:
```

NOTE   The IP Relay (nwip) address, if configured, must be on a separate subnet from that used for the LAN port IP address configured with **cnflan**.

Also, you must have SuperUser access to use the **cnflan** command.

To display the LAN port parameters, use the **dsplancnf** command.

Configuring Network IP: cnfnwip

Example 10-19 shows the screen display for the **cnfnwip** command.

Example 10-19 *cnfnwip Command*

```
SantRosa     TN    SuperUser      BPX 8620  9.3.XX    Apr. 10 200X 18:10 PST

Active Network IP Address:           10.10.4.11
Active Network IP Subnet Mask:       255.255.255.0


Last Command: cnfnwip 10.10.4.11 255.255.255.0

Changing current Network IP configuration
Next Command:
```

The **cnfnwip** command configures the address and subnet mask for the Network IP (or IP Relay). The IP Relay address can be used to Telnet to a node in-band through the network trunks and is required by Cisco WAN Manager for node management and statistics collection.

NOTE   You must have SuperUser access to use the **cnfnwip** command.

Displaying the Network IP Address: dspnwip

Example 10-20 shows the screen display for the **dspnwip** command.

Example 10-20 dspnwip *Command*

```
hei1bpx1        TRM    Teacher:1        BPX 8620  9.3.XX    May  11 200X 13:12 G+12

Active Network IP Address:             10.10.80.202
Active Network IP Subnet Mask:         255.255.255.0

NodeName   IP Address
hei1bpx1 10.10.80.202
         10.10.80.214
hei2bpx1 10.10.80.211
         10.10.80.214
hei3bpx1 10.10.80.220


Last Command: dspnwip

Next Command:
```

The **dspnwip** command screen lists the current IP Relay addresses of all nodes in the
network.

Any feeder device (such as MGX 8220 shelves or IGX feeder nodes) IP Relay address is
also displayed on the **dspnwip** screen. All feeder devices are listed under the associated
routing BPX node. Note that because they are edge devices, feeders do not provide their
node name.

Summary

In this chapter, you learned how to log into and out of the BPX system and how to use online
help. BPX access methods were presented, and command syntax, entry modes, and privilege
levels were explained. You should be able to add users, change passwords, configure a node
name, and set the system date, time, and time zone.

You should be able to display and monitor system data and configure serial ports. You saw
how to change printing capabilities and how to communicate with external devices through
the external device window. Given the information in this chapter, you should now be able
to configure nodes and network IP addresses.

Review Questions

1 Which of the following is not a valid choice of access method for a first-time installation?

A. Cisco WAN Manager

B. PC with terminal emulation

C. VT100-compatible terminal

D. UNIX workstation with a serial interface

2 What are the default settings for the control and auxiliary ports?

A. 9600, odd, 8, and 1

B. 9600, even, 7, and none

C. 9600, none, 8, and none

D. 9600, none, 8, and 1

3 Commands are a combination of _____ and _____. The < > brackets indicate _____ parameters, and the [ ] brackets represent _____ parameters.

4 What are the four categories of command privilege levels?

5 Which of the following devices *cannot* be attached to the auxiliary port?

A. Serial printer

B. Dumb terminal

C. Dial-out modem

D. Router console port

E. Cisco WAN Manager workstation

F. PC running VT100 terminal emulation

6 Which command lists recently issued commands?

7 Match the command-line access method with its definition.

1. _____ IP Relay   A. A 15-pin AUI port connected to Ethernet

2. _____ LAN port   B. The default CLI access using a VT100 terminal

3. _____ Control port   C. A secondary serial port often used for a dial-in modem

4. _____ Auxiliary port D. A method to Telnet to a node in-band through the BPX network

8 Mark the following statements as true or false.

A. _____ The **Esc** key aborts a command.

B. _____ All commands have required and optional parameters.

C. _____ Most commands consist of an abbreviated verb and noun.

D. _____ A command is complete when all required parameters have been defined with appropriate values.

E. _____ The BPX node prompts you for all required and optional parameters when you use the prompted entry mode.

9 What is the purpose of the **help** command?

A. To teach you how to configure a BPX node

B. To identify a command's definition and syntax

C. To define the value range of a connection's required parameters

D. To provide a detailed description of the use of each command

10 Which of the following requirements must be met when you assign a BPX node name?

A. Node names are case-sensitive.

B. Node names must start with a letter.

C. A node name can contain up to ten characters.

D. Node names must be unique within the network.

E. Any keyboard character can be used in a node name.

11 Mark the following statements as true or false.

A. _____ User IDs and passwords are network-specific.

B. _____ The default password is newuser.

C. _____ You can display the password of any user who has an equal or lower access privilege than yourself.

D. _____ A user ID with a privilege level of 1 can perform all of the commands available to a user ID with a privilege level of 0.

12 Which of the following commands display the current cabinet temperature?

A. **dspasm**

B. **dspcd**

C. **cnfasm**

D. **dsppwr**

13 Mark the following statements as true or false.

A. _____ Cabinet temperature in excess of the configured threshold generates a major alarm.

B. _____ If the **dspcds** command shows a front card type of BDR, the firmware revision is R.

    C. _____ Cards can be in an active and failed condition at the same time.

    D. _____ All cards provide the same information when you use the **dspcd** command.

    E. _____ Cabinet temperature in excess of the configured threshold generates a minor alarm.

14 Mark the following statements as true or false.

    A. _____ You can attach a printer to either the control or auxiliary port.

    B. _____ A printer configured for log printing prints events for its local node only.

    C. _____ Configuring a node for remote printing redirects all log events for printing at that node.

    D. _____ The remote print option only applies to CLI print commands.

    E. _____ You can have multiple log printers in the network.

15 Which of the following devices should you be able to access using the **window** command?

A. The control port on a BPX switch

B. The auxiliary port on a BPX switch

C. The Ethernet port on a Cisco router

D. The console port on a Cisco router

E. The Ethernet port on a BPX switch

16 When defining the IP addresses for a network with CWM, which of the following are required?

A. LAN port, IP Relay, and default gateway addresses on the same subnet

B. LAN port, IP Relay, and default gateway addresses on different subnets

C. IP Relay addresses for all nodes

D. LAN port addresses for all nodes

E. LAN port and IP Relay addresses on separate subnets

F. LAN port address on at least one node

17 Match the command with its primary function.

1. _____	**bye**	A.	Ends the CLI session
2. _____	**dspcd**	B.	Modifies your password
3. _____	**dspcds**	C.	Lists all cards in the node
4. _____	**cnfasm**	D.	Modifies the environmental alarm thresholds
5. _____	**dspasm**	E.	Shows a card's status and serial number
6. _____	**cnfpwd**	F.	Shows the status of the power supplies and fans

18 Mark the following statements as true or false.

A. _____ The **Delete** key can be used to abort a command.

B. _____ The abbreviation "dis" means "display" on the BPX CLI.

C. _____ Cards can be in both an active and failed condition at the same time.

D. _____ All cards provide the same information when you use the **dspcd** command.

19 Assume that a card is reporting QRS as the revision when you use the **dspcds** or **dspcd** command. Match each letter with the information it provides.

1. _____ Q   A. Hardware revision

2. _____ R   B. Firmware revision, which is a variation on the model

3. _____ S   C. Model, which determines the feature set on the card

This chapter covers the following key topics:

- What Is a Trunk?
- What Is a Virtual Trunk?
- Trunk Resource Partitions
- Dynamic Partitioning
- Activating, Configuring, and Deactivating Network Trunks
- How to Activate, Configure, and Deactivate Network Trunks
- Steps Used to Activate, Configure, and Deactivate Network Trunks
- What Is a Line?
- Activating, Configuring, and Deactivating Access Lines
- Steps Used to Activate, Configure, and Deactivate Access Lines

CHAPTER 11

Configuring Network Trunks and Access Lines

This chapter introduces the concept of trunking in a network. You will learn how to configure and activate the trunks that connect the BPX nodes into a single network. You will learn about physical and virtual trunks and the applications for each type. Trunks are also used to connect MGX feeder shelves or IGX feeder nodes to the BPX network nodes.

As soon as the network trunks are in place and operational between the BPX nodes, the network is ready to provision user services. Properly functioning network trunks also allow you to verify that internode communication is possible.

In this chapter, you will learn how to configure and activate the ATM access lines that connect a BPX node to external user equipment. ATM access lines need to be configured and activated correctly to support user connections. As soon as the lines have been brought up, you can configure the ports that form the interface between the BPX network and user devices.

What Is a Trunk?

This section defines the function of a trunk in a Cisco WAN switching network. The focus is on physical trunks; virtual trunks are covered in a separate section.

Trunk Definition

A *trunk* is a high-speed digital transport facility that carries user and management information in ATM cells between any two nodes (Cisco WAN switches). It also connects feeder shelves to routing nodes. A physical trunk must terminate on the same type of physical interface at each end node, such as T3. Trunks can directly connect nodes, perhaps in a campus network. More commonly, however, a trunk uses a public wide-area network (WAN), in which case, the carrier equipment provides a termination point at each end.

Trunks can differ in technology and format and may be physical or virtual. (Virtual trunks are discussed in the next section.) The actual trunk layout that is implemented usually represents a balance between redundancy and cost. A network could be implemented using a fully meshed design in which every node is physically connected via a trunk to every other node. In most cases, however, this would be cost-prohibitive, so a partial-mesh approach is typically used. As a rule of thumb, every node should be connected to the network by at least two trunks, each of which should terminate on a different node, similar to a hub-and-spoke configuration.

Trunks are used between a BPX node and any of the following equipment:

- Another BPX node
- MGX 8220/8230/8250 ATM interface shelf
- IGX multiservice switch
- MGX 8850 Release 1 (with PXM1 processor) edge switch (MGX 8850-PXM1 switch)
- MGX 8850 Release 2 (with PXM45 processor) core switch (MGX 8850-PXM45 switch)

NOTE   Trunks support a proprietary, multifunctional implementation called *statistical reserve* between Cisco WAN switches in a flat network and switches and feeders in a tiered network.

BPX Card Modules That Support Trunks

Both the BXM and BNI card modules on the BPX node support trunks. Because the BNI cards are being discontinued, we will focus on the BXM cards. The following BXM trunk card types are supported:

- Eight or 12 T3 interfaces
- Eight or 12 E3 interfaces
- Four or eight OC3-c/STM-1 single-mode, single-mode long-reach, or multimode fiber interfaces
- One or two OC12-c/STM-4 single-mode, single-mode long-reach, or multimode fiber interfaces

Both BXM and BNI card modules are responsible for managing and queuing network traffic between nodes.

What Is a Virtual Trunk?

This section introduces the concept of virtual trunks and contrasts the characteristics and applications of virtual trunks with those of physical trunks.

Figure 11-1 shows a sample network layout that includes both physical and virtual trunks.

Figure 11-1 *Virtual Trunks*

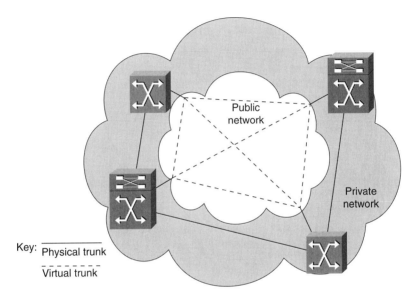

Virtual Trunk Definition

A *virtual trunk* is an ATM trunk that is defined over a public ATM network in the form of a virtual path connection (VPC). Multiple virtual trunks can terminate on a single physical trunk interface. Each virtual trunk corresponds to a single VPC and is identified by a unique VPI provided by the ATM network administrator (for example, the service provider).

In Figure 11-1, six virtual trunks (indicated by broken lines) are configured in the network. Notice that multiple virtual trunks terminate on each of the physical interfaces. Physical trunks also terminate on the nodes (such as the lower two) shown in this figure.

For service provider customers who already have a core ATM network infrastructure with no Cisco products in place, virtual trunking provides the ability to expand the network using a Cisco solution while making use of the existing network for transport in the core. Using virtual trunking over an ATM network with no Cisco products instead of connecting to such a network via NNI (network-to-network interface) not only preserves the advanced BPX networking and traffic management features but also allows all the BPX switches to be managed as a single network. Virtual trunks facilitate the logical subdivision of broadband services such as E3/T3 and STM-1 or STM-4 for dedicated use in a public environment.

Physical and Virtual Trunk Differences

Table 11-1 summarizes the major functional differences between physical and virtual trunks as implemented on the BXM card. Physical trunks and virtual trunks allow the logical subdivision of broadband services such as E3/T3 and STM-1 or STM-4 for dedicated use in a public environment.

Table 11-1 *Physical and Virtual Trunk Differences*

Feature or Function	BXM Physical Trunks	BXM Virtual Trunks
Number of trunks per physical interface port	One	Up to 31
Number of VPCs per trunk	Up to 4095	One
VPC type configurable	No	Yes: CBR, VBR, or ABR
Number of Virtual Interfaces per physical port	One	Up to 31 (one per virtual trunk)
Terminating interfaces on the trunk	Both must be the same type— for example, both T3	Might be different at each end—for example, T3 at one end and OC-3c at the other end
ATM cell types supported	NNI only	UNI or NNI
Support for MGX feeder trunks	Yes	No
Routing of external VPCs	Yes	No

BXM Virtual Interface

Each BXM module has up to 31 Virtual Interfaces (VIs) associated with the egress to a network trunk. Activation of a trunk, whether physical or virtual, results in the creation of a logical trunk by the system software. The new logical trunk is assigned one of the available VIs. Figure 11-2 shows the 31 VIs on a BXM card and how they might be assigned to a set of physical and logical trunks.

Figure 11-2 *BXM Virtual Interface*

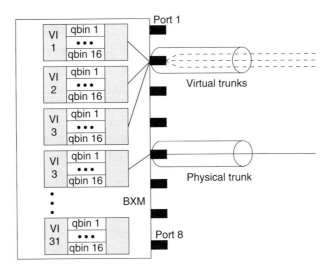

Each of the 31 VIs constitutes a set of class of service (CoS) buffers called *QBins*. Each VI has 16 QBins, allowing for up to 16 different types of traffic.

AutoRoute connections use QBins 0 through 9. Virtual Switch Interfaces (VSIs) that support master controllers use QBins 10 through 15, as applicable. Other queuing structures on the BXM card, such as the egress queues for connections, also use QBin structures. These are discussed in other sections of this book.

You can configure trunk QBins using the SuperUser **cnftrkparm** command or, in the case of QBins 10 through 15, by using the **cnfqbin** command.

BPX Support for Virtual Trunks

Virtual trunks can be implemented on BPX nodes between any two BXM trunk ports. Note that virtual trunks between BXM and BNI cards are not supported. BXM virtual trunks use standard UNI or NNI cells—whichever is required by the service provider. The range of VPI values supported differs by interface type, as follows:

- **UNI**—1 to 255
- **NNI**—1 to 4095

Each virtual trunk must be configured as a CBR, VBR, or ABR trunk to correspond with the type of service purchased from the ATM service provider. There are limitations on the number of trunks that can be supported on a per-node-basis type and a per-card-basis type:

- **BPX node**—Up to 50 (32 MB processor) or 64 (64 MB processor) trunks, physical or virtual

- **BXM**—Up to 31 virtual trunks per physical port, with a maximum of 31 per card

Trunk Resource Partitions

Why is it necessary to define resource partitions when activating a physical or virtual trunk?

Trunks have limited resources, such as bandwidth, the number of Logical Channel Numbers (LCNs), and VPI/VCI space. Three controllers compete for these resources—Portable AutoRoute (PAR) (using PVCs), PNNI (using SVCs), and MPLS or TAG (using LVCs or TVCs). The PNNI and MPLS controllers reside on external equipment, and PAR is integrated with the BCC. Virtual trunks are used to attach these external controllers to the VPX network. By setting limits on these controllers, you eliminate competition for trunk resources. The following sections discuss trunk resource partitions and BPX VSI controllers and show you how resources are allocated to controllers at the card and port level.

Virtual Switch Interface Controllers

The following is a brief overview of Virtual Switch Interface (VSI) controller functionality. It leads into a discussion of resource partitioning for trunks.

The VSI protocol is used in MPLS between the external router (LSC) and the BXM ports on the BPX. This interface allows the VSI master controller to control the BXM slave ports.

Figure 11-3 shows how multiple VSI controllers can be supported with the BPX switch software. Here, multiple VSI controllers are set to share resources on the BPX switch with the traditional Automatic Routing Management system AR (formerly known as Portable AutoRoute [PAR]). Each controller operates independently of the others and is unaware that the other controllers exist. To ensure that the controllers can function without interference, you must allocate certain physical resources to each controller. Each set of such resources represents a *resource partition*. Each partition can be viewed as a *logical switch*, independent from the other logical switches. Together, they constitute the physical BPX switch.

Figure 11-3 *BPX VSI Controllers*

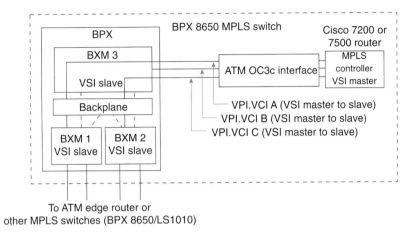

To ATM edge router or
other MPLS switches (BPX 8650/LS1010)

Figure 11-4 shows a VSI functional block diagram.

Figure 11-4 *VSI Functional Block Diagram*

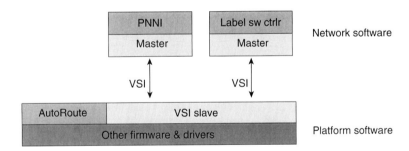

Which Resources Are Partitioned?

On the BPX switch, resources are allocated to controllers at the card and port level, as shown in Figure 11-5. (The BW in this figure stands for bandwidth.)

Figure 11-5 *Resource Partitioning*

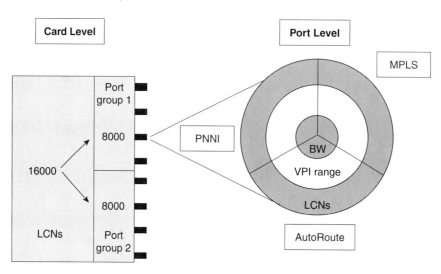

Card-Level Resources

Each BXM card can support a finite number of connection channels, varying from 16,000 to 32,000, depending on the card type. Each connection channel is associated with an LCN. The pool of card LCNs is shared among all controllers. You can see how many LCNs are supported by the BXM card using the **dspcd** command.

Additionally, some models of the BXM card support more than one port group. The **dspcd** command indicates how many port groups are supported. Although each card supports a given number of channels, hardware limitations on some card types do not permit all the channels to be assigned to a single port. An example is the BXM eight-port OC-3c card, which has two port groups, consisting of ports 1 to 4 and 5 to 8, respectively. The card firmware defines the maximum number of channels each port group can support.

Port-Level Resources

Each port on a BXM card includes the following resources, which can be partitioned among the controllers:

- **Bandwidth**—The available port bandwidth in cells per second. Dependent on the card type.

- **VPI address range**—Specifies the VPI range that the controller can use. The range is 1 to 255 for each UNI port or 1 to 4095 for each NNI port.

- **Channels (LCNs)**—Defines the number of channels per controller from the card-level pool.

Example of Trunk Resource Partitioning

The following example walks through the process of activating trunks on a BXM card that has the following attributes:

- Eight T3 ports, each with an available bandwidth of 96,000 cps
- Support for 16,000 channels
- A single port group per card

Later in this chapter, you will learn how to use the **cnfrsrc** command to define resource partitions for physical and virtual trunks. In this example, we will focus on the process and on understanding how resources are allocated to different partitions.

The BPX switch supports resource partitioning between AR and up to two VSI controllers. Assume in the example that the BXM card needs to support the following:

- Two physical trunks, each supporting AR, MPLS, and PNNI
- A virtual trunk supporting AR only (multiple partitions are not supported on virtual trunks)
- A virtual trunk supporting MPLS only

Step 1: Partition the First Physical Trunk

Assume that the BXM is in slot 5 and that the physical interface is port 1. Using the **cnfrsrc** command, request three partitions with the values shown in Table 11-2 on port 5.1.

Table 11-2 *Partitioning of the First Physical Trunk*

Interface 5.1	AR	MPLS	PNNI
Enable partition?	Yes	Yes	Yes
LCNs	2000	1000	1600
Bandwidth (cps)	40,000	20,000	24,000
VPI range	1 to 99	100 to 199	200 to 249

- System response to this request: ACCEPTED
- Next step: Define the next interface

Step 2: Partition the Second Physical Trunk

Using the **cnfrsrc** command, request three partitions with the values shown in Table 11-3 on port 5.2.

Table 11-3 *Partitioning of the Second Physical Trunk*

Interface 5.2	AR	MPLS	PNNI
Enable partition?	Yes	Yes	Yes
LCNs	1600	2000	1200
Bandwidth (cps)	24,000	60,000	16,000
VPI range	1 to 99	100 to 199	200 to 249

- System response to this request: REJECTED
- Reason for rejection: The requested bandwidth allocations exceed the port rate.
- How to correct: Modify one of the partitions to allocate less bandwidth. For example, you might consider lowering the MPLS bandwidth to 20000.

Step 3: Partition the First Virtual Trunk

Using the **cnfrsrc** command, request two partitions with the values shown in Table 11-4 on port 5.3.1.

Table 11-4 *Partitioning of the First Virtual Trunk*

Interface 5.3.1	AR	MPLS	PNNI
Enable partition?	Yes	No	Yes
LCNs	1600		8000
Bandwidth (cps)	24,000		72,000
VPI range	1 to 99		200

- System response to this request: REJECTED
- Reasons for rejection:
  — You requested an illegal VPI range for the AR partition; virtual trunks can have only a single VPI.
  — You attempted to add a second partition to a virtual trunk.
- How to correct: Select a single VPI value for the AR partition, and abandon the attempt to add the PNNI partition.

Step 4: Partition the Second Virtual Trunk

Using the **cnfrsrc** command, request two partitions with the values shown in Table 11-5 on port 5.3.2.

Table 11-5 *Partitioning of the Second Virtual Trunk*

Interface 5.3.2	AR	MPLS	PNNI
Enable partition?	No	No	Yes
LCNs			8000
Bandwidth (cps)			72,000
VPI range			200

- System response to this request: REJECTED
- Reason for rejection: The accumulated total requested allocation of LCNs exceeds the card limit of 16000.
- How to correct: Reduce the requested allocation of LCNs.

Summary of Enabled Partitions

Table 11-6 summarizes the three logical switches that were created in this example and identifies the interfaces that are part of each switch.

Table 11-6 *Summary of Enabled Partitions*

Interface	AR Partition	MPLS Partition	PNNI Partition
5.1	Yes	Yes	Yes
5.2	Yes	Yes	Yes
5.3.1	Yes		
5.3.2			Yes

Dynamic Partitioning

When you add PNNI to an existing network, you can either add ports and trunks as new interfaces or configure existing interfaces to allow PNNI traffic. When you add PNNI to existing interfaces, bandwidth and a VPI/VCI range must be made available to PNNI. This is called *partitioning* because these resources are allocated to AR and PNNI.

After partitioning, both AR and PNNI have a defined bandwidth available to their respective CAC algorithms for adding new connections. Each has a pool of available VPI/VCI to assign to new connections. The total bandwidth assigned to all protocols in use on a port (AR, PNNI, MPLS) cannot exceed the physical port bandwidth. The allocated (or partitioned) bandwidth for each protocol impacts only the CAC bandwidth. Existing connections can use available bandwidth on each port as dictated by their respective CoS without regard to partitioning.

Dynamic partitioning lets you add a PNNI partition to existing interfaces (both ports and trunks) without affecting any of the existing AR connections on that interface. The VPI/VCI range assigned to PNNI can contain existing AR connections, but no new AR connections may be made in the PNNI range. Similarly, new PNNI connections can be made only in the newly partitioned PNNI VPI/VCI range. Dynamic partitioning also enables the expansion of the PNNI VPI/VCI range into the AR partition without impacting existing connections.

Allowing overlapping of VPI/VCI ranges between existing AR connections and new PNNI connections simplifies the conversion of AR connections to PNNI by allowing new PNNI connections to assume the VPI/VCI of the AR connection they replace.

You can add PNNI partitioning remotely through the CWM Service Agent Interface or locally at the BPX switch's CLI. With the PNNI partition in place, CWM allows the user to provision new SPVC connections.

For future migration phases, planned enhancement to dynamic partitioning will allow not only the addition and expansion of PNNI ranges, but also the expansion of the AR range at the expense of the PNNI partition.

Activating, Configuring, and Deactivating Network Trunks

In this section, you will learn how to use the CLI to activate and configure a network trunk between two BPX switches.

Activating (or *upping*) a trunk activates the hardware and physical characteristics that support the trunk. This includes sending out the correct frame format and a signal (idle code). Even after you issue the **uptrk** command, there are no intelligent communications between the two nodes.

The **uptrk** command must be issued from both ends of the trunk. If the trunk is in alarm after it has been upped, this could be due to a physical failure or configuration mismatch. Typically many other devices are on a trunk between two nodes, and all must be compatible. For example, an OC-3c card can support Physical Layer Convergence Protocol (PLCP) or Header Error Correction (HEC) framing; the card must be configured using the **cnftrk** command to match the framing method actually being used.

The **addtrk** command introduces the trunk as a bandwidth resource in the network. When a trunk is added, intelligent communication (in the form of ATM cells) begins between the two nodes. This activity adds the switch to the network if it was not already part of the network. It is *generally a better idea* to do the **addtrk** from the new node in certain cases, and it is also *generally a better idea* to delete a trunk (**deltrk**) from the network side.

The trunk must be out of alarm before you issue the **addtrk** command. If the trunk is still in alarm, the command fails. Some configuration parameters might also affect the success of the **addtrk** command. For example, if the payload or frame scrambling options are inconsistent at both ends, the **addtrk** operation does not succeed. Use the **dsptrkcnf** command, at both ends if necessary, to verify that the trunk is correctly configured. Make any changes using the **cnftrk** command. The **addtrk** command needs to be issued from only one side.

The nodes initially exchange their node name, node number, and trunk number when the **addtrk** command is issued. For the **addtrk** to be successful, the two nodes must have unique node names and numbers. A database exchange occurs afterward that includes the network topology, user IDs and passwords, network synchronization, and trunk-loading information.

Table 11-7 describes some commands used throughout this book and lists the privilege level necessary to issue each command.

Table 11-7   *Commands for Trunks*

Command	Description	Privilege Level
uptrk	Up trunk. Activates trunk hardware and physical-layer characteristics.	2
cnftrk	Configure trunk. Modifies trunk configuration parameters.	1
addtrk	Add trunk. Introduces the trunk as a network resource and begins intelligent communications between nodes.	1
dsptrks	Display trunks. Displays summary information for all trunks on the node.	6
dsptrkcnf	Display trunk configuration. Displays configuration parameters for a particular trunk.	6
dspnw	Display network. Displays the network topology.	6
deltrk	Delete trunk. Removes the trunk from the network.	1
dntrk	Down trunk. Deactivates the trunk hardware.	2
vt	Virtual terminal. Creates a virtual link to another node in the network to access the remote user interface.	6

How to Activate, Configure, and Deactivate Network Trunks

You must follow several steps to activate and introduce trunks into the network. You must follow these steps in a specific order, beginning with trunk activation using the **uptrk** command.

uptrk Command

The **uptrk** command activates, or "ups," a physical or virtual network trunk. The BXM supports trunks and lines on the same card.

The **uptrk** command syntax for the different trunk types supported on the BXM is as follows:

- **Physical trunk—uptrk** *<slot.port>*
- **Virtual trunk—uptrk** *<slot.port.vtrk>*

NOTE   As soon as a trunk has been upped as a physical trunk, it cannot support virtual trunks. The trunk must be downed using the **dntrk** command and then upped as a virtual trunk.

Example 11-1 shows the effect of issuing the **uptrk** command on a node where the other end of the trunk has not yet been activated. Immediately after you issue this command, the trunk appears to be clear, but after several seconds, it goes into major alarm, as shown here. This example shows a virtual trunk being upped.

Example 11-1 uptrk *Command*

```
hei1bpx1           TN      Teacher:1       BPX 8620  9.3.XX      Feb. 14 200X 13:16 PST

TRK        Type       Current Line Alarm Status              Other End
  1.1.1    T3         Major - Loss of Sig (RED)              -




Last Command: uptrk 1.1.1

256 PVCs allocated. Use 'cnfrsrc' to configure PVCs
Next Command:
```

A trunk cannot be upped if the required cards are unavailable. Furthermore, if a card is executing a background self-test, a "card in test" message might appear on the screen. If this message appears, wait a moment and then reenter the **uptrk** command.

cnftrk Command

The **cnftrk** command configures parameters for physical and virtual trunks. A trunk has a default configuration after activation "upping" with the **uptrk** command. Beyond this default configuration, **cnftrk** lets you configure trunk parameters. You must use **uptrk** to up the trunk, use **cnftrk** to configure trunk parameters, and then use **addtrk** to add the trunk to the network. You must execute **cnftrk** at both ends of a trunk. For virtual trunks, define the bandwidth and VPI number.

Here is the **cnftrk** command syntax:

```
cnftrk <slot.port>[.vtrk] <options for | E3 | T3 | OC-3 | OC-12>
```

Example 11-2 shows that the trunk has been reconfigured to do the following:

- Define the transmit cell rate
- Set CBR as the traffic type for the virtual trunk (this is normally set to match the service provided by the public carrier)
- Specify the specific VPI needed for a virtual trunk

All other parameters remain at the default values for the particular type of trunk—in this case, a T3 trunk on a BXM.

Example 11-2 cnftrk *Command*

```
hei1bpx1         TN    Teacher:1      BPX 8620  9.3.XX    Feb. 14 200X 13:16 PST

TRK  1.1.1 Config   T3      [24000 cps]  BXM slot:      3
Transmit Rate:        24000            VPC Conns disabled:    --
Protocol By The Card:  --              Line framing:          PLCP
VC Shaping:           No                 coding:              --
Hdr Type NNI:         No                 recv impedance:      --
Statistical Reserve:  1000      cps      cable type:          --
Idle code:            7F hex                   length:        0-225 ft.
Connection Channels:  256             Pass sync:             No
Traffic:V,TS,NTS,FR,FST,CBR,N&RT-VBR,ABR  Loop clock:        No
SVC Vpi Min:          --              HCS Masking:           Yes
SVC Channels:         --              Payload Scramble:      No
SVC Bandwidth:        --       cps     Frame Scramble:        --
Restrict CC traffic:  No              Virtual Trunk Type:    ABR
Link type:            Terrestrial     Virtual Trunk VPI:     100
Routing Cost:         10              Deroute delay time:    0 seconds

Last Command: cnftrk 1.1.1 24000 n 1000 7F V,TS,NTS,FR,FST,CBR,NRT-VBR,ABR,RT-VB
R N TERRESTRIAL 10 0 0 N N N ABR 100

Next Command:
```

Detailed information on the configurable trunk parameters for each type of BXM trunk is included in the **dsptrkcnf** command description.

NOTE	Later software releases have increased the number of parameters that can be configured after a trunk has been added. Refer to the **cnftrk** command summary on your Cisco Documentation CD for details.

Configurable parameter options are listed in Table 11-8. Although all trunk types use a common screen template to display configuration parameters and values, there are differences between trunk types for certain parameters, such as trunk framing. Table 11-8 is valid for BXM cards only.

Table 11-8 *Configurable Parameter Options for BXM Cards*

Parameter	Description	Usage and Modification Limitations
Transmit Rate	The maximum rate at which cells can be sent out on the trunk (display only).	Cannot be changed with **cnftrk**. Use the **cnfrsrc** command.
Protocol By The Card	Defines whether the LMI protocol runs on the BXM card (set to yes) or on the BCC (set to no). The default is no.	
VC Shaping	Defines whether traffic shaping is enabled for the trunk. The default is no.	
Hdr Type NNI	Cell header type—UNI or NNI.	For physical trunks, the header type is always NNI. Virtual trunks can be UNI or NNI, depending on the service provider interface.
Statistical Reserve	Bandwidth reserved for statistical variations. Connections routing over the trunk cannot be allocated to the statistical reserve, although the bandwidth is available for traffic to use as needed. The default is 1000 cells per second.	The configured value is applied to the transmit direction only. Increasing the statistical reserve significantly after the trunk is added might cause all connections to reroute.
Idle code	The hexadecimal character placed in the cell payload during idle periods. The range is 0 through FF. The default is 7F.	

Table 11-8   *Configurable Parameter Options for BXM Cards (Continued)*

Parameter	Description	Usage and Modification Limitations
Connection Channels	The number of channels permitted on this virtual trunk. The total number of channels on a port cannot exceed the number of channels supported on the card.	Virtual trunks only.
Valid traffic classes	The connection types permitted to route across this trunk. The default setting includes all the standard connection types (voice, time-stamped, non-time-stamped, Frame Relay, and Frame Relay with ForeSight), plus CBR, VBR, and ABR.	Virtual trunks only.
SVC Vpi Min	The minimum VPI value for SVCs. The default is 0.	
SVC Channels	The number of channels reserved for SVCs. The range is 0 to 1771 for T3 and E3 and 0 to 16199 for OC-3c. The default is 0.	
SVC Bandwidth	The amount of bandwidth reserved for SVCs. The range is 0 to 96000 cells per second for T3, 0 to 80000 for E3, and 0 to 353208 for OC-3c. The default is 0 in all cases.	
Restrict CC traffic	Limits control/management traffic on this trunk. The default is no.	SuperUser only.
Link type	Restricts certain connections from routing across the trunk. Does not affect traffic processing. Choices are satellite or terrestrial. The default is terrestrial.	Cannot be changed after **addtrk**.
Routing Cost	The user-defined cost of a trunk when cost-based routing is configured. The range is 1 to 50. The default is 10.	

continues

Table 11-8 *Configurable Parameter Options for BXM Cards (Continued)*

Parameter	Description	Usage and Modification Limitations
Line framing	HEC for E3; HEC or PLCP for T3; STS3c or STM-1 for OC3/STM-1; STS12c or STM-4 for OC12/STM-4. The default depends on the back card.	Cannot be changed after **addtrk**.
Cable length	The length of the cable used for line build-out. Entered as a number (0 or 1). The default is 0, representing 0 to 255 feet.	T3 only. Cannot be changed after **addtrk**.
Pass sync	Specifies whether this trunk is allowed to pass synchronization signals from a clock source to another node. The default is no. The pass synchronization should be set to no for virtual trunks.	
Loop clock	Loops the receive clock to the transmit clock. The default is no.	
HCS Masking	HCS masking (add 55 hex to all HCS fields) to facilitate cell delineation. Be sure to configure this parameter the same on both ends of the trunk; otherwise, the **addtrk** fails. The default is yes.	Cannot be changed after **addtrk**.
Payload Scramble	The ATM standard payload scramble. Be sure this parameter is the same on both ends; otherwise, the trunk fails. The default is yes for BNI-E3; otherwise, it is no.	Cannot be changed after **addtrk**.
Frame Scramble	The standard SONET frame scramble. This must be the same on both ends; otherwise, the trunk fails. The default is yes.	OC-3c and OC-12c only. Cannot be changed after **addtrk**.
Virtual Trunk Type	The type of service provided by the public ATM network for this trunk—CBR, VBR, or ABR. The default is CBR.	Virtual trunks only. Cannot be changed after **addtrk**.

Table 11-8   *Configurable Parameter Options for BXM Cards (Continued)*

Parameter	Description	Usage and Modification Limitations
Virtual Trunk VPI	The VPI address used for the virtual trunk. This parameter must be a nonzero number and must match the VPI used on the public network. The range is 1 to 255 for UNI and 1 to 4095 for NNI.	Virtual trunks only. Cannot be changed after **addtrk**.
Deroute delay time	The amount of time in seconds that connections will wait before derouting when the trunk fails. This parameter prevents connections from derouting (and therefore failing) when a trunk experiences a brief outage. The range is 0 to 600 seconds. The default is 0.	

addtrk Command

The **addtrk** command adds a trunk between nodes. You must add a trunk to the network before it can carry traffic. You need to execute **addtrk** at only one of the nodes terminating the trunk. Before you add a trunk to the network, you must have activated (upped) the trunk at both ends using **uptrk**. A trunk must be free of major alarms before you can add it. Most configured options can't be changed after an **addtrk**.

Here is the addtrk command syntax:

```
addtrk <slot.port>[.vtrk]
```

Example 11-3 shows the virtual trunk that was previously activated and configured being added using the **addtrk** command. The **uptrk** command must have been used at the other end of the trunk in order for the **addtrk** to be successful.

Example 11-3 addtrk *Command*

```
hei1bpx1          TN    Teacher:1       BPX 8620  9.3.XX    Feb. 14 200X 13:16 PST

TRK      Type   Current Line Alarm Status          Other End
1.1.1    T3/159 Clear - OK                         Seattle/1.1.1




Last Command: addtrk 1.1.1

Next Command:
```

If the **addtrk** command is used to join two previously separate networks, the local node verifies that all node names in both networks are unique before the trunk is added.

The **addtrk** command cannot be executed in the following situations:

- Another node is simultaneously attempting to change the network topology by adding or deleting a trunk.

- Another node is notifying all nodes that it has been renamed.

- Another node is adding or deleting a connection in the network with the **addcon** or **delcon** command.

- There is an unreachable node in the network.

- Two networks are to be joined, and the node names are not unique across both networks.

dsprtks Command

The **dsprtks** command displays basic trunk information for all trunks (physical and virtual) on a node. Information displayed includes trunk number, line type (E3, T3, OC3, or OC12), and alarm status.

Here is the **dsprtks** command syntax:

```
dsptrks
```

The **dsptrks** screen, shown in Example 11-4, provides summary information on the status of all active trunks that terminate on this node. Trunks appear when the **uptrk** command is issued. Use the **dsptrks** command to see which trunks are active, their current state, and the name and trunk number of the remote node.

Example 11-4 dsptrks *Command*

```
hei1bpx1          TN    Teacher:1      BPX 8620  9.3.XX   Feb. 14 200X 13:16 PST

TRK        Type      Current Line Alarm Status        Other End
 1.1.1     T3        Clear - OK                        Seattle/1.1
 3.1       OC3       Clear - OK                        Sacmento/3.1




Last Command: dsptrks

Next Command:
```

Possible trunk states are as follows:

- **Not upped**—The trunk does not appear on the **dsptrks** screen.
- **Upped**—Monitors the trunk for physical layer status but has no traffic on the trunk. An upped trunk has a Current Line Alarm status reported but no Other End information.
- **Added**—Monitors the trunk for physical layer status as well as other possible errors and alarms (for example, dropped cells) that are associated with cell transmission. An added trunk reports a destination node name and trunk number at the other end.

The **dsptrks** screen is also displayed if you issue the **uptrk**, **dntrk**, **addtrk**, or **deltrk** commands.

dsptrkcnf Command

The **dsptrkcnf** command provides detailed configuration information about a trunk. Use **dsptrkcnf** to display the current configuration of a trunk on a card module.

Here is the **dsptrkcnf** command syntax:

```
dsptrkcnf <slot.port>[.vtrk]
```

The **dsptrkcnf** screen, shown in Example 11-5, provides detailed configuration information about a particular trunk. This example shows the **dsptrkcnf** screen for an OC-3c trunk on a BXM card.

Example 11-5 dsptrkcnf *Command*

```
hei1bpx1        TN     Teacher:1      BPX 8620  9.3.XX    Feb. 14 200X 13:16 PST

TRK  3.1 Config   OC3    [353207cps]     BXM-155 slot: 3
Transmit Rate:          353208          Line framing:         STS-3C
Protocol By The Card:   --                coding:             --
VC Shaping:             --              CRC:                  --
Hdr Type NNI:           --                recv impedance:     --
Statistical Reserve:    2000     cps     cable type:          --
Idle code:              7F hex                 length:        --
Connection Channels:    16050           Pass sync:            No
Traffic:V,TS,NTS,FR,FST,CBR,N&RT-VBR,ABR  Loop clock:         No
SVC Vpi Min:            --              HCS Masking:          Yes
SVC Channels:           --              Payload Scramble:     No
SVC Bandwidth:          --     cps      Frame Scramble:       Yes
Restrict CC traffic:    No              Virtual Trunk Type:   --
Link type:              Terrestrial     Virtual Trunk VPI:    --
Routing Cost:           10              Deroute delay time:   0 seconds

Last Command: dsptrkcnf 3.1


Next Command:
```

Parameters can fall into several categories:

- Does not apply to this trunk type (identified with -- as the value)
- Cannot be modified—informational only
- Can be modified by SuperUser only
- Can be modified only when the trunk is upped but not added
- Can always be modified

The **dsptrkcnf** screen appears as the result of the **dsptrkcnf** or **cnftrk** commands.

deltrk Command

The previous sections discussed activating and introducing trunks into the network. The following sections discuss the **deltrk** and **dntrk** commands, which are used to deactivate network trunks.

The **deltrk** command deletes a trunk. Because deleting a trunk removes the communication path between two nodes, using the **deltrk** command might split a network into two separate networks. (You should delete a trunk from the network side.)

After you delete a trunk, it still carries framing signals but no traffic. After you add a trunk, some configuration parameters cannot be changed. If a change must be made to such a parameter, you must delete the trunk using the **deltrk** command before modifying the configuration.

Here is the **deltrk** command syntax:

```
deltrk <slot.port>[.vtrk]
```

The deltrk screen is shown in Example 11-6.

Example 11-6 deltrk *Command*

```
hei1bpx1          TN     Teacher:1        BPX 8620  9.3.XX    Feb. 14 200X 13:16 PST

TRK       Type     Current Line Alarm Status          Other End
1.1.1     T3       Clear - OK                          Seattle/1.1.1




This Command: deltrk 1.1.1

Warning: Connections may be deleted if the network is split
Delete this trunk (y/n)? n


                                                                Minor Alarm
```

If the **deltrk** command execution splits the network, it deletes any connections using the deleted trunk. After deletion, the trunk still carries framing signals and can generate alarms, but no traffic can pass across it. To remove the trunk completely, use the **dntrk** command after the **deltrk** command.

dntrk Command

The **dntrk** command downs a trunk, after which it no longer carries framing. Before you can down a trunk with **dntrk**, you must remove it from the network using **deltrk**.

Here is the **dntrk** command syntax:

```
dntrk <slot.port>[.vtrk]
```

vt Command

As soon as you establish trunks between nodes, you can use the **vt** command to create a virtual terminal connection to a remote node. This connection establishes a virtual terminal (vt) session that lets you access a remote node inband through the BPX network. During a vt session, the remote node name and date are displayed on the local terminal screen, and Virtual Terminal appears in the lower-left corner. The **bye** command terminates a virtual terminal session and returns the terminal to local usage. After a default timeout of 4 minutes of inactivity, a vt connection automatically reverts to a local connection. This timeout is the equivalent of using the **bye** command. Note that, after you **vt** to a remote node, you cannot **vt** to a different remote node. You must first end the vt session and then **vt** to the other node.

Here is the **vt** command syntax:

```
vt <node name>
```

To access a remote BPX node, both nodes must be in the network, although a trunk does not need to be established directly between the two nodes. User IDs and passwords are network-wide, so you do not need to log in when a vt session is established to another node.

By default, only one vt session can be active on a node at a time. Up to six vt sessions can be established, provided that you have purchased the appropriate software license for the node.

Vt sessions cannot be chained. In other words, if you establish a vt session to one node, you cannot establish a second vt session to a second node. Also, keep in mind that you cannot **vt** to feeder nodes.

Steps Used to Activate, Configure, and Deactivate Network Trunks

The following section describes the steps used to activate, configure, and deactivate network trunks.

Steps Used to Activate and Configure Network Trunks

Follow these steps to activate and configure a network trunk between two BPX switches:

Step 1 At the Next Command prompt, enter **dsptrks**. This displays the trunks that are currently in the node database. For a newly added switch, the display is empty.

Step 2 Enter **uptrk** <*slot.port*> [.*vtrk*] at one of the BPX nodes. This displays the newly upped trunk. Initially the Alarm Status indicates clear, but this changes to a Loss of Signal state after about 10 seconds.

Step 3 Review the trunk configuration to ensure compatibility at both ends. If necessary, enter the **cnftrk** command to make any changes. This displays the modified trunk configuration.

Step 4 At the BPX node at the other end of the trunk, enter **uptrk** <*slot.port*> [.*vtrk*]. This displays the newly upped trunk. Initially the Alarm Status indicates the Loss of Signal (LOS) state, but this should change to clear after about 10 seconds.

Step 5 At either of the BPX nodes, enter **addtrk** <*slot.port*> [.*vtrk*]. This displays the other end of the trunk: node name/trunk ID.

Step 6 To confirm connectivity between the two nodes, enter **vt** <*nodename*>, where ***nodename*** is the name of the BPX node at the other end of the trunk. Your session is transferred by the virtual terminal protocol across the network trunk(s) to the target node.

Step 7 Enter **bye**. You are returned to the command prompt at your original node.

Step 8 Enter **dspnds** [+*n*]. This displays a list of all network nodes and their node numbers.

Step 9 Enter **dspnw**. This displays all network nodes and the trunks that connect them.

Step 10 Enter **deltrk** <*slot.port*> [.*vtrk*], referring to the trunk you added earlier. This displays a warning message that deleting the trunk might partition the network and that connections might be lost.

Step 11 Enter **Y** to confirm that you want to delete the trunk. The trunk is deleted from the node database, and the **dsptrks** screen shows that the other end is no longer present.

Step 12 Enter **dntrk** <*slot.port*> [.*vtrk*], referring to the trunk you just deleted. This deactivates the trunk port and displays the **dsptrks** screen indicating that the trunk is no longer present.

Step 13 At the other BPX node, enter **dsptrks**. The display indicates that the trunk is still activated at this end but is in red alarm state.

Step 14 Enter **dntrk** <*slot.port*> [.*vtrk*]. This deactivates the trunk port and displays the **dsptrks** screen indicating that the trunk is no longer present.

Step 15 Enter **bye**. This terminates your CLI session and returns you to the login prompt.

Deactivating Network Trunks

Follow these steps to deactivate a network trunk between two BPX switches:

Step 1 At the Next Command prompt, enter **deltrk** <*slot.port*> [.*vtrk*], referring to the trunk you added earlier. This displays a warning message that deleting the trunk might partition the network and that connections might be lost.

Step 2 Enter **Y** to confirm that you want to delete the trunk. The trunk is deleted from the node database, and the **dsptrks** screen shows that the other end is no longer present.

Step 3 Enter **dntrk** <*slot.port*> [.*vtrk*], referring to the trunk you just deleted. This deactivates the trunk port and displays the **dsptrks** screen indicating that the trunk is no longer present.

Step 4 At the other BPX node, enter **dsptrks**. This display indicates that the trunk is still activated at this end but is in red alarm state.

Step 5 Enter **bye**. This terminates your CLI session and returns you to the login prompt.

What Is a Line?

This section describes the function of an ATM access line in a Cisco WAN switching network.

An *access line*, or line, is a digital transport facility that carries information in ATM cells between an external user device and a Cisco WAN switch.

The external user device can be a router, another ATM switch (Cisco or third-party), an access concentrator, or any other specialized gateway device that supports an ATM interface. However, it does not support a proprietary implementation of the statistical reserve that trunks support.

BPX Modules Supporting Access Lines

In BPX nodes, both BXM and BME card modules support lines. Both card modules provide broadband lines that bring in ATM cells from attached user equipment and are responsible for processing the cells by applying the appropriate policing, queuing, and traffic shaping.

The following list summarizes the BXM line card types supported in the system software:

- Eight or 12 T3 interfaces
- Eight or 12 E3 interfaces
- Four or eight OC3-c/STM-1 single-mode, single-mode long-reach, or multimode fiber interfaces
- One or two OC12-c/STM-4 single-mode, single-mode long-reach, or multimode fiber interfaces

The BME provides multicast services in the BPX switch. It is used in conjunction with a two-port OC-12 back card. Note that BMEs have no physical connection to external equipment because the ports are cabled together.

Commands for Access Lines

Table 11-9 describes the BPX CLI commands for activating and configuring access lines and lists the privilege level necessary to issue each command.

Table 11-9 *Commands for Access Lines*

Command	Description	Privilege Level
dsplns	Display lines. Displays summary information on all lines on the node.	6
upln	Up line. Activates a line.	2
cnfrsrc	Configure resource. Partitions resources.	6
dsplncnf	Display line configuration. Displays detailed configuration information on a particular line.	6
cnfln	Configure line. Modifies the line configuration parameters.	2
dnln	Down line. Deactivates a line.	2

Activating, Configuring, and Deactivating Access Lines

This section describes how commands are used to activate, configure, and deactivate access lines.

dsplns Command

The **dsplns** screen provides summary information on the status of all lines that terminate on your node. Lines appear when the **upln** command is issued. Use this command when you want to learn which lines are active and their current alarm status.

This screen also appears if you issue the **upln** or **dnln** command to activate or deactivate one of the lines.

Here is the **dsplns** command syntax:

```
dsplns
```

The **dsplns** screen is shown in Example 11-7. Lines appear when the upln command is issued.

Example 11-7 dsplns *Command*

```
hei1bpx1          TN     Teacher:1      BPX 8620  9.3.XX    Feb. 14 200X 13:16 PST

Line
    Type        Current Line Alarm Status
   4.6    T3         Major - Loss of Sig (RED)
   9.1    E3         Clear - OK
   9.2    E3         Clear - OK
  13.1    OC3        Clear - OK
  13.2    OC3        Clear - OK


Last Command: dsplns

Next Command:

                                                            MAJOR ALARM
```

The **dsplns** command displays basic configuration and status information for all the lines on the node. This information includes the line number, type of line, and line alarm status. The line type shows whether the line is E3, T3, OC-3c/STM-1, or OC-12/STM-4.

Line status categories include

- Clear
- Major alarm
- Minor alarm

upln Command

The **upln** command activates (ups) a line. Use the **upln** command to make the line available for configuring and to start gathering statistics. If the line terminates at another Cisco WAN switch, you must execute the **upln** command at both ends of the line. Configure the line's signal characteristics for the data you intend for the line by using the **cnfln** command.

Here is the **upln** command syntax:

upln *<slot.line>*

If you issue the **upln** command at a card where no other lines currently exist, the system prompts you with the message "No channel stat level configured, ok (y/n)?". Respond yes to the prompt to enable multilevel statistics at the card level. All ports and user connections that you add later on this card will be enabled for multilevel statistics. Note that, unlike trunks, there is no "addln" requirement.

NOTE   Changing the channel statistics level resets the card.

Immediately after you issue the **upln** command, the line appears to be clear, but after several seconds, it goes into major alarm unless the line achieves frame synchronization with the attached device. Example 11-8 shows an OC-3c line being upped. The message "256 PVCs allocated..." indicates that the line is enabled with support for 256 AutoRoute connections by default.

Example 11-8 upln *Command*

```
hei1bpx1          TN    Teacher:1       BPX 8620  9.3.XX   Feb. 14 200X 13:16 PST

Line      Type      Current Line Alarm Status
10.1      OC3       Clear - OK



Last Command: upln 10.1

256 PVCs allocated. Use 'cnfrsrc' to configure PVCs
Next Command:

                                                                  MAJOR ALARM
```

cnfrsrc Command

The **cnfrsrc** command partitions resources for the following:

- Automatic Routing Management PVCs
- VSI-MPLS (Multiprotocol Label Switching)
- VSI-PNNI (Private Network-to-Network Interface)

To configure resources for a VSI-MPLS controller or PNNI SVCs, refer to the subsequent BPX-specific command definitions.

Up to two controllers of the same type can be attached to a node and assigned the same partition to provide controller redundancy on that partition. A different set of controllers can be attached to the node and assigned a different partition to provide controller redundancy on this second partition.

You can configure a virtual trunk to be dedicated to VSI or to Automatic Routing Management. You cannot configure a virtual trunk for both VSI and Automatic Routing Management.

This command supports physical trunks and virtual trunks. After VSI is enabled, the virtual trunk becomes a dedicated VSI virtual trunk.

The switch software does the following:

- Allows start VPI = 0 for a VSI partition on a port interface or for a feeder trunk interface
- Prevents a second VSI partition from being enabled on a port interface if the first VSI partition uses a start VPI = 0

Here is the **cnfrsrc** command syntax:

```
cnfrsrc <slot.port> <parameters>
```

If more than a certain number of PVCs are expected, you must use the **cnfrsrc** command to increase the number. Example 11-9 shows the number increased to 1024. The **cnfrsrc** command is also used to define VSI resource partitions, but this is not shown in this example.

Example 11-9 cnfrsrc *Command*

```
hei1bpx1          TN    Teacher:1       BPX 8620  9.3.XX    Feb. 14 200X 13:16 PST

Port : 10.1
                                        Full Port Bandwidth: 353208
Maximum PVC LCNS:              1024     Maximum PVC Bandwidth: 353208
                                        (CAC Reserve: 0)

PVC VPI RANGE [1]:    -1    /-1         PVC VPI RANGE [2]: -1    /-1
PVC VPI RANGE [3]:    -1    /-1         PVC VPI RANGE [4]: -1    /-1
```

continues

Example 11-9 cnfrsrc *Command (Continued)*

```
               Partition :  1              2              3
         Partition State :  Disabled       Disabled       Disabled
       VSI LCNS (min/max):  0      /0      0      /0      0      /0
     VSI VPI (start/end):   0      /0      0      /0      0      /0
         VSI BW (min/max):  0      /0      0      /0      0      /0
          VSI ILMI Config:  CLR            CLR            CLR


Last Command: cnfrsrc 10.1 1024 353208 N N


Next Command:

                                                            MAJOR ALARM
```

dsplncnf Command

The **dsplncnf** command provides detailed configuration information about a particular line. The display fields that actually contain data depend on the type of line.

Here is the **dsplncnf** command syntax:

```
dsplncnf <slot.port>
```

Example 11-10 shows the display for the **dsplncnf** command. This example shows the default configuration for an OC-3c.

Example 11-10 dsplncnf *Command*

```
hei1bpx1          TN    Teacher:1      BPX 8620  9.3.XX    Feb. 14 200X 13:16 PST

LN
   10.1 Config     OC3    [353208cps]   BXM slot:     10
Loop clock:               No                 Idle code:            7F hex

Line framing:             --
     coding:              --

     recv impedance:      --
     E1 signalling:       --
     encoding:            --            cable type:           --
     T1 signalling:       --                length:           --
                                        HCS Masking:          Yes
                                        Payload Scramble:     Yes
     56KBS Bit Pos:       --            Frame Scramble:       Yes
     pct fast modem:      --            Cell Framing:         STS-3C
```

Example 11-10 **dsplncnf** *Command (Continued)*

```
Last Command: dsplncnf 10.1


Next Command:

                                                            MAJOR ALARM
```

The **dsplncnf** command provides detailed configuration information about a particular line. This screen is a template for any type of line that may exist in a BPX network. Use this command to display the current configuration of a line on a BXM card module.

Example 11-10 shows the OC-3c being configured for payload scrambling and STS-3C cell framing, with the other parameters remaining at the defaults.

cnfln Command

The **cnfln** command configures a line to be compatible with the ATM device to which it connects.

Here is the **cnfln** command syntax:

> **cnfln** *<slot.line> <parameters>*

Because of the variety of line types and characteristics, separate parameter sections are included in this command description to define the parameters for specific line types. The system automatically presents the correct options on the command line for each line type. If a parameter is not applicable to a card type, the system displays the parameter in half-tone or the parameter value field with dashed lines.

You modify line parameters for the BXM cards using the **cnfln** command, as shown in Example 11-11. Parameters with -- for the value do not apply to this type of line. (Many of the unconfigurable line parameters are associated with narrowband lines that are supported on the IGX node.)

Example 11-11 **cnfln** *Command*

```
hei1bpx1          TN     Teacher:1        BPX 8620   9.3.XX    Feb. 14 200X 13:16 PST

LN  10.1 Config      OC3    [353208cps]    BXM slot:      10
Loop clock:          No                    Idle code:            7F hex

Line framing:        --
     coding:         --

     recv impedance: --
     E1 signalling:  --
     encoding:       --                     cable type:    --
```

continues

Example 11-11 **cnfln** *Command (Continued)*

```
        T1 signalling:    --                length:       --
                                           HCS Masking:      Yes
                                           Payload Scramble: No
        56KBS Bit Pos:    --               Frame Scramble:   Yes
        pct fast modem:   --               Cell Framing:     STM-1



 Last Command: cnfln 10.1 N 7F Y n Y 1



 Next Command:


                                                          MAJOR ALARM
```

Configurable line parameter options are listed in Table 11-10. These are physical characteristics only. Although all types of lines use a common screen template to display configuration parameters and values, there are differences between line types for certain parameters, such as line framing. (This table is valid for BXM cards only; many of the parameters shown apply to narrowband lines on IGX nodes only.)

Table 11-10 *Configurable Line Parameter Options*

Parameter	Description	Default
Loop clock	Loops the receive clock to the transmit clock. Set this to yes to isolate the line clocking from the BPX system clock.	No
Idle code	The idle character placed into idle cells. This value is rarely changed.	7F
Cable length	The cable length for T3 lines only. Choices are 0 to 225 feet or greater than 225 feet. This value must be set correctly for line build-out. Failure to do so might cause line errors or a line failure.	0 for 0 to 225 feet
HCS Masking	Add hexadecimal 55 to all Header Error Correction (HEC)/Header Check Sum (HCS) fields for cell delineation. This value cannot be configured for T3/E3 lines. Be sure to have both the BPX switch and user equipment interfaces set the same; otherwise, all the cells will be dropped due to HEC/HCS errors, and a line alarm will occur.	Yes

Table 11-10 *Configurable Line Parameter Options (Continued)*

Parameter	Description	Default
Payload Scramble	Optional standard payload scramble. Be sure to have both the BPX switch and user equipment interfaces set either with or without payload scrambling; otherwise, all the cell payloads will be in error. This will not result in an alarm, but the end-user devices will be unable to communicate with each other.	T3/E3: No OC-3c/OC-12c: Yes
Frame Scramble	Optional standard frame scramble for Synchronous Optical Network (SONET) interfaces only. Like cell scrambling, it is vital to have both the BPX and user equipment interfaces set either with or without frame scrambling.	Yes
Cell Framing	PLCP or HEC (for self-delineated cells) on BXM-T3. STS-3C (for OC-3c) or STM-1 (for STM-1) on BXM-155. STS-12C (for OC-12c) or STM-4 (for STM-4) on BXM-622.	Card-dependent

Steps Used to Activate, Configure, and Deactivate Access Lines

In this section, you will learn how to use the CLI to activate and configure an access line on a BPX switch.

How to Activate and Configure Access Lines

Follow these steps to activate and configure an access line:

Step 1 At the Next Command prompt, enter **dsplns**. This displays the lines that are currently activated. For a newly added switch, the display is empty.

Step 2 Enter **upln** *<slot.line>* at one of the BPX nodes. This displays the newly upped line. Initially the Alarm Status indicates clear, but this changes to a Loss of Signal state after about 10 seconds.

NOTE   To increase the number of PVCs supported, use the **cnfrsrc** command.

Step 3   Review the line configuration to ensure compatibility with the attached user equipment. If necessary, use the **cnfln** command to make any changes. This displays the modified line configuration.

Step 4   Enter **dsplncnf** *<slot.line>* to review the line configuration. This displays the line configuration.

Step 5   Enter **bye**. This returns you to the login command prompt.

Deactivating Access Lines

Follow these steps to deactivate access lines:

Step 1   At the Next Command prompt, enter **upln** *<slot.line>* at one of the BPX nodes. This displays a warning message that deleting the line might partition the network and that connections might be lost.

Step 2   Enter **Y** to confirm that you want to delete the line. The line is deleted from the node database, and the **dsplns** screen shows that the line is no longer present.

Step 3   Enter **bye**. This terminates your CLI session and returns you to the login prompt.

Summary

After reading this chapter, you should be able to define a trunk and a virtual trunk and understand the differences between them. You should be able to explain what trunk resource partitions and dynamic partitioning are used for, and you should be able to identify, modify, and describe the impact of trunk configurations. You should be able to verify trunk operation and internode communication and know how to remotely access other nodes using a virtual terminal. You should also be able to activate and deactivate network trunks.

You should understand how to identify and modify line configuration parameters, describe the impact of line configurations, and know how to activate and deactivate access lines.

Review Questions

1   How many virtual trunks can you terminate on a single port on a BXM card?

   A. 4

   B. 11

   C. 31

   D. 32

   E. 64

2 What is a virtual trunk?

A. A way to remotely log into another BPX service node in the network

B. A trunk that attaches a BPX service node to another vendor's ATM switch

C. An ATM connection in a BPX network that carries traffic for another switch network

D. A trunk that utilizes a public ATM service to carry the cell traffic from one BPX service node to another BPX service node

3 What is the purpose of resource partitioning on a trunk?

A. To allocate the available port groups to different VSI controllers

B. To allocate specific resources between VSI controllers and AutoRoute PVCs

C. To ensure that physical and virtual trunks do not compete for physical interfaces on the BXM card

D. To provide guaranteed bandwidth for different traffic types such as CBR, VBR, and ABR

4 Mark the following statements as true or false.

A. _____ All models of BXM cards support two port groups.

B. _____ You can allocate more LCNs to multiple partitions than are shown by the **dspcd** command.

C. _____ Virtual trunks cannot support both AutoRoute PVCs and MPLS VCs.

D. _____ As soon as a resource is allocated to one VSI partition, it is unavailable for use by a different controller.

E. _____ Only physical trunks support multiple partitions.

5 You have successfully upped the trunk, but the **addtrk** command fails. What could be possible reasons for this?

A. ATM cell scrambling is configured differently at each end.

B. The other end of the trunk has not been upped.

C. The transmit rate has been configured differently at each end.

D. There is a mismatch in the cell-framing configuration.

6 Mark the following statements as true or false.

A. _____ Some trunk parameters do not apply to all trunk types.

B. _____ Cell scrambling affects the alarm condition of an upped trunk.

C. _____ The **addtrk** command must be issued before the **uptrk** command.

D. _____ All configuration parameters can be configured when a trunk is added.

E. _____ When deactivating a trunk, you must delete a trunk before it can be downed.

7 Which of the following events generates a major network alarm?

A. Card self-test failure

B. ATM port communication failure due to ILMI breakdown

C. Loss of signal on a network trunk

D. Missing processor in a redundant configuration

E. Cabinet temperature above the configured threshold

8 Mark the following statements as true or false.

A. The ASM reports MGX shelf alarms.

B. The **dspalms** screen summarizes all alarms on a node.

C. You can clear statistical trunk alarms with the **clrtrkalm** command.

D. The **cnftrkalm** command allows you to define major and minor alarm thresholds on a trunk.

E. A large value in the ETS indicates the presence of a momentary fault condition.

9 Match each of the following trunk configuration parameters with its description.

1. _____ Loop clock   A. A portion of trunk bandwidth reserved for SVCs

2. _____ SVC bandwidth   B. The number of connections allowed on a virtual trunk

3. _____ Statistical reserve   C. A way to use the receive clock in the transmit direction

4. _____ Frame scrambling   D. A portion of bandwidth that cannot be allocated to connections

5. _____ Transmit trunk rate   E. A standards-based method for rearranging the SONET trunk frame

6. _____ Connection channels   F. The maximum number of data cells permitted on a trunk per second

10 What is the difference between a UNI cell and an NNI cell?

A. A UNI cell has a bigger payload than an NNI cell.

B. The UNI cell is defined by the ATM Forum, and the NNI cell is not.

C. The UNI cell has an 8-bit VPI field, and the NNI cell has a 12-bit VPI field.

D. UNI cells are created only by routers; NNI cells are created only by switches.

11 What is a QBin?

    A. An egress per PVC queue

    B. An ingress per PVC queue

    C. An egress per traffic type queue

    D. An ingress per traffic type queue

12 Mark the following statements as true or false.

    A. _____ A line failure causes user connections to reroute in the network.

    B. _____ The **dspalms** command displays the lines that are in alarm.

    C. _____ You can clear statistical line alarms with the **clrlnalm** command.

    D. _____ The **cnflnalm** command allows you to define major and minor alarm thresholds on a line.

    E. _____ Unavailable line seconds statistics are accumulated for all BXM lines.

This chapter covers the following key topics:

- SONET APS
- APS Implementation on BPX
- Activating and Configuring APS
- Configuring and Verifying APS Operation

CHAPTER 12

Configuring SONET APS

In this chapter, you will learn about the operation of the SONET Automatic Protection Switching (APS) feature, which is supported on the BPX switch. An understanding of how APS works is important background knowledge for activating and configuring the APS feature on BPX trunks and access lines.

SONET APS

APS is a standards-based redundancy scheme that enhances network reliability by protecting against the effects of card or line failure. APS is defined in Bellcore and ITU standards for North American SONET and international Synchronous Digital Hierarchy (SDH) optical network links. SDH is a set of international fiber-optic transmission standards developed by the CCITT (Consultative Committee on International Telegraphy and Telephony), which is now known as the ITU-T (International Telecommunications Union-Telecommunications Services Sector). SDH was based on the North American SONET standards, which are now considered to be a subset of SDH. The relevant standards discussed in this chapter are Bellcore GR-253 and ITU-T G.783. The term SONET includes SDH.

In the BPX switch, APS implementation is supported for OC-3c/STM-1 and OC-12c/STM-4 interfaces. Further details of the BPX implementation are described in the section, "APS Implementation on BPX."

Basic APS Operation

In its basic form, APS allows a pair of SONET lines to be configured for line redundancy. One line is active, and the other is a backup. Whether or not the backup passes real traffic while in standby mode depends on which version of APS is implemented, as described later in this chapter.

If the fiber-optic carrier for the active line is severed or damaged, the user traffic switches automatically to the standby line within 60 milliseconds. Some versions of APS can be configured with a *revertive* option, in which the hardware automatically switches back to the active line after it is repaired and a defined time period has elapsed.

In APS terminology, the active line is called the *working* (W) line, and the standby line is the *protection* (P) line. Coordination of line switching in the event of failure or repair happens under the control of an in-band signaling protocol.

APS Versions

The standards define two basic forms of APS:

- **APS 1:*n***—Provides line redundancy in which one line supports one or more other lines. In APS 1:*n*, the protection line does not carry traffic when the working line is active.

- **APS 1+1**—Provides line and card redundancy in which one line supports one other line. In APS 1+1, both the working and protection lines carry traffic.

The BPX switch supports the following:

- APS 1:1, which is a subset of APS 1:*n*
- APS 1+1
- APS 1+1 G.783 Annex B
- APS 1+1 ignore K1K2 bytes

APS 1:1 Line Redundancy

APS 1:1 protects against fiber cuts, but not against card failures. Each working line requires a dedicated protection line, and both lines terminate on a single card. In normal operation, user traffic is carried only on the active line, which is initially the working line. If the working line fails, the protection line switches on. However, user traffic does not flow on the protection line until the transmit end recognizes that a failure has occurred and initiates the switchover.

Figure 12-1 shows the system components required for APS 1:1 implementation. Notice that these components are contained on a single card at each end of the SONET line. This figure shows the working line as the active line.

Figure 12-2 shows system operation in the event of failure of the working line. Following an interval during which the transmit and receive ends coordinate using the SONET K1K2 APS control protocol, traffic switches over to the protection line, as shown in the figure.

If the revertive option is enabled, the hardware attempts to switch back to the working line from the protection line after a configurable time period (Wait to Restore [wtr]) has elapsed.

Figure 12-1 *APS 1:1 Line Redundancy*

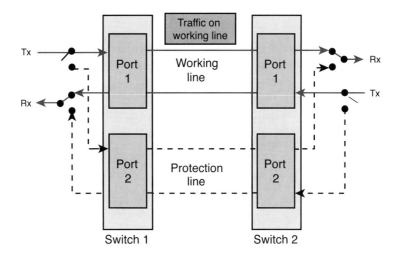

Figure 12-2 *APS 1:1 Line Failure*

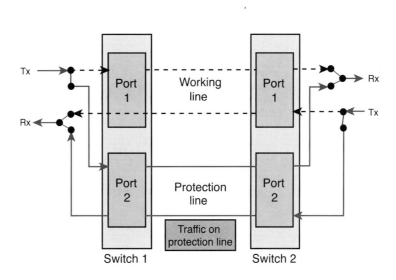

APS 1+1 Card and Line Redundancy

APS 1+1 expands the capabilities provided by APS 1:1 to include protection against both line and card failures. As with APS 1:1, APS 1+1 requires a redundant protection line for every working line. Additionally, the working and protection lines must terminate on different cards.

Unlike APS 1:1, the working and protection lines carry user traffic simultaneously. Because traffic is carried simultaneously by the working and protection lines, the receiver that terminates the APS 1+1 must select cells from either line and continue to forward one consistent traffic stream. The receiving-end cards can switch from working to protection line without coordination at the transmit end, because both lines transmit the same information. This capability simplifies and accelerates the switching process compared to APS 1:1.

Figure 12-3 shows the system components required for an APS 1+1 implementation. Notice that these components are contained on separate cards at each end of the SONET line. In Figure 12-3, the working line is the active line.

Figure 12-3 *APS 1+1 Redundancy*

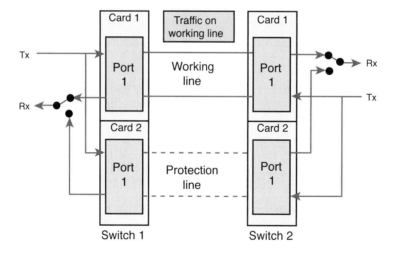

Figure 12-4 shows system operation in the event of failure of the working line, with traffic switched over to the protection line.

Figure 12-4 *APS 1+1 Line Failure*

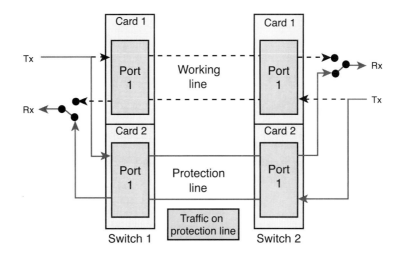

APS Automatic Operation

Upon detection of failure of a line or card or degradation of the signal beyond a user-configurable threshold, the APS system attempts to switch automatically from the current active line to the standby. Line or card failures are indicated by an excessive Bit Error Rate (BER) or by physical alarm conditions, including the following:

- Loss of Signal (LOS)
- Loss of Frame (LOF)
- Alarm Indication Signal (AIS), or by signal degradation such as excessive BER

APS Manual Operation

In addition to automatic switching mode, the APS standards also include provisions for operator-controlled manual switching. The command set lets the user switch operation from the working line to the protection line, and vice versa. Refer to the section, "Activating and Configuring APS" for details on the manual APS control interface commands.

K1K2 Control Protocol

APS channel information is transported between the SONET/SDH interfaces using the K1 and K2 control bytes that are located in the Line Overhead portion of the OC-3c/STM-1 frame.

The two control bytes are carried on the protection channel. They are interpreted as shown in Table 12-1.

Table 12-1 *K1K2 Control Protocol*

Control Byte (Bits)	Definition
K1 (1 to 4)	Requests automatic or manual switching, such as a signal failure (automatic) or forced switchover (manual). The default is no request.
K1 (5 to 8)	Defines the channel making the request; the default is null. The K1 byte carries the type of switch request and the channel number.
K2 (1 to 4)	Channel definition. The same as K1 bits 5 to 8.
K2 (5)	APS architecture. Either 1:1 or 1+1 (the default).
K2 (6 to 8)	Mode of operation—either unidirectional (the default) or bidirectional. The AIS is carried in bits 6 to 8 of the K2 byte when set to 111 or Line FERF if set to 110.

APS Implementation on BPX

APS is supported on the OC-3c/STM-1 and OC-12c/STM-4 versions of the BXM card modules. Using this standard's compliant line and card redundancy scheme, the BPX switch operates seamlessly with SONET/SDH Add/Drop Multiplexers (ADMs) and with other equipment that supports APS, such as the MGX 8850 edge switch and the MGX 8240 private line gateway.

Figure 12-5 shows an optical SONET/SDH line connecting the network with an external user device.

In Figure 12-5, the user device interfaces with Line Terminating Equipment (LTE). The SONET line can consist of multiple concatenated sections, each of which can include Section Terminating Equipment (STE), such as an optical signal regenerator. The optical access line terminates at a port on another LTE, such as a BPX switch, as shown in the figure.

Figure 12-5 *APS Implementation*

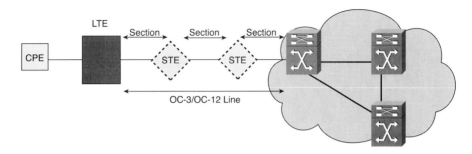

APS 1:1

APS version 1:1 can be implemented using all variants of BXM cards with the appropriate fiber-optic interfaces. Because APS 1:1 uses adjacent ports on a single BXM card, no additional hardware is required. However, it might be necessary to update the BXM firmware. Refer to the Software Release Notes on your Cisco Documentation CD for further details.

Figure 12-6 shows an example of APS 1:1 involving two BPX nodes. Notice that more than one APS line can be configured on a card provided that the ports are paired sequentially, as shown here.

Figure 12-6 *APS 1:1 in Two BPX Nodes: Example 1*

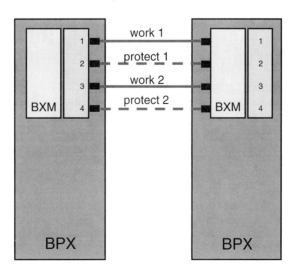

APS 1+1

APS version 1+1 requires a special paired back card with an APS daughter backplane. The paired back card occupies two adjacent rear slots. The two BXM front cards must have firmware support for APS and occupy the corresponding front slots. With some earlier versions of the BPX chassis, stiffeners in the card cage limit the placement of the paired back cards to certain slots. This restriction is not present in current production versions. Figure 12-7 shows an example of APS 1+1 involving two BPX nodes. Again, more than one APS line can be configured on a card provided that the working and protection lines use the same numbered port on each card pair, as shown in the figure. As soon as a port on a BXM card has been configured for APS, the card pair operates as a set, and independent usage of the two cards is not possible. If no port is configured for APS, the two card sets can be used independently in normal non-APS fashion.

Figure 12-7 *APS 1+1 in Two BPX Nodes: Example 2*

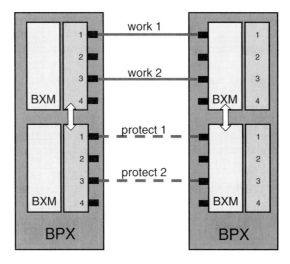

Figure 12-8 shows an example of APS 1+1 with a BPX switch and another compliant device that supports APS—in this case, the MGX 8240 Private Line Service gateway. The MGX 8240 connects to the BPX switch via an access line rather than a trunk.

APS 1+1 G.783 Annex B

The BXM can be configured for this version of APS with System Software release 9.2.10 and later. There are no additional hardware or firmware requirements. APS 1+1 Annex B provides the fastest switching by limiting the configurable options to bidirectional with nonrevertive protection switching.

Figure 12-8 *APS 1+1 with MGX*

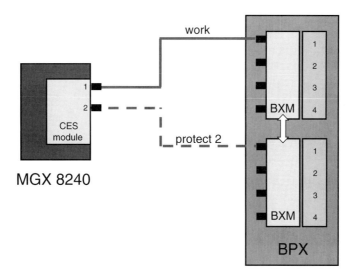

For Annex B, the active line is called the primary section, and the standby line is called the secondary section. Manual switching is not supported in the APS 1+1 Annex B implementation.

APS Compared to Y-Redundancy

Most trunk and line service cards available for Cisco WAN switches also support an earlier proprietary form of redundancy called Y-redundancy. This scheme provides card but not line redundancy.

APS performs switchovers at the physical layer, which is significantly faster than at Layer 2 or Layer 3. For example, an APS switchover is accomplished in less than 60 ms, whereas a Y-cable redundancy switchover (done at the ATM layer) requires approximately 250 ms. Fast switchovers are becoming increasingly more critical as traffic speeds approach OC-12c/STM-4 and higher.

Activating and Configuring APS

In this section, you will learn how to use the CLI to activate and configure APS on a network trunk or access line.

APS Configuration

The BPX switch supports two versions of APS: APS 1+1 and APS 1:1. Both GR-253 and ITU-T G.783 are APS 1:1. GR-253 (Annex A) is the default used for SONET interfaces. ITU-T G.783 (Annex B) is for SDH interfaces. If Annex B is required, you must have Service-level access to configure each BXM front card using the **cnfcdaps** command. For APS to work, the equipment on both ends of the physical cable needs to use the same protocol. APS uses signaling bytes (K1 and K2 bytes, described earlier in this chapter) in the SONET overhead to determine which line is active. When both ends of the cable are attached to BPX equipment, only one type needs to be supported (the same is true for BPX and MGX feeders), but when the configuration is BPX-SONET-SONET-BPX, the APS switching is between SONET and BPX and requires that each use exactly the same protocol to work.

If Annex B is selected, several parameters (such as selection of the 1:1 protocol) are blocked at the command line.

Before you add APS, the working and protection lines must be physically cabled, and in the case of APS 1:1, the trunks or lines must be downed and free of active connections. With APS 1+1, the trunks or lines might be up or down (causing service interruption) and might carry user traffic when APS is added.

The APS protocols are differentiated by the following parameters:

- **Directional switching mode**—Defines whether the switching is unidirectional or bidirectional. Unidirectional means that the end of the line detecting the failure switches, but the remote end does not. The result is that transmit and receive traffic can travel on different lines and on different cards; bidirectional means that transmit and receive traffic can travel in at least one direction, assuming that there is no more than one break in a fiber. With bidirectional switching, half of the working network is sent counter-clockwise over one fiber and the other half is sent clockwise over another fiber, carrying traffic in either direction but not in both simultaneously.

- **Revertive switching**—Defines whether the standby line automatically switches back to the original working line as soon as the latter returns to service following a failure.

Table 12-2 lists the valid settings of these parameters for the four APS protocols supported on the BXM.

Table 12-2 *APS Protocols Supported on the BXM*

Directional	Revertive	APS 1:1	APS 1+1 APS 1+1 Ignore K1K2	APS 1+1 Annex B
Unidirectional	Revertive	No	Yes	No
Unidirectional	Nonrevertive	No	Default	No
Bidirectional	Revertive	Yes	Yes	No
Bidirectional	Nonrevertive	No	Yes	Yes

APS 1+1 Implementation on BXM

The implementation of APS 1:1 on the BXM is quite straightforward in that failure of the working line causes a revertive switchover to the protection line. Because card redundancy is not a feature of APS 1:1, failure of either the front card or the back card at either end of the line causes the trunk to fail.

With APS 1+1, the situation is more complex because you need to consider separately the effect of failures of the line, back card, and front card. You also need to take into account the directional switching mode.

Figure 12-9 shows an APS 1+1 setup, including two BXM card modules with the redundant paired back cards. The back cards are cross-coupled as shown so that the transmit data from one front card is electrically bridged to both back cards.

Figure 12-9 *APS 1+1 on BXM*

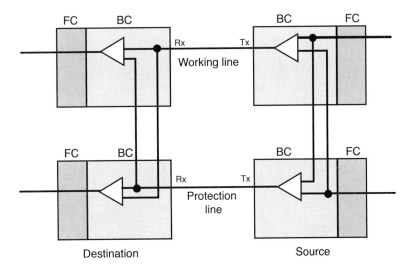

NOTE   Figure 12-9 depicts only one end of the APS line; the complete depiction would show source and destination at both ends. Also, unidirectional switching is not a valid option for 1+1 Annex B.

Using this basic schematic, we will walk through each of the three failure scenarios in turn. The first case is a physical line failure, which could be the result of a fiber cut or failure of the optical transceiver at either end of the working line. Assuming the default configuration of unidirectional switching, the line failure causes the user traffic to travel through the protection line, as shown in Figure 12-10. Notice that the front cards do not switch.

Figure 12-10 *APS 1+1 Case 1*

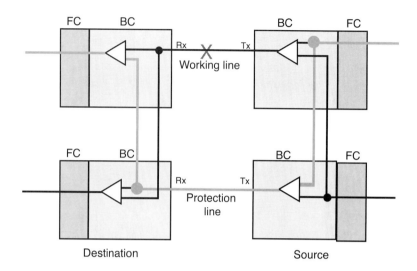

Figure 12-11 depicts the second case, a total failure of the working line back card, again with unidirectional switching. Here, the source end switches to the protection front card, but because bidirectional switching is not enabled, traffic from the protection line is switched to the destination front card of the working line.

Figure 12-11 *APS 1+1 Case 2*

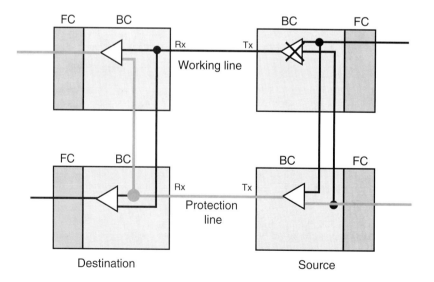

Figure 12-12 depicts the third case, involving failure of the source end working front card. Traffic switches to the protection front card and line, but with unidirectional switching, the working line front card at the destination still carries the user traffic.

Figure 12-12 *APS 1+1 Case 3*

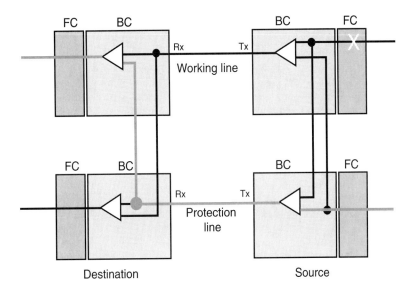

Now we will consider the previous failure modes with bidirectional swiching enabled. As previously discussed, bidirectional means that transmit and receive traffic can travel in at least one direction, assuming that there is no more than one break in a fiber. Figure 12-13 shows a failure of the source end working front card with bidirectional switching enabled. Traffic automatically switches to the source end protection front card and line, and then switches to the protection front card at the destination.

Figure 12-14 shows a total failure of the source end working back card with bidirectional switching enabled. Again, traffic automatically switches to the source end protection front card and line and then switches to the protection front card at the destination.

Commands for APS

This section describes the BPX CLI commands for activating and configuring APS on a BPX network trunk or access line.

Figure 12-13 *APS 1+1 Case 1 with Bidirectional Signaling*

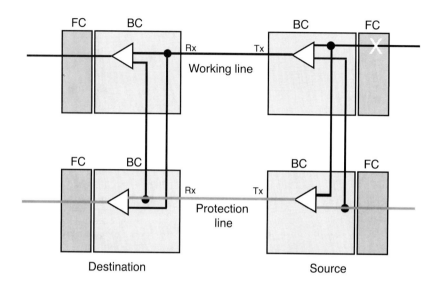

Figure 12-14 *APS 1+1 Cases 2 and 3 with Bidirectional Signaling*

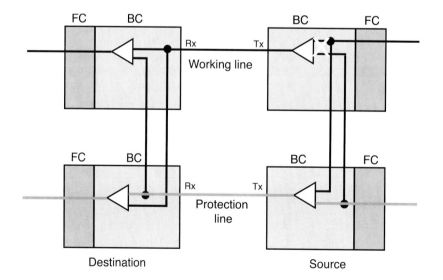

Table 12-3 describes the commands used in this chapter. It gives a brief description of the command and the privilege level necessary to issue it.

Table 12-3   *Commands for APS*

Command	Description	Privilege Level
addcdred	Add card redundancy. Enables card and line redundancy for APS.	4
addapsln	Add APS line pair. Defines the working and protection lines and the APS protocol.	1
dspapsln	Display APS line. Displays the current configured APS lines and their status.	6
cnfapsln	Configure APS line. Configures APS line parameters.	4
switchapsln	Switch APS line. Controls the user interface for manual APS switching.	1
dsplog	Display log. Displays the system log.	6
delapsln	Delete APS line. Deletes the APS line.	1

NOTE   The term *APS line* used in Table 12-3 and throughout this section refers to a trunk or line on the BPX node.

addcdred Command

The **addcdred** command enables card and line redundancy for the cards on the BPX switch. You can use **addcdred** to add card and line redundancy for APS 1+1 across two BXM OC-3 and OC-12 cards. You also use it before enabling APS 1:1 line redundancy. Use the **addcdred** command to specify the slots of the primary and secondary (standby) cards that form the redundant pair.

Here is the command syntax:

```
addcdred <primary slot> <secondary slot>
```

addapsln Command

The **addapsln** command adds SONET APS for BXM OC-3 or OC-12 trunks or lines. You must specify the desired APS protocol when adding a new APS line pair.

Here is the command syntax:

```
addapsln <slot.port1> <slot.port2> <protocol>
```

Table 12-4 lists the parameter options.

Table 12-4   **addapsln** *Command Parameter Options*

Parameter	Description
slot.port1	The working line number.
slot.port2	The protection line number. For APS 1:1, the slot number must be the same for both the working and protection lines, and the port numbers must be in consecutive sequence. For APS 1+1, the slot numbers must be adjacent for the working and protection lines, and the port numbers must be the same.
protocol	The APS mode to use on the line pair. Entered as a value from 1 to 4: 1 = 1+1 2 = 1:1 3 = 1+1 Annex B 4 = 1+1 ignore K1K2 bytes The 1+1 ignore K1K2 is used when the BXMs are connected by a Y-cable to a feeder device that does not support APS.

dspapsln Command

This command lists the configuration for all APS lines. Use this command to learn how APS is set up on a line.

Command syntax:

```
dspapsln
```

cnfapsln Command

This command changes the APS configuration. The APS options on both ends of the line must match.

Command syntax:

```
cnfapsln <slot.port> <SF ber> <SD ber> <revertive mode> <WTR> <direction>
```

Table 12-5 lists the parameter options.

Table 12-5   **cnfapsln** *Command Parameter Options*

Parameter	Description
slot.port	The working line number.
SF ber	Signal Fail Bit Error Rate. The bit error rate threshold at which the system attempts to perform an APS switchover. Entered as a value from 3 to 12 (the default is 3), where 3 represents 10^{-3}.

Table 12-5 **cnfapsln** *Command Parameter Options (Continued)*

Parameter	Description
SD ber	Signal Degrade Bit Error Rate. The bit error rate threshold at which the system attempts to perform an APS switchover. Entered as a value from 5 to 12 (the default is 5), where 5 represents 10^{-5}.
revertive mode	Reverts to the working line after the Wait To Restore interval expires. Choices are 0 (revertive) or 1 (nonrevertive). For Annex A, the default is nonrevertive. For Annex B, the default and only option is nonrevertive.
	Revertive switching applies to automatic switches only; it cannot occur as the result of a user-initiated switch.
WTR	Wait To Restore. After a switch from a working to a protection line, the Wait To Restore interval is the interval in minutes to wait before attempting to switch back to the working line. This parameter is not applicable if the revertive mode option is disabled. The range is 1 to 12 minutes; the default is 5.
direction	The direction of switching. Choices are 0 (unidirectional) and 1 (bidirectional). The default is unidirectional, except for 1+1 Annex B, which is bidirectional only.

switchapsln Command

This command allows operator control of the APS switching interface.

Here is the command syntax:

```
switchapsln <slot.port> <switch option> [S]
```

Table 12-6 lists the parameter options.

Table 12-6 **switchapsln** *Command Parameter Options*

Parameter	Description
slot.port	The working line number.
switch option	Defines the manual switch option. Choices are 1 to 6:
	1 Clear—Clears the last user request, switches back to the working line, resets to all defaults, and sets BXM to fully automatic APS control.
	2 Lockout—Prevents a switchover to the protection line. If the protection line is already active, switches back to the working line.
	3 Forced working-to-protection line switch—If the working line is active, switches to the protection line unless the protection line is locked out, in the FS condition, or a Forced Switch is already in effect. Forces hardware to switch to the protection line even if it is in alarm.

continues

Table 12-6 **switchapsln** *Command Parameter Options (Continued)*

Parameter	Description
switch option	4 Forced protection-to-working line switch—If the protection line is active, switches to the working line. This parameter is invalid if a request of equal or higher priority is in effect. A protection-to-working switch applies only in the 1+1 architecture.
	5 Manual switch (working-to-protection line)—Switches from the working line to the protection line. This parameter is invalid if a request of equal or higher priority is in effect. Does not switch if other line is in alarm. Not applicable to APS 1+1, Annex B.
	6 Manual switch (protection-to-working line)—Not applicable to APS 1+1, Annex B.
S	If you enter **S** as an additional parameter, a service switch is performed for all ports on the card such that all lines are forcibly switched to one back card so that the other back card of the pair can be removed for service. Be sure that the associated front card is active for the back card that is to remain in the chassis. You might have to perform a **switchcdred** command so that the back card that the service switch changes to has an associated active front card.

dsplog Command

You can view events and alarms associated with APS switching and problems in the system log by using the **dsplog** command.

delapsln Command

This command removes an APS line pair. When you enter the command, the line you deleted is gone. (The display is empty or shows only the remaining APS lines.) The **delapsln** command parameters include the working line number (*<slot.port1>*), the protection line number (*<slot.port2>*), and the APS mode (*<protocol>*).

Here is the command syntax:

```
delapsln <slot.ort1> <slot.port2> <protocol>
```

Configuring and Verifying APS Operation

Follow these steps to configure and verify APS operation on a network trunk between two BPX switches. The example in this procedure is APS 1+1:

Step 1 At the next command prompt, enter **dspcd** *<slot>*, where *<slot>* is the slot number of one of the two BXM cards on which you are configuring APS. This displays details of the card hardware and firmware.

Step 2   Verify that the front card includes firmware and hardware support for APS.

Step 3   Verify that the back card is one of a redundant pair. Back card information should indicate the slot number of the companion paired back card, which will be in an adjacent slot.

Step 4   Repeat Steps 1 through 3 for the other BXM in the APS set.

Step 5   Enter **addcdred** *<primary slot> <secondary slot>*, where the *slot* numbers are the adjacent BXM cards. This configures the lines associated with the adjacent cards as redundant lines.

Step 6   Enter **addapsln** *<primary slot.port> <secondary slot.port>* **1**, where the integer 1 defines the APS 1+1 protocol. This adds an APS redundant pair; the first *slot.port* listed on the command line is the working line.

Step 7   Enter **dspapsln**. This displays all currently configured APS lines on the node and their status.

Step 8   Enter **cnfapsln** *<slot.port>*, where *<slot.port>* is the working line. This displays the current APS configuration.

Step 9   Verify that the APS protocol is shown as APS 1+1. This displays all network nodes and the trunks connecting them.

Step 10 Enter **cnfapsln** *<slot.port>*, and press the **Return** key five times until Direction appears on the command line.

Step 11 Enter **1** to select bidirectional switching. The APS configuration screen changes to reflect the modification to bidirectional switching.

Step 12 Enter **uptrk** *<slot.port>* at one of the BPX nodes. This displays the newly upped trunk. Initially the Alarm Status indicates clear, but this changes to a Loss of Signal state after about 10 seconds.

Step 13 Review the trunk configuration to ensure compatibility at both ends; if necessary, enter the **cnftrk** command to make any changes. This displays the modified trunk configuration.

Step 14 At the BPX node at the other end of the trunk, enter **uptrk** *<slot.port>*. This displays the newly upped trunk. Initially the Alarm Status indicates the Loss of Signal state, but this should change to clear after about 10 seconds.

Step 15 At either of the BPX nodes, enter **addtrk** *<slot.port>*. This displays the other end of the trunk: node name/trunk ID.

Step 16 Enter **switchapsln** <*slot.port*> **1** to clear the APS command line and reset the defaults. This displays the current configuration for this APS line pair: **Last User Switch Request = "clear"**.

Step 17 Enter **switchapsln** <*slot.port*> **3** to force a switchover to the protection line. This displays the active line as PROT.

Step 18 Enter **dsplog.** The system log confirms the manual switch action.

Step 19 Enter **switchapsln** <*slot.port*> **1** to clear the APS command line and reset the defaults.

Step 20 Enter **dsplog.** The system log confirms the manual switch action.

Step 21 Enter **switchapsln** <*slot.port*> **4** to force a switchback to the working line. This displays the active line as WORK.

Step 22 Enter **bye**. This terminates your CLI session and returns you to the login prompt.

Displaying Cards: dspcd

Example 12-1 shows the effect of issuing the **dspcd** command at a BXM card. This screen confirms that the card has hardware and firmware support for APS and that the back card is paired with a redundant back card in slot 5.

Example 12-1 dspcd *Command*

```
hei1bpx1          TN     Teacher:1        BPX 8620  9.3.XX    Feb. 14 200X 13:16 PST

Detailed Card Display for BXM-155 in slot 4
Status:          Active
Revision:        EJC              Backcard Installed
Serial Number:   914685            Type:        LM-BXM
Fab Number:      28-2158-02        Revision:    BA
Queue Size:      228300            Serial Number: 888319
Support: 8 Pts, OC3, FST, VcShp    Supp: 8 Pts,OC3,SMF,RedSlot:5
Support: VT,
    ChStLv 1, VSIlvl 2
Support: APS(FW,HW1+1)
Support: LMIver 1, ILMIver 1
Support: OAMLp, TrfcGen
#Ch:16320,PG[1]:8160,PG[2]:8160
PG[1]:1,2,3,4,
PG[2]:5,6,7,8,
#Sched_Ch:16384


Last Command: dspcd 4


Next Command:
```

Adding Card Redundancy: addcdred

Example 12-2 shows the **addcdred** command, which is used to add card redundancy. The two BXM card modules in these adjacent slots are now recognized as a redundant pair by the system software.

Example 12-2 addcdred *Command*

```
hei1bpx1          TN     Teacher:1       BPX 8620  9.3.XX    Feb. 14 200X 13:16 PST

        Slot Other Front    Back
Slot Type Slot  Card     Card
4    Pri  5     BXM      LM-BXM
5    Sec  4     BXM      LM-BXM


Last Command: addcdred 4 5

Next Command:

                                                               MAJOR ALARM
```

Adding APS Line Pairs: addapsln

Example 12-3 shows the **addapsln** command, with port 4.1 as the working line, port 5.1 as the protection line, and the APS protocol configured as 1+1. If the selected protocol is 1:1, the **addapsln** command must be issued while the trunk is down.

Example 12-3 addapsln *Command*

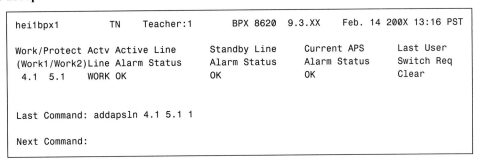

```
hei1bpx1          TN     Teacher:1       BPX 8620  9.3.XX    Feb. 14 200X 13:16 PST

Work/Protect Actv Active Line    Standby Line    Current APS    Last User
(Work1/Work2)Line Alarm Status   Alarm Status    Alarm Status   Switch Req
  4.1  5.1   WORK OK             OK              OK             Clear


Last Command: addapsln 4.1 5.1 1

Next Command:
```

Configuring APS Lines: cnfapsln

Example 12-4 shows the use of the **cnfapsln** command to modify APS line parameters. In this example, revertive switching is being enabled with a Wait to Restore timer value of two minutes, and the direction of switching is being set to bidirectional.

Example 12-4 cnfapsln *Command*

```
hei1bpx1          TN    Teacher:1       BPX 8620  9.3.XX    Feb. 14 200X 13:16 PST

APS Configuration parameters for Working, Protection lines 4.1, 5.1

APS Protocol:                                         1+1

Signal Fail BER threshold (10 to the -n):            3
Signal Detect BER threshold (10 to the -n):          5
Revertive Switching:                                 Yes
Wait to Restore Timer:                               2 minutes
Uni/Bi Directional Switching:                        Bidirectional
Command: cnfapsln 1.1

Last Command: cnfapsln 4.1 3 5 y 2 b

Next Command:
```

Switching APS Lines: switchapsln

You can use the **switchapsln** command to control APS switching from the user interface. User-initiated switching is not supported for 1+1 Annex B. The **switchapsln** command allows you to do the following:

- Reset the APS system defaults

- Disable switching

- Manually initiate switchover from the working to the protection line and vice versa

Example 12-5 shows the effect of issuing a **switchapsln** command to initiate a switch to the protection line.

Example 12-5 switchapsln *Command*

```
hei1bpx1           TN     Teacher:1       BPX 8620  9.3.XX    Feb. 14 200X 13:16 PST

Work/Protect Actv Active Line     Standby Line    Current APS     Last User
(Work1/Work2)Line Alarm Status    Alarm Status    Alarm Status    Switch Req
 4.1  5.1    PROT OK              OK              APS OK          Forced W->P

Last Command: switchapsln 4.1 3

  Please confirm APS switch.
Next Command:
```

Command Precedence

Automatic and manual switching commands comply with a set of precedence rules to avoid conflicts and possible indeterminate states. Conditions that can cause or prevent a switchover are listed here in order of precedence from highest to lowest:

1 **Lockout of protection**—A user-initiated command (**switchapsln**) that prevents switching from working line to protection line.

2 **Forced switch**—A user-initiated request to force a switch from working line to protection line or vice versa, regardless of the alarm condition of the destination line.

3 **Signal fail**—An automatically initiated switch caused by a signal failure on the incoming line. Signal failures include loss of signal, loss of frame, alarm indication signal, and a bit error rate exceeding the configured threshold (**cnfapsln**).

4 **Signal degrade**—An automatically initiated switch due to a "soft failure" resulting from the line bit error rate exceeding the configured threshold (**cnfapsln**).

5 **Manual switch**—A user-initiated request to switch from working line to protection line or vice versa, but only if no alarm is on the destination line.

6 **Wait to restore**—An automatically initiated request for revertive switchback to the working line following expiration of the wait to restore timer.

7 **Reverse request**—An automatically initiated request to switch, resulting from a switch at the remote-end APS bidirectional line.

8 **Do not revert**—An automatically initiated request following a manual user request (such as a forced switch) being cleared while using nonrevertive switching.

9 **No request**—An automatically initiated request following a manual user request (such as a forced switch) being cleared while using revertive switching.

You can view events and alarms associated with APS switching and problems in the system log using the **dsplog** command, as shown in Example 12-6.

Example 12-6 dsplog *Command*

```
hei1bpx1        TN    Teacher:1      BPX 8620  9.3.XX    Feb. 14 200X 13:16 PST

Most recent log entries (most recent at top)
Class  Description                                     Date      Time
Info   User requested APS Clear LN 4.1                 02/14/01  13:36:21
Info   APS Lockout switch from LN 5.1 to 4.1           02/14/01  13:35:23
Info   User requested APS Lockout LN 4.1               02/14/01  13:35:23
Info   APS Forced switch from LN 4.1 to 5.1            02/14/01  13:34:49
Info   User requested APS Forced Work->Prot Switch LN 4.1  02/14/01  13:34:48
Clear  Y-Redundancy Alarm in slot 4                    02/14/01  13:30:48
Info   BXM 4 Up                                        02/14/01  13:30:48
```
                                                                    continues

Example 12-6 dsplog *Command (Continued)*

```
Info   APS Init, Clear, or Revert on LN 4.1              02/14/01 13:29:40
Minor  Y-Redundancy Alarm in slot 4                      02/14/01 13:29:40
Info   BXM 4 Down - Activated BXM 5                      02/14/01 13:29:40
Info   Clock switch to oscillator of SaltLake via TRK 3.1  02/14/01 13:29:40
Info   Clock switch to oscillator of CC                  02/14/01 13:29:40
Clear  APS OK on Lines 4.1, 5.1                          02/14/01 13:28:41

This Command: dsplog

Continue?

                                                            MAJOR ALARM
```

Summary

After completing this chapter, you should be able to configure and verify the operation of SONET APS on the trunks and use the CLI to configure BXM ports for APS 1+1 and/or 1:1 operation. You should also understand the differences between APS 1+1 and 1:1 operation and be able to describe the configuration rules that apply to BXM APS operation.

Review Questions

1 How do the APS 1:1 and 1+1 protocols differ?

A. APS 1:1 provides card redundancy only.

B. APS 1+1 provides card and line redundancy.

C. APS 1+1 requires a dedicated protection line; APS 1:1 does not.

D. APS 1+1 can carry user traffic simultaneously on both lines.

E. The BXM supports multiple pairs of 1:1 lines but only one pair of 1+1 lines per card.

2 Which of the following network events can trigger an automatic switchover to the APS protection line?

A. Cutting the fiber trunk between two BPX nodes

B. Loss of framing on a line or trunk

C. Excessive cell discards in the trunk queues

D. A bit error rate exceeding a preset limit

E. The wait to restore timer expiring in revertive switching mode

3 Which of the following is not supported on the BXM?

   A. APS 1:1 with revertive and bidirectional switching

   B. APS 1+1 with nonrevertive and unidirectional switching

   C. APS 1+1 Annex B with nonrevertive and unidirectional switching

   D. APS 1:1 with nonrevertive switching

4 What command would you use to define the APS protocol?

   A. **cnfcdaps**

   B. **addcdred**

   C. **addapsln**

   D. **cnfapsln**

5 Which types of APS provide line and card protection?

   A. 1+1

   B. 1+1, Annex B

   C. 1:1

   D. 1:1, Annex B

6 Which type of APS is never revertive?

   A. 1+1

   B. 1+1, Annex B

   C. 1:1

   D. 1:1, Annex B

7 Which type of APS provides line protection only?

   A. 1+1

   B. 1+1, Annex B

   C. 1:1

   D. 1:1, Annex B

8 Regarding APS 1:1, which of the following is true?

   A. Redundant lines must be on adjacent ports.

   B. Redundant lines need not be on adjacent ports.

   C. Redundant lines must be on adjacent back cards.

   D. Redundant lines need not be on adjacent back cards.

9 Which of the following statements is true?

A. APS information is carried by the K1-K1 bytes of the section overhead.

B. APS information is carried by the K1-K2 bytes of the line overhead.

C. APS information is carried by the K1-K2 bytes of the path overhead.

D. APS information is not carried by the K1-K1 bytes.

10 Which of the following bytes indicates the line AIS?

A. A1

B. A2

C. K1

D. K2

11 Which byte does the SONET line interface use to determine BER?

A. H1

B. B2

C. K1

D. E2

This chapter covers the following key topics:

- What Is an ATM Port?
- What Is a Port Queue?
- What Is Traffic Shaping?
- Signaling Protocols
- Activating, Configuring, and Deactivating ATM Ports
- Steps for Activating, Configuring, and Deactivating ATM Ports
- Monitoring and Resolving ATM Port Failures
- Steps for Monitoring and Resolving ATM Port Failures

CHAPTER 13

Configuring ATM Ports

In this chapter, you learn how to configure and activate the ATM ports that support user connections on a BPX node. ATM ports need to be configured and activated correctly to support user connections. As soon as the ports have been brought up, you can verify that the switch and the attached user device are communicating properly and then provision the user connections.

What Is an ATM Port?

This section defines the function of an ATM port in a Cisco WAN switching network.

Port Definition

A *port* is the interface between the BPX switch and a single ATM user device. Ports on the BPX switch are located on the BXM card module and can be activated as either *physical* or *virtual* ports. With physical ports, there is a one-to-one relationship between BXM ports and the physical access line. If virtual ports are used, there can be more than one port per access line, as shown in Figure 13-1. Ports are the originating and terminating entities for connections in the BPX.

The number of physical ports activated on a BXM card is restricted to the number of physical interfaces, which depends on the card type and particularly the back card. The number of virtual ports is limited by the number of Virtual Interfaces (VIs) supported by the BXM card, which is 31. You can mix and match physical and virtual ports on a single card, up to a total of 31 ports. Physical and virtual ports cannot exist on the same physical interface.

When configuring an ATM port, you must define several characteristics, including interface type, signaling protocol, port queue sizes, and thresholds.

The external user device could be a router, another ATM switch (Cisco or third-party), an access concentrator, or any other specialized gateway device that supports an ATM interface.

Figure 13-1 *Port Description*

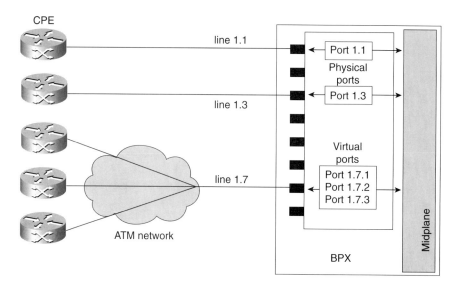

Virtual Port Applications

Virtual ports can be considered the user-side equivalent of virtual trunks, and they exist for similar reasons. Having both virtual ports and virtual trunks together in a system allows service providers to offer enhanced flexibility to their customers.

Figure 13-2 shows how virtual trunks and virtual ports are deployed by a service provider in key points of presence (POPs) using third-party ATM virtual path connections (VPCs) for core trunking and user access.

Virtual ports can extend the core ATM infrastructure to end-user organizations via a third-party network cloud. In this way, customers who require ATM connectivity can access services through a cost-effective permanent virtual circuit (PVC) or private virtual path (PVP) facility that terminates at a virtual port on a BPX switch in the provider's network. As ATM services become more prevalent, the virtual trunk/port capability offers advantages to both second- and third-tier providers as well as to enterprises that want to interconnect user networks to a BPX switch across an ATM service. The feature can also extend IP services through a public ATM service with Multiprotocol Label Switching (MPLS).

Figure 13-2 *Virtual Trunk and Port Deployment*

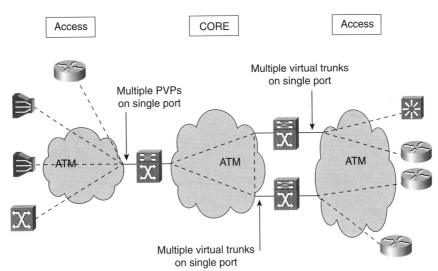

Physical and Virtual Port Differences

In most major respects, virtual and physical ports operate in the same manner. However, there are some important functional differences; they are summarized in Table 13-1. Also see the section, "What Is Traffic Shaping?"

Table 13-1 *Physical and Virtual Port Differences*

Feature or Function	BXM Physical Ports	BXM Virtual Ports
Number of ports per physical interface port	One	Up to 31
Support for VSI partitions?	Yes	No
Support for LMI/ILMI?	Yes	No (supported in a future release)
Requires a specific VPI range to be assigned?	No	Yes
Number of VIs per physical port (see the next section for a definition of VI)	One	Up to 31 (one per virtual port)

BXM Virtual Interface

Each BXM module has 31 VIs associated with the egress from the card via a trunk or access port. Activation of a trunk or port, whether physical or virtual, results in the creation of a logical port by the system software. The new logical port is assigned one of the 31 available VIs. There is a system software limitation of 254 BXM ports on a single node.

What Is a Port Queue?

This section defines the function of an ATM port queue in a BPX switch.

Port Queue Definition

Each physical and virtual interface is associated with a single set of port queues. The port queues form a shared buffer space that serves all user connections terminating at that port. The port queue structure is used only for cells traveling out of the network to a user device—the *egress* direction. Cells entering the network in the *ingress* direction do not use the port queues; a separate system of *per-VC* (virtual circuit) *queues* is used for ingress traffic. VC queues are discussed with ATM connections in Chapter 21, "ATM Ports and Connections."

BXM Port Queues

Each physical (not virtual) port is associated with a single physical line on the BXM module, as shown in Figure 13-3. In general, each port queue on the BXM consists of 16 subqueues called QBins. Four of these QBins are assigned to ATM traffic—one for each of the following traffic types: CBR, real-time VBR (rt-VBR), non-real-time VBR (nrt-VBR), and a shared QBin for UBR and ABR. ABR connection types use the UBR/ABR QBin. ATM-FR types use the VBR-nrt QBin.

Configurable Thresholds

Associated with each QBin is a set of configurable thresholds that play a role in traffic management for the switch. The thresholds are as follows:

- **Queue depth**—This is the maximum number of cells that can be admitted to the QBin. The BXM card module has a fixed, dedicated amount of buffer space that can be allocated to the port queues, ranging from 128 to 512 KB cells, depending on the card type. If the QBin fills up to the configured maximum queue depth, any subsequent cells arriving from the network for that port QBin are dropped.

- **CLP High**—Cell Loss Priority (CLP) is a bit in the ATM cell header that is set either by the originating CPE or by a network switch. It identifies the cell to be discarded. Cells with CLP set to 1 are *tagged* as being eligible for discard. If traffic enters a particular QBin at a rate higher than the CPE can accept, the queue fills up. If the queue reaches the CLP High threshold level (expressed as a percentage of the maximum queue depth), any cells arriving from the network with CLP = 1 are discarded.

- **CLP Low**—As soon as the QBin drains (empties) to the CLP Low threshold level, arriving CLP-tagged cells are no longer discarded and are once more admitted to the queue.

- **EFCI**—The Explicit Forward Congestion Indicator (EFCI) bit in the cell header indicates the presence (or absence) of congestion in the network. As soon as the port QBin fills to the EFCI threshold level, all cells entering the QBin are *marked* by setting the EFCI bit. Networks can include advanced traffic management schemes that monitor the congestion state in the network and adjust traffic flows accordingly. EFCI is one of several mechanisms in these networks that assists with congestion management.

Figure 13-3 *BXM Port Queues*

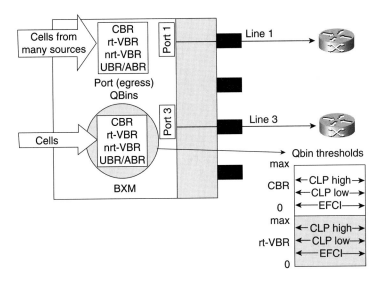

What Is Traffic Shaping?

This section defines the implementation of traffic shaping at egress ports on a BPX switch.

Definition

Traffic shaping (sometimes called VC shaping) smoothes the delivery of cells to the port by avoiding excessive burstiness and by reducing the variation in cell delivery rate or jitter. Traffic shaping works by applying upper and lower cell rates for each user connection, as defined when the connection is provisioned. If traffic shaping is enabled for the port, all cells arriving from the network are placed in individual shaping queues for each user connection.

Implementation

Traffic shaping in the BPX switch must be enabled for each connection. It is enabled when you configure the egress queues for a specific port and is disabled by default for connections (PVP or PVC).

Figure 13-4 shows a simplified view of where egress (or VC) traffic shaping takes place on the BXM card. In this example, traffic shaping is enabled for port (line) 1, but not for port 3. Notice that VC shaping is enabled by traffic type. For example, you can enable shaping for ABR or UBR connections and leave it disabled for other types.

Figure 13-4 *BXM Traffic Shaping*

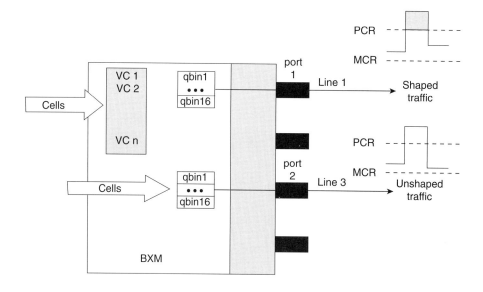

The rate at which the VC queues are serviced depends on the traffic type, as shown in Table 13-2.

Table 13-2   *VC Queue Service Types and Cell Rates*

Service Type	Minimum Cell Rate (MCR)	Peak Cell Rate (Maximum Service Rate) (PCR)
CBR	PCR	PCR
rt-VBR, nrt-VBR	SCR × utilization %	PCR
UBR	Zero	PCR
ABR	MCR × utilization %	PCR

As you can see from Table 13-2, the maximum cell rate at which a VC queue is serviced is the configured PCR for that connection. The minimum rate depends on the traffic type. SCR is the configured sustained cell rate for VBR. The utilization factor is a percentage from 1 through 100 and is defined by the network administrator when provisioning a VBR or ABR connection.

Virtual Port Traffic Shaping

Virtual ports allow you to implement *hierarchical* traffic shaping—that is, traffic shaping at more than one level.

Shaping at the port level is automatically enabled when you activate a virtual port. This means that the aggregate throughput of all the PVPs and PVCs on the port cannot exceed the configured port speed.

You enable shaping at the connection level by service type, just as for physical ports, by using the **cnfportq** command. As previously mentioned, connection-level shaping is disabled by default.

Signaling Protocols

This section presents an overview of the LMI and ILMI signaling protocols.

LMI/ILMI Overview

A signaling protocol is used to exchange PVC status and configuration information between two devices. Typically, there are periodic keepalive or heartbeat messages in addition to status information.

Two signaling protocols are defined for ATM interfaces—the Local Management Interface (LMI) and the Integrated Local Management Interface (ILMI). LMI is an implementation of the ITU-T Q.2931 (Annex G) standard, whereas the ILMI implementation is based on the ATM Forum ILMI 4.0 Specification af-ilmi-0065.000. Neither protocol is required for a BPX ATM port to transmit and receive traffic, although some user equipment might depend on either the LMI or ILMI to maintain an active interface. Figure 13-5 shows the operation of LMI and ILMI.

Figure 13-5 *LMI and ILMI*

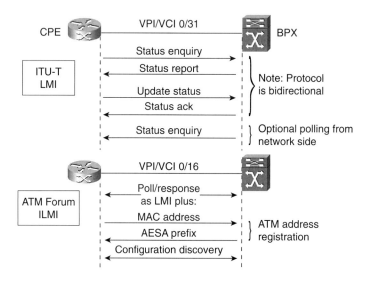

The most important concern when defining a signaling protocol is to ensure that the BPX port and the user equipment interface are configured to use the same protocol. In addition, you need to configure the protocol timers so that they are compatible across the interface because failure to do so might cause a minor "ATM Port Communications Failure" alarm. You configure the signaling protocol and the timers associated with it for each BPX ATM port using the **cnfport** command.

LMI Signaling Protocol

The LMI signaling protocol is bidirectional in that both the user device and the network side participate as peers. Each side communicates periodically with the other side of the interface to exchange status information and to verify active operation. The LMI signaling protocol includes configurable VPI and VCI. The basic message streams are as follows:

- **Status Inquiry**—As soon as the interface is activated, each side starts to send Status Inquiry messages to the other side to request the current status of one or more PVCs. The sender expects to receive a Status Report containing the same Transaction Number as the inquiry message within a time period defined by the T393 timer (the default is

10 seconds). If no response is received, a retry is made using the original transaction number. When the maximum number of retries has been sent, as defined by the N394 counter (the default is 5), the BPX switch assumes that the protocol has broken down and posts a minor alarm indicating "ATM Port Communication Failed." If a timely Status Report is received and if it includes the correct, original transaction number, the receiver decodes the Information Elements in the report to determine the current status of each PVC.

- **Update Status**—The Update Status message is sent asynchronously to advise the other side of a change in status on one or more PVCs. The sender expects to receive a response (the Update Status Ack) within the period defined by timer T394 (the default is 10 seconds). If no response is received, the retry counter is incremented, and a retry is made. If no response is received after N395 retires (the default is 5), the BPX switch posts the "ATM Port Communications Failed" minor alarm.

- **LMI Status Poll**—This applies to the network side only and is a configurable parameter for the BXM port. If LMI polling is enabled, the BPX switch checks for receipt of Status Updates from the user device. If no message is received within a period defined by T396 (the default is 10 seconds), the BXM port sends a Status Inquiry message.

ILMI Signaling Protocol

An ILMI is a peer-to-peer protocol that uses Simple Network Management Protocol (SNMP) packets to carry bidirectional messages across the ATM interface. Both the user and network sides of the interface include a Management Information Base (MIB) that contains configuration and other data accessible via SNMP. In addition to the keepalive and status update messages similar to LMI, the ILMI protocol and MIB support a growing number of extended functions, including ATM address registration and autodiscovery of configuration parameters such as the UNI signaling version in use and the VPI/VCI ranges.

The keepalive procedure used in ILMI is based on the AT&T InterSpan ATM Service UNI Specification. The network side of the UNI (the BPX switch) may be configured to send periodic polls to the user side. A poll usually consists of an SNMP Get Request. A Get Response is expected from the attached ATM device before the next poll is sent.

A polling timer (T491; the default is 30 seconds) defines the maximum interval between Get Requests from the network side of the UNI. If the number of Get Responses defined by N491 (the default is 3) is not received out of a number of Get Requests (N492; the default is 4), the protocol fails, and the BPX switch posts a minor alarm. Traps may be enabled for the ATM interface, in which case an event or status change results in an SNMP trap message's being sent to the attached device.

Activating, Configuring, and Deactivating ATM Ports

This section describes the commands and parameters used to activate, configure, and deactivate an ATM port on a BPX switch.

Commands for ATM Ports

This section describes the BPX CLI commands for activating and configuring ATM ports.

The commands listed in Table 13-3 are discussed in this chapter. The table describes each command and the privilege level necessary to issue it.

Table 13-3 *Commands for ATM Ports*

Command	Description	Privilege Level
addport	Add port. Creates a physical or virtual port.	2
cnfrsrc	Configure resource. Modifies the number of PVCs allocated to a port.	2
cnfport	Configure port. Modifies the port configuration parameters.	2
upport	Up port. Activates a port.	2
dspports	Display ports. Displays port status information for a node or for an individual card.	6
dspport	Display port. Displays status information for a single port.	6
cnfportq	Configure port queues. Modifies the egress port queue (QBin) configuration.	2
dspportq	Display port queues. Displays the egress port queue (QBin) configuration for a particular port.	6
dnport	Down port. Deactivates a port.	2
delport	Delete port. Deletes a physical or virtual port.	2

addport Command

The **addport** command creates a single physical or virtual port on a BXM card.

Here is the **addport** command syntax:

```
addport <slot.port>
```

Example 13-1 shows the effect of the **addport** command for a physical port. The **addport** command fails if the corresponding physical line has not been activated with the **upln** command. The new port is shown with the status Inactive, with the other parameters at the system defaults.

Example 13-1 addport *Command*

```
hei1bpx1         TN    Teacher:1        BPX 8620  9.3.XX    Feb. 14 200X 13:16 PST

Port configuration for ATM 6

From         VPI Min/Max     Bandwidth    Interface   State      Protocol  Type
6.1              0 /  255    348207 (cps) LM-BXM      INACTIVE   NONE      UNI




Last Command: addport 6.1

256 PVCs allocated. Use 'cnfrsrc' to configure PVCs
Next Command:

                                                                    MAJOR ALARM
```

After you enter the **addport** command, a prompt indicates that the system defaults to 256 PVCs on the port. This is the maximum number of AutoRoute connections that can be placed on this port by default. If this number is too high or too low, you can use the **cnfrsrc** command to modify the number of PVCs, as shown in the next section.

cnfrsrc Command

Example 13-2 shows the result of using the **cnfrsrc** command to allocate 1024 PVCs to a port. The bandwidth available for AutoRoute PVCs has been configured the same as the physical port speed (348,207 cells per second). The N in the command line appears because the system defaults were accepted to not modify the VSI parameters associated with the port.

Example 13-2 cnfrsrc *Command*

```
hei1bpx1         TN    Teacher:1        BPX 8620  9.3.XX    Feb. 14 200X 13:16 PST

Port/Trunk : 6.1

Maximum PVC LCNS:              1024    Maximum PVC Bandwidth:348207
                                      (Statistical Reserve: 5000)

Partition 1
```

continues

Example 13-2 **cnfrsrc** *Command (Continued)*

```
Partition State :            Disable




Last Command: cnfrsrc 6.1 1024 348207 N


Next Command:


                                                      MAJOR ALARM
```

cnfport Command

The **cnfport** command configures a port to be compatible with the ATM device with which it interfaces.

Here is the **cnfport** command syntax:

```
cnfport <slot.port> <parameters>
```

If you are activating a virtual port, the next step is to use the **cnfport** command to define the range of VPI values that can be used on the port. Example 13-3 shows the previously created virtual port 1.5.1 being configured with one SVC channel and the VPI range from 1 (minimum) to 100 (maximum).

Example 13-3 **cnfport** *Command*

```
hei1bpx1         TN    Teacher:1      BPX 8620  9.3.XX   Feb. 14 200X 13:16 PST

Port:        1.5.1   [FAILED  ]
Interface:           LM-BXM                 CAC Override:     Enabled
Type:                UNI                    %Util Use:        Disabled
Shift:               SHIFT ON HCF (Normal Operation)
SIG Queue Depth:     640                    Port Load:        0 %

Protocol:            NONE                   Protocol by Card: Yes
  SVC Channels:                  1            SVC Channels:   0
  SVC VPI Min:                   1            SVC VPI Min:    0
  SVC VPI Max:                 100            SVC VPI Max:    0
  SVC Bandwidth:                 0 (cps)      VC Bandwidth:   0 (cps)
  T396 Polling Timer:           10
  N394 Max Status Enquiry Retry: 5
  N395 Max Update Status Retry:  5


Last Command: cnfport 1.5.1 n h n n n Y 1 1 100 0

Next Command:

                                                      MAJOR ALARM
```

Example 13-3 shows a returned status of FAILED. In this case, the port was not configured correctly to be compatible with the ATM device with which it interfaces.

The next step is to use the **cnfport** command to modify the port configuration to match the characteristics of the attached user device. Example 13-4 shows port 6.1 after modification to activate ILMI and to specify that the ILMI agent and protocol for this port should be run from the BXM firmware rather than from the switch software on the BCC controller. Other parameters remain at the system defaults.

Example 13-4 **cnfport** *Command*

```
hei1bpx1          TN     Teacher:1        BPX 8620   9.3.XX    Feb. 14 200X 13:16 PST


Port:        6.1     [ACTIVE  ]
Interface:           LM-BXM                     CAC Override:     Enabled
Type:                NNI                        %Util Use:        Disabled
Shift:               SHIFT ON HCF (Normal Operation)
SIG Queue Depth:     640                        Port Load:        0 %

Protocol:            ILMI                       Protocol by Card: Yes
  VPI.VCI:                           0.16         Addr Reg Enab:  N
  ILMI Polling Enabled:              N            SVC Channels:   0
  Trap Enabled:                      N            SVC VPI Min:    1
  T491 Polling Interval:             30           SVC VPI Max:    100
  N491 Error Threshold:              3            SVC Bandwidth:  0 (cps)
  N492 Event Threshold:              4
  N395 Max Update Status Retry:      5



Last Command: cnfport 2.1 N H i 0 16 N N N 30 3 4 N N Y 0 1 100 0

Next Command:

                                                              MAJOR ALARM
```

There are two main advantages to enabling Protocol by Card. First, processor loading is reduced. Second, the ILMI protocol running in firmware on the BXM can respond faster to interface messages, which can be important for attached CPEs with the stringent timing requirements. The overall benefit is increased scalability.

Configurable Port Parameters

Configurable port parameter options are listed in Table 13-4. Certain value fields, such as those for the LMI/ILMI parameters, are displayed for configuration only if other parameters have been previously selected and modified.

Table 13-4 *Configurable Port Parameter Options for the* **cnfport** *Command*

Parameter	Description	Default
slot.port[.*vport*]	Specifies the BXM card slot and port number. Also indicates the port status as Active, Inactive, or Failed.	Display only
Interface	The type of back card.	Display only
VPI Range	Physical port. Defaults to 0 to 255 (UNI) or 0 to 4095 (NNI). Virtual port. Configurable in the range from 0 to 255 for UNI or 0 to 4095 for NNI.	0 to 255 or 0 to 4095
Type	Specifies whether the cell header format is NNI or UNI.	UNI
Shift	If the attached device is a Cisco WAN switch that has virtual trunks tunneled through this network (the node is part of the SP cloud), you must select N (shift off). In all other cases, select H (the default, or shift on).	H (shift on)
SIG queue depth	Queue depth in cells for the signaling traffic on the port.	640
Protocol	For physical ports only. Specifies the use of either an LMI protocol or an ILMI protocol, or no specified protocol. No specified protocol is the default. Protocol values are one of the following: N (none) L (LMI) I (ILMI) See Tables 13-5 and 13-6 for parameter descriptions for LMI and ILMI.	N (none)
Bandwidth/AR BW	Configurable for all port types up to the maximum bandwidth available. The sum of all the configured bandwidths for virtual ports cannot exceed the maximum bandwidth for the physical interface.	Varies by card
CAC Override	If this is enabled, new connections that cause the port to be oversubscribed are permitted. If this is disabled, new connections that cause the port to be oversubscribed are rejected and are not added to the port.	Enabled

Table 13-4   *Configurable Port Parameter Options for the* **cnfport** *Command (Continued)*

Parameter	Description	Default
CAC Reserve	CAC Reserve is configurable on all ports but is valid only if CAC Override is disabled. If CAC Override is disabled, this parameter specifies the amount of AutoRoute Port Bandwidth that is unavailable for booking by connections. If CAC Override is enabled, overbooking is permitted. This parameter reserves some bandwidth to handle bursts of traffic without cell discards. This parameter is configurable in all ports. CAC Override is entered in cells per second.	0
%util	Determines whether the configured percent utilization specified for a connection (with the **addcon** command) is used as a factor determining egress QBin service rates and oversubscription warnings. Applicable only for VBR and ABR connections.	Disabled
Port Load	Indicates the percentage of the port bandwidth allocated to connections.	Display only
Protocol by Card	Defines whether the LMI/ILMI signaling protocol runs on the BCC controller or on the BXM service module. Not configurable for virtual ports.	No (runs on BCC)

LMI Port Parameters

Table 13-5 describes the LMI parameters for a port.

Table 13-5   *LMI Port Parameters*

Parameter	Description	Default
VPI.VCI	The VPI and VCI reserved for the LMI protocol messages. This VPI/VCI pair cannot be used for a connection terminating on this port.	0.31
LMI Polling Enabled	Enables or disables periodic status inquiries.	Disabled
T393 Status Inquiry Timer	The timeout period, in seconds, for expected responses to be received from the attached device as the result of the port's sending out a status inquiry. If the timer expires, the port attempts to transmit another inquiry.	10

continues

Table 13-5 *LMI Port Parameters (Continued)*

Parameter	Description	Default
T394 Update Status Timer	The timeout period, in seconds, for expected responses to be received from the attached device as the result of the port's sending out an update status message. If the timer expires, the port attempts to transmit another update status message.	10
T396 Polling Timer	The time between status inquiries, in seconds, sent by the port if polling is enabled.	10
N394 Max Status Inquiry Retry	The maximum number of status inquiry retries sent by the port before an "ATM Port Communications Failure" alarm is declared.	5
N395 Max Update Status Retry	The maximum number of update status retries sent by the port before an "ATM Port Communications Failure" alarm is declared.	5

ILMI Port Parameters

Table 13-6 provides the ILMI parameter descriptions for a port.

Table 13-6 *ILMI Port Parameters*

Parameter	Description	Default
VPI.VCI	The VPI and VCI reserved for the ILMI protocol messages. This VPI/VCI pair cannot be used for a connection terminating on this port.	0.16
ILMI Polling Enabled	Enables or disables periodic status polls.	Disabled
Trap Enabled	Enables or disables unsolicited event or alarm transmission.	Disabled
T491 Polling Interval	The time period, in seconds, between status polls sent by the port if polling is enabled.	20
N491 Error Threshold	If N491 messages out of N492 messages do not receive a response from the attached device, an "ATM Port Communications Failure" alarm is declared.	4
N492 Event Threshold	The number of attempted messages, in conjunction with the N491 threshold, that determines an alarm condition.	5
Address Registration	Enables and disables ILMI address registration. Address registration is supported only for ports that are under the control of a Virtual Switch Interface (VSI).	Disabled

upport Command

The **upport** command activates a single port on a BXM card. The port must have been previously added with the **addport** command. In the case of a virtual port, it must have been assigned a VPI range using the **cnfport** command. If the port was not previously added and configured, the default configuration values are applied to it.

Here is the **upport** command syntax:

```
upport <slot.port> [.vport]
```

vport is a VI identifier from 1 to 31.

As soon as the port is created, the next step is to activate it using the **upport** command. This is shown in Example 13-5 for the previously created physical port 6.1.

Example 13-5 upport *Command*

```
hei1bpx1           TN    Teacher:1      BPX 8620  9.3.XX    Feb. 14 200X 13:16 PST

Port:      6.1     [ACTIVE  ]              Bandwidth/AR BW:  1412830/1412830
Interface:         LM-BXM                  CAC Override:     Enabled
VPI Range:           0  -  255            CAC Reserve:      0
Type:              UNI                     %Util Use:        Disabled
Shift:             SHIFT ON HCF (Normal Operation)
SIG Queue Depth:   640                     Port Load:        0 %

Protocol:          NONE                    Protocol by Card: No




Last Command: upport 6.1


Next Command:

                                                                  MAJOR ALARM
```

dspports Command

The **dspports** command, without any additional parameters, displays a list of all ports that have been added on that node. The **dspports** command with the card slot number displays summary information for all ports added on that particular card.

Here is the **dspports** command syntax:

```
dspports
dspports <slot>
```

The **dspports** command with the slot number parameter, as shown in Example 13-6, summarizes the configured parameters for each port that has been added on that card. A port does not need to be upped to be displayed.

Example 13-6 dspports *Command*

```
hei1bpx1          TN    Teacher:1       BPX 8620  9.3.XX    Feb. 14 200X 13:16 PST

Port configuration for ATM 6

Port   Chan      Speed      Interface      State      Protocol    Type
1      1         353208 (cps) LM-BXM        INACTIVE   NONE        UNI


Last Command: dspports 6
```

Information provided by **dspports** *<slot>* includes the following:

- **Port number**
- **Channel number**
- **Speed**—The port speed based on line type in cells per second. Here, 1412830 cps indicates an OC-12c/STM-4 line with a nominal bit rate of 622 Mbps.
- **Interface**—The interface or line type. BXMs show LM-BXM as the interface type.
- **State**—The state of the port, which is one of the following:
  - **ACTIVE**—The port is up and free of alarms.
  - **INACTIVE**—The port has not been activated with the **upport** command.
  - **FAILED**—The port is active and has a failure condition—either a signaling protocol failure or a line failure.
  - **LOOPED**—The port has been looped using the **addloclp** command. This requires a **dellp** command to remove an added loopback.
- **Protocol**—The configured signaling protocol—LMI, ILMI, or none.
- **Type**—The cell header type—either UNI or NNI.

Example 13-7 shows the **dspports** *<slot>* command for a BXM card in which one of the ports has failed due to a physical line failure. This is indicated by the Major Alarm message.

Example 13-7 dspports *Command*

```
hei1bpx1          TN    Teacher:1       BPX 8620  9.3.XX    Feb. 14 200X 13:16 PST

Port configuration for ATM 1

Port   Chan      Speed      Interface      State      Protocol    Type
2      2         353208 (cps) LM-BXM        INACTIVE   ILMI        UNI
```

Example 13-7 **dspports** *Command (Continued)*

```
Last Command: dspports 1

Next Command:
                     SW CD                                    MAJOR ALARM
```

dspport Command

The **dspport** command displays detailed configuration information for a single ATM port.

Here is the **dspport** command syntax:

dspport *<slot.port>*

cnfportq Command

The **cnfportq** command is used to modify port queue (QBin) parameters on the BXM card.

Here is the **cnfportq** command syntax:

cnfportq *<slot.port> <parameters>*

The **cnfportq** command allows you to configure QBins associated with an ATM port, as shown in Example 13-8.

Example 13-8 **cnfportq** *Command*

```
hei1bpx1          TN    Teacher:1       BPX 8620  9.3.XX   Feb. 14 200X 13:16 PST

Port:         6.1      [ACTIVE  ]
Interface:           LM-BXM
Type:                UNI
AR Bandwidth:        1412830 (cps)
SVC Queue Pool Size:        0
          QUEUE    DEPTH    CLP HI   CLP LO   EFCI   VC SHAPE
                                     /EPD
            CBR    1200      80%      60%      60%   ENABLED
         rt-VBR   10000      80%      60%      60%   DISABLED
        nrt-VBR   10000      80%      60%      60%   DISABLED
        UBR/ABR   40000      80%      60%      20%   DISABLED



Last Command: cnfportq 6.1 0 1200 80 60 60 e 10000 80 60 60 D 10000 80 60 60 D 4
0000 80 60 20 D

Next Command:

                                                             MAJOR ALARM
```

Using the **cnfportq** command, the following values may be configured for each QBin:

- Queue Depth
- CLP High Threshold
- CLP Low/EPD Threshold
- EFCI Threshold
- VC Traffic Shaping

Note that setting a threshold to 100% of the queue depth disables the cell discard or congestion marking associated with that threshold.

dspportq Command

The **dspportq** command displays the detailed queue configuration for a single ATM port.

Here is the **dspportq** command syntax:

> **dspportq** <*slot.port*>

The **dspportq** screen, shown in Example 13-9, provides configuration information on the QBins associated with an ATM port. Queue depths are displayed in cells, and thresholds are defined as a percentage of the configured queue depth.

Example 13-9 dspportq *Command*

```
hei1bpx1          TN     Teacher:1      BPX 8620  9.3.XX    Feb. 14 200X 13:16 PST

Port:        1.2    [ACTIVE  ]
Interface:          LM-BXM
Type:               UNI
Speed:              353208 (cps)


SVC Queue Pool Size:           0
CBR Queue Depth:              600     rt-VBR Queue Depth:             5000
CBR Queue CLP High Threshold: 80%     rt-VBR Queue CLP High Threshold:  80%
CBR Queue CLP Low Threshold:  60%     rt-VBR Queue CLP Low/EPD Threshold: 60%
CBR Queue EFCI Threshold:     60%     rt-VBR Queue EFCI Threshold:       60%
nrt-VBR Queue Depth:         5000     UBR/ABR Queue Depth:            20000
nrt-VBR Queue CLP High Threshold: 80% UBR/ABR Queue CLP High Threshold:  80%
nrt-VBR Queue CLP Low Threshold:  60% UBR/ABR Queue CLP Low/EPD Threshold:60%
nrt-VBR Queue EFCI Threshold: 60%     UBR/ABR Queue EFCI Threshold:      20%



Last Command: dspportq 1.2

Next Command:
```

Configurable Port Queue Parameters

Configurable port queue parameter options are listed in Table 13-7.

Table 13-7   *Configurable Port Queue Parameters*

Parameter	Description	Default
slot.port[*.vport*]	The BXM card slot and port number. Also indicates the port status as Active, Inactive, or Failed.	Display only
Interface	The type of back card.	Display only
Type	Specifies whether the cell header format is NNI or UNI.	Display only
Bandwidth	Configured port speed in cps.	Display only
CBR Queue Depth	Maximum depth of the CBR QBin. The range is 0 to 228,300 cells for OC-3c/ and 0 to 195,500 cells for T3/E3 and STM1OC-12c/STM4.	E3/T3: 400 cells OC-3c/STM-1: 600 cells OC-12c/STM-4: 1200 cells
rt-VBR Queue Depth	Maximum depth of the rt-VBR QBin. The range is 0 to 228,300 cells for OC-3c/ and 0 to 195,500 cells for T3/E3 and STM1OC-12c/STM4.	E3/T3: 5000 cells OC-3c/STM-1: 5000 cells OC-12c/STM-4: 10,000 cells
nrt-VBR Queue Depth	Maximum depth of the nrt-VBR QBin. The range is 0 to 228,300 cells for OC-3c/ and 0 to 195,500 cells for T3/E3 and STM1OC-12c/STM4.	E3/T3: 5000 cells OC-3c/STM-1: 5000 cells OC-12c/STM-4: 10,000 cells
UBR/ABR Queue Depth	Maximum depth of the UBR/ABR QBin. The range is 0 to 228,300 cells for OC-3c/ and 0 to 195,500 cells for T3/E3 and STM1OC-12c/STM4.	E3/T3: 10,000 cells OC-3c/STM-1: 20,000 cells OC-12c/STM-4: 40,000 cells
CLP High Threshold	Threshold above which arriving cells tagged with CLP = 1 are discarded. Defined as a percentage of the queue depth (0 to 100).	80%

continues

Table 13-7   *Configurable Port Queue Parameters (Continued)*

Parameter	Description	Default
CLP Low/EPD Threshold	Threshold below which arriving cells tagged with CLP = 1 are enqueued. Or, if Early Packet Discard is enabled, invokes frame discard. Defined as a percentage of the queue depth (0 to 100).	60%
EFCI Threshold	Threshold above which arriving cells are marked with EFCI = 1. Defined as a percentage of the queue depth (0 to 100).	60% for CBR, rt-VBR, nrt-VBR 20% for ABR/UBR
VC Shape	Defines whether VC traffic shaping is enabled or disabled by QBin type.	Disabled

dnport Command

If you want to down (deactivate) a port, use the **dnport** command. Note that before you down a port, all connections must be removed from the port.

delport Command

If you want to delete a downed (deactivated) port, use the **delport** command on the downed port. You must first down the port using the **dnport** command (as just described) before you can delete it.

Steps for Activating, Configuring, and Deactivating ATM Ports

Follow these steps to activate, configure, and deactivate an ATM port on a BXM card:

Step 1   At the Next Command prompt, enter **dspcd** *<slot>* to verify that features such as VC (traffic) shaping and BXM firmware-resident LMI/ILMI support are available. This displays a card's status, revision, and serial number. If a back card is present, its type, revision, and serial number appear.

Step 2   Enter **dsplns** to verify that the line you want to use is active and free of alarms. This displays the access lines that are currently activated.

Step 3   Enter **addport** <*slot.port*>[.<*vport*>], where **port** is the physical line number and **vport** is the virtual port identifier (1 to 31). For now, you can accept all the defaults, because you will configure the port in Step 7. This creates a new physical or virtual port with a status of Inactive.

Step 4   If you have created a virtual port, enter **cnfport** <*slot.port*>[.<*vport*>] [*VPI range*] [<*parameters*>] to configure it. This defines the range of VPIs that are associated with the virtual port.

Step 5   Enter **upport** <*slot.port*>[.<*vport*>] to activate the port. This displays the newly upped port. Initially the Status is Active, but this changes to a Failed state after about 10 seconds if the line is in alarm.

Step 6   Enter **dspport** <*slot.port*>[.<*vport*>] for the port you just upped. This displays the port's detailed configuration. A new port has the default values.

Step 7   Enter **dspports** <*slot*> to review the card's port configuration summary. This displays the port's detailed configuration. A new port has the default values.

Step 8   Review the port configuration to ensure compatibility with the attached user equipment. If necessary, use the **cnfport** command to make any changes. This displays the modified port configuration.

Step 9   Enter **dspportq** <*slot.port*>[.<*vport*>]. This displays a detailed configuration for the port queues (QBins). A new port has the default values.

Step 10   Review the port queue configuration to ensure correct settings of queue depths, thresholds, and VC traffic shaping. If necessary, use the **cnfportq** command to make any changes. This displays the modified port queue configuration.

Step 11   Repeat Steps 1 through 10 for each ATM port that is to be activated on the card.

Step 12   If you want to down the port, enter **dnport** <*slot.port*>[.<*vport*>]. This deactivates the port.

Step 13   If you want to delete the port, enter **delport** <*slot.port*>[.<*vport*>] on the downed port. This deletes the deactivated port.

Step 14   Enter **bye**. You are returned to the login command prompt.

Monitoring and Resolving ATM Port Failures

In this section, you learn how to use the CLI to monitor and resolve failures and alarms on a BPX ATM port.

A failure of an ATM port is failure of the physical access line. Line failure can be caused by any of several physical problems that result in a major alarm.

If a port is configured for a signaling protocol (LMI or ILMI) and the attached device is either unconfigured or configured incorrectly, eventually the signal protocol will fail and the BPX switch will indicate a minor alarm for "ATM Port Communication Failed." Although this causes port failures, user traffic can still pass between the switch and the CPE.

Commands for Monitoring ATM Port Failures

This section describes the BPX CLI commands for monitoring and resolving BPX ATM port alarms.

The commands listed in Table 13-8 are discussed in this section. The table describes each command and the privilege level necessary to issue it.

Table 13-8   *ATM Port Commands*

Command	Description	Privilege Level
dspalms	Display alarms. Displays an alarm summary for the node.	6
dspportstats	Display port statistics. Displays historical and real-time ATM port statistics.	6
dsplmistats	Display LMI statistics. Displays LMI or ILMI statistics for a port that has been configured with a signaling protocol.	6
clrportstats	Clear ATM port statistics. Clears ATM statistics counters for one or all ports on a node.	5

dspalms Command

The **dspalms** command displays major and minor alarms throughout the network and more specific alarms at the local node.

Here is the **dspalms** command syntax:

```
dspalms
```

After dealing with a line failure, our sample node still has a minor alarm, so we use the **dspalms** command, as shown in Example 13-10. This command shows that one or more ATM ports are reporting a communications failure due to a breakdown of the signaling protocol.

Example 13-10 dspalms *Command*

```
hei1bpx1          TN     Teacher:1      BPX 8620  9.3.XX    Feb. 14 200X 13:16 PST

Alarm summary    (Configured alarm slots: None)
Connections Failed:       None
TRK Alarms:               None
Line Alarms:              None
Cards Failed:             None                  ATM Port Communication Failed
Slots Alarmed:            None
Missing Cards:            None
Remote Node Alarms:       None
APS Alarms:               None

Interface Shelf Alarms: None
ASM Alarms:               None




Last Command: dspalms


Next Command:

                  SW CD                                        MINOR ALARM
```

dspportstats Command

This command displays the accumulated statistics for a single port.

Here is the **dspportstats** command syntax:

```
dspportstats <slot.port> [interval]
```

interval is the refresh rate in seconds. The default is 10 seconds; the range is 1 to 60 seconds.

The **dspportstats** screen, shown in Example 13-11, provides detailed historical and real-time statistics for an ATM port. Use this command to display the traffic being transmitted to and received from the attached end-user device. By default, all statistics screens update every 10 seconds. An optional parameter entered after the port number can define an update interval in seconds.

Because the statistics are historical, you might want to clear them using the **clrportstats** command before beginning your testing or troubleshooting.

Example 13-11 dspportstats *Command*

```
hei1bpx1          TN    Teacher:1        BPX 8620  9.3.XX    Feb. 14 200X 13:16 PST

Port Statistics for 1.2           Cleared: Mar.  8 2001 14:48
Port Speed: 353208 cps  Collection Time: 0 day(s) 00:15:06      Corrupted: NO


              Cells           CLP          (EFCI)
Rx Port:          0             0            --
Tx Port:        276             0            --

Unknown Addr  :         2  Rx OAM Cells  :       0  Rx Clp 0 Cells:        0
Rx Clp 0 Dscd :         0  Rx Clp 1 Dscd :       0  Tx Clp 0 Cells:      276
Tx OAM Cells  :       278  Rx RM Count   :       0  Tx RM Count   :        0
Lst Unk VpiVci:     0.0


This Command: dspportstats 1.2 1


Hit DEL key to quit:

                  SW CD                                        MAJOR ALARM
```

Information provided by the **dspportstats** screen is as follows:

- **Cleared**—The time since the port statistics were last cleared with the **clrportstats** command.

- **Collection time**—The time since the port was initially activated (**upport**) or since the last **clrportstats** command.

- **Corrupted**—A Yes in this field indicates that a software loopback or a test has been run on this port. In such a case, the statistics might not be 100 percent reliable. (This can be cleared using the **clrportstats** command.)

- **Rx Port Cells**—The number of cells received from the end-user device.

- **Tx Port Cells**—The number of cells transmitted to the end-user device.

- **Rx Port CLP**—The number of cells received from the end-user device with the CLP bit set to 1.

- **Tx Port CLP**—The number of cells transmitted to the end-user device with the CLP bit set to 1. This number does not imply that the BPX node has set the CLP bit to 1.

- **Unknown Addr**—A received cell was discarded because the VPI and VCI were unknown. Discard often happens because the end-user equipment has a PVC specified that has not been added to the BPX network. A mismatch in signaling protocols is also indicated by an unknown VPI/VCI.

- **Rx and Tx OAM Cells**—A count of the OAM cells received from and transmitted to the attached equipment. This count includes any type of OAM cell, such as Alarm Indicator Signal (AIS) and Far-End Receive Failure (FERF).

- **Rx and Tx CLP 0 Cells**—The number of cells received and transmitted with the CLP bit set to 0.

- **Rx CLP 0 Dscd**—The number of cells discarded by the port that had the CLP bit set to 0. These cells were discarded as the result of per-card QBin (slot server) overflows.

- **Rx CLP 1 Dscd**—The number of cells received with the CLP bit set to 1 that were discarded. This number implies that the cells were tagged with the CLP bit outside the BPX network, not by the BPX network.

- **Rx and Tx RM Count**—The number of Resource Management (RM) cells received and transmitted. These RM cells are used if the Flow Control External Segment (FCES) feature is enabled on a standard ABR connection.

- **Lst Unk VpiVci**—The VPI and VCI of the last unknown cell with a VPI/VCI that is unknown (to the BPX switch).

dsplmistats Command

The **dsplmistats** command displays the accumulated LMI or ILMI statistics for a single port.

Here is the **dsplmistats** command syntax:

```
dsplmistats <slot.port> [interval]
```

interval is the refresh rate in seconds. The default is 10 seconds; the range is 1 to 60 seconds.

You can use the **dsplmistats** command to verify the operation of the signaling protocol. The same command is used for ports that are configured for the LMI or ILMI protocol. Example 13-12 shows the **dsplmistats** screen for a port configured with LMI. The lack of any statistics in the Receive direction (from the CPE) indicates that there is a mismatch in the protocol control configuration.

Example 13-12 dsplmistats *Command*

```
hei1bpx1          TN    Teacher:1        BPX 8620  9.3.XX    Feb. 14 200X 13:16 PST

LMI Statistics for slot:1 port:2   Cleared:  Mar. 7 200X  14:48
Collection Time:   0 day(s) 00:19:20   Corrupted: :        NO
VPI.VCI:        0.31
Status     Rx:              0         Status     Tx:              0
UpdtStatus Rx:              0         UpdtStatus Tx:              5
Status Enq Rx:             0         Status Enq Tx:            117
Status Ack Rx:             0         Status Ack Tx:              0
```

continues

Example 13-12 dsplmistats *Command (Continued)*

```
Invalid PDU Rx:              0      ==Debug Info==
Invalid PDU Len Rx:          0      Egress Status:      31607C0C
Unknown PDU Rx:              0      Ingress Status:     315E1970
Invalid I.E. Rx:             0
Invalid Transaction:         0




This Command: dsplmistats 1.2 1


Hit DEL key to quit:

                                                        MAJOR ALARM
```

The **dsplmistats** screen provides the following information for an LMI port (this list also includes command output information that is not shown in Example 13-12):

- **Cleared**—The time since the port statistics were last cleared with the **clrportstats** command.

- **Collection time**—The time since the port was initially activated (**upport**) or since the last **clrportstats** command.

- **Corrupted**—A Yes in this field indicates that a software loopback or a test has been run on this port. In such a case, the statistics might not be 100 percent reliable. The test in this case is the test connection command.

- **VPI.VCI**—The channel dedicated for the ILMI protocol; 0.16 is the default.

- **GetRequest Rx and Tx**—The number of Get messages received from and sent to the attached end-user device.

- **GetResp Rx and Tx**—The number of Response messages received and transmitted. A Get Response message is expected after the transmission of a Get Request, a Get Next, or a Set message.

- **GetNextReq Rx and Tx**—The number of Get Next messages received and transmitted.

- **SetRequest Rx and Tx**—The number of Set messages received and transmitted. A Set operation is used to modify information in the MIB.

- **Trap Rx and Tx**—The number of traps received and transmitted. Traps are used to report extraordinary events.

- **Unknown PDU received**—An SNMP message received from the attached end-user device that was in error.

clrportstats Command

The **clrportstats** command clears the accumulated statistics counts for a single port or for all ports on a node. Statistics collection then resumes for the port(s).

Here is the **clrportstats** command syntax:

```
clrportstats <slot.port | *>
```

* indicates all ports on this node.

Steps for Monitoring and Resolving ATM Port Failures

Follow these steps to monitor and resolve port failure and alarms on a BPX node. This procedure assumes that at least one node in the network has a current active port failure or alarm:

Step 1 At the Next Command prompt, enter **dspports**. Verify which ports, if any, have failed. This displays a summary status of all ports activated on the node.

Step 2 Enter **dsplns** to verify whether the associated line(s) have a major alarm. This displays the current status of all lines on the node: Clear, Major, or Minor alarm.

Step 3 If the line has failed, resolve the cause before proceeding.

Step 4 Enter **dspalms** and verify whether the node has an ATM Port Communication Failed minor alarm. ATM port communication failure is indicated by a message on the right side of the **dspalms** screen.

Step 5 If no ATM port failure is indicated, proceed to Step 10; otherwise, continue with Step 6.

Step 6 Enter **cnfport** <*slot.port*> * * **n** to turn off the signaling protocol on the port. This displays the modified port configuration with Protocol NONE.

Step 7 Wait about 15 seconds, and then enter **dspalms**. This displays the current alarm status.

Step 8 Verify that the Port Communication Failure alarm has disappeared.

Step 9 Investigate the signaling protocol configuration at the CPE, and make any necessary changes at the CPE.

Step 10 To display the accumulated statistics for a single port, enter **dspportstats** <*slot.port*>. Examine the statistics. When finished, enter **clrportstats** <*slot.port*> to clear the statistics. This displays the accumulated statistics counters for the port, including LMI/ILMI statistics.

Step 11 If necessary, re-enable the signal protocol on the BXM port. Ensure that polling is enabled, and for ILMI, enable traps. This displays the modified port configuration with Protocol LMI or ILMI.

Step 12 Enter **dsplmistats** *<slot.port>* **1** to display the LMI/ILMI statistics with a 1-second refresh rate. This displays the LMI/ILMI statistics for the port.

Step 13 Verify that the statistics increment at the correct intervals according to the protocol timer settings.

Step 14 Enter **bye**. This terminates your CLI session and returns you to the login prompt.

Summary

After completing this chapter, you should be able to activate and configure ATM ports on the BPX switch and describe the operation of the LMI and ILMI signaling protocols. You should be able to monitor and resolve port failures and alarms and verify that a port is operating correctly.

Review Questions

1 Mark the following statements as true or false.

A. _____ Each BXM port has 16 QBins.

B. _____ Each BPX ATM port has four QBins.

C. _____ The CLP and EFCI threshold both control congestion marking.

D. _____ The CLP threshold controls cell discard, and the EFCI threshold controls congestion marking.

E. _____ Egress and ingress queues share a common buffer space.

F. _____ Dedicated ATM QBins are provided for CBR, VBR, UBR, and ABR traffic.

2 What is the purpose of traffic shaping?

A. To eliminate congestion at the egress port

B. To eliminate excessive burstiness and jitter

C. To ensure that QBin thresholds are not exceeded

D. To guarantee that traffic is delivered to the CPE at PCR

E. To separate CBR, VBR, ABR, and UBR traffic in the egress queues

3 You have upped the port, but it fails after several seconds. What could be the possible reasons for this?

A. A breakdown of the LMI or ILMI.

B. The LMI or ILMI is not activated.

C. The port is UNI but the attached router is NNI.

D. The line is in alarm.

4 Mark the following statements as true or false.

A. _____ LMI is based on SNMP.

B. _____ Both LMI and ILMI are signaling protocols.

C. _____ A signaling protocol must be activated on an ATM port.

D. _____ On the BXM, ILMI has a fixed, preset VPI and VCI.

E. _____ The purpose of a signaling protocol is to exchange alarm information between two BPX nodes.

5 Match the following commands with their functions:

A. **dnln**   1. Activates a port

B. **upport**   2. Deactivates a line

C. **dsplns**   3. Lists all lines on the node

D. **cnfport**   4. Displays the QBin characteristics

E. **dsplncnf**   5. Shows the configuration of a single line

F. **dspports**   6. Displays all ports on the node or on a card

G. **dspportq**   7. Modifies a port, including the signaling protocol

6 For which of the following reasons would you display port statistics?

A. To find out if a user connection is in alarm

B. To check if LMI frames or OAM cells are being received by the port

C. To learn the number of cells transmitted on a given network trunk

D. To confirm that frames or cells are being sent to the attached user equipment

7 What does it mean when the corrupted field on the port or channel statistics screens is Yes?

A. The port has an LMI failure.

B. The statistics were collected too long ago and are no longer correct.

C. A loopback or test has been run since the last time the statistics were cleared.

D. The node has had a major alarm since the last time the statistics were cleared.

8   Why would a BPX ATM port report an unknown VPI/VCI cell?

A. The attached end-user equipment has failed.

B. The attached end-user equipment has sent a cell using a reserved VPI or VCI.

C. A connection on the BPX service node is not routed through the network because no addressing resources are available.

D. The attached end-user equipment has sent a cell with a VPI/VCI, and there is no corresponding connection on the port.

9   Mark the following statements as true or false.

A. _____ When a statistics field reaches its maximum size, it resets to 0.

B. _____ You can display detailed signaling protocol statistics using the **dspportstats** command.

C. _____ Both the port and channel statistics can be viewed using an optionally configurable update timer.

D. _____ All port and channel statistics are cleared automatically based on a configurable network timer.

10   What does a channel's percent utilization statistic measure?

A. The connection's configured percent utilization

B. A comparison of the traffic rate to the PCR

C. A comparison of the traffic rate to the MCR

D. A comparison of the traffic rate to the PCR or MCR, depending on the connection type

This chapter covers the following key topics:

- ATM Connections
- ATM Connection Types
- Traffic Management Overview
- Traffic Policing
- VC Queues
- Frame-Based Traffic Control
- Standard ABR
- ABR with ForeSight
- ATM-to-Frame Relay Interworking
- Multicast Services
- Establishing and Configuring ATM Connections
- Monitoring ATM Connections
- Determining Connection Routes

Configuring ATM Connections and Routing AutoRoute Connections

In this chapter, you will learn how to establish, configure, and monitor the ATM and interworking connections that transport user traffic across the BPX backbone network. Connections need to be established and correctly configured to support user traffic.

This chapter introduces you to how the BPX node uses AutoRoute to determine how a connection routes in the network, and what the bandwidth requirements are for a connection.

This chapter also explores the trunk load model and its role in allocating connection bandwidth. It examines automatic connection routing and the assigning of specific routes for connections.

NOTE   This chapter deals primarily with AutoRoute. Other types of routing across a BPX network (such as MPLS and PNNI) are handled by external controllers (such as the SES and LSC) and are covered in other books and in Cisco training courses.

ATM Connections

This section introduces the term *ATM connection* as used in a BPX switch.

ATM Connection Definition

A *connection* is a point-to-point permanent virtual circuit (PVC). A PVC is a static connection (it does not change, regardless of network events or changes) between two ports on an ATM switch or between two ports on separate switches. A PVC requires administrative action to be established, typically by a network administrator using a command-line interface (CLI) or network management tool such as a Cisco WAN Manager (CWM) station. As soon as a

PVC is in place, it remains in place unless specifically removed by management action. The switch ports and the set of resources on the ports that have been allocated to the connection also remain dedicated for the lifetime of the PVC.

To confuse matters, many Frame Relay and ATM networks use the term *PVC* to refer to a dynamically routed virtual circuit. The BPX is an example of such a network.

ATM connections that originate on a BXM port on a BPX switch can terminate on another BXM port or on an ATM or Frame Relay port on edge switches (MGX 8220, 8230, 8250, 8850 PXM1, or IGX) on ATM or FR ports. Multiple connections can terminate on a single port and are differentiated by their assigned VPI and VCI.

Figure 14-1 shows some of the connection types that can be provisioned. This chapter is concerned with PVCs only. Other connection types, including Switched Virtual Circuits (SVCs) and Soft PVCs (SPVCs), are described in Chapter 19, "Connection Types."

Figure 14-1 *ATM Connection Definition*

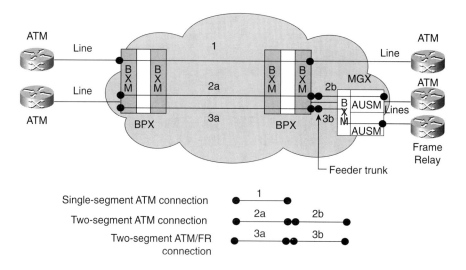

Figure 14-1 shows three types of ATM connections:

- **Single-segment connection**—This connection links two channels on BXM ports. A *channel* defines one end of a PVC, so a connection links a *local channel* and a *remote channel,* each of which is identified by a VPI/VCI. In this example, the channels are defined on different BXM ports on different switches. This need not be the case; the local and remote channels could be defined on the same BPX switch—even on the same port (as long as the VPI and VCI assigned to each channel are unique). The connection terminates at the BXM port; it does not extend to the user device. In fact, a user device need not even be attached for a connection to be configured and activated.

- **Two-segment ATM connection**—This connection originates on a BXM port and terminates at an ATM port on an MGX 8230/8250/8220 feeder node (or vice versa). This really consists of two concatenated PVCs—one between the local BXM port and the port at which the MGX feeder trunk is connected (2a in the figure), and a second (2b) between the Processor Switch Module (PXM) trunk port on the feeder node and the ATM UNI Service Module (AUSM) port.

- **Two-segment ATM interworking connection**—This connection originates on a BXM port and terminates at a Frame Relay port on an MGX 8230/8250 feeder node (or vice versa). This also consists of two concatenated PVCs, with the second one terminating at a port on a Frame Relay Service Module. Interworking defines the process by which ATM cells are converted into Frame Relay frames, and vice versa. It is described in the section, "ATM-to-Frame Relay Interworking."

A connection segment in a BPX network can consist of many underlying, concatenated logical connections if the data path traverses multiple switches. For example, even if there are five intermediate switches between the originating and terminating BPX ports, the switch software still treats this as a single-segment connection.

There can also be three-segment connections, in which the connection originates on an MGX feeder port, travels via a BPX network, and terminates at a feeder port on a different MGX concentrator. In this case, the connection consists of two feeder segments and a switch (BPX) segment.

NOTE   Connections can be configured using the CLI or the graphical Connection Manager application included with the Cisco WAN Manager (CWM) station.

ATM Connection Types

Several different types of ATM connections are supported on the BPX node. When a connection is added to the network, a connection type must be specified. The type depends on the device that created the ATM cells and the applications that are carried in the cells. It is important to remember that the network is responsible for transporting and managing the user data, but it does not have any knowledge of the cell payload or the end-user application. It is up to you, as the administrator, to appropriately define the connection type.

Connection types are not specifically dependent on the ATM Adaptation Layer (AAL) used to create the cells. However, because the different AALs are defined for use with particular types of traffic, such as voice or LAN interconnect, you will often apply similar AALs to the same connection type.

Constant Bit Rate

Constant Bit Rate (CBR) traffic is used for time-dependent constant-rate traffic, such as uncompressed voice, video, or synchronous data. A few allowances are made to accommodate burstiness on CBR connections. Most often, CBR connections carry cells that were created using AAL1.

Variable Bit Rate

Variable Bit Rate (VBR) traffic is used for bursty traffic that might have some time dependency, such as compressed voice, video, or synchronous data. Traffic is permitted to burst within set limitations. VBR connections can support any variable-rate application, but they are used most often for AAL5 cells.

Two types of VBR traffic exist: nonreal-time VBR (nrt-VBR) and real-time VBR (rt-VBR). Nrt-VBR is appropriate for applications that can tolerate some delay, and rt-VBR is for traffic that cannot tolerate delay.

Available Bit Rate

Available Bit Rate (ABR) traffic is a variation on VBR. It is most commonly used for LAN-WAN services, such as router traffic. ABR traffic, like VBR traffic, supports variable-rate applications. The added function of ABR connections allows you to adjust the data rates to accommodate for congestion and bandwidth availability in the network.

There are two types of ABR connections in a BPX network: standard ABR and ForeSight. Both types of ABR connections are typically used to support AAL5 ATM cells.

- **Standard ABR**—The BXM card module supports standard ABR connections as defined by the ATM Forum's Traffic Management 4.0 (TM 4.0) recommendation.

- **ForeSight**—BXM cards support the Cisco prestandard ABR using the ForeSight feature. Similar to standard ABR, the ForeSight feature dynamically manages variable-rate traffic based on the availability of network resources.

Unspecified Bit Rate

Unspecified Bit Rate (UBR) connections are variable-rate connections without a guaranteed service rate. In other words, if there is congestion or no available bandwidth, a UBR connection is not given bandwidth in the network. UBR connections are for variable-rate applications that can tolerate zero-transmission periods, such as batch-processed e-mail or LAN emulation services.

Traffic Management Overview

This section provides an overview of the various mechanisms for ATM traffic management that are supported on the BPX switch. More detailed descriptions of certain functions are included in other chapters.

The Role of Traffic Management

For most service providers today, the great majority of applications running over their networks, whether data, video, or voice, are based on traffic flows that tend to be bursty in nature rather than constant and predictable. The challenge for the network designer is to engineer a backbone network that accommodates these statistical traffic bursts while minimizing data loss (in other words, while maintaining a low Cell Loss Ratio [CLR]).

Consequently, sophisticated traffic management schemes are important to control access to the network (traffic control) and to deal with any congestive conditions that might result from excess bursts (congestion control).

Traffic Control Mechanisms

Traffic control is primarily concerned with ensuring that user connections are "well-behaved," in the sense of verifying that a connection is eligible for admittance to the network, and that once admitted, it remains in compliance with the agreed-upon traffic contract.

Traffic Contract

The traffic contract is specific to a particular user connection and consists of several parameters that describe the characteristics of the traffic source. The traffic contract defines the following:

- **Traffic class or category**—The ATM service type or category described earlier: CBR, rt-VBR, nrt-VBR, ABR, or UBR.

- **Traffic parameters**—Depending on the traffic class, these parameters include the Peak Cell Rate (PCR), Sustainable Cell Rate (SCR), Maximum Burst Size (MBS), Minimum Cell Rate (MCR), and Cell Delay Variation Tolerance (CDVT). Traffic parameters are agreed on with the user and can be configured by the network administrator.

- **Quality of service (QoS) parameters**—Depending on the traffic class, one or more of these parameters apply: peak-to-peak Cell Delay Variation (CDV), Cell Transfer Delay (CTD), Cell Loss Ratio (CLR), and Cell Error Ratio (CER). QoS parameter values are implicit in the network design for each traffic class and typically cannot be configured.

ATM Service Categories

The following summarizes the application of ATM service categories:

- CBR service is typically used for uncompressed voice and video.
- rt-VBR service is typically used for compressed voice.
- nrt-VBR service is typically used for LAN traffic.
- ABR service is typically used for Frame Relay.
- UBR service is typically used for file transfer.

Connection Admission Control

Connection Admission Control (CAC) is the process taken by the network at the time of connection setup (or during a subsequent configuration change) to determine whether the connection can be accepted into the network given the available bandwidth, the requested QoS, and the QoS requirements of the existing connections. CAC is applied on ports and trunks in the network, as shown in Figure 14-2.

Figure 14-2 *CAC Process*

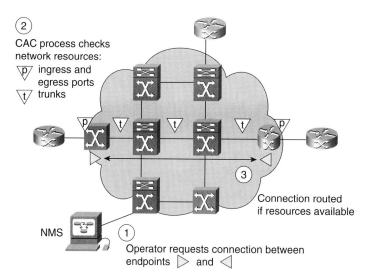

The BPX switch implements a CAC scheme that varies according to the requested service type.

BXM ports have a CAC override function that, if enabled, allows oversubscription of the port. This means that you can add more connections than the physical bandwidth of the port can support. If CAC override is disabled, the switch software does not permit you to add a new connection or change an existing one if the new total bandwidth in cells per second becomes greater than the configured port rate.

CAC override is enabled or disabled using the **cnfport** command. You can optionally oversubscribe ports. All trunks also use CAC and can be oversubscribed through the use of percentage utilization on connections.

Usage Parameter Control

As soon as a connection is admitted to the network, it can optionally be subjected to Usage Parameter Control (UPC), which is the standard term for network policing. UPC is a set of algorithms performed by an ATM switch upon the receipt of cells within a connection that determines whether the cell stream complies with the traffic contract. Cells on compliant connections might be discarded immediately or *tagged* for potential discard elsewhere in the network.

The policing function is at the ingress point to the network. If enabled for the particular connection, it occurs prior to any buffering or queuing. Figure 14-3 shows the location of the policing function in relation to the ingress queue structures on the BXM card.

Figure 14-3 *BXM Ingress Queues*

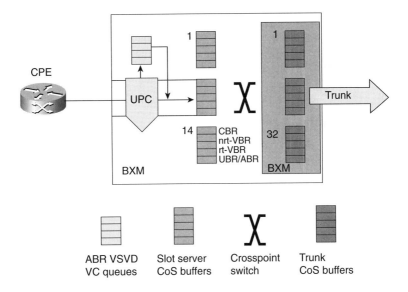

Traffic Shaping

Traffic shaping is the metering or smoothing of the flow of cells into (or out of) the network so that a connection conforms to its defined traffic parameters. Traffic shaping increases the efficiency of allocating network resources by introducing a more deterministic traffic pattern and a reduction in burstiness. It also reduces intercell jitter (variability of arrival times) by controlling the CDV.

Many ATM user devices, including Cisco LAN switches and routers, include traffic shaping. The BPX switch implements traffic shaping at the egress ports, as shown in Figure 14-4.

Figure 14-4 *Traffic Shaping Functions*

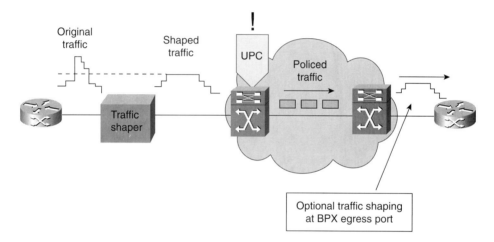

Congestion Control Mechanisms

Although CAC, policing, and traffic shaping are important to ensure that individual user connections remain compliant with their traffic contracts, they are effectively network-admission policies that do not consider the actual congestion in the network.

Even in very large networks, there can be periods when all active users individually comply with their contracts but the offered traffic load exceeds the available network resources. In such circumstances, internal network congestion can occur. It is the role of the more sophisticated congestion control schemes to resolve this contention for resources fairly and efficiently.

Several different congestion control mechanisms can be used. These types are listed in ascending order of effectiveness and complexity. The basic objective of congestion control is to minimize the severity and duration of events in the network that cause congestion.

Such events include erratic and unpredictable traffic flows and network faults such as trunk failures.

- **Selective cell discard**—Sometimes called Priority Control, cell discard uses the Cell Loss Priority (CLP) bit in the header of every ATM cell to define the cell's discard eligibility. Cells in which the CLP bit is set to 1 (CLP = 1) are considered lower-priority and therefore are more eligible for discard in cases of network congestion. The CLP bit can be set by the source user end station (SUES) or as a result of policing in the ingress BPX switch.

- **Frame discard**—Frame discard seeks to avoid the worst side effect of cell discard— excessive retransmissions and a high risk of congestive network collapse. It does this by discarding a partial or complete frame rather than individual cells. Whereas dropping random individual cells can affect multiple higher-layer frames and, effectively, multiple users, dropping a single frame tends to result in fewer retransmissions. Two basic forms of frame discard are supported: Partial Packet Discard (PPD) and Early Packet Discard (EPD). PPD is also called Tail Packet Discard (TPD) in some documentation. Both PPD and EPD are also sometimes called Frame-Based Traffic Control (FBTC).

- **Explicit Forward Congestion Indicator (EFCI)**—If the EFCI bit in the cell header is set, network switches can notify the destination end station (DES) of current congestion. Additionally, using a feedback mechanism (described in the section, "ABR Feedback Mechanism"), the system can use EFCI to signal the SES, which (hopefully) will reduce its transmission rate.

- **Relative Rate (RR) EFCI**—Because there is a high probability that the SES might not respond appropriately to EFCI congestion signals, the BPX switch can use the RR messages from the destination side of the network to throttle back the rate at which user cells are accepted (the Allowed Cell Rate [ACR]) into the network on an individual connection basis. RR refers to the difference between the previous ACR and the new ACR, dependent on congestion conditions. The RR approach allows the new ACR to be higher than the old as long as the congestion is absent or below a defined threshold.

- **Explicit Rate (ER)**—The ER approach differs from RR in that the new ACR is an exact cell rate rather than a preconfigured percentage of the old. ER congestion control is quite complex, because each switch in the network path must accurately assess the real-time resource loadings and calculate the ER for each connection. In the BPX switch, ER traffic management is handled by dedicated hardware on the BXM cards.

- **Virtual Source Virtual Destination (VS/VD)**—VS/VD is an extension of the ER scheme in which the network is defined in terms of flow control segments and each segment has a VS and a VD. This allows greater control over traffic management and provides the ability to isolate users and network segments, such as short- and long-haul segments.

The last four schemes listed here are defined as implementation options in the ATM Forum's Traffic Management 4.0 specification. Details of implementing each of these schemes in the BPX switch are discussed in the following sections.

Traffic Policing

This section provides detailed information on how ingress policing is implemented for ATM connections in the BPX switch. All connections, regardless of type, are subjected to policing as the cells enter the network. *Policing* is the process of monitoring ingress traffic to determine whether the traffic can enter and how that traffic is handled as soon as it is inside the network. Each connection has several policing parameters that can include characteristics such as burst sizes and data rates. The end-user device is responsible for meeting the defined policing requirements; otherwise, the traffic is deemed *noncompliant* and can be dropped by the network.

Leaky Bucket Model

The *leaky bucket* model defines policing on ingress for ATM connections on the node. Remember that the leaky bucket is not a queue structure, but a means of describing how the network monitors and controls incoming user cells. The leaky bucket model is discussed in Chapter 5, "Frame Relay Ports and Connections."

Think of the model as a test on the traffic that answers two questions:

- Should the cell be allowed into the network?

- If so, should it be given a normal or low priority (set the CLP bit to 1)?

The implementation of traffic policing in the BPX switch is based on a single or dual leaky bucket implementation, depending on the type of service. In all cases, the underlying algorithm is the Generic Cell Rate Algorithm (GCRA) as defined in the ATM Forum Traffic Management Specification 4.0 (TM 4.0).

The leaky bucket model has three basic components:

- **Token**—Arrives in the bucket at a rate defined by the incoming traffic. For ATM traffic, each cell is represented in the leaky bucket model as a single token. The rate at which the tokens fill the bucket is variable. The actual user-data cell does *not* go into the bucket.

- **Bucket size**—Determines how many tokens can be held before the bucket is full. When the bucket is full, any new tokens represent cells that are noncompliant. Noncompliant cells may be dropped or tagged with a 1 in the CLP field, depending on the situation.

- **Leak rate**—Determines the average acceptable token rate to maintain compliance. If the tokens arrive at approximately the same rate as the leak rate, the bucket never fills up. If the tokens arrive at a rate greater than the leak rate, they eventually become noncompliant. If the tokens arrive at a rate less than the leak rate, the bucket is always empty.

Dual Leaky Bucket Model

Several ATM connection types use a dual leaky bucket model for policing. A dual leaky bucket consists of two different leaky bucket models, each with its own configurable characteristics.

In general, the first leaky bucket is set to discard any noncompliant cells, which means that all incoming traffic must meet the requirements of the first leaky bucket in order to be accepted by the network.

The second leaky bucket can be disabled, it can drop noncompliant cells, or it can *tag* noncompliant cells with CLP = 1. The behavior of the second bucket depends on the configured policing type.

Policing Types

Table 14-1 summarizes the policing types applicable to each ATM service type. This table can be viewed as progressing from most restrictive (type 1) to least restrictive (type 5).

Default policing is type 3 for all connection types except CBR, which is type 4.

The policing types listed in Table 14-1 are associated with connections on the BPX switch only. These types map to the ATM Forum standard service types such as VBR.1, VBR.2, VBR.3, UBR.2, and CBR.1.

Table 14-1 *Policing Types*

BPX Type	Cells Tested in First Bucket	First Bucket Noncompliance Result	Cells Tested in Second Bucket	Second Bucket Noncompliance Result	ATM Forum Equivalent Types
1	All	Discard	CLP = 0 or 1	Discard	VBR.1
2	All	Discard	CLP = 0 only	Discard	VBR.2
3	All	Discard	CLP = 0 only	Tag with CLP	VBR.3, UBR.2
4	All	Discard	None		CBR.1, UBR.1
5	None		None		No policing

Policing Implementation for Different Service Types

The remainder of this section describes how the single or dual leaky bucket policing mechanism is implemented for several of the different ATM service types. In most cases, the same BPX switch policing type can be applied to different service types. For example, Type 4 policing applies for both CBR.1 and UBR.1.

The conformance definition for ABR traffic is left as "implementation-specific" in the TM 4.0 Specification. In the BPX switch, ABR traffic can be policed as type 1, 2, or 3.

CBR Policing Example

CBR traffic is most often configured to use policing type 4, in which the traffic is policed using a single leaky bucket that discards all noncompliant cells. Another option is to use policing type 5, which disables all policing and results in all cells being accepted into the network.

The nature of CBR traffic implies that cells arrive at a constant rate. In other words, the inter-cell time is expected to be constant. However, demanding that cells arrive exactly as expected is unreasonable, because traffic on one physical line might be from many different sources.

Two values determine compliance for CBR cells:

- **Peak Cell Rate (PCR)**—Defines the bucket leak rate
- **Cell Delay Variation Tolerance** (CDVT)—Determines the bucket size

Cells are expected to arrive, on average, at the PCR. However, if they exceed the PCR, the cells are limited to the following variation tolerance defined by the CDVT:

- **Size of first bucket**—CDVT(0 + 1) for cells with CLP = 0 or 1, in microseconds
- **Leak rate of first bucket**—PCR(0 + 1) for cells with CLP = 0 or 1, in cells per second

Time-Based Policing Example

Because it is difficult to visualize a bucket whose size is configured as a time period, you can look at the policing mechanism using the theoretical arrival time. As each cell arrives in the network, it is compared to the expected arrival time (1/PCR), as shown in Figure 14-5. If the cell is early, a penalty is added to the total penalty. The penalty is based on how early the cell is. If the cell is late, a credit is given and is subtracted from the total penalty. If the total penalty exceeds the configured limit (CDVT), the cell is noncompliant and is discarded without adding to the total penalty. The next cell to arrive continues to accumulate penalties or credits.

Figure 14-5 *Time-Based Policing Model*

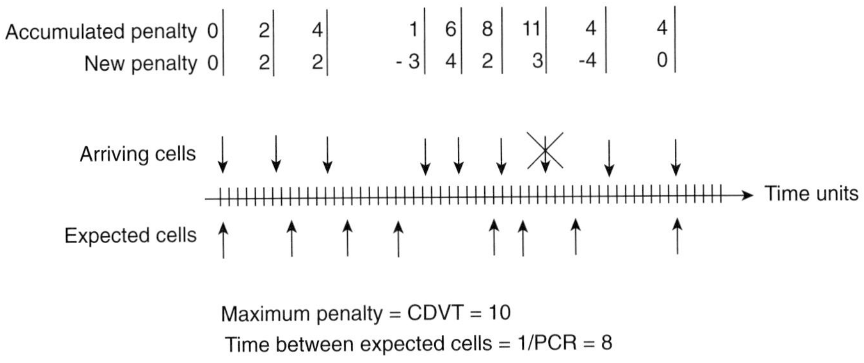

CBR Policing Calculation

When you assign policing values to a connection, it helps if you can determine how large a burst of cells will be allowed into the network at a certain rate before the traffic becomes noncompliant. By using the following equation, you can check whether the values for the CDVT and PCR are reasonable (AR stands for arrival rate):

Number of cells until noncompliance = 1 + CDVT / [1 / PCR − 1 / AR]

This calculation can determine the results of setting the policing parameters (CDVT and PCR). For example, if

- CDVT (0 + 1) = 10,000 microseconds (use seconds in the equation)
- PCR (0 + 1) = 20,000 cells per second

the information in Table 14-2 is true.

Table 14-2 *CBR Policing Calculation*

Arrival Rate (Cells Per Second)	Compliant	Comments
19,000	—	If AR < PCR(0 + 1), no cells are dropped.
21,000	4201	If AR > PCR(0 + 1), a limited number of cells are allowed in before some cells are dropped.
40,000	401	As AR increases, the number of compliant cells decreases.

When the traffic reaches the point where cells are being dropped due to noncompliance, some of the traffic at a rate of the configured PCR is still compliant. However, in most situations, the application fails if any portion of the cells is not successfully transported across the network.

VBR Policing Examples

The three types of policing most often used for VBR connections are 1, 2, and 3, all of which use a dual leaky bucket model. These types are called VBR.1, VBR.2, and VBR.3.

VBR.1

As shown in Figure 14-6, VBR traffic with policing type 1 is implemented using two leaky bucket models, both of which discard noncompliant cells.

Figure 14-6 *VBR.1 Policing*

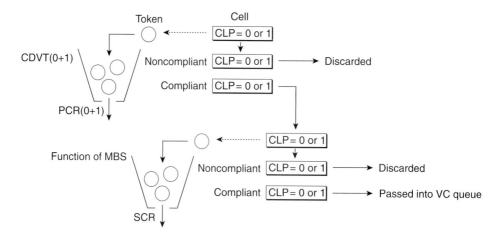

The first leaky bucket functions like CBR traffic, using the PCR(0 + 1) and CDVT(0 + 1) values to limit the flow of cells into the network. The bucket ensures that the network does not receive cells in excess of the peak rate allowed for a given PVC. All noncompliant cells are discarded at the first leaky bucket. Compliant cells are checked by the second leaky bucket.

The second leaky bucket uses the maximum burst size (MBS) and the Sustainable Cell Rate (SCR). The second leaky bucket maintains an average cell rate of SCR while still allowing some burstiness up to the PCR. The MBS is the number of cells that are compliant on the second leaky bucket if the cells arrive at a rate of PCR(0 + 1). All noncompliant cells on the second leaky bucket are discarded.

Here is a summary of the VBR policing parameters:

- **Size of first bucket**—CDVT(0 + 1) for cells with CLP = 0 or CLP = 1, in microseconds
- **Leak rate of first bucket**—PCR(0 + 1) for cells with CLP = 0 or CLP = 1, in cells per second
- **Size of the second bucket**—Based on the MBS, in cells
- **Leak rate of the second bucket**—SCR, in cells per second

VBR.2

Figure 14-7 shows the VBR.2 policing model. VBR traffic configured with policing type 2 uses a dual leaky bucket model, in which both buckets discard noncompliant cells. Unlike VBR.1, VBR.2 checks only cells with CLP set to 0 on the second leaky bucket. As a result, cells tagged with CLP = 1 have an advantage on ingress over cells with CLP = 0. Of course, in the event of network congestion, cells with CLP = 1 are discarded before cells with CLP = 0. In all other ways, VBR.1 and VBR.2 are identical.

Figure 14-7 *VBR.2 Policing*

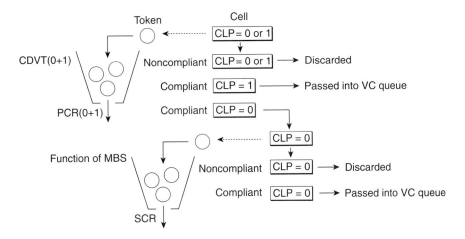

VBR.3

The most commonly used policing type for VBR traffic is type 3, which also uses the dual leaky bucket model, as shown in Figure 14-8. The first bucket checks all cells and discards any that are noncompliant. The second bucket polices cells with CLP = 0 only and tags any noncompliant cells with CLP = 1. Cells already tagged with CLP = 1 are not checked on the second leaky bucket, because they cannot be tagged again. VBR.3 is similar to VBR.2, except that cells are tagged, not dropped on the second leaky bucket.

Figure 14-8 *VBR.3 Policing*

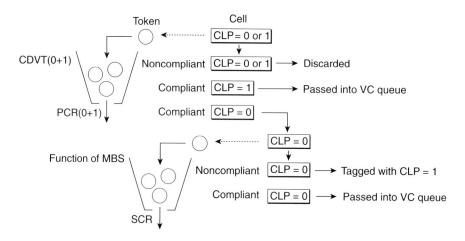

VBR Policing Calculations

All three types of VBR connections—VBR.1, VBR.2, and VBR.3—can use the same equations to determine the effect of configuring the various policing parameters. Similar to the calculation described for CBR traffic earlier in this section, the following equations determine how many cells can enter the network at a defined rate before becoming noncompliant. The results of being noncompliant differ, depending on the policing type applied to the connection.

On the first (PCR) bucket:

Number of cells until noncompliance = 1 + CDVT / [1 / PCR − 1 / AR]

On the second (SCR) bucket:

Number of cells until noncompliance = 1 + {[(MBS − 1) * (1 / SCR − 1 / PCR)] + CDVT} / [1 / SCR − 1 / AR]

These equations can determine the results of setting the policing parameters (CDVT, PCR, MBS, and SCR). For example, if

- Policing type = 3
- CDVT (0 + 1) = 10,000 microseconds (note that this is in seconds in the calculations)
- PCR (0 + 1) = 20,000 cells per second

- MBS = 501 cells
- SCR (0) = 10,000 cells per second

the information in Table 14-3 is true.

NOTE	The CDVT used in these equations is in seconds. In other words, with a CDVT of 10,000 microseconds, you plug in the number .01, not 10000.

Table 14-3   *VBR Policing Calculations*

Arrival Rate (Cells Per Second)	Compliant on First Bucket	Compliant on Second Bucket	Comments
9000	—	—	If AR < PCR(0 + 1) and SCR, all cells are compliant.
11,000	—	2751	If PCR(0 + 1) > AR > SCR, no cells are dropped on the first bucket, but some are tagged CLP = 1 on the second bucket.
19,000	—	528	As the arrival rate increases, the number of cells compliant on the second bucket decreases.
21,000	4201	478	If AR > PCR(0 + 1), a limited number of cells are allowed on the first bucket, and a portion of those go on to be tagged CLP = 1 on the second bucket.
40,000	401	334	As AR increases, the number of compliant cells on the first bucket decreases.

VBR Policing Results

The results of VBR policing can be summarized in graphical form. Figure 14-9 shows the cell rates over time and how the network for a VBR.3 connection treats them if the cell arrival rate (AR) is greater than the configured PCR.

Figure 14-9 *VBR Policing Results with AR > PCR*

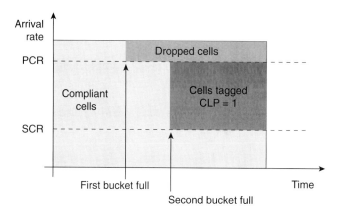

Figure 14-10 shows the results of policing a VBR.3 connection when the arrival rate is less than or equal to the configured PCR. No cells are dropped in this example because the first leaky bucket never fills up at a rate less than the PCR.

Figure 14-10 *VBR Policing Results with AR ≤ PCR*

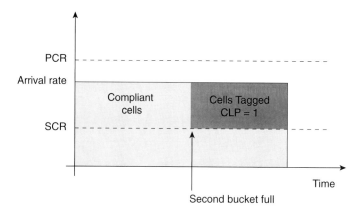

ABR Policing Example

ABR connections, both standard and with the ForeSight feature, are policed in the same fashion as VBR connections based on the policing type selected for the connection. Figure 14-11 shows the policing model for an ABR connection using policing type 3. Notice that the cells are put into a VC queue after being subjected to admission control. The VC queue is used to shape the ABR traffic based on network availability.

Figure 14-11 *ABR Connection Using Policing Type 3*

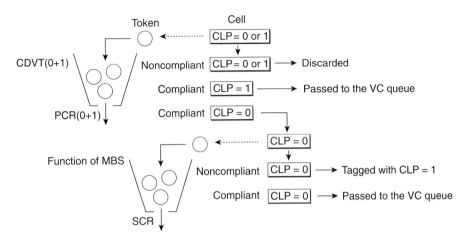

UBR Policing

UBR connections are policed using a single or dual leaky bucket, either with or without CLP tagging enabled.

UBR.2 with CLP Tagging

If a UBR connection is configured with CLP tagging enabled (UBR.2), as shown in Figure 14-12, it is policed like a VBR.3 connection, with an SCR of 0 cells per second. As a result, all cells are tagged with CLP = 1 on the second leaky bucket, giving them a low priority in the network.

Figure 14-12 *UBR.2 with CLP Tagging*

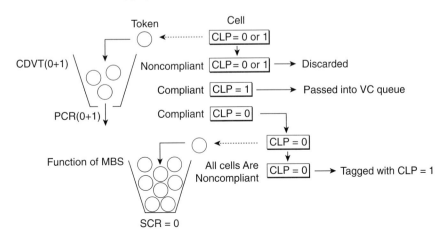

UBR.1 Without CLP Tagging

A UBR connection with CLP tagging disabled (UBR.1) does not use the second leaky bucket (see Figure 14-13). Similar to CBR connections, only the first leaky bucket is used for policing, and all noncompliant cells are dropped.

Figure 14-13 *UBR.1 Without CLP Tagging*

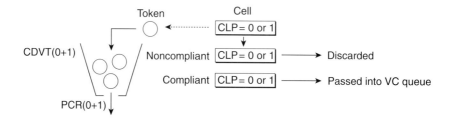

Avoid using UBR.1 if your network supports both UBR and ABR traffic because both service types use the same QBins in the BXM, and UBR.1 can potentially overrun the ABR traffic.

VC Queues

A separate VC queue buffers the cells for each connection after they are policed and before they are switched through the BPX node toward their final destination, as shown in Figure 14-14. The VC queue shapes the traffic as it enters the network. The rate at which the VC queue is serviced is determined by the congestion control messages that are (or should be) received from the destination side of the network.

Figure 14-14 *VC Queue Operation on a BXM Card*

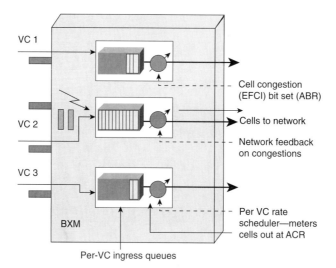

VC Queue Thresholds

The VC queue has several thresholds to mark and respond to congestion:

- **Congestion marking**—The EFCI threshold defines the point where the BPX node tags incoming cells with the EFCI bit.

- **Tagging**—The CLP high and CLP low thresholds determine when CLP tagged cells (CLP = 1) are discarded in the VC queue.

In summary, configurable VC queuing characteristics include the following:

- **VQ queue depth**—The size of the VC queue, in cells, up to approximately 64,000. When the VC queue reaches its configured depth, all arriving cells are discarded.

- **CLP high threshold**—Cell Loss Priority (CLP) is a bit in the ATM cell header that is set either by the originating CPE or by a network switch to identify the cell as being eligible for discard. Cells with CLP set to 1 are *tagged* as being eligible for discard. If traffic enters a particular VC queue at a rate faster than the queue can be serviced, eventually the queue fills up. If the queue reaches the CLP high threshold level (expressed as a percentage of the maximum queue depth), any further cells arriving from the user device with CLP = 1 are discarded. CLP1 cells that are already in the queue are not discarded.

- **CLP low threshold**—Determines when to stop dropping CLP tagged cells. After the VC queue reaches the CLP high threshold, CLP tagged cells are dropped until the queue has been emptied to the level determined by the CLP low threshold. The CLP low threshold is a percentage of the VC queue depth.

- **EFCI threshold**—Determines congestion marking for ABR. When the VC queue reaches the EFCI threshold, the EFCI bit of all cells arriving in the VC queue is set to 1 to notify the end-user equipment of congestion in the network. The EFCI threshold is a percentage of the VC queue depth.

VC queue thresholds are also described in Chapter 6, "ATM Ports and Connections and ATM-to-Frame Relay Interworking."

Frame-Based Traffic Control

Frame-based traffic control (FBTC) allows an ATM device to discard part or all of an AAL5 frame based on predefined criteria. FBTC can be enabled or disabled on VBR, ABR, and UBR connections on the BPX node.

ATM cells that are segmented using AAL5 carry frame-based data. Examples of this data include Frame Relay, TCP/IP, X.25, and HDLC. As shown in Figure 14-15, the cell header format for AAL5 cells includes a single bit that identifies the location of that cell within the original frame. This is the third bit in the Payload Type Indicator (PTI) field of both the UNI and NNI cell headers. If the bit is 0, the cell is either the beginning or continuation of a frame. If the bit is 1, the cell marks the end of the frame.

Figure 14-15 *PTI Field of the ATM Cell Header*

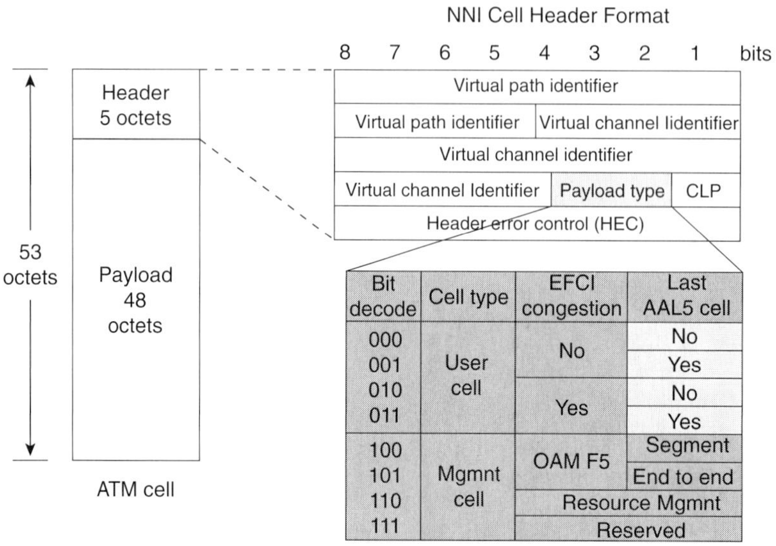

FBTC requires this ability in order to locate the frame boundary—hence the limitation to AAL5, which is the only ATM adaptation layer that currently includes a "last cell of frame" indication.

In general, the motivation behind FBTC is that if part of a frame is discarded (due to policing), the rest of the frame is of no value to the destination device and should also be discarded. Because the destination device depends on the last cell from a frame to delineate between frames, in most cases this cell is not dropped and is sent through to its final destination.

FBTC Implementation on BXM

On the BPX node, FBTC is implemented on the BXM card. The three different implementations of FBTC are described next.

Partial Packet Discard

If a cell must be discarded due to congestion inside the network, Partial Packet Discard (PPD) ensures that subsequent cells of the frame, except for the last cell (marked in the PTI field), are also discarded, as shown in Figure 14-16. PPD is implemented on VC queues, ingress, trunk, and egress QBins. Another variant of PPD is implemented on BXM ingress ports at the VC queues.

Figure 14-16 *Partial Packet Discard*

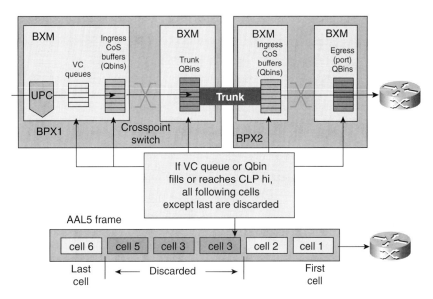

Cells are dropped if the start-of-frame cell arrives when the queue is below the CLP low threshold and subsequent cells fill the queue, or the queue fills to the CLP high threshold and the CLP bit is set to 1 on the cell.

PPD offers better congestion control than cell discard (CLP tagging and discard) for AAL5-based traffic flows. However, it has the inherent inefficiency of allowing partial frames to traverse the network before they get discarded.

Early Packet Discard

If congestion occurs at the beginning of a frame, the entire frame, including the last cell, is discarded. Early Packet Discard (EPD), shown in Figure 14-17, is implemented on the BXM VC queue or QBin if the start-of-frame cell arrives after the queue has filled to the EPD threshold. There is no explicit start-of-frame cell with AAL5; the system deduces the start-of-frame by referring to the previous end-of-frame (EOF) cell.

The EPD threshold is numerically the same value as the configured CLP low threshold on a BXM queue. If the queue depth is below the EPD threshold when the start-of-frame cell arrives, the frame is accepted even if the EPD threshold is subsequently exceeded.

Figure 14-17 *Early Packet Discard*

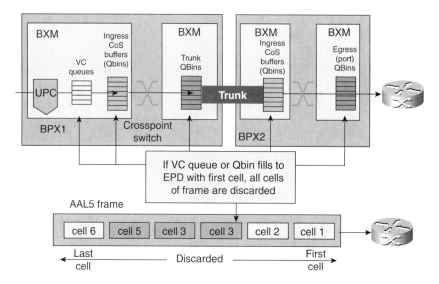

EPD avoids the inefficiency of PPD by attempting to drop complete rather than partial frames. However, in some circumstances, such as very long frames, one or more cells might be accepted into the queue before EPD discard activates. In these cases, the system reverts to the PPD process and discards all subsequent cells except the EOF cell.

Frame-Based Generic Cell Rate Algorithm

The BXM card can optionally be configured to perform PPD as the result of cell discard caused by ingress policing. The PPD operation is the same as previously discussed, except that as soon as PPD is activated on a connection, the discarded cells are not policed (except the first one) and do not enter the VC queue.

This feature, shown in Figure 14-18, is called *FBTC with PPD policing*. It is enabled on a per-node basis using the SuperUser **cnfnodeparm** command.

Figure 14-18 *FBTC with PPD Policing*

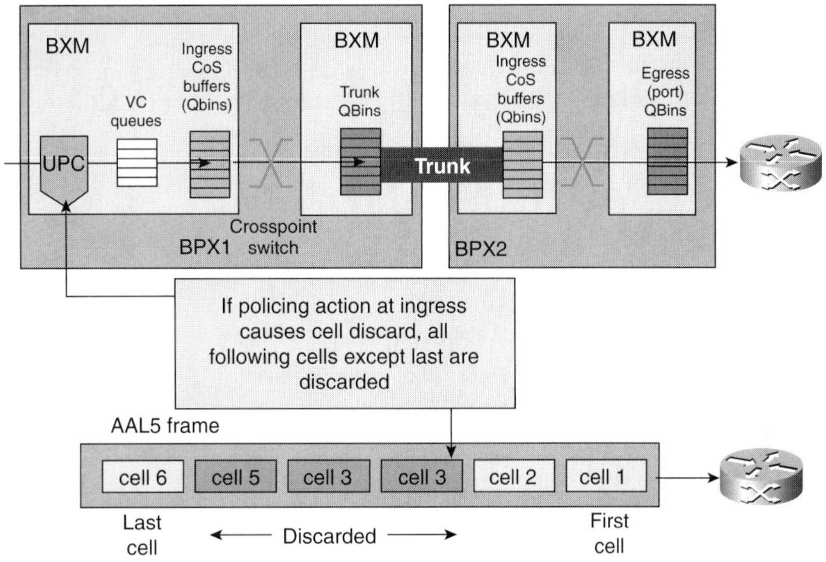

Standard ABR

This section describes the implementation and operation of traffic shaping at ATM Forum Standard ABR Standard on a BPX switch.

ABR is fundamentally different from the other service types in that it includes a feedback mechanism to control network congestion during periods of heavy load. It also optimizes the use of network resources during quieter periods. In the network, ABR traffic is intended to use bandwidth that has not been allocated to CBR and VBR connections.

Each service category is assigned a guaranteed minimum bandwidth to ensure deterministic behavior even under a very heavy load. If additional bandwidth is available, it is dynamically assigned to the service categories that will benefit.

ABR Feedback Mechanism

Two types of ABR connections can be defined in a BPX network: ABR with ForeSight (ABRFST) and standard ABR (ABRSTD). These types differ in the method used to determine the VC queue service rate. Before examining these methods, you should understand how congestion is measured and reported in the BPX network for ABR connections.

ABR connections use a closed-loop mechanism to report and respond to congestion. ABR performs the following functions:

- Data moves from the source to the destination. In addition, control messages flow from source to destination.

- As the traffic (both data and control) travels through the network, the various network elements may mark congestion and other control fields in the cells.

- The destination device collects the congestion and control information and reports this information to the source device.

- The source, after receiving the congestion and control information from the destination, makes the required adjustments in the VC queue service rate.

Resource Management Cells

The feedback mechanism that is implemented for ABR Standard (and ABR ForeSight) in the BPX switch uses a special type of control cell called the Resource Management (RM) cell.

Standard ABR uses an RM cell to measure and report network conditions to determine the virtual circuit queue service rate. Periodically, the source sends an RM cell in the data stream to the destination. Along the way, the BPX network might alter bits in the RM cell to report network conditions and availability. When the destination receives the RM cell, it turns it around and sends it back to the source. When the source receives the RM cell, it adjusts the queue service rate accordingly.

RM cells originate from the source, which, depending on how the network is configured, can be an end station outside the network or an ingress switch. These cells are sometimes called Forward RM (FRM) cells. At the destination (end station or switch), the RM cell is turned around to return on the same connection, but in the reverse direction. These reversed cells are called Backward RM (BRM) cells.

RM Cell Format

Figure 14-19 shows the RM cell format.

Figure 14-19 *RM Cell Format*

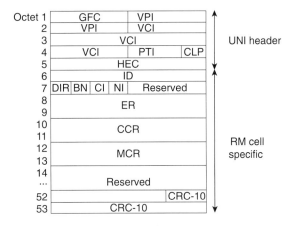

The fields in the RM cell include the following:

- **Generic Flow Control (GFC)**—Always set to 0000.

- **Virtual Path Identifier (VPI)**—The same VPI that the connection uses.

- **Virtual Channel Identifier (VCI)**—If the connection is a virtual channel, the VCI is the same as the connection uses. If the connection is virtual path, the VCI is 6.

- **Payload Type Identifier (PTI)**—Always set to 110 for RM cells.

- **Cell Loss Priority (CLP)**—Set to 0 for in-rate RM cells. Set to 1 for out-of-rate RM cells. Out-of-rate RM cells exceed the Allowed Cell Rate (ACR).

- **Header Error Check (HEC)**—8-bit CRC on cell header only.

- **Protocol Identifier (ID)**—Set to hexadecimal 1 for a standard ATM RM cell. Set to hexadecimal FF for an STI supervisory cell.

- **Direction (DIR)**—Determines the cell's direction, either from source to destination (set to 1) or destination to source (set to 0).

- **Backward Explicit Congestion Notification (BN)**—Determines whether the cell is a switch-generated backward congestion cell (set to 1) or not (set to 0). A BN RM cell is generated by a network element to notify the source of congestion. A BN cell must have either CI or NI set to 1.

- **Congestion Indicator (CI)**—The CI bit is set to 1 by the network if the RM cell experiences congestion.

- **No Increase (NI)**—The NI bit is set to 1 by a network element that cannot allow the connection to increase in rate.

- **Explicit Rate (ER)**—An ER can be defined by a network element to tell the source to use a particular rate.

- **Current Cell Rate (CCR)**—Placed in the RM cell by the source, the CCR is the rate currently being used for the connection.

- **Minimum Cell Rate (MCR)**—Placed in the RM cell by the source, the MCR is the configured minimum allowable rate for the connection.

- **CRC-10**—A 10-bit error detection field on the entire cell.

- **Reserved**—Some bits might be defined but not implemented or might be reserved for future use. Unused octets are set to 6A hex.

RM Cell Generation

RM cells are inserted into the cell stream by the source based on several parameters, some of which can be configured per connection. Figure 14-20 shows how RM and BRM cells are generated.

Figure 14-20 *RM Cell Generation*

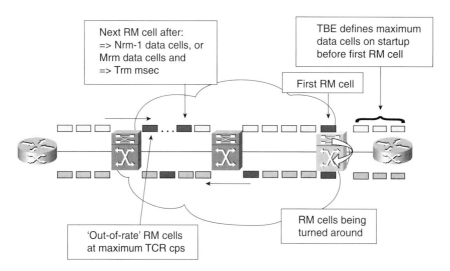

Parameters that determine RM/BRM cell generation are as follows:

- **Transient Buffer Exposure (TBE)**—Defines the number of user cells that can initially be sent by the source at startup before it must wait for a BRM cell from the network. The TBE is configured per PVC and defaults to 1,048,320 cells.

- **Number per RM (Nrm)**—Determines the maximum number of cells a source can send for each forward RM cell. An RM cell must be sent for every Nrm – 1 data cells. The Nrm is configured per PVC and defaults to 32.

- **Minimum per RM (Mrm)**—Defines the minimum number of user cells that can be sent between RM cells. The Mrm cannot be configured and is set to two cells.

- **Time RM (Trm)**—Defines the maximum time between RM cells for an active source. The default is 100 ms.

- **Tagged Cell Rate (TCR)**—The rate at which the source can send out-of-rate RM cells. Out-of-rate RM cells exceed the Allowed Cell Rate (ACR) and are always tagged with a CLP of 1. RM cells are usually sent with CLP = 0 so that out-of-rate RM cells can be generated as "probes" for connections that have a low ACR. The TCR cannot be configured and is set to 10 cells per second.

Operation of Standard ABR in BPX

Operation of standard ABR in the BPX switch uses one or more of the following methods of congestion control:

- EFCI control
- Relative Rate (RR) control
- Explicit Rate (ER) control
- Virtual Source Virtual Destination (VS/VD) control

Each method is described further in the following sections.

EFCI Control

EFCI is the simplest of the four traffic management procedures specified in TM 4.0. In the event of congestion in any of the BXM queues, as indicated by the queue filling to the configured EFCI threshold, the switch starts to set the EFCI bit in the PTI field of the cell header, as shown in Figure 14-21.

The destination end station can modify its cell transmission rate in response to the cells arriving with the active congestion indication. An end station that implements ABR also generates a BRM cell with CI = 1 to tell the source end station to lower its transmission rate to a lower value.

In the case of the BPX network, it is not a wise policy to rely on end stations to respond properly to EFCI. Consequently, this method is implemented, but only for backward compatibility with earlier traffic management schemes.

Figure 14-21 *EFCI Congestion Control*

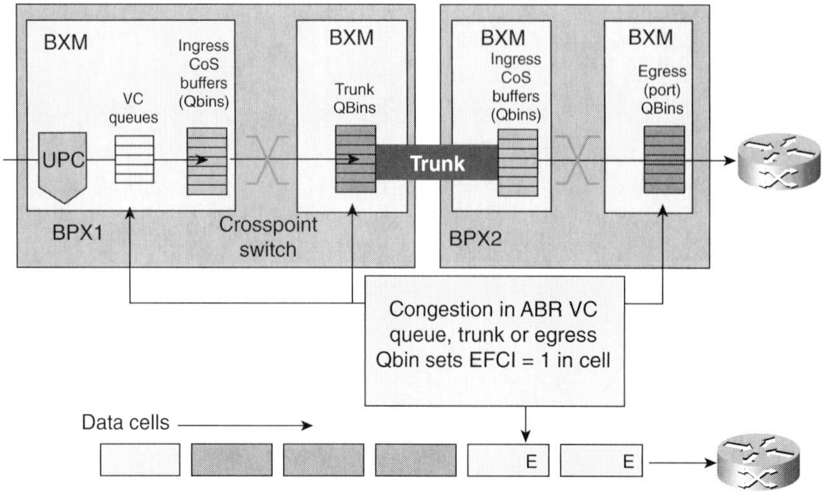

Relative Rate Control

The Relative Rate (RR) control method is an extension of EFCI control that uses the RM/BRM cell to convey congestion information within the network. A network consisting of ATM switches, like the BPX switch, that implements RR control does not depend on the end stations being well-behaved.

As mentioned earlier, the RM cell includes several control bits that assist in congestion control. These are the NI, CI, and BN bits, and their functions are discussed next.

ABR Cell Flow: No Congestion

Figure 14-22 shows the cell flow on a single connection. In this figure, the CPE on the left is the source for data cells and RM cells that are traveling east, and the CPE on the right is the source for data cells that are traveling west. The BRM cells, generated by the destination BPX switch, turn around the forward RM cells. In this case, the BPX switch is acting as the destination and is actually the virtual destination, as explained in a moment.

In this example, there is no congestion within the network, so the BRM cells arrive at the source (the BPX switch acting as a virtual source) with the CI bit set to 0. Consequently, the VC queue service rate for this connection is increased to allow a higher cell into the ABR/UBR QBin. The actual rate increase is a configurable option, as discussed later in this chapter. The increase is a proportion of the current rate—hence the term relative rate.

Figure 14-22 *ABR Cell Flow with No Congestion*

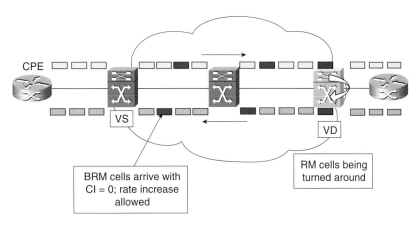

ABR Cell Flow: QBin Congestion

At some point, the network load could increase to the point where one or more of the switches start to register an impending congestion. That switch, which could be an intermediate node or the destination node, sets the NI bit = 1 in either a forward RM cell or in a BRM. When the BRM returns to the source, this is interpreted as "no increase," and the ACR for that connection cannot be increased (it could be reduced)—at least until the next BRM cell arrives.

The BPX node monitors the VC queues and QBins on every BXM card to detect the onset of congestion. Figure 14-23 shows a QBin on an intermediate switch that has filled up to the EFCI congestion-marking threshold. As a result, both the EFCI bit in the data cells and the CI bit in the RM cells are set to 1.

The RM cell is turned around at the destination and converted into a BRM cell (DIR = 1). The source BPX switch, on receipt of the BRM cell with CI = 1, reduces the VC queue service rate for the connection to reflect a lower ACR.

ABR Cell Flow: Loss of BRM Cells

From time to time, congestion might become severe enough that many data cells and several interleaved RM cells are discarded, as shown in Figure 14-24. Consequently, no BRM cells are generated by the destination. If this continues for a long-enough period, the source switch assumes that there is congestion downstream in the network and unilaterally reduces the connection to a new, lower ACR. This process repeats until the RM cell flow resumes.

Figure 14-23 *ABR Cell Flow with QBin Congestion*

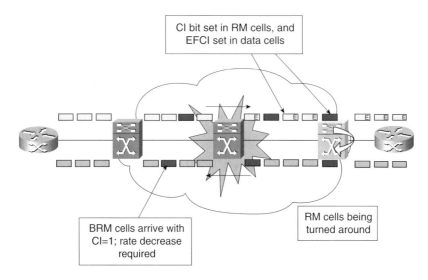

CI bit set in RM cells, and
EFCI set in data cells

RM cells being
turned around

BRM cells arrive with
CI=1; rate decrease
required

Figure 14-24 *ABR Cell Flow with Loss of BRM Cells*

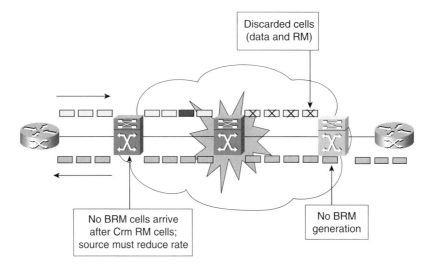

Discarded cells
(data and RM)

No BRM cells arrive
after Crm RM cells;
source must reduce rate

No BRM
generation

The amount of time that the source waits before forcing the rate reduction is defined indirectly by the Cutoff RM factor (Crm), which is the maximum number of RM cells that can be sent before a BRM returns. Crm is not a configurable parameter; the system calculates it for each connection, as follows:

Crm = TBE / Nrm

TBE is the transient buffer exposure in cells, and Nrm is the maximum number of user cells per RM cell.

ABR Cell Flow: QBin Congestion

In addition to setting the CI and NI in RM cells, intermediate and destination BPX switches can also generate BRM cells. These cells are not "turned around" RM cells. They are independently created to provide faster feedback and notification to the source that the node is experiencing some congestion. A switch-generated BRM cell must have the BN bit and the CI and/or NI bit(s) set to 1. As with all BRM cells, the DIR bit is also set to 1. Figure 14-25 shows this ABR cell flow.

Figure 14-25 *ABR Cell Flow: QBin Congestion with BECN*

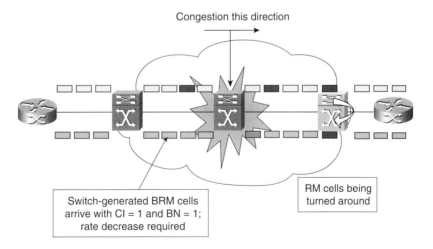

Congestion this direction

Switch-generated BRM cells
arrive with CI = 1 and BN = 1;
rate decrease required

RM cells being
turned around

NOTE   Switch-generated BRM cells are subject to the TCR limit of 10 cps.

Explicit Rate Control

BPX switches that are configured for ER control use a sophisticated hardware-based process to determine the highest cell rate that can be supported given the current network loading and congestion (see Figure 14-26). Explicit rate refers to the specific ACR for a connection, compared to relative rate, in which the new ACR is a percentage of the old one.

Figure 14-26 *ABR Cell Flow: Explicit Rate Stamping*

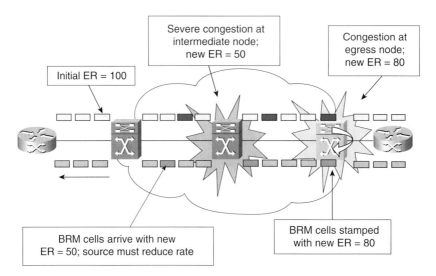

For a new connection, or for an existing one that has been idle, the source sets the ER field in the first RM to the PCR for the connection. The RM cell is turned around at the destination, and each ER-enabled switch on the return path through the network can modify the ER in the BRM cell. If congestion is experienced, as shown here, the switch *stamps* a new, lower ER in the BRM cell, overwriting the current ER value. By the time the BRM returns to the source, its ER field contains the ACR as calculated by the most constricted switch in the connection path. The source switch is required to reduce the queue service rate to the received ER.

ER calculation is performed on the BXM card and involves the following:

- MCR for the connection
- Calculated Congestion Factor (CF), which reflects the actual current status
- Connection Weight (CW) factor

The algorithm is based on the Congestion Avoidance using Proportional Control (CAPC) procedure described in the TM 4.0 specification. Each ER-enabled BXM must repeat the ER calculation approximately every 10 ms to provide real-time updates.

Virtual Source Virtual Destination Control

When adding an ABR connection in the BPX network, you must enable or disable several parameters that affect where congestion is measured and reported on a connection.

A *segment* is a portion of a connection that can be managed separately from other segments. At each end of a segment is a virtual source (VS) and virtual destination (VD). The VS and VD might not be the actual endpoints of the connection, but they are considered endpoints of the congestion control segment. In the simplest case, an ATM connection has one segment between the PVC terminating devices and therefore a VS and VD at each end. More often, a connection is viewed as three segments—two outside the network at either end, and one inside the BPX network. A single PVC can have many segments, especially when other networks (public or private) transport the traffic to the BPX node.

Figure 14-27 shows the various ABR connection types that can be configured, with or without VS/VD.

Figure 14-27 *Congestion Control Segments*

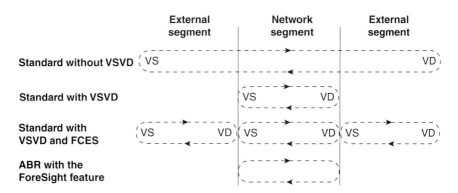

The following characteristics can be set for ABR connections on the BPX switch:

- **ABR connection type**—Either ABR Standard or ABR with the proprietary ForeSight feature. ABR ForeSight is discussed more in the section "Comparison of ABR Standard and ABR ForeSight."

- **ABR Standard with VS/VD**—When VS/VD defines a standard ABR connection, the endpoints of the connection become virtual sources and destinations. If VS/VD is not enabled, the BPX network is simply part of a larger connection segment where the VS and VD are external to the network.

- **FCES (Flow Control External Segment)**—In a multisegment environment, the BPX node can view the external segment as having another VS and VD. In this case, congestion control messaging occurs out toward the end-user equipment as well as within the BPX network.

ABR Standard Implementation on BXM

This section describes the cell flow for an ABR connection using BXM cards. Figure 14-28 shows two BPX nodes that form a single VS/VD control segment. External control segments are included for Cisco routers with ABR support.

Figure 14-28 *Source BXM Line Card: ABRSTD*

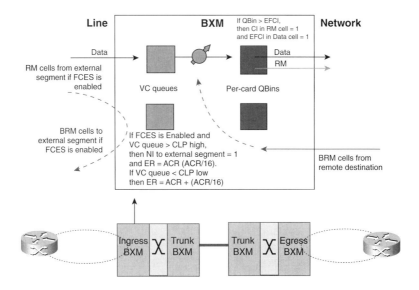

Each element (line and trunk cards) in the BPX network participates in the ABR process to notify the source device of network congestion.

The source BXM line card is the card receiving ATM user traffic from the line. It is responsible for the following:

- **Virtual circuit queues**—Buffers incoming data for traffic shaping. The VC queue receives BRM cells from the network and adjusts the VC queue service rate based on congestion information in the BRM cell, or the ER if it is enabled.

- **Per-card QBin**—Buffers ingress cells before they are passed to the crosspoint node. There is a QBin for each destination BXM card. If VSVD is enabled and the QBin exceeds the EFCI threshold, all data cells have their EFCI bit set to 1, and all RM cells have CI set to 1. Per-card QBins cannot be configured.

- **VD of external segment**—RM cells received are turned from the CPE back toward the external segment if FCES is enabled. If FCES is enabled and the VC queue has exceeded the CLP high threshold, NI in the RM cell from the external segment is set to 1 and ER = ACR − (ACR / 16). This signals a "rate down" to the external segment when the RM cell is turned around. If FCES is enabled and the VC queue is less than the CLP low threshold, ER = ACR + (ACR / 16). This signals a "rate up."

Figure 14-29 shows the functions performed by a BXM trunk card on an ABRSTD connection. In this example, the trunk originates at the source node.

Figure 14-29 *Intermediate BXM Trunk Card 1: Standard ABR*

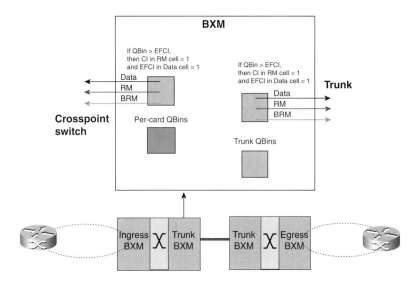

All BXM trunk cards that support an ABR connection are responsible for the following:

- **Trunk QBins**—Buffers for traffic going out on the trunk to another BPX node. If the QBin exceeds the EFCI threshold, all data cells have the EFCI bit set to 1, and all RM cells have CI set to 1. Trunk QBins can be configured with the **cnftrkparm** SuperUser command.

- **Per-card QBins**—Buffers ingress cells before they are passed to the crosspoint switch. If the QBin exceeds the EFCI threshold, all data cells have the EFCI bit set to 1, and all RM cells have CI set to 1.

Figure 14-30 shows the BXM trunk at the destination end. The source trunk card uses the trunk QBins, and the destination trunk card QBin uses the per-card QBin.

The destination BXM line card receives user data from the network and passes it to the end-user device attached on the line, as shown in Figure 14-31.

Figure 14-30 *Intermediate BXM Trunk Card 2: Standard ABR*

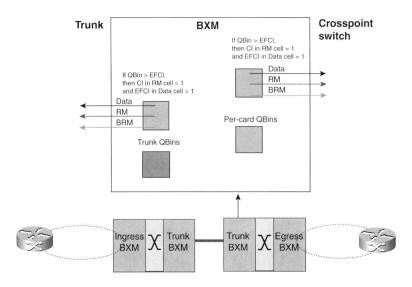

Figure 14-31 *Destination BXM Line Card: Standard ABR*

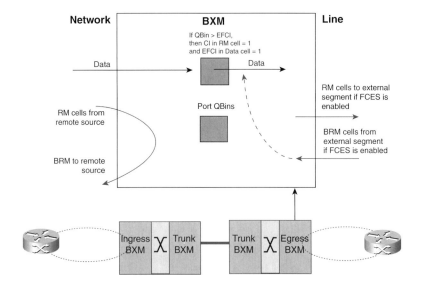

In Figure 14-31, data and RM cells go source-to-destination, and BRM cells go destination-to-source. Approaching the sample network from the other side (source becomes destination and destination becomes source), the figure then shows simultaneous, bidirectional flow of data, RM, and BRM cells.

The destination BXM is responsible for the following:

- **Port QBins**—Buffers outgoing traffic from the network. If FCES is enabled, BRM cells are received from the external segment (the dotted line in Figure 14-31), and the congestion information is used to determine the traffic's service rate. If the QBin exceeds the EFCI threshold, all data cells have the EFCI bit set to 1, and all RM cells have the CI bit set to 1.

- Turns around RM cells from the network if VSVD is enabled.

Figure 14-32 summarizes the various queuing structures on the BXM card that are involved in ABR connections.

Figure 14-32 *ABR Example: FCES and VS/VD Enabled*

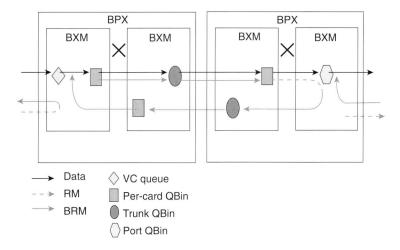

ABR Standard Rate Adjustments

As a result of measuring and reporting congestion using RM and BRM cells, the source BXM card must adjust the VC queue service rate accordingly. Table 14-4 describes the rate adjustments made by the BXM card on an ABR Standard connection.

Table 14-4   *ABR Standard Rate Adjustments*

Congestion Information	Result
No BRM cells received after CRM cells have been sent	New ACR = ACR – (ACR * CDF)
No congestion; both CI and NI are 0 in the BRM cell	New ACR = ACR + (PCR * RIF)
NI in BRM cell is set to 1	New ACR = ACR
CI in BRM cell is set to 1	New ACR = ACR - (ACR * RDF)
If the EFCI bit in the most recent cell when a BRM cell arrives is set to 1	New ACR = ACR - (ACR * RDF)
The ER is set	New ACR = ER

CRM is the cutoff RM. It is not a user-configurable parameter; it is calculated by the system using CRM = (TBE / Nrm).

CDF is the cutoff decrease factor. It is hard-coded in the system as 1 / 16.

RIF is the rate increase factor, and RDF is the rate decrease factor. RIF and RDF are both user-configurable parameters. Refer to the **addcon** command parameter tables later in this chapter for further descriptions, defaults, and value ranges for configurable parameters.

BXM Configuration for RR or ER Control

The BXM cards in a BPX switch can be configured to operate with RR, ER, or both. The default is RR. Use the SuperUser **cnfabrparm** command to enable or disable the control type(s) as required.

Rate Adjustment Example

As BRM cells are received by the source device, the VC queue service rate is adjusted accordingly. Figure 14-33 shows the changes in ACR for a single ABR standard connection as a result of changes in network congestion. The figure includes the following parameters:

- **PCR**—The maximum rate at which the source can generate traffic into the network.

- **MCR**—The minimum rate at which the source can generate traffic into the network.

- **Initial Cell Rate (ICR)**—The rate at which the source transmits traffic after an idle period defined by the ADTF.

- **Allowed-cell-rate decrease time factor (ADTF)**—The time between RM cells before the source rate returns to the ICR.

- **TRM**—The maximum time between RM cells.

- **RIF**—A percentage that determines the rate increase when there is no congestion.

- **RDF**—A percentage that determines the rate decrease when there is congestion.
- **CDF**—A percentage that determines the rate decrease when BRM cells are not being received from the network.

Figure 14-33 *ABR Standard Rate Adjustment Example*

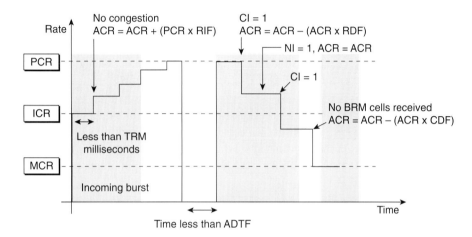

Assuming that this is the first burst of traffic on this connection, the VC queue service rate begins at the initial cell rate (ICR).

After a period of time no greater than the TRM, a BRM cell arrives from the network. In this case, the BRM cell does not have the CI or NI bits set (no congestion), and the ACR increases by the percentage defined by RIF × the previous ACR.

If the BRM cells continue to have CI and NI = 0, the rate continues to increase. The rate cannot exceed the PCR, regardless of network conditions. When the VC queue is empty and no new cells are arriving, the connection is idle.

If the connection has been idle for a relatively short period, as indicated by the time between RM cells being less than the allowed-cell-rate decrease time factor (ADTF), the rate returns to the most recently used rate—in this example, the PCR. If the idle period is greater than the ADTF, the rate goes back to the ICR.

After an initial burst at the PCR, a BRM cell returns from the network with CI = 1, so the rate must decrease. The next BRM cell has the NI bit set to 1, so the rate does not change.

The BRM cell arrives with CI = 1, indicating congestion somewhere in the network.

If, after cutoff RM (CRM), several RM cells are sent without a response BRM, the rate decreases based on the cutoff decrease factor (CDF). The rate cannot be less than the minimum cell rate (MCR), regardless of network conditions. The process continues in this manner as long as there are cells to send.

Often, the rate reaches a steady state and remains constant if the network is stable. If an ER is stamped in a BRM cell, the ACR is set to that ER.

ABR with ForeSight

This section defines the implementation of ABR with ForeSight at egress ports on a BPX switch.

Comparison of ABR Standard and ABR ForeSight

ABR ForeSight (ABRFST) and ABR Standard (ABRSTD) are similar in operation and implementation in BPX switches equipped with BXM cards. ABRFST is the Cisco prestandard version of ABR, and many aspects of ForeSight were incorporated by the ATM Forum as part of the traffic management 4.0 specification. Here are some of the main differences between ABRFST and ABRSTD:

- Implementation of ABRFST is restricted to Cisco routers and WAN switches.
- ABRFST on the BXM uses a modified version of the standard RM cell format; there is no corresponding BRM cell.
- ABRFST uses RR control only; there is no support for ER control.
- The ABRFST rate adjustment messages are implemented differently, as discussed in a moment.

ABRFST RM Cell

Figure 14-34 shows the special RM cell format used with ABRFST. The cell header is standard UNI or NNI, with the same VPI/VCI rules as the ABRSTD RM cell, which is that it has the same VPI/VCI as the connection for a virtual channel connection (VCC) or VCI = 6 for a virtual path connection (VPC).

Other fields following the header are as follows:

- **Protocol identifier**—Sets the hex F1 for a ForeSight RM cell (hex 01 for standard RM).
- **ForeSight rate adjustment (RA) message**—This octet serves the same purpose as the CI and NI bits in the standard RM cell. There are four ForeSight RA message types:
  - No change (hex F4)
  - Adjust rate up (hex F5)
  - Adjust rate down (hex F6)
  - Adjust rate fast down (hex F7)

Figure 14-34 *RM Cell Format*

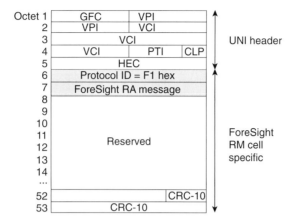

ForeSight RM cells are generated by the destination BXM card at a fixed rate. This rate is defined by the fixed round-trip delay, which can be configured using the SuperUser **cnffstparm** command. All RM cells are "out-of-band" cells and represent additional system overhead. You should be cautious about modifying the fixed round-trip delay from the default values.

ABRFST Rate Adjustments

As a result of measuring and reporting congestion using the EFCI in the last received user cell and/or the RA message in the RM cell, the BXM card must adjust the VC queue service rate accordingly. Table 14-5 lists the conditions necessary for the ForeSight feature to declare a congested, severely congested, or not congested condition.

Table 14-5 *ABRFST Congestion Criteria*

Conditions	Congestion Control State
Last sampled data cell, EFCI = 1	Congestion 10
Port QBin > EFCN threshold	Congestion 10
Last sampled data cell, EFCI = 1 and port QBin = queue depth	Severe congestion 11
Last sampled data cell, EFCI = 0 and port QBin < EFCN threshold	No congestion 01

Rate adjustments are relative to the current ACR and can be configured using the **cnffstparm** command. The adjustments for each congestion condition are as follows:

- **Congestion**—New ACR = present ACR × Rate Decrease Factor (RDF). RDF defaults to 93%.

- **Severe congestion**—New ACR = present ACR × Cutoff Decrease Factor (CDF). CDF defaults to 50%.

- **No congestion**—New ACR = present ACR × Rate Increase Factor (RIF). RIF defaults to PCR / 128 or 10% of present ACR—whichever is less.

ABRFST Rate Adjustment Example

As RM cells with RA messages (and data cells marked with EFCI) are received by the source device, the VC queue service rate is adjusted accordingly. Figure 14-35 shows the changes in ACR for a single ABR ForeSight connection as the result of changes in network congestion with the following parameters:

- **PCR**—The maximum rate at which the source can generate traffic into the network.

- **ICR**—The rate at which the source transmits traffic after an idle period defined by the ADTF.

- **MCR**—The minimum rate at which the source can generate traffic into the network.

- **ADTF**—The idle timeout period before the source rate returns to the ICR.

- **TRM**—The maximum time between RM cells.

- **RIF**—A percentage that determines the rate increase when there is no congestion.

- **RDF**—A percentage that determines the rate decrease when there is congestion.

- **CDF**—A percentage that determines the rate decrease when there is severe congestion.

- **CC**—Reports congestion back to the source using CC bits in data cells traveling back on the PVC.

- **ACR**—The current rate in cells per second at which a source is allowed to send.

Assuming that this is the first burst of traffic on this connection, the VC queue service rate begins at the initial cell rate (ICR).

After a period of time no greater than the TRM, an RM cell arrives from the network. In this case, the RM cell does not contain an RA message indicating congestion or server congestion, and the ACR increases by the percentage defined by the RIF.

If the no congestion RA messages continue, the rate continues to increase. The rate will never increase above the PCR, regardless of network conditions.

When the VC queue is empty and no new cells are arriving, the connection is idle. If the time until the next cell arrives is less than the ADTF, the rate returns to the most recently used rate—in this case, the PCR. If the time is greater than the ADTF, the rate returns to the ICR.

Figure 14-35 *ABRFST Rate Adjustment*

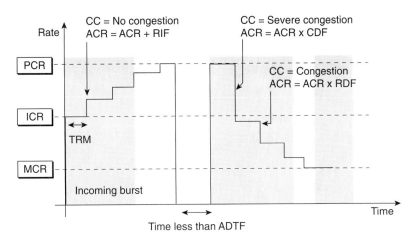

After the connection restarts with an initial burst at the PCR, an RA message returns from the destination with a severe congestion indication. The rate must decrease based on the CDF.

The next RA message reports congestion (but not severe congestion), and the rate decreases based on the rate decrease factor (RDF).

If the congestion continues, the rate continues to decrease. The rate will not decrease below the MCR, regardless of network conditions.

ATM-to-Frame Relay Interworking

ATM-to-Frame Relay interworking allows users to retain their existing Frame Relay services. As their needs expand, it also allows them to migrate to the higher-bandwidth capabilities provided by BPX switch ATM networks. ATM-to-Frame Relay interworking allows Frame Relay traffic to be connected across high-speed ATM trunks using Frame Relay Forum standards-based interworking procedures.

The key element in ATM-to-Frame Relay interworking is the Interworking Function (IWF). It has two possible implementations:

- **Network Interworking (NIW)**—Facilitates the transparent transport of Frame Relay traffic over ATM. One important application of NIW is to connect two Frame Relay networks over an ATM backbone network. The Frame Relay network takes Frame Relay frames and segments them into cells using AAL5 for transport across an ATM backbone. The frames are kept intact and are reassembled at the remote destination.

- **Service Interworking (SIW)**—Used when traffic originates as Frame Relay frames but terminates on an ATM interface. In this case, frames are not left intact.

Network interworking and service interworking are shown in Figure 14-36.

Figure 14-36 *Interworking ATM and Frame Relay*

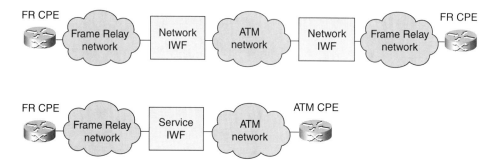

NIW and SIW Implementation

The NIW and SIW implementations are based on the Frame Relay Forum Implementation Agreements FRF.5 and FRF.8, respectively. In effect, both NIW and SIW processes are implemented in the Frame Relay Service Modules (FRSM) of the MGX 8230 and MGX 8250 concentrators.

The BPX switch does nothing for ATM-FR connections. In fact, in most situations, they are treated the same as ATM connections. It is the FR end (which is external to the BPX switch) that does the work.

Interworking connections originating on an FRSM port can terminate on any other Frame Relay port in the network or on an ATM port.

BPX Interworking Connection Types

The following connection types are available to provision interworking connections on the BPX switch. These connection types are relevant when using the CLI to configure connections. When using a CWM station to provision multisegment connections, the connection type is transparent to the user.

- **ATFR**—NIW connection without ForeSight
- **ATFST**—NIW connection with ForeSight
- **ATFT**—SIW transparent connection without ForeSight
- **ATFTFST**—SIW transparent connection with ForeSight

- **ATFX**—SIW translational connection without ForeSight
- **ATFXFST**—SIW translational connection with ForeSight

Figure 14-37 shows the application of BPX Interworking Connection Types 1.

Figure 14-37 *BPX Interworking Connection Types 1*

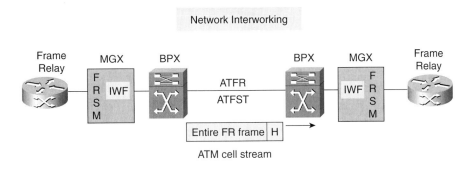

Figure 14-38 shows the application of BPX Interworking Connection Types 2.

Figure 14-38 *BPX Interworking Connection Types 2*

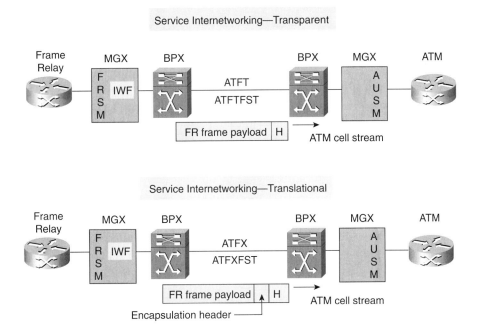

The NIW connection types (ATFR and ATFST) are for the BPX switch segment of multi-segment Frame Relay connections between MGX concentrators. Each of the FRSMs that terminate the connection perform the NIW function.

SIW connections are used when the BPX switch provides the trunk segment for connections originating on an FRSM port and terminating on an ATM port on an ATM UNI Service Module (AUSM). SIW can be transparent or translational, depending on the encapsulation method used by the CPE. The FRSM also performs the SIW function.

NIW Operation

Figure 14-39 shows in more detail the components of the NIW function. These include the following:

- Link-Access Procedure Frame Relay (LAP-FR)
- Frame Relay service-specific
- FR-SSCS frame
- Common Part Convergence Sublayer (CPCS)
- Segmentation and Reassembly sublayer (SAR)
- ATM layer

Figure 14-39 *Network Interworking (NIW)*

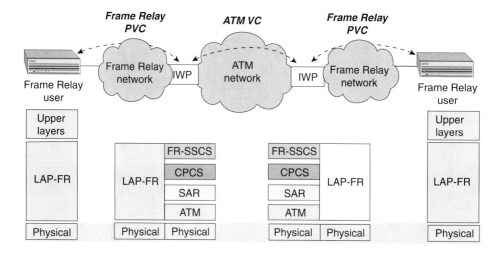

NIW encapsulates the standard Frame Relay header and payload sections in an FR-SSCS PDU, which is then converted to an AAL5 frame, and finally into ATM cells. This process is shown in Figure 14-40:

1 The leading and trailing flags and the Frame Check Sequence (FCS) are stripped off and discarded.

2 The resulting FR-SSCS PDU is passed to the CPCS, where the AAL5 trailer is appended, forming the CPCS PDU. The trailer includes control information, such as the PDU length and a CRC, plus a padding field to make the PDU a multiple of 48 bytes.

3 The CPCS PDU (AAL5 frame) is then sent to the SAR, where it is segmented into 48-byte fields that will form the payload section of ATM cells.

4 The ATM layer appends the cell header before passing the cell to the physical layer for transmission.

Figure 14-40 *NIW Frame-to-Cell Conversion*

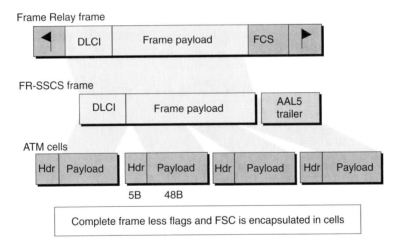

SIW Operation

Service interworking carries Frame Relay traffic between Frame Relay and ATM users. The following two forms of SIW are supported:

- *Transparent* SIW forwards frames and cells transparently with no further modification. Transparent SIW is used to transport protocols known to both endpoints—typically proprietary ones such as digitized voice.

• *Translational* SIW maps standard protocol encapsulations between ATM and Frame Relay. Frame Relay encapsulations are translated from RFC 1490 to RFC 1483, with the reverse translation occurring when converting from cells to frames. This method is most often used for standard protocols such as 802.3, FDDI, and IP (for example, in LAN-to-LAN connections).

Figure 14-41 shows the components of the SIW function.

Figure 14-41 *Service Interworking Components*

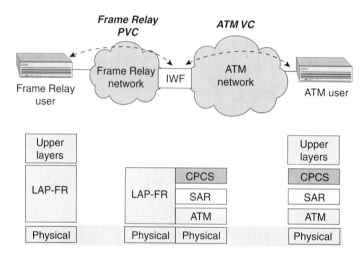

The SIW function is performed on the MGX FRSM cards; no interworking is performed in the BPX switch or on the MGX AUSM card. The main difference between NIW and SIW is that the frame header including the DLCI is mapped to corresponding fields in the ATM cell header. It is not transported across the network with the frame payload. This process is shown in Figure 14-42.

Header mapping is performed from Frame Relay to ATM as follows:

1 The Data Link Connection Identifier (DLCI) is mapped to a VPI/VCI.

2 The Discard Eligibility (DE) bit is mapped to the CLP bit.

3 The Forward Explicit Congestion Notification (FECN) bit is mapped to the EFCI bit.

NOTE   No mapping is specified for the Backward Explicit Congestion Notification (BECN) bit, because no equivalent exists in the ATM header.

Additionally, for translational SIW only, an additional conversion is performed on the encapsulation header from RFC 1490 format to RFC 1483 and vice versa.

Figure 14-42 *Service Interworking Process*

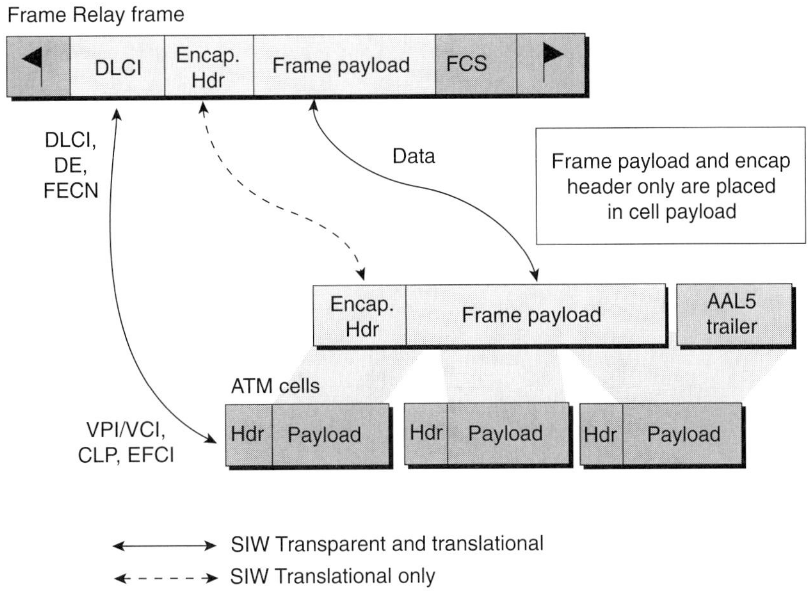

Multicast Services

Multicast services is another type of connection that uses a single primary source of traffic and duplicates that traffic to multiple destinations. An example of a multicast application is a videoconference, in which one site is being videotaped and many other sites are receiving that video signal. The Broadband Multicast Engine (BME) also supports VC merge, which allows any traffic from the destination sites to be sent back to the single primary source.

Adding BME Multicast Connections

There are two types of multicast connections: roots and leaves. A *root* is the single primary source of the multicast group; the *leaves* are the multiple destination connections in the group. Each group has one root connection and multiple leaf connections. Figure 14-43 shows an example of a multicast group with one root and three leaf connections.

The non-BME end of any multicast connection terminates on a BXM or BNI port and is added to the network using the **addcon** command. In most respects, a multicast connection is the same as any other ATM connection in the network.

Figure 14-43 *Multicast Connections*

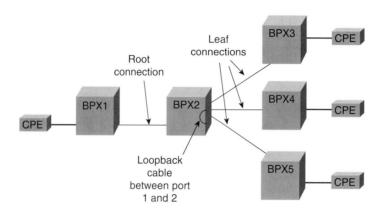

Ingress admission control or policing occurs on the non-BME end of all connections and on the BME end of leaf connections. Because only a minimal amount of traffic is expected back from the leaf connections, there is no policing on the BME end of the root connection.

For multicast connections, if the following are true:

• CPE on BPX1 is attached to BXM port 2.1

• BME on BPX2 is in card slot 5

• CPEs on BPX3, BPX4, and BPX5 are attached to BXM port 3.4

creating the appropriate connections requires the following four **addcon** commands:

• From BPX1, **addcon 2.1.200.0 BPX2 5.2.100.0 5** to add the root

• From BPX2, **addcon 5.1.100.1 BPX3 3.4.50.55 5** to add one leaf

• From BPX2, **addcon 5.1.100.2 BPX4 3.4.53.21 5** to add a second leaf

• From BPX2, **addcon 5.1.100.3 BPX5 3.4.48.2 5** to add a third leaf

In this example, all four connections are added using connection class 5. The VPI and VCI at the non-BME ends of the connections are not restricted to any particular VPI and VCI. Also, the connections could have been added from either the BME or non-BME end of the connection. Restrictions that are imposed on the BME end of the connection include that the VPI of the leaf source must match the VPI of the root destination. In this example, VPI = 100.

Multicast Addressing Conventions

The BPX supports multisegment multicast connections, which means that a multisegment multicast connection uses the leaf of one multicast group as the root of another multicast group.

The addressing conventions used in a multicast group are as follows:

- Root and leaves share a common VPI.

- Root uses VCI 0; leaves use nonzero VCI.

- Root terminates on one BME port; leaves must terminate on the other port. For example, if root is on port 2, all leaves must be on port 1.

- Root and leaves can be added or deleted in any order and at any time.

Establishing and Configuring ATM Connections

In this section, you will learn how to use the CLI to establish and configure ATM connections on a BPX switch.

From the BPX command line, you can establish three types of ATM connections in a network:

- Connection between two BXM ports

- Two-segment connection between a BXM port and a port on an ATM UNI Service Module (AUSM) on an MGX concentrator

- Interworking connection between a BXM port and a Frame Relay Service Module (FRSM) port on an MGX concentrator

Figure 14-44 shows the threes types of connections.

Figure 14-44 *ATM Connection Definition*

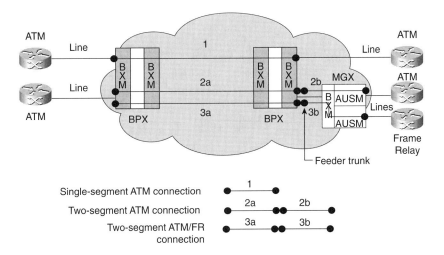

Commands for Establishing and Configuring ATM Connections

Table 14-6 describes the BPX CLI commands for activating and configuring ATM connections, along with the privilege levels necessary to issue them.

Table 14-6 *Commands for ATM Connections*

Command	Description	Privilege Level
dspatmcls	Display connection class. Displays all connection classes in the network.	6
addcon	Add connection. Adds a connection to the network using a connection class or by specifying all connection parameters.	2
dspcon	Display specific connection. Displays details for a particular connection, including route and endpoint status.	6
cnfatmcls	Configure connection class. Modifies the connection parameters associated with a connection class.	2
dspcons	Display all connections. Displays all connections on this node.	6
delcon	Delete connection. Removes a connection from the network.	2
cnfcon	Configure connection. Modifies connection configuration parameters.	3
dspconcnf	Display connection configuration. Displays detailed configuration information for a connection, including policing and ForeSight characteristics.	6

dspatmcls Command

The **dspatmcls** command displays the current configuration of each of the ten ATM connection classes. The screen cycles through the ten classes in turn in response to a screen prompt.

Here is the **dspatmcls** command syntax:

```
dspatmcls [class number]
```

The **dspcls** and **cnfcls** commands perform the same function as **dspatmcls**. Here is their syntax:

```
dspcls [class number]
cnfcls [class number]
```

addcon Command

The **addcon** command establishes an ATM connection between two BXM ports, or a trunk and a port, or between two trunks, but only if the trunks are feeder trunks from an MGX. There is no connection from a BPX to an MGX card. However, there are MGX connections from the MGX card to the PXM trunk, which feeds to the BPX.

The general **addcon** command syntax is as follows:

```
addcon <local channel> <remote node> <remote channel> <connection class or type>
   [connection parameters] [route avoid]
```

Configurable connection parameters are listed in Table 14-7. Certain value fields, such as those for the LMI/ILMI parameters, are displayed for configuration only if other parameters have been previously selected and modified.

delcon is a related command. It deletes a connection.

Here is the **delcon** command syntax:

```
delcon <local channel>
```

Example 14-1 shows the **addcon** command being used to add a CBR connection between two BPX ports using connection class 10. This is the first of three connections you will add.

Example 14-1 addcon *Command*

```
hei1bpx1        TRM     Teacher:1     BPX 8620   9.3.XX      May  11 200X 12:35 G+12

  Local          Remote        Remote                            Route
  Channel        NodeName      Channel       State  Type      Avoid COS O
  1.2.1.1        hei1bpx3      2.1.1.1       Failed cbr              0  L
  1.2.1.100      hei1bpx2      2.1.1.100     Failed rt-vbr
  2.1.1.1        hei1bpx2      1.2.1.1       Failed cbr
  2.1.1.100      hei1bpx2      1.2.1.100     Failed rt-vbr
  12.2.9.32      hei1bpx3      1.2.12.32     Failed atfr             0  L
  12.2.10.32     hei1bpx2      12.2.10.38    Ok     nrt-vbr
  12.2.10.38     hei1bpx2      12.2.10.32    Ok     nrt-vbr
  12.2.11.32     hei1bpx3      1.2.11.32     Failed cbr              0  L




Last Command: addcon 1.2.1.1 hei1bpx3 2.1.1.1 10 y


Next Command:

               SW                                            MAJOR ALARM
```

Table 14-7 lists the general parameters that apply to all connection types.

Table 14-7 *General **addcon** Parameters*

Parameter	Description
local channel	The local channel is identified as *slot.port.VPI.VCI* for a VC switched connection and as *slot.port.VPI.** for a VP switched connection. The VPI range is 1 to 255 for a UNI connection and 1 to 4095 for an NNI connection. The VCI range is 1 to 65,535.

continues

Table 14-7 *General* **addcon** *Parameters (Continued)*

Parameter	Description
remote node	The name of the destination node.
remote channel	The local channel is identified as *slot.port.VPI.VCI* for a VC switched connection and as *slot.port.VPI.** for a VP switched connection.
connection class	The ATM connection class, from 1 to 10. The class defines many of the parameters associated with the connection. Classes are listed in software with the **dspatmcls** command.
connection type	The type of connection to be added—CBR, rt-VBR, nrt-VBR, ABRSTD, ABRFST, or UBR. If you try to add an unsupported connection to a card, the **addcon** command fails, and an error message appears.
VC queue depth	The size of the ingress VC queue used for traffic shaping. The VC queue depth is configured in cells and can be the same or different at each end of the connection. The default is 16,000 cells, and the value range is 0 to 61,440 cells.
CLP high	The high threshold on the VC queue for determining when to discard CLP tagged cells. The CLP high is configured as a percentage of the VC queue depth. The default is 80%.
CLP low/EPD	The low threshold on the VC queue for determining when to stop discarding CLP tagged cells. The CLP low is configured as a percentage of the VC queue depth and must be less than the CLP high threshold. The default is 35%.
	If FBTC is enabled for the connection, the CLP low threshold is used as the EPD threshold.
connection parameters	If a connection type is used instead of a connection class, each appropriate connection parameter must be entered during the **addcon** command. Most of the connection-specific parameters can be entered as a single number that applies the same value to the local and remote sides. To apply different values to each end, enter the local value followed by a slash and the remote value (for example, 10/50). Detailed descriptions of all connection-specific parameters are provided on the following pages.
route avoid	Restricts the connection from routing over certain types of trunks. Choices are *s (no satellite) or *t (no terrestrial).

CBR **addcon** Parameters

Here is the CBR **addcon** command syntax:

```
addcon <local channel> <remote node> <remote channel> cbr <PCR(0+1)>
  <percent utilization> <CDVT(0+1)> <policing type> <VC queue depth> <CLP high>
  <CLP low> [route avoid]
```

The **addcon** parameters that are specific to CBR connections are listed in Table 14-8.

Table 14-8   **addcon** *Parameters Used for CBR Connections*

Parameter	Description
PCR(0+1)	The average maximum rate for all cells (CLP = 0 and CLP = 1) on the connection. The PCR is defined in cells per second.
percent utilization	Determines the necessary bandwidth for a connection. CBR connections require PCR × *percent utilization* cells per second of bandwidth on a trunk to route through the network. It is recommended that CBR connections use the default percent utilization of 100.
CDVT(0+1)	Policies the connection for all cells (CLP = 0 and CLP = 1). The range is 0 to 5,000,000 microseconds. The default for CBR is 10,000 microseconds.
policing type	For a CBR connection, this can be either 4 or 5. Type 4 uses a single leaky bucket and discards all noncompliant cells. Type 5 disables all policing functions. The default is Type 4.

VBR **addcon** Parameters

Here is the VBR **addcon** command syntax:

```
addcon <local channel> <remote node> <remote channel> rt-vbr | nrt-vbr <PCR(0+1)>
    <percent utilization> <CDVT(0+1)> <FBTC> <SCR> <MBS> <policing type>
    <VC queue depth> <CLP high> <CLP low> [route avoid]
```

The **addcon** parameters that are in addition to those for CBR or that have a specific interpretation for VBR connections are listed in Table 14-9.

Table 14-9   *VBR* **addcon** *Parameters*

Parameter	Description
AAL5 FBTC	Enables or disables Frame-Based Traffic Control, which includes PPD/EPD and FGCRA, depending on the BXM card firmware. FBTC is disabled by default for all VBR connections.
SCR	Defines the average rate of cells that will be compliant on the second leaky bucket. The SCR must be equal to or less than the PCR and is defined in cells per second. The default is 50 cps.
MBS	Defines the number of cells that are compliant on the second leaky bucket if the cells arrive at the PCR. The MBS is defined as a number of cells. The range is 1 to 5,000,000 cells. The default is 1000 cells.
policing type	For a VBR connection, this can be set to 1, 2, or 3. The default for VBR connections is Type 3.

ABRSTD **addcon** Parameters

Here is the ABRSTD **addcon** command syntax:

```
addcon <local channel> <remote node> <remote channel> abrstd <PCR(0+1)>
    <percent utilization> <MCR> <CDVT(0+1)> <FBTC> <VSVD> <FCES>
    <default parameters> <SCR> <MBS> <policing type> <VC queue depth> <CLP high>
    <CLP low> <EFCI> <ICR> <ADTF> <Trm> <RIF> <RDF> <Nrm> <FRTT> <TBE>
    [route avoid]
```

The **addcon** parameters that are in addition to CBR/VBR or that have a specific interpretation for ABRSTD connections are listed in Table 14-10.

Table 14-10 *ABRSTD* **addcon** *Parameters*

Parameter	Description
MCR	Used by the ABR algorithm. Must be equal to or less than the PCR. For ABR connections, the MCR defaults to 50 cps.
CDVT(0+1)	Polices the connection for all cells (CLP = 0 and CLP = 1). The range is 0 to 5,000,000 microseconds. The default for ABR is 10,000 microseconds.
AAL5 FBTC	Enables or disables Frame-Based Traffic Control, which includes PPD/EPD and FGCRA, depending on the BXM card firmware. FBTC is enabled by default for all ABR connections.
VSVD	Enables or disables VSVD. If enabled, the BXM acts as a VS and a VD. If disabled, the BXM is considered an intermediate hop, and the VS and VD are external to the BPX network. When VSVD is disabled (the default), you are not prompted for the FCES parameter.
FCES	Specifies whether a congestion control segment exists outside the BPX network. The default is disabled.
default parameters	If this is enabled, defaults are used for all subsequent ABR connection parameters, and the command is complete. If it is disabled, you are prompted to enter the subsequent parameters for the connection.
policing type	For an ABR connection, this can be set to 1, 2, 3, 4, or 5. The default is Type 3.
EFCI	Determines when to start marking the EFCI congestion bit on incoming cells. The EFCI is configured as a threshold of the VC queue depth. The default value is 20%.
ICR	Determines the starting queue service rate after an idle period. The ICR must be less than or equal to the PCR and greater than or equal to the MCR. The default value is 50 cps.
ADTF	Defines the idle time necessary to return the queue service rate to the ICR. The ADTF range is 62 to 8000 milliseconds. The default value is 1000.
Trm	The maximum time between RM cells. For ABRSTD, the range is 1 to 100 ms. The default is 100 ms.

Table 14-10 *ABRSTD* **addcon** *Parameters (Continued)*

Parameter	Description
RIF	Determines how much to increase the queue service rate if the connection is not congested. For ABRSTD, RIF is defined as an integer power of 2 from 1 to 32,768. The default is 128. RIF is applied by the system as a negative power of 2, such as 1/128.
RDF	Determines how much to decrease the queue service rate if the connection is congested. The units and range for RDF are the same as for RIF for ABRSTD, except that the default is 16 (applied as 1/16).
Nrm	The maximum number of data cells between RM cells. The range is 2 to 256. The default is 32.
FRTT	The sum of the fixed and propagation delays through the BPX network. The range is 0 to 16,700 ms. The default is 0.
TBE	Determines the number of cells that can be sent by the source before the first RM cell returns from the destination. The range is 0 to 1,048,320. 1,048,320 is the default.

ABRFST **addcon** Parameters

Here is the ABRFST **addcon** command syntax:

```
addcon <local channel> <remote node> <remote channel> abrfst <PCR(0+1)>
   <percent utilization> <MCR> <CDVT(0+1)> <FBTC> <default parameters>
   <SCR> <MBS> <policing type> <VC queue depth> <CLP high> <CLP low> <EFCI>
   <ICR> <ADTF> <Trm> <RIF> <RDF> [route avoid]
```

The **addcon** parameters that are in addition to the preceding connection types or that have a specific interpretation for ABRFST connections are listed Table 14-11.

Table 14-11 *ABRFST* **addcon** *Parameters*

Parameter	Description
Trm	The time between RM cells. For ForeSight connections, the Trm determines the time period between CC messages from the destination to the source. The Trm range is 3 to 255 ms. The default is 100 ms.
RIF	Determines how much to increase the queue service rate if the connection is not congested. For ABRFST, RIF is defined in cells per second. The default is the greater of PCR/128 and 10.
RDF	Determines how much to decrease the queue service rate if the connection is congested. For ABRFST, RDF is a percentage and defaults to 93%.

UBR **addcon** Parameters

Here is the UBR **addcon** command syntax:

```
addcon <local channel> <remote node> <remote channel> ubr <PCR(0+1)>
    <percent utilization> <CDVT(0+1)> <FBTC> <CLP setting>
```

The **addcon** parameters that are specific to UBR connections are listed in Table 14-12.

Table 14-12 *UBR* addcon *Parameters*

Parameter	Description
percent utilization	For UBR connections, this is often set low. The default value is 1 percent.
CLP setting	Enables or disables CLP tagging during UBR policing. If this is disabled, the second leaky bucket is disabled, and no cells are tagged by the BPX node with a CLP of 1. If enabled, the second leaky bucket is defined with an SCR of 0 cells per second, and all cells are tagged with a CLP of 1.

ATFR/ATFT/ATFX **addcon** Parameters

The ATFR, ATFT, and ATFX connection types use an nrt-VBR connection at the ATM end. Several of the parameters (*VC queue depth, EFCI,* and *IBS*) are mapped to their Frame Relay equivalents.

Here is the ATFR/ATFT/ATFX **addcon** command syntax:

```
addcon <local channel> <remote node> <remote channel> atfr | aftf | atfx
    <PCR(0+1)> <percent utilization> <CDVT(0+1)> <SCR> <MBS> <policing type>
    <VC queue depth> <EFCI> <IBS> [route avoid]
```

The **addcon** parameters that are in addition to nrt-VBR or that have a specific interpretation, ranges, or defaults for ATFT, ATFT, and ATFX connections are listed in Table 14-13.

Table 14-13 *ATFR/ATFT/ATFX* addcon *Parameters*

Parameter	Description
remote channel	Identified as *slot.port.DLCI.*
VC queue depth	The size of the ingress VC queue used for traffic shaping. The VC queue depth is configured in cells and can be the same or different at each end of the connection. The value range is 0 to 61440 cells. The default is 1280 cells.
EFCI	Determines when to start marking the EFCI congestion bit on incoming cells. The EFCI threshold is configured as a percentage of the VC queue depth. The default value is 35%.
IBS	Initial Burst Size is a parameter on MGX Frame Relay modules that allows short initial bursts at port speed. The IBS range is 0 to 24,000 cells. The default is 1 cell.

ATFST/ATFTFST/ATFXFST **addcon** Parameters

The ATFST, ATFTFST, and ATFXFST connection types use an ABRFST connection at the ATM end.

Here is the ATFST/ATFTFST/ATFXFST **addcon** command syntax:

```
addcon <local channel> <remote node> <remote channel> atfst | atftfst | atfxfst
    <PCR(0+1)> <percent utilization> <MCR> <CDVT(0+1)> <FBTC>
    <default parameters> <SCR> <MBS> <policing type> <VC queue depth> <CLP high>
    <CLP low> <EFCI> <ICR> <ADTF> <Trm> <RIF> <RDF> <IBS> [route avoid]
```

Several of the parameters (*VC queue depth, EFCI,* and *IBS*) are mapped to their Frame Relay equivalents. The **addcon** parameters that are in addition to ABRFST or that have specific interpretation, ranges, or defaults for ATFST, ATFTFST, and ATFXFST connections are listed in Table 14-14.

Table 14-14 *ATFST/ATFTFST/ATFXFST* **addcon** *Parameters*

Parameter	Description
remote channel	Identified as *slot.port.DLCI.*
VC queue depth	The size of the ingress VC queue used for traffic shaping. The VC queue depth is configured in cells and can be the same or different at each end of the connection. The default is 1280 cells. The value range is 0 to 61,440 cells.
EFCI	Determines when to start marking the EFCI congestion bit on incoming cells. The EFCI threshold is configured as a percentage of the VC queue depth. The default value is 35%.
IBS	Initial Burst Size is a parameter on MGX Frame Relay modules that allows short initial bursts at port speed. The IBS range is 0 to 24,000 cells. The default is 1 cell.

dspcon Command

The **dspcon** screen, shown in Example 14-2, provides detailed information for a given connection. Use this command to display connection configuration, the connection route through the network, and endpoint alarm status.

Example 14-2 dspcon *Command*

```
hei1bpx1        TRM       Teacher:1     BPX 8620  9.3.XX      May  11 200X 12:35 G+12


Conn:  1.2.1.100        hei1bpx3    2.1.1.100         rt-vbr     Status:Ok
   PCR(0+1)     % Util    CDVT(0+1)      FBTC       SCR          MBS       PLC
   4000/4000    100/100   10000/10000     n      4000/4000    1000/1000    3
Owner: LOCAL   Restriction: NONE   COS: 0
TestRTD: 0 msec
Path:    hei1bpx112.2-- 1.2hei1bpx3
```

continues

Example 14-2 dspcon *Command (Continued)*

```
Pref:   Not Configured


hei1bpx1       BXM      : OK      hei1bpx1 BXM      : OK
               Line  1.3 : OK              Line 10.2 : OK
               OAM Cell RX: Clear          NNI      : OK
               NNI      : OK

This Command: dspcon 1.2.1.100


Continue?

                    SW CD
```

The following fields (in addition to the information provided in the **dspcons** screen) are included in the first of the two screens for the **dspcon** command:

- Parameters defined during the **addcon** command, such as PCR(0+1), CDVT (0+1), and percent utilization.

- **Test RTD**—The most recent result of the **tstdelay** command.

- **Path**—The connection route currently in use by the connection, including the node names and trunk numbers of all intermediate hops. If the connection originates and terminates on the same node, there is no routing information.

- **Preferred route**—The user-configured preferred route, if configured (defined using the **cnfpref** command).

- **Local and remote card status**—OK or failed status of the local and remote line cards.

- **Local and remote line status**—OK or failed status of the local and remote access lines.

- **Local OAM cell Rx**—Clear or Failed, indicating the receipt of OAM Alarm Indicator Status (AIS) cells from the attached ATM user device.

The second screen of the **dspcon** command, shown in Example 14-3, provides detailed configuration information for a connection. Information includes parameter values defined using the **addcon** or **cnfcon** commands. Use this command to display the configured values of the connection parameters.

Example 14-3 dspcon *Command, Part 2*

```
hei1bpx1        TRM      Teacher:1    BPX 8620  9.3.XX    May  11 200X 12:35 G+12

Conn:  1.2.1.100         hei1bpx3  2.1.1.100       rt-vbr     Status:Ok
   PCR(0+1)    % Util    MCR         CDVT(0+1)      FCES        SCR
   5000/5000   100/100   1200/1200   250000/250000   n         5000/5000
```

Example 14-3 dspcon *Command, Part 2 (Continued)*

```
        MBS         Policing   VC Qdepth   CLP Hi CLP Lo/EDP    EFCI         ICR
    1000/1000           5      1280/1280    80/80     35/35    35/35    1200/1200


    ADTF   Trm      RIF        RDF         IBS
    1000   100        39        93         1/1




    Last Command: dspcon 1.2.1.100


    Next Command:

                    SW CD
```

This same information can be displayed with the **dspconcnf** and **cnfcon** commands. (The **cnfcon** command can modify any of the connection parameters.)

dspcons Command

The **dspcons** command is used to display summary information about all connections that terminate on this node.

Here is the **dspcons** command syntax:

```
dspcons [start channel] [nodename] [-f] [-v] [-d] [-atfr] [-abit] [-fabit]
    [-fail] [-down]
```

The **dspcons** command parameters are as follows:

- [*start channel*]—Starts listing the connections, beginning with the specified channel.
- [*nodename*]—Lists the connections that terminate on the specified node name.
- [-f]—Displays only frame relay connections
- [-v]—Displays only voice connections
- [-d]—Displays only data connections
- [-atfr]—Displays only NIW connections without ForeSight
- [-abit]—Displays the connection A-bit states at both the local and remote ends. The A-bit state is determined by either the interface signaling protocol (LMI or ILMI) or as the result of Operation, Administration, and Maintenance (OAM) cells received by the network from the attached end-user device.
- [-fabit]—Displays only connections that have failed A-bits.
- [-fail]—Displays only connections that are in a failed state.
- [-down]—Displays only connections that are in a downed state.

The **dspcons** screen, shown in Example 14-4, displays the status of all connections that terminate on the node. Use this command to list all connections, their endpoints, connection type, and status. The **dspcons** screen is also displayed as the result of many other commands, including **addcon**, **delcon**, **upcon**, and **dncon**.

Example 14-4 dspcons *Command*

```
hei1bpx1        TRM      Teacher:1      BPX 8620  9.3.XX     May  11 200X 12:35 G+12

 Local          Remote       Remote                            Route
 Channel        NodeName     Channel        State  Type        Avoid COS O
 1.2.1.1        hei1bpx3     2.1.1.1        Failed cbr
 1.2.1.100      hei1bpx2     2.1.1.100      Failed rt-vbr
 2.1.1.1        hei1bpx2     1.2.1.1        Failed cbr
 2.1.1.100      hei1bpx2     1.2.1.100      Failed rt-vbr
 12.2.9.32      hei1bpx3     1.2.12.32      Failed atfr                0   L
 12.2.10.32     hei1bpx2     12.2.10.38     Ok     nrt-vbr
 12.2.10.38     hei1bpx2     12.2.10.32     Ok     nrt-vbr
 12.2.11.32     hei1bpx3     1.2.11.32      Failed cbr                 0   L




 Last Command: dspcons


 Next Command:
                 SW CD
```

The following fields are included in the **dspcons** screen:

- Local Channel
- Remote Node
- Remote Channel
- **State**—OK means that the connection is routed and there are no endpoint card or line alarms. Failed means that the connection cannot route or that an endpoint card or line is in alarm. Down means that the connection has been brought out of service using the **dncon** command.
- **Type**—CBR, rt-VBR, nrt-VBR, ABRFST, ABRSTD, UBR, ATFR, ATFST, ATFT, ATFTFST, ATFX, or ATFXFST.
- **Route Avoid**—Any trunk type that the connection cannot route across. *s for satellite or *t for terrestrial.
- **COS**—Class of service used during rerouting to give an advantage to some connections (low CoS) over others (high CoS). If a connection originates and terminates on the same node, there is no CoS. The CoS is measured in seconds, from 0 to 15.

- **Owner**—Determines the connection end from which the **addcon** command was issued. "Local" means that the connection was added from this node. "Remote" means that the connection was added from the remote node. The local owner of a connection is responsible for determining the route through the network. If the connection originates and terminates on the same node, the connection has no owner.

dspcon and **dspconcnf** are related commands.

The **dspcon** command displays a single connection. **dspcon** requires two screens for most connection types.

Here is the **dspcon** command syntax:

```
dspcon <slot.port.vpi.vci>
```

The **dspconcnf** command displays a single connection on a single screen, with a subset of the parameters of the **dspcon** command.

Here is the **dspconcnf** command syntax:

```
dspconcnf <slot.port.vpi.vci>
```

cnfatmcls Command

The **cnfatmcls** command modifies any of the ten preconfigured class templates for ATM connections. When you enter the number of the class to configure, the display shows the current value of each parameter in the class. For each item in the class, a prompt appears for changing or keeping the current value.

The **cnfatmcls** parameters are the same as for the **addcon** command; therefore, see the **addcon** command section for a list and descriptions.

Here is the **cnfatmcls** command syntax:

```
cnfatmcls <class number> [class parameters]
```

The **cnfcls** command performs the same function as **cnfatmcls**. It also can be used to modify Frame Relay classes.

The **cnfatmcls** screen, shown in Example 14-5, allows you to modify the connection parameters associated with a connection class.

Example 14-5 **cnfatmcls** *Command*

```
hei1bpx1        TRM      Teacher:1     BPX 8620  9.3.XX    May  11 200X 12:35 G+12

 ATM Connection Classes
 Class: 10                                                     Type: rt-VBR
    PCR(0+1)       % Util       CDVT(0+1)       AAL5 FBTC       SCR
    4000/4000      100/100      10000/10000        n         4000/4000
```

continues

Example 14-5 cnfatmcls *Command (Continued)*

```
       MBS            Policing
   1000/1000             3

          Description: "Default CBR 4000"




This Command: cnfatmcls 10 rt-vbr * * * * * * *


Do you want this change (y/n)?

                  SW CD
```

cnfcon Command

The **cnfcon** command modifies ATM connection parameters.

Here is the **cnfcon** command syntax:

```
cnfcon <slot.port.vpi.vci> [parameters]
```

Parameters can be entered in response to system prompts or may be entered directly on the command line. Use *, n/*, or */n to retain existing values for specific parameters when in direct entry mode. The * symbol retains the existing values in transmit and receive directions, whereas n/* and */n retain the receive and transmit values, respectively.

How to Establish and Configure ATM Connections

Follow these steps to establish and configure the ATM connection types described earlier:

Step 1   At the Next Command prompt, enter **dspports**. This displays the BXM ports that are currently activated. Verify that the port you want to use is active and free of alarms.

Step 2   Enter **dspcons**. This displays any connections that currently terminate at this node. Verify that the local and remote VPI/VCI (or DLCI for ATM/FR) that you want to use are not already assigned.

If the connection terminates on a remote BPX switch, log into the remote BPX node (**vt**) and enter **dspports**. This displays the BXM ports that are currently activated on the remote node. Verify that the port you want to use is active and free of alarms. If it is, enter **bye** to terminate the **vt** session and return to your original node; otherwise, correct the configuration.

Step 3   Enter **dspatmcls** to display configurations that you can use as a template when adding your connection. This displays the current configuration of the ten ATM connection classes.

To add an ATM connection between your local and remote BXM channels, use the **addcon** command with the appropriate parameters. The system prompts you to confirm the connection addition.

Step 4   Enter **y** to confirm the **addcon** command. This displays the modified port configuration in summary form with the connection status. If the connection is invalid, this displays an error message. Verify that the connection status is OK.

Step 5   Enter **dspcon** <*slot.port.vpi.vci*> for the connection you just added. This displays the detailed configuration. Verify that the connection endpoints and other parameters are correct. Check the path on which the connection has been routed.

A connection copies the information from a class at the time of the **addcon**. After that, the class can be changed without affecting the connections that were made from it, and the connection can be changed without affecting the class.

The remaining steps show you how to configure an ATM class.

Step 6   Enter **cnfatmcls** <*number*>, where *number* is the class you used to add the first connection. This displays the parameters for modification.

Step 7   Select a parameter to modify. For example, increase the PCR by 50%.

Step 8   Enter **dspconcnf** <*slot.port.vpi.vci*> for the connection you just added. This displays the detailed configuration, minus the endpoint status and routing information. Verify that altering the connection class has not modified the PCR on the existing connection.

If the connection you added terminates on a remote BPX switch, log into the remote BPX node (**vt**) and enter **dspatmcls** <*number*>, where *number* is the class you altered on the first node. This displays the ATM connection class configuration so that you can verify that the connection class you modified on the other node has the new PCR value. If so, enter **bye** to terminate the **vt** session and return to your original node; otherwise, correct the configuration.

Ten classes are available for adding a new connection to the network. The connection classes can be changed using the **cnfatmcls** command without affecting existing connections. The new class configuration applies network-wide for any subsequent connection, and connections can be changed without affecting the classes.

Table 14-15 lists the ten ATM classes by connection type, with PCR or MCR identified for each type.

Table 14-15 *ATM Preconfigured Classes*

ATM Class Number	Connection Type	PCR or MCR (ABRSTD) in cps
1	ABRSTD	96,000
2	nrt-VBR	1000
3	rt-VBR	4000
4	nrt-VBR	8000
5	nrt-VBR	16,000
6	nrt-VBR	32,000
7	nrt-VBR	96,000
8	CBR	500
9	CBR	1000
10	CBR	4000

Verifying That BXM Lines and Ports Are Free of Alarms

Prior to configuring the connections, you must verify that the BXM lines and ports you intend to use are active and free of alarms. You need to also verify the configurations of the user devices and verify that the lines, ports, and feeder connections are correctly configured and active. (You can do this by using the **dspports** and **dspcons** commands.)

To make it easier to correctly configure a new connection, you can enter the **dspatmcls** command to display any of ten preconfigured ATM connection classes. You can then use one of these connection classes as a template for adding a new connection to the network.

Monitoring ATM Connections

In this section, you will learn how to use the CLI to monitor connections on a BPX ATM port.

Channel Statistics

On a BPX node, real-time statistics can be viewed for both ports and channels. Earlier, you learned that a port is the interface between the network and a single end-user device, such as a router. You also learned that a channel is the endpoint designator for a connection. The channel is identified in different ways, depending on the line card involved, as shown in Figure 14-45.

Figure 14-45 *Port and Channel Definitions*

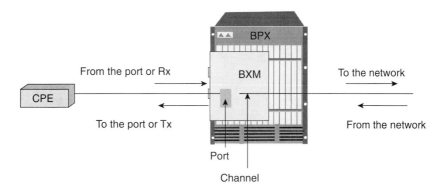

When displaying port statistics on the node, traffic is defined as follows:

- **Rx port**—Received from the attached user device
- **Tx port**—Transmitted to the attached user device

When displaying channel statistics, traffic is defined as follows:

- **From port**—Received from the attached user device
- **To network**—Transmitted to the network (Cellbus or crosspoint switch)
- **From network**—Received from the network (Cellbus or crosspoint switch)
- **To port**—Transmitted to the attached user device

Statistics Applications

The channel statistics discussed in this section are *summary* statistics. They are accumulated in 32-bit counters on each BXM module and are retrieved using CLI commands such as **dspportstats** and **dspchstats**. Summary statistics counters are cleared only by operator action (**clrportstats**, **clrchstats**). Unless they are cleared manually, the counters eventually wrap around. Monitoring summary statistics on a node can be very useful for determining the amount of traffic being sent by the attached device, as well as for determining whether packets or cells are being dropped because they are in error.

Another class of statistics, *interval* statistics, can also be collected automatically by the Cisco WAN Manager (CWM) system. Interval statistics are stored in temporary *buckets* on the BPX BCC controller module. After periodic collection by the CWM system, the interval statistics are stored in a relational database for longer-term historical trend analysis, capacity planning, and management reporting. The BPX switch discards any statistics buckets not collected by the CWM system after a defined time period.

Testing

Summary statistics can be used during testing to monitor user traffic while adjusting the connection parameters. The **cnfcon** command can modify the connection characteristics without bringing the connection out of service. For example, what affect does increasing the sustainable cell rate (SCR) have on a variable bit rate (VBR) connection that is being used to transfer a file?

Often, it is useful to determine an application's type of traffic patterns. You can monitor channel statistics such as FTP to learn an application's average throughput. This can help you determine reasonable policing values for the permanent virtual circuit (PVC).

Because ABR adjusts the service rate for the user data, it might be wise to test whether an application performs well using an ABR (either Standard or with the ForeSight feature) connection. Monitoring the channel statistics can give you an idea of how ABR is adjusting the traffic rate.

Troubleshooting

Real-time statistics monitoring can also help you troubleshoot network problems. For example, if a signaling protocol (LMI or ILMI) is enabled on a port and the node is not receiving the expected messages from the attached device, a Port Communications Failure alarm is declared. These port statistics can help you determine whether any traffic is coming in from the end-user device so that you can see whether it has failed.

You can monitor port and channel statistics to determine whether data is being discarded and, if ATM cells *are* being dropped, possible reasons. These reasons can include the following:

- Failed Header Error Check (HEC) fields
- Unknown VPI and VCI
- Buffer overflows
- Policing

In addition, cell drops can also result in low or no user traffic throughput.

Multilevel Channel Statistics

The Multilevel Channel Statistics feature lets you extend the traditional summary statistics. *Summary* statistics are derived from real-time event counters that record accumulated totals of specific network events, such as the number of cells transmitted or received on a particular port. Summary statistics should not be confused with the historical or *interval* statistics that are collected from network nodes by the CWM system.

The Multilevel Channel Statistics feature allows you to configure and display additional levels of statistics beyond Level 1 statistics (for example, Levels 2 and 3). Channel statistics for BXM cards are defined in four levels: 0, 1, 2, and 3. Level 0 means that statistics collection is disabled. A larger set of statistics is collected as the level increases from 1 to 2, and even larger from 2 to 3. At the same time, the maximum number of channels that can be supported on the card decreases as the statistics level increases.

The relationship between statistics level and supported channels for the current generation of BXM cards is as follows:

- **Statistics Level 0**—61,440 channels are supported in the BXM hardware, although the actual limit imposed by switch software is 32,768.
- **Level 1**—32,768 channels are supported.
- **Level 2**—16,384 channels are supported.
- **Level 3**—8192 channels are supported.

For example, if you configure slot 5 to support Level 3 channel statistics, all connections on that particular card are set to provide Level 3 statistics. Switch software collects, displays, and propagates to the CWM system the various statistics types. The channel statistics types vary in number and type based on the level of support provided by the BXM cards. Use the **dspchstats** and **clrchstats** commands to display and clear the statistics.

The maximum number of supported channels includes the 64 reserved channels that are needed by the switch software for various purposes. The number of channels available (displayed by the **dspcd** command) reflects the lower number, which is the number actually available for user connections.

Before you up the line, use the **dspcd** command to verify that the BXM supports Multilevel Statistics. If a BXM card has firmware that supports Multilevel Statistics, the first time you activate a line on a standby card, you are prompted to initialize the Multilevel Statistics. After responding Yes, you can use the SuperUser **cnfcdparm** command to define which of the three levels of statistics you want to activate for this card.

NOTE   Changing the statistics level resets the card, which might disrupt user service.

Commands for Monitoring ATM Connections

Table 14-16 describes the commands used to monitor BPX ATM connections, along with their privilege levels.

Table 14-16 *Commands for Monitoring ATM Connections*

Command	Description	Privilege Level
dspchstats	Display port statistics. Displays historical and real-time ATM channel statistics.	6
clrchstats	Clear ATM channel statistics. Clears ATM statistics counters for one channel or for all channels on a node.	5

dspchstats Command

The **dspchstats** command displays the accumulated statistics for a single channel.

Here is the **dspchstats** command syntax:

```
dspchstats <slot.port.vpi.vci> [interval]
```

interval is the refresh rate in seconds. The range is 1 to 60 seconds. The default is 10 seconds.

clrchstats Command

The **clrchstats** command clears the accumulated statistics counts for a single channel or for all channels on a node. Statistics collection then resumes for the channel(s).

Here is the **clrchstats** command syntax:

```
clrchstats <slot.port.vpi.vci | *>
```

* indicates all channels on this node.

How to Monitor ATM Connections

Follow these steps to monitor ATM connections on a BPX node. The procedure assumes that at least one node in the network has a current active port failure or alarm:

Step 1   At the Next Command prompt, enter **dspcons**. This displays a summary status of all connections terminating on the node. Verify which connections are active. If any connection is listed as Failed, enter **dspcon** *<slot.port.vpi.vci>*. This displays the connection's status. Determine the cause of failure, and correct it if possible.

Step 2 Enter **dspcd** <*slot*>. This displays the status, revision, and serial number of the specified card. Verify the statistics level configured for the BXM card.

Step 3 Enter **dspchstats** <*slot.port.vpi.vci*> **1**, where **1** specifies the refresh rate as 1 second. This displays in real time the accumulating statistics for the selected channel.

Step 4 Verify that traffic is passing from the port to the network and vice versa.

Step 5 Verify that the From Port and To Network cell counts are the same or nearly so.

Step 6 Verify that the From Network and To Port cell counts are the same or nearly so.

Step 7 Verify that the % utilization and average cps statistics agree with the configured PCR or MCR, depending on traffic type. If cells are being discarded, note the statistics counts for discards and congestion (EFCI) indications. If the card is configured for Level 2 or Level 3 statistics, you might need to display the second or third screens to determine the error statistics.

Step 8 After you examine the statistics and made the necessary corrections, enter **clrchstats** <*slot.port.vpi.vci*>. This clears the accumulated statistics counters for all connections on the node.

Step 9 Enter **bye**. This terminates your CLI session and returns you to the login prompt.

Verifying the Card Statistics Level

Display a summary of all connections on the node by using the **dspcons** command to see if any connections have failed. If they have, display a failed connection by using the **dspcon** command and then determine the cause of failure and correct it if possible.

Before initiating statistics monitoring, you should verify the statistics level configured for the BXM card. Example 14-6 shows a BXM configured for Level 1 statistics that supports up to 16,320 user connections. The Scheduled Channel value includes the 64 management channels reserved by the switch software.

Example 14-6 *Verify Card Statistics Level:* **dspcd**

```
hei1bpx1        TRM      Teacher:1      BPX 8620  9.3.XX     May  11 200X 12:35 G+12

Detailed Card Display for BXM-155 in slot 1
Status:          Active
```

continues

Example 14-6 *Verify Card Statistics Level:* **dspcd** *(Continued)*

```
Revision:        FHA              Backcard Installed
Serial Number:   836752           Type:         LM-BXM
Top Asm Number:  28215802         Revision:      BA
Queue Size:      228300           Serial Number: 693990
Support: 8 Pts, OC3, FST, VcShp   Supp: 8 Pts,OC3,SMF,RedSlot:NO
Supp: VT,ChStLv 1,VSI(Lv 2,I,T,M)
Support: APS(FW)
Support: LMIver 1, ILMIver 1
Support: OAMLp, TrfcGen
#Ch:16320,PG[1]:8160,PG[2]:8160
PG[1]:1,2,3,4,PG[2]:5,6,7,8,
#Sched_Ch:16384




Last Command: dspcd 1


Next Command:

                    SW CD
```

ATM Channel Statistics Descriptions: Level 1

Example 14-7 shows the accumulated channel statistics for a channel on the preceding card. This is the only screen that is displayed for Level 1 statistics.

The statistics on this screen are common to all levels, but they are the only ones provided for Level 1. These statistics allow you to determine the following:

- Total number of cells received from and transmitted to the user device on this connection
- Utilization of the bandwidth allocated to the connection
- Instantaneous state of the ingress and egress VC queues for ABR connections
- Number of cells that have been discarded because of noncompliance and congestion

Example 14-7 *ATM Channel Statistics: Level 1*

```
hei1bpx1        TRM      Teacher:1      BPX 8620  9.3.XX     May  11 200X 12:35 G+12

Channel Statistics for 1.1.1.100   Cleared: June 26 200X 15:03  (|)
PCR: 4000/4000 cps        Collection Time: 0 day(s) 00:00:30      Corrupted: NO
   Traffic      Cells      CLP       Avg CPS   %util  Chan Stat Addr: 31136AD0
From Port   :        0          0         0        0  OAM Cell RX: Clear
To Network  :        0        ---         0        0
From Network:        0          0         0        0
To Port     :        0          0         0        0
```

Example 14-7 *ATM Channel Statistics: Level 1 (Continued)*

```
Rx Frames Rcv :      0  NonCmplnt Dscd:    0  Rx Q Depth   :      0
Tx Q Depth    :      0  Rx CLP0      :     0  Rx Nw CLP0   :      0
Igr VSVD ACR  :      0  Egr VSVD ACR :     0  Tx Clp0 Port :      0
Rx Clp0+1 Port:      0  NCmp CLP0 Dscd:    0  NCmp CLP1 Dscd:     0
Oflw CLP0 Dscd:      0  Oflw CLP1 Dscd:    0



This Command: dspchstats 1.1.1.100 1 1



Hit DEL key to quit:
                    SW CD
```

Table 14-17 describes the statistics that apply to Level 1.

Table 14-17 *ATM Channel Statistics: Level 1*

Parameter	Description
Cleared	The last time the **clrchstats** command was issued.
Collection Time	The time period since the **clrchstats**, **upcon**, or **addcon** command was issued.
PCR or MCR	The configured PCR or MCR. All percent utilization statistics are based on this value. The Peak Cell Rate (PCR) is used for all connection types except ABR, which uses the Minimum Cell Rate (MCR). These cell rates are also used when allocating bandwidth on network trunks for the connection.
Corrupted	Lets you determine whether a test or software loop was issued since the statistics were cleared that might have corrupted the information displayed on the screen.
From/To Port: Cells	The number of cells received and transmitted by the channel.
From/To Port: CLP	The number of cells transmitted and received with the CLP bit set to 1. This number does not imply that the BPX node changed the CLP bit to 1.
From/To Port: Avg CPS	The average traffic rate received and transmitted in cells per second.
From/To Port: %util	The traffic received and transmitted, described as a percentage of the PCR or MCR. The percent utilization can be used to determine whether the channel uses the expected amount of resources in the network.

continues

Table 14-17 *ATM Channel Statistics: Level 1 (Continued)*

Parameter	Description
To/From Network: Cells	The number of cells received and transmitted by the channel.
To/From Network: Avg CPS	The average traffic rate received and transmitted in cells per second.
To/From Network: % util	The traffic received and transmitted, described as a percentage of the PCR or MCR.
Rx Frames Rcv	The number of AAL5 frames received by the channel.
NonCmplnt Dscd	The number of received cells that were dropped due to the policing process.
Rx Q depth	A snapshot of the receive virtual circuit queue depth, in cells.
Tx Q depth	A snapshot of the transmit virtual circuit queue depth, in cells. The transmit queue is used on BXM cards when implementing standard ABR FCES.
Rx CLP0	The number of cells received from the attached end-user device with CLP set to 0.
Rx network CLP 0	The number of cells received from the network (crosspoint switch) with CLP set to 0.
Igr VSVD ACR	On a standard ABR connection, the Allowed Cell Rate (ACR) used by the ingress VC queue.
Egr VSVD ACR	On a standard ABR connection, the ACR used by the egress VC queue. The ACR on egress changes if FCES is enabled for the connection.
Tx Clp0 Port	The number of cells transmitted to the user device with CLP = 0.
Rx Clp0+1 Port	The number of cells with CLP = 0 or CLP = 1 received from the user device.
NCmp CLP0 Dscd	The number of noncompliant cells with CLP = 0 discarded by policing.
NCmp CLP1 Dscd	The number of noncompliant cells with CLP = 1 discarded by policing.
Oflw CLP0 Dscd	The number of cells with CLP = 0 discarded due to congestion.
OflwCLP1 Dscd	The number of cells with CLP = 1 discarded due to congestion.

ATM Channel Statistics Descriptions: Level 2

Level 2 includes all the statistics provided in Level 1, plus additional statistics that allow you to determine the following:

- The number of cells that have been received and transmitted with the EFCI congestion indicator bit set

- The number of EOF cells that have been discarded, which indicates FBTC action

- The number of cells that have been sent into the network with the CLP bit set to 1

Example 14-8 shows the first of the two screens for Level 2 statistics. It includes all the Level 1 statistics plus the additional statistics just mentioned.

Example 14-8 *ATM Channel Statistics: Level 2, Screen 1*

```
hei1bpx1        TRM     Teacher:1     BPX 8620   9.3.XX     May  11 200X 12:35 G+12

Channel Statistics for 1.1.1.100   Cleared: July 31 2000 06:09  (-)
PCR: 4000/4000 cps        Collection Time: 0 day(s) 00:02:32       Corrupted: NO
___Traffic      Cells       CLP      Avg CPS   %util  Chan Stat Addr: 31136AD0
From Port  :         0          0         0        0  OAM Cell RX: Clear
To Network :         0        ---         0        0
From Network:        0          0         0        0
To Port    :         0          0         0        0

Rx Frames Rcv :      0  NonCmplnt Dscd:      0  Rx Q Depth   :         0
Tx EFCI Port  :      0  Tx Q Depth    :      0  Rx CLP0      :         0
Rx Nw CLP0    :      0  Igr VSVD ACR  :      0  Egr VSVD ACR :         0
Tx Clp0 Port  :      0  Rx Clp0+1 Port:      0  NCmp CLP0 Dscd:        0
NCmp CLP1 Dscd:      0  Oflw CLP0 Dscd:      0  Oflw CLP1 Dscd:        0
Tx CLP1 Net:         0  Tx EFCI0 Net:        0  Tx EFCI1 Net:         0


This Command: dspchstats 1.1.1.100 1



Next page? (+/-/DEL key to quit)

                  SW CD 13
```

Example 14-9 shows the second screen for Level 2 statistics.

Example 14-9 *ATM Channel Statistics: Level 2, Screen 2*

```
hei1bpx1        TRM     Teacher:1       BPX 8620  9.3.XX     May  11 200X 12:35 G+12

Channel Statistics for 1.1.1.100   Cleared: July 31 2000 06:09   (/)
PCR: 4000/4000 cps       Collection Time: 0 day(s) 00:02:56       Corrupted: NO
___Traffic      Cells      CLP      Avg CPS   %util  Chan Stat Addr: 31136AD0
From Port   :       0         0       0        0  OAM Cell RX: Clear
To Network  :       0       - - -     0        0
From Network:       0         0       0        0
To Port     :       0         0       0        0

Tx EFCI0 Port:      0  Oflw EOF Dscd:      0  Tx EOF Port:         0




This Command: dspchstats 1.1.1.100 1


Next page? (+/-/DEL key to quit)

                SW CD
```

Table 14-18 lists the Level 2 statistics.

Table 14-18 *ATM Channel Statistics: Level 2*

Parameter	Description
Tx EFCI Port	The number of cells with EFCI = 1 transmitted to the user device. This number does not imply that the BPX network has changed the EFCI bit to 1.
Tx CLP1 Net	The number of cells received with CLP = 1.
Tx EFCI0 Net	The number of cells received with EFCI = 0.
Tx EFCI1 Net	The number of cells received with EFCI = 1.
Tx EFCI0 Port	The number of cells with EFCI = 0 transmitted to the user device.
Oflw EOF Dscd	The number of EOF cells discarded at the ingress due to congestion.
Tx EOF Port	The number of EOF cells transmitted to the user device.

ATM Channel Statistics Descriptions: Level 3

Level 3 includes all the statistics provided in Level 2, plus statistics that allow you to determine the following:

- The number of management cells that have been received and transmitted. These include RM, BRM, OAM, and the special BRM cells for connections with the ForeSight feature.

- The number of RM and OAM cells that have been discarded due to congestion.

- The number of cells that have been discarded due to congestion in the egress QBins.

Example 14-10 shows the first of three screens for Level 3 channel statistics.

Example 14-10 *ATM Channel Statistics: Level 3, Screen 1*

```
hei1bpx1        TRM      Teacher:1      BPX 8620  9.3.XX     May  11 200X 12:35 G+12

Channel Statistics for 1.1.1.100   Cleared: July 31 2000 06:09  (-)
PCR: 4000/4000 cps       Collection Time: 0 day(s) 00:04:40       Corrupted: NO
___Traffic      Cells        CLP      Avg CPS   %util  Chan Stat Addr: 31136AD0
From Port   :        0           0         0        0  OAM Cell RX: Clear
To Network  :        0         - - -       0        0
From Network:        0           0         0        0
To Port     :        0           0         0        0

Rx Frames Rcv :      0  NonCmplnt Dscd:     0  Rx Q Depth    :          0
Tx EFCI Port  :      0  Tx Q Depth    :      0  Rx CLP0       :          0
Rx Nw CLP0    :      0  Igr VSVD ACR  :      0  Egr VSVD ACR  :          0
Tx Clp0 Port  :      0  Rx Clp0+1 Port:      0  NCmp CLP0 Dscd:          0
NCmp CLP1 Dscd:      0  Oflw CLP0 Dscd:      0  Oflw CLP1 Dscd:          0
Tx CLP1 Net:         0  Tx EFCI0 Net:        0  Tx EFCI1 Net:           0


This Command: dspchstats 1.1.1.100 1


Next page? (+/-/DEL key to quit)

                SW CD
```

Example 14-11 shows the second of three screens for Level 3 channel statistics.

Example 14-11 *ATM Channel Statistics: Level 3, Screen 2*

```
hei1bpx1        TRM      Teacher:1      BPX 8620  9.3.XX     May  11 200X 12:35 G+12

Channel Statistics for 1.1.1.100   Cleared: July 31 2000 06:09  (-)
PCR: 4000/4000 cps       Collection Time: 0 day(s) 00:04:50       Corrupted: NO
___Traffic      Cells        CLP      Avg CPS   %util  Chan Stat Addr: 31136AD0
From Port   :        0           0         0        0  OAM Cell RX: Clear
```

continues

Example 14-11 *ATM Channel Statistics: Level 3, Screen 2 (Continued)*

```
To Network  :        0    ---           0       0
From Network:        0         0        0       0
To Port     :        0         0        0       0

Tx EFCI0 Port:      0  Oflw EOF Dscd:      0  Tx EOF Port:          0
Tx RM Port:         0  Rx EFCI0 Port:      0  Rx EFCI1 Port:        0
Rx OAM Port:        0  Rx RM Port:         0  Ofl EFCI0 Dscd:       0
Ofl EFCI1 Dscd:     0  Oflw OAM Dscd:      0  Oflw RM Dscd:         0
Tx FRM Net:         0  Tx BRM+FST Net:     0  Rx EFCI0 Net:         0
Rx EFCI1 Net:       0  Rx Egr OAM:         0  Rx Egr RM:            0



This Command: dspchstats 1.1.1.100 1


Next page? (+/-/DEL key to quit)

               SW CD
```

Example 14-12 shows the third of three screens for Level 3 channel statistics.

Example 14-12 *ATM Channel Statistics: Level 3, Screen 3*

```
hei1bpx1         TRM      Teacher:1     BPX 8620  9.3.XX      May  11 200X 12:35 G+12

Channel Statistics for 1.1.1.100   Cleared: July 31 2000 06:09  (-)
PCR: 4000/4000 cps      Collection Time: 0 day(s) 00:05:16      Corrupted: NO
___Traffic      Cells      CLP      Avg CPS   %util  Chan Stat Addr: 31136AD0
From Port   :        0         0        0       0  OAM Cell RX: Clear
To Network  :        0    ---           0       0
From Network:        1         0        0       0
To Port     :        1         0        0       0

TxOfl EFCI0 Dd:     0  TxOfl EFCI1 Dd:      0  TxOfl RM Dscd:        0
TxOfl OAM Dscd:     0




This Command: dspchstats 1.1.1.100 1


Next page? (+/-/DEL key to quit)

               SW CD
```

Table 14-19 lists the Level 3 channel statistics.

Table 14-19 *ATM Channel Statistics: Level 3*

Parameter	Description
Tx RM Port	The number of RM cells transmitted to the user device.
Rx EFCI0 Port	The number of cells received with EFCI = 0.
Rx EFCI1 Port	The number of cells received with EFCI = 1.
Rx OAM Port	The number of OAM cells received.
Rx RM Port	The number of RM cells received.
Ofl EFCI0 Dscd	The number of cells with EFCI = 0 discarded at the ingress due to congestion.
Oflw OAM Dscd	The number of cells with EFCI = 0 discarded at the ingress due to congestion.
Oflw RM Dscd	The number of cells with EFCI = 0 discarded at the ingress due to congestion.
Tx FRM Net	The number of Forward RM cells transmitted to the user device.
Tx BRM+FST Net	The number of BRM/ForeSight RM cells transmitted to the user device.
Rx EFCI0 Net	The number of cells received from the network with EFCI = 0.
Rx EFCI1 Net	The number of cells received from the network with EFCI = 1.
Rx Egr OAM	The number of RM cells received from the network.
Rx Egr RM	The number of OAM cells received from the network.
TxOfl EFCI0 Dd	The number of cells with EFCI = 0 discarded due to congestion at the egress.
TxOfl EFCI1 Dd	The number of cells with EFCI = 1 discarded due to congestion at the egress.
TxOfl RM Dscd	The number of RM cells discarded due to congestion at the egress.
TxOfl OAM dscd	The number of OAM cells discarded due to congestion at the egress.

Determining Connection Routes

In Figure 14-46, the following possible routes for a connection between node A and node F can be identified:

- A to B to C to F
- A to B to C to E to F
- A to B to E to F
- A to B to E to C to F
- A to B to D (3.3) to (3.1) E to F
- A to B to D (2.1) to (4.1) E to F
- A to B to D (3.3) to (3.1) E to C to F

- A to B to D (2.1) to (4.1) E to C to F
- A to D to B to C to F
- A to D to B to C to E to F
- A to D to B to E to F
- A to D to B to E to C to F
- A to D (3.3) to (3.1) E to F
- A to D (2.1) to (4.1) E to F
- A to D (3.3) to (3.1) E to C to F
- A to D (2.1) to (4.1) E to C to F
- A to D (3.3) to (3.1) E to B to C to F
- A to D (2.1) to (4.1) E to B to C to F

Figure 14-46 *Connection Route*

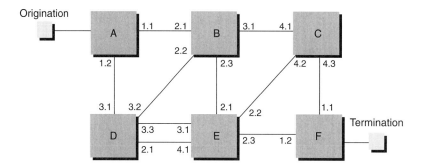

The following sections look at how to determine which of these routes are the best ones to use.

BPX Routing Criteria

In the following sections, rules 1 through 3 limit the trunks that can be used to route a connection, and rules 4 through 6 are used to select the best route from the available routes in the network.

Rule 1: Trunk Restrictions

Any of the following trunk restrictions can prevent a connection from routing across the trunk:

- A connection was added with the ***s** optional parameter to restrict it from routing across satellite hops, and the trunk is a satellite trunk.

- A connection was added with the ***t** optional parameter to restrict it from routing across terrestrial hops, and the trunk is a terrestrial trunk.
- The trunk is a virtual trunk, and the connection type is not supported on the trunk.

Rule 2: Connection IDs

A limited number of connections can route on a trunk. This number is defined by the number of connection IDs (ConnIDs) assigned to the trunk. The number of ConnIDs is hard-coded on physical trunks and can be configured on virtual and BXM trunks. Also, if a number of switched virtual circuit (SVC) channels have been defined for the trunk, the number of available permanent virtual circuits (PVCs) is reduced by that number.

Each connection that is allocated to a trunk is assigned one ConnID.

Rule 3: Bandwidth

A connection's expected bandwidth must be available on the trunk for the connection to route across that trunk.

Rule 4: Hops/Cost

To reduce network delay and the utilization of network resources (bandwidth), the BPX node attempts to limit the number of hops used by a connection.

Out of the possible routes through the network, cross out all the routes except those with three hops (two intermediate nodes). (Note that in hop-based routing, the maximum number of hops is 10.)

Rule 5: Bandwidth Bottlenecks

To evenly distribute the bandwidth in the network, the BPX node avoids bandwidth bottlenecks in the network. It examines the available bandwidth on each trunk of a route and identifies the bottleneck (the trunk with the least available bandwidth). The BPX node eliminates the routes with the smallest bottlenecks and selects the route with the largest bottleneck.

In the sample network, assume that the trunks in the remaining routes have the following bandwidth available:

- A to B—20,000 cps
- A to D—50,000 cps
- B to C—10,000 cps
- B to E—20,000 cps

- C to F—5000 cps
- E to F—50,000 cps
- D (3.3) to (3.1) E—50,000 cps
- D (2.1) to (4.1) E—5000 cps

Cross out all the routes that would have the smallest bottlenecks.

Rule 6: Trunk Number

If a single route has not been selected, the BPX node selects the route that leaves the node on the lowest trunk number. The trunk number is used only as a tiebreaker after all reasonable factors have been considered.

Considering all these criteria, the route our sample BPX network would use for the connection is A to B to E to F.

AutoRoute Routing

To simplify the routing process, two route-selection algorithms are available to the AutoRoute feature of the BPX switch:

- Fewest hops
- Lowest cost

Hop-Based Routing

In hop-based routing, the path with the fewest number of hops to the destination node is chosen as the best route. Each node along the path uses its own routing knowledge to determine the next hop in the route. The nodes choose consistent hops such that the call reaches the desired destination. Hop-based routing is the default.

Cost-Based Routing

Cost-based routing is an optional variation on the existing AutoRoute algorithm used by the BPX switches. The best route is determined based on the cost to the destination, not on the number of hops to the destination.

The **cnfcmparm** SuperUser command enables or disables cost-based routing on a per-node basis. The connection owner determines which routing algorithm is used, either cost- or hop-based. Because cost-based routing is configured per node, there is no restriction that all nodes in a network use cost-based routing.

Each trunk in the network is assigned a cost from 1 to 50 (the default is 10). The **cnftrk** command modifies the trunk's cost. Figure 14-47 illustrates the process of cost based routing.

Figure 14-47 *Cost-Based Routing*

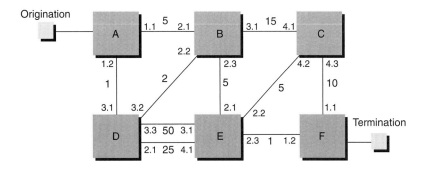

Each connection is also assigned a maximum cost route from 1 to 100 (the default is 100) that cannot be exceeded by the connection's route. The **cnfrtcost** command modifies the maximum cost route for a connection.

Based on the aggregate trunk cost and the maximum cost route for the connections, the BPX switch determines the best route for the connection.

In Figure 14-47, node A owns a connection to node F. If node A is using cost-based routing, it would choose route A to D to B to E to F with a cost of 9 over a shorter-hop route such as A to B to E to F with a cost of 11. If there were equal-cost routes, then, as with the hop-based AutoRoute scheme, the available bandwidth and the trunk numbers would be considered in the route-determination process.

Types of Routes

Three routing types are available on the BPX including network-assigned, preferred, and directed. These types are discussed in the following sections.

Network-Assigned Route

When the connection is added, the owning BPX node calculates and assigns the route. The connection remains on this initial route until one of the following occurs:

- A new route is selected.

- The route fails.

- The connection is taken out of service.

Preferred Route

A preferred, or operator-specified, route is configured using the **cnfpref** command. After it is configured, the switch attempts to keep the connection on that preferred route. If the preferred route fails and the connection is rerouted, it returns to the preferred route when the route recovers.

Directed Route

A directed route is a preferred route that does not reroute under any circumstance. If the preferred route is unavailable, the connection fails.

Reasons for Rerouting

When a trunk fails, all connections using that trunk must find new routes through the network. When a trunk failure is detected, the connection status indicates the following in succession:

- The connection has been derouted.
- Looking for a route. The owning switch checks the trunk load model and attempts to reroute the connection.

If the reroute attempt is unsuccessful, the connection goes into a failed status.

When a preferred route is configured by using the **cnfpref** command, the connection owner checks to see if the route is available. If the preferred route is available, the connection is rerouted. If, for any reason, a connection is not using its preferred route (due to a trunk failure, no bandwidth, and so on) and the preferred route becomes available, it reroutes.

When connections are downed using the **dncon** command, they are removed from the current route and remain idle until they are upped using the **upcon** command. When the connection is upped, the node must determine the best available route. The **dncon** command can affect either a single connection or an entire class.

Rules for Rerouting

Rules for rerouting are as follows:

- **Class of service**—CoS can be configured from 0 to 15. It is modified using the **cnfcos** command. CoS defines how many seconds a connection must wait after a trunk failure before the owning switch attempts to find a new route. In this way, connections might be given an advantage by being assigned a low CoS. The CoS, however, does not guarantee routing order.

NOTE	The **cnfcos** command must be issued from the connection owner.

- **Bandwidth requirements**—Higher-bandwidth connections are routed before lower-bandwidth connections to increase the possibility of rerouting the connection.
- **Bundling connections during reroute**—As soon as a connection route is determined, the switch checks for other connections that terminate on the same destination node. Multiple connections are then routed simultaneously to speed up the reroute process.

All the connections of one CoS are rerouted before the BPX switch attempts to reroute the next CoS.

Optional Routing Schemes

The BPX switch uses two schemes to reroute connections—concurrent routing and priority bumping. These schemes are used after an original route has been selected. They allow the BPX switch to more intelligently choose routes when massive numbers of connections are trying to reroute at the same time.

Concurrent Routing

Concurrent routing allows multiple route requests to be accepted and serviced without blocking, which shortens the network settling time. *Settling time* is the time required for all connections in the network to reroute.

Concurrent routing allows the degree of route concurrency to be configured on a node-by-node basis, allowing you to tailor the application of the enhancement to a specific network topology.

Concurrent routing allows multiple route requests to be concurrently active on a node. With this feature, the switch's processor can be more effectively utilized, which results in better reroute performance.

Priority Bumping

Priority bumping allows connections for the BPX node that are classified as more important (through CoS value) to bump existing connections that are of lesser importance. Priority bumping is useful when there are insufficient resources (for example, bandwidth) to route these important connections due to trunk failures in the network.

Trunk Bandwidth Allocation

When routing a connection, you must consider both the required bandwidth to support the connection and the available bandwidth on the trunks.

When a connection is routed over a trunk, the node must allocate some bandwidth to the connection on that trunk. This allocated bandwidth is used to determine how many connections can route over the trunk and how the trunk queues should be serviced. Bandwidth is allocated based on a minimum "guaranteed" rate for each connection. The load model provides a guideline to manage the traffic on the trunk.

Load Model Versus Actual Utilization

Trunk usage is based on the instantaneous traffic flow on the trunk. Because many connections are bursty in nature, they will not always have cells to send. As a result, multiple connections might share the same bandwidth. In this way, bandwidth is not assigned to a particular connection, but is offered to traffic as it arrives.

To prevent certain types of traffic from taking over all the trunk bandwidth, the traffic is controlled based on the load model. Cells of a particular type (CBR, VBR, or ABR) are serviced from their OptiClass queues based on the expected load. If a large burst of ABR traffic occurs, the CBR traffic is still given its allocated portion of the trunk. OptiClass uses a weighted-queue implementation to ensure that each type of traffic has fair access to trunk bandwidth. The weights are dynamic, based on configured connections.

NOTE   The load model considers only the AutoRoute partition. AutoRoute is unaware of the presence of other partitions.

Handling Bursts

What happens if several connections burst beyond their predicted bandwidth? For example, variable bit rate (VBR) connections are allocated bandwidth based on the Sustainable Cell Rate (SCR). What happens to the connection's cells or FastPackets when it sends at the *peak* cell rate (PCR)? Bursts are accommodated through a process of preserving bandwidth that is called the *statistical reserve*. Figure 14-48 illustrates the handling of bursty traffic.

Refer to Chapter 7, "Connection Routing, Synchronizing the Network, and Managing Jobs," for more information on handling bursts.

Figure 14-48 *Handling Bursts*

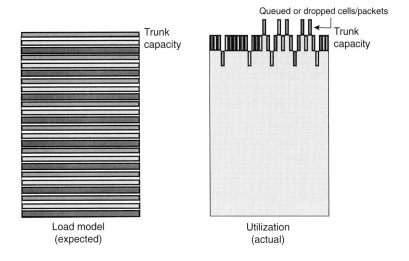

Statistical Reserve

The statistical reserve is a portion of bandwidth that cannot be allocated in the load model. The statistical reserve is designed to accommodate statistical variations in traffic but is not assigned to any specific connection, as shown in Figure 14-49. Having a statistical reserve reduces the possibility of dropped packets due to short-term bursts of traffic.

Figure 14-49 *Statistical Reserve*

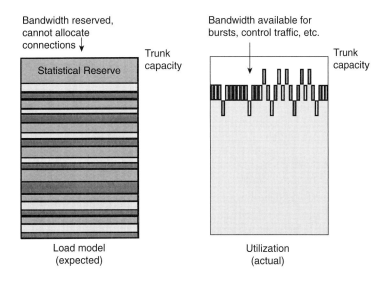

The statistical reserve carries the following traffic:

- BPX control traffic
- User traffic bursts
- Resources to allow time for the ABR feature to respond to trunk congestion with a low probability of cell loss

The size of the statistical reserve is set using the **cnftrk** command, and the total trunk capacity of the statistical reserve can be calculated using the following formula:

Total trunk capacity = current load + available bandwidth + statistical reserve

Connection Load

When you add connections to the BPX network, you define connection parameters that define the connection's policing, congestion control, and processing. For each connection type, a guaranteed rate is specified as part of the policing or queue servicing characteristics.

For example, a VBR connection is permitted to burst at the PCR for a limited time. If the connection is allocated less than the PCR, cells that are compliant on ingress might not have enough bandwidth on the trunks. However, because a VBR connection is permitted to burst for only a fixed amount of time, one connection does not need its PCR of bandwidth all the time. The percent utilization scales the allocated bandwidth to account for a connection's burstiness.

The required load for an ATM connection is based on the expected bandwidth multiplied by the configured percent utilization, which provides each connection a minimum rate on the trunk.

Connection Characteristics

The following connection characteristics affect bandwidth allocation:

- **CBR**—PCR(0+1) and percent utilization
- **VBR**—PCR(0+1) and percent utilization
- **ABR**—MCR and percent utilization
- **UBR**—PCR(0+1) and percent utilization

CBR and VBR connection bandwidth is based on their PCR. ABR connections need to be allocated only their minimum cell rate (MCR), because the Standard ABR or ForeSight congestion control algorithms always maintain the MCR for a connection. Unavailable bit rate (UBR) connections are also allocated their PCR. UBR connections, however, have a default percent utilization of 1 percent.

Connection Load Uses

The connection load calculated for a connection is used for the following:

- **Bandwidth needed to route the connection**—When a connection is routed or rerouted in the BPX network, the connection load (as determined by the CAC process) determines the bandwidth necessary on all trunks in the route to support the connection.

- **Bandwidth available on a trunk, based on connections routed on the trunk**—The sum of the connection load of all connections routed on a trunk determines the allocated bandwidth on a trunk. The trunk capacity minus the allocated bandwidth and statistical reserve determines the bandwidth still available on a trunk.

- **Queue service rate for each connection type on the trunk**—The aggregate of all connections for a given traffic type (such as VBR) determines the rate at which that OptiClass queue is serviced. This way, the BPX node always offers a guaranteed amount of bandwidth to a particular traffic type. If fewer than the expected number of cells are in the OptiClass queue, the bandwidth is made available to one of the other traffic types. Queue servicing is credit-based. Each credit is worth one cell.

A traffic type earns credits based on the aggregate of all connections of that type that are routed across the trunk. For example, if 5 VBR connections with PCRs of 5000 cps and percent utilizations of 50 are routed across a trunk, the VBR queue is issued 12,500 cps. If there is a credit and there is a cell to send, the queue gets served—12,500 cps of VBR traffic is guaranteed. If there is a credit for a traffic type but there is not a cell (underutilized), another traffic type gets a "free" credit. If there is free bandwidth, each queue is checked, and free credits are offered.

Expected Versus Actual Trunk Loading

The *load model* is a database that describes the expected amount of traffic on network trunks. The expected traffic is based on the rate and configured percent utilization of the connections routed on the trunks.

As stated earlier in this chapter, the *statistical reserve* is a portion of bandwidth that cannot be allocated in the load model.

Assume that one VBR connection has been routed across the trunk. In Figure 14-50, the box on the left shows the load model, and the box on the right shows the utilization.

As more connections are routed across the trunk (assume that they are all the same), the load model changes. The utilization reflects the actual traffic on the trunk, as shown in Figure 14-51.

Figure 14-50 *Expected Versus Actual Trunk Loading*

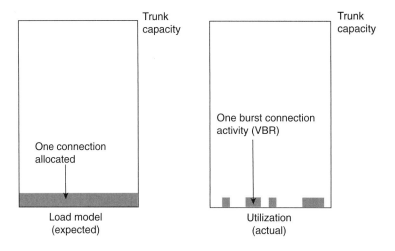

Figure 14-51 *Expected Versus Actual Trunk Loading, Continued*

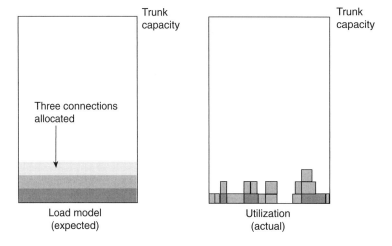

When enough connections have been routed across the trunk, it no longer accepts any additional connections. For example, if each VBR connection has a PCR of 1000 cps and the trunk is an E3 format (80,000 cps), 80 connections could route over the trunk.

Although the trunk will not accept any more connections, the bandwidth is not fully utilized because the burstiness of the VBR traffic has not been accounted for. The allocation assumes that the traffic is constant and needs the PCR all the time, as shown in Figure 14-52.

Figure 14-52 *Expected Versus Actual Trunk Loading, Continued*

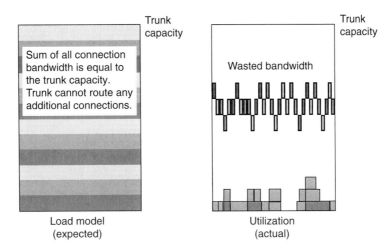

The percent utilization scales the amount of bandwidth necessary to route the connections. In this case, a 50 percent utilization should allow twice the number of connections to route on the trunk. Unfortunately, cells are being dropped.

Cells are dropping because statistically there is still a chance that 51 percent of the connections are transmitting at the PCR at the same time, as shown in Figure 14-53. Also, there is control and management traffic that is not accounted for.

Figure 14-53 *Expected Versus Actual Trunk Loading, Continued*

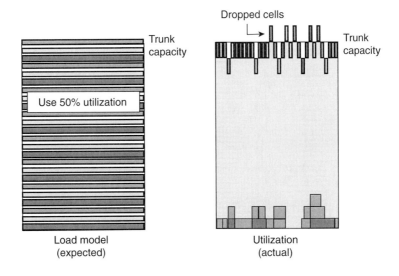

The statistical reserve protects the trunk from dropping cells by reducing the amount of bandwidth that can be allocated on the trunk. In Figure 14-54, the reserved bandwidth can be used but cannot be allocated to connections.

Figure 14-54 *Expected Versus Actual Trunk Loading, Continued*

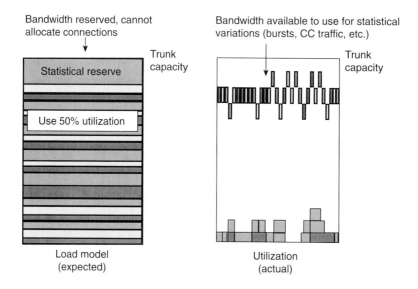

Commands for Routing Networks

Table 14-20 describes the BPX CLI commands for routing BPX AutoRoute connections in a BPX switch, along with their privilege levels.

Table 14-20 *Commands for Routing Networks*

Commands	Description	Privilege Level
dspload	Display load model. Displays the expected load on all or one trunk on the local or remote BPX node.	6
dsptrkutl	Display trunk utilization. Displays the real-time traffic utilization on a trunk.	6
cnfcos	Configure CoS. Defines the CoS for a locally owned connection.	2
cnfpref	Configure preferred route. Defines a preferred route for one or all locally owned connections.	2
cnfrtcost	Configure connection cost. Configures the cost cap for a connection when cost-based routing is configured.	2

Table 14-20 *Commands for Routing Networks (Continued)*

Commands	Description	Privilege Level
dsprts	Display routes. Displays all routes for connections that terminate on this node.	6
dncon	Down connection. Brings a connection or all network connections of a particular CoS out of service.	2
upcon	Up connection. Brings a connection or all network connections of a particular CoS back into service.	2
cnfcmparm	Configure connection management parameters. Configures various connection management parameters for the node.	SuperUser

How to Route and Configure Connections

Follow these steps to route and configure connections in a BPX switch:

Step 1   At the Next Command prompt, enter **dspload** to display the bandwidth for all the trunks. This displays the allocated and available transmit and receive bandwidth for each trunk.

Step 2   Enter **dspload** [*node name*] [*trunk id*]. This displays any connections that currently terminate at this node. Verify the bandwidth for the trunk.

If the connection terminates on a remote BPX switch, log into the remote BPX node (**vt**) and enter **dspload** [*node-name*] [*trunk-id*]. This displays the bandwidth of the trunk on the remote node. Verify the bandwidth, then enter **bye** to terminate the session and return to your original node.

Step 3   Enter **dspcons** to display the connections and identify a VBR or available bit rate (ABR) connection. This displays summary information on all connections on the node.

Step 4   Enter **dspcon** <*slot.port.vpi.vci*> for the connection you want to route. This displays the detailed configuration. Identify the route, the PCR or minimum cell rate (MCR), and the percent utilization. Determine how much bandwidth the connection should be allocated.

Step 5   Enter **dsptrkutl** <*trunk id*> [*interval*] for the connection you just routed. This displays trunk usage statistics.

Step 6   Enter **cnfcos** <*channel*> [*node name*] to determine the priority for rerouting this connection. This specifies the delay in seconds before the network reroutes this connection in the event of a failure.

Step 7   Enter **cnfpref** <*channel*> <*+1 - 1 route*> [d] for the connection. This specifies the preferred route.

Step 8 Enter **cnfrtcost** *<con id> <cost>* for the connection. This sets the maximum route cost the connection.

Step 9 Enter **dsprts**. This displays the current routing information for all connections.

dspload Command

The **dspload** command displays the allocated and available transmit and receive bandwidth for each trunk at the specified switch. The transmit direction is from the node specified to the node at the other end of the trunk. Failed trunks appear in dim reverse video on the screen. The **dspload** command displays the following summary information:

- Trunk number
- **Transmit and receive units**—Packets or cells
- **Transmit and receive used**—Bandwidth allocated to connections
- **Transmit and receive available**—Bandwidth available to route additional connections
- **Transmit and receive reserved**—Statistical reserve

The local trunk card (BXM or BNI) is responsible for servicing the egress queues based on the transmit bandwidth requirements.

Here is the **dspload** command syntax:

```
dspload [node-name] [trunk-id]
```

Table 14-21 describes the parameters for the **dspload** command.

Table 14-21 dspload *Command*

Parameter	Description	Required/Optional
node-name	Displays the load model for a specific switch. If a node is not specified, the display shows loading on the local node.	Optional
trunk-id	Displays the load model for a specific trunk.	Optional

dspload [*trunk*] Command

The **dspload** command with a trunk ID lists the following detailed load characteristics for that trunk:

- Local and remote node names and trunk IDs
- Non-time-stamped (NTS) allocated traffic
- Time-stamped (TS) allocated traffic
- Voice allocated traffic

- Frame Relay without ForeSight traffic (BDataA) allocated traffic
- Frame Relay with ForeSight traffic (BDataB) allocated traffic
- CBR allocated traffic
- Real-time and nonreal-time variable bit rate (VBR) allocated traffic
- ABR allocated traffic
- Total FastPackets or cells in use
- Available FastPackets or cells
- Statistical reserve
- Total capacity
- Connection identifiers in use, available and total capacity
- Miscellaneous trunk characteristics

NOTE   The **dspload** screen display is a template used on the IGX and is why Frame Relay, voice, and data connections are shown.

dsptrkutl Command

The **dsptrkutl** command displays real-time trunk usage statistics for a specified trunk. Unlike some of the other statistics screens, the **dsptrkutl** command display does not provide any historical information. Before you use this command, the trunk must be upped and added. Disabled trunks have their trunk number displayed in dim reverse video on the screen.

Comparing the load model and utilization for a particular trunk can provide insight into bandwidth efficiency and capacity requirements for the network.

Here is the **dsptrkutl** command syntax:

```
dsptrkutl <trunk-id> [interval]
```

Table 14-22 describes the command parameters for the **dsptrkutl** command.

Table 14-22   **dsptrkutl** *Command*

Parameter	Description	Required/Optional
trunk-id	Displays a trunk's current bandwidth usage.	Required
interval	Time, in seconds, between screen updates. If no value is specified, the command defaults to 20 seconds.	Optional

Parameter and statistic descriptions for the **dsptrkutl** command are described in Table 14-23.

Table 14-23 *Parameter and Statistic Descriptions*

Parameter and Statistic	Description
Elapsed Time (seconds)	Elapsed time, in seconds, since the command was started.
Total Packets Transmitted	Number of cells/packets transmitted during the elapsed time.
Overall Packet Rate	Number of cells/packets transmitted per second during the elapsed time.
Overall utilization	Bandwidth used, expressed as a percentage of the available bandwidth during the elapsed time: $100 \times$ (total packets transmitted / elapsed time $\times$ bandwidth in packets per second).
Peak Interval Utilization	Bandwidth used, expressed as a percentage of the available bandwidth during the *peak* interval: $100 \times$ (total packets transmitted / peak interval $\times$ bandwidth in packets per second).
Last Interval (seconds)	Elapsed time, in seconds, for the last screen update interval.
Interval packets generated	Number of packets transmitted during the last interval.
Interval packet rate (pkts/sec)	Number of packets transmitted per second during the last interval.
Interval utilization	The used bandwidth, expressed as a percentage of the available bandwidth during the last interval. The derivation of interval utilization is as follows: $100 \times$ (interval packets transmitted) / (last interval $\times$ bandwidth in packets per second).
Total Connections	Total number of connections routed over the trunk.
Terminated/Via	Terminated: Number of connections routed over the trunk that terminates at this node.
	Via: Number of connections routed over the trunks that do not terminate at this node.

Table 14-24 describes terminated connection statistics for the **dsptrkutl** command.

Table 14-24 *Terminated Connection Statistic Descriptions*

Terminated Connection Statistic	Description
Voice terminated	Number of voice connections terminated at this node that are routed over this trunk.
Data terminated	Number of data connections terminated at this node that are routed over this trunk.
Frame Relay terminated	Number of Frame Relay connections terminated at this node that are routed over this trunk.

Table 14-24 *Terminated Connection Statistic Descriptions (Continued)*

Terminated Connection Statistic	Description
Num voice off-hook	Number of voice connections off-hook that are terminated at this node and are routed over this trunk.
Connection Type	Voice connection types: c, a, v, p, or t.
Connection Num	Number of terminated voice connections of each type: c, a, v, p, and t.
Modem On	Number of terminated connections with a modem detected.
Modem V.25	Number of terminated connections with a V.25 modem detected.
VAD Enabled	Number of terminated connections with VAD enabled.

cnfcos Command

The **cnfcos** command determines the priority for rerouting a connection. You determine the priority by specifying a 0- to 15-second delay before the network reroutes one or more failed connections. The CoS applies to the following:

- Single connection
- Range of connections
- Connection group

The CoS is the delay in seconds before the network reroutes a connection in the event of a trunk failure.

Here is the **cnfcos** command syntax:

```
cnfcos <channel(s)> <CoS>
```

Table 14-25 describes the parameters for the **cnfcos** command.

Table 14-25 **cnfcos** *Command*

Parameter	Description	Required/Optional
channel(s)	Specifies the channel to configure.	Required
CoS	Delay in seconds before rerouting starts for this channel. CoS can range from 0 to 15 seconds.	Required

cnfpref Command

The **cnfpref** command specifies the preferred route for a connection, connection group, or range of connections. Use this command to add, remove, or modify a connection's preferred route. The **cnfpref** command must be issued from the connection owner.

The preferred route for a connection is used when possible. If the preferred route is different from the existing route, the connection automatically moves to the preferred route whenever network conditions allow (for example, when trunks are out-of-alarm and sufficient bandwidth exists).

Here is the **cnfpref** command syntax:

```
cnfpref <channel | * > <+ | - | route> [d]
```

Table 14-26 describes the parameters for the **cnfpref** command.

Table 14-26 cnfpref *Command*

Parameter	Description	Required/Optional
channel | *	Specifies the channel or range of channels for preferred route configuration. * specifies all locally owned connections.	Required
+ | - | *route*	Designates a specific preferred route through the network in the format *trunk/node name*. + makes the current route the preferred route. - removes the current route as the preferred route.	Required
d	Specifies directed routing. If the preferred route is unavailable, the connection fails.	Optional

Configure Preferred Route Example

In Example 14-13, a preferred route between bpx1 and bpx2 is configured for connection 3.1.1. (The **cnfpref** command specifies 14/hei1bpx2.) Trunk 14 is the interface on hei1bpx2, *not* hei1bpx1. For longer routes, specify multiple trunk/node pairs. For example:

```
cnfpref 3.1.1 14/hei1bpx2 16/hei1bpx6 12.2/bpx4
```

Example 14-13 cnfpref *Command*

```
hei1bpx1        TRM     Teacher:1      BPX 8620  9.3.XX   May  11 200X 12:35 G+12

Conn    Route
3.1.1
        hei1bpx1        13--   14hei1bpx2
Pref:   hei1bpx1        13--   14hei1bpx2
3.1.2-6
        hei1bpx1        15--   15hei1bpx2
Pref:   Not Configured
5.1
        hei1bpx1        12--   13hei1bpx4      15--   15bpx3
Pref:   Not Configured
16.10.100
        hei1bpx1        12--   13hei1bpx4
```

Example 14-13 cnfpref *Command (Continued)*

```
Pref:   Not Configured




Last Command: cnfpref 3.1.1 14/hei1bpx2


Next Command:
```

cnfrtcost Command

The **cnfrtcost** command sets the maximum route cost for a connection, as shown in Example 14-14. The maximum route cost is not enforced until the connection is rerouted. If all available routers exceed the configured route cost, the connection fails.

Example 14-14 cnfrtcost *Command*

```
hei1bpx1      TRM     Teacher:1    BPX 8620  9.3.XX   May  11 200X 12:35 G+12

Conn:  9.1.10.100        hei1bpx3    9.1.100.32000     cbr      Status:OK
   PCR(0+1)     % Util    CDVT(0+1)     Policing
   2000/2000   100/100   15000/15000      4/4

Owner: LOCAL  Restriction: NONE  COS: 0 Pri: L  Test-RTD: 0 msec  Max Cost: 10
Path:    bpx4      14--  13bpx3
Pref:    Not Configured




bpx4      UXM:   OK                   bpx3      UXM:   OK
          Line  9.1 : OK                        Line  9.1 : OK
          OAM Cell RX: Clear                    NNI:   OK
          NNI:   OK

Last Command: cnfrtcost 9.1.10.100 10


Next Command:
```

Here is the **cnfrtcost** command syntax:

```
cnfrtcost <con-id> <cost>
```

Table 14-27 describes the parameters for the **cnfrtcost** command.

Table 14-27 cnfrtcost *Command*

Parameter	Description	Required/Optional
con-id	The connection ID.	Required
cost	The maximum route cost. Cost values range from 1 to 500.	Required

dsprts Command

The **dsprts** command shows the current routing information for all connections on a switch. A blinking trunk indicates a failed circuit. A tilde (~) indicates a satellite trunk.

The routing information for each connection includes the following:

- Connection or channel number
- Node name and trunk number of the local, intermediate, and remote nodes in the route
- Preferred route, if configured
- Route cost, if enabled. The route cost is calculated by adding the costs for all trunks in the trunk route. (Individual trunk costs are set using the **cnftrk** command.)

The **dsprts** screen is also displayed if you use the **cnfpref** command to define a preferred route.

Here is the **dsprts** command syntax:

```
dsprts [start-channel] [node-name]
```

Table 14-28 describes the parameters for the **dsprts** command.

Table 14-28 dsprts *Command*

Parameter	Description	Required/Optional
start-channel	Specifies the starting channel with which to begin the display. If you do not specify a starting channel, the display begins with the first connected channel.	Optional
node-name	Displays only connections from the local switch to the specified node. If the node name is omitted, this displays all connections.	Optional

dncon Command

The **dncon** command deactivates a connection, a group of connections, or all connections that have a specific CoS or CoS range. Use this command to bring the connection out of service, make room for other connections on a trunk, or reroute the connection. When a connection is downed, the system removes it from the route and releases its bandwidth in the trunk load model.

Voice connections can be downed immediately or with courtesy. With courtesy downing, the system waits until the connection is on-hook before downing it. Courtesy downing is possible only if the on-hook status has been configured with the **cnfvchtp** command.

The State display column in the **dspcons** screen has the following values:

- **Ok**—Routed
- **Down**—Downed
- **Ok(Dn)**—Voice connections that have been courtesy downed are waiting for on-hook
- **Failed**—Not routed, but trying

Here is the **dncon** command syntax:

```
dncon <channel(s) | cos> [cos-range] [c | i]
```

Table 14-29 describes the parameters for the **dncon** command.

Table 14-29 dncon *Command*

Parameter	Description	Required/Optional
channel(s) | cos	The channel(s) of the connection to deactivate. Alternatively, you can specify cos followed by a CoS number to deactivate all connections that have that CoS. You can down a connection from either the local or remote owner BPX node.	Required
cos-range	The CoS number or range to deactivate. Determines which connections will be downed based on their CoS. Use this parameter with caution, because it deroutes *all* connections in the BPX network within the CoS range.	Optional
c | *i*	Immediate (i) or courtesy (c) down off-hook voice connections. For voice connections only. The node monitors the state of the voice connection (on- or off-hook) when you choose a courtesy and waits until the connection is on-hook before bringing it down.	Optional

upcon Command

The **upcon** command ups a downed connection, a group of connections, or all connections that have a specific CoS or CoS range. When a connection is upped, the system tries to route. If the connection cannot immediately be routed, the system marks the connection as failed and generates a major alarm.

Here is the **upcon** command syntax:

```
upcon <channel(s) | cos> [cos-range]
```

Table 14-30 describes the parameters for the **upcon** command.

Table 14-30 **upcon** *Command*

Parameter	Description	Required/Optional
channel(s) | cos	The channel or range of channels to activate. Alternatively, you can specify cos followed by a CoS number to activate all connections that have that CoS.	Required
cos-range	The CoS number or range to activate.	Optional

Summary

In this chapter, you learned how to define and modify ATM connections. You should now understand traffic policing in the BPX switch and the function of VC queues. You should be able to explain frame-based traffic control and describe how standard ABR and ABR with ForeSight are implemented in the BPX switch.

You learned how to establish, configure, and monitor ATM and interworking connections on the BPX switch. You should be able to describe the impact on traffic throughput of modifying connection parameters. This chapter also covered observing and manipulating connection routes and predicting network routes.

Statistical reserve and bandwidth requirements for connections also were described. You should be able to identify and describe the trunk load model and contrast the trunk load model and actual trunk utilization. You should also be able to display connection routes and select preferred connection routes.

Review Questions

1 Mark the following statements as true or false.

A. _____ The default BPX policing type is 3 for CBR and 4 for all other service.

B. _____ Noncompliant cells are discarded at the first bucket.

C. _____ CDVT defines the depth of the PCR bucket.

D. _____ BPX policing type 5 is the same as no policing.

E. _____ Any BPX policing type can be configured for an ABR connection.

2 Given the following parameters, how many cells will be received before a CBR.1 connection becomes noncompliant?

CDVT (0 + 1) = 10,000 microseconds

PCR (0 + 1) = 4,000 cells per second

AR = 5,000 cells per second

A. 200

B. 2,000,000

C. 2,000,001

D. 201

3 How does ABR differ from other ATM service types?

A. Only ABR incorporates a feedback mechanism.

B. ABR uses AAL5.

C. ABR circuits are guaranteed a bandwidth of MCR.

D. A and B only.

E. A and C only.

F. All of the above.

4 What values would the DIR, BN, CI, and NI bits have in a BRM cell generated by an intermediate switch?

A. 0, 1, 1, 1

B. 1, 1, 1, 0

C. 1, 1, 1, 1

D. 1, 0, 1, 1

5 In the BXM card, which of the following queue structures does not have a configurable EFCI threshold?

A. Trunk QBin

B. Per-card QBin

C. Port QBin

D. VC queue

6 Mark the following statements as true or false.

A. _____ The maximum time between RM cells in normal operation is defined by Trm.

B. _____ On startup, the ER field is set to MCR.

C. _____ BPX nodes do not generate RM or BRM cells in ABR without VS/VD.

D. _____ By default, a BRM cell is expected after no more than 32,760 RM cells have been sent.

E. _____ With ER control, the arriving BRM cell always contains the ER as calculated by the previous node in the connection path.

F. _____ A connection idle for more than the ADTF resumes transmission at the ICR.

7 Select the correct definitions for NIW and SIW from the following list.

A. **NIW**—Interworking function for Frame Relay-to-ATM adaptation. Implemented on BXM trunk cards.

B. **SIW**—Interworking function that supports the connection of two endpoints with different service types, such as ATM and Frame Relay.

C. **NIW**—Interworking function that supports the transport of complete Frame Relay frames across an ATM backbone.

D. **SIW**—Interworking function that converts protocols, such as IP to FDDI.

8 Match the following commands with their function.

1. _____ **addcon**   A. Modifies connection parameters

2. _____ **dspcon**   B. Lists all connections on the node

3. _____ **dspatmcls** C. Creates a new ATM connection in the network

4. _____ **dspcons**   D. Displays connection configuration status and routing

5. _____ **cnfcon**   E. Shows the parameters associated with a connection class

9 What is a leaky bucket?

A. A model used for policing

B. A queue used for policing

C. A per-connection ingress queue

D. A way to determine the connection type

10 Mark the following statements as true or false.

A. _____ ATM cells are never dropped if they are noncompliant.

B. _____ ATM cells are always dropped if they are noncompliant.

C. _____ ATM cells are always tagged with the CLP bit if they are noncompliant.

D. _____ ATM cells can be dropped or tagged with the CLP bit if they are noncompliant.

11 Which type of traffic uses an ingress virtual circuit queue?

A. CBR

B. VBR

C. ABR

D. UBR

12 Which of the following statements are true for a connection with a preferred route?

A. The connection load-shares on multiple trunks between nodes.

B. The connection cannot route on any path other than the preferred route.

C. The connection uses less bandwidth than a connection without a preferred route.

D. The preferred route can be configured for a path that is not the best possible route in the network.

E. The connection returns to its preferred route if it was rerouted because of a trunk failure and the trunk has been repaired.

13 Which of the following are considered when routing or rerouting a connection?

A. Number of hops

B. Delay on a trunk

C. CoS

D. Distance to the destination node

E. Connection bandwidth requirements

F. The connection's service type, such as ABR or CBR

G. Route restrictions, such as no satellite or terrestrial trunks

14 Of the following commands, which three display route cost information?

A. **dspcon**

B. **dsprts**

C. **dspload**

D. **dsptrkcnf**

E. **dspconcnf**

F. **dspchstats**

15 What is the load model?

A. The amount of traffic being used on a trunk

B. A model that describes the expected traffic on a trunk

C. The amount of bandwidth necessary to route a connection

D. The amount of bandwidth that is reserved for management traffic

16 What is the statistical reserve? (Choose all that apply.)

A. A management channel on a trunk

B. Bandwidth that is reserved for SVCs to route over a trunk

C. Bandwidth that is reserved on a trunk so that ABR connections can burst

D. Bandwidth on a trunk that is reserved for control traffic and cannot be used by connections

E. Bandwidth that cannot be allocated to connections, but can be used to accommodate statistical variations in the traffic

This chapter covers the following key topics:

- Network Synchronization
- What Is an Alarm?
- Monitoring and Resolving BPX Trunk Alarms
- Monitoring and Resolving BPX Line Alarms
- Locating Alarms
- Monitoring Multicast Connections
- Commands for Troubleshooting

CHAPTER 15

Synchronizing the Network and Troubleshooting

BPX switches must be synchronized to a common network clock to avoid data loss. This chapter introduces you to the methods and concepts of network synchronization in a BPX network. It describes how to select potential clock sources and how to discover which clock source is used by the network.

This chapter covers possible alarm conditions and examines the commands required to locate, monitor, and resolve BPX trunk and line alarms, monitor multicast connections, and set up connection loopback tests.

Many of the commands and concepts discussed in this chapter were introduced in other chapters.

Network Synchronization

Network synchronization depends on a reliable and accurate clocking scheme that ensures that all nodes in the network automatically synchronize to the nearest, most stable clock available (as discussed in the following sections). No time-division multiplexing (TDM) facilities are attached to the BPX switch. If there are any TDM circuits, they are attached to MGX feeders and sent as ATM to the BPX switch. The **dspcurclk** command displays the current clock source for a BPX switch and the trunk path between the source and the local switch. Synchronization is essential if end-user equipment is using TDM-based access lines for time-dependent traffic, such as voice or synchronous data.

Carrier Network Timing

Carrier central offices use a clocking hierarchy called the Building Integrated Timing Supply (BITS), in which each carrier device can trace its clock source back to a Stratum 1 or Stratum 2 clock. Clocks are described in terms of their stability—their ability to maintain framing consistency without slips for a defined interval. The highest level is a Stratum 1 clock, which may be a Cesium atomic clock, a ground station interface for a Global Positioning System (GPS) clock, and so on. A Stratum 1 clock provides timing for lower-stability clocks such as Stratum 2 clocks. Stratum 2 clocks provide timing for other Stratum 2, Stratum 3, or Stratum 4 clocks. The BPX switch has a Stratum 3 clock. All timing sources should be traceable back to a Stratum 1 source to ensure its own stratum level stability. Stratum clock intervals are discussed in Chapter 7, "Connection Routing, Synchronizing the Network, and Managing Jobs."

Clock Sources

Node clocking is generated by the BCC. Because the BPX switch resides as an element in a telecommunications network, it can synchronize to higher-stratum clocking devices in the network and provide synchronization to lower-stratum devices. The BCC can be synchronized to any of three different sources under software control:

- Internal, high-stability oscillator

- Derived clock from a BXM module

- External clock source connected directly to the BPX switch

The BCC clock circuits provide clocking signals to every other card slot. If a function card needs to synchronize its physical interface to the BPX switch clock, it can use this timing signal to derive the proper reference frequency. These reference frequencies include DS1, E1, DS3, and E3.

Clock sources in a BPX network are defined using the **cnfclksrc** command as primary, secondary, or tertiary sources. Any type of clock source can be configured as any of the three levels.

A BPX switch can derive timing from a clock attached to any of the following:

- **External**—An external clock source is a T1 or E1 alternate mark inversion (AMI) bipolar signal typically purchased as a service from the carrier. An external clock source is the most common type in BPX networks. The BCC back card has either one (on the BCC-32) or two (on the BCC-4) clock input connectors to attach external clock sources to the BPX node. The external clock source can be an EIA/TIA-422 square wave at 1.544 kHz or 2048 kHz.

- **Trunk**—Framed T3, E3, OC-3/STM-1, or OC-12/STM-4 trunks, as well as virtual trunks, can be used as a clock source. In order to provide clocking, the trunk parameter "pass synch" should be set to "No." If a trunk provides timing, it cannot pass timing (synch) over the trunk. For example, if it provides timing, pass synch = no; if it doesn't, pass synch = yes (which is the default setting on the **cnftrk** command). It is common for the carrier to expect the end-user equipment to provide the clocking for the trunk.

- **Line**—A framed T3, E3, OC-3/STM-1, or OC-12/STM-4 line can also be used as a network clock source. Similar to a trunk, the carrier might expect the BPX node to provide the clock.

BPX Trunks as Clock Sources

Trunks that "pass sync" (or "pass clock") are not allowed to be clock sources. Use the **cnftrk** command to change this option. If a trunk does not pass sync, it may be configured as a clock source. A trunk passes sync if the clock information transmitted from one end arrives as the identical clock at the other end. Normal T3 or E3 trunks pass clock. Before selecting a circuit as either a clock source or clock path, ask your carrier how it is timed. Figure 15-1 illustrates passing sync on BPX trunks.

Figure 15-1 *Passing Sync on BPX Trunks*

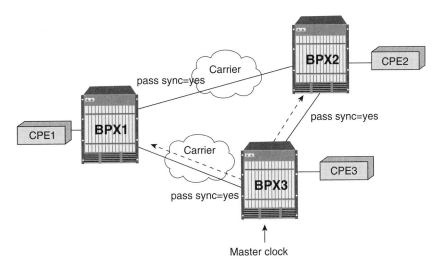

Rules for Selecting a Clock Reference

Clock sources in a BPX network are defined as primary, secondary, or tertiary sources. The primary should be the most stable clock source. If multiple clock sources are defined in the BPX network, a node chooses the primary source over a secondary and a secondary over a tertiary.

Clock stability is determined by using a continuous clock test to compare the frequency of the node clock source to a reference on the control card. If a clock source is outside the preset frequency limits, the controller declares the source defective and selects another source.

This clocking scheme ensures that all nodes in the network automatically synchronize to the nearest, most stable clock available. After you specify a clock source using the **cnfclksrc** command, the location and type of the network clock source go out to all nodes in the network. This synchronization remains in effect despite line failures, power outages, controller card switchovers, line repairs, and all other network topology changes.

The **dspclksrcs** command displays all clock sources in a network. If multiple sources of the same level (primary, secondary, or tertiary) are available in the network, each node chooses the closest one (measured in number of hops). If multiple equal clock sources still exist, the BPX node chooses, in order, the external sources, and then the lines (lowest number first), and finally the trunks (lowest number first). If two equal hop count routes exist, the lowest node number path is chosen.

Clock sources can be changed manually or automatically by a node. If no primary, secondary, or tertiary clock sources are defined or working in a network, the internal oscillator of the highest node number is automatically selected as the active network clock source. Whenever a clock source changes, the node ensures that the clock path remains hierarchical. Clock source rules are as follows:

- In a BPX network, a clock source functions as a source for the entire network.

- To avoid unnecessary clock disruptions, all primary clock sources should be configured for the network first.

- A line must be upped and not in alarm before it is configured as a network clock source.

- Defining a trunk as a clock source is incompatible with defining it as passing sync. Before you define a trunk as a clock source, use the **cnftrk** command to specify that the trunk does not pass synchronization.

Carrier limitations might restrict clocking options. Here are some possible restrictions:

- Trunks and lines must be clocked

- Trunks and lines cannot be clocked ("loop" the clock)

- Multiple carrier facilities in a single network

Synchronization Example

Figures 15-2 through 15-12 present synchronization examples to illustrate how the BPX nodes choose from the configured clock sources.

Before any clock sources are configured in the network, the BPX nodes use the internal oscillator of the highest numbered node, as illustrated in Figure 15-3. The highest numbered node is represented in Figures 15-3 through 15-12 by the letter F as a clock source. The letter P represents the primary clock source.

Figure 15-2 *Synchronization Example*

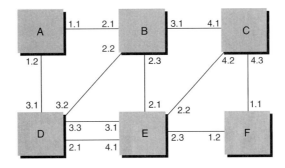

Figure 15-3 *Synchronization Example, Continued*

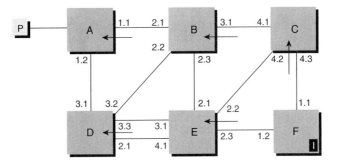

Node A, which is directly attached to the external clock source, as illustrated in Figure 15-4, extracts the signal from the source and compares it to its own internal oscillator. Provided that the signal is within the required frequency range, the signal is divided and propagated across the BPX node's timing bus.

Figure 15-4 *Synchronization Example, Continued*

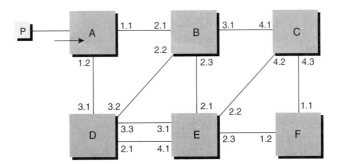

When the network clock sources or topology change, each BPX node must decide which clock source to use and how to reference it.

Figure 15-5 illustrates the paths used by each node back to the primary external clock source on node A. For example, node F's path to the clock source is A to B to C to F. Note that two primary sources are introduced in this figure. They are discussed in greater detail in the following paragraph.

Figure 15-5 *Synchronization Example, Continued*

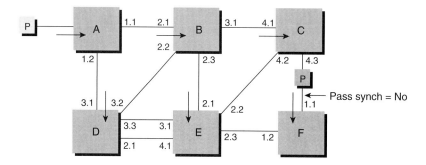

With two primary clock sources in the network, each BPX node must determine the best source to use and the path to that source. Figure 15-6 illustrates two different clock sources being used in the network and both nodes E and F using the new primary source. The letter S represents the secondary clock source.

Figure 15-6 *Synchronization Example, Continued*

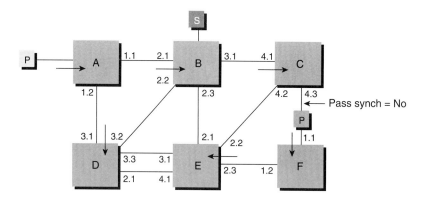

In a cell-based network, frame slips are not as damaging, because often idle cells can be removed and inserted between the cells that are carrying data. Synchronization is essential if end-user equipment is using TDM-based access lines for time-dependent traffic, such as voice or synchronous data. In this case, end-to-end synchronization must be configured.

In this example, if both primary sources were referenced to the same source, there would not be a problem.

Figure 15-7 illustrates that node B has discovered that the clock signal it is receiving across trunk 2.1 is no longer within the required frequency range.

Figure 15-7 *Synchronization Example, Continued*

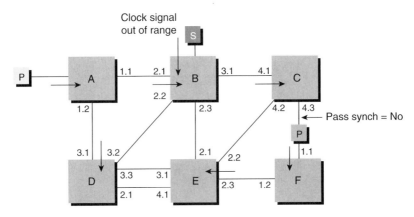

Because node B is not directly attached to the clock source, as shown in Figure 15-8, it assumes that the clocking problem is with the trunk that is carrying the clock signal. A minor bad clock path alarm is declared by node B, and the trunk can no longer be used to pass synchronization. The trunk, however, can still carry user traffic.

Figure 15-8 *Synchronization Example, Continued*

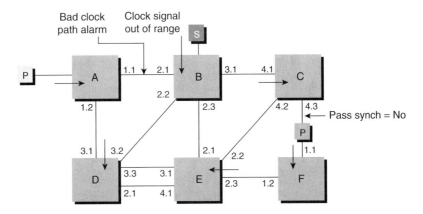

Node B reassesses the clock sources in the network. In Figure 15-9, it uses the primary source from trunk 1.1 on node F. Node C must also change its clock source, because the source at node F is now closer than the source at node A.

Figure 15-9 *Synchronization Example, Continued*

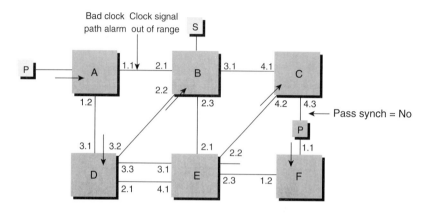

If node A also discovers that the clock signal is no longer within the required frequency, a bad clock source alarm is declared, as shown in Figure 15-10.

Figure 15-10 *Synchronization Example, Continued*

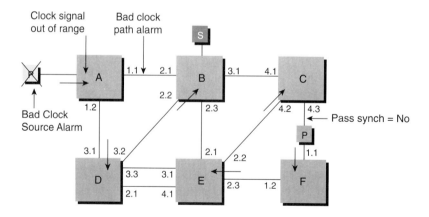

The bad clock source alarm is reported to all nodes, as shown in Figure 15-11, and the external primary clock source at node A can no longer be used. Node B, now informed that the clock source is bad, should clear the bad clock path alarm.

Figure 15-11 *Synchronization Example, Continued*

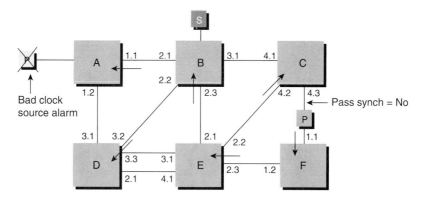

The bad clock source alarm at node A does not clear automatically, even if the source has recovered. To clear the alarm, use the **clrclkalm** command.

If the trunk between node F and node C fails, as shown in Figure 15-12, the clock source is unavailable, and all the nodes need to decide which source to use. The secondary source at node B is available, so all nodes switch to that source.

Figure 15-12 *Synchronization Example, Continued*

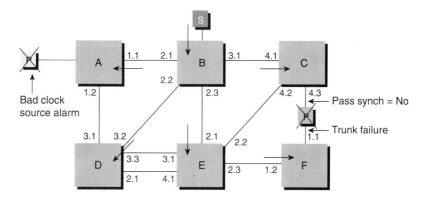

If the trunk recovers, the clock source automatically recovers, unlike the previous example with the external clock source at node A.

Commands for Synchronizing Networks

Table 15-1 describes the commands that are used for network synchronization, along with their privilege levels.

Table 15-1 *Network Synchronization Commands*

Command	Description	Privilege Level
dspclksrcs	Display clock sources. Displays all configured network clock sources.	6
dspcurclk	Display current clock source. Displays the clock source used by the BPX node.	6
dspnds	Display nodes. Displays all nodes in the network. For information flow, **dspnds** shows which nodes have alarms and their highest level (such as MAJOR). The **dspnds** command is described in greater detail in the "Locating Alarms" section.	6
cnfclksrc	Configure clock source. Adds or removes a network clock source. Specifies a primary, secondary, or tertiary clock source in a network.	1
dspalms	Display alarms. Displays a count of alarm conditions by category on this switch and a total count of remote switch alarms.	6
clrclkalm	Clear clock alarm. Clears a bad clock source or bad clock path alarm.	5
dsptrks	Display trunks. Determines which trunk has an alarm.	6

How to Synchronize Networks

Follow these steps to synchronize BPX networks:

Step 1 At the Next Command prompt, enter **dspclksrcs** to display the clock sources. This displays the current clock reference for the node and the path. The BPX node should be using the internal oscillator of the highest numbered node.

Step 2 Enter **dspcurclk**. This displays the clock source used by the BPX node. To display the current clock of a remote BPX switch, log into the remote BPX node (**vt**) and then enter **dspcurclk**.

Step 3 Enter **dspnds** [+*n*], where *n* is the command option used to display the node numbers. This displays summary information for the node. Confirm that the clock source is the highest numbered node.

Step 4 Enter **cnfclksrc** *<line type> <line number> <source type>* [*frequency*]. This creates or removes the clock source.

Step 5 To modify the trunk to pass synch = no, enter **cnftrk** *<slot.port>*[*.vtrk*] *<options>*. This configures parameters for the trunk.

Step 6 Enter **dspcurclk**. This displays the current clock for the trunk. Verify that the node is using the trunk as its clock source.

Step 7 To see if any clock sources have failed, enter **dspalms**. This displays local alarms by category.

Step 8 If any clock sources have failed, correct the problem. To clear the specific clock source, enter **clrclkalm** *<line type> <line number>*. Wait a few minutes to make sure that the alarm has not returned. Use the **dspalms** command to display local alarms by category.

Step 9 To remove clock sources, enter **cnfclksrc** *<line type> <line number> <source type>* [*frequency*].

Step 10 To return a trunk to its original condition, enter **cnftrk** *<slot.port>*[*.vtrk*] *<options>*. This configures parameters for the trunk.

dspclksrcs Command

The **dspclksrcs** command, shown in Example 15-1, lists all *potential* network clock sources and their levels (primary, secondary, or tertiary). The display for unreachable or failed clock sources flashes on and off. Clock sources are defined using the **cnfclksrc** command. The **dspcurclk** command displays the *current* network clock source.

Example 15-1 **dspclksrcs** *Command*

```
hei1bpx1          TN     Teacher:1       BPX 8620  9.3.XX   June 12 200X 03:31 PDT

                            Network Clock Sources

Primary
hei1bpx1 EXT-2 1.544 MHz

Secondary
Brussels TRNK  10.1

Tertiary
None


```

continues

Example 15-1 *dspclksrcs Command (Continued)*

```
Last Command: dspclksrcs


Next Command:
```

dspcurclk Command

The **dspcurclk** command screen in Example 15-2 shows the current clock reference for the node and the path to the clock reference.

Example 15-2 *dspcurclk Command*

```
hei1bpx1          TN    Teacher:1      BPX 8620  9.3.XX   June 12 200X 03:31 PDT



                             Current Clock Source

Source Node        : hei1bpx1
Source Line        : Internal (CC)
Source Type        : Primary
Local Clock Format: T3
Clock Deviation    : -8.78 ppm relative to active BCC's oscillator

Node is currently receiving clock from its internal oscillator.



Last Command: dspcurclk

Next Command:
```

Table 15-2 describes the fields associated with the **dspcurclk** command output, as shown in Example 15-2.

Table 15-2 *dspcurclk Fields and Descriptions*

Field	Description
Source Node	The BPX switch where the clock source originates.
Source Line	The type of line used as the clock source and its back slot and interface number (for example, CLN 15, TRK 9.1, EXTERNAL 1, or INTERNAL).
Source Type	The clock type configured for the source clock (primary, secondary, or tertiary). If the source clock is an internal oscillator, no clock type is given.
Local Clock Format	The local clock format. In Example 15-2, the clock format is a T3.

Table 15-2 **dspcurclk** *Fields and Descriptions (Continued)*

Field	Description
Clock Deviation	This is a timing measurement that indicates the amount of deviation for the clock.
Path to Source	The trunk path from the current node to the clock source. This path to the source includes all intermediate nodes and trunks. In Example 15-2, the node is currently receiving clock from its internal oscillator and there is no Path to Source.

cnfclksrc Command

The **cnfclksrc** command is used to create or remove a network-wide clock source. The clocking scheme ensures that all nodes in the network automatically synchronize to the nearest, most stable clock available. After you specify a clock source, the location and type of the network clock source goes out to all nodes in the network. To remove a clock source, enter **r** as the source type. You must be logged into the node where the clock source is located to add it to or delete it from the network. Example 15-3 shows an example of the **cnfclksrc** command.

Example 15-3 cnfclksrc *Command*

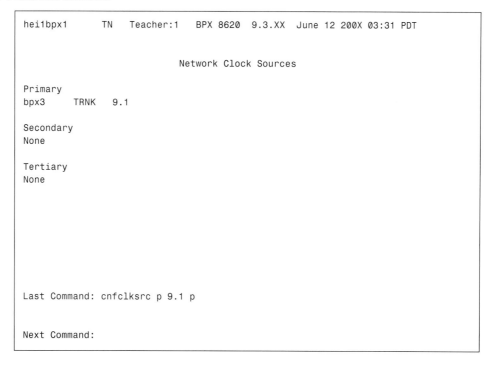

```
hei1bpx1      TN   Teacher:1   BPX 8620  9.3.XX  June 12 200X 03:31 PDT



                        Network Clock Sources

Primary
bpx3      TRNK    9.1

Secondary
None

Tertiary
None







Last Command: cnfclksrc p 9.1 p


Next Command:
```

The p in Example 15-3 stands for Packet Line. Multiple primary, secondary, and tertiary clock sources can be defined. The network regards all primary clocks as equal in the network clocking hierarchy, all secondary clocks as equal, and all tertiary clocks as equal. If multiple equal clock sources are available, the node synchronizes to the closest source (the fewest hops away). If none of the clock sources are available, the network synchronizes to the internal oscillator of one of the BPX switches in the network through the lowest-numbered node path.

Here is the **cnfclksrc** command syntax:

```
cnfclksrc <line-type> <line-number> <source-type> [frequency]
```

Table 15-3 describes the required parameters for the **cnfclksrc** command.

Table 15-3   **cnfclksrc** *Command Parameters*

Parameter	Description	Required/Optional
line-type	The clock source line type: trunk (t), line (l), or external clock interface (e).	Required
line-number	The clock source line number, formatted as *slot* or *slot.interface*. For external clock sources, enter **1** or **2** to identify the external clock interface.	Required
source-type	The clock source type: primary (p), secondary (s), or tertiary (t). Enter **r** to remove the clock source.	Required
frequency	The clock source frequency for an external clock only. Enter **1** for 1.544 MHz or **2** for 2.048 MHz.	Optional

dspalms Command

The **dspalms** screen, shown in Example 15-4, provides summary information on all alarms on the node. Use this command to see the number and type of alarms on a node. To learn which nodes are in alarm, use the **dspnw** or **dspnds** commands, described in the section, "Remote Alarms."

Example 15-4 dspalms *Command*

```
hei1bpx1         TN    Teacher:1      BPX 8620  9.3.XX    Feb. 14 200X 13:16 PST


Alarm summary    (Configured alarm slots: None)
Connections Failed:      None
TRK Alarms:              None
Line Alarms:             3 Majors
Cards Failed:            None              ATM Port Communication Failed
Slots Alarmed:           None
Missing Cards:           2
APS Alarms:              None
```

Example 15-4 dspalms *Command (Continued)*

```
ASM Alarms:              None


Last Command: dspalms

Next Command:
```

Miscellaneous alarms are displayed on the right side of the screen, as you can see with ATM Port Communication Failed. Additional alarms that are not shown here include clock source failure, connection A bit/AIS alarms, temperature alarms, power failures, and fan failures.

Alarms are listed by category. The additional categories not shown in Example 15-4 are the following:

- **Slots Alarmed**—Slot alarms on the BPX node.
- **Bus Failed**—Indicates a control bus failure.
- **Bus Needs Diagnostics**—Indicates a control bus problem that is not severe enough to cause a bus failure. However, please note that any bus diagnostic affects bus traffic, effectively taking the node out of service. This should be done only at TAC's request or in an extreme service emergency!
- **Ext Clk Src Alm (Bad Clk)**—Indicates a bad clock.
- **Ext Clk Src Alm (LOS)**—Indicates a loss of signal (LOS).
- **Ext Clk Src Alm (OOF)**—Indicates out of frame (OOF).

clrclkalm Command

The **clrclkalm** command clears a clock alarm state for a specific clock source, as shown in Example 15-5.

Example 15-5 clrclkalm *Command*

```
hei1bpx1      TN    Teacher:1    BPX 8620  9.3.XX  June 12 200X 03:31 PDT

TRK
          Type    Current Line Alarm Status              Other End
    9.1   E3/530 Clear - OK                              bpx4/9.1
    9.2   E3/530 Clear - OK                              bpx4/9.2
    9.3   E3/530 Clear - OK                              bpx4/9.3
    12    T1/24  Clear - OK                              bpx2/13
    13    E1/32  Clear - OK                              bpx4/14




```

continues

Example 15-5 clrclkalm *Command (Continued)*

```
Last Command: clrclkalm t 9.1

Next Command:
```

Here is the **clrclkalm** command syntax:

```
clrclkalm <line-type> <line-number>
```

Table 15-4 describes the required parameters for the **clrclkalm** command.

Table 15-4 **clrclkalm** *Command Parameters*

Parameter	Description	Required/Optional
line-type	Specifies the type of line as circuit line (c), external clock interface (e), or trunk (t).	Required
line-number	Specifies the line number, formatted as slot or *slot.interface*.	Required

dsptrks Command

The **dsptrks** command lists trunks and their alarm states, as shown in Example 15-6. Use the **dsptrks** command to identify trunks that are in alarm. This command displays all trunks upped on the node and their alarm status.

Example 15-6 dsptrks *Command*

```
hei1bpx1      TN    Teacher:1    BPX 8620  9.3.XX  June 12 200X 03:31 PDT

TRK        Type    Current Line Alarm Status          Other End
 2.1       OC3     Clear - OK                          VSI(VSI)
 2.2       OC3     Clear - OK                          bpxny/2.2
 2.4       OC3     Clear - OK                          bpxla/2.4
 2.7       OC3     Clear - OK                          MGXSF(AAL/5)
 2.8.11    OC3     Clear - OK                          VSI only
 2.9       T3      Clear - OK                          pubsaxi1(AXIS)
```

Example 15-6 dsptrks *Command (Continued)*

```
Last Command: dsptrks


Next Command:

                    SW                                          MAJOR ALARM
```

The **dsptrks** command displays basic trunk information and alarm states for all trunks on a node. This command applies to both physical and virtual trunks. For disabled trunks, the trunk numbers appear in dim reverse video on the screen. The next section describes both line and trunk alarms and errors. It defines the functions and types of alarms that can occur in a BPX switch and shows how these alarms might affect services.

What Is an Alarm?

Many line and trunk alarms and errors are caused by failed error-checking bits in the framing structure, misconfiguration of the framing type, or incorrect configuration of ones density. Other errors, such as line-code violations (LCVs), are caused by incorrect bit polarities. An understanding of the line or trunk's physical-layer characteristics is necessary to troubleshoot statistical errors.

Previously, we discussed the different types of alarms that can occur in a BPX switch. By way of review, the two main types of alarms are major and minor.

Major alarms always affect service and can result from failed connections, trunks, or lines, and also from missing cards.

Minor alarms might affect service and can include port signaling failures, degraded trunks or lines, card self-test failures, cabinet temperature problems, and failed power supplies.

This section defines the functions and types of alarms that can occur in a BPX switch. For information on troubleshooting, see the section, "Commands for Troubleshooting."

Node and Network Alarms

If an individual BPX node experiences a problem that is likely to affect service on the network, that node generates an alarm signal that is registered locally and broadcast across the network. Other nodes recognize the alarm signal and post a local notification that a remote node is in an alarm condition. If the network is being managed with Cisco WAN Manager (CWM), the CWM station registers the alarm in its event log and in the database and flags the node in alarm on its topology map display. Figure 15-13 shows the alarm process.

Figure 15-13 *Node and Network Alarms*

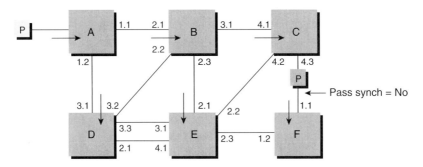

When you log into a node, the network alarm status is always displayed in the lower-right corner of the screen. The network alarm status reports the most severe alarm in the network. If one node has a major alarm and all others have minor alarms, the network alarm status reports a major alarm. To determine which nodes are in alarm, use the **dspnw** or **dspnds** command.

Major Alarms Always Affect Service

Major alarms always affect traffic, primarily because they often result in failed user connections. It is important to remember that a failed connection is frequently the result of another major alarm, such as a failed trunk, line, or card.

When a network trunk experiences a condition that prevents traffic from being carried over that trunk, the trunk is declared failed, and all connections routing over the trunk are rerouted. Use the **dsptrks** command to display the status of all trunks on a node. Examples of trunk failures include LOS, OOF, or a communications failure. A communications failure occurs when a node does not receive acknowledgments to trunk keepalive messages from the neighbor node. Figure 15-14 shows the effect on user connections in a network where a trunk fails.

A line might also experience LOS or OOF conditions that cause it to fail. Connections that enter the network on a failed line cannot be rerouted, so all connections on the line fail and are not recovered until the line failure is resolved. Use the **dsplns** command to display the states of the lines on your node.

A severe card failure on an active card causes a missing card alarm. A missing card is one that supports services (such as a BXM card with active trunks on it) that can no longer perform its functions. Most often, hardware failures cause cards to be in a missing state. Not all card failures cause a card to be declared missing. Some self-test failures, failures on active cards with Y-cable redundancy, or failures on standby cards do not generate major alarms. The **dspcds** or **dspcd** command shows the status of a card module.

Figure 15-14 *Connection Paths Before and After Trunk Failure*

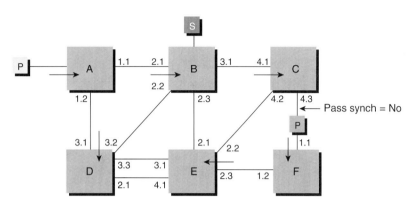

If, for any reason, a connection fails, it generates a major alarm. The major alarm is declared at both terminating ends of the connection, but not on any intermediate nodes. The **dspcons** command lists all the connections on the node and the status of each connection. If you want to list only the failed connections, use the **dspcons** command with the [*-fail*] option. Use the **dspcon** command to determine the cause of a connection failure.

Unreachable Node: The Network Is Split

An unreachable node occurs as a result of a complete failure of control communications between a node or nodes and the rest of the network. This results in a partitioned network. An unreachable condition is serious and requires immediate action to remedy the situation.

If the node is unreachable because of a local hardware or software failure, the problem should be corrected as soon as possible, usually with the assistance of Cisco TAC. If the problem cannot be fixed quickly, the recommended short-term remedy is to delete the trunk(s) connecting the unreachable node(s) to the main network.

An unreachable node severely impacts the network, generally because many operations that affect the network topology or have network-wide implications cannot be implemented. This includes adding or deleting trunks and modifying connection classes.

Minor Alarms Might Affect Service

Minor alarms do not result in failed connections and do not necessarily affect traffic. However, a degraded trunk or line might create problems on a connection (usually from the end user's perspective), such as retransmissions or low throughput.

A port signaling failure occurs when the configured signaling protocol (LMI or ILMI) breaks down. Each protocol has configurable error threshold parameters that determine whether the protocol is communicating correctly. In general, the signaling protocol fails if responses are not received from the attached CPE within specified time periods.

A degraded trunk or line can generate an alarm in the network. Statistical alarm thresholds determine the error rate for determining both major and minor alarms. To display the errors on a trunk or line, use the **dsptrkerrs** or **dsplnerrs** command, respectively. Connections are never rerouted because of a statistical alarm, even if it is a major alarm. However, often a high error rate on a trunk causes communications to break down between the two nodes, which generates a communication failure.

On the BPX node, the interface between a card module and the backplane is monitored for slot errors. Slot errors, like trunk and line errors, can generate major or minor alarms based on configured alarm thresholds. Use the **dspslotalms** command to display the alarm status of each card slot. The **dspsloterrs** command displays the error counters for each slot. Note that these commands apply only to the BPX node.

On the BPX node, environmental measurements are made by the Alarm/Status Monitor (ASM) card module and are displayed using the **dspasm** command. Cabinet temperature, power supply voltages, and fan RPMs are all compared to configured thresholds to determine a minor alarm condition.

Monitoring and Resolving BPX Trunk Alarms

In this section, you learn how to use the CLI to monitor and resolve alarms on network trunks between BPX switches.

Statistical and Physical Trunk Errors

Trunk alarms on the BPX switch can result from either of the following:

- An accumulated number of short-duration events (statistical errors) that exceed a user-configurable threshold

- Longer-duration events (physical errors) that cause the trunk to fail and connections to be rerouted

Statistical errors can result in a minor or major alarm, because separate threshold levels can be configured for each. (See the description of the **cnflnalm** command later in this chapter.) Trunk alarms resulting from statistical errors can be cleared by operator action using the **clrtrkalm** command.

Physical errors always result in a major alarm and cannot be cleared by operator action. It is possible using the SuperUser **cnftrkparm** command to modify the system timer that determines how long the system waits following the detection of a physical error before declaring a major physical trunk alarm. Conversely, you can also use the **cnftrkparm** command to modify the timer that defines how long the system waits after a local physical problem is cleared before clearing the alarm condition.

Commands for BPX Trunk Alarms

Table 15-5 describes the BPX CLI commands for monitoring and resolving BPX trunk alarms, along with their privilege levels.

Table 15-5 *Commands for BPX Trunk Alarms*

Command	Description	Privilege Level
dsplnalmcnf	Display line alarm configuration. Displays line and trunk alarm configuration and thresholds.	6
cnflnalm	Configure line alarm. Sets trunk and line alarm values for failures that are statistical in nature.	3
dsplog	Display log. Displays alarm and event log for the node.	6
clrlog	Clear log. Clears entries from the alarm and event log.	5
dsptrkerrs	Display trunk errors. Displays errors on all trunks on the node or for a particular trunk.	6
clrtrkerrs	Clear trunk errors. Clears error statistics for one or all trunks on the node.	5
clrtrkalm	Clear trunk alarm. Clears a statistical alarm from a trunk.	5
cnftrkalm	Configure trunk alarm. Enables or disables alarm reporting on a trunk.	1

dsplnalmcnf Command

Use the **dsplnalmcnf** command to display line and trunk alarm configuration by alarm type. Each alarm type defines the minor and major alarm thresholds, alarm integration, and clearing periods.

Here is the **dsplnalmcnf** command syntax:

```
dsplnalmcnf
```

Example 15-7 shows the effect of issuing the **dsplnalmcnf** command. On the BPX switch, this command displays three screens that list all the alarm types for which statistical error count thresholds can be defined for minor and major alarms.

Example 15-7 dsplnalmcnf *Command*

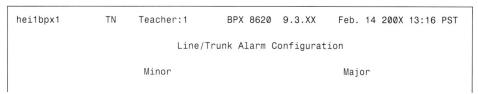

```
hei1bpx1        TN    Teacher:1      BPX 8620  9.3.XX    Feb. 14 200X 13:16 PST


                         Line/Trunk Alarm Configuration


            Minor                                    Major
```

continues

Example 15-7 dsplnalmcnf *Command (Continued)*

```
     Violation             Rate    Alarm Time  Clear   Rate    Alarm Time  Clear
      3) Lof              .0001%   10 min      3 min   .01%    30 sec      10 sec
      4) BNI:Tx V OCD        2%     5 min      3 min     5%    60 sec      10 sec
      5) BNI:Tx TS OCD     .01%     5 min      3 min    .1%    60 sec      10 sec
      6) BNI:Tx NTS OCD    .01%     5 min      3 min    .1%    60 sec      10 sec
      8) Los              .0001%   10 min      3 min   .01%    30 sec      10 sec
     14) BNI:TX BDA OCD   .001%     5 min      3 min    .1%    60 sec      10 sec
     15) BNI:TX BDB OCD   .001%     5 min      3 min    .1%    60 sec      10 sec
     17) BNI:TX HP OCD    .001%     5 min      3 min    .1%    60 sec      10 sec




     This Command: dsplnalmcnf


     Continue?

                                                                MAJOR ALARM
```

The **dsplnalmcnf** screen provides configured statistical alarm thresholds for all lines and trunks on the node. Use this command to determine how many errors over what time period are needed to generate a major or minor statistical alarm.

Thresholds are divided into major and minor alarms and include the following:

- **Violation**—Error type.

- **Rate**—Error rate/frequency.

- **Alarm time**—Duration of the configured error rate for declaring an alarm. The errors need not occur for the full alarm time provided that the concentration of errors (based on the rate) would be met after the prescribed alarm time. For example, if the rate is 1% and the alarm time is 10 minutes, an error rate of 10 percent over 1 minute would justify declaring the alarm.

- As soon as the alarm (mathematically) reaches its percent level, it goes into alarm immediately. For example, if 10% over 1 minute could be achieved with 20% over 30 seconds, the system would go into alarm at the 30 second mark and would wait for the 1 minute period to elapse.

- **Clear**—The alarm clears after this amount of time if the alarm threshold is no longer met.

cnflnalm Command

This command sets the trunk and line alarm values for failures that are statistical in nature. The switch software declares statistical alarms when a card supporting these trunks or lines reports too many errors. The switch declares an alarm if the detected error rate equals the

cnflnalm parameter *error rate* for the period of time designated by the *alarm time* parameter. Error rates that exceed the specified error rate cause an alarm in a proportionately shorter period of time. An alarm is cleared when the error rate remains below the rate specified by *error rate* for the period of time designated by the *clear time*.

Here is the **cnflnalm** command syntax:

```
cnflnalm <failure type> <alarm class> <rate> <alarm time> <clear time>
```

The major and minor alarm thresholds can be modified using the **cnflnalm** command, as shown in Example 15-8.

Example 15-8 cnflnalm *Command*

```
hei1bpx1          TN     Teacher:1        BPX 8620  9.3.XX    Feb. 14 200X 13:16 PST

                               Line/Trunk Alarm Configuration

                       Minor                                    Major

Violation              Rate    Alarm Time  Clear     Rate    Alarm Time  Clear
  8) Los               .0001%  10 min       3 min    .01%    30 sec       30 sec




Last Command: cnflnalm 8 2 3 30 30


Next Command:

                                                                    MAJOR ALARM
```

The **cnflnalm** command modifies the minor and major alarm thresholds for both lines and trunks. Example 15-8 shows alarm type 8 (Los) being configured. The other parameters on the command line are as follows:

- Alarm class (2, for major)
- Alarm rate (3, representing 0.001%)
- A new value for the alarm time of 30 seconds
- Alarm clear time of 30 seconds

This modification makes the criteria for a major alarm of this type more stringent than the defaults.

Table 15-6 lists the alarm failure types that can be configured on a BXM card. Refer to the *Cisco WAN Switching Command Reference* for the **cnflnalm** command's full syntax.

Table 15-6 *Alarm Failure Types for a BXM Card*

Failure Type	Name	Description
3	Lof	Loss of frame
8	Los	Loss of signal
18	Lcv	Line code violations
19	Pcvl	P-bit parity code violations
20	Pcvp	C-bit parity code violations
21	Bcv	PLCP BIP-8 code violations
28	Hcserr	Cell header HEC errors
29	FSyncerr	Frame synchronization errors
34	Tx NTS CDscd	Non-time-stamped cells discarded
35	Tx HP CDscd	High-priority cells discarded
36	Tx V CDscd	Voice cells discarded
37	Tx TS CDscd	Time-stamped cells discarded
38	Tx BDA CDscd	Bursty data A cells discarded
39	Tx BDB CDscd	Bursty data B cells discarded
40	Tx CBR CDscd	CBR cells discarded
41	Tx ABR CDscd	ABR cells discarded
42	Tx VBR CDscd	VBR cells discarded

dsplog Command

The **dsplog** screen, shown in Example 15-9, provides a node event and alarm log. This event log is one of several available to you in the network. Because the log is stored on the node, it provides a filtered list of all events on the node. The event log that is sent to a printer that is attached to the auxiliary port, or the log on the WAN Manager workstation, is more complete.

Example 15-9 dsplog *Command*

```
hei1bpx1        TN     Teacher:1      BPX 8620  9.3.XX    Feb. 14 200X 13:16 PST

Most recent log entries (most recent at top)
Class   Description                                      Date      Time
Info    User SuperUser logged in (Local)                 02/14/01  16:53:01
Info    User StrataCom logged out (Local)                02/14/01  16:52:51
```

Example 15-9 dsplog *Command (Continued)*

```
Clear  Comm Break with Sacmento Cleared          02/14/01 16:46:53
Clear  TRK 3.1 OK                                 02/14/01 16:46:41
Major  TRK 3.1 Communication Failure              02/14/01 16:46:40
Clear  BXM-155 3 Up - Activated                   02/14/01 16:46:40
Clear  Comm Break with SaltLake Cleared           02/14/01 16:46:23
Minor  Comm Break with SaltLake                   02/14/01 16:45:46
Minor  Comm Break with Sacmento                   02/14/01 16:45:46
Major  TRK 3.1 Front Card Missing                 02/14/01 16:45:35
Major  BXM-155 3 Down - No backup available       02/14/01 16:45:35
Info   Port 12.1 Activated                        02/14/01 16:11:08
Major  LN 12.1 Loss of Sig (RED)                  02/14/01 16:11:03

This Command: dsplog


Continue?

                                                      MAJOR ALARM
```

The log can hold up to 500 messages before it overwrites the oldest events. Use the **clrlog** command to clear the events in the event log. Log messages can be sent to the WAN Manager to be stored for extended periods of time.

NOTE   Connection event logging such as failures and reroutes can be enabled or disabled with the **cnffunc** command. If connection events are not being reported, check that logging is enabled. In large networks, connection event logging can fill the event log quickly.

Log information includes the following:

- Event class—Major, Minor, Info, Clear
- Event description
- Date
- Time

clrlog Command

The **clrlog** command clears the event log. When the log is cleared, one entry remains—Info Log Cleared. Before the event log is cleared, you are prompted to confirm the clearing activity.

dsptrkerrs Command

The **dsptrkerrs** command displays the accumulated line error counts, by failure type, for the specified trunk(s). If you do not enter a trunk number, this command displays a one-line summary of errors for all trunks at the local node. If you enter a specific trunk number with this command, it displays a detailed analysis, including error threshold (ETH).

Here is the **dsptrkerrs** command syntax:

dsptrkerrs [*slot.port | slot.port.vtrk*]

The **dsptrkerrs** screen, shown in Example 15-10, provides a summary of historical statistical errors that have occurred on all trunks on the node. Use this command when you suspect that trunk errors are degrading service on a connection. Degraded service does not result in an alarm on the node, so you know about it only if an end user reports the problem. Displaying the trunk errors is not useful if the trunk has failed.

Example 15-10 dsptrkerrs *Command*

```
hei1bpx1      TN      Teacher:1      BPX 8620  9.3.XX   June 12 200X   03:31 PDT

Total Errors

         Code    Out of  Loss of HCS     Unavail Ln Unav Path Un Tx Cell
 TRK     Errors  Frames  Signal  Errors  Seconds Seconds Seconds Dropped
 2.1       -       0       0       0        -       51      51       0
 2.2       -       0       0       0        -        2       2      15K
 2.4       -       0       0       0        -        9       9       0
 2.7       -       0       0       7        -        0       0       0
 2.8.11    -       0       0       5        -        4       4       0




Last Command: dsptrkerrs


Next Command:

                  SW                                        MAJOR ALARM
```

BXM errors include the following:

- **Code errors**—Bipolar or line-code violations.

- **Out of frames**—Statistical out of frames. Short duration.

- **Loss of signal**—Statistical loss of signal. Short duration.

- **HCS errors**—Cell header CRC did not match the trunk card's calculated CRC. Performed on receive cells only.

- **Tx cell dropped**—Cells dropped due to egress trunk queue overflow or expiration.

In the case of broadband trunks, this command has two screens, which might differ slightly depending on the type of trunk you are looking at. The display screens are laid out in two sections. The left section (or column) lists statistical errors, or errors that occur for a short duration. The right section (or column) lists physical errors that result in trunk failure and that occur for a longer period of time. You can configure the alarm time per trunk using the **cnftrkparm** SuperUser command. Some types of errors, such as OOF and LOS, appear twice—as statistical and physical errors.

Error counts and errored ten seconds (ETS) are provided for each type of statistical error. The ETS field indicates during how many 10-second periods the errors occurred, which helps you determine how the errors were distributed over time. For example, if 2000 HCS errors occurred in one 10-second period (ETS = 1), you can assume that the errors were a single short-lived event (a *burst* or *hit* on the trunk). However, if the 2000 HCS errors occurred in 500 different 10-second periods (ETS = 500), you can assume that the errors were spread over a longer period of time (*dribbling* or ongoing) and probably need to be monitored.

Error counts that show an ETS might cause major or minor alarms if they exceed the configured alarm thresholds. Error counts that do not indicate an ETS are physical errors; in other words, the trunk experienced an error that caused it to fail and traffic to be rerouted. These physical errors always generate major alarms.

clrtrkerrs Command

The **clrtrkerrs** command clears the statistical error counters at the node for a specified physical or virtual trunk, or for all trunks on the node.

Command syntax:

   clrtrkerrs *<slot.port | slot.port.vtrk | *>*

* indicates all trunks on this node.

Example 15-11 shows the **clrtrkerrs** command being used to clear error counters.

Example 15-11 **clrtrkerrs** *Command*

```
hei1bpx1          TN     Teacher:1       BPX 8620  9.3.XX    Feb. 14 200X 13:16 PST

Trunk   3.1      Status: Clear - OK                   Clrd: 02/14/01 16:24:49
Type             Count ETS    Status   Type              Count ETS    Status
Out of Frms          0    0            Comm Fails            0      -
Loss of Sig          0    0            Loss of Sig (RED)     0      -
Tx V Ovfl C Drp      0    0            AIS         (BLU)     0      -
Tx TS Ovfl C Drp     0    0            Out of Frms (RED)     0      -
Tx NTS Ovfl C Drp    0    0            Rmt Oof     (YEL)     0      -
Tx HP Ovfl C Drp     0    0
Tx BDA Ovfl C Drp    0    0
```

continues

Example 15-11 **clrtrkerrs** *Command (Continued)*

```
Tx BDB Ovfl C Drp    0    0
Line Code Errs       0    0
P-bit Parity Errs    0    0
C-bit Parity Errs    0    0
BIP-8 Code Errs      0    0


Last Command: clrtrkerrs 3.1


Next Command:
```

clrtrkalm Command

The **clrtrkalm** command clears statistical alarms associated with either a physical or virtual trunk. Because the statistical alarms associated with a trunk have associated integration times, they can keep a major or minor alarm active for some time after the cause has been identified and resolved.

Here is the **clrtrkalm** command syntax:

```
clrtrkalm <slot.port | slot.port.vtrk> <failure type>
```

The **clrtrkalm** command clears these alarms, allowing any new alarms to be quickly identified, as shown in Example 15-12. However, this command can clear only alarms caused by the collection of statistical data. Alarms caused by a network failure cannot be cleared. For example, an alarm caused by a series of bipolar errors can be cleared, but an alarm caused by a card failure cannot. Example 15-12 represents just one page of a multipage display.

Example 15-12 **clrtrkalm** *Command*

```
hei1bpx1    TN   Teacher:1   BPX 8620  9.3.XX  June 12 200X 03:31 PDT

                        Line Alarm Configuration

                  Minor                           Major

   Violation    Rate    Alarm Time  Clear      Rate    Alarm Time  Clear
   1) Bpv       10E-7   10 min      3 min      10E-3   30 sec      10 sec
   2) Fs          .01%  10 min      3 min        .1%   30 sec      10 sec
   3) Oof       .0001%  10 min      3 min        .01%  30 sec      10 sec
   4) Los       .0001%  10 min      3 min        .01%  30 sec      10 sec
   5) Fer         .01%  10 min      3 min        .1%   200 sec     10 sec
   6) CRC         .01%  10 min      3 min        .1%   200 sec     10 sec
   7) Oom        .001%  10 min      3 min        .1%   30 sec      10 sec
   8) Ais16     .0001%  10 min      3 min        .01%  30 sec      10 sec
```

Example 15-12 **clrtrkalm** *Command (Continued)*

```
This Command: clrtrkalm 15 3


Next Command:


                                                       MAJOR ALARM
```

cnftrkalm Command

The **cnftrkalm** command configures trunk alarm reporting, as shown in Example 15-13. When trunks are upped and added to the network, alarm reporting is enabled by default. The **cnftrkalm** command lets you disable alarms on a trunk. This might be useful during installation or maintenance activities to avoid spurious alarms. Disabling alarms is also useful for trunks that are connected to the node but not yet in service, or for nodes that are experiencing occasional bursts of errors but are still operational.

Here is the **cnftrkalm** command syntax:

```
cnftrkalm <trunk number> <enable | disable>
```

Example 15-13 **cnftrkalm** *Command*

```
hei1bpx1      TN    Teacher:1    BPX 8620   9.3.XX   June 12 200X 03:31 PDT


Last Command: cnftrkalm 15 d


Next Command:


                                                       MAJOR ALARM
```

How to Monitor and Resolve BPX Trunk Alarms

Follow these steps to monitor and resolve trunk alarms on a BPX node. This procedure assumes that at least one trunk in the network has a current active alarm.

Step 1 At the Next Command prompt, enter **dspnds**. This displays a list of all nodes in the network and their current alarm status.

Step 2 Identify any nodes with major alarms; if necessary, use **vt** to access a remote node.

Step 3 Enter **dspalms** and verify whether this node has a major trunk alarm; if necessary, use **vt** to navigate through the network to locate a node with an active trunk alarm. This displays a summary list of all current alarm conditions present on the node.

Step 4 Enter **dsptrks** and identify the trunk(s) in alarm. This displays all trunks upped on the node and their alarm status.

Step 5 Enter **cnftrkalm** *<slot.port>* **d** to disable alarm reporting on the trunk in alarm. This displays the selected trunk and current alarm status.

Step 6 Enter **dspalms**. This displays "disabled" after TRK Alarms.

Step 7 Enter **cnftrkalm** *<slot.port>* **e** to re-enable alarm reporting on the trunk, and then enter **dspalms**. This displays the original status after TRK Alarms.

Step 8 Enter **dsplog**. This displays the most recent system log entries. Verify that the alarm status and trunk alarm configuration actions appear in the log.

Step 9 Enter **dsptrkerrs**. This displays the statistical error counts for all trunks on the node.

Step 10 Select a trunk with a current error count, and then enter **dsptrkerrs** *<slot.port>*. This displays the trunk's statistical and physical error counts.

NOTE   If you want to know how many errors are needed to declare an alarm, use the **dsplnalmcnf** command. To change the thresholds, use the **cnflnalm** command.

Step 11 To clear error counts for a specific trunk, enter **clrtrkerrs** *<slot.port>*. This clears the statistical error counts for the specified trunk, but not the physical error counts, and also refreshes the error count screen. To clear all the error counts, enter **clrtrkerrs** *. Enter **yes** in response to the Clear all trunk errors? prompt. This clears the statistical error counts and refreshes the **dsptrkerrs** error count screen.

Step 12 After a few minutes, re-enter the **dsptrkerrs** command and verify whether any of the trunks report new errors. This displays the statistical error counts for all trunks on the node.

Step 13 Enter **clrtrkalm** *<slot.port>* to clear statistical alarms on each trunk in turn. This displays the trunks and their alarm status.

Step 14 Enter **bye**. This terminates your CLI session and returns you to the login prompt.

Monitoring and Resolving BPX Line Alarms

In this section, you learn how to use the CLI to monitor and resolve alarms on BPX access lines.

Statistical and Physical Line Errors

Line alarms on the BPX switch can result from an accumulated number of short-duration events (statistical errors) that exceed a user-configurable threshold. They can also result from a longer-duration event (physical error) that causes the line and any user connections to fail.

Statistical errors can result in a minor or major alarm because separate threshold levels can be configured for each; see the description of the **cnflnalm** command earlier in this chapter. Line alarms resulting from statistical errors can be cleared by the **clrlnalm** command.

Physical errors always result in a major alarm and cannot be cleared by operator action. You can use the SuperUser **cnflnparm** command to modify the system timer that determines how long the system waits following the detection of a physical error before declaring a major physical line alarm. Conversely, you can also use the **cnflnparm** command to modify the timer that defines how long the system waits after a local physical problem is cleared before clearing the alarm condition.

Commands for BPX Line Alarms

Table 15-7 describes the BPX CLI commands for monitoring and resolving BPX line alarms that were not already described in the previous section on trunk alarms. Most of the commands presented in this chapter serve a dual purpose of monitoring and resolving both trunk and line alarms.

Table 15-7 *Commands for BPX Line Alarms*

Command	Description	Privilege Level
dsplnerrs	Display line errors. Displays errors on all lines on the node or for a particular line.	6
clrlnerrs	Clear line errors. Clears error statistics for one or all lines on the node.	5
clrlnalm	Clear line alarm. Clears a statistical alarm from a line.	5

dsplnerrs Command

The **dsplnerrs** displays the accumulated line error counts by failure type for the specified line(s). If you do not enter a line number, this command displays a one-line summary of errors for all lines at the local node. If you enter a specific line number with this command, it displays a detailed analysis, including error threshold (ETH).

Here is the **dsplnerrs** command syntax:

```
dsplnerrs [slot.line]
```

The **dsplnerrs** screen also provides a summary of historical statistical errors that have occurred on all lines on the node. Use this command when a line has a major or minor statistical alarm, or when you suspect that line errors are causing degraded service on a connection. Degraded service does not result in an alarm on the node, so you will know about it only if an end user reports the problem. If the line fails, usually it is not useful to display the line errors.

To clear the counters, use the **clrlnerrs** command.

Example 15-14 shows the line errors screen for a node. In this example, line 3.3 is a T3 line, whereas line 10.3 is an OC-3c line.

Example 15-14 dsplnerrs *Command*

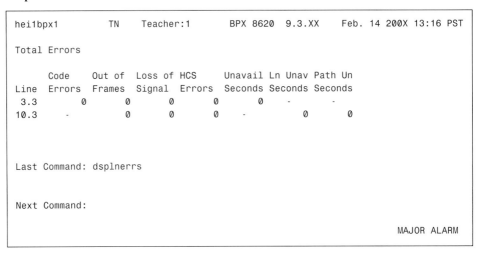

BXM line errors include the following:

- **Code errors**—Bipolar or line-code violations (T3/E3 only).
- **Out of frames**—Statistical out of frames. Short duration.
- **Loss of signal**—Statistical loss of signal. Short duration.
- **HCS errors**—Cell header CRC did not match the line card's calculated CRC. Performed on receive cells only.
- Unavailable seconds (T3/E3 only)
- Line and path unavailable seconds (SONET/SDH only)

The **dsplnerrs** command, when used with an optional line number parameter, provides detailed error statistics for a line. Example 15-15 shows the **dsplnerrs** command used for an OC-3c line.

Example 15-15 dsplnerrs *[line #] Command*

```
hei1bpx1          TN    Teacher:1        BPX 8620  9.3.XX    Feb. 14 200X 13:16 PST

Line 10.3          Status: Major - Loss of Sig (RED)       Clrd: 04/22/00 02:28:37
Type              Count ETS   Status    Type                 Count ETS    Status
Out of Frms          0     0            Loss of Sig (RED)      1      -
Loss of Sig          0     0            AIS         (BLU)      0      -
HCS Errors           0     0            Out of Frms (RED)      0      -
Line Unavail Secs    0     0            Rmt Oof     (YEL)      0      -
Path Unavail Secs    0     0






Last Command: dsplnerrs 10.3


Next Command:

                                                                      MAJOR ALARM
```

The **dsplnerrs** display screen is laid out in two sections. The left section (or column) lists statistical errors or errors that occur for a short duration. The right section (or column) lists physical errors that result in line failure and that occur for a longer period of time. The alarm time period can be configured using the **cnflnparm** SuperUser command. Some types of errors, such as OOF and LOS, appear twice—as statistical and physical errors.

Error counts and errored ten seconds (ETS) are provided for each type of statistical error. The ETS field indicates the number of 10-second periods during which the errors occurred, which helps you determine how the errors were distributed over time. For example, if 2000 HCS errors occurred in one 10-second period (ETS = 1), you can assume that the errors were a single short-lived event (a burst or hit on the line). However, if the 2000 HCS errors occurred in 500 different 10-second periods (ETS = 500), you can assume that the errors were spread over a longer period of time (dribbling, or ongoing) and will probably need to be monitored.

Error counts that show an ETS might cause major or minor alarms if they exceed the configured alarm thresholds. Error counts that do not indicate an ETS are physical errors; in other words, the line experienced an error that caused the line and associated connections to fail. These physical errors always generate major alarms.

clrlnerrs Command

The **clrlnerrs** command clears the statistical error counters at the node for a specified line or for all lines on the node.

Here is the **clrlnerrs** command syntax:

```
clrlnerrs <slot.line | *>
```

* indicates all lines on this node.

clrlnalm Command

The **clrlnalm** command clears statistical alarms associated with an access line. Because the statistical alarms have associated integration times, they can keep a major or minor alarm active for some time after the cause has been rectified. The **clrlnalm** command clears these alarms, allowing any new alarms to be quickly identified.

Here is the **clrlnalm** command syntax:

```
clrlnalm <slot.line> <failure type>
```

The **clrlnalm** command only clears alarms caused by the collection of statistical data. Alarms caused by a network failure are not cleared. For example, it can clear an alarm caused by a series of bipolar errors but cannot clear an alarm caused by a card failure.

How to Monitor and Resolve BPX Line Alarms

Follow these steps to monitor and resolve line alarms on a BPX node. This procedure assumes that at least one node in the network has a current active line alarm:

Step 1 At the Next Command prompt, enter **dsplnalmcnf**. This displays details of the minor and major alarm thresholds for statistical alarms for lines.

Step 2 Enter **cnflnalm 3 1 5 5 2**. This command modifies alarm type 3 (Lof), retaining the default rate (5, representing .0001%), but changing the alarm integration time to 5 minutes and the alarm clear time to 2 minutes. This displays the modified alarm threshold.

Step 3 Enter **dspnds**. This displays a list of all nodes in the network and their current alarm status.

Step 4   Identify any nodes with major alarms; if necessary, use **vt** to access a remote node.

Step 5   Enter **dspalms**. This displays a summary list of all current alarm conditions present on the node. Verify whether this node has a major line alarm; if necessary, use **vt** to navigate through the network to locate a node with an active line alarm.

Step 6   Enter **dsplns** and identify the line(s) in alarm. This displays all lines upped on the node and their alarm status.

Step 7   Enter **dsplnerrs**. This displays the statistical error counts for all lines on the node.

Step 8   Select a line with a current error count, and enter **dsplnerrs** <*slot.line*>. This displays the line's statistical and physical error counts.

Step 9   To clear line errors for a specific line, enter **clrlnerrs** <*slot.line*>. This clears the statistical error counts for this line, but not the physical error counts, and also refreshes the error count screen. To clear all line errors, enter **clrlnerrs ***. Enter **yes** in response to the Clear all line errors? prompt. This clears the statistical error counts and refreshes the **dsplnerrs** error count screen.

Step 10   After a few minutes, re-enter the **dsplnerrs** command and verify whether any of the lines report new errors. This displays the statistical error counts for all lines on the node.

Step 11   Enter **clrlnalm** <*slot.line*> to clear statistical alarms on each line in turn. This displays the lines and their alarm status.

Step 12   Enter **bye**. This terminates your CLI session and returns you to the login prompt.

Locating Alarms

The **dspalms** command is typically the first command used to troubleshoot the BPX node, because it lists alarm counts by category for the local switch. Remote switch alarms are counted but not identified.

Local Alarms

The **dspalms** command identifies the alarm category. For a historical view, the switch log file indicates when the alarm occurred and which resource entered an alarm state. The **dsplog** command displays the log file. The **clrlog** command clears the log file.

Remote Alarms

The **dspnds** command displays the name, type, and alarm status of all nodes. The **dspnw** and **dspnds** commands indicate only the general alarm state of a remote node. Use the **vt** command to access the remote node and display specific alarm information. The **dspnds** command is the quickest way to determine which node has an error because of its compact display. The **dspnw** command is best used in a small network when you suspect trunk problems. Otherwise, it can be too cumbersome as an initial alarm tool.

NOTE   If you use a communications package to Telnet into the CLI, the Telnet session might not support a blinking node display.

---

dspnds Command

The **dspnds** screen, shown in Example 15-16, provides a summary list of all nodes in the network and their current alarm status. The optional +n parameter can be used to display the node numbers.

Example 15-16 dspnds *Command*

```
hei1bpx1          TN     Teacher:1      BPX 8620  9.3.XX    Feb. 14 200X 13:16 PST

NodeName Alarm
SantRosa/1
Sacmento/3
Seattle/4


Last Command: dspnds +n

Next Command:
```

dspnw Command

The **dspnw** command displays the network topology in table form, as shown in Example 15-17, providing summary information about all nodes and trunks in the network. Each node is listed, followed by the trunk number, remote node name, and remote trunk number of every trunk terminating on the node. Use this command to display the network topology and status.

Example 15-17 dspnw *Command*

```
hei1bpx1         TN     Teacher:1       BPX 8620  9.3.XX    Feb. 14 200X 13:16 PST


NodeName     Alarm                 Trunk
SantRosa
      1.1.1-1.1.1/Seattle       3.1-3.1/Sacmento
Sacmento
      3.1-3.1/SantRosa
Seattle
      1.1.1-11..1/SantRosa






This Command: dspnw


Next Command:
```

The alarm status for each node is reported to the right of the node name:

- **Unrch**—The node is unreachable from this node. An unreachable node is a node that is no longer in communication with the other nodes in the network. This state can be caused by a failure of all trunks in the node, a loss of power, or a severe processor failure without an available redundant processor.
- **Major**—There is a major alarm at this node. Further investigation is needed.
- **Minor**—There is a minor alarm at this node. Further investigation is needed.

These are the command display conventions:

- ~ indicates that the trunk is a satellite line.
- A flashing entry indicates a failed line.

If the network has more nodes and trunk connections than can be displayed on a single screen, a Continue? prompt appears, asking whether you want the remaining network topology to be displayed. If you do, press the **Return** key. If no, enter **n** and press the **Return** key.

Hardware LEDs

Hardware alarms are triggered by any of the following:

- Card failures

- Fan or power supply failures
- Bus errors

The BPX switch has LEDs on the cards to indicate card and line states.

Alarm Categories

As indicated by the **dspalms** command, alarms fall into the following general categories:

- Card
- Bus
- Connection
- Trunk (trunk alarms were discussed in the section, "Monitoring and Resolving BPX Trunk Alarms")
- Line (line alarms were discussed in the section, "Monitoring and Resolving BPX Line Alarms")
- Port (port alarms were discussed in Chapter 13, "Configuring ATM Ports")

Card Alarms

Card information and alarm states are indicated with the **dspcds** and **dspcd** commands. The **dspcds** command displays the cards in a shelf, front and back, with their type, revision, and status. For front and back card sets, the status field applies to the cards as a set. The letter T opposite a card indicates that it is running a self-test. The letter F indicates that it has failed a test. If lines or connections have been configured for a slot, but no suitable card is present, the missing cards are displayed at the top of the screen. If a card was previously installed, empty slots are identified as being reserved.

The **resetcd** command resets the hardware and software for a specified card. A hardware reset is equivalent to physically removing and reinserting the front card of a card group and resets the card's logic.

The **switchcc** command switches the standby BCC processor card to active and the active card to standby. If a standby processor is unavailable, the command is not executed. If a standby processor is available but is not ready to go active, you are prompted to confirm or abort the operation. The **switchcc** command should cause little or no interruption of service.

Executing **switchcc** has the following effects:

- Transfers control to the standby controller card.
- Aborts any job currently running.
- Logs off the user.

- Reverts the new standby processor to a download mode indicated by the flashing FAIL lamp. The system software image stored in ROM is downloaded to RAM in the event that the system software was corrupted.

- After these transitions are complete, the configuration database is downloaded from the newly active controller card to complete the download. This process takes several minutes, so this controller card is unavailable for standby operation until the download is complete.

NOTE	Do not perform **switchcc** if the processor cards contain different software levels, such as 9.2.12 and 9.3. The **dsprevs** command displays the software revision level on each processor card in the network. Never issue the **switchcc** command before **resetcd** <*standby*>. Make sure that no errors are in the **dspswlog** and **dspswlogs** command outputs. Also make sure that "Standby CC Connection Database Updates Pending: No" is returned for the **dspqs** command.

Bus Alarms

The BPX switch features a redundant bus structure known as the A and B buses. Only one bus actively carries traffic at a time.

The **dspbuses** command indicates the active and standby bus.

The **cnfbus** command switches the indicated bus to the active state or toggles the bus states.

The **diagbus** command may be used to diagnose bus problems. Use the **diagbus** command only if indicated by the **dspbuses** command because this command disrupts service. All bus commands require major caution, because they can cause the node to drop out of service.

Connection Alarms

The **dspcons** command lists all connections terminating at the local node. The display includes the connection state, loopback state, and test state if present.

The **dspcon** command displays detailed information for a specific connection.

The **dsprts** command displays routing information for all connections terminating at the local node.

The end-user equipment attached to a BPX node can be a router, switch, or any device that can send and receive ATM cells. The BPX network has limited information about the external devices that use the connection.

Figure 15-15 shows an external device experiencing a permanent virtual circuit (PVC) or other failure.

Figure 15-15 *External Connection Alarms*

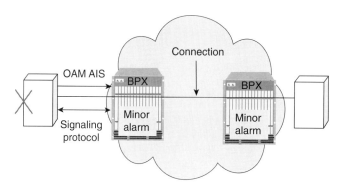

Here are some examples of external failures:

- PVC outage in a remote Asynchronous Transfer Mode (ATM) network
- Customer premises equipment (CPE) failure
- Line failure into remote CPE

If a failure occurs outside the BPX network, the following two methods can be used to report the failures:

- Signaling protocols to provide failed PVC status
- Operations, Administration, and Maintenance (OAM) alarm indicator signal (AIS) generated by the attached device

Use the **dspcons** command with the [*-abit*] option to display the state of the local and remote external connection segment failures.

Multicast Connection Alarms

Like standard ATM connections in the BPX network, multicast connections report their alarm status (okay, failed, or down) on the **dspcons** and **dspcon** screens. In fact, you cannot tell the difference between a multicast and nonmulticast connection on the BPX command-line interface (CLI) without knowing that the terminating end of the connection is a BME card module. Figure 15-16 illustrates OAM alarm notification for multicast connections.

Figure 15-16 *OAM Alarm Notification*

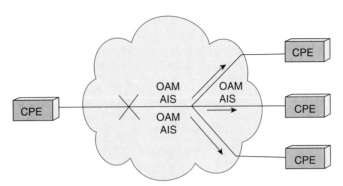

Because the leaf connections are dependent on the root connection for the traffic, OAM cells are sent down the leaf connections to the attached CPE if the root connection is unavailable for any of the following reasons:

- The root does not exist.

- The root has been brought out of service with the **dncon** command.

- The access line on the non-BME end of the root has failed.

- The root connection cannot find a route through the network because of a trunk outage or insufficient routing resources (such as bandwidth, conids, and restrictions).

If a leaf connection fails, the only alarm is the failure of the single leaf connection. If end-to-end OAM cells are sent on a root from outside the network, those OAM cells are propagated to all leaf connections.

Monitoring Multicast Connections

Use the **dspportstats** command, described in Chapter 13, and the **dspchstats** command to monitor the traffic on multicast ports and channels. The following apply to the use of the **dspchstats** command:

- The channels at both ends of a leaf connection can be monitored.

- The channel at the non-BME end of the root connection can be monitored.

- The channel at the BME end of the root connection *cannot* be monitored.

NOTE   The **dspchstats** command can be issued on the BME end of the root connection. However, all values are set to 0.

Connection Testing

Connections can be tested via the **tstconseg** command or by using local, remote, or external loopback tests. The loopback commands only create a loopback *condition;* therefore, external test equipment is required to generate a test pattern. In contrast, the BPX switch can generate its own test patterns for the **tstconseg** command.

The following types of loopbacks are available on the BPX switch:

- **Local loopback**—Tests continuity up to the local interface. A local loop can be added to any connection or ATM port.

- **Remote loopback**—Tests continuity through the network on a given connection from the local to the remote interface. Remote loops can be added to any connection that terminates on a remote node.

- **Local-remote loopback**—Tests continuity through the network on a given connection from the remote to the local interface. The local-remote connection loop is identical to the remote connection loop but is added from the other end of the connection. Remote loops can be added to any connection that terminates on a remote switch.

- **External loopback**—Tests continuity through the network on a given connection from the local interface to the remote user. The external user equipment is looped and must return the test pattern.

Local Loopback

The local loopback tests the front and back card pairs by looping incoming traffic back out for a port or data interface, as shown in Figure 15-17. External test equipment, such as a Bit Error Rate Tester (BERT), must be used to generate the test pattern and to analyze the traffic for errors. Local loopback checks the traffic path from the electrical interface at the port through the card set to the CellBus in both directions of transmission.

Figure 15-17 *Local Loopback*

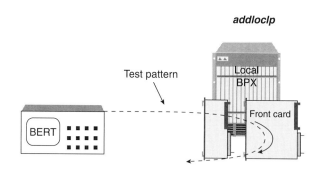

NOTE Because this test is disruptive, notify your network administrator before performing it.

Performing Local Loopback Testing

To perform a local loopback, follow these steps:

Step 1 Disconnect the data cable connection to the card to be tested, and connect the test equipment in its place.

Step 2 Set up an internal loopback on the ATM port or connection to be tested using the **addloclp** command.

Step 3 Turn on the test equipment. Make sure it indicates circuit continuity. Observe the indicated error rate.

Step 4 If any unexpected errors are detected, replace the back card and retest. If the errors remain after retesting, replace the front card and retest. Cisco strongly recommends downing a card (use the **dncd** command) before removing it.

Step 5 When the test is complete, disconnect the test equipment and reconnect the data cable. Release the local loopback using the **dellp** command. If necessary, repeat at the node at the other end of the connection.

Step 6 While testing, use the **dspcons** command to see which connections are looped back. A flashing right parenthesis [ )] or left parenthesis [( ] indicates a loopback.

A local loopback can simultaneously exist at both ends of a connection. However, a local loopback and a remote loopback cannot coexist on a connection. Prior to executing a loopback, the BPX node performs signal and code conditioning to remove the connection from service. The loopback remains in place until it is removed by the **dellp** command.

The **dspcons** screen provides current loopback and testing information on the connections on the local node. Possible states are listed in Table 15-8.

Table 15-8 dspcons *Command Loopback Types and Display*

Loopback Type	Added By	Symbol	dspcons Display
Local connection loop	Local BPX	)	Left of remote node name
Remote connection loop	Local BPX	)	Right of remote node name
Local connection loop	Remote BPX	(	Right of remote node name
Remote connection loop or local remote loop	Remote BPX	(	Left of remote node name

continues

Table 15-8 **dspcons** *Command Loopback Types and Display (Continued)*

Loopback Type	Added By	Symbol	dspcons Display
Frame Relay local port loop	Local BPX	]	Left of remote node name
Frame Relay local port loop	Remote BPGX	[	Right of remote node name
Connection in test	—	T	Right of local channel

Remote Loopback

The **addrmtlp** command transmits an information stream over a channel across the network and loops it back to the local transmitting interface by way of the remote front card. External test equipment is used to generate and analyze a test pattern.

Prior to executing remote loopback on a voice channel, the remote BPX node tells the remote end to remove the connection from service. The loopback remains in place until it is removed by the **dellp** command. You cannot establish a remote loopback on a connection that is already looped back, either locally or remotely. Figure 15-18 illustrates the remote loopback feature.

Figure 15-18 *Remote Loopback*

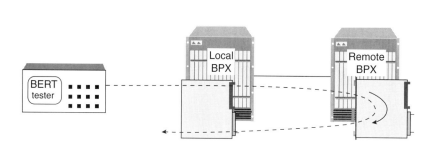

NOTE Because this test is disruptive, notify your network administrator before performing it.

Testing Connection Integrity

The **tstconseg** command externally tests a connection's integrity by sending OAM segment loopback cells over the specified channel the specified number of times.

You can use this command to test a connection segment's integrity by inserting test data generated by the BPX switch. Although the **tstconseg** command is intrusive, connection service is affected for only a few seconds. Because service is disrupted for only a short time, no conditioning is normally applied during the test.

If a failure is detected, the fault is isolated to a specific BPX node and card. If a standby card is available, it automatically goes into service. During fault isolation, conditioning is applied to both ends of the connection.

A connection can be repaired if the network can detect and resolve a problem. Repairing might include clearing buffers or switching to a redundant card. (Loopbacks and external test equipment provide more complete testing capabilities.) The **tstconseg** command reports the following results:

- **Completed**—Total number of tests that were run.
- **Aborted**—Number of tests that did not run because of loopbacks or missing or failed hardware.
- **Failed**—Number of tests that failed.
- **Repaired**—A connection that failed a previous test but passed the current test.

A T after the Local Channel under test indicates that the test is currently running on that channel. When the first test is completed, a message appears, indicating the results of the tests. As each test is completed, the T moves to the next channel to be tested, and the message is updated to include the cumulative results of the tests. When the test is completed for all the specified connections, the T disappears, and the message indicates the total number of tests and the cumulative results of the test. Example 15-18 shows an example of the **tstconseg** command output.

Example 15-18 tstconseg *Command*

```
heiligx1    TN    Teacher:1    IGX1      9.3.XX  June 12 200X  03:31 PDT

External
      Connection Segment Test

Status: Test Complete

Connection ID      Test Count     Failure Count  Success Count
1.2.1.100             1               1               0
```

continues

Example 15-18 tstconseg *Command (Continued)*

```
Last Command: tstconseg 1.2.1.100 1 a

Test aborted
Next Command:


                          SW                                    MAJOR ALARM
```

Repaired connections indicate that a test failed previously but the current test succeeded.

Here is the **tstconseg** command syntax:

```
tstconseg <channel> <loop count> [A]
```

Table 15-9 describes the required and optional parameters for the **tstconseg** command.

Table 15-9   tstconseg *Command Parameters*

Parameter	Description	Required/Optional
channel	Tests the specified channel or all channels (*).	Required
loop count	The number of times to repeat the tests, from 1 through 10.	Required
A	If A is entered and the test fails, aborts the **tstconseg** command.	Optional

In addition, the **tstdelay** command can be used to test the delay in a connection. This command puts the remote end of the connection into a loopback state, generates a test packet, and calculates and displays the round-trip delay (RTD). This delay includes module and trunk queuing and processing delays throughout the network.

Commands for Troubleshooting

Table 15-10 describes the network alarms and troubleshooting commands that have not yet been discussed in this chapter or previous chapters.

Table 15-10   *Troubleshooting and Alarm Commands*

Command	Description	Privilege Level
dspslotalms	Display slot alarms. Displays the alarm summary for all card slots in the node.	6
dspsloterrs	Display slot errors. Displays errors on all card slots on the node or for a particular card slot.	6
dspslotalmcnf	Display slot alarm configuration. Displays the major and minor alarm thresholds for statistical slot alarms.	6
addloclp	Add local loopback. Adds a loop at the local port or channel.	2

Table 15-10 *Troubleshooting and Alarm Commands (Continued)*

Command	Description	Privilege Level
addrmtlp	Add remote loopback. Adds a loop at the remote channel.	2
dellp	Delete loopback. Removes any type of loop.	2
resetcd	Reset card. Performs either a failure or hardware reset on a card to clear a failure condition or to switch from an active to a standby card with Y-cable redundancy.	3

dspslotalms Command

The **dspslotalms** command shows the current alarm state (most severe) for each card slot, as shown in Example 15-19. Use this command when the BPX node is reporting a slot alarm to determine the slot number and alarm type.

Example 15-19 **dspslotalms** *Command*

```
hei1bpx1      TN      Teacher:1      BPX 8620  9.3.XX   June 12 200X   03:31 PDT

Slot  Type        Current Slot Alarm Status
   1 BXM          Clear - Slot OK
   2 BXM          Clear - Slot OK
   4 ASI-E3       Clear - Slot OK
   5 BNI-155      Clear - Slot OK
   6 BNI-T3       Minor - PRBS Error
   7 BCC3         Clear - Slot OK
   9 ASI-T3       Clear - Slot OK
  12 BNI-T3       Clear - Slot OK



Last Command: dspslotalms


Next Command:                                              Minor Alarm
```

In general, slot alarms indicate one of the following:

- **A bad card**—A card cannot communicate with the processor or exchange data across the backplane.

- **A bad backplane**—The entire backplane or part of it cannot carry data as expected.

- **A bad processor**—A processor card cannot communicate with the other card modules or exchange data across the backplane. If slot errors occur for several cards, switching to the standby BCC using the **switchcc** command helps isolate the errors.

- **A firmware/hardware/software mismatch**—A card whose firmware or hardware is not supported by the BPX system software might report slot errors and alarms.

dspsloterrs Command

The **dspsloterrs** command provides a summary of historical statistical errors that have occurred on all card slots on the node, as shown in Example 15-20. These errors relate to card interface functions such as bus and BFrame transmit and receive errors. Use this command to see the number of errors of each type reported by the card slots. Use the **clrsloterrs** command to clear the counters. A line with a lot of errors horizontally can indicate a bad card. A line of vertical errors tends to indicate a midplane (backplane) problem.

Example 15-20 dspsloterrs *Command*

```
 hei1bpx1      TN      Teacher:1      BPX 8620  9.3.XX    June 12 200X    03:31 PDT

                         Summary of Slot Errors

             Invld Poll  Poll                    B-   Rx
       Stdby Rx    A Bus B Bus Bad   Tx   Rx          Frame FIFO Poll  CK-
       PRBS  Port  Par   Par   Grant BIP- BIP-  SIU   Par   Sync Clk   192
 Slot  Errs  Errs  Errs  Errs  Errs  16   16    Phase Errs  Errs Errs  Errs
                                     Errs Errs  Errs
 1     560K  1     0     0     0     0    1     1     0     0    0     0
 2     0     0     0     0     0     0    0     0     0     0    0     0
 4     0     0     0     0     0     0    0     0     0     0    0     0
 7     0     0     0     0     0     0    0     0     0     0    0     0
 9     0     0     0     0     0     0    0     0     0     0    0     0
 13    0     0     0     0     0     0    0     0     0     0    0     0




 Last Command: dspsloterrs


 Next Command:

                                                           Minor ALARM
```

Historical statistical errors provided by the **dspsloterrs** command include the following:

- **Standby PRBS errors**—Errors running a pseudo-random bit sequence test on the standby bus.
- **Receive port errors**—Cells from the crosspoint switch for an unknown or inactive port.
- **A bus parity errors**—Parity errors occurred on the A polling bus (BCC in slot 7).
- **B bus parity errors**—Parity errors occurred on the B polling bus (BCC in slot 8).
- **Bad grant errors**—The arbiter did not issue a grant to send a cell to the crosspoint switch within a set time period.

- **Transmit BIP-16 errors**—The transmit (to crosspoint switch) BFrame had a BIP 16 error on the cell header or payload.

- **Receive BIP-16 errors**—The receive (from crosspoint switch) BFrame had a BIP 16 error on the cell header or payload.

- **SIU phase errors**—The serial interface unit (SIU) on the card could not synch up on the BFrame from the crosspoint switch.

- **BFrame parity errors**—An error occurred in the parity bits of the BFrame header.

- **Receive FIFO synchronization errors**—The receive buffer could not synchronize to the BFrame.

- **Polling clock errors**—The arbiter polling clock is not present.

- **CK 192 errors**—The synchronization clock from the BCC is not present.

The **dspsloterrs** command, when used with an optional slot number parameter, provides detailed error statistics for a particular card slot, as shown in Example 15-21. Use this command to determine the frequency of the slot errors. Error counters are arranged in a fashion similar to those provided on the **dsptrkerrs** and **dsplnerrs** screens.

Example 15-21 **dspsloterrs** *[slot number] Command*

```
hei1bpx1        TN      Teacher:1       BPX 8620  9.3.XX   June 12 200X    03:31 PDT

BXM 2             Status: Clear - Slot OK                Clrd: 05/29/0X 01:50:30
Type              Count ETS   Status    Type              Count ETS   Status
Stby PRBS Errs     506K    200
Rx Invld Prt Errs     0      0
Poll Bus A Parity     0      0
Poll Bus B Parity     0      0
Bad Grant Errs        0      0
Tx BIP-16 Errs        0      0
Rx BIP-16 Errs        0      0
SIU Phase Errs        0      0
Bfrm. Par. Errs       0      0
Rx FIFO Sync Errs     0      0
Poll Clk Errs         0      0
CK 192 Errs           0      0
BXM Errs              0      0


Last Command: dspsloterrs 2

Next Command:

                                                                   Minor Alarm
```

dspslotalmcnf Command

The **dspslotalmcnf** command provides configured statistical alarm thresholds for all card slots in the node, as shown in Example 15-22. Use this command to see how many errors are needed to generate a major or minor slot alarm. The major and minor alarm thresholds can be modified using the **cnfslotalm** command.

Example 15-22 **dspslotalmcnf** *Command*

```
hei1bpx1     TN     Teacher:1      BPX 8620  9.3.XX   June 12 200X   03:31 PDT

                        Slot Alarm Configuration

                 Minor                              Major

Violation       Rate   Alarm Time  Clear   Rate   Alarm Time  Clear
1) SPRBS          .1%   10 min       3 min    1%   100 sec     100 sec
2) InvP           .1%   10 min       3 min    1%   100 sec     100 sec
3) PollA          .1%   10 min       3 min    1%   100 sec     100 sec
4) PollB          .1%   10 min       3 min    1%   100 sec     100 sec
5) BGE            .1%   10 min       3 min    1%   100 sec     100 sec
6) TBip           .1%   10 min       3 min    1%   100 sec     100 sec
7) RBip           .1%   10 min       3 min    1%   100 sec     100 sec
8) Bfrm           .1%   10 min       3 min    1%   100 sec     100 sec
9) SIU            .1%   10 min       3 min    1%   100 sec     100 sec
10) RFifo         .1%   10 min       3 min    1%   100 sec     100 sec

This Command: dspslotalmcnf


Continue?
```

Thresholds are divided into major and minor alarms and include the following:

- **Violation**—Error type.
- **Rate**—Error rate or frequency.
- **Alarm Time**—Duration of the configured error rate for declaring an alarm. The errors do not need to occur for the full alarm time, provided that the concentration of errors (based on the rate) would be met after the prescribed alarm time.
- **Clear**—If the alarm threshold is no longer met, the alarm clears after this amount of time.

addloclp Command

The **addloclp** command places ATM connections in local loopback mode. Example 15-23 shows an example of the **addloclp** command output.

Example 15-23 **addloclp** *Command*

```
hei1bpx1     TN    Teacher:1    BPX 8620  9.3.XX  June 12 200X 03:31 PDT

   Local            Remote       Remote                              Route
   Channel          NodeName     Channel        State  Type      Avoid COS O
   1.2.1.100        )hei1bpx2    2.1.1.100      Failed rt-vbr
   2.1.1.100        hei1bpx2     (1.2.1.100     Failed rt-vbr
   12.2.9.32        hei1bpx3     1.2.12.32      Failed atfr                0  L
   12.2.10.32       hei1bpx2     12.2.10.38     Ok     nrt-vbr
   12.2.10.38       hei1bpx2     12.2.10.32     Ok     nrt-vbr
   12.2.11.32       hei1bpx3     1.2.11.32      Failed cbr                 0  L



   This Command: addloclp 1.2.1.100



                                                      MAJOR ALARM
```

Use the **dspcons** command to learn which connections are looped back. A flashing close parenthesis [ )] or open parenthesis [( ] in the connections display indicates a loopback. The direction and location of the parenthesis depend on whether the loopback is local or remote and which end of the connection was used to establish the loopback.

Here is the **addloclp** command syntax:

```
addloclp <connection | port>
```

addrmtlp Command

The **addrmtlp** command places ATM connections in remote loopback mode. Example 15-24 shows an example of the **addrmtlp** command output.

Example 15-24 **addrmtlp** *Command*

```
hei1bpx1     TN    Teacher:1    BPX 8620  9.3.XX  June 12 200X 03:31 PDT

   Local
                    Remote       Remote                              Route
   Channel          NodeName     Channel        State  Type      Avoid COS O
   1.2.1.100        pubsbpx2     2.1.1.100      Failed rt-vbr
   2.1.1.100        pubsbpx2     1.2.1.100      Failed rt-vbr
```

continues

Example 15-24 addrmtlp *Command (Continued)*

```
12.2.9.32        pubsbpx3    1.2.12.32      Failed atfr              0  L
12.2.10.32       )pubsbpx2   12.2.10.38     Ok     nrt-vbr
12.2.10.38       pubsbpx2    (12.2.10.32    Ok     nrt-vbr
12.2.11.32       pubsbpx3    1.2.11.32      Failed cbr               0  L




This Command: addrmtlp 12.2.10.32


Loopback these connections (y/n)?
```

Both local and remote loopbacks are removed using the **dellp** command (discussed next). Loopbacks for data channels can also be initiated by pressing a button on the front of the associated data card.

Here is the **addrmtlp** command syntax:

```
addrmtlp <connection | port>
```

dellp Command

The **dellp** command deletes an external, local, remote, or local-remote loopback from the designated channel, set of channels, or port. After the loopback is deleted, any conditioning applied during the loopback process is removed, and service is restored. A local loop can be deleted only from the node that added it. However, a remote loop can be deleted from the node at either end of the connection. Local-remote loopbacks are added with the **addlocrmtlp** command. With local-remote loopbacks, execution of **dellp** is mandatory after testing is complete; otherwise, continuity errors follow. Example 15-25 shows an example of the **dellp** command output.

Example 15-25 dellp *Command*

```
hei1bpx1       TN      Teacher:1     BPX 8620  9.3.XX    June 12 200X  03:31 PDT

   Local         Remote      Remote                              Route
   Channel       NodeName    Channel       State  Type     Avoid COS O
   1.2.1.100     pubsbpx2    2.1.1.100     Ok     rt-vbr
   2.1.1.100     pubsbpx2    1.2.1.100     Ok     rt-vbr
   12.2.9.32     pubsbpx3    1.2.12.32     Failed atfr              0  L
   12.2.10.32    pubsbpx2    12.2.10.38    Ok     nrt-vbr
   12.2.10.38    pubsbpx2    12.2.10.32    Ok     nrt-vbr
   12.2.11.32    pubsbpx3    1.2.11.32     Failed cbr               0  L
```

Example 15-25 dellp *Command (Continued)*

```
Last Command: dellp 1.2.1.100

Next Command:
                                                          MAJOR ALARM
```

Here is the **dellp** command syntax:

```
dellp <channel>
```

resetcd Command

The **resetcd** command resets the hardware and software for a specified card. A hardware reset is equivalent to physically removing and reinserting the front card of a card group and resets the card's logic. When you reset the hardware of an active card other than a controller card (BCC), a standby card takes over if one is available. A failure reset clears the card failures associated with the specified slot. If a slot contains a card set, both the front and back cards are reset.

Do not use **resetcd** on an *active* BCC processor card, because a temporary interruption of all traffic can occur while the card is rebooting. (Resetting a controller card does not destroy configuration information.) When a redundant BCC is available, the **switchcc** command switches the active controller card to standby and the standby controller card to active. If a standby card is available, resetting an active card (except for BCC) does not cause a system failure. A hardware (h) or background test (f) that resets an active card that is not in standby disrupts service until the self-test finishes.

Here is the **resetcd** command syntax:

```
resetcd <slot> <h | f>
```

Table 15-11 describes the required parameters for the **resetcd** command.

Table 15-11 resetcd *Command Parameters*

Parameter	Description	Required/Optional
slot	Specifies the card to be reset based on the slot location.	Required
*h	f*	Indicates a hardware (h) reset or test failure (f) reset.	Required

Summary

In this chapter, you learned how to configure network clock sources, predict and identify node clock references, and monitor and resolve clocking alarms. You also learned how to locate and display network alarms and identify alarm types.

Troubleshooting trunk, line, and port alarms and errors was described in detail. You should know how to troubleshoot card failures and connection alarms and set up connection loopbacks. You should also understand how to monitor the BPX alarm and event log.

Review Questions

1 Mark the following statements as true or false.

A. _____ External clock sources are attached to the BCC back card.

B. _____ Only one clock source can be configured on each BPX node.

C. _____ Only external sources can be primary network clock sources.

D. _____ Trunks cannot pass synchronization signals to other BPX nodes.

2 Which of the following are possible clock sources for the BPX switch?

A. T3 lines

B. T1 lines

C. E1 lines

D. OC-3 lines

E. STM-1 lines

3 What is the meaning of a major alarm status on the bottom-right corner of the BPX console screen?

A. The local BPX node has a major alarm.

B. The BPX network has at least one major alarm.

C. All nodes in the BPX network have major alarms.

D. A major alarm has occurred in the last five minutes on a remote BPX node.

4 Of the following events, which four can generate a major alarm in the BPX network?

A. Fan failure

B. LMI failure on a port

C. Loss of frame on a line

D. Connection cannot route

E. Loss of signal on a trunk

F. Cell header CRC errors on a line

G. AIS OAM cells received from a CPE

H. Unknown virtual path identifier (VPI) and virtual channel identifier (VCI) on a connection

5 Of the following events, which six can generate a minor alarm in the BPX network?

A. LMI failure on a port

B. Fan failure

C. Loss of frame on a line

D. Connection cannot route

E. Loss of signal on a trunk

F. Cell header CRC errors on a line

G. AIS OAM cells received from a CPE

H. Unknown VPI and VCI on a connection

6 Which of the following events can cause a connection to fail and generate a major alarm?

A. No route is available in the network

B. An incorrect policing configuration

C. A statistical alarm on the access line

D. Dropped cells on an intermediate trunk

E. A failed card at either end of the connection

F. No LMI messages coming in from the CPE on the port

7 Mark the following statements as true or false.

A. _____ You use the **resetcd** <*f*> command to clear a self-test failure alarm on a card.

B. _____ You use the **resetcd** <*h*> command to clear a self-test failure alarm on a card.

C. _____ You use the **resetcd** <*h*> command to switch from the active to the standby processor.

D. _____ You use the **resetcd** <*f*> command to switch from an active to a standby Y-cabled card module.

8 Which two commands display the alarm status of all nodes in the network?

9 Which command displays a history of alarms and when they occurred?

10 Which command would you use to clear accumulated statistics on trunks?

11 The four loopback connection types are local, remote, external, and what?

12 When you test connections, what are the four possible results?

PART IV

MGX ATM Concentrator Configuration

Chapter 16   MGX Product Overview and System Hardware

Chapter 17   The User Interface and MGX Network Configuration

Chapter 18   Lines, Feeder Nodes, and SONET APS

Chapter 19   Connection Types

Chapter 20   Frame Relay Ports and Connections

Chapter 21   ATM Ports and Connections

Chapter 22   Voice, IP, and ATM MPLS Features

Appendix A   Answers to Review Questions

This chapter covers the following key topics:

- The MGX Product Family
- MGX Product Features
- Network Management
- MGX Networking
- MGX 8850 Processor Cards
- The SRM Card
- The RPM Card
- MGX Service Modules
- MGX Required Features and Hardware

CHAPTER 16

MGX Product Overview and System Hardware

This chapter presents Cisco's MGX product family, which includes multiservice edge concentrators and switches and a variety of low-speed and high-speed card modules designed for interfacing ATM backbone networks. All MGX devices transport network traffic on broadband ATM facilities. This chapter also presents MGX product features and discusses network management, including the tools available for the MGX 8230, 8250, and 8850-PXM1 switches.

MGX networking is presented, along with instructions for installing MGX switches into a network. This chapter discusses MGX processor cards, Service Resource Module (SRM), Route Processor Module (RPM), and MGX service modules, including the Circuit Emulation Service Module (CESM), Frame Relay Service Module (FRSM), ATM User Service Module (AUSM), and Voice Interworking Service Module (VISM). MGX required features and hardware guidelines are also presented.

The MGX Product Family

The MGX product family includes multiservice edge concentrators and switches. All MGX devices transport network traffic on broadband ATM facilities. Many MGX hardware modules are interchangeable among the different MGX devices. For example, the Frame Relay service module (FRSM) is supported on the MGX 8220, 8230, 8250, and 8850 devices.

MGX devices include the following:

- The MGX 8220 edge concentrator supports circuit emulation, Frame Relay, and ATM services.

- The MGX 8230 edge switch supports circuit emulation, Frame Relay, ATM, Layer-3 LAN, and voice services.

- The MGX 8250 edge switch supports circuit emulation, Frame Relay, ATM, Layer-3 LAN, and voice services.

NOTE   The MGX 8250 is physically identical to an MGX 8850 Release 1 feeder (MGX 8850-PXM1 switch).

- The MGX 8850 Release 1 (with PXM1 processor) edge switch supports circuit emulation, Frame Relay, ATM, Layer-3 LAN, and voice services. In this chapter, this switch is called the MGX 8850-PXM1 switch.

- The MGX 8850 Release 2 (with PXM45 processor) core switch supports ATM services. In the near future, the MGX 8850 switch will support a full complement of user services. The MGX 8850 and 8250 chassis are identical. In this chapter, the MGX 8850 Release 2 switch is called the MGX 8850-PXM45 switch.

MGX Feature Comparison

The features of each member of the MGX product family are described in Table 16-1.

Table 16-1   *Feature Comparison*

Feature	8220	8230	8250 and 8850-PXM1	8850-PXM45
Multiple trunks	No	No	No	Yes
Switching capacity	320 Mbps	1.2 Gbps	1.2 Gbps	45 Gbps
Local switching	No	Yes	Yes	Yes
User services	Circuit emulation	Circuit emulation	Circuit emulation	ATM
	Frame Relay	Frame Relay	Frame Relay	Layer 3
	ATM	ATM	ATM	
		Layer 3	Layer 3	
		Voice	Voice	

MGX Product Features

This section describes the features of the MGX 8230, 8250, and 8850-PXM1 edge switches.

The MGX 8230/8250/8850-PXM1 switch, shown in Figure 16-1, is an ATM edge concentrator that supports a single T3, E3, OC-3c, STM1, OC-12c, or STM4 ATM trunk to an ATM backbone network. Except for local traffic (traffic that originates and terminates on the same switch), all traffic on the MGX 8230/8250/8850-PXM1 switch is sent across the ATM trunk. The ATM backbone network can comprise BPX switches, MGX 8850-PXM45 switches, or any other vendor's ATM switch.

Figure 16-1 *MGX 8250/8850-PXM1*

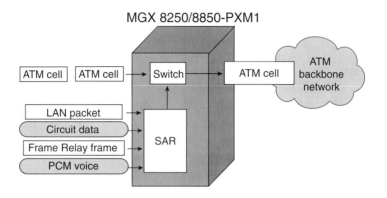

NOTE   The PXM-1 can have multiple lines active, but only one can be configured as a trunk.

MGX User Services

The MGX 8230/8250/8850-PXM1 switch provides the following user services:

- **Circuit emulation**—The MGX switch receives structured or unstructured bit-stream data and converts the data into ATM cells using AAL1 for transport through the network. Synchronization options are available for circuit emulation services, and idle suppression based on signaling bits is available for voice services. The MGX switch supports T1, E1, Nx64 Kbps, T3, and E3 circuit emulation interfaces.

- **Frame Relay**—The MGX switch receives Frame Relay, FUNI, or frame-based data traffic and converts it into ATM cells using AAL5 for transport through the network. ForeSight and standard Available Bit Rate (ABR) congestion management services are available on all frame-based services. The MGX 8850 switch supports T1, E1, Nx64 Kbps, T3, E3, HSSI, and V.35 Frame Relay interfaces.

- **ATM**—The MGX switch supports ATM traffic with six ATM services: constant bit rate (CBR), real-time variable bit rate (rt-VBR), non-real-time variable bit rate (nrt-VBR), ForeSight ABR, Standard ABR, and undefined bit rate (UBR). The MGX 8850 switch supports T1, E1, T3, E3, OC-3c, STM1, OC-12c, and STM4 ATM interfaces.

- **Layer-3 LAN**—The MGX switch provides Layer 3 LAN services similar to a Cisco 7000-series router. Ethernet and Fast Ethernet LAN interfaces are supported, as well as Multiprotocol Label Switching (MPLS) services. The MGX switch can be configured as a Label Switch Router (LSR) or Label Edge Router (LER).

- **Voice**—The MGX switch receives PCM voice traffic and transports it through the network using Voice over IP (VoIP) or Voice over AAL2 (VoAAL2). An external server handles call management for VoIP.

MGX Optional Features

The MGX switch supports optional features that require the purchase of special software licenses. These features are enabled by Cisco or authorized resellers. The optional MGX features include the following:

- **Service module redundancy**—1-to-1 and 1-to-N service module redundancy is available on the MGX switch. It requires that one or more Service Resource Modules (SRMs) be installed in the switch.

- **ForeSight for Frame Relay and ATM**—The ForeSight congestion-management feature is available on a per-card basis for both Frame Relay and ATM services.

- **Channelized Frame Relay or circuit emulation ports**—Multiple channelized Frame Relay or circuit emulation ports are optionally available on T1 or E1 service modules.

- **Inverse multiplexed ATM (IMA) ports**—IMA services are available on the T1 and E1 ATM service modules.

Network Management

This section describes the network management tools available for the MGX 8230, 8250, and 8850-PXM1 switches. Network management encompasses a wide variety of functions:

- Element display and configuration
- Connection display and configuration
- Alarm and event notification
- Topology information
- Statistics collection and display

The MGX switch can be managed using the command-line interface (CLI) or the Cisco WAN Manager (CWM) workstation. In addition, customized SNMP management tools can be used to manage the MGX switch.

CLI

The CLI provides all the information required to manage an MGX switch. However, the CLI is a text-based tool, so accessing the information requires familiarity with the command structure and output screens. You can use any dumb terminal, PC, or workstation to access the CLI, making it a versatile management tool. You can access the CLI using the following methods:

- A VT100 terminal or PC running terminal emulation software attached to a serial port on the PXM1

- A PC or workstation running Serial Line Internet Protocol (SLIP) attached to a serial port on the PXM1, provided that a valid IP address is configured on the PXM1

- A PC or workstation attached to a LAN can Telnet to the LAN port on the PXM1, provided that a valid IP address is configured on the PXM1

- A console port to terminal server

- A PC or workstation communicating with the MGX switch via a BPX backbone network

CWM

CWM is a LAN-attached network and element-management system that addresses operations, maintenance, and management of WAN multiservice networks consisting of ATM and Frame Relay switching products. The CWM station provides a number of graphical user interfaces (GUIs) for configuring and monitoring the network.

CWM software supports MGX switches and includes the following features:

- Network Topology
- Alarm and Event Log
- Statistics management
- Equipment management
- Connection management
- Cisco View for device management
- Permanent Virtual Circuit (PVC) connection management
- Firmware download
- Configuration Save and Restore
- SNMP Service Agent support

Customized SNMP Management Tools

CWM uses SNMP for element configuration and the customization of management tools. These customized tools can be developed to use SNMP to manage the MGX switch. For example, a tool could query a customer's database and translate the information so that new services can be automatically established in the network without additional steps. It is common for service providers to develop customized management tools to tie existing configuration and billing applications to the MGX network.

MGX Networking

This section describes the ways in which MGX switches can be installed in a network. For continuity, some MGX 8850-PXM45 topologies are also described.

MGX switches can be installed in a number of network topologies, depending on the software and hardware release in use and the application it supports. Supported networks include

- MGX 8220, 8230, 8250, or 8850-PXM1 feeder nodes in a tiered network supported by BPX switches
- MGX 8230, 8250, or 8850-PXM1 feeder nodes in a tiered network supported by MGX 8850-PXM45 switches

---

NOTE   These feeders support T1/E1 Frame Relay and ATM services, and T1/E1 circuit emulation.

- A standalone MGX 8220, 8230, 8250, or 8850-PXM1 concentrator attached to an ATM backbone network
- MGX 8230 feeder nodes in a tiered network supported by IGX switches
- A homogenous MGX 8850-PXM45 PNNI network
- A mixed-device PNNI network that includes the MGX 8850-PXM45 switch and other PNNI-capable switches

MGX 8850-PXM45/8230 Tiered Network

An MGX 8850-PXM45/8230 tiered network, shown in Figure 16-2, comprises an MGX 8850-PXM45 backbone network and MGX 8230 feeder shelves. The MGX 8230 feeders support Frame Relay and ATM user services when attached to MGX 8850-PXM45 backbone switches.

Figure 16-2 *MGX 8850-PXM45/8230 Tiered Network*

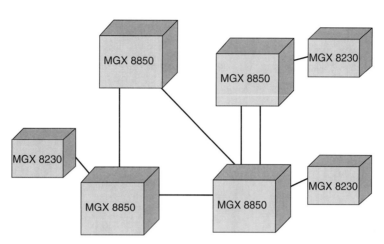

BPX/MGX 8250 Tiered Network

A BPX/MGX tiered network comprises geographically dispersed MGX 8250 edge switches attached to a BPX ATM backbone network. The MGX 8250 switches provide multiservice access to the ATM network, including broadband and narrowband Frame Relay and circuit emulation, narrowband ATM, and Layer 3 routing access. Alarm and management information is shared between the MGX 8250 switches and the BPX network. Figure 16-3 shows an MGX 8250 network supported by BPX switches and a single CWM station.

Figure 16-3 *BPX/MGX 8250 Tiered Network with a CWM Station*

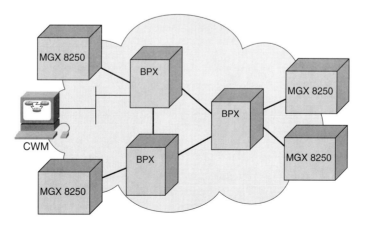

MGX Standalone Devices

Figure 16-4 shows MGX 8850-PXM1, 8250, and 8230 switches as standalone devices attached to a public ATM network. In this example, the MGX devices are attached to the ATM network on UNIs and are treated like CPE by the backbone network. In this case, limited CWM management is supported for the switches.

Figure 16-4 *MGX Standalone Devices*

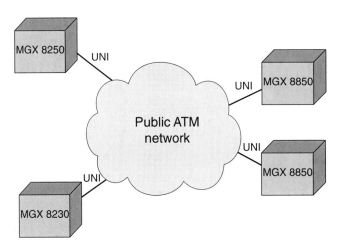

MGX 8850-PXM45 and a BPX/SES PNNI Network

MGX 8850-PXM45 switches and BPX switches (with attached Service Expansion Shelf [SES]) can be used to form a single integrated PNNI network, as shown in Figure 16-5. Notice the MGX 8250 feeder nodes attached to the MGX 8850-PXM45 switches.

Figure 16-5 *MGX 8850-PXM45 Switches and a BPX/SES PNNI Network*

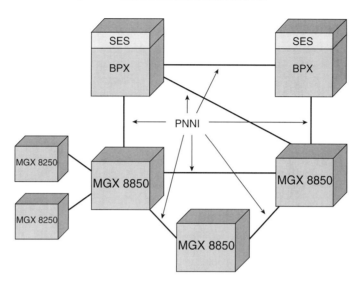

MGX 8850 Processor Cards

This section describes the Processor Switch Module 1 (PXM1) for the MGX 8230/8250/8850-PXM1 switch.

The PXM1

The PXM1 is a double-height card that is the central processor for the MGX switch. The PXM1 is responsible for switching cells and storing configuration and firmware images for the other card modules installed on the switch. The PXM1 is also responsible for network management, including the CLI, and communicating with CWM stations. In addition to processor and management functions, the PXM also supports one or more UNI ATM ports.

Three PXM1 models are available:

- PXM-2-T3E3 supports two T3 or E3 lines
- PXM-4-155 supports four OC-3c or STM1 lines
- PXM-1-622 supports one OC-12c or STM4 line

The MGX switch can run with one or two PXM1s installed in card slots 7 and 8 on the MGX 8250/8850-PXM1 or in card slots 1 and 2 on the MGX 8230 switch. If two PXM1s are installed, one is active and the other is a hot standby. All configuration and management information is updated on both PXM1s. If the active PXM1 fails, the standby takes over the switch operation.

Figure 16-6 shows the PXM1 front cards installed in an MGX 8250/8850-PXM1 and 8230 chassis.

Figure 16-6 *PXM1 Front Cards*

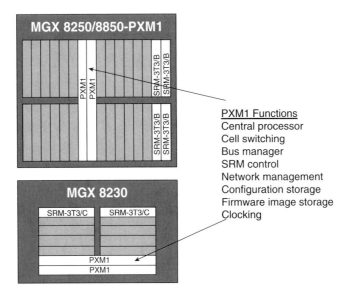

NOTE   Processor Switch Modules (PXM45 and PXM1) perform similar functions, including scalable nonblocking switching capacity from 1.2 Gbps to 45 Gbps, shelf control, and housing the PNNI.

PXM1 Back Cards

The double-height PXM1 front card supports two back cards—one for user interface ports and the other for line interfaces. Figure 16-7 shows a block diagram of the PXM1 and its back cards.

Figure 16-7 *PXM1 Back Cards*

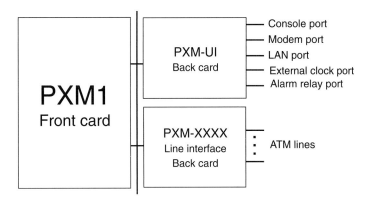

The PXM-UI provides serial and LAN ports for managing the switch using the CLI or CWM station. The PXM-UI also provides an external timing input (T1 or E1) and an alarm relay output connector.

The ports on the PXM-UI back card are as follows:

- **Console port**—An RJ-45 DTE port that is used to attach a VT100 terminal or a PC running terminal emulation for CLI access.

- **Modem port**— An RJ-45 DTE port that supports SLIP for command-line access.

- **LAN port**— An RJ-45 802.3 LAN attachment unit interface (AUI) port that provides CWM station access for network management and Telnet access for other LAN devices to the CLI. If redundant PXM1s are installed in the switch, do not Y-cable the two LAN ports together—each LAN port should be attached to the network.

- **External timing**—An RJ-45 or SMB port that accepts a T1 or E1 signal as an external clock source for the switch.

- **Alarm relay**—A DB-15 port that provides dry-contact relays for local major and minor alarm reporting.

A variety of PXM line interface cards are available. The back card type used depends on the front card type (T3/E3, 155, or 622) and the physical interface or connector type. For example, the BNC-2E3 back card provides two grounded BNC E3 connectors, and the SMFLR-4-155/B provides four SC-type long-reach single-mode fiber 155 Mbps connectors.

NOTE   Care is required when matching front and back cards. Verify the accuracy of the intended slot for each card before beginning to install the cards. This includes verifying that the daughter card type on the PXM back card corresponds to the uplink card type by executing the **dspcd** command. If you receive a "mismatch" response, remove the daughter card and replace it with the proper daughter card.

WARNING   Do not install an OC-48 back card with any card other than an OC-48 front card, or you will damage the cards.

Figure 16-8 shows a back view of the MGX 8850 chassis with PXM1 back cards installed.

Figure 16-8 *PXM1 User and Line Interface Back Cards*

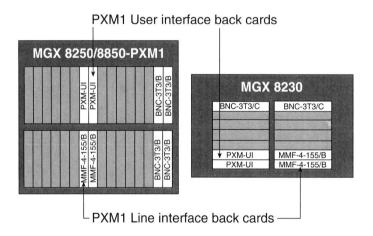

Two different models of the PXM-UI are available: The PXM-UI and the PXM-UI-S3. The PXM-UI-S3 provides Stratum 3 clock support for the MGX switch, and the PXM-UI provides Stratum 4 clock support for the MGX switch.

NOTE   The PXM-UI-S3 back card has two LAN ports and two external timing ports. Only one of the ports (the top one) is supported for each type.

PXM1 Functions

The PXM1 performs the following functions:

- **Shelf management**—The PXM1 monitors and controls the card modules in the MGX switch.

- **Cell switches**—The PXM1 houses the shared-memory switch that sends and receives ATM cells to and from the network trunk and the service modules.

- **Bus master**—All ATM cells created by the service modules are sent to the PXM1 card to be switched to other service modules or the attached ATM network. The PXM1 manages the flow of cells on the cell bus for the MGX switch.

- **SRM control**—The PXM1 and SRM(s) form a single logical card on the MGX switch. The PXM1 card manages all SRM firmware and configuration.

- **Network management**—Network management devices (such as a CWM work-station, PC, or dumb terminal) communicate directly with the PXM1. When logging into an MGX switch to access the CLI, you are communicating with the PXM1.

- **Service module configuration and firmware image storage**—A copy of the config-uration database and firmware image for each service module installed in the MGX switch is stored on the PXM1 on an ATAID disk drive. If a service module is replaced, the configuration and firmware are downloaded from the PXM1. RPM configuration is not automatically saved on the PXM1 but can be manually saved onto the disk.

- **Shelf timing**—The PXM1 extracts a clock signal from either an external clock source or the trunk to the ATM network. The PXM1 propagates the timing signals across the switch's timing bus.

- **Environmental alarms monitoring**—Chassis temperature and fan and power supply status are monitored by the PXM. You can display environmental alarms from the PXM with the **dspshelfalm** command.

- **Local alarm reporting**—Local major and minor alarms are reported by the PXM1 via front-card LEDs or dry-contact relays on the PXM-UI back card.

- **UNI ports**—The PXM1 performs all ATM interface functions, including CAC, policing, and queuing.

The SRM Card

The SRM manages 1-to-N service module redundancy and can perform bit error-rate tests (BERTs) on service module lines and ports. The SRM-3T3 can manage T3 to T1 line distribution on the shelf.

The SRM-3T3/B (Model B) is supported on MGX 8250 and 8850-PXM1 switches only. The SRM-3T3/B provides T1 bulk distribution to all service module slots except slots 9, 10, 25, and 26.

The SRM-3T3/C (Model C) is supported on MGX 8230, 8250, and 8850-PXM1 switches. The SRM-3T3/C provides T1 bulk distribution to all service module slots except slots 9, 10, 25, and 26. Any service module that uses bulk distribution or relies on the distribution bus for redundancy cannot reside in these slots.

Figure 16-9 shows an SRM-3T3/B and its back card.

Figure 16-9 *SRM-3T3/B Front and Back Cards*

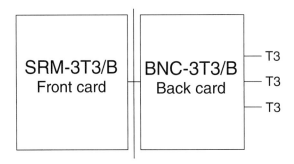

On MGX 8250 and 8850-PXM1 switches, a pair of SRMs can be installed in both the upper bay (slots 15 and 16) and lower bay (slots 31 and 32) of the chassis. If SRM functions are needed on a bay, SRMs must be installed in that bay. Like PXM1s, one SRM is active and a second can be installed as a hot standby. Each SRM is assigned to a PXM1 card for re-dundancy purposes. SRMs in slots 15 and 31 are associated with the PXM1 in slot 7; SRMs in slots 16 and 32 are associated with the PXM1 in slot 8. Whichever PXM is active deter-mines which SRMs are active. If PXM1 redundancy is unavailable, only one SRM needs to be installed in each bay. Be sure to install the SRM in the appropriate card slot depending on the location of the PXM1.

On the MGX 8230 switch, SRMs are installed in slots 7 and 14. Both SRMs support the entire chassis. One is active, and the other is a hot standby. The SRM in slot 7 is tied to the PXM1 in slot 1; the SRM in slot 14 is tied to the PXM1 in slot 2. Unlike the PXM1, the SRM is not required for an MGX switch to function. Figure 16-10 shows the SRMs installed in MGX switches.

Figure 16-10 *SRMs in MGX Switches*

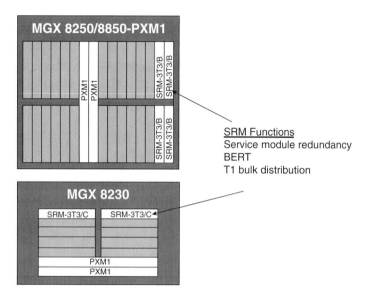

SRM Functions
Service module redundancy
BERT
T1 bulk distribution

NOTE   If redundant PXMs are installed on a switch with SRM cards, you must have redundant SRMs installed on the switch as well.

NOTE   Two SRM cards are supported in the MGX 8220 concentrator: SRM-T1E1 and SRM-3T3. Only the SRM-3T3 is supported on the MGX 8230/8250/8850-PXM1 switch.

SRM Functions

The SRM-3T3 performs the following functions:

- **Service module redundancy**—The SRM manages the optional 1-to-N and 1-to-1 service module redundancy on the MGX switch. 1-to-N redundancy is when a single service module is installed as a backup card for a number of like cards in the MGX chassis. 1-to-1 redundancy is when two like cards are attached to each other using a Y-cable. The SRM reroutes the incoming traffic to the backup card in the event of a failure.

- **BERT**—The SRM can perform service module line and port BERT functions to isolate transmission errors between MGX service modules and the attached equipment. The SRM BERT function also includes local, remote, and far-end loopback activation.

- **T1 line distribution**—The SRM-3T3 can accept up to three T3 lines that comprise multiplexed T1 lines. The SRM demultiplexes the T3 lines into T1 lines (up to 80) and forwards the traffic on the T1 lines across the backplane to specified service module interfaces.

The RPM Card

The Route Processor Module (RPM) card is a double-height MGX card module that is equivalent to a Cisco 7000 series router. The RPM can support Ethernet, Fast Ethernet, or Fiber Distributed Data Interface (FDDI) LAN interfaces. The RPM runs Cisco IOS Software and can be configured from the MGX command line using IOS commands. Traffic from the RPM LAN interfaces can be routed to any of the trunk or line ports on the MGX switch. Figure 16-11 shows RPMs installed in the MGX 8250/8850-PXM1 chassis.

Figure 16-11 *RPMs in the MGX 8250/8850-PXM1 Chassis*

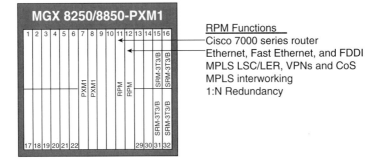

RPM Functions

The RPM performs the following functions:

- The RPM is a Cisco Series 7000 router that runs a customized version of Cisco IOS Release 12.0 Software.

- Up to two LAN interface cards can be installed on the RPM. Each interface card has four Ethernet ports, one Fast Ethernet port, or one FDDI port.

- The RPM communicates with the other MGX card modules via a high-speed ATM cell bus interface.

- Multiprotocol Label Switching (MPLS)—The RPM can be configured as a Label Switch Router (LSR) or a Label Edge Router (LER) and supports virtual private networks (VPNs) and Class of Service (CoS) features.

- MPLS networks comprising MGX 8850-PXM45 switches, MGX 8230/8250/8850-PXM1 switches, and BPX switches are supported.

- 1-to-N redundancy

- Software and configuration can be stored on a PXM1 hard drive.

Types of RPM

There are two RPM card modules:

- **RPM/B**—The standard RPM on the MGX 8230, 8250, and 8850-PXM1 platforms can support 150 KB packets per second, 150 MHz processing, 128 MB memory, 16MB Flash memory, and IOS 12.0(7)T or higher.

- **RPM-PR**—The premium RPM-PR on the MGX 8230, 8250, 8850-PXM1, and 8850-PXM45 platforms can support 350 KB packets per second, 350 MHz processing, 256/512 MB memory, 32 MB Flash memory, and IOS 12.1(5.3)T_XT or higher.

RPM Front and Back Cards

The RPM front card is a double-height card module that can be installed in any card slot except those reserved for processor, switch, or SRM cards. The RPM front card supports three LAN interface back cards, as follows:

- Four-port Ethernet card. There are two versions of the Ethernet back card. Model A can be used only with the RPM/B, and Model B can be used with the RPM/B or RPM-PR

- One-port Fast Ethernet card

- One-port FDDI card

MGX Service Modules

Service modules for the MGX switch interface with end-user equipment and perform ingress and egress processing on the user traffic. Service module functions can include ingress and egress queuing, ingress policing, segmentation and reassembly (SAR), idle suppression, interface alarm reporting, and network-to-CPE signaling. These features are discussed in detail later in this chapter.

MGX service modules include

- Circuit Emulation Service Module (CESM)

- Frame Relay Service Module (FRSM)

- ATM User Service Module (AUSM)
- Voice Interworking Service Module (VISM)

Each service module has several types. Each type supports a different line interface, such as FRSM-8T1, FRSM-T3E3, FRSM-HS2, and so on.

Figure 16-12 shows the low-speed service modules. Low-speed service modules can be installed in the upper or lower bay of the MGX chassis.

Figure 16-12 *Low-Speed Service Modules*

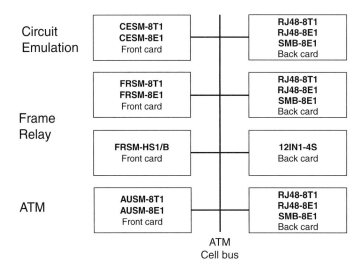

Figure 16-13 shows the high-speed service modules. High-speed service modules should be installed in the upper bay of the MGX 8250/8850-PXM1 chassis to ensure expected card throughput. High-speed cards can be installed in any single-height card slot in the MGX 8230 chassis. The number of card slots supported by a bus determines the bus bandwidth that is accessible by each card module. For this reason, high-speed cards should be installed in the upper bay, and low-speed cards should be installed in the lower bay.

NOTE   Card slots on the MGX are numbered from 1 to 16 on the upper bay and from 17 to 32 on the lower bay. If a double-height card is installed, it is defined by the upper bay card slot number. For example, the PXM is a double-height card that is installed in slots 7 and 8 of the MGX switch.

Figure 16-13 *High-Speed Service Modules*

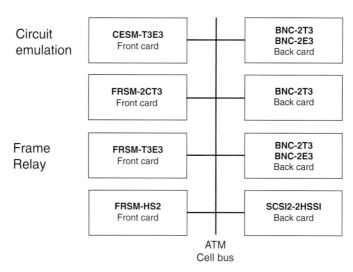

Table 16-2 summarizes the MGX service module features.

Table 16-2 *MGX Service Module Features*

Front Card	Back Cards	Number of Line Interfaces	Number of Logical Ports	Number of Connections
CESM-8T1	RJ48-8T1	8	8 (unchannelized)	1000
			192 (channelized)	
CESM-8E1	RJ48-8E1	8	8 (unchannelized)	1000
	SMB-8E1		248 (channelized)	
CESM-T3	BNC-2T3	1	1	1
CESM-E3	BNC-2E3	1	1	1
FRSM-8T1	RJ48-8T1	8	8 (unchannelized)	1000
			192 (channelized)	898 (with LMI)
FRSM-8E1	RJ48-8E1	8	8 (unchannelized)	1000
	SMB-8E1		192 (channelized)	898 (with LMI)
FRSM-HS1/B	12IN1-4S	4	4	200
FRSM-T3E3	BNC-2T3	2	2	2000
	BNC-2E3			

continues

Table 16-2 *MGX Service Module Features (Continued)*

Front Card	Back Cards	Number of Line Interfaces	Number of Logical Ports	Number of Connections
FRSM-2CT3	BNC-2T3	2	256	4000
FRSM-HS2	SCSI2-2HSSI	2	2	2000
AUSM-8T1	RJ48-8T1	8	8	1000
				898 (with LMI)
AUSM-8E1	RJ48-8T1	8	8	1000
				898 (with LMI)

CESM Features

The CESM segments and reassembles channelized or unchannelized user traffic using ATM Adaptation Layer 1 (AAL1). All incoming traffic, including signaling and framing bits, is segmented and transported through the network to a destination CESM.

Three CESM models are supported on MGX switches:

- **CESM**—8T1 with a DB-15 back card
- **CESM**—8E1 with a DB-15 or BNC back card
- **CESM**—T3E3 with a BNC-2T3 or BNC-2E3 back card. The back cards provide two line interfaces. Only line 1 (on the top) is supported on the CESM-T3E3.

CESM features include the following:

- **Structured or unstructured data mode**—The CESM supports structured data transfer that identifies framing and signaling bits in the data stream. Unstructured mode treats all bits as part of the data stream.

NOTE   T3 and E3 do not support structured data mode.

- **Multiplexing and demultiplexing T1 and E1 timeslots**—If the optional channelized feature is available on T1 or E1 CESMs, the individual timeslots are multiplexed and demultiplexed on the CESM.

- **Segmenting and reassembling traffic streams using AAL1**—The CESM takes bit-stream traffic and segments it into ATM cells using AAL1. All traffic is forwarded to the ATM network and transported on a constant bit rate (CBR) circuit to the destination MGX CESM.

- **Monitoring on-hook and off-hook signaling states**—CESMs that support channelized T1 or E1 lines can monitor Channel Associated Signaling (CAS) for channel signaling states. These signaling states are used to turn on and off the SAR process, eliminating the transmission of traffic during on-hook periods. This feature is available only on 64 Kbps structured connections.

- **Clock recovery**—The T1 and E1 CESM can use one of two methods for clock recovery that enable end-to-end timing between the two circuit-terminating devices. Clock recovery is available only on full-unstructured T1 or E1 connections.

- **Physical layer**—The CESM performs all necessary physical-layer functions on the attached access lines.

FRSM Features

The FRSM converts Frame Relay frames into ATM cells using AAL5. The FRSM performs policing and congestion management functions on all incoming user traffic.

Six FRSM models are supported on an MGX device:

- FRSM-8T1 with RJ-48 back card

- FRSM-8E1 with RJ-48 or SMB back card

- FRSM-HS1/B with X.21/V.35 back card

- FRSM-HS2 with HSSI back card

- FRSM-2CT3 with T3 back card

- FRSM-T3E3 with T3 or E3 back card

The FRSM performs the following functions:

- **Segmenting and reassembling Frame Relay frames using AAL5**—The FRSM converts Frame Relay frames into ATM cells using AAL5 for transport across the ATM network.

- **Signaling protocols**—The FRSM supports all Frame Relay signaling protocols, including the Enhanced Local Management Interface (ELMI).

- **Policing**—The FRSM supports ingress policing based on configurable burst sizes and data rates.

- **ForeSight feature**—The FRSM can optionally support congestion management using the ForeSight feature.

- **Standard ABR for Frame Relay**—The FRSM-8T1 and FRSM-8E1 cards support congestion management using standard ABR services.

- **ATM-Frame Relay interworking**—ATM-Frame Relay interworking, both transparent and translational, is supported on the FRSM.

- **Frame forwarding**—An FRSM port can support a frame forwarding connection. Frame forwarding takes frames (HDLC, SDLC, X.25, and so on) and forwards them to the destination Frame Relay interface. A frame forwarding port supports only a single connection.

- **Physical layer**—The FRSM performs all necessary physical-layer functions on the attached access line.

AUSM Features

The AUSM provides narrowband (T1 or E1) ATM UNI services. The AUSM also supports Inverse Multiplexing over ATM (IMA) services.

Two AUSM models are supported on MGX switches:

- AUSM-8T1 with a DB-15 back card
- AUSM-8E1 with a DB-15 or BNC back card

The AUSM supports the following functions:

- **User-Network Interface (UNI) or Network-Node Interface (NNI) cell format**—The ATM ports on the AUSM card can be configured to accept either the UNI or NNI cell header formats.

- **CBR, rt-VBR, nrt-VBR, standard ABR, ForeSight ABR, and UBR services**—The AUSM supports all six types of ATM services.

- **Policing**—Single and dual leaky-bucket models are used to police ingress ATM traffic on the AUSM. Policing is defined on a per-channel basis.

- **Virtual path or virtual channel connections**—The AUSM supports both virtual path (VP) and virtual channel (VC) connections.

- **Inverse multiplexed ATM (IMA) access lines**—Multiple T1 or E1 lines can form a single ATM port using IMA.

- **ILMI signaling protocol**—The Integrated Local Management Interface (ILMI) signaling protocol can be configured on the AUSM on a per-port basis. ATM LMI is not supported.

- **Physical layer**—All necessary physical-layer functions are performed by the AUSM.

VISM Features

The VISM provides T1 and E1 digital voice services in the MGX network. Currently, the VISM supports Voice over IP (VoIP) services in conjunction with the Cisco VSC2700 voice switch controller and the Route Processor Module (RPM).

Two VISM models are supported on MGX switches:

- VISM-8T1 with a DB-15 back card
- VISM-8E1 with a DB-15 or BNC back card

The VISM performs the following functions:

- **Voice over IP**—Support for VoIP to RFC 1889
- **Voice over ATM**—Using standards-compliant AAL2 adaptation
- **PCM voice coding**—Support for both pulse-code modulation (PCM) a-law and mu-law
- **Compression**—G.726 and G.729a/b
- **Built-in echo cancellation**—Programmable 16-, 32-, 64-, or 128-millisecond near-end echo cancellation
- **Voice activity detection (VAD)** and comfort noise generation using variable threshold energy (Cisco proprietary)
- **Signaling**—The VISM in AAL2 mode facilitates transport of DTMF and CAS signaling information.
- **Fax/modem detection**
- **Physical layer**—Similar to other MGX service modules, all necessary physical-layer functions are performed by the VISM.

Reserved Card Slots

The MGX card modules should be installed into the correct card slot locations in order for them to perform correctly. The MGX 8250/8850-PXM1 switch has six reserved card slots:

- Slots 7 and 8 for PXM1s
- Slots 15 and 16 for SRMs in the upper bay
- Slots 31 and 32 for SRMs in the lower bay

The MGX 8230 switch has four reserved card slots:

- Slots 1 and 2 for PXM1s
- Slots 7 and 14 for SRMs

High and Low-Speed Card Modules

The MGX 8250/8850-PXM1 switch has eight cell buses, each running at 155 Mbps. The upper bay has six buses and the lower bay has two buses.

The MGX 8230 switch has eight cell buses—one to each service module slot, each running 155 Mbps.

Although each cell bus runs at the same speed, the number of card slots that a bus supports determines the bus bandwidth that is accessible by each card module. For this reason, high-speed cards should be installed in the upper bay, and low-speed cards should be installed in the lower bay. You can optionally double the cell buses' clock speed (on the MGX 8250/8850-PXM1 switch, only the upper-bay buses support this feature). Increasing the clock speed provides more bandwidth to high-speed service modules. Figure 16-14 shows the cell bus configuration on the MGX switches.

Figure 16-14 *MGX Cell Bus Configuration*

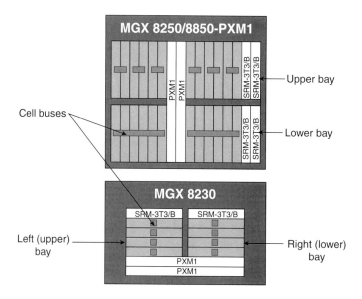

There is nothing to stop you from putting cards in either the upper or lower bays. There are some instances when low-speed cards are installed in the upper bay, such as in a heavily populated switch with only low-speed cards in use.

MGX card modules are grouped as high- or low-speed cards, depending on the card's maximum traffic throughput. In general, T1 and E1 cards are low-speed, and T3, E3, and HSSI cards are high-speed.

Low-speed cards include

- CESM-8T1 and CESM-8E1
- FRSM-8T1 and FRSM-8E1
- FRSM-HS1/B (X.21/V.35 interface)

- AUSM-8T1 and AUSM-8E1
- VISM-8T1 and VISM-8E1

High-speed cards include

- FRSM-2CT3
- FRSM-T3E3
- FRSM-HS2
- CESM-T3E3

Configuring Double-Height Card Slots

Initially, all card slots except those reserved for PXM1s are single-height. Dividers between the upper and lower bay must be removed to accommodate double-height card modules.

On the MGX 8250/8850-PXM1 chassis, each divider is two card slots wide; removing the divider changes four single-height slots into two double-height slots. Dividers must be removed from the left to the right starting from card slot 1 or card slot 9.

On the MGX 8230 chassis, each divider is one card slot wide; removing the divider changes two single-height slots into one double-height slot. Dividers must be removed from the bottom (left) to the top (right) starting from card slot 3. Figure 16-15 shows card slots 9 to 12 as double-height card slots on an MGX 8250 chassis.

Figure 16-15 *Double-Height Card Slots*

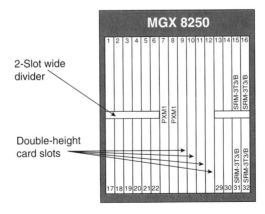

MGX Required Features and Hardware

This section describes the guidelines used to determine the features and hardware needed for an MGX 8230/8250/8850-PXM1 switch.

Guidelines

In order to determine which features and hardware are required for an MGX switch, follow these steps:

Step 1 Decide which optional features are required. (1-to-1 and 1-to-N service module redundancy, ForeSight for Frame Relay and ATM—Channelized Frame Relay or circuit emulation ports—Multiple channelized Frame Relay or circuit emulation ports, and Inverse multiplexed ATM (IMA) ports—IMA services.)

Step 2 Identify the user services that are needed (Layer 3 LAN, circuit emulation, Frame Relay, ATM, and voice) to determine the required service modules.

Step 3 Identify the quantity and type of each service interface—for example, how many Nx64 Kbps Frame Relay ports are needed.

Step 4 Identify the connector types for each interface to determine back card requirements.

Step 5 Consider card placement and chassis card capacity. Know where to install double- and single-height cards and high- and low-speed cards. More than one MGX switch might be needed.

Step 6 Consider expansion. Higher-density cards might provide future services without your having to add new hardware.

Step 7 Examine relative costs for cards that provide similar services. For example, an external TDM used with a channelized FRSM-8T1 might cost less than multiple FRSM-HS1/B cards with V.35 interfaces.

Frame Relay Only Example

You are responsible for ordering a new MGX 8250 switch for your customer, Earth Telecom, to provide public Frame Relay services in Bangkok. They have provided you with these requirements:

- Processor redundancy
- Service module redundancy
- E3 trunk interface

- 117 Frame Relay customer ports—five full E3, 18 full E1, 42 64 Kbps, 15 128 Kbps, 20 256 Kbps, 12 512 Kbps, and five 1024 Kbps

- All E1 interfaces with SMB connectors

- Congestion management on all Frame Relay services

- All user traffic (except E3) is multiplexed onto E1 lines

Figure 16-16 shows Earth Telecom's new Bangkok switch.

Figure 16-16 *Earth Telecom's New Bangkok Switch*

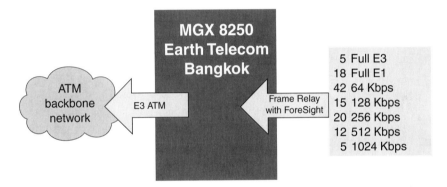

This example is straightforward because the user traffic and interface requirements do not vary significantly. It's obvious that a number of E3 and E1 FRSM cards are needed.

All MGX switches must have at least one PXM1 installed. In this case, two PXM1s are needed for processor redundancy. SRMs must be installed in pairs if you have redundant PXM1s. You need to see if service modules using 1-to-N redundancy are installed in one or both bays. If only one bay has service modules, two SRMs are needed. If there are service modules in both the upper and lower bays, four SRMs are needed.

Three FRSM-T3E3 cards that provide two E3 lines each can support the five E3 lines. These cards should be installed in the upper bay of the chassis. 1-to-1 redundancy is available on the FRSM-T3E3, so six cards are needed.

The full E1 and all Nx64 Kbps ports can be supported on FRSM-8E1 cards. Channelized line support is an optional feature on the FRSM-8E1. It is more cost-effective to put the full E1 ports on unchannelized cards and the Nx64 Kbps ports on channelized cards. However, as new customers are added to the switch, the flexibility of the channelized cards might outweigh the cost increase. In this case, two unchannelized FRSM-8E1 cards are used for 16 of the full E1 ports. The extra two E1 lines are supported by channelized FRSM-8E1.

The Nx64 Kbps ports add up to 232x64 Kbps. For E1 lines, you must know whether channel-associated signaling (CAS) or common-channel signaling (CCS) line coding is required in order to decide whether 30 or 31 timeslots are available on each E1 line. Although voice signaling is not required for Frame Relay, some E1 transmission systems might reserve timeslot 16. If you don't know, assume that only 30 timeslots are available. Based on this assumption, eight E1s are needed.

To support the two full E1 lines and the Nx64 Kbps ports, you need two more FRSM-8E1 cards. Only one of these two cards needs to be channelized, but to support any new Nx64 Kbps customers, both of them should be channelized. In total, two unchannelized, two channelized, and one redundant (also channelized) FRSM-8E1s are needed.

All the FRSM-8E1 cards will fit in the lower bay, so two SRMs are needed. The FRSM-T3E3 cards are installed in the upper bay but do not need SRMs to support their 1-to-1 redundancy.

Table 16-3 lists the required hardware and software licenses needed for your MGX 8850 switch.

NOTE   Software, power supplies, racks, and cables are not included in this list.

Table 16-3   *Required Hardware and Software Licenses*

Quantity	Description	Part Number
1	MGX 8250 chassis (comes with one PXM1 and PXM-UI)	MGX8850
1	Redundant PXM1 with T3E3 daughter card option (for both PXMs) and one PXM-UI	PXM1-2-T3E3-R
2	PXM E3 back cards with BNC connectors	MGX-BNC-2E3
2	SRM-3T3 front cards	MGX-SRM-3T3/B
2	Software license for 1-to-N redundancy using SRM	AX-SR-8
2	SRM-3T3 back cards	MGX-BNC-3T3-M
2	Unchannelized FRSM-8E1 front cards	AX-FRSM-8E1
3	Channelized FRSM-8E1 front cards	AX-FRSM-8E1-C
5	Software license for ForeSight on FRSM-8E1s	AX-FS-8
4	FRSM E1 back cards with SMB connectors	AX-SMB-8E1
1	FRSM E1 redundant back card	AX-R-SMB-8E1
6	FRSM-T3E3 front card	MGX-FRSM-2T3E3
6	FRSM E3 back cards with BNC connectors	MGX-BNC-2E3
6	ForeSight license (per card) for FRSM-T3E3s	AX-FS-HS

Figure 16-17 shows the hardware installed in the MGX 8250 chassis.

Figure 16-17 *MGX 8250 Chassis*

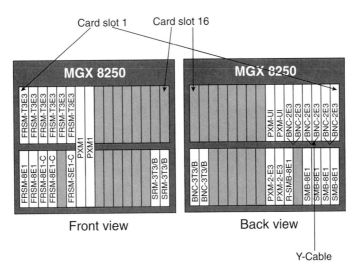

Multiservice Example

You are responsible for ordering a new MGX 8850-PXM1 switch for your customer, ABC Technology, in Denver. This switch will be installed in the existing MGX network that carries their corporate voice and data traffic. They have provided you with these requirements:

- No processor or service module redundancy
- OC-3c trunk interface
- 214 circuit emulation ports—three full T1 and 210 64 Kbps
- 47 Frame Relay ports—15 64 Kbps, 21 128 kbps, eight 256 Kbps, three 8 Mbps
- Six T1 ATM ports
- 11 Layer 3 LAN interfaces—10 Ethernet, 1 Fast Ethernet
- All Nx64 Kbps services transported on T1 lines
- All T1 interfaces with RJ-48 connectors
- Congestion management on 8 Mbps Frame Relay services only

Figure 16-18 shows ABC Technology's new Denver switch.

Figure 16-18 *ABC Technology's New Denver Switch*

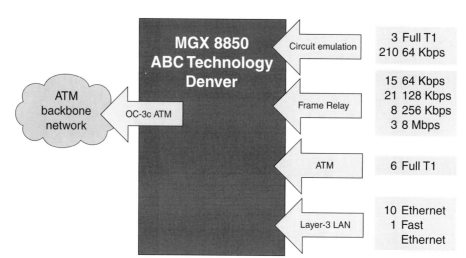

This MGX 8850-PXM1 switch requires only one PXM1 and no SRM cards. The PXM1 needs a 155 Mbps daughter card and a line interface back card. Because the customer did not specify the interface type for the OC-3c line, you should find out which type they need.

Twelve channelized CESM-8T1 cards are needed for the circuit emulation services, and one AUSM-8T1 card is needed for the ATM services.

The Nx64 Kbps Frame Relay services will fit onto one channelized FRSM-8T1. The three 8 Mbps Frame Relay ports require two FRSM-HS2 cards with ForeSight software licenses.

RPMs are needed to support the Layer 3 LAN services. Each Ethernet back card has four ports; each FDDI back card has one port. To meet ABC Technology's requirements, you need to order two RPMs, three Ethernet back cards, and one Fast Ethernet back card.

The customer did not specify the interface type for the OC-3c line or the LAN ports, so you must find out which type they need before you order the hardware.

Table 16-4 lists the required hardware for ABC Technology's Denver switch. Some assumptions have been made regarding the unspecified interface types.

NOTE Software, power supplies, racks, and cables are not included in this list.

Table 16-4 *Required Hardware for ABC Technology's Denver Switch*

Quantity	Description	Part Number
1	MGX 8850 chassis (comes with one PXM1 and PXM-UI)	MGX8850
1	PXM 155 Mbps daughter card option	PXM1-4-155
1	PXM 155 Mbps back card with multimode fiber interface	MGX-MMF-4-155/B
2	CESM-8T1 front cards	AX-CESM-8T1
2	Software licenses for structure circuit emulation services	AX-SDT-8
1	Channelized FRSM-8T1 front card	AX-FRSM-8T1-C
1	AUSM-8T1 front card	AX-AUSM-8T1
4	RJ-48 T1 back cards for CESM, FRSM, and AUSM T1 cards	AX-RJ48-8T1
2	FRSM-HS2 front cards	MGX-FRSM-HS2
2	Software licenses for ForeSight	AX-FS-HS
2	SCSI2 HSSI back cards	MGX-SCSI2-2HSSI/B
2	RPM front cards with 64 MB of DRAM	MGX-RPM-64M
3	RJ-45 Ethernet LAN interface back cards	MGX-RJ45-4E
1	Multimode fiber FDDI LAN interface back card	MGX-MMF-FE

Figure 16-19 shows the hardware installed in the MGX 8850-PXM1 chassis.

Figure 16-19 *MGX 8850-PXM1 Chassis*

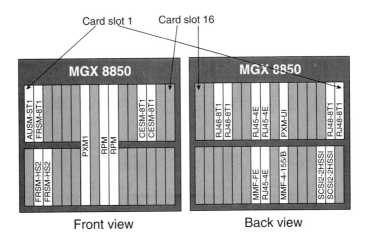

Summary

This chapter provided an overview of the MGX products and discussed the network management tools that are available for the MGX 8230, 8250, and 8850-PXM1 switches. MGX networking was discussed, along with instructions for installing MGX switches in a network.

The functions and features of the MGX processor cards, the SRM card, the RPM card, and the MGX service modules were detailed. MGX card slots and the cell bus structure were described, and high- and low-speed card module features were discussed.

Also presented in this chapter were MGX required features and hardware guidelines, including Frame Relay and multiservice switch installation examples.

Review Questions

1 Which of the following best describes the MGX 8250 concentrator?

A. A core switch that supports broadband ATM interfaces

B. A multiservice edge device that supports circuit emulation, Frame Relay, and ATM services

C. An enterprise switch with multiple narrow or broadband trunks that supports voice, data, and Frame Relay services

D. A multiservice edge switch that supports a variety of narrow and broadband services, including circuit emulation, voice, Frame Relay, ATM, and Layer 3 LAN services

2 Which of the following best describes the MGX 8850-PXM45 switch?

A. A core switch that supports broadband ATM interfaces

B. A multiservice edge device that supports circuit emulation, Frame Relay, and ATM services

C. An enterprise switch with multiple narrow or broadband trunks that supports voice, data, and Frame Relay services

D. A multiservice edge switch that supports a variety of narrow and broadband services, including circuit emulation, Frame Relay, ATM, and Layer 3 LAN services

3 Which MGX platform does *not* support local switching?

4 Which of the following optional MGX features requires a purchased software license?

A. IP routing

B. Channelized Frame Relay

C. ATM variable bit rate services

D. T3 and E3 Frame Relay services

5 Of the following services, which two are available on the MGX switch?

A. HSSI ATM

B. Analog voice

C. T3 Frame Relay

D. Nx64 Kbps ATM

E. E1 circuit emulation

6 Which feature is an optional congestion management feature available for Frame Relay and ATM services on the MGX switch?

7 What is the CLI?

A. A GUI on the CWM station

B. A text-based command interface

C. A tool that allows a PC to Telnet to the CWM station

D. A PC-based application for configuring Cisco WAN switches

8 Which of the following MGX networks are supported?

A. A PNNI network of MGX 8250 switches

B. A PNNI network of MGX 8850-PXM45 switches

C. A tiered network of BPX switches and MGX 8220 concentrators

D. A tiered network of BPX switches and MGX 8850-PXM1 switches

E. A PNNI network of MGX 8850-PXM45 switches with 8220 feeders

9 Of the following functions, which three are performed by the PXM1?

A. Cell switching

B. Network management

C. AAL5 SAR for Frame Relay

D. Storing the service module configuration

E. Voice signaling and call management

10 Of the following PXM1 models, which three are available for the MGX 8850 switch?

A. PXM-4-155

B. PXM-8-155

C. PXM-1-622

D. PXM-8-T1E1

E. PXM-2-T3E3

F. PXM-4-T3E3

11 You have a PXM-1-622 installed in your MGX 8250 switch. Of the following back cards, which two must be installed with your PXM1?

A. PXM-UI

B. BNC-2T3

C. PXM-CLK

D. MMF-4-155/B

E. SMFIR-1-622/B

12 Which type of SRMs is supported on the MGX 8250 switch?

A. SRM-3E3

B. SRM-T1E1

C. SRM-2-155

D. SRM-3T3/B

E. SRM-3T3/C

13 Of the following functions, which two are performed by the SRM-3T3 (Model B or C) for the MGX switch?

A. Alarm reporting

B. 1-to-N redundancy

C. T1 line distribution

D. ATM cell switching

E. Node synchronization

14 What are two rules for installing SRMs in the MGX 8250/8850-PXM1 chassis?

A. SRMs can only be installed in slots 7 and 14.

B. SRMs can only be installed in slots 15, 16, 31, and 32.

C. If you have redundant PXMs, you must install four SRMs.

D. Four SRMs must be installed for the MGX switch to function properly.

E. SRMs can be installed in just the upper or lower bay, depending on where service modules are installed.

15 What are two rules for installing SRMs in the MGX 8230 chassis?

A. SRMs can only be installed in slots 7 and 14.

B. SRMs can only be installed in slots 15, 16, 31, and 32.

C. If you have redundant PXMs, you must install two SRMs.

D. Four SRMs must be installed for the MGX switch to function properly.

E. SRMs can be installed in just the left or right bay, depending on where service modules are installed.

16 What is the RPM? (Choose all that apply.)

A. A Cisco router

B. An MPLS LSR

C. A switch module

D. A single-height card module

17 An RPM front card can support up to how many back cards?

18 Of the following back cards, which two are supported for the RPM?

A. One-port FDDI

B. Four-port FDDI

C. Four-port Ethernet

D. Eight-port Ethernet

E. One-port Fast Ethernet

F. Two-port Fast Ethernet

19 A T1 Frame Relay router interface is attached to a _____ card installed in the MGX 8850 chassis.

20 What does the CESM do?

A. Converts digital voice samples into IP packets

B. Converts Frame Relay frames into ATM cells using AAL5

C. Converts a 64 Kbps, T1, or E1 traffic stream into ATM cells using AAL1

D. Transports a T3 or E3 ATM traffic stream across multiple T1 or E1 lines

21 You have an empty MGX 8250 chassis. Which card slot is the best choice in which to install an FRSM-2CT3?

A. 1

B. 6

C. 7

D. 22

22 You are installing cards in an MGX 8850-PXM1 chassis. There are PXM1s installed in slots 7 and 8 and SRM-3T3s installed in slots 31 and 32. In order to best utilize the card slots and to provide 1-to-N redundancy on all E1 cards, choose the best location for the following card modules:

Two FRSM-8E1s:

A. 1 and 2

B. 17 and 18

C. 29 and 30

Four CESM-8E1s:

A. 1 to 4

B. 3 to 6

C. 17 to 20

D. 19 to 22

Two RPMs:

A. 1 and 2

B. 5 and 6

Six FRSM-HS1/Bs:

A. 3, 4, 5, 6, 9, and 10

B. 9 to 14

23   Which card slots are reserved in the MGX 8230 switch?

This chapter covers the following key topics:

- Methods for Connecting to the Command-Line Interface
- MGX Command Syntax
- MGX User IDs and Passwords
- Card and Port Resource Partitions
- MGX Node Configuration Commands
- Redundancy on the MGX Switch
- MGX Card Redundancy Commands

CHAPTER 17

The User Interface and MGX Network Configuration

This chapter presents the MGX user interface, including methods for connecting to the command-line interface (CLI), the command syntax, and help commands that are available on the MGX. User passwords and IDs for the MGX are discussed, and the range of command privilege levels is presented.

How to log into and out of the MGX is covered in this chapter, and a list of the steps, actions, and results of logging into and out of the MGX CLI is provided. Card and port resource partitions are discussed, and MGX node configuration commands are detailed.

Redundancy capabilities on the MGX switch are described, as well as how the MGX supports both 1-to-1 and 1-to-N redundancy, with the cards that support this feature and the MGX card redundancy commands used. Information about how to set up MGX node characteristics is presented, including procedures for setting up service module redundancy.

Methods for Connecting to the Command-Line Interface

You can use four methods to access the MGX CLI, which is the interface used to monitor and configure the MGX platform, including shelf, trunk, line, port, connection, and channel characteristics. These access methods are described as follows:

- **Console port**—The Console port is an RJ-45 DTE interface on the PXM-UI back card. Initially, the Console port is the only method available to access the switch. You can use a dumb terminal or a PC running a VT100 terminal emulation program.

- **Modem port**—The Modem port is an RJ-45 DTE Serial Line Internet Protocol (SLIP) interface on the PXM-UI back card. To use the Modem port, you must configure an IP address and use a PC or workstation running a SLIP application.

- **LAN port**—The LAN port allows the switch to communicate with other devices, such as PCs, workstations, and Cisco WAN Manager, across a LAN. The LAN port is an RJ-45 connector, 10BaseT, 802.3 Ethernet port.

- **IP forwarding**—IP forwarding is a method to propagate IP traffic (Telnet, SNMP, FTP, and TFTP) in-band through a BPX/MGX network. The originating workstation communicates with one of the BPX switches in the network via a LAN port. If you're using a Cisco WAN Manager station, this is one way it communicates with the MGX switch.

Figure 17-1 illustrates the console, modem and LAN ports on an MGX switch.

Figure 17-1 *CLI Access Methods*

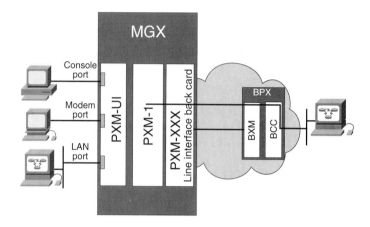

MGX Command Syntax

All commands on the MGX CLI are a single word comprising a combination of abbreviated verbs and nouns. Commands might be followed by any number of required and optional parameters. Commands can have both optional and required parameters, only one type of parameter, or no parameters.

Issuing a command without any parameters prompts the MGX CLI to return the correct syntax, including all parameters. Command syntax is also described in this book where appropriate. In this book, and in the MGX command reference manuals, required parameters are enclosed in angle brackets, and optional parameters are enclosed in square brackets. The brackets are used in the documentation to differentiate between the two types of parameters; they should not be typed on the command line.

The general command format is as follows:

```
command <required parameter> ... [optional parameter]
```

Some commands follow this format:

```
command -keyword <required parameter> ... [-optional keyword <optional parameter>]
```

In either format, all required parameters must be entered; optional parameters (and keywords) do not need to be entered. Many parameters are numbers that represent the parameter options. For example, a 1 might represent "yes" and a 2 might represent "no."

All required keywords and parameters must follow the command in order, separated by a single space. Optional parameters preceded by keywords can usually be entered in any order.

You will need a reference (either from the CLI or documentation) for most commands, because the MGX CLI does not provide parameter prompting.

NOTE   The MGX CLI is case-sensitive. It is recommended that you use uppercase and lowercase exactly as described. Otherwise, you might not get the expected results. For example, if you are prompted for a "Yes/No" response, type the response exactly as it is printed in the prompt.

The MGX CLI command prompt provides information about the switch you are logged into. The command prompt is in this form:

```
node name.card slot.card type.card status
```

card status is either active (**a**) or standby (**s**).

Add Port Command Example

The **addport** command is used to activate and configure an ATM port on the AUSM.

The command syntax is

```
addport <port number> <port type> <line number>
```

Here are the parameter options:

- *port number*—The assigned port number can be between 1 and 8. If the port is assigned to a single line (a non-IMA port), the port number does not need to be the same as the line number. Each assigned port number must be unique on the AUSM.

- *port type*—The ATM cell header used by the port; 1 = UNI, 2 = NNI.

- *line number*—The line number associated with the ATM port.

For example, type **addport 1 1 1** to add UNI port 1 to line number 1. Type **addport 3 2 6** to add NNI port 3 to line number 6.

Configure Line Command Example

The **cnfln** command is used to modify the characteristics of service module lines. The command varies depending on the line type (serial, T1, E1, T3, E3, and so on). The command syntax for a T1 or E1 line is

```
cnfln <line number> <line code> <line length> <clock source> [E1 signaling]
```

The parameters are as follows:

- *line number*—The line number.
- *line code* (T1)—2 = B8ZS (also makes line type ESF), 4 = AMI (also makes line type D4).
- *line code* (E1)—3 = HDB3, 4 = AMI.
- *line length* (T1)—Defines multiples of 131 feet for line build-out; 10 to 15.
- *line length* (E1)—8 = 75-ohm impedance for SMB connectors, 9 = 120 ohm impedance for RJ-48 connectors.
- *clock source*—1 = loop timing (the line uses the receive clock to transmit data), 2 = local timing (the line uses the MGX clock to transmit data).
- *signaling* (E1)—CAS = Channel Associated Signaling (CAS) without CRC checking, CAS_CRC = CAS with CRC checking, CCS = Common Channel Signaling (CCS) without CRC checking, CCS_CRC = CCS with CRC checking, CLEAR = clear E1—no framing or signaling.

NOTE   Not all E1 lines support all signaling configurations. For example, the AUSM-8E1 does not allow any configuration other than CCS.

Help Command

The **Help** command (you can also type **?**) on the MGX CLI lists the valid commands for your access level on the local card. Some card modules output a simple alphabetical list of the commands; others output additional information about the commands.

NOTE   The **Help** command has an uppercase H when used on most service modules.

You can use the **Help** (or **?**) command to search for commands using a character string. For example, if you type **Help ln** on the PXM1, the output will list all commands with "ln" in the command.

Finding Command Syntax

The MGX **Help** command only lists valid commands; it does not provide any assistance with command syntax or usage. The only tool available to you is to type the command without any parameters. This method works only if parameters are associated with the command.

WARNING   Some commands do not have required parameters or do not require confirmation. Be careful when typing unfamiliar commands; you could accidentally misconfigure the node and cause a loss of service to the users.

For example, if you type **cnfln** on an FRSM-8T1, the command syntax is output by the MGX CLI. Example 17-1 shows the output for the **cnfln** command.

Example 17-1 *The* **cnfln** *command on the MGX*

```
SJ8850.1.20.FRSM.a > cnfln

ERR : incorrect number of parameters (not enough)
Syntax : cnfln "line_num line_code line_len clk_src [E1-signalling]"
         line number -- values ranging from 1-8 are accepted, for FRSM_8
         line code -- 2 for B8ZS (T1),
                      3 for HDB3 (E1),
                      4 for AMI (T1/E1)
         line length -- 10-15 for T1,
                        8 for E1 with SMB line module,
                        9 for E1 with RJ48 line module
         clock source -- clock source : 1 for loop clock, 2 for local clock
         E1 signalling -- CAS: CAS, no CRC;    CAS_CRC: CAS, with CRC;
                          CCS: CCS, no CRC;    CCS_CRC: CCS, with CRC
                          CLEAR : Clear E1

         possible errors are :
         a) illegal/invalid parameters
         b) line doesn't exist, use addln to add line first
         c) loopback/bert is on

SJ8850.1.20.FRSM.a >
```

Here are some helpful hints:

- The syntax quotations and brackets are shown. You do not type these on the command line when issuing the command.

- Read the parameter options carefully. Often the text formatting and wording are difficult to understand.

- Not all listed parameters apply in all cases. In the output just shown, some parameters are for T1 lines, and others are for E1 lines.

MGX CLI Error Messages

The MGX CLI provides minimal error messaging if you type a command or any parameters incorrectly. In many cases, the command syntax is output with some possible error causes. Some errors generate helpful messages, as shown in Example 17-2.

Example 17-2 *MGX CLI Error Messages*

```
SJ8850.1.20.FRSM.a > cnfln 2 2 10 1

  Error occurred during the SNMP SET operation !!
  Probable Reason : "Line does not exist"
  SNMP Error Code : 25

Set failed due to illegal parameter(s)

Syntax : cnfln "line_num line_code line_len clk_src [E1-signalling]"
         line number -- values ranging from 1-8 are accepted, for FRSM_8
         line code --  2 for B8ZS (T1),
                       3 for HDB3 (E1),
                       4 for AMI (T1/E1)
         line length -- 10-15 for T1,
                        8 for E1 with SMB line module,
                        9 for E1 with RJ48 line module
         clock source -- clock source : 1 for loop clock, 2 for local clock
         E1 signalling -- CAS: CAS, no CRC;    CAS_CRC: CAS, with CRC;
                          CCS: CCS, no CRC;    CCS_CRC: CCS, with CRC
                          CLEAR : Clear E1

         possible errors are :
         a) illegal/invalid parameters
         b) line doesn't exist, use addln to add line first
         c) loopback/bert is on

         line len : 1) 000-110ft 2) 110-220ft 3) 220-330ft
                    4) 330-440ft 5) 440-550ft 6) 550-660ft
                    7) > 655ft
```

In Example 17-2, the **cnfln** command is issued for an inactive line. Just below the command line at the top of the screen is a message that indicates why the command failed.

MGX User IDs and Passwords

Each MGX command falls into a range of command privilege levels. When a user ID is created, it is assigned a privilege level and can only issue commands allowed by that level.

For example, the **addport** command can be issued by user level 1. If a user has been assigned a user ID of level 2, he or she would be unable to issue this command. Preconfigured user IDs include superuser, service, and cisco, which are above levels 1 through 6.

NOTE   On the MGX CLI, user level 6 is called ANYUSER.

When a new user ID is added to an MGX switch, it can be assigned a specific password or the default password. The default password is "newuser" and should be changed after you log in for the first time.

All user IDs and passwords are case-sensitive. User IDs are strings between 1 and 12 characters in length; passwords are strings between 6 and 15 characters in length. Any ASCII keyboard characters are supported.

Commands for Managing User IDs and Passwords

The following commands are used to create and display user IDs on the MGX CLI:

- **adduser**—Creates a new user ID (level 1 to 6).
- **deluser**—Removes a user ID.
- **dspusers**—Lists all the user IDs configured on the switch.
- **users**—Lists all the user IDs logged into the switch and tells you how they are accessing the CLI.
- **cnfpass**—Changes a password.

Add User Command

The **adduser** command is used to create new user IDs on the MGX switch. The command syntax is

```
adduser <user ID> <access level> [password]
```

The parameter options are as follows:

- *user ID*—A character string between 1 and 12 characters in length.
- *access level*—The user's privilege level: GROUP1, GROUP2, GROUP3, GROUP4, or ANYUSER.

- *password*—A character string from 6 to 15 characters in length. The *password* is not typed on the command line; you are prompted for it after you enter the *user ID* and *access level* parameters. The default password is newuser. You can type the password or press **Enter** to apply the default password.

The **deluser** command is used to delete a user ID on the MGX switch.

Display Users Command

The **dspusers** command lists the user IDs configured on the switch, as shown in Example 17-3.

Example 17-3 *The* **dspusers** *Command on the MGX*

```
SJ8850.1.7.PXM.a > dspusers

    UserId          AccessLevel
    - - - - - - - - - - - - - - - - - - - - - - - -
    cisco           CISCO_GP
    service         SERVICE_GP
    superuser       SUPER_GP
    manager         GROUP1
    student1        GROUP2
    <temp>          ANYUSER

SJ8850.1.7.PXM.a >
```

Users Command

The **users** command shows the user ID and how the user is logged into the MGX switch, as shown in Example 17-4. The star (*) marks the user ID.

Example 17-4 *The* **users** *Command on the MGX*

```
hei1pop1.1.7.PXM.a > users

    Port        Slot     Idle       UserId      From
    - - - - - - - - - - - - - - - - - - - - - - - - - - - - - - - - - - - - - - - - - - - - -
    console   *   7      0:00:00    manager     console port
    telnet.01     7      0:00:04    cisco       10.21.64.108
```

Configure Password Command

The **cnfpass** command is used to change a user's password. You can change your password or the password belonging to any user who has an access level below yours. For example, if you are a GROUP1 user, you can change the password for a GROUP4 user.

The command syntax is

```
cnfpass [user ID]
```

When you use this command, you are prompted to type your old password and then your new password. You are also prompted to confirm your new password. If you are changing the password for another user, you are only prompted to type the new password and confirm it.

You can press the **Enter** key instead of typing a new password to apply the default newuser password.

The MGX CLI has no way to display a user's password. If you forget your password, a user with a higher access level needs to log in and give you a new password using the **cnfpass** command.

Logging into and out of the MGX CLI

This section describes the steps, actions, and results of logging into and out of the MGX switch:

Step 1   Connect to the MGX CLI using whichever method is available to you (direct connection, Telnet application, and so on). The MGX login prompt appears.

Step 2   Type in your user ID. The password prompt appears.

Step 3   Type in your password. The card selection prompt appears. The active PXM card slot number is displayed in brackets.

Step 4   Type in the card slot number you want to use. If you want to log in to the active PXM, just press the **Enter** key. The MGX CLI prompt appears.

Step 5   Use the CLI to complete your task.

Step 6   If you need to log in to another card, type **cc** *<card slot>* to switch card slots. You are logged in to the specified card.

Step 7   Type **bye**. You are logged off of the MGX CLI. If you are using a Telnet session, the session will end.

You have successfully completed the steps necessary for logging into and out of the MGX switch.

Card and Port Resource Partitions

The MGX switch uses the Virtual Switch Interface (VSI) architecture to manage and control user services on the switch. The three VSI controllers that exist on the MGX switch are as follows:

- **Portable AutoRoute (PAR)**—For PVCs that are added using the CLI or Cisco WAN Manager station's Connection Manager GUI.

- **Multiprotocol Label Switching (MPLS)**—For Label Virtual Circuits (LVCs) that are added from a Label Switch Controller (LSC) such as the RPM.

- **Private Network-to-Network Interface (PNNI)**—For SVCs that are added from an external PNNI server.

NOTE   In Release 1.x PXM1 firmware, only the PAR and MPLS controllers are supported.

Both card- and port-level resource partitioning can be defined on the MGX switch. Card-level partitions define the total number of connections of each type (PAR, MPLS, or PNNI) that are allowed on a particular card module. Port-level partitions define the bandwidth, addressing ranges (for example, VPI, VCI, DLCI), and number of connections of each type that are allowed on a particular logical port. A logical port can be a trunk on the PXM or a port on any of the service modules.

When a connection is added, both the port and card resources are checked. If the necessary resources are unavailable, the connection addition is rejected.

Figure 17-2 shows the resource partitions on an MGX card module.

Figure 17-2 *Card and Port Resource Partitions*

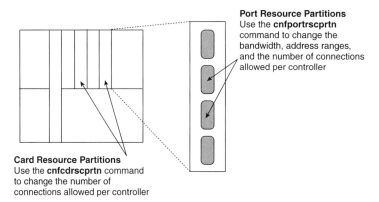

Port Resource Partitions
Use the **cnfportrscprtn** command to change the bandwidth, address ranges, and the number of connections allowed per controller

Card Resource Partitions
Use the **cnfcdrscprtn** command to change the number of connections allowed per controller

If you do not configure the card- or port-level resource partitions, all controllers are given equal access to all resources. In other words, the default values for all partitions are equal to the maximum allowable resource. Remember that restrictions might still apply to the total allowable bandwidth, the number of connections, and the addressing ranges, depending on the hardware and firmware you are using.

FRSM Example

In Figure 17-3, an FRSM card has card- and port-level resource partitions configured for each of the three controller types (PAR, MPLS, and PNNI).

Figure 17-3 *FRSM Resource Partitions Configured for PAR, MPLS, and PNNI*

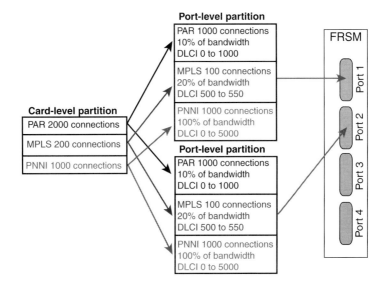

Each port has resource partitions configured for some or all controllers.

NOTE   Many of the resources can overlap. For example, both the PAR and MPLS controllers on port 1 can use DLCIs between 500 and 550.

If a PVC is added from the CLI to port 1, it must meet the requirements defined by the resource partitions. For example, if port 1 is a 64 Kbps port and it already has PAR connections whose bandwidth adds up to 30 Kbps, a 4 Kbps PAR connection would not be allowed, because the bandwidth would exceed the 50 percent (32 Kbps) permitted for PAR.

Even though the physical capacity of the port is 64 Kbps, the PAR connections are allowed only half of that bandwidth. So, even if there are no MPLS or PNNI connections, the PAR connections could not use the remaining bandwidth.

MGX Node Configuration Commands

This section describes the commands used to configure MGX node characteristics:

- **dspcds**—Lists the type and status of front and back cards installed in the switch
- **dspcd**—Displays detailed status information for a specific card
- **dspifip**—Displays the IP configuration for the LAN, SLIP, and internal ATM interfaces
- **cnfname**—Changes the name of the MGX switch
- **dspcdrscprtn**—Displays the card resource partition configuration
- **cnfcdrscprtn**—Changes the card resource partitioning

Display Cards Command

The **dspcds** command provides summary information on the status of all cards installed in the MGX chassis. Cards are autodetected and need not be installed or defined in software. Use this command to learn what kinds of cards are installed in your shelf and what their status is. The output of the **dspcds** command is shown in Examples 17-5 and 17-6.

Example 17-5 *The* **dspcds** *Command on the MGX, Page 1*

```
SJ8850.1.7.PXM.a > dspcds

   Slot  CardState    CardType    CardAlarm  Redundancy
   ----  -----------  --------    ---------  -----------
   1.1   Empty                    Clear
   1.2   Empty                    Clear
   1.3   Empty                    Clear
   1.4   Active       FRSM-2T3    Clear
   1.5   Active       FRSM-2CT3   Clear
   1.6   Active       FRSM-HS2    Clear
   1.7   Active       PXM1-T3E3   Minor
   1.8   Empty                    Clear
   1.9   CardInit     RPM         Clear
   1.10  Empty                    Clear
   1.11  Empty                    Clear
   1.12  Empty                    Clear
   1.13  Empty                    Clear
   1.14  Empty                    Clear
   1.15  Empty                    Clear
   1.16  Empty                    Clear
   1.17  Empty                    Clear
   1.18  Empty                    Clear
   1.19  Active       CESM-8T1    Clear

Type <CR> to continue, Q<CR> to stop:
```

The **dspcds** output includes the following information:

- Card number
- Card state
    - **Active**—The card is available for use and is free of alarms.
    - **Standby**—The card is serving as a backup or redundant card for an active card.
    - **Failed**—The card is out of service due to a failure.
    - **Mismatch**—There is a front-back card mismatch or PXM-service module configuration mismatch.
    - **Empty**—The card slot is empty.
    - **CardInit**—The RPM is downloading an image. It will remain in the CardInit state until the image download is complete, and then it will report a Standby state.
- Card type
- Card alarm status
    - **Minor**
    - **Major**
    - **Clear**
- **Redundancy**—When a secondary (redundant) card is active and is replacing a primary card, it reports which card it is replacing. The primary card reports which card is replacing it.

Example 17-6 shows the second page of the **dspcds** output.

Example 17-6 *The **dspcds** Command on the MGX, Page 2*

```
Slot  CardState    CardType    CardAlarm  Redundancy
----  -----------  --------    ---------  -----------
1.20  Active       FRSM-8T1    Clear
1.21  Active       CESM-8T1    Clear
1.22  Active       AUSMB-8T1   Clear
1.25  Empty                    Clear
1.26  Empty                    Clear
1.27  Standby      FRSM-8T1    Clear
1.28  Empty                    Clear
1.29  Empty                    Clear
1.30  Empty                    Clear
1.31  Active       SRM-3T3     Clear
1.32  Empty                    Clear

NumOfValidEntries:    32
NodeName:             MGX8850
```

continues

Example 17-6 *The* **dspcds** *Command on the MGX, Page 2 (Continued)*

```
      Date:                 04/01/2001
      Time:                 11:38:52
      TimeZone:             GMT
      TimeZoneGMTOff:       12
      StatsMasterIpAddress: 172.10.10.2
      shelfIntegratedAlarm: Minor
      BkplnSerialNum:       SAA03180840

Type <CR> to continue, Q<CR> to stop:

      BkplnType:            0
      BkplnFabNumber:       28-2681-02
      BkplnHwRev:           B0
      ChassisType:          MGX8250
      Power Supply Wattage  1200
```

The second and third page (not shown) of the **dspcds** output on the MGX switch provide information about higher-numbered card slots and the following shelf-level information:

- Backplane serial number

- Node name

- **Date**—In a tiered network, the date is determined by the attached BPX switch and the configured time zone. For standalone nodes, the date can be changed using the **cnfdate** superuser command.

- **Time**—In a tiered network, the time is determined by the attached BPX switch and the configured time zone. For standalone nodes, the time can be changed using the **cnftime** superuser command.

- **Time zone**—The U.S. time zone name. The time zone can be changed with the **cnftmzn** superuser command.

- **Time zone GMT offset**—The configured time zone based on a number of hours before or after GMT. The number of hours before or after GMT can be configured with the **cnftmzngmt** superuser command.

- **Statistics master IP address**—Cisco WAN Manager (CWM) Statistics Master identification. The Statistics Master is the CWM station that is responsible for enabling statistics collection on the switch.

- **Shelf integrated alarm**—The highest-level alarm currently on the shelf. The alarm status is reported to the attached BPX switch and the CWM station.

- **Backplane**—Specific information such as serial and fabrication numbers.

- **Chassis type**—Either MGX 8230, 8250, or 8850.

- **Power supply wattage**—The power supported by the installed power supply in watts.

Display Card Command

The **dspcd** command provides detailed information on a particular card module. PXM1 and SRM cards are displayed from the appropriate PXM1 on the MGX switch. All other cards can be displayed only when you are logged into that card. Use the **cc** command to move from one card to another. Example 17-7 shows the **dspcd** output for a PXM1.

Example 17-7 *The* **dspcd** *Output for a PXM1*

```
SJ8850.1.7.PXM.a > dspcd

    ModuleSlotNumber:           7
    FunctionModuleState:        Active
    FunctionModuleType:         PXM1-T3E3
    FunctionModuleSerialNum:    SBK0306002E
    FunctionModuleHWRev:        22
    FunctionModuleFWRev:        1.1.32
    FunctionModuleResetReason:  Clrallcnf
    LineModuleType:             PXM-UI
    LineModuleState:            Present
    SecondaryLineModuleType:    LM-BNC-2T3
    SecondaryLineModuleState:   Present
    mibVersionNumber:           0.0.20
    configChangeTypeBitMap:     No changes
    cardIntegratedAlarm:        Clear
    cardMajorAlarmBitMap:       Clear
    cardMinorAlarmBitMap:       Clear
    BkCardSerialNum:            SBK02420129
    TrunkBkCardSerialNum:       SAK02380044
    FrontCardFabNumber:         800-04003-03
    TrunkBkCardFabNumber:       800-04057-02
    UIBkCardFabNumber:          800-03688-01
```

The card information provided depends on the card type and can include the following:

- Slot number
- **State**—Active, Standby, Failed, or Mismatch.
- **Type**—The card type.
- Serial number
- **Hardware revision**—The two-letter hardware revision identifier.
- **Firmware revision**—The three-field firmware revision. The firmware is associated with the shelf and card feature set. You can modify it using TFTP to transfer new firmware code to the card from a PC or workstation.
- **Reset reason**—The last reset cause.
- **LM type**—The line module (back card) type.

- **LM state**—The line module state.

- **Card integrated alarm**—The most severe alarm level associated with the card, either major or minor.

Display Interface IP Command

The **dspifip** command provides the following IP configuration information for the three IP interfaces available on the MGX switch:

- **Ethernet/lnPci0**—The LAN port on the PXM-UI.

- **SLIP/sl0**—The Control port on the PXM-UI.

- **ATM/atm0**—In-band access from the backbone network.

If an interface has not been configured, it might not be listed on the **dspifip** command output. The IP addresses can be changed using the **cnfifip** superuser command.

Example 17-8 shows the **dspifip** command output.

Example 17-8 *The* **dspifip** *Command on the MGX*

```
SJ8850.1.7.PXM.a > dspifip

    Interface      Flag  IP Address      Subnetmask       Broadcast Addr
    --------------  ----  --------------  ---------------  ---------------
    Ethernet/lnPci0 UP    172.21.115.214  255.255.255.192  172.21.115.255
    SLIP/sl0        DOWN  0.0.0.0         255.0.0.0        (N/A)
    ATM/atm0        UP    10.10.80.214    255.255.255.0    10.10.80.255
```

Configure Name Command

The **cnfname** command is used to change the node name of your MGX switch. You must set up the node name when the switch is installed. Do not change the node name after you have added connections. Changing the node name can result in lost data on your CWM station.

The command syntax is

```
cnfname <node name>
```

node name is a string between 1 and 8 characters in length. The node name must start with a letter and can include the _ (underscore) or . (period, decimal, full stop, dot) characters. Node names on the MGX switch are case-sensitive.

For example, valid node names are SanJose, san.jose, SJ1, sanjose, and San_Jose. Invalid node names are SanJose! (the "!" is not a valid character), 1SJ (the node name must be a string between 1 and 8 characters), San Jose (no spaces are allowed), and SANJOSE123 (this node name exceeds 8 characters).

Display Card Resource Partitions Command

The **dspcdrscprtn** command is used to list the configured resource partitions for the card. Use this command to learn how many of each connection type (PAR, MPLS [Tag], or PNNI) you can add to the card. The total number of connections includes terminating and pass-through connections. Example 17-9 shows the **dspcdrscprtn** output on a PXM1 and an FRSM.

Example 17-9 *The* **dspcdrscprtn** *Command on the MGX*

```
hei1pop1.1.7.PXM.a > dspcdrscprtn

   Controller  Status   Number of Available LCNs
   ---------------------------------------------
   PAR         Enabled    32767
   PNNI        Enabled    32767
   TAG         Enabled    32767

hei1pop1.1.7.PXM.a > cc 11

(session redirected)

hei1pop1.1.11.FRSM.a > dspcdrscprtn

   User    Status   NumOfLcnAvail
   ------  ------   -------------
   PAR     Add        1000
   PNNI    Add        1000
   TAG     Add        1000
```

NOTE   To change the card resource partitions, use the **cnfcdrscprtn** command.

Redundancy on the MGX Switch

This section describes the service module redundancy process on the MGX switch.

The MGX switch supports both 1-to-1 and 1-to-N redundancy for service modules provided that an SRM card is installed. The **addred** command links redundant cards; the **dspred** command displays the redundancy configuration.

Service Module Redundancy

The following features apply to MGX service module redundancy:

- **1-to-1 on serial and broadband service modules**—The FRSM-HS2, FRSM-2CT3, FRSM-T3E3, and CESM-T3E3 card modules support 1-to-1 redundancy. One card module is defined as the primary and the other as the secondary.

- **Identical primary and secondary cards (front and back)**—All front and back card characteristics must be identical (for example, the same optional features must be enabled).

- **Cards installed in adjacent slots**—The primary and secondary cards must be installed in adjacent card slots.

- **External Y-cable**—External Y-cables must be installed on all active ports between the primary and secondary cards for 1-to-1 redundancy.

- **1-to-N on all T1 and E1 service modules**—All T1 and E1 service modules (FRSM, AUSM, CESM, and VISM) support 1-to-N redundancy. Multiple primary cards are linked to a single secondary card.

- **Requires SRM-3T3**—In order to establish service module redundancy on an MGX switch, SRM cards must be installed in the shelf. You must install your SRM card(s) in the bay that contains service modules that require 1-to-N redundancy.

- **Primary cards must be identical**—All primary card modules that share a secondary card module must have identical characteristics. The secondary card must support the same or a superset of the primary card characteristics. Characteristics include the front card type, the back card type, the card feature set (channelized, the ForeSight feature, and so on), and the bulk or nonbulk card status. Cards that have the T1 and E1 access lines physically connected to their back cards are in nonbulk mode. Cards that receive T1 access lines from an SRM-3T3 across the backplane are in bulk mode.

- **Secondary card has special back card**—The secondary card must have a special redundant back card that is specific to the interface type. Secondary cards supporting primary cards that are in bulk mode do not require a back card.

- **Only one secondary card can be active in nonbulk mode**—For nonbulk mode cards, 1-to-N redundancy uses the redundancy bus on the backplane to pass the user traffic from the back card of the failed primary card to the active secondary front card. In this situation, only one secondary card can be active on the shelf at a time.

- **Multiple secondary cards can be active in bulk mode**—For cards in bulk mode, the T1 distribution bus is used to pass the user traffic to the secondary card. Because the T1 distribution bus can handle multiple T1s, multiple secondary cards can be active at the same time.

Figure 17-4 shows 1-to-1 and 1-to-N redundancy on the MGX switch.

Figure 17-4 *Redundancy on the MGX*

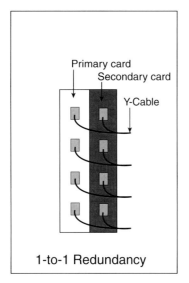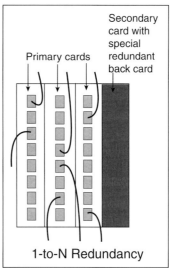

1-to-N Redundancy Process

The three stages of 1-to-N redundancy are described in Table 17-1.

Table 17-1 *1-to-N Redundancy Process*

Stage	Description
1	User traffic comes from the CPE on the T1 line to the back card.
2	User traffic moves from the back card to the primary front card for processing.
3	Cells move across the cell bus to the destination card module (PXM1 or other service module).

The six stages of front card failure and redundancy are described in Table 17-2.

Table 17-2 *Card Failure and Redundancy*

Stage	Description
1	A primary card fails.
2	The secondary card changes from standby to active.
3	All other active primary cards are blocked. A blocked card is one that has 1-to-N redundancy configured but cannot be replaced by its redundant card. In the case of T1 cards, the secondary card is active. In the case of E1 cards, the redundancy bus is in use by the other group and cannot be used to pass traffic for another group. If one of the primary E1 cards fails, it will not be replaced by its secondary card.
4	The user traffic is sent from the primary back card across the redundancy bus to the secondary back card.
5	The user data is sent from the secondary back card to the secondary front card for processing.
6	The cells are sent across the cell bus to their destination.

MGX Card Redundancy Commands

This section describes the commands used to display and set up service module redundancy on the MGX switch:

- **addred**—Defines a primary and secondary card slot of a redundant pair.
- **delred**—Removes redundancy between two card slots.
- **dspred**—Displays the redundancy configuration for all cards in the node.
- **softswitch**—Switches between the active and standby cards in a redundant pair.
- **dspcds**—Lists the type and status of front and back cards installed in the switch.

Add Redundancy Command

The **addred** command defines a primary and secondary pair of redundant service modules. (Use the **delred** command to remove card redundancy on a primary card.)

The command syntax for the **addred** command is

```
addred <primary slot> <secondary slot> <type>
```

The parameters are as follows:

- *primary slot*—The primary card slot number.

- *secondary slot*—The secondary card slot number. For cards in nonbulk mode using 1-to-N redundancy, the secondary card must have the appropriate redundant back card installed.

- *type*—The redundancy type; 1 = 1-to-1 Y-cable redundancy, 2 = 1-to-N redundancy.

For example, type **addred 2 5 2** to make card slot 5 the secondary for card slot 2 using 1-to-N redundancy.

Display Redundancy Command

The **dspred** command lists all cards that are configured with redundancy on the MGX switch. Use this command to learn which cards have redundancy and what the redundancy status is.

The **dspred** output provides the following information:

- Primary card slot number

- Primary card type

- **Primary state**—Active, Fail, Empty, or Standby. If the card has failed, the secondary card should have taken over. If the card is in standby, it is no longer failed, and you should use the **softswitch** command to return the primary card to an active state.

- Secondary slot number

- Secondary card type

- **Secondary state**—Standby, Active, or Blocked. If the secondary card is currently replacing a primary card, it will be in an active state. All other 1-to-N cards in nonbulk mode will report a blocked state. A blocked state means that if the primary card fails, the secondary cannot take over its functions.

- **Redundancy type**—1:1 (1-to-1) or 1:N (1-to-N).

- **Redundant slot coverage**—The primary card slot currently being replaced by the secondary card.

Summary

This chapter provided an overview of the methods used to connect to the MGX CLI. It also discussed the MGX command syntax. The help commands available on the MGX CLI were presented, along with an explanation of acceptable MGX user IDs and passwords. The variations in command privilege levels, and how to log in to and out of the MGX CLI, were also discussed.

Card and port resource partitions were presented, including the MGX switch VSI architecture. This chapter also described how to manage and control user services on the switch with the three VSI controllers, including Portable AutoRoute (PAR), Multiprotocol Label Switching (MPLS), and Private Network-to-Network Interface (PNNI).

Commands used for MGX node configuration and MGX switch support for 1-to-1 and 1-to-N redundancy, and the associated commands, were detailed. Also, the procedures for setting up MGX node characteristics were presented, with the associated steps, actions, and results explained.

Review Questions

1 You want to dial up from home and use a Telnet session to access the MGX CLI. Your PC has a SLIP communications package installed. Which PXM-UI port do you connect to?

A. In-band IP

B. LAN port

C. Modem port

D. Console port

2 Your PC is attached to a LAN. One of your associates has given you an IP address to access the MGX CLI using a Telnet session. How are you connected to the MGX switch? (Choose two.)

A. LAN port

B. Modem port

C. Console port

D. IP forwarding

3 The command syntax for the **addred** command on the PXM1 card is shown in Example 17-10.

Example 17-10 *Command Syntax for the* **addred** *Command*

```
SJ8850.1.7.PXM.a > addred

ERR: incorrect number of parameters: (not enough)
Syntax:
  addred <redPrimarySlotNum> <redSecondarySlotNum> <redType>
  redPrimarySlotNum -- <redPrimarySlotNum>
        where redPrimarySlotNum = 1-6|9-14|17-22|25-30
  redSecondarySlotNum -- <redSecondarySlotNum>
        where redSecondarySlotNum ranges from 1-6|9-14|17-22|25-30
  redType -- <redType> where redType = 1(1:1 Y-Cable) or 2(1:N)
```

You must configure the following card redundancy:

- Primary card slot 3
- Secondary card slot 10
- 1-to-N redundancy

What is the command and all parameters to complete this task?

4 The command syntax to add a new user ID is **adduser** *<user ID> <access level>*, where *user ID* is a character string of 1 to 12 characters and *access level* is GROUP1, GROUP2, GROUP3, GROUP4, GROUP5, or ANYUSER. Which of the following commands is valid?

A. **adduser myID group1**

B. **adduser myID GROUP3**

C. **add user myID ANYUSER**

D. **adduser myID <access level> GROUP1**

5 You are logged in to the MGX CLI and are configuring a CESM-8E1 card. You need to change a port on the card but do not know the exact command to use. What command(s) should you type to help you find the command?

A. **?**

B. **Help**

C. **? port**

D. **Help port**

6 You are logged into an FRSM-HS2 card, and you want to see a list of all valid commands. What command would you type to accomplish this task?

7 Of the following user IDs, which three are valid?

A. teacher

B. group5a

C. 22.COMM

D. ThisIsMyUserID

8 Of the following passwords, which two are valid?

A. pass

B. password

C. $$$airplane$$$

D. PASSWORD123password

9 Which command would you type to learn which user IDs are configured for your MGX switch?

10 Of the following virtual switch interface (VSI) controllers, which three are supported by the MGX switch?

A. Portable AutoRoute (PAR)

B. User Network Interface (UNI)

C. Voice Switch Controller (VSC)

D. Multiprotocol Label Switching (MPLS)

E. Private Network-to-Network Interface (PNNI)

11 You are adding new connections to the AUSM-8E1 shown in Figure 17-5. Assuming that there are no connections on the card, which of the following connections can you add on port 1?

Figure 17-5 *Adding New Connections to the AUSM-8E1*

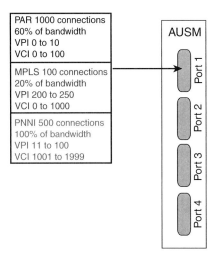

A. A 1 Mbps PAR PVC with a VPI of 5 and a VCI of 20

B. A 1 Mbps PAR PVC with a VPI of 5 and a VCI of 200

C. A 1.8 Mbps PAR PVC with a VPI of 5 and a VCI of 50

D. A 1 Mbps PAR PVC with a VPI of 200 and a VCI of 1000

12 You are adding a new PAR PVC to port 2 on the AUSM-8T1 shown in Figure 17-6. For each connection characteristic, select the value that is supported on this port.

Figure 17-6 *Adding a New PAR PVC to Port 2 on the AUSM-8T1*

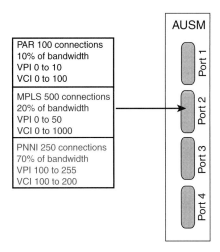

A. Connection bandwidth requirement: 200 Kbps or 100 Kbps

B. VPI value: 0 or 100

C. VCI value: 100 or 1000

13 Of the following statements, which two correctly describe MGX node commands?

A. The **dspifip** command output lists the IP addresses configured on the switch.

B. The **dspcds** command output provides card- and node-level status information.

C. The **cnfname** command must be issued on both the active and standby PXM1 cards.

D. The **dspcdrscprtn** command output shows the configuration of all cards installed in the shelf.

14 Of the following node names, which three can be used on the MGX switch?

A. 8850_A

B. lab12_A

C. MY8250

D. mgx.lab1

15 You want to use a Telnet application to access the CLI on your MGX switch. The PXM-UI LAN port is connected to the LAN. Based on the output from the **dspifip** command shown in Example 17-11, what IP address must you use?

Example 17-11 *Output from the* **dspifip** *Command*

```
SJ8850.1.7.PXM.a > dspifip

    Interface        Flag  IP Address       Subnetmask       Broadcast Addr
    --------------   ----  --------------   ---------------  --------------
    Ethernet/lnPci0  UP    10.10.51.62      255.255.255.000  10.10.51.255
    Slip/sl0         UP    10.10.12.25      255.255.255.000  (N/A)
    ATM/atm0         UP    10.10.48.2       255.255.255.000  10.10.48.255
```

A. 10.10.48.2

B. 10.10.51.62

C. 10.10.12.25

D. 255.255.255.000

16 You are logged in to the active PXM1 on your MGX switch. You want to know what firmware revision is loaded on the card. What command must you use to get this information?

17 You have redundant PXM1s installed in your MGX 8250 switch. You also have four FRSM-8E1 cards (one with a redundant back card) installed in card slots 19 to 22 and FRSM-HS1/B cards installed in card slots 5 and 6. If you want to have 1-to-N redundancy on your E1 cards and 1-to-1 Y-cable redundancy on your HS1/B cards, in which card slot(s) must you install SRM-3T3 cards?

A. 15

B. 32

C. 15 and 16

D. 15 and 31

E. 31 and 32

F. 15, 16, 31, and 32

18 Based on the redundancy configuration shown in Figure 17-7, which three of the following statements are true?

Figure 17-7 *Redundancy Configuration*

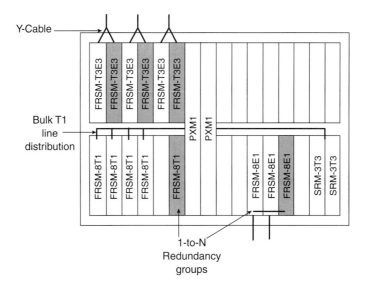

A. If the FRSM-T3E3 in slot 1 fails, card slot 2 can take over.

B. If the FRSM-8E1 in slot 27 fails, the secondary FRSM-8T1 in slot 22 can take over for slots 17 to 20.

C. If the FRSM-8T1 in slot 17 fails, the secondary FRSM-8E1 in slot 29 cannot take over for slots 27 or 28.

D. If the FRSM-8T1s in slots 17 and 18 fail, the traffic for one of the cards will be redirected to slot 22, and the traffic from the other card will fail.

19 Which command must you use to learn which service module is the primary and which is the secondary when you are using 1-to-N redundancy?

A. **dspcd**

B. **dspcds**

C. **dspred**

D. **dspslots**

20 You are looking at the **dspred** output on your MGX switch. What does it mean when a card module reports that the secondary state is "blocked"?

A. The card is in bulk mode.

B. The secondary card has failed.

C. The active card has failed and the secondary has taken over.

D. A secondary card is active and this primary card is not protected.

This chapter covers the following key topics:

- Lines
- MGX Commands
- Commands for Displaying, Adding, and Configuring Lines
- Commands for Monitoring Line Alarms and Errors
- How to Add Lines to an MGX Service Module
- SRM-3T3 Distribution of T1 Lines
- TI Line Distribution Process
- How to Test T1 and E1 Lines on MGX Service Modules
- Feeder Nodes
- SONET APS

CHAPTER 18

Lines, Feeder Nodes, and SONET APS

This chapter covers Cisco MGX lines, including service module lines on the PXM1, CESM, FRSM, AUSM, and VISM. It discusses Cisco MGX feeder nodes, including the MGX 8220, 8230, 8250, and 8850-PXM1, and backbone nodes, including the MGX 8850-PXM45. It also describes the MGX commands.

The SONET Automatic Protection Switching (APS) feature that is supported on PXM1 cards in the MGX switch is described, along with commands for configuring SONET APS. This chapter also discusses how to add a feeder node to a BPX network and an MGX 8850-PXM45 network and details the procedures for setting up an MGX standalone switch.

How the SRM-3T3 distributes T1 lines is discussed, and the commands for line distribution are presented, along with the commands for displaying, adding, and configuring lines and monitoring line alarms and errors. This chapter also discusses how to test E1 and T1 lines on service modules using the bit error rate test (BERT) feature on the SRM.

Lines

A line, on the MGX switch, is a physical digital transport facility that carries information between the switch and an external piece of equipment. Regardless of the card module supporting the line on the shelf, all like lines are configured in the same way.

Physically, there is no difference between a line going to CPE and a line going to the ATM backbone network. The line to the ATM backbone network requires additional configuration to identify it as a trunk. External equipment may include the following:

- PXM1

    — A BPX, MGX 8850-PXM45, or other-vendor ATM network with a T3, E3, OC-3c, STM1, OC-12c, or STM4 interface

    — Any ATM device with a T3, E3, OC-3c, STM-1, OC-12c, or STM4 interface

- CESM
  - A PBX with a T1 or E1 tie line
  - A router with a T1 or E1 HDLC interface
  - A video CODEC with a T1 or E1 interface
  - A channel bank with data and voice services multiplexed onto a T1 or E1 line
  - Any device that sends traffic on a T1, E1, T3, or E3 line
- FRSM
  - A router with a T1, E1, T3, or E3 Frame Relay interface
  - A T1 or E1 TDM with Frame Relay routers attached
  - A T1 or E1 TDM with any Frame Relay Access Devices (FRADs) attached
  - A router with an HSSI or high-speed V.35 or X.21 Frame Relay interface
  - A T3 TDM with T1 TDMs or T1 Frame Relay devices attached
- AUSM
  - Any ATM device with a T1 or E1 interface
  - Any ATM device with up to eight T1 or E1 ATM inverse multiplexed interfaces
- VISM
  - A PBX or PABX with a T1 or E1 interface
  - A T1 or E1 voice trunk line from the public telephone network
  - Any device that sends Pulse Code Modulation (PCM) voice on a multiplexed T1 or E1 line

PXM1 OC-3c Example

The PXM-4-155 supports four 155 Mbps ATM lines. One of these lines may be configured as the feeder trunk to the ATM backbone network.

NOTE   If you're connecting into a BPX or IGX as a feeder node, one of the PXM-4-155 ATM lines *must* be configured as the feeder trunk to the ATM backbone network.

The other three lines may be configured as User-Network Interface (UNI) lines to CPE. Figure 18-1 shows the PXM1 and the lines it supports.

Figure 18-1 *PXM1 Lines*

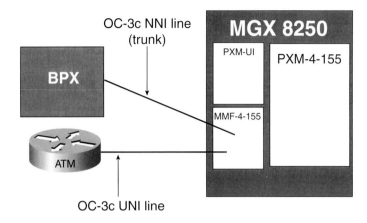

FRSM-8T1 Example

The FRSM-8T1 card supports eight T1 lines. These lines are multiplexed using time-division multiplexing (TDM) and can support much customer premises equipment (CPE) on one line. FRSM-8E1, CESM-8T1, CESM-8E1, VISM-8T1, and VISM-8E1 lines are all similar to the FRSM-8T1 lines.

Figure 18-2 shows an FRSM-8T1 card installed in an MGX 8250 switch with one attached line.

Figure 18-2 *FRSM-8T1 Example*

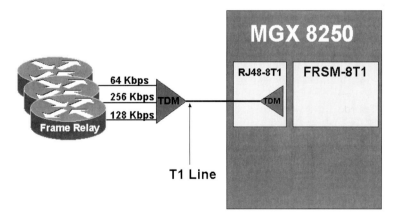

MGX Commands

This section describes the commands used to display and configure MGX network interfaces:

- **dsplns**—Lists summary status and configuration information for all lines on the card.
- **dspln**—Lists detailed configuration information for a line.
- **addln**—Activates a physical line.
- **delln**—Deactivates a physical line.
- **cnfln**—Changes the line characteristics.
- **dspalms**—Lists the alarm status of all lines on the card.
- **dspalm**—Lists detailed alarm status for a line.
- **dspatmlncnf**—Shows the ATM cell header used on the line.
- **cnfatmln**—Changes the ATM cell header used on the line.
- **addport**—Creates a new logical port.
- **delport**—Removes a logical port.
- **cnfport**—Modifies the logical port characteristics, including the bandwidth and VPI range.
- **dspports**—Lists all logical ports on the card.
- **dspportrscprtns**—Lists the resource partition configuration for all ports on the card.
- **cnfportrscprtns**—Modifies the port resource partition characteristics.
- **dsptrks**—Lists the feeder trunks on the node.
- **cnfifastrk**—Defines a logical port as a trunk.
- **uncnfifastrk**—Unconfigures a logical port as a trunk.

Display Lines Command

The **dsplns** command provides summary configuration information for the PXM1 lines on an MGX switch, as shown in Example 18-1. The information output with the **dsplns** command depends on the platform and interface type used.

Here is the **dsplns** command syntax:

```
dsplns {-ds3 | -e3 | -sonet} <slot number>
```

The parameter and keyword options are as follows:

- **-ds3**—Use this keyword when adding a T3 line.
- **-e3**—Use this keyword when adding an E3 line.
- **-sonet**—Use this keyword when adding a 155 Mbps or 622 Mbps optical line.
- *slot number*—The card slot number.

Example 18-1 **dsplns** *Command Output for a T3 PXM1 Line*

```
SJ8850.1.7.PXM.a > dsplns -ds3 7

Line Type Status/Coding Length Criteria AIScBitsCheck
---- ------------- -------------- ----------- --------- -------------
1 dsx3CbitParity Ena / dsx3B3ZS lessThan225 fBits3Of8 Check C-bits
2 dsx3CbitParity Dis / dsx3B3ZS lessThan225 fBits3Of8 Check C-bits
```

Display Line Command

The **dspln** command provides configuration information for the PXM1 line on the MGX switch. The information output with the **dspln** command is very similar to the information output with the **dsplns** command. Example 18-2 shows the **dspln** output for a T3 PXM1 line.

Here is the **dspln** command syntax:

dspln {**-ds3** | **-e3** | **-sonet**} *<line number>*

line number is in the format *slot.line*.

Example 18-2 **dspln** *Output for a T3 PXM1 Line*

```
My8250.1.7.PXM.a > dspln -ds3 7.1

LineNum:                1
LineType:               dsx3CbitParity
LineCoding:             dsx3B3ZS
LineLength:             lessThan225
LineOOFCriteria:        fBits3Of8
LineAIScBitsCheck:      Check C-bits
LineLoopbackCommand:    NoLoop
LineRcvFEACValidation:  4 out of 5 FEAC codes
LineXmtFEACCode:        SendNoCode
FarEndLoopbkLineNum:    0
LineEnable:             Enable
LinePayloadScramble:    Disabled
```

The **dspln** command provides configuration information for the 155 Mbps PXM1 line on the MGX switch as shown in Example 18-3.

Example 18-3 dspln *Output for a 155 Mbps PXM1 Line*

```
mgx8800b.1.7.PXM.a > dspln -sonet 7.2

  sonetLineNum:              2
  sonetLineType:             sonetSts3c
  sonetLineLoopback:         NoLoop
  sonetHCSmasking:           Enabled
  sonetPayloadScramble:      Enabled
  sonetFrameScramble:        Enabled
  sonetLineEnable:           Disable
  sonetMediumType:           sonet
  sonetMediumTimeElapsed:    0
  sonetMediumValidIntervals: 0
  sonetMediumLineCoding:     Other
  sonetMediumLineType:       MultiMode
  sonetMediumCircuitIdentifier: Sonet Line
```

Add Line Command

The **addln** command activates a line on the PXM1. Add a line before making any changes to its configuration. Use the **delln** command to deactivate a PXM1 line.

Here is the **addln** command syntax:

```
addln {-ds3 | -e3 | -sonet} <line number>
```

The parameter and keyword options are as follows:

- **-ds3**—Use this keyword when adding a T3 line.
- **-e3**—Use this keyword when adding an E3 line.
- **-sonet**—Use this keyword when adding a 155 Mbps or 622 Mbps optical line.
- *line number*—The line number in the format *slot.line*. Specify the card slot 7 or 8, depending on which PXM1 is active.

For example, type **addln -ds3 7.1** to add DS3 line 1 on card slot 7.

Configure Line Command

Use the **cnfln** command to modify the characteristics of the lines on the MGX PXM1 card. Different characteristics can be set, depending on the specified line type.

Here is the **cnfln** command syntax:

```
cnfln -ds3 <line number> [-lc <line coding>] [-len <line length>]
    [-oof <line OOF criteria>] [-cb <line AIS C-bit check>]
    [-lpb <loop>] [-felpnum <far-end loop line number>]
    [-rfeac <receive FEAC validation>] [-teac <transmit FEAC code>]
    [-pls <DS3 PLCP payload scramble>]
cnfln -e3 <line number> [-lc <line coding>] [-len <line length>]
    [-lpb <loop>] [-topt <trail trace option>] [-txtt <transmit trail trace>]
    [-txma <transmit timing marker>] [-rxma <receive timing marker>]
    [-txpt <transmit payload type>]
cnfln -sonet <line number> [-slt <line type>] [-lpb <loop>]
    [-smask <HCS masking>] [-sps <payload scramble>]
    [-sfs <frame scramble>]
```

The T3 line configuration parameter options are as follows:

- *line number*—The line number in the format *slot.port*. Specify card slot 7 or 8, depending on which PXM1 is active.

- *line coding*—The ones-density enforcement used on the line. For a DS3, the line coding is always 1 = B3ZS.

- *line length*—The length of cable used for line build-out purposes. 1 = less than 225 feet, 2 = greater than 225 feet.

- *line OOF criteria*—The number of errored frames necessary to declare an out of frame (OOF) condition. 1 = 3 out of 8, 2 = 3 out of 16.

- *line AIS C-bit check*—The C-bits in the DS3 frame can be used to pass an alarm indicator signal (AIS) from one device to another. 1 = check C-bits, 2 = ignore C-bits.

- *loop*—Creates a loop on the line for testing purposes. 1 = no loop, 2 = remote loop (loop facing out toward the line), 3 = local loop (loop facing toward the MGX switch), 4 = in-band local loop.

- *far-end loop line number*—The DS1 line number. 1 to 28 = DS1 line number, 29 = all DS1 lines, 30 = DS3 line.

- *receive FEAC validation*—The required number of Far-End Alarm Codes (FEACs) before declaring an alarm. 1 = 4 out of 5, 2 = 8 out of 10.

- *transmit FEAC code*—The far-end alarm code. 1 = send no code, 2 = send line code, 3 = send payload code, 4 = send reset code, 5 = send DS1 loopback code, 6 = send test pattern.

- *DS3 PLCP payload scramble*—Enables or disables payload scramble. 1 = enable, 2 = disable.

The E3 line configuration parameter options are as follows:

- *line number*—The line number in the format *slot.port*. Specify card slot 7 or 8, depending on which PXM1 is active.

- *line coding*—The ones-density enforcement used on the line. For an E3, the line coding is always 2 = HDB3.

- *line length*—The length of cable used for line build-out purposes. 1 = less than 225 feet, 2 = more than 225 feet.

- *loop*—Create a loop on the line for testing purposes. 1 = no loop, 2 = remote loop (loop facing out toward the line), 3 = local loop (loop facing toward the MGX switch), 4 = in-band local loop.

The SONET line configuration parameter options are as follows:

- *line number*—The line number in the format *slot.port*. Specify card slot 7 or 8, depending on which PXM1 is active.

- *line type*—The optical line framing type. 1 = OC-3c, 2 = STM-1, 3 = OC-12c, 4 = STM-4.

- *loop*—Creates a loop on the line for testing purposes. 1 = no loop, 2 = remote loop (loop facing out toward the line), 3 = local loop (loop facing toward the MGX switch).

- *HCS masking*—HCS masking (add hexadecimal 55 to all HEC/HCS fields) in order to facilitate cell delineation. Be sure to configure this parameter the same on both ends of the trunk; otherwise, the cell framing might fail. 1 = disable, 2 = enable.

- *payload scramble*—Enables or disables standard cell payload scrambling. Be sure to configure this parameter the same on both ends of the trunk; otherwise, the **addshelf** command will fail. 1 = disabled, 2 = enabled.

- *frame scramble*—Standard frame scrambling for optical lines. Be sure to configure this parameter the same on both ends of the trunk; otherwise, the trunk will fail. 1 = disabled, 2 = enabled.

Here are some examples:

- Type **cnfln -ds3 7.1 -len 2 -cb 2** to configure T3 line 1 on the PXM1 with a length of greater than 225 feet and to ignore C-bits.

- Type **cnfln -sonet 7.3 -sps 1** to disable payload scrambling on line 3.

Display Alarm(s) Commands

The **dspalms** command lists the alarm conditions of the lines on the PXM1 card and gives a summary alarm status for all lines on the card. Example 18-4 shows the **dspalms** output for 155 Mbps PXM1 lines.

Here is the **dspalms** command syntax:

```
dspalms {ds3 | e3 | sonet} <card slot>
```

NOTE   No dash or hyphen (-) precedes the **ds3**, **e3**, and **sonet** keywords.

Example 18-4 dspalms *Output for 155 Mbps PXM1 Lines*

```
mgx8800b.1.7.PXM.a > dspalms sonet 7

Line :  1
   AlarmStatus
      Section : Clear
      Line    : Clear
      Path    : Clear
   StatisticalAlarmStatus
      Section : Clear
      Line    : Clear
      Path    : Clear
Line :  2
   AlarmStatus
      Section : Clear
      Line    : Clear
      Path    : Clear
   StatisticalAlarmStatus
      Section : Clear
      Line    : Clear
      Path    : Clear
```

Example 18-5 shows the **dspalms** output for T3 PXM1 lines.

Example 18-5 dspalms *Output for T3 PXM1 Lines*

```
NZ_8850.1.8.PXM.a > dspalms ds3 7

Line : 1
AlarmState : No Alarms
StatisticalAlarmState : UAS24hrAlarm
Line : 2
AlarmState : No Alarms
StatisticalAlarmState : No Statistical Alarms
```

The **dspalm** command lists the alarm conditions of the lines on the PXM1 card and gives a detailed alarm status for a specified line. Use the **dspalms** or **dspalm** commands to confirm that the line is free of alarms. Example 18-6 shows the **dspalm** output for a 155 Mbps PXM1 line.

Example 18-6 dspalm *Output for a 155 Mbps PXM1 Line*

```
mgx8800b.1.7.PXM.a > dspalm -sonet 7.3

 LineNum:                      3
 SectionCurrentStatus:         Clear
 LineCurrentStatus:            Clear
```

continues

Example 18-6 dspalm *Output for a 155 Mbps PXM1 Line (Continued)*

```
PathCurrentStatus:              Clear
SectionStatAlarmStatus:         Clear
LineStatAlarmStatus:            Clear
PathStatAlarmStatus:            Clear
```

Example 18-7 shows the **dspalm** output for a T3 PXM1 line.

Example 18-7 dspalm *Output for a T3 PXM1 Line*

```
NZ_8850.1.8.PXM.a > dspalm -ds3 7.1

LineNum:                        1
LineAlarmState:                 Alarm(s) On --
                                    RcvRAI
LineStatisticalAlarmState:      No Statistical Alarms
```

Display and Configure ATM Line Commands

The **dspatmlncnf** command shows the cell header type used on a PXM1 line on the MGX switch. The cell header type can be changed using the **cnfatmln** command. Cell header choices include UNI and NNI. Example 18-8 shows the **dspatmlncnf** output.

Example 18-8 dspatmlncnf *Output*

```
mgx8800b.1.7.PXM.a > dspatmlncnf 3

lineNum atmLineInterfaceFormat
---------------------------------
3 NNI
```

Here is the **cnfatmln** command syntax:

```
cnfatmln <line number> <type>
```

The parameter options are as follows:

- *line number*—The PXM1 line number.
- *type*—The ATM cell header type. 2 = UNI, 3 = NNI. When attaching the MGX switch to a BPX network as a feeder node, use the NNI cell header. When setting up a standalone MGX switch, use either the UNI or NNI cell header, depending on the configuration of the ATM network interface your switch is connected to.

Add Port, Configure Port, and Delete Port Commands

The **addport** command creates a new logical port on a physical line. When you activate a trunk on the MGX switch, at least one logical port must be defined for each physical line. The port characteristics can be changed using the **cnfport** command. Delete a port using the **delport** command.

Consider the cell type (UNI or NNI) used on the line and how you want to limit traffic based on the bandwidth and VPI values allowed when creating a new logical port. Later, when connections are added to the port, you must remember these limitations. Misconfiguration can result in failed or rejected connections.

Here is the **addport** command syntax:

```
addport <port number> <line number> <percent bandwidth>
  <minimum VPI> <maximum VPI>
```

The parameter options are as follows:

- *port number*—A unique number between 1 and 32 that identifies the logical port.
- *line number*—The physical line number that the logical port is associated with. PXM1 firmware limits you to one logical port per line.
- *percent bandwidth*—The percentage of the physical line's bandwidth that the logical port can use. It is recommended that you use 100 percent of the bandwidth.
- *minimum VPI*—The minimum value for the VPI on cells that use the port. If the line uses the UNI cell header, this value must be less than or equal to 255. If the line uses the NNI cell header, this value must be less than or equal to 4095. It is recommended that you use the full range of VPI values. You should set the *minimum VPI* to 0.
- *maximum VPI*—The maximum value for the VPI on cells that use the port. This value must be greater than or equal to the minimum VPI. It is recommended that you use the full range of VPI values. You should set the *maximum VPI* to 255 or 4095, depending on the cell header type.

For example, type **addport 1 1 100 0 4095** to add port 1 to line 1 using all the available bandwidth and VPI values (assuming that the cell header type is NNI).

Display Ports Command

The **dspports** command lists all logical ports on the MGX PXM1 card, including their configuration details. The **dspports** output is shown in Example 18-9.

Example 18-9 dspports *Output*

```
mgx8800b.1.7.PXM.a > dspports

Port Status Line PctBw minVpi maxVpi
3 ON 3 100 0 255
4 ON 4 100 0 4095
```

Display Port Resource Partition Command

Resource partitions are defined for all logical ports. By default, all connection types are given equal access to a port for all card types except the RPM. If you need to modify an existing partition, use the **cnfportrscprtn** command. To display port resource partitions, use the **dspportrscprtn** command. The **dspportrscprtn** output shown in Example 18-10 shows that the different partitions overlap in all the resource categories. In this configuration, all connection types are given free access to all resources.

Example 18-10 **dspportrscprtn** *Output*

```
mgx8800b.1.7.PXM.a > dspportrscprtn

   Port  Ctrlr  Row   PctBw      VPI          VCI        Max
   Num   Type   Stat  In/Out   min/max      min/max     GLCNs
   -------------------------------------------------------------
     3   PAR    ON    100/100   0/255        0/65535    32767
     3   PNNI   ON    100/100   0/255        0/65535    32767
     3   TAG    ON    100/100   0/255        0/65535    32767
     4   PAR    ON    100/100   0/4095       0/65535    32767
     4   PNNI   ON    100/100   0/4095       0/65535    32767
     4   TAG    ON    100/100   0/4095       0/65535    32767
```

Display Trunks Command

The **dsptrks** command on the MGX switch lists all the trunks on the switch, their status, and what is attached to the remote end of each trunk. Trunks are defined using the **cnfifastrk** command. Only one trunk can be defined on the PXM1. The **dsptrks** output is shown in Example 18-11.

Example 18-11 **dsptrks** *Output*

```
mgx8800b.1.7.PXM.a > dsptrks

TRK        Current Alarm Status      Other End

7.3        CLEAR                     bpx1
```

The **dsptrks** output lists the following information:

- **Trunk number**—The trunk number in the format *slot.port*. The slot number is always 7 for PXM1 trunks, regardless of which PXM1 is active.

- **Current alarm status**—CLEAR means the trunk is active and free of alarms. Major means the trunk is active with a major alarm. Minor means the trunk is active with a minor alarm.

- **Other end**—The node name of the attached ATM backbone switch.

Configure Interface as Trunk Command

The **cnfifastrk** command defines a port as a trunk. You are limited to one trunk per switch. If you want to remove the trunk, use the **uncnfifastrk** command.

Here is the **cnfifastrk** command syntax:

```
cnfifastrk <port number> {ftrk | rtrk | vtrk}
```

The parameter and keyword options are as follows:

- *port number*—The port number in the format *slot.port*.
- **ftrk**—The trunk is a feeder trunk. This is the only option supported by the PXM1.
- **rtrk**—The trunk is a routing trunk. This option is not supported by the PXM1.
- **vtrk**—The trunk is a virtual trunk. This option is not supported by the PXM1 firmware.

For example, type **cnfifastrk 7.3 ftrk** to make port 3 on card 7 a feeder trunk.

Commands for Displaying, Adding, and Configuring Lines

This section describes the commands used to display, add, and configure MGX service modules:

- **dsplns**—Lists summary status and configuration information for all lines on the card.
- **dspln**—Lists detailed configuration information for a line.
- **dspds3lns**—Lists summary status and configuration information for all T3 and E3 lines on the card (FRSM-T3E3, FRSM-2CT3, and CESM-T3E3 cards).
- **dspds3ln**—Lists detailed configuration information for a T3 or E3 line (FRSM-T3E3, FRSM-2CT3, and CESM-T3E3 cards).
- **addln**—Activates a physical line.
- **delln**—Deactivates a physical line.
- **cnfln**—Changes the characteristics of the physical line.

The Display Lines Command

The **dsplns** command output lists summary configuration and status information for all narrowband and serial lines terminating on the service module. The **dsplns** command is also used to display the broadband lines on the PXM1. Use this command to learn the line type and status of an MGX service module. Use the **dspds3lns** command to output similar information for T3 and E3 lines on the FRSM-2CT3, FRSM-T3E3, and CESM-T3E3 cards. The **dsplns** output from a CESM-8T1 is shown in Example 18-12.

Example 18-12 dsplns *Output from a CESM-8T1*

```
SJ8850.1.19.CESM.a > dsplns

  Line  Conn     Type  Status/Coding    Length     XmtClock Alarm Stats
        Type                                       Source         Alarm
  ----  -----  --------  ------ --------  -----------  --------  -----  -----
  19.1  RJ-48  dsx1ESF        Ena/dsx1B8ZS   0-131  ft   LocalTim  No     Yes
  19.2  RJ-48  dsx1ESF        Mod/dsx1B8ZS   0-131  ft   LoopTime  No     No
  19.3  RJ-48  dsx1ESF        Dis/dsx1B8ZS   0-131  ft   LocalTim
  19.4  RJ-48  dsx1ESF        Dis/dsx1B8ZS   0-131  ft   LocalTim
  19.5  RJ-48  dsx1ESF        Dis/dsx1B8ZS   0-131  ft   LocalTim
  19.6  RJ-48  dsx1ESF        Dis/dsx1B8ZS   0-131  ft   LocalTim
  19.7  RJ-48  dsx1ESF        Dis/dsx1B8ZS   0-131  ft   LocalTim
  19.8  RJ-48  dsx1ESF        Dis/dsx1B8ZS   0-131  ft   LocalTim

  LineNumOfValidEntries: 8
```

For T1 and E1 lines, the following information is provided:

- **Line number**
- **Connector type**—Based on the line module type. RJ-48 for TI, RJ-48 or SMB for E1.
- **Line type**—ESF or D4 for T1, CAS or CCS for E1. If CAS is configured, timeslot 16 is reserved for signaling purposes and cannot be used for data.
- **Line status**—Disabled, enabled, or modified. If the line has been added and changed, it reports a modified state.
- **Coding**—Ones-density enforcement. B8ZS or AMI for T1, HDB3 or AMI for E1.
- **Length**—Multiples of 131 feet for T1, impedance of 75 ohms or 120 ohms for E1.
- **Transmit clock source**—Local or looped timing. Local timing uses the MGX backplane clock source in the transmit direction; looped timing uses the receive clock.
- **Alarm**—Is the line currently in physical alarm (loss of signal, out of frame, and so on)? Use the **dspalms** and **dspalm** commands to determine the alarm type.
- **Statistical alarm**—Does the line have statistical alarms (BPV, CRC, and so on)? Use the **dspalms** and **dspalm** commands to determine the alarm type.

The **dsplns** output on the FRSM-2CT3 is similar to that of other T1 service modules.

The **dsplns** output on a serial interface (HSSI) is shown in Example 18-13.

Example 18-13 dsplns *Output from an HSSI*

```
SJ8850.1.6.VHSHS2.a > dsplns

 Line  Type     Rate        Status     Alarm

 ----  ----  -----------  --------  ---------
 6.1   DCE   2048 Kbps    Modify       Yes
 6.2   DCE   52 Mbps      Disable

 LineNumOfValidEntries: 2
```

NOTE   In the first line of Example 18-13, VHS stands for Very High Speed.

For all serial lines, the following information is provided:

- **Line number**
- **Type**—Either data terminal equipment (DTE) or data communications equipment (DCE).
- **Rate**—The data rate in kbps or Mbps.
- **Status**—Disable, enable, or modify.
- **Alarm**—Specifies whether the line is currently in physical alarm (loss of control signal). Use the **dspalms** and **dspalm** commands to determine the alarm type.

The Display DS3 Lines Command

The **dspds3lns** output lists the summary status and configuration information for all T3 or E3 lines on the FRSM-2CT3, FRSM-T3E3, and CESM-T3E3 card modules. Example 18-14 shows the **dspds3lns** output on an FRSM-2CT3 card.

Example 18-14 dspds3lns *Output from an FRSM-2CT3*

```
SJ8850.1.4.VHS2T3.a > dspds3lns

 Line  Type   Status/Coding    Length    XmtClock   Alarm  Stats
                                                    Source Alarm
 ----  ----  ------ ------    -------   --------   -----  -----
 4.1   c-bit  Enable/dsx3B3ZS  LT225ft   localClk    No     No
 4.2   c-bit  Disabl/dsx3B3ZS  LT225ft   localClk

 LineNumOfValidEntries: 2
```

The following information is provided in the **dspds3lns** output:

- Line number
- **Type**—The line type. In Example 18-14, the line is a T3 with C-bit parity checking enabled.
- **Line status**—Disabled, enabled, or modified. If the line has been added and changed, it reports a modified state.
- **Coding**—The ones-density enforcement technique used on the line.
- **Length**—The line length. Either greater than or less than 225 feet.
- **Transmit clock**—The clock source used on the line. Options include local (the clock is generated from the MGX backplane) or loop (line receive clock).
- **Alarm source**—Specifies whether there is a physical line alarm such as loss of signal or out of frame.
- **Statistical alarm**—Specifies whether an alarm is generated because a statistical error threshold has been exceeded.

Display DS3 Line Command

The **dspds3ln** output shows detailed information about a given broadband line on the FRSM-2CT3 and FRSM-T3E3 card modules. The **dspds3ln** output for an FRSM-2CT3 card module is shown in Example 18-15.

Example 18-15 dspds3ln *Output from an FRSM-2CT3*

```
SJ8850.1.4.VHS2T3.a > dspds3ln 1

  LineNum:                1
  LineEnable:             Enabled
  LineType:               c-bit
  LineCoding:             dsx3B3ZS
  LineLength:             LT225ft
  LineSubRateEnable:      Disable
  LineDsuSelect:          dl3100Mode
  LineRate:               44736kbps
  LineOOFCriteria:        3 out of 8
  LineAIScBitsCheck:      Ignore C-bits
  LineLoopbackCommand:    NoLoop
  LineRcvFEACValidation:  4 out of 5 FEAC codes
  LineXmitClockSource:    localClk
  LineEqualizer:          internal equalizer
  LineBertEnable:         Disable

  LineNumOfValidEntries: 2
```

The Add Line Command for MGX Service Modules

The **addln** command activates a line on all MGX service modules, regardless of line type. The line must be active before you can make any configuration changes or add user services to the line.

Here is the **addln** command syntax:

```
addln <line number>
```

For example, type **addln 2** to activate line 2 on a service module.

For all line types, use the **delln** command to delete the line. When adding user services to the line (ports and connections), you must delete them before you can delete the line.

The Configure Line Command

The **cnfln** command is used to modify serial or narrowband line characteristics on service modules. The command syntax differs depending on the card and line type in use. The **cnfln** command applies to all T1 and E1 lines and all serial lines. There are no configuration options for T3 and E3 lines on the FRSM-T3E3 and CESM-T3E3 card modules. Use the **cnfds3ln** command to configure other T3 and E3 cards.

Here is the **cnfln** command syntax for T1 and E1 lines on eight-port T1 or E1 service modules:

```
cnfln <line number> <line code> <line length> <clock source> [E1 signaling]
```

Here is the **cnfln** command syntax for T1 lines on the FRSM-2CT3:

```
cnfln <line number> <DS1 line type> <clock source>
```

Here is the **cnfln** command syntax for serial lines:

```
cnfln <line number> <line type> <line rate>
```

The parameter options are as follows:

- *line number*—The line number.
- *line code* (T1)—2 = B8ZS (also makes *line type* ESF), 4 = AMI (also makes *line type* = D4).
- *line code* (E1)—3 = HDB3, 4 = AMI.
- *line length* (T1)—Defines multiples of 131 feet for line build-out. 10 to 15.
- *line length* (E1)—8 = 75-ohm impedance for SMB connectors, 9 = 120 ohm impedance for RJ-48 connectors.
- *clock source*—1 = loop timing (the line uses the receive clock to transmit data), 2 = local timing (the line uses the MGX clock to transmit data).

- *E1 signaling*—CAS = Channel Associated Signaling (CAS) without CRC checking, CAS_CRC = CAS with CRC checking, CCS = Common Channel Signaling (CCS) without CRC checking, CCS_CRC = CCS with CRC checking, CLEAR = clear E1 (no framing or signaling).

NOTE   Not all E1 lines support all signaling configurations. For example, the AUSM-8E1 does not allow any configuration other than CCS.

- *DS1 line type* (FRSM-2CT3 card)—1 = ESF, 2 = D4.
- *line type* (FRSM-HS2 and FRSM-HS1/B cards)—1 = DTE, 2 = DCE.
- *line rate* (FRSM-HS2 and FRSM-HS1/B cards)—The supported line rates are represented by a number from 1 to 50. Some commonly used rates include 2 = 56 kbps, 3 = 64 kbps, 5 = 128 kbps, 9 = 256 kbps, 16 = 512 kbps, 18 = 1024 kbps, 20 = 1.544 Mbps, and 24 = 2.048 Mbps. For FRSM-HS2 lines, only rates above 1.544 Mbps (option 20) are supported.

Commands for Monitoring Line Alarms and Errors

This section describes the commands used to monitor line errors and alarms on the MGX switch:

- **dspalms**—Summarizes the alarm status of all lines on a card module.
- **dspalm**—Lists alarm details on a line.
- **clralm**—Clears a statistical alarm on a line.
- **dspalmcnt**—Lists the statistical line alarm counters.
- **clralmcnt**—Clears the statistical line alarm counters.
- **dspalmcnf**—Shows the alarm thresholds for statistical line alarms.
- **cnfbert**—Enables the BERT on a line or port, including looping or unlooping the line or port.
- **dspbert**—Displays the BERT results.
- **modbert**—Inserts an error in the BERT.
- **delbert**—Ends the BERT in progress.

The Display Alarms Command

The **dspalms** command output summarizes the alarm status of all lines on a card module. The **dsplns** command on many service modules can also be used to determine the line alarm status. Example 18-16 shows the **dspalms** output for the T3 and T1 lines on an FRSM-2CT3 card.

Example 18-16 **dspalms** *Output from an FRSM-2CT3*

```
SJ8850.1.5.VHS2T3.a > dspalms -ds3

  Line  AlarmState   StatisticalAlarmState
  ----  -----------  ---------------------
  5.1   No Alarms    No Statistical Alarms
  5.2   No Alarms    No Statistical Alarms

SJ8850.1.5.VHS2CT3.a > dspalms -ds1

  Line  AlarmState           StatisticalAlarmState
  ----  -----------          ---------------------
  5.1   No Alarms            No Statistical Alarms
  5.2   No Alarms            No Statistical Alarms
  5.3   No Alarms            No Statistical Alarms
  5.4   No Alarms            No Statistical Alarms
  5.5   No Alarms            No Statistical Alarms
  5.6   No Alarms            No Statistical Alarms
  5.7   No Alarms            No Statistical Alarms
  5.8   No Alarms            No Statistical Alarms
  5.9   No Alarms            No Statistical Alarms
  5.10  No Alarms            No Statistical Alarms
  5.11  No Alarms            No Statistical Alarms
  5.12  No Alarms            No Statistical Alarms
  5.13  No Alarms            No Statistical Alarms
  5.14  No Alarms            No Statistical Alarms
  5.15  No Alarms            No Statistical Alarms
  5.16  No Alarms            No Statistical Alarms
  5.17  No Alarms            No Statistical Alarms
  5.18  No Alarms            No Statistical Alarms
  5.19  No Alarms            No Statistical Alarms
  5.20  No Alarms            No Statistical Alarms

Type <CR> to continue, Q<CR> to stop: q
```

The **dspalms** output for an FRSM-HS2 card is shown in Example 18-17.

Example 18-17 **dspalms** *Output from an FRSM-HS2*

```
SJ8850.1.6.VHSHS2.a > dspalms -x21

  Line  AlarmState
  ----  -----------
  6.1   Alarm(s) On
```

The Display Alarm Command

The **dspalm** command output shows the alarms on a specified line type and number. Use this command to learn what type of alarm is active on a line. The **clralm** command is used to clear any line alarms and the line alarm counters. If an alarm is in progress, the line alarm returns after it is cleared. The **dspalm** output for T3, T1, and HSSI lines is shown in Example 18-18.

Example 18-18 dspalm *Output*

```
SJ8850.1.4.VHS2T3.a > dspalm -ds3 1

  LineNum:                  1
  LineAlarmState:           No Alarms
  LineStatisticalAlarmState: No Statistical Alarms


SJ8850.1.4.VHS2T3.a > cc 22

SJ8850.1.22.AUSMB8.a > dspalm -ds1 2

  LineNum:                  2
  LineAlarmState:           No Alarms
  LineStatisticalAlarmState: Alarm(s) On --
                                CRC24hrAlarm
                                CRCES24hrAlarm
                                SEFS24hrAlarm

SJ8850.1.22.VHS2T3.a > cc 6

SJ8850.1.6.VHSHS2.a > dspalm -x21 1

  LineNum:                     1
  LineAlarmState:              Alarm(s) On --
                                Rcv TA- or CA-lead Off
```

The Display Alarm Counter Command

The **dspalmcnt** command output lists statistical line alarm counters. Use this command to learn how many statistical errors have occurred on a line. The **clralmcnt** command is used to clear the counters. To determine the alarm thresholds for declaring an alarm because of statistical line errors, use the **dspalmcnf** command. Example 18-19 shows the **dspalmcnt** output for a T1 on an AUSM-8T1.

Example 18-19 dspalmcnt *Output for a T1 on an AUSM-8T1*

```
SJ8850.1.22.AUSMB8.a > dspalmcnt -ds1 1

  LineNum:                  1
  lCVCurrent:               0
  lCVLast15minBucket:       0
  lCVLast24hrBucket:        32
  lESCurrent:               0
  lESLast15minBucket:       0
  lESLast24hrBucket:        0
  lSESCurrent:              0
  lSESLast15minBucket:      0
  lSESLast24hrBucket:       0
  cRCCurrent:               2
  cRCLast15minBucket:       12
  cRCLast24hrBucket:        0
  cRCESCurrent:             0
  cRCESLast15minBucket:     0
  cRCESLast24hrBucket:      0
  cRCSESCurrent:            0
  cRCSESLast15minBucket:    0
  cRCSESLast24hrBucket:     0
  sEFSCurrent:              0
  sEFSLast15minBucket:      0

Type <CR> to continue, Q<CR> to stop: q
```

Example 18-20 shows the **dspalmcnt** output for a T1 on an FRSM-2CT3. The information output for the FRSM-2CT3 is the same as that for the FRSM-8T1, FRSM-8E1, CESM-8T1, CESM-8E1, VISM-8T1, and VISM-8E1 cards.

Example 18-20 dspalmcnt *Output for a T1 on an FRSM-2CT3*

```
SJ8850.1.5.VHS2CT3.a > dspalmcnt -ds1 1

  Line  RcvLOSCount   RcvOOFCount   RcvRAICount   RcvFECount
  ----  -----------   -----------   -----------   ----------
  5.1             0             1             0            2
```

The Configure Bit Error Rate Test Command

The **cnfbert** command initiates a menu-driven function that is used to add and remove loops and run bit error rate tests (BERTs) on MGX service module lines and ports. The menu choices are dependent on the service module and interface type. For example, the AUSMs do not have a port option, because each port is associated with a single line. The far-end loopback is not supported on every interface type.

As soon as a BERT is in progress, you can view the results using the **dspbert** command. Errors can be injected into the bit stream using the **modbert** command. The BERT does not time out automatically; you must use the **delbert** command to end the test.

NOTE   The BERT function is not supported on serial, T3, or E3 service modules. This includes the CESM-T3E3, FRSM-HS1/B, FRSM-HS2, FRSM-2CT3, and FRSM-T3E3 card modules.

Example 18-21 shows some of the menu options for the **cnfbert** command. In this example, card 22 is an FRSM-8T1.

Example 18-21 *Menu Options for* **cnfbert** *on an FRSM-8T1*

```
SJ8850.1.7.PXM.a > cnfbert 22

        ** T1/E1 DIAGNOSTIC TESTS PACKAGE **
        =====================================

This is a package of Bit Error Rate Tests as well as
other associated operations such as loopbacks.  This
package is menu driven and can be used for any T1/E1
Service Module in the shelf.

Test Medium Is:
---------------
Line.

                LINE
                ----
        r. Redo From Start
        p. Previous Menu
        q. Quit Menu

            Line number to test please: 2




--------
        r. Redo From Start
        p. Previous Menu
        q. Quit Menu

        1. BERT Pattern Test
        2. Loopback

            Please Enter Choice[1-2]: 2

            LOOPBACK
            --------
```

Example 18-21 *Menu Options for* **cnfbert** *on an FRSM-8T1 (Continued)*

```
            r. Redo From Start
            p. Previous Menu
            q. Quit Menu

            1. Far End Loopback
            2. Remote Loopback
            3. Local Loopback

                    Please Enter Choice[1-3]: 3
```

The Display BERT Command

The **dspbert** command output reports the results of a BERT in progress. Use this command to learn how the line test is performing. Example 18-22 shows the **dspbert** output for an FRSM T1 line.

Example 18-22 **dspbert** *Output for an FRSM T1 Line*

```
SJ8850.1.7.PXM.a > dspbert 22

        User                      : Teacher
        Start Date                : 02/24/2000
        Current Date              : 02/24/2000
        Start Time                : 16:56:30
        Current Time              : 16:59:15
        Physical Slot Number      : 22
        Logical Slot Number       : 22
        Line Number               : 2 (Line test)
        Device To Loop            : Far End ESF Loopback
        BERT Pattern              : Alternate One Zero Pattern
        Error Inject Count        : 1
        Bit Count                 : 247226255
        Bit Error Count           : 242641
        Bit Error Rate (BER)      : 0.00098

              BERT is in sync.
```

The **dspbert** command provides the following information:

- The user ID that initiated the BERT
- The test's start date and time
- The current date and time
- **The physical and logical slot numbers**—The physical slot number might be different if a redundant card is active in place of the primary card.
- Line number

- **DS0 (timeslot) speed**—56 or 64 kbps (for port testing)
- **Test type**—BERT pattern or loopback (for port testing)
- Device to loop if a loop has been established
- BERT pattern in use
- **Error inject count**—The number of errors injected into the bit stream using the **modbert** command
- **Bit count**—The total number of bits sent during this test
- **Bit errors**—The number of bits received in error
- **Bit error rate**—The ratio of the errored bits to the total number of bits sent

How to Add Lines to an MGX Service Module

This section describes the procedure used to add and configure lines on MGX service modules and the PXM1.

The following steps show the actions and results associated with adding lines to an MGX service module or the PXM1. When using the SRM-3T3 for T1 bulk line distribution, start with Step 1; otherwise, start with Step 10.

Step 1   On the active PXM1, type **dsplns -ds3** {**15** | **16** | **31** | **32**} and verify that the T3 line is disabled. This outputs the SRM T3 line status.

Step 2   If the T3 is disabled, type **addln -ds3** *<slot.line>*. The T3 line is activated.

Step 3   Type **dspln -ds3** *<slot.line>* and verify the line configuration. This outputs the SRM T3 line status and configuration information.

Step 4   If you need to change the T3 line configuration, type **cnfln -ds3** *<slot.line>*. This changes the T3 line configuration.

Step 5   Type **dspsrmclksrc** *<slot.line>* and verify the SRM clock source configuration. This outputs the SRM T3 line clock source—either the MGX backplane or the T3.

Step 6   If you need to change the SRM T3 clock source, type **cnfsrmclksrc -ds3** *<slot.line>* **-srmclk** *<clock source>*.

Step 7   Type **addlink** *<T3 line number> <T1 line number> <number of T1s> <target slot number> <slot line number>*. This links one or more T1s on the SRM to a service module.

Step 8   Type **dsplink** *<slot.line>* or **dspslotlink** *<slot number>* and verify that the links are correct. This outputs the T1 links to the service module.

Step 9   Type **cc** <*slot number*> where *slot number* is the service module that the line is on. This logs you into the service module.

Step 10   On your service module, type **addln** <*line number*>. This activates the line.

Step 11   Type **dsplns** or **dspds3lns** and verify that the line is active. This outputs the line status.

Step 12   Type **dspln** <*line number*> and verify the line configuration. This outputs the line configuration information.

Step 13   If you need to change your line configuration, type **cnfln** <*line number*>. This changes the line configuration. Type **dspln** <*line number*> and verify the line configuration. This outputs the line configuration information.

You have now successfully completed the steps necessary for adding lines to an MGX service module or PXM1.

SRM-3T3 Distribution of T1 Lines

This section describes how the SRM-3T3 distributes T1 lines to MGX service modules.

SRM-3T3 Features

The SRM-3T3 T1 line distribution feature has the following capabilities and limitations:

- Up to 80 T1 lines from three T3 lines are supported.

- A service module must have all T1 lines coming from the SRM-3T3 or all T1 lines coming from the back card.

- Service module back cards are not required if bulk T1 line distribution is in use.

- Service modules in bulk mode with 1:N redundancy configured use the T1 distribution bus (not the redundancy bus) when a secondary card is active.

NOTE   The SRM-3T3/B (Model B) does not support T1 line distribution to slots 9, 10, 25, and 26 on the MGX 8250/8850-PXM1 switch.

The SRM-3T3/C (Model C) is supported on MGX 8230, 8250, and 8850-PXM1 switches. It provides T1 bulk distribution to all service module slots except slots 9, 10, 25, and 26. Any service module that uses bulk distribution or that relies on the distribution bus for redundancy cannot reside in these slots.

T1 Line Distribution Process

Figure 18-3 shows the different stages of user traffic flow through the SRM-3T3 to an MGX service module (FRSM-8T1).

Figure 18-3   *User Traffic Flow from SRM-3T3 to FRSM-8T1*

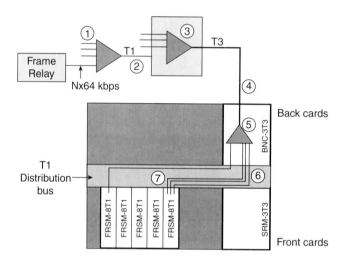

NOTE	Stage 1 applies only to channelized service modules (FRSM-8T1, CESM-8T1, and VISM-8T1).

Table 18-1 describes the stages associated with user traffic flow through the SRM-3T3 to an MGX service module (FRSM-8T1) that are shown in Figure 18-3.

Table 18-1   *Stages Associated with User Traffic Flow Through the SRM-3T3*

Stage	Description
1	Up to 24 Frame Relay CPE interfaces are attached to a TDM. Each interface has one or more 64 kbps timeslots.
2	The Nx64 kbps timeslots are multiplexed onto a T1.
3	The T1 is multiplexed with up to 27 other T1s to form a T3 line. The device that performs this function is often called an M13.
4	The T3 line is attached to the SRM-3T3 back card.
5	The SRM-3T3 demultiplexes the T3 line back into its component T1 lines.
6	The T1 lines are sent across the T1 distribution bus.
7	The T1s are received, and the service modules process the traffic.

Commands for T1 Line Distribution

This section describes the commands used to set up and display T1 bulk line distribution on the MGX switch using the SRM-3T3:

- **dsplns**—Lists summary status and configuration information for all lines on the card.
- **dspln**—Lists detailed configuration information for a line.
- **addln**—Activates a physical line.
- **delln**—Deactivates a physical line.
- **cnfln**—Changes the characteristics of the physical line.
- **dspsrmclksrc**—Shows the configured clock source for the SRM card.
- **cnfsrmclksrc**—Changes the clock source for the SRM card.
- **addlink**—Links a T1 line from the SRM-3T3 to a service module.
- **dellink**—Unlinks a T1 line from the STM-3T3 to a service module.
- **delslotlink**—Unlinks all lines from the SRM-3T3 to a service module.
- **dsplink**—Lists the T1 lines linked from the SRM-3T3 to all the service modules on the node.
- **dspslotlink**—Lists the T1 lines linked from the SRM-3T3 to a service module.

The Display Lines Command

The **dsplns** command output lists summary status and configuration information for the three T3 lines on the SRM-3T3. The **dsplns** command is issued from the active PXM1 on the MGX switch. Example 18-23 shows the **dsplns** output for an SRM-3T3 card.

Here is the **dsplns** command syntax:

```
dsplns -ds3 <slot number>
```

Example 18-23 **dsplns** *Output for an SRM-3T3 Card*

```
SJ8850.1.7.PXM.a > dsplns -ds3 31

  Line     Type       Status/Coding     Length      Criteria   AIScBitsCheck
  ----  -------------  --------------  ------------  ---------- -------------
    1   dsx3CbitParity Ena / dsx3B3ZS  lessThan225  fBits3Of8  Check C-bits
    2   dsx3CbitParity Dis / dsx3B3ZS  lessThan225  fBits3Of8  Check C-bits
    3   dsx3CbitParity Dis / dsx3B3ZS  lessThan225  fBits3Of8  Check C-bits
```

SRM line information includes the following:

- **Line number**
- **Type**—The line type. In Example 18-23, the line is a T3 with C-bit parity checking enabled.

- **Line status**—Disabled, enabled, or modified. If the line has been added and changed, it reports a modified state.

- **Coding**—The ones-density enforcement technique used on the line.

- **Length**—The line length. In Example 18-23, the line length is less than 225 feet for each line that is listed in the output.

- **Criteria**—The loss of frame criteria. In Example 18-23, the line fails if three out of eight frames are in error.

- **AIS C-bit check**—Determines whether T3 C-bits are used to determine a line failure.

The Display Line Command

The **dspln** command output shows the configuration information for a specified SRM-3T3 broadband line. The **dspln** command is issued from the active PXM1 on the MGX switch. Example 18-24 shows the **dspln** command output.

Here is the **dspln** command syntax:

```
dsplns -ds3 <slot.line>
```

Example 18-24 **dspln** *Output*

```
SJ8850.1.7.PXM.a > dspln -ds3 31.1

  LineNum:                1
  LineType:               dsx3CbitParity
  LineCoding:             dsx3B3ZS
  LineLength:             lessThan225
  LineOOFCriteria:        fBits3Of8
  LineAISCbitsCheck:      Check C-bits
  LineLoopbackCommand:    NoLoop
  LineRcvFEACValidation:  4 out of 5 FEAC codes
  LineEnable:             Enabled
  LinePayloadScramble:    Disabled
```

The Add Line Command

The **addln** command activates a T3 line on the SRM-3T3 card. Here is the **addln** command syntax:

```
addln -ds3 <slot.line>
```

slot is the card slot number of the SRM-3T3 (15, 16, 31, or 32, depending on which SRM-3T3 is currently active), and *line* is the line number you want to activate (1, 2, or 3).

For example, type **addln -ds3 15.2** to activate line 2 on the SRM-3T3 in slot 15 (and slot 16 if you have redundant SRMs).

Use the **delln** command to deactivate the line.

The Configure Line Command

Use the **cnfln** command to modify the characteristics of the lines on the SRM-3T3 card.

Here is the **cnfln** command syntax:

```
cnfln -ds3 <line number> [-lc <line coding>] [-len <line length>]
  [-oof <line OOF criteria>] [-cb <line AIS C-bit check>] [-lpb <loop>]
  [-felpnum <far-end loop line number>] [-rfeac <receive FEAC validation>]
  [-teac <transmit FEAC code>] [-pls <DS3 PLCP payload scramble>]
```

The parameter options are as follows:

- *line number*—The line number in the format *slot.port*. The SRM-3T3 line is on slot 15, 16, 31, or 32, depending on the active SRM-3T3 card slot number.

- *line coding*—The ones-density enforcement used on the line. For a DS3, the line coding is always 1 = B3ZS.

- *line length*—The length of cable used for line build-out purposes. 1 = less than 225 feet, 2 = greater than 225 feet.

- *line OOF criteria*—The number of errored frames necessary to declare an out of frame (OOF) condition. 1 = 3 out of 8, 2 = 3 out of 16.

- *line AIS C-bit check*—The C-bits in the DS3 frame can be used to pass an alarm indicator signal (AIS) from one device to another. 1 = check C-bits, 2 = ignore C-bits.

- *loop*—Creates a loop on the line for testing purposes. 1 = no loop, 2 = remote loop (loop facing out toward the line), 3 = local loop (loop facing toward the MGX switch), 4 = in-band local loop.

- *far-end loop line number*—The DS1 line number. 1 to 28 = DS1 line number, 29 = all DS1 lines, 30 = DS3 line.

- *receive FEAC validation*—The required number of FEACs before declaring an alarm. 1 = 4 out of 5, 2 = 8 out of 10.

- *transmit FEAC code*—The far-end alarm code. 1 = send no code, 2 = send line code, 3 = send payload code, 4 = send reset code, 5 = send DS1 loopback code, 6 = send test pattern.

- *DS3 PLCP payload scramble*—Enables or disables payload scramble. 1 = enable, 2 = disable.

The Display SRM Clock Source Command

The **dspsrmclksrc** command shows the configured clock source for an SRM T3 line. The **cnfsrmclksrc** command is used to change the transmit clock source to either the MGX backplane or the DS3 receive clock. Example 18-25 shows the **dspsrmclksrc** command output.

Here is the **dspsrmclksrc** command syntax:

```
dspsrmclksrc -ds3 <slot.line>
```

Example 18-25 dspsrmclksrc *Output*

```
SJ8850.1.7.PXM.a > dspsrmclksrc -ds3 15.1

  LineNum:              1
  LineXmtClockSource:   backplane clock
```

The Add Link Command

The **addlink** command links a T1 line on the SRM-3T3 to a specific service module card slot number and line number. The **dellink** command is used to remove specific T1 links, and **delslotlink** removes all links to a specified slot number.

Here is the **addlink** command syntax:

```
addlink <T3 line number> <T1 line number> <number of T1s>
  <target slot number> <slot line number>
```

The parameter options are as follows:

- *T3 line number*—The source T3 line. The line number is entered as *slot.line*.

- *T1 line number*—The starting line number of the T1 line(s) on the SRM-3T3.

- *number of T1s*—The number of T1s that are distributed to the service module, starting with the specified T1 starting line number.

- *target slot number*—The service module that will receive the T1 lines.

- *slot line number*—The starting line number on the target service module.

For example, type **addlink 15.1 1 4 20 1** to link T1 lines 1 to 4 on T3 line 1 on SRM-3T3 in slot 15 to T1 lines 1 to 4 on the service module in slot 20.

The Display Link Command

The **dsplink** command output lists the links between the demultiplexed T1s and the service module card slots. The **dsplink** command output is shown in Example 18-26.

Example 18-26 dsplink *Output*

```
SJ8850.1.7.PXM.a > dsplink 31.1

  T3Line  T1Slot  T1RowStatus  TargetSlot  TargetSlotLine
  ------  ------  -----------  ----------  --------------
     1       1        Add          19            1
     1       2        Add          19            2
     1       3        Add          19            3
     1       4        Add          19            4
```

The information that is output with the **dsplink** command includes the following:

- T3 line number
- T1 slot number
- **T1 row status**—The status of the T1, either Add or Modify
- **Target slot**—The card slot number of the service module receiving the T1 line
- **Target slot line**—The line number on the service module receiving the T1 line

The Display Slot Link Command

The **dspslotlink** command output shows the T1 lines distributed from the SRM-3T3 to a specific card slot. The **dspslotlink** command is issued from the active PXM1 on the MGX switch. Example 18-27 shows the output for the **dspslotlink** command.

Example 18-27 dspslotlink *Output*

```
SJ8850.1.7.PXM.a > dspslotlink 19

Slot Num : 19
Max Lines   : 8
Link Counter: 4

Slot  Line#  T3 Line#  T1 Slot#
====  =====  ========  =========
 19     1       1          1
 19     2       1          2
 19     3       1          3
 19     4       1          4
 19     5       0          0
 19     6       0          0
 19     7       0          0
 19     8       0          0
```

How to Test T1 and E1 Lines on MGX Service Modules

This section describes the procedure used to test T1 and E1 lines on MGX service modules using the bit error rate test (BERT) feature on the SRM.

Bit Error Rate Testing

The SRM line testing features include

- **Line loopback initiation**—The SRM initiates local, remote, and far-end loops to test continuity. You can test to these loops using local or remote external BERT devices.

- **BERT**—The SRM sends a test pattern to an SRM-initiated or manual far-end loop and reports the results to the MGX CLI.

Figure 18-4 shows the location of local, remote, and far-end loops initiated by the SRM.

Figure 18-4 *Locations of Loops Initiated by the SRM*

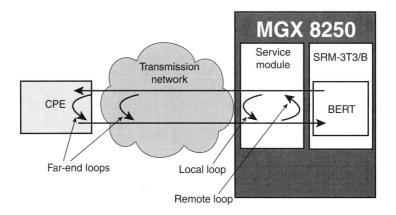

NOTE   Far-end loops can occur on any external device that responds to the transmitted loopback code.

Procedures for Testing T1 and E1 Lines on MGX Service Modules

The following steps show you the actions and results associated with Bit Error Rate Testing (BERT). This procedure requires that you have an active SRM card installed in the same bay as your service module.

Step 1   Log on to your service module and type **dsplns** to determine whether the line is in alarm. This outputs line alarm status for all lines on the card.

Step 2   If there is an alarm, type **dspalm -ds1** *<line number>* to determine the alarm type. This outputs alarm information for the line.

Step 3   To check if there are errors that might not be causing alarms, type **dspalmcnt -ds1** *<line number>*. This command is most effective on AUSM cards. It outputs a list of errors on the line.

Step 4   Type **cc** *<slot number>* to log into the active PXM1.

Step 5 Type **dspbert** <*slot number*> to confirm that the BERT is not in progress. If it is, use the **delbert** <*slot number*> command to end the test. This outputs BERT status and results.

Step 6 If you are planning to run a BERT to a manual loopback, place the loop on your equipment as required, and then type **cnfbert** <*slot number*>. This starts the BERT menu on the CLI.

Step 7 Select Line. For AUSMs, the Line option is selected automatically, because the line and port are the same. This continues the menu with the line options and formats the menu choices based on the card and line type.

Step 8 Enter the line number as prompted by the CLI. This selects the line to test.

Step 9 Select Loopback or BERT Pattern Test. If you select Loopback, proceed with Step 10; if you select BERT Pattern Test, go to Step 14. This continues the menu with loopback or BERT options.

Step 10 Depending on the card and line type, you may select far-end, remote, or local loopbacks. This continues the menu with loopback options.

Step 11 Select Loop Up. For local and remote loops, go to Step 13; for far-end loops, proceed with Step 12. This initiates the local or remote loop or continues the menu for far-end loops.

Step 12 Select the loop type. This initiates the far-end loopback.

Step 13 Type **dspbert** <*slot number*> to confirm that the loop was successful. If you are testing using an external BERT device, proceed with your testing. When you are finished, go to Step 19. This outputs the result of the loopback request.

NOTE   The loop described in Step 13 does not time out; you must remove it as described in Step 19.

Step 14 Select the loop type (the selection depends on the card and line type). If you are using a manual loop, select No Loopback. This initiates a far-end loopback.

Step 15 Select the pattern test (the selection depends on the card and line type). This begins the BERT.

Step 16 Type **dspbert** <*slot number*> to monitor the BERT status. The output does not update automatically; you must type **dspbert** <*slot number*> to view the current results. This outputs the results of the BERT.

Step 17 Type **modbert** <*slot number*> to inject errors into the bit stream. The resulting errors are shown in the **dspbert** output. When you are finished testing, continue to the next step.

NOTE The BERT does not time out in Step 17; you must remove it as described in Step 18.

Step 18 Type **delbert** <*slot number*> to end the BERT. The procedure is complete.

Step 19 To remove a far-end, remote, or local loopback, type **cnfbert** <*slot number*>. This starts the BERT menu on the CLI.

Step 20 Enter the line number that the loop is on. This selects the line and formats the menu choices based on the card and line type.

Step 21 Select Loopback. This continues the menu with loopback options.

Step 22 Select the loop type that is in progress. This continues the menu with loopback options.

Step 23 Select Loop Down. The procedure is complete. The loop on the line is removed.

You have now successfully completed the steps associated with Bit Error Rate Testing of T1 and E1 lines on service modules using the SRM.

Feeder Nodes

A *feeder node* is a multiservice device that concentrates multiple streams of traffic across a single link to an ATM backbone network. In the strictest sense, a feeder node does not make routing or switching decisions. It relies on the backbone network to send the traffic to the appropriate destination. Some feeder nodes might perform local switching; others might send all traffic (local and remote) to the backbone network.

Having feeder nodes effectively reduces the network size to simplify network control and management. A feeder node can be considered an extension of the backbone node (also called a *routing* or *core* node) it is attached to. In most cases, visibility to the feeder nodes is limited to the locally attached backbone node.

A Cisco WAN network comprising feeder nodes and backbone nodes is called a *tiered network*. In contrast, a *flat network* comprises nodes that are visible to all other nodes. Feeder and backbone nodes are managed by one or more network management stations in a Cisco WAN network. A special kind of feeder node, a *standalone feeder*, is attached to a non-Cisco backbone network as a generic UNI device. In this case, management might be limited to the standalone feeders. All feeder devices can be installed as standalone feeders.

Figure 18-5 shows a Cisco tiered network with feeder and backbone nodes.

Figure 18-5 *Cisco Tiered Network with Feeder and Backbone Nodes*

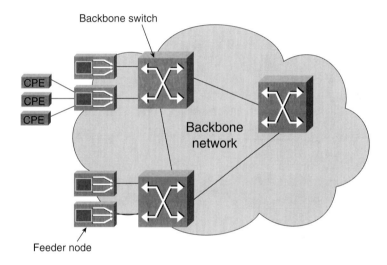

Types of Feeder and Backbone Nodes

The following devices are Cisco MGX feeder nodes:

- MGX 8220
- MGX 8230
- MGX 8250
- MGX 8850-PXM1

The following devices are Cisco backbone nodes:

- **MGX 8850-PXM45**—Supports MGX 8230, 8250, and 8850-PXM1 feeders
- **BPX**—Supports MGX 8220, 8230, 8250, and 8850-PXM1 feeders
- **IGX**—Supports MGX 8230 feeders

How to Add a Feeder to a BPX Network

This section shows the steps, actions, and results associated with adding an MGX feeder node to a BPX network.

Step 1 Type **addln** {**-ds3** | **-e3** | **-sonet**} 7.<*line number*> to activate a PXM1 line.

Step 2 Type **dsplns** {**-ds3** | **-e3** | **-sonet**} 7 and **dspln** {**-ds3** | **-e3** | **-sonet**} 7.<*line number*> to verify the line configuration. This outputs the line status and configuration information.

Step 3 Type **cnfln** {**-ds3** | **-e3** | **-sonet**} 7.<*line number*> if you need to make changes to the line configuration.

Step 4 Type **dsplns** {**-ds3** | **-e3** | **-sonet**} 7 and **dspln** {**-ds3** | **-e3** | **-sonet**} 7.<*line number*> to verify the configuration changes. This outputs the line status and configuration information.

Step 5 Type **dspatmlncnf** <*line number*> to verify the ATM cell header type (UNI or NNI). You must use NNI cells between the MGX switch and the BPX network. Use the **cnfatmln** command to change the configuration.

Step 6 Type **addport** <*port number*> <*line number*> <*percent bandwidth*> <*minimum VPI*> <*maximum VPI*>. A new logical port is created on the line.

Step 7 Type **dspports** and verify the port configuration. If you need to make any changes, use the **cnfport** command. This outputs the port configuration.

Step 8 Type **dspportrscprtn** and the verify port resource partition configuration.

Step 9 If you need to make changes to the port resource partitions, use the **cnfportrscprtn** command.

Step 10 Type **cnfifastrk** <*port number*> **ftrk**. This defines the logical port as a trunk.

Step 11 Log on to the BPX node that your MGX switch is attached to and type **uptrk** <*slot.port*>. The BPX trunk is activated.

Step 12 On your BPX node, type **dsptrkcnf** <*slot.port*> and verify trunk configuration.

Step 13 If your BPX trunk needs to be changed, use the **cnftrk** command.

Step 14 On your BPX node, type **dsptrks** and verify that the trunk is clear of alarms. This outputs a list of the trunks on the node and their alarm status.

Step 15 If the BPX is reporting alarms, log back into the MGX CLI and check the alarm status by typing **dspalm** {**-ds3** | **-e3** | **-sonet**} **7.**<*line number*>. Troubleshoot the line as necessary.

Step 16 Type **cnfrsrc** <*slot.port*> <*number of PVCs*> <*bandwidth*> **n** and increase the number of PVCs supported on the trunk from the default of 256. This changes the resource configuration on the trunk.

Step 17 On your BPX node, type **addshelf** <*slot.port*>. This adds the MGX feeder node to the BPX node.

Step 18 Log back into your MGX switch, and type **dsptrks** to verify that the trunk is active. This outputs a list of trunks on the MGX switch.

You have now successfully completed the steps necessary for adding an MGX feeder node to a BPX network.

How to Add a Feeder to an MGX 8850-PXM45 Network

This section shows the steps, actions, and results associated with adding an MGX feeder node to an MGX 8850-PXM45 network.

Step 1 Type **addln** {**-ds3** | **-e3** | **-sonet**} **7.**<*line number*> to activate a PXM1 line.

Step 2 Type **dsplns** {**-ds3** | **-e3** | **-sonet**} **7** and **dspln** {**-ds3** | **-e3** | **-sonet**} **7.**<*line number*> to verify the line configuration. This outputs the line status and configuration information.

Step 3 Type **cnfln** {**-ds3** | **-e3** | **-sonet**} **7.**<*line number*> if you need to make changes to the line configuration.

Step 4 Type **dsplns** {**-ds3** | **-e3** | **-sonet**} **7** and **dspln** {**-ds3** | **-e3** | **-sonet**} **7.**<*line number*> to verify the configuration changes. This outputs the line status and configuration information.

Step 5 Type **dspatmlncnf** <*line number*> to verify the line's ATM cell header type (UNI or NNI). You can use UNI or NNI cells between the MGX feeder and the MGX 8850-PXM45 network. Use the **cnfatmln** command if you need to change the configuration.

Step 6 Type **addport** <*port number*> <*line number*> <*percent bandwidth*> <*minimum VPI*> <*maximum VPI*> to create a new logical port on the line.

Step 7 Type **dspports** and verify the port configuration. If you need to make any changes, use the **cnfport** command.

Step 8 Type **dspportrscprtn** and verify the port resource partition configuration.

Step 9   If you need to make changes to the port resource partitions, use the **cnfportrscprtn** command.

Step 10   Type **cnfifastrk** *<port number>* **ftrk**. This defines the logical port as a trunk.

Step 11   Log in to the MGX 8850-PXM45 switch that your MGX feeder is attached to. This starts a CLI session.

Step 12   Type **cc** *<slot>*, where *slot* is the card slot of the AXSM attached to the MGX feeder. This transfers the CLI session to the AXSM.

Step 13   Type **upln** *<bay.line>*. This activates the AXSM line.

Step 14   Type **dspln** *<bay.line>* and verify the line configuration parameters. This outputs the line configuration and status information. Make sure that frame scrambling, payload scrambling, and line framing match the other end. If you want to change the line configuration, use the **cnfln** command.

Step 15   Type **addport** *<bay.line> <guaranteed rate> <maximum rate> <SCT ID> <interface type>*. This creates a logical port. Make sure the *interface type* (cell header type) matches the MGX feeder configuration from Step 5.

Step 16   Type **dspport** *<interface number>* to verify that the port is configured correctly. This outputs the port configuration and status information. Use the **cnfport** command to make any changes.

Step 17   Type **addpart** *<if number> <partition ID>* **2** *<egress minimum BW> <egress maximum BW> <ingress minimum BW> <ingress maximum BW> <minimum VPI> <maximum VPI> <minimum VCI> <maximum VCI> <minimum connections> <maximum connections>*. Be sure to match the bandwidth and VPI ranges with the feeder port configured in Steps 6 and 9. This creates a PNNI partition on the port.

Step 18   Type **addfdr** *<interface number>*. This adds the feeder node to the MGX 8850-PXM45 switch.

Step 19   Type **dspfdrs** or **dspfdr** *<interface number>* to verify the feeder status.

Step 20   Type **bye.** This ends your MGX 8850-PXM45 CLI session.

Step 21   Log back into your MGX feeder and type **dsptrks** to verify that the trunk is active. This outputs a list of trunks on the MGX switch.

You have now successfully completed the steps necessary for adding an MGX feeder node to an MGX 8850-PXM45 network.

Setting Up an MGX 8850 Standalone Switch

This section shows the steps, actions, and results associated with setting up an MGX 8850 standalone MGX switch.

Step 1   Type **addln** {**-ds3** | **-e3** | **-sonet**} **7.**<*line number*> to activate a PXM1 line.

Step 2   Type **dsplns** {**-ds3** | **-e3** | **-sonet**} **7** and **dspln** {**-ds3** | **-e3** | **-sonet**} **7.**<*line number*> to verify the line configuration. This outputs the line status and configuration information.

Step 3   Type **cnfln** {**-ds3** | **-e3** | **-sonet**} **7.**<*line number*> if you need to make changes to the line configuration.

Step 4   Type **dsplns** {**-ds3** | **-e3** | **-sonet**} **7** and **dspln** {**-ds3** | **-e3** | **-sonet**} **7.**<*line number*> to verify the configuration changes. This outputs the line status and configuration information.

Step 5   Type **dspatmlncnf** <*line number*> to verify the line's ATM cell header type.

Step 6   If you need to change the ATM cell header type, use the **cnfatmln** command.

Step 7   Type **addport** <*port number*> <*line number*> <*percent bandwidth*> <*minimum VPI*> <*maximum VPI*>. This creates a new logical port on the line.

Step 8   Type **dspports** and verify the port configuration. If you need to make any changes, use the **cnfport** command.

Step 9   Type **dspportrscprtn** and verify the port resource partition configuration.

Step 10   If you need to make changes to the port resource partitions, use the **cnfportrscprtn** command.

Step 11   Activate and configure the ATM interface on the attached ATM switch. This procedure will vary depending on the type of equipment in use.

Step 12   Log back in to the MGX CLI and check the alarm status by typing **dspalm** {**-ds3** | **-e3** | **-sonet**} **7.**<*line number*>. Troubleshoot the line as necessary. This outputs the line alarm status.

You have now successfully completed the steps necessary for setting up an MGX 8850 standalone MGX switch.

Sonet APS

The SONET Automatic Protection Switching (APS) feature is supported on PXM1 cards in the MGX switch. APS is a standards-based redundancy scheme that enhances network reliability by protecting against the effects of line failure. APS is defined in Bellcore and ITU standards for North American SONET and international Synchronous Data Hierarchy (SDH) optical network links. The relevant standards are Bellcore GR-253 and ITU-T G.783. For the purposes of this book, the term SONET is understood to include SDH as well.

In its basic form, APS lets a pair of SONET lines be configured for line redundancy, where one line is active and the other is a backup. Whether the backup passes real traffic while in standby mode depends on the version of APS that is implemented, as described in a moment.

If the fiber-optic carrier for the active line is severed or damaged, the user traffic switches automatically to the standby line within 60 milliseconds. Some versions of APS can be configured with a *revertive* option, in which the hardware switches back to the active line automatically after it is repaired and as soon as a defined time period has elapsed.

In APS terminology, the active line at the time of initial configuration is called the *working* (W) line, and the standby line is the *protection* (P) line. Coordination of line switching in the event of failure or repair happens under the control of an in-band signaling protocol.

In the MGX, PXM1 implementation of APS is supported for OC-3c and OC-12c fiber-optic interfaces. APS is not supported on E3 or T3 interfaces. Additional implementation details are included later in this section.

APS Versions

The standards define two basic forms of APS:

- **APS 1:N**—Provides line redundancy, in which one line supports one or more other lines. In APS 1:N, the protection line does not carry traffic when the working line is active.

- **APS 1+1**—Provides line redundancy. In APS 1+1, both the working and protection lines carry traffic.

The PXM1 supports intercard APS 1+1, in which the working and protection lines are on different PXM1 cards. Model B PXM1 back cards must be used (for example, SMLR-1-622/B). No other hardware is required.

NOTE   When you configure APS on the MGX switch, a number of APS options are provided. Only APS 1+1 with two back cards (APS mode 2) is supported.

Figure 18-6 shows APS 1+1 supported on an MGX feeder attached to an MGX 8850-PXM45 backbone switch.

Figure 18-6 *APS 1+1 on an MGX*

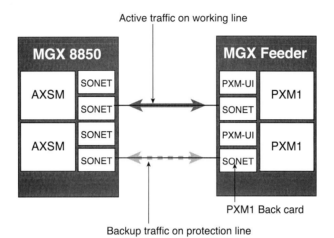

The PXM1 supports two switching directions for APS 1+1: unidirectional and bidirectional. *Bidirectional* means that when a failure is detected, the line (both transmit and receive directions) and the cards switch. *Unidirectional* means that the end of the line detecting the failure switches but the remote end does not. The result is that transmit and receive traffic may travel on different lines and on different cards.

Upon detection of a line or card failure, or in the event of the degradation of the signal beyond a user-configurable threshold, the APS system attempts to switch automatically from the current active line to the standby. Line or card failures are indicated by physical alarm conditions including Loss of Signal (LOS), Loss of Frame (LOF), and Alarm Indication Signal (AIS), or by an excessive Bit Error Rate (BER).

If revertive switching is enabled, the hardware attempts to switch back to the working line from the protection line after a configurable "Wait to Restore" time period has elapsed. The working line must be in a clear state for this to occur.

In addition to the automatic switching mode, the APS standards also include provisions for operator-controlled manual switching. The AXSM command set lets the user switch operation from the working line to the protection line, and vice versa.

APS channel information is transported between the SONET/SDH interfaces using the K1 and K2 control bytes, which are located in the Line Overhead portion of the OC-3c/STM1 frame. The two control bytes are carried on the protection channel and are interpreted as shown in Table 18-2.

Table 18-2 *APS Channel Information*

Control Byte (Bits)	Definition
K1 (1 to 4)	Used to request an automatic or manual switch action, such as a signal failure (automatic) or forced switchover (manual). The default is no request.
K1 (5 to 8)	Defines the channel making the request; the default is null. The K1 byte carries the type of switch request and the channel number.
K2 (1 to 4)	Channel definition. Same as K1 bits 1 to 4.
K2 (5)	APS architecture. Either 1:1 or 1+1 (the default).
K2 (6 to 8)	Mode of operation, either unidirectional (default) or bidirectional.

Most trunk and line service cards available for Cisco WAN switches, including the MGX 8230/8250/8850-PXM1 switch, also support Y-cable redundancy. The PXM1 has this redundancy built in, which provides card but not line redundancy. APS performs switchovers at the physical layer, which is significantly faster than at Layer 2 or Layer 3. For example, an APS switchover is accomplished in less than 60 ms, whereas a Y-cable redundancy switchover, done at the ATM layer, requires approximately 250 ms. Fast switchovers are becoming increasingly critical as traffic speeds approach OC-12c/STM4 and higher.

APS 1+1 Unidirectional Example

Figure 18-7 shows an APS 1+1 setup, including two card modules with the redundant paired back cards.

Figure 18-7 *APS 1+1 Setup*

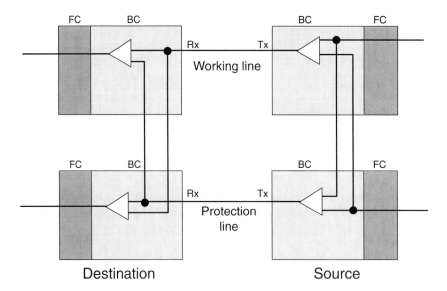

NOTE   Figure 18-7 shows only one end of the APS line. The complete depiction would show source and destination at both ends.

The back cards are cross-coupled as shown in Figure 18-7 so that the transmit data from one front card is electrically bridged to both back cards.

Using this basic schematic, we will step through three failure scenarios. The first case is a physical line failure, as shown in Figure 18-8. This type of failure could be the result of a fiber cut or a failure of the optical transceiver at either end of the working line. Assuming the default configuration of unidirectional switching, the line failure causes the user traffic to travel via the protection line as shown.

Figure 18-8 *Physical Line Failure*

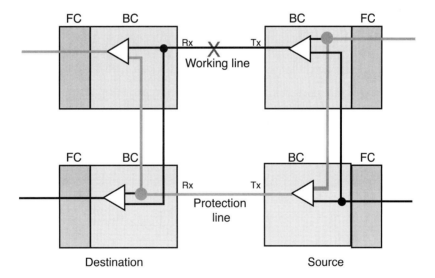

NOTE   The front cards do not switch.

The second case, shown in Figure 18-9, is a total failure of the working line back card, again with unidirectional switching. Here the source end switches to the protection front card, but because bidirectional switching is not enabled, traffic from the protection line is switched to the working line destination front card.

Figure 18-9 *Total Failure of the Working Line Back Card*

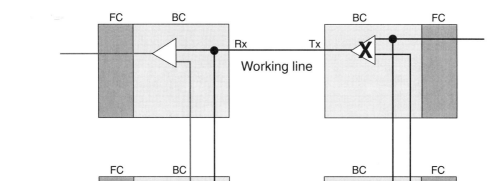

The third case, shown in Figure 18-10, involves failure of the source end working front card. Traffic switches to the protection front card and line, but with unidirectional switching. The working line front card at the destination still carries the user traffic.

Figure 18-10 *Failure of the Source End Working Front Card*

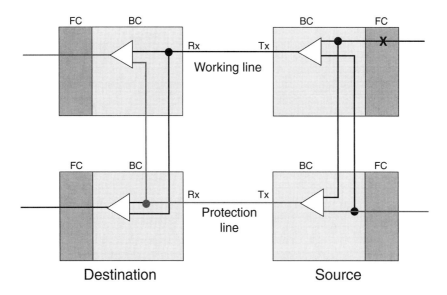

Now we will consider the previous failure modes with bidirectional switching enabled. Figure 18-11 shows a failure of the source end working front card with bidirectional switching enabled. Traffic automatically switches to the source end protection front card and line, and then switches to the protection front card at the destination. Because no card switching is required, the working source and destination card sets remain in service, although traffic travels over the protection line.

Figure 18-11 *APS 1 + 1 Case 1 with Bidirectional Signaling*

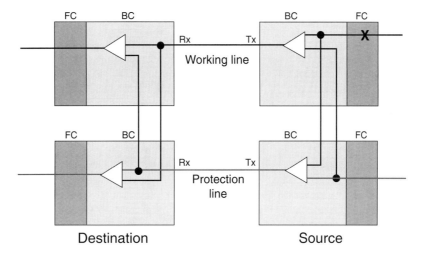

Figure 18-12 shows a total failure of the source end working back card with bidirectional switching enabled. Again, traffic automatically switches to the source end protection front card and line, and then switches to the protection front card at the destination.

Figure 18-12 *APS 1 + 1 Case 2 with Bidirectional Signaling*

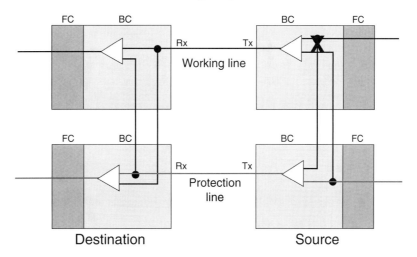

Commands for Configuring SONET APS on a PXM1 Line

This section describes the commands used to configure Automatic Protection Switching (APS) on a PXM1 line:

- **dspapsln**—Lists the configured APS lines on the PXM1.
- **addapsln**—Defines an APS line pair.
- **delapsln**—Removes an APS line pair.
- **cnfapsln**—Modifies the APS line configuration, including direction, revertive, and K1K2 options.
- **switchapsln**—Manually controls the APS switching options.

The Display APS Line Command

The **dspapsln** command lists the configuration for all PXM1 APS lines. Use this command to learn how APS is set up on a line. Example 18-28 shows an example of the **dspapsln** output.

Example 18-28 dspapsln *Output*

```
NODENAME.1.7.PXM.a > dspapsln

SlotLine Type  Act W_LINE P_LINE APS_ST CDType Dirc Revt LastUsrSwReq
-------- ----- --- ------ ------ ------ ------ ---- ---- --------------
7.1&8.1  1+1_2 7.1 OK     OK     OK     OC-12  UNI  NRV  NO_REQUEST
```

Information provided by the **dspapsln** command includes the following:

- **Slot and line**—The line numbers of the APS pair.
- **Type**—The APS mode. The PXM1 supports only APS 1+1 using two back cards. This is identified as 1+1_2 in Example 18-28.
- **Active**—The line that is currently active.
- **Working line**—The status of the working line. Status can be okay (OK), remote-end signal degrade (R_SD), signal degrade (SigD), remote-end signal failure (R_AM), line alarm (ALM), signal failure (SigF), back card mismatch or missing (MIS), or line in loopback (LOOPBK).
- **Protection line**—The status of the protection line. Status types include those supported for the working line, as well as protocol defection (P_D) and protection byte failure (P_B).
- **APS status**—Okay (OK), architecture mismatch (AR_MIS), direction mismatch (DI_MIS), channel mismatch (CH_MIS), or line alarm on protection line (PL_ALM).
- **Back card type**—OC-3 or OC-12.

- **Direction**—The switching direction, either unidirectional (UNI) or bidirectional (BI).

- **Revertive**—Specifies whether the revertive (RV) or nonrevertive (NRV) option is set for the APS line pair.

- **Last user switching request**—The most recent manual switch request using the **switchapsln** command.

The Add and Delete APS Line Command

The **addapsln** SuperUser command defines the APS line pair on the PXM1. Use this command to set the working and protection lines. Use **delapsln** to remove the APS line pair.

Here is the **addapsln** command syntax:

```
addapsln <working line> <working slot> <protection line>
    <protection slot> <architecture mode>
```

The parameter options are as follows:

- *working line*—The line number of the working line.

- *working slot*—The card slot number of the working line.

- *protection line*—The line number of the protection line.

- *protection slot*—The card slot number of the protection line.

- *architecture mode*—The APS mode to use on the line pair. 1 = 1+1 with one back card (this mode is not supported), 2 = 1+1 with two back cards, 3 = 1:1 with one back card (this mode is not supported), 4 = 1+1 Annex B (this mode is not supported).

For example, type **addapsln 1 7 1 8 2** to set up APS 1+1 with two back cards with line 1 on card 7 as the working line and line 1 on card 8 as the protection line.

The Configure APS Line Command

The **cnfapsln** command is used to change the APS configuration. The APS options on both ends of the line must match. Enter this command from the PXM1 that owns the working line.

Here is the **cnfapsln** command syntax:

```
cnfapsln <working line> <signal fail BER> <signal degrade BER>
    <WTR> <direction> <revertive> <K1K2>
```

The parameter options are as follows:

- *working line*—The working line number.

- *signal fail BER*—The bit error rate (BER) threshold for the line to report a signal failure. $3 = 10^{-3}$, $4 = 10^{-4}$, $5 = 10^{-5}$.

- *signal degrade BER*—The BER threshold for the line to report a signal degrade. $5 = 10^{-5}, 6 = 10^{-6}, 7 = 10^{-7}, 8 = 10^{-8}, 9 = 10^{-9}$.
- *WTR*—The wait to restore (WTR) timer value in minutes. 1 to 12.
- *direction*—The switching direction. 1 = unidirectional, 2 = bidirectional.
- *revertive*—Enables or disables the revertive option. 1 = disable, 2 = enable.
- *K1K2*—Enables or disables the in-band K1K2 option. 1 = enable, 2 = disable. You should always enable K1K2.

For example, type **cnfapsln 1 4 8 4 1 2 1** to configure APS line 1 for a signal failure BER of 10^{-4}, a signal degrade BER of 10^{-8}, a WTR timer of 4 minutes, unidirectional switching, the revertive option enabled, and in-band K1K2 enabled.

The Switch APS Line Command

The **switchapsln** command is used to manually control the APS lines. For example, you can force a switch from the working line to the protection line using the **switchapsln** command.

Here is the **switchapsln** command syntax:

```
switchapsln <line number> <operation>
```

The parameter options are as follows:

- *line number*—The working line number of the APS pair.
- *operation*—The switch operation. 1 = clears the last user request, 2 = forced switch without regard to any outstanding commands, 3 = manual switch that will not occur if there are outstanding commands, 4 = lockout to prevent a switch from occurring, 5 = service that forces all lines to switch to one back card.

Summary

This chapter provided an overview of the Cisco MGX switch, including service module lines on the PXM1, CESM, FRSM, AUSM, and VISM. It discussed Cisco MGX feeder nodes, including the MGX 8220, 8230, 8250, and 8850-PXM1, and backbone nodes, including the MGX 8850-PXM45.

You learned about the SONET Automatic Protection Switching (APS) feature, supported on PXM1 cards in the MGX switch. You also read about MGX commands and commands for configuring SONET APS. This chapter also discussed how to add a feeder node to a BPX network and an MGX 8850-PXM45 network and detailed the procedures for setting up an MGX standalone switch.

How the SRM-3T3 distributes T1 lines was discussed, and the commands for line distribution were presented, along with the commands for displaying, adding, and configuring lines and monitoring line alarms and errors. You should understand how to test E1 and T1 lines on service modules using the BERT feature on the SRM.

Review Questions

1 What is different about a standalone feeder node?

A. Standalone feeders do not support network management.

B. Only one standalone feeder can be attached to a BPX switch.

C. A standalone feeder can be attached to a non-Cisco backbone network.

D. The MGX 8220 concentrator can be installed only as a standalone feeder.

E. The backbone node treats a standalone feeder like a generic UNI device.

2 In Figure 18-13, identify each element as one of the following:

Figure 18-13 *Identify Each Element*

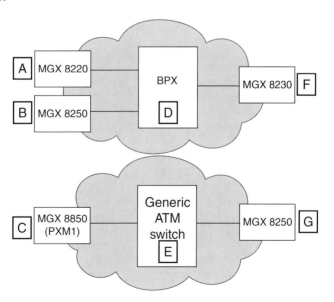

A. Feeder node

B. Backbone node

C. Standalone feeder node

3 Which of the images in Figure 18-14 depict a line?

Figure 18-14 *Which of the Images Depict a Line?*

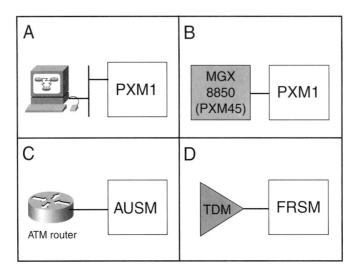

4 What kinds of devices can be attached to a PXM1 line?

A. A T1 PBX

B. A BPX switch

C. An ATM router with a T3 interface

D. A Frame Relay router with an E1 interface

5 On the MGX 8230, what is a line?

A. An Ethernet LAN segment

B. A T3 or E3 attached to an ATM switch

C. A multiplexed T1 that carries up to 24 different user circuits

D. Any digital transmission facility that carries traffic between a CPE and an MGX service module

6 Which of the following network events can trigger an automatic switchover to the APS protection line?

A. Loss of framing on a line or trunk

B. Bit error rate exceeding a preset limit

C. Excessive cell discards in the trunk queues

D. Cutting the fiber trunk between two MGX nodes

E. Wait to restore timer expiring in revertive switching mode

7 Which of the following APS protocols are supported on the PXM1?

A. 1:1 intracard

B. 1:1 intercard

C. 1+1 intracard

D. 1+1 intercard

8 Select the correct command for each function by choosing one of the commands enclosed in brackets.

A. To learn how many connections a card can support, use the {**dspcd** | **cnfcdrscprtn** | **dspcds** | **dspcdrscprtn**} command.

B. To learn whether a PXM1 line is in alarm, use the {**dsplns** | **dspalms** | **dsptrks**} command.

C. To learn the cell header type on a PXM1 line, use the {**dspln** | **dspport** | **dspatmlncnf**} command.

9 You have typed **dsplns -sonet 7** on your PXM1 card. What information is output on the CLI?

A. Line status

B. Payload scramble

C. Framing (OC-X/STM-X)

D. Line speed in cells per second

10 What can you conclude about the ports when looking at the output from the **dspports** command shown in Example 18-29?

Example 18-29 **dspports** *Output*

```
mgx8800b.1.7.PXM.a > dspports

 Port  Status  Line  PctBw  minVpi  maxVpi
 ------------------------------------------------
   3     ON      3    100      0      255
   4     ON      4    100      0      4095
```

A. Port 3 has failed.

B. Port 3 is an NNI.

C. Port 4 is an NNI.

D. Port 4 allows all VPI values.

11 Which of the following commands is valid?

A. **addapsln 1 7 1 8 1**

B. **addapsln 1 7 2 7 3**

C. **addapsln 2 7 2 8 2**

D. **addapsln 1 7 1 10 2**

12 You want to switch from the protection line to the working line only if there are no outstanding commands. The working line is line 2 on card 7. What command must you type on the CLI to accomplish this task?

13 You type **cnfapsln 2 5 6 5 2 1 1** on the CLI. Which of the following statements are true?

A. In-band K1K2 is enabled.

B. The revertive option is enabled.

C. The working line is on card slot 8.

D. The switching direction is bidirectional.

E. A signal failure will be reported when the bit error rate reaches 10^{-5}.

F. A signal degrade will be reported when the bit error rate reaches 10^{-5}.

14 You are using an SRM-3T3 to distribute T1 lines on your MGX switch. One of the T1 lines on your FRSM-8T1 card is reporting a loss of signal. Where is the most likely cause of this problem?

A. On the FRSM back card

B. On the MGX T1 distribution bus

C. On the T3 coming into the SRM-3T3 back card

D. On the T1 facility attached to the end-user equipment

15 You have an MGX 8250 switch, and you require 22 E1 circuit emulation lines and 12 T1 circuit emulation lines from a variety of customer locations. Would T1 bulk distribution be beneficial to this installation?

16 How many T1 lines can be distributed using an SRM-3T3?

A. 24

B. 28

C. 80

D. 84

E. 192

17 You are logged into an FRSM-HS1/B card module. Write the command and all required parameters you would use to see the line rate of line 1.

18 On which cards would you use the **dspds3lns** command?

A. PXM

B. CESM-8E1

C. FRSM-8T1

D. FRSM-2CT3

E. FRSM-T3E3

19 What command do you use to map a T1 line on the SRM to a service module?

A. **addln**

B. **addlink**

C. **cnflink**

D. **addslotlink**

20 What command must you type (including all required parameters) to learn which SRM T1 lines are linked to card 18?

21 The command syntax for the **addlink** command is shown in Example 18-30. If you need to link T1 lines 20 to 23 of T3 line 3 to T1 lines 5 to 8 on an AUSM-8T1 in slot 5, what must you type on the command line?

Example 18-30 addlink *Command*

```
SJ8850.1.7.PXM.a > addlink

ERR: incorrect number of parameters: (not enough)
Syntax: addlink <T3LineNum> <T1Slot> <NumberOfT1s> <TargetSlotNum>
                <TargetSlotLineNum> <T3LineNum>
                   where T3LineNum = Slot.Line
                        where Slot = 15,16,31,32
                        Line = 1 - 3
                <T1Slot> where T1Slot = 1 - 28
                <NumberOfT1s> where NumberOfT1s = 1-8
                <TargetSlotNum> where TargetSlotNum = 1-6¦11-14¦17-22¦27-30
                <TargetSlotLineNum> where TargetSlotLineNum = 1-8
```

A. **addlink 31.3 20 4 5**

B. **addlink 31.3 20 4 5 5**

C. **addlink 15.3 20 4 5 5**

D. **addlink 15.3 5 20 5 8**

22 You want to know which lines on your CESM-8E1 card are in alarm. Which commands would you use?

A. **dspln**

B. **dspalm**

C. **dspalms**

D. **dspalmcnt**

23 What is the purpose of the **modbert** command?

A. It ends the BERT.

B. It changes the BERT pattern.

C. It injects an error into the BERT.

24 Which command would you use to learn how many times line 1 on your FRSM-8T1 has experienced a loss of signal?

A. **dspln 1**

B. **dspalm -ds1 1**

C. **dspalms -ds1**

D. **dspalmcnt -ds1 1**

This chapter covers the following key topics:

- Supported VC Types: PVCs, SPVCs, and SVCs
- Connection Types in the Backbone Network
- MGX Connections
- Commands for Adding, Configuring, and Displaying MGX 8850-PXM45 Connections
- How to Add a Connection in an MGX 8850-PXM45 Network
- Circuit Emulation Ports
- Circuit Emulation Connections
- Circuit Emulation Clocking Modes
- How the CESM Manages Traffic
- Commands for Adding, Configuring, and Displaying Circuit Emulation Ports
- Commands for Adding, Configuring, and Displaying Circuit Emulation Connections
- Commands for Verifying Circuit Emulation Connections
- How to Create Circuit Emulation Services in an MGX Network

CHAPTER 19

Connection Types

This chapter presents the different virtual circuit (VC) types supported on MGX switches, including PVCs, SPVCs, and SVCs, and gives examples of each of these types of connections. It discusses ATM connection types available on the BPX and MGX 8850-PXM45 switches that are used to support MGX connections. It also shows you how, in an MGX network, all connections carry ATM cells.

You will read about slave and master connections, as well as commands for adding, configuring, and displaying BPX connections. You will also see how to add a connection in a BPX backbone network and MGX 8850-PXM45 network. Commands for adding, configuring, and displaying MGX 8850-PXM45 connections are presented.

Circuit emulation ports, connections, and clocking modes are presented, with a detailed discussion of how the CESM manages user traffic. You will learn the commands used to add, configure, and display circuit emulation ports and connections, and you will see how to verify these connections. Finally, you'll see how to create circuit emulation services in an MGX network.

Supported VC Types: PVCs, SPVCs, and SVCs

This section describes the different VC types supported on MGX switches, including the Permanent Virtual Circuit (PVC), Soft Permanent Virtual Circuit (SPVC), and Switched Virtual Circuit (SVC). It also compares how each is implemented in a network.

PVC Definition

A Permanent Virtual Circuit (PVC) is a static connection between two ports on an ATM switch or between two ports on separate switches. A PVC is established by an administrative action, typically by a network administrator using a command-line interface (CLI) or network management tool such as a Cisco WAN Manager (CWM) station. As soon as a PVC is in place, it remains in place unless it is specifically removed by a management action. The switch ports, or the set of resources on the ports that have been allocated to the connection, also remain dedicated for the PVC's lifetime.

Strictly speaking, a PVC is a static connection in the network. In other words, the connection does not change, regardless of network events or changes. To confuse matters, many Frame Relay and ATM networks use the term PVC to refer to a dynamically routed virtual circuit.

Figure 19-1 highlights the generic characteristics of PVCs.

Figure 19-1 *Permanent Virtual Circuit (PVC)*

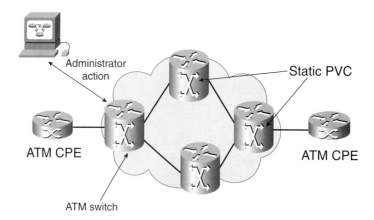

Provisioning of a PVC involves careful planning prior to the actual configuration steps. Connection identifiers are required on each link along the complete end-to-end network path. Connection identifiers are the VPI in the case of a VPC (path) connection or the VPI and VCI in the case of a VCC (channel) connection. Also, any Quality of Service or traffic-contract parameters that differ from the system defaults need to be defined by the administrator on a per-connection basis.

On an MGX switch, a PVC may originate and terminate on a service module or modules within the same switch (local switching) or may terminate on the ATM feeder trunk for a PVC that is part of a multisegment network connection. Figure 19-2 illustrates and contrasts the forms of PVC that can exist in a network comprising MGX 8250 switches and BPX switches.

Figure 19-2 *PVCs in a Network with MGX and BPX Switches*

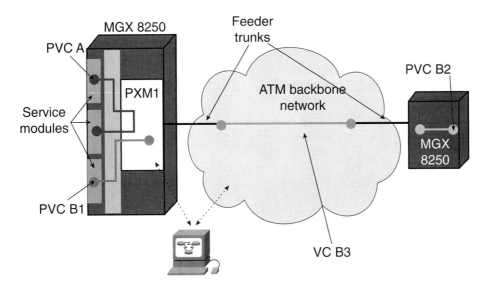

PVC A represents a local connection between two service modules on the same MGX 8250 concentrator. PVC B1 is a feeder PVC that terminates at the feeder trunk port on the PXM1. This forms one segment of a multisegment connection that links service module ports on two different MGX 8250 switches. Similarly, the MGX 8250 switch on the right has another feeder PVC segment, PVC B2. The two MGX segments are linked by a third segment, VC B3, in the attached ATM backbone network that transports traffic between the switches. VC B3 could be an SPVC or PVC or could comprise several PVCs. The figure also shows the feeder trunks that extend the backbone segment to the PXM1 trunk ports.

SPVC Definition

A Soft Permanent Virtual Circuit (SPVC) provides a means of providing PVC-like characteristics as viewed from the end systems while using a dynamic routing mechanism within the ATM backbone. Figure 19-3 highlights the generic characteristics of SPVCs.

NOTE   Cisco uses Portable Autoroute to manage PVCs, making them similar to SPVCs.

Figure 19-3 *Soft Permanent Virtual Circuit (SPVC)*

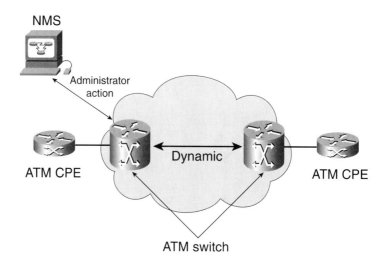

SPVCs are configured similarly to PVCs but do not strictly reserve bandwidth in the backbone switches when the connection is added—only when data is transported across the connection. However, in most networks, some sort of allocation scheme is required to monitor and control routing resources. The major advantage of SPVCs over PVCs is that they dynamically reroute based on changes in traffic parameters and network failures.

An end-to-end SPVC comprises three distinct segments. At each end, an ATM PVC is provisioned between each CPE end system and the ingress port on a network switch. In the middle, a switched connection is initiated administratively to provide a third SPVC segment between the switch ports. Because the SPVC must be provisioned manually, there is no need for the end systems to signal a setup request. Figure 19-4 shows an SPVC between two MGX 8850-PXM45 ATM interfaces.

In the MGX 8850-PXM45 (Release 2), the SPVCs use Private Network-Network Interface Specification Version 1.0 (PNNI 1.0) for route selection. PNNI 1.0 includes both routing and signaling protocols. The routing protocol is based on dynamic link-state routing similar to OSPF, and signaling is based on the widely used ATM Forum UNI standards.

In an MGX 8850-PXM45 network, SPVCs can be provisioned and managed using either the switch-level CLI or the graphical Connection Manager application provided with the CWM network management system (NMS).

NOTE   SPVCs are *not* supported on PXM1-based MGX switches running Release 1.x firmware.

Figure 19-4 *SPVC Between Two MGX 8850-PXM45 ATM Interfaces*

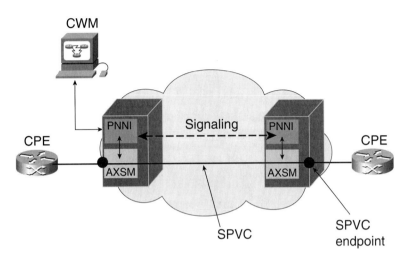

SVC Definition

Switched Virtual Circuits (SVCs) are dynamically established in an ATM network for on-demand connections. They are set up as needed and are torn down when no longer required. As a simple analogy, you might compare an SVC to a call in the public switched telephone network. To initiate a call, you (the calling party) must have the telephone number (address) of the person you want to reach, and the network must have the intelligence to determine the best path to reach the called party. Figure 19-5 highlights the generic characteristics of SVCs.

Figure 19-5 *Switched Virtual Circuit (SVC)*

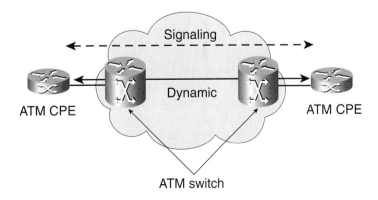

Call setup starts when an ATM endpoint signals that a connection should be established to another ATM endpoint. An endpoint is a user device outside the MGX 8850-PXM45 network, such as a router. Particular traffic parameters and QoS characteristics can be included in the signaling request. Successful connection establishment occur only when the called endpoint accepts and confirms the call. As soon as the call is complete, the SVC is taken down, and the network resources are freed up for use by another call.

Given the presence in the network of an active signaling and routing mechanism such as PNNI, setup and teardown of an SVC requires no administrative intervention. SVCs are flexible, simple to administer, and relatively tolerant of network disruptions, but they do require both a carefully planned ATM addressing scheme and an efficient dynamic routing protocol such as PNNI. In the MGX 8850-PXM45 switch, the PNNI software runs on the PXM controller.

The process starts with a Call Setup Request message from the CPE. The request is routed across the UNI interface on the AXSM card and is directed to the PNNI controller. The controller software attempts to route the call across the PNNI network to the destination port. From here, the setup request is relayed via UNI messaging to the called CPE. If the called CPE accepts the call, a Connect message is returned to the ingress PNNI controller, following the same path as the original messages. The controller then activates the connection and signals the calling CPE that the call is in place.

NOTE   SVCs are *not* supported on PXM1-based MGX switches running Release 1.x firmware.

PVC Example

Great Western Aerospace (GWA) Inc. is an aircraft and space vehicle manufacturer with major production facilities in four locations in the Western United States (see Figure 19-6). GWA is the result of several industry mergers in which the existing communications networks of the individual companies have been merged or grafted onto existing networks with little long-range planning. Consequently, GWA is struggling with the management and scalability problems associated with having several different network infrastructures based on incompatible technologies.

GWA has decided to consolidate its multiple separate networks into one ATM multiservice network based on MGX 8250 concentrators. Traffic from each of the four locations is concentrated at local MGX 8250 concentrators. ATM trunks at OC-12c rates to a central ATM switch connect the four concentrators that are located in the San Francisco facility. The new network architecture is shown in Figure 19-7.

Figure 19-6 *PVC Example*

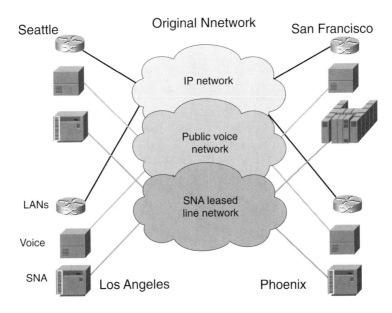

Figure 19-7 *GWA's New Network*

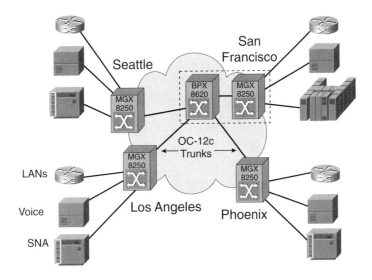

Each concentrator includes a set of service modules that convert incoming traffic, such as IP packets or SDLC frames, into ATM cells. The cells are then switched within the MGX 8250 concentrators for local traffic or are directed onto the backbone trunk for transmission to the San Francisco backbone switch. The interconnections between the MGX 8250 user ports are PVCs, set up by the network administrator to support anticipated traffic patterns within the network. For example, digital voice or circuit emulation PVCs would connect the four PBXs, with an appropriate number of voice channels between each PBX pair to support the required service level.

By using MGX 8250 concentrators, GWA can maintain the user equipment essentially unaltered and realizes significant cost savings in line charges and support personnel by having only a single backbone network to maintain and administer. By adding additional service modules or trunk ports to the switches, GWA can handle anticipated future growth in traffic and services.

SPVC Example

ABC Bank has four main sites in Canada. All of their traffic is routed through Cisco Series 7000 routers with ATM connectivity through a public ATM network, as shown in Figure 19-8.

Figure 19-8 *SPVC Example*

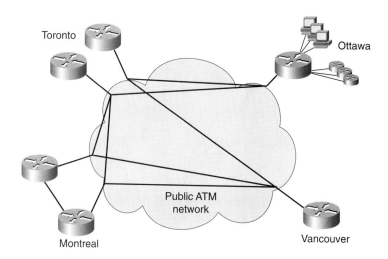

ABC Bank's business is growing, and it has decided to install its own ATM backbone network. ABC Bank hopes to take advantage of future MGX 8850-PXM45 features, especially to fulfill its voice needs.

Without redesigning the existing ABC Bank network, MGX 8850-PXM45 switches are installed at the network's demarcation points. SPVCs are created in the MGX 8850-PXM45 network to replace those that were in the public ATM network. In addition, full-mesh connectivity between the main routers is possible without significant added expense. ABC Bank can consolidate equipment to take advantage of the MGX 8850-PXM45 switches' high port density. Additionally, the bank is positioning itself for future growth and the addition of voice traffic. Figure 19-9 shows ABC Bank's network after the MGX 8850-PXM45 switches have been installed.

Figure 19-9 *ABC Bank's New Network*

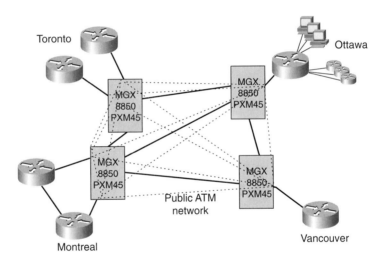

SVC Example

The GoodFoods Company has been leasing bandwidth from its local carrier, TelcoUK, to send sales, inventory, and production information to the main office. This information is usually sent three times a day during the week and once daily on weekends and holidays. Figure 19-10 shows how the network is set up.

Figure 19-10 *SVC Example*

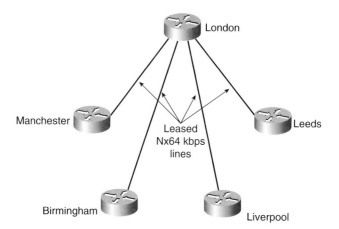

TelcoUK has just installed an MGX 8850-PXM45 network to provide customers with on-demand ATM services. GoodFoods is planning a change in how it does business, so it requires that its sites have higher-speed connectivity with each other. Having leased lines does not meet GoodFoods' bandwidth requirements when it needs the network, and it is paying for them even when they are not in use. To meet GoodFoods' needs, TelcoUK has offered GoodFoods SVC services in its ATM network. Figure 19-11 shows an example of GoodFoods' SVC connectivity.

Figure 19-11 *GoodFoods' New Network*

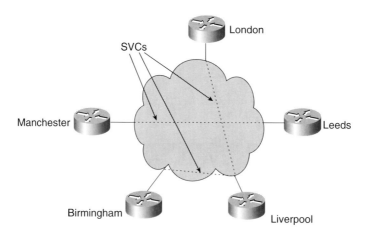

NOTE   Connectivity between sites is possible at any time.

Connection Types in the Backbone Network

When adding an end-to-end connection terminating on an MGX service module, you must also create a connection through the ATM backbone network. The MGX connection characteristics determine the type of connection that is needed in the ATM backbone.

This section describes the ATM connection types available on the BPX and MGX 8850-PXM45 switches used to support MGX connections.

BPX Connection Types

The BPX switch supports the following connection types:

- Constant bit rate (CBR)
- Real-time variable bit rate (rt-VBR)
- Nonreal-time variable bit rate (nrt-VBR)
- Unspecified bit rate (UBR)
- **Available bit rate standard (ABRSTD)**—ABR per the ATM Forum standard, with the option of enabling virtual source-virtual destination (VSVD) congestion control.
- **Available bit rate with ForeSight (ABRFST)**—Prestandard ABR with Cisco ForeSight congestion control.
- **ATM-Frame Relay (ATFR)**—ATM-to-Frame Relay network interworking.
- **ATM-Frame Relay with ForeSight (ATFST)**—ATM-to-Frame Relay network interworking with ForeSight congestion control.
- **ATM-Frame Relay transparent (ATFT)**—ATM-to-Frame Relay transparent service interworking for BPX-IGX connections.
- **ATM-Frame Relay transparent with ForeSight (ATFTFST)**—ATM-to-Frame Relay transparent service interworking with ForeSight congestion control for BPX-IGX connections.
- **ATM-Frame Relay translated (ATFX)**—ATM-to-Frame Relay translated service interworking for BPX-IGX connections.
- **ATM-Frame Relay translated with ForeSight (ATFXFST)**—ATM-to-Frame Relay translated service interworking with ForeSight congestion control for BPX-IGX connections.

MGX 8850-PXM45 Connection Types

The MGX 8850-PXM45 switch supports the following connection types:

- CBR
- rt-VBR

- nrt-VBR
- UBR
- Available Bit Rate (ABR)

Connection Types for MGX Feeder Connections

The function of the connection in the ATM backbone network is to provide bandwidth for the traffic and to route the traffic to the destination MGX feeder switch. It is necessary to create the appropriate backbone connection for each pair of MGX connection segments so that the traffic is processed with like traffic. For example, a VBR connection should be created in the backbone network to support MGX VBR ATM connections.

Table 19-1 lists the required connection types and connection configuration parameters for BPX and MGX 8850-PXM45 connections. Use these characteristics when adding a backbone connection to support MGX feeder connections.

NOTE If you're using standalone MGX feeders, the connection type in the backbone network should be the same as that specified for MGX 8850-PXM45 switches.

Table 19-1 uses the following abbreviations:

- **PCR**—The connection's configured peak cell rate
- **MCR**—The connection's configured minimum cell rate
- **MIR**—The Frame Relay connection's minimum information rate

Table 19-1 *Connection Types for MGX Feeder Connections*

MGX Feeder	BPX	MGX 8850-PXM45	PCR	MCR	Example
Circuit emulation	CBR	CBR	Data rate/ payload	—	One timeslot (64 kbps) with 20-byte partially filled cells. PCR = 400 cells per second (cps).
Frame Relay	ATFR	nrt-VBR	MIR × scale	—	A 42 cps (16 kbps) MIR and a scaling factor of 120 percent. PCR = 50 cps.

Table 19-1 *Connection Types for MGX Feeder Connections (Continued)*

MGX Feeder	BPX	MGX 8850-PXM45	PCR	MCR	Example
Frame Relay with ForeSight	ATFST	ABR	Greater than the MCR	MIR × scale	A 63 cps (24 bps) MIR and a scaling factor of 110 percent. MCR = 69 cps.
ATM	ATFST	ABR	Greater than the MCR	MIR × scale	A 63 cps (24 bps) MIR and a scaling factor of 110 percent. MCR = 69 cps.
Voice over ATM	CBR or rt-VBR	CBR or rt-VBR	Data rate/ payload	—	—

The MIR in Table 19-1 is in cells per second (cps). If you are using a MIR in bps, divide the value by 384 to convert it to cps. The scaling factor in Table 19-1 for Frame Relay connections accommodates for the inefficiency of the frame-to-cell conversion, which is the result of creating partially filled cells. In most cases, a 120 percent scaling factor is sufficient. If extremely small frames (less than 100 bytes) are used, a higher scaling factor might be required.

MGX Connections

A *connection* is an end-to-end virtual circuit that carries user data from one interface to another in the network. In an MGX network, all connections carry ATM cells. These cells might have been created on an MGX service module. For example, Frame Relay frames are segmented into ATM cells by the FRSM card. A connection is defined by its termination points (usually a port on a service module), its type (voice, Frame Relay, and so on), and its characteristics (rate, cell payload size, compression, and so on).

Network Connections

Connections in the MGX network comprise multiple connection segments. A connection *segment* is one portion of the end-to-end connection, such as a connection segment from an MGX service module port to the PXM1 trunk interface.

MGX connections include the following:

- Three-segment connection in a tiered network comprising MGX feeders and BPX or MGX 8850-PXM45 backbone switches
- Local (or DAX) connection between two interfaces on the same MGX switch

- Multisegment connection between standalone MGX switches
- Two-segment connection in a tiered network between the MGX feeder and the BPX or MGX 8850-PXM45 backbone switch
- Three-segment connection in a tiered network comprising MGX and IGX feeders and BPX backbone switches
- Two-segment connection in a tiered network comprising MGX feeders and BPX and IGX backbone switches

The different MGX connections are shown in Figure 19-12. Each connection segment (shown as a line with endpoint dots) requires a CLI command to create. For example, to create a local connection on the 8250 switch, you must type two commands—one to add each connection segment. If you're using CWM, you can add all connections except those on the standalone MGX switch using the Connection Manager graphical user interface (GUI) application.

Figure 19-12 *MGX Connections*

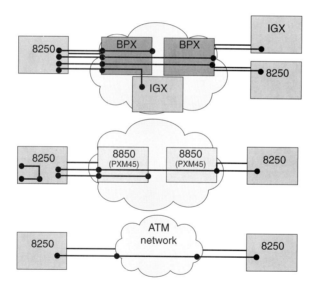

Slave and Master Connection Definitions

The MGX switch has slave and master connections, as shown in Figure 19-13. When adding a connection segment using the CLI, you must specify if the connection is a slave or a master.

Figure 19-13 *Slave and Master Connections*

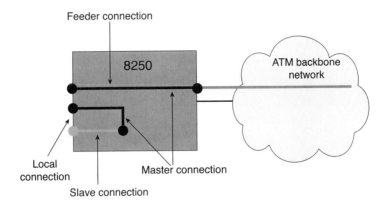

A *slave* connection is an endpoint without a specified destination. A *master* connection includes an endpoint and information about the destination. The role of the master connection is to route the connection from one end to the other.

A *feeder* connection is one that originates on a service module such as the FRSM and terminates on the PXM1 trunk attached to the ATM backbone network. Feeder connections are always master connections.

A *local* (or DAX) connection is one that originates and terminates on a service module such as the AUSM. A local connection has a slave connection at one end and a master connection at the other. You must add the slave end first before you can add the master end.

Commands for Adding, Configuring, and Displaying MGX 8850-PXM45 Connections

This section describes the commands used to add, configure, and display connections using the CLI on the MGX 8850-PXM45 switch that supports MGX feeder connections. This section does not attempt to provide an in-depth explanation of all connection features. Only SPVCs are discussed.

This section covers the following commands:

- **addcon**—Creates a new master or slave segment for a connection.
- **delcon**—Deletes a master or slave segment.
- **delcons**—Deletes a range of connection endpoints.
- **cnfcon**—Changes the connection parameters, including policing and queuing.
- **dspcons**—Lists all SPVCs that terminate on the AXSM card.
- **dspcon**—Lists detailed configuration information for a connection.

Each port on an AXSM card has a unique identifier ranging from 1 to 60. When you enter port commands at the AXSM command line, it is usually sufficient to provide the identifier, which is called the *interface number* in the command syntax and examples in this section.

However, when you use PXM45 commands that reference AXSM PNNI ports, you must provide an extended identifier, which is called the *port ID*. It has the format *<slot:subslot.port:subport>*, where

- *slot*—The slot number of the AXSM card.

- *subslot*—The back card on the AXSM. Use 1 for the back card in the upper bay and 2 for the back card in the lower bay. The default is 1.

- *port*—The physical line number on the AXSM card. The range is from 1 to 8, depending on the card type.

- *subport*—The logical port (or interface) number. The range is 1 to 60.

Add Connection Command

You use the **addcon** command to provision SPVCs using the CLI. To provision an SPVC, you perform the **addcon** command twice—once for each of the connection's two endpoints. One endpoint is the slave, and the other is the master. The master endpoint is the owner of the connection after it is established. The master endpoint is responsible for initiating the rerouting process if the SPVC needs to be rerouted in the event of a network disruption.

Here is the **addcon** command syntax:

```
addcon <interface number> <vpi> <vci> <service type> <mastership> [-slave
    <atmaddress.vpi.vci>] [-lpcr <local PCR>] [-rpcr <remote PCR>]
    [-lscr <local SCR>] [-rscr <remote SCR>] [-lmbs <local MBS>]
    [-rmbs <remote MBS>] [-lcdvt <local CDVT>] [-rcdvt <remote CDVT>]
    [-lcdv <local CDV>] [-rcdv <remote CDV>] [-lctd <local CTD>]
    [-rctd <remote CTD>] [-cc <OAM option>] [-stat <statistics option>]
    [-frame <frame discard option>] [-aw <admin weight>]
```

A number of the optional parameters for the **addcon** command have preassigned values derived from the Service Class Template (SCT) applied to the card (with **cnfcdsct**) and the logical port (with **addport**). You might not need to modify the default values. Use the **dspcdsct** and **dspportsct** commands to view the preassigned parameter values for card and port SCTs, respectively.

Parameter options for **addcon** are as follows. Except where stated, each parameter must be defined for the slave and master endpoints.

- *interface number*—The interface number for the AXSM logical port. The range is 1 to 60.

- *vpi*—The VPI for this endpoint. The range is 0 to 255 for UNI and 0 to 4095 for NNI.

- *vci*—The VCI for this endpoint. The range is 32 to 65535 for an SPVC. 0 is the only valid VCI value for a soft permanent virtual path (SPVP).

- *service type*—The requested ATM service type for this connection. For each service type, enter the number in parentheses: cbr1 (**1**), cbr2 (**11**), cbr3 (**12**), vbr1rt (**2**), vbr2rt (**3**), vbr3rt (**4**), vbr1nrt (**5**), vbr2nrt (**6**), vbr3nrt (**7**), ubr1 (**8**), ubr2 (**9**), abrstd (**10**). The service type you select causes appropriate preassigned optional parameters to be applied for this connection as defined by the card and port SCTs. The service type must be the same for the slave and master endpoints.

- *mastership*—Defines the endpoint as a slave or master. Enter **1** for master and **2** for slave.

NOTE	You must add an endpoint before you define it as a slave or master.

- **-slave**—For the master endpoint only, follow the **-slave** keyword with the parameter *atmaddress.vpi.vci*, where *atmaddress* is the slave endpoint's 20-byte ATM address, *vpi* is the slave endpoint's configured VPI value, and *vci* is the slave endpoint's VCI.

NOTE	The periods are required in *atmaddress.vpi.vci*. When adding a slave connection, the *atmaddress.vpi.vci* is output by the CLI. You must enter this exact value when you add the master end.

A number of the following optional parameters have local and remote options for the same parameter, such as Peak Cell Rate (PCR). For these parameters, you are required to use the same parameter value at both the master and slave endpoints. For example, if when adding the slave endpoint you set the local PCR (**lpcr**) to, say, 10,000 cps, you must ensure that the remote PCR (**rpcr**) at the master endpoint is set to the same cell rate.

- **-lpcr**—The local PCR. The range is from 7 to 5,651,320 cps.
- **-rpcr**—The remote PCR. The range is from 7 to 5,651,320 cps.
- **-lscr**—The local Sustained Cell Rate (SCR). The range is from 7 to 5,651,320 cps.
- **-rscr**—The remote SCR. The range is from 7 to 5,651,320 cps.
- **-lmbs**—The local Maximum Burst Size (MBS) at the peak rate. The range is 1 to 5,000,000 cells.
- **-rmbs**—The remote MBS at the peak rate. The range is 1 to 5,000,000 cells.

- **-lcdvt**—The local Cell Delay Variation Tolerance (CDVT). It represents the acceptable amount of change in the variance of the cell transfer delay. The range is 1 to 5,000,000 microseconds.

- **-rcdvt**—The remote Cell Delay Variation Tolerance. It represents the acceptable amount of change in the variance of the cell transfer delay. The range is 1 to 5,000,000 microseconds.

- **-lcdv**—The local Cell Delay Variation (CDV). The range is 1 to 16,777,215 microseconds.

- **-rcdv**—The remote CDV. The range is 1 to 16,777,215 microseconds.

- **-lctd**—The local Cell Transfer Delay (CTD). The range is 1 to 65,535 milliseconds.

- **-rctd**—The remote CTD. The range is 1 to 65,535 milliseconds.

- **-cc**—This option enables or disables the flow of Operation, Administration, and Maintenance Continuity Check (OAM CC) cells on the connection. Enter 1 to enable or 0 to disable. The default is disabled.

- **-stat**—This option enables or disables statistics collection for the connection. Enter 1 to enable or 0 to disable. The default is disabled.

- **-frame**—This option enables or disables frame discard for the connection. Enter 1 to enable or 0 to disable. The default is disabled.

- **-aw**—This option assigns an administrative weight, or a maximum cost, to the connection. When the connection is routed or rerouted, the end-to-end cost of each possible route is compared to the configured maximum cost, and the lowest-cost route is selected. Any route with a cost above the administrative weight is not considered. The value is entered as an integer from 0 to 2,147,483,647. If you do not enter a value for maximum cost, the default value of –1 is used. This means that the lowest-cost available route is selected.

NOTE Setting the maximum cost to an unrealistically low value might prevent the connection from being routed. For reference, the default cost per link is 5040, which can be modified with the **cnfpnni-intf** command.

For example, type **addcon 5 23 1002 11 2 -lpcr 1000 -rpcr 2000** to add a slave endpoint to logical port 5, with service type cbr2, a VPI of 23, a VCI of 1023, a local PCR of 1000 cps, and a remote PCR of 5000 cps. To configure a master endpoint for the same connection, type **addcon 6 10 501 11 1 -slave 450073130000001010101010101000000000000100.23.1002**. In this case, the endpoint is logical port 6, the VPI is 10, and the VCI is 501.

Delete Connection Command

Use the **delcon** command to delete a connection endpoint. To completely remove a connection, you must delete both the local and remote endpoints by using the **delcon** command twice—once each at the local and remote AXSM ports. You must delete the master endpoint before deleting the slave.

Here is the **delcon** command syntax:

```
delcon <interface number> <vpi> <vci>
```

The parameter options are as follows:

- *interface number*—The interface number for the AXSM logical port. The range is 1 to 60.

- *vpi*—The VPI for this endpoint. The range is 0 to 255 for UNI and 0 to 4095 for NNI.

- *vci*—The VCI for this endpoint. The range is 32 to 65535 for an SPVC. 0 is the only valid VCI value for an SPVP.

For example, type **delcon 5 23 1002** to remove a connection endpoint with a VPI of 23 and a VCI of 1023 from logical port 5. The system responds to a successful endpoint deletion with a "Deletion successful" message.

Delete Connections Command

Use the **delcons** command to delete a range of connection endpoints on a single AXSM card. To completely remove a range of connections, you need to delete both the local and remote endpoints by using the **delcons** command twice—once each at the local and remote AXSM ports.

Here is the **delcons** command syntax:

```
delcons <interface number> <vpi> <vci> [-num <number>] [-verbose <option>]
```

The parameter options are as follows:

- *interface number*—The interface number for the AXSM logical port. The range is 1 to 60.

- *vpi*—The VPI for this endpoint. The range is 0 to 255 for UNI and 0 to 4095 for NNI.

- *vci*—The VCI for this endpoint. The range is 32 to 65535 for an SPVC. 0 is the only valid VCI value for an SPVP.

- **-num**—The value *number* specifies the number of connections to delete, starting from the connection defined by *vpi* and *vci*.

- **-verbose**—If enabled, this option causes the system to display the endpoint deleted in turn. 1 enables and 0 disables.

For example, type **delcons 5 23 1002 5 1** to remove five connection endpoints on this AXSM starting at the endpoint with a VPI of 23 and a VCI of 1002. The system deletes this connection and up to four other connections in ascending order of VPI and VCI. If less than four connections with higher VPI/VCI values exist, only those connections are deleted.

Configure Connection Command

Use the **cnfcon** command to modify parameters for an existing connection. You must execute the **cnfcon** command at the master endpoint.

Here is the **cnfcon** command syntax:

```
cnfcon <interface number> <vpi> <vci> [-lpcr <local PCR>] [-rpcr <remote PCR>]
   [-lscr <local SCR>] [-rscr <remote SCR>] [-lmbs <local MBS>]
   [-rmbs <remote MBS>] [-cdvt <local CDVT>] [-lcdv <local CDV>]
   -rcdv <remote CDV>] [-lctd <local CTD>] [-rctd <remote CTD>]
   [-cc <OAM option>] [-stat <statistics option>]
   [-frame <frame discard option>] [-mc <admin weight>]
```

The parameter options are the same as those described for the **addcon** command.

For example, type **cnfcon 5 23 1002 -lpcr 500 -rpcr 1000** to set the PCR cell rate at the master (local) endpoint to 500 cps and at the slave (remote) endpoint to 100 cps for the connection terminating at logical port 5 with VPI = 23 and VCI = 1002.

Display Connections Command

The **dspcons** command is used to display summary status and configuration information for connections on a switch. This command may be entered at the active PXM45 or at any AXSM on the switch; no additional parameters are required. When issued on the PXM45, the **dspcons** command lists all SPVC/SPVPs on the switch. When this command is issued on an AXSM, the display is limited to connections that terminate on that card.

The **dspcons** output differs depending on whether the command is issued on an AXSM card or the active PXM45, as shown in Example 19-1.

Example 19-1 **dspcons** *Output on AXSM and PXM45 Cards*

```
pop20one.10.AXSM.a > dspcons

record    Identifier   Type   SrvcType   M/S    Upld     Admn   Alarm
------    ----------   ----   --------   ---    ----     ----   -----
     0   04 0100 00100  VCC       cbr1    M   0167bf01     UP    none
     1   05 0021 00210  VCC       cbr1    M   016d3fa8     UP    none

pop20one.10.AXSM.a > cc 7

(session redirected)

pop20one.7.PXM.a > dspcons
```

Example 19-1 **dspcons** *Output on AXSM and PXM45 Cards (Continued)*

```
Local Port        Vpi.Vci  Remote Port       Vpi.Vci  State   Owner
--------------------------+--------------------------+-------+------
10:2.1:5            21 210   Routed             22 220   OK      MASTER
Local  Addr: 47.00918100000000107b65f33c.0000010a1805.00
Remote Addr: 47.00918100000000001a531c2a.00001a531c2a.01
10:2.2:4           100 100   Routed            100 100   OK      MASTER
Local  Addr: 47.00918100000000107b65f33c.0000010a1804.00
Remote Addr: 47.00918100000000001a531c2a.000001011804.00
```

The following information is provided when the **dspcons** command is issued on an AXSM card:

- **Record**—An internal system identifier for the connection endpoint. Record numbers are assigned sequentially as new connections are created.

- **Identifier**—Displays the interface number, VPI, and VCI for this endpoint.

- **Type**—Indicates whether the connection is a Virtual Channel Connection (VCC) or Virtual Path Connection (VPC).

- **Service type**—The configured service type as defined in the **addcon** command.

- **Upload**—A timestamp value encoded in hexadecimal. This timestamp is used by the Cisco WAN Manager application.

- **Administrative status**—Up or Down.

- **Alarm status**—The connection's alarm status.

The following information is provided when the **dspcons** command is issued on the active PXM45 card:

- **Local port**—The local port ID in the format *slot:bay.line.logical port.*

- **Local VPI.VCI**—The VPI and VCI at the local end of the connection.

- **Remote port**—The remote port ID in the format *slot:bay.line.logical port.*

- **Remote VPI.VCI**—The VPI and VCI at the remote end of the connection.

- **State**—The connection state: OK or Failed.

- **Owner**—Indicates whether the local endpoint is the master or the slave.

- **Local address**—ATM Network Service Access Point (NSAP) address for the local endpoint.

- **Remote address**—ATM NSAP address for the remote endpoint.

Display Connection Command

The **dspcon** command is used to display detailed status and configuration information for a particular SPVC or SPVP. This command may be entered at the active PXM45 or at any AXSM on the switch. The command syntax differs slightly, as follows:

On the AXSM: **dspcon** *<interface number> <vpi> <vci>*
On the PXM45: **dspcon** *<port ID> <vpi> <vci>*

The **dspcon** output differs depending on whether the command is issued on an AXSM card or on the active PXM45. For an AXSM card, you can use the **dspcon** command to view only connections that terminate on that card. Example 19-2 shows the output of the command issued on an AXSM card.

Example 19-2 **dspcon** *Output on an AXSM Card*

```
pop20one.10.AXSM.a > dspcon 5 21 210
----------------------------------------------------------------
Local   :              NSAP  Address                 vpi      vci
(M)       47009181000000000107B65F33C0000010A180500   21      210
Remote  :              NSAP  Address                 vpi      vci
(S)       470091810000000000001A531C2A00001A531C2A01  22      220
----------------------------------------------------------------
Conn. Type    :    VCC                 Admn Status  :  ADMN-UP
Service Type  :    cbr1                Oper Status  :     OK
Controller    :     2                  Record #     :      1
----------------------------------------------------------------
Local PCR     :     50                 Remote PCR   :     50
Local SCR     :     N/A                Remote SCR   :     N/A
Local CDV     :     -1                 Remote CDV   :     -1
Local CTD     :     -1                 Remote CTD   :     -1
Local MBS     :     N/A                Remote MBS   :     N/A
Max Cost      :     -1                 Frame discard:     N
Local CDVT    :   250000
----------------------------------------------------------------
OAM CC Config : DISABLED               Statistics   : DISABLED
----------------------------------------------------------------
Loopback Type : No  Lpbk ¦ Dir: N/A    ¦ Status: No Lpbk ¦ RTD:    0us
----------------------------------------------------------------
Port side Tx  :     AIS                Swth side Tx : normal
Port side Rx  :  normal                Swth side Rx : normal
----------------------------------------------------------------
I-AIS/RDI   E-AIS/RDI   CONDITIONED   CCFAIL   IfFail   Mismatch  LMI-ABIT
   NO         NO           NO           NO       NO        NO        NO
----------------------------------------------------------------
```

The information provided when the **dspcon** command is issued on an AXSM card is organized into several sections:

- Local and remote endpoint identifiers:

    — Mastership of endpoint—Master (M) or slave (S).

    — NSAP address.

    — VPI and VCI.

- Provisioning and status parameters:

    — Connection type—VCC or VPC.

    — Service type—As defined by the **addcon** command.

    — Controller ID—The network controller ID, fixed at 2 for the PNNI controller in Release 2.

    — Administrative status—Up or Down.

    — Operational status—OK or Failed.

    — Record number—Internal connection identifier.

- Local and remote traffic management parameters:

    — PCR, SCR, CDV, MBS, and CDVT—Unless modified with the **addcon** or **cnfcon** command, these fields contain the default values assigned by the service class template (SCT) for the AXSM card. A value of –1 means that the parameter was not specified. N/A means that the parameter does not apply to the service type.

    — Frame discard—Specifies whether frame discard is enabled. Y (yes) or N (no).

- Management option settings:

    — OAM continuity check—Enabled or disabled.

    — Statistics collection—Enabled or disabled.

- Loopback status:

    — Loopback type and status—Indicates whether a software loop is in place on the connection.

    — Round-trip delay—Indicates the round-trip delay in milliseconds as measured by the **tstdelay** command.

- Alarm and fault indicators:

    — Port side

    — Switch side

— Ingress AIS/RDI

— Egress AIS/RDI

— Conditioned

— CC failure

— Interface failure

— Mismatch

— LMI A-bit

Example 19-3 shows the output of the **dspcon** command issued on the active PXM45 for the same connection.

Example 19-3 **dspcon** *Output on a PXM45 Card*

```
pop20one.7.PXM.a > dspcon 10:2.1:5 21 210

Port                  Vpi Vci                    Owner     State
----------------------------------------------------------------
Local  10:2.1:5        21.210                    MASTER    OK
        Address: 47.00918100000000107b65f33c.0000010a1805.00
Remote Routed          22.220                    SLAVE     OK
        Address: 47.00918100000000001a531c2a.00001a531c2a.01


------------------- Provisioning Parameters -------------------
Connection Type: VCC          Cast Type: Point-to-Point
Service Category: CBR         Conformance: CBR.1
Bearer Class: BCOB-X
Last Fail Cause: SPVC Established              Attempts: 0
Continuity Check: Disabled    Frame Discard: Disabled
L-Utils: 100   R-Utils: 100   Max Cost: -1   Routing Cost: 0

---------- Traffic Parameters ----------
Tx PCR:  50          Rx PCR:  50
Tx CDV:  N/A         Rx CDV:  N/A
Tx CTD:  N/A         Rx CTD:  N/A
```

Additional information is provided when the **dspcon** command is issued on the active PXM45:

- Remote endpoint identifiers:

    — Connection status at remote endpoint.

- Provisioning and status parameters:

    — Bearer Class—Reserved for future voice service.

    — Last Fail Cause—If the connection has failed since its initial establishment, a failure cause is indicated here.

— Attempts—Indicates the number of attempts, if any, the system has made to re-establish a failed SPVC.

— Local and remote utilization—Defaults to 100% and cannot be changed in Release 2.0.

— Max Cost—The maximum cost per link (administrative weight), as configured with the **addcon** or **cnfcon** command. A value of –1 indicates that the administrative weight is not defined, in which case maximum cost is not a factor in route selection.

— Routing Cost—The product of the number of links in a connection route and the Max Cost. A routing cost of 0 indicates that a value for Max Cost has not been defined.

How to Add a Connection in an MGX 8850-PXM45 Network

This section describes the procedures you follow to create an SPVC using the MGX 8550-PXM45 CLI.

Step 1   Using the SuperUser ID and password, log into the active PXM45 on the MGX 8850-PXM45 switch that is connected to your MGX feeder. This begins the CLI session.

Step 2   Type **cc** *<slot>*, where *slot* is the card slot number of the AXSM that your MGX feeder is attached to. This transfers the CLI session to the AXSM card.

Step 3   Type **dspfdrs** and verify the port number associated with your MGX feeder. This lists all feeders attached to the card.

Step 4   Type **addcon** *<interface number> <vpi> <vci> <service type>* **2** [*parameters*], where *interface number* is the logical port number, *service type* is the ATM service type, and **2** indicates the slave endpoint. This adds the slave endpoint for the SPVC. The system responds with "Slave endpoint added successfully" and displays the slave endpoint ID in the format *atmaddress.vpi.vci*. Take note of the slave endpoint ID for later use when configuring the master endpoint. It is a good idea to copy the *atmaddress.vpi.vci* to your computer's Clipboard or a separate text file to reduce the chance of errors when creating the master connection.

Step 5   Type **dspcon** *<interface number> <vpi> <vci>*. This displays a summary listing of the SPVCs terminating on this AXSM card. Verify that the slave endpoint you just configured is configured correctly. If you need to change the connection, use the **cnfcon** command.

Step 6 Repeat Steps 1 through 4 at the MGX 8850-PXM45 that will support the other end of the SPVC, the master endpoint. This creates and configures the master end of the connection. Use the slave endpoint ID (*atmaddress.vpi.vci*) that you saved in Step 4 when creating the master connection.

Step 7 Type **addcon** <*interface number*> <*vpi*> <*vci*> <*service type*> **1** <**-slave** *slave endpoint ID*> [*parameters*], where *interface type* is the logical port number, *service type* is the ATM service type, **1** indicates the master endpoint, and the *slave endpoint ID* is as previously noted. This adds the master endpoint for the SPVC. The system responds with "Master endpoint added successfully" and displays the master endpoint ID in the format *atmaddress.vpi.vci*.

Step 8 Type **dspcon** <*interface number*> <*vpi*> <*vci*>. This displays a summary listing of the SPVCs terminating on this AXSM card. Verify that the master endpoint you just configured is configured correctly. Make sure that the remote QoS parameters on this end match the local QoS parameters at the other end, and vice versa. These include the PCR, CDV, and CDT. If they do not match, the connection will not route. Use the **cnfcon** command to make any changes.

Step 9 Type **dspcon** <*interface number*> <*vpi*> <*vci*> for the master endpoint. This displays detailed information for the SPVC, including both master and slave endpoints. Verify that the slave NSAP address is correct and that the SPVC operational status is OK.

Step 10 Type **cc** <*slot*>, where *slot* is the slot number of the active PXM45. This displays the command-line prompt for the PXM45.

Step 11 Type **dspcon** <*port ID*> <*vpi*> <*vci*> for the master endpoint. This displays detailed information for the SPVC, including both master and slave endpoints. Verify that both endpoint NSAP addresses are displayed and that the Last fail Cause field indicates "SPVC established."

Step 12 Type **bye**. This terminates your CLI session and returns you to the login prompt.

You have completed the steps necessary for adding an SPVC in an MGX 8550-PXM45 network.

Circuit Emulation Ports

A circuit emulation port is a virtual interface on the CESM that sends and receives traffic to and from a single end-user device. A port is not the same as a line, which is the physical transport facility for user traffic. There are two types of ports: structured and unstructured.

An *unstructured* port uses all timeslots on the line. The signaling and framing bits are sent transparently through the network with the data.

A *structured* port uses one or more timeslots and interprets the framing and signaling bits. The framing bits are used to determine the timeslot boundaries for multiplexing and demultiplexing. The signaling bits are extracted on ingress and reinserted on egress. Signaling bits can be used to start and stop data transfer based on an on- or off-hook condition. Figure 19-14 shows both structured and unstructured circuit emulation ports on a CESM.

Figure 19-14 *Structured and Unstructured Circuit Emulation Ports on a CESM*

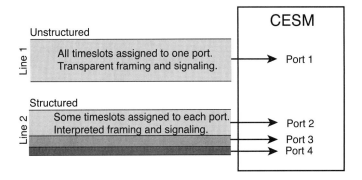

Support of Unstructured and Structured Ports

The following card modules support unstructured circuit emulation ports:

- CESM-8T1
- CESM-8E1
- CESM-8T1-C
- CESM-8E1-C
- CESM-T3
- CESM-E3

The following card modules support structured circuit emulation ports:

- CESM-8T1-C
- CESM-8E1-C

The C designator that follows the card module name indicates that the card supports channelized ports. On a channelized card, multiple ports are supported on a single line; on an unchannelized card, only one port is supported per line.

Unstructured Example

You would use an unstructured circuit emulation port to transport the circuit data for an entire T1, E1, T3, or E3 line. If you want to use the MGX network to tunnel the trunk line between two T1 multiplexers, you need to configure unstructured ports at each end on the CESMs. Figure 19-15 shows two CESM ports and the attached equipment.

Figure 19-15 *Unstructured Circuit Emulation Ports*

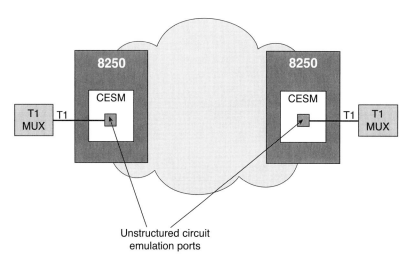

Unstructured circuit
emulation ports

Structured Example

You would use a structured circuit emulation port to transport the circuit data for a portion of a T1 or E1 line. All structured ports are configured at speeds that are multiples of 64 kbps. In other words, a structured port comprises one or more timeslots of a T1 or E1 line.

If you want to use the MGX network to transport multiplexed voice and data services to diverse destinations in the network, you need to configure unstructured ports on the CESMs at each end. Figure 19-16 shows a number of structured data ports configured on three CESMs in the network.

Figure 19-16 *Structured Circuit Emulation Ports*

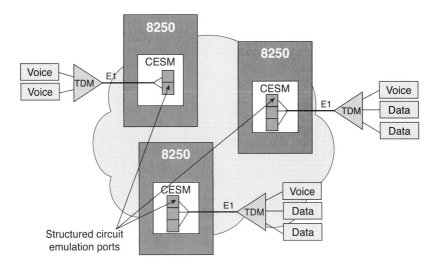

Structured circuit
emulation ports

Circuit Emulation Connections

A circuit emulation connection is an end-to-end PVC that originates and terminates on
MGX CESM circuit emulation ports. The connection receives circuit data, converts it into
ATM cells using AAL1, and transports the cells to the remote port. All circuit emulation
connections are bidirectional; traffic flows in both directions.

You can add two types of circuit emulation connections in an MGX network: feeder and
local. Feeder connections go from the CESM to the PXM trunk and are transported through
the ATM backbone network (BPX or other) to the destination MGX 8850 switch. Local
connections go from one port on an MGX switch to another port on the same switch. Local
connections can be between ports on the same or different CESM cards. Both feeder and
local connections perform the same functions.

Signaling on Connections

When creating a new circuit emulation connection, you must specify the signaling type you
want to use. Unstructured circuit emulation connections forward all signaling bits in-band
to the destination. Structured circuit emulation connections can extract and insert the signaling bits into the appropriate bit location. The signaling bits can also be used for idle
suppression.

The four signaling options are as follows:

- Basic—All data and signaling bits are passed transparently through the network. This is the only option for unstructured connections.

- E1 CAS—Signaling bits are extracted from timeslot 16 on ingress and are inserted into the appropriate bit position in timeslot 16 on egress.

- DS1 SF CAS—Used on T1 superframe (D4) lines. Two signaling bits (A and B) are extracted from the robbed-bit position on ingress and are inserted into the appropriate bit position on egress.

- DS1 ESF CAS—Used on T1 extended superframe (ESF) lines. Four signaling bits (A, B, C, and D) are extracted from the robbed-bit position on ingress and are inserted into the appropriate bit position on egress.

NOTE   All connections on a given line must be configured for the same signaling type.

Feeder Example

A circuit emulation feeder connection has three connection segments:

- A master connection between the CESM and PXM trunk on one MGX switch
- A CBR routing connection through the ATM backbone network
- A master connection between the CESM and PXM trunk on the other MGX switch

Figure 19-17 shows a feeder connection in an MGX/BPX network.

Figure 19-17 *Circuit Emulation Feeder Connection*

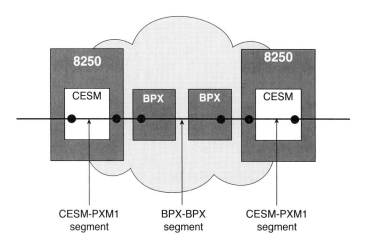

Local Example

A circuit emulation local connection has two connection segments:

- A slave connection on one CESM. The slave connection must be added first.
- A master connection on the other CESM pointing to the slave connection.

Figure 19-18 shows a local connection on an MGX switch.

Figure 19-18 *Circuit Emulation Local Connection*

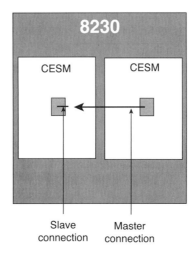

Circuit Emulation Clocking Modes

Circuit emulation services require that end-to-end clocking be available to prevent data loss. Depending on the installation, one of three methods can be used. The clocking method is defined for each connection using the **cnfcon** command.

Three clock modes are available for circuit emulation connections:

- Synchronous clocking for structured or unstructured connections (this is the default clock mode)
- Synchronous Residual Time Stamp (SRTS) asynchronous clocking for unstructured connections
- Adaptive asynchronous clocking for unstructured connections

Synchronous Clocking

Synchronous clocking is available on structured and unstructured circuit emulation ports. The circuit data leaving the network uses the same clock as the MGX switch. This clock signal is available via the timing bus on the MGX backplane. Provided that the MGX network is synchronized, the ingress and egress data are also synchronized.

SRTS Clocking

If the end-user devices are clocked independently of the MGX network, an asynchronous clocking method might be more effective. The two asynchronous methods are SRTS and adaptive clocking. They are supported on unstructured ports only.

SRTS clocking is used when the attached end-user devices are synchronized to each other but do not use the same clock source as the MGX network. On ingress, the CESM measures the rate of the clock received and periodically reports this rate to the destination CESM using bits in the AAL1 SAR-PDU header. The destination CESM uses this rate for the clock in the transmit direction. In this way, the data is synchronized between ingress and egress in the MGX network.

Adaptive Clocking

Adaptive clocking does not require network or end-user synchronization. The average rate of the data coming from the network is used to generate the transmit clock on egress. An egress queue on the CESM is used to buffer data before it leaves the network. If the queue begins to fill up, the transmit clock rate is increased; if the queue begins to empty, the transmit clock rate is decreased. In this way, the clock rate dynamically adjusts to match the traffic rate in the network.

How the CESM Manages Traffic

The main function of the Circuit Emulation Service Module (CESM) is to provide a constant bit rate (CBR) circuit emulation service by converting data streams into CBR AAL1 cells for transport across an ATM network. The CESM supports the CES-IS specifications of the ATM Forum.

The CESM manages traffic using both egress and ingress queues, as described next.

CESM Egress Queues

The CESM has an egress queue that eliminates the effect of delay variation between cells. All ports, regardless of type, have egress queues. Figure 19-19 shows the CESM egress queue.

Figure 19-19 *The CESM Egress Queue*

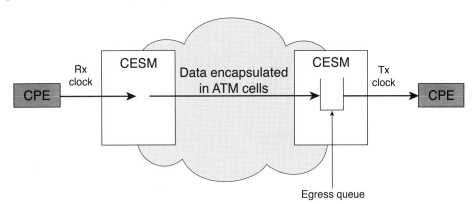

Egress queue

Initially, as traffic arrives from the network to be sent out of the CESM to the end-user equipment, the egress buffer is partially filled, up to the amount defined by the Cell Delay Variation Tolerance (CDVT). The CDVT is configured in microseconds, but you can convert it to bytes or bits by multiplying the CDVT by the port rate. For example, if the CDVT is 10,000 microseconds, the queue fills to 1930 bytes on a full T1 or 2560 bytes on a full E1.

As soon as the queue fills to the amount defined by the CDVT, data is sent from the queue out on the line. This mechanism smoothes out the delay variations caused by the network.

If the queue underruns, "dummy" data is sent out on the line. After underrunning for a defined period of time called the Cell Loss Integration Period (CLIP), the MGX switch generates a trap to notify network management devices that an underrun has occurred. An underrun does not cause an alarm on the CESM. If the buffer overruns, arriving cells are dropped until the queue empties back down to the CDVT level. As soon as this level is reached, cells are admitted into the queue.

The buffer size, the CDVT, and the CLIP are configured after you add a connection to the network using the **cnfcon** command.

Ingress Traffic

Ingress traffic is defined as traffic entering a network. Table 19-2 describes the stages in the ingress process on the CESM.

Table 19-2 *Stages in the Ingress Process on the CESM*

Stage	Description
1	Circuit data arrives on the T1, E1, T3, or E3 line.
2	On a channelized T1 or E1 card, the line is demultiplexed into Nx64 kbps traffic streams based on the port configuration.
3	Traffic is *not* buffered in the egress queue.
4	If SRTS clocking is configured, the clock rate is extracted from the data stream.
5	The circuit data is segmented into ATM cells using AAL1. If no data is received (the line is failed), "dummy" cells are created.
6	The SRTS clock information is inserted into the ATM cells.
7	The ATM cells are sent to the cell bus and are switched by the PXM1 to their destination.

Egress Traffic

Egress traffic is defined as traffic leaving a network. Table 19-3 describes the stages in the egress process on the CESM.

Table 19-3 *Stages in the Egress Process on the CESM*

Stage	Description
1	ATM cells are received from the PXM1 on the cell bus.
2	If SRTS clocking is configured, the time stamp is extracted from the cells.
3	ATM cells are reassembled into circuit data using AAL1.
4	Circuit data is buffered in the egress queue.
5	If SRTS clocking is configured, the time stamp clock rate is used to determine the queue service rate.
6	Circuit data is released from the queue based on the specified rate. The service rate is determined by the MGX clock source, the SRTS rate, or the received data rate, depending on the configured clock mode.
7	On channelized T1 and E1 CESMs, the Nx64 kbps traffic streams are multiplexed to reform the T1 or E1 line.

Commands for Adding, Configuring, and Displaying Circuit Emulation Ports

This section describes the commands used to add, configure, and display ports on the CESM:

- **addport**—Creates a new circuit emulation port on the CESM.
- **delport**—Removes a circuit emulation port from the CESM.
- **dspports**—Lists summary information for all ports on the CESM.
- **dspport**—Lists detailed information for a port.

Add Port Command

The **addport** command is used to create new ports on the CESM. You must use the **delport** command if you want to delete a port.

Here is the **addport** command syntax:

```
addport <port number> <line number> <beginning timeslot>
    <number of timeslots> <port type>
```

The parameter options are as follows:

- *port number*—The logical port number. You must assign a unique port number to each port you create. 1 to 192 for T1, 1 to 248 for E1, always 1 for T3 and E3.
- *line number*—The line that carries the traffic from the end-user device. 1 to 8 for T1 and E1, always 1 for T3 and E3.
- *beginning timeslot* (T1 and E1 only)—The beginning timeslot assigned to this port. On T1 lines, timeslots are numbered 1 to 24. On E1 lines, timeslots are numbered 1 to 32, which means that timeslot 1 is for framing and timeslot 17 is for CAS signaling.
- *number of timeslot* (T1 and E1 only)—The total number of timeslots assigned to this port. This number determines the port's speed.
- *port type* (T1 and E1 only)—The port type, either structured or unstructured. A special unstructured port type (framing on VC disconnect) prevents a remote-end CPE from going to loss of frame (LOF) by placing the line in remote loopback when a connection deletion or failure has occurred in the ATM network. 1 = structured, 2 = unstructured, 3 = framing on VC disconnect.

For example, type **addport 1 1 1 4 1** to add structured port number 1 to line 1 using timeslots 1 to 4 of a T1 or E1 card. Type **addport 1 1** to add an unstructured port number 1 to line 1 on a T3 or E3 card.

Display Ports Command

The **dspports** command lists all the circuit emulation ports on the CESM. Use this command to learn which ports have been defined and what type of port they are. Example 19-4 shows the **dspports** output.

Example 19-4   **dspports** *Output*

```
hei1pop1.1.3.CESM.a > dspports

  Port    Ena/Speed   Type
  ------  --- ------ --------
  3.1.1   Add/ 512k structur
  3.1.2   Add/ 128k structur
  3.2.3   Add/1544k unstruct

  Number of ports:    3

  PortDs0UsedLine1:          0x000003ff
  PortDs0UsedLine2:          0x00ffffff
  PortDs0UsedLine3:          0x00000000
  PortDs0UsedLine4:          0x00000000
  PortDs0UsedLine5:          0x00000000
  PortDs0UsedLine6:          0x00000000
  PortDs0UsedLine7:          0x00000000
  PortDs0UsedLine8:          0x00000000
  PortNumNextAvailable:      12
```

The **dspports** output includes the following information:

- **Port number**—The port number in the form *slot.line.port*
- **Enable**—Added or Modified
- **Speed**—The port speed in kbps
- **Type**—The port type, either structured or unstructured
- Total number of ports
- **Timeslots allocated**—At the bottom of the **dspports** output is a hexadecimal number that describes the timeslots in use on each line. This number should be converted into binary, where each bit represents a timeslot on the line. The least-significant bit (on the right) is timeslot 1 on the line. A 1 means that the timeslot is in use; a 0 means that the timeslot is not in use.

For example:

0x1e07f8ff = 0001 1110 0000 0111 1111 1000 1111 1111

means that timeslots 1 to 8, 12 to 19, and 26 to 29 are in use on an E1 line. Timeslot 1 is reserved for framing, and timeslot 17 may be used for signaling if the line is configured for CAS.

Display Port Command

The **dspport** command shows the configuration details of a port on the CESM. Use this command to learn how a port has been configured. Port characteristics are defined when you add a port using the **addport** command. Example 19-5 shows the **dspport** output for a structured port and an unstructured port.

Example 19-5 **dspport** *Output for a Structured Port and an Unstructured Port*

```
hei1pop1.1.3.CESM.a > dspport 1

  SlotNum:                       3
  PortLineNum:                   1
  PortNum:                       1
  PortRowStatus:                 Add
  PortNumOfSlots:                8
  PortDs0ConfigBitMap(1stDS0):   0xff(1)
  PortSpeed:                     512kbps
  PortType:                      structured
  PortState:                     Active


hei1pop1.1.3.CESM.a > dspport 3

  SlotNum:                       3
  PortLineNum:                   2
  PortNum:                       3
  PortRowStatus:                 Add
  PortNumOfSlots:                24
  PortDs0ConfigBitMap(1stDS0):   0xffffff(1)
  PortSpeed:                     1544kbps
  PortType:                      unstructured
  PortState:                     Active
```

The **dspport** output provides the following information (in addition to that provided in the **dspports** output):

- **DS0 configuration bitmap and first DS0**—A hexadecimal representation of the timeslots used for this port. This number is formatted in the same way the allocated timeslots for the line are displayed at the bottom of the **dspports** output. The number in parentheses is the first timeslot (in decimal form) used by the port.
- **Port state**—The port's current state.

Commands for Adding, Configuring, and Displaying Circuit Emulation Connections

This section describes the commands you use to add, configure, and display connections on the CESM:

- **addcon**—Creates a new circuit emulation connection on the CESM.
- **delcon**—Removes a circuit emulation connection from the CESM.
- **dspcons**—Lists summary information for all connections on the card.
- **dspcon**—Lists detailed information for a connection.
- **cnfcon**—Modifies the connection characteristics.

Add Connection Command

The **addcon** command is used to add local and feeder circuit emulation connections on the CESM. Use the **delcon** command to delete a connection.

Remember that a feeder connection requires additional connection segments on the ATM backbone network and the remote MGX feeder switch.

Here is the **addcon** command syntax for T1 and E1 cards:

```
addcon <port number> <signaling type> <partial fill>
  <conditioning data> <conditioning signaling> [<controller type>
  <mastership> <remote connection ID>]
```

Here is the **addcon** command syntax for T3 and E3 cards:

```
addcon <port number> [mastership <remote connection ID>]
```

The parameter options are as follows:

- *port number*—The port number that terminates the connection. 1 to 192 for T1 cards, 1 to 248 for E1 cards, always 1 for T3 and E3 cards.
- *signaling type* (T1 and E1)—All connections on the same line must be configured with the same signaling type. 1 = basic, 2 = E1 CAS, 3 = T1 superframe CAS, 4 = T1 extended superframe (ESF) CAS.
- *partial fill* (T1 and E1)—The number of data bytes put into the cell. 0 for fully filled, 20 to 47 for structured E1, 25 to 47 for structured T1, 33 to 47 for unstructured T1/E1.
- *conditioning data* (T1 and E1)—The bit pattern that is used in the data timeslots during an underflow or outage condition. The data pattern is configured as a base-10 number to represent an 8-bit binary code. Always 255 for unstructured data transfer (UDT), 0 to 255 for structured data transfer (SDT).

- *conditioning signaling* (T1 and E1)—The signaling bits that are used in the event of an underflow or outage. The signaling bits are configured as a base-10 number to represent the four binary signaling bits (A, B, C, and D) 0 to 15.

- *controller type* (T1 and E1)—1 = PVC/PAR (default), 2 = SPVC/PNNI. Only option 1 is supported.

- *mastership*—1 = master, 2 = slave. When you add a slave connection, do not enter the *mastership* value. Eliminating this parameter automatically makes the connection a slave.

- *remote connection ID*—The destination connection ID for master connections in the form *node.slot.port.VPI.VCI*. For MGX feeder connections, the slot number is 0 for the PXM1. For MGX local connections, the VPI and VCI are always 0.

Display Connections Command

The **dspcons** command lists all connections on the CESM. Use this command to learn which connections have been added and how they are configured. Example 19-6 shows the **dspcons** output on the CESM.

Example 19-6   **dspcons** *Output on the CESM*

```
hei1pop1.1.3.CESM.a > dspcons

 Line     ConnId          ChNum Status CDVT  BufSize CLIP  CBRserv  Alarm
 ----  ------------------- ----- ------ ----- ------- ----- -------- -----
    2 hei1pop1.3.3.0        34   Add    1000   384    2500 unstruct alarm
    3 hei1pop1.3.10.0       41   Add    1000   152    2500   struct alarm
    4 hei1pop1.3.20.0       51   Add    1000   102    2500   struct okay
    4 hei1pop1.3.21.0       52   Add    1000   102    2500   struct okay

 ChanNumNextAvailable:  34
```

The **dspcons** output shows the following information on the CESM:

- Line number

- **Connection ID**—The connection ID in the form *node.slot.port*.0.

- **Channel number**—A unique channel identifier that is chosen by the CESM. The channel number is used to modify local channel characteristics such as the CDVT and buffer size using the **cnfcon** command.

- **Status**—Added or modified.

- **CDVT**—Cell delay variation tolerance.

- Maximum buffer size

- **CLIP**—Cell loss integration period.

- **CBR service type**—Structured, unstructured, or framing on VC disconnect.

- **Alarm**—Specifies whether the line is in alarm.

On the MGX PXM1 card, all connections (local or remote) are listed using the **dspcons** command. Example 19-7 shows the **dspcons** output on the PXM1.

NOTE   Connection 3.3.0.0 is a feeder connection, and 3.20.0.0 and 3.21.0.0 are opposite ends of a local connection.

Example 19-7   **dspcons** *Output on the PXM1*

```
hei1pop1.1.7.PXM.a > dspcons

This End        Node Name       Other End       Status

3.3.0.0         hei1pop1        7.1.40.45       OK
3.10.0.0        hei1pop1        7.1.40.40       FAILED   ABIT ALARM
3.20.0.0        hei1pop1        3.21.0.0        OK
3.21.0.0        hei1pop1        3.20.0.0        OK
7.1.40.40       hei1pop1        3.10.0.0        FAILED   ABIT ALARM
7.1.40.45       hei1pop1        3.3.0.0         OK
```

The following information is provided in the **dspcons** output from the PXM1:

- **This End**—The local end of the connection in one of the following formats:
  - *slot.port.VPI.VCI* for PXM1 trunk connections
  - *slot.port*.0.0 for circuit emulation connections
  - *slot.port*.0.*DLCI* for Frame Relay connections
  - *slot.port.VPI.VCI* for ATM connections
- **Node Name**—The node name of the destination MGX switch
- **Other End**—The remote end of the connection using the same format as the local end
- **Status**—The connection status, either OK or FAILED

Display Connection Command

The **dspcon** command provides detailed configuration and status information for a given circuit emulation connection. There are two pages to the **dspcon** output; the second page follows. Example 19-8 shows the **dspcon** output for a circuit emulation feeder connection.

Example 19-8 **dspcon** *Output for a Circuit Emulation Feeder Connection*

```
hei1pop1.1.3.CESM.a > dspcon 10

  ChanNum:                   41
  ChanRowStatus:             Add
  ChanLineNum:               3
  ChanMapVpi:                3
  ChanMapVci:                41
  ChanCBRService:            struct
  ChanClockMode:             Synchronous
  ChanCAS:                   Basic
  ChanPartialFill:           47
  ChanMaxBufSize:            152 bytes
  ChanCDVT:                   1000 micro seconds
  C L I P:                   2500 milliseconds
  ChanLocalRemoteLpbkState: Disabled
  ChanTestType:              TestOff
  ChanTestState:             NotInProgress
  ChanRTDresult:             65535 ms
  ChanPortNum                10
  ChanConnType               PVC
  ISDetType                  DetectionDisabled
  CondData                   255
  CondSignalling             12

Type <CR> to continue, Q<CR> to stop:
```

The first page of the **dspcon** output shows the following information (in addition to that provided for the **dspcons** command):

- **Channel map VPI**—Significant only on MGX 8220 CESMs.
- **Channel map VCI**—Significant only on MGX 8220 CESMs.
- **Clock mode**—Synchronous, SRTS, or adaptive.
- **CAS**—Basic, DS1 SF, DS1 ESF, or E1 timeslot 16.
- **Partial fill**—The number of data octets in the ATM cell.
- Maximum buffer size in bytes
- CDVT in microseconds
- CLIP in milliseconds
- **Remote loopback state**—Specifies whether a channel loop is enabled or disabled.

- **Test type**—If a test is in progress, the type of test is listed.

- **Test state**—Specifies whether a test is in progress.

- **Round-trip delay test result**—The result of the most recent round-trip delay test (use the **tstdelay** command). If the test has never been run, the test result reports 65,535 milliseconds.

- **Idle suppression detection type**—Either enabled or disabled.

Example 19-9 shows the second page of the **dspcon** output for a CESM feeder connection.

Example 19-9 **dspcon** *Output for a CESM Feeder Connection*

```
ExtISTrig              DisableIdleSupression
  ISIntgnPeriod        3 seconds
  ISSignallingCode     0
  OnHookCode           1
  ChanLocalVpi:        0
  ChanLocalVci:        0
  ChanLocalNSAP:       68656931706f703100000000000000000003000a00
  ChanRemoteVpi:       40
  ChanRemoteVci:       40
  ChanRemoteNSAP:      68656931706f7031000000000000000000000000100
  ChanMastership:      Master
  ChanVpcFlag:         Vcc
  ChanConnServiceType: CBR
  ChanRoutingPriority: 1
  ChanMaxCost:         255
  ChanRestrictTrunkType: No Restriction
  ChanConnPCR:         1366
  ChanConnMCR:         1366
  ChanConnPercentUtil: 100

  ChanNumNextAvailable:  36
```

The second page of the **dspcon** output shows the following information (in addition to that provided for the **dspcons** command):

- **External idle suppression trigger**—Enabled or disabled.

- **Idle suppression integration period**—How long the idle on-hook condition must exist before idle suppression begins.

- **Idle suppression signaling code**—A hexadecimal number that represents the 4-bit signaling code sent out on a channel during idle-suppression periods.

- **On-hook code**—The on-hook signaling bit pattern that triggers idle suppression on the connection.

- **Local VPI and VCI**—Always 0 for circuit emulation connections.

- **Local NSAP**—The NSAP address uniquely identifies this interface (port) in the network. The 20-byte hexadecimal address comprises the following fields:
  - The most significant 8 bytes (16 digits) is the node name in ASCII. The connection shown is on node hei1pop1.
  - The card slot number is the fourth byte from the right. The connection shown is on card 19.
  - The port number is the second byte from the right. The connection shown is on port 1.
- **Remote VPI and VCI**—Always 0 for circuit emulation connections.
- **Remote NSAP**— The remote NSAP address is in the same format as the local NSAP address. If this connection terminates on the PXM, the card slot field is 0. The slave end of an MGX local connection does not have a remote NSAP and is reported as NULL NSAP.
- **Mastership**—Master or slave.
- **VPC flag**—VPC or VCC. A CESM connection is always a VCC.
- **Connection service type**—The service type that is used in the ATM network. A CESM connection always uses a CBR service.
- **Routing priority, Max cost, and Restrict trunk type**—Not applicable.
- **PCR, MCR, and Percent utilization**—The peak and minimum cell rate and the percent utilization of the connection on the network trunk.

Configure Connection Command

The **cnfcon** command is used to modify the connection. The connection characteristics are associated with the connection's local ingress and egress processing and do not have any network impact.

Here is the **cnfcon** command syntax for a T1 or E1 card:

```
cnfcon <port number> <CDVT> <CLIP> <buffer size> <clock mode>
  <idle suppression> <force idle suppression>
```

Here is the **cnfcon** command syntax for a T3 or E3 card:

```
cnfcon <port number> <CDVT> <CLIP> <buffer size>
```

The parameter options are as follows:

- *port number*—The connection's port number.
- *CDVT*—Determines the amount of delay variation in the network that the egress buffer can accommodate. The CDVT is how much the egress buffer is filled before cells are sent to the attached end-user equipment. 125 to 24000 (for T1) or 26000 (for E1) microseconds in 125-microsecond increments.

- *CLIP*—When the egress buffer is empty for the time specified by the CLIP, a trap is sent to the Cisco WAN Manager station reporting the condition. 1000 to 65535 milliseconds.

- *buffer size*—The egress buffer size. 0 = calculated automatically by the CESM, 1 to 9216 bytes for structured T1, 1 to 16384 bytes for all other lines. The CESM calculates the buffer size automatically based on the CDVT and the connection rate.

- *clock mode*—The connection's clock mode. 1 = synchronous (structured or unstructured), 2 = SRTS (unstructured only), 3 = adaptive (unstructured only).

- *idle suppression*—Enables or disables idle suppression. 1 = disable, 2 = enable.

- *force idle suppression*—Forces the connection into idle suppression mode. 1 = disable, 2 = enable.

Commands for Verifying Circuit Emulation Connections

This section describes the commands used to verify connections on the CESM:

- **tstcon**—Tests the continuity on a connection.

- **tstdelay**—Tests the continuity and the round-trip delay on a connection.

- **dspchancnt**—Lists the statistics counters for a channel.

- **clrchancnt**—Clears the statistics counters for a channel.

- **clrchancnts**—Clears the statistics counters for all channels.

Test Connection Command

The **tstcon** command tests continuity on MGX network connections. If connection segments are failed or misconfigured, the **tstcon** command fails.

NOTE   The **tstcon** command does *not* test quality of service or connectivity beyond the MGX network.

Here is the **tstcon** command syntax:

```
tstcon <port number>
```

The MGX CLI returns a pass or fail message after a few seconds, as shown in Example 19-10.

Example 19-10 *Pass or Fail Message*

```
hei1pop1.1.3.CESM.a > tstcon 10

TestCon in progress.

TestCon Passed.

hei1pop1.1.3.CESM.a > tstcon 3

TestCon in progress.

TestCon Failed !

hei1pop1.1.3.CESM.a >
```

The **tstcon** command has some limitations:

- It works only for local connections or connections in a tiered MGX network with BPX or MGX 8850-PXM45 backbone switches.

- It should be issued from both ends to completely verify connectivity.

- A passing result of the test does not guarantee the connection's end-to-end performance.

Test Delay Command

The **tstdelay** command is similar to the **tstcon** command, because it also checks connection continuity. The **tstdelay** command also measures the round-trip delay through the network, and the results are output on the CLI. The most recent delay measurement is also reported in the **dspcon** output.

Here is the **tstdelay** command syntax:

```
tstdelay <channel number>
```

channel number is a channel index number. You can learn the channel number for a connection from the **dspcons** output. The **tstdelay** command and its results are shown in Example 19-11.

Example 19-11 **tstdelay** *Command Results*

```
hei1pop1.1.3.CESM.a > tstdelay 41

TestDelay in progress.

TestDelay Passed with 2 ms.

hei1pop1.1.3.CESM.a > tstdelay 34

TestDelay in progress.

TestDelay Failed !

hei1pop1.1.3.CESM.a >
```

NOTE   The limitations on the **tstcon** command also apply to the **tstdelay** command.

Display Channel Count Command

The **dspchancnt** command lists historical channel statistics counters on the CESM. Use this command to learn how much traffic has been sent, received, or dropped on the circuit emulation connection.

NOTE   The **dspchancnt** command requires you to specify the connection's channel number.

Use the **dspchancnt** command to clear the counters on a specific channel; use the **clrchancnts** command to clear the counters for all channels on the card. Example 19-12 shows the **dspchancnt** output.

Example 19-12 **dspchancnt** *Output*

```
hei1pop1.1.3.CESM.a > dspchancnt 41

ChanNum:                 41
Chan State:              okay
Chan RCV ATM State:      Normal
Chan XMT ATM State:      Normal
Cell Loss Status:        No Cell Loss
Reassembled Cells:       389887
Generated Cells:         144810078
Header Errors:           0
```

Example 19-12 *dspchancnt Output (Continued)*

```
Seqence Mismatches :      0
Lost Cells:               2
Channel Uptime (secs.)    106061
Signalling Status         Offhook
```

The **dspchancnt** output shows the following information:

- **Channel number**—If you do not know the channel number, use the **dspcons** command, which lists the connection and channel numbers.

- **Channel state**—The channel's current state, based on the local or network status.

- **Channel receive ATM state**—Indicates whether the channel is receiving OAM cells from the remote MGX device or the ATM backbone network.

- **Channel transmit ATM state**—Indicates whether the channel is sending OAM cells to the remote MGX device through the ATM backbone network.

- **Cell loss status**—If cells are not received from the ATM backbone network, a cell loss status is reported.

- **Reassembled cells**—Cells received from the ATM backbone network and reassembled back into circuit data.

- **Generated cells**—Cells created from the end-user circuit data and sent into the ATM backbone network.

- **Header errors**—If there are errors in the AAL1 CS-PDU, the cells are discarded.

- **Sequence mismatches**—AAL1 cells received from the network (ATM backbone trunk) in the wrong sequence.

- **Lost cells**—The number of cells lost in the network determined by missing AAL1 sequence numbers.

- **Channel uptime**—The number of seconds that the channel has been active.

- **Signaling status**—The channel's on- or off-hook state.

How to Create Circuit Emulation Services in an MGX Network

This section describes the procedure used to create new circuit emulation services on the CESM. This procedure includes adding circuit emulation ports, adding and configuring circuit emulation connections on the CESM, adding and configuring the appropriate BPX routing connection, and verifying and testing the end-to-end connection through the network.

Implement the following steps to create circuit emulation services in your network. This procedure includes the command syntax for T1 and E1 cards. The T3 and E3 cards have fewer parameters associated with some of the commands.

Step 1 On your CESM, type **dsplns** to verify that your line is active. This outputs line summary information.

Step 2 Type **dspports** to verify that the port number and timeslots you want to use are available. This outputs port summary and line timeslot information.

Step 3 Type **addport** *<port number> <line number> <beginning timeslot> <number of timeslots> <port type>*. A new circuit emulation port is created.

Step 4 Type **dspports** to confirm that the port was added. This outputs port summary information.

Step 5 If you are adding a local connection, type **addcon** *<port> <signaling type> <partial fill> <conditioning data> <conditioning signaling>* to create a slave connection. This adds a slave connection and outputs the connection ID.

Step 6 If you are adding a feeder connection, type **addcon** *<port> <signaling type> <partial fill> <conditioning data> <conditioning signaling>* [*<controller type> <mastership> <remote connection ID>*], specifying the PXM trunk in the *remote connection ID*. This adds a master connection.

Step 7 Type **dspcons** to verify that your connection was added. This outputs connection summary information.

Step 8 Type **dspcon** *<port number>* to verify the connection configuration. This outputs the connection's configuration details.

Step 9 If you need to change the connection configuration, type **cnfcon** *<port number> <CDVT> <CLIP> <buffer size> <clock mode> <idle suppression> <force idle suppression>* to make the change. This modifies the connection configuration parameters.

Step 10 If you are adding a local connection, type **cc** *<slot number>* and follow Steps 1 through 4. Then follow Step 6, specifying the connection ID of the slave connection on the other CESM. Continue with Steps 7 through 9 to display and configure your connection, and then go to Step 15 to test your connection.

Step 11 If you are adding a feeder connection, log into the remote MGX switch and CESM card and follow Steps 1 through 4 and Steps 6 through 9. This adds the circuit emulation port and connection to the other end of the end-to-end connection.

Step 12 If you have standalone MGX switches, you need to add, configure, and verify the routing connection in the ATM network. You have completed the procedure. If you do not have standalone MGX switches, proceed with Step 13.

Step 13 If you have a BPX backbone network, log into the BPX switch attached to one of your MGX switches. Type **addcon** *<local channel>* *<remote node> <remote channel> <connection class | connection type>* *[connection parameters] [route avoid]* to add a CBR routing connection through the BPX network. Be sure to match the VPI and VCI values in the BPX network with the values you used when you added the MGX connection segments. Use the **dspcons** and **dspcon** commands to verify the connection status.

Step 14 If you have an MGX 8850-PXM45 backbone network, log into the AXSM on the local switch, and type **addcon** *<interface number> <vpi> <vci> <service type>* **2** *[parameters]*, where **2** indicates the slave endpoint. This adds a routing connection through the MGX 8850-PXM45 network. Be sure to write down the endpoint ID (NSAP address, VPI, and VCI). Log into the AXSM on the remote switch and type **addcon** *<interface number> <vpi> <vci> <service type>* **1** *<-slave slave endpoint ID> [parameters]*, where **1** indicates the master endpoint, and the *slave endpoint ID* is as previously noted. Use the **dspcons** and **dspcon** commands to verify the connection status.

Step 15 Log back into the CESM on one of your MGX switches. Use the **tstcon** or **tstdelay** command to verify the continuity on the connection.

Step 16 Type **dspchancnt** *<channel number>* to verify that there is traffic on the connection. This outputs the channel counters.

Step 17 Complete Steps 15 and 16 on the other end of the connection.

You have completed the steps necessary for creating circuit emulation services in your network.

Summary

This chapter provided an overview of the different virtual circuit (VC) types supported on MGX switches, including PVCs, SPVCs, and SVCs. It discussed ATM connection types available on the MGX 8850-PXM45 switches used to support MGX connections and how in an MGX network all connections carry ATM cells.

This chapter discussed slave and master connections and showed you how to add a connection in an MGX 8850-PXM45 network. You learned commands for adding, configuring, and displaying MGX 8850-PXM45 connections.

Circuit emulation ports, connections, and clocking modes were presented, with a detailed discussion of how the CESM manages user traffic. You learned the commands used to add, configure, and display circuit emulation ports and connections. You saw how to verify these connections. Also, procedures for creating circuit emulation services in an MGX network were presented.

Review Questions

1 Which of the following VCs require administrative action to set up and take down?

   A. SVC

   B. PVC

   C. SPVC

2 Mark the following statements as true or false.

   A. _____ MGX Frame Relay services are supported by VBR connections in the BPX network.

   B. _____ ATFR and ATFST connections are added in the BPX network to support MGX Frame Relay services.

   C. _____ A CBR connection segment in the ATM backbone network supports MGX circuit emulation services.

   D. _____ MGX feeder Frame Relay connections are supported by UBR connections in the MGX 8850-PXM45 backbone network.

3 A scaling factor is recommended when you add backbone connections that support MGX feeder Frame Relay services to increase the required bandwidth allocated in the network. Why is this scaling factor necessary?

   A. To accommodate for frames greater than 1000 bytes in length

   B. To accommodate for the additional traffic generated by the LMI protocol

   C. To ensure that the backbone network does not police the cells coming from the MGX feeder node

D. To accommodate for partially filled cells that are created when frames are encapsulated into ATM cells

E. To reduce the amount of congestion that might occur in the backbone network because Frame Relay traffic is bursty

4 What is a local connection?

A. Any MGX connection

B. A connection that routes through a single BPX switch

C. A connection that originates and terminates on a Frame Relay port

D. A connection that originates and terminates on the same MGX switch

E. A connection that originates and terminates on the same service module on an MGX switch

5 You want to create a connection between an AUSM ATM port on one MGX 8230 switch and an AUSM ATM port on another MGX 8230 switch. The backbone network includes BPX switches. How many connection segments must you add to accomplish this task?

6 The connection segments for three end-to-end connections are shown in Figure 19-20. Which graphic is correct?

Figure 19-20 *Connection Segments for Three End-to-End Connections*

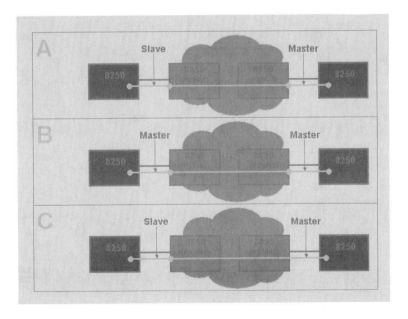

7 Mark the following statements as true or false.

A. _____ When you create a local connection, you must add the slave end first.

B. _____ You can terminate MGX 8230 connections on IGX and BPX switches.

C. _____ Local connections must originate and terminate on the same service module.

D. _____ Each connection segment addition requires you to type a command on the CLI.

E. _____ CWM is used to add connections on all MGX switches, including standalone switches.

8 Which command(s) would you use to modify the service type of an existing connection?

A. **cnfcon**

B. **addcon**

C. **delcon**, **cnfcon**

D. You cannot modify the service type.

9 When provisioning the master endpoint for an SPVC, which parameters must you specify with the **addcon** command?

A. Mastership

B. Service type

C. VPI and VCI

D. Remote PCR

E. Interface number

F. Slave endpoint interface number

10 Which command syntax would you use to verify the VPI and VCI for both SPVC endpoints?

A. AXSM.a > **dspcons**

B. PXM.a > **dspcon** *port ID*

C. AXSM.a > **dspcon** *portID vpi vci*

D. PXM.a > **dspcon** *interface number vpi vci*

E. AXSM.a > **dspcon** *interface number vpi vci*

11 You have created a 512 kbps circuit emulation port on your CESM. Is this a structured or unstructured port?

12 How many unstructured ports can you have on an E1 line?

13 What are two features of a structured port?

A. All timeslots are assigned to one port.

B. The port comprises one or more timeslots.

C. Signaling and framing bits are sent with the user data.

D. Signaling bits are extracted on ingress and reinserted on egress.

14 How many connection segments are required for a local circuit emulation connection between two adjacent CESM cards?

15 You are adding an unstructured circuit emulation connection to your MGX network. What kind of signaling can you use on this connection?

A. Basic

B. E1 CAS

C. E1 CCS

D. DS1 SF CAS

E. DS1 ESF CAS

16 Mark the following statements as true or false.

A _____ Slave connections always use basic signaling.

B. _____ Up to ten local connections can be added to a CESM.

C. _____ All structured connections must be configured for CAS signaling.

D. _____ All connections on the same line must use the same signaling method.

E. _____ You must add the slave end of a local connection before the master end.

17 When would you use SRTS clocking?

A. When the MGX network is not synchronized

B. When neither CPE nor the MGX network is synchronized

C. When the CPEs and the MGX are using the same clock source

D. When the CPEs are synchronized to each other but the MGX network is using a different clock source

18 What is the default clock mode for all CESM connections?

A. SRTS

B. Adaptive

C. Synchronous

D. Asynchronous

E. There is no default.

19 Which of the following statements is *not* true?

A. Adaptive clocking is asynchronous.

B. SRTS clocking uses a time stamp in the AAL1 SAR-PDU header.

C. Unstructured ports support only synchronous and adaptive clocking.

D. Adaptive clocking uses an egress buffer to accommodate clock changes.

20 You want to monitor when underruns occur for more than 5 seconds on a circuit emulation connection. What should you change to make sure you are notified?

A. CLIP

B. CDVT

C. Buffer size

D. Statistics timer

21 Which of the following statements is true?

A. During an underrun, there are no cells across the connection.

B. You might experience underruns if the buffer size is too small.

C. You might experience underruns if the CDVT value is too small.

D. When the buffer underruns, the CESM declares a minor alarm.

22 You want to find out if port 5 is failed. What command and any required parameters must you type to find out the port's state?

23 When you use the **addport** command to create a new port, you must specify the port type. Which of the following are valid port types?

A. Structured

B. T1 ESF CAS

C. Unstructured

D. Asynchronous

E. Framing on VC disconnect

F. E1 CCS with CRC checking

24 For each function, select the appropriate command:

A. To create a new circuit emulation connection, use the {**addport** | **addcon**} command.

B. To find out whether a connection is a master or slave connection, use the {**dspcon** | **dspcons**} command.

C. To change the CLIP, use the {**cnfcon** | **cnfport**} command.

25 What is the function of the **tstcon** command?

A. To check for connection alarms

B. To test the connection's continuity

C. To test the connection's quality

D. To measure the round-trip delay on the connection

E. To confirm that the connection is configured correctly

26 Mark the following statements as true or false.

A. _____ The **dspchancnt** output updates automatically.

B. _____ The channel number is the same as the port number.

C. _____ The most recent **tstdelay** result is shown in the **dspchancnt** output.

D. _____ The **clrchancnts** command clears all the channel counters on the card.

E. _____ The **dspchancnt** command shows historical statistics counters for a channel.

This chapter covers the following key topics:

- Frame Relay Ports
- FRSM Port Queues
- How Traffic Moves Through the FRSM
- Commands for Adding, Configuring, and Displaying Frame Relay Ports
- Commands for Monitoring Frame Relay Ports
- Configuring a Frame Relay Port on an FRSM
- Frame Relay Connections
- Interworking
- Frame Relay Policing
- ForeSight on Frame Relay Connections
- ABR for Frame Relay
- VC Queues on the FRSM
- Commands for Adding, Configuring, and Displaying Frame Relay Connections
- Commands for Verifying Frame Relay Connections
- Creating Frame Relay Connections in an MGX Network

CHAPTER 20

Frame Relay Ports and Connections

This chapter presents Frame Relay ports and describes FRSM port queues. How traffic moves through the FRSM in both the ingress and egress directions is discussed in detail for both high-speed and low-speed FRSMs. Commands for adding, configuring, displaying, and monitoring Frame Relay ports are presented, and configuring a Frame Relay port on an FRSM card is described.

This chapter also discusses Frame Relay connections and the two kinds of interworking supported on the FRSM: network interworking and service interworking. The Frame Relay policing process is also detailed. You'll see how the ForeSight feature works on Frame Relay connections and how ABR dynamically adjusts the rate that traffic enters the network.

You'll learn how virtual circuit (VC) queues are used to shape ingress traffic and how the FRSM buffers ingress traffic in VC queues. You'll also read about the commands used to add, configure, display, and verify Frame Relay connections in an MGX network.

Frame Relay Ports

A Frame Relay port is the interface between the network and a single Frame Relay device. The number of ports on an FRSM depends on the FRSM model and the line type in use. After the line is enabled and configured, the port is created. Frame Relay connections and channels terminate on a port. The port must be created before connections can be added.

Port Types

Regardless of the card type or physical characteristics of a port (speed, timeslots, and so on), each port can be configured as the following:

- **A Frame Relay port**—A port that sends and receives standard Frame Relay frames as defined by ITU-T Q.922. Multiple virtual circuits (VCs) can terminate on a single Frame Relay port and are differentiated by their data-link connection identifiers (DLCIs).

- **A frame forwarding port**—A port that sends and receives frame-based traffic that is similar to Frame Relay frames such as HDLC, SDLC, and X.25. Because the port is unable to read the address and control information in the frame, all traffic must be forwarded to a single destination frame forwarding port. Only one frame forwarding PVC is allowed per port.

- **Frame-based user-network interface (FUNI) ports**—A port that sends and receives standard FUNI frames. FUNI frames are similar to Frame Relay frames and are designed to interwork with ATM interfaces. Like a Frame Relay port, a FUNI port supports multiple PVCs that are differentiated by their frame address.

Serial Frame Relay Ports

A serial port is associated with a single line, and its speed is defined by the line rate. The FRSM-HS1/B and FRSM-HS2 cards support serial Frame Relay ports. Although a T3 or E3 line is not strictly serial, the FRSM-T3E3 has ports that are like other serial ports. Figure 20-1 shows an example of two serial ports on an FRSM-HS2. In this figure, FRAD stands for Frame Relay Access Device. FRAD is responsible for framing data with header and trailer information prior to delivery of the frame to a Frame Relay switch.

Figure 20-1 *Serial Frame Relay Ports*

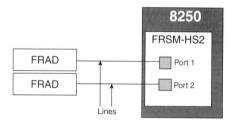

Narrowband Channelized Frame Relay Ports

Channelized narrowband FRSMs can support up to 24 (T1) or 31 (E1) Frame Relay ports per line. The FRADs are attached to a time-division multiplexer (TDM) that aggregates multiple subrate traffic streams onto a single T1 or E1 line. Channelized ports are associated with one or more consecutive timeslots on the line. The FRSM-8T1, FRSM-8E1, and FRSM-2CT3 support channelized Frame Relay ports. Figure 20-2 shows an FRSM-8E1 with three channelized Frame Relay ports.

Figure 20-2 *Channelized Narrowband Frame Relay Ports*

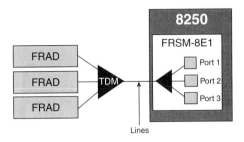

NOTE	The three channelized ports (ports 1, 2, and 3) shown in Figure 20-2 are from a single line.

Narrowband Fractional Frame Relay Ports

On a fractional (unchannelized) FRSM, each line can support a single port. The end-user equipment either has a T1, E1 interface or uses multiple timeslots on a T1 or E1 line. Like channelized Frame Relay ports, fractional ports are defined by consecutive timeslots on the line. The FRSM-8T1, FRSM-8E1, and FRSM-2CT3 support fractional Frame Relay ports. Figure 20-3 shows an FRSM-8T1 with two fractional Frame Relay ports.

Figure 20-3 *Narrowband Fractional Frame Relay Ports*

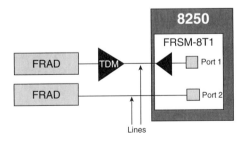

NOTE	The two fractional Frame Relay ports (ports 1 and 2) shown in Figure 20-3 are from two separate lines.

FRSM Port Queues

The FRSM buffers egress (from the network to the CPE) traffic in port queues. The purpose of the port queues is to prevent frames from being dropped as they leave the MGX network. Each port terminates a number of VCs. At any given time, the port can receive frames from multiple VCs that must all be sent across a physical line with a fixed amount of available bandwidth. In order to compensate for these potential bursts of traffic, the queues must buffer the frames and service them at the port rate.

Each logical port has several subqueues. These subqueues all have three characteristics:

- The queue depth defines the maximum amount of data that can be buffered at any time.

- The DE threshold defines when DE-marked frames are discarded. If the queue fills up beyond the DE threshold, any newly arriving frames with the DE bit set to 1 are not allowed into the queue and are discarded. Any frames already in the queue are not discarded.

- The ECN threshold defines when congestion bits (FECN and BECN) are set on the frames. If the queue fills up beyond the ECN threshold, any newly arriving frames have their FECN bit set to 1. Any frames traveling in the opposite direction (ingress) have their BECN bit set to 1.

Figure 20-4 shows a Frame Relay ingress port queue.

Figure 20-4 *FRSM Ingress Port Queue*

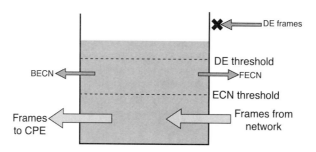

Low-Speed FRSM Port Queues

The low-speed FRSM cards (FRSM-8T1, FRSM-8E1, and FRSM-HS1/B) have three subqueues for each logical port:

- **A high-priority queue for management traffic**—Signaling traffic such as the Local Management Interface (LMI) and Consolidated Link-Layer Management (CLLM) are queued in a high-priority egress port queue. These frames are always serviced when they are in the queue.

- **Queue 1 for high-priority data frames**—High-priority data frames are buffered in queue 1. Queue 1 is served at regular intervals. After queue 1 is served n times, queue 2 is served. If you want the connection to use the high-priority data queue, you must change the connection parameter from the default normal-priority queue to the high-priority data queue.

- **Queue 2 for normal-priority frames**—Normal-priority data frames are buffered in queue 2. Queue 2 is served after queue 1 is served n times. By default, all connections are configured to use the normal-priority queue.

Figure 20-5 shows the three subqueues on a low-speed FRSM logical port.

Figure 20-5 *Subqueues on a Low-Speed FRSM Logical Port*

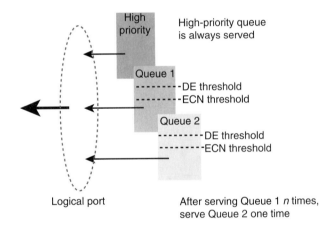

High-Speed FRSM Port Queues

The high-speed FRSM cards (FRSM-2CT3, FRSM-T3E3, and FRSMHS2) have four class of service (CoS) egress queues for each logical port:

- A high-priority queue for management traffic—LMI and CLLM frames are queued in the high-priority egress queue. These frames are always serviced when they are in the queue.

- Real-time variable bit rate (rt-VBR)

- Nonreal-time variable bit rate (nrt-VBR) and available bit rate (ABR)

- Unspecified bit rate (UBR)

Figure 20-6 shows the four subqueues on a high-speed FRSM logical port.

Figure 20-6 *Subqueues on a High-Speed FRSM Logical Port*

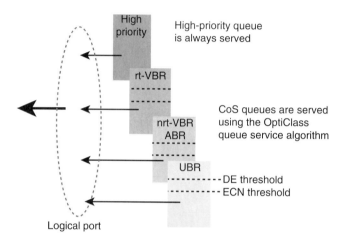

VCs are configured as rt-VBR, nrt-VBR, ABR, or UBR. Each of the three CoS queues buffer frames from like VCs so that bursty time-independent traffic does not adversely affect time-dependent traffic.

The OptiClass queue service algorithm is a credit-based process that gives equal and fair access to the port bandwidth. Each CoS has an expected traffic rate based on the aggregate rate of the terminating VCs. The CoS queue is served at this rate using a credit system. Each queue earns credits at a fixed rate and can spend the credits when it has traffic to send. A queue that has more data than expected will eventually fill up but will not affect the other queues.

When a queue has a credit and no traffic to send, the other queues are given the opportunity to send traffic. The rt-VBR queue is given the first opportunity to send traffic. The nrt-VBR/ABR queue is next, and the UBR queue is last.

The OptiClass algorithm is also used on the IGX and BPX switches for egress trunk and port queues.

How Traffic Moves Through the FRSM

This section describes the traffic process on the FRSM in both the ingress and egress directions.

Ingress Frame Relay Traffic for Low-Speed FRSMs

The following steps describe how traffic is processed in the ingress direction (from the CPE to the network) on the FRSM-8T1 and FRSM-8E1 cards:

1   The frame comes in from the CPE on the line. On channelized ports, the line is demultiplexed, and the frames for each logical port are processed.

2   The frames are *not* buffered in any of the port queues. If data traveling in the egress direction is congested, the BECN bit can be set on the ingress frames.

3   The frames go through the usage parameter control (UPC) process (policing) to determine whether the cell is allowed into the network and to determine whether the DE bit is set to 1. The UPC process is performed independently for each VC.

4   The frames are segmented into ATM cells.

5   The ATM cells are sent to the appropriate VC queue. The VC queue can discard the cell if the DE threshold is met. The VC queue can also mark congestion on the cell (EFCI bit) if the ECN threshold is met.

6   The ATM cell is sent to the cell bus to be switched by the PXM1 to the destination card slot.

Ingress Frame Relay Traffic for High-Speed FRSMs

The following steps describe how traffic is processed in the ingress direction (from the CPE to the network) on the FRSM-2CT3, FRSM-T3E3, and FRSM-HS2 cards:

1   The frame comes in from the CPE on the line. On channelized ports, the line is demultiplexed, and the frames for each logical port are processed.

2   The frames are *not* buffered in any of the port queues. If data traveling in the egress direction is congested, the BECN bit can be set on the ingress frames.

3   The frames go through the UPC process to determine whether the cell is allowed into the network and to determine whether the DE bit is set to 1. The UPC process is performed independently for each VC.

4   The frames are segmented into ATM cells.

5   The ATM cells are sent to the appropriate VC queue. Each connection has a CoS associated with it that determines the queue's service priority. The VC queue can discard the cell if the DE threshold is met. The VC queue can also mark congestion on the cell (EFCI bit) if the ECN threshold is met.

6   The ATM cell is sent to the cell bus to be switched by the PXM1 to the destination card slot.

Egress Frame Relay Traffic for Low-Speed FRSMs

The following steps describe how traffic is processed in the egress direction (from the network to the CPE) on the FRSM-8T1, FRSM-8E1, and FRSM-HS1/B cards:

1 The cells come in from the cell bus.

2 The cells are *not* buffered in any of the VC queues. If data traveling in the ingress direction is congested, the BECN bit can be set on the egress frames.

3 The cells are reassembled into frames.

4 The frames are sent to the appropriate port queue based on the traffic's priority. The port queue can discard the frame if the DE threshold is met. The port queue can also mark congestion on the frame (EFCI bit) if the ECN threshold is met.

5 If the port is channelized, the traffic streams are multiplexed onto the line. In all cases, the frames are sent out on the line to the CPE.

Egress Frame Relay Traffic for High-Speed FRSMs

The following steps describe how traffic is processed in the egress direction (from the network to the CPE) on the FRSM-2CT3, FRSM-T3E3, and FRSM-HS2 cards:

1 The cells come in from the cell bus.

2 The cells are *not* buffered in any of the VC queues. If data traveling in the ingress direction is congested, the BECN bit can be set on the egress frames.

3 The cells are reassembled into frames.

4 The frames are sent to the appropriate port queue based on the connection's configured CoS. The port queue can discard the frame if the DE threshold is met. The port queue can also mark congestion on the frame (EFCI bit) if the ECN threshold is met.

5 If the port is channelized, the traffic streams are multiplexed onto the line. In all cases, the frames are sent out on the line to the CPE.

Commands for Adding, Configuring, and Displaying Frame Relay Ports

The following commands are used when adding, configuring, and displaying Frame Relay ports on the FRSM:

- **dspports**—Lists the status of all logical ports on the FRSM card.

- **dspport**—Lists detailed status and configuration information for a logical port.

- **addport**—Creates a new logical port on the FRSM.

- **delport**—Removes a logical port from the FRSM.

- **cnfport**—Modifies a logical port, including signaling protocol characteristics.

- **xcnfport**—Creates and modifies a logical Frame Relay port. Includes configuration parameters that are not part of the **addport** and **cnfport** commands.

- **cnfportcllm**—Changes the consolidated link-layer management (CLLM) characteristics of a logical port.

Display Ports Command

The **dspports** command shows summary configuration and status information on all ports defined on an FRSM card. Use this command to learn which ports have been created and how they are configured. Example 20-1 shows an example of the **dspports** output for an FRSM-8T1 card.

Example 20-1 **dspports** *Output*

```
hei1pop1.1.11.FRSM.a > dspports

   Port  Ena/Speed EQServ  SignalType  T391 T392 N391 N392 N393   Type   Alarm ELMI
                   Ratio
 ------- --- ----- ------  ------------ ---- ---- ---- ---- ---- -------- ----- ----
 11.1.1  Mod/ 512k   1     NoSignalling  10   15    6    3    4 frameRel  No    Off
 11.1.2  Add/ 112k   1     NoSignalling  10   15    6    3    4 funi-mod  No    Off
 11.2.3  Add/1536k   1     NoSignalling  10   15    6    3    4 frForwar  No    Off
 11.1.4  Add/ 224k   1     NoSignalling  10   15    6    3    4 frameRel  No    Off
 11.3.10 Add/ 224k   1     NoSignalling  10   15    6    3    4 frameRel  No    Off
 11.3.11 Add/ 112k   1     StrataLMI     10   15    6    3    4 frameRel  No    On

   Number of ports:          6

   PortDs0UsedLine1:         0x00003fff
   PortDs0UsedLine2:         0x00ffffff
   PortDs0UsedLine3:         0x000006f0
   PortDs0UsedLine4:         0x00000000
   PortDs0UsedLine5:         0x00000000
   PortDs0UsedLine6:         0x00000000
   PortDs0UsedLine7:         0x00000000
   PortDs0UsedLine8:         0x00000000
   PortNumNextAvailable:     64
```

The information shown in the **dspports** output includes the following:

- **Port number**—The port number, identified as *slot.line.port*.

- **Enable**—The state of the port, either Add or Modify.

- **Speed**—The port rate based on timeslot assignation or the specified line rate (FRSM-HS1/B and FRSM-HS2 only).

- **Egress queue service ratio**—Determines the queue's service priority.

- **Signaling protocol type**—The signaling protocol defined for the port. Choices include none, StrataCom (Cisco) LMI, Annex D UNI, Annex D NNI, Annex A UNI, and Annex A NNI.

- **T391, T392, N391, N392, N393**—The signaling protocol timers.

- **Type**—The port type, either Frame Relay, FUNI, or frame forwarding.

- **Alarm**—Specifies whether an alarm is present, due to a signaling protocol or a line failure.

- **ELMI**—Specifies whether the enhanced LMI option is on or off.

- **Timeslots allocated (FRSM-8T, FRSM-8E1, and FRSM-2CT3 only)**—At the bottom of the **dspports** output is a hexadecimal number that describes the timeslots in use on each line. The number should be converted to binary, where each bit represents a timeslot on the line. The least-significant bit (on the right) is timeslot 1 on a T1 and timeslot 0 on an E1. A 1 means that the timeslot is in use; a 0 means that the timeslot is not in use.

  For example:

  0x1e07f8ff = 0001 1110 0000 0111 1111 1000 1111 1111

  means that timeslots 1 to 8, 12 to 19, and 26 to 29 are in use on an E1 line. Timeslot 0 is reserved for framing, and timeslot 16 may be for signaling if the line is configured for CAS. Otherwise, it is used for data.

NOTE   Keep in mind that the **dspports** output shows a hexadecimal number that describes the timeslots in use on each line. After this number is converted to binary, with each bit representing a timeslot on the line, the least-significant bit represents timeslot 1 on a T1 or timeslot 0 on an E1. A 1 means that the timeslot is in use; a 0 means that the timeslot is not in use.

Display Port Command

The **dspport** command provides configuration and status information for a particular port. Use this command to learn additional configuration details about a port. The **dspport** output shown in Example 20-2 is from a channelized T1 FRSM card module.

Example 20-2 dspport *Output, Page 1*

```
hei1pop1.1.11.FRSM.a > dspport 11

  SlotNum:                       11
  PortLineNum:                   3
```

Example 20-2 **dspport** *Output, Page 1 (Continued)*

```
        PortNum:                        11
        PortRowStatus:                  Mod
        PortDs0Speed:                   56k
        PortDs0ConfigBitMap(1stDS0):    0x600(10)
        PortEqueueServiceRatio:         1
        PortFlagsBetweenFrames:         1
        PortSpeed:                      112kbps
        SignallingProtocolType:         StrataLMI
        AsynchronousMsgs:               UPD enabled
        T391LineIntegrityTimer:         10
        T392PollingVerificationTimer:   15
        N391FullStatusPollingCounter:   6
        N392ErrorThreshold:             3
        N393MonitoredEventCount:        4
        EnhancedLmi:                    On
        PortState:                      FailedDuetoSignallingFailure
        PortSignallingState:            LMI Failure
        CLLMEnableStatus:               Disable
        CLLMxmtStatusTimer:             0

Type <CR> to continue, Q<CR> to stop:
```

The following information is provided in Example 20-2, which shows the **dspport** output (in addition to that using the **dspports** command):

- **Port DS0 speed**—Either 56 kbps or 64 kbps.

- **Port DS0 configuration bit map and 1st DS0**—A hexadecimal representation of the port's timeslot usage, similar to the line timeslot usage just described. In addition, the first timeslot in use is listed (in base 10) in parentheses.

- **Flags between frames**—The minimum number of idle flags (hexadecimal 7E) required between consecutive frames leaving the port.

- **Asynchronous messages**—Enables or disables signaling protocol asynchronous updates.

- **Port state**—Active or failed due to line or port (LMI) failure.

- **Signaling state**—Indicates LMI failures.

- **CLLM**—Enables or disables ForeSight messages across an NNI to an attached Cisco Frame Relay network (MGX or IGX) or router. CLLM is enabled using the **cnfportcllm** command.

- **CLLM timer**—The frequency of CLLM messages.

Example 20-3 shows the second page of the **dspport** output from an FRSM-8T1 card.

Example 20-3 dspport *Output, Page 2*

```
portType:                  frameRelay
PortIngrPercentUtil:       0
PortEgrPercentUtil:        0
PortOversubscribed:        False
PortSvcStatus:             Disable
PortSvcInUse:              Not In-Use
PortSvcShareLcn:           Card-based
PortSvcLcnLow:             0
PortSvcLcnHigh:            0
PortSvcDlciLow:            0
PortSvcDlciHigh:           0

PortDs0UsedLine1:          0x00003fff
PortDs0UsedLine2:          0x00ffffff
PortDs0UsedLine3:          0x000006f0
PortDs0UsedLine4:          0x00000000
PortDs0UsedLine5:          0x00000000
PortDs0UsedLine6:          0x00000000
PortDs0UsedLine7:          0x00000000
PortDs0UsedLine8:          0x00000000
PortNumNextAvailable:      82
```

The following information is provided in Example 20-3, which shows the **dspport** output (in addition to that using the **dspports** command):

- **Port ingress percent utilization**—The percentage of the ingress bandwidth used on the port, based on the aggregate of all PVCs' minimum rates that terminate on the port.

- **Port egress percent utilization**—The percentage of the egress bandwidth used on the port, based on the aggregate of all PVCs' egress service rates that terminate on the port.

- **Port oversubscribed**—Specifies whether the port has more traffic terminating on it than the configured port speed can support.

- **Port SVC status**—Specifies whether this port supports SVCs.

- **Port SVC in use**—Specifies whether SVCs are active on this port.

- **Port SVC LCN low**—The low end of the range of logical channel numbers (LCNs) reserved for switched virtual circuits (SVCs).

- **Port SVC LCN high**—The high end of the range of LCNs reserved for SVCs.

- **Port SVC DLCI low**—The low end of the range of DLCIs reserved for SVCs.

- **Port SVC DLCI high**—The high end of the range of DLCIs reserved for SVCs.

Add Port Command

The **addport** command defines the timeslots associated with a port on a multiplexed line and activates a serial port. (Use the **delport** command to delete a Frame Relay port.)

On the FRSM-8T1, FRSM-8E1, and FRSM-2CT3, the command syntax is

```
addport <port number> <line number> <DS0 speed> <beginning timeslot>
    <number of timeslots> <port type>
```

On the FRSM-HS1/B, FRSM-HS2, and FRSM-T3E3, the command syntax is

```
addport <port number> <line number> <port type>
```

The parameter options are as follows:

- *port number*—The logical port number: 1 to 192 on T1, 1 to 248 on E1, 1 to 2 on HSSI, 1 to 256 on channelized T3, and 1 to 2 on unchannelized T3 and E3. On the FRSM-HS1/B card, port numbers 1 to 4 are allowed. Each port corresponds to a line number.

- *line number*—The line that carries the traffic from the end-user device.

- *DS0 speed*—The timeslot's data rate: 1 = 56 kbps for use on single-timeslot 56 kbps ports, and 2 = 64 kbps.

- *beginning timeslot*—The beginning timeslot defined for the port: 1 to 24 for T1 and 1 to 32 for E1.

NOTE On E1 lines, the timeslot numbering is from 1 to 32, not 0 to 31. This means that timeslot 1 is reserved for framing and timeslot 17 is reserved for signaling on CAS lines. Be sure to double-check the timeslots you are using. A mistake can result in the port's being unable to process frames.

- *number of timeslots*—The total number of timeslots used by the port.
- *port type*—The type of traffic transmitted and received by the port. 1 = Frame Relay, 2 = FUNI, 3 = frame forwarding.

For example, type **addport 1 1 2 1 4 2** to add FUNI port 1 to line 1 using timeslots 1 to 4. Type **addport 2 1 3** to add frame forwarding port 2 on line 1 on an FRSM-HS2 card.

NOTE On the FRSM-2CT3, only 128 ports can be added per T3 line. In addition, ports must be distributed across the two T3 lines as follows: T1 lines 1 to 14 and 43 to 56 can support a total of 128 ports, and T1 lines 15 to 28 and 29 to 42 can support a total of 128 ports. You must take these limitations into account when you are adding ports on the card.

Configure Port Command

The **cnfport** command is used to modify the most commonly changed characteristics of an FRSM port.

The command syntax is

```
cnfport <port number> <signaling> <asynchronous updates> <ELMI>
  [T391] [T392] [N391] [N392] [N393]
```

The parameter options are as follows:

- *port number*—The logical port number you want to modify.

- *signaling*—The signaling protocol used by the port. N = none, S = Cisco (StrataCom) LMI, AU = Annex A UNI, DU = Annex D UNI, AN = Annex A NNI, DN = Annex D NNI.

- *asynchronous updates*—Enables or disables asynchronous updates. 1 or N = disable all updates, 2 or Y = enable status updates only, 3 = enable unsolicited full status updates only, 4 = enable all updates.

- *ELMI*—Enable ELMI. Y = yes, N= no.

- *T391*—5 to 30 seconds.

- *T392*—5 to 30 seconds.

- *N391*—1 to 255.

- *N392*—1 to 10.

- *N393*—1 to 10 and greater than N392.

Extended Configure Port Command

The **xcnfport** command can be used to modify all the port characteristics, including those using the **cnfport** and **cnfportcllm** commands. The **xcnfport** command can also be used to create new Frame Relay ports. All parameters are optional and are preceded by a keyword. They may be typed in any order.

The command syntax is

```
xcnfport -pt <port number> [-keyword <parameter value>]
```

The keyword/parameter options are as follows:

- *port number*—The logical port number you want to modify.

- **ln**—The line number associated with the logical port.

- **en**—The port state. 1 = add, 2 = modify, 3 = delete.

- **sp**—The DS0 speed. 1 = 56 kbps, 2 = 64 kbps. The DS0 speed cannot be changed on an existing port.

- **ts**—A binary number, where each bit represents a timeslot on the T1 or E1 line. The least-significant bit is the lowest timeslot number. A 1 bit signifies that the timeslot is used; a 0 bit signifies that the timeslot is not used. 0 to $2^{32}-1$. The DS0 bitmap cannot be changed on an existing port.

- **rat**—Egress queue service ratio. Determines the queue service priority on egress. 1 to 15.

- **flag**—The minimum number of hexadecimal 7E flags inserted between frames leaving the FRSM. 1 to 255.

- **sig**—The signaling protocol. 1 = none, 2 = Cisco LMI, 3 = Annex A UNI, 4 = Annex D UNI, 5 = Annex A NNI, 6 = Annex D NNI.

- **asy**—Enables or disables asynchronous updates. 1 or N = disable all updates, 2 or Y = enable status updates only, 3 = enable unsolicited full status updates only, 4 = enable all updates.

- **t391**—T391 timer. 5 to 30 seconds.

- **t392**—T392 timer. 5 to 30 seconds.

- **n391**—N391 counter. 1 to 255.

- **n392**—N392 counter. 1 to 10.

- **n393**—N393 counter. 1 to 10 and greater than N392.

- **enhancedLMI**—Enables or disables enhanced LMI (ELMI). 1 = disabled, 2 = enabled.

- **cllmen**—Enables or disables consolidated link layer management (CLLM). CLLM allows the ForeSight congestion management feature to extend beyond the boundaries of the MGX network. 1 = disabled, 2 = enabled.

- **cllmtm**—CLLM status time. The amount of time between CLLM messages sent by the port. 40 to 5000 milliseconds.

- **ptp**—Port type. 1 = Frame Relay, 2 = FUNI, 3 = frame forwarding.

- **pta**—Port administrative state. 1 = up, 2 = down.

- **svcen**—SVC status. 1 = disabled, 2 = enabled.

- **svcuse**—Specifies whether SVCs are in use. 1 = not in use, 2 = in use.

- **pbe**—Enables or disables BERT. 1 = disabled, 2 = enabled.

Configure Port CLLM Command

The **cnfportcllm** command is used to modify a port's CLLM configuration. CLLM allows the ForeSight feature to extend beyond network boundaries to another Cisco network attached via an NNI or a Cisco router that supports the ForeSight feature.

The command syntax is

```
cnfportcllm <port number> <CLLM enable> <CLLM timer>
```

The parameter options are as follows:

- *port number*—The logical port number you want to configure.
- *CLLM enable*—Enables or disables the CLLM feature. 1 = disable, 2 = enable.
- *CLLM timer*—The time period between CLLM messages. 40 to 5000 milliseconds.

Commands for Monitoring Frame Relay Ports

This section covers the commands used to monitor Frame Relay ports on the MGX switch:

- **dspportcnt**—Lists the statistical counters for a logical port on the FRSM.
- **clrportcnt**—Clears the statistical counters on a logical port.
- **clrportcnts**—Clears the statistical counters on all logical ports on the FRSM.

Display Port Counter Command

The **dspportcnt** command provides detailed historical statistics for a Frame Relay port. Use this command to view the traffic being transmitted to and received from the attached end-user equipment. Because the statistics are historical, you might want to clear them using the **clrportcnt** or **clrportcnts** command before beginning your testing or troubleshooting.

Example 20-4 shows the **dspportcnt** output.

Example 20-4 dspportcnt *Output*

```
POPEYE3.1.20.FRSM.a > dspportcnt 1

  PortNum: 1
                                    Tx                 Rx
                             - - - - - - - - - -    - - - - - - - - - -
    Total Frames:            354243                 347208
    Total Bytes:             9400584                9031591
    Frames FECN:             0                      0
    Frames BECN:             0                      0
    Frames Abort:            0                      2
    Buf Not Available:       0                      0
    KbpsAIR:                 0                      0
    XmtFramesDiscXceedQDepth:  0
    XmtBytesDiscXceedQDepth:   0
    XmtFramesDuringLMIAlarm:   17
    XmtByteDuringLMIAlarm:     791
    XmtFramesUnderrun:         0
    RcvFramesDE:                                    0
    RcvFramesDiscCRCError:                          0
    RcvFramesDiscIllegalHeader:                     0
    RcvFramesDiscAlignmentError:                    0
    RcvFramesDiscIllegalLen:                        0
```

Example 20-4 dspportcnt *Output (Continued)*

```
Type <CR> to continue, Q<CR> to stop:

Tx                      Rx
                         - - - - - - - - - - - - - -         - - - - - - - - - - - - - -
RcvFramesDiscXceedDEThresh:                          0
RcvFramesDiscNoChan:                                 0
RcvFramesUnknownDLCI:                                2
RcvLastUnknownDLCI:                                  0
RcvFramesTaggedFECN:                                 0
RcvFramesTaggedBECN:                                 0
RcvFramesTaggedDE:                                   0
Status:                 256020                        0
StatusInquiry:          0                        256020
AsynchUpdate:           0                             0
RcvInvalidRequest:                                   0
RcvUNISeqMismatch:                                   1
RcvNNISeqMismatch:                                   0
UNISignallingTimeout:                                3
NNISignallingTimeout:                                0
FramesCLLM:             0                             0
BytesCLLM:              0                             0
CLLMFailures:                        0
```

The **dspportcnt** output includes the following information:

- **Total frames**—The number of frames transmitted and received on the port.

- **Total bytes**—The number of bytes transmitted and received on the port.

- **Frames FECN**—The number of frames transmitted and received with the FECN bit set. This number does not imply that the MGX switch set the FECN bit.

- **Frames BECN**—The number of frames transmitted and received with the BECN bit set. This number does not imply that the MGX switch set the BECN bit.

- **Frames abort**—The number of frames that were aborted in the transmit and receive directions.

- **Buffer not available**—The number of times the pooled transmit and receive buffers overflowed.

- **Kbps AIR**—The average information rate (AIR) of traffic transmitted and received in kbps.

- **Transmit frames discarded because of exceeded queue depth**—The number of frames dropped because the egress VC queue was full.

- **Transmit bytes discarded because of exceeded queue depth**—The number of bytes dropped because the egress VC queue was full.

- **Transmit frames during LMI alarm**—The number of frames transmitted during an LMI alarm. The MGX switch did not drop these frames, but the end-user equipment might have been unavailable at the time.

- **Transmit bytes during LMI alarm**—The number of bytes transmitted during an LMI alarm.

- **Transmit frames underrun**—The number of times the frames were underrun.

- **Receive frames DE**—The number of frames received with the DE bit set. This number does not imply that the MGX switch set the DE bit.

- **Receive frames discarded because of a CRC error**—The number of frames dropped because the frame's CRC field was incorrect.

- **Receive frames discarded because of an illegal header**—The number of frames dropped because the EA bits were incorrect.

- **Receive frames discarded because of an alignment error**—The number of frames dropped because the payload was not byte-aligned.

- **Receive frames discarded because of an illegal length**—The number of frames dropped because they were fewer than 5 bytes long or greater than 4510 bytes long.

- **Receive frames discarded because exceeded queue DE threshold**—The number of DE frames dropped because the VC queue DE threshold was exceeded.

- **Receive frames discarded because there was no channel**—The number of received frames dropped because the ATM backbone connection was inactive.

- **Receive frames discarded because of an unknown DLCI**—The number of receive frames dropped with an invalid or unknown DLCI.

- **Receive last unknown DLCI**—The DLCI of the last dropped "unknown DLCI" frame.

- **Receive frames tagged FECN**—The number of frames received that were tagged FECN by the FRSM because the ingress VC queue ECN threshold was exceeded.

- **Receive frames tagged BECN**—The number of frames received that were tagged BECN by the FRSM because the egress VC queue ECN threshold was exceeded.

- **Receive frames tagged DE**—The number of frames received that were tagged DE by the FRSM based on the configured policing characteristics (CIR and Bc).

- **Status**—The number of short or long status messages transmitted (UNI or NNI) and received (NNI only).

- **Status inquiry**—The number of short or long status inquiries transmitted (NNI only) and received (UNI or NNI).

- **Asynchronous update**—The number of asynchronous updates transmitted (UNI or NNI) and received (NNI only).

- **Receive invalid request**—The number of invalid or unrecognizable LMI messages received.

- **Receive UNI sequence mismatch**—The number of UNI inquiry messages received with skipped or repeated sequence numbers.
- **Receive UNI signaling timeout**—The number of expected status inquiry messages that were not received from the attached equipment.
- **Receive NNI signaling timeout**—The number of expected status messages that were not received from the attached equipment.
- **Frames CLLM**—The number of ForeSight update frames transmitted and received.
- **Bytes CLLM**—The number of ForeSight update bytes transmitted and received.
- **CLLM failures**—The number of times that expected ForeSight updates were not received.

Configuring a Frame Relay Port on an FRSM

This section shows you the procedures for adding, configuring, and monitoring Frame Relay ports on an FRSM:

Step 1   Type **dsplns**. This outputs the line configuration and status information. Confirm that the line you want to use is active. Also check that the timeslots you want to use for your port are available.

Step 2   Type **dspports**. This outputs the port configuration and status information. Confirm that the port number you want to use does not already exist on the card.

Step 3   Type **addport** *<port number> <line number> <DS0 speed> <beginning timeslot> <number of timeslots> <port type>* on FRSM-8T1, FRSM-8E1, and FRSM-2CT3 cards, or type **addport** *<port number> <line number> <port type>* on FRSM-HS1/B, FRSM-HS2, and FRSM-T3E3 cards. This creates a new Frame Relay port.

Step 4   Type **dspports** to confirm that your port has been added.

Step 5   Type **dspport** *<port number>* to verify the port configuration.

Step 6   If you want to change the port signaling options, type **cnfport** *<port number> <signaling> <asynchronous updates> <ELMI> [T391] [T392] [N391] [N392] [N393]* and make the necessary changes. You could also use the **xcnfport** command.

Step 7   If you want to change the CLLM configuration, type **cnfportcllm** *<port number> <CLLM enable> <CLLM timer>*. You could also use the **xcnfport** command.

Step 8   Type **dspport** *<port number>* to verify your changes.

Step 9   Type **dspportcnt** *<port number>* to verify that signaling and data frames are being exchanged with the CPE.

You have successfully completed the steps necessary for adding, configuring, and monitoring Frame Relay ports on an FRSM.

Frame Relay Connections

A Frame Relay connection is an end-to-end permanent virtual circuit (PVC) that originates and terminates on MGX FRSM Frame Relay ports. The connection receives frames, converts them into ATM cells using AAL5, and transports the cells to the remote port. All Frame Relay connections are bidirectional: Traffic flows in both directions.

You can add two kinds of Frame Relay connections in an MGX network: feeder and local. Feeder connections go from the FRSM to the PXM trunk and are transported through the ATM backbone network to the destination MGX switch. Local connections go from one port on an MGX switch to another port on the same switch. Local connections can be between ports on the same or different FRSM cards. Both feeder and local connections perform the same functions.

Connection Types

The FRSM supports three connection types that align with the three port types: Frame Relay, frame forwarding, and Frame-based User-Network Interface (FUNI) (see Figure 20-7). A connection must terminate on the appropriate port type. For example, frame forwarding connections must terminate on frame forwarding ports.

Figure 20-7 *The Three Connection Types Supported on the FRSM*

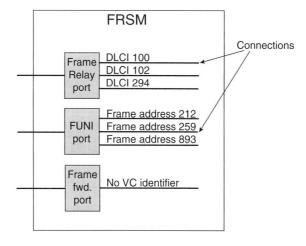

Frame Relay connections support standard ITU-T Q.922 frames. Multiple Frame Relay connections can terminate on a single port. The data-link connection identifier (DLCI) differentiates traffic between connections.

Frame forwarding connections support frame-based traffic such as X.25, HDLC, and SDLC. Only one frame forwarding connection can terminate on a port. The FRSM does not look at any addressing information in the frame and cannot make switching decisions.

FUNI connections support standard FUNI frames. Multiple FUNI connections can terminate on a single port. The frame address is used to send the frames on the appropriate connection.

NOTE   Figure 20-7 illustrates FRSM connections on Frame Relay ports and FUNI ports. Be aware that the main difference between standard Frame Relay and FUNI is the DLCI/Frame address.

Feeder Example

A Frame Relay feeder connection comprises three connection segments (see Figure 20-8):

- A master connection between the FRSM and PXM trunk on one MGX switch.

- A variable-rate routing connection through the ATM backbone network. The ATM connection type depends on the backbone network. If there is a BPX backbone network, you need an ATM-Frame Relay (ATFR) or ATM-Frame Relay with ForeSight (ATFST) connection. If there is a nonBPX backbone network, you need an nrt-VBR or ABR connection.

- A master connection between the FRSM and PXM trunk on the other MGX switch.

Figure 20-8 *Feeder Connection in an MGX Network*

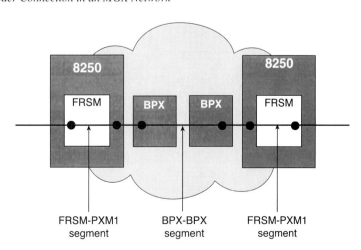

Local Example

A Frame Relay local connection comprises two connection segments (see Figure 20-9):

- A slave connection on one FRSM. This connection must be added first.
- A master connection on the other FRSM pointing to the slave connection.

Figure 20-9 *Local Connection on an MGX Switch*

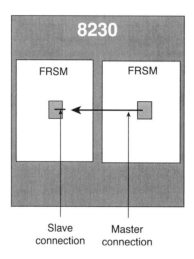

NOTE Note that the local connection (from master to slave) illustrated in Figure 20-9 runs through the PXM.

Interworking

ATM-Frame Relay interworking on the FRSM allows Frame Relay traffic to travel through or terminate in an ATM network. The interworking function on the FRSM must convert frames into ATM cells so that the ATM network can process and terminate the cells.

Two kinds of interworking are supported on the FRSM: network interworking and service interworking.

Network Interworking

Network interworking (NIW) is the most commonly used interworking method on the FRSM. The source FRSM takes the Frame Relay frames and segments them into cells using AAL5 for transport across an ATM backbone. The frames are kept intact and are reassembled at the destination FRSM. Network interworking can also be used between the FRSM and other Frame Relay interfaces. Figure 20-10 shows a NIW connection. Note that the entire frame, including the header and CRC, is segmented into ATM cells using AAL5.

Figure 20-10 *Network Interworking Connection*

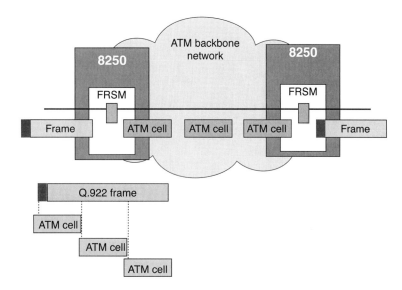

Service Interworking

Service interworking (SIW) is used when traffic originates as Frame Relay frames on an FRSM but terminates on an ATM interface either on a remote MGX switch or somewhere on the ATM backbone network. In this case, the frames are not left intact but are transformed so that the ATM side of the connection can process the data.

Transparent SIW takes the frame and removes the header and CRC. The payload is then segmented into cells using AAL5. This method is most often used to provide voice and data services between a device with a Frame Relay interface and a device with an ATM interface across the WAN. Figure 20-11 shows a transparent SIW connection. Note that the frame payload, but not the header or CRC, is encapsulated into ATM cells using AAL5.

Translated SIW expects the incoming frame payload to be in a format defined by RFC 1490. The frame header and CRC are removed, and the payload is converted to a new format (RFC 1483) prior to segmentation using AAL5.

Figure 20-11 *Service Interworking Connection*

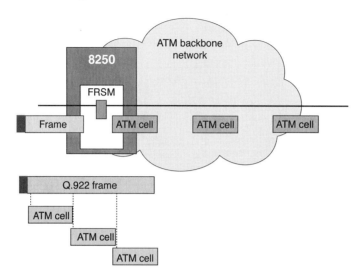

Translated SIW is most often used between a Frame Relay router and an ATM router configured with AAL5SNAP. Figure 20-12 shows a translated SIW connection. Note that the frame header and CRC are removed and that the payload is translated from RFC 1490 to RFC 1483 and is then encapsulated into ATM cells using AAL5.

Figure 20-12 *Translated Service Interworking Connection*

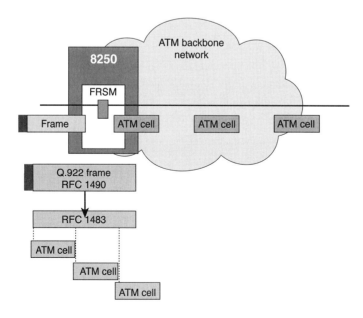

Frame Relay Policing

Policing is the process of monitoring ingress traffic to determine whether the traffic can enter and how that traffic is handled as soon as it is inside the network. Each connection has a number of policing parameters that can include characteristics such as burst sizes and data rates. The end-user device is responsible for meeting the defined policing requirements. Otherwise, the traffic is deemed noncompliant and can be dropped by the network.

A *leaky bucket* is a model used to define policing on ingress for Frame Relay connections on the MGX switch. It is important to remember that the leaky bucket is not a queue structure, but a way to describe how the network monitors and controls incoming user cells.

It is easiest to think of the model as a test that is done on the traffic to answer two questions:

- Should the frame be allowed into the network?
- If so, should it be given a normal or low priority (set the DE bit to 1)?

Low-Speed FRSM Policing

The low-speed FRSM cards (FRSM-8T1, FRSM-8E1, and FRSM-HS1/B) use a single leaky bucket model to police ingress traffic (see Figure 20-13). The bucket fills up based on the incoming traffic—one token for each byte in the incoming frame. The bucket leaks at a rate defined as the Committed Information Rate (CIR). Two thresholds on the leaky bucket define the policing results:

- **Bc (committed burst size)**—If the bucket is less than Bc full when a frame arrives, the frames are sent into the network without any modification. If the frame arrives and the bucket is greater than Bc full, the frames are tagged for possible discard (the cells created from the frame are marked with CLP = 1).
- **Be (excess burst size)**—If the bucket is full (Bc + Be) when a frame arrives, the frames are immediately dropped.

In other words, bursts up to the Bc are committed or guaranteed. Bursts in excess of the Bc by an amount Be are permitted but not guaranteed. Bursts beyond the Be are not permitted. The CIR, Bc, and Be values are configurable per connection on the FRSM.

Low-Speed FRSM Example

A 256 kbps Frame Relay port supports several connections. One connection has the following policing characteristics:

- Bc is 1000 bytes or 8000 bits
- Be is 1000 bytes or 8000 bits
- CIR is 64 kbps

Figure 20-13 *Leaky Bucket Policing Model for Low-Speed FRSMs*

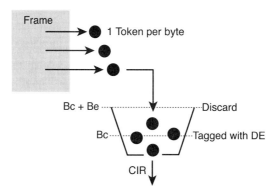

To gain a better understanding of how the traffic is handled as it enters the network, it is useful to calculate the amount of time and the number of bytes that are compliant when the traffic arrives at some defined rate.

In this example, the frames arrive at the port speed, 256 kbps. Assuming that the leaky bucket is empty, the following equation applies:

$$Bc + Be = T \times (AR - CIR)$$

Bc + Be represents the number of bytes in the bucket, T is the time period, and AR is the arrival rate.

With Bc + Be solved for T, the following equations result:

Time until frames are marked with DE = Bc / (AR – CIR)
Time until frames are discarded = (Bc + Be) / (AR – CIR)

When the example numbers are plugged into the equations, the time until frames are marked with DE is 41.7 milliseconds, and the time until frames are discarded is 83.3 milliseconds. Another way of looking at these numbers is that a burst of 1334 bytes can enter before the frames are marked with DE, and a burst of 2668 bytes can enter before the frames are discarded. Figure 20-14 shows how the traffic is policed over time.

In order to guarantee that all frames are compliant, bursts less than 41.67 milliseconds (or 1334 bytes) must be followed by a gap of the same time period before another burst is sent.

Figure 20-14 *Traffic Policed Over Time*

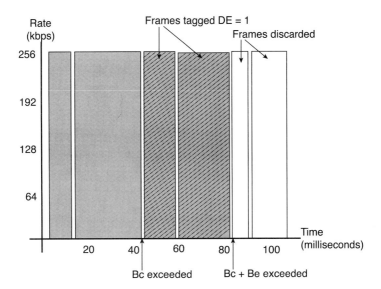

High-Speed FRSM Policing

The high-speed FRSM cards (FRSM-2CT3, FRSMT3E3, and FRSM-HS2) use a dual leaky bucket model to police ingress traffic (see Figure 20-15).

Figure 20-15 *Dual Leaky Bucket Policing Model for High-Speed FRSMs*

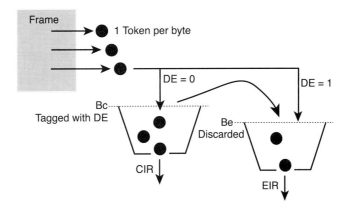

Only frames with the DE set to 0 are checked on the first bucket. The first bucket fills up to the Bc and empties out at the CIR. Noncompliant frames are sent on to the second bucket.

The second bucket checks all frames. The second bucket fills up to the Be and empties out at the excess information rate (EIR). The EIR is calculated as follows:

$$EIR = (Be / Bc) \times CIR$$

Noncompliant frames on the second bucket are discarded.

High-Speed FRSM Example

A 256 kbps Frame Relay port supports several connections. One connection has the following policing characteristics:

- Bc is 1000 bytes or 8000 bits
- Be is 2000 bytes or 16,000 bits
- CIR is 64 kbps

The EIR is therefore 128 kbps. Using equations for T that are similar to those for the low-speed example discussed a moment ago, the following equations apply:

Time until frames are marked with DE = Bc / (AR – CIR)
Time until frames are discarded = Be / (AR – EIR)

When the example numbers are plugged into the equations, the time until frames are marked with DE is 41.7 milliseconds, and the time until frames are discarded is 125 milliseconds. Another way of looking at these numbers is that a burst of 1334 bytes can enter before the frames are marked with DE, and a burst of 4000 bytes can enter before the frames are discarded. Figure 20-16 shows how the traffic is policed over time.

NOTE   Notice that with similar policing values, the end result of policing on high-speed FRSM cards is different than with low-speed cards. Be aware of this when you are configuring connections on different card types.

Figure 20-16 *Traffic Policed Over Time*

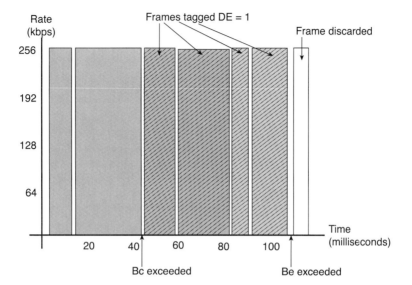

ForeSight on Frame Relay Connections

The ForeSight feature is a closed-loop feedback mechanism that predicts and adjusts network traffic to avoid congestion and subsequent data loss and to fully utilize available bandwidth. ForeSight is a congestion-management feature. It is a prestandard version of available bit rate (ABR) implemented on Frame Relay connections. The ForeSight feature is enabled per connection and controls the VC queue service rate. When congestion occurs on a connection, the queue service rate decreases; when there is no congestion, the queue service rate increases. By dynamically adjusting the rate at which traffic enters the network, the ForeSight feature prevents data loss and offers the connection the maximum bandwidth available in the network.

The ForeSight feature relies on measuring network congestion along the data path and reporting the congestion to the source end of the connection. Figure 20-17 shows the following:

- Data moves from the source to the destination. Control messages may also flow from source to destination.

- As the traffic (both data and control) travels through the network, the various network elements may mark congestion and other control fields in the cells.

- The destination device collects the congestion and control information and reports the information back to the source device. The source, after receiving the congestion and control information from the destination, makes the required adjustments in the VC queue service rate.

Figure 20-17 *The ForeSight Feature*

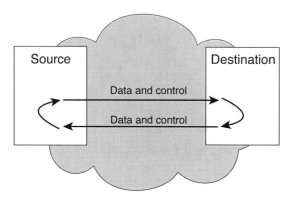

Potential Congestion Locations

Congestion is measured on egress queues both on the FRSM and on intermediate trunk queues in the BPX network (if you are using a BPX backbone network). For local connections or when the MGX switch is attached to a non-BPX network, only the FRSM egress queue congestion is considered.

NOTE   The MGX 8850-PXM45 does not support the ForeSight feature. It is recommended that you use standard ABR (if available) on Frame Relay connections that route through MGX 8850-PXM45 backbone networks.

The thresholds for determining congestion in an MGX/BPX tiered network are

- The ECN threshold on the egress FRSM port
- The EFCN threshold on the egress BPX, BXM, or BNI trunks (the default value is approximately 10 percent of the queue depth)
- The EFCI threshold on the ingress BXM card (the threshold is hard-coded)

Figure 20-18 shows the queues where congestion can occur on a Frame Relay connection in a tiered network.

Figure 20-18 *Queues Where Congestion Can Occur on a Frame Relay Connection*

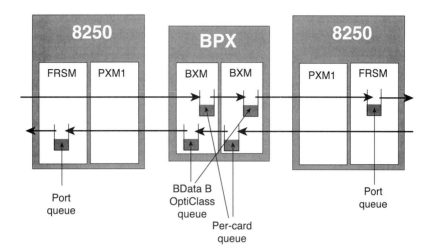

ForeSight Congestion Criteria

As a result of measuring and reporting congestion in the data cells (EFCI bit) and control cells, the source FRSM card must adjust the VC queue service rate accordingly. Table 20-1 lists the conditions required for the ForeSight feature to declare a congested, severely congested, or not congested state, and the resulting VC queue service rate change.

Table 20-1 *ForeSight Congestion Conditions, States, and Results*

Condition	Congestion State	Result
Last sampled data cell, EFCI = 1 or port queue > ECN threshold	Congested	New rate = (old rate) × (rate down)
Last sampled data cell, EFCI = 1 and port queue > queue depth	Severely congested	New rate = (old rate) × (rate fast down)
Last sampled data cell, EFCI = 0 and port queue < ECN threshold	Not congested	New rate = (old rate) + (MIR rate up)

The information in Table 20-1 is applicable when the MIR is the configured minimum information rate and rate up, rate down, and rate fast down are the configured ForeSight adjustment rates.

ForeSight Configurable Characteristics

The following ForeSight characteristics are configured per connection:

- **Peak Information Rate (PIR)**—The maximum connection rate that the source can allow.

- **Minimum Information Rate (MIR)**—The minimum connection rate that the source can allow.

- **Quiescent Information Rate (QIR)**—The connection rate that the source uses after a set idle period (QIR timeout).

The following ForeSight characteristics are configured per FRSM (see Figure 20-19):

- **Rate up**—A percentage of the configured MIR that the connection rate increases if there is no congestion. By default, rate up is 10 percent.

- **Rate down**—A percentage of the current connection rate that the connection rate drops to if there is congestion. By default, rate down is 87 percent (which is equivalent to a 13% reduction).

- **Rate fast down**—A percentage of the current connection rate that the connection rate drops to if there is severe congestion. By default, rate fast down is 50 percent.

- **QIR timeout**—The idle period after which the connection rate is reset to the QIR. By default, QIR timeout is 10 seconds.

Figure 20-19 *Foresight Characteristics Configured Per FRSM*

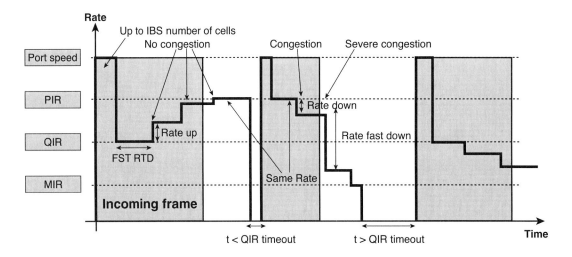

Example of a Congested Network

You have added a Frame Relay connection to an FRSM that uses the ForeSight feature and has been configured with the following:

- MIR 8 kbps
- QIR 16 kbps
- PIR 24 kbps

Assuming that the ForeSight adjustment rates and the QIR timeout are set to the defaults, how will the connection behave when there is network congestion? Figure 20-20 shows the connection rate over time.

Figure 20-20 *Connection Rate Over Time in a Congested Network*

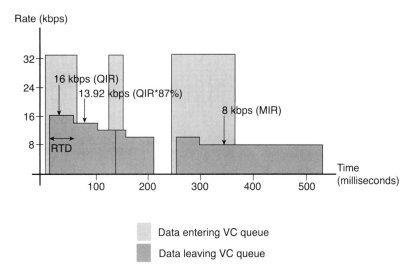

In this example, the data leaving the VC queue is initially served at the QIR, which means that the connection was idle for at least the QIR timeout period (10 seconds). The queue service rate decreases to 87 percent of the QIR when a congestion control message is returned to the source, indicating that there is network congestion. If the network remains in a congested state, the rate continues to decrease. Notice that the MIR is the lowest rate that is allowed, regardless of the congestion control messages received.

Example of an Uncongested Network

You have added a Frame Relay connection to an FRSM that uses the ForeSight feature and has been configured with the following:

- MIR 8 kbps
- QIR 16 kbps
- PIR 24 kbps

Assuming that the ForeSight adjustment rates and the QIR timeout are set to the defaults, how will the connection behave when there is no network congestion? Figure 20-21 shows the connection rate over time.

Figure 20-21 *Connection Rate Over Time in an Uncongested Network*

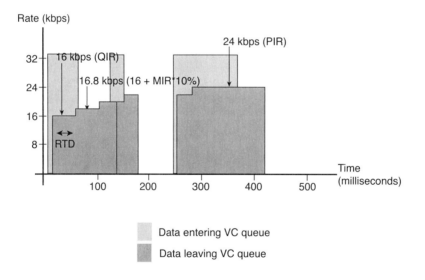

In this example, the data leaving the VC queue is initially served at the QIR, which means that the connection was idle for at least the QIR timeout period (10 seconds). The queue service rate increases by 10 percent of the MIR when a congestion control message is returned to the source, indicating that there is no network congestion. If the network remains in an uncongested state, the rate continues to increase. Notice that the PIR is the highest rate that is allowed, regardless of the congestion control messages received.

ABR for Frame Relay

Available bit rate (ABR) connections include a closed-loop feedback mechanism that predicts and adjusts network traffic to avoid congestion and subsequent data loss. ABR is enabled per connection and controls the VC queue service rate. When congestion occurs on a connection, the queue service rate decreases; when there is no congestion, the queue service rate increases. By dynamically adjusting the rate at which traffic enters the network, ABR prevents data loss and offers the connection the maximum bandwidth available in the network.

Standard ABR utilizes a resource management (RM) cell to measure and report network conditions to determine the virtual circuit queue service rate. Periodically, the source sends an RM cell in the data stream to the destination. Along the way, the network might alter bits in the RM cell to report network conditions and availability. When the destination receives the RM cell, it turns it around and sends it back to the source. This is called a backward RM (BRM) cell. When the source receives the BRM cell, it is required to adjust the queue service rate accordingly. On the FRSM, the Frame Relay port is both virtual source and virtual destination. In other words, the port performs the role of the source and destination in the ABR feedback loop.

The RM Cell

RM cells are standard UNI cells with a payload comprising control fields that are used to mark and report network congestion. The key control fields are as follows:

- **Direction (DIR)**—Determines the cell's direction, either from source to destination (set to 1) or destination to source (set to 0).

- **Backward Explicit Congestion Notification (BECN)**—Determines whether the cell is a switch-generated backward congestion cell (set to 1) or not (set to 0). A BECN RM cell is generated by a network element and is used to notify the source of congestion. A BECN cell must have either CI or NI set to 1.

- **Congestion Indicator (CI)**—The CI bit is set to 1 by the network if the RM cell experiences congestion.

- **No Increase (NI)**—The NI bit is set to a 1 by a network element that cannot allow the connection to increase in rate.

- **Explicit Rate (ER)**—In most cases, the RM cell reports whether a connection can increase or decrease its rate. An ER may be defined by a network element to tell the source to use a particular rate.

- **Current Cell Rate (CCR)**—Placed in the RM cell by the source, the CCR is the rate currently being used for the connection.

- **Minimum Cell Rate (MCR)**—Placed in the RM cell by the source, the MCR is the configured minimum allowable rate for the connection.

When Are RM Cells Sent?

The virtual source determines when RM cells are sent on the connection based on the following configurable characteristics:

- **Number per RM (NRM)**—The maximum number of cells a source can send for each forward RM cell. In other words, an RM cell must be sent for every NRM – 1 data cells. The NRM is configured per connection.

- **Minimum per RM (MRM)**—The minimum number of cells that can be sent between RM cells. The MRM cannot be configured and is set to two cells.

- **Time RM (TRM)**—The maximum time between RM cells, which can be configured per connection.

- **Fixed Round-Trip Time (FRTT)**—The amount of time it takes for an RM cell to travel through the network from the source to the destination and back again. The FRTT can be configured per connection.

- **Transient Buffer Exposure (TBE)**—The number of RM cells that can initially be sent by the source before it must wait for a BRM cell from the network. The TBE can be configured per PVC.

Potential Congestion Locations

Congestion is measured on egress queues on both the FRSM and the intermediate trunk queues in the ATM network. The FRSM egress queue congestion is considered for local connections only. Here are the thresholds for determining congestion in an MGX/BPX tiered network:

- The ECN threshold on the egress FRSM port

- The EFCN threshold on the egress BPX, BXM, or BNI trunks (the default value is approximately 10 percent of the queue depth)

- The EFCI threshold on the ingress BXM card (the threshold is hard-coded)

Refer again to Figure 20-18, which shows the queues where congestion can occur on a Frame Relay connection in a tiered network. If the backbone network comprises MGX 8850-PXM45 switches, the network congestion points are similar, except that the AXSM, not the BXM, supports the lines between switches. ATM switches from other vendors have similar queuing schemes.

ABR Rate Adjustments

As a result of measuring and reporting congestion utilizing RM and BRM cells, the source must adjust the VC queue service rate accordingly. Table 20-2 describes the rate adjustments made on an ABR connection.

NOTE   Neither the PXM1 nor the AUSM can perform the functions of the virtual source.

Table 20-2   *ABR Congestion Information and Results*

Congestion Information	Result
No BRM cells are received after CRM cells have been sent	New ACR = ACR – (ACR × CDF)
No congestion; both CI and NI are 0 in the BRM cell	New ACR = ACR + (PCR × RIF)
CI in the BRM cell is set to 1	New ACR = ACR – (ACR × RDF)
NI in the BRM cell is set to 1	New ACR = ACR
The EFCI bit in the most recent data cell when a BRM cell arrives is set to 1	New ACR = ACR – (ACR × RDF)
The ER is set	New ACR = ER

Rate adjustment characteristics include the following:

- **ACR**—Allowed cell rate
- **CRM**—Cutoff RM
- **CDF**—Cutoff decrease factor
- **RIF**—Rate increase factor
- **RDF**—Rate decrease factor
- **PCR**—Peak cell rate
- **ER**—Explicit rate

Configurable ABR Connection Parameters

In summary, the following ABR connection characteristics can be configured:

- **Minimum cell rate (MCR)**—The minimum connection rate that the source can allow in cells per second
- **Peak cell rate (PCR)**—The maximum connection rate that the source can allow in cells per second
- **Initial cell rate (ICR)**—The initial cell rate after timeout period ADTF
- **RIF**—A factor that determines the rate increase when there is no congestion

- **RDF**—A factor that determines the rate decrease when there is congestion
- **CDF**—A factor that determines the rate decrease when BRM cells are not being received from the network
- **NRM**—A factor that determines the maximum number of cells a source can send for each forward RM cell
- **TRM**—The maximum time between RM cells
- **TBE**—The number of RM cells that can initially be sent by the source before it must wait for a BRM cell from the network
- **FRTT**—The amount of time it takes for an RM cell to travel through the network from the source to the destination and back again
- **Allowed-cell-rate decrease time factor (ADTF)**—The amount of time between RM cells before the source rate returns to the ICR

Example of a Congested Network

A standard ABR connection has been added to a network. It is configured with the following:

- MCR 20 cps
- ICR 40 cps
- PCR 60 cps
- RDF 16 percent

How will the connection behave when there is network congestion? Figure 20-22 shows the connection rate over time.

In this example, the data leaving the VC queue is initially served at the ICR, which means that the ADTF time has passed since the last RM cell was received. The queue service rate decreases by the RDF (16 percent) when an RM cell with CI set to 1 is returned to the source, indicating that there is network congestion. If the network remains in a congested state, the rate continues to decrease.

NOTE   The MCR is the lowest rate that is allowed, regardless of the congestion reported in the RM cells.

Figure 20-22 *Standard ABR Connection in a Congested Network*

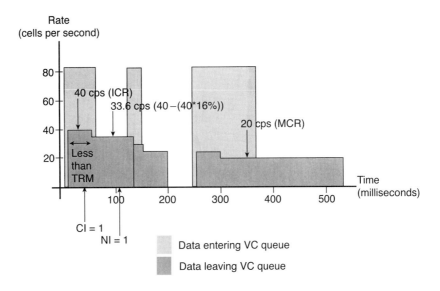

Example of an Uncongested Network

A standard ABR connection has been added to a network. It is configured with the following:

- MCR 20 cps
- ICR 40 cps
- PCR 60 cps
- RIF 8 percent

How will the connection behave when there is no network congestion? Figure 20-23 shows the connection rate over time.

In this example, the data leaving the VC queue is initially served at the ICR, which means that the ADTF time has passed since the last RM cell was received. The queue service rate increases based on the RIF (8 percent) when no congestion is reported in the network (RM cell with both CI and NI set to 0). If the network remains in an uncongested state, the rate continues to increase. Notice that the PCR is the highest rate that is allowed, regardless of the lack of congestion reported in the RM cells.

Figure 20-23 *Standard ABR Connection in an Uncongested Network*

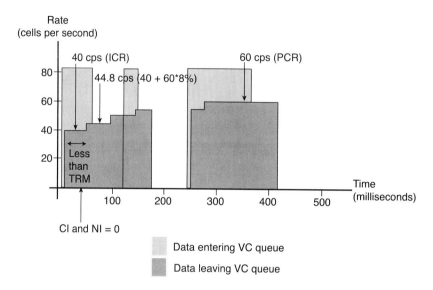

VC Queues on the FRSM

The FRSM buffers ingress (from the CPE to the network) traffic in virtual circuit (VC) queues. VC queues are used to shape the ingress traffic. The FRSM serves the data in the queues based on the connection's expected rate (usually the CIR). Connections that use ABR or ForeSight congestion management features are served at a variable rate, depending on network availability.

Each VC queue has the following configurable characteristics:

- The queue depth that defines the maximum amount of data that can be buffered at any time.

- The DE threshold that defines when DE-marked frames are discarded. If the queue fills up beyond the DE threshold, any newly arriving frames with the DE bit set to 1 are not allowed into the queue and are discarded. Any frames already in the queue are not discarded.

- The ECN threshold that defines when congestion bits (FECN and BECN) are set on the frames. If the queue fills up beyond the ECN threshold, any newly arriving frames have their FECN bit set to 1. Any frames traveling in the opposite direction (egress) have their BECN bit set to 1.

On low-speed FRSM cards (FRSM-8T1, FRSM-8E1, and FRSM-HS1/B), all VC queues are equal; no VC has priority over another. On high-speed FRSM cards (FRSM-2CT3, FRSM-T3E3, and FRSM-HS2), each VC is assigned a class of service (CoS). The CoS determines how the data is serviced on ingress and egress. There are four different classes of service:

- Real-time variable bit rate (rt-VBR)
- Nonreal-time variable bit rate (nrt-VBR)
- Available bit rate (ABR)
- Unspecified bit rate (UBR)

The ingress VC queue service algorithm gives priority to the queues in the order they are listed here (rt-VBR has the highest priority, and UBR has the lowest). Figure 20-24 shows the VC queues on a high-speed FRSM card.

Figure 20-24 *VC Queues on a High-Speed FRSM*

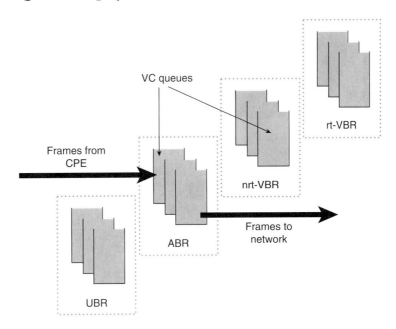

Initial Burst Size Definition

An Initial Burst Size (IBS) is defined for each connection. The IBS function determines whether the data is allowed to burst at a rate greater than the usual VC queue service rate. A burst must be earned or accrued over time. When a connection is silent (not sending frames), it earns credits at the queue service rate. The IBS is the maximum number of credits that can be earned by a connection and sent to the network at the full port speed. Setting the IBS value to 0 disables the IBS function.

Initial Burst Size Example

For example, if the CIR is 8 kbps, 8000 bits (1000 bytes) are earned per second when the connection is silent. If the IBS is 100 bytes, the maximum burst is earned in one-tenth of a second (100 milliseconds). Figure 20-25 shows how the traffic is handled in the VC queue for this example.

Figure 20-25 *VC Queue Traffic*

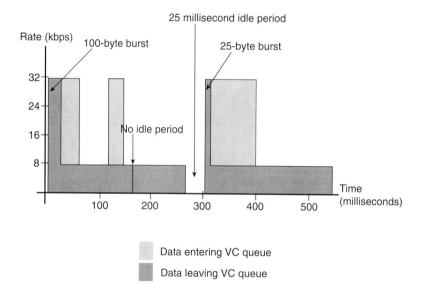

Commands for Adding, Configuring, and Displaying Frame Relay Connections

This section describes the commands used to add, configure, and display Frame Relay connections on the FRSM:

- **addcon**—Creates a new connection on the FRSM.
- **delcon**—Removes a connection from the FRSM.
- **dspcons**—Lists summary information for all connections on the card.

- **dspcon**—Lists detailed status and configuration information for a connection.
- **cnfchanpol**—Modifies the policing characteristics of a connection, including CIR and burst sizes.
- **cnfchaneir**—Modifies the excess information rate (EIR) for a connection that has a CIR of 0.
- **cnfchanabrparams**—Modifies the standard ABR rate adjustment characteristics of a connection, including increase and decrease factors and RM cell timers.
- **cnfchanabrrates**—Modifies the standard ABR traffic rates for a connection, including the peak, minimum, and initial cell rates.
- **cnfchanstdabr**—Modifies all the standard ABR characteristics of a connection, including those modified using the **cnfchanabrparams** and **cnfchanabrrates** commands.
- **cnfchanfst**—Modifies the ForeSight characteristics of a connection, including the peak, minimum, and initial cell rates.
- **cnfchanmap**—Modifies the control bitmapping on a connection.
- **cnfchaningressq**—Modifies the ingress queue characteristics of a connection.
- **cnfchanegressq**—Modifies the egress queue characteristics of a connection.

Add Connection Command

The **addcon** command is used to create a new Frame Relay connection on the MGX FRSM. Remember that multiple Frame Relay and FUNI connections can be added to a single port, but only one frame forwarding connection can be added to a port. (You can use the **delcon** command to remove the connection.)

The command syntax is

```
addcon <port> <DLCI> <CIR> <channel type> [egress service type] [CAC]
    [controller type] [mastership] [remote connection ID] [service type]
```

The parameter options are as follows:

- *port*—The Frame Relay port number that terminates the connection. 1 to 192 for T1 cards or 1 to 248 for E1 cards.
- *DLCI*—The DLCI of the Frame Relay connection. 0 to 1023.
- *CIR*—The committed information rate for the connection. 0 to 1536000 bps for T1 lines or 0 to 2048000 bps for E1 lines.
- *channel type*—1 = network interworking (NIW), 2 = transparent service interworking (SIW), 3 = translated SIW, 4 = FUNI, 5 = frame forwarding.

- *egress service type* (FRSM-HS2, FRSM-2CT3, and FRSM-T3E3 only)—The egress service type of the connection. 1 = high priority, 2 = rt-VBR, 3 = nrt-VBR, 4 = ABR, 5 = UBR.

- *CAC*—Enables or disables connection admission control (CAC). 1 = enable, 2 = disable.

- *controller type*—1 = PAR, 2 = PNNI. The controller type is not specified on the slave end of MGX local connections.

- *mastership*—1 = master, 2 = slave. When you add a slave connection on an MGX FRSM, do not enter the mastership value. Eliminating this parameter automatically makes the connection a slave. If you want to specify a service type for a slave connection, you must enter 2.

- *remote connection ID*—The destination connection ID for master connections in the form *node.slot.port.VPI.VCI*. For MGX feeder connections, the slot number is 0 for the PXM. For MGX local connections, the VPI is always 0 and the VCI is the remote DLCI value. If you want to specify a service type, you must enter the correct information for master and slave connections.

- *service type* (FRSM-8T1 and FRSM-8E1 only)—The service type used on the PXM1 trunk. 1 = high priority, 2 = rt-VBR, 3 = nrt-VBR, 4 = ForeSight ABR, 5 = UBR, 9 = Standard ABR.

Display Connections Command

The **dspcons** command provides summary status and configuration information for all connections on the card. Use this command to learn which connections have been added and how they are configured. Example 20-5 shows an example of the **dspcons** output.

NOTE   Because the output is very wide, the lines have been divided in Example 20-5.

Example 20-5 dspcons *Output*

```
hei1pop1.1.11.FRSM.a > dspcons

  Line       ConnId          Chan EQ ServType I/EQDepth    I/EQDEThre
  --- --------------------   ---- -- -------- ----- ----- ----- -----
   1   hei1pop1.11.1.0.100    16   2  fstABR   65535/65535 32767/32767
   1   hei1pop1.11.1.0.101    17   2  stdABR   65535/65535 32767/32767
   1   hei1pop1.11.1.0.102    18   1  rtVBR    65535/65535 32767/32767
   1   hei1pop1.11.1.0.202    20   2  nrtVBR   65535/65535 32767/32767
   1   hei1pop1.11.1.0.203    21   2  nrtVBR   65535/65535 32767/32767
```

Example 20-5 dspcons *Output (Continued)*

```
            I/EECNThre  Fst/ DE Type  Alarm
            ----- ----- --- --- ----- -----
            6553/6553  Ena/Dis NIW   Yes
            6553/6553  Dis/Dis NIW   Yes
            6553/6553  Dis/Dis NIW   Yes
            6553/6553  Dis/Dis NIW   Yes
            6553/6553  Dis/Dis NIW   Yes
```

The following information is listed in the **dspcons** output:

- Line number

- **Connection ID**—Connection identification in the form of *nodename.slot.port.0.DLCI*.

- Channel number

- **Egress queue select**—The priority of the channel in the egress queue (1 = high, 2 = low).

- **Service type**—The configured service type (ForeSight ABR, standard ABR, rt-VBR, nrt-VBR, or UBR).

- Ingress/egress VC queue depth

- Ingress/egress VC queue ECN threshold

- Ingress/egress VC queue DE threshold

- **ForeSight**—Specifies whether the ForeSight feature is enabled or disabled on this channel.

- **DE**—Specifies whether CLP-to-DE mapping is enabled or disabled on this channel.

- **Type**—NIW, SIW-t (transparent), SIW-x (translational), FUNI, frame forwarding.

- **Alarm**—The connection alarm indication, either yes or no. Connection alarms are the result of local line or port failures or remote connection alarms reported via OAM cells or the ATM LMI protocol.

Display Connection Command

The **dspcon** command shows detailed configuration and status information on a given Frame Relay connection. There are three pages in the **dspcon** output. Example 20-6 shows an example of the **dspcon** output on a feeder connection.

NOTE   A number of fields only apply standard ABR or ForeSight connections.

Example 20-6 dspcon *Output, Page 1*

```
hei1pop1.1.11.FRSM.a > dspcon 1.101

  ChanNum:                  17
  ChanRowStatus:            Add
  ChanPortNum:              1
  ChanDLCI:                 101
  EgressQSelect:            2
  ChanServType:             stdABR
  IngressQDepth:            65535
  IngressQDEThresh:         32767
  IngressQECNThresh:        6553
  EgressQDepth:             65535
  EgressQDEThresh:          32767
  EgressQECNThresh:         6553
  DETaggingEnable:          Disabled
  CIR:                      16000
  Bc:                       5100
  Be:                       5100
  IBS:                      100
  ForeSightEnable:          Disabled
  QIR:                      50
  MIR:                      41
  PIR:                      82
Type <CR> to continue, Q<CR> to stop:
```

Many of the fields shown using the **dspcon** command can be modified using a number of configuration commands that are discussed later in this section. Example 20-7 shows the second page of the **dspcon** output.

Example 20-7 dspcon *Output, Page 2*

```
  ICR:                         50
  MCR:                         41
  PCR:                         82
  RIF:                         128
  RDF:                         32
  Nrm:                         64
  Trm:                         255 ms
  TBE:                         16777215 Cells
  FRTT:                        10000 ms
  ADTF:                        10000 ms
  CDF:                         8
  ChanLocalRemoteLpbkState: Disabled
  ChanTestType:                TestOff
  ChanTestState:               NotInProgress
  ChanRTDresult:               65535 ms
  ChanType:                    NIW
  ChanFECNmap:                 setEFCIzero
  ChanDEtoCLPmap:              mapCLP
```

Example 20-7 dspcon *Output, Page 2 (Continued)*

```
    ChanCLPtoDEmap:          mapDE
    ChanFrConnType:          PVC
    ChanIngrPercentUtil:     100

Type <CR> to continue, Q<CR> to stop:
```

Information of interest in Example 20-7 includes the following:

- **Channel loopback state**—Specifies whether the channel loop is enabled or disabled. The local remote loopback faces toward the backbone network and is created using the **addchanloop** command.

- **Test type**—The type of test if a test is in progress.

- **Test state**—The result of the most recent test, either passed or failed.

- **RTD result**—The result of the most recent round-trip delay test (use the **tstdelay** command). If the test has never been run, the test reports 65,535 milliseconds.

- **Channel Frame Relay connection type**—The connection type, either permanent (PVC) or switched (SVC).

- **Channel ingress percent utilization**—Used in the CAC calculation to determine whether a port is oversubscribed in the ingress direction. The expected ingress traffic for a channel = (Minimum Information Rate) × (percent utilization).

Example 20-8 shows the third page of the **dspcon** output.

Example 20-8 dspcon *Output, Page 3*

```
    ChanEgrPercentUtil:      100
    ChanEgrSrvRate:          16000
    ChanOvrSubOvrRide:       Enabled
    ChanLocalVpi:            0
    ChanLocalVci:            101
    ChanLocalNSAP:           68656931706f7031000000000000000000b000100
    ChanRemoteVpi:           100
    ChanRemoteVci:           102
    ChanRemoteNSAP:          68656931706f70310000000000000000000000100
    ChanMastership:          Master
    ChanVpcFlag:             Vcc
    ChanConnServiceType:     ABRSTD
    ChanRoutingPriority:     1
    ChanMaxCost:             255
    ChanRestrictTrunkType:   No Restriction
    ChanConnPCR:             82
    ChanConnMCR:             41
    ChanConnPercentUti:      100
    ChanServiceTypeOverride: disabled
    ChanServiceRate:         41 cps
    ChanZeroCirEir:          0 bps
```

Information of interest in Example 20-8 includes the following:

- **Channel egress percent utilization**—Used in the CAC calculation to determine whether a port is oversubscribed in the egress direction. The expected egress traffic for a channel = (egress service rate) × (percent utilization).

- **Channel oversubscribe override**—If CAC is disabled, the channel oversubscribe override is enabled, which means that the port can be oversubscribed. If CAC is enabled, the port cannot be oversubscribed.

- **Channel local VPI**—This value is always 0 on Frame Relay connections.

- **Channel local VCI**—This value is the same as the DLCI on Frame Relay connections.

- **Channel local NSAP**—The network service access point (NSAP) address uniquely identifies this interface (port) in the network. The 20-byte hexadecimal address comprises the following fields:

  — The most significant 8 bytes (16 digits) is the node name in ASCII. The connection in Example 20-8 is on node hei1pop1.

  — The card slot number is the fourth byte from the right. The connection in Example 20-8 is on card 11.

  — The port number is the second byte from the right. The connection in Example 20-8 is on port 1.

- **Channel remote VPI**—The VPI value at the remote end. In this case, the connection terminates on the PXM, so the VPI value is used on all cells at the ATM trunk interface. A local connection to another FRSM would have a VPI value of 0.

- **Channel remote VCI**—The VCI value at the remote end. In this case, the connection terminates on the PXM, so the VCI value is used on all cells at the ATM trunk interface. A local connection to another FRSM would have a VCI equal to the remote DLCI.

- **Channel remote NSAP**—The remote NSAP address is in the same format as the local NSAP address. If this connection terminates on the PXM, the card slot field is 0. The slave end of a local connection does not have a remote NSAP and is reported as "NULL NSAP."

- **Channel mastership**—The connection's mastership, either master or slave.

- **Channel connection service type**—The service type (ATFR or ATFST) used for the connection in the ATM backbone network.

- **Routing priority, Max cost, and Restrict trunk type**—Not applicable at this time.

- **PCR**—The peak cell rate (PCR) used on the ATM trunk interface for this connection.

- **MCR**—The minimum cell rate (MCR) on the ATM trunk interface for this connection.

- **Percent utilization**—The percentage of on-time cells expected for this connection.

Configure Channel Policing Command

The **cnfchanpol** command is used to modify the policing characteristics of a Frame Relay connection.

The command syntax is

```
cnfchanpol <connection number> <CIR> <Bc> <Be> <IBS> <DE tag> <egress service rate>
```

The parameter options are as follows:

- *connection number*—The connection number in the form *port.DLCI.*

- *CIR*—Determines the rate at which the Frame Relay connection is policed. 0 to the configured port speed.

- *Bc*—Committed burst size. 0 to 65,535 bytes (FRSM-8T1, FRSM-8E1, and FRSM-HS1/B) or 0 to 2,097,151 bytes (FRSM-HS2, FRSM-2CT3, and FRSM-T3E3).

- *Be*—Excess burst size. 0 to 65,535 bytes (FRSM-8T1, FRSM-8E1, and FRSM-HS1/B) or 0 to 2,097,151 bytes (FRSM-HS2, FRSM-2CT3, and FRSM-T3E3).

- *IBS*—The maximum initial burst size that is permitted through the VC queue at the access rate. 0 to 65,535 bytes (FRSM-8T1, FRSM-8E1, and FRSM-HS1/B) or 0 to 2,097,151 bytes (FRSM-HS2, FRSM-2CT3, and FRSM-T3E3) and greater than the Bc.

- *DE tag*—Enables or disables the tagging of the DE bit on ingress frames as the result of the policing mechanism. 1 = enable, 2 = disable.

- *egress service rate*—The rate at which the connection should be serviced on the egress queue. This value is used to determine whether the Frame Relay port is oversubscribed. 0 to the configured port speed.

Configure Channel Excess Information Rate Command

The **cnfchaneir** command sets the excess information rate (EIR) for a connection that has a CIR of 0. The EIR is the second bucket leak rate in the dual leaky bucket policing model.

The command syntax is

```
cnfchaneir <channel number> <zero CIR EIR>
```

The parameter options are as follows:

- *channel number*—The connection's channel number. Use the **dspcons** command to learn your connection's channel number.

- *zero CIR EIR*—The EIR in bits per second for the zero CIR connection.

For example, type **cnfchaneir 20 64000** to set the EIR of channel 20 to 64 kbps.

Configure Channel ABR Parameters Command

The **cnfchanabrparams** command is used to modify the standard ABR connection characteristics of a Frame Relay connection. The **cnfchanabrrates** and **cnfchanstdabr** commands are subsets of the **cnfchanabrparams** command.

The command syntax is

```
cnfchanabrparams <connection number | channel number> <RIF> <RDF> <NRM>
  <TRM> <TBE> <FRTT> <ADTF> <CDF>
```

The parameter options are as follows:

- *connection number*—The connection number in the form *port.DLCI*.
- *channel number*—Alternatively, you can use the connection's channel number.
- *RIF*—Rate increase factor. For cells per second, a factor from 1 to 32,768 in steps of power of 2. For example, you can type 2, 4, 8, 16, or 32 but not 3 or 35.
- *RDF*—Rate decrease factor. For cells per second, a factor from 1 to 32,768 in steps of power of 2.
- *NRM*—Number per RM. From 2 to 256 in steps of power of 2.
- *TRM*—Time between RM. From 3 to 255 milliseconds.
- *TBE*—Transient buffer exposure. From 0 to 1,677,7215 cells.
- *FRTT*—Fixed round-trip time. From 0 to 16,700 milliseconds.
- *ADTF*—Allowed-cell-rate decrease time factor. From 10 to 10,230 milliseconds.
- *CDF*—Cutoff decrease factor. A percentage from 0 to 64 in steps of power of 2.

Configure Channel ForeSight Command

The **cnfchanfst** command is used to modify the ForeSight characteristics on a Frame Relay connection.

The command syntax is

```
cnfchanfst <connection number> <ForeSight enable> <MIR> <PIR> <QIR>
```

The parameter options are as follows:

- *connection number*—The connection number in the form *port.DLCI*.
- *ForeSight enable*—Enables or disables the ForeSight feature on the connection. 1 = enable, 2 = disable.
- *MIR*—The Minimum Information Rate in cells per second (cps).
- *PIR*—The Peak Information Rate in cps.
- *QIR*—The Quiescent Information Rate in cps.

For example, type **cnfchanfst 1.100 1 25 1334 167** to enable the ForeSight feature on connection 1.100 with an MIR of 25 cps, a PIR of 1334 cps, and a QIR of 167 cps.

Configure Channel Mapping Command

The **cnfchanmap** command is used to modify the congestion and priority mapping between the Frame Relay frames and ATM cells.

The command syntax is

```
cnfchanmap <connection number | channel number> <type> <FECN to EFCI>
  <DE to CLP> <CLP to DE>
```

The parameter options are as follows:

- *connection number*—The connection number in the form *port.DLCI.*

- *channel number*—The connection's channel number. Use the **dspcons** command to learn your connection's channel number.

- *type*—The channel type. 1 = NIW, 2 = SIW-transparent, 3 = SIW-translational, 4 = FUNI, 5 = frame forwarding.

- *FECN to EFCI*—Maps the Frame Relay FECN bit to the ATM Explicit Forward Congestion Indication (EFCI) bit. 1 = map EFCI, 2 = EFCI is always set to 0. FECN-to-EFCI mapping should be enabled only on Frame Relay-ATM service interworking connections.

- *DE to CLP*—Maps the Frame Relay DE bit to the ATM Cell Loss Priority (CLP) bit. 1 = map DE, 2 = CLP is always set to 0, 3 = CLP is always set to 1.

- *CLP to DE*—Maps the ATM CLP bit to the Frame Relay DE bit. 1 = map DE, 2 = DE is always set to 0, 3 = DE is always set to 1, 4 = ignore CLP bit.

For example, type **cnfchanmap 2.150 2 1 2 4** to configure the mapping on DLCI 150 on port 2. This transparent service interworking connection maps the FECN bit to the EFCI bit, sets the CLP bit to 0 regardless of the DE bit, and ignores the CLP bits.

Configure Channel Ingress and Egress Queue Commands

The **cnfchaningressq** and **cnfchanegressq** commands are used to modify the ingress and egress VC queues on a Frame Relay connection.

The command syntax is

```
cnfchaningressq <connection number> <queue depth> <ECN threshold> <DE threshold>

cnfchanegressq <connection number> <queue select> <queue depth> <ECN threshold>
  <DE threshold>
```

The parameter options are as follows:

- *connection number*—The connection number in the form *port.DLCI.*

- *queue depth*—Depth of the queue. 0 to 65,535 bytes (FRSM-8T1, FRSM-8E1, and FRSM-HS1/B) or 4095 to 2,097,151 bytes (FRSM-HS2, FRSM-2CT3, and FRSM-T3E3).

- *queue select* (egress only)—The egress queue priority. A connection that has a high priority is given a queue service advantage over the low-priority channels. 1 = high, 2 = low.

- *ECN threshold*—Depth of the queue to begin marking congestion (FECN and BECN). 0 to 65,535 bytes (FRSM-8T1, FRSM-8E1, and FRSM-HS1/B) or 0 to 2,097,151 bytes (FRSM-HS2, FRSM-2CT3, and FRSM-T3E3).

- *DE threshold*—Depth of the queue to begin dropping DE frames. 0 to 65,535 bytes (FRSM-8T1, FRSM-8E1, and FRSM-HS1/B) or 0 to 2,097,151 bytes (FRSM-HS2, FRSM-2CT3, and FRSM-T3E3).

Commands for Verifying Frame Relay Connections

Here are the commands used to verify connections on the FRSM:

- **tstcon**—Checks a connection's continuity.

- **tstdelay**—Checks a connection's continuity and measures the round-trip delay.

- **dspchancnt**—Lists a connection's statistical counters.

- **clrchancnt**—Clears a connection's statistical counters.

- **clrchancnts**—Clears the statistical counters for all connections on the FRSM.

Test Connection Command

The **tstcon** command tests continuity on MGX network connections. If connection segments fail or are misconfigured, the **tstcon** command fails. MGX CLI returns a pass or fail message after a few seconds.

NOTE   The **tstcon** command does *not* test quality of service or connectivity beyond the MGX network.

The command syntax is

```
tstcon <connection number>
```

connection number is in the form *port.DLCI*.

The **tstcon** command limitations are as follows:

- This command works only for local connections or connections in a tiered network comprising a Cisco backbone network.

- This command should be issued from both ends to completely verify connectivity.
- A passing result for the test does not guarantee the connection's end-to-end performance.

Test Delay Command

The **tstdelay** command is similar to the **tstcon** command in that it also checks connection continuity. The **tstdelay** command also measures the round-trip delay through the network, and the results are output on the CLI. The most recent delay measurement is also reported in the **dspcon** output.

The command syntax is

```
tstdelay <connection number>
```

connection number is in the form *port.DLCI*.

NOTE	The limitations on the **tstcon** command also apply to the **tstdelay** command. Also be aware that both of these commands might be disruptive to traffic.

Display Channel Count Command

The **dspchancnt** command shows detailed historical statistics for an MGX Frame Relay connection. Use this command to view the traffic being processed on a specific connection.

The command syntax is

```
dspchancnt <channel number>
```

You can learn a connection's *channel number* by using the **dspcons** command.

Because the statistics are historical, you might want to clear them using the **clrchancnt** or **clrchancnts** command before beginning your testing or troubleshooting.

The **dspchancnt** output shows the following information:

- **Channel state**—The current connection state. Either okay or failed.
- **Channel up time**—The number of minutes that the channel has been active.
- **A-bit state**—The a-bit state for the connection that is being transmitted to and received from the Frame Relay CPE via the signaling protocol status messages.

- **ATM state**—The OAM VC status that is being transmitted to and received from the remote MGX switch.

- **Total Frames**—The total number of frames traffic transmitted and received on the connection.

- **Total Bytes**—The total number of bytes transmitted and received.

- **Frames DE**—The number of frames transmitted and received with DE = 1. This number does not imply that the MGX FRSM set the DE bit.

- **Bytes DE**—The number of bytes transmitted and received with DE = 1.

- **Frames Discarded**—The number of frames dropped in the transmit and receive directions.

- **Bytes Discarded**—The number of bytes dropped in the transmit and receive directions.

- **Frames discarded exceeded queue depth**—The number of transmit and receive frames discarded because the VC queue exceeded the configured depth.

- **Bytes discarded exceeded queue depth**—The number of transmit and receive bytes discarded because the VC queue exceeded the configured depth.

- **Frames discarded exceeded DE threshold**—The number of transmit and receive DE frames discarded because the VC queue exceeded the configured DE threshold.

- **Frames FECN**—The number of frames transmitted and received with the FECN bit set to 1. This number does not imply that the MGX FRSM set the FECN bit.

- **Frames BECN**—The number of frames transmitted and received with the BECN bit set to 1. This number does not imply that the MGX FRSM set the FECN bit.

- **Frames tagged FECN**—The number of frames tagged with the FECN bit by the MGX FRSM in the transmit and receive directions because the VC queue exceeded the configured ECN threshold.

- **Frames tagged BECN**—The number of frames tagged with the BECN bit by the MGX FRSM in the transmit and receive directions because the VC queue exceeded the configured ECN threshold.

- **kbps AIR**—The average transmit and receive information rate in kbps.

- **Frames tagged DE**—The number of frames tagged with the DE bit because of ingress policing in the transmit and receive directions.

- **Bytes tagged DE**—The number of bytes tagged with the DE bit because of ingress policing in the transmit and receive directions.

- **Receive frame discarded shelf alarm**—The number of receive frames discarded while the shelf was in alarm (the PXM line to the ATM network failed).

- **Transmit frames discarded physical layer failure**—The number of transmit frames discarded while the access line was in physical alarm (either a red or yellow alarm).

- **Transmit frames discarded CRC error**—The number of transmit frames discarded during reassembly because the CRC was incorrect.

- **Transmit frames discarded reassembly failure**—The number of transmit frames discarded because of a reassembly failure. This is usually the result of missing cells that were dropped in the backbone network.

- **Transmit frames discarded source abort**—The number of transmit frames discarded due to source abort. The frame aborted during the segmentation at the source MGX concentrator.

- **Transmit frames during LMI alarm**—The number of frames transmitted during an LMI failure.

- **Receive frames discarded UPC**—The number of receive frames discarded because of usage parameter control (policing).

Creating Frame Relay Connections in an MGX Network

This section describes the procedure used to create new Frame Relay connections on the FRSM. This procedure includes adding and configuring Frame Relay connections on the FRSM, adding and configuring the appropriate routing connection, and verifying and testing the end-to-end connection through the network. Follow these steps to create circuit emulation services in a network:

Step 1   Type **dspports** to verify that the port you want to use exists and is the correct type (Frame Relay, frame forwarding, or FUNI).

Step 2   If you are adding a local connection, type **addcon** *<port> <DLCI> <CIR> <channel type>* [*egress service type*] [*CAC*] [*controller type*] [*mastership*] [*remote connection ID*] [*service type*] to create a slave connection. This adds a slave connection and outputs the connection ID.

Step 3   If you are adding a feeder connection, type **addcon** *<port> <DLCI> <CIR> <channel type>* [*egress service type*] [*CAC*] [*controller type*] [*mastership*] [*remote connection ID*] [*service type*], specifying the PXM trunk in the *remote connection ID*. This adds a master connection.

Step 4   Type **dspcons** to verify that your connection has been added. This outputs connection summary information.

Step 5   Type **dspcon** *<connection number>* to verify the connection configuration. This outputs the connection's configuration details.

Step 6   If you need to change the policing parameters, type **cnfchanpol** *<connection number> <CIR> <Bc> <Be> <IBS> <DE tag> <egress service rate>*. This changes the connection's policing characteristics.

Step 7   If you have a zero CIR connection, type **cnfchaneir** *<channel number> <zero CIR EIR>*. This changes the connection's excess information rate (EIR).

Step 8   If you need the connection to use the ForeSight feature, type **cnfchanfst** *<connection number> <ForeSight enable> <MIR> <PIR> <QIR>* and proceed to Step 10. This enables the ForeSight feature and sets the ForeSight connection characteristics.

Step 9   If you have created a standard ABR connection on an FRSM-8T1 or 8E1, type **cnfchanabrparams** *<connection number | channel number> <RIF> <RDF> <NRM> <TRM> <TBE> <FRTT> <ADTF> <CDF>*. This changes the standard ABR connection characteristics.

Step 10 If you have an ATM-Frame Relay service interworking connection and you need to change the congestion and priority bitmapping, type **cnfchanmap** *<connection number | channel number> <type> <FECN to EFCI> <DE to CLP> <CLP to DE>*. This changes the congestion (FECN and EFCI) and priority (DE and CLP) bitmapping.

Step 11 If you want to change the ingress or egress queues, type **cnfchaningressq** *<connection number> <queue depth> <ECN threshold> <DE threshold>* or **cnfchanegressq** *<connection number> <queue select> <queue depth> <ECN threshold> <DE threshold>*. This changes the ingress and egress queue characteristics.

Step 12 If you are adding a local connection, type **cc** *<slot number>* and complete Step 1. Then complete Step 3, specifying the connection ID of the slave connection on the other CESM. Continue with Steps 4 through 11, and then go to Step 17. This changes to the remote card slot and adds the master connection.

Step 13 If you are adding a feeder connection, log into the remote MGX switch and FRSM card and complete Step 1 and Steps 3 through 11. This adds the Frame Relay connection to the other end of the end-to-end connection.

Step 14 If you have standalone MGX switches, you need to add, configure, and verify the routing connection in the ATM network. Continue with Step 18. This creates a routing connection in the ATM backbone network.

Step 15 If you have a BPX backbone network, log into the BPX switch attached to one of your MGX switches. Type **addcon** *<local channel> <remote node> <remote channel> <connection class | connection type> [connection parameters] [route avoid]* to add an ATFR, ATFST, or ABRSTD routing connection. Be sure to match the VPI and VCI values in the BPX network with the values you used when you added the MGX connection segments. Use the **dspcons** and **dspcon** commands to verify the connection status. Continue with Step 17. This adds a routing connection through the BPX network.

Step 16 If you have an MGX 8850-PXM45 backbone network, log into the AXSM on the local switch and type **addcon** *<interface number> <VPI> <VCI> <service type>* **2** *[parameters]*, where **2** indicates the slave endpoint. Be sure to write down the endpoint ID (NSAP address, VPI, and VCI). Log into the AXSM on the remote switch and type **addcon** *<interface number> <VPI> <VCI> <service type>* **1** **<-slave** *slave endpoint ID> [parameters]*, where **1** indicates the master endpoint and the *slave endpoint ID* is as previously noted. Use the **dspcons** and **dspcon** commands to verify the connection status. This adds a routing connection through the MGX 8850-PXM45 network.

Step 17 Log back in to the FRSM on one of your MGX switches. Use the **tstcon** or **tstdelay** command to verify the continuity on the connection. This tests the connection's end-to-end continuity.

Step 18 Type **dspchancnt** *<channel number>* to verify that there is traffic on the connection. This outputs the channel counters.

Complete Steps 17 and 18 on the other end of the connection. This tests the remote end of the connection.

You have successfully completed the steps necessary for creating new Frame Relay connections on the FRSM.

Summary

This chapter provided an overview of Frame Relay ports and FRSM port queues. It discussed how traffic moves through the FRSM in both the ingress and egress directions for both high-speed and low-speed FRSMs. Commands for adding, configuring, displaying, and monitoring Frame Relay ports were presented, and you saw how to configure a Frame Relay port on an FRSM card.

This chapter also discussed Frame Relay connections and the two kinds of interworking supported on the FRSM: network interworking and service interworking. The Frame Relay policing process was also discussed. You saw how the ForeSight feature works on Frame Relay connections and how ABR dynamically adjusts the rate at which traffic enters the network.

This chapter also discussed how VC queues are used to shape ingress traffic and how the FRSM buffers ingress traffic in virtual circuit (VC) queues. You learned the commands that are used to add, configure, display, and verify Frame Relay connections in an MGX network.

Review Questions

1 How many fractional Frame Relay ports are allowed on an E1 line?

2 Which card modules support serial Frame Relay ports?

A. FRSM-8E1

B. FRSM-8T1

C. FRSM-HS2

D. FRSM-2CT3

3 What is a channelized Frame Relay port?

A. A port comprising multiple T1 or E1 lines

B. A port that provides access to multiple FRADs

    C. The only port on a line that uses one or more timeslots

    D. One of several ports on a line that uses one or more timeslots

4 Mark the following statements as true or false.

    A. _____ The High Priority queue is for LMI and CLLM traffic.

    B. _____ On low-speed FRSMs, Queue 1 is served more often than Queue 2.

    C. _____ All queues on the FRSM-8E1 are served using a round-robin algorithm.

    D. _____ The FRSM-8T1 card has one High Priority queue and three CoS queues per virtual port.

5 What is the purpose of the DE threshold on a queue?

    A. It is part of the policing algorithm.

    B. It determines when the DE bit is set on a frame.

    C. It determines when congestion occurs on the queue.

    D. It determines when DE frames are not allowed into the queue.

    E. It controls when ABR connections increase or decrease their rate.

6 A port queue buffers traffic coming from or going to the CPE?

7 At which two places on the FRSM could ingress traffic get dropped?

    A. UPC

    B. SAR

    C. VC queue

    D. Port queue

8 A Frame Relay port is reporting a large number of cells being transmitted with the DE bit set to 1. Assuming that all the frames are coming from the remote CPE with the DE bit set to 0, where are the DE bits being set?

    A. On the ingress VC queue

    B. On the egress port queue

    C. By the ingress UPC algorithm

9 What is the main difference between traffic flow on low-speed FRSMs and traffic flow on high-speed FRSMs?

    A. The low-speed cards have a set number of port queues.

    B. The high-speed cards have ingress and egress VC queues.

    C. The high-speed cards have CoS queues in both directions.

    D. The low-speed cards buffer traffic in only the egress direction.

    E. The low-speed cards support only VBR and UBR queue servicing.

10 Which command is used to determine the cause of a port alarm?

A. **dspcd**

B. **dsplns**

C. **cnfport**

D. **dspport**

E. **dspports**

11 Of the following commands, which two are used to enable CLLM on a Frame Relay port?

A. **cnfcllm**

B. **cnfport**

C. **addport**

D. **xcnfport**

E. **cnfportcllm**

12 How would you define a port as a UNI or NNI?

A. Use the **cnfint** command and set the interface type to UNI or NNI.

B. Use the **cnfport** command and set the interface type to UNI or NNI.

C. Use the **xcnfport** command and set the interface type to UNI or NNI.

D. Use the **cnflmi** command and set the signaling protocol to AU or DU.

E. Use the **cnfport** command and set the signaling protocol to S, AU, DU, AN, or DN.

F. The port cannot be configured; it automatically detects the interface type using ELMI.

13 Of the following, which two are reasons why Frame Relay port statistics would be displayed?

A. To learn if a channel is in alarm

B. To check if OAM cells are being sent to the ATM network

C. To learn the number of frames transmitted and received on a port

D. To confirm that LMI messages are being sent to the attached user equipment

14 Why would a Frame Relay port report an unknown DLCI frame?

A. The attached end-user equipment has failed.

B. The attached end-user equipment has sent a frame using a reserved DLCI.

C. The attached end-user equipment has sent a frame with a DLCI, and there is no corresponding connection on the port.

D. A connection on the ATM backbone switch is not routed through the network because no addressing resources are available.

15 How many connection segments are required for a local Frame Relay connection between two adjacent FRSM cards?

16 You are adding a Frame Relay connection between two Frame Relay ports, as shown in Figure 20-26. Which connection segments must you add?

Figure 20-26 *Which Connection Segments Must You Add?*

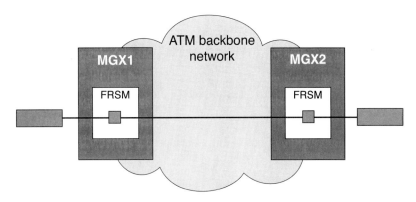

A. A slave connection on the FRSM on MGX1

B. A master connection on the FRSM on MGX1

C. A master connection on the FRSM on MGX2

D. A CBR connection in the ATM backbone network

E. A variable-rate connection in the ATM backbone network

17 You are adding a frame forwarding connection. How many connections can terminate on the port?

A. 1

B. 2

C. 256

D. 1000

18 Mark the following statements as true or false.

A. _____ Multiple FUNI connections can terminate on a port.

B. _____ Up to ten local connections can be added to an FRSM.

C. _____ Connections that share a line must all be of the same type.

D. _____ You must add the slave end of a local connection before the master end.

E. _____ All frame forwarding connections are supported by ABR connections in the ATM backbone network.

19 You have added a network interworking connection on your FRSM. Where can the connection terminate?

A. On a PXM1 trunk

B. On any ATM interface

C. On an MGX FRSM port

D. On an MGX AUSM port

20 Which configurable Frame Relay connection parameters affect the ingress policing on the connection?

A. Bc

B. Be

C. AR

D. CIR

E. EIR

F. DE threshold

G. VC queue depth

21 What is the difference between Bc and Be?

A. Bc is for ingress traffic; Be is for egress traffic.

B. Bc is configured per port; Be is configured per channel.

C. Bc determines whether frames are dropped; Be determines whether frames are congested.

D. Bc determines whether frames are discard-eligible; Be determines whether frames are dropped.

22 Under what conditions can the connection rate drop below the configured MIR?

A. If frames have the DE bit set to 1

B. When data is being dropped on egress

C. When there is severe congestion in the network

D. The connection rate cannot drop below the configured MIR under any conditions.

E. When there is an alarm on the line between the MGX switch and the ATM backbone network

23 A Frame Relay connection is configured with an MIR of 64 kbps, a QIR of 64 kbps, and a PIR of 512 kbps on an FRSM with the ForeSight rate adjustment parameters set at their default values. If the VC queue service rate is currently 274 kbps and the network reports severe congestion, what is the new queue service rate in kbps?

24 A Frame Relay connection is configured with an MIR of 64 kbps, a QIR of 64 kbps, and a PIR of 512 kbps on an FRSM with the ForeSight rate adjustment parameters set at their default values. If the VC queue service rate is currently 510 kbps and the network reports no congestion, what is the new queue service rate in kbps?

A. 510 kbps

B. 512 kbps

C. 516.4 kbps

D. 561.2 kbps

25 Mark the following statements as true or false.

A. _____ The ICR is the rate used when NI is set to 1.

B. _____ The ICR is the rate used after timeout period ADTF.

C. _____ An ABR source can send data at rates less than the PCR and greater than the MCR.

D. _____ An ABR source can send data at rates less than the MCR and greater than the PCR.

E. _____ An ABR connection source can send data at any rate between 0 cps and the line speed.

26 Mark the following statements as true or false.

A. _____ The FRSM-2CT3 card has four CoS queues per virtual circuit.

B. _____ On low-speed FRSMs, all VC queues are of equal priority.

C. _____ All VC queues on the FRSM-HS2 are served using a round-robin algorithm.

D. _____ The IBS is the maximum number of bytes that can burst out of the VC queue.

27 What is the purpose of the ECN threshold on a VC queue?

A. It is part of the policing algorithm.

B. It determines when FECN frames are discarded.

C. It determines when the FECN bit is set on a frame.

D. It determines when FECN frames are not allowed into the queue.

E. It controls when ABR connections increase or decrease their rate.

28 What command must you type (without required or optional parameters) to enable the ForeSight feature on a connection?

29 Which command must you use to set the committed and excess burst sizes?

A. **cnfcon**

B. **cnfpolicing**

    C. **cnfchanpol**

    D. **cnfchanmap**

    E. **cnfchanburst**

    F. **cnfchanstdabr**

30 Mark the following statements as true or false.

    A. _____ The **dspchancnt** output updates automatically.

    B. _____ The channel number is the same as the port number.

    C. _____ The most recent **tstdelay** result is shown in the **dspchancnt** output.

    D. _____ The **clrchancnts** command clears all the channel counters on the card.

    E. _____ The **dspchancnt** command shows historical statistical counters for a channel.

This chapter covers the following key topics:

- ATM Ports
- Inverse Multiplexing Over ATM
- AUSM Port Queues
- How Cells Move Through the AUSM
- Commands for Adding, Configuring, and Displaying ATM Ports on the AUSM
- Commands for Adding, Configuring, and Displaying ATM Ports on the PXM1
- Commands for Monitoring ATM Ports
- How to Configure an ATM Port on the AUSM and PXM1
- ATM Connections
- ATM Class of Service
- ATM Policing
- ForeSight on ATM Connections
- ABR for ATM
- VC Queues on the AUSM
- Commands for Adding, Configuring, and Displaying ATM Connections on the AUSM
- Commands for Adding, Configuring, and Displaying ATM Connections on the PXM1
- Commands for Verifying ATM Connections
- How to Create ATM Connections on the AUSM and PXM1

CHAPTER 21

ATM Ports and Connections

This chapter presents ATM ports and Inverse Multiplexing over ATM (IMA). It shows you how IMA distributes an ATM traffic stream across multiple narrowband T1 or E1 lines. AUSM port queues are discussed, along with how cells move through the AUSM card in both the ingress and egress directions.

Commands for adding, configuring, displaying, and monitoring ATM ports on the AUSM and PXM1 are presented, along with information about how to configure an ATM port on the AUSM and PXM1.

ATM connections, ATM class of service (CoS), and ATM policing are presented and discussed in detail. You'll see how the ForeSight feature and ABR are used on ATM connections, as well as how VC queues buffer and shape ingress traffic.

Procedures and commands for adding, configuring, displaying, and verifying ATM connections on the AUSM and PXM1 are presented, and you'll see how to configure an ATM port on the AUSM and PXM1.

ATM Ports

An ATM port is the interface between the AUSM or PXM1 and a single ATM device. There is usually one port per line. An IMA port supports multiple lines. Up to eight ports can exist on an AUSM-8T1 or AUSM-8E1 card module; one to four ports can exist on a PXM1, depending on the front and back card type.

ATM Port

Figure 21-1 shows an example of an ATM port on the AUSM. Notice that a single router is attached to the line, which terminates on the port. The port number is assigned when the port is activated. The port number is not necessarily the same as the line number. In Figure 21-1, port 2 is associated with line 1. This port is not an IMA port.

Figure 21-1 *AUSM ATM Port*

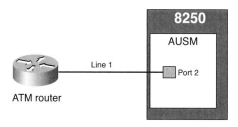

IMA Port

Figure 21-2 shows an example of an IMA port on an AUSM. Notice that a single router is attached to multiple lines that terminate on the port. The IMA group number that is assigned when the IMA group is established is used as the ATM port number. In Figure 21-2, IMA group 3 comprises lines 2, 3, and 4.

Figure 21-2 *AUSM IMA Port*

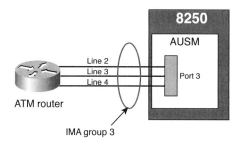

IMA and non-IMA ATM ports share many common features; the primary difference is the way in which the cells are transported from the CPE to the AUSM.

Inverse Multiplexing Over ATM

Inverse Multiplexing over ATM (IMA) is a process that distributes an ATM traffic stream across multiple narrowband (T1 or E1) lines. An IMA group comprises up to eight narrowband lines that carry ATM cells between two devices. By default, if any of the lines fails, the IMA group fails. Optional resiliency can be set up so that a defined number of lines can fail before the IMA group fails.

Figure 21-3 shows how cells are distributed in an IMA group. The stream of cells, numbered 1 to 9, is shown in order as they travel from right to left.

Figure 21-3 *Inverse Multiplexing Over ATM*

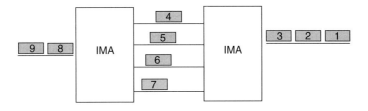

IMA is supported on a number of Cisco products:

* AUSM on MGX 8230, 8250, and 8850-PXM1 switches and MGX 8220 concentrators
* IMATM on the MGX 8220 concentrator
* UXM on the IGX switch
* Catalyst 8500 and 5500 series switches
* LightStream 1010 switches
* Cisco 2600, 3600, and 7000 series routers

AUSM Port Queues

The egress port queues on the AUSM provide traffic management for multiple virtual circuits terminating on a single physical interface. They also serve as buffers that store ATM cells before they leave the MGX network. Before you configure a port queue on the AUSM, you should know the queue's characteristics in order to set the proper feature configurations and threshold values.

A port QBin is a subqueue on an ATM port that buffers a specific type of traffic. Each port has five QBins: CBR, rt-VBR, nrt-VBR, ABR, and UBR. The **xcnfportq** command, discussed later in this chapter, modifies the QBin characteristics, including the queue depth, the CLP high and low thresholds, and the EFCI threshold.

QBin Characteristics

The following characteristics define a port QBin on the AUSM:

- Port number

- **Queue number**—1 is for CBR, 2 is for ABR, 3 is for nrt-VBR, 4 is for UBR, and 5 is for rt-VBR

- **Depth maximum**—The maximum number of cells that can be stored in the QBin

- **CLP high**—The queue depth at which CLP tagged cells (CLP set to 1) are not allowed into the queue and are dropped

- **CLP low**—The queue depth at which point CLP tagged cells are allowed into the queue and are no longer dropped

- **EFCI threshold**—The point at which cells are marked as congested

QBin Configuration Example

Figure 21-4 shows an example of a VBR QBin, including the queue size, CLP high and low, and EFCI configuration.

Figure 21-4 *QBin Configuration*

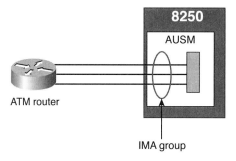

What happens as cells come from the network and are queued in the QBin? Suppose the nrt-VBR QBin shown in Figure 21-4 has 500 cells. If new cells arrive at the queue faster than they are serviced and sent out on the line, the queue begins to fill. When the queue has 650 (EFCI threshold) cells in it, all subsequent cells have their EFCI bit set to 1. If the queue reaches 800 cells (CLP high threshold), any new cells with a CLP of 1 are discarded and are not allowed into the queue. Any existing cells in the queue remain there. If the queue reaches 1000 cells, all new cells are dropped.

If the QBin services cells at a rate faster than it is filling, the queue empties. When the queue has fewer than 800 cells (CLP high threshold), CLP tagged cells are dropped. Only when the queue depth reaches 500 cells (CLP low threshold) does it begin accepting cells that have a CLP of 1.

Virtual Circuit Queues

On an AUSM card, each port has many ingress VC queues—one VC queue is used for every VC that terminates on the port, and it buffers only the cells arriving into the network on a particular VC.

Each VC queue is dedicated to a single VC, so there is no concept of QBins as described in the context of egress port queues.

How Cells Move Though the AUSM

When you configure and monitor ATM ports and connections, it is important to understand how cells move through the card in both the ingress and egress directions.

Ingress ATM Traffic

For each connection, a VC queue buffers the cells after they are policed and before they are sent to the cell bus. The purpose of the VC queue is to manage the traffic as it moves from the AUSM to the PXM, but it also has the function of shaping ingress traffic (from the CPE to the network).

Several stages are involved as ATM cell traffic moves in the ingress direction toward the cell bus, where the cell ultimately will be switched by the PXM to the destination card slot.

First, the ATM cell traffic moves from the CPE to the AUSM in the ingress direction. The cell does not get buffered in a port QBin, but instead moves through the usage parameter control (UPC) process to determine whether the cell is allowed into the network, and also to determine whether the CLP bit is set to 1. Note that the UPC process is performed independently for each virtual circuit.

The cell is then sent to the appropriate VC queue, where the cell can be discarded if the CLP threshold is met, or where the cell can be marked for congestion (EFCI bit) if the EFCI threshold is met.

Finally, the cell is sent to the cell bus to be switched by the PXM to the destination card slot.

Table 21-1 describes the stages of ATM cell traffic movement in the ingress direction.

Table 21-1 *Stages of Ingress ATM Traffic*

Stage	Description
1	The ATM cell comes in from the CPE.
2	The cell does *not* get buffered in a port QBin.

continues

Table 21-1   *Stages of Ingress ATM Traffic (Continued)*

Stage	Description
3	The cell goes through the UPC process to determine whether the cell is allowed into the network and whether the CLP bit is set to 1. The UPC process is performed independently for each VC.
4	The cell is sent to the appropriate VC queue. The VC queue can discard the cell if the CLP threshold is met. The VC queue can mark congestion on the cell (EFCI bit) if the EFCI threshold is met.
5	The cell is sent to the cell bus to be switched by the PXM to the destination card slot.

Egress ATM Traffic

AUSM egress (from the network to the CPE) port queues provide traffic management for multiple virtual circuits terminating on a single physical interface.

Several stages are involved as ATM cell traffic moves in the egress direction, with cells moving from the cell bus through the AUSM, ultimately to be sent along the line to the attached CPE.

First, the ATM cell traffic comes in from the cell bus without getting buffered in a VC queue and without getting processed by the UPC. The cell is instead sent directly to the appropriate QBin based on its traffic type. The QBin can then discard the cell if the cell has its CLP bit set to 1 and if the CLP threshold is met. The QBin can also mark congestion on the cell (EFCI bit) if the EFCI threshold is met. If the QBin overflows, the arriving cells are dropped.

Finally, the cell is sent along the line to the attached CPE.

Table 21-2 describes the stages of ATM cell traffic movement in the egress direction.

Table 21-2   *Stages of Egress ATM Traffic*

Stage	Description
1	The ATM cell comes in from the cell bus.
2	The cell does *not* get buffered in a VC queue.
3	The UPC algorithm does *not* process the cell.
4	The cell is sent to the appropriate QBin based on the traffic type (CBR, rt-VBR, nrt-VBR, ABR, or UBR). The QBin can discard the cell if the cell has its CLP bit set to 1 and he CLP threshold is met. The QBin can mark congestion on the cell (EFCI bit) if the EFCI threshold is met. If the QBin overflows, the arriving cells are dropped.
5	The cell is sent on the line to the attached CPE.

Commands for Adding, Configuring, and Displaying ATM Ports on the AUSM

This section describes the commands used to add, configure, and display an ATM port on the AUSM:

- **dspports**—Lists summary status information for all ports on the AUSM.
- **dspport**—Lists detailed status and configuration information for a port.
- **addport**—Creates a new port on the AUSM.
- **delport**—Removes a port from the AUSM.
- **addimagrp**—Creates a IMA port on the AUSM.
- **delimagrp**—Removes an IMA port from the AUSM.
- **addlns2imagrp**—Adds one or more lines to an existing IMA port.
- **dellnsfmimagrp**—Removes one or more lines from an existing IMA port.
- **cnfimagrp**—Modifies a port's IMA characteristics.
- **dspportqs**—Lists summary information for all QBins on the card.
- **dspportq**—Lists the configuration information for a QBin.
- **xcnfportq**—Modifies the port QBin characteristics.
- **dspilmi**—Lists a port's signaling protocol configuration.
- **cnfilmi**—Modifies a port's signaling protocol configuration.

Display Ports Command

The **dspports** command provides summary information about the ATM ports (IMA and non-IMA) on the card. You use it to learn which ports are active. The **dspports** command does not have any required or optional parameters.

Example 21-1 shows the **dspports** output on an AUSM. Notice that one ATM port and one IMA port are configured on the card.

Example 21-1 **dspports** *Output*

```
hei1pop1.1.1.AUSMB8.a > dspports

  List of ATM ports:
  ==================

  Port PortType Line# Portenable  Speed  PortState
  ---- -------- ----- ----------  -----  ---------
  1.1   UNI      1     UP          3622   Active
```

continues

Example 21-1 dspports *Output (Continued)*

```
List of IMA groups:
===================

ImaGrp PortType Conf  Avail  Lines        Lines     Tol Diff  Port State
                rate  rate   configured   present   Delay(ms)
------ -------- ----- -----  -----------  --------- --------- ----------
 1.4    UNI    14364 14364  5.6.7.8      5.6.7.8   275       Active

  NextPortNumAvailable:  5
```

The **dspports** output lists the following information for ATM (non-IMA) ports:

- **Port number**—Identified as *slot.port*.
- **Port type**—UNI or NNI.
- **Port enable**—The port enable state. Either UP or DOWN.
- **Speed**—The port speed in cells per second, depending on the line type and configuration.
- **Port state**—The port alarm state. Either Active or a failure cause.

The **dspports** output lists the following information for IMA ports:

- **IMA group**—Identified as *slot.group*.
- **Port type**—UNI or NNI.
- **Configured rate**—The port rate based on the line type and configuration and the number of lines in the group.
- **Available rate**—The current port rate based on the active lines in the IMA group.
- **Lines configured**—A list of the lines in the IMA group, separated by dots. For example, 5.6.7.8 means that lines 5 through 8 are assigned to the IMA group.
- **Lines present**—A list of the active lines in the IMA group, separated by dots.
- **Total differential delay**—The configured differential delay between the lines in the IMA group.
- **Port state**—The IMA group state.

Display Port Command

The **dspport** command lists detailed status and configuration information about a particular ATM port. Use this command to learn the configuration of an ATM port.

Here is the **dspport** command syntax:

```
dspport <port number | IMA group number>
```

Example 21-2 shows the **dspport** output for port number 1.

Example 21-2 dspport *Output*

```
hei1pop1.1.1.AUSMB8.a > dspport 1
  LogicalPortNumber:          1
  Port Enable:                UP
  Port State:                 Active
  PortType:                   UNI
  PhysicalPortNumber:         1
  CellFraming:                ATM
  CellScramble:               No Scramble
  Plpp Loopback:              No Loopback
  Single-bit error correction:  Disabled
```

The **dspport** output for an ATM (non-IMA) port provides the following information:

- Port number
- **Port enable**—UP or DOWN.
- **Port state**—The port alarm state, either Active or a failure cause.
- **Port type**—UNI or NNI.
- **Physical port number**—The line associated with the port.
- **Cell framing**—The cell framing method used on the port, either ATM (self-delineated cells) or Physical Layer Convergence Protocol (PLCP).
- **Cell scramble**—Specifies whether cell scrambling is enabled. Either Yes or No.
- **PLPP loopback**—Specifies whether Physical Layer Protocol Processor (PLPP) loopback is enabled. Either No or the loopback type.
- **Single-bit error correction**—The header error control (HEC) field in the ATM cell header can be used to detect errors and correct a single-bit error in the cell header. This field shows whether the error-correcting capability is enabled for the port.

Example 21-3 shows the **dspport** output for IMA port number 4. The **dspimagrp** command provides the same output.

Example 21-3 dspport *Output for an IMA Port*

```
hei1pop1.1.1.AUSMB8.a > dspport 4

  IMA Group number            : 4
  Port type                   : UNI
  Lines configured            : 5.6.7.8
  Enable                      : Enabled
  IMA Port state              : Active
```

continues

Example 21-3 dspport *Output for an IMA Port (Continued)*

```
    IMA Group Ne state               : operational
    PortSpeed (cells/sec)            : 14364
    GroupTxAvailCellRate (cells/sec) : 14364
    ImaGroupTxFrameLength(cells)     : 128
    LcpDelayTolerance (IMA frames)   : 1
    ReadPtrWrPtrDiff  (cells)        : 4
    Minimum number of links          : 4
    MaxTolerableDiffDelay (msec)     : 275
    Lines Present                    : 5.6.7.8
    Observed Diff delay (msec)       : 0
    Clock Mode                       : CTC
    GroupAlpha                       : 2
    GroupBeta                        : 2
    GroupGamma                       : 1
    GroupConfiguration               : 1
    IMAGrp Failure status            : No Failure

Type <CR> to continue, Q<CR> to stop:

    Timing reference link            : 5
    ImaGroupTxImaId                  : 0x3
    ExpectedGroupRxImaId             : 0x3
```

The **dspport** output for an IMA port provides the following information:

- IMA group number

- **Port type**—The ATM cell header configured for the group. UNI or NNI.

- **Lines configured**—The list of lines in the IMA group, separated by dots.

- **Enable**—The IMA group's enable state.

- **IMA port state**—The port state.

- **Port speed**—The port rate in cells per second based on the line type and configuration and the number of lines in the group.

- **Group transmit available cell rate**—The current port rate in cells per second based on the active lines in the IMA group.

- **IMA group transmit frame length**—The frequency, in cells, of IMA control cells. This frequency defines the length of an IMA frame.

- **Link Control Protocol (LCP) Delay Tolerance**—The number of missed IMA frames before the IMA group fails the line.

- **Read Pointer Write Pointer Differential**—The difference between the read and write pointer of a line in the common cell buffer.

- **Minimum number of links**—The configured number of lines that must be active for the IMA group to stay active.

- **Maximum tolerable differential delay**—The configured maximum differential delay permitted between consecutive cells carried across different lines in the IMA group.

- **Receive IMA ID**—The identifier of the remote IMA group used to differentiate between IMA groups.

- **Transmit IMA ID**—The identifier of the local IMA group used to differentiate between IMA groups.

- **Observed Differential Delay**—The number of milliseconds measured between arriving cells on different lines in the IMA group.

- **Clock mode**—Transmit clocking mode used by the near end of the IMA group. Common timing clock (CTC) is a clocking mode defined by the ATMF in the IMA specification. In the current implementation, only the default value of CTC is supported on the AUSM/B. With CTC, all transmit clocks of the links in the group are derived from the same source.

- **Group alpha**—Indicates the alpha value, used to specify the number of consecutive invalid ICP cells.

- **Group beta**—Indicates the beta value, used to specify the number of consecutive errored ICP cells.

- **Group gamma**—Indicates the gamma value, used to specify the number of consecutive valid ICP cells.

- **Group configuration**—Indicates the symmetry mode with which the IMA group is configured. The current implementation supports only one mode—symmetric configuration and operation. This is represented by the value 1.

- **IMA group failure status**—Indicates the IMA group's current failure status and helps determine the reason for the failure.

- **Timing reference link**—The line in the IMA group that is used as a clock reference for the rest of the group.

Add Port Command

The **addport** command assigns a port number, associates the port with a line, and activates the port on the AUSM. For IMA ports, use the **addimagrp** command; to delete ports, use the **delport** command.

Here is the **addport** command syntax:

```
addport <port number> <port type> <line number>
```

The parameter options are as follows:

- *port number*—The assigned port number can be between 1 and 8. If the port is assigned to a single line (non-IMA port), the port number does not need to be the same as the line number. Each assigned port number must be unique on the AUSM.

- *port type*—The ATM cell header used by the port. 1 = UNI, 2 = NNI.
- *line number*—The line number associated with the ATM port.

For example, type **addport 1 1 1** to add UNI port 1 to line number 1; type **addport 3 2 6** to add NNI port 3 to line number 6.

Add IMA Group Command

The **addimagrp** command is used to create a new IMA group on the AUSM. As soon as an IMA group exists, you can add additional lines to the group using the **addlns2imagrp** command or delete lines from the group using the **dellnsfmimagrp** command. To delete an IMA group, use the **delimagrp** command.

Here is the **addimagrp** command syntax:

```
addimagrp <group number> <port type> <list of lines> <minimum number of links>
```

The parameter options are as follows:

- *group number*—The IMA group number. This number is used as the port number on the AUSM. The port number must be unique on the AUSM card.
- *port type*—The cell header type used on the group. 1 = UNI, 2 = NNI.
- *list of lines*—The lines assigned to the IMA group. If more than one line is in the IMA group, type the line numbers separated by dots.
- *minimum number of links*—The minimum number of lines that must be active for the IMA group to stay active. From 1 to $n-1$, where n is the number of lines in the IMA group.

For example, type **addimagrp 1 1 1.2.3.4 3** to add IMA group 1 using lines 1, 2, 3, and 4. The lines carry UNI cells, and the group will fail if fewer than three lines are active. Type **addimagrp 2 2 5.6 2** to add IMA group 2 using lines 5 and 6. These lines carry NNI cells, and the group will fail if fewer than two lines are active.

Configure IMA Group Command

The **cnfimagrp** command is used to modify an IMA group's characteristics.

Here is the **cnfimagrp** command syntax:

```
cnfimagrp <group number> <maximum differential delay> <minimum number of links>
```

The parameter options are as follows:

- *group number*—The IMA group number or the port number.

- *maximum differential delay*—The maximum amount of time permitted between consecutive cells carried on adjacent lines is 275 milliseconds. If the maximum differential delay is exceeded, the offending line is not used by the IMA group. The IMA group will not fail if the minimum number of links is still available.

- *minimum number of links*—The minimum number of lines that must be active for the IMA group to stay active. From 1 to *n*–1, where *n* is the number of lines in the IMA group. The IMA group fails if fewer than the minimum number of lines are available to the IMA group.

For example, type **cnfimagrp 1 20 2** to change IMA group 1 to have a differential delay of 20 milliseconds and to require two active lines to remain active. Type **cnfimagrp 2 5 1** to change IMA group 2 to have a differential delay of 5 milliseconds and to require one active line to remain active.

Display Port Queues Command

The **dspportqs** command shows the egress port queue (QBin) configuration. No required or optional parameters are associated with the **dspportqs** command. Example 21-4 shows the **dspportqs** output.

Example 21-4 dspportqs *Output*

```
hei1pop1.1.1.AUSMB8.a > dspportqs

Port Q Num  State   Q-Algo Service-Seq Depth-Max CLP-High CLP-Low EFCI-Thrsh
---- -----  -----   ------ ----------- --------- -------- ------- ----------
  1    1    Enabled   3         1          200      180      160      160
  1    2    Enabled   3         4          900      800      700      700
  1    3    Enabled   3         3          900      800      700      700
  1    4    Enabled   3         5          200      180      160      160
  1    5    Enabled   3         2          900      800      700      700
  4    1    Enabled   3         1          200      180      160      160
  4    2    Enabled   3         4          900      800      700      700
  4    3    Enabled   3         3          900      800      700      700
  4    4    Enabled   3         5          200      180      160      160
  4    5    Enabled   3         2          900      800      700      700
```

The **dspportqs** output lists the following information:

- Port number
- **Queue number**—1 is for CBR, 2 is for ABR, 3 is for nrt-VBR, 4 is for UBR, and 5 is for rt-VBR.
- **State**—Always enabled.
- **Queue algorithm**—The queue service algorithm determines how the QBin is serviced. All queues are set for 3, which is first in, first out (FIFO).

- **Service sequence**—The order in which the queues are serviced. The service sequence determines the queues' priority based on the traffic type's quality of service requirements. Queue service rates are dependent on the connections that terminate on the port and the rate associated with those connections.

- **Depth maximum**—The maximum number of cells that can be queued in the QBin.

- **CLP high**—The queue depth at which CLP tagged cells are not allowed into the queue and are dropped.

- **CLP low**—The queue depth at which CLP tagged cells are allowed into the queue.

- **EFCI threshold**—The point at which cells are marked as congested.

Display Port Queue Command

The **dspportq** command provides detailed information about a particular QBin on a port.

Here is the **dspportq** command syntax:

dspportq <port number> <QBin number>

Example 21-5 shows the **dspportq** output for the CBR QBin on port 1.

Example 21-5 dspportq *Output*

```
hei1pop1.1.1.AUSMB8.a > dspportq 1 1

   ServicePortNum:              1
   QueueNumber:                 1
   PortBinState:                Enabled
   ServiceSequence:             1
   QueueDepth(cells):           200
   CLPThresholdHigh(cells):     180
   CLPThresholdLow(cells):      160
   EFCIThreshold(cells):        160
   QueueAlgorithm:              3
   MaxBandwidthIncrement:       0
   MinBandwidthIncrement:       0
   QCLPState:                   Low
   QFullDiscardedCells:         0
   CLPSetDiscardedCells:        0
```

Most of the fields in the **dspportq** output are identical to those displayed in the **dspportqs** output. Additional information includes the following:

- **Queue CLP state**—The CLP dropping state of the QBin. Either Low (the queue is below the CLP low threshold) or High (the queue is above the CLP high threshold).

- **Queue full discarded cells**—The number of cells discarded because the QBin exceeded its maximum configured depth.

- **CLP set discarded cells**—The number of CLP tagged cells dropped because the QBin exceeded the configured CLP high threshold.

Extended Configure Port Queue Command

The **xcnfportq** command is used to modify QBin characteristics, including the queue depth, the CLP high and low thresholds, and the EFCI threshold.

Here is the **xcnfportq** command syntax:

```
xcnfportq -pt <port number> -pqn <queue number> [-e <enable>]
    [-sn <sequence number>] [-qdm <queue depth maximum>] [-clph <CLP high>]
    [-clpl <CLP low>] [-clpt <EFCI threshold>] [-qa <queue algorithm>]
```

The parameter options are as follows:

- *port number*—The port number.
- *queue number*—The QBin number. 1 = CBR, 2 = ABR, 3 = nrt-VBR, 4 = UBR, 5 = rt-VBR.
- *enable*—This parameter enables the port queue.
- *sequence number*—The order in which the queues are serviced. It is strongly recommended that you do not change this value. 1 to 16.
- *queue depth maximum*—The maximum QBin depth, up to 16,000 cells deep.
- *CLP high*—Determines the queue depth required to start dropping CLP tagged cells. 1 to the queue depth maximum.
- *CLP low*—Determines the queue depth required to stop dropping CLP tagged cells. 1 to the CLP high threshold.
- *EFCI threshold*—Determines the queue depth required to start marking the congestion bits on the cells. 1 to the queue depth maximum.
- *queue algorithm*—Determines how the queue is served. It is strongly recommended that you do not change this value. 1 to 5, or 0 to disable the queue.

For example, type **xcnfportq -pt 1 -pqn 1 -qdm 5000** to set the maximum queue depth to 5000 cells on the CBR QBin on port 1. Type **xcnfportq -pt 2 -pqn 2 -clpt 7500** to set the EFCI threshold to 7500 on the ABR QBin on port 2.

Display ILMI Command

The **dspilmi** command provides detailed ILMI configuration information for a particular ATM port. Example 21-6 shows the **dspilmi** output for port 1.

Example 21-6 dspilmi *Output*

```
hei1pop1.1.1.AUSMB8.a > dspilmi 1

 PortNum:                       1
 Signalling:                    ILMI
 SignallingVPI:                 0
 SignallingVCI:                 16
 ILMITrap:                      Disable
 ILMI-Min-Trap-Interval(secs):  5
 KeepAlivePolling:              Disable
 ErrorThreshold:                3
 EventThreshold:                4
 PollingInterval(secs):         30
 MinimumEnquiryInterval(secs):  10
 AddressRegistration:           Disable
```

The **dspilmi** output lists the following information:

- Port number

- **Signaling**—The type of signaling configured for this port. Either ILMI or none.

- **Signaling VPI**—The VPI used by the signaling protocol.

- **Signaling VCI**—The VCI used by the signaling protocol.

- **ILMI trap**—Specifies whether ILMI trap messages are enabled or disabled. Traps are asynchronous event messages sent by the port to the attached CPE.

- **ILMI minimum trap interval**—The minimum time, in seconds, between trap messages sent by the port.

- **Keepalive polling**—Specifies whether keepalive polling is enabled or disabled. Keepalives or polls are sent periodically to the attached CPE.

- **Error threshold**—The number of timeouts (missed messages) needed to declare a port alarm. This field is also called N491.

- **Event threshold**—The number of attempted messages, in conjunction with the error threshold, that determines a port alarm condition. This field is also called N492.

- **Polling interval**—The amount of time, in seconds, between keepalive messages. This field is also called T491.

- **Minimum enquiry interval**—The minimum time allowed between received ILMI inquiries from the attached CPE.

- **Address registration**—Specifies whether the address registration is enabled or disabled. Address registration is used to assign ATM addresses to an attached CPE that can ask SVCs to terminate on the port.

Configure ILMI Command

The **cnfilmi** command is used to modify the signaling protocol and timers on an ATM port.

Here is the **cnfilmi** command syntax:

```
cnfilmi <port number> <signaling type> [VPI] [VCI] [trap enable]
   [minimum trap interval] [keep alive] [address registration]
```

The parameter options are as follows:

- *port number*—The port number.
- *signaling type*—The port signaling type. 1 = other, 2 = none, 3 = ILMI.
- *VPI*—The VPI used for the signaling protocol. 0 to 255.
- *VCI*—The VCI used for the signaling protocol. 0 to 65,535, or * for a virtual path connection.
- *trap enable*—Enables or disables the sending of trap messages. 1 = disable, 2 = enable.
- *minimum trap interval*—The minimum time between trap messages. 1 to 10 seconds.
- *keep alive*—Enables or disables keepalive messages (polls). 1 = disable, 2 = enable.
- *address registration*—Enables or disables address registration. 1 = disable, 2 = enable.

For example, type **cnfilmi 1 3 0 16 2 10 2 1** to enable ILMI on port 1 using VPI 0 and VCI 16. This port has traps enabled, with a minimum of 10 seconds between traps, and it has keepalives enabled and address registration disabled. Type **cnfilmi 2 2** to disable ILMI on port 2.

Commands for Adding, Configuring, and Displaying ATM Ports on the PXM1

This section describes the commands used to add, configure, and display ATM ports on the PXM1:

- **dspports**—Lists summary status information for all ports on the PXM1.
- **addport**—Creates a new port on the PXM1.
- **delport**—Removes a port from the PXM1.
- **cnfport**—Modifies a port on the PXM1.
- **dspportrscprtns**—Lists the resource partitions for all ports on the PXM1.
- **cnfportrscprtns**—Modifies a port's resource partitions.
- **cnfilmi**—Modifies a port's signaling protocol configuration.
- **dspilmis**—Lists the signaling protocol configuration information for all ports on the PXM1.
- **dspilmi**—Lists a port's signaling protocol configuration information.

Display Ports Command

The **dspports** command lists all logical ports on the MGX PXM1 card, including their configuration details. The **dspports** output is shown in Example 21-7.

Example 21-7 dspports *Output*

```
mgx8800b.1.7.PXM.a > dspports

   Port  Status  Line  PctBw  minVpi  maxVpi
   --------------------------------------------------------
       3    ON      3    100       0     255
       4    ON      4    100       0    4095
```

The **dspports** output lists the following information for ATM ports:

- **Port**—The logical port or interface number.
- **Status**—The port status. Either ON or OFF.
- **Line**—The line number that supports the port.
- **Percent bandwidth**—The percentage of the line bandwidth assigned to the port.
- **Minimum and maximum VPI**—The VPI range supported on the port.

Add Port Command

The **addport** command creates a new logical port on a physical line. The port characteristics can be changed using the **cnfport** command. You can delete a port using the **delport** command.

You must consider the cell type (UNI or NNI) used on the line (use the **dspatmlncnf** command to verify) and how you want to limit traffic based on the bandwidth and VPI values allowed when creating a new logical port. Later, when connections are added to the port, you must remember these limitations. Misconfiguration can result in failed or rejected connections.

Here is the **addport** command syntax:

```
addport <port number> <line number> <percent bandwidth> <minimum VPI> <maximum VPI>
```

The parameter options are as follows:

- *port number*—A unique number between 1 and 32 that identifies the logical port.
- *line number*—The physical line number that the logical port is associated with. PXM1 firmware limits you to one logical port per line.
- *percent bandwidth*—The percentage of the physical line's bandwidth that the logical port can use. It is recommended that you use 100 percent of the bandwidth.

- *minimum VPI*—The minimum value for the VPI on cells that use the port. If the line uses the UNI cell header, this value must be less than or equal to 255. If the line uses the NNI cell header, this value must be less than or equal to 4095. It is recommended that you use the full range of VPI values. You should set the *minimum VPI* to 0.

- *maximum VPI*—The maximum value for the VPI on cells that use the port. This value must be greater than or equal to the minimum VPI. It is recommended that you use the full range of VPI values. You should set the *maximum VPI* to 255 or 4095, depending on the cell header type.

For example, type **addport 1 1 100 0 255** to add port 1 to line 1 using all the available bandwidth and VPI values (assuming that the cell header type is UNI).

Display Port Resource Partition Command

Resource partitions are defined for all logical ports. By default, all connection types are given equal access to a port. If you need to modify an existing partition, use the **cnfportrscprtn** command. To display the port resource partitions, use the **dspportrscprtns** command. The **dspportrscprtns** output lists the following information:

- Port number

- **Controller type**—Portable AutoRoute (PAR), Private Network Node Interface (PNNI), or Multiprotocol Label Switching (MPLS or TAG).

- **Row status**—Always ON.

- **Percent bandwidth in and out**—The percentage of the ingress and egress port bandwidth available to the resource partition.

- **VPI minimum and maximum**—The VPI range used by the resource partition.

- **VCI minimum and maximum**—The VCI range used by the resource partition.

- **Maximum global logical connections (GLCONS)**—The maximum number of connections available to the resource partition.

Configure ILMI Command

The **cnfilmi** command modifies a port's ILMI configuration. Use this command to enable or disable ILMI and to change the polling and timer options.

Here is the **cnfilmi** command syntax:

```
cnfilmi <interface number> <ILMI enable> <signaling protocol type>
    <signaling VPI> <signaling VCI> <ILMI trap> <minimum trap interval>
    <keep alive> <error threshold N491> <polling interval T491>
    <event threshold N492> <minimum enquiry interval T493> <address registration>
```

The parameter options are as follows:

- *interface number*—The logical port or interface number between 1 and 32.
- *ILMI enable*—Enables or disables ILMI. 1 = disable, 2 = enable.
- *signaling protocol type*—1 = other, 2 = no signaling, 3 = ILMI.
- *signaling VPI*—The VPI used by the signaling protocol. 0 to 255 for UNI ports, 0 to 4095 for NNI ports.
- *signaling VCI*—The VCI used by the signaling protocol. 0 to 4095.
- *ILMI trap*—Enables or disables traps. 1 = disable, 2 = enable.
- *minimum trap interval*—The minimum time between trap messages. 1 to 10 seconds.
- *keep alive*—Enables or disables keepalive messages. 1 = disable, 2 = enable.
- *error threshold N491*—The number of timeouts (missed messages) needed to declare a port alarm. 1 to 10 seconds.
- *polling interval T491*—The time between keepalive messages. v1 to v12.
- *event threshold N492*—The number of attempted messages, in conjunction with the error threshold N491, that determines a port alarm condition. 1 to 10.
- *minimum enquiry interval T493*—The minimum time between inquiries. 1 to 2 seconds.
- *address registration*—Enables or disables address registration. 1 = disable, 2 = enable.

Display ILMIs Command

The **dspilmis** command lists the signaling protocol configuration information for all ports on the PXM1. The only supported signaling protocol is the Integrated Local Management Interface (ILMI). Example 21-8 shows an example of the **dspilmis** output.

Example 21-8 dspilmis *Output*

```
hei1pop1.1.7.PXM.a > dspilmis

  Sig.   Ilmi      Sig Sig  Ilmi           T491     T492   T493   Addr
  Port State/Type  Vpi Vci Trap/Int KA ErrTh/Pollint EvntTh EnqInt Reg.
  ----  ---------  ---- ---- --------- --- ------------- ------ ------ ----
     1 Off/none      0   16 Off/01    Off    3/v6         4     10    Off
     2 On/iLMI       0   16 Off/05    On     3/v6         4     10    Off
     3 Off/none      0   16 Off/01    Off    3/v6         4     10    Off
```

Refer to the preceding section on the **cnfilmi** command syntax for descriptions of the display fields.

Commands for Monitoring ATM Ports

This section describes the commands you use to monitor ATM ports on the AUSM and PXM1:

- **dspportcnt**—Lists a port's statistics counters.
- **clrportcnt**—Clears a port's statistics counters.
- **clrportcnts**—Clears the statistics counters for all ports on the card.
- **dspilmicnt**—Lists a port's ILMI statistics counters.
- **clrilmicnt**—Clears a port's ILMI statistics counters.

Display Port Counter Command

The **dspportcnt** command provides detailed historical statistics for an ATM port. Use this command to view the traffic being transmitted to and received from the attached end-user equipment. Because the statistics are historical, you might want to clear the counters using the **clrportcnt** *<port number>* or **clrportcnts** command before beginning your testing or troubleshooting. Example 21-9 shows the **dspportcnt** output for AUSM port number 2.

Example 21-9 **dspportcnt** *Output for an AUSM Port*

```
NZ_8850.1.22.AUSM8.a > dspportcnt 2

PortNum:                                2
PortState:                              Okay
IngressRcvCells:                        423980
IngressRcvCellRate (cells/sec):         423
IngressRcvUtilization (percentage):     12
IngressXmtCells:                        423875
IngressGFCErrorCells:                   0
IngressVpiVciErrCells:                  5
IngressUnknownVpiVci:                   0x0e34a
IngressRcvClpSetCells:                  23
EgressRcvCells:                         5231
EgressRcvCellRate (cells/sec):          26
EgressRcvUtilization (percentage):      1
EgressXmtCells:                         5231
EgressXmtCellRate (cells/sec):          26
EgressXmtUtilization (percentage):      1
EgressPortAlarmDiscardCells:            0
EgressXmtClpSetCells:                   2
EgressXmtEfciSetCells:                  0
PortXmtAisCells:                        0
PortXmtSgmtLpbkCells:                   0
PortRcvAisCells:                        0
PortRcvFerfCells:                       0
```

continues

Example 21-9 dspportcnt *Output for an AUSM Port (Continued)*

```
PortRcvSgmtLpbkCells:              0
PortRcvCrcErrOAMCells:             0
TotalIngressQFullDiscardCells:     0
TotalIngressClpSetDiscardCells:    0
TransmitFIFOFullCount (per card):  0
ReceivedHECErrorCells:             1
HECErroredSeconds:                 1
SeverelyHECErroredSeconds:         0
```

The **dspportcnt** output for AUSM ATM (non-IMA) ports lists the following information:

- **Port state**—The current port state. Active, Line Failure, or ILMI Failure.

- **Ingress receive cells**—The number of cells received from the attached end-user device.

- **Ingress receive cell rate**—The average rate of cells received by the port from the end-user device in cells per second.

- **Ingress receive utilization**—The average percentage of the port rate that is being used.

- **Ingress transmit cells**—The number of cells received from the end-user equipment and passed to the cell bus.

- **Ingress GFC errored cells**—The number of cells received from the attached end-user device with the nonzero Generic Flow Control (GFC) field (UNI only).

- **Ingress VPI and VCI errored**—The number of cells received with valid VPI and VCI values that do not have a channel created for that VPI and VCI.

- **Ingress unknown VPI and VCI**—The number of cells received that have invalid VPI and VCI values.

- **Ingress receive CLP-set cells**—The number of cells entering the port with the CLP bit set. This number does not imply that the AUSM set the CLP bit.

- **Egress receive cells**—The number of cells received from the cell bus.

- **Egress receive cell rate**—The average rate of cells received from the cell bus in cells per second.

- **Egress receive utilization**—The average percentage of the port rate that is being used.

- **Egress transmit cells**—The number of cells sent to the attached end-user device from the AUSM.

- **Egress transmit cell rate**—The average rate of cells sent to the end-user equipment in cells per second.

- **Egress transmit utilization**—The average percentage of the port rate that is being used.

- **Egress port alarm discard cells**—The number of transmit cells discarded because the port was in alarm.

- **Egress transmit CLP set cells**—The number of cells leaving the AUSM with the CLP bit set. This number does not imply that the AUSM set the CLP bit.

- **Egress transmit EFCI set cells**—The number of cells leaving the network with the EFCI bit set. This number does not imply that the AUSM set the EFCI bit.

- **Port transmit AIS cells**—The number of Operation, Administration, and Maintenance (OAM) Alarm Indicator Signal (AIS) cells sent to the attached end-user device during a network alarm condition.

- **Port transmit segment loopback cells**—The number of segment loopback cells sent from the MGX concentrator to the end-user device. The **tstconseg** command is used to create a segment loopback and test the continuity to it. Testing the continuity of a segment loopback allows you to validate its reliability.

- **Port receive AIS cells**—The number of OAM AIS cells received from the attached end-user device during a remote alarm condition.

- **Port receive FERF cells**—The number of OAM far-end receive failure (FERF) cells received from the attached end-user device by the MGX concentrator in response to transmitted AIS cells.

- **Port receive segment loopback cells**—The number of segment loopback cells received from the attached end-user device.

- **Port receive CRC errored OAM cells**—The number of OAM cells received from the attached end-user device that had CRC errors.

- **Total ingress queues full discarded cells**—The number of cells discarded because the ingress queue was full.

- **Total ingress CLP set discarded cells**—The number of cells discarded because they had a CLP of 1 and the ingress queue had exceeded the configured CLP threshold.

- **Transmit FIFO full count**—The number of times the pooled egress buffers on the AUSM card were full.

- **Received HEC errored cells**—The total number of received cells that had Header Error Control (HEC) errors. These cells were discarded.

- **HEC errored seconds**—The number of seconds during which at least one HEC errored cell occurred.

- **Severely HEC errored seconds**—The number of seconds during which the HEC error rate exceeded ten errors per second.

Example 21-10 shows the **dspportcnt** output for PXM1 port number 1.

Example 21-10 **dspportcnt** *Output for a PXM1 Port*

```
hei1pop1.1.7.PXM.a > dspportcnt 1

Interface Num                  :           1
Interface State                : Active
Current Cells in Qbins         :           0
OAM   Cells Received to XmtQ    :          84
RM    Cells Received to XmtQ    :           4
CLP=0 Cells Received to XmtQ    :      142488
CLP=1 Cells Received to XmtQ    :          84
CLP=0 Discard Cells at XmtQ     :           0
CLP=1 Discard Cells at XmtQ     :           0
Transmitted OAM Cells          :          84
Transmitted RM Cells           :           4
Transmitted CLP0 Cells         :      142494
Transmitted CLP1 Cells         :          84
```

The **dspportcnt** output for PXM1 ATM ports lists the following information:

- **Port state**—The current port state. Active, Line Failure, or ILMI Failure.

- **Current cells in QBins**—The number of cells currently in the port QBins.

- **OAM cells received to transmit queue**—The number of OAM cells received from the network and sent to the port egress queue.

- **RM cells received to transmit queue**—The number of resource management (RM) cells received from the network and sent to the port egress queue.

- **CLP 0 cells received to transmit queue**—The number of cells with a CLP of 0 received from the network and sent to the transmit queue.

- **CLP 1 cells received to transmit queue**—The number of cells with a CLP of 1 received from the network and sent to the transmit queue.

- **CLP 0 discard cells at transmit queue**—The number of cells with a CLP of 0 discarded by the transmit queue.

- **CLP 1 discard cells at transmit queue**—The number of cells with a CLP of 1 discarded by the transmit queue.

- **Transmitted OAM cells**—The number of OAM cells sent to the CPE.

- **Transmitted RM cells**—The number of RM cells sent to the CPE.

- **Transmitted CLP 0 cells**—The number of cells with a CLP of 0 sent to the CPE.

- **Transmitted CLP 1 cells**—The number of cells with a CLP of 1 sent to the CPE.

Example 21-11 shows the **dspportcnt** output for AUSM IMA port number 1.

Example 21-11 dspportcnt *Output for an AUSM IMA Port*

```
NZ8850.1.10.AUSM8.a > dspportcnt 1

PortNum:                          1
PortState:                        Active
IngressRcvCells:                  135
IngressVpiVciErrCells:            0
IngressUnknownVpiVci:             0x0
EgressXmtCells:                   129
EgressPortAlarmDiscardCells:      0
EgressXmtEfciSetCells:            0
ReceivedHECErrorCells:            0
HECErroredSeconds:                0
SeverelyHECErroredSeconds:        0
```

The **dspportcnt** output for IMA ports lists the following information:

- **Ingress receive cells**—The total number of cells received from the port (the aggregate of all narrowband lines).

- **Ingress VPI/VCI errored cells**—All cells coming from the remote IMA device (IMATM or AUSM) should have cells within the range specified for the IMA group. Any cells that have invalid or unknown VPIs are dropped.

- **Ingress unknown VPI/VCI**—The VPI and VCI of the last unknown cell. This number is a hexadecimal number that represents the cell's VPI and VCI.

- **Egress transmit cells**—The total number of cells transmitted to the port.

- **Egress port alarm discard cells**—The number of cells discarded while the IMA port (group) was in alarm.

- **Egress transmit EFCI set cells**—The total number of cells transmitted with the EFCI bit set.

- **Received HEC errored cells**—The number of cells received that had invalid HEC. These cells were discarded.

- **HEC errored seconds**—The number of seconds in which at least one line had invalid HECs.

- **Severely HEC errored seconds**—The number of seconds in which greater than $10 \times n$ (where n is the number of lines in the AIM group) cells had invalid HECs.

Display ILMI Counter Command

The **dspilmicnt** command provides historical statistics counters of ILMI messages between the ATM port and the attached CPE. Because the statistics are historical, you might want to clear them using the **clrilmicnt** <*port number*> command before beginning your testing or troubleshooting.

Example 21-12 shows the **dspilmicnt** output for AUSM port number 4.

Example 21-12 **dspilmicnt** *Output for an AUSM Port*

```
hei1pop1.1.1.AUSMB8.a > dspilmicnt 4

 PortNum:                          4
 SNMPPDUsReceived:                 9
 GetRequestReceived:               2
 GetNextRequestReceived:           2
 SetRequestReceived:               0
 TrapReceived:                     1
 GetResponseReceived:              4
 GetResponseTransmitted:           4
 GetRequestTransmitted:            2
 TrapsTransmitted:                 1
 InvalidPDUReceived:               0
 Asn1ParseError:                   0
 NoSuchNameError:                  0
 TooBigError:                      0
```

The **dspilmicnt** output shows the following information:

- **SNMP PDUs received**—The total number of ILMI SNMP protocol data units (PDUs) received from the attached end-user device.

- **Get request received**—The number of "Get" messages received from the attached end-user device.

- **Get next request received**—The number of "Get Next" messages received from the attached end-user device.

- **Set request received**—The number of "Set" messages received from the attached end-user device.

- **Trap received**—The number of traps received from the attached end-user device.

- **Get response received**—The number of messages received from the attached end-user device in response to a "Get" message sent by the MGX switch.

- **Get response transmitted**—The number of messages sent to the attached end-user device in response to a received "Get" message.

- **Get request transmitted**—The number of "Get" messages sent to the attached end-user device from the MGX switch.

- **Traps transmitted**—The number of trap messages sent to the attached end-user device from the MGX switch.

- **Invalid PDU received**—An SNMP message received from the attached end-user device was in error.

- **ASN1 parse error**—The number of errors resulting from faulty Abstract Syntax Notation 1 (ASN1) parsing of incoming PDUs.

- **No such name error**—The number of PDUs received that have a "NoSuchName" error, indicating that the ILMI peer does not support ILMI 4.0 address registration.

- **PDU too big error**—PDUs received where the message length exceeds the value in the length field of the PDU header.

Example 21-13 shows the **dspilmicnt** output for PXM1 port number 2.

Example 21-13 **dspilmicnt** *Output for a PXM1 Port*

```
hei1pop1.1.7.PXM.a > dspilmicnt 2

        PortNum:                        2
        SNMPPDUsReceived:               4492
        GetRequestReceived:             2246
        GetNextRequestReceived:         0
        SetRequestReceived:             0
        TrapReceived:                   0
        GetResponseReceived:            2246
        GetResponseTransmitted:         2246
        GetRequestTransmitted:          2246
        TrapsTransmitted:               0
        InvalidPDUReceived:             0
        Asn1ParseError:                 0
        NoSuchNameError:                0
        TooBigError:                    0
```

NOTE   The fields in the **dspilmicnt** output for a PXM1 port are similar to those for an AUSM port.

How to Configure an ATM Port on the AUSM and PXM1

This section describes the steps you follow to create and configure ATM ports on AUSM and PXM1 cards:

Step 1   Type **dsplns** or **dsplns** {**-ds3** | **-e3** | **-sonet**} *<slot number>* and confirm that the line(s) you want to use for your port are active. This outputs the line status for all lines on the card. If the line(s) are not active, use the **addln** command.

Step 2   Type **dspports** and confirm that the port does not already exist on the card. This outputs a list of ports on the card.

Step 3   If you are adding an IMA port on an AUSM, type **addimagrp** *<group number> <port type> <list of lines> <minimum number of links>* to create an IMA group on the AUSM, and then go to Step 5. Otherwise, proceed with Step 4.

Step 4   Type **addport** *<port number> <port type> <line number>* or **addport** *<port number> <line number> <percent bandwidth> <minimum VPI> <maximum VPI>* to create an ATM port.

Step 5   Type **dspportrscprtn** to determine whether the resource partition configuration is correct.

Step 6   If you want to change the port resource partitions, use the **cnfportrscprtn** command. Otherwise, go to Step 7.

Step 7   If you want to enable ILMI, use the **cnfilmi** command. For AUSM ports, proceed with Step 8. For PXM1 ports, go to Step 10.

Step 8   Type **dspportqs** and verify the QBin configuration.

Step 9   If you want to change a QBin configuration, type **xcnfportq -pn** *<port number>* **-pqn** *<queue number>* [**-qdm** *<queue depth maximum>* **-clph** *<CLP high>* **-clpl** *<CLP low>* **-clpt** *<EFCI threshold>*]. Otherwise, proceed with Step 10.

Step 10   If you enabled ILMI, type **dspilmicnt** *<port number>* and verify that ILMI messages are being exchanged between the port and the attached CPE. Otherwise, proceed with Step 11.

Step 11   Type **dspportcnt** *<port number>* and verify that cells are being sent to and received by the port.

You have completed the steps necessary to create and configure ATM ports on AUSM and PXM1 cards.

ATM Connections

For the purposes of this section, an ATM connection is an end-to-end permanent virtual circuit (PVC) that originates and terminates on MGX ATM ports. The connection receives ATM cells, polices them, and transports them to the remote port. All ATM connections are bidirectional: Traffic flows in both directions.

You can add two kinds of ATM connections in an MGX network: feeder and local. Feeder connections go from the ATM port on the AUSM or PXM1 to the PXM1 trunk and are transported through the ATM backbone network to the destination MGX switch. Local connections go from one port on an MGX switch to another port on the same switch. Local connections can be between ports on the same or different cards. Both feeder and local connections perform the same functions.

In addition to local and feeder connections, you can terminate ATM connections on other Cisco switches, such as the BPX and the MGX 8850-PXM45. For example, if you have a backbone network comprising MGX 8850-PXM45 switches, you can create a two-segment ATM connection from the AUSM to an AXSM port.

Connection Types

The MGX switch supports a number of ATM connection types, including CBR, rt-VBR, nrt-VBR, ABRFST, and ABRSTD, as listed in Table 21-3. The connection type, or class of service (CoS) type, determines how the cells are policed, queued, and processed in the network. CoS types are described in greater detail in the section "ATM Class of Service."

In general, there are no limitations when you add connections to an AUSM or PXM1 port. Any combination of connection types (provided that they are supported) can coexist on the same port. The number of connections supported on a port is determined by the software release and the port and resource partition configuration.

Table 21-3 summarizes the connection types supported on the AUSM and PXM1.

Table 21-3   *Connection Types Supported on the AUSM and PXM1*

Connection Type	Abbreviation	PXM1	AUSM
Constant Bit Rate	CBR	Yes	Yes
Real-time Variable Bit Rate	rt-VBR	Yes	Yes
Nonreal-time Variable Bit Rate	nrt-VBR/VBR	Yes	Yes
ForeSight Available Bit Rate	ABRFST	No	Yes
Standard Available Bit Rate	ABRSTD/ABR	Yes (no VSVD)	Yes (no VSVD)

When the ABR feedback loop terminates on a device, it is considered a Virtual Source-Virtual Destination (VSVD) and is responsible for sending resource management (RM) cells and responding to them by performing the appropriate traffic shaping. The PXM1 and AUSM do not support this feature; they are intermediate elements in a larger feedback loop. The PXM1 and AUSM recognize RM cells and mark the appropriate control information in them.

ATM Feeder Connection

An ATM feeder connection has three connection segments:

- A master connection between the AUSM or PXM1 port and PXM1 trunk on one MGX switch.

- A routing connection through the ATM backbone network. The routing connection should be of the same CoS type as the MGX connection.

- A master connection between the AUSM or PXM1 and the PXM1 trunk on the other MGX switch.

ATM Local Connection

An ATM local connection has two connection segments:

- A slave connection on one AUSM or PXM1. The slave connection must be added first.

- A master connection on the other AUSM or PXM1 pointing to the slave connection.

ATM Class of Service

An ATM class of service (CoS) is a group of connections or virtual circuits (VCs) that share common traffic characteristics. Traffic characteristics include policing definitions, congestion management, time sensitivity, and so on. A CoS is defined to best support traffic with particular needs. By identifying a CoS for a connection, the network can prevent like traffic from having to compete with other traffic that might have conflicting requirements. For example, uncompressed voice traffic is time-sensitive and needs a fixed, guaranteed amount of bandwidth. Voice traffic must be managed differently than another traffic type, such as Internet e-mail services.

ATM Classes of Service

ATM networks support the following classes of service:

- **Constant Bit Rate (CBR)**—CBR traffic is used for time-dependent constant-rate traffic, such as uncompressed voice, video, or synchronous data. Few allowances are made to accommodate burstiness on CBR connections. Most often, CBR connections carry cells that are created using AAL1.

- **Variable Bit Rate (VBR)**—VBR traffic is used for bursty traffic that might have some time dependency, such as compressed voice, video, or synchronous data. Traffic is permitted to burst within set limitations. VBR connections can support any variable-rate application but are used most often for AAL5 cells.

  Variable Bit Rate traffic has two variations:

  - **Real-time VBR (rt-VBR)**—Used when there is a fixed timing relationship between bursts.

  - **Nonreal-time VBR (nrt-VBR)**—Used when there is no fixed timing relationship between bursts, but a guaranteed quality of service is still required.

- **Available Bit Rate (ABR)**—ABR traffic is a variation on VBR and is most commonly used for LAN-WAN services such as router traffic. ABR traffic, like VBR traffic, supports variable-rate applications. The added function of ABR connections is the ability to adjust the data rates in order to accommodate for congestion and bandwidth availability in the network.

  Available Bit Rate traffic has two variations:

  - **Standard**—The ATM-Forum standardized ABR service type. The MGX switch supports ABR services but does not support VSVD connections. ABR connections are marked with the appropriate congestion and rate stamps, but traffic shaping is not performed on ingress to or egress from the MGX network.

  - **ForeSight**—Cisco prestandard ABR using the ForeSight feature. Like standard ABR, the ForeSight feature is used to dynamically manage variable-rate traffic based on the availability of network resources. The AUSM supports ForeSight ABR services; the PXM1 does not.

- **Unspecified Bit Rate (UBR)**—UBR connections are variable-rate connections without a guaranteed service rate. In other words, if there is congestion or no available bandwidth, a UBR connection is not given bandwidth in the network. UBR connections are used for variable-rate applications that are tolerant of zero-transmission periods such as batch-processed e-mail or LAN emulation services.

ATM Policing

Policing is the process of monitoring ingress traffic to determine whether the traffic can enter and how that traffic is handled as soon as it is inside the network. Each connection has a number of policing parameters that can include characteristics such as burst sizes and data rates. The end-user device is responsible for meeting the defined policing requirements. Otherwise, the traffic is deemed noncompliant and can be dropped by the network.

The *leaky bucket* model defines policing on ingress for ATM connections on the MGX switch. It is important to remember that the leaky bucket is not a queue structure, but a way to describe how the network monitors and controls incoming user cells.

It is easiest to think of this model as a test that is done on the traffic to answer two questions:

- Should the cell be allowed into the network?
- If so, should it be given a normal or low priority (set the CLP bit to 1)?

Leaky Bucket Model

The leaky bucket model has three basic components:

- **Token**—Arrives in the bucket at a rate defined by the incoming traffic. For ATM traffic, each cell is represented in the leaky bucket model as a single token. The rate at which the tokens fill the bucket is variable. The actual user-data cell does not go into the bucket.

- **Bucket size**—Determines how many tokens can be held before the bucket is full. As soon as the bucket reaches its capacity, any new tokens represent cells that are noncompliant. Noncompliant cells may be dropped or tagged with a 1 in the CLP field, depending on the situation.

- **Leak rate**—Determines the average acceptable token rate to maintain compliance. If the tokens arrive at approximately the same rate as the leak rate, the bucket never fills up. If the tokens arrive at a rate greater than the leak rate, they eventually become noncompliant. If the tokens arrive at a rate less than the leak rate, the bucket is always empty.

Dual Leaky Bucket Model

Many ATM classes of service use a dual leaky bucket model for policing. A dual leaky bucket is made up of two different leaky bucket models, each with its own configurable characteristics.

In general, the first leaky bucket is set to discard any noncompliant cells, which means that all incoming traffic must meet the requirements of the first leaky bucket in order to be accepted by the network. If a cell is dropped at the first leaky bucket, the second leaky bucket does not check it.

The second leaky bucket can be disabled, drop on noncompliance, or tag with CLP on noncompliance. The behavior of the second bucket is dependent on the configured policing type.

Leaky Bucket Characteristics

For all traffic types, the size and leak rate of the two leaky bucket models are defined by the following:

- The size of the first bucket is the Cell Delay Variation Tolerance (CDVT) in microseconds.
- The leak rate of the first bucket is the Peak Cell Rate (PCR) in cells per second.
- The size of the second bucket is a function of the Maximum Burst Size (MBS) in cells. If traffic is running at exactly the PCR, the second bucket size is the MBS.
- The leak rate of the second bucket is the Sustainable Cell Rate (SCR) in cells per second.

NOTE   For a graphical representation of the leaky bucket characteristics, refer to Chapter 6, "ATM Ports and Connections and ATM-to-Frame Relay Interworking."

The PCR is the maximum average rate that a connection is allowed. Rates higher than the PCR are allowed provided that the CDVT is not exceeded.

The SCR is the average rate that a connection is guaranteed. The MBS is the number of cells that are guaranteed if a connection is going at exactly the PCR. At other rates, the burst might be bigger or smaller than the MBS.

The PCR, CDVT, SCR, and MBS are configured for each end of a connection in the network. All policing characteristics affect the ingress traffic and can be configured differently at each end (asymmetric configuration). For example, you might have a T3 interface on one end and an OC-3c interface on the other.

Policing Based on Class of Service

The dual leaky bucket model can be applied to each ATM CoS. For each CoS, policing conventions define how the policing is done and what the results of policing are.

Many traffic types have several variations based on the policing options. For example, there are three commonly used CBR types: CBR.1, CBR.2, and CBR.3. The policing options include the following:

- Disable or enable the policing process
- Use only the first leaky bucket or both leaky buckets in the model
- Check all cells, only CLP 0 cells, or no cells on the second bucket
- Discard or tag with CLP on each bucket

When you add an ATM connection, you can specify the SCR/MCR policing type as 1, 2, or 3. In addition, you can disable the policing process entirely.

Table 21-4 lists the standard policing definitions for each CoS. The most commonly used types are highlighted.

Table 21-4   *Standard Policing Definitions*

	First Bucket		Second Bucket	
CoS	**Cells**	**Result**	**Cells**	**Result**
CBR.1	All	Discard	None	—
CBR.2	All	Discard	CLP 0	Discard
CBR.3	All	Discard	CLP 0	Tag
rt-VBR.1	All	Discard	All	Discard
rt-VBR.2	All	Discard	CLP 0	Discard
rt-VBR.3	All	Discard	CLP 0	Tag
nrt-VBR.1	All	Discard	All	Discard
nrt-VBR.2	All	Discard	CLP 0	Discard
nrt-VBR.3	All	Discard	CLP 0	Tag
ABR	All	Discard	All	Discard
UBR.1	All	Discard	None	—
UBR.2	All	Discard/CLP	None	—

NOTE   Standard ABR and ForeSight ABR are policed in the same way. For UBR.2 connections, noncompliant cells are discarded, and compliant cells are all tagged with the CLP bit.

Time-Based Model for PCR and CDVT

In most cases, the PCR is defined in cells per second, and the CDVT is defined in microseconds. You might find it difficult to conceptualize a bucket whose size is configured as a time period.

Another way to look at the policing mechanism is using the theoretical arrival time. As each cell arrives in to the network, it is compared to the expected arrival time (1/PCR). If the cell is early, a penalty is added to the total penalty. The penalty is based on how early the cell is.

If the cell is late, a credit is given and is subtracted from the total penalty. If the total penalty exceeds the configured limit (CDVT), the cell is noncompliant and is discarded without adding to the total penalty. The next cell to arrive continues to accumulate penalties or credits. You can see the similarities between the time-based and leaky bucket models as time accumulates and leaks when cells arrive early or late, based on the PCR.

NOTE   For a graphical representation of the time-based model for PCR and CDVT, refer to Chapter 6.

CBR Example

When you assign policing values to a connection, it is helpful if you can determine how large of a cell burst is allowed into the network at a certain rate before the traffic becomes noncompliant. By using the following equation, you can check to see whether the values you have used for the CDVT and PCR are reasonable:

Allowable burst size = 1 + [CDVT / (1 / PCR – 1 / AR)]

AR is the cell arrival rate.

For example, if CDVT is 100,000 microseconds and PCR is 2000 cells per second, the results for a single leaky bucket are shown in Table 21-5.

Table 21-5 *CBR Results*

AR (Cells Per Second)	Burst Size (Cells)	Comments
1900	—	If the AR is less than the PCR, no cells are dropped.
2100	4201	If the AR is greater than the PCR, a limited number of cells are allowed in before some cells get dropped.
4000	401	As the AR increases, the burst size decreases.

When the traffic reaches the point where cells are being dropped due to noncompliance, some of the traffic, at the rate of the configured PCR, is still compliant. However, in most situations, the end-user application fails if any of the cells are not successfully transported across the network.

VBR Example

Both real-time VBR (rt-VBR) and nonreal-time VBR (nrt-VBR) services are policed using a dual leaky bucket model. The first leaky bucket is identical to that used for policing CBR connections. The second bucket is defined by the SCR and MBS. The following equation can check the configuration of the second leaky bucket:

$$\text{Allowable burst size} = 1 + \{[(MBS-1) \times (1/SCR - 1/PCR) + CDVT]/[1/SCR - 1/AR]\}$$

AR is the cell arrival rate.

For example, if CDVT is 100,000 microseconds, PCR is 2000 cells per second, MBS is 501 cells, and SCR is 1000 cells per second, the results are as described in Table 21-6.

Table 21-6   *VBR Results*

AR (Cells Per Second)	Compliant on First Bucket	Compliant on Second Bucket	Comments
900	—	—	If the AR is less than the PCR and the SCR, all cells are compliant.
1100	—	3851	If the PCR is greater than the AR and the AR is greater than the SCR, no cells are dropped on the first bucket, but some are tagged CLP = 1 on the second bucket.
1900	—	740	As the AR increases, the number of cells compliant on the second bucket decreases.
2100	4201	669	If the AR is greater than the PCR, a limited number of cells are allowed in the first bucket, and a portion of those go on to be tagged CLP = 1 on the second bucket.
4000	401	468	As the AR increases, the number of compliant cells in both buckets decreases.

NOTE   The CDVT used to calculate the results in Table 21-6 is described in seconds. Therefore, you would use 1 second in the calculation, not 100,000.

ForeSight on ATM Connections

The *ForeSight* feature is a prestandard version of ABR implemented on ATM connections. It is a closed-loop feedback mechanism that predicts and adjusts network traffic to avoid congestion and subsequent data loss. The ForeSight feature is enabled per connection and controls the VC queue service rate. When congestion occurs on a connection, the queue service rate decreases; when there is no congestion, the queue service rate increases. By dynamically adjusting the rate at which traffic enters the network, the ForeSight feature prevents data loss and offers the connection the maximum bandwidth available in the network.

The ForeSight feature relies on measuring network congestion along the data path and reporting the congestion to the source end of the connection using the following criteria:

- Data moves from the source to the destination. Control messages can also flow from source to destination.

- As the traffic (both data and control) travels through the network, the various network elements can mark congestion and other control fields in the cells.

- The destination device collects the congestion and control information and reports it back to the source device.

- The source, after receiving the congestion and control information from the destination, makes the required adjustments in the VC queue service rate.

Potential Congestion Locations

Congestion is measured on egress queues both on the AUSM and on intermediate trunk queues in the BPX network (if you are using a BPX backbone network). For local connections or when the MGX switch is attached to a non-BPX network, only the AUSM egress queue congestion is considered.

Here are the thresholds for determining congestion in an MGX/BPX tiered network:

- The EFCI threshold on the egress ATM port

- The EFCN threshold on the egress BPX BXM trunks (the default value is approximately 10 percent of the queue depth)

- The EFCI threshold on the ingress BXM card (the threshold is hard-coded)

Figure 21-5 shows the queues where congestion can occur on an ATM connection in a tiered network.

Figure 21-5 *Congestion Locations*

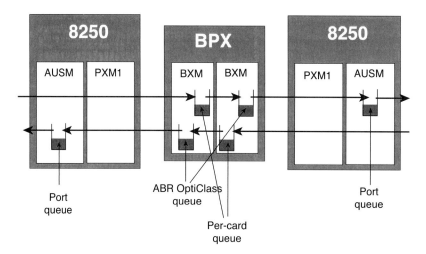

ForeSight Congestion Criteria

As a result of measuring and reporting congestion in the data cells (EFCI bit) and control cells, the source AUSM card must adjust the VC queue service rate accordingly. Table 21-7 lists the conditions required for the ForeSight feature to declare a congested, severely congested, or not congested state, and the resulting VC queue service rate change. MCR is the configured minimum information rate, and rate up, rate down, and rate fast down are the configured ForeSight adjustment rates.

Table 21-7 *ForeSight Congestion States and Results*

Condition	Congestion State	Result
Last sampled data cell, EFCI = 1, or port queue > EFCI threshold	Congested	New rate = (old rate) × (*rate down*)
Last sampled data cell, EFCI = 1, and port queue > queue depth	Severely congested	New rate = (old rate) × (*rate fast down*)
Last sampled data cell, EFCI = 0, and port queue < EFCI threshold	Not congested	New rate = (old rate) + [(MCR) × (*rate up*)]

ForeSight Configurable Characteristics

The following ForeSight characteristics are configured per connection:

- **Peak Cell Rate (PCR)**—The maximum connection rate that the source can allow.
- **Minimum Cell Rate (MCR)**—The minimum connection rate that the source can allow.

- **Initial Cell Rate (ICR)**—The connection rate that the source uses after a set idle period (ICR timeout).

The following ForeSight characteristics are configured per AUSM:

- **Rate up**—The percentage of the configured MCR by which the connection rate increases if there is no congestion. By default, rate up is 10 percent.

- **Rate down**—The percentage of the current connection rate that the connection rate drops to if there is congestion. By default, rate down is 87 percent.

- **Rate fast down**—The percentage of the current connection rate that the connection rate drops to if there is severe congestion. By default, rate fast down is 50 percent.

- **ICR timeout**—The idle period after which the connection rate is reset to the ICR. By default, the ICR timeout is 10 seconds.

ABR for ATM

This section describes standard Available Bit Rate (ABR) in an ATM network. Standard ABR is supported on both PXM1 and AUSM ATM ports, but in a limited capacity. Neither the PXM1 nor the AUSM can function as an ABR Virtual Source-Virtual Destination (VSVD). ABR connections include a closed-loop feedback mechanism that predicts and adjusts network traffic to avoid congestion and subsequent data loss. ABR is enabled per connection and controls the VC queue service rate. When congestion occurs on a connection, the queue service rate decreases; when there is no congestion, the queue service rate increases. By dynamically adjusting the rate at which traffic enters the network, the ABR prevents data loss and offers the connection the maximum bandwidth available in the network.

Standard ABR utilizes a resource management (RM) cell to measure and report network conditions to determine the virtual circuit queue service rate. Periodically, the source sends an RM cell in the data stream to the destination. Along the way, the network can alter bits in the RM cell to report the network conditions and availability. The destination, when it receives the RM cell, turns it around and sends it back to the source. This is called a backward RM (BRM) cell. The source, when it receives the BRM cell, is required to adjust the queue service rate accordingly.

On the PXM1 and AUSM, the ATM port is neither virtual source nor virtual destination. In other words, the ports do *not* perform the role of the source and destination in the ABR feedback loop. The MGX portion of a larger ABR connection provides congestion and explicit rate (ER) marking on RM cells that are passed on the connection. For more information on RM cells, see the section "The RM Cell" in Chapter 20, "Frame Relay Ports and Connections."

Potential Congestion Locations

Congestion is measured on egress queues both on the PXM1 or AUSM ATM port and on intermediate trunk queues in the ATM network. PXM1 and AUSM egress queue congestion is considered for local connections only. The thresholds for determining congestion in an MGX/BPX tiered network are as follows:

- The EFCI threshold on the egress AUSM port
- The EFCN threshold on the egress BPX BXM trunks (the default value is approximately 10 percent of the queue depth)
- The EFCI threshold on the ingress BXM card (the threshold is hard-coded)

VC Queues on the AUSM

A virtual circuit (VC) queue buffers ingress (from the CPE to the network) traffic. VC queues are used to shape the ingress traffic. The AUSM serves the data in the queues based on the connection's expected rate (usually the PCR or SCR). ABR connections are served at a variable rate, depending on network availability. Figure 21-6 shows VC queues on the AUSM card.

Figure 21-6 *AUSM VC Queues*

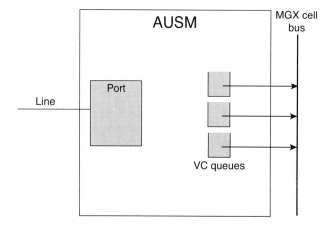

Frame-Based Traffic Control

Frame-based traffic control is a mechanism that lets an ATM device discard part or all of an AAL5 frame based on predefined criteria. ATM cells that are segmented using AAL5 carry frame-based data. This data could be in the form of Frame Relay, TCP/IP, X.25, HDLC, and so on. The cell header format for AAL5 cells includes a single bit that identifies the location of that cell within the original frame. This bit is the third bit in the Payload Type Indicator (PTI) field of both the UNI and NNI cell headers. If the bit is 0, the cell is either the beginning or continuation of a frame. If the bit is 1, the cell marks the end of the frame.

In general, the motivation behind frame-based traffic control is that if a part of a frame is discarded, the rest of the frame is of no value to the destination device and should also be discarded. Because the destination device depends on the last cell from a frame to delineate between frames, in most cases this cell is not dropped and is sent through to its final destination.

Early packet discard (EPD) is when congestion occurs at the beginning of a frame, and the entire frame, including the last cell, is discarded. There are two EPD thresholds:

- EPD0 is the threshold to drop either CLP 1 or CLP 0 cells.

- EPD1 is the threshold to drop CLP 1 cells. EPD1 is less than or equal to EPD0.

Figure 21-7 shows how EPD is implemented.

Figure 21-7 *Early Packet Discard*

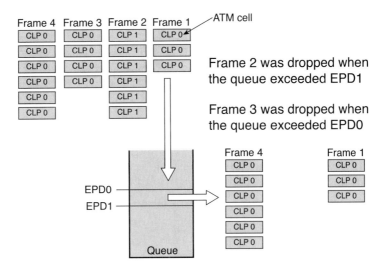

Configuration Example

Figure 21-8 shows an example of a VC queue, including the queue size, CLP high and low, and EFCI configuration. In this example, EPD is disabled.

Figure 21-8 *VC Queue Configuration Example*

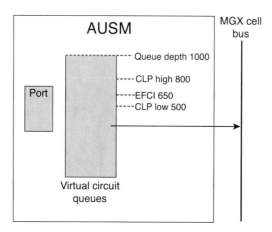

What happens as cells come from the CPE and are queued in the VC queue? Suppose the VC queue shown in Figure 21-8 has 400 cells. If new cells arrive in the queue faster than they are serviced and sent out on the line, the queue begins to fill. When the queue contains 500 (EFCI threshold) cells, all subsequent cells have their EFCI bit set to 1. If the queue reaches 800 cells (CLP high threshold), any new cells with a CLP of 1 are discarded and are not allowed into the queue. Any existing cells in the queue remain there. If the queue reaches 1000 cells, all new cells are dropped.

If the VC queue services cells at a rate faster than it is filling, the queue empties. When the queue has fewer than 800 cells (CLP high threshold), CLP tagged cells still are not accepted into the queue. Only when the queue depth reaches 500 cells (CLP low threshold) does the queue begin accepting cells with a CLP of 1.

Queue Characteristics

The following characteristics define a port or VC queue:

- **Queue depth maximum**—The maximum number of cells that can be stored in the queue.

- **CLP high**—The queue depth at which CLP tagged (CLP set to 1) cells are not allowed into the queue and are dropped.

- **CLP low**—The queue depth at which CLP tagged cells are allowed into the queue and are no longer dropped. If EPD is enabled, the CLP low threshold defines the EPD0 threshold.
- **EPD1**—The queue threshold that determines when to start EPD on CLP 1 and CLP 0 cells.
- **EFCI threshold**—The point at which cells are marked as congested.

Commands for Adding, Displaying, and Configuring ATM Connections on the AUSM

This section describes the commands used to add, display, and configure ATM connections on the AUSM:

- **addcon**—Creates a new ATM connection.
- **delcon**—Removes an ATM connection.
- **dspcons**—Lists summary status information for all connections on the card.
- **dspcon**—Lists detailed configuration and status information for an ATM connection.
- **cnfchanfst**—Modifies a connection's ForeSight characteristics. Also modifies the initial burst size (IBS) and Frame-based Generic Cell Rate Algorithm (FGCRA) on all connection types.
- **cnfupccbr**—Modifies the CBR connection characteristics of an ATM connection.
- **cnfupcvbr**—Modifies the nrt-VBR connection characteristics of an ATM connection.
- **cnfupcrtvbr**—Modifies the rt-VBR connection characteristics of an ATM connection.
- **cnfupcabr**—Modifies the ForeSight ABR connection characteristics of an ATM connection.
- **cnfupcubr**—Modifies the UBR connection characteristics of an ATM connection.
- **cnfconabrparams**—Modifies the standard ABR connection parameters.
- **cnfconabrrates**—Modifies the standard ABR traffic rates for a connection, including the peak, minimum, and initial cell rates.
- **cnfconstdabr**—Modifies all the standard ABR characteristics of a connection, including those modified using the **cnfchanabrparams** and **cnfchanabrrates** commands.
- **dspconstdabr**—Lists a connection's standard ABR characteristics.
- **cnfchanq**—Modifies the VC queue characteristics.

Add Connection Command

Use the **addcon** command to create a new ATM connection on the MGX AUSM. You can use the **delcon** command to remove the connection.

Here is the **addcon** command syntax:

```
addcon <port number> <VPI> <VCI> <connection type> <service type>
  [controller type] [mastership] [remote connection ID]
```

The parameter options are as follows:

- *port number*—The ATM port that the connection uses.
- *VPI*—The VPI of the incoming user cells on this connection. 0 to 255.
- *VCI*—The VCI of the incoming user cells on this connection. 0 to 65,535 or * for VPC channels.
- *connection type*—Determines whether both the VPI and VCI of the incoming cells are used to switch the cells (VCC), or just the VPI (VPC). 0 = VCC, 1 to 1000 = VP ID.
- *service type*—The connection's service type. 1 = CBR, 2 = nrt-VBR, 3 = standard ABR, 4 = UBR, 5 = rt-VBR, 6 = ForeSight ABR.
- *controller type*—1 = PVC (PAR), 2 = SPVC (PNNI). The controller type is not specified on the slave end of a local connection.
- *mastership*—1 = master, 2 = slave. When you add a slave connection, do not enter the mastership value. Eliminating this parameter automatically makes the connection a slave.
- *remote connection ID*—The destination connection ID for master connections in the form *node.slot.port.VPI.VCI*. For feeder connections, the slot number is 0 for the PXM1.

Display Connections Command

The **dspcons** command provides summary status and configuration information for all connections on the card. Use this command to learn which connections have been added and how they are configured. Example 21-14 shows an example of the **dspcons** output.

Example 21-14 **dspcons** *Output*

```
hei1pop1.1.1.AUSMB8.a > dspcons

ConnId                  Chan ConnType Serv Type    PCR[0+1]  Q-Depth State
-------------------     ---- -------- ---------    --------- ------- -------
hei1pop1.1.1.20.20      17   VCC      VBR          3622      1000    Active
hei1pop1.1.1.20.30      19   VCC      ABR          3622      1000    Alarm
hei1pop1.1.4.56.*       24   VPC      UBR          14364     1000    Active

ChanNumNextAvailable    :  25
Local VpId NextAvailable :  4
```

The **dspcons** command provides the following information:

- **Connection ID**—In the form *nodename.slot.port.VPI.VCI.* The VCI value is always *
  on VP connections.
- **Channel number**—An identifier used internally by the switch.
- **Connection type**—VCC or VPC.
- **Service type**—CBR, VBR (nrt-VBR), rt-VBR, ABR (there is no differentiation
  between standard and ForeSight ABR), or UBR.
- **PCR[0+1]**—Can be configured from 10 to the port speed in cells per second.
- **Queue depth**—Ingress VC queue depth in cells.
- **State**—Alarm or Active.

Display Connection Command

The **dspcon** command lists detailed configuration information for a specified connection.
The **dspcon** output shows some policing parameters that do not apply to the connection
type (such as MBS for a UBR connection). To determine which parameters do apply, use
the appropriate UPC configuration command (such as **cnfupcubr**).

Example 21-15 shows the first page of the **dspcon** output. (This command's output has four
pages. The second, third, and fourth follow.)

Example 21-15 dspcon *Output, Page 1*

```
hei1pop1.1.1.AUSMB8.a > dspcon 4.56.0

  ChanNum:                          24
  RowStatus:                        Add
  ConnectionType:                   VPC
  ServiceType:                      UBR
  ChanSvcFlag:                      PVC
  PortNum:                          4
  VPI:                              56
  VCI (For VCC):                    *
  Local VPId(for VPC):              56
  EgressQNum:                       4
  IngressQDepth(cells):             1000
  IngressDiscardOption:             CLP hysterisis
  IngressFrameDiscardThreshold      1000
  IngressQCLPHigh(cells):           900
  IngressQCLPLow(cells):            800
  QCLPState:                        LOW
  IngressEfciThreshold(cells):      1000
  UPCEnable:                        Enabled
  PeakCellRate[0+1](cells/sec):     14364
```

continues

Example 21-15 *dspcon Output, Page 1 (Continued)*

```
    CellDelayVariation[0+1]:            10000 (micro secs)
    PeakCellRate[0](cells/sec):        14364

Type <CR> to continue, Q<CR> to stop:
```

Many of the fields listed in the **dspcon** output can be modified using a number of
configuration commands discussed later in this section. Other information in the **dspcon**
output includes the following:

- **Row status**—The connection's administrative status. Either Add or Modify.

- **Queue CLP state**—If the ingress VC queue is below the CLP low threshold, the CLP
  state is LOW. If the ingress VC queue is above the CLP high threshold, the CLP state
  is HIGH.

Example 21-16 shows the second **dspcon** output screen.

Example 21-16 *dspcon Output, Page 2*

```
    CellDelayVariation[0]:             250000 (micro secs)
      SustainedCellRate(cells/sec):    14364
      MaximumBurstSize(cells):         1000
      SCRPolicing:                     CLP[0]
      CLPTagEnable:                    Enabled
      FrameGCRAEnable:                 Disable

      ForesightEnable:                 Disable
      InitialBurstSize(cells):         0
      ForeSightPeakCellRate(cells/sec): 14364
      MinimumCellRate(cells/sec):      0
      InitialCellRate(cells/sec):      0

      LocalRemoteLpbkState:            Disable
      ChanTestType:                    No Test
      ChanTestState:                   Not In Progress
      ChanRTDresult:                   65535 ms

      Ingress percentage util:         100
      Egress percentage util :         0
      Egress Service Rate:             0

Type <CR> to continue, Q<CR> to stop:
```

Information on the second **dspcon** output screen includes the following:

- **Local remote loopback state**—Specifies whether the channel loop is enabled or
  disabled. The local remote loopback faces toward the backbone network and is
  created using the **addchanloop** command.

- **Test type**—The type of test if a test is in progress.

- **Test state**—The result of the most recent test. Either passed or failed.

- **RTD result**—The result of the most recent round-trip delay test (use the **tstdelay** command). If the test has never been run, the test reports 65,535 milliseconds.

Example 21-17 shows the third **dspcon** output screen.

Example 21-17 dspcon *Output, Page 3*

```
LocalVpi:                      56
  LocalVci:                     *
  LocalNSAP:                   68656931706f70310000000000000000001000400
  RemoteVpi:                   56
  RemoteVci:                    *
  RemoteNSAP:                  68656931706f70310000000000000000000000100
  Mastership:                  Master
  VpcFlag:                     Vpc
  ConnServiceType:             UBR
  RoutingPriority:             1
  MaxCost:                     255
  RestrictTrunkType:           No Restriction
  ConnPCR:                     14364
  ConnMCR:                     0
  ConnPercentUtil:             100
  ChanOvrSubOvrRide:           Enabled
  Stdabr Parameters:
  Minimum Cell Rate:           10 Cells per second
  Peak Cell Rate:              10 Cells per second
  Initial Cell rate:           10 Cells per second
  Rate Increase Factor:        64

Type <CR> to continue, Q<CR> to stop:
```

Information on the third **dspcon** output screen includes the following:

- **Channel local NSAP**—The Network Service Access Point (NSAP) address uniquely identifies this interface (port) in the network. The 20-byte hexadecimal address contains the following fields:

  — The most significant 8 bytes (16 digits) spell out the node name in ASCII. The connection in Example 21-17 is on node hei1pop1.

  — The card slot number is the fourth byte from the right. The connection in Example 21-17 is on card 1.

  — The port number is the second byte from the right. The connection in Example 21-17 is on port 4.

- **Channel remote VPI**—The VPI value at the remote end.

- **Channel remote VCI**—The VCI value at the remote end. In this case, the connection is a VPC, so a * is reported in this field.

- **Channel remote NSAP**—The remote NSAP address is in the same format as the local NSAP address. If this connection terminates on the PXM1, the card slot field is 0. The slave end of a local connection does not have a remote NSAP and is reported as NULL NSAP.

Example 21-18 shows the fourth **dspcon** output screen.

Example 21-18 dspcon *Output, Page 4*

```
Rate Decrease Factor:              16
  Nrm -- Inrate Cell Count:        64
  Trm -- Time limit for Frm:       255 milliseconds
  Transient Buffer Exposure:       16777215 Cells
  Fixed Round Trip Time:           0 milliseconds
  ACR Decrease Time Factor:        500 milliseconds
  Cutoff Decrease Factor:          16
  AbrType:                         Switch behavior without VS/VD

ChanNumNextAvailable     : 28
Local VpId NextAvailable : 8
```

Configure Channel ForeSight Command

The **cnfchanfst** command is used to modify a connection's ForeSight ABR characteristics. You must use this command to enable ForeSight on a connection even though you specified the connection type when the connection was added. You must also use this command to change the FGCRA and IBS parameters for all connections, regardless of their service type.

Here is the **cnfchanfst** command syntax:

```
cnfchanfst <connection> <ForeSight> <FGCRA> <IBS> <PCR> <MCR> <ICR>
```

The parameter options are as follows:

- *connection*—The connection to be modified, in the form *port.VPI.VCI*.
- *ForeSight*—1 = disable, 2 = enable.
- *FGCRA*—FGCRA (early packet discard [EPD]). 1 = disable, 2 = enable.
- *IBS*—Initial burst size. 0 to 5000 cells.
- *PCR*—Peak cell rate. 10 to the port rate.
- *MCR*—Minimum cell rate. 0 to 8000 cells per second.
- *ICR*—Initial cell rate. 0 to 8000 cells per second.

Configure UPC CBR Command

The **cnfupccbr** command is used to modify a connection's CBR policing characteristics. The **dspcon** command shows all policing parameters (CBR and others). The **cnfupccbr** command filters out values that do not apply.

Here is the **cnfupccbr** command syntax:

```
cnfupccbr <connection> <UPC enable> <PCR(0+1)> <CDVT(0+1)> <ingress utilization>
  <egress service rate> <egress utilization>
```

The parameter options are as follows:

- *connection*—The connection to be modified, in the form *port.VPI.VCI*.

- *UPC enable*—Enables or disables the policing process on the connection. 1 = disable, 2 = enable.

- *PCR(0+1)*—Can be configured from 10 to the port speed in cells per second.

- *CDVT(0+1)*—1 to 250,000 microseconds.

- *ingress utilization*—A connection's expected utilization. Used to determine the port's ingress bandwidth capacity. The expected bandwidth = PCR × utilization. 1 to 127 percent, or 0 for the default (100 percent for CBR connections).

- *egress service rate*—Determines the rate at which this connection should be serviced on egress from the port queue. 1 to the port speed.

- *egress utilization*—A connection's expected utilization. Used to determine the port's egress bandwidth capacity. The expected bandwidth = egress service rate × utilization. 1 to 127 percent, or 0 for the default (100 percent for CBR channels).

For example, type **cnfupccbr 1.10.100 2 1000 200000 50 1000 50** to enable policing, set the PCR to 1000 cps, set the CDVT to 200,000 microseconds, set the ingress utilization to 50 percent, set the egress service rate to 1000 cps, and set the egress utilization to 50 percent.

Configure UPC VBR Command

The **cnfupcvbr** command is used to modify the VBR policing characteristics on an nrt-VBR connection. (Use the **cnfupcrtvbr** command for rt-VBR connections, as described in the following section.) The **dspcon** command shows all policing parameters (VBR and others). The **cnfupcvbr** command filters out values that do not apply.

Here is the **cnfupcvbr** command syntax:

```
cnfupcvbr <connection> <UPC enable> <PCR(0+1)> <CDVT(0+1)> <SCR> <SCR policing>
  <MBS> <ingress utilization> <egress service rate> <egress utilization>
  <CLP tagging>
```

The parameter options are as follows (parameters that were described previously for the **cnfupccbr** command are not repeated):

- *SCR*—Sustainable cell rate. Can be configured from 10 to the port rate in cells per second.

- *SCR policing*—Determines which cells are policed on the second leaky bucket. 1 = CLP 0 cells only, 2 = all cells, 3 = no cells.

- *MBS* —Maximum burst size. 1 to 5000 cells.

- *CLP tagging*—Determines whether noncompliant cells on the second leaky bucket are tagged or discarded. 1 = disable (discard noncompliant cells), 2 = enable (tag non-compliant cells with CLP).

Configure UPC rt-VBR Command

The **cnfupcrtvbr** command is used to modify a connection's rt-VBR policing characteristics. The **cnfupcrtvbr** command has the same parameter options as the **cnfupcvbr** command just described.

Configure UPC ABR Command

The **cnfupcabr** command is used to modify a connection's ABR policing characteristics. The **cnfupcabr** command has the same parameter options as the **cnfupcvbr** command just described.

Configure UPC UBR Command

The **cnfupcubr** command is used to modify a connection's UBR policing characteristics. The **dspcon** command shows all policing parameters (UBR and others). The **cnfupcubr** command filters out values that do not apply.

Here is the **cnfupcubr** command syntax:

```
cnfupcubr <connection> <UPC enable> <PCR(0+1)> <CDVT(0+1)>
    <ingress utilization> <CLP tagging>
```

All the parameters in the **cnfupcubr** command are described in the previous **cnfupccbr** and **cnfupcvbr** command sections.

Configure Connection ABR Parameters Command

The **cnfconabrparams** command is used to modify a connection's standard ABR connection characteristics. The **cnfconabrrates** and **cnfconstdabr** commands are subsets of the **cnfconabrparams** command.

Here is the **cnfconabrparams** command syntax:

```
cnfconabrparams <connection number | channel number> <ABR type>
   <RIF> <RDF> <NRM> <TRM> <TBE> <FRTT> <ADTF> <CDF>
```

The parameter options are as follows:

- *connection number*—The connection number, in the form *port.VPI.VCI*.

- *channel number*—Alternatively, you can use the connection's channel number.

- *ABR type*—The type of ABR service. 1 = switch behavior, 2 = virtual source virtual destination (not supported).

- *RIF*—Rate increase factor. A percentage from 1 to 32,768 in steps of power of 2. For example, you can type 2, 4, 8, 16, or 32, but not 3 or 35.

- *RDF*—Rate decrease factor. A percentage from 1 to 32,768 in steps of power of 2.

- *NRM*—Number per RM. From 2 to 256 in steps of power of 2.

- *TRM*—Time between RM. From 3 to 255 milliseconds.

- *TBE*—Transient buffer exposure. From 0 to 16,777,215 cells.

- *FRTT*—Fixed round-trip time. From 0 to 16,700 milliseconds.

- *ADTF* —Allowed-cell-rate decrease time factor. From 10 to 10,230 milliseconds in multiples of 10.

- *CDF*—Cutoff decrease factor. A percentage from 0 to 64 in steps of power of 2.

Display Connection Standard ABR Command

The **dspconstdabr** command is used to list a connection's standard ABR characteristics.

Example 21-19 shows the **dspconstdabr** output.

Example 21-19 dspconstdabr *Output*

```
hei1pop1.1.1.AUSMB8.a > dspconstdabr 1.20.30

     ChannelNumber               :  19
     Minimum Cell Rate           :  3622 Cells per second
     Peak Cell Rate              :  3622 Cells per second
     Initial Cell rate           :  3622 Cells per second
     Rate Increase Factor        :  64
     Rate Decrease Factor        :  16
     Nrm -- Inrate Cell Count     :  64
     Trm -- Time limit for Frm    :  255 milliseconds
     Transient Buffer Exposure   :  16777215 Cells
     Fixed Round Trip Time       :  0 milliseconds
     ACR Decrease Time Factor    :  500 milliseconds
     Cutoff Decrease Factor      :  16
     ABRType                     :  Switch behavior without VS/VD
```

All the fields are described in the **cnfconabrparams** command in the preceding section.

Configure Channel Queue Command

The **cnfchanq** command is used to modify the ingress VC queue characteristics, including the congestion and discard thresholds.

Here is the **cnfchanq** command syntax:

```
cnfchanq <connection> <discard option> <VC queue depth> <CLP high>
  <CLP low | EPD threshold> <EFCI threshold>
```

The parameter options are as follows:

- *connection*—The connection to be modified, in the form *port.VPI.VCI*.

- *discard option*—Defines whether the connection will discard based on the CLP high and low thresholds or use EPD. 1 = CLP hysteresis, 2 = EPD.

- *VC queue depth*—The maximum number of cells permitted to be buffered on ingress for this channel. 0 to 16,000 cells.

- *CLP high*—The threshold at which CLP = 1 cells are no longer accepted into the VC queue and are discarded. 1 to 16,000 cells.

- *CLP low*—The threshold, after reaching CLP high, at which CLP = 1 cells are again allowed into the VC queue and are no longer discarded. 1 to 16,000 cells.

- *EPD threshold*—When the VC queue reaches this threshold, any new AAL5 frame is dropped in its entirety. 1 to 16,000 cells.

- *EFCI threshold*—The threshold on the VC queue where congestion tagging begins by setting the EFCI bit to 1. 1 to 16,000 cells.

Commands for Adding, Displaying, and Configuring ATM Connections on the PXM1

This section describes the commands used to add, display, and configure ATM connections on the PXM1:

- **addcon**—Creates a new ATM connection.

- **delcon**—Removes an ATM connection.

- **dspcons**—Lists summary status information for all connections on the card, including feeder connections and local connections on service modules.

- **dspcon**—Lists limited configuration and status information for an ATM connection.

- **dspchans**—Lists summary status information for connections that terminate on PXM1 UNI ports.

- **dspchan**—Lists configuration and status information for an ATM connection that terminates on a PXM1 UNI port.

- **cnfupccbr**—Modifies the CBR connection characteristics of an ATM connection.
- **cnfupcvbr**—Modifies the nrt-VBR connection characteristics of an ATM connection.
- **cnfupcabr**—Modifies the ForeSight ABR connection characteristics of an ATM connection.
- **cnfupcubr**—Modifies the UBR connection characteristics of an ATM connection.
- **cnfchanq**—Modifies the VC queue characteristics.

Add Connection Command

Use the **addcon** command to create a new ATM connection on the MGX PXM1. You can use the **delcon** command to remove the connection.

Here is the **addcon** command syntax:

```
addcon <port number> <connection type> <VPI> <VCI> <service type> <CAC>
   [mastership] [remote connection ID]
```

The parameter options are as follows:

- *port number*—The ATM port that the connection uses.
- *connection type*—1 = VPC, 2 = VCC.
- *VPI*—The VPI of the incoming user cells on this connection. 0 to 255.
- *VCI*—The VCI of the incoming user cells on this connection. 0 to 65,535.
- *service type*—The connection's service type. 1 = CBR, 2 = nrt-VBR, 3 = standard ABR, 4 = UBR, 5 = rt-VBR.
- *CAC*—Enables or disables connection admission control (CAC). 1 = enable, 2 = disable.
- *mastership*—1 = master, 2 = slave. When you add a slave connection, do not enter the mastership value. Eliminating this parameter automatically makes the connection a slave.
- *remote connection ID*—The destination connection ID for master connections, in the form *node.slot.port.VPI.VCI*. For feeder connections, the slot number is 0 for the PXM1.

Display Connections Command

The **dspcons** command lists all the connections that terminate on the PXM1 (including feeder connections to the PXM1 trunk) and all local connections between service modules on the switch. Use the **dspchans** command to learn about the connections that terminate on PXM1 UNI ports.

Example 21-20 shows the **dspcons** output. Notice that connections are listed twice—once in each direction. For example, 1.1.20.20 goes to 7.2.21.21, and vice versa.

Example 21-20 dspcons *Output*

```
hei1pop1.1.7.PXM.a > dspcons

This End         Node Name       Other End        Status

1.1.20.20        hei1pop1        7.2.21.21        FAILED
1.1.20.30        hei1pop1        7.1.21.31        FAILED
1.4.56.*         hei1pop1        7.1.56.*         FAILED  ABIT ALARM
3.1.0.0          hei1pop1        7.1.50.50        OK
3.3.0.0          hei1pop1        7.1.40.45        FAILED
3.10.0.0         hei1pop1        7.1.40.40        OK
3.20.0.0         hei1pop1        3.21.0.0         OK
3.21.0.0         hei1pop1        3.20.0.0         OK
7.1.21.31        hei1pop1        1.1.20.30        FAILED
7.1.40.40        hei1pop1        3.10.0.0         OK
7.1.40.45        hei1pop1        3.3.0.0          FAILED
7.1.50.50        hei1pop1        3.1.0.0          OK
7.1.56.*         hei1pop1        1.4.56.*         FAILED  ABIT ALARM
7.1.100.101      hei1pop1        11.1.0.100       FAILED
7.1.100.102      hei1pop1        11.1.0.101       FAILED
7.1.100.103      hei1pop1        11.1.0.102       FAILED
7.1.120.120      hei1pop1        7.2.0.100        FAILED
7.2.0.100        hei1pop1        7.1.120.120      FAILED
7.2.21.21        hei1pop1        1.1.20.20        FAILED
11.1.0.100       hei1pop1        7.1.100.101      FAILED

Type <CR> to continue, Q<CR> to stop:
```

Information listed in the **dspcons** output includes the following:

- **This End**—The local connection identifier, in the form *slot.port.VPI.VCI*.
- **Node Name**—The destination node name. For feeder nodes, the node name is always the local node.
- **Other End**—The remote connection identifier.
- **Status**—The connection state. OK, FAILED, or FAILED ABIT ALARM.

Display Connection Command

The **dspcon** command is used to list details about any of the connections listed in the **dspcons** output. If you are working with a connection that terminates on a PXM1 UNI port, it is a good idea to use the **dspchan** command, because it shows you additional details pertaining to this type of connection. Example 21-21 shows the **dspcon** output.

Example 21-21 dspcon *Output*

```
hei1pop1.1.7.PXM.a > dspcon 7.2.21.21

  Conn Par Addr        : 7.2.21.21
  Vc Index             : 805306377
  Conn SM Addr         : Ept:     vpi = 21 vci = 21 vpc = 0
  ifNum = 0x2          conNum = 0x7ff4     glcn = 0x800b     lcn = 19
  qosFwd = 1027 qosBwd = 1027 pcrFwd = 50 pcrBwd = 50 mcrFwd = 7 mcrBwd = 7
  Remote Node Name     : hei1pop1
  Remote Conn PAR Addr: 1.1.20.20
  Remote Conn SM  Addr: Ept:     vpi = 20 vci = 20 vpc = 0
  ifNum = 0x10001      conNum = 0x7ff4     glcn = 0x2cd      lcn = 17
  qosFwd = 1027 qosBwd = 1027 pcrFwd = 50 pcrBwd = 50 mcrFwd = 7 mcrBwd = 7
  OE VC Index          : 805306377
  Oper Status          : FAILED
  Conn Failure Reason :
  RRT Failure Reason   : local interface failure
  Admin Status         : UP
  Route                :
```

Many of the fields displayed in the **dspcon** output are for the switch's internal use or for features not yet supported on the switch. The most useful information is the reason for the reroute failure (RRT Failure Reason), which gives you additional information about why a connection has failed. Example 21-21 shows that a "local interface failure" is the reason why the RRT failed.

Display Channels Command

The **dspchans** command lists all the channels (connections) that terminate on PXM1 UNI ports (ports other than those identified as trunks). Use this command to learn summary configuration and status information for PXM1 connections. Example 21-22 shows the **dspchans** output.

Example 21-22 dspchans *Output*

```
hei1pop1.1.7.PXM.a > dspchans

Chan Stat Intf locVpi locVci conTyp srvTyp PCR[0+1] Mst rmtVpi rmtVci State
-------------------------------------------------------------------------
  18 MOD   2      0    100   VCC   ABR      50 Mst   120    120 normal
  19 ADD   2     21     21   VCC   VBR      50 Mst    20     20 alarm
```

Information listed in the **dspchans** output includes the following:

- **Channel number**—Assigned by the switch when you add a connection.
- **Status**—Either ADD if no changes have been made or MOD if the channel configuration has been modified since it was first added.
- **Interface**—The logical port number.
- Local VPI and VCI
- **Connection type**—VCC or VPC.
- **Service type**—CBR, VBR, rt-VBR, ABR, or UBR.
- **PCR (0+1)**—The configured PCR.
- **Mastership**—Mst (master) or Slv (Slave).
- Remote VPI and VCI
- **Connection state**—Normal or alarm.

Display Channel Command

The **dspchan** command lists detailed status and configuration information for a channel. Use the **dspchans** command to learn the channel number for a connection.

Example 21-23 shows the **dspchan** output. There are three pages. The second and third follow.

Example 21-23 dspchan *Output, Page 1*

```
hei1pop1.1.7.PXM.a > dspchan 19

bbChanCnfNum               : 19
bbChanRowStatus            : ADD
bbChanConnType             : VCC
bbChanServiceType          : VBR
bbChanConnDesc             : 0x0000000000000000000000000000000000000000
bbChanSvcFlag              : PVC
bbChanIfNum                : 2
bbChanVpi                  : 21
bbChanVci                  : 21
bbChanUpcEnable            : ENA
bbChanUpcPCR               : 50
bbChanUpcCDVT              : 250000
bbChanUpcSCR               : 7
bbChanUpcMBS               : 1000
bbChanUpcMCR               : 7
bbChanGcra1Action          : Discard All NonConform Cells
bbChanGcra2Action          : No Action
bbChanUpcSCRPolicing       : CLP0+1
bbChanEfciThreshold        : 98304
```

Example 21-23 dspchan *Output, Page 1 (Continued)*

```
bbChanDiscardOption       : CLP Hysteresis
bbChanFrmDiscardThreshold : 0
bbChanClpHiThreshold      : 0

Type <CR> to continue, Q<CR> to stop:
```

Many of the fields listed in the **dspchan** output can be modified using a number of configuration commands discussed later in this section. Example 21-24 shows the second page of the **dspchan** output.

Example 21-24 dspchan *Output, Page 2*

```
bbChanClpLoThreshold      : 0
bbChanCongstUpdateCode    : Dont Update
bbChanMaxCellMemThreshold : 131072
bbChanIngrPercentUtil     : 100
bbChanEgrPercentUtil      : 100
bbChanEgrSrvRate          : 50
bbChanOvrSubOvrRide       : Enable
bbChanLocalVpi            : 21
bbChanLocalVci            : 21
bbChanLocalNsapAddr       : 0x68656931706F7031000000000000000000000200
bbChanRemoteVpi           : 20
bbChanRemoteVci           : 20
bbChanRemoteNsapAddr      : 0x68656931706F7031000000000000000001000100
bbChanMaster              : Mst
bbChanRtePriority         : 1
bbChanMaxCost             : 255
bbChanRestrictTrkType     : No Restriction
bbChanTestType            : 3
bbChanTestState           : Not In Progress
bbChanTestResult          : 0
bbChanTestTypeCPESide     : 2
bbChanTestStateCPESide    : Not In Progress

Type <CR> to continue, Q<CR> to stop:
```

Useful information includes the following:

- **Channel local NSAP**—The Network Service Access Point (NSAP) address uniquely identifies this interface (port) in the network. The 20-byte hexadecimal address comprises the following fields:

  — The most significant 8 bytes (16 digits) spell out the node name in ASCII. The connection in Example 21-24 is on node hei1pop1.

  — The card slot number is the fourth byte from the right. The connection in Example 21-24 is on card 0 (PXM1).

— The port number is the second byte from the right. The connection in Example 21-24 is on port 2.

- **Channel remote NSAP**—The remote NSAP address is in the same format as the local NSAP address. The slave end of a local connection does not have a remote NSAP and is reported as NULL NSAP.

Example 21-25 shows the third page of the **dspchan** output.

Example 21-25 dspchan *Output, Page 3*

```
bbConnVpcFlag              : VCC
bbConnServiceType          : VBR
bbConnPCR                  : 50
bbConnSCR                  : 7
bbConnPercentUtil          : 100
bbRemoteConnPCR            : 50
bbRemoteConnSCR            : 7
bbRemoteConnPercentUtil    : 100
```

Configure UPC CBR Command

The **cnfupccbr** command modifies the CBR policing characteristics on a connection. The **dspcon** command shows all policing parameters (CBR and others). The **cnfupccbr** command filters out values that do not apply.

Here is the **cnfupccbr** command syntax:

```
cnfupccbr <connection> <policing type> <PCR(0+1)> <CDVT(0+1)>
  <ingress utilization> <egress service rate> <egress utilization>
```

The parameter options are as follows:

- *connection*—The connection to be modified, in the form *port.VPI.VCI*.

- *policing type*—4 = single leaky bucket and discard all noncompliant cells, 5 = no policing.

- *PCR(0+1)*—Can be configured from 10 to the port speed in cells per second.

- *CDVT(0+1)*—1 to 5,000,000 microseconds.

- *ingress utilization*—A channel's expected utilization. Used to determine the port's ingress bandwidth capacity. The expected bandwidth = PCR × utilization. 1 to 100 percent.

- *egress service rate*—Determines the rate at which this connection should be serviced on egress from the port queue. 50 to the port speed.

- *egress utilization*—A connection's expected utilization. Used to determine the port's egress bandwidth capacity. The expected bandwidth = egress service rate × utilization. 1 to 100 percent.

For example, type **cnfupccbr 1.10.100 4 1000 200000 50 1000 50** can enable policing, set the PCR to 1000 cps, set the CDVT to 200,000 microseconds, set the ingress utilization to 50 percent, set the egress service rate to 1000 cps, and set the egress utilization to 50 percent.

Configure UPC VBR Command

The **cnfupcvbr** command modifies the VBR policing characteristics on an nrt-VBR connection (use the **cnfupcrtvbr** command for rt-VBR connections). The **dspcon** command shows all policing parameters (VBR and others). The **cnfupcvbr** command filters out values that do not apply.

Here is the **cnfupcvbr** command syntax:

```
cnfupcvbr <connection> <policing type> <PCR(0+1)> <CDVT(0+1)>
  <SCR> <MBS> <ingress utilization> <egress service rate> <egress utilization>
```

The parameter options are as follows (parameters that were described previously for the **cnfupccbr** command are not repeated):

- *policing type*—Determines which cells are policed on which bucket and the resulting action of the policing. Table 21-8 describes the policing types.

Table 21-8   *Policing Types*

Type	Police in First Bucket	Noncompliance Action	Police in Second Bucket	Noncompliance Action
1	All	Discard	CLP 0 and 1	Discard
2	All	Discard	CLP 0 only	Discard
3	All	Discard	CLP 0 only	Tag with CLP
4	All	Discard	None	—
5	None	—	None	—

- *SCR*—Sustainable cell rate. Can be configured from 50 to the port rate in cells per second.
- *MBS*—Maximum burst size. 1 to 5,000,000 cells.

Configure UPC ABR Command

The **cnfupcabr** command modifies the ABR policing characteristics on a connection. The **cnfupcabr** command has the same parameter options as the **cnfupcvbr** command.

Configure UPC UBR Command

The **cnfupcubr** command modifies the UBR policing characteristics on a connection. The **dspcon** command shows all policing parameters (UBR and others). The **cnfupcubr** command filters out values that do not apply.

Here is the **cnfupcubr** command syntax:

```
cnfupcubr <connection> <policing type> <PCR(0+1)> <CDVT(0+1)>
    <ingress utilization>
```

All the parameters in the **cnfupcubr** command are described in the previous **cnfupccbr** and **cnfupcvbr** command sections.

For the **cnfupcubr** command, you can select options 3, 4, or 5 for the *policing type* parameter.

Configure Channel Queue Command

The **cnfchanq** command modifies the ingress VC queue characteristics, including the congestion and discard thresholds.

Here is the **cnfchanq** command syntax:

```
cnfchanq <channel> <discard option> <CLP high> <CLP low> <EFCI threshold>
    <congestion update> <max cell count>
```

The parameter options are as follows:

- *connection*—The channel number of the connection to be modified. Use the **dspchans** command to learn the connection's channel number.

- *discard option*—Defines whether the connection will discard based on the CLP high and low thresholds or use EPD. 1 = CLP hysteresis, 2 = EPD.

- *CLP high*—The threshold when CLP = 1 cells are no longer accepted into the VC queue and are discarded. 1 to 491,520 cells.

- *CLP low*—The threshold, after reaching CLP high, when CLP = 1 cells are again allowed into the VC queue and are no longer discarded. 1 to 491,520 cells.

- *EFCI threshold*—The threshold on the VC queue where congestion tagging begins by setting the EFCI bit to 1. 1 to 491,520 cells.

- *congestion update*—The resulting action for queue congestion notification. 1 = do not update the cell, 2 = set the CI bit in RM cells when congested, 3 = set the EFCI bit when congested, 4 = clear the EFCI bit when not congested.

- *Max cell count*—Specifies the queue depth measured in cells.

Commands for Verifying ATM Connections

This section describes the commands used to verify ATM connections on AUSM and PXM1 ports:

- **dspchancnt**—Lists a connection's statistics counters.
- **clrchancnts**—Clears statistics counters for all connections on the card.
- **clrchancnt**—Clears a connection's statistics counters.
- **tstcon**—Tests continuity on a connection through the network.
- **tstdelay**—Tests a connection's continuity and the round-trip delay time.
- **tstconseg**—Tests continuity on a connection toward the CPE.

Display Channel Count Command

The **dspchancnt** command provides detailed historical statistics for an ATM connection. Use this command to view the traffic being processed on a specific connection. Because the statistics are historical, you might want to clear them using the **clrchancnt** or **clrchancnts** command before beginning your testing or troubleshooting.

Example 21-26 shows the first of two pages for the **dspchancnt** output from an AUSM connection. The second page follows.

Example 21-26 dspchancnt *Output, Page 1*

```
hei1pop1.1.1.AUSMB8.a > dspchancnt 1.1.20.30

   ChanNum:                              19
   ChannelState:                         Alarm
   ChannelEgressRcvState:                Normal
   ChannelEgressXmitState:               Normal
   ChannelIngressRcvState:               Alarm
   ChannelIngressXmtState:               Sending OAM AIS
   ChanInServiceSeconds:                 5485
   ChanIngressPeakQDepth(cells):         1508
   ChanIngressCurrQDepth(cells):         64
   ChanIngressReceiveCells:              289413
   ChanIngressClpSetCells:               12
   ChanIngressEfciSetRcvCells:           2
   ChanIngressEfciSetXmtCells:           11
   ChanIngressUpcClpSetCells:            71
   ChanIngressQfullDiscardCells:         0
   ChanIngressClpSetDiscardCells:        1
   ChanIngressTransmitCells:             289408
   ChanShelfAlarmDiscardCells:           0
   ChanEarlyPacketDiscardCells:          0
```

continues

Example 21-26 dspchancnt *Output, Page 1 (Continued)*

```
    ChanPartialPacketDiscardCells:                0
    ChanIngressTransmitAAL5Frames:                687

Type <CR> to continue, Q<CR> to stop:
```

The **dspchancnt** output provides the following information:

- **Channel state**—The channel state. Ok or Alarm.

- **Egress receive state**—The current connection state based on information received from the attached end-user equipment. The alarm indication can be the result of a physical line failure or OAM AIS received from the attached end-user device.

- **Egress transmit state**—The current connection state being sent to the attached end-user equipment. A failure indication is sent out as OAM AIS cells.

- **Ingress receive state**—The current connection state received from the ATM backbone network, indicating an outage on the network routing connection segment or the remote MGX concentrator, card, or port.

- **Ingress transmit state**—The current connection state being sent in the form of OAM AIS cells to the ATM backbone network to indicate to the network and remote MGX device that there is an outage on the local line or port.

- **In service seconds**—The number of seconds that the connection has been in service since the last time the counters were cleared.

- **Ingress peak queue depth**—The peak number of cells that have been in the ingress VC queue at any one time.

- **Ingress receive cells**—The total number of cells received by the connection from the attached end-user equipment.

- **Ingress CLP set cells**—The total number of cells received from the attached end-user equipment with the CLP bit set to 1. This number does not imply that the MGX AUSM set the CLP bit.

- **Ingress EFCI set receive cells**—The total number of cells received from the attached end-user equipment with the EFCI bit set to 1. This number does not imply that the MGX AUSM set the EFCI bit.

- **Ingress EFCI set transmit cells**—The total number of cells transmitted to the cell bus from the attached end-user equipment with the EFCI bit set to 1. This number does not imply that the MGX AUSM set the EFCI bit.

- **Ingress UPC CLP set cells**—The number of cells that the AUSM has set the CLP bit, based on the channel's configured policing characteristics.

- **Ingress queue full discard cells**—The number of cells dropped on ingress because the VC queue was full.

- **Ingress CLP set discard cells**—The number of cells with the CLP bit set that were discarded on ingress because the VC queue has exceeded the CLP high threshold.

- **Ingress transmit cells**—The number of cells sent to the ATM backbone network from this connection. Provided that no cells were dropped on ingress, this should be the same as the number of ingress receive cells.

- **Shelf alarm discard cells**—The number of cells dropped on ingress because the MGX device was in alarm. A shelf alarm is usually the result of an outage on the trunk between the MGX device and the ATM backbone network.

- **Early packet discard cells**—The number of ingress cells discarded because the early packet discard (EPD) threshold on the VC queue was exceeded.

- **Partial packet discard cells**—The number of ingress cells discarded because of the partial packet discard (PPD) feature on the VC queue.

- **Ingress transmit AALS frames**—The number of AALS frames sent to the cell bus.

Example 21-27 shows the second page of the **dspchancnt** output for an AUSM connection.

Example 21-27 dspchancnt *Output, Page 2*

```
ChanIngressReceiveCellRate(cells/sec):        53
  ChanIngressReceiveUtilization(percentage):  34
  ChanIngressTransmitCellRate(cells/sec):     53
  ChanIngressTransmitUtilization(percentage): 34
  ChanEgressReceiveCellRate(cells/sec):       41
  ChanEgressReceiveUtilization(percentage):   29
  EgressPortQFullDiscardCells:                0
  EgressPortQClpThreshDiscardCells:           2
  ChanTransmitFifoFullCount (per card):       0
```

The **dspchancnt** output provides the following information:

- **Ingress receive cell rate**—The average rate of cells received in cells per second.

- **Ingress receive utilization**—The connection's average utilization as a percentage of the PCR (CBR, VBR, and UBR connections) or MCR (ABR connections). This counter is for traffic received from the CPE.

- **Ingress transmit cell rate**—The average rate of cells transmitted to the cell bus in cells per second.

- **Ingress transmit utilization**—The connection's average utilization as a percentage of the PCR or MCR. This counter is for traffic sent to the cell bus.

- **Egress receive cell rate**—The average rate of cells received from the cell bus in cells per second.

- **Egress receive utilization**—The connection's average utilization as a percentage of the PIR or MIR. This counter is for traffic received from the cell bus.

- **Egress port queue full discard cells**—The number of cells on this connection discarded because the egress QBin was full.

- **Egress port queue CLP threshold discard cells**—The number of CLP = 1 cells on this connection discarded because the egress QBin exceeded its configured CLP threshold.

- **Transmit FIFO full count**—The number of times the pooled memory on the AUSM was fully allocated.

Example 21-28 shows the **dspchancnt** output for a PXM1 connection.

Example 21-28 dspchancnt *Output*

```
hei1pop1.1.7.PXM.a > dspchancnt 19

Channel Number              :           19
Channel State               :        alarm
Channel Ingress State       :       rcvAIS
Channel Egress State        :        other
CLP=0  Rcvd. Cells          :       100904
CLP=1  Rcvd. Cells          :            0
GCRA1  Non Conforming Cells :            0
GCRA2  Non Conforming Cells :            0
EOF    Cells Rcvd.,  to CBus :           0
CLP=0  Discard Cells to CBus :           0
CLP=1  Discard Cells to CBus :           0
CLP=0+1 Xmtd. Cells  to CBus :      100905
CLP=0  Xmtd. Cells   to Port :      100905
CLP=1  Xmtd. Cells   to Port :           0
CLP=0  Discard Cells to Port :           0
CLP=1  Discard Cells to Port :           0
```

The **dspchancnt** output provides the following information:

- **Channel state**—The connection state. Either normal or in alarm.

- **Channel ingress state**—The connection state on the network side.

- **Channel egress state**—The connection state on the CPE side.

- **CLP 0 received cells**—The number of cells with CLP 0 received from the CPE.

- **CLP 1 received cells**—The number of cells with CLP 1 received from the CPE.

- **Generic Cell Rate Algorithm 1 (GCRA1) nonconforming cells**—The number of cells that were noncompliant on the first leaky bucket.

- **GCRA2 nonconforming cells**—The number of cells that were noncompliant on the second leaky bucket.

- **End of frame (EOF) cells received and sent to cell bus**—The number of EOF AAL5 cells.

- **CLP 0 discard cells to cell bus**—The number of CLP 0 cells discarded before being sent to the cell bus.

- **CLP 1 discard cells to cell bus**—The number of CLP 1 cells discarded before being sent to the cell bus.

- **CLP 0+1 transmitted cells to cell bus**—The total number of cells sent to the cell bus.

- **CLP 0 transmitted cells to cell bus**—The number of CLP 0 cells sent to the cell bus.

- **CLP 1 transmitted cells to cell bus**—The number of CLP 1 cells sent to the cell bus.

- **CLP 0 discarded cells to port**—The number of CLP 0 cells discarded before being sent to the CPE.

- **CLP 1 discarded cells to port**—The number of CLP 1 cells discarded before being sent to the CPE.

Test Connection Command

The **tstcon** command tests continuity on MGX network connections. If connection segments are failed or misconfigured, the **tstcon** command fails. Note that the **tstcon** command does *not* test quality of service or connectivity beyond the MGX network.

Here is the **tstcon** command syntax:

```
tstcon <connection number>
```

connection number is in the form *port.VPI.VCI*. For VPC connections, specify the VPI and use VCI 0.

The MGX CLI returns a pass or fail message after a few seconds.

The **tstcon** command has some limitations:

- It works only for local connections or connections in a tiered network comprising a Cisco backbone network.

- It should be issued from both ends to completely verify connectivity.

- A passing result of the test does not guarantee the connection's end-to-end performance.

Test Delay Command

The **tstdelay** command is similar to the **tstcon** command in that it also checks connection continuity. The **tstdelay** command also measures the round-trip delay through the network, and the results are output on the CLI. The most recent delay measurement is also reported in the **dspcon** output.

Here is the **tstdelay** command syntax:

```
tstdelay <connection number>
```

connection number is in the form *port.VPI.VCI*. For VPC connections, specify the VPI and use VCI 0.

NOTE   The limitations on the **tstcon** command also apply to the **tstdelay** command.

Test Connection Segment Command

The **tstconseg** command tests continuity between the MGX ATM port and the CPE or other attached equipment. The **tstconseg** command initiates an OAM loopback request to the attached device and reports whether it was successful. You should make sure that the attached device can respond to the OAM cells before attempting this test.

Here is the **tstconseg** command syntax:

```
tstconseg <connection number | channel number>
```

connection number is in the form *port.VPI.VCI*. On the PXM1, you must use the *channel number;* on the AUSM, you can use either the *connection number* or the *channel number.*

How to Create ATM Connections on the AUSM and PXM1

This section describes the steps you must follow to create ATM connections on AUSM and PXM1 cards.

AUSM Procedure

Follow these steps to create connections on the AUSM:

Step 1   Type **dspports** to confirm that the ATM port that you want to terminate your connection on is active. This outputs the summary status of all the ports on the card.

Step 2   If you are adding a local connection, type **addcon** *<port number> <VPI> <VCI> <connection type> <service type>* [*controller type*] to create a slave connection. If you are adding a feeder connection, type **addcon** *<port number> <VPI> <VCI> <connection type> <service type>* [*controller type*] [*mastership*] [*remote connection ID*], specifying the

PXM1 trunk in the *remote connection ID*. Type **dspcons** to verify that your connection was added. This outputs connection summary information.

Step 3 Type **dspcon** <*connection number*> to verify the connection configuration. If you have added a standard ABR connection, type **dspconstdabr** <*connection number*> to verify the ABR configuration. Otherwise, go to Step 8. If you need to change the standard ABR characteristics, type **cnfconabrparams** <*connection number | channel number*> <*ABR type*> <*RIF*> <*RDF*> <*NRM*> <*TRM*> <*TBE*> <*FRTT*> <*ADTF*> <*CDF*>.

Step 4 If you need to change the initial burst size (IBS) or frame-based generic cell rate algorithm (FGCRA) on the connection, or if you need to enable the ForeSight feature on a connection, use the **cnfchanfst** command. This modifies the ForeSight connection characteristics.

Step 5 If you need to change the VC queue characteristics, use the **cnfchanq** command. This modifies the VC queue characteristics.

Step 6 If you need to change the policing characteristics, use the **cnfupccbr**, **cnfupcvbr**, **cnfupcrtvbr**, **cnfupcabr**, or **cnfupcubr** command, depending on the connection service type.

Step 7 If you are adding a local connection, type **cc** <*slot number*>. This changes to the remote card slot and adds the master connection. Follow Step 1. Then follow Step 3, specifying the connection ID of the slave connection on the other AUSM. Continue with Steps 4 through 10, and then go to Step 16.

Step 8 If you are adding a feeder connection, log into the remote MGX switch and the AUSM card, and then follow Step 1 and Steps 3 through 10. This adds the ATM connection to the other end of the end-to-end connection.

Step 9 If you have standalone MGX switches, you need to add, configure, and verify the routing connection in the ATM network. Continue with Step 12.

Step 10 If you have a BPX backbone network, log into the BPX switch attached to one of your MGX switches. Type **addcon** <*local channel*> <*remote node*> <*remote channel*> <*connection class | connection type*> [*connection parameters*] [*route avoid*] to add an ATM routing connection through the BPX network. Be sure to match the VPI and VCI values in the BPX network with the values you used when you added the MGX connection segments. Use the **dspcons** and **dspcon** commands to verify the connection status. Continue with Step 12.

Step 11 If you have an MGX 8850-PXM45 backbone network, log into the AXSM on the local switch and type **addcon** <*interface number*> <*vpi*> <*vci*> <*service type*> **2** [*parameters ...*], where **2** indicates the slave endpoint.

This adds a routing connection through the MGX 8850-PXM45 network. Be sure to write down the endpoint ID (NSAP address, VPI, and VCI). Log into the AXSM on the remote switch and type **addcon** <*interface number*> <*vpi*> <*vci*> <*service type*> **1** <**-slave** *slave endpoint ID*> [*parameters* ...], where **1** indicates the master endpoint, and the *slave endpoint ID* is as previously noted. Use the **dspcons** and **dspcon** commands to verify the connection status.

Step 12 Log back into the AUSM on one of your MGX switches. Use the **tstcon** or **tstdelay** command to verify the connection's end-to-end continuity.

Step 13 Type **tstconseg** <*connection number*>. This tests continuity between the MGX switch and the CPE.

Step 14 Type **dspchancnt** <*channel number*> to verify that there is traffic on the connection. This outputs the channel counters.

Step 15 Complete Steps 12, 13, and 14 on the other end of the connection. This tests the remote end of the connection.

Step 16 Log out of the MGX CLI.

You have completed the steps necessary for creating ATM connections on the AUSM.

PXM1 Procedure

Follow these steps to create connections on the PXM1:

Step 1 Type **dspports** to confirm that the ATM port that you want to terminate your connection on is active. This outputs the summary status of all ports on the card.

Step 2 If you are adding a local connection, type **addcon** <*port number*> <*connection type*> <*VPI*> <*VCI*> <*service type*> <*CAC*> to create a slave connection.

Step 3 If you are adding a feeder connection, type **addcon** <*port number*> <*connection type*> <*VPI*> <*VCI*> <*service type*> <*CAC*> [*mastership*] [*remote connection ID*], specifying the PXM1 trunk in the *remote connection ID*. This adds a master connection.

Step 4 Type **dspchans** to verify that your connection has been added. This outputs connection summary information.

Step 5 Type **dspchan** <*channel number*> to verify the connection configuration.

Step 6 If you need to change the VC queue characteristics, use the **cnfchanq** command.

Step 7   If you need to change the policing characteristics, use the **cnfupccbr**, **cnfupcvbr**, **cnfupcabr**, or **cnfupcubr** command, depending on the connection service type. This modifies the connection policing characteristics.

Step 8   If you are adding a local connection, type **cc** *<slot number>*. This changes to the remote card slot and adds the master connection. Follow Step 1. Then follow Step 3, specifying the connection ID of the slave connection on the other PXM1. Continue with Steps 4 through 7 and then go to Step 13.

Step 9   If you are adding a feeder connection, log into the remote MGX switch and PXM1 card, and complete Step 1 and Steps 3 through 7. This adds the ATM connection to the other end of the end-to-end connection.

Step 10 If you have standalone MGX switches, you need to add, configure, and verify the routing connection in the ATM network. Continue with Step 14.

Step 11 If you have a BPX backbone network, log into the BPX switch attached to one of your MGX switches. Type **addcon** *<local channel> <remote node> <remote channel> <connection class | connection type>* [*connection parameters*] [*route avoid*] to add an ATM routing connection through the BPX network. Be sure to match the VPI and VCI values in the BPX network with the values you used when you added the MGX connection segments. Use the **dspcons** and **dspcon** commands to verify the connection status. Continue with Step 13.

Step 12 If you have an MGX 8850-PXM45 backbone network, log into the AXSM on the local switch and type **addcon** *<interface number> <vpi> <vci> <service type>* **2** [*parameters ...*], where **2** indicates the slave endpoint. This adds a routing connection through the MGX 8850-PXM45 network. Be sure to write down the endpoint ID (NSAP address, VPI, and VCI). Log into the AXSM on the remote switch, and type **addcon** *<interface number> <vpi> <vci> <service type>* **1** **<-slave** *slave endpoint ID>* [*parameters ...*], where **1** indicates the master endpoint, and the *slave endpoint ID* is as previously noted. Use the **dspcons** and **dspcon** commands to verify the connection status.

Step 13 Log back into the PXM1 on one of your MGX switches. Use the **tstcon** or **tstdelay** command to verify the continuity on the connection.

Step 14 Type **tstconseg** *<channel number>*. This tests continuity between the MGX switch and the CPE.

Step 15 Type **dspchancnt** *<channel number>* to verify that there is traffic on the connection. This outputs the channel counters.

Step 16 Complete Steps 13 through 15 on the other end of the connection. This tests the remote end of the connection.

Step 17 Log out of the MGX CLI.

You have completed the steps necessary for creating ATM connections on the PXM1.

Summary

This chapter provided an overview of ATM ports and Inverse Multiplexing over ATM (IMA). It showed you how IMA distributes an ATM traffic stream across multiple narrowband T1 or E1 lines. AUSM port queues were discussed, along with how cells move through the AUSM card in both the ingress and egress directions.

Commands for adding, configuring, displaying, monitoring, and verifying ATM ports and connections on the AUSM and PXM1 were presented. You learned how to configure an ATM port on the AUSM and PXM1.

ATM connections, ATM CoS, and ATM policing were discussed in detail. You learned how the ForeSight feature and ABR are used on ATM connections and how VC queues buffer and shape ingress traffic.

Review Questions

1 For which of the following situations would you use an IMA port on an AUSM?

   A. A Frame Relay router with an unchannelized E1 interface

   B. A router with four T1 ATM interfaces to four other ATM routers

   C. A virtual trunk between two BPX switches with E3 line interfaces

   D. A router with four T1 lines used to carry 6 Mbps of traffic between it and another router

2 Which of the graphics shown in Figure 21-9 best depicts an inverse multiplexing over ATM service?

Figure 21-9 *Which Shows Inverse Multiplexing Over ATM?*

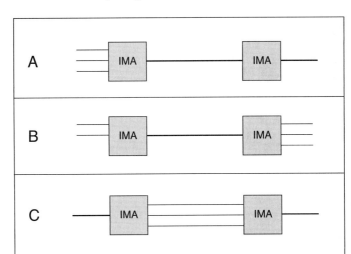

3 How many QBins are on an ATM port on the AUSM?

4 Your AUSM port 1 VBR QBin is set as follows:

Maximum queue depth 500 cells
CLP high 400 cells
CLP low 250 cells
EFCI threshold 280 cells

Which two of the following statements are true?

A. When 250 cells are in the QBin, all CLP tagged cells are discarded.

B. When 280 cells are in the QBin, all EFCI tagged cells are discarded.

C. When 280 cells are in the QBin, new cells are marked with congestion (EFCI bit set to 1).

D. When 400 cells are in the QBin, all arriving CLP tagged cells are not queued and are discarded.

5 An end user is complaining that there is congestion on his nrt-VBR ATM services. Although he is not experiencing poor performance, he reports that many of his cells are being marked with the EFCI bit. You look at his port QBin configuration and note that the VBR QBin is set for the following:

Queue depth 1000 cells
CLP high 500 cells
CLP low 100 cells
EFCI threshold 50 cells

Which of the following changes might resolve this problem?

A. Change the CLP high to 750 cells.

B. Decrease the queue depth to 600 cells.

C. Increase the queue depth to 1500 cells.

D. Increase the EFCI threshold to 750 cells.

6 At which of the following locations could an egress cell on the AUSM get dropped?

A. The UPC

B. The QBin

C. The VC queue

7 You are troubleshooting an ATM port that is reporting a large number of cells being transmitted with the CLP bit tagged. Assuming that all of the cells are coming from the remote CPE with the CLP bit set to 0, where are the cells being tagged?

A. On the ingress VC queue

B. By the ingress UPC algorithm

C. On the egress QBin

8 An end user is complaining that there is congestion in the network. Cells sent from the New York office to the Paris office are leaving the MGX network with the EFCI bit set to 1; traffic in the other direction is not reporting congestion. Where should you look for congestion?

A. On the QBin in Paris

B. On the VC queue in Paris

C. On the QBin in New York

D. On the VC queue in New York

9 What is the maximum differential delay on an IMA group?

A. The maximum delay between ATM cells on any one line

B. The maximum number of links that can be active at any one time

C. The amount of time before a trap is sent to the CWM if the IMA group fails

D. The maximum amount of time permitted between consecutive cells carried on adjacent lines

10 You need to enable the ILMI signaling protocol on a port. Which command (without any required or optional parameters) must you use to make this change?

11 What functions are performed when you use the **addport** command?

A. The IMA group is created.

B. The ILMI protocol is enabled.

C. The VC queues are configured.

D. The ATM cell header type is defined.

E. A logical port number is assigned to a line.

12 Which of the following commands must you use if you want to learn the number of ATM and IMA ports on an AUSM?

A. **dspport**

B. **dspports**

C. **dspportcnt**

D. **dspimagrps**

13 What command must you type (including all required parameters) to find out the CLP high threshold of the CBR QBin on port 2?

14 Based on the port information shown in Example 21-29, which two of the following statements are true?

Example 21-29 dspports *Output*

```
NZ_8850.1.22.AUSM8.a > dspports

  List of ATM ports:
  ==================

  Port PortType Line# Portenable  Speed  PortState
  ---- -------- ----- ----------  -----  ---------
  22.2  UNI       5   UP           3622  Line alarm
  22.4  NNI       6   UP           3622  Active

  List of IMA groups:
  ==================

  ImaGrp PortType Conf  Avail  Lines       Lines     Tol Diff   Port State
                  rate  rate   configured  present   Delay(ms)
  ------ -------- ----- -----  ----------  --------  ---------  ----------
  22.1    UNI     14364 10773  1.2.4.3     1.2.3       275      B/w changed
  22.3    NNI     7182  0      7.8                              Sig. failure
```

A. Line 5 is in alarm.

B. IMA port 3 is failed.

C. Port 4 is using line 4.

D. All lines on IMA group 1 are active.

15 You need to create a new logical port (number 4) on line 2 of your PXM1 card. Assuming that the line is configured for UNI and you want to use all the line bandwidth and the full addressing range, what command (including all required parameters) must you type to accomplish this task?

16 What command (with all required parameters) must you use to learn how many ILMI messages have been sent by port 2 on an AUSM?

17 The **dspportcnt** output is shown in Example 21-30. Based on this information, which two of the following statements are true?

Example 21-30 dspportcnt *Output*

```
NZ_8850.1.22.AUSM8.a > dspportcnt 4

  PortNum:                                4
  PortState:                              Okay
  IngressRcvCells:                        23486
  IngressRcvCellRate (cells/sec):         1022
  IngressRcvUtilization (percentage):     23
  IngressXmtCells:                        23429
  IngressGFCErrorCells:                   0
  IngressVpiVciErrCells:                  55
  IngressUnknownVpiVci:                   0x010066
  IngressRcvClpSetCells:                  23
  EgressRcvCells:                         21065
  EgressRcvCellRate (cells/sec):          986
  EgressRcvUtilization (percentage):      19
  EgressXmtCells:                         21064
  EgressXmtCellRate (cells/sec):          986
  EgressXmtUtilization (percentage):      19
  EgressPortAlarmDiscardCells:            0
  EgressXmtClpSetCells:                   2
  EgressXmtEfciSetCells:                  0
  PortXmtAisCells:                        0
  PortXmtSgmtLpbkCells:                   0
  PortRcvAisCells:                        0
  PortRcvFerfCells:                       0
  PortRcvSgmtLpbkCells:                   0
  PortRcvCrcErrOAMCells:                  0
  TotalIngressQFullDiscardCells:          0
  TotalIngressClpSetDiscardCells:         0
  TransmitFIFOFullCount (per card):       0
  ReceivedHECErrorCells:                  1
  HECErroredSeconds:                      1
  SeverelyHECErroredSeconds:              0
```

A. These counters apply to a PXM1 port.

B. These counters apply to port number 4.

C. The port received a cell with a VCI value of 10066.

D. The ingress VC queues associated with this port are congested.

E. Cells are arriving from the CPE with unknown VPI and VCI values.

18 Which command must you use to monitor the traffic on an IMA port on an AUSM?

A. **dspport**

B. **dspimagrp**

C. **dspportcnt**

D. **dspimagrpcnt**

19 How many connection segments are required for a local ATM connection between two adjacent AUSM cards?

20 Mark the following statements as true or false.

A. _____ All ATM service types are supported on the AUSM.

B. _____ ForeSight and Standard ABR are supported on the PXM1.

C. _____ Connections that share a port all must be of the same service type.

D. _____ CBR connections can terminate on AUSM and PXM1 ATM ports.

E. _____ You cannot add a connection between two ports on the same AUSM card.

21 Which CoS type does not offer any service guarantee?

A. ABR

B. UBR

C. rt-VBR

D. nrt-VBR

22 What is the difference between real-time and nonreal-time VBR?

A. rt-VBR has a service guarantee; nrt-VBR does not.

B. rt-VBR has end-to-end timing standards; nrt-VBR does not.

C. rt-VBR is not supported on the AUSM; nrt-VBR is supported.

D. rt-VBR is for uncompressed voice and video; nrt-VBR is for compressed voice and video.

23 What is policing?

A. A queue service algorithm

B. A traffic-shaping algorithm that determines how cells leave an ATM network

C. A process that determines whether cells are accepted into the network or tagged with the CLP bit

D. A method to determine whether a new connection can be added to the network based on the bandwidth requirements and maximum burst size

24 Figure 21-10 shows how a burst of cells is policed using the dual leaky bucket model. Identify the two rates and the two events shown in the figure.

Figure 21-10 *Dual Leaky Bucket Model*

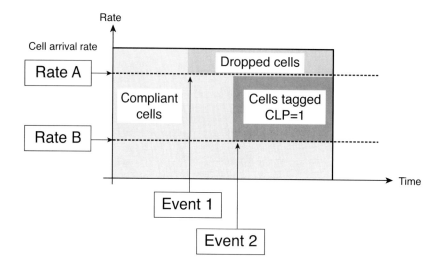

Rate A: _____

Rate B: _____

Event 1: _____

Event 2: _____

A. SCR

B. PCR

C. MBS

D. CDVT

E. Port congestion

F. First bucket full

G. Second bucket full

H. Network congestion

25 Which of the following statements is false?

A. UBR connections are policed using a single leaky bucket.

B. Cells are always discarded if the second leaky bucket is full.

C. The configuration of one leaky bucket is independent of the other.

D. A cell with the CLP bit set to 1 is discarded in the network if there is sufficient congestion.

26 Under what conditions can the ForeSight connection rate drop below the configured MCR?

A. If cells have the CLP bit set to 1

B. When data is being dropped on egress

C. When there is severe congestion in the network

D. The connection rate cannot drop below the configured MCR under any conditions

E. When there is an alarm on the line between the MGX switch and the ATM backbone network

27 A ForeSight ABR connection is configured with an MCR of 170 cps, an ICR of 170 cps, and a PCR of 1400 cps on an AUSM, with the ForeSight rate adjustment parameters set at their default values. If the VC queue service rate is currently 500 cps and the network reports severe congestion, what will the new queue service rate be in cps?

28 A ForeSight ABR connection is configured with an MCR of 170 cps, an ICR of 170 cps, and a PCR of 1400 cps on an AUSM, with the ForeSight rate adjustment parameters set at their default values. If the VC queue service rate is currently 1390 cps and the network reports no congestion, what will the new queue service rate be in cps?

A. 1390 cps

B. 1400 cps

C. 1407 cps

D. 1395 cps

29 Your VC queue is set as follows:

Maximum queue depth 500 cells
CLP high 400 cells
CLP low 250 cells
EFCI threshold 280 cells

Which two of the following statements are true?

A. When 250 cells are in the queue, all CLP tagged cells are discarded.

B. When 280 cells are in the queue, all EFCI tagged cells are discarded.

C. When 280 cells are in the queue, new cells are marked with congestion (EFCI bit set to 1).

D. When 400 cells are in the queue, all arriving CLP tagged cells are not queued and are discarded.

30 You have EPD enabled on a VC queue. The EPD0 threshold is 500 cells, the EPD1 threshold is 400 cells, and the CLP high threshold is 550 cells. If the queue is filled up to 450 cells, what will happen?

A. A new CLP 0 cell will be discarded.

B. A new CLP 1 cell will be discarded.

C. A new CLP 0 frame will be discarded.

D. A new CLP 1 frame will be discarded.

31 You want to know the rate decrease factor (RDF) for a standard ABR connection. Which commands can you use to learn this information?

A. **dspfst**

B. **dspcon**

C. **dspcons**

D. **dspabrcon**

E. **dspconstdabr**

32 Which of the following statements are true of the **dspcon** command?

A. Connection routing details are listed.

B. Standard ABR parameters are not listed.

C. The most recent **tstdelay** results are listed.

D. Only CBR policing parameters are listed for CBR connections.

E. A master connection lists both a local and remote NSAP address.

F. A slave connection lists both a local and remote NSAP address.

33 You are configuring an nrt-VBR connection using the **cnfupcvbr** command. You set the policing type to 3. What does this do? (Choose all that apply.)

A. Disables all policing

B. Disables the second leaky bucket

C. Enables policing using both leaky buckets

D. Checks all cells on the second leaky bucket

E. Tags noncompliant cells on the second leaky bucket

F. Checks only CLP 0 cells on the second leaky bucket

G. Discards noncompliant cells on the second leaky bucket

34 You want to know how many connections terminate on the UNI ports on your PXM1. Which command should you use to quickly learn this information?

35 You want to test the continuity between the MGX ATM port and the CPE. Which command must you use to accomplish this task?

   A. **tstcon**

   B. **tstdelay**

   C. **tstconseg**

   D. **dspchancnt**

   E. **addchanloop**

36 Example 21-31 shows the **dspchancnt** output for a PXM1 connection. Based on this information, which of the following statements are true?

Example 21-31 **dspchancnt** *Output*

```
hei1pop1.1.7.PXM.a > dspchancnt 20

Channel Number              :         20
Channel State               :      alarm
Channel Ingress State       :     normal
Channel Egress State        :     rcvAIS
CLP=0  Rcvd. Cells          :       5412
CLP=1  Rcvd. Cells          :          0
GCRA1  Non Conforming Cells :          0
GCRA2  Non Conforming Cells :        242
EOF    Cells Rcvd.,  to CBus :         0
CLP=0  Discard Cells to CBus :         0
CLP=1  Discard Cells to CBus :        19
CLP=0+1 Xmtd. Cells  to CBus :      5398
CLP=0  Xmtd. Cells   to Port :     10654
CLP=1  Xmtd. Cells   to Port :         4
CLP=0  Discard Cells to Port :         0
CLP=1  Discard Cells to Port :         0
```

   A. Channel 20 is passing traffic.

   B. Channel 20 is not passing traffic.

   C. The channel does not have policing enabled.

   D. Cells are being marked with CLP as a result of policing.

   E. Egress cells are being dropped because the queue is congested.

   F. Ingress cells are being dropped because the queue is congested.

This chapter covers the following key topics:

- VISM Overview
- MPLS Overview
- RPM Overview
- VISM Voice Features
- Voice Connections
- Voice Over AAL2 Network
- Voice Over IP Network
- Voice Over ATM Services on the VISM
- Digital Signal Processors
- VISM Clocking
- Commands for Adding, Configuring, and Displaying Voice Connections
- Commands for Verifying Voice Connections
- Introduction to Multiprotocol Label Switching
- ATM MPLS Technical and Business Benefits
- Label Switching Advantages
- The Problem of Persistent Loops Due to Protocol Conflicts
- Cisco WAN Switches with MPLS Support
- Setting Up MPLS on the MGX Switch
- MPLS and Virtual Private Networks Using the
  Route Processor Module
- RPM Memory Locations
- RPM Port Numbering
- The Cisco IOS Command-Line Interface
- Commands for Configuring the RPM
- Commands for Setting Up the RPM ATM Switch Interface
- How to Set Up the RPM
- Configuring Subinterfaces
- PVCs on the RPM
- Commands for Creating and Displaying PVCs on the RPM
- Creating Connections on the RPM

CHAPTER 22

Voice, IP, and ATM MPLS Features

This chapter presents the Cisco Voice Interworking Service Module (VISM) set of features and the solutions provided by this voice card, including Voice Over AAL2, Voice over ATM, and Voice over IP (VoIP) networks. This chapter shows you how to add, configure, display, and verify voice connections. It describes VISM clocking, including clocking options and configuration procedures.

Multiprotocol Label Switching (MPLS) is introduced, with the steps required to set up MPLS on the RPM. The MPLS section does not provide detailed configuration information; it is intended only as a guide for planning for MPLS in your network.

The RPM, including memory locations and port numbering, is also described, and the Cisco IOS command-line interface is introduced. Commands for configuring the RPM and for setting up the RPM ATM switch interface are explained. This chapter also discusses permanent virtual circuits (PVCs) on the RPM, including commands for creating and displaying these PVCs.

VISM Overview

The first key topic discussed in this chapter is the Cisco Voice Interworking Service Module (VISM). The VISM consists of a front and back card set designed to operate on the Cisco MGX 8250/8850-PXM1 switches for Releases 1.5 and 2.0. For VISM services on MGX 8230 switches, you must use VISM Release 2.0 or 2.1. The VISM provides interfaces to an ATM packet network and to TDM (time-division multiplexing) T1/E1 lines.

VISM Release 2.1 is a single-height Cisco MGX front card. As many as 24 cards can be installed in a Cisco MGX 8250 or Cisco MGX 8850 shelf, and as many as 8 cards can be installed in a Cisco MGX 8230 shelf. Each VISM supports either eight T1 lines or eight E1 lines. There are two hardware versions of the card—one for T1 lines and one for E1 lines. T1 and E1 lines cannot be mixed on a VISM card. (VISM is not supported on the Cisco MGX 8260 platform.)

A Cisco MGX 8850 Wide Area Edge Switch, when equipped with one or more VISM card sets, can transport digitized voice signals across a packet network. Thus, the VISM/MGX 8850 combination provides an interface or gateway between conventional voice TDM networks and networks based on packet-switching technology.

VISM employs the concept of operating modes, which permit it to be used in a variety of applications. Releases 1.5 and 2.0 have two operating modes—VoIP and AAL2 trunking. These modes support three major applications:

- **Switching**—Using VoIP mode, this application provides the emulation of many of the functions of a tandem (Class 4) switch. In this application, VISM functions as voice gateway (also called a media gateway) to an IP network and performs call control in conjunction with a call agent. The call agent (also called a media gateway controller) initiates and controls the call control functions. VISM transmits the voice payload through a bearer circuit using VoIP and ATM AAL5 network protocols.

- **Multiservice Access with Call Control**—This application also uses VoIP mode. In this application, the VISM/MGX 8850 combination is used to concentrate voice and user data services onto a single broadband circuit for transmission over the packet network, again using VoIP and ATM AAL5 techniques. As with the switching application, VISM can function with a call agent to perform call control. In this application, VISM can function as a front-end to a voice gateway.

- **AAL2 trunking**—This application uses AAL2 trunking mode. In this application, a VISM/MGX 8850 combination is used to concentrate voice (and fax/modem) user services over a preprovisioned AAL2 trunk. VISM merely passes (tunnels) bearer and signaling data across a packet network. It plays no part in call setup and teardown.

VISM architecture provides the following benefits:

- Technology flexibility that allows the incorporation of new or improved technology as it becomes available

- Application flexibility such that it can be used in a range of situations, providing interoperability with a wide variety of equipment types

- Modularity that allows equipment to be purchased and installed as it is needed in a step-by-step manner

Equipped with eight T1 or E1 ports, an array of Digital Signal Processors (DSPs), an HDLC (High-Level Data Link Control) framer, and a broadband interface to the packet network, VISM is ideally suited to processing high-density digital voice circuits providing compression, echo cancellation, dejittering, and packetization on-the-fly.

MPLS Overview

The second key topic discussed in this chapter is Multiprotocol Label Switching (MPLS). MPLS is an improved and efficient method for forwarding packets through a network. One of the most important applications of MPLS is in IP+ATM networks. IP+ATM is Cisco's trade name for equipment that simultaneously supports traditional ATM services (PVCs, SVCs, SPVCs, PVPs, and so on), and optimized IP transport using MPLS.

These networks offer traditional ATM and Frame Relay services while providing optimized IP support using ATM MPLS. MPLS also brings important new services, such as IP Virtual Private Networks (VPNs), to both IP+ATM networks and router networks.

IP-based services, such as IP VPNs and VoIP, are increasingly carried on ATM or Frame Relay networks to meet greater demands. Internet service providers (ISPs) are adding traditional Layer 2 capabilities and services, such as traffic engineering and VPNs, to their IP networks. Cisco addresses this problem with MPLS.

Integrating ATM infrastructures into the Internet model is as simple as providing IP continuity between the ATM network and the rest of the IP world. IP is integrated over ATM inside the autonomous system (AS) using MPLS, and the AS is connected to the rest of the Internet via BGP. This is done using IP+ATM, in which the ATM switches can continue to operate according to the ATM Forum and ITU-T standards while running MPLS in parallel. This means that other network applications such as PNNI, SVC, and AutoRoute can still operate independently of the MPLS application offering routed services.

MPLS is increasingly important as the building of internets on ATM expands and develops across the globe. The Internet is a collection of service providers offering IP services to their customers, all interconnected either directly or via high-speed network access points (NAPs). The NAPs are usually managed by a dedicated provider acting as a point of contact for coordination and connectivity purposes.

Each ISP maintains multiple Points of Presence (PoPs) that serve as concentration points for customer connectivity in multiple regions. PoPs can be interconnected via an ATM infrastructure or via direct high-speed leased-line connections. Currently, ISPs use Border Gateway Protocol version 4 (BGP4) for the purposes of interdomain connectivity. BGP4 offers a wide range of capabilities in segmenting providers' networks and offering routing policies that define the providers' administrative and political boundaries.

RPM Overview

The third key topic discussed in this chapter is the RPM. The RPM is a high-performance router module based on the Cisco 7200 NPE-150 router that has been modified to fit into a 32-slot, full-height MGX 8850 switch. The RPM substantially enhances the MGX 8850 product. The Cisco 7200 NPE-150 router engine can process up to 140 k packets per second (pps). It is a double-height service module that can be placed in any of the MGX 8850 service module slots.

The RPM provides integrated IP in an ATM platform, enabling services such as integrated Point-to-Point (PPP), Frame Relay termination, and IP VPNs using MPLS technology. It provides Cisco IOS-based multiprotocol routing over ATM, Frame Relay and ATM Interface Layer 3 termination, local server interconnect over high-speed LANs, access concentration, and switching between Ethernet LANs and the WAN facilities of the MGX 8850.

The RPM includes interprocessor communication with the main processor switch control module (called the PXM) in the MGX 8850 for management, including configuration, mode supervision (such as redundancy and load-sharing control), and software and configuration file management.

VISM Voice Features

This section provides an overview of the features supported in VISM Releases 1.5, 2.0, and 2.1. VISM firmware releases are not coupled with PXM1 firmware releases, unlike other service modules.

VISM Release 1.5 Features

VISM Release 1.5 is supported on MGX 8250/8850-PXM1 switches. For VISM services on MGX 8230 switches, you must use VISM Release 2.0.

VISM Release 1.5 supports the following voice features:

- **Voice over IP (VoIP) using real-time transport protocol (RTP)**—VISM Release 1.5 supports standards-based VoIP using RTP (see RFC 1889) and real-time transport control protocol (RTCP) protocols. This allows VISM to interwork with other VoIP gateways.

- **Multiservice Access with Call Control**—This application also uses VoIP mode. In this application, the VISM/MGX 8850 combination is used to concentrate voice and user data services onto a single broadband circuit for transmission over the packet network using VoIP and ATM AAL5 techniques. VISM can also function with a call agent to perform call control.

- **Voice over AAL2 (VoAAL2) with subcell multiplexing PVC**—The VISM supports standards-compliant AAL2 adaptation for the transport of voice over an ATM infrastructure. The AAL2 trunking mode is supported.

- **Codec support**—G.711 Pulse Code Modulation (PCM) A-law and μ-law, G.726 Adaptive Differential PCM (ADPCM), and G.729a/b Conjugate Structure Algebraic Code Excited Linear Predictive (CS-CELP) coding.

- **Eight T1/E1 lines**—The VISM supports eight T1 or eight E1 interfaces when G.711 PCM coding is used. For higher-complexity coders such as G.726-32K and G.729a-8K, the density drops to six T1 or five E1 interfaces and a maximum of 145 connections.

- **Echo cancellation**—The VISM provides on-board echo cancellation on a per-connection basis. Up to 128 milliseconds of user-configurable near-end delay can be canceled. Echo cancellation is compliant with ITU G.165 and G.168 specifications.

- **Voice Activity Detection (VAD)**—VISM uses VAD to distinguish between silence and voice on an active connection. VAD reduces a voice connection's bandwidth requirements by not generating traffic during periods of silence in an active voice connection. At the far end, comfort noise is generated.

- **Fax/modem detection for echo cancellation and VAD control**—The VISM continually monitors and detects fax and modem carrier tones. When carrier tone from a fax or modem is detected, the connection is upgraded to full PCM to ensure transparent connectivity. Fax and modem tone detection ensures compatibility with all voice-grade data connections.

- **Channel Associated Signaling (CAS) tunneling via AAL2 (for AAL2 trunking mode)**—The VISM in AAL2 mode facilitates transport of CAS signaling information. CAS signaling information is carried transparently across the AAL2 connection using Type 3 packets. In this mode, VISM does not interpret any of the signaling information.

- **Primary Rate Interface (PRI) tunneling via AAL5 (for AAL2 trunking mode)**—VISM supports transport of D-channel signaling information over an AAL5 VC. The signaling channel is transparently carried over the AAL5 VC and is delivered to the far end. In this mode, VISM does not interpret any of the signaling messages.

- **Voice connection admission control (CAC)**—VISM can be configured to administer CAC so that the bandwidth distribution between voice and data can be controlled in AAL2 mode.

- **Type 3 Packet for dual tone multifrequency (DTMF)**—The VISM in AAL2 mode facilitates transport of DTMF signaling information. DTMF information is carried transparently across the AAL2 connection using Type 3 packets.

- **Dual (redundant) PVCs for bearer/control**—The VISM can configure two PVCs for bearer/signaling traffic terminating on two external routers (dual-homing). VISM continually monitors the status of the active PVC by using OAM loopback cells. Upon detection of failure, the traffic is automatically switched over to the backup PVC.

- **64 kbps clear channel transport**—The VISM supports 64 kbps clear-channel support. In this mode, all codecs are disabled, and the data is transparently transported through the VISM.

- **DTMF relay for G.729**—In VoIP mode, DTMF signaling information is transported across the connection using RTP named signaling event (NSE) packets.

- **Media Gateway Control Protocol (MGCP) Version 0.1 for VoIP with Softswitch control**—VISM supports MGCP Version 0.1. This open protocol allows any Softswitch to interwork with the VISM module.

- Support for call agent Simple Gateway Control Protocol (SGCP) version 1.0, SGCP 1.1+

- **Resource Coordination via Simple Resource Control Protocol (SRCP)**—SRCP provides a heartbeat mechanism between the VISM and the Softswitch. In addition, SRCP also provides the Softswitch with gateway auditing capabilities.

- Courtesy downing of ongoing voice calls when the VISM is taken out of service for maintenance or other reasons

- Support for CCS (Common Channel Signaling) transport across an AAL5 trunk

- **Support for full continuity testing (COT)**—Supports origination and terminating loopback and transponder COT toward the packet bearer and the TDM sides.

- **1:N cold redundancy using SRM-3T3 capabilities (bulk mode support for T1 lines only)**—Calls do not persist during switchover.

VISM Release 2.0 Features

VISM Release 2.0 supports the VISM Release 1.5 features just listed, in addition to the features listed in this section. VISM Release 2.0 is supported on MGX 8230, 8250, and 8850-PXM1 switches.

Here are the key features of the VISM Release 2.0 card set:

- **PRI backhaul to the Softswitch using Reliable User Data Protocol (RUDP)**—The PRI backhaul capability provides PRI termination on the VISM with the Softswitch providing call control. ISDN Layer 2 is terminated on the VISM, and Layer 3 messages are transported to the Softswitch using RUDP.

- **Codecs preference**—VISM provides the capability to have the codecs negotiated between a call's two endpoints. The VISM can be configured, for a given endpoint, to have a prioritized list of codecs. Codec negotiation can be directly between the endpoints or can be controlled by a Softswitch.

- **31 timeslots for E1 with 240 channels only**—Although all 31 timeslots on an E1 port can be used, there is a limitation of 240 connections per card.

VISM Release 2.1 Features

VISM Release 2.1 supports the VISM Release 1.5 and 2.0 features listed previously. It also includes voice compression to G.711, G.726-16k, 24k, 32k, 40k, G.729a, and G.729ab standards.

VISM offers different solutions for carrying voice traffic, including Voice Over AAL2 network, VoIP network, and Voice Over ATM services, as described in the following sections. An introductory discussion of voice connections is presented first.

Voice Connections

A voice connection is an end-to-end permanent virtual circuit (PVC) that originates and terminates on MGX VISM endpoints. The connection receives PCM voice samples and signaling and converts them into ATM cells using AAL2 (voice traffic and CAS signaling) or AAL5 (CCS signaling) and transports the cells to the remote endpoint. All voice connections are bidirectional, meaning that traffic flows in both directions.

A single AAL2 voice connection can carry multiple voice calls. This is called AAL2 multiplexing. The channel identifier (CID) differentiates voice traffic streams on the connection.

You can add two types of voice connections in an MGX network: feeder and local. Feeder connections go from the VISM to the PXM trunk and are transported through the ATM backbone network (BPX or other) to the destination MGX switch. Local connections go from one endpoint on an MGX switch to another endpoint on the same switch. Local connections can be between endpoints on the same or different VISM cards. Feeder and local connections perform the same functions.

Endpoints

All VISM connections terminate on endpoints. An endpoint is a channel (DS0 or timeslot) on a T1 or E1 line. An endpoint is defined by its endpoint number and the T1 or E1 line and channel number. You must create VISM endpoints before you can terminate connections on them.

Channel Identifiers

A CID identifies a specific voice traffic stream. You use it when multiplexing multiple voice calls across a single ATM connection. On the MGX switch, the CID also links the connection to the endpoint. When you create a CID, you identify the compression type and other voice processing characteristics, such as echo cancellation and dual-tone multifrequency (DTMF) transport. Figure 22-1 shows the VISM with endpoints, connection, and CIDs.

Figure 22-1 *Channel Identifiers*

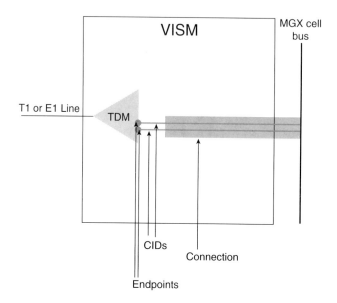

Feeder Example

A voice feeder connection has three connection segments:

- A master connection between the VISM endpoint and PXM1 trunk on one MGX switch.
- A routing connection through the ATM backbone network. The routing connection should be rt-VBR for voice traffic and nrt-VBR for signaling traffic.
- A master connection between the VISM and PXM1 trunk on the other MGX switch.

Figure 22-2 shows a voice feeder connection in an MGX network.

Local Example

An ATM local connection has two connection segments:

- A slave connection on one VISM. The slave connection must be added first.
- A master connection on the other VISM pointing to the slave connection.

Figure 22-2 *Feeder Example*

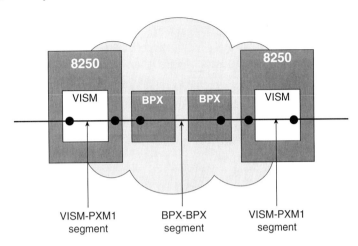

How PCM Samples Are Converted into ATM Cells

How are ATM cells created on Voice over AAL2 (VoAAL2) services on the VISM?

Figure 22-3 shows a high-level view of the traffic flow of voice traffic on the VISM.

Figure 22-3 *Traffic Flow*

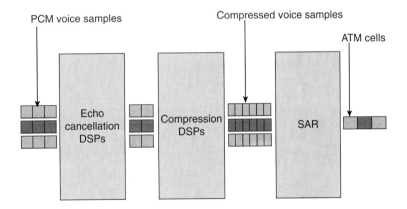

Pulse Code Modulation (PCM) voice samples come in from the line and are processed by echo cancellation digital signal processors (DSPs) to eliminate any echo (if echo cancellation is enabled). Next, the PCM samples are processed by the compression DSPs. This is where the 8-bit PCM samples are converted into a variety of different samples (length and frequency), depending on the compression method in use. The compressed samples go to the segmentation and reassembly (SAR) processor to be loaded into ATM cells for transport to the cell bus and across the network.

AAL2 Segmentation

ITU-T Recommendation I.363.2 specifies the basic AAL2 structure for VoAAL2. Figure 22-4 shows three voice samples (from the same or different voice calls) and how they are made into an ATM cell.

Figure 22-4 *Voice Sample Conversion to ATM Cell*

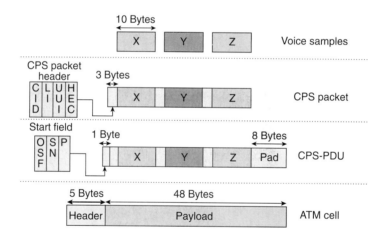

Table 22-1 describes each stage of the AAL2 segmentation process.

Table 22-1 *AAL2 Segmentation Process*

Stage	Description
Voice samples	The fixed-length voice samples come from the codec. In this example, each voice sample is 10 bytes long, but the length depends on the compression method used.
CPS (Common Part Sublayer) packet	A 3-byte CPS header is added to each voice sample. Because the voice samples could come from different traffic streams (channels or calls), the CPS header differentiates the channels with the CID.

Table 22-1   *AAL2 Segmentation Process (Continued)*

Stage	Description
CPS-PDU	The CPS-PDU includes a 1-byte start field at the beginning of the CPS packets. Padding is added to the data to make the CPS-PDU exactly 48 bytes long.
ATM cell	The 5-byte ATM header is added to the CPS-PDU (ATM cell payload), and the cell is then ready to transport through the network.
LI (Length Indicator)	The number of cells with a payload length that does not match the LI in the CPS packet header.

AAL2 Coding

Here are the coding or compression methods supported on the VISM:

- G.711u—PCM with μ-law coding
- G.711a—PCM with A-law coding
- G.726—ADPCM
- G.729—CS-CELP with 10-, 20-, and 30-millisecond (ms) cell times

The coding type you use affects the voice sample size and the sample and cell frequency. Ultimately, this determines how much bandwidth the voice traffic utilizes. Figure 22-5 shows each coding type and the ATM cell created from the voice samples, assuming that multiplexing (multiple voice streams on the same ATM connection) is not in use.

Figure 22-5   *AAL2 Coding Types*

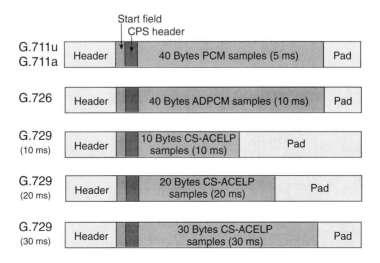

Voice Over AAL2 Network

The Voice over AAL2 (VoAAL2) solution with VISM is used to replace trunk lines between voice switches. A separate PVC is needed for voice channels destined for a specific remote endpoint. Signaling information is sent using one of two methods: CAS signaling is sent with voice traffic, and CCS signaling is sent on a separate AAL5 connection. Except for signaling extraction and insertion, the VISM does not participate in the signaling process.

- As described with the previous VISM features, the VISM supports standards-compliant AAL2 adaptation for the transport of voice over an ATM infrastructure with AAL2 trunking mode.

Here are the major features of AAL2 trunking mode:

- The voice payload is transported across the packet network using an AAL2 PVC. Multiple voice channels are supported in a single PVC using CIDs (channel identifiers) and subcell multiplexing. A single VISM supports up to 64 AAL2 PVCs.

- Call setup through a call agent is not supported. All bearer paths are provisioned using either the command-line interface (CLI) or Simple Network Management Protocol (SNMP).

- If CAS signaling is used, the signaling is transported across the packet network along with the voice payload using AAL2 Type 3 packets.

- CCS signaling channels are supported and are transported across the packet network using a separate AAL5 PVC.

In AAL2 trunking mode, VISM provides a set of AAL2 trunks carrying the voice payload over the packet network. Figure 22-6 shows a high-level view of VoAAL2 between two voice switches.

Figure 22-6 *VoAAL2 with VISM*

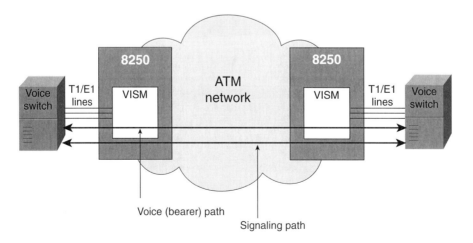

Voice (bearer) path

Signaling path

Voice payloads and CAS signaling are transported across the AAL2 trunk. If a channel is configured for CCS signaling, the signaling is transmitted by extracting HDLC frames and forwarding them over preprovisioned AAL 5 virtual circuits (the voice payload is still transmitted using AAL 2).

In this role, the VISM merely passes signal traffic to and from the trunk.

VoIP Network

The VoIP solution with VISM requires one or more (up to eight) call agents to manage signaling for the voice calls. The Cisco Virtual Switch Controller (VSC) is one such call agent. Other call agents might be supported. The call agent receives call requests and other signaling messages from the voice switch and converts these to Simple Gateway Control Protocol (SGCP) or MGCP and sends them to the VISM. The VISM uses the signaling messages to set up or break down voice calls. Multiple call agents communicate with each other using Enhanced ISDN User Part (E-ISUP).

Here are the major features of VoIP mode:

- Calls are set up under the control of one or more (up to eight) call agents using SGCP or MGCP protocol (CLI-configurable).

- CAS signaling can be extracted from the voice payload and backhauled to the call agent using either SGCP or MGCP.

- CCS signaling on an ISDN D-channel can be backhauled as Q.931 to the call agent using RUDP protocol.

- The voice payload is converted to IP packets, which are then tunneled through an AAL5 PVC to the IP network.

- A single PVC for both signaling and data can be configured with a second (redundant) channel together with automatic switchover in the event of a failure. Alternatively, AAL5 PVCs can be configured to provide a split into control and bearer streams, each on a separate PVC. If the signal and data streams are split, one of the PVCs (but not both) can be provided with a second redundant PVC.

- In VoIP mode, VISM operates in conjunction with a call agent.

Briefly, the call setup procedure consists of the following steps:

Step 1   The calling party lifts the handset and dials a number. The resulting on/off hook and digit signaling are sent to the call agent either directly or by VISM through CAS backhauling over SGCP.

Step 2   The call agent at the originating end looks up the called number in a table and locates the remote call agent that manages the called number. It forwards the IP address of the calling VISM to the remote call agent using C-ISUP.

Step 3 The remote call agent responds by providing the IP address of the remote VISM to the originating VISM.

Step 4 With the exchange of IP addresses, a bearer circuit is set up across the IP/ATM network between the calling and the called VISMs. This procedure also involves the negotiation of coding, compression, and so on. Endpoints that identify the two ends of the call to the VISM/DS1/DS0 level are identified with the bearer circuit so that a complete end-to-end bearer circuit is established between the calling and called parties. At this point, the voice call can proceed.

Step 5 CAS signaling is sent to the call agent for processing. Any resulting action required of VISM is executed by commands from the call agent.

In VoIP mode, a single AAL5 PVC is set up for communication with the packet-switching network. All calls use this single PVC. It is the responsibility of the network edge router to extract the IP addresses from the voice payloads and route the traffic across the IP network.

Figure 22-7 *VoIP Network*

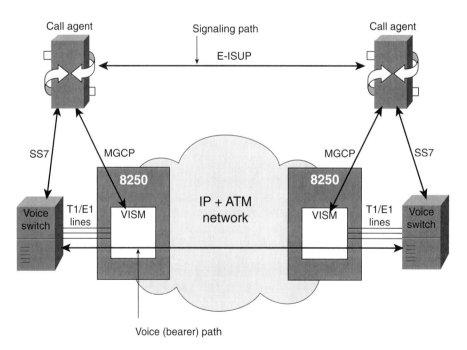

The network connecting VISMs is IP. This can be an IP-only network (for example, Cisco 7500 series routers) or an IP+ATM network (for example, MGX RPMs with an ATM back-bone network). The VISMs have PVCs between them to carry control and voice (bearer)

traffic. These PVCs use AAL5 for segmentation and reassembly (SAR) of the IP packets to ATM. Figure 22-7 shows a high-level view of a VoIP network using VISM. You can use the same PVC or separate PVCs for control and voice traffic.

Voice Over ATM Services on the VISM

A Cisco MGX 8850 Wide-Area Edge Switch, when equipped with one or more VISM cards, can transport digitized voice signals across a packet network while providing voice quality and reliability equal to the quality expected on the public telephone network. By transporting the voice traffic over ATM packet networks instead of traditional time-division multiplexing (TDM) networks, you realize considerable savings in network bandwidth requirements. Thus, the VISM/MGX 8850 combination provides an interface or voice gateway between conventional voice TDM networks and networks based on packet-switching technology.

The MGX network supports VISM-to-ATM connections. The primary use of this type of connection is to provide interworking with Cisco 3810 voice services.

Figure 22-8 shows an example of VISM and 3810 voice interworking.

Figure 22-8 *VISM and Voice Interworking*

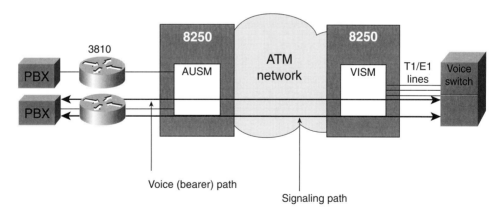

Follow these steps to create Voice over ATM (VoATM) services in the MGX network on VISM:

Step 1   Type **dspvismparam** and confirm that the VISM mode is aal2Trunking. If it isn't, type **cnfvismmode 2**. This outputs the VISM voice mode and changes the voice mode to AAL2 trunking.

Step 2   Type **dsplns**. This outputs summary information for all lines on the card. Confirm that the line you want to use is enabled and free of alarms.

Step 3 Type **dspln** <*line number*> and verify the line signaling type. If you need to change it, use the **cnflnsig** command. This outputs the line configuration and changes the signaling type.

Step 4 Type **dspport**. If no port exists, type **addport**. This outputs the port information and creates a new logical port between the VISM and the PXM1.

Step 5 Type **dsprscprtn**. If no resource partitions exist, type **addrscprtn 1**. This outputs the resource partition information and creates a new portable AutoRoute (PAR) resource partition on the port.

Step 6 Type **dsplndsp** <*line number*> and review the digital signal processor (DSP) configuration. If you want to make any changes, use the **cnfecanenable**, **cnfecanrec**, **cnfecantail**, or **cnfcompvad** commands. This outputs the line DSP configuration and changes the line echo cancellation and VAD settings.

Step 7 Type **dspendpts** to identify an endpoint. If the endpoint you want to use is not listed, use the **addendpt** or **addendpts** command to create new endpoints. This outputs a list of all endpoints on the VISM and adds one or more new endpoints.

Step 8 Type **dspendpt** <*endpoint number*> and verify that the endpoint is using the appropriate line and timeslot. This outputs the endpoint configuration.

Step 9 To add a local connection, type **addcon** <*local VCI*> <*preference*> <*PVC type*> <*application*> <*PCR*>. Go to Step 11 and note the connection ID.

Step 10 To add a feeder connection, type **addcon** <*local VCI*> <*preference*> <*PVC type*> <*application*> <*PCR*> <*mastership*> [*remote connection ID*], specifying the PXM1 trunk in the *remote connection ID*. This creates a new master connection.

Step 11 Type **dspcons** and **dspcon** <*channel number*> and verify the connection configuration. This outputs the connection status and configuration information.

Step 12 Type **addcid** <*endpoint number*> <*LCN*> <*CID number*> <*codec type*> [*profile type*] [*profile number*] [*VAD*] [*VAD initialization timer*] [*echo cancellation*] [*triple redundancy protection*] [*CAS transport*] [*DTMF transport*] [*ICS*] [*packet period*], specifying the endpoint and connection channel number (LCN) you identified in Step 7 and Step 9 or 10. This creates a CID on the connection.

Step 13 If multiple CIDs are using the same connection, repeat Step 12 for each CID. Specify the same LCN and a different CID and endpoint. This creates additional CIDs.

Step 14 Log into the remote VISM if you are adding a local connection and type **cc** <*card slot*>. This transfers the CLI to another card slot.

Step 15 Repeat Steps 1 through 8. This configures the VISM, line, and endpoint(s).

Step 16 If you are adding a local connection, type **addcon** <*local VCI*> <*preference*> <*PVC type*> <*application*> <*PCR*> <*mastership*> [*remote connection ID*], specifying the *remote connection ID* you noted in Step 9. Then go to Step 18. This creates a master connection.

Step 17 If you are adding a feeder connection, type **addcon** <*local VCI*> <*preference*> <*PVC type*> <*application*> <*PCR*> <*mastership*> [*remote connection ID*], specifying the PXM1 trunk in the *remote connection ID*. This creates a master connection.

Step 18 Complete Steps 11 through 13 on this VISM. This adds one or more CIDs.

Step 19 If you have a BPX backbone network, log into the BPX switch attached to one of your MGX switches. Type **addcon** <*local channel*> <*remote node*> <*remote channel*> <*connection class | connection type*> [*connection parameters*] [*route avoid*] to add an ATM routing connection through the BPX network. Be sure to match the VPI and VCI values in the BPX network with the values you used when you added the MGX connection segments. Use the **dspcons** and **dspcon** commands to verify the connection status. Proceed to Step 21.

Step 20 If you have an MGX 8850-PXM45 backbone network, log into the AXSM on the local switch and type **addcon** <*interface number*> <*vpi*> <*vci*> <*service type*> **2** [*parameters*], where **2** indicates the slave endpoint. Be sure to write down the endpoint ID (NSAP address, VPI, and VCI). Log into the AXSM on the remote switch and type **addcon** <*interface number*> <*vpi*> <*vci*> <*service type*> **1** <-**slave** *slave endpoint ID*> [*parameters*], where **1** indicates the master endpoint and the *slave endpoint ID* is as previously noted. This adds a routing connection through the MGX 8850-PXM45 network. Use the **dspcons** and **dspcon** commands to verify the connection status.

Step 21 Use the **tstcon** or **tstdelay** command to verify connectivity. This tests end-to-end connectivity in the network.

Step 22 Type **dspconcnt** *<channel number>* and **dspmngcidcnt** *<CID>* and verify that there is traffic. This outputs connection and CID statistics counters.

Step 23 Log into the original VISM and repeat Steps 21 and 22. This confirms that the connection and CID are functioning correctly at the other end.

Step 24 Type **bye.** This logs you off the CLI.

You have completed the steps necessary to create Voice over ATM (VoATM) services in the MGX network on VISM.

Digital Signal Processors

A major feature of VISM is the array of Digital Signal Processors (DSPs) that provide extensive voice signal processing capability.

Each VISM contains 37 DSPs. Twelve are general-purpose and can be configured to perform echo cancellation or data compression. Twenty-four can be used for data compression only. One DSP is a Jukebox DSP that is used to load code (program) overlays to the other 36 DSPs.

In addition to the DSPs, one HDLC controller is used for CCS signal processing.

Together, the DSPs support the DS0 channels of the eight T1/E1 lines.

A timeslot interchanger routes the DS0s to

- A data compression DSP or
- An echo cancellation DSP and then a data compression DSP or
- The HDLC controller (for CCS processing)

DSPs are loaded with their programs at boot time.

VISM Clocking

This section describes the options and procedures for setting up the clocking on a VISM-equipped MGX 8850 shelf.

VISM Clocking Options

VISM cards and MGX 8850 PXM cards each provide multiple clocking options. To avoid conflicts and to ensure proper operation, it is important that the settings for clocking options in both card types be considered together.

An overriding principle is that an MGX 8850 shelf consisting of PXM and VISM cards should have *one and only one* primary clocking source.

A second principle is that at the VISM/MGX 8850 PXM interface there are two options:

- The MGX 8850 PXM card provides clock for all the VISM cards in the shelf.
- One of the VISM cards on the shelf provides clock for the PXM (and hence the remainder of the shelf).

The user must choose one of these options.

Using the first option, in which the clock source originates at the PXM side of the VISM/PXM interface, the source stems from one of the following:

- An external BITS clock on the PXM's T1 or E1 backcard port
- An external OC3 signal on a PXM SONET backcard port
- The PXM's internal crystal

The internal crystal is the default and is automatically set as the primary clock source at power-on. The user can use one of the other two clock sources by executing the **cnfclksrc** (configure clock source) command.

Also, in this situation, the PXM becomes the clock source for the entire shelf. As such, it uses its clock source to provide clocking for all the VISM cards in the shelf. The VISM cards, in turn, use this clock to provide clocking for their T1 or E1 lines. In order for this situation to operate correctly, all the VISM lines must be configured for local clocking using the **cnfln** (configure line) command.

Moving on to the second option, the clock source originates on the VISM side of the VISM/PXM interface. It stems from one of the T1 or E1 lines on one of the VISM cards (the line receiving the clock signal on the selected VISM card must be line number 1). The line number 1 that is receiving the clock source must be configured for loop clocking using the **cnfln** command. All the remaining T1 or E1 lines on all the VISM cards in the shelf must be configured for local clocking.

Also, in this situation, the VISM becomes the clock source for the PXM and hence the entire shelf, including the remaining VISM cards. In order for this situation to operate correctly, the PXM must be configured for a service module as the clocking source with the selected VISM and its clock line specified in the **cnfclksrc** command.

Configuration Procedures

Follow these steps to set up clocking on a VISM-equipped MGX 8850 shelf:

Step 1   Examine the entire configuration of the MGX 8850 shelf and determine the single clock source. The type of equipment connected to the VISM's T1 or E1 lines might dictate this choice. If the selected clock source is from one of the VISM's T1 or E1 lines, that line must be connected to the physical port 1 on the VISM backcard.

Step 2   Configure the clocking option on the PXM card using the **cnfclksrc** command:

```
cnfclksrc <slot.port> <clktype>
```

The *slot.port* parameter specifies the clock source. The **clktype** parameter is either **p** for primary, **s** for secondary, or **null** for no external clock source. The following configurations show the criteria used to specify these parameters:

(a)   If the clock source is the external BITS clock (a T1 or E1 port on the PXM backcard), specify the configuration as

```
cnfclksrc 7.35 p
```

Use slot 7 whether the PXM is in slot 7 or 8. The BITS port is always numbered port 35.

(b)   If the clock source is an external signal on one of the PXM OC3 ports, specify the configuration as

```
cnfclksrc 7.n p
```

Use slot 7 whether the PXM is in slot 7 or 8. *n* is the OC3 port number in the range 1 to 4.

(c)   If the clock source is the PXM's internal crystal and no other clock source has been specified, there is no need to configure the clock source, because the crystal is the automatic default. However, if another clock source is specified and you want to change to the crystal, specify the configuration as

```
cnfclksrc 7.x null
```

Use slot 7 whether the PXM is in slot 7 or 8. *x* is either 35 or the OC3 port number, depending on which is the currently specified source. The **null** value cancels the previous configuration and returns the clocking source to the default crystal.

(d) If the clock source is from the a line on a VISM card, specify the configuration as

> **cnfclksrc** *y.z* **p**

y is the slot number of the VISM card, and z is the line number (which must be 1).

Step 3   Configure the clocking option on the VISM card(s) using the **cnfln** command:

> **cnfln** *<line_num> <line_code> <line_len> <clk_src>*
>   *<line_type> <loopback_detection>*

You must enter all the parameters, but for clocking purposes, only *line_num* and *clk_src* are relevant. The line number is the physical port number on the VISM backcard. The clock source can be specified as either loop clock or local. Loop clock is clocking from a T1 or E1 line, and local clock is clocking from the PXM.

(a) If the clock source to the VISM is from the PXM, all lines on all VISM cards must be configured as local using the **cnfln** command.

(b) If the clock source is from a line on a VISM card, specify that line (which must be line 1) as loop clock, and configure all remaining lines on the VISM and all lines on all the other cards as local.

You have successfully set up clocking on a VISM-equipped MGX 8850 shelf.

Commands for Adding, Configuring, and Displaying Voice Connections

This section describes the commands you use to add, configure, and display voice connections on the VISM:

- **dspvismparam**—Displays the VISM configuration, including the voice mode (VoIP or VoAAL2).
- **cnfvismmode**—Changes the VISM configuration, including the voice mode.
- **addport**—Creates a logical port on the VISM. This command must be used only once on the VISM.
- **delport**—Removes the logical port from the VISM.
- **dspport**—Lists the logical port on the VISM.

- **addrscprtn**—Creates a resource partition. This command must be used only once on the VISM.

- **delrscprtn**—Removes a resource partition.

- **dsprscprtn**—Displays the resource partition configuration.

- **cnflnsig**—Changes a line's signaling type.

- **dsplndsp**—Displays the line digital signal processor (DSP) configuration, including echo cancellation and voice activity detection (VAD).

- **cnfecanenable**—Enables or disables a line's echo cancellation.

- **cnfecanrec**—Sets a line's residual echo control.

- **cnfecantail**—Sets the maximum echo cancellation tail length between 24 and 128 milliseconds.

- **cnfcompvad**—Enables VAD on a line.

- **addendpt**—Creates an endpoint on the VISM.

- **delendpt**—Removes an endpoint from the VISM.

- **addendpts**—Adds multiple, contiguous endpoints on the VISM.

- **delendpts**—Removes multiple, contiguous endpoints from the VISM.

- **dspendpts**—Lists all endpoints on the VISM.

- **dspendpt**—Lists detailed information for an endpoint.

- **addcon**—Creates a new voice connection on the VISM.

- **delcon**—Removes a voice connection from the VISM.

- **dspcons**—Lists summary status and configuration information for all connections on the VISM.

- **dspcon**—Lists detailed configuration information for a connection.

- **addcid**—Creates a new CID on the VISM that associates a connection with an endpoint.

- **delcid**—Removes a CID from the VISM and disassociates a connection with an endpoint.

- **dspcids**—Lists configuration information for all CIDs on a connection.

- **dspcid**—Lists configuration information for a CID.

Display VISM Parameter Command

The **dspvismparam** command shows the voice mode configuration for the VISM. Use this command to learn whether the VISM is configured for VoIP or VoAAL2 services. You can change the VISM's voice mode using the **cnfvismmode** command. Example 22-1 shows the **dspvismparam** output.

Example 22-1 dspvismparam *Output*

```
smoke.1.3.VISM8.a > dspvismparam


VISM mode:                    aal2Trunking
CAC flag:                     enable
DS0s available:               240
Template number:              2
Percent of functional DSPs: 100
IP address:                   0.0.0.0
Subnet mask                   0.0.0.0
RTCP report interval:         1000
RTP receive timer:            disable
ControlPrecedence/Tos:        0x60
BearerPrecedence/Tos:         0xa0
Aal2 muxing status:           disable
Tftp Server Dn                TFTPDOMIAN
```

The information shown in the **dspvismparam** output includes the following:

- **VISM mode**—Either AAL2 trunking or VoIP switching.

- **Connection Admission Control (CAC) flag**—Specifies whether CAC is enabled or disabled on the VISM. This field applies only to VoIP mode.

- **DS0s available**—The number of channels available on the card. This number depends on the card type (T1 or E1) and the template in use. This field applies only to VoAAL2 mode.

- **Template number**—Specifies which template (1 or 2) is configured for the VISM. Template number 1 supports G.711u, G.711a, G.729a, G.729ab, G.726/32, and clear-channel codecs. Template 1 is not allowed in VoIP mode and reduces the number of channels supported on the card. Template number 2 supports G.711u, G.711a, and clear channel only. You can change the template using the **cnfcodectmpl** command.

NOTE   Template number 1 in VISM Release 2.1 supports G.711u, G.711a, G.729a, G.729ab, G.726/32, and clear-channel codecs, plus G.726 16K, 24K, 32K, and 40K codecs.

- **Percent of functional DSPs**—The percentage of DSPs that are fully functional on the VISM.

- **IP address**—The IP address of the VISM used in VoIP mode.

- **Subnet mask**—The subnet mask that the VISM uses in VoIP mode.

- **Real-time Transport Control Protocol (RTCP) report interval**—The amount of time between RTCP messages for VoIP.

- **Real-time Transport Protocol (RTP) receive timer**—The amount of time between expected RTP messages.

- **Control precedence**—Control precedence for IP packets is a type of service (ToS) that conforms to RFC 1349. It determines which IP packets have higher priority as defined by the bearer precedence.

- **Bearer precedence**—Bearer precedence for IP packets conforms to RFC 791. It can be in the priority range of 0 to 7. You can adjust the precedence of the bearer IP packets as follows: 0 = low priority, 7 = high priority. The priority levels help ensure timely delivery of all traffic in a heterogeneous network.

- **AAL2 multiplexing status**—Specifies whether multiple voice streams can be multiplexed onto the same AAL2 connection. You can change this field using the **cnfaal2subcellmuxing** command.

- **TFTP server domain name**—The domain name of the TFTP server.

Configure VISM Mode Command

The **cnfvismmode** command changes the VISM card's voice mode. Use this command if you need to change the VISM to or from VoIP or VoAAL2.

Here is the **cnfvismmode** command syntax:

```
cnfvismmode <mode>
```

mode is either 1 for VoIP or 2 for VoAAL2.

For example, type **cnfvismmode 2** to change the mode from VoIP to VoAAL2.

Add Port Command

The **addport** command creates a logical interface between the VISM and the PXM1. You must type this command before you add any endpoints, connections, or CIDs on the VISM. This command has no required or optional parameters.

Display Port Command

The **dspport** command shows the VISM port status. Use this command to verify that the port was added. You can delete the port using the **delport** command.

Example 22-2 shows the **dspport** output.

Example 22-2 **dspport** *Output*

```
smoke.1.3.VISM8.a > dspport

    vismPortNum:            1
    vismPortRowStatus:      add
    vismPortSpeed:          60000
    vismPortState:          active
```

The information shown in the **dspport** output includes the following:

- **Port number**—Always 1.

- **Port row status**—The row status is add unless the port is modified. In that case, the status is mod.

- **Port speed**—Indicates the amount of voice traffic that the VISM can send to the PXM1.

- **Port state**—In most cases, the port state is active.

Add Resource Partition Command

The **addrscprtn** command creates resource partitions on the VISM port. You must issue this command after adding the port and before you add any endpoints, connections, or CIDs to the VISM. You can remove the resource partition using the **delrscprtn** command.

Here is the **addrscprtn** command syntax:

addrscprtn *<controller ID>*

controller ID is 1 for Portable AutoRoute (PAR).

For example, type **addrscprtn 1** to add the PAR resource partition to the VISM port.

Display Resource Partition Command

The **dsprscprtn** command shows the resource partition configuration. Note that the resource partition cannot be configured. Example 22-3 shows the **dsprscprtn** output.

Example 22-3 **dsprscprtn** *Output*

```
smoke.1.1.VISM8.a > dsprscprtn

    vismResPartPortNum:     1
    vismResPartCtrlrNum:    par
    vismResPartRowStatus:   add
```

continues

Example 22-3 dsprscprtn *Output (Continued)*

```
vismResPartNumOfLcnAvail:    72
vismResPartLcnLow:           131
vismResPartLcnHigh:          510
vismResPartIngrPctBW:        100
vismResPartEgrPctBW:         100
vismResPartCtrlrID:          1
```

The information shown in the **dsprscprtn** output includes the following:

- **Port number**—Always 1.
- **Controller number**—Always par.
- **Row status**—Always add.
- **Number of logical connection numbers (LCNs) available**—The number of channels that you can add on the VISM.
- **LCN low**—The minimum LCN or channel number allowed.
- **LCN high**—The maximum LCN or channel number allowed.
- **Ingress percent bandwidth**—The percentage of the ingress port bandwidth allocated to this resource partition.
- **Egress percent bandwidth**—The percentage of the egress port bandwidth allocated to this resource partition.
- **Controller ID**—Always 1 for PAR.

Configure Line Signaling Command

The **cnflnsig** command sets the signaling method of a T1 or E1 line. Use this command to enable CAS or CCS signaling on the line. Even if the physical line is set for CCS using the **cnfln** command, you must use the **cnflnsig** command to set up the signaling method. Use the **dspln** command to learn the line-signaling configuration.

Here is the **cnflnsig** command syntax:

```
cnflnsig <line number> <signaling type>
```

The parameter options are as follows:

- *line number*—The T1 or E1 line number. 1 to 8.
- *signaling type*—The voice signaling type. 1 = CAS, 2 = CCS, 3 = no signaling.

For example, type **cnflnsig 2 1** to enable CAS signaling on line number 2.

Display Line DSP Command

The **dsplndsp** command shows the DSP configuration for a line. Use this command to learn the echo cancellation and VAD settings. Example 22-4 shows the **dsplndsp** output.

Example 22-4 dsplndsp *Output*

```
smoke.1.1.VISM8.a > dsplndsp 8

  VismLineNum:         8
  ECANEnable:          enable
  MaximumTail:         32 milliseconds
  ResidualEcho:        SuppressResidual
  VoiceDetection:      Enable
```

The information shown in the **dsplndsp** output includes the following:

- **VismLineNum**—Represents the VISM card line number.

- **Echo cancel enable**—Enabled or disabled. Use the **cnfecanenable** command to change this field.

- **Maximum tail**—The maximum tail length (delay) for the echo canceller. Choices include 24, 32, 48, 64, 80, 96, 112, and 128 milliseconds. Use the **cnfecantail** command to change this field.

- **Residual echo**—The echo canceller's action for residual echo. Residual echo is what is left over after the echo is cancelled due to the echo model's being imperfect. Choices include cancel only, suppress residual, or inject comfort noise. Use the **cnfecanrec** command to change this field.

- **Voice detection**—Specifies whether VAD is enabled or disabled. Use the **cnfcompvad** command to change this field.

Add Endpoint and Add Endpoints Commands

The **addendpt** and **addendpts** commands are used to add new endpoints on the VISM. The **addendpt** command creates one endpoint, and the **addendpts** command creates multiple contiguous endpoints. It is recommended that you use the **addendpts** command to create endpoints on all available channels when you start configuring your VISM. You must add endpoints before adding connections and CIDs to the VISM. Use the **delendpt** and **delendpts** commands to delete endpoints on the VISM.

Here is the **addendpt** command syntax:

```
addendpt <endpoint number> <DS1 number> <DS0 number>
```

Here is the **addendpts** command syntax:

```
addendpts <endpoint number> <DS1 number> <DS0 number> <number of endpoints>
```

The parameter options are as follows:

- *endpoint number*—Used when you add a CID. 1 to 192 for T1, 1 to 240 for E1.

- *DS1 number*—The T1 or E1 line number. 1 to 8.

- *DS0 number*—The DS0 or (starting) timeslot number. 1 to 24 for T1, 1 to 31 for non-CAS E1, 1 to 15 and 17 to 31 for CAS E1.

- *number of endpoints* (**addendpts** only)—The number of contiguous endpoints you want to add. 1 to 192 for T1, 1 to 240 for E1.

For example, type **addendpt 1 4 8** to add endpoint 1 to timeslot 8 on line 4; type **addendpts 2 4 9 10** to add 10 endpoints starting with endpoint number 2 on timeslot 9 on line 4.

Display Endpoints Command

The **dspendpts** command lists all the endpoints configured on the VISM. Use this command to learn which endpoints exist. Example 22-5 shows the **dspendpts** output.

Example 22-5 dspendpts *Output*

```
smoke.1.3.VISM8.a > dspendpts

    EndptNum  Ena/Speed
    --------  --- -----
    1         act/  64k
    2         act/  64k
    3         act/  64k
    4         act/  64k
    5         act/  64k
    6         act/  64k
    7         act/  64k
    8         act/  64k
    9         act/  64k
    10        act/  64k
    11        act/  64k
    12        act/  64k
    13        act/  64k
    14        act/  64k
    15        act/  64k
    16        act/  64k
    17        act/  64k
    18        act/  64k
    19        act/  64k
    20        act/  64k

Type <CR> to continue, Q<CR> to stop:
```

Display Endpoint Command

The **dspendpt** command shows detailed information about an endpoint. Use this command to learn which line and timeslot an endpoint is associated with. Example 22-6 shows the **dspendpt** output.

Example 22-6 dspendpt *Output*

```
smoke.1.1.VISM8.a > dspendpt 1

    EndptNum:       1
    EndptLineNum:   8
    EndptName:      E1-8/1@cisco.com
    EndptSpeed:     64 kbps
    EndptState:     active
    EndptChannelMap: 2
    EndptEnable:    active
    EndptLoopback:  disabled
```

The **dspendpt** output includes the following information:

- **EndptNum**—The endpoint number.

- **EndptLineNum**—The line an endpoint is associated with.

- **EndptName**—The endpoint name in the form *line type-line number/endpoint number@domain name. line type* is T1 or E1, and *domain name* is the VISM domain name that is used for VoIP signaling messages. The default domain name is cisco.com. In Example 22-6, E1-8/1@cisco.com is endpoint 1 on E1 line 8.

- **EndptSpeed**—The endpoint speed. Either 56 or 64 kbps.

- **EndptState**—The endpoint state, usually active.

- **EndptChannel Map**—A hexadecimal number representing the timeslot assigned to the endpoint. If you convert this number into a binary number, each bit represents a timeslot. The least-significant digit (on the right) is timeslot 1; the most-significant digit (on the left) is the highest timeslot number. Notice that leading zeros are not shown. In Example 22-6, the channel map is 2, which is a binary 10. This means that timeslot 1 is assigned to this endpoint. (Because this is an E1, timeslot 0, the least-significant bit is reserved for framing.)

- **EndptEnable**—Usually active.

- **EndptLoopback**—The endpoint loopback state, either enabled or disabled. You can loop the endpoint using the **addendptloop** command and remove an endpoint using the **delendptloop** command.

Add Connection Command

The **addcon** command is used to create a new voice connection on the VISM. You can use the **delcon** command to remove the connection.

Here is the **addcon** command syntax:

```
addcon <local VCI> <preference> <PVC type> <application> <PCR> <mastership>
  [remote connection ID]
```

The parameter options are as follows:

- *local VCI*—The LCN number. You use this number when you configure a CID. 131 to 510.

- *preference*—Specifies a primary or secondary channel for redundancy purposes. 1 = primary, 2 = secondary.

- *PVC type*—1 = AAL5 used for VoIP and signaling channels, 2 = AAL2 for VoAAL2 channels, 3 = AAL1 (not supported).

- *application*—Specifies how the connection is used. 1 = control for VoIP when a separate control channel is used, 2 = bearer for voice traffic, 3 = signaling for VoAAL2.

- *PCR*—The connection's Peak Cell Rate (PCR). For connections in which multiple voice circuits are multiplexed onto one connection, you need to calculate the PCR based on the aggregate rate of the supported voice calls. 1 to 75,600 cells per second (cps) for AAL5 bearer PVC, 1 to 24,400 cps for AAL5 control PVC, 1 to 50,000 cps for T1 AAL2 bearer PVC, 1 to 60,000 cps for E1 AAL2 bearer PVC, 1 to 400 cps for signaling PVC in AAL2 trunking mode.

- *mastership*—1 = master, 2 = slave. If you are adding a slave connection, you do not need to specify the mastership or the remote connection ID.

- *remote connection ID*—The destination connection ID for master connections in the form *node name.card slot.port.VPI.VCI*. If you are adding a feeder connection to the PXM1, *card slot* must be 0. If you are adding a local connection to another VISM, *port* is always 1, *VPI* is always 0, and *VCI* is the remote LCN. If you are adding a local connection to an ATM interface, you must specify the port, VPI, and VCI on the ATM side.

Display Connections Command

The **dspcons** command lists summary status information for all connections on the VISM. Example 22-7 shows the **dspcons** output.

Example 22-7 dspcons *Output*

```
smoke.1.3.VISM8.a > dspcons

  ConnId         ChanNum Status  Preference Protection  Active  Locking
  -------        ------- ------  ---------- ----------  ------- --------
  smoke.3.1.0.131    131   Mod          1   unprotected unknown unlock
  smoke.3.1.0.132    132   Add          1   unprotected unknown unlock
  smoke.3.1.0.133    133   Add          1   unprotected unknown unlock
```

The **dspcons** output includes the following information:

- **Connection ID**—The local connection ID in the form *node name.card slot*.1.0.*LCN*
- **Channel number**—The local VCI or LCN
- **Status**—Add or Mod (modify)
- **Preference**—Specifies a primary (1) or secondary (2) channel
- **Protection**—The redundancy protection type
- **Active**—The redundancy state
- **Locking**—The redundancy locking

Display Connection Command

The **dspcon** command shows detailed configuration information for a connection. Example 22-8 shows the **dspcon** output. There are two pages to the **dspcon** output; the second page is shown in Example 22-9.

Example 22-8 dspcon *Output, Page 1*

```
smoke.1.3.VISM8.a > dspcon 131

  ChanNum:                131
  ChanRowStatus:          Mod
  ChanLocalRemoteLpbkState: Disabled
  ChanTestType:           TestOff
  ChanTestState:          NotInProgress
  ChanRTDresult:          65535 ms
  ChanPortNum:            1
  ChanPvcType:            AAL2
  ChanConnectionType:     PVC
  ChanLocalVpi:           0
  ChanLocalVci:           131
  ChanLocalNSAP:          736d6f6b6500000000000000000000000003000100
  ChanRemoteVpi:          0
  ChanRemoteVci:          131
```

continues

Example 22-8 dspcon *Output, Page 1 (Continued)*

```
      ChanRemoteNSAP:            736d6f6b65000000000000000000000001000100
      ChanMastership:            Master
      ChanVpcFlag:               Vcc
      ChanConnServiceType:       CBR
      ChanRoutingPriority:       1
      ChanMaxCost:               4294967295
      ChanRestrictTrunkType:     No Restriction

    Type <CR> to continue, Q<CR> to stop:
```

Many of the fields listed in the **dspcon** output can be modified using a number of configuration commands discussed in this section. Other information in the **dspcon** output includes the following:

- **RTD result**—The result of the most recent round-trip delay test (use the **tstdelay** command). If the test has never been run, it reports 65,535 milliseconds.

- **Channel local NSAP**—The network service access point (NSAP) address uniquely identifies this interface (port) in the network. The 20-byte hexadecimal address has the following fields:

  — The most-significant 8 bytes (16 digits) spell out the node name in ASCII. The connection in Example 22-8 is on node smoke.

  — The card slot number is the fourth byte from the right. The connection in Example 22-8 is on card 3.

  — The port number is the second byte from the right. All VISM connections are on port 1.

Example 22-9 shows the second page of the **dspcon** output.

Example 22-9 dspcon *Output, Page 2*

```
  ChanConnPCR:              100
    ChanConnPercentUtil:     100
    ChanPreference:          1
    ChanRemotePCR:           100
    ChanRemotePercentUtil:   100
    ChanProtection:          unprotected
    ChanActivityState:       unknown
    ChanLockingState:        unlock
    ChanApplication:         bearerf
    ChanServiceType:         cbr
    ChanScrIngress:          100
    ChanMbsIngress:          100

    ChanNumNextAvailable:  132
```

Add CID Command

The **addcid** command creates a new CID that associates a connection with an endpoint. You can add multiple CIDs to a connection, but each must have a different endpoint and CID. Use the **delcid** command to delete a CID from the VISM.

Here is the **addcid** command syntax:

```
addcid <endpoint number> <LCN> <CID number> <codec type> [profile type]
    [profile number] [VAD] [VAD initialization timer] [echo cancellation]
    [triple redundancy protection] [CAS transport] [DTMF transport] [ICS]
    [packet period]
```

The parameter options are as follows:

- *endpoint number*—The endpoint associated with this CID. Only one CID can be associated with an endpoint. 1 to 192 for T1 cards, 1 to 240 for E1 cards.

- *LCN*—The logical connection number. 131 to 510.

- *CID number*—The CID must be unique per connection (LCN). 9 to 255.

- *codec type*—The voice compression type. 1 = G.711u, 2 = G.711a, 3 = G.726/32, 4 = G.729a, 5 = G.729ab, 6 = clear channel. (VAD must be off when the codec is clear-channel.)

- *profile type*—1 = ITU, 3 = custom. This parameter is required if *codec type* is G.729a/ab.

- *profile number*—1, 2, or 7 for ITU. 100 or 101 for custom. Use the **dspaal2profile** command to see the profile characteristics. Be sure to use a profile that supports the compression type (codec type) you are using. This parameter is required if *codec type* is G.729a/ab.

- *VAD*—Enables or disables VAD. 1 = VAD on, 2 = VAD off (the default).

- *VAD initialization timer*—Determines how long to wait after a speech burst before starting VAD. If this time is too short, you might experience clipping. If it is too long, you might not get the bandwidth savings you require. 250 to 65,535 milliseconds.

- *echo cancellation*—Enables or disables echo cancellation. 1 = on (default), 2 = off.

- *triple redundancy protection*—Enables or disables triple redundancy protection. 1 = on, 2 = off.

- *CAS transport*—Enables or disables the transport of CAS signaling bits in the AAL2 traffic stream. 1 = on (default), 2 = off.

- *DTMF transport*—Enables or disables the transport of DTMF tones in the AAL2 traffic stream (inband). 1 = on (default), 2 = off.

- *Integrated Communications System (ICS)*—1 = enable, 2 = disable.

- *packet period*—The amount of time between G.729a packets. 10, 20, 30, or 40 milliseconds.

For example, type **1131 9 1 1 1 1 300 1 2 1 1 1** to create CID number 9 associated with endpoint 1 and LCN 131. This CID is set for G.711u and uses ITU profile number 1.

Display CIDs Command

The **dspcids** command lists all the CIDs on a specified LCN. Use this command to learn which CIDs are on a connection and how they are configured. Example 22-10 shows the **dspcids** command output.

Example 22-10 dspcids *Output*

```
smoke.1.1.VISM8.a > dspcids 132

LCN CID Endpt  Cid    Type3     VAD  Prof  Prof  Codec Cas  DTMF      ICS    Pkt
Num Num Num    Status Redun VAD Timer Type  Num   Type  Tran Tran Ecan Enable Per.
--- --- ----- ------ ----- --- ----- ----- ---- ------ ---- ---- ---- ------ ----
132 10  2      active ena   ena 250 ITU   1     G.711u ena  ena  ena  Dis    5
132 22  3      active ena   ena 250 ITU   1     g.711u ena  ena  ena  Dis    5
```

The **dspcids** output shows all the characteristics you set using the **addcid** command.

Display CID Command

The **dspcid** command shows the same information as the **dspcids** output, but for a specific CID. Example 22-11 shows the **dspcid** output.

Example 22-11 dspcid *Output*

```
smoke.1.3.VISM8.a > dspcid 131 9

    LCN number :        131
    CID number:         9
    Endpoint number :   50
    CidRowStatus:       active
    Type3redundancy:    enabled
    VAD:                disabled
    VADInitTimer:       200
    Profile type:       Custom
    Profile number:     100
    Codec type:         clr chan
    Cas transport:      enabled
    DTMF transport:     enabled
    Ecan on/off:        enabled
    ICS enable:         Disabled
    pkt period:         5
```

Commands for Verifying Voice Connections

This section describes the commands you use to verify voice connections in the MGX network:

- **tstcon**—Tests a connection's continuity
- **tstdelay**—Tests a connection's continuity and the round-trip delay
- **dspconcnt**—Lists a channel's statistics counters
- **dspmngcidcnt**—Lists an endpoint's managed CID counters

Test Connection Command

The **tstcon** command tests continuity on MGX network connections. If connection segments are failed or misconfigured, the **tstcon** command fails. The **tstcon** command does *not* test quality of service or connectivity beyond the MGX network.

Here is the **tstcon** command syntax:

```
tstcon <channel number>
```

The **tstcon** command has some limitations:

- It works only for local connections or connections in a tiered MGX network with BPX or MGX 8850-PXM45 backbone switches.
- It should be issued from both ends to completely verify connectivity.
- A passing result of the test does not guarantee the connection's end-to-end performance.

Test Delay Command

The **tstdelay** command is similar to the **tstcon** command in that it checks connection continuity. The **tstdelay** command also measures the round-trip delay through the network. The results are output on the CLI. The most recent delay measurement is also reported in the **dspcon** output.

Here is the **tstdelay** command syntax:

```
tstdelay <channel number>
```

The **tstdelay** output is shown in Example 22-12.

Example 22-12 tstdelay *Output*

```
smoke.1.3.VISM8.a > tstdelay 131

test type is..... 2

TestDelay in progress.

TestDelay Passed with 54 us.
```

NOTE The limitations on the **tstcon** command also apply to the **tstdelay** command.

Display Connection Count Command

The **dspcncnt** command lists historical connection statistics counters on the VISM. Use this command to learn how much traffic has been sent, received, or dropped on the voice connection. The cells reported in the **dspcncnt** output are counted at the segmentation and reassembly (SAR) processor in the VISM. Example 22-13 shows the **dspcncnt** output.

Example 22-13 **dspcncnt** *Output*

```
smoke.1.3.VISM8.a > dspcncnt 131

ChanNum:                          131
Chan State:                       okay
Chan XMT ATM State:               Normal
Chan RCV ATM State:               Normal
OAM Lpb Lost Cells:                      0
AAL2 HEC Errors:                         0
AAL2 CRC Errors:                         0
AAL2 Invalid OSF Cells:                  0
AAL2 Invalid Parity Cells:               0
AAL2 CPS Packet Xmt:                     70327
AAL2 CPS Packet Rcv:                     124971
AAL2 Invalid CID CPS:                    0
AAL2 Invalid UUI CPS:                    0
AAL2 Invalid Len. CPS:                   0
AAL5 Invalid CPI:                        0
AAL5 oversized SDU PDU:                  0
AAL5 Invalid Len. PDU:                   0
AAL5 PDU CRC32 Errors:                   0
AAL5 Reassembly Timer expired PDU:   0
```

The **dspcncnt** output shows the following information:

- **Channel state**—okay or failed.
- **Channel transmit ATM state**—The channel state as reported to the ATM network and the remote end of the connection. For example, if the local line fails, the connection sends Operation, Administration, and Maintenance (OAM) alarm indicator signal (AIS) cells to the remote end (VISM or ATM interface) of the connection.
- **Channel receive ATM state**—The channel state reported from the ATM network.
- **OAM loopback lost cells**—The number of cells dropped while an OAM loopback was in progress.
- **HEC errors**—The number of cells with incorrect header error check (HEC) values.

- **CRC errors**—Cyclic Redundancy Check errors. This is a process that is used to check the integrity of a block of data. CRC is a common method of establishing that data was received correctly.

- **Invalid OSF cells**—The number of cells with an invalid offset field (OSF) in the start field of the common part sublayer protocol data unit (CPS-PDU).

- **Invalid CID CPS**—The number of cells with invalid CIDs in the CPS packet header.

- **Invalid UUI CPS**—The number of cells with invalid User-to-User Interface (UUI) fields in the CPS packet header.

- **Invalid length**—The number of cells with a payload length that does not match the length indicator (LI) in the CPS packet header.

- **Invalid CPI**—Invalid computer-to-PBX interface.

- **Length Indicator (LI)**—The number of cells with a payload length that does not match the LI in the CPS packet header.

- **Sequence Number (SN)**—The order in which the queues are serviced. It is strongly recommended that you do not change this value. 1 to 16.

- **Parity (P)**—The process of detecting whether bits of data were altered during transmission of that data.

- **Oversize SDU PDU**—Oversized service data unit (interface information that is unchanged from layer to layer) protocol data unit (packet).

- **Invalid length PDU**—Invalid protocol data unit (packet) length.

- **PDU CRC32 errors**—Protocol data unit for CRC errors.

- **Reassembly timer expired PDU**—A PDU can span multiple ATM cells. If the remainder of the PDU does not arrive within a set time period, the reassembly timer expires, and the PDU is discarded.

Display Managed CID Counter Command

Use the **dspmngcidcnt** command to display the managed CID count for a specified endpoint. Example 22-14 shows the **dspmngcidcnt** output.

Example 22-14   dspmngcidcnt *Output*

```
smoke.1.3.VISM8.a > dspmngcidcnt 50

  EndptNum:          50
  Lcn:               131
  Cid:               9
  SentPkts:          76843
  RcvdPkts:          76844
```

continues

Example 22-14 **dspmngcidcnt** *Output (Continued)*

```
SentOctets:        3301527
RcvdOctets:        3301570
LostPkts:          0
Jitter:            0
Latency:           0
Ext AIS Rcvd:      0
Ext RAI Rcvd:      0
Ext Conn AIS Rcvd: 0
Ext Conn RDI Rcvd: 0
```

The **dspmngcidcnt** output includes the following information:

- **Sent packets**—The number of packets sent to the network.

- **Received packets**—The number of packets received from the network.

- **Sent octets**—The number of octets sent to the network.

- **Received octets**—The number of octets received from the network.

- **Lost packets**—The number of packets lost during transmission.

- **Jitter**—The phase shift of digital pulses over a transmission medium.

- **Latency**—The time it takes to get information through a network; waiting time or time delay.

- **External AIS received**—The number of alarm indicator signals received from the line.

- **External RAI received**—The number of remote alarm indicators (RAIs) received from the line.

- **External connection AIS received**—An external connection AIS has been received.

- **External connection RAI received**—An external connection RAI has been received.

Introduction to Multiprotocol Label Switching

Multiprotocol Label Switching (MPLS) is a method of switching IP packets through a network by applying simple labels to packets. This allows devices in the network core to switch packets according to these labels with minimal lookup activity. Besides the obvious advantage of faster network transit, MPLS also provides the privacy and quality of service (QoS) advantages of connection-oriented services such as ATM without the complexity of manually creating fully-meshed PVCs.

MPLS integrates the performance and traffic-management capabilities of the data link layer (Layer 2) with the scalability and flexibility of network layer (Layer 3) routing. MPLS is applicable to networks using any Layer 2 switching, but it has particular advantages when applied to ATM networks. It integrates IP routing with ATM switching to offer scalable IP-over-ATM networks.

In contrast to label switching, conventional Layer 3 IP routing is based on the exchange of network reachability information. As a packet traverses the network, each router extracts all the information relevant to forwarding from the Layer 3 header. This information is then used as an index for a routing table lookup to determine the packet's next hop. This is repeated at each router across the network. At each hop in the network, the packet's optimal forwarding must again be determined.

The information in IP packets, such as information on IP Precedence and Virtual Private Network (VPN) membership, is usually not considered when packets are forwarded. To get maximum forwarding performance, typically only the destination address is considered. However, because other fields could be relevant, a complex header analysis must be done at each router the packet meets.

The main concept of MPLS is to include a *label* on each packet. Packets or cells are assigned short, fixed-length labels. Switching entities perform table lookups based on these simple labels to determine where data should be forwarded.

The label summarizes essential information about routing the packet:

- Destination
- Precedence
- VPN membership
- QoS information from Resource Reservation Protocol (RSVP)
- The packet's route, as chosen by traffic engineering (TE)

With label switching, the complete analysis of the Layer 3 header is performed only once: at the edge label switch router (LSR), which is located at each edge of the network. At this location, the Layer 3 header is mapped to a fixed-length label.

At each router across the network, only the label need be examined in the incoming cell or packet in order to send the cell or packet on its way across the network. At the other end of the network, an edge LSR swaps the label out for the appropriate header data linked to that label.

A key result of this arrangement is that forwarding decisions based on some or all of these different sources of information can be achieved by means of a single table lookup from a fixed-length label. For this reason, label switching makes it feasible for routers and switches to make forwarding decisions based on multiple destination addresses.

Label switching integrates switching and routing functions, combining the reachability information provided by the router function with the traffic engineering benefits achieved by the optimizing capabilities of switches.

ATM MPLS Technical and Business Benefits

MPLS, in conjunction with other standard technologies, offers many features that are critical for service providers:

- MPLS, in combination with the standard IP routing protocols OSPF and IS-IS, provides full, highly scalable support of IP routing within an ATM infrastructure.

- MPLS, in combination with Border Gateway Protocol (BGP), provides support for highly scalable IP VPN services. IP VPN services are an invaluable development in provider networks, giving enterprise customers a service that meets their needs for private, connectionless delivery of IP services.

- Service-Level Agreements (SLAs) can be provided in a form suitable for connection-less traffic. Cisco networks assist the process of providing SLAs by supporting MPLS in combination with forthcoming standards. Along with supporting VPNs, the ability to offer SLAs suitable for IP traffic is a critical requirement to meet new demands for IP services.

- Cisco's implementation of MPLS allows support for harder QoS where required using full ATM switch capabilities.

Cisco IP+ATM networks fully support all relevant IP routing protocols and MPLS while fully supporting traditional ATM services. MPLS and IP routing can readily be introduced into traditional ATM networks by using permanent virtual path (PVP) or PVC tunnels since MPLS-capable switches are continuously being introduced.

Cisco IP+ATM switches allow carriers to continue meeting their existing demands for virtual circuit services while adding optimized support for critically important new services: IP and IP VPNs. Furthermore, Cisco supports all the standards relevant to carrier-class IP services: MPLS, Multiprotocol BGP, other standard routing protocols, and MPLS traffic engineering.

Label Switching Advantages

MPLS offers many advantages over traditional IP over ATM.

When integrated with ATM switches, label switching uses switch hardware optimized to take advantage of the fixed length of ATM cells and to switch the cells at high speeds. For multiservice networks, label switching allows the Cisco WAN switch to provide ATM, Frame Relay, and IP Internet service all on a single platform in a highly scalable way. Support of all these services on a common platform provides operational cost savings and simplifies provisioning for multiservice providers.

For ISPs using ATM switches at the core of their networks, label switching allows the Cisco BPX 8600 series, the 8540 Multiservice Switch Router, MGX 8850-PXM45 (discussed in a moment), and other Cisco ATM switches to provide a more scalable and manageable networking solution than overlaying IP over an ATM network. Label switching avoids the scalability problem of too many router peers and provides support for a hierarchical structure within an ISP's network.

These MPLS benefits are analyzed in greater detail in the following list:

- **Integration**—When applied to ATM, MPLS integrates IP and ATM functionality rather than overlaying IP on ATM. This makes the ATM infrastructure visible to IP routing and removes the need for approximate mappings between IP and ATM features. MPLS does not need ATM addressing and routing techniques such as PNNI, although these can be used in parallel if required.

- **Greater reliability**—In wide-area networks (WANs) with ATM infrastructures, MPLS is an easy solution for integrating routed protocols with ATM. Traditional IP over ATM involves setting up a mesh of PVCs between routers around an ATM cloud, and the Next-Hop Resolution Protocol (NHRP) achieves a similar result with switched virtual circuits (SVCs). But a number of problems exist with this approach, all arising from the fact that the PVC links between routers are overlaid on the ATM network. This makes the ATM network structure invisible to the routers. A single ATM link failure could make several router-to-router links fail, creating problems with large amounts of routing update traffic and subsequent processing. (See the next section for details.)

- **Better efficiency**—Without extensive tuning of routing weights, all PVCs are seen by IP routing as single-hop paths with the same cost. This might lead to inefficient routing in the ATM network.

- **Direct CoS implementation**—When used with ATM hardware, MPLS makes use of the ATM queueing and buffering capabilities to provide different classes of service. This allows direct support of IP precedence and CoS on ATM switches without complex translations to the ATM Forum service classes.

- **More elegant support of multicast and RSVP**—In contrast to MPLS, overlaying IP on ATM has other disadvantages, particularly in support of advanced IP services such as IP multicast and RSVP. Support of these services entails much time and work in the standards bodies and implementation; the resulting mapping between IP features and ATM features is often approximate.

- **VPN scalability and manageability**—MPLS can make IP VPN services highly scalable and very easy to manage. VPN services are an important way to provide enterprises with private IP networks within their infrastructures. When an ISP offers a VPN service, the carrier supports many individual VPNs on a single infrastructure. With an MPLS backbone, VPN information can be processed only at the ingress and exit points, with MPLS labels carrying packets across a shared backbone to their correct exit point. In addition to MPLS, Multiprotocol (BGP) is used to deal with information about the VPNs. The combination of MPLS and Multiprotocol BGP makes MPLS-based VPN services easier to manage, with straightforward operations to manage VPN sites and VPN membership. It also makes MPLS-based VPN services extremely scalable, with one network able to support hundreds of thousands of VPNs.

- **Reduces the load on network cores and is more robust**—VPN services demonstrate how MPLS supports a hierarchy of routing knowledge. Additionally, you can isolate Internet routing tables from service provider network cores. Similar to VPN data, MPLS allows access to the Internet routing table only at the ingress and egress points of a service provider network. With MPLS, transit traffic entering at the edge of the provider's autonomous system can be given labels that are associated with specific exit points. As a result, internal transit routers and switches need only process the connectivity with the provider's edge routers, shielding the core devices from the overwhelming routing volume exchanged on the Internet. This separation of interior routes from full Internet routes also provides better fault isolation and improved stability.

- **Traffic engineering capabilities**—Other benefits of MPLS include traffic engineering capabilities needed for the efficient use of network resources. Traffic engineering lets you shift the traffic load from overutilized portions of the network to underutilized portions, according to traffic destination, traffic type, traffic load, time of day, and so on.

The Problem of Persistent Loops Due to Protocol Conflicts

If n routers are running OSPF and are connected in a full mesh over ATM PVCs, a single physical ATM link failure might result in ATM-layer rerouting of a large number of PVCs. If this takes too long, or if the ATM network cannot reroute PVCs, a large number of PVCs effectively fails.

The number of PVCs involved might be of the same order magnitude as n, and even $n2$ in some cases. In any case, it is likely to be seen by $O(n)$ routers, where $O(n)$ means "a number proportional to n." So, a single ATM link failure causes each of $O(n)$ routers to send a link-state advertisement (LSA) of size (at least) $O(n)$ to $n - 1$ neighbors. Thus, a single event in the ATM network results in $O(n3)$ to $O(n4)$ traffic.

When a router receives an LSA, it must immediately recalculate its routing table because it must not forward packets based on old routing information. The processor load caused by a storm of routing updates might cause the routers to drop or not send keepalive packets. This appears to the neighboring routers as further link failures. These lead to further LSAs being sent, which perpetuates the problem.

The net result is that a full-mesh network can become persistently unstable after a single network event.

This critical failure occurs because the routers do not see the state of the ATM links and switches directly. IS-IS has somewhat better performance than OSPF in full-mesh conditions because IS-IS has more sophisticated flooding capabilities. (These capabilities, especially the ability to pace and block flooding on some interfaces, are also becoming available on OSPF.) However, this does not address the underlying problem.

The solution is to enable IP routing to directly see the state of ATM links, which is what ATM MPLS does.

MPLS addresses the fundamental problem underlying the instability of the full-mesh network: the basic conflict between routing protocols. PNNI routing at the ATM layer can make decisions that conflict with OSPF or similar routing at the IP layer. These conflicting decisions can lead to persistent loops. The only reliable solution to this problem is to use the same routing protocol at the IP layer and ATM layer. This is exactly what MPLS does in ATM networks.

Cisco WAN Switches with MPLS Support

Figure 22-9 shows an example of an MPLS network.

Figure 22-9 *MPLS Network Example*

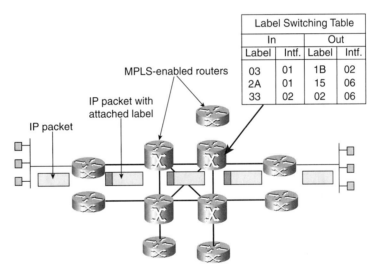

Based on the network routing protocol, a path (or route) is set up to all reachable IP networks. Simple label-switching tables identifying the labels and the destination interface are set up on all intermediate nodes. The nodes at the edge of the MPLS network attach the appropriate labels to the IP packets. The nodes in the network core simply switch the packets from one interface to the next based on the label. For example, if a packet with label 2A comes in on interface 01, it is switched to interface 06, and the label is changed to 15.

Label switching is similar to switching cells in an ATM network: Instead of a VPI and a VCI, there is a label. Because of this similarity, using an MPLS-enabled ATM network in the core is the ideal solution, especially in cases where ATM networks are already deployed.

An LSR is a core device that switches labeled packets according to predefined switching tables. An LSR can be a switch or a router. BPX 8650 switches (a BPX switch plus a 7200-series router) and MGX 8850-PXM45 switches (with RPM installed) are examples of LSRs.

An Edge LSR (ELSR) or Label Edge Router (LER) is an edge device that performs initial packet processing and classification and applies the first label. An ELSR can be either a router or a switch with built-in routing. The RPM installed in an MGX switch is an example of an ELSR.

A Label Switch Controller (LSC) is an MPLS router that controls the operation of an ATM switch in such a way that the two function together as a single ATM-LSR. An LSR comprises a switch and an LSC. A 7200 series router is an LSC for the BPX switch; an RPM is an LSC for the MGX 8850-PXM45 switch.

MPLS Features Supported on the MGX Switch

This section provides a high-level description of the MPLS features supported on the RPM installed in an MGX switch running Release 1.1.x firmware.

The RPM supports the following MPLS features:

- The RPM as an ELSR or LER
- Support for MPLS VPNs
- Support for QoS
- Support for MGX switches (with PXM1) interworking with MGX 8850-PXM45 switches via MPLS Virtual Switch Interface (VSI) virtual trunks
- Support for MGX switches (with PXM1) interworking with BPX 8650 switches via MPLS VSI virtual trunks

The RPM as an Edge Label Switch Router

The RPM installed in an MGX switch is an ELSR or LER. As an ELSR, the RPM is responsible for initial packet processing and classification. It also applies the first label to the packets.

MPLS VPN Support on RPM

MPLS VPN support on RPM is described in greater detail in the upcoming section, "MPLS and Virtual Private Networks Using the Route Processor Module."

The VPN offers private connectivity over a public infrastructure. Each customer is assigned a VPN ID. You can think of the VPN ID as a prefix or extension of the IP address. For example, if a destination IP address is 10.10.15.2 and the VPN ID is 243, the packet destination is effectively 243.10.10.15.2, uniquely identifying the destination. Even if another customer is using the same IP address, the VPN ID is different, making the packet address different as well. In the MPLS network, the VPN identifier and the destination IP address are associated with a label.

The VPN is also isolated by the routing protocol (BGP) so that routing updates are exchanged only between members of the same VPN. The router at one customer's site does not even know about another customer's routers.

Figure 22-10 shows an example of VPNs in the MPLS network. Company A and Company B are connected to the same public network; however, they each have a VPN that behaves like a private network.

Figure 22-10 *Example of VPNs in the MPLS Network*

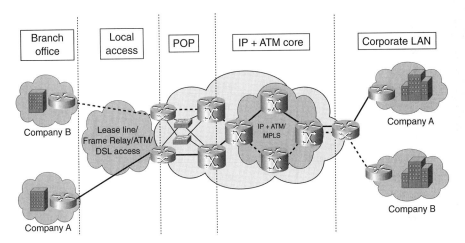

MPLS QoS Support on RPM

Customers have different types of traffic that they want to send to the service provider. MPLS allows the service provider to assign a different label to each traffic class. This label determines how traffic will be handled in the network.

The MPLS QoS solution does not map different traffic classes into different virtual circuits, as is done in ATM. MPLS simply applies a different label. These labels move the packet from end to end, maybe over a different path. Each switch along the way has a label that tells it the packet's CoS.

MGX PXM1 MPLS Interworking with MGX 8850-PXM45 and BPX Switches

This feature allows RPMs as ELSRs in PXM1-based platforms to interwork with the MGX 8850-PXM45 or BPX 8650 LSC function. The MPLS VSI virtual trunks feature enables the definition of one virtual path (VP) tunnel per ELSR on a PXM1-based platform to be mapped to one VSI virtual trunk under the control of the LSC on the attached backbone switch.

Figure 22-11 shows the MPLS interworking feature for MGX 8850-PXM45 switches.

Figure 22-11 *The MPLS Interworking Feature*

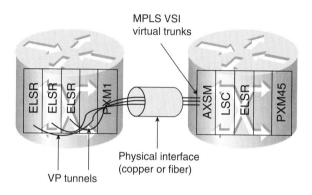

MPLS Networks Using the MGX Switch

This section describes how the MGX switch is placed in an MPLS network. It shows how the MGX switches with the BPX ATM MPLS core, the MGX 8850-PXM45 ATM MPLS core, and the IP MPLS core.

MGX Switches with the BPX ATM MPLS Core

This ATM MPLS architecture uses BPX 8650 ATM LSRs. The ELSR or LERs in this network are RPMs installed in MGX 8230/8250/8850-PXM1 switches.

The MGX switches are connected to the BPX switches by T3, E3, OC-3/STM1, or OC-12/STM4 ATM links.

Figure 22-12 shows an ATM MPLS core with MGX switches with RPMs as ELSRs.

Figure 22-12 *ATM MPLS Core with MGX Switches*

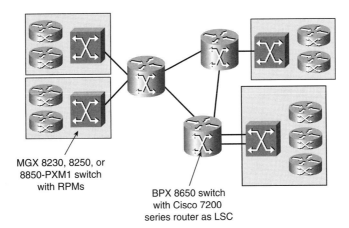

MGX 8230, 8250, or
8850-PXM1 switch
with RPMs

BPX 8650 switch
with Cisco 7200
series router as LSC

Cisco MGX 8230, 8250, and 8850-PXM1 switches do not yet support LSCs. This means that all MPLS traffic to RPMs must be carried inside a PVC or a PVP. PVCs are used with packet-based MPLS. If an MGX switch is used with ATM MPLS, the connections to the RPMs must be PVPs, which are used as MPLS VP tunnels.

Two options exist for the PVP connections, as shown in Figure 22-13. In the first option, at least two separate ATM lines are used between the MGX switch and the BPX switch. One line is the feeder trunk, which carries all but MPLS traffic, and the second line carries PVPs from the RPMs to the BPX switch. The second line is a UNI or NNI port on the MGX switch, with several VSI virtual trunk endpoints on the BPX switch.

Figure 22-13 *PVP Connections*

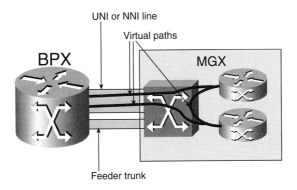

UNI or NNI line

Virtual paths

BPX

MGX

Feeder trunk

The second line is required because the BPX switch does not support virtual trunk endpoints on interfaces that are configured as feeder trunks. Another option involves using three or four lines with the PVPs distributed across them, increasing the available bandwidth. In this topology, additional lines are configured in the same fashion as the second UNI or NNI (nonfeeder trunk) link.

If two or three UNI or NNI lines are used to carry MPLS PVPs, these can be connected from one MGX switch to two or three different BPX nodes. Non-MPLS traffic from the MGX switch is still carried on the feeder trunk to a single BPX switch.

It is possible to carry all traffic (MPLS and non-MPLS) on the feeder trunk between the MGX and BPX switches. This option requires loopback cables on the BPX node and additional connections between the BPX feeder trunk and UNI or NNI ports.

MGX Switches with the MGX 8850-PXM45 ATM MPLS Core

Using an MGX 8850-PXM45 ATM MPLS core for MGX switches is similar to using a BPX core. The main difference is that the LSC for the MGX 8850-PXM45 switch is an RPM card module rather than an external router.

Figure 22-14 shows MGX 8850-PXM45 switches and MGX PXM1 switches in an ATM MPLS network.

Figure 22-14 *Cisco Switches in an ATM MPLS Network*

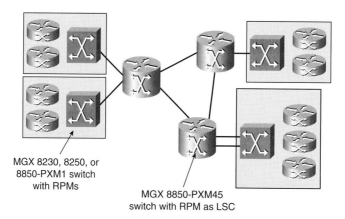

MGX 8230, 8250, or
8850-PXM1 switch
with RPMs

MGX 8850-PXM45
switch with RPM as LSC

Like a BPX ATM MPLS core, you must set up a second line between the MGX PXM1 and the MGX 8850-PXM45 switches to carry the PVPs from the RPM ELSR.

MGX Switches with the IP MPLS Core

It is possible to set up the MGX switches without an ATM MPLS core. In this case, PVCs are required between RPMs in the network that need to pass traffic between them. The ATM backbone can be BPX, MGX 8850-PXM45, or other-vendor switches, but it is not an MPLS-enabled network. The ATM backbone network simply transports ATM cells from one RPM to another without any knowledge of MPLS.

Figure 22-15 shows an example of MGX switches and an IP MPLS core.

Figure 22-15 *Cisco Switches in an IP MPLS Core*

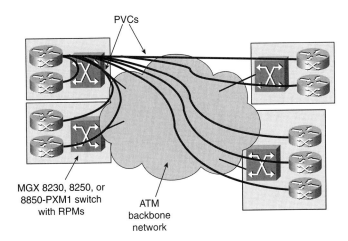

Refer to this Web site for more information on the benefits of MPLS: www.ciscopress.com/book.cfm?series=1&book=168.

Setting Up MPLS on the MGX Switch

This section describes the steps required to set up MPLS on the RPM. This section does not provide detailed configuration information. It is intended as a guide for you to plan for MPLS in your network.

Network Topology

Use Figure 22-16 as a reference for the steps described in this section.

Figure 22-16 *Setting Up MPLS on the MGX Switch*

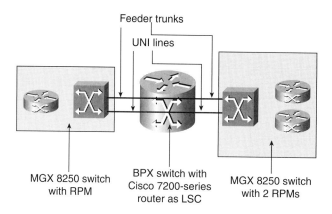

Feeder trunks

UNI lines

MGX 8250 switch
with RPM

BPX switch with
Cisco 7200-series
router as LSC

MGX 8250 switch
with 2 RPMs

Follow these steps to set up MPLS on the MGX switch:

Step 1 The Cisco 7200 series router is cabled to the BPX, added as a shelf, and configured as the LSC.

Step 2 The MGX 8250 PXM1 is cabled to the BPX (this is in addition to the feeder trunk).

Step 3 The MGX 8250 PXM1 line is configured as a UNI or NNI line. An AutoRoute port and resource partition are added to the line.

Step 4 The BPX virtual trunk (the other end of the PXM1 line) is activated (upped) and added. MPLS partitions must be configured on the virtual trunks. A VPI is assigned to the virtual trunk.

Step 5 The BPX virtual trunks are identified to the LSC as MPLS trunks.

Step 6 The RPM on the MGX 8250 switch is initialized: The IOS image is loaded, and the ATM switch interface is active.

Step 7 Enable OSPF or IS-IS routing on the RPM. These are the recommended routing protocols for interior routing in MPLS networks.

Step 8 Activate Cisco Express Forwarding (CEF) on the RPM.

Step 9 Assign an area to the RPM. This area defines which devices this RPM can communicate with in the network. For example, if you assign area 100 to this RPM, all other RPMs it communicates with must also be assigned area 100.

Step 10 Create an MPLS subinterface on the RPM ATM switch interface.

Step 11 Assign an IP address to the subinterface.

Step 12 Enable MPLS on the subinterface.

Step 13 Create a VP tunnel on the subinterface. The VP tunnel is assigned a VPI number, which must be the same at both ends of the tunnel. The VPI number must also match the VPI assigned to the BPX virtual trunk in Step 4.

Step 14 Add an ATM PVP on the subinterface. The VPI for the PVP must match that of the VP tunnel.

Step 15 Add a VP connection to the PXM1 UNI or NNI line that is attached to the PXM switch. Make sure the connection VPI matches that of the PVP and VP tunnel. You must add both a master and a slave connection (one on the RPM, the other on the PXM1), because this is a local connection.

Step 16 Your RPM is now ready to function as an ELSR in the network.

You have completed the steps necessary for setting up MPLS on the MGX switch.

MPLS and Virtual Private Networks Using the Route Processor Module

Virtual Private Networks (VPNs) provide the appearance, functions, and usefulness of a dedicated private network. The VPN feature for MPLS allows a Cisco IOS network to deploy scalable IPv4 Layer 3 VPN backbone service with private addressing, controlled access, and service-level guarantees between sites.

VPNs are supported by service provider networks over which labeled packets are forwarded from RPM ELSRs to other RPM ELSRs. A VPN service creates multiple private network environments within the public infrastructure. Service providers can use VPNs to target a given clientele and to deliver individualized private network services to that clientele in a secure IP environment by using the public infrastructure.

VPN Requirements

Here are the requirements for an effective VPN:

- **Privacy**—All IP VPN services offer privacy over a shared (public) network infrastructure, the most well-known solution of which is an encrypted tunnel. An IP VPN service must offer private addressing, in which addresses within a customer private network do not need to be globally unique.

- **Scalability**—IP VPN services must scale to serve hundreds of thousands of sites and users. An IP VPN service should also serve as a management tool for service providers to control access to services, such as closed user groups for data and voice services. Controlled access places performance limits on authorized programs, processes, or other systems in a network.

- **Flexibility**—IP VPN services must accommodate any-to-any traffic patterns and be able to accept new sites quickly, connect users over different media, and meet transport and bandwidth requirements of new intranet applications.

- **Predictable performance**—Intranet applications supported by an IP VPN service require different classes of service. The service level performance between customer sites must be guaranteed. Examples include widespread connectivity required by remote access for mobile users and sustained performance required by interactive intranet applications in branch offices.

MPLS VPN Features

Beyond the functions of an IP VPN, the VPN features for MPLS allow a Cisco IOS network to deploy the following scalable IPv4 Layer 3 VPN backbone services:

- **Connectionless service**—MPLS VPNs are connectionless. They also are significantly less complex because they do not require tunnels or encryption to ensure network privacy.

- **Centralized service**—VPNs in Layer 3 privately connect users to intranet services and allow flexible delivery of customized services to the user group represented by a VPN. VPNs deliver IP services such as multicast, QoS, and telephony support within a VPN, and centralized services such as content and Web hosting. Combinations of services can be customized for individual customers.

- **Scalability**—MPLS-based VPNs use a Layer 3 connectionless architecture and are highly scalable.

- **Security**—MPLS VPNs provide the same security level as connection-based VPNs. Packets from one VPN cannot accidentally go to another VPN. At the edge of a provider network, incoming packets go to the correct VPN. On the backbone, VPN traffic remains separate.

- **Easy to create**—Because MPLS VPNs are connectionless, it is easy to add sites to intranets and extranets and to form closed user groups. A given site can have multiple memberships.

- **Flexible addressing**—MPLS VPNs provide a public and private view of addresses, allowing customers to use their own unregistered or private addresses. Customers can freely communicate across a public IP network without network address translation (NAT).

- **Straightforward migration**—MPLS VPNs can be built over multiple network architectures, including IP, ATM, Frame Relay, and hybrid networks. There is no requirement to support MPLS on the customer edge (CE) router.

Supported Platforms

The MGX 8850 node with RPM supports VPNs, as do all Cisco routers from the 3600 series up, the 6400 series, and several other devices. Any LSR-capable platform can serve in the backbone including the LS 1010 ATM switch, the 8540 MSR, and the BPX 8650 switch. Non-MPLS-capable switches can also be used, because they can carry MPLS over PVCs or PVPs.

How Do VPNs Work?

Each VPN is associated with one or more VPN routing/forwarding instances (VRFs), which define a VPN at a customer site attached to a PE router. A VRF table consists of the following:

- IP routing table
- Derived Cisco Express Forwarding table
- Set of interfaces that use the forwarding table
- Set of rules and routing protocol variables that determine what goes into the forwarding table

VPNs for MPLS

A customer site can be a member of multiple VPNs. However, a site can be associated with only one VRF. A customer site's VRF contains all routes available to the site from the associated VPNs.

The IP routing table and CEF table for each VRF store packet-forwarding information. (Together, these tables are analogous to the forwarding information base [FIB] used in MPLS.) A logically separate set of routing and CEF tables is constructed for each VRF. These tables prevent packets from being forwarded outside a VPN and prevent packets outside a VPN from being forwarded to a router within the VPN.

VPN Route-Target Communities and Export and Import Lists

The distribution of VPN routing information is controlled through the use of VPN route-target communities, implemented by BGP extended communities. Distribution works as follows:

- When a VPN route is injected into BGP, it is associated with a list of VPN route-target communities. This list is set through an export list associated with the VRF from which the route was learned.

- Associated with each VRF is an import list of route-target communities that defines values to be verified by the VRF table before a route is deemed eligible for import into the VPN routing instance. For example, if a given VRF's import list includes community distinguishers A, B, and C, any VPN route carrying A, B, or C is imported into the VRF.

IBGP Distribution of VPN Routing Information

A PER learns an IP prefix from a CE router through static configuration, a BGP session, RIP, or OSPF. The PER then generates a VPN-IPv4 (vpnv4) prefix by linking an 8-byte route distinguisher to the IP prefix. The VPN-IPv4 address uniquely identifies hosts within each VPN site, even if the site uses globally nonunique (unregistered private) IP addresses. The route distinguisher used to create the VPN-IPv4 prefix is specified by a configuration command on the PER.

BGP uses VPN-IPv4 addresses to distribute network reachability information for each VPN within a service provider network. In building and maintaining routing tables, BGP sends routing messages within (interior BGP [IBGP]) or between (exterior BGP or [EBGP]) IP domains.

BGP propagates vpnv4 information using BGP multiprotocol extensions to handle extended addresses. Refer to RFC 2283, "Multiprotocol Extensions for BGP-4." BGP propagates reachability information (expressed as VPN-IPv4 addresses) among PE routers; reachability information for a given VPN is propagated only to members of that VPN. BGP multiprotocol extensions identify valid recipients of VPN routing information.

Label Forwarding

Based on the routing information stored in each VRF's IP routing and CEF tables, Cisco MPLS uses extended VPN-IPv4 addresses to forward packets to their destinations.

To achieve this, an MPLS label is associated with each customer route. The PE router assigns the route originator's label and directs data packets to the correct CE router. Tag forwarding across the provider backbone is based on dynamic IP paths or traffic-engineered paths.

A customer data packet has two levels of labels attached when it is forwarded across the backbone:

- The top label directs the packet to the correct PE router.
- The second label indicates how that PE router should forward the packet.

The PE router associates each CE router with a forwarding table that contains only the set of routes that are available to that CE router.

RPM Memory Locations

The RPM card module has several memory locations that it uses to store and manage software code, configuration information, and other information.

The RPM boot Flash is used to store a boot image. This boot image is used by the RPM if a suitable IOS image is unavailable. When you install a new RPM, the boot image is loaded, and you must configure the RPM to upload the IOS image from the PXM1 hard drive.

The startup configuration file is stored in nonvolatile random-access memory (NVRAM).

Dynamic random-access memory (DRAM) on the RPM is used to run the IOS software, and it stores a working copy of the configuration files. As soon as the initial RPM configuration is done, the RPM uploads the IOS image into DRAM.

Static random-access memory (SRAM) on the RPM is used for shared-memory switching of packets. This memory is used when routing data packets from one interface to another.

NOTE	Unlike many Cisco routers, the RPM does not support optional Flash cards.

The PXM1 has an IDE hard drive that the MGX switch uses to store firmware and configuration files. The RPM also utilizes this drive for IOS image and configuration storage. If you want to store the IOS image or RPM configuration file on the PXM hard drive, you must do so manually from the RPM CLI.

RPM Port Numbering

This section describes how RPM ports are numbered so that when you configure the RPM you can correctly identify the interfaces.

Definition

The port-numbering scheme on the RPM is as follows:

- LAN interfaces are identified as *chassis-slot/slot/port*.
- The top-rear interface card is slot 1.
- The bottom-rear interface card is slot 2.
- Ports are numbered 1 to 4 from top to bottom.
- The ATM cell bus interface is always port 1.

Cisco IOS Command-Line Interface

This section describes how to use the Cisco IOS command-line interface (CLI). This section is not intended to be a complete tutorial on IOS commands. Instead, it provides novice users with the fundamental skills to use the CLI.

It is assumed that you do not have experience on Cisco IOS products. However, it is highly recommended that you attend appropriate Cisco training courses before attempting to configure an RPM in a live network environment.

RPM CLI Access

The RPM CLI can be accessed using any of the following three methods:

- **Console port on the front of the RPM**—The RPM has an RJ-45 connector on the front of the card module. A PC or dumb terminal can be directly attached to this port with an EIA/TIA-232 to RJ-45 cable for CLI access. The console port is the only way to access the RPM CLI when the card module is first installed into an MGX chassis.

- **cc from another MGX card**—You can access the RPM CLI using the **cc** (change card) command from any of the other cards in the MGX switch. The ATM switch interface on the RPM must be enabled before you can use the **cc** command.

- **Telnet from a workstation, PC, or another router**—The RPM CLI can be accessed from a PC or workstation on any of the LANs attached to the RPM. Also, after the RPM is installed and has PVCs to other RPMs or routers in the network, you can Telnet to the RPM CLI remotely from these other devices.

CLI Modes

The RPM, like all Cisco routers, has seven modes of operation:

- **User EXEC mode**— Once you have logged into the router CLI, be aware that you will have limited read access to the status and configuration of the router in this mode.

- **Privileged EXEC mode**—In privileged EXEC mode, you can access detailed status and configuration information and modify the router's configuration files. To enter privileged EXEC mode, use the **enable** command. An additional password might be required to access privileged EXEC mode.

- **ROM monitor mode**—ROM monitor mode is used when a router is first initialized and does not have a configuration file. Interrupting the boot process with a keyboard break sequence also starts ROM monitor mode.

- **Setup mode**—Setup mode is a prompted configuration sequence that is used when a router is first initialized.

- **RX boot mode**—The boot helper software that is used if the router cannot access the Cisco IOS image.
- **Global configuration mode**—A mode in which configuration changes can be made that affect the general router operation. For example, changing the router host name is a global configuration command.
- **Other configuration modes**—Other configuration modes for modifying specific router elements are accessed from configuration mode. For example, to make configuration changes on an Ethernet interface, enter **interface ethernet 9/1/1** while in configuration mode.

Entering Commands

When you are logged into the RPM, you enter commands at the command prompt. Most commands can be abbreviated using a few letters, provided that the abbreviation is unique. For example, you can enter **sho int** instead of **show interface**. Entering **sho i** is not enough, because several keywords start with the letter i, such as **ip** and **ipx**. In this book, all commands and keywords are spelled out in their entirety.

The **Tab** key completes an abbreviated word or provides you with choices based on the letters you have entered. For example, if you enter **sho** and then press **Tab**, the system spells out **show** on the command line.

The **?** key provides the next keyword or parameter if you are unsure of your options. For example, if you enter **show ?**, the system displays a list of possible choices, such as **interface**, **configuration**, and **memory**.

Preceding a command with **no** negates most configuration commands. For example, to assign an IP address to an interface, use the **ip address** command. To remove an IP address from an interface, use the **no ip address** command.

Changing the RPM Configuration

Before making changes to a configuration file, you should view the file using one of the following commands:

- **show running-config**
- **show startup-config**

When you enter **configure terminal**, you execute the configuration commands from the terminal. In this case, you make changes to the running configuration.

If you want to make changes to a configuration file other than the current running configuration, you need to copy the file into the running configuration by entering one of the following commands:

- **copy startup-config running-config**—Copies the startup configuration into the running configuration. When this command is complete, you can use the **configure terminal** command to enter configuration mode.

- **copy c:***filename* **running-config**—Copies the configuration file named *filename* that is stored on the PXM hard drive into the running configuration. When this command is complete, you can use the **configure terminal** command to enter configuration mode.

NOTE   The configuration file named *filename* is stored in the RPM directory of the PXM hard drive.

- **copy tftp running-config**—Copies a configuration file from a Trivial File Transfer Protocol (TFTP) server into the running configuration. You are prompted for the server name or address and the filename. When this command is complete, you can use the **configure terminal** command to enter configuration mode.

If you want to go from a specific configuration mode (for example, interface configuration mode) to global configuration mode, use the **exit** command. From any configuration mode, press **Ctrl-Z** to exit. The changes you made are automatically stored in the running configuration file in RAM.

After you determine that the new configuration is correct, you must save your changes to the startup configuration file. Saving the changes ensures that the router uses the changes when you copy the startup configuration file into memory or perform a reload. Save the configuration using one of the following methods:

- **copy running-config startup-config**—Saves the configuration variables to the startup configuration file in NVRAM.

- **copy running-config c:***filename*—Saves the configuration variables to a file named *filename* on the PXM hard drive.

- **copy running-config** *tftp*—Saves the configuration variables to a remote server on the network. The variable *tftp* represents the target server type.

Example 22-15 shows an example of making a configuration change to the RPM.

Example 22-15 *Making a Configuration Change to the RPM*

```
RPM-PR_NY_9>enable
Password:

RPM-PR_NY_9#configure terminal
Enter configuration commands, one per line.  End with CNTL/Z.

RPM-PR_NY_9(config)#interface switch 9/1

RPM-PR_NY_9(config-if)#ip address 10.10.12.34 ?
  A.B.C.D  IP subnet mask

RPM-PR_NY_9(config-if)#ip address 10.10.12.34 255.255.255.0 ?
  secondary  Make this IP address a secondary address
  <cr>

RPM-PR_NY_9(config-if)#ip address 10.10.12.34 255.255.255.0

RPM-PR_NY_9(config-if)#^Z

RPM-PR_NY_9#copy running-config startup-config
Destination filename [startup-config]?
Building configuration...
[OK]

RPM-PR_NY_9#
```

Commands for Configuring the RPM

This section describes the commands you use to configure the RPM:

- **enable**—Accesses privileged EXEC mode. This command might require a password.
- **show running-config**—Displays the running configuration file.
- **show startup-config**—Displays the startup configuration file.
- **copy**—Copies a configuration file from one location to another.
- **reload**—Resets the RPM and loads the Cisco IOS image.
- **configure terminal**—Enters configuration mode so that you can modify a configuration file.
- **boot system**—Defines the location and filename of the IOS image for the RPM to boot from.
- **hostname**—Sets the RPM host name.
- **enable password**—Defines an enable password.

- **line**—Defines a user access line.
- **password**—Defines a user access line password.
- **rpmrscprtn**—Defines the resource partitions on the RPM.

Enable Command

The **enable** command starts privileged EXEC mode on the IOS CLI. Many of the commands for the RPM require that you be in privileged EXEC mode. The **enable** command might require a password.

When you enter privileged EXEC mode, the CLI prompt changes from *hostname>* to *hostname#*.

Show Running Configuration and Show Startup Configuration Commands

The **show running-config** and **show startup-config** commands output the running or startup configuration files. Use these commands to verify the RPM's configuration.

The output is often several screens in length. Use the **Spacebar** to move forward one screen; use the **Enter** key to move forward one line.

Example 22-16 shows the first of three screens for the **show running-config** output.

Example 22-16 show running-config *Output, Page 1*

```
Current configuration:
!
version 12.1
no service pad
service timestamps debug uptime
service timestamps log uptime
no service password-encryption
!
hostname rpm01
!
boot system c:rpm-js-mz.120-2.5.T
boot system c:rpm-js-mz.121-3.T
enable password cisco
!
!
!
!
!
ip subnet-zero
```

Example 22-16 show running-config *Output, Page 1 (Continued)*

```
!
cns event-service server
!
!
!
```

Example 22-17 shows the second of three screens for the **show running-config** output.

Example 22-17 show running-config *Output, Page 2*

```
interface Ethernet2/1
 no ip address
 no ip route-cache
 no ip mroute-cache
 shutdown
!
interface Ethernet2/2
 no ip address
 no ip route-cache
 no ip mroute-cache
 shutdown
!
interface Ethernet2/3
 no ip address
 no ip route-cache
 no ip mroute-cache
 shutdown
!
interface Ethernet2/4
 no ip address
 no ip route-cache
 no ip mroute-cache
 shutdown
!
```

Example 22-18 shows the third of three screens for the **show running-config** output.

Example 22-18 show running-config *Output, Page 3*

```
interface Switch1
 no ip address
 no ip route-cache
 no ip mroute-cache
 no atm ilmi-keepalive
!
!
ip classless
no ip http server
```

continues

Example 22-18 **show running-config** *Output, Page 3 (Continued)*

```
!
!
!
line con 0
 transport input none
line aux 0
line vty 0 4
 password cisco
 no login
!
rpmrscprtn PAR 100 100 0 255 0 3840 4000
addcon auto_synch off
end
```

Copy Command

The **copy** command copies a configuration file to a specified location. For example, you can save the running configuration file to the PXM1 hard drive. Use this command to save changes to the running configuration. In some cases, you are prompted to confirm the **copy** command.

Here is the **copy** command syntax:

```
copy <source> <destination>
```

Both the *source* and *destination* can be specified as the following:

- **running-config**—The running configuration stored in RAM.
- **startup-config**—The startup configuration stored in NVRAM.
- **c:***filename*—A configuration file named *filename* is stored on the PXM1 hard drive in the RPM subdirectory.
- *tftp*—A configuration file stored on a remote TFTP server. If you use this keyword, you are prompted for additional information, including the server's name or IP address and the filename.

For example, type **copy running-config startup-config** to copy the running configuration to the startup configuration. Type **copy startup-config c:start_lab_test** to copy the startup configuration to the PXM1 hard drive with a filename of start_lab_test.

Reload Command

The **reload** command reboots the RPM and loads the IOS image as specified in the startup configuration. Use this command after you configure the RPM to load the IOS image from the PXM1 hard drive.

You are prompted to confirm the reload. If the new IOS image is significantly different from the previous one, some configuration on the RPM might be changed or lost. Use caution when using this command.

Configure Terminal Command

The **configure terminal** command starts configuration mode from the terminal (CLI). Use this command when you want to change the RPM running configuration. When you start configuration mode, the CLI prompt changes from *hostname*# to *hostname* (config)#. You must be in privileged EXEC mode to issue the **configure terminal** command.

When you start configuration mode, you can make general configuration changes that affect the RPM as a whole (global configuration mode). You can make specific configuration changes by specifying an element on the RPM, such as an Ethernet interface. The CLI prompt changes to reflect the specific configuration mode. For an interface, the CLI prompt changes to *hostname*(config-if)#. Use the **exit** command to end a specific configuration mode.

After you finish making configuration changes, press **Ctrl-Z** to exit configuration mode. Remember to use the **copy** command if you want to save the changes to anywhere other than the running configuration.

Boot System Command

The **boot system** command specifies the IOS image that the RPM should load on startup. In most cases, you configure the RPM to load the IOS image from the PXM1 hard drive. It is possible to store the IOS image at other locations, such as a TFTP server. You must be in global configuration mode to use the **boot system** command.

Here is the **boot system** command syntax:

```
boot system c:filename
```

filename is the name of the IOS image on the PXM1 hard drive. The file must be in the RPM subdirectory on the PXM1.

For example, type **boot system c:rpm-js-mz.121-5.3.T_XT** to load the IOS image file rpm-js-mz.121-5.3.T_XT from the PXM1 hard drive.

Hostname Command

The **hostname** command sets the RPM host name. You must be in global configuration mode to use the **hostname** command.

Here is the **hostname** command syntax:

```
hostname <hostname>
```

hostname is a character string less than 63 characters in length. The host name must start with a letter, end with a letter or number, and have as interior characters only letters, digits, and hyphens. Valid host names are router, RPM-cardslot9, and San-Jose5. Host names 5-san-jose, san jose 5, and RPM#9.2 are invalid.

Enable Password Command

The **enable password** global configuration command sets a privileged EXEC password. It is recommended that you set up an enable password to prevent unauthorized users from changing the RPM configuration. You must set up an enable password if you want to remotely access the RPM CLI in any way (from the PXM1 or using Telnet) except from the console port on the RPM front card.

Here is the **enable password** command syntax:

```
enable password {0 | 7 | level} [level-number] <password>
```

The keyword and parameter options are as follows:

- **0**—An unencrypted password follows. If no option is specified, the password is encrypted and is not hidden.

- **7**—A hidden password follows. If no option is specified, the password is encrypted and is not hidden.

- **level**—Specifies a user EXEC-level password.

- *level-number*—The user EXEC level between 1 and 15.

- *password*—The password character string.

For example, type **enable password 0 cisco=enable** to change the enable password (unencrypted) to cisco=enable; type **enable password 123dog** to change the enable password (encrypted) to 123dog.

Line Command

The **line** global configuration command sets up user access lines on the RPM. The **line** command also starts line-specific configuration mode. When you are in this mode, you can change the access characteristics, such as the password, session timers, and event logging. You must set up user access lines to remotely access the RPM CLI.

NOTE   Vty ports must be configured with a password before you can **cc** to the RPM card.

Here is the **line** command syntax:

```
line {aux | console | vty} <first-line-number> <last-line-number>
```

The keyword and parameter options are as follows:

- **aux**—Configures the RPM auxiliary port.

- **console**—Configures the RPM console port.

- **vty**—Configures a virtual terminal. Virtual terminal lines include Telnet and PXM1 CLI sessions.

- *first-line-number*—The first line number of a range. Up to six virtual terminal lines are supported. The RPM auxiliary and console ports are always line number 0.

- *last-line-number*—The last line number of a range. This parameter is not specified for RPM auxiliary and console ports.

For example, type **line vty 0 4** to configure virtual terminal lines 0 to 4; type **line console 0** to configure the RPM console port.

Password Command

The **password** line-specific configuration command sets a password for accessing the RPM CLI from a line (auxiliary, console, or virtual terminal). You must specify a password for virtual terminal lines on the RPM if you want to remotely access the RPM CLI.

Here is the **password** command syntax:

```
password {0 | 7} <password>
```

The keyword and parameter options are as follows:

- **0**—An unencrypted password follows. If no option is specified, the password is encrypted and is not hidden.

- **7**—A hidden password follows. If no option is specified, the password is encrypted and is not hidden.

- *password*—The password character string.

For example, type **password 0 CLIpassword** to change the password (unencrypted) to CLIpassword; type **password mgx8850-2** to change the enable password (encrypted) to mgx8850-2.

RPM Resource Partition Command

Similar to other card modules in the MGX switch, the RPM must have resource partitions configured. The **rpmrscprtn** global configuration command sets up the partitions on the RPM. You must set up partitions before you can configure any connections on the RPM.

Here is the **rpmrscprtn** command syntax:

```
rpmrscprtn {par | tag | pnni} <ingress-percent> <egress-percent>
   <minimum-VPI> <maximum-VPI> <minimum-VCI> <maximum-VCI> <LCNS>
```

The keyword and parameter options are as follows:

- **par** (Portable AutoRoute), **tag** (MPLS), or **pnni**—The controller type you want to define.

- *ingress-percent*—The percentage of the ingress bandwidth on the ATM switch interface that can be allocated by the controller type. The aggregate of the ingress bandwidth across all three controllers can exceed 100 percent.

- *egress-percent*—The percentage of the egress bandwidth on the ATM switch interface that can be allocated by the controller type. The aggregate of the egress bandwidth across all three controllers can exceed 100 percent.

- *minimum-VPI*—The minimum VPI value that can be assigned on PVCs on this controller. The VPI ranges on the three controllers can overlap. Valid values are from 0 to 255.

- *maximum-VPI*—The maximum VPI value that can be assigned on PVCs on this controller. The VPI ranges on the three controllers can overlap. Valid values are from 0 to 255.

- *minimum-VCI*—The minimum VCI value that can be assigned on PVCs on this controller. The VCI ranges on the three controllers can overlap. Valid values are from 0 to 3840.

- *maximum-VCI*—The maximum VCI value that can be assigned on PVCs on this controller. The VCI ranges on the three controllers can overlap. Valid values are from 0 to 3840.

- *LCNS*—The total number of logical connections that can use this controller. Valid values are from 0 to 4047.

For example, type **rpmrscprtn par 100 100 0 255 0 3840 4047** to allow the PAR controller access to the full range of resources.

Commands for Setting Up the RPM ATM Switch Interface

This section describes the commands you use to set up the RPM ATM switch interface. The switch interface is the ATM interface between the RPM and the cell bus (PXM1).

- **show interface**—Displays the status of a specific interface or all interfaces on the RPM.

- **interface**—Creates or accesses the configuration of an interface or subinterface.

- **shutdown**—Disables an interface. The **no shutdown** command activates an interface.

Show Interface Command

The **show interface** command output lists detailed interface configuration and status information. You can specify a particular interface. Otherwise, all interfaces are listed.

Here is the **show interface** command syntax:

```
show interface [switch <slot-number>/<interface-number>.[subinterface-number]]
```

The keyword and parameter options are as follows:

- **switch**—This optional keyword shows the switch interface. If you do not specify a keyword, all interfaces are listed.

- *slot-number*—If you specify the **switch** keyword, you must specify the RPM card slot number.

- *interface-number*—If you specify the **switch** keyword, you must specify the interface number. For the RPM switch interface, the only valid value is 1.

- *subinterface-number*—You can also specify a subinterface number.

For example, type **show interface 9/1** to list information on the ATM switch interface of the RPM in slot 9. Type **show interface** to list information on all interfaces on the RPM.

Example 22-19 shows the **show interface switch** output.

Example 22-19 show interface switch *Output*

```
rpm01#sho int switch 9/1

Switch1 is up, line protocol is up
  Hardware is ENHANCED ATM PA
  MTU 4470 bytes, sub MTU 4470, BW 149760 Kbit, DLY 100 usec,
     reliability 255/255, txload 1/255, rxload 1/255
  Encapsulation ATM, loopback not set
  Keepalive not supported
  Encapsulation(s): AAL5
  4096 maximum active VCs, 6 current VCCs
  VC idle disconnect time: 300 seconds
  0 carrier transitions
  Last input never, output 00:00:00, output hang never
  Last clearing of "show interface" counters never
  Input queue: 0/75/0/0 (size/max/drops/flushes); Total output drops: 0
  Queueing strategy: Per VC Queueing
  5 minute input rate 0 bits/sec, 1 packets/sec
  5 minute output rate 1000 bits/sec, 1 packets/sec
     2090 packets input, 101234 bytes, 0 no buffer
     Received 0 broadcasts, 0 runts, 0 giants, 0 throttles
     0 input errors, 0 CRC, 0 frame, 0 overrun, 0 ignored, 0 abort
     2118 packets output, 179057 bytes, 0 underruns
     0 output errors, 0 collisions, 1 interface resets
     0 output buffer failures, 0 output buffers swapped out
```

Useful information in the **show interface switch** output includes the following:

- **Interface status**—Up or down
- **Line protocol status**—Up or down
- **Maximum Transmission Size (MTU)**—The largest packet size, in bytes, permitted on the interface
- **Bandwidth (BW)**—The interface bandwidth, in kbps
- **Encapsulation**—Always ATM
- Maximum number of virtual circuits (VCs) allowed
- **Current number of VCs**—The current number of VCs being used
- **Queue status**—The current queue status
- Ingress and egress traffic counters

You can clear the traffic counters using the **clear counters switch** command.

Interface Command

The **interface** global configuration command accesses interface-specific configuration mode. You also use the **interface** command to create a new subinterface. When you use the **interface** command, the CLI prompt changes from *hostname*(config)# to *hostname*(config-if)#.

Here is the **interface** command syntax:

```
interface [switch <slot-number>/<interface-number>.[subinterface-number]]
```

The keyword and parameter options are as follows:

- **switch**—This optional keyword shows the switch interface.
- *slot-number*—If you specify the **switch** keyword, you must specify the RPM card slot number.
- *interface-number*—If you specify the **switch** keyword, you must specify the interface number. For the RPM switch interface, the only valid value is 1.
- *subinterface-number*—You can also specify a subinterface number.

For example, type **interface switch 9/1** while in global configuration mode to configure the ATM switch interface on the RPM in card slot 9.

Shutdown Command

The **shutdown** interface-specific configuration command is used to deactivate an interface. Use the **no shutdown** command to activate an interface. By default, the ATM switch interface is inactive. You must activate it using the **no shutdown** command before the RPM can send and receive cells to and from the cell bus.

How to Set Up the RPM

This section describes the steps you must follow to set up the RPM in your MGX switch. This procedure assumes that the RPM is newly installed and is set with the factory defaults:

Step 1 Log into the active PXM1 using your user ID and password. This begins a CLI session.

Step 2 Type **cd C:/RPM**. This changes to the RPM directory on the PXM1 hard drive**.**

Step 3 Type **ll**. This lists the contents of the E:/RPM directory. Verify that the IOS image is on the PXM1 hard drive. The IOS image will have a name such as rpm-js-mz.121-5.3.T_XT.

Step 4 If the IOS runtime image you need is not on the PXM1 hard drive, download it from its source (such as PC or workstation) using a TFTP application. Make sure the file is put into the C:/RPM directory. This copies the IOS image to the PXM1 hard drive.

Step 5 Log into the RPM using the RPM console port. This starts a CLI session on the RPM.

Step 6 Type **enable**. This puts you in privileged EXEC mode.

Step 7 Type **configure terminal**. This starts global configuration mode.

Step 8 Type **boot system c:**<*filename*>, where *filename* is the IOS runtime image filename described in Step 3. This configures the RPM to download the IOS image from the PXM1 hard drive.

Step 9 Type **interface switch** <*slot-number*>**/1**. This starts interface-specific configuration mode.

Step 10 Type **no shutdown.** This brings up the RPM ATM switch interface.

Step 11 Press **Ctrl-Z**. This ends configuration mode.

Step 12 Type **copy running-config start-config**. This copies the running configuration to the startup configuration and saves the configuration changes you have made.

Step 13 Type **reload**. You are prompted to confirm the reload. The RPM reboots and loads the IOS image. This process takes a few minutes. If you are not directly attached to the RPM console, your CLI session ends.

Step 14 Log back into the PXM1. This starts a CLI session.

Step 15 Monitor the RPM using the **dspcds** command. This outputs the card status. The RPM becomes active when the process is complete.

Step 16   Log into the RPM using the RPM console port. This starts a CLI session on the RPM.

Step 17   Type **show interface switch** *<slot-number>*/**1** and verify that the ATM switch interface is up.

Step 18   Type **enable**. This puts you in privileged EXEC mode.

Step 19   Type **configure terminal**. This starts global configuration mode.

Step 20   Type **hostname** *<hostname>*. This configures the RPM host name.

Step 21   Type **enable password** {**0** | **7** | **level**} [*level-number*] *<password>*. This sets the enable password.

Step 22   Type **line vty** *<first-line-number> <last-line-number>*. This creates virtual terminal lines and starts line-specific configuration mode.

Step 23   Type **password** {**0** | **7**} *<password>*. This sets the virtual terminal access password.

Step 24   Type **exit**. This exits line-specific configuration mode and returns you to global configuration mode.

Step 25   Type **rpmrscprtn par** *<ingress-percent> <egress-percent> <minimum-VPI> <maximum-VPI> <minimum-VCI> <maximum-VCI> <LCNS>*. This creates a PAR partition on the RPM.

Step 26   Press **Ctrl-Z**. This ends configuration mode.

Step 27   Type **copy running-config start-config**. This copies the running configuration to the startup configuration and saves the configuration changes you have made.

Step 28   Log back into the PXM1. This starts a CLI session.

Step 29   Log into the RPM CLI by typing **cc** *<slot number>*. This starts a CLI session on the RPM and confirms communication on the cell bus between the PXM1 and RPM.

You have completed the steps necessary to set up the RPM in your MGX switch.

Configuring Subinterfaces

A *subinterface* is a logical interface on a physical interface such as the RPM ATM switch interface. Multiple subinterfaces can exist on a single physical interface.

A permanent virtual circuit (PVC) on the RPM is associated with a subinterface. You cannot terminate a PVC on the ATM switch interface. Some subinterfaces support multiple PVCs (multipoint); others support only one PVC (point-to-point). Figure 22-17 shows a multipoint subinterface and a point-to-point subinterface.

Figure 22-17 *Multipoint and Point-to-Point Subinterfaces*

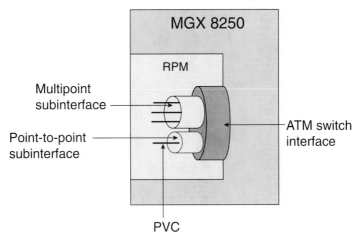

A subinterface is assigned one IP address regardless of the number of PVCs that terminate on it. In order for multiple PVCs to terminate on one subinterface, the IP addresses of all meshed subinterfaces must be on the same network or subnetwork.

Subinterface Example

Figure 22-18 shows two subinterfaces on the RPM. Each subinterface is identified as *chassis-slot/interface.subinterface*. The *chassis-slot* is the RPM's card slot number, the *interface* is always 1, and the *subinterface* is a number that identifies the subinterface.

Figure 22-18 *Subinterfaces on the RPM*

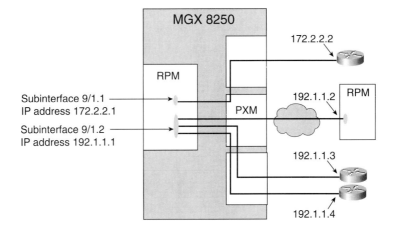

In Figure 22-18, one of the subinterfaces is point-to-point (9/1.1), and the other is multipoint (9/1.2). Notice how all interfaces that terminate PVCs on a subinterface share the same IP network address. For example, 192.1.1.2, 192.1.1.3, and 192.1.1.4 are the IP addresses on interfaces attached to subinterface 2, which has an IP address of 192.1.1.1.

PVCs on the RPM

In general, a PVC is a static connection between two interfaces on an ATM switch or between two ports on separate switches. A PVC requires an administrative action to establish, typically by a network administrator using a CLI or network management tool. As soon as a PVC is in place, it remains in place unless specifically removed by management action. The switch ports, or the set of resources on the ports that have been allocated to the connection, also remain dedicated for the lifetime of the PVC.

Strictly speaking, a PVC is a static connection in the network. In other words, the connection does not change, regardless of network events or changes. To confuse matters, many Frame Relay and ATM networks use the term PVC to refer to a dynamically routed virtual circuit. The BPX is an example of such a network. On the RPM, two configured elements comprise a PVC: the PVC and the ATM connection. The PVC is associated with a subinterface and is assigned a local identifier, VPI, and VCI. The PVC is often associated with an IP address for Layer 3 routing purposes. An ATM connection links the PVC to a destination endpoint such as another RPM, the PXM1 trunk, or any Frame Relay or ATM port on the MGX switch.

Figure 22-19 shows PVCs and ATM connections on the RPM.

Figure 22-19 *PVCs and ATM Connections*

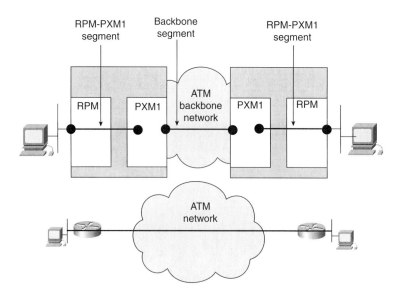

RPM connections can terminate on PXM1, FRSM, or AUSM cards, as shown in Figure 22-20.

Figure 22-20 *Terminating RPM Connections*

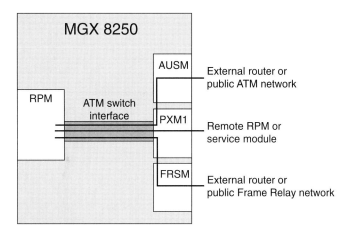

Similar to other MGX service modules, ATM connections on the RPM are either master or slave segments. A local connection has a slave connection at one end and a master connection on the other. A feeder connection has a master connection to the PXM1 trunk, a routing connection through the ATM backbone network, and a master connection on the remote MGX switch.

Commands for Configuring Subinterfaces

This section describes the commands you use to create and configure subinterfaces on the RPM ATM switch interface:

- **show interface**—Displays the status of a specific interface or all interfaces on the RPM.
- **interface**—Creates or accesses the configuration of an interface or subinterface.
- **shutdown**—Disables an interface or subinterface. The **no shutdown** command activates an interface.
- **ip address**—Assigns an IP address and subnet mask to a subinterface.

Show Interface Command

The **show interface** command output lists detailed interface and subinterface configuration and status information. You can specify a particular interface. Otherwise, all interfaces are listed.

Here is the **show interface** command syntax:

```
show interface [switch <slot-number>/<interface-number>.[subinterface-number]]
```

The keyword and parameter options are as follows:

- **switch**—This optional keyword shows the switch interface. If you do not specify a keyword, all interfaces are listed.

- *slot-number*—If you specify the **switch** keyword, you must specify the RPM card slot number.

- *interface-number*—If you specify the **switch** keyword, you must specify the interface number. For the RPM switch interface, the only valid value is 1.

- *subinterface-number*—You can also specify a subinterface number.

For example, type **show interface 9/1.100** to list information for subinterface 100 on the ATM switch interface of the RPM in slot 9. Type **show interface** to list information for all interfaces on the RPM. Example 22-20 shows the **show interface switch** output for a subinterface.

Example 22-20 show interface switch *Output*

```
rpm01>sho int switch 9/1.100

Switch1.100 is up, line protocol is up
  Hardware is ENHANCED ATM PA
  Internet address is 10.100.100.2/24
  MTU 4470 bytes, BW 149760 Kbit, DLY 100 usec,
     reliability 255/255, txload 1/255, rxload 1/255
  Encapsulation ATM
  0 packets input, 0 bytes
  9 packets output,531 bytes
  0 OAM cells input, 0 OAM cells output
```

Useful information in the **show interface switch** output includes the following:

- **Interface status**—Up or down
- **Line protocol status**—Up or down
- IP address
- **Maximum Transmission Size (MTU)**—The largest packet size, in bytes, permitted on the interface
- **Bandwidth (BW)**—The interface bandwidth in kbps
- **Encapsulation**—Always ATM
- Ingress and egress traffic counters

You can clear the traffic counters by using the **clear counters switch** command.

Interface Command

The **interface** global configuration command accesses interface-specific configuration mode. You also use the **interface** command to create a new subinterface.

When you use the **interface** command, the CLI prompt changes from *hostname*(config)# to *hostname*(config-if)#.

Here is the **interface** command syntax:

```
interface [switch <slot-number>/<interface-number>.[subinterface-number]]
    {point-to-point | multipoint | tag}
```

The keyword and parameter options are as follows:

- **switch**—This optional keyword shows the switch interface.

- *slot-number*—If you specify the **switch** keyword, you must specify the RPM card slot number.

- *interface-number*—If you specify the **switch** keyword, you must specify the interface number. For the RPM switch interface, the only valid value is 1.

- *subinterface-number*—You can also specify a subinterface number.

- **point-to-point**—Creates a point-to-point subinterface that supports only one PVC. You need to specify this keyword only when you are creating a new subinterface.

- **multipoint**—Creates a multipoint subinterface that supports multiple PVCs. You need to specify this keyword only when you are creating a new subinterface.

- **tag**—Creates a tag (MPLS) subinterface. You need to specify this keyword only when you are creating a new subinterface.

Shutdown Command

The **shutdown** interface-specific configuration command deactivates an interface. Use the **no shutdown** command to activate an interface. By default, a subinterface is active when you create it using the **interface** command.

IP Address Command

The **ip address** interface-specific configuration command is used to assign an IP address to a subinterface.

Here is the **ip address** command syntax:

```
ip address <IP-address> <subnet-mask>
```

The parameter options are as follows:

- *IP-address*—The IP address assigned to the subinterface. Remember when choosing an IP address that subinterfaces with PVCs between them must be on the same IP network. The IP address is entered in dotted-decimal format, such as 172.100.100.54.

- *subnet-mask*—The subnet mask used on the subinterface. Subinterfaces with PVCs between them should all be configured with the same subnet mask. The subnet mask is entered in dotted-decimal format, such as 255.255.255.0.

Commands for Creating and Displaying PVCs on the RPM

This section describes the commands you use to create, configure, and display PVCs and connections on the RPM:

- **atm pvc**—Creates an ATM PVC on an interface
- **show atm vc**—Displays the status of one or all ATM VCs on the RPM
- **map-group**—Assigns a map group to an interface
- **map list**—Creates or accesses the configuration of a map list
- **ip**—Assigns IP addresses to PVCs in a map list
- **show atm map**—Lists ATM mapping information
- **addcon**—Creates a connection between an RPM PVC and the PXM card
- **show switch connections**—Lists summary or detailed information for the connections on the RPM

ATM PVC Command

The **atm pvc** interface-specific configuration command adds a new PVC to a subinterface on the RPM. Remember that point-to-point subinterfaces support only one PVC; multipoint subinterfaces support multiple PVCs. You must create a PVC on the subinterface before you can add the ATM connection.

Here is the **atm pvc** command syntax:

```
atm pvc <VCD> <VPI> <VCI> <AAL-encapsulation> [inarp]
```

The keyword and parameter options are as follows:

- *VCD*—The virtual circuit descriptor is a unique number that identifies the PVC. Do not use VCD 1 or 2 because these are hard-coded for RPM management.
- *VPI*—The VPI value on the ATM cells created from the IP packets on this PVC. A VPI of 0 indicates that this PVC is a virtual channel connection (VCC). A nonzero value indicates that this is a virtual path connection (VPC). VPCs are used for MPLS edge routing. Remember to restrict VPI values to the range defined by the resource partitions.

- *VCI*—The VCI value on the ATM cells created from the IP packets on this PVC. Remember to restrict VCI values to the range defined by the resource partitions. Use VCI 0 for VPCs.

- *AAL-encapsulation*—The encapsulation method used by the RPM. The encapsulation options are aal5snap, used for ATM or translated ATM-Frame Relay services; aal5nlpid, used for transparent ATM-Frame Relay services; and aal5ciscoppp, used for PPP applications—usually frame forwarding connections from the FRSM.

- **inarp**—Enables inverse Address Resolution Protocol (ARP) updates on aal5snap PVCs.

NOTE   Additional options apply to the **atm pvc** command. For details, refer to the Cisco IOS documentation.

Show ATM Virtual Circuit Command

The **show atm vc** command lists summary or detailed information about the virtual circuits (VCs) on the RPM. Use this command to learn which VCs are configured on the RPM and their status.

Here is the **show atm vc** command syntax:

```
show atm vc [VCD]
```

If you type **show atm vc**, a summary of all VCs is output. If you specify a VCD, detailed information on the specified VC is output. Example 22-21 shows the **show atm vc** output.

Example 22-21 show atm vc *Output*

```
rpm01#sho atm vc

            VCD /                                 Peak  Avg/Min Burst
Interface   Name VPI   VCI  Type   Encaps    SC   Kbps  Kbps   Cells  Sts
1.1         11    0     11  PVC    SNAP      UBR  155000               UP
1.2         12    0     12  PVC    SNAP      UBR  149760               UP
1.66        66    0     66  PVC    SNAP      UBR  149760               UP
1.100       99    0     99  PVC    SNAP      UBR  149760               UP
1           1     0  65526  PVC    IPC       UBR  149760               UP
1           2     0  65528  PVC    IPC       UBR  149760               UP
1.101       101   6    400  PVC    SNAP      ABR   1200   500          UP
1.101       102   6    401  PVC    SNAP      ABR   1200   500          UP
1.101       400  10      0  PVC    CISCOPPP  UBR  149760               UP
```

The **show atm vc** output provides the following information:

- The interface or subinterface the VC is on

- The VCD, VPI, and VCI assigned to the VC

- The type of VC—PVC or tag
- The encapsulation method
- The service class
- The configured Peak Cell Rate (PCR)
- The average and minimum traffic rate
- The burst size in cells
- The VC status (UP or DOWN)

Example 22-22 shows the **show atm vc** output when a VCD is specified.

Example 22-22 show atm vc *Output*

```
rpm01#sho atm vc 102

Switch1.101: VCD: 102, VPI: 6, VCI: 401
ABR, PeakRate: 1200, Minimum Rate: 500, Initial Rate: 1200, Current Rate: 0
RIF: 16, RDF: 16
FRM cells received: 0, BRM cells received: 0
RM cells sent: 0
AAL5-LLC/SNAP, etype:0x0, Flags: 0x10820, VCmode: 0x0
OAM frequency: 0 second(s)
InARP frequency: 15 minute(s)
Transmit priority 3
InPkts: 0, OutPkts: 6, InBytes: 0, OutBytes: 168
InPRoc: 0, OutPRoc: 0, Broadcasts: 0
InFast: 0, OutFast: 0, InAS: 0, OutAS: 0
InPktDrops: 0, OutPktDrops: 0
CrcErrors: 0, SarTimeOuts: 0, OverSizedSDUs: 0, LengthViolation: 0,
CPIErrors: 0
Out CLP=1 Pkts: 0
OAM cells received: 0
OAM cells sent: 0
Status: UP
```

Map Group Command

The **map-group** interface-specific configuration command identifies a map group for a subinterface. Each multipoint subinterface must refer to a map group name. The associated map list identifies the destination IP addresses for each PVC that terminates on the subinterface. Use the **map-list** global configuration command to define the map list. Remember that PVCs on a subinterface terminate on interfaces that share the same IP network or subnetwork address.

Here is the **map-group** command syntax:

```
map-group <group-name>
```

group-name is a character string naming the map group. For example, type **map-group FRport5** to associate the subinterface with a map group named FRport5.

Map List Command

The **map-list** global configuration command is used to create a map list and to start map-list-specific configuration mode. When you use the **map-list** command, the CLI prompt changes from *hostname*(config)# to *hostname*(config-map-list)#.

Here is the **map-list** command syntax:

```
map-list <list-name>
```

list-name is the same as the group name specified for the subinterface using the **map-group** command. For example, type **map-list FRport5** to create or access the map list named FRport5.

IP Command

The **ip** map-list-specific configuration command associates an IP address with a VCD.

Here is the **ip** command syntax:

```
ip <IP-address> atm-vc <VCD> [broadcast]
```

The parameter options are as follows:

- *IP-address*—The IP address assigned to the VC. Remember when choosing an IP address that subinterfaces with PVCs between them must be on the same IP network. The IP address is entered in dotted-decimal format, such as 172.100.100.54.

- *VCD*—The VCD of the PVC.

Show ATM Map Command

The **show atm map** command lists the ATM mapping on the RPM. If you have map lists configured or are using ARP, you will have VCD-to-IP address mapping. Example 22-23 shows the **show atm map** output.

Example 22-23 show atm map *Output*

```
rpm01#show atm map

Map list port101 : PERMANENT
ip 10.10.15.2 maps to VC 101
        , broadcast
ip 10.10.15.3 maps to VC 102
        , broadcast
```

Add Connection Command

The **addcon** command adds an ATM connection on the RPM. This connection is similar to a connection on any other service module, such as the FRSM or AUSM. A number of optional parameters are supported for the **addcon** command. These optional parameters control ATM network routing and are not supported on PXM1 platforms.

Here is the **addcon** command syntax:

```
addcon vcc switch <slot-number>/<interface-number>.[subinterface-number]
  <VCI> [rname remote-name] rslot <remote-slot> <remote-interface>
  <remote-VPI> <remote-VCI> [master local]

addcon vpc switch <slot-number>/<interface-number>.[subinterface-number]
  <VPI> [rname remote-name] rslot <remote-slot> <remote-interface>
  <remote-VPI> [master local]
```

The keyword and parameter options are as follows:

- *VCI*—The VCI value defined for the ATM PVC. This parameter applies only to VCCs and should match the VCI of the ATM PVC that is already added to the RPM.

- *VPI*—The VPI value defined for the ATM PVC. This parameter applies only to VPCs and should match the VPI of the ATM PVC that is already added to the RPM.

- *remote-name*—The node name of the destination MGX switch. For PXM1 MGX switches, all connections terminate on the local switch, so this parameter is not used.

- *remote-slot*—The destination card slot number. 0 for the PXM1.

- *remote-interface*—The remote interface (port) number.

- *remote-VPI*—The remote VPI value on the destination card slot. If the destination service type is ATM, the VPI value can be any number that falls within the configured resource partitions on the destination card. If the destination card is an FRSM, the value is 0.

- *remote-VCI*—The remote VCI value on the destination card slot. This parameter applies only to VCCs. If the destination card is an FRSM, this parameter is the DLCI at the remote end.

- **master local**—These optional keywords identify the connection as a master connection. If you do not type **master**, the connection is a slave. Remember that all feeder connections to the PXM1 must be master connections. If this is a local connection, one end must be the master and the other end the slave. The slave end of the connection (whether on the RPM or a service module) must be added first. Only the **master local** keyword combination is used. Do not use the **master remote** keyword combination.

Show Switch Connections Command

The **show switch connections** command lists summary or detailed information about the connections on the ATM switch interface. Use this command to learn which connections are on the RPM and to learn how they are configured.

Here is the **show switch connections** command syntax:

```
show switch connections {vpc | vcc} [VPI] [VCI]
```

The keyword and parameter options are as follows:

- *vpc*—Use this keyword to show a specific VPC.
- *vcc*—Use this keyword to show a specific VCC.
- *VPI*—The VPI of the VPC you want to show. Use this optional parameter with the *vpc* keyword.
- *VCI*—The VCI of the VCC you want to show. Use this optional parameter with the *vcc* keyword.

Example 22-24 shows the **show switch connections** output.

Example 22-24 show switch connections *Output*

```
rpm01#show switch connections
                                                             Synch
lVpi   lVci   remoteNodeName   remoteSlot remoteIf  rVpi   rVci   Status

  0     11                         0        1        10    243    inSynch
 10      0                         0        1       200      0    inSynch
```

Example 22-25 shows the **show switch connections** output for a specified VCC.

Example 22-25 show switch connections *Output*

```
rpm01#show switch connections vcc 11

------------------------------------------------------------
Local Sub-Interface   : 1
Local VPI             : 0
Local VCI             : 11
Remote Node Name      :
Remote Slot           : 0
Remote Interface      : 1
Remote VPI            : 10
Remote VCI            : 243
Routing Priority      : 0
Max Cost              : 255
Restricted Trunk Type : none
Percent Util          : 100
Remote PCR            : 353208
```

continues

Example 22-25 **show switch connections** *Output (Continued)*

```
Remote MCR          : 353208
Remote Percent Util : 100
Connection Master   : Local
Synch Status        : inSynch
Auto Synch          : OFF
```

Creating Connections on the RPM

Follow these steps to create a connection on the RPM:

Step 1 Log into the RPM CLI.

Step 2 Type **show switch partitions** to confirm that there is a PAR resource partition on the RPM. Note the VPI and VCI ranges. If the partition is not there, use the **rpmrscprtn** global configuration command to create one. This outputs a list of all resource partitions on the RPM.

Step 3 Type **enable**. This prompts you for the enable password.

Step 4 Type the password. You enter privileged EXEC mode. The command prompt changes from > to #.

Step 5 Type **configure terminal**. This starts the configuration mode from the terminal.

Step 6 Type **interface switch** *<slot-number>* **/1.**[*subinterface-number*] {**point-to-point** | **multipoint**}, where *subinterface-number* is either an existing interface or a new subinterface. This enters interface configuration mode and creates a new subinterface.

Step 7 If you need to assign an IP address to the subinterface, type **ip address** *<IP-address> <subnet-mask>*. This assigns an IP address and subnet mask to the subinterface.

Step 8 Type **atm pvc** *<VCD> <VPI> <VCI> <AAL-encapsulation>* [**inarp**], where the *VPI* and *VCI* values are within the specified range of the PAR partition. For a VCC, the VPI must be 0; for a VPC, the VCI must be 0. This creates an ATM PVC on the subinterface.

Step 9 If you need to customize the PVC (for example, to set traffic shaping), refer to the IOS configuration guide for assistance.

Step 10 If this is a point-to-point subinterface, type **exit** and go to Step 15. If this is a multipoint subinterface and a map group is not already defined, type **map-group** *<group-name>*. This associates a map group to the subinterface.

Step 11 Type **exit**. You exit interface-specific configuration mode.

Step 12 Type **map-list** <*list-name*>, where *list-name* is the same as the map group name from Step 10. This adds a slave (master remote) connection on the RPM subinterface.

Step 13 Type **ip** <*IP-address*> **atm-vc** <*VCD*> [**broadcast**] for the VCD you created in Step 8. This associates an IP address to the ATM PVC.

Step 14 Type **exit**. This ends map-list-specific configuration mode.

Step 15 If you are adding a VCC, type **addcon vcc switch** <*slot-number*> **/1.**[*subinterface-number*] <*VCI*> [**rslot** <*remote-slot*> <*remote-interface*> <*remote-VPI*> <*remote-VCI*> [**master local**]. If you are adding a VPC, type **addcon vpc switch** <*slot-number*>**/1.**[*subinterface-number*] <*VPI*> **rslot** <*remote-slot*> <*remote-interface*> <*remote-VPI*> [**master local**]. This adds an ATM connection from the RPM PVC.

Step 16 Press **Ctrl-Z**. If you want to save the changes, type **copy running-config start-config**. This exits configuration mode and saves the configuration to the startup configuration.

Step 17 Type **show switch connection** {**vcc** | **vpc**} [*VPI*] [*VCI*]. This outputs the connection information. Verify the connection configuration.

Step 18 If the remote end of the connection is an RPM, log into the remote RPM and follow Steps 1 through 17. If the remote end is an FRSM or AUSM, create a connection on the remote card module as required. This creates a logical port and a master connection on the AXSM.

Step 19 If you are adding a local connection, you are finished. If you are adding a feeder connection, continue with Step 20.

Step 20 If you have a BPX backbone network, log into the BPX switch attached to one of your MGX switches. Type **addcon** <*local channel*> <*remote node*> <*remote channel*> <*connection class* | *connection type*> [*connection parameters*] [*route avoid*] to add an ATM routing connection through the BPX network. Be sure to match the VPI and VCI values in the BPX network with the values you used when you added the MGX connection segments. Use the **dspcons** and **dspcon** commands to verify the connection status.

Step 21 If you have an MGX 8850-PXM45 backbone network, log into the AXSM on the local switch and type **addcon** <*interface number*> <*vpi*> <*vci*> <*service type*> **2** [*parameters*], where **2** indicates the slave endpoint. Be sure to write down the endpoint ID (NSAP address, VPI, and VCI). Log into the AXSM on the remote switch and type **addcon**

<interface number> <vpi> <vci> <service type> **1** *<-***slave** *slave endpoint ID> [parameters]*, where **1** indicates the master endpoint, and the *slave endpoint ID* is as previously noted. This adds a routing connection through the MGX 8850-PXM45 network. Use the **dspcons** and **dspcon** commands to verify the connection status.

You have completed the steps necessary for creating a connection on the RPM.

Summary

This chapter provided an overview of VISM voice features, including voice over AAL2 and IP networks. It showed you how to add, configure, display, and verify voice connections. Voice over ATM on the VISM was discussed, and RPM memory locations were identified.

RPM port numbering was described, and the Cisco IOS CLI was presented. You learned commands for configuring the RPM and commands for setting up the RPM ATM switch interface. This chapter discussed PVCs on the RPM and how to configure subinterfaces. You also saw commands for creating connections and for creating and displaying PVCs on the RPM.

MPLS was introduced, with an outline and discussion of its business and technical advantages. The benefits of label switching were presented, with a discussion of the problems inherent in persistent loops due to network protocol conflicts. Cisco WAN switching products and features with MPLS support were also presented.

Review Questions

1 Mark the following statements as true or false.

A. _____ VISM supports both A-law and μ-law PCM encoding.

B. _____ VISM-Frame Relay connections are supported in the MGX network.

C. _____ Regardless of the configuration, VISM supports eight T1s or E1s per card.

D. _____ CAS signaling is sent on an AAL5 PVC when you are using VoAAL2.

E. _____ VoIP voice signaling is sent with voice traffic through the MGX network.

2 VISM-to-ATM connections are designed to support voice traffic between the VISM and a _____.

A. CESM

B. IGX UVM

C. Cisco 3810

D. TDM switch

E. Class 4 voice switch

3 What is the purpose of a connection identifier (CID)?

A. To associate an endpoint with a connection

B. To identify the IP address of the destination VISM

C. To determine the connection's destination node

D. To specify the number of channels assigned to a connection group

4 How are PCM voice samples segmented and reassembled into ATM cells?

A. AAL1

B. AAL2

C. AAL5

5 An AAL2 CPS-PDU is how many bytes in length?

6 How many PCM voice samples are transported in one ATM cell, assuming that multiplexing is not being done on the connection?

A. 10

B. 3

C. 48

D. It varies.

7 Match the command with its function.

_____ Enables VAD

_____ Creates a new connection identifier

_____ Creates an AAL2 PVC

_____ Configures a line for CAS or CCS

_____ Shows the VISM's voice mode

_____ Creates a voice channel and specifies the compression type

A. **cnfcompvad**

B. **addcid**

C. **addcon**

D. **dspcons**

E. **cnflnsig**

F. **addendpt**

G. **dspvismparam**

8 You want to create 16 endpoints on T1 line number 5, starting with timeslot 4. What must you type to accomplish this task?

A. **addendpt 1 5 4**

B. **addendpt 1 5 4 16**

C. **addendpts 1 1 16 4**

D. **addendpts 1 5 4 16**

E. **addendpts 5 5 1 16**

9 You want to test the time it takes for a voice cell to travel through the MGX network. Which command must you use?

10 You have tested a connection using the **tstcon** command. The test has failed. What could be the causes of the failure? (Choose three.)

A. The PXM1 trunk is failed.

B. The remote PXM1 card is failed.

C. The local VISM line is in alarm.

D. The remote VISM line is in alarm.

E. The multisegment connection is incomplete.

11 Where is the startup configuration usually stored?

A. DRAM

B. NVRAM

C. On an external TFTP server

D. On the hard drive on the PXM1

E. In Flash memory on a PCMCIA card

12 Where is the Cisco IOS image usually stored?

A. DRAM

B. NVRAM

C. On an external TFTP server

D. On the hard drive on the PXM1

E. In Flash memory on a PCMCIA card

13 An RPM Ethernet interface is referred to as 1/2/3. Which three of the following statements are true?

A. The RPM is in MGX card slot 1.

B. The RPM is in MGX card slot 3.

C. The Ethernet card is installed in the upper bay.

D. The Ethernet card is installed in the lower bay.

E. The Ethernet interface is the first one from the top.

F. The Ethernet interface is the second one from the top.

G. The Ethernet interface is the third one from the top.

14 You have an RPM installed in MGX card slot 11. How would you refer to the switch interface?

A. interface ATM11

B. interface switch 11

C. interface switch 11/1

D. interface switch 11:0

E. interface ATM0:11.1

15 How do you enter privileged EXEC mode?

A. Type **exec**.

B. Type **enable**.

C. Press Ctrl-Z.

D. You do nothing. This is the mode when you log in.

16 What must you type to save your configuration changes so that they are used when the RPM starts up?

A. **save startup**

B. **save running-config**

C. **copy running-config c:startup_file**

D. **copy running-config startup-config**

17 What command must you type to configure the RPM from the CLI?

18 Based on the portion of the **show running-config** output shown in Example 22-26, which of the following statements are true?

Example 22-26 show running-config *Output*

```
version 12.0
no service pad
service timestamps debug uptime
service timestamps log uptime
no service password-encryption
!
hostname rpm01
!
boot system c:rpm-js-mz.120-2.5.T
enable password cisco
!
ip subnet-zero
!
!
!
interface Ethernet9/2/1
 no ip address
 no ip directed-broadcast
 no ip route-cache
 shutdown
!
```

A. The enable password is hidden.

B. The enable password in encrypted.

C. The enable password is unencrypted.

D. The RPM loads the IOS image from a TFTP server.

E. The RPM loads the IOS image from its Flash memory.

F. The RPM loads the IOS image from the PXM1 hard drive.

19 You want to set up remote access to the RPM CLI from the PXM1. Which of the following configuration commands must you use?

A. **reload**

B. **line vty 0 4**

C. **line console 0**

D. **password 0 cisco**

E. **enable password cisco**

F. **boot system c:ios_image_file**

20 You need to save your configuration changes to a remote location for disaster recovery purposes. Which command must you use?

A. **copy startup-config running-config**

B. **copy running-config startup-config**

C. **copy RPM_config_june19 startup-config**

D. **save running-config c:RPM_config_june19**

E. **copy running-config c:RPM_config_june19**

F. **save running-config PXM RPM_config_june19**

21 You need to configure the RPM ATM switch interface. Which three commands must you use to start interface-specific configuration mode?

A. **enable**

B. **interface atm 0**

C. **configure terminal**

D. **interface switch 1/1**

E. **show interface switch 1/1**

F. **configure interface switch 1/1**

22 You are in interface-specific configuration mode for your RPM ATM switch interface. What command must you type to activate the interface?

23 How many PVCs can terminate on a point-to-point subinterface?

24 You are configuring a subinterface on your RPM. You want to terminate PVCs on two other subinterfaces in the network. These other subinterfaces are assigned IP addresses 10.10.15.6 and 10.10.15.7. What IP address should you assign to your subinterface?

A. 10.10.15.6

B. 10.10.15.8

C. 10.15.15.2

D. Any valid IP address

25 You are working on subinterface 2/1/25. Which of the following statements are true?

A. The RPM is in card slot 1.

B. The RPM is in card slot 2.

C. The RPM is in card slot 25.

D. This is subinterface number 1.

E. This is subinterface number 2.

F. This is subinterface number 25.

G. The RPM is installed in the upper bay.

H. The RPM is installed in the lower bay.

26 Identify which of the following characteristics are associated with a PVC and which are associated with the connection on an RPM.

_____ Local VPI

_____ Local VCI

_____ Subinterface

_____ Destination card module

27 On which card modules can you terminate RPM connections?

A. RPM

B. SRM

C. PXM1

D. FRSM

E. CESM

F. AUSM

28 Which of the following subinterfaces are valid?

A. interface switch 5

B. interface switch 1:1.1

C. interface switch 9.1.1

D. interface switch 9/2.63

E. interface switch 12/1.1

F. interface switch 7/0.100

G. interface switch 2/1.105

29 You want to find out if subinterface 25 on the RPM installed in slot 3 is up. What command and parameters must you type to accomplish this?

30 You want to learn how many PVCs are configured on your RPM. Which command should you use?

A. **dspcons**

B. **dsppvcs**

C. **show atm vc**

D. **show atm map**

E. **display atm pvcs**

F. **show switch connections**

31 You are adding a new connection from the RPM to the PXM1 feeder trunk. Which of the following commands is valid?

A. **addcon vpc switch 1 40 rslot 7 50 master local**

B. **addcon vcc switch 9/1.101 533 rslot 0 1 43 452**

C. **addcon vpc switch 9/1.2 32 rslot 7 43 master remote**

D. **addcon vcc switch 9/1.100 235 rslot 0 1 50 500 master local**

32 What is an Edge Label Switch Router or Label Edge Router?

A. A Cisco 4000 series router

B. A virtual path between two MGX switches

C. An MPLS router that controls the operation of an ATM switch

D. A core device that switches labeled packets according to predefined switching tables

E. An edge device that performs initial packet processing and classification and applies the first label

33 What is a Label Switch Router?

A. A Cisco 4000 series router

B. A virtual path between two MGX switches

C. An MPLS router that controls the operation of an ATM switch

D. A core device that switches labeled packets according to predefined switching tables

E. An edge device that performs initial packet processing and classification and applies the first label

34 Which of the following MPLS features are *not* supported on the RPM installed in an MGX PXM1 switch?

A. LSC function

B. 16 classes of service

C. The MGX switch as an LSR

D. The MGX switch as an LER

E. Interworking with the BPX switch

F. Interworking with PXM45 platforms

35 How many QoS classes are supported in the MPLS network?

36 Mark the following statements as true or false.

A. _____ VPNs allow different customers to use the same IP address.

B. _____ All packets for a given IP address are assigned the same label.

C. _____ When using VPNs, customers must have unique IP addressing schemes.

D. _____ A different label is assigned to packets in different traffic classes, even when they have the same IP address.

37 Mark the following statements as true or false.

A. _____ You cannot send MPLS traffic on the MGX feeder trunk.

B. _____ PVPs from RPM ELSRs terminate on a virtual trunk interface on the BPX switch.

C. _____ You must have an MPLS-enabled core network to support MPLS on an RPM installed in an MGX 8250 switch.

D _____ If you have a BPX ATM MPLS core network, you need to create full-mesh PVCs between all ELSRs in the network.

38 How many UNI or NNI (nonfeeder) lines can you set up on your MGX switch to carry MPLS traffic?

A. Only one.

B. Up to four.

C. It depends on the PXM1 hardware.

Answers to Review Questions

Chapter 2

1 What characteristic of cell or FastPacket traffic results in lower network delay?

Answer: Fixed-length cells require less processing to switch.

2 The IGX supports what kinds of services?

Answer: Voice, legacy data, Frame Relay, ATM

3 The IGX converts incoming voice, data, and Frame Relay user traffic into what?

Answer: FastPackets

4 What are circuits between IGX switches called?

Answer: Trunks

5 Which IGX reliability features protect against hardware and network failures?

Answer: Optional 1:1 redundancy, any topology is supported, distributed network database

6 List the five automatic fault-management features of IGX switches.

Answer: Hardware diagnostics, card and bus switchover, trunk diagnostics, dynamic rerouting, and alarm reporting

7 Why is it important to know which node is the "owner" of a connection?

Answer: Because the owner node determines the routing and rerouting in case of trunk failures.

8 The originating end card _____ the incoming data, and the receiving card _____.

Answers: packetizes, reassembles the FastPackets or cells into the original format

9 The Cellbus is what kind of bus?

Answer: Time-division multiplexed

Chapter 3

1 Commands are a combination of _____ and _____. The < > brackets indicate _____ parameters, and the [ ] brackets indicate _____ parameters.

Answers: nouns, verbs, required, optional

2 What are the four categories of command privilege levels?

Answers: StrataCom, Service, SuperUser, levels 1 to 6

3 Which command would you use to view summary information about the status of all node interfaces?

Answer: dspnds

4 Which command would you use to view a node's environmental conditions?

Answer: dsppwr

5 In checking the interfaces' status, you see that one interface displays "Standby-F." This indicates that the card is what?

Answer: idle (self-test failure)

6 To define the node name, you use the _____ command and specify a name that is _____ characters long.

Answers: cnfname, one to eight

7 To define the date, you use the _____ command. To define the local time zone, you use the _____ command.

Answers: cnfdate, cnftmzn

8 Which command would you use to specify the control and auxiliary port configuration parameter?

Answer: cnfterm

9 Which command would you use to specify printer characteristics and modes?

Answer: cnfprt

10 What are the three printer modes?

Answers: local, remote, none

11 Which command would you use to discover which trunks exist in the network?

Answer: dspnw

12 To display trunk configuration details, use the _____ or _____ command, and to modify them, use the _____ command.

Answers: dsptrkcnf, dsptrk, cnftrk

13 In what order do you use the **dntrk** and **deltrk** commands in order to deactivate a trunk?

Answer: deltrk, dntrk

14 True or false: The **addcon** command is used to activate a trunk, but not until both ends of the trunk have been enabled with the **uptrk** command.

Answer: False

15 Which command would you use to determine the status of all lines on the node?

Answer: dsplns

16 The _____ command activates a line, and the _____ command modifies a line's configuration parameters.

Answers: upln, cnfln

17 In an IGX network, a _____ is defined as a T1, E1, T3, E3, or OC3c/STM1 digital transport facility, carrying information between the node and an _____.

Answers: line, external device

18 What are the total user channels available on T1, E1, and J1 voice or data lines?

Answer: 24, 30, or 31

Chapter 4

1 What is a point-to-point PVC that provides service for user devices in an IGX network?

Answer: connection

2 What is the silence-suppression technique supported on CVM and UVM cards?

Answer: Voice Activity Detection (VAD)

3 Which command creates a new connection in the network?

Answer: addcon

4 Which command checks all the connections on a node?

Answer: dspcons

5   What is the endpoint of a voice connection?

Answer: channel

6   The item that defines the on-hook condition and conditioning template is the
_____, which is defined using the _____ command.

Answers: signaling type, cnfvchtp

7   What command would you use to view the configuration of a range of voice channels
on a single line?

Answer: dspchcnf

8   What two commands would you use to modify receive and transmit signaling?

Answers: cnfrcvsig, cnfxmtsig

9   Which command displays a channel's echo canceller configuration?

Answer: dspchec

10   What is the algorithm used to minimize the transmission of repetitive data patterns in
the incoming data stream?

Answer: Data Frame Multiplexing (DFM)

11   Which command eliminates a connection?

Answer: delcon

12   What command would you use to configure the control signal sampling rate?

Answer: cnfcheia

13   What command would you use to configure channel bandwidth allocation?

Answer: cnfchutl

14   Which command modifies an interface control template?

Answer: cnfict

15   What command would you use to modify a data channel's clock mode?

Answer: cnfdclk

16   What command would you use to view the current settings of an interface control
template?

Answer: dspict

Chapter 5

1 What is the interface between the network and a single external Frame Relay device?

Answer: Frame Relay port

2 List the steps to activate a Frame Relay port on a UFM-C card.

Answers: 1. Confirm that the line is enabled (dsplns), 2. Create a logical Frame Relay port (addport), 3. Configure the port (cnfport), 4. Activate the port (upport).

3 To verify line configuration, use the _____ command, and to check an individual port, use the _____ command.

Answers: dsplns (or dspln), dspport

4 Which command would you use to modify port parameters?

Answer: cnfport

5 Which command would you use to create a logical Frame Relay port?

Answer: addport

6 List the command and parameters used to display the Port, ID, Speed, Interface, State, and Protocol fields in the display.

Answer: dspport [*slot*]

7 While displaying port statistics, some ports might have corrupt statistics. What might be the cause?

Answer: A loopback might have occurred since the statistics were last cleared. If so, the display would indicate "yes" in the Corrupt field.

8 When a frame is received with a CRC error, is the CRC regenerated correctly before the frame is passed on?

Answer: CRC errors are not corrected. Frames received with CRC errors are discarded.

9 When clearing port statistics, some statistics cannot be cleared. Why?

Answer: The clrportstats command can clear only statistics that are present longer than 1 minute.

10 What is a point-to-point VC that provides transport services for an attached user device in an IGX network?

Answer: connection

11   What is ForeSight?

Answer: It is a closed-loop, relative-rate traffic management mechanism designed to adjust network Frame Relay traffic to efficiently utilize available bandwidth without loss.

12   Which commands modify and display connection parameters?

Answers: cnfcon, dspcon

13   Which commands modify and display the ten Frame Relay classes?

Answers: cnfcls, dspcls

14   Which command would you use to specify high- or low-priority connections?

Answer: cnfchpri

Chapter 6

1   Which command lists all ATM and Frame Relay ports?

Answer: dspports

2   Which command displays port details?

Answer: dspport

3   Which command activates an ATM port?

Answer: upport

4   List the port queues available on a UXM port.

Answer: CBR, rt-VBR, nrt-VBR, ABR

5   Which command modifies ATM port queues?

Answer: cnfportq

6   UXM supports which ATM connection types?

Answer: CBR, rt-VBR, nrt-VBR, ABR, UBR

7   What three things locally identify an ATM connection associated with a UXM card?

Answer: port, VPI, VCI

8   Which command establishes an ATM connection between two lines in the network?

Answer: addcon

9   Which command displays ATM connections?

Answer: dspcons

10 Which command sets the ABR VC queue depth?

Answer: cnfcon

11 Which command modifies the percent utilization of the connection bandwidth?

Answer: cnfcon

12 What does standards-based ABR use to carry flow control information?

Answer: RM cells

13 Which feature allows an IGX to insert RM cells into a user's traffic stream?

Answer: VSVD

14 True or false: The rate increase factor and rate decrease factor must be the same size.

Answer: False

Chapter 7

1 How is **dspload** information different from **dsptrkutl** information?

Answer: dspload describes allocated bandwidth for connection admission control purposes, and dsptrkutl shows the actual trunk usage.

2 What is the purpose of the statistical reserve?

Answer: Statistical reserve is a portion of bandwidth used to carry IGX common control traffic and to accommodate user bursts.

3 Which command specifies a certain route for a connection?

Answer: cnfpref

4 True or false: The **dsprts** command shows all terminating or through connections on this node.

Answer: False. The dsprts command displays routes for terminating connections only.

5 Connections in CoS Class 10 have a _____ connection rerouting priority than connections in CoS Class 1.

Answer: lower

6 What are the three IGX network clock source levels?

Answer: primary, secondary, tertiary

7 By default, which trunks pass clock?

Answer: T-1, E-1

8 Which command would you use to view clock sources in the network?

Answer: dspclksrcs

9 To avoid unnecessary clock disruptions, configure the _____ clock source for the network first.

Answer: primary

10 What are the clock line types?

Answers: line (l), external (e), trunk (t)

11 Which command would you use to delete the clock alarm on circuit line 7.1?

Answer: clrclkalm c 7

12 True or false: Using a specific job number as part of the **stopjob** command causes only that job to be stopped.

Answer: False. The stopjob command stops *all* executing or waiting commands.

13 The **deljobtrig** command deletes how many job trigger(s) at a time?

Answer: 1

Chapter 8

1 Contrast the effects of major and minor alarms.

Answer: A major alarm affects service and traffic due to failed connections. A minor alarm might affect service, but it does not necessarily affect traffic. Minor alarms do not result in failed connections.

2 Which two commands display the alarm status of all nodes in the network?

Answers: dspnw, dspnds

3 Which command displays a history of alarms and when they occurred?

Answer: dsplog

4 Which command would you use to clear accumulated statistics on trunks?

Answer: clrtrkerrs

5 Which command sets line and trunk alarm thresholds for statistical alarms?

Answer: cnflnalm

6 When you test connections, what are the possible results?

Answers: completed, aborted, failed, repaired

7 If an external device supports loopback, the loopback is configured using which command?

Answer: addextlp

8 When loopback testing is complete, you should use which command to delete the loop?

Answer: dellp

9 Which command indicates that a connection is looped?

Answer: dspcons

10 How will you know when the testing of connections is finished?

Answer: The T disappears.

Chapter 9

1 What is a BPX node?

A. ATM switch

B. ATM access device

C. Multiprotocol access device

D. Multiprotocol packet switch

Answer: A

2 Which of the following functions does the BPX node perform?

A. Switches ATM cells

B. Can be a feeder node in a tiered network

C. Segments and reassembles Frame Relay frames

D. Supports CBR, VBR, ABR, and UBR ATM traffic

E. Communicates with a CWM network management station

F. Can provide PNNI signaling and routing

G. Performs MPLS switching

Answers: A, D, E, F, G

3 Match the service type with its definition.

1. _____ CBR   A. Variable-rate traffic without a service guarantee

2. _____ rt-VBR   B. Bursty traffic with low delay sensitivity

3. _____ ABR   C. Time-dependent variable-rate traffic—compressed voice, data, and video

4. _____ nrt-VBR   D. Variable-rate traffic with congestion avoidance—router LAN-WAN traffic

5. _____ UBR   E. Time-dependent constant-rate traffic—uncompressed voice, data, and video

Answers: 1 E, 2 C, 3 D, 4 B, 5 A

4 Which one of the following fault management functions does the BPX node *not* perform?

A. Bus switchover

B. Card module self-tests

C. N:1 card module redundancy

D. Dynamic connection rerouting

E. Automatic alarm reporting to CWM stations

Answer: C

5 Of the following elements, which three are part of the BPX switch?

A. Fan assembly

B. AC power shelf

C. Crosspoint switch

D. 32-card slot chassis

E. Multishelf bus cable

F. Standalone cabinet with front and back doors

Answers: A, B, C

6 Which card slots are reserved for the BCCs and the ASM?

A. 1, 2, and 3

B. 7, 8, and 11

C. 7, 8, and 15

D. 1, 2, and 15

Answer: C

7 Of the following devices, which two use a BXM card to attach to a BPX switch?

A. Cisco 7000 router

B. Cisco LightStream 1010 ATM switch

C. MGX shelf with a BXM trunk card

D. IGX switch with a BTM or ALM/B trunk card

E. BPX switch with a BXM trunk card

Answers: B, E

8 Mark the following statements as true or false.

A. _____ BPX nodes support up to 15 service modules.

B. _____ The maximum number of trunks on a single BXM card is 12.

C. _____ Slots 7, 8, and 15 are reserved for core controller cards.

D. _____ APS 1:1 provides card and line redundancy.

E. _____ APS 1+1 provides card and line redundancy.

Answers: F, F, T, F, T

9 The BME back card connects to which of the following?

A. Another BME with a 622 Mbps back card

B. BXM with a 622 Mbps back card

C. Itself

D. None of the above

Answer: C

10 Which of the following are features of the BPX system software?

A. Support for routing and feeder nodes

B. Connection admission control for PVCs, SVCs, and SPVCs

C. Automatic routing and rerouting of trunks following a node failure

D. IP routing with MPLS

E. VSI master capability

F. Automatic bus switchover

Answers: A, B, C, F

11 Mark the following statements as true or false.

A. _____ PPD, EPD, and CAC are examples of FBTC.

B. _____ All cells entering the network are subject to policing.

C. _____ QBins service up to 16 different traffic types.

D. _____ ForeSight and ABR Standard both cause cell discard in trunk queues.

Answer: F, T, F, F

12 Which of the following are functions of the ASM?

A. Monitors DC power voltage thresholds

B. Senses the presence of other cards in the chassis

C. Generates a major alarm in the event of a fan failure

D. Transmits alarm messages to an external device

E. Notifies the network administrator if the cabinet temperature exceeds the configured threshold

Answers: A, D, E

13 How many crosspoints are used in the BCC-4 crosspoint switch matrix?

A. 256

B. 392

C. 196

D. 512

Answer: B or D

14 When does the BBC-4 arbiter permit two cells to be transmitted to a single card?

A. Only when source and destination cards are all BXMs

B. Whenever two cards ask to transmit to the same BXM card

C. When two cards ask to transmit to the same BXM during the same polling cycle

D. If a card received a Wait command during the previous cycle

Answer: C

15 Which of the following are functions of the BXM?

A. Ingress policing for ABR connections

B. Signaling protocols on UNI interfaces

C. Generation of RM cells for ABR VS/VD

D. CAC for new PVCs and SVCs

E. Trunk interface to any Cisco WAN switch trunk card

Answers: A, B, C

16 Which of the following BXM card modules support APS?

A. BXM-155-8

B. BXM-622-1

C. BXM-622-2

D. BXM-E3-12

E. BXM-155-4

F. All of the above

Answers: A, B, C, E

17 What is the major difference between the BCC-4 and the other BCC card modules?

A. The BCC-4 is less expensive.

B. The BCC-4 has a faster polling cycle.

C. The BCC-4 has a 16×32 crosspoint switch.

D. The BCC-4 is needed to support the system software.

E. The BCC-4 allows all cards to transmit and receive two cells simultaneously.

Answer: C

18 Mark the following statements as true or false.

A. _____ You must use a BCC-4 if you have BXM cards.

B. _____ Up to 32 cells can be switched at the same time.

C. _____ Only the BXM card can receive two cells at a time.

D. _____ The crosspoint switch can support 14 input paths and 28 output paths.

E. _____ The arbiter polls each active card module once every 200 microseconds.

F. _____ Up to three cards can transmit cells to the same destination card simultaneously.

Answers: F, F, T, T, F, F

19 Mark the following statements as true or false.

A. _____ PNNI uses distance-vector routing.

B. _____ PNNI is based on newly developed protocols and standards.

C. _____ PNNI uses link-state routing.

D. _____ PNNI is based on existing protocols and standards.

Answers: F, F, T, T

20 Which of the following is *not* specified by the PNNI standard?

A. Network topology

B. UNI cell format

C. Network routing

D. All of the above

Answer: B

Chapter 10

1 Which of the following is not a valid choice of access method for a first-time installation?

A. Cisco WAN Manager

B. PC with terminal emulation

C. VT100-compatible terminal

D. UNIX workstation with a serial interface

Answer: A

2 What are the default settings for the control and auxiliary ports?

A. 9600, odd, 8, and 1

B. 9600, even, 7, and none

C. 9600, none, 8, and none

D. 9600, none, 8, and 1

Answer: D

3 Commands are a combination of _____ and _____. The < > brackets indicate _____ parameters, and the [ ] brackets represent _____ parameters.

Answers: verbs, nouns, required, optional

4 What are the four categories of command privilege levels?

Answers: 1 to 6, Cisco, Service, SuperUser

5 Which of the following devices *cannot* be attached to the auxiliary port?

A. Serial printer

B. Dumb terminal

C. Dial-out modem

D. Router console port

E. Cisco WAN Manager workstation

F. PC running VT100 terminal emulation

Answer: E

6 Which command lists recently issued commands?

Answer: .

7 Match the command-line access method with its definition.

1. _____ IP Relay   A. A 15-pin AUI port connected to Ethernet

2. _____ LAN port   B. The default CLI access using a VT100 terminal

3. _____ Control port   C. A secondary serial port often used for a dial-in modem

4. _____ Auxiliary port D. A method to Telnet to a node inband through the BPX network

Answers: 1 D, 2 A, 3 B, 4 C

8 Mark the following statements as true or false.

A. _____ The **Esc** key aborts a command.

B. _____ All commands have required and optional parameters.

C. _____ Most commands consist of an abbreviated verb and noun.

D. _____ A command is complete when all required parameters have been defined with appropriate values.

E. _____ The BPX node prompts you for all required and optional parameters when you use the prompted entry mode.

Answers: F, F, T, T, F

9 What is the purpose of the **help** command?

A. To teach you how to configure a BPX node

B. To identify a command's definition and syntax

C. To define the value range of a connection's required parameters

D. To provide a detailed description of the use of each command

Answer: B

10 Which of the following requirements must be met when you assign a BPX node name?

A. Node names are case-sensitive.

B. Node names must start with a letter.

C. A node name can contain up to ten characters.

D. Node names must be unique within the network.

E. Any keyboard character can be used in a node name.

Answers: A, B, D

11 Mark the following statements as true or false.

A. _____ User IDs and passwords are network-specific.

B. _____ The default password is newuser.

C. _____ You can display the password of any user who has an equal or lower access privilege than yourself.

D. _____ A user ID with a privilege level of 1 can perform all of the commands available to a user ID with a privilege level of 0.

Answers: T, T, F, F

12 Which of the following commands display the current cabinet temperature?

A. **dspasm**

B. **dspcd**

C. **cnfasm**

D. **dsppwr**

Answers: A, C, D

13 Mark the following statements as true or false.

A. _____ Cabinet temperature in excess of the configured threshold generates a major alarm.

B. _____ If the **dspcds** command shows a front card type of BDR, the firmware revision is R.

C. _____ Cards can be in an active and failed condition at the same time.

D. _____ All cards provide the same information when you use the **dspcd** command.

E. _____ Cabinet temperature in excess of the configured threshold generates a minor alarm.

Answers: F, T, T, F, T

14 Mark the following statements as true or false.

A. _____ You can attach a printer to either the control or auxiliary port.

B. _____ A printer configured for log printing prints events for its local node only.

C. _____ Configuring a node for remote printing redirects all log events for printing at that node.

D. _____ The remote print option only applies to CLI print commands.

E. _____ You can have multiple log printers in the network.

Answers: F, F, T, F, T

15 Which of the following devices should you be able to access using the **window** command?

A. The control port on a BPX switch

B. The auxiliary port on a BPX switch

C. The Ethernet port on a Cisco router

D. The console port on a Cisco router

E. The Ethernet port on a BPX switch

Answers: A, B, D

16 When defining the IP addresses for a network with CWM, which of the following are required?

A. LAN port, IP Relay, and default gateway addresses on the same subnet

B. LAN port, IP Relay, and default gateway addresses on different subnets

C. IP Relay addresses for all nodes

D. LAN port addresses for all nodes

E. LAN port and IP Relay addresses on separate subnets

F. LAN port address on at least one node

Answers: C, E, F

17 Match the command with its primary function.

1. _____ **bye**   A. Ends the CLI session

2. _____ **dspcd**   B. Modifies your password

3. _____ **dspcds**   C. Lists all cards in the node

4. _____ **cnfasm**   D. Modifies the environmental alarm thresholds

5. _____ **dspasm**   E. Shows a card's status and serial number

6. _____ **cnfpwd**   F. Shows the status of the power supplies and fans

Answers: 1 A, 2 E, 3 C, 4 D, 5 F, 6 B

18 Mark the following statements as true or false.

A. _____ The **Delete** key can be used to abort a command.

B. _____ The abbreviation "dis" means "display" on the BPX CLI.

C. _____ Cards can be in both an active and failed condition at the same time.

D. _____ All cards provide the same information when you use the **dspcd** command.

Answers: T, F, T, F

19 Assume that a card is reporting QRS as the revision when you use the **dspcds** or **dspcd** command. Match each letter with the information it provides.

1. _____ Q   A. Hardware revision

2. _____ R   B. Firmware revision, which is a variation on the model

3. _____ S   C. Model, which determines the feature set on the card

Answers: 1 C, 2 A, 3 B

Chapter 11

1 How many virtual trunks can you terminate on a single port on a BXM card?

A. 4

B. 11

C. 31

D. 32

E. 64

Answer: C

2 What is a virtual trunk?

A. A way to remotely log into another BPX service node in the network

B. A trunk that attaches a BPX service node to another vendor's ATM switch

C. An ATM connection in a BPX network that carries traffic for another switch network

D. A trunk that utilizes a public ATM service to carry the cell traffic from one BPX service node to another BPX service node

Answer: D

3 What is the purpose of resource partitioning on a trunk?

A. To allocate the available port groups to different VSI controllers

B. To allocate specific resources between VSI controllers and AutoRoute PVCs

C. To ensure that physical and virtual trunks do not compete for physical interfaces on the BXM card

D. To provide guaranteed bandwidth for different traffic types such as CBR, VBR, and ABR

Answer: B

4 Mark the following statements as true or false.

A. _____ All models of BXM cards support two port groups.

B. _____ You can allocate more LCNs to multiple partitions than are shown by the **dspcd** command.

C. _____ Virtual trunks cannot support both AutoRoute PVCs and MPLS VCs.

D. _____ As soon as a resource is allocated to one VSI partition, it is unavailable for use by a different controller.

E. _____ Only physical trunks support multiple partitions.

Answers: F, F, T, T, F

5 You have successfully upped the trunk, but the **addtrk** command fails. What could be possible reasons for this?

A. ATM cell scrambling is configured differently at each end.

B. The other end of the trunk has not been upped.

C. The transmit rate has been configured differently at each end.

D. There is a mismatch in the cell-framing configuration.

Answer: A

6 Mark the following statements as true or false.

A. _____ Some trunk parameters do not apply to all trunk types.

B. _____ Cell scrambling affects the alarm condition of an upped trunk.

C. _____ The **addtrk** command must be issued before the **uptrk** command.

D. _____ All configuration parameters can be configured when a trunk is added.

E. _____ When deactivating a trunk, you must delete a trunk before it can be downed.

Answers: T, T, F, F, T

7 Which of the following events generates a major network alarm?

A. Card self-test failure

B. ATM port communication failure due to ILMI breakdown

C. Loss of signal on a network trunk

D. Missing processor in a redundant configuration

E. Cabinet temperature above the configured threshold

Answer: E

8 Mark the following statements as true or false.

A. The ASM reports MGX shelf alarms.

B. The **dspalms** screen summarizes all alarms on a node.

C. You can clear statistical trunk alarms with the **clrtrkalm** command.

D. The **cnftrkalm** command allows you to define major and minor alarm thresholds on a trunk.

E. A large value in the ETS indicates the presence of a momentary fault condition.

Answers: T, T, T, F, F

9 Match each of the following trunk configuration parameters with its description.

1. _____ Loop clock	A. A portion of trunk bandwidth reserved for SVCs
2. _____ SVC bandwidth	B. The number of connections allowed on a virtual trunk
3. _____ Statistical reserve	C. A way to use the receive clock in the transmit direction
4. _____ Frame scrambling	D. A portion of bandwidth that cannot be allocated to connections
5. _____ Transmit trunk rate	E. A standards-based method for rearranging the SONET trunk frame
6. _____ Connection channels	F. The maximum number of data cells permitted on a trunk per second

Answers: 1 C, 2 A, 3 D, 4 E, 5 F, 6 B

10 What is the difference between a UNI cell and an NNI cell?

A. A UNI cell has a bigger payload than an NNI cell.

B. The UNI cell is defined by the ATM Forum, and the NNI cell is not.

C. The UNI cell has an 8-bit VPI field, and the NNI cell has a 12-bit VPI field.

D. UNI cells are created only by routers; NNI cells are created only by switches.

Answer: C

11 What is a QBin?

A. An egress per PVC queue

B. An ingress per PVC queue

C. An egress per traffic type queue

D. An ingress per traffic type queue

Answer: C

12 Mark the following statements as true or false.

A. _____ A line failure causes user connections to reroute in the network.

B. _____ The **dspalms** command displays the lines that are in alarm.

C. _____ You can clear statistical line alarms with the **clrlnalm** command.

D. _____ The **cnflnalm** command allows you to define major and minor alarm thresholds on a line.

E. _____ Unavailable line seconds statistics are accumulated for all BXM lines.

Answers: F, T, T, F, F

Chapter 12

1 How do the APS 1:1 and 1+1 protocols differ?

A. APS 1:1 provides card redundancy only.

B. APS 1+1 provides card and line redundancy.

C. APS 1+1 requires a dedicated protection line; APS 1:1 does not.

D. APS 1+1 can carry user traffic simultaneously on both lines.

E. The BXM supports multiple pairs of 1:1 lines but only one pair of 1+1 lines per card.

Answers: B, D

2 Which of the following network events can trigger an automatic switchover to the APS protection line?

A. Cutting the fiber trunk between two BPX nodes

B. Loss of framing on a line or trunk

C. Excessive cell discards in the trunk queues

D. A bit error rate exceeding a preset limit

E. The wait to restore timer expiring in revertive switching mode

Answers: A, B, D, E

3 Which of the following is not supported on the BXM?

A. APS 1:1 with revertive and bidirectional switching

B. APS 1+1 with nonrevertive and unidirectional switching

C. APS 1+1 Annex B with nonrevertive and unidirectional switching

D. APS 1:1 with nonrevertive switching

Answer: D

4 What command would you use to define the APS protocol?

  A. **cnfcdaps**

  B. **addcdred**

  C. **addapsln**

  D. **cnfapsln**

  Answer: D

5 Which types of APS provide line and card protection?

  A. 1+1

  B. 1+1, Annex B

  C. 1:1

  D. 1:1, Annex B

  Answers: A, B

6 Which type of APS is never revertive?

  A. 1+1

  B. 1+1, Annex B

  C. 1:1

  D. 1:1, Annex B

  Answer: B

7 Which type of APS provides line protection only?

  A. 1+1

  B. 1+1, Annex B

  C. 1:1

  D. 1:1, Annex B

  Answer: C

8 Regarding APS 1:1, which of the following is true?

  A. Redundant lines must be on adjacent ports.

  B. Redundant lines need not be on adjacent ports.

  C. Redundant lines must be on adjacent back cards.

  D. Redundant lines need not be on adjacent back cards.

  Answer: A

9 Which of the following statements is true?

A. APS information is carried by the K1-K1 bytes of the section overhead.

B. APS information is carried by the K1-K2 bytes of the line overhead.

C. APS information is carried by the K1-K2 bytes of the path overhead.

D. APS information is not carried by the K1-K1 bytes.

Answer: B

10 Which of the following bytes indicates the line AIS?

A. A1

B. A2

C. K1

D. K2

Answer: D

11 Which byte does the SONET line interface use to determine BER?

A. H1

B. B2

C. K1

D. E2

Answer: B

Chapter 13

1 Mark the following statements as true or false.

A. _____ Each BXM port has 16 QBins.

B. _____ Each BPX ATM port has four QBins.

C. _____ The CLP and EFCI threshold both control congestion marking.

D. _____ The CLP threshold controls cell discard, and the EFCI threshold controls congestion marking.

E. _____ Egress and ingress queues share a common buffer space.

F. _____ Dedicated ATM QBins are provided for CBR, VBR, UBR, and ABR traffic.

Answers: T, F, F, T, F, F

2 What is the purpose of traffic shaping?

A. To eliminate congestion at the egress port

B. To eliminate excessive burstiness and jitter

C. To ensure that QBin thresholds are not exceeded

D. To guarantee that traffic is delivered to the CPE at PCR

E. To separate CBR, VBR, ABR, and UBR traffic in the egress queues

Answer: B

3 You have upped the port, but it fails after several seconds. What could be the possible reasons for this?

A. A breakdown of the LMI or ILMI.

B. The LMI or ILMI is not activated.

C. The port is UNI but the attached router is NNI.

D. The line is in alarm.

Answers: A, B

4 Mark the following statements as true or false.

A. _____ LMI is based on SNMP.

B. _____ Both LMI and ILMI are signaling protocols.

C. _____ A signaling protocol must be activated on an ATM port.

D. _____ On the BXM, ILMI has a fixed, preset VPI and VCI.

E. _____ The purpose of a signaling protocol is to exchange alarm information between two BPX nodes.

Answers: F, T, F, F, F

5 Match the following commands with their functions:

A. _____ **dnln**   1. Activates a port

B. _____ **upport**   2. Deactivates a line

C. _____ **dsplns**   3. Lists all lines on the node

D. _____ **cnfport**   4. Displays the QBin characteristics

E. _____ **dsplncnf**   5. Shows the configuration of a single line

F. _____ **dspports**   6. Displays all ports on the node or on a card

G. _____ **dspportq**   7. Modifies a port, including the signaling protocol

Answers: A 2, B 1, C 3, D 7, E 5, F 6, G 4

6 For which of the following reasons would you display port statistics?

  A. To find out if a user connection is in alarm

  B. To check if LMI frames or OAM cells are being received by the port

  C. To learn the number of cells transmitted on a given network trunk

  D. To confirm that frames or cells are being sent to the attached user equipment

  Answers: B, D

7 What does it mean when the corrupted field on the port or channel statistics screens is Yes?

  A. The port has an LMI failure.

  B. The statistics were collected too long ago and are no longer correct.

  C. A loopback or test has been run since the last time the statistics were cleared.

  D. The node has had a major alarm since the last time the statistics were cleared.

  Answer: C

8 Why would a BPX ATM port report an unknown VPI/VCI cell?

  A. The attached end-user equipment has failed.

  B. The attached end-user equipment has sent a cell using a reserved VPI or VCI.

  C. A connection on the BPX service node is not routed through the network because no addressing resources are available.

  D. The attached end-user equipment has sent a cell with a VPI/VCI, and there is no corresponding connection on the port.

  Answer: D

9 Mark the following statements as true or false.

  A. _____ When a statistics field reaches its maximum size, it resets to 0.

  B. _____ You can display detailed signaling protocol statistics using the **dspportstats** command.

  C. _____ Both the port and channel statistics can be viewed using an optionally configurable update timer.

  D. _____ All port and channel statistics are cleared automatically based on a configurable network timer.

  Answers: F, F, T, F

10 What does a channel's percent utilization statistic measure?

  A. The connection's configured percent utilization

  B. A comparison of the traffic rate to the PCR

C. A comparison of the traffic rate to the MCR

D. A comparison of the traffic rate to the PCR or MCR, depending on the connection type

Answer: D

Chapter 14

1 Mark the following statements as true or false.

A. _____ The default BPX policing type is 3 for CBR and 4 for all other service.

B. _____ Noncompliant cells are discarded at the first bucket.

C. _____ CDVT defines the depth of the PCR bucket.

D. _____ BPX policing type 5 is the same as no policing.

E. _____ Any BPX policing type can be configured for an ABR connection.

Answers: F, F, T, F, F

2 Given the following parameters, how many cells will be received before a CBR.1 connection becomes noncompliant?

CDVT (0 + 1) = 10,000 microseconds

PCR (0 + 1) = 4,000 cells per second

AR = 5,000 cells per second

A. 200

B. 2,000,000

C. 2,000,001

D. 201

Answer: D

3 How does ABR differ from other ATM service types?

A. Only ABR incorporates a feedback mechanism.

B. ABR uses AAL5.

C. ABR circuits are guaranteed a bandwidth of MCR.

D. A and B only.

E. A and C only.

F. All of the above.

Answer: E

4 What values would the DIR, BN, CI, and NI bits have in a BRM cell generated by an intermediate switch?

A. 0, 1, 1, 1

B. 1, 1, 1, 0

C. 1, 1, 1, 1

D. 1, 0, 1, 1

Answer: B

5 In the BXM card, which of the following queue structures does not have a configurable EFCI threshold?

A. Trunk QBin

B. Per-card QBin

C. Port QBin

D. VC queue

Answer: B

6 Mark the following statements as true or false.

A. _____ The maximum time between RM cells in normal operation is defined by Trm.

B. _____ On startup, the ER field is set to MCR.

C. _____ BPX nodes do not generate RM or BRM cells in ABR without VS/VD.

D. _____ By default, a BRM cell is expected after no more than 32,760 RM cells have been sent.

E. _____ With ER control, the arriving BRM cell always contains the ER as calculated by the previous node in the connection path.

F. _____ A connection idle for more than the ADTF resumes transmission at the ICR.

Answers: F, F, F, F, F, T

7 Select the correct definitions for NIW and SIW from the following list.

A. **NIW**—Interworking function for Frame Relay-to-ATM adaptation. Implemented on BXM trunk cards.

B. **SIW**—Interworking function that supports the connection of two endpoints with different service types, such as ATM and Frame Relay.

C. **NIW**—Interworking function that supports the transport of complete Frame Relay frames across an ATM backbone.

D. **SIW**—Interworking function that converts protocols, such as IP to FDDI.

Answers: B, C

8 Match the following commands with their function.

1. _____ **addcon**   A. Modifies connection parameters

2. _____ **dspcon**   B. Lists all connections on the node

3. _____ **dspatmcls** C. Creates a new ATM connection in the network

4. _____ **dspcons**   D. Displays connection configuration status and routing

5. _____ **cnfcon**   E. Shows the parameters associated with a connection class

Answers: 1 C, 2 D, 3 E, 4 B, 5 A

9 What is a leaky bucket?

A. A model used for policing

B. A queue used for policing

C. A per-connection ingress queue

D. A way to determine the connection type

Answer: A

10 Mark the following statements as true or false.

A. _____ ATM cells are never dropped if they are noncompliant.

B. _____ ATM cells are always dropped if they are noncompliant.

C. _____ ATM cells are always tagged with the CLP bit if they are noncompliant.

D. _____ ATM cells can be dropped or tagged with the CLP bit if they are noncompliant.

Answers: F, F, F, T

11 Which type of traffic uses an ingress virtual circuit queue?

A. CBR

B. VBR

C. ABR

D. UBR

Answer: C

12 Which of the following statements are true for a connection with a preferred route?

A. The connection load-shares on multiple trunks between nodes.

B. The connection cannot route on any path other than the preferred route.

C. The connection uses less bandwidth than a connection without a preferred route.

D. The preferred route can be configured for a path that is not the best possible route in the network.

E. The connection returns to its preferred route if it was rerouted because of a trunk failure and the trunk has been repaired.

Answers: D, E

13 Which of the following are considered when routing or rerouting a connection?

A. Number of hops

B. Delay on a trunk

C. Class of Service (CoS)

D. Distance to the destination node

E. Connection bandwidth requirements

F. The connection's service type, such as ABR or CBR

G. Route restrictions, such as no satellite or terrestrial trunks

Answers: A, C, E, G

14 Of the following commands, which three display route cost information?

A. **dspcon**

B. **dsprts**

C. **dspload**

D. **dsptrkcnf**

E. **dspconcnf**

F. **dspchstats**

Answers: A, D, E

15 What is the load model?

A. The amount of traffic being used on a trunk

B. A model that describes the expected traffic on a trunk

C. The amount of bandwidth necessary to route a connection

D. The amount of bandwidth that is reserved for management traffic

Answer: B

16 What is the statistical reserve? (Choose all that apply.)

A. A management channel on a trunk

B. Bandwidth that is reserved for switched virtual circuits (SVCs) to route over a trunk

      C. Bandwidth that is reserved on a trunk so that ABR connections can burst

      D. Bandwidth on a trunk that is reserved for control traffic and cannot be used by connections

      E. Bandwidth that cannot be allocated to connections, but can be used to accommodate statistical variations in the traffic

      Answers: C, D, E

Chapter 15

1 Mark the following statements as true or false.

      A. _____ External clock sources are attached to the BCC back card.

      B. _____ Only one clock source can be configured on each BPX node.

      C. _____ Only external sources can be primary network clock sources.

      D. _____ Trunks cannot pass synchronization signals to other BPX nodes.

      Answers: T, F, F, F

2 Which of the following are possible clock sources for the BPX switch?

      A. T3 lines

      B. T1 lines

      C. E1 lines

      D. OC-3 lines

      E. STM-1 lines

      Answers: A, D, E

3 What is the meaning of a major alarm status on the bottom-right corner of the BPX console screen?

      A. The local BPX node has a major alarm.

      B. The BPX network has at least one major alarm.

      C. All nodes in the BPX network have major alarms.

      D. A major alarm has occurred in the last five minutes on a remote BPX node.

      Answer: B

4 Of the following events, which four can generate a major alarm in the BPX network?

      A. Fan failure

      B. LMI failure on a port

      C. Loss of frame on a line

D. Connection cannot route

E. Loss of signal on a trunk

F. Cell header CRC errors on a line

G. AIS OAM cells received from a CPE

H. Unknown virtual path identifier (VPI) and virtual channel identifier (VCI) on a connection

Answers: B, C, D, E

5 Of the following events, which six can generate a minor alarm in the BPX network?

A. LMI failure on a port

B. Fan failure

C. Loss of frame on a line

D. Connection cannot route

E. Loss of signal on a trunk

F. Cell header CRC errors on a line

G. AIS OAM cells received from a CPE

H. Unknown VPI and VCI on a connection

Answers: B, E, F, G, H

6 Which of the following events can cause a connection to fail and generate a major alarm?

A. No route is available in the network

B. An incorrect policing configuration

C. A statistical alarm on the access line

D. Dropped cells on an intermediate trunk

E. A failed card at either end of the connection

F. No LMI messages coming in from the CPE on the port

Answers: A, E

7 Mark the following statements as true or false.

A. _____ You use the **resetcd** <*f*> command to clear a self-test failure alarm on a card.

B. _____ You use the **resetcd** <*h*> command to clear a self-test failure alarm on a card.

C. _____ You use the **resetcd** <*h*> command to switch from the active to the standby processor.

      D. _____ You use the **resetcd** *<f>* command to switch from an active to a standby Y-cabled card module.

    Answers: T, F, F, F

8 Which two commands display the alarm status of all nodes in the network?

    Answers: dspnw, dspnds

9 Which command displays a history of alarms and when they occurred?

    Answer: dspalms

10 Which command would you use to clear accumulated statistics on trunks?

    Answer: clrtrkerrs

11 The four loopback connection types are local, remote, external, and what?

    Answer: local-remote

12 When you test connections, what are the four possible results?

    Answers: completed, aborted, failed, repaired

Chapter 16

1 Which of the following best describes the MGX 8250 concentrator?

A. A core switch that supports broadband ATM interfaces

B. A multiservice edge device that supports circuit emulation, Frame Relay, and ATM services

C. An enterprise switch with multiple narrow or broadband trunks that supports voice, data, and Frame Relay services

D. A multiservice edge switch that supports a variety of narrow and broadband services, including circuit emulation, voice, Frame Relay, ATM, and Layer 3 LAN services

    Answer: D

2 Which of the following best describes the MGX 8850-PXM45 switch?

A. A core switch that supports broadband ATM interfaces

B. A multiservice edge device that supports circuit emulation, Frame Relay, and ATM services

C. An enterprise switch with multiple narrow or broadband trunks that supports voice, data, and Frame Relay services

D. A multiservice edge switch that supports a variety of narrow and broadband services, including circuit emulation, Frame Relay, ATM, and Layer 3 LAN services

Answer: A

3 Which MGX platform does *not* support local switching?

Answer: 8220

4 Which of the following optional MGX features requires a purchased software license?

A. IP routing

B. Channelized Frame Relay

C. ATM variable bit rate services

D. T3 and E3 Frame Relay services

Answer: B

5 Of the following services, which two are available on the MGX switch?

A. HSSI ATM

B. Analog voice

C. T3 Frame Relay

D. Nx64 Kbps ATM

E. E1 circuit emulation

Answers: C, E

6 Which feature is an optional congestion management feature available for Frame Relay and ATM services on the MGX switch?

Answer: ForeSight

7 What is the CLI?

A. A GUI on the CWM station

B. A text-based command interface

C. A tool that allows a PC to Telnet to the CWM station

D. A PC-based application for configuring Cisco WAN switches

Answer: B

8 Which of the following MGX networks are supported?

A. A PNNI network of MGX 8250 switches

B. A PNNI network of MGX 8850-PXM45 switches

C. A tiered network of BPX switches and MGX 8220 concentrators

D. A tiered network of BPX switches and MGX 8850-PXM1 switches

E. A PNNI network of MGX 8850-PXM45 switches with 8220 feeders

Answers: B, C, D

9 Of the following functions, which three are performed by the PXM1?

A. Cell switching

B. Network management

C. AAL5 SAR for Frame Relay

D. Storing the service module configuration

E. Voice signaling and call management

Answers: A, B, D

10 Of the following PXM1 models, which three are available for the MGX 8850 switch?

A. PXM-4-155

B. PXM-8-155

C. PXM-1-622

D. PXM-8-T1E1

E. PXM-2-T3E3

F. PXM-4-T3E3

Answers: A, C, E

11 You have a PXM-1-622 installed in your MGX 8250 switch. Of the following back cards, which two must be installed with your PXM1?

A. PXM-UI

B. BNC-2T3

C. PXM-CLK

D. MMF-4-155/B

E. SMFIR-1-622/B

Answers: A, E

12 Which type of SRMs is supported on the MGX 8250 switch?

A. SRM-3E3

B. SRM-T1E1

C. SRM-2-155

D. SRM-3T3/B

E. SRM-3T3/C

Answer: E

13 Of the following functions, which two are performed by the SRM-3T3 (Model B or C) for the MGX switch?

A. Alarm reporting

B. 1-to-N redundancy

C. T1 line distribution

D. ATM cell switching

E. Node synchronization

Answers: B, C

14 What are two rules for installing SRMs in the MGX 8250/8850-PXM1 chassis?

A. SRMs can only be installed in slots 7 and 14.

B. SRMs can only be installed in slots 15, 16, 31, and 32.

C. If you have redundant PXMs, you must install four SRMs.

D. Four SRMs must be installed for the MGX switch to function properly.

E. SRMs can be installed in just the upper or lower bay, depending on where service modules are installed.

Answers: B, E

15 What are two rules for installing SRMs in the MGX 8230 chassis?

A. SRMs can only be installed in slots 7 and 14.

B. SRMs can only be installed in slots 15, 16, 31, and 32.

C. If you have redundant PXMs, you must install two SRMs.

D. Four SRMs must be installed for the MGX switch to function properly.

E. SRMs can be installed in just the left or right bay, depending on where service modules are installed.

Answers: A, E

16 What is the RPM? (Choose all that apply.)

A. A Cisco router

B. An MPLS LSR

C. A switch module

D. A single-height card module

Answers: A, B

17 An RPM front card can support up to how many back cards?

Answer: Two

18 Of the following back cards, which two are supported for the RPM?

A. One-port FDDI

B. Four-port FDDI

C. Four-port Ethernet

D. Eight-port Ethernet

E. One-port Fast Ethernet

F. Two-port Fast Ethernet

Answers: A, C, E

19 A T1 Frame Relay router interface is attached to a _____ card installed in the MGX 8850 chassis.

Answer: FRSM-8T1

20 What does the CESM do?

A. Converts digital voice samples into IP packets

B. Converts Frame Relay frames into ATM cells using AAL5

C. Converts a 64 Kbps, T1, or E1 traffic stream into ATM cells using AAL1

D. Transports a T3 or E3 ATM traffic stream across multiple T1 or E1 lines

Answer: C

21 You have an empty MGX 8250 chassis. Which card slot is the best choice in which to install an FRSM-2CT3?

A. 1

B. 6

C. 7

D. 22

Answer: B

22 You are installing cards in an MGX 8850-PXM1 chassis. There are PXM1s installed in slots 7 and 8 and SRM-3T3s installed in slots 31 and 32. In order to best utilize the card slots and to provide 1-to-N redundancy on all E1 cards, choose the best location for the following card modules:

Two FRSM-8E1s:

A. 1 and 2

B. 17 and 18

C. 29 and 30

Answer: C

Four CESM-8E1s:

A. 1 to 4

B. 3 to 6

C. 17 to 20

D. 19 to 22

Answer: D

Two RPMs:

A. 1 and 2

B. 5 and 6

Answer: A

Six FRSM-HS1/Bs:

A. 3, 4, 5, 6, 9, and 10

B. 9 to 14

Answer: B

23 Which card slots are reserved in the MGX 8230 switch?

Answers: 1, 2, 7, 14

Chapter 17

1 You want to dial up from home and use a Telnet session to access the MGX CLI. Your PC has a SLIP communications package installed. Which PXM-UI port do you connect to?

A. In-band IP

B. LAN port

C. Modem port

D. Console port

Answer: C

2 Your PC is attached to a LAN. One of your associates has given you an IP address to access the MGX CLI using a Telnet session. How are you connected to the MGX switch? (Choose two.)

A. LAN port

B. Modem port

C. Console port

D. IP forwarding

Answers: A, D

3 The command syntax for the **addred** command on the PXM1 card is shown in Example 17-10.

Example 17-10 *Command Syntax for the **addred** Command*

```
SJ8850.1.7.PXM.a > addred

ERR: incorrect number of parameters: (not enough)
Syntax:
   addred <redPrimarySlotNum> <redSecondarySlotNum> <redType>
  redPrimarySlotNum -- <redPrimarySlotNum>
          where redPrimarySlotNum = 1-6¦9-14¦17-22¦25-30
  redSecondarySlotNum -- <redSecondarySlotNum>
          where redSecondarySlotNum ranges from 1-6¦9-14¦17-22¦25-30
  redType -- <redType> where redType = 1(1:1 Y-Cable) or 2(1:N)
```

You must configure the following card redundancy:

• Primary card slot 3

• Secondary card slot 10

• 1-to-N redundancy

What is the command and all parameters to complete this task?

Answer: addred 3 10 2

4 The command syntax to add a new user ID is **adduser** *<user ID> <access level>*, where *user ID* is a character string of 1 to 12 characters and *access level* is GROUP1, GROUP2, GROUP3, GROUP4, GROUP5, or ANYUSER. Which of the following commands is valid?

A. **adduser myID group1**

B. **adduser myID GROUP3**

C. **add user myID ANYUSER**

D. **adduser myID <access level> GROUP1**

Answer: B

5 You are logged in to the MGX CLI and are configuring a CESM-8E1 card. You need to change a port on the card but do not know the exact command to use. What command(s) should you type to help you find the command?

A. **?**

B. **Help**

C. **? port**

D. **Help port**

Answers: C, D

6 You are logged into an FRSM-HS2 card, and you want to see a list of all valid commands. What command would you type to accomplish this task?

Answers: Help, ?

7 Of the following user IDs, which three are valid?

A. teacher

B. group5a

C. 22.COMM

D. ThisIsMyUserID

Answers: A, B, C

8 Of the following passwords, which two are valid?

A. pass

B. password

C. $$$airplane$$$

D. PASSWORD123password

Answers: B, C

9 Which command would you type to learn which user IDs are configured for your MGX switch?

Answer: dspusers

10 Of the following virtual switch interface (VSI) controllers, which three are supported by the MGX switch?

A. Portable AutoRoute (PAR)

B. User Network Interface (UNI)

C. Voice Switch Controller (VSC)

D. Multiprotocol Label Switching (MPLS)

E. Private Network-to-Network Interface (PNNI)

Answers: A, D, E

11 You are adding new connections to the AUSM-8E1 shown in Figure 17-5. Assuming that there are no connections on the card, which of the following connections can you add on port 1?

Figure 17-5 *Adding New Connections to the AUSM-8E1*

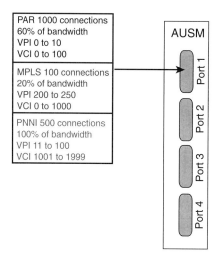

A. A 1 Mbps PAR PVC with a VPI of 5 and a VCI of 20

B. A 1 Mbps PAR PVC with a VPI of 5 and a VCI of 200

C. A 1.8 Mbps PAR PVC with a VPI of 5 and a VCI of 50

D. A 1 Mbps PAR PVC with a VPI of 200 and a VCI of 1000

Answer: A

12 You are adding a new PAR PVC to port 2 on the AUSM-8T1 shown in Figure 17-6. For each connection characteristic, select the value that is supported on this port.

Figure 17-6 *Adding a New PAR PVC to Port 2 on the AUSM-8T1*

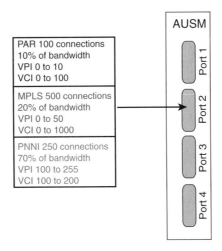

A. Connection bandwidth requirement: 200 Kbps or 100 Kbps

B. VPI value: 0 or 100

C. VCI value: 100 or 1000

Answers: A. 100 Kbps, B. 0, C. 100

13 Of the following statements, which two correctly describe MGX node commands?

A. The **dspifip** command output lists the IP addresses configured on the switch.

B. The **dspcds** command output provides card- and node-level status information.

C. The **cnfname** command must be issued on both the active and standby PXM1 cards.

D. The **dspcdrscprtn** command output shows the configuration of all cards installed in the shelf.

Answers: A, B

14 Of the following node names, which three can be used on the MGX switch?

A. 8850_A

B. lab12_A

C. MY8250

D. mgx.lab1

Answers: B, C, D

15 You want to use a Telnet application to access the CLI on your MGX switch. The PXM-UI LAN port is connected to the LAN. Based on the output from the **dspifip** command shown in Example 17-11, what IP address must you use?

Example 17-11 *Output from the* **dspifip** *Command*

```
SJ8850.1.7.PXM.a > dspifip

   Interface        Flag  IP Address       Subnetmask        Broadcast Addr
   --------------   ----  ---------------   ---------------   --------------
   Ethernet/lnPci0   UP    10.10.51.62       255.255.255.000   10.10.51.255
   Slip/sl0          UP    10.10.12.25       255.255.255.000   (N/A)
   ATM/atm0          UP    10.10.48.2        255.255.255.000   10.10.48.255
```

A. 10.10.48.2

B. 10.10.51.62

C. 10.10.12.25

D. 255.255.255.000

Answer: B

16 You are logged in to the active PXM1 on your MGX switch. You want to know what firmware revision is loaded on the card. What command must you use to get this information?

Answer: dspcd

17 You have redundant PXM1s installed in your MGX 8250 switch. You also have four FRSM-8E1 cards (one with a redundant back card) installed in card slots 19 to 22 and FRSM-HS1/B cards installed in card slots 5 and 6. If you want to have 1-to-N redundancy on your E1 cards and 1-to-1 Y-cable redundancy on your HS1/B cards, in which card slot(s) must you install SRM-3T3 cards?

A. 15

B. 32

C. 15 and 16

D. 15 and 31

E. 31 and 32

F. 15, 16, 31, and 32

Answer: E

18 Based on the redundancy configuration shown in Figure 17-7, which three of the following statements are true?

Figure 17-7 *Redundancy Configuration*

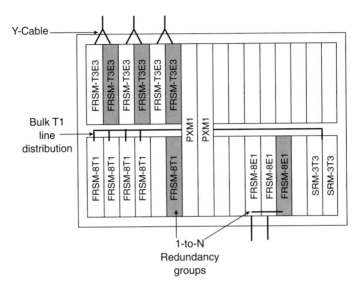

A. If the FRSM-T3E3 in slot 1 fails, card slot 2 can take over.

B. If the FRSM-8E1 in slot 27 fails, the secondary FRSM-8T1 in slot 22 can take over for slots 17 to 20.

C. If the FRSM-8T1 in slot 17 fails, the secondary FRSM-8E1 in slot 29 cannot take over for slots 27 or 28.

D. If the FRSM-8T1s in slots 17 and 18 fail, the traffic for one of the cards will be redirected to slot 22, and the traffic from the other card will fail.

Answers: A, B, D

19 Which command must you use to learn which service module is the primary and which is the secondary when you are using 1-to-N redundancy?

A. **dspcd**

B. **dspcds**

C. **dspred**

D. **dspslots**

Answer: C

20 You are looking at the **dspred** output on your MGX switch. What does it mean when a card module reports that the secondary state is "blocked"?

A. The card is in bulk mode.

B. The secondary card has failed.

C. The active card has failed and the secondary has taken over.

D. A secondary card is active and this primary card is not protected.

Answer: D

Chapter 18

1   What is different about a standalone feeder node?

A. Standalone feeders do not support network management.

B. Only one standalone feeder can be attached to a BPX switch.

C. A standalone feeder can be attached to a non-Cisco backbone network.

D. The MGX 8220 concentrator can be installed only as a standalone feeder.

E. The backbone node treats a standalone feeder like a generic UNI device.

Answers: C, E

2   In Figure 18-13, identify each element as one of the following:

Figure 18-13 *Identify Each Element*

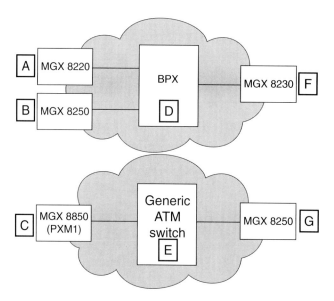

A. Feeder node

B. Backbone node

C. Standalone feeder node

Answers: Feeder nodes: A, B, F; backbone nodes: D, E; standalone feeder nodes: C, G

3 Which of the images in Figure 18-14 depict a line?

Figure 18-14 *Which of the Images Depict a Line?*

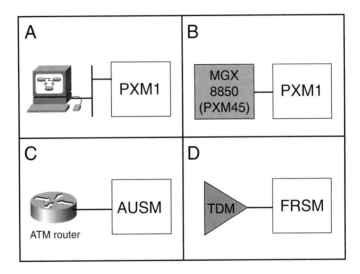

Answers: B, C, D

4 What kinds of devices can be attached to a PXM1 line?

A. A T1 PBX

B. A BPX switch

C. An ATM router with a T3 interface

D. A Frame Relay router with an E1 interface

Answers: B, C

5 On the MGX 8230, what is a line?

A. An Ethernet LAN segment

B. A T3 or E3 attached to an ATM switch

C. A multiplexed T1 that carries up to 24 different user circuits

D. Any digital transmission facility that carries traffic between a CPE and an MGX service module

Answers: B, C, D

6 Which of the following network events can trigger an automatic switchover to the APS protection line?

A. Loss of framing on a line or trunk

B. Bit error rate exceeding a preset limit

C. Excessive cell discards in the trunk queues

D. Cutting the fiber trunk between two MGX nodes

E. Wait to restore timer expiring in revertive switching mode

Answers: A, B, D, E

7 Which of the following APS protocols are supported on the PXM1?

A. 1:1 intracard

B. 1:1 intercard

C. 1+1 intracard

D. 1+1 intercard

Answer: D

8 Select the correct command for each function by choosing one of the commands enclosed in brackets.

A. To learn how many connections a card can support, use the {**dspcd** | **cnfcdrscprtn** | **dspcds** | **dspcdrscprtn**} command.

B. To learn whether a PXM1 line is in alarm, use the {**dsplns** | **dspalms** | **dsptrks**} command.

C. To learn the cell header type on a PXM1 line, use the {**dspln** | **dspport** | **dspatmlncnf**} command.

Answers: A: dspcdrscprtn; B: dspalms; C: dspatmlncnf

9 You have typed **dsplns -sonet 7** on your PXM1 card. What information is output on the CLI?

A. Line status

B. Payload scramble

C. Framing (OC-X/STM-X)

D. Line speed in cells per second

Answers: B, C

10 What can you conclude about the ports when looking at the output from the **dspports** command shown in Example 18-29?

Example 18-29 *dspports Output*

```
mgx8800b.1.7.PXM.a > dspports

  Port  Status  Line  PctBw  minVpi  maxVpi
  - - - - - - - - - - - - - - - - - - - - - - - - - - - - - - - - - - - - - - - - -
     3    ON      3    100      0      255
     4    ON      4    100      0      4095
```

A. Port 3 has failed.

B. Port 3 is an NNI.

C. Port 4 is an NNI.

D. Port 4 allows all VPI values.

Answer: C

11 Which of the following commands is valid?

A. **addapsln 1 7 1 8 1**

B. **addapsln 1 7 2 7 3**

C. **addapsln 2 7 2 8 2**

D. **addapsln 1 7 1 10 2**

Answer: C

12 You want to switch from the protection line to the working line only if there are no outstanding commands. The working line is line 2 on card 7. What command must you type on the CLI to accomplish this task?

Answer: switchapsln 2 3

13 You type **cnfapsln 2 5 6 5 2 1 1** on the CLI. Which of the following statements are true?

A. In-band K1K2 is enabled.

B. The revertive option is enabled.

C. The working line is on card slot 8.

D. The switching direction is bidirectional.

E. A signal failure will be reported when the bit error rate reaches 10^{-5}.

F. A signal degrade will be reported when the bit error rate reaches 10^{-5}.

Answers: A, D, E

14 You are using an SRM-3T3 to distribute T1 lines on your MGX switch. One of the T1 lines on your FRSM-8T1 card is reporting a loss of signal. Where is the most likely cause of this problem?

  A. On the FRSM back card

  B. On the MGX T1 distribution bus

  C. On the T3 coming into the SRM-3T3 back card

  D. On the T1 facility attached to the end-user equipment

  Answer: D

15 You have an MGX 8250 switch, and you require 22 E1 circuit emulation lines and 12 T1 circuit emulation lines from a variety of customer locations. Would T1 bulk distribution be beneficial to this installation?

  Answer: No

16 How many T1 lines can be distributed using an SRM-3T3?

  A. 24

  B. 28

  C. 80

  D. 84

  E. 192

  Answer: C

17 You are logged into an FRSM-HS1/B card module. Write the command and all required parameters you would use to see the line rate of line 1.

  Answer: dsplns

18 On which cards would you use the **dspds3lns** command?

  A. PXM

  B. CESM-8E1

  C. FRSM-8T1

  D. FRSM-2CT3

  E. FRSM-T3E3

  Answers: D, E

19 What command do you use to map a T1 line on the SRM to a service module?

  A. **addln**

  B. **addlink**

C. **cnflink**

D. **addslotlink**

Answer: B

20 What command must you type (including all required parameters) to learn which SRM T1 lines are linked to card 18?

Answer: dspslotlink 18

21 The command syntax for the **addlink** command is shown in Example 18-30. If you need to link T1 lines 20 to 23 of T3 line 3 to T1 lines 5 to 8 on an AUSM-8T1 in slot 5, what must you type on the command line?

Example 18-30 addlink *Command*

```
SJ8850.1.7.PXM.a > addlink

ERR: incorrect number of paramters: (not enough)
Syntax: addlink <T3LineNum> <T1Slot> <NumberOfT1s> <TargetSlotNum>
                <TargetSlotLineNum> <T3LineNum>
            where T3LineNum = Slot.Line
                  where Slot = 15,16,31,32
                        Line = 1 - 3
            <T1Slot> where T1Slot = 1 - 28
            <NumberOfT1s> where NumberOfT1s = 1-8
            <TargetSlotNum> where TargetSlotNum = 1-6¦11-14¦17-22¦27-30
            <TargetSlotLineNum> where TargetSlotLineNum = 1-8
```

A. **addlink 31.3 20 4 5**

B. **addlink 31.3 20 4 5 5**

C. **addlink 15.3 20 4 5 5**

D. **addlink 15.3 5 20 5 8**

Answer: C

22 You want to know which lines on your CESM-8E1 card are in alarm. Which commands would you use?

A. **dspln**

B. **dspalm**

C. **dspalms**

D. **dspalmcnt**

Answers: A, C

23 What is the purpose of the **modbert** command?

A. It ends the BERT.

B. It changes the BERT pattern.

C. It injects an error into the BERT.

Answer: C

24 Which command would you use to learn how many times line 1 on your FRSM-8T1 has experienced a loss of signal?

A. **dspln 1**

B. **dspalm -ds1 1**

C. **dspalms -ds1**

D. **dspalmcnt -ds1 1**

Answer: D

Chapter 19

1 Which of the following VCs require administrative action to set up and take down?

A. SVC

B. PVC

C. SPVC

Answers: B, C

2 Mark the following statements as true or false.

A. _____ MGX Frame Relay services are supported by VBR connections in the BPX network.

B. _____ ATFR and ATFST connections are added in the BPX network to support MGX Frame Relay services.

C. _____ A CBR connection segment in the ATM backbone network supports MGX circuit emulation services.

D. _____ MGX feeder Frame Relay connections are supported by UBR connections in the MGX 8850-PXM45 backbone network.

Answers: F, T, T, F

3 A scaling factor is recommended when you add backbone connections that support MGX feeder Frame Relay services to increase the required bandwidth allocated in the network. Why is this scaling factor necessary?

A. To accommodate for frames greater than 1000 bytes in length

B. To accommodate for the additional traffic generated by the LMI protocol

C. To ensure that the backbone network does not police the cells coming from the MGX feeder node

D. To accommodate for partially filled cells that are created when frames are encapsulated into ATM cells

E. To reduce the amount of congestion that might occur in the backbone network because Frame Relay traffic is bursty

Answer: D

4 What is a local connection?

A. Any MGX connection

B. A connection that routes through a single BPX switch

C. A connection that originates and terminates on a Frame Relay port

D. A connection that originates and terminates on the same MGX switch

E. A connection that originates and terminates on the same service module on an MGX switch

Answer: D

5 You want to create a connection between an AUSM ATM port on one MGX 8230 switch and an AUSM ATM port on another MGX 8230 switch. The backbone network includes BPX switches. How many connection segments must you add to accomplish this task?

Answer: Three

6 The connection segments for three end-to-end connections are shown in Figure 19-20. Which graphic is correct?

Figure 19-20 *Connection Segments for Three End-to-End Connections*

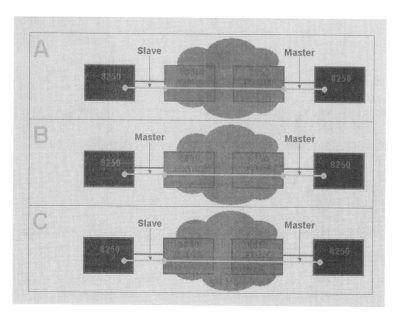

Answer: B

7 Mark the following statements as true or false.

A. _____ When you create a local connection, you must add the slave end first.

B. _____ You can terminate MGX 8230 connections on IGX and BPX switches.

C. _____ Local connections must originate and terminate on the same service module.

D. _____ Each connection segment addition requires you to type a command on the CLI.

E. _____ CWM is used to add connections on all MGX switches, including standalone switches.

Answers: T, T, F, T, F

8 Which command(s) would you use to modify the service type of an existing connection?

A. **cnfcon**

B. **addcon**

C. **delcon**, **cnfcon**

D. You cannot modify the service type.

Answer: A

9 When provisioning the master endpoint for an SPVC, which parameters must you specify with the **addcon** command?

A. Mastership

B. Service type

C. VPI and VCI

D. Remote PCR

E. Interface number

F. Slave endpoint interface number

Answers: A, B, C, E, F

10 Which command syntax would you use to verify the VPI and VCI for both SPVC endpoints?

A. AXSM.a > **dspcons**

B. PXM.a > **dspcon** *port ID*

C. AXSM.a > **dspcon** *portID vpi vci*

D. PXM.a > **dspcon** *interface number vpi vci*

E. AXSM.a > **dspcon** *interface number vpi vci*

Answer: E

11 You have created a 512 kbps circuit emulation port on your CESM. Is this a structured or unstructured port?

Answer: Structured

12 How many unstructured ports can you have on an E1 line?

Answer: One

13 What are two features of a structured port?

A. All timeslots are assigned to one port.

B. The port comprises one or more timeslots.

C. Signaling and framing bits are sent with the user data.

D. Signaling bits are extracted on ingress and reinserted on egress.

Answers: B, D

14 How many connection segments are required for a local circuit emulation connection between two adjacent CESM cards?

Answer: Two

15 You are adding an unstructured circuit emulation connection to your MGX network. What kind of signaling can you use on this connection?

A. Basic

B. E1 CAS

C. E1 CCS

D. DS1 SF CAS

E. DS1 ESF CAS

Answer: A

16 Mark the following statements as true or false.

A. _____ Slave connections always use basic signaling.

B. _____ Up to ten local connections can be added to a CESM.

C. _____ All structured connections must be configured for CAS signaling.

D. _____ All connections on the same line must use the same signaling method.

E. _____ You must add the slave end of a local connection before the master end.

Answers: F, T, F, T, T

17 When would you use SRTS clocking?

A. When the MGX network is not synchronized

B. When neither CPE nor the MGX network is synchronized

C. When the CPEs and the MGX are using the same clock source

D. When the CPEs are synchronized to each other but the MGX network is using a different clock source

Answer: D

18 What is the default clock mode for all CESM connections?

A. SRTS

B. Adaptive

C. Synchronous

D. Asynchronous

E. There is no default.

Answer: C

19 Which of the following statements is *not* true?

   A. Adaptive clocking is asynchronous.

   B. SRTS clocking uses a time stamp in the AAL1 SAR-PDU header.

   C. Unstructured ports support only synchronous and adaptive clocking.

   D. Adaptive clocking uses an egress buffer to accommodate clock changes.

   Answer: C

20 You want to monitor when underruns occur for more than 5 seconds on a circuit emulation connection. What should you change to make sure you are notified?

   A. CLIP

   B. CDVT

   C. Buffer size

   D. Statistics timer

   Answer: A

21 Which of the following statements is true?

   A. During an underrun, there are no cells across the connection.

   B. You might experience underruns if the buffer size is too small.

   C. You might experience underruns if the CDVT value is too small.

   D. When the buffer underruns, the CESM declares a minor alarm.

   Answer: C

22 You want to find out if port 5 is failed. What command and any required parameters must you type to find out the port's state?

   Answer: dspport 5

23 When you use the **addport** command to create a new port, you must specify the port type. Which of the following are valid port types?

   A. Structured

   B. T1 ESF CAS

   C. Unstructured

   D. Asynchronous

   E. Framing on VC disconnect

   F. E1 CCS with CRC checking

   Answers: A, C, E

24 For each function, select the appropriate command:

A. To create a new circuit emulation connection, use the {**addport** | **addcon**} command.

B. To find out whether a connection is a master or slave connection, use the {**dspcon** | **dspcons**} command.

C. To change the CLIP, use the {**cnfcon** | **cnfport**} command.

Answers: A: addcon; B: dspcon; C: cnfcon

25 What is the function of the **tstcon** command?

A. To check for connection alarms

B. To test the connection's continuity

C. To test the connection's quality

D. To measure the round-trip delay on the connection

E. To confirm that the connection is configured correctly

Answer: B

26 Mark the following statements as true or false.

A. _____ The **dspchancnt** output updates automatically.

B. _____ The channel number is the same as the port number.

C. _____ The most recent **tstdelay** result is shown in the **dspchancnt** output.

D. _____ The **clrchancnts** command clears all the channel counters on the card.

E. _____ The **dspchancnt** command shows historical statistics counters for a channel.

Answers: F, F, F, T, T

Chapter 20

1 How many fractional Frame Relay ports are allowed on an E1 line?

Answer: 1

2 Which card modules support serial Frame Relay ports?

A. FRSM-8E1

B. FRSM-8T1

C. FRSM-HS2

D. FRSM-2CT3

Answer: C

3 What is a channelized Frame Relay port?

A. A port comprising multiple T1 or E1 lines

B. A port that provides access to multiple FRADs

C. The only port on a line that uses one or more timeslots

D. One of several ports on a line that uses one or more timeslots

Answer: D

4 Mark the following statements as true or false.

A. _____ The High Priority queue is for LMI and CLLM traffic.

B. _____ On low-speed FRSMs, Queue 1 is served more often than Queue 2.

C. _____ All queues on the FRSM-8E1 are served using a round-robin algorithm.

D. _____ The FRSM-8T1 card has one High Priority queue and three CoS queues per virtual port.

Answers: T, T, F, F

5 What is the purpose of the DE threshold on a queue?

A. It is part of the policing algorithm.

B. It determines when the DE bit is set on a frame.

C. It determines when congestion occurs on the queue.

D. It determines when DE frames are not allowed into the queue.

E. It controls when ABR connections increase or decrease their rate.

Answer: D

6 A port queue buffers traffic coming from or going to the CPE?

Answer: going to

7 At which two places on the FRSM could ingress traffic get dropped?

A. UPC

B. SAR

C. VC queue

D. Port queue

Answers: A, C

8 A Frame Relay port is reporting a large number of cells being transmitted with the DE bit set to 1. Assuming that all the frames are coming from the remote CPE with the DE bit set to 0, where are the DE bits being set?

A. On the ingress VC queue

B. On the egress port queue

C. By the ingress UPC algorithm

Answer: C

9 What is the main difference between traffic flow on low-speed FRSMs and traffic flow on high-speed FRSMs?

A. The low-speed cards have a set number of port queues.

B. The high-speed cards have ingress and egress VC queues.

C. The high-speed cards have CoS queues in both directions.

D. The low-speed cards buffer traffic in only the egress direction.

E. The low-speed cards support only VBR and UBR queue servicing.

Answer: C

10 Which command is used to determine the cause of a port alarm?

A. **dspcd**

B. **dsplns**

C. **cnfport**

D. **dspport**

E. **dspports**

Answer: D

11 Of the following commands, which two are used to enable CLLM on a Frame Relay port?

A. **cnfcllm**

B. **cnfport**

C. **addport**

D. **xcnfport**

E. **cnfportcllm**

Answers: A, D

12 How would you define a port as a UNI or NNI?

A. Use the **cnfint** command and set the interface type to UNI or NNI.

B. Use the **cnfport** command and set the interface type to UNI or NNI.

C. Use the **xcnfport** command and set the interface type to UNI or NNI.

D. Use the **cnflmi** command and set the signaling protocol to AU or DU.

E. Use the **cnfport** command and set the signaling protocol to S, AU, DU, AN, or DN.

F. The port cannot be configured; it automatically detects the interface type using ELMI.

Answer: D

13 Of the following, which two are reasons why Frame Relay port statistics would be displayed?

A. To learn if a channel is in alarm

B. To check if OAM cells are being sent to the ATM network

C. To learn the number of frames transmitted and received on a port

D. To confirm that LMI messages are being sent to the attached user equipment

Answers: C, D

14 Why would a Frame Relay port report an unknown DLCI frame?

A. The attached end-user equipment has failed.

B. The attached end-user equipment has sent a frame using a reserved DLCI.

C. The attached end-user equipment has sent a frame with a DLCI, and there is no corresponding connection on the port.

D. A connection on the ATM backbone switch is not routed through the network because no addressing resources are available.

Answer: C

15 How many connection segments are required for a local Frame Relay connection between two adjacent FRSM cards?

Answer: Two

16 You are adding a Frame Relay connection between two Frame Relay ports, as shown in Figure 20-26. Which connection segments must you add?

Figure 20-26 *Which Connection Segments Must You Add?*

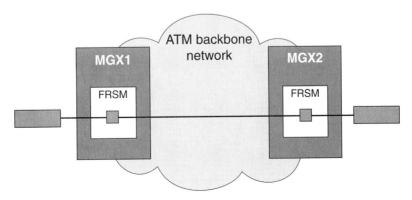

A. A slave connection on the FRSM on MGX1

B. A master connection on the FRSM on MGX1

C. A master connection on the FRSM on MGX2

D. A CBR connection in the ATM backbone network

E. A variable-rate connection in the ATM backbone network

Answers: B, C, E

17 You are adding a frame forwarding connection. How many connections can terminate on the port?

A. 1

B. 2

C. 256

D. 1000

Answer: A

18 Mark the following statements as true or false.

A. _____ Multiple FUNI connections can terminate on a port.

B. _____ Up to ten local connections can be added to an FRSM.

C. _____ Connections that share a line must all be of the same type.

D. _____ You must add the slave end of a local connection before the master end.

E. _____ All frame forwarding connections are supported by ABR connections in the ATM backbone network.

Answers: T, F, F, T, F

19 You have added a network interworking connection on your FRSM. Where can the connection terminate?

A. On a PXM1 trunk

B. On any ATM interface

C. On an MGX FRSM port

D. On an MGX AUSM port

Answer: C

20 Which configurable Frame Relay connection parameters affect the ingress policing on the connection?

A. Bc

B. Be

C. AR

D. CIR

E. EIR

F. DE threshold

G. VC queue depth

Answers: A, B, D

21 What is the difference between Bc and Be?

A. Bc is for ingress traffic; Be is for egress traffic.

B. Bc is configured per port; Be is configured per channel.

C. Bc determines whether frames are dropped; Be determines whether frames are congested.

D. Bc determines whether frames are discard-eligible; Be determines whether frames are dropped.

Answer: D

22 Under what conditions can the connection rate drop below the configured MIR?

A. If frames have the DE bit set to 1

B. When data is being dropped on egress

C. When there is severe congestion in the network

D. The connection rate cannot drop below the configured MIR under any conditions.

E. When there is an alarm on the line between the MGX switch and the ATM backbone network

Answer: D

23 A Frame Relay connection is configured with an MIR of 64 kbps, a QIR of 64 kbps, and a PIR of 512 kbps on an FRSM with the ForeSight rate adjustment parameters set at their default values. If the VC queue service rate is currently 274 kbps and the network reports severe congestion, what is the new queue service rate in kbps?

Answer: 137.5 kbps

24 A Frame Relay connection is configured with an MIR of 64 kbps, a QIR of 64 kbps, and a PIR of 512 kbps on an FRSM with the ForeSight rate adjustment parameters set at their default values. If the VC queue service rate is currently 510 kbps and the network reports no congestion, what is the new queue service rate in kbps?

A. 510 kbps

B. 512 kbps

C. 516.4 kbps

D. 561.2 kbps

Answer: C

25 Mark the following statements as true or false.

A. _____ The ICR is the rate used when NI is set to 1.

B. _____ The ICR is the rate used after timeout period ADTF.

C. _____ An ABR source can send data at rates less than the PCR and greater than the MCR.

D. _____ An ABR source can send data at rates less than the MCR and greater than the PCR.

E. _____ An ABR connection source can send data at any rate between 0 cps and the line speed.

Answers: F, T, T, F, F

26 Mark the following statements as true or false.

A. _____ The FRSM-2CT3 card has four CoS queues per virtual circuit.

B. _____ On low-speed FRSMs, all VC queues are of equal priority.

C. _____ All VC queues on the FRSM-HS2 are served using a round-robin algorithm.

D. _____ The IBS is the maximum number of bytes that can burst out of the VC queue.

Answers: F, T, F, T

27 What is the purpose of the ECN threshold on a VC queue?

A. It is part of the policing algorithm.

B. It determines when FECN frames are discarded.

C. It determines when the FECN bit is set on a frame.

D. It determines when FECN frames are not allowed into the queue.

E. It controls when ABR connections increase or decrease their rate.

Answer: C

28 What command must you type (without required or optional parameters) to enable the ForeSight feature on a connection?

Answer: cnfchanfst

29 Which command must you use to set the committed and excess burst sizes?

A. **cnfcon**

B. **cnfpolicing**

C. **cnfchanpol**

D. **cnfchanmap**

E. **cnfchanburst**

F. **cnfchanstdabr**

Answer: C

30 Mark the following statements as true or false.

A. _____ The **dspchancnt** output updates automatically.

B. _____ The channel number is the same as the port number.

C. _____ The most recent **tstdelay** result is shown in the **dspchancnt** output.

D. _____ The **clrchancnts** command clears all the channel counters on the card.

E. _____ The **dspchancnt** command shows historical statistical counters for a channel.

Answers: F, F, F, T, T

Chapter 21

1 For which of the following situations would you use an IMA port on an AUSM?

A. A Frame Relay router with an unchannelized E1 interface

B. A router with four T1 ATM interfaces to four other ATM routers

C. A virtual trunk between two BPX switches with E3 line interfaces

D. A router with four T1 lines used to carry 6 Mbps of traffic between it and another router

Answer: D

2 Which of the graphics shown in Figure 21-9 best depicts an inverse multiplexing over ATM service?

Figure 21-9 *Which Shows Inverse Multiplexing Over ATM?*

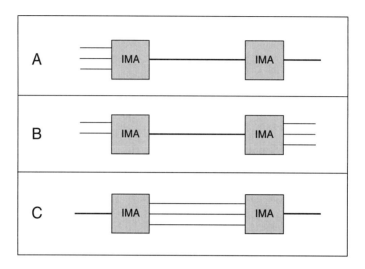

Answer: C

3 How many QBins are on an ATM port on the AUSM?

Answer: 5

4 Your AUSM port 1 VBR QBin is set as follows:

Maximum queue depth 500 cells
CLP high 400 cells
CLP low 250 cells
EFCI threshold 280 cells

Which two of the following statements are true?

A. When 250 cells are in the QBin, all CLP tagged cells are discarded.

B. When 280 cells are in the QBin, all EFCI tagged cells are discarded.

C. When 280 cells are in the QBin, new cells are marked with congestion (EFCI bit set to 1).

D. When 400 cells are in the QBin, all arriving CLP tagged cells are not queued and are discarded.

Answers: C, D

5 An end user is complaining that there is congestion on his nrt-VBR ATM services. Although he is not experiencing poor performance, he reports that many of his cells are being marked with the EFCI bit. You look at his port QBin configuration and note that the VBR QBin is set for the following:

Queue depth 1000 cells
CLP high 500 cells
CLP low 100 cells
EFCI threshold 50 cells

Which of the following changes might resolve this problem?

A. Change the CLP high to 750 cells.

B. Decrease the queue depth to 600 cells.

C. Increase the queue depth to 1500 cells.

D. Increase the EFCI threshold to 750 cells.

Answer: D

6 At which of the following locations could an egress cell on the AUSM get dropped?

A. The UPC

B. The QBin

C. The VC queue

Answer: B

7 You are troubleshooting an ATM port that is reporting a large number of cells being transmitted with the CLP bit tagged. Assuming that all of the cells are coming from the remote CPE with the CLP bit set to 0, where are the cells being tagged?

A. On the ingress VC queue

B. By the ingress UPC algorithm

C. On the egress QBin

Answer: B

8 An end user is complaining that there is congestion in the network. Cells sent from the New York office to the Paris office are leaving the MGX network with the EFCI bit set to 1; traffic in the other direction is not reporting congestion. Where should you look for congestion?

A. On the QBin in Paris

B. On the VC queue in Paris

C. On the QBin in New York

D. On the VC queue in New York

Answers: A, D

9 What is the maximum differential delay on an IMA group?

A. The maximum delay between ATM cells on any one line

B. The maximum number of links that can be active at any one time

C. The amount of time before a trap is sent to the CWM if the IMA group fails

D. The maximum amount of time permitted between consecutive cells carried on adjacent lines

Answer: D

10 You need to enable the ILMI signaling protocol on a port. Which command (without any required or optional parameters) must you use to make this change?

Answer: cnfilmi

11 What functions are performed when you use the **addport** command?

A. The IMA group is created.

B. The ILMI protocol is enabled.

C. The VC queues are configured.

D. The ATM cell header type is defined.

E. A logical port number is assigned to a line.

Answers: D, E

12 Which of the following commands must you use if you want to learn the number of ATM and IMA ports on an AUSM?

A. **dspport**

B. **dspports**

C. **dspportcnt**

D. **dspimagrps**

Answer: B

13 What command must you type (including all required parameters) to find out the CLP high threshold of the CBR QBin on port 2?

Answer: dspportq 2 1

14 Based on the port information shown in Example 21-29, which two of the following statements are true?

Example 21-29 *dspports* Output

```
NZ_8850.1.22.AUSM8.a > dspports

  List of ATM ports:
  ==================

  Port PortType Line# Portenable  Speed  PortState
  ---- -------- ----- ----------  -----  ---------
  22.2  UNI      5     UP          3622  Line alarm
  22.4  NNI      6     UP          3622  Active

  List of IMA groups:
  ===================

  ImaGrp PortType Conf  Avail Lines       Lines    Tol Diff  Port State
                  rate  rate  configured  present  Delay(ms)
  ------ -------- ----- ----- ----------- -------- --------- ----------
   22.1  UNI      14364 10773 1.2.4.3     1.2.3     275       B/w changed
   22.3  NNI      7182  0     7.8                             Sig. failure
```

A. Line 5 is in alarm.

B. IMA port 3 is failed.

C. Port 4 is using line 4.

D. All lines on IMA group 1 are active.

Answers: A, B

15 You need to create a new logical port (number 4) on line 2 of your PXM1 card. Assuming that the line is configured for UNI and you want to use all the line bandwidth and the full addressing range, what command (including all required parameters) must you type to accomplish this task?

Answer: addport 4 2 100 0 255

16 What command (with all required parameters) must you use to learn how many ILMI messages have been sent by port 2 on an AUSM?

Answer: dspilmicnt 2

17 The **dspportcnt** output is shown in Example 21-30. Based on this information, which two of the following statements are true?

Example 21-30 dspportcnt *Output*

```
NZ_8850.1.22.AUSM8.a > dspportcnt 4

  PortNum:                              4
  PortState:                            Okay
  IngressRcvCells:                      23486
  IngressRcvCellRate (cells/sec):       1022
  IngressRcvUtilization (percentage):   23
  IngressXmtCells:                      23429
  IngressGFCErrorCells:                 0
  IngressVpiVciErrCells:                55
  IngressUnknownVpiVci:                 0x010066
  IngressRcvClpSetCells:                23
  EgressRcvCells:                       21065
  EgressRcvCellRate (cells/sec):        986
  EgressRcvUtilization (percentage):    19
  EgressXmtCells:                       21064
  EgressXmtCellRate (cells/sec):        986
  EgressXmtUtilization (percentage):    19
  EgressPortAlarmDiscardCells:          0
  EgressXmtClpSetCells:                 2
  EgressXmtEfciSetCells:                0
  PortXmtAisCells:                      0
  PortXmtSgmtLpbkCells:                 0
  PortRcvAisCells:                      0
  PortRcvFerfCells:                     0
  PortRcvSgmtLpbkCells:                 0
  PortRcvCrcErrOAMCells:                0
  TotalIngressQFullDiscardCells:        0
  TotalIngressClpSetDiscardCells:       0
  TransmitFIFOFullCount (per card):     0
  ReceivedHECErrorCells:                1
  HECErroredSeconds:                    1
  SeverelyHECErroredSeconds:            0
```

A. These counters apply to a PXM1 port.

B. These counters apply to port number 4.

C. The port received a cell with a VCI value of 10066.

D. The ingress VC queues associated with this port are congested.

E. Cells are arriving from the CPE with unknown VPI and VCI values.

Answers: B, E

18 Which command must you use to monitor the traffic on an IMA port on an AUSM?

A. **dspport**

B. **dspimagrp**

C. **dspportcnt**

D. **dspimagrpcnt**

Answer: C

19 How many connection segments are required for a local ATM connection between two adjacent AUSM cards?

Answer: Two

20 Mark the following statements as true or false.

A. _____ All ATM service types are supported on the AUSM.

B. _____ ForeSight and Standard ABR are supported on the PXM1.

C. _____ Connections that share a port all must be of the same service type.

D. _____ CBR connections can terminate on AUSM and PXM1 ATM ports.

E. _____ You cannot add a connection between two ports on the same AUSM card.

Answers: T, F, F, T, F

21 Which CoS type does not offer any service guarantee?

A. ABR

B. UBR

C. rt-VBR

D. nrt-VBR

Answer: B

22 What is the difference between real-time and nonreal-time VBR?

A. rt-VBR has a service guarantee; nrt-VBR does not.

B. rt-VBR has end-to-end timing standards; nrt-VBR does not.

C. rt-VBR is not supported on the AUSM; nrt-VBR is supported.

D. rt-VBR is for uncompressed voice and video; nrt-VBR is for compressed voice and video.

Answer: B

23 What is policing?

A. A queue service algorithm

B. A traffic-shaping algorithm that determines how cells leave an ATM network

C. A process that determines whether cells are accepted into the network or tagged with the CLP bit

    D. A method to determine whether a new connection can be added to the network based on the bandwidth requirements and maximum burst size

Answer: C

24 Figure 21-10 shows how a burst of cells is policed using the dual leaky bucket model. Identify the two rates and the two events shown in the figure.

Figure 21-10 *Dual Leaky Bucket Model*

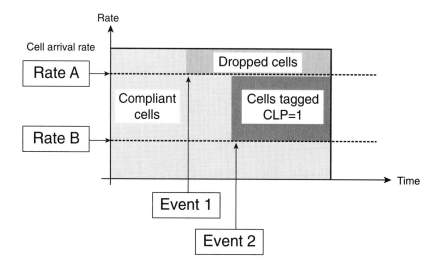

Rate A: _____

Rate B: _____

Event 1: _____

Event 2: _____

A. SCR

B. PCR

C. MBS

D. CDVT

E. Port congestion

F. First bucket full

G. Second bucket full

H. Network congestion

Answers: B, A, F, G

25 Which of the following statements is false?

A. UBR connections are policed using a single leaky bucket.

B. Cells are always discarded if the second leaky bucket is full.

C. The configuration of one leaky bucket is independent of the other.

D. A cell with the CLP bit set to 1 is discarded in the network if there is sufficient congestion.

Answer: B

26 Under what conditions can the ForeSight connection rate drop below the configured MCR?

A. If cells have the CLP bit set to 1

B. When data is being dropped on egress

C. When there is severe congestion in the network

D. The connection rate cannot drop below the configured MCR under any conditions

E. When there is an alarm on the line between the MGX switch and the ATM backbone network

Answer: D

27 A ForeSight ABR connection is configured with an MCR of 170 cps, an ICR of 170 cps, and a PCR of 1400 cps on an AUSM, with the ForeSight rate adjustment parameters set at their default values. If the VC queue service rate is currently 500 cps and the network reports severe congestion, what will the new queue service rate be in cps?

Answer: 250

28 A ForeSight ABR connection is configured with an MCR of 170 cps, an ICR of 170 cps, and a PCR of 1400 cps on an AUSM, with the ForeSight rate adjustment parameters set at their default values. If the VC queue service rate is currently 1390 cps and the network reports no congestion, what will the new queue service rate be in cps?

A. 1390 cps

B. 1400 cps

C. 1407 cps

D. 1395 cps

Answer: C

29 Your VC queue is set as follows:

Maximum queue depth 500 cells
CLP high 400 cells
CLP low 250 cells
EFCI threshold 280 cells

Which two of the following statements are true?

A. When 250 cells are in the queue, all CLP tagged cells are discarded.

B. When 280 cells are in the queue, all EFCI tagged cells are discarded.

C. When 280 cells are in the queue, new cells are marked with congestion (EFCI bit set to 1).

D. When 400 cells are in the queue, all arriving CLP tagged cells are not queued and are discarded.

Answers: C, D

30 You have EPD enabled on a VC queue. The EPD0 threshold is 500 cells, the EPD1 threshold is 400 cells, and the CLP high threshold is 550 cells. If the queue is filled up to 450 cells, what will happen?

A. A new CLP 0 cell will be discarded.

B. A new CLP 1 cell will be discarded.

C. A new CLP 0 frame will be discarded.

D. A new CLP 1 frame will be discarded.

Answer: D

31 You want to know the rate decrease factor (RDF) for a standard ABR connection. Which commands can you use to learn this information?

A. **dspfst**

B. **dspcon**

C. **dspcons**

D. **dspabrcon**

E. **dspconstdabr**

Answers: B, E

32 Which of the following statements are true of the **dspcon** command?

A. Connection routing details are listed.

B. Standard ABR parameters are not listed.

C. The most recent **tstdelay** results are listed.

D. Only CBR policing parameters are listed for CBR connections.

E. A master connection lists both a local and remote NSAP address.

F. A slave connection lists both a local and remote NSAP address.

Answers: A, D

33 You are configuring an nrt-VBR connection using the **cnfupcvbr** command. You set the policing type to 3. What does this do? (Choose all that apply.)

A. Disables all policing

B. Disables the second leaky bucket

C. Enables policing using both leaky buckets

D. Checks all cells on the second leaky bucket

E. Tags noncompliant cells on the second leaky bucket

F. Checks only CLP 0 cells on the second leaky bucket

G. Discards noncompliant cells on the second leaky bucket

Answers: C, E, F

34 You want to know how many connections terminate on the UNI ports on your PXM1. Which command should you use to quickly learn this information?

Answer: dspchans

35 You want to test the continuity between the MGX ATM port and the CPE. Which command must you use to accomplish this task?

A. **tstcon**

B. **tstdelay**

C. **tstconseg**

D. **dspchancnt**

E. **addchanloop**

Answer: C

36 Example 21-31 shows the **dspchancnt** output for a PXM1 connection. Based on this information, which of the following statements are true?

Example 21-31 dspchancnt *Output*

```
hei1pop1.1.7.PXM.a > dspchancnt 20

Channel Number              :       20
Channel State               :    alarm
Channel Ingress State       :   normal
Channel Egress State        :   rcvAIS
CLP=0  Rcvd. Cells          :     5412
CLP=1  Rcvd. Cells          :        0
GCRA1  Non Conforming Cells :        0
GCRA2  Non Conforming Cells :      242
EOF    Cells Rcvd.,  to CBus :       0
CLP=0  Discard Cells to CBus :       0
```

continues

Example 21-31 dspchancnt *Output (Continued)*

```
CLP=1  Discard Cells to CBus :        19
CLP=0+1 Xmtd. Cells  to CBus :      5398
CLP=0  Xmtd. Cells   to Port :     10654
CLP=1  Xmtd. Cells   to Port :         4
CLP=0  Discard Cells to Port :         0
CLP=1  Discard Cells to Port :         0
```

A. Channel 20 is passing traffic.

B. Channel 20 is not passing traffic.

C. The channel does not have policing enabled.

D. Cells are being marked with CLP as a result of policing.

E. Egress cells are being dropped because the queue is congested.

F. Ingress cells are being dropped because the queue is congested.

Answers: A, D

Chapter 22

1 Mark the following statements as true or false.

A. _____ VISM supports both A-law and μ-law PCM encoding.

B. _____ VISM-Frame Relay connections are supported in the MGX network.

C. _____ Regardless of the configuration, VISM supports eight T1s or E1s per card.

D. _____ CAS signaling is sent on an AAL5 PVC when you are using VoAAL2.

E. _____ VoIP voice signaling is sent with voice traffic through the MGX network.

Answers: T, F, F, T, F

2 VISM-to-ATM connections are designed to support voice traffic between the VISM and a _____.

A. CESM

B. IGX UVM

C. Cisco 3810

D. TDM switch

E. Class 4 voice switch

Answer: C

3 What is the purpose of a connection identifier (CID)?

A. To associate an endpoint with a connection

B. To identify the IP address of the destination VISM

C. To determine the connection's destination node

D. To specify the number of channels assigned to a connection group

Answer: A

4 How are PCM voice samples segmented and reassembled into ATM cells?

A. AAL1

B. AAL2

C. AAL5

Answers: B, C

5 An AAL2 CPS-PDU is how many bytes in length?

Answer: 48

6 How many PCM voice samples are transported in one ATM cell, assuming that multiplexing is not being done on the connection?

A. 10

B. 3

C. 48

D. It varies.

Answer: B

7 Match the command with its function.

_____ Enables VAD

_____ Creates a new connection identifier

_____ Creates an AAL2 PVC

_____ Configures a line for CAS or CCS

_____ Shows the VISM's voice mode

_____ Creates a voice channel and specifies the compression type

A. **cnfcompvad**

B. **addcid**

C. **addcon**

D. **dspcons**

E. **cnflnsig**

F. **addendpt**

G. **dspvismparam**

Answers: B, F, C, E, G, B

8 You want to create 16 endpoints on T1 line number 5, starting with timeslot 4. What must you type to accomplish this task?

A. **addendpt 1 5 4**

B. **addendpt 1 5 4 16**

C. **addendpts 1 1 16 4**

D. **addendpts 1 5 4 16**

E. **addendpts 5 5 1 16**

Answer: D

9 You want to test the time it takes for a voice cell to travel through the MGX network. Which command must you use?

Answer: tstdelay

10 You have tested a connection using the **tstcon** command. The test has failed. What could be the causes of the failure? (Choose three.)

A. The PXM1 trunk is failed.

B. The remote PXM1 card is failed.

C. The local VISM line is in alarm.

D. The remote VISM line is in alarm.

E. The multisegment connection is incomplete.

Answers: A, B, E

11 Where is the startup configuration usually stored?

A. DRAM

B. NVRAM

C. On an external TFTP server

D. On the hard drive on the PXM1

E. In Flash memory on a PCMCIA card

Answer: B

12 Where is the Cisco IOS image usually stored?

A. DRAM

B. NVRAM

C. On an external TFTP server

D. On the hard drive on the PXM1

E. In Flash memory on a PCMCIA card

Answer: D

13 An RPM Ethernet interface is referred to as 1/2/3. Which three of the following statements are true?

A. The RPM is in MGX card slot 1.

B. The RPM is in MGX card slot 3.

C. The Ethernet card is installed in the upper bay.

D. The Ethernet card is installed in the lower bay.

E. The Ethernet interface is the first one from the top.

F. The Ethernet interface is the second one from the top.

G. The Ethernet interface is the third one from the top.

Answers: A, D, G

14 You have an RPM installed in MGX card slot 11. How would you refer to the switch interface?

A. interface ATM11

B. interface switch 11

C. interface switch 11/1

D. interface switch 11:0

E. interface ATM0:11.1

Answer: C

15 How do you enter privileged EXEC mode?

A. Type **exec**.

B. Type **enable**.

C. Press Ctrl-Z.

D. You do nothing. This is the mode when you log in.

Answer: B

16 What must you type to save your configuration changes so that they are used when the RPM starts up?

A. **save startup**

B. **save running-config**

C. **copy running-config c:startup_file**

D. **copy running-config startup-config**

Answer: D

17   What command must you type to configure the RPM from the CLI?

Answer: configure terminal

18   Based on the portion of the **show running-config** output shown in Example 22-26, which of the following statements are true?

Example 22-26 show running-config *Output*

```
version 12.0
no service pad
service timestamps debug uptime
service timestamps log uptime
no service password-encryption
!
hostname rpm01
!
boot system c:rpm-js-mz.120-2.5.T
enable password cisco
!
ip subnet-zero
!
!
!
interface Ethernet9/2/1
 no ip address
 no ip directed-broadcast
 no ip route-cache
 shutdown
!
```

A. The enable password is hidden.

B. The enable password in encrypted.

C. The enable password is unencrypted.

D. The RPM loads the IOS image from a TFTP server.

E. The RPM loads the IOS image from its Flash memory.

F. The RPM loads the IOS image from the PXM1 hard drive.

Answers: C, F

19 You want to set up remote access to the RPM CLI from the PXM1. Which of the following configuration commands must you use?

A. **reload**

B. **line vty 0 4**

C. **line console 0**

D. **password 0 cisco**

E. **enable password cisco**

F. **boot system c:ios_image_file**

Answers: B, D, E

20 You need to save your configuration changes to a remote location for disaster recovery purposes. Which command must you use?

A. **copy startup-config running-config**

B. **copy running-config startup-config**

C. **copy RPM_config_june19 startup-config**

D. **save running-config c:RPM_config_june19**

E. **copy running-config c:RPM_config_june19**

F. **save running-config PXM RPM_config_june19**

Answer: E

21 You need to configure the RPM ATM switch interface. Which three commands must you use to start interface-specific configuration mode?

A. **enable**

B. **interface atm 0**

C. **configure terminal**

D. **interface switch 1/1**

E. **show interface switch 1/1**

F. **configure interface switch 1/1**

Answers: A, C, D

22 You are in interface-specific configuration mode for your RPM ATM switch interface. What command must you type to activate the interface?

Answer: no shutdown

23 How many PVCs can terminate on a point-to-point subinterface?

Answer: One

24 You are configuring a subinterface on your RPM. You want to terminate PVCs on two other subinterfaces in the network. These other subinterfaces are assigned IP addresses 10.10.15.6 and 10.10.15.7. What IP address should you assign to your subinterface?

A. 10.10.15.6

B. 10.10.15.8

C. 10.15.15.2

D. Any valid IP address

Answer: B

25 You are working on subinterface 2/1/25. Which of the following statements are true?

A. The RPM is in card slot 1.

B. The RPM is in card slot 2.

C. The RPM is in card slot 25.

D. This is subinterface number 1.

E. This is subinterface number 2.

F. This is subinterface number 25.

G. The RPM is installed in the upper bay.

H. The RPM is installed in the lower bay.

Answers: B, F

26 Identify which of the following characteristics are associated with a PVC and which are associated with the connection on an RPM.

_____ Local VPI

_____ Local VCI

_____ Subinterface

_____ Destination card module

Answers: PVC, PVC, PVC, connection

27 On which card modules can you terminate RPM connections?

A. RPM

B. SRM

C. PXM1

D. FRSM

E. CESM

F. AUSM

Answers: A, C, D, F

28 Which of the following subinterfaces are valid?

A. interface switch 5

B. interface switch 1:1.1

C. interface switch 9.1.1

D. interface switch 9/2.63

E. interface switch 12/1.1

F. interface switch 7/0.100

G. interface switch 2/1.105

Answers: E, G

29 You want to find out if subinterface 25 on the RPM installed in slot 3 is up. What command and parameters must you type to accomplish this?

Answer: show interface switch 3/1.25

30 You want to learn how many PVCs are configured on your RPM. Which command should you use?

A. **dspcons**

B. **dsppvcs**

C. **show atm vc**

D. **show atm map**

E. **display atm pvcs**

F. **show switch connections**

Answer: C

31 You are adding a new connection from the RPM to the PXM1 feeder trunk. Which of the following commands is valid?

A. **addcon vpc switch 1 40 rslot 7 50 master local**

B. **addcon vcc switch 9/1.101 533 rslot 0 1 43 452**

C. **addcon vpc switch 9/1.2 32 rslot 7 43 master remote**

D. **addcon vcc switch 9/1.100 235 rslot 0 1 50 500 master local**

Answer: D

32   What is an Edge Label Switch Router or Label Edge Router?

     A. A Cisco 4000 series router

     B. A virtual path between two MGX switches

     C. An MPLS router that controls the operation of an ATM switch

     D. A core device that switches labeled packets according to predefined switching tables

     E. An edge device that performs initial packet processing and classification and applies the first label

     Answer: E

33   What is a Label Switch Router?

     A. A Cisco 4000 series router

     B. A virtual path between two MGX switches

     C. An MPLS router that controls the operation of an ATM switch

     D. A core device that switches labeled packets according to predefined switching tables

     E. An edge device that performs initial packet processing and classification and applies the first label

     Answer: D

34   Which of the following MPLS features are *not* supported on the RPM installed in an MGX PXM1 switch?

     A. LSC function

     B. 16 classes of service

     C. The MGX switch as an LSR

     D. The MGX switch as an LER

     E. Interworking with the BPX switch

     F. Interworking with PXM45 platforms

     Answers: A, B, C

35   How many QoS classes are supported in the MPLS network?

     Answer: Four

36   Mark the following statements as true or false.

     A. _____ VPNs allow different customers to use the same IP address.

     B. _____ All packets for a given IP address are assigned the same label.

C. _____ When using VPNs, customers must have unique IP addressing schemes.

D. _____ A different label is assigned to packets in different traffic classes, even when they have the same IP address.

Answers: T, F, F, T

37 Mark the following statements as true or false.

A. _____ You cannot send MPLS traffic on the MGX feeder trunk.

B. _____ PVPs from RPM ELSRs terminate on a virtual trunk interface on the BPX switch.

C. _____ You must have an MPLS-enabled core network to support MPLS on an RPM installed in an MGX 8250 switch.

D. _____ If you have a BPX ATM MPLS core network, you need to create full-mesh PVCs between all ELSRs in the network.

Answers: F, T, F, F

38 How many UNI or NNI (nonfeeder) lines can you set up on your MGX switch to carry MPLS traffic?

A. Only one.

B. Up to four.

C. It depends on the PXM1 hardware.

Answer: B

INDEX

Symbols

< > (angle brackets), command parameter syntax, 43
[ ] (square brackets), command parameter syntax, 43
? (question mark)
    BPX CLI help system, 420–422
    IGX CLI help system, 44–45

Numerics

1-to-N redundancy, 785
7/8 embedded coding, 153
8/8 inverted coding, 153

A

AAL2 multiplexing, 1059
ABR (Available Bit Rate), 244, 363, 566, 940–941, 1003, 1011. *See also* ABRFST; ABRSTD; Foresight
    characteristics, modifying, 1022–1023
    configurable parameters, 943–944
    congestion, 944–945
        monitoring, 1012
        potential locations for, 942
    ForeSight, 1009
    on UXM cards, 259
    policing, 580
    rate adjustments, 942–943
    RM cells, 941–942
    standard, 587–588
    traffic policing, 251, 254
    VC queuing, 254
ABRFST
    characteristics, 1010
    configurable parameters, 621
    congestion
        criteria for, 1008–1010
        monitoring potential locations, 1009
    parameters, 266
    rate adjustments, 260–261, 605–607
    RM cell, 604–605
    versus ABR Standard, 604

ABRSTD, 260
    implementing on BXM, 598–601
    operation in BPX, 591–592, 595–597
    rate adjustment, 601–604, 620
    RM cells, 588–591
    parameters, 267
    versus ABRFST, 604
AC power supply, IGX switches, 23
access lines
    activating, 495–496
    deactivating, 496
    statistical alarms, clearing, 704
accessing
    BPX CLI
        with auxiliary port, 412
        with control port, 411–412
        with IP Relay, 413
        with LAN port, 413
    IGX CLI, 39
        with auxiliary port, 40
        with control port, 39
        with LAN port, 40
    MGX CLI, 732–733, 767
    RPM CLI, 1108
acquisition of Stratacom, Inc., 6
activating
    ATM ports, 238, 550–551
    downed connections, 303
    Frame Relay ports, 188
    lines, 490
        IGX, 87–88
        on MGX service modules, 811
        on PXM1, 800
    logical Frame Relay ports, 192–193
    physical Frame Relay ports, 192–193
    ports
        on AUSM, 983–984
        on BXM card, 545
    trunks, 474–476, 486–487
active control templates, 192
actual trunk loading versus expected, 286
adaptive clocking, 882
Adaptive Differential Pulse Code Modulation, 103-104
Adaptive VAD, 117
    configuring, 118

addapsln command, 515, 521, 841

addcdred command, 521

addcid command, 1085–1086

addcon command, 106–112, 144–145, 224–225, 262–268, 616–617, 866–868, 888–889, 949–950, 1016, 1025, 1132

added trunks, 66

addendpt command, 1079–1080

addextlp command, 348, 355

addimagrp command, 984

adding

    ATM-Frame Relay connections, 278–279

    connections

        BME, 613

        CBR, 262–264

        data connections, 144–145

        Frame Relay, 224–225

        to AUSM card, 1038–1040

        to MGX 8850-PXM45, 875–876

        to PXM1 card, 1025, 1038–1042

        UBR, 268

        VBR, 264–267

    feeder nodes

        to BPX networks, 830

        to MGX networks, 831–832

    gain to voice circuits, 121

    lines to MGX service modules, 818–819

    trunks, 474–475

        between nodes, 481

        IGX, 67

    users to network, 435

    voice connections, 106–108, 111–112

        to VISM, 1082

addjob command, 318–319

addjobtrig command, 324–325

addln command, 800, 811, 822

addloclp command, 346–347, 721

addport command, 538–539, 769, 885, 919, 983–984, 990–991, 1076

addred command, 786

addressing, multicast, 615

addrmtlp command, 347–348, 354, 721

addrscprtn command, 1077

addtrk command, 58, 67, 474–475, 481

adduser command, 773

addyred command, 28

adjusting VC queues, 216

ADPCM (Adaptive Differential Pulse Code Modulation), 103–104

alarms, 329, 687

    ATM port failures, displaying, 552

    BPX, resolving, 691–699

    bus alarms, 331, 709

    card alarms, 330, 708

    clearing, 314

    connection alarms, 333, 709

    displaying counts of, 313

    event logging, 694–695

    identifying, 329

    line alarms, 332

        resolving, 701

        summarizing historical statistical errors, 702–703

    local, locating, 705

    major, 329, 688

    minor, 329, 689

    multicast connection, 710–711

        monitoring, 711

    port, 332

    remote, locating, 706–707

    slots

        statistical alarm thresholds, 720

        troubleshooting, 717

    statistical error counters, clearing, 697

    status monitor,

        configuring, 440–441

        displaying, 439–440

    summary information, displaying, 684–685

    trunk alarms, 332, 690

        displaying configuration, 691–692

        resolving, 699–700

        statistical thresholds, 692

    types of failures reported, 688

    unreachable nodes, 689

allocating

    bandwidth, statistical reserve, 650–652

    controller resources, 469

        card-level, 470

        port-level, 470

    PVCs for ports, 539

angle brackets (< >), command parameter syntax, 43

APS (Automatic Protection Switching), 368, 501
    automatic operation, 505
    basic operation, 501
    cards
        adding line pairs, 521
        adding redundancy, 521
        displaying, 520
        line configuration, 522
        switching lines, 522
    configuring, 510
    directional switching mode, 510
    implementing on BPX, 506
    K1K2 protocol, 506
    manual operation, 505
    revertive switching, 510
    verifying operation, 518–520
    version 1+1, implementing on BPX, 508,
        511–513
    versions, 502–504
    versus Y-cable redundancy, 509
APS 1+1 Annex B, implementing on BPX
    networks, 508
arbiter polling, 392–393
ARM (Alarm Relay Module) front card, 21
ASM (Alarm/Status Monitor) card, 378–379
    parameters, configuring, 429
assigning
    names
        to BPX nodes, 441–442
        to IGX nodes, 55–56
    port number to AUSM port, 983–984
Asynchronous status field (dspport command
    output), 195
asynchronous update mode, 185
AT&T, Frame Relay network meltdown, 8–9
ATM (Asynchronous Transfer Mode), 27
    ABR connections, 1011
        monitoring potential congestion, 1012
        VC queueing, 254
    AUSM cards
        adding connections, 1038–1040
        configuration example, 1014
        port configuration, 1000
        QBins, 975–976
        traffic flow, 977–978
        VC queues, 977, 1012

BPX
    closed-loop congestion avoidance, 402
    commbus, 391–392
    connections, 362, 861
    crosspoint switch, 389–390
    FBTC, 401
    functions, 371–372
    lines, 362
    network types, 369–370
    product family, 361–362
    QoS, 402
    queuing architectures, 403–404
    reliability, 368–369
    service types, 363–366
    SES, 371
    system hardware, 372–392
    system software, 394–399
    trunks, 362
    UPC, 400
cell relay switching, 366–367
cells
    CLP, 533
    format, 365
    payloads for IGX networks, 61
    transmission over framed trunks, 63
    transmission over unframed trunks, 63
Cisco BPX 8600 switch, 8
connections, 243, 563, 1001–1002
    ABR, 259, 566
    ABRFST, 604–605
        rate adjustment, 605–607
    CBR, 566
    configurable parameters, 617–618
    creating on AUSM, 1016
    displaying channel status, 1028–1029
    establishing, 628–630
    feeder, 1002
    gateways, 274–276
    local, 1002
    modifying CBR characteristics, 1021
    monitoring, 630–635
    policing, 245–254
    segments, 256
    standard ABR, 256–258
    statistics monitoring, 635–643
    UBR, 566
    VBR, 566

CoS, 1003
    CBR example, 1007
    ForeSight, 1008–1010
    VBR example, 1008
encapsulation, 276
endpoints, 856
Frame Relay interworking, 34, 270–271, 608
    SIW, 273–275
ILMI
    configuration information, displaying,
      987–988
    historical statistics counters, displaying,
      998–999
    enabling, 991
IMA, 975
    group characteristics, modifying, 984
    groups,creating, 984
IMA trunks, 63
interworking
    NIW, 928
    SIW, 929–930
lines, configuring, 804
MGX 8850-PXM45 connection types, 861
MPLS, 8
packet flow on IGX switches, 34
ports, 973
    activating, 238, 550–551
    characteristics, displaying, 237
    configuring, 239–240, 550–551
    deactivating, 550–551
    deleting, 550
    detailed information, displaying, 238
    device compatibility, configuring,
      540–541
    egress queue thresholds, displaying, 241
    failures, troubleshooting, 552–558
    IMA, 974
    physical versus virtual, 531
    queue configuration, displaying, 548–549
    queue depth, modifying, 242
    statistics, displaying, 553–555, 993–997
    status, displaying, 980–983
    summary information, displaying,
      979–980
PXM1 cards
    adding connections, 1038–1042
    port configuration, 1000

services, 568
    ABR policing, 580
    CBR policing, 574–575
    time-based policing, 574
    UBR policing, 581–582
    VBR policing, 576–580
signaling protocols, 239, 535–536
    ILMI, 537
    LMI, 536–537
    statistics, displaying, 555–556
timers, modifying, 989
traffic policing, 1004–1006
traffic management, 567
    CAC, 568–569
    traffic control, 567
    traffic shaping, 570
    UPC, 569
traffic shaping, 534
    implementing, 534–535
    port level, 535
virtual ports, 530
virtual trunks, 465–466
ATM card group, Cisco IGX switches, 23
atm pvc command, 1128
AUI (Attachment Unit Interface), LAN port,
    accessing IGX CLI, 40
AUSM cards, 750
    connections
      adding, 1016
      creating, 1038–1040
    ports
      activating, 983–984
      configuring, 1000
    QBins, 975–976
    traffic flow
      egress ATM traffic, 978
      ingress ATM traffic, 977–978
    VC queues, 977, 1012
      characteristics, 1014
      configuration example, 1014
      frame-based traffic control, 1012
automatic fault management, 369
automatic operation, APS, 505
Automatic Routing Management, PVC resource
    partitioning, 491

AutoRoute routing, 7
    BPX switches, 395
    determining potential connection routes,
      646–647
auxiliary ports
    BPX
        CLI, accessing, 412
        configuration, displaying, 450
        external device window, 452–453
        print modes, configuring, 451–452
    data transmission parameters, configuring,
      430–431
    IGX
        CLI, accessing, 40
        configuring, 51–52
        listing functions of, 52–53
    port functions, configuring, 432–433
average utilization rate
    data channels, configuring, 162
    voice channels, configuring, 117
AXSM card, removing connection endpoints, 869

B

back cards
    IGX switches, 20
    RPM, 745
    summary information, 45–47
    UFM-U
        active ports, displaying, 201
        mode, displaying, 200
        mode, selecting, 201–202
bandwidth
    allocating on trunks, 650
    connection load, calculating, 653
    managing on Cisco IGX switches, 30
    of NTM trunks, calculating, 64
    of UXM trunks, calculating, 64
    statistical reserve, 288, 650–652
BCC (Broadband Controller Card), 375–376
    back cards, 376–377
    functions, 377–378
BdataA queues, 215
BdataB queues, 215

BERTs
    results, reporting, 817–818
    running on MGX service modules, 815–817
BGP (Border Gateway Protocol)
    APS, verifying operation, 518–520
bit conversions
    receive, configuring, 137–138
    transmit, configuring, 139
bit error correction, ZCS, 152
BITS (Building Integrated Timing Supply), 305, 671
BME (Broadband Multicast Engine), 384–386
    adding connections, 613
BNI (Broadband Network Interface)
    arbiter polling, 392–393
    BPX switches, 386–392
boot Flash (RPM), 1107
boot images, storing, 1107
boot system command, 1115
BOP (Bit-Oriented Protocol) frame structure,
    217–219
BPX switches
    8600 series switches, 10
    administrative access, 367
    alarms, 687
        locating, 705–707
        major, 688
        minor, 689
        unreachable nodes, 689
    APS
        adding card redundancy, 521
        adding line pairs, 521
        automatic operation, 505
        basic operation, 501
        cards, displaying, 520
        configuring, 510
        implementing, 506–508
        K1K2 protocol, 506
        line configuration, 522
        manual operation, 505
        switching lines, 522
        versions, 502–504
        versus Y-cable redundancy, 509
    ATM
        ABRFST, 604–605
        cell-based switching, 366–367
        cell format, 365
        connections, 861

rate adjustment, 605–607
standard ABR, 591–592, 595–604
auxiliary ports, external device window,
452–453
bus architecture, 388–389
BXM card module, 380–381
ports, activating, 545
cards
line support, 488
trunk support, 464
CLI
accessing with auxiliary port, 412
accessing with control port, 411–412
accessing with IP Relay, 413
accessing with LAN port, 413
command entry modes, 416
command privilege levels, 416
command structure, 415
command syntax, 413–414
editing, 423
help system, 420–422
keyboard shortcuts, 419
logging out, 423
menu-driven interface, 416
repeating commands, 422–423
screen information, 418
commands
addapsln, 515
cnfapsln, 516–517
delapsln, 518
dspapsln, 516
dsplog, 518
precedence rules, 523–524
switchapsln, 517–518
commbus, 391–392
common core card group, BCC, 375–378
concurrent routing, 649
connections, 362
required load, calculating, 652
crosspoint switch, 389–390
date/time, configuring, 443–445
directed routes, 648
environmental measurements,
alarm conditions, 690
FBTC, 401
feeder nodes, adding, 830

functions, 371–372
initial configuration
adduser commands, 425
cnfasm commands, 429
cnfdate commands, 430
cnflan commands, 433
cnfname commands, 429
cnfnwip commands, 434
cnfpwd commands, 426
cnfterm commands, 430
cnftermfunc commands, 432–433
cnftime commands, 430
cnftmzn commands, 430
commands, 423–424
dspcd commands, 428
dspcds commands, 427–428
dspnds commands, 430
dsppwr commands, 428
IP addressing schemes
configuring, 453–456
LAN port, 455–456
line alarms, resolving, 701, 704–705
lines, 362
logging in, requirements, 417
network synchronization, 671
carrier network timing, 671
clock sources, 672
example, 674, 677–679
guidelines, 680–686
selecting clock sources, 673
network types, 369–370
network-assigned routes, 647
nodes
assigning names, 441–442
displaying, 442–443
IP relay addresses, listing, 457
names, verifying, 442
polling, 392–393
ports, 529
physical versus virtual, 531
preferred routes, 648
print modes, configuring, 451–452
printer configuration, displaying, 451
priority bumping, 649
product family, 361–362
reliability, 368–369

serial ports
    communications parameters, configuring, 446–448
    functions of, 446–447
service types, 363
    QoS parameters, 364–366
SES PNNI Controller, 371
slot errors, 690
system data, monitoring, 436–439
system hardware, 372
    BNI, 386–392
    card groups, 374–385
    chassis, 373
system software, 394
    AutoRoute, 395
    CAC, 399
    MPLS, 397–399
    NOS, 394
    PNNI, 396
    VSI, 395
terminal port configuration, displaying, 448–449
tiered networks, 735
time/date, configuring, 443–445
traffic management
    closed-loop congestion avoidance, 402
    QoS, 402
    queuing architectures, 403–404
traffic shaping, 534
    implementing, 534–535
    port level, 535
trunks, 362, 464
    alarms, 690–700
    physical errors, 690
UPC, 400
users, adding to network, 435
virtual ports, 530
virtual trunks, 467
VSI controllers, 468–469
BRM (backward RM), 1011
building data FastPackets, 143
bursts
    handling, 288, 650–652
    signaling delay, 126
bus alarms, 331, 709
BXE cards, line support, 488

BXM (Broadband Switch Module) card module, 380–381
    APS 1+1, implementing, 511–513
    BME, 384–386
    channels, statistics levels, 633
    configurable parameters, 478–481
    enhanced models, 382–383
    FBTC, implementing, 584–586
    line support, 488
    ports
        activating, 545
        creating, 538
        queues, 532
    standard ABR
        implementing, 598–601
        rate adjustments, 601, 604
    statistics level, verifying, 635–643
    trunk errors, 697
    trunk support, 464
    VIs, 532
        QBins, 466–467
bye command, 423, 485

C

CAC (Connection Admission Control), 568–569
    BPX switches, 399
calculating
    connection load, 653
        on BPX connections, 652
    ER, 596
    NTM trunk capacity, 64
    UXM trunk capacity, 64
call agents (VISM), VoIP mode, 1065–1067
capacity calculations, NTM/UXM trunks, 64
CAPC (Congestion Avoidance using Proportional Control), 596
card alarms, 330
card groups
    BPX switches, 374–385
    for routing trunks, 60
Card Type field (dspport command output), 197
card-level resource partitions (MGX), 776–777
cards
    alarms, 708
    ASM, configuring parameters, 429

AXSM, removing endpoints, 869

BPX
    trunk support, 464
    verifying installation, 436–439

BXM
    configurable parameters, 478–481
    FBTC, 584–586
    line support, 488
    port queues, 532
    resource allocation, 470
    standard ABR, implementing, 598, 601
    standard ABR, rate adjustments, 601, 604
    statistics level, verifying, 635–643
    trunk support, 464
    VIs, 466–467, 532

CVM, voice connection types, 107

data faceplate, 356

FRM, 180

FRSM-2CT3, displaying broadband line
    configuration information, 810

hardware, resetting, 723

IGX
    state descriptions, 46–47
    status, displaying, 47–48, 236–237

MGX, high-speed, 752

PXM1 processor card, 737–738
    back card, 738–740
    functions, 741

reserved slots, 427

RPM, 745
    functions, 744
    memory locations, 1107
    port numbering, 1107

slots
    errors, 690, 717
    historical statistical errors, summarizing,
        718–719
    statistical alarm thresholds, 720

SRM card, 741–743
    functions, 743–744

statistics, displaying, 427–428

UFM, 180
    leaky bucket policing, 213–214

UVM
    Fax Relay, 109
    line pass-through state, displaying, 111
    voice connection types, 108

UXM
    ABR, 259
    supported ATM connections, 244
    VISM, clocking options, 1070–1073

carrier network timing, 671
    clock sources, 672–673
    IGX, 305

CAS (Channel Associated Signaling), 125

Cascade, 6

CBR (Constant Bit Rate), 566, 1003
    characteristics, modifying, 1021
    configurable parameters, 618
    connections, adding, 262–264
    example, 1007
    policing, 248, 574–575
        characteristics, modifying, 1030

CCS (Common Channel Signaling), 125

CDVT (Cell Delay Variation Tolerance), 364, 883,
    1005
    time-based model, 1007

cell delay, 364

Cell Delay Variation Tolerance, 364, 883, 1005

cell loss, 364

cell loss priority (CLP), 210

cell rate, 364

Cellbus (Cisco IGX switches), 30–31

cells (ATM), 365–367
    AUSM traffic flow
        egress traffic, 978
        ingress traffic, 977–978
    CLP (Cell Loss Priority), threshold level, 533
    payloads for IGX networks, 61
    traffic shaping, 534
        implementing, 534–535
        port level, 535
    transmission over unframed trunks, 63

CESM (Circuit Emulation Service Module),
    748–749
    circuit emulation ports, listing, 886
    circuit emulation services, creating, 897–899
    egress queues, 882–884
    historical channel statistics counters, listing,
        896–897
    ingress traffic, 883
    ports, displaying configuration information,
        887

changing BPX CLI passwords, 426

Channel Associated Signaling, 125
Channel Range field (dspport command output), 197
Channel Speed field (dspport command output), 197
channelized narrowband FRSMs, 908
channels, 564
    listing on PXM1 UNI ports, 1027–1028
    statistics levels, 633
    utilization, 285
characteristics
    of ABR, modifying, 1022–1023
    of CBR, modifying, 1021, 1030
    of connections, 285–286
        data connections, 143
    of ForeSight, modifying, 1020
    of ingress VCs
        modifying, 1024
        queues, 1032
    of leaky bucket models, 1005
    of QBins, 975–976
        modifying, 987
    of UBR, modifying, 1032
    of VBR, modifying, 1021–1022, 1031
    of VC queues, 254, 1014
chassis, BPX switches, 373
CIDs
    adding to connections, 1085–1086
    displaying for specified LCN, 1086
circuit emulation connections, 879
    clocking modes, 882
    configuring, 893–894
    deleting, 888–889
    detailed status, displaying, 891–893
    signaling, 880
    testing, 894–896
circuit emulation ports, 876
    creating, 885
    listing on CESM, 886
Cisco BPX 8600 switch. *See* BPX switches
Cisco IGX switches, 15
    8410 rack-mount chassis, 16–17
        standalone system, 16
    8420 standalone chassis, 17–19
    8430 standalone chassis, 19–20
    ATM card group, 23
    back card, 20
    bandwidth management, 30
    Cellbus, 30

    data card group, 22
    fault management, 29
    Frame Relay card group, 22
    front card, 20
    lanes, 31
    lines, 25
    message formats, 25–27
    NPM card redundancy, 28
    packet flow
        ATM, 34
        data packets, 32
        Frame Relay, 33
        voice packets, 31
    power supplies, 23
    processor card group, 21
    trunk card group, 21
    trunks, 24
    voice card group, 22
    Y-cable redundancy, 28
Cisco WAN Manager, 733
clearing
    alarms, 314
    BPX CLI display information, 421
    clock alarms, 685
    event log, 695
    Frame Relay connection statistics, 231–232
    Frame Relay port statistics, 206–207
    statistical error counters, 697
CLI (command-line interface)
    BPX
        accessing with auxiliary port, 412
        accessing with control port, 411–412
        accessing with IP Relay, 413
        accessing with LAN port, 413
        clearing display information, 421
        command entry modes, 416
        command privilege levels, 416
        command structure, 415
        command syntax, 413–414
        editing, 423
        help system, 420–422
        keyboard shortcuts, 419
        logging in, 417
        logging out, 423
        menu-driven interface, 416
        monitoring ATM channel statistics, 630
        repeating commands, 422–423
        screen information, 418

IGX
    accessing, 39–40
    CLI shortcuts, 42
    command syntax, 43
    direct entry, 43
    menu-driven interface, 44
    privilege levels, 43
    screen display, 41
MGX, 732–733
    error messages, 772
    login process, 775
RPM
    accessing, 1108
    changing configuration file, 1109–1110
    entering commands, 1109
    modes, 1108
CLLM status /x Timer field (dspport command output), 197
clocking
    BITS, 305
    data channels, 171
        isochronous data clocking, 172–173
        looped clocking mode, 172
        normal clocking mode, 172
        split clock mode, 172
    network synchronization, 671
        carrier network timing, 671
        clock sources, 672
        example, 674, 677–679
        guidelines, 680–686
        selecting clock sources, 673
    on VISM, 1070–1071
        configuring, 1072–1073
    reference selection, 308–309
    sources, 305–307
        alarms, clearing, 314
        listing, 309
        network-wide, specifying, 311–313
    stability, 671
clocking field (dspport command output), 194
closed-loop congestion-avoidance, 402
CLP (cell loss priority), 210
    tagging on UBR connections, 253
    threshold level, 533
clrchstats command, 231, 634
clrclkalm command, 314, 685
clrlnalm command, 344, 704

clrlnerrs command, 332, 704
clrlog command, 329, 336, 695
clrportstats command, 206–207, 557
clrtrkalm command, 332, 339, 698
clrtrkerrs command, 332, 697
cnfapsln command, 516–517, 522, 841–842
cnfasm command, 429, 440–441
cnfatmcls command, 627, 628
cnfbert command, 815–817
cnfbus command, 331
cnfcdaps command, 510
cnfchadv command, 118
cnfchanabrparams command, 956
cnfchanegressq command, 957
cnfchaneir command, 955
cnfchanfst command, 956, 1020
cnfchaningressq command, 957
cnfchanmap command, 957
cnfchanpol command, 955
cnfchanq command, 1024, 1032
cnfchdfm command, 159
cnfchdl command, 128
cnfchec command, 124
cnfchfax command, 119–120
cnfchgn command, 121
cnfchpri command, 228–229
cnfchutl command, 116–117, 285
cnfclksrc command, 311–313, 683–684
cnfcls command, 221–224, 269
cnfcon command, 225–226, 269, 628, 870, 893–894
cnfconabrparams command, 1022–1023
cnfcond command, 135–136
cnfcos command, 301, 661
cnfdate command, 50, 445–446
cnfdclk command, 173
cnfifastrk command, 807
cnfilmi command, 989–991
cnfimagrp command, 984
cnflan command, 433, 455–456
cnfln command, 58, 89–90, 493–495, 800–802, 811–812
cnflnalm command, 332, 342–343, 693–694
cnflnpass command, 109–110
cnflnsig command, 1078
cnfmode command, 201–202
cnfname command, 55–56, 442, 782
cnfnwip command, 434, 456

cnfpass command, 774

cnfport command, 190–192, 239–240, 536, 540–541, 920

    ILMI parameters, 544

    LMI parameters, 543–544

    parameters, 541–543

cnfportcllm command, 921

cnfportq command, 242, 535

cnfportrscprtn command, 806

cnfpref command, 297–300, 661–662

cnfprt command, 53–54, 451–452

cnfpwd command, 49

cnfrcvsig command, 137–138

cnfrsrc command, 491, 539

cnfrtcost command, 300, 663

cnfterm command, 51–52, 449

cnftermfunc command, 432

cnftime command, 50

cnftmzn command, 51, 443–444

cnftrk command, 58, 69–70, 477

cnftrkalm command, 338, 699

cnfupcabr command, 1022

cnfupccbr command, 1021, 1030

cnfupcrtvbr command, 1022

cnfupcubr command, 1022, 1032

cnfupcvbr command, 1021–1022, 1031

cnfvchtp command, 130–132

cnfvismmode command, 1076

cnfxmtsig command, 138–139

coding data FastPackets, 153

commands, 430

    addapsln, 515, 521, 841

    addcid, 1085–1086

    addcon, 106–108, 111–112, 144–145, 224–225, 262–268, 616–617, 866–889, 949–950, 1016, 1025, 1132

    addcred, 521

    addendpt, 1079–1080

    addextlp, 348, 355

    addimagrp, 984

    addjob, 318–319

    addjobtrig, 324–325

    addln, 800, 811, 822

    addloclp, 346–347, 721

    addport, 538–539, 769, 885, 919, 983, 984, 990–991, 1076

    addred, 786

addrmtlp, 347–348, 354, 721

addrscprtn, 1077

addtrk, 58, 67, 474–475, 481

adduser, 773

addyred, 28

atm pvc, 1128

boot system, 1115

bye, 423

clrchstats, 231, 634

clrclkalm, 314, 685

clrlnalm, 344, 704

clrlnerrs, 332

clrlog, 329, 336, 695

clrnerrs, 704

clrportstats, 206–207, 557

clrtrkalm, 332, 339, 698

clrtrkerrs, 332, 697

cnfapsln, 516–517, 522, 841–842

cnfasm, 429, 440–441

cnfatmcls, 627–628

cnfbert, 815–817

cnfbus, 331

cnfchadv, 118

cnfchanabrparams, 956

cnfchanegressq, 957

cnfchaneir, 955

cnfchanfst, 956, 1020

cnfchaningressq, 957

cnfchanmap, 957

cnfchanpol, 955

cnfchanq, 1024, 1032

cnfchdfm, 159

cnfchdl, 128

cnfchec, 124

cnfchfax, 119–120

cnfchgn, 121

cnfchpri, 228–229

cnfchutl, 116–117, 285

cnfclksrc, 311–313

cnfcls, 221–224, 269

cnfcon, 225–226, 269, 628, 870, 893–894

cnfconabrparams, 1022–1023

cnfcond, 135–136

cnfcos, 301, 661

cnfdate, 50, 445–446

cnfdclk, 173

cnfifastrk, 807

cnfilmi, 989–991

cnfimagrp, 984

cnflan, 433, 455–456

cnfln, 58, 89–90, 493–495, 800–802, 811–812

cnflnalm, 332, 342–343, 693–694

cnflnpass, 109–110

cnflnsig, 1078

cnfmode, 201–202

cnfname, 55–56, 442, 782

cnfnwip, 434, 456

cnfpass, 774

cnfport, 53–54, 190–192, 239–240, 536, 540–541, 920

    ILMI parameters, 544

    LMI parameters, 543–544

cnfportcllm, 921

cnfportq, 535

cnfportrscprtn, 806

cnfpref, 297–300, 661–662

cnfprt, 451–452

cnfrcsig, 137–138

cnfrsrc, 491, 539

cnfrtcost, 663

cnfrtcost command, 300

cnfterm, 51–52, 449

cnftermfunc, 432

cnftime, 50

cnftmzn, 51, 443–444

cnftrk, 58, 69–70, 477

cnftrkalm, 338–699

cnfupcabr, 1022

cnfupccbr, 1021, 1030

cnfupcrtvbr, 1022

cnfupcubr, 1022, 1032

cnfupcvbr, 1021–1022, 1031

cnfvchtp, 130–132

cnfvismmode, 1076

cnfwd, 49

cnfxmtsig, 138–139

configure terminal, 1115

copy, 1114

cpyict, 171

cspcd, 520

csprts, 664

delapsln, 518

delcon, 115, 155, 229–230, 268, 869

delcons, 869

deljob, 323

deljobtrig, 325

dellp, 349, 722

delport, 203, 550

deltrk, 58, 81–82, 484–485

dncon, 302–303, 664–665

dnfportq, 242

dnln, 58

dnport, 202–203, 550

dntrk, 58, 82, 485

dspalm, 814

dspalmcnt, 814–815

dspalms, 313, 329, 334–335, 552, 684–685, 802–804, 813

dspapsln, 516, 840

dspasm, 439–440

dspatmcls, 616

dspbert, 817–818

dspbob, 174–175, 332

dspbuses, 331

dspcd, 47–48, 236–237, 428, 438, 781–782

dspcdrscprtn, 783

dspcds, 45–47, 427–428, 436–437, 778–780

dspchan, 1028–1029

dspchancnt, 896–897, 959–961, 1033–1037

dspchans, 1027–1028

dspchcnf, 175–176

dspchdlcnf, 129–130

dspchec, 123–124

dspchstats, 219, 230–231, 634

dspcid, 1086

dspcids, 1086

dspclksrcs, 309, 681

dspcls, 220–221, 269

dspcon, 114, 154–155, 227–228, 269, 623–625, 872–875, 891–893, 951–954, 1017–1019, 1026–1027, 1083–1084

dspconcnt, 1088–1089

dspcond, 134

dspcons, 112–113, 154, 227, 269, 333, 625, 626–627, 870–871, 889–890, 950–951, 1016–1017, 1025–1026, 1082

dspconst, 132–133

dspconstdabr, 1023

dspcurclk, 310, 682

dspds3ln, 810

dspds3lns, 809

dspendpt, 1081
dspendpts, 1080
dspict, 167–168
dspifip, 782
dspilmi, 987–988
dspilmicnt, 998–999
dspilmis, 992
dspjob, 320–321
dspjobs, 319–320
dsplancnf, 56–57
dsplink, 824
dsplmistats, 555–556
dspln, 58, 111, 799–800, 822
dsplnalmcnf, 332, 341–342, 691–692
dsplncnf, 58, 88–89, 492–493
dsplndsp, 1079
dsplnerrs, 332, 340–341, 702–703
dsplns, 58, 87, 188, 332, 489, 798,
    807–809, 821
dspload, 292–293, 658
dsplog, 329, 335, 518, 694–695
dspmngcidcnt, 1089–1090
dspmode, 200
dspmodes, 201
dspnds, 54–55, 330, 442–443, 706
dspnw, 79–80, 329, 706–707
dspnwip, 57–58, 457
dspport, 193– 200, 238, 887, 980–983, 1076
dspportcnt, 922–925, 993–997
dspportq, 241, 548–549, 986
    parameters, 549
dspportrscprtns, 991
dspports, 198, 237, 332, 545–547, 805, 886,
    979–980, 990
dspportsqs, 985
dspportstats, 204–206, 332, 553–555
dspprtcnf, 451
dspppwd, 49–50, 427
dspppwr, 48
dspred, 787
dsprscprtn, 1077–1078
dsprtks, 482–483
dsprts, 296–297
dspsigqual, 140
dspslotalmcnf, 720
dspslotalms, 717
dspsloterrs, 718–719

dspslotlink, 825
dsptermcnf, 448–449
dsptermfunc, 52–53, 450
dsptrk, 58, 68–69
dsptrkcnf, 58, 68–69, 483–484
dsptrkerrs, 332, 336–337, 696
dsptrks, 58, 65–66, 314, 332, 686, 806
dsptrkutl, 294–296, 659– 660
dspusers, 774
dspvismparam, 1074–1075
dssport, 916–918
dssports, 915–916
editjob, 321
enable, 1112
enable password, 1116
help, 44
help (BPX CLI), 420–421
hostname, 1115
IGX CLI syntax, 43
interface, 1120, 1127
ip, 1131
ip address, 1127
line, 1116–1117
map-group, 1130
map-list, 1131
password, 1117
reload, 1114
repeating, 422–423
resetcd, 330, 345, 723
rpmrscprtn, 1117–1118
runjob, 322
show atm map, 1131
show atm vc, 1129–1130
show interface, 1119–1120, 1125–1126
show running-config, 1112–1114
show startup-config, 1112–1114
show switch connections, 1133–1134
shutdown, 1127
snfclksrc, 683–684
stopjob, 323
switchapsln, 517–518, 522, 842
switchcc, 331, 708
troubleshooting, 333
tstcon, 350–354, 894–895, 958, 1037, 1087
tstconseg, 712–714, 1038
tstdelay, 232, 895–896, 959, 1037–1087
upcon, 303, 665

upln, 58, 87–88, 490
upport, 192–193, 238, 545
uptrk, 58, 66, 474–476
users, 774
vt, 58, 80–81, 485
window, 453
xcnfport, 920–921
xcnfportq, 987
commbus, 391–392
Common Channel Signaling, 125
common core card group (BPX), BCC, 375–376
    back cards, 376–377
    functions, 377–378
Communicate priority field (dspport command
    output), 196
communication failures, 688
    unreachable nodes, 689
comparing virtual and physical trunks, 466
complex gateways, 274–276
compression schemes, 103
    ADPCM, 103–104
    CS-ACELP, 104
    LD-CELP, 104
    PCM, 103
concurrent routing, 649
conditioning templates, 133
    configuring, 135–136
    displaying, 134
configurable parameters
    ABRFST, 621
    ABRSTD, 620
    ATM connections, 617–618
    BXM cards, 478–481
    CBR, 618
    data channels
        DFM, 159–160
        ICS, 160–161
        utilization, 162
    IGX lines, 90–92
        frame scramble, 96
        HCS masking, 96
        idle code, 96
        IMA clock mode, 93
        IMA group member, 93
        IMA max. diff. dly, 93
        IMA protocol option, 93
        line 56KBS bit pos, 95

line cable type, 95
line coding, 94
line CRC, 94
line DS-0, 93
line encoding, 94
line length, 95
line pct fast modem, 95
line recv impedance, 94
line T1 signaling, 95
loop clock, 93
retained links, 93
IGX trunks, 70–72
    deroute delay time, 78
    frame scramble, 78
    gateway channels, 77
    HCS masking, 77
    header type, 75
    idle code, 75
    IMA clock code, 78
    IMA group member, 73
    IMA max. diff. dly, 78
    IMA protocol option, 78
    line cable length impedance, 77
    line cable type impedance, 76
    line coding, 76
    line CRC, 76
    line DS-0, 73
    line framing, 76
    line recv impedance, 76
    line type, 75
    loop clock, 74
    pass sync, 74
    payload scramble, 77
    rcv trunk rate, 73
    restrict PCC traffic, 75
    retained links, 73
    routing cost, 75
    statistical reserve, 74
    subrate data rate, 74
    subrate interface, 73
    traffic, 77
    transit trunk rate, 73
    VC shaping, 79
    virtual trunk type, 78
    virtual trunk VPI, 78
    VPC conns, 79
    VPI address, 75

port queues, 183
UBR, 622
VBR, 619
VC queues, 212
configuration files, copying, 1114
configure terminal command, 1115
configuring
    access lines, 495–496
    Adaptive VAD, 118
    alarm status monitor, 440–441
    APS, 510, 518–520
    ATM
        lines, 804
        ports, 239–240, 550–551
    BPX switches
        adduser command, 425
        cnfasm command, 429
        cnfdate command, 430
        cnflan command, 433
        cnfname command, 429
        cnfnwip command, 434
        cnfpwd command, 426
        cnfterm command, 430
        cnftermfunc command, 432–433
        cnftime command, 430
        cnftmzn command, 430
        commands, 423–424
        date/time, 443–445
        dspcd command, 428
        dspcds command, 427–428
        dspnds command, 430
        dsppwr command, 428
        IP addressing schemes, 453–456
        print modes, 451–452
        serial port communications parameters,
            446–448
        terminal ports, 449
    circuit emulation connections, 893–894
    data channels, clock mode, 173
    data connections
        ICT, 169
        input control signal transport, 165
        output control signal transport, 166
    echo canceller parameters, 124
    Fax Relay, 119–120

Frame Relay
    connections, 220–232
    ports, 925–926
    signaling parameters, 190–192
IGX switches
    auxiliary port, 51–52
    control port, 51–52
    print modes, 53–54
    trunks, 69–70
lines, 89–90
    ATM device compatibility, 493–495
MGX switches
    RPM, 1121–1122
ports
    on AUSM cards, 1000
    on PXM1 cards, 1000
QBins, 976
    thresholds, 532–533
routes
    direct, 290
    IGX, 290, 304
    preferred, 290
RPM, hostname, 1115
subinterfaces, 1122
trunks, 486–487
    alarm reporting, 699
UVM cards, line pass-through, 109–110
VISM
    clocking options, 1072–1073
    VoATM services, 1067–1070
voice channels, 130–132
    conditioning template, 135–136
    dial types, 127–129
    gain, 121
    receive signaling bit conversion, 137–138
    signaling bit conversion, 136–139
    transmit signaling bit conversion, 138–139
    utilization, 116–117
congestion, 215
    ABR, 944–945
    ABRFST rate adjustment, 261
    ATM
        EPD, 1012
        monitoring potential locations, 1012
    control mechanisms, 570–572
    EFCI, 533
    example, 939

ForeSight, 935, 1009
    configurable characteristics, 938, 1010
    criteria for, 937, 1008–1010
    monitoring potential congestion,
        936, 1009
    rate adjustment, 216
    VC queue servicing, 216
Conjugate Structure Algebraic Code Excited Linear
    Prediction, 104
connecting to MGX CLI, 767
connection admission control, 283
connection alarms, 333
connection load, estimating, 285
connection-oriented protocols, encapsulation, 278
connections
    ABRFST
        rate adjustment, 605–607
        RM cell, 604–605
    activating, 303
    adding to MGX 8850-PXM45, 875–876
    alarms, 709
    ATM, 243, 563, 861, 1001–1002
        ABR, 259, 566
        CBR, 566
        channel status, displaying, 1028–1029
        configurable parameters, 617–618
        CoS, 1003
        creating on AUSM, 1016
        displaying configuration information,
            1017–1019
        displaying standard ABR characteristics,
            1023
        establishing, 628–630
        feeder connections, 1002
        gateways, 274–276
        local connections, 1002
        monitoring, 630–635
        policing, 245–254
        removing, 268
        segments, 256
        single-segment, 564
        standard ABR, 256–258
        two-segment, 565
        UBR, 566
        VBR, 566
        VC queuing, 254
    ATM-Frame Relay, adding, 278–279

BME Multicast, adding, 613
BPX, 362
bursts, handling, 288, 650–652
CBR, adding, 262–268
characteristics, 285–286
CIDs, adding, 1085–1086
circuit emulation connections, 879
    clocking modes, 882
    configuring, 893–894
    deleting, 888–889
    detailed status, displaying, 891–893
    signaling, 880
    testing, 894–896
continuity testing, 1037–1087
creating on RPM, 1134–1135
data, 142, 153
    adding, 144–145
    detailed information, displaying, 154–155
    DFM, 144
    ICT, configuring, 167–170
    removing, 155
    subrate, 151
    summary information, displaying, 154
    super-rate, 151
    transparent, 152
    transporting control signal states, 148–150
    types of, 146–147
deactivating, 302–303
displaying routing information, 296–297
endpoints
    managed CID count, displaying,
        1089–1090
    removing, 869
event logging, 695
failures, alarms, 687
feeder nodes on MGX switches, 862–863
Frame Relay, 207
    ABR, 940–945
    adding, 224–225
    class, specifying, 220–221
    CLP bit, 210
    configuring, 220–232
    creating in MGX network, 962–964
    customizing, 225–226
    EFCN bit, 210
    FR-SSCS, 272
    global addressing, 208

parameters, 213
  removing, 229–230
  setting channel priority, 228–229
  UFM leaky bucket policing, 213–214
FRSM, 926–927
  feeder connections, 927
  local connections, 928
integrity, testing, 714–716
load model, statistical reserve, 288
load, calculating, 653
local loopback
  removing, 722
  testing, 712–713
maximum route cost, setting, 300
multicast services, 613
parameters, modifying, 870
PNNI, dynamic partitioning, 473–474
potential routes, identifying, 643–647
preferred routes, specifying, 297–300
remote loopback, testing, 714
rerouted, prioritizing, 301
routing, 657–658
  displaying statistics, 664
segments, 565
standard ABR, 587–588
  implementing on BXM, 598, 601
  operation in BPX, 591–592, 595–597
  rate adjustments, 601–604
  RM cells, 588–591
  versus ABRFST, 604
statistics monitoring, 635–643
testing, 352–353, 632
  external loopback, 355
  local loopback, 353–354
  remote loopback, 354
VCs
  PVCs, 851–858
  SPVCs, 853–854, 858
  SVCs, 855–856, 859
voice, 1059
  AAL2 segmentation, 1062–1063
  adding to UVM/CVM cards, 106–108,
    111–112
  CIDs, 1059
  deleting, 115

detailed parameters, 114
displaying, 112–113
endpoints, 1059
vt, creating, 485
continuity of connections, verifying, 1037
control port
  BPX configuration, displaying, 450
  CLI, accessing
    BPX, 411–412
    IGX, 39
  data transmission parameters, configuring,
    430–431
  IGX
    configuring, 51–52
    listing functions of, 52–53
  port functions, configuring, 432–433
control signal transport (IGX), 148–150
  interleaved, 149–150
  normal, 149
  partially interleaved, 150
control terminal port, 430
conventions
  BPX CLI command structure, 415
  BPX node names, 441–442
converting Frame Relay frames to FastPackets, 209
copy command, 1114
copying data channels, 170
CoS (class of service), 1003
  ABR, 1011
    ForeSight, 1008–1010
    monitoring potential congestion, 1012
  BPX switch buffers, 403
  CBR, example, 1007
  traffic policing, 1005–1006
  VBR, example, 1008
counters
  for signaling protocols, 185
  of summary statistics, 631
cpyict command, 171
creating
  circuit emulation ports, 885
  connections
    Frame Relay connections in MGX
      network, 962–964
    on AUSM card, 1038–1040
    on PXM1 card, 1038–1042

data FastPackets, 143
IGX jobs, 318–319
IMA groups, 984
jobs
  IGX, 316
  triggers, 318
logical ports
  Frame Relay ports, 189–190
  on physical lines, 805, 990–991
MGX user IDs, 773
service emulation services on MGX, 897–899
SPVCs with MGX 8850-PXM45 CLI, 875–876
virtual ports, 538
vt connections, 485
criteria for reporting ATM congestion locations with
  ForeSight, 1008–1010
crosspoint switche, 389–390
CS-ACELP (Conjugate Structure Algebraic Code
  Excited Linear Prediction), 104
cspcds command, 436–437
customizing Frame Relay connections, 225–226
Cutoff RM factor, 595
CVM (Channelized Voice Module) cards, 101
  card group (IGX), 84
  front card, 22
  subrate data connections, 151
  super-rate data connections, 151
  transparent data connections, 152
  voice connections, adding, 106–108, 111–112
CWM (Cisco WAN Manager), 10

D

data card group, Cisco IGX switches, 22
data channels, 142, 156
  clocking, 171
    configuring, 173
    isochronous data clocking, 172–173
    looped clocking mode, 172
    normal clocking mode, 172
    split clocking mode, 172
  DFM, 159–160
  ICS, configuring, 160–161
  serial, 163
  utilization, configuring, 162

data connections, 142
  adding, 144–145
  characteristics, 143
  control signal states, transporting on IGX,
    148–150
  data channels, 156
    EIA/TIA-232, 157
    EIA/TIA-449, 158
    serial, 163
    subrate, 158
    super-rate, 158
    transparent, 158
    V.35, 157
    X.21, 158
  deleting, 155
  ICTs
    configuring, 169
    copying, 170
    displaying, 167–168
  input control signal sampling, configuring, 165
  output control signals, specifying, 166
  subrate, 151
  summary information, displaying, 154
  super-rate, 151
  transparent, 152
  types of, 146–147
data faceplate buttons, 356
data FastPackets
  building, 143
  coding, 153
  DFM, 144
  partially filled, 147
data networks, private line replacement, 141
data packet flow on IGX switches, 32
data transmission parameters, configuring control/
  auxiliary ports, 430–431
date/time, setting on IGX nodes, 50
DC power supply on IGX switches, 23
DCE (Data Communication Equipment), 164
DE threshold field (dspport command output), 195
deactivating
  access lines, 496
  ATM ports, 550–551
  connections, 302–303
  Frame Relay ports, 202–203
  trunks, 485–487
delapsln command, 518

delcon command, 115, 155, 229–230, 268, 869
delcons command, 869
deleting
    ATM connections, 268
    circuit emulation connections, 888–889
    data connections, 155
    Frame Relay connections, 229–230
    loopbacks, 722
    network-wide clock sources, 683–684
    trunks, 484–485
        between nodes, 81–82
    voice connections, 115
deljob command, 323
deljobtrig command, 325
dellp command, 349, 722
delport command, 203, 550
deltrk command, 58, 81–82, 484–485
demand for Frame Relay services, 5
deroute delay time parameter (IGX trunks), 78
devices
    CIDs, 1059
    DCE, 164
    DTE, 164
    endpoints, 856, 1059
        removing, 869
    FRADs, 180
    MGX, 729–730, 736
        features, 730
        optional features, 732
        user services, 731
    modems, 64 kbps upgrade, 119
DFM (Data Frame Multiplexing), 7, 30–32, 144
    configuring, 159–160
dial types for voice channels, configuring, 127–129
dialing protocols, timing, 126
direct command entry mode, 416
direct entry of IGX commands, 43
Direct NLPID encapsulation, 278
directed routes, 290, 648
directional switching mode, APS, 510
displaying, 545–547
    alarms, 313
        ATM port-related, 552
        status monitor, 439–440

ATM ports
    characteristics, 237
    queue configuration, 548–549
    statistics, 553–555
auxiliary port functions (IGX), 52–53
BPX
    nodes, 442–443
    port functions, 450
    printer configuration, 451
    terminal port configuration, 448–449
card status, 330, 427–428
connections
    configuration information, 1017–1019
    routing information, 296–297, 664
control port functions (IGX), 52–53
current network clock sources, 682
data connections
    detailed information, 154–155
    ICTs, 167–168
    summary information, 154
echo canceller parameters, 123–124
egress port queue configuration, 985
external device window, 452–453
Frame Relay port parameters, 193–197
Frame Relay port statistics, 204–206
front/back card summary information, 45–47
IGX switches
    card status, 47–48, 236–237
    environmental measurements, 48
    job statistics, 319–321
    line configuration, 88–89
    line summary information, 87
    nodes, 54–55
    tabular network summary, 79–80
    trunk configuration, 68–69
    trunk summary information, 65–66
    user password, 49–50
ILMI configuration information, 987–988
IP relay address of IGX nodes, 57–58
lines
    detailed configuration information,
        492–493
    pass-through state (UVM cards), 111
    status information, 489
LMI/ILMI statistics per port, 555–556
logical ports on MGX PXMI card, 990
network users, 435

node status, 430
port resource partitions, 991
potential network clock sources, 681
power supply status, 428
QBin statistics, 986
serial port configurations, 447–448
signaling protocol configuration on PXMI, 992
standard ABR characteristics of connections, 1023
system data, 436–439
system power status, 439
trunks
    alarm state, 314, 686
    bandwidth, 292–293
    usage statistics, 294–296
UFM-U back card mode, 200
voice channels
    conditioning template, 134
    connection state, 132–133
    signaling bit conversion, 140
    signaling timing parameters, 129–130
    summary configuration information, 140–141
voice connections, detailed parameters, 112–114
distribution process of T1 lines, 820–825
DLCIs (data-link connection identifiers), 207, 927
dncon command, 302–303, 664–665
dnln command, 58
dnport command, 202–203, 550
dntrk command, 58, 82, 485
double-height card slots, configuring, 753
downing
    Frame Relay ports, 202–203
    IGX lines, 97
    trunks, 485
        IGX, 82
DRAM (dynamic random-access memory), 1107
DS0A subrate connections, 151
DSPs (Digital Signal Processors)
    echo cancellers, 123
    PCM, converting voice samples to ATM cells, 1061
    voice compression, 103
        ADPCM, 103–104
        CS-ACELP, 104

LD-CELP, 104
PCM, 103
dspalm command, 814
dspalmcnt command, 814–815
dspalms command, 313, 329, 334–335, 552, 684–685, 802–804, 813
dspapsln command, 516, 840
dspasm command, 439–440
dspatmcls command, 616
dspbert command, 817–818
dspbob command, 174–175, 332
dspbuses command, 331
dspcd command, 47–48, 236–237, 428, 438, 520, 781–782
dspcdrscprtn command, 783
dspcds command, 45,–47, 427–428, 778– 780
dspchan command, 1028–1029
dspchancnt command, 896–897, 959–961, 1033–1037
dspchans command, 1027–1028
dspchcnf command, 175–176
dspchdlcnf command, 129–130
dspchec command, 123–124
dspchstats command, 219, 230–231, 634
dspcid command, 1086
dspcids command, 1086
dspclksrcs command, 309, 681
dspcls command, 220–221, 269
dspcon command, 114, 154–155, 227–228, 269, 623–625, 872–875, 891–893, 951–954, 1017–1019, 1026–1027, 1083–1084
dspconcnt command, 1088–1089
dspcond command, 134
dspcons command, 112–113, 154, 227, 269, 333, 625–627, 870–871, 889–890, 950–951, 1016–1017, 1025–1026, 1082
dspconst command, 132–133
dspconstdabr command, 1023
dspcurclk command, 310, 682
dspds3ln command, 810
dspds3lns command, 809
dspendpt command, 1081
dspendpts command, 1080
dspict command, 167–168
dspifip command, 782
dspilmi command, 987–988
dspilmicnt command, 998–999

dspilmis command, 992

dspjob command, 320–321

dspjobs command, 319–320

dsplancnf command, 56–57

dsplink command, 824

dsplmistats command, 555–556

dspln command, 58, 111, 799–800, 822

dsplnalmcnf command, 332, 341–342, 691–692

dsplncnf command, 58, 88–89, 492–493

dsplndsp command, 1079

dsplnerrs command, 332, 340–341, 702–703

dsplns command, 58, 87, 188, 332, 798,
    807–809, 821

dsplns commnad, 489

dspload command, 292–293, 658

dsplog command, 329, 335, 518, 694–695

dspmngcidcnt command, 1089–1090

dspmode command, 200

dspmodes command, 201

dspnds, 430

dspnds command, 54–55, 330, 430, 442–443, 706

dspnw command, 79–80, 329, 706–707

dspnwip command, 57–58, 457

dspport command, 193–200, 238, 887, 980–982,
    983, 1076

dspportcnt command, 922–925, 993–997

dspportq command, 241, 548–549, 986

dspportrscprtns command, 991

dspports command, 198, 237, 332, 545–547, 805,
    886, 979–980, 990

dspportsqs command, 985

dspportstats command, 204–206, 332, 553–555

dspprtcnf command, 451

dsppwd command, 49–50, 427

dsppwr command, 48

dspred command, 787

dsprscprtn command, 1077–1078

dsprtks command, 482–483

dsprts command, 296–297, 664

DSPs (Digital Signal Processors), 1070

dspsigqual command, 140

dspslotalmcnf command, 720

dspslotalms command, 717

dspsloterrs command, 718–719

dspslotlink command, 825

dsptermcnf command, 448–449

dsptermfunc command, 52–53, 450

dsptrk command, 58, 68–69

dsptrkcnf command, 58, 68–69, 483–484

dsptrkerrs command, 332, 336–337, 696

dsptrks command, 58, 65–66, 314, 332, 686, 806

dsptrkutl command, 294–296, 659–660

dspusers command, 774

dspvismparam command, 1074–1075

dssport command, 916–918

dssports command, 915–916

DTE (Data Terminal Equipment), 164

dual leaky bucket model, 573, 1004
    ATM connection policing, 246–247
    CoS, policing, 1005–1006

dynamic partitioning, 473–474

dynamic rate control, Frame Relay services, 7

E

E-1, 7

E1 format (CAS), 126

E1 lines, signaling methods, 1078

E3 lines, listing summary configuration information,
    809

echo, 122

echo cancellers, 123
    parameters
        configuring, 124
        displaying, 123–124

echo perception, 122

Echo Return Loss (ERL), 122

ECN queue threshold field (dspport command
    output), 194

editing
    BPX CLI, 423
    IGX jobs, 317–318

editjob command, 321

EFCI (Explicit Forward Congestion Indicator), 533,
    571, 591
    threshold, 242

EFCN (Explicit Forward Congestion
    Notification), 210

egress port queues
    displaying configuration, 985
    on CESM, 882–883

egress traffic
AUSM cell flow, 978
on CESM, 884
EIA/TIA-232 data channels, 157
EIA/TIA-449 data channels, 158
enable command, 1112
enable password command, 1116
enabling
Frame Relay ports, 188
ILMI, 991
encapsulation
ATM, 276
Frame Relay, 277–278
simple gateway process, 61
endpoints, 856, 1059
adding to VISM, 1079–1080
deleting, 869
detailed information, displaying, 1081
listing on VISM, 1080
managed CID count, displaying, 1089–1090
end-to-end connections, segments, 863–864
end-to-end SPVCs, 854
enhanced BXM cards, 382–383
Enter User ID prompt (IGX), 40
entering commands
in RPM CLI, 1109
partial command entry, IGX help system, 44–45
entry modes for BPX CLI commands, 416
environmental measurements (IGX), displaying, 48
EPD (Early Packet Discard), 585, 1012
ER (Explicit Rate) control, 571, 596
calculating, 596
ERL (echo return loss), 122
error counts, dsptrkerrs command output, 337–338
Error threshold field (dspport command output), 195
errors
BERTs
reporting results, 817–818
running on MGX service modules, 815–817
message reporting, MGX CLI, 772
establishing
ATM connections, 628–630
vty sessions with remote nodes, 80–81
estimating connection load, 285

ETS (errored ten seconds), 697
line alarms, 704
event log
alarms, 694–695
clearing, 695
examples
of CBR, 1007
of VBR, 1008
of network synchronization, 674, 677–679
of trunk resource partitioning, 471–473
executing IGX jobs, 317
expected trunk loading versus actual, 286
Explicit Forward Congestion Notification (EFCN), 210
external device window, 452–453
external loopbacks, IGX, 352

F

failed connection alarms, 687
failed trunks, 688
rerouting, 648
failure resets, 723
FastPackets, 6
coding, 153
converting from Frame Relay frames, 209
creating, 143
data, 143
DFM, 144
last header fields, 211–212
message format, 25–27
partially filled, 147
transmission over framed trunks, 63
transmission over unframed trunks, 63
voice, 102
fault management
BPX switches, 369
IGX switches, 29
Fax Relay, 109
configuring, 119–120
FBTC (Frame-Based Traffic Control), 253, 401, 583
implementing on BXM, 584–586

features
    of MGX product family, 730
    of MPLS, 1092, 1104–1105
    of VISM
        Release 1.5, 1056–1058
        Release 2.0, 1058
        Release 2.1, 1058
feedback, 364
feeder connections, 926–927, 1002
    example, 927
    MGX, 862–864
feeder nodes, 828–829
    adding to BPX networks, 830
    adding to MGX networks, 831–832
FGCRA (Frame-Based Generic Cell Rate
    Algorithm), 586
fields
    of Frame Relay header, 182
    of last FastPacket header, 211–212
finding MGX command syntax, 771
first FastPacket header, 209–210
five nines, 9
flat networks, 369, 828
ForeSight, 7, 215, 364, 566, 935, 1003, 1009.
    See also ABR; ABRFST
    configurable characteristics, 938, 1010
    congestion criteria, 937, 1008–1010
    modifying connection characteristics, 1020
    monitoring potential congestion, 1009
    potential congestion locations, 936
    rate adjustment, 216, 260–261
    VC queue servicing, 216
formats
    of ATM cells, 365
    of IGX lines, 84
    of routing trunks, 60
forwarding packets, MPLS, 1055
fractional FRSMs, 909
fractional trunks, 62
FRAD (Frame Relay access device), 180
frame discard, 571
frame forwarding, 217–219, 927
frame forwarding ports, 908

Frame Relay
    AT&T network meltdown, 8–9
    ATM interworking, 34, 270–271, 608
        SIW, 273–275
    cards, 180
    Cascade, 6
    channel statistics, 219
    connections, 207
        ABR, 940–945
        adding, 224–225
        channel priority, setting, 228–229
        class, specifying, 220–221
        CLP bit, 210
        configuring, 220–232
        creating in MGX network, 962–964
        customizing, 225–226
        EFCN bit, 210
        global addressing, 208
        parameters, 213
        removing, 229–230
        statistics, clearing, 231–232
    demand for services, 5
    dynamic rate control, 7
    encapsulation, 277–278
    frames, 182
        converting to FastPackets, 209
    logical ports, creating, 189–190
    packet flow on IGX switches, 33
    port queues, 182
        configurable parameters, 183
    ports, 181, 907–908
        card module information, displaying,
            199–200
        configuring, 925–926
        displaying detailed information, 198
        downing, 202–203
        fractional FRSMs, 909
        narrowband channelized, 908
        parameters, displaying, 193–197
        statistics, clearing, 206–207
        statistics, displaying, 204–206
    serial ports, 908
    signaling protocols
        counters, 185
        NNI, 186
        timers, 185
    UFM, leaky bucket policing, 213–214

UNI, 184
VC queue parameters, 212
Frame Relay card group (Cisco IGX switches), 22
frame scramble parameter (IGX trunks), 78
frame-based traffic control (FBTC), 253, 1012
framed trunks (IGX), 62
cell transmission, 63
FastPacket transmission, 63
frames, converting to FastPackets, 209
framing, 86
T1 D4, 125
T1 ESF, 125
FRM (Frame Relay Module), 180
back card, 23
logical Frame Relay ports
creating , 189–190
removing, 203
front card, 23
FRM-31 card group (IGX), 84
front cards
IGX switches, 20
summary information, displaying, 45– 47
FRSM (Frame Relay Switch Module), 749–750
connection types, 926–927
feeder connections, 927
high-speed FRSM
policing, 934
traffic flow, 913–914
local connections, 928
low-speed
policing, 931–932
traffic flow, 912
NIW, 928
port queues, 910
high-speed, 911–912
low-speed, 910
ports, configuring, 925–926
SIW, 929–930
VC queues, 946–947
FRSM-2CT3 card modules, displaying broadband
line configuration information, 810
FR-SSCS (Frame Relay Service-Specific
Convergence Sublayer), 272
full status poll, 185
Full Status Polling Cycle field (dspport command
output), 197

full-mesh networks, resolving persistent loops with
MPLS, 1094–1095
functions
of BPX serial ports, 446–447
of BPX switches, 371–372
of voice channel conditioning template, 133
of VSI controllers, 468–469
FUNI (Frame-based user-network interface)
ports, 908, 927
future of WAN technologies, 9
MPLS VPN over ATM, 10

G

gain, configuring on voice channels, 120–121
Gang of Four, 5
gateway channels parameter (IGX trunks), 77
generating
loopback test patterns
local loopback, 712–713
remote loopback, 714
RM cells, 590–591
global addressing, 208

H

handling bursts, 288
hardware
BPX, 372
BNI, 386–392
card groups, 374–385
chassis, 373
failures, 688
MGX, selecting, 755–758
resetting for cards, 330, 723
HCS masking parameter (IGX trunks), 77
HDM (High-Speed Data Module) front card, 22
header type parameter (IGX trunks), 75
HEC framing, 63
help command, 44, 420–421, 770–771
help system
BPX CLI, 420–422
IGX CLI, 44–45
high availability services, necessity of, 9
high-speed card modules, MGX, 752

high-speed FRSMs
 ingress traffic flow, 913–914
 policing, 934
 port queues, 911–912
hop count, 211
hostname command, 1115

I

IBGP distribution of VPN routing information, 1106
IBS (initial burst size), 947
ICS (Idle Code Suppression), configuring, 160–161
ICT (Interface Control Template), 166
 configuring, 169
 copying, 170
 displaying, 167–168
IDE to DE Mapping field (dspport command
 output), 197
identifying
 alarms, 329
 connection routes, 643
  AutoRoute routing, 646–647
  BPX routing, 644–646
idle code parameter (IGX trunks), 75
IGX switches
 8410 rack-mount chassis, 16–17
 8420 standalone chassis, 17–19
 8430 standalone chassis, 19–20
 Adaptive VAD, 117–118
 alarms
  bus alarms, 331
  card alarms, 330
  connection alarms, 333
  identifying, 329
  line alarms, 332
  port alarms, 332
  trunk alarms, 332
 ATM card group, 23
 ATM connections
  cell payloads, 61
  congestion control segments, 256
  removing, 268
 auxiliary port
  configuring, 51–52
  listing functions of, 52–53

back cards, displaying summary information,
 45–47
bandwidth management, 30
card states, displaying, 46–47, 236–237
Cellbus, 30–31
CLI
 accessing, 39–40
 directy entry, 43
 menu-driven command interface, 44
 privilege levels, 43
connections
 ATM, 243
 testing, 352–355
control port
 configuring, 51–52
 listing functions of, 52–53
control signal states, transporting, 148–150
CVM cards, voice connection types, 107
data card group, 22
data channels, clocking, 171–172
data connections, 142
 adding, 144–145
 characteristics, 143
 removing, 155
 subrate, 151
 super-rate, 151
 transparent, 152
 types of, 146, 147
displaying network in tabular form, 79–80
environmental measurements, displaying, 48
fault management, 29
Frame Relay card group, 22
front cards, displaying summary information,
 45–47
help system, 44–45
jobs
 creating, 316
 deleting, 323
 editing, 317–318
 executing, 317
 managing, 316
 planning, 317
 statistics, displaying, 319–321
 stopping, 318, 323
LAN interfaces, displaying screen information,
 56–57
LEDs, 330

lines, 83
  card group hardware, 84
  configurable parameters, 90–96
  configuring, 89–90
  displaying configuration, 88–89
  displaying summary information, 87
  downing, 97
  formats, 84
  multiplexed, 85
  notation, 86
  technologies, 84
  unmultiplexed, 85
  upping, 87–88
login procedures, 40
  CLI screen, 41
  CLI shortcuts, 42
  command syntax, 43
message formats, 25
  FastPacket, 25–27
network synchronization
  carrier network timing, 305
  clock reference selection, 308–309
  clocking sources, 305–307
  commands, 304
NPM cards, redundancy, 28
nodes
  displaying, 54–55
  IP relay address, 57–58
  naming, 55–56
packet flow
  ATM, 34
  data packets, 32
  Frame Relay, 33
  voice packets, 31
passwords, changing, 49
power supplies, 23
print modes, configuring, 53–54
processor card group, 21
route configuration, 290–304
  direct routes, 290
  network-assigned routes, 290
  preferred routes, 290
routing trunks, 59
  card groups, 60
  formats, 60
  technologies, 60
  transmission facilities, 60–61

serial ports, DCE/DTE selection, 164
simple gateway process, 61
T1/12 trunks, 62
time zone, modifying, 51
troubleshooting commands
  addextlp, 348
  addloclp, 346–347
  addrmtlp, 347–348
  clrlnalm, 344
  clrlog, 336
  clrtrkalm, 339
  cnflnalm, 342–343
  cnftrkalm, 338
  dellp, 349
  dspalms, 334–335
  dsplnalmcnf, 341–342
  dsplnerrs, 340–341
  dsplog, 335
  dsptrkerrs, 336–337
  resetcd, 345
  tstcon, 350–351
trunk card group, 21
trunks
  adding, 67
  configurable parameters, 70–79
  configuring, 69–70
  displaying configuration, 68–69
  downing, 82
  framed versus unframed, 62
  notation, 63–64
  removing between nodes, 81–82
  upping, 66
UVM cards
  Fax Relay, 119–120
  line pass-through configuration, 109–110
  voice connection types, 108
UXM cards
  ABR, 259
  supported ATM connections, 244
voice card group, 22
voice channels
  conditioning templates, 133
  configuring, 130–132
  connection state, displaying, 132–133
  signaling bit conversion, 136–140
  signaling bit interpretation, 126, 130

voice connections, 101
Y-cable redundancy, 28
ILMI (Integrated Local Management Interface), 537
enabling, 991
field descriptions, 240–241
historical statistics counters, displaying, 998–999
IMA (Inverse Multiplexing over ATM), 975
groups
characteristics, modifying, 984
creating, 984
ports, 973–974
displaying status information, 982–983
trunks, 63
IMA clock code parameter (IGX trunks), 78
IMA group member parameter (IGX trunks), 73
IMA max. diff. dly parameter (IGX trunks), 78
IMA protocol option parameter (IGX trunks), 78
implementing
APS on BPX networks, 506
version 1+1, 508, 511–513
FBTC on BXM cards, 584–586
level loss plans, 121
MGX switches on MPLS networks
as ELSRs, 1098–1100
IP MPLS core, 1101
MGX 8850-PXM45 ATM MPLS core, 1100
standard ABR on BXM card, 598–601
traffic shaping, 534–535
port level, 535
in-band dialing, 126
index number, command history function (BPX CLI), 423
indicator LEDs, IGX, 330
ingress ATM traffic, AUSM cell flow, 977–978
ingress port queues, Frame Relay, 910
ingress traffic
high-speed FRSMs, 913–914
low-speed FRSMs, 912
on CESM, 883
policing, 1004
CoS-based, 1005–1006
dual leaky bucket model, 1004
leaky bucket model, 1004
ingress VC queues, modifying characteristics, 1032

initial BPX configuration
adduser command, 425
cnfasm command, 429
cnfdate command, 430
cnflan command, 433
cnfname command, 429
cnfnwip command, 434
cnfpwd command, 426
cnfterm command, 430
cnftermfunc command, 432–433
cnftime command, 430
cnftmzn command, 430
commands, 423–424
dspcd command, 428
dspcds command, 427–428
dspnds command, 430
dsppwr command, 428
input control signal transport, configuring, 165
integrity of connections, testing, 714–716
interface command, 1120, 1127
interleaved control signal transport, 149–150
interpreting voice channel signaling bit on IGX, 130
interpretive DS0A data connections, 151
interval statistics, monitoring, 631
interworking
ATM and Frame Relay, 270–271
NIW, 928
FR-SSCS, 272
SIW, 273–275, 929–930
translational, 273
transparent, 273
IOS images, loading on startup, 1115
ip address command, 1127
IP addressing schemes (BPX)
configuring, 453–456
LAN port, 455–456
ip command, 1131
IP Relay, 40
accessing BPX CLI, 413
displaying address for IGX nodes, 57–58
IPX
DFM, 7
E-1, 7
FastPacket, 6
Frame Relay service integration, 7
voice/data integration, 7
isochronous data clocking, 172–173

ISPs, PoPs, 1055
IWF (Interworking Function)
    BPX connection types, 608
    BPX interworking connection types, 608
    NIW, 608–611
    SIW, 608–612

J

J1 format, CAS signaling, 126
jobs (IGX)
    creating, 318–319
    deleting, 323
    editing, 317–318
    executing, 317
    managing, 316
    planning, 317
    privilege levels, 316
    statistics, displaying, 319–321
    stopping, 318, 323
    triggers, creating, 318

K

K1K2 protocol (APS), 506
keepalive procedure, ILMI, 537
keyboard shortcuts
    BPX CLI, 419
    IGX CLI, 42

L

label switching, MPLS, 1091
    configuring on MGX switch, 1101–1103
    features, 1092
    resolving persistent loops in full-mesh
        networks, 1094–1095
    versus IP over ATM, 1092–1093
    VPNs, 1103–1106
LAN interfaces (IGX), displaying screen
    information, 56–57

LAN port
    BPX
        CLI, accessing , 413
        configuring, 455–456
    IGX CLI, accessing, 40
last FastPacket header, 211–212
LD-CELP (Low-Delay Code Excited Linear
    Prediction), 104
LDI (Low-Speed Data Interface) back card, 22
LDM (Low-Speed Data Module) front card, 22
leaky bucket model, 572–573, 1004
    ATM connection policing, 245–246
    high-speed FRSM policing, 934
    low-speed FRSM policing, 931–932
    time-based, 1007
    UFM policing, 213–214
leaves, 613
LED indicators, IGX, 330
Level 1 channel statistics, 636–638
Level 2 channel statistics, 639–640
Level 3 channel statistics, 641–643
level loss plans, implementing, 121
line alarms, 332
line cable length parameter (IGX trunks), 77
line cable type parameter (IGX trunks), 76
line coding parameter (IGX trunks), 76
line command, 1116, 1117
line CRC parameter (IGX trunks), 76
line DS-0 parameter (IGX trunks), 73
line framing, 86
line framing parameter (IGX trunks), 76
line pass-through
    configuring on UVM card, 109–110
    displaying on UVM card, 111
line recv impedance parameter (IGX trunks), 76
line type parameter (IGX trunks), 75
lines, 487
    activating on PXM1, 800
    adding to MGX service modules, 818–819
    alarms
        on PXM1 (MGX), displaying, 802–804
        resolving, 701–705
        statistical thresholds, 692
        summarizing historical statistical errors,
            702–703

ATM
 configuring, 804
 device compatibility, 493–495
BPX, 362
configuring, 89–90
detailed configuration information, displaying,
 492–493
DSP configuration, displaying, 1079
errors, displaying, 689
IGX, 25, 83
 card group hardware, 84
 configurable parameters, 90–96
 configuring, 89–90
 displaying configuration, 88–89
 displaying summary information, 87
 downing, 97
 formats, 84
 multiplexed, 85
 notation, 86
 technologies, 84
 unmultiplexed, 85
 upping, 87–88
LOS, 688
MGX, 795–796
 FRSM-8T1, 797
 PXM1 OC-3c, 796
narrowband, modifying characteristics,
 811–812
OOF (out of frame), 688
physical, creating logical ports, 805
PXM1, displaying summary information, 798
serial, modifying characteristics, 811–812
status, displaying, 489
upping, 490
voice lines, 101
link integrity timer, 185
Link Integrity Timer field (dspport command
 output), 197
listing
 BPX nodes, IP relay addresses, 457
 clock sources, 309
 connections on PXM1, 1025–1026
 current network clock sources, 682
 network users, 435
 potential network clock sources, 681
Littlewood, Morgan, 5

LLC/ISO (Logical Link Control/International
 Standards Organization), 277
LLC/SNAP (Logical Link Control/Subnetwork
 Access Protocol), 277
LMI (Local Management Interface), 536–537
load model, 653
 bursts, handling, 288
 expected versus actual trunk loading, 286
 statistical reserve, 288
 versus actual usage, 284
local alarms, locating, 705
local connections, 864, 926–928, 1002
local loopback
 IGX, 352
 performing, 353–354
locating alarms, 329
 local, 705
 remote, 706–707
logging in
 to BPX switch, requirements, 417
 to IGX switch, 40
  CLI screen, 41
  CLI shortcuts, 42
  command syntax, 43
 to MGX switch, 775
logging out of BPX CLI, 423
logical Frame Relay ports, 181
 activating, 192–193
logical ports, 532
 creating on physical lines, 805, 990–991
 displaying on MGX PXMI cards, 990
 on MGX PXM1, listing, 805
 removing from FRM/UFM-C cards, 203
 resource partitions, displaying, 806
loop clock parameter (IGX trunks), 74
loopback testing
 local loopback, 712–713
 remote loopback, 714
looped clocking mode, 172
LOS (Loss of Signal), 688
Low-Delay Code Excited Linear Prediction,
 (LD-CELP), 104
low-speed card modules, MGX, 752
low-speed data connections, partially filled
 FastPackets, 147

low-speed FRSMs
    ingress traffic flow, 912
    policing, 931–932
    port queues, 910
LSRs (label switch routers), 1091

M

major alarms, 329, 687–688
managing traffic on CESM, 882–884
mandatory framing structure, IGX transmission
  facilities, 62
manual operation of APS, 505
map-group command, 1130
map-list command, 1131
master connections, MGX, 864
maximum route cost
    configuring, 663
    setting for connections, 300
MBS (Maximum Burst Size), 1005
measuring echo perception, 123
memory, DRAM, 1107
menu-driven command interface, 416
    IGX, 44
message formats, IGX switches, 25
    FastPacket, 25–27
MGX switches, 729–730
    8800 series switches, 10
    8850-PXM45/8230 tiered network, 734
    ATM connections, 1001–1002
        feeder, 1002
        local, 1002
    ATM lines, configuring, 804
    card modules, high-speed, 752
    card-level resource partitions, 776–777
    circuit emulation services, creating, 897–899
    CLI, 732–733
        accessing, 767
        error messages, 772
        login process, 775
    commands
        Help, 770–771
        syntax, 768–770
    connections
        network connections, 863–864
        slave/master connections, 864
        testing network continuity, 1037, 1087

double-height card slots, configuring, 753
features, 730
feeder connections, 862–863
feeder nodes, 828–829
    adding, 831–832
Frame Relay connections, creating, 962–964
hardware, selecting, 755–758
implementing on MPLS networks
    as ELSRs, 1098–1100
    IP MPLS core, 1101
    MGX 8850-PXM45 ATM MPLS
      core, 1100
lines, 795, 796
    FRSM-8T1, 797
    PXM1 OC-3c, 796
MGX 8550-PXM45
    adding connections, 875–876
    ATM connection types, 861
    standalone switches, configuring, 833
MPLS support, 1096
    configuring, 1101–1103
    QoS, 1097
    RPM as ELSR, 1096
    VPNs, 1097
network management, 733–734
optional features, 732
PXM1 processor cards, 737–738
    back card, 738–740
    characteristics, modifying, 800–802
    functions, 741
    lines, activating, 800
    logical ports, displaying, 990
    logical ports, listing, 805
    SONET APS, 834–836, 839
required features, 754
RPM card, 745–745, 1055
    configuring, 1121–1122
    connections, creating, 1134–1135
    PVCs, 1124
service modules, 745–746
    adding lines, 818–819
    AUSM, 750
    BERTs, running, 815–817
    CESM, 748–749
    E1 lines, testing, 825–828
    FRSM, 749–750

lines, activating, 811
redundancy, 783–785
reserved card slots, 751
SRM-3T3 T1 line distribution, 819
T1 line distribution process, 820–825
T1 lines, testing, 825–828
VISM, 750
SRM card, 741–744
standalone devices, 736
supported VCs
PVCs, 851–858
SPVCs, 853–858
SVCs, 855–859
trunks, displaying, 806
user IDs, 773
user services, 731
middle FastPacket header, 209–210
Min. flags/frame field (dspport command output), 196
minimum wink, 128–129
minor alarms, 687–689
modems, 64 kbps upgrade, 119
modes of RPM CLI, 1108
modifying
ABR connection characteristics, 1022–1023
ATM
port queue depth, 242
signaling protocols, 989
timers, 989
BPX CLI passwords, 426
CBR characteristics, 1021, 1030
ForeSight connection characteristics, 1020
igress VC characteristics, 1024
IGX trunk parameters, 69–70
IMA group characteristics, 984
ingress VC queue characteristics, 1032
QBin characteristics, 987
serial port configurations, 447–448
UBR policing characteristics, 1032
VBR policing characteristics, 1031
VGR policing characteristics, 1021–1022
Monitored events count field (dspport command output), 196
monitoring
alarms, multicast connection, 711

ATM
connections, 630–635
port failures, 552–558
traffic, potential congestion locations, 1009
BPX
line alarms, 704–705
trunk alarms, 691–699
system data, 436– 439
voice channel signaling bit on IGX, 130
MPLS (Multiprotocol Label Switching), 8, 1055, 1091
BPX switches, 397–399
configuring on MGX switch, 1101–1103
features, 1092
MGX switches
as ELSRs, 1098–1100
IP MPLS core, 1101
MGX 8850-PXM45 ATM MPLS core, 1100
resolving persistent loops in full-mesh networks, 1094–1095
support on MGX switches, 1096
QoS, 1097
RPM as ELSR, 1096
VPNs, 1097
versus IP over ATM, 1092–1093
VPNs, 1103, 1104
features, 1104–1105
IBGP distribution of routing information, 1106
label forwarding, 1106
operation, 1105
over ATM, 10
route-target communities, 1105
multicast connection alarms, 710–711
multicast services, 613
addressing, 615
BME connections, adding, 613
Multilevel Channel Statistics, 632–633
multiplexing, 85
AAL2, 1059
DFM, 144
line framing, 86
TDM, 85
voice FastPackets, 102

N

N392 Error Threshold field (dspport command output), 197
N393 Monitored Events Count field (dspport command output), 197
naming
    IGX nodes, 55–56
    network nodes, 429, 441–442
    trunk nodes, 475
NAPs (network access points), 1055
narrowband IMA, 975
narrowband channelized Frame Relay ports, 908
narrowband lines
    modifying characteristics, 811–812
    summary configuration information, listing, 807–809
network management
    BPX, 367
    MGX switches
        Cisco WAN Manager, 733
        CLI, 732–733
        connections, 863–864
        SNMP management tools, 734
network synchronization, 671
    carrier network timing, 671
    clock alarms, clearing, 685
    clock sources, 672
        listing, 682
        removing, 683–684
        selecting, 673
    example, 674, 677–679
    guidelines, 680–686
    IGX
        clock reference selection, 308–309
        commands, 304
network topologies
    BPX/MGX tiered networks, 735
    MGX 8850-PXM45/8230 tiered networks, 734
    PNNI networks, 736
network types, BPX, 369–370
network-assigned routes, 290, 647
network-wide clock source, specifying, 311–313
network-wide BPX configuration, date & time, 445–446

NIW (network interworking), 270–271, 608, 928.
    See also SIW
    FR-SSCS, 272
    operation, 610–611
NNI (Network-Node Interface) cell headers, 366
NNI (Network-to-Network Interface), 186
nodes
    BPX
        date/time configuration, 443–445
        displaying, 442–443
        naming, 429, 441–442
        status, displaying, 430
normal clocking mode, 172
normal control signal transport, 149
NOS (Network Operating System), BPX switches, 394
NPM (Nodal Processor Module) front card, 21
    redundancy, 28
    toggling between active and standby, 331
nrt-VBR (nonreal-time VBR), 363, 1003
    configurable parameters, 622–623
NTM (Network Trunk Module) front card, 21, 60
    capacity, calculating, 64
NTS (non-time-stamped) data FastPackets, 143
    DFM, 144

O

OAM FastPacket Threshold field (dspport command output), 196
OAM segment loopback, testing connection integrity, 714–716
ones density, ZCS, 152
OOF (out of frame), 688
operating modes (VISM), 1053–1054
optional features of MGX switches, 732
optional framing structures of IGX transmission facilities, 62
optional parameters of BPX CLI command syntax, 414
output control signal transport, configuring, 166

P

Packet Technologies, 6
packets
    Cisco IGX switches
        ATM, 34
        data packets, 32
        Frame Relay, 33
        voice packets, 31
    encapsulation, simple gateway process, 61
    forwarding, MPLS, 1055
parameters
    addcon command, 106–107, 111–112
    addjob command, 319
    addjobtrig command, 325
    BPX CLI command syntax, 414
    BPX serial ports, configuring, 446–448
    clrlnalm command, 344
    cnfasm command, 429
    cnfchdl command, 129
    cnfchgn command, 122
    cnfclksrc command, 311–312
    cnfcls command, 221–224
    cnfcond command, 136
    cnfcos command, 302
    cnflan command, 434
    cnflnalm command, 343
    cnfnwip command, 434
    cnfport command, 541–544
    cnfpref command, 298
    cnfrtcost command, 301
    cnfterm command, 52, 431
    cnftermfunc command, 432–433
    cnftmzn command, 444
    cnfxmtsig command, 139
    command syntax, 770
    dncon command, 303
    dspcons command, 112–113
    dspnds command, 55
    dspportq command, 549
    dsptrk command, 69
    dsptrkutl command, 295
    for ABR, 943, 944
    for ABRFST, 266, 621
    for ABRSTD, 260, 267, 620
    for CBR, 618
    for echo cancellers

        configuring, 124
        displaying, 123–124
    for Frame Relay
        connections, 213
        ports, displaying, 193–197
    for IGX lines, 90–92
        frame scramble, 96
        HCS masking, 96
        idle code, 96
        IMA clock mode, 93
        IMA group member, 93
        IMA max. diff. dly, 93
        IMA protocol option, 93
        line 56 KBS bit pos, 95
        line cable type, 95
        line coding, 94
        line CRC, 94
        line DS-0, 93
        line encoding, 94
        line length, 95
        line PCT fast modem, 95
        line recv impedance, 94
        line T1 signaling, 95
        loop clock, 93
        retained links, 93
    for IGX trunks
        configuring, 70–72
        deroute delay time, 78
        frame scramble, 78
        gateway channels, 77
        HCS masking, 77
        header type, 75
        idle code, 75
        IMA clock code, 78
        IMA group member, 73
        IMA max. diff. dly, 78
        IMA protocol option, 78
        line cable length, 77
        line cable type, 76
        line coding, 76
        line CRC, 76
        line DS-0 map, 73
        line framing, 76
        line recv impedance, 76
        line type, 75
        loop clock, 74
        pass sync, 74

payload scramble, 77
rcv trunk rate, 73
restrict PCC traffic, 75
retained links, 73
routing cost, 75
statistical reserve, 74
subrate data rate, 74
subrate interface, 73
traffic, 77
transit trunk rate, 73
VC shaping, 79
virtual trunk type, 78
virtual trunk VPI, 78
VPC conns, 79
VPI address, 75
for ports, displaying summary, 545–547
for UBR, 622
for VBR, 619
for VC queues, 212
resetcd command, 345
tstcon command, 351
tstdelay command, 232
partial command entry, IGX help system, 44–45
partially interleaved control signal transport, 150
partially filled FastPackets, 147
pass sync parameter (IGX trunks), 74
passing sync, 673
pass-through mode, UVM card configuration, 109–110
password command, 1117
passwords
BPX CLI, changing, 426
entering for BPX login, 417
IGX
changing, 49
displaying, 49–50
payload (ATM cells)
for IGX networks, 61
partially filled FastPackets, 147
payload scramble parameter (IGX trunks), 77
PCM (Pulse Code Modulation) algorithm, 102–103
voice samples, conversion to ATM cells, 1061
PCR (Peak Cell Rate), 364, 1005
time-based model, 1007
performance, traffic shaping, 534
implementing, 534–535
port level, 535

physical errors
on BPX lines, 701
on trunks, 690
physical lines, creating logical ports, 805
physical ports, 529
creating, 538
Frame Relay, 181
activating, 192–193
port queues, 532
QBins, 532–533
versus virtual ports, 531
physical trunks
displaying statistics, 482–483
parameters, configuring, 477
resource partitions, 468
example, 471–473
resource allocation, 469–470
statistical alarms, clearing, 698
versus physical trunks, 466
planning IGX jobs, 317
playout delay, 128–129
PNNI (Private Network to Network Interface), 10, 371, 736
BPX switches, 396
dynamic partitioning, 473–474
policing
ABR, 580
ATM connections, 245–247, 1004
ABR traffic policing, 251, 254
CBR traffic policing, 248
CoS-based, 1005–1006
dual leaky bucket model, 246–247, 1004
leaky bucket model, 246, 1004
time-based leaky bucket models, 1007
UBR traffic policing, 252–253
VBR traffic policing, 248–250
CBR traffic, 574–575
dual leaky bucket model, 573
high-speed FRSM policing, 934
leaky bucket model, 572–573
low-speed FRSM policing, 931–932
time-based, 574
UBR, 581–582
VBR, 576–580
polling, 392–393

polling timer,
  ILMI, 537
  verification timer, 185
Polling verify timer field (dspport command
  output), 195
PoPs (points of presence), 1055
port alarms, 332
Port ID field (dspport command output), 194
port level traffic shaping, 535
Port queue depth field (dspport command
  output), 194
port queues, 182, 532
  configurable parameters, 183
  Frame Relay
    high-speed, 911–912
    low-speed, 910
  QBins
    configurable thresholds, 532–533
    displaying statistics, 986
port summary information, 545–547
Port type field (dspport command output), 194
port-level resource partitions, MGX, 776–777
ports, 529
  activating on BXM cards, 545
  ATM, 973
    activating, 238, 550–551
    characteristics, displaying, 237
    configuring, 239–240, 550–551
    deactivating, 550–551
    deleting, 550
    detailed information, displaying, 238
    device compatibility, configuring,
      540–541
    displaying queue configuration, 548–549
    displaying statistics, 993–997
    displaying status, 980–983
    displaying summary information,
      979–980
    egress queue thresholds, displaying, 241
    failures, troubleshooting, 552–558
    QBins, 975–976
    queue depth, modifying, 242
    signaling protocol statistics, displaying,
      555–556
    statistics, displaying, 553–555
  AUSM, activating, 983–984

circuit emulation ports, 876
  creating, 885
  listing on CESM, 886
configuring on PXM1 cards, 1000
Frame Relay, 181, 907–908
  activating, 188, 192–193
  card module information, displaying,
    199–200
  configuring, 925–926
  displaying detailed information, 198
  downing, 202–203
  narrowband fractional Frame Relay
    ports, 909
  serial, 908
  signaling parameters, configuring,
    190–192
  statistics, clearing, 206–207
  statistics, displaying, 204–206
IMA, 974
logical, creating, 189–190, 805, 990–991
multicast, monitoring alarms, 711
physical, 529
  creating, 538
  versus virtual, 531
PVCs, allocating, 539
resource partitions, displaying, 991
serial, DCE, 164
signaling failure, 689
summary information, displaying, 545–547
virtual ports, 529–530
  creating, 538
  versus physical, 531
VIs, 532
potential congestion locations, ABR, 942
potential connection routes, identifying, 643
  AutoRoute routing, 646–647
  on BPX switches, 644–646
power supplies
  IGX switches, 23
  status, displaying, 428
precedence rules for BPX switching commands,
  523–524
preferred routes, 290, 648
  configuring, 662
  specifying, 298–300
previous commands, listing, 422–423
print modes (IGX), configuring, 53–54

prioritizing rerouted connections, 301
priority bumping, 649
private line replacement, 141
privilege levels
    BPX CLI, 416
    IGX CLI, 43
    IGX jobs, 316
    MGX CLI, 773
processor cards
    IGX switches, 21
    PXM1, 737–738
        back cards, 738–740
        functions, 741
    switching between active and standby, 331
Proctor, Don, 5
prompts, BPX CLI, 416
protection (P) line, APS, 502
protocol-independent data connections, 143
provisioning
    PVCs, 852
    SPVCs, 866–868
Pulse Code Modulation. *See* PCM
pulse dialing, 126
PVCs (permanent virtual circuits), 207, 563,
    851–853
    circuit emulation connections, 879–880
    data connections, 142
    example, 856–858
    on RPM, 1124
    port allocation, 539
    provisioning, 852
    signaling protocols, 535–536
        ILMI, 537
        LMI, 536–537
    Status Inquiry messages, 536
    UNI signaling, asynchronous update mode, 185
    Update Status messages, 537
    voice connections, 101, 1059
        AAL2 segmentation, 1062–1063
        CIDs, 1059
        endpoints, 1059
PXM1 processor card, 737–738, 741
    back cards, 738–740
    connections
        adding, 1025
        creating, 1038–1042
        listing, 1025–1026

ports
    configuring, 1000
    displaying signaling protocol
        configuration, 992
  on MGX switch
    displaying configuration information,
        799–800
    displaying summary line information, 798
    displaying line alarm conditions, 802–804
    logical ports, listing, 805
    SONET APS, 834–839
  UNI ports, listing channels, 1027–1028

Q

Q.2931 code points, 277
QBins, 467, 532, 975–976
    characteristics, modifying, 987
    configurable thresholds, 532–533
    displaying statistics, 986
QoS (quality of service), 402
    BPX service type parameters, 364–366
    queuing architectures, 403–404
question mark (?), IGX help system, 44–45
queuing architectures
    BPX switches, 403–404
    congestion, 215

R

RA (Rate Adjustment) bits, 210
rate adjustments
    ABR, 942–943
    ABR ForeSight, 260–261
rcv trunk rate parameter (IGX trunks), 73
rebooting RPM processor card, 1114
receive signaling bit conversion, configuring,
    137–138
redundancy
    MGX service module, 783–784
        1-to-N redundancy, 785
    NPM cards, 28

SONET APS, 834
    1+1 setup, 836, 839
    versions, 834–835
  Y-cable, 28
Relative Rate EFCI, 571
reliability
  BPX, 368–369
  five nines, 9
reload command, 1114
remote alarms, locating, 706–707
remote loopback
  IGX, 352
  performing, 354–355
remote nodes, establishing vty sessions, 80–81
removing
  ATM connections, 268
  circuit emulation connections, 888–889
  connection endpoints from AXSM card, 869
  data connections, 155
  downed ATM ports, 550
  Frame Relay connections, 229–230
  logical ports from FRM/UFM-C cards, 203
  loopback connections, 722
  network-wide clock sources, 683–684
  trunks, 484–485
    between nodes, 81–82
  voice connections, 115
repeating commands, 422–423
reporting
  BERT test results, 817–818
  trunk alarms, 699
required features of MGX switches, 754
required parameters, BPX CLI command
  syntax, 414
rerouting
  failed trunk connection routes, 648
  prioritizing connections, 301
  rules, 291
reserved card slots, 427, 751
resetcd command, 330, 345, 723
resolving
  alarms
    bus, 709
    card, 708
    connection, 709

line, 701, 704–705
  multicast connection, 710–711
  trunk, 691–700
ATM port failures, 557–558
resource partitions, 468, 491
  displaying, 991
  example, 471–473
  on logical ports, displaying, 806
  resource allocation, 469
    card-level, 470
    port-level, 470
restrict PCC traffic parameter (IGX trunks), 75
retained links parameter (IGX trunks), 73
revertive option, APS configuration, 501, 510
RM (resource management), 1011
  cells, 588–591, 941–942
  Cutoff RM factor, 595
roots, 613
route-target communities, 1105
routing connections, 657–658
routing cost parameter (IGX trunks), 75
routing trunks, 59
  card groups, 60
  formats, 60
  technologies, 60
  transmission facilities, 60–61
RPM (Route Processing Module), 745, 1055
  access lines, configuring, 1116–1117
  ATM switch interface, configuring, 1119–1120
  CLI
    accessing, 1108
    changing configuration file, 1109–1110
    entering commands, 1109
    modes, 1108
  configuring, 1121–1122
  connections, creating, 1134–1135
  functions, 744
  hostname, setting, 1115
  memory locations, 1107
  MPLS support, 1096–1097
  port numbering, 1107
  PVCs, 1124
  rebooting, 1114
rpmrscprtn command, 1117–1118
RPS (Repetitive Pattern Suppression) algorithms,
  DFM (Data Frame Multiplexing), 144
RR (Relative Rate) control, 592

rt-VBR (real-time VBR), 363, 1003
rules for rerouting traffic, 291
runjob command, 322

S

sample WAN network, 370
SCM (System Clock Module) back card, 21
SCR (Sustainable Cell Rate), 364, 1005
screen information, BPX CLI, 418
SDH (Synchronous Digital Hierarchy), 501
SDI (Synchronous Data Interface) back card, 22
security, IGX switches
  user privilege levels, 43
  changing passwords, 49
segments, 256, 565, 863–864
selecting
  clock reference, 308–309, 673
  commands from menu-driven interface, 416
  control signals for data connections, 150
  MGX hardware, 755–758
  UFM-U card mode, 201–202
  VISM clocking option, 1070–1071
  voice channel type, 131–132
selective cell discard, 571
serial data channels, 163
serial interfaces, active control templates, 192
serial lines
  characteristics, modifying, 811–812
  summary configuration information, listing,
    807–809
serial ports
  communications parameters, configuring,
    446–448
  DCE, 164
  Frame Relay, 908
service interworking, FR-SSCS, 272
service modules
  CESM
    egress queues, 882–883
    egress traffic, 884
    ingress traffic, 883
  E1 lines, testing, 825–828
  MGX, 745–746
    adding lines, 818–819
    AUSM, 750

CESM, 748–749
FRSM, 749–750
high-speed card modules, 752
redundancy, 783–785
reserved card slots, 751
T1 line distribution process, 820–825
VISM, 750
T1 lines, testing, 825–828
VISM, 1053–1054
  AAL2 coding schemes, 1063
  adding endpoints, 1079–1080
  adding voice connections, 1082
  clocking options, 1070–1073
  DSPs, 1070
  listing historical connection statistics
    counters, 1088–1089
  port status, displaying, 1076
  Release 1.5 features, 1056–1058
  Release 2.0 features, 1058
  Release 2.1 features, 1058
  resource partitions, creating, 1077
  VoATM services, creating, 1067–1070
  voice mode configuration, displaying,
    1074–1075
  voice mode, changing, 1076
  VoIP mode, 1065–1067
service types, BPX, 363–366
SES (Service Expansion Shelf), 371
setting date/time on IGX nodes, 50
shelf units
  cards
    alarms, 330
    statistics, displaying, 427–428
  spacer brackets, 17
shortcuts
  BPX CLI cursor movement, 419
  IGX CLI keyboard sequences, 42
show atm map command, 1131
show atm vc command, 1129–1130
show interface command, 1119–1120, 1125–1126
show running-config command, 1112–1114
show startup-config command, 1112–1114
show switch connections command, 1133–1134
shutdown command, 1127

signaling
  bit conversion, 136–139
    displaying, 140
  bit interpretation on IGX, 130
  bit timing, 126
    dial type configuration, 127–129
  bit transport, 126
  CAS, 125
  delay, 126
  on circuit emulation connections, 880
  UNI, 184
signaling protocol field (dspport command output),
  195
signaling protocols, 184, 535–536
  asynchronous update mode, 185
  ATM, 239
  counters, 185
  ILMI, 537
    field descriptions, 240–241
  LMI, 536–537
    field descriptions, 240–241
  NNI, 186
  port signaling failures, 689
  timers, 185
silence suppression
  Adaptive VAD, 117–118
  VAD, 116
simple gateway process, 61, 274–276
single-segment connections, 564
SIW (service interworking), 270–275, 608, 929–930
  adding ATM-Frame Relay connections,
    278–279
  operation, 611–612
  translational, 273
  transparent, 273
SLAs (Service-Level Agreements), 1092
slave/master connections, MGX, 864
slot errors, 690
slot.port field (dspport command output), 194
slot.port.line field (dspport command output), 194
slots
  alarms
    statistical thresholds, 720
    troubleshooting, 717
  historical statistical errors, summarizing,
    718–719
SNAP encapsulation, 278

SNMP (Simple Network Management Protocol)
  management tools, 734
software
  BPX, 394
    AutoRoute, 395
    CAC, 399
    MPLS, 397–399
    NOS, 394
    PNNI, 396
    VSI, 395
  resetting for cards, 723
SONET APS (Automatic Protection Switching), 834
  1+1 setup, 836, 839
  versions, 834–835
sources of BPX network clocks, 672–673
spacer brackets, 17
specifying
  BPX network node names, 442
  network-wide clock sources, 311–313
  preferred routes for connections, 297–300
Speed field (dspport command output), 194
split clocking mode, 172
SPVCs (Soft Permanent Virtual Circuits), 853–854
  example, 858
  provisioning, 866–868
  status information, displaying, 872–875
SRAM (static random-access memory), 1107
SRM processor card, 741–744
SRM-3T3, T1 line distribution, 819
SRTS clocking, 882
stability of clocking mechanisms, 671
stages of ATM cell egress traffic, 978
standalone chassis
  IGX 8410 rack-mount chassis, 16
  IGX 8420 switch, 17–19
  IGX 8430 switch, 19–20
  MGX switches, 736, 833
standalone feeders, 829
standard ABR, 256–258, 566, 587–588, 1003, 1011
  displaying characteristics per connection, 1023
  implementing on BXM, 598, 601
  rate adjustments, 601–604
  RM cells, 588–590
    generation, 590–591
    operation in BPX, 591–592, 595–597
  versus ABRFST, 604

standby NPM processor card, switching to active, 331
static PVC connections, 851, 853, 856–858
statistical alarm thresholds for lines/trunks, 692
statistical errors
    counters, clearing, 697
    on BPX lines, 701
statistical reserve, 288, 650–653
statistical reserve parameter (IGX trunks), 74
Status Inquiry messages, 536
status LEDs, Cisco IGX 8420 standalone system, 18
STI (StrataCom Trunk Interface) cells, 366
stopjob command, 323
stopping IGX jobs, 318
StrataCom
    acquisition by Cisco, 6
    development of Frame Relay services, 6
    MPLS, 8
Stratum 1 clocks, 672
Stratum 2 clocks, 672
    BITS, 305
structure of BOP frames, 217–219
structured ports, card module support, 876
subinterfaces, configuring, 1122
subrate data channels, 158
subrate data connections, 151
subrate data rate parameter (IGX trunks), 74
subrate interface parameter (IGX trunks), 73
summary statistics
    counters, 631
    extending, 632–633
super-rate data channels, 158
super-rate data connections, 151
suppressing data FastPackets, 144
SVCs (Switched Virtual Circuits), 855–856
    example, 859
switchapsln command, 517–518, 522, 842
switchcc command, 331, 708
switches
    BPX. *See* BPX switches
    IGX. *See* IGX switches
    MGX. *See* MGX switches
    VT, 25
switching, cell-based, 366–367
synchronization
    carrier network timing, 305
    clock sources, 305–307

synchronous clocking, 882
synchronous data connections, 143
syntax
    addexlp command, 348
    addloclp command, 347
    addport command, 538–539
    addrmtlp command, 348
    BPX CLI commands, 413–414
    clrlnalm command, 344
    clrtrkalm command, 339
    cnflnalm command, 343
    cnftrkalm command, 338
    dsplnerrs command, 341
    dsptrkerrs command, 337
    IGX CLI commands, 43
    MGX commands, 768–771
    resetcd command, 345
    tstcon command, 351
system data, monitoring, 436–439
system hardware, BPX, 372
    BNI, 386–392
    card groups, 374–385
    chassis, 373
system power, displaying status, 439
system software, BPX, 394
    AutoRoute, 395
    CAC, 399
    MPLS, 397–399
    NOS, 394
    PNNI, 396
    VSI, 395
system time, configuring on BPX nodes, 443–445

T

T1 D4 framing, 125
T1 ESF framing, 125
T1 lines
    CAS, 126
    distribution, 820–825
    signaling method, configuring, 1078
    SRM-3T3 distribution, 819
T1/12 trunk, 62
T3 lines, listing summary configuration
   information, 809

Tag Switching, 8
TDM (time-division multiplexing), 85
technologies for routing trunks, 60
terminating virtual terminal sessions, 485
testing
    circuit emulation connections, 894–896
    connections, 352–353, 632
        external loopback, 355
        integrity, 714–716
        local loopback, 353–354, 712–713
        remote loopback, 354, 714
    E1 lines on MGX service modules, 825–828
    MGX network continuity, 1087
    T1 lines on MGX service modules, 825–828
thresholds
    for EPD (early packet discard), 1013
    for QBins, configuring, 532–533
    for VC queues, 583
tiered networks, 370, 828
    BPX/MGX tiered network, 735
    MGX 8850-PXM45/8230 tiered network, 734
time zones
    setting for BPX nodes, 444
    setting for IGX nodes, 50–51
time-based policing, 574
timers
    ATM, modifying, 989
    for signaling protocols, 185
timing
    tone dialing, 126
    voice channel signaling, displaying parameters,
        129–130
toggling NPM processor card between active and
    standby, 331
tone detection, 123
topologies
    BPX/MGX tiered network, 735
    MGX 8850-PXM45/8230 tiered network, 734
    PNNI networks, 736
traffic
    ABRFST, 935
        configurable parameters, 621, 938
        congestion criteria, 937
        potential congestion locations, 936
    ABRSTD
        configurable parameters, 620
        rate adjustment, 260–261

ATM
    ABR, 1011–1012
    ABR policing, 580
    CAC, 568–569
    CBR policing, 574–575
    CoS, 1003
    ForeSight, 1008–1010
    management, 567
    policing, 245–254, 1004–1006
    shaping, 570
    time-based policing, 574
    UBR policing, 581–582
    UPC, 569
    VBR policing, 576–580
    VC queuing, 254
AUSM cell flow
    egress traffic, 978
    ingress traffic, 977–978
CBR, configurable parameters, 618
congestion, 215, 570–572
    EFCI, 533
    example, 939
    ForeSight rate adjustment, 216
    ForeSight VC queue servicing, 216
controlling, FBTC, 583–586
FBTC, 583–586
flow through FRSM, 912–914
high-speed FRSM policing, 934
ingress, VC queues, 946–947
low-speed FRSM policing, 931–932
management on BPX switches
    closed-loop congestion avoidance, 402
    FBTC, 401
    QoS, 402
    queuing architectures, 403–404
    UPC, 400
policing
    dual leaky bucket model, 573
    leaky bucket model, 572–573
rerouting, 291
UBR, configurable parameters, 622
VBR, configurable parameters, 619
traffic contracts, 567
traffic descriptors, BPX service types, 364–366
traffic parameter (IGX trunks), 77

traffic shaping, 534
  implementing, 534–535
  port level, 535
  VC queues, 1012
    configuration example, 1014
    frame-based traffic control, 1012
transit trunk rate parameter (IGX trunks), 73
translational SIW, 273, 612
transmission facilities
  IGX framing structures, 62
  of routing trunks, 60–61
transmit signaling bit conversion, configuring,
  138–139
transparent data channels, 158
transparent data connections, 143, 152
transparent SIW, 273, 611
TransPath, 11
transporting control signal states on IGX, 148–150
triggers for IGX jobs
  creating, 318
  deleting, 325
troubleshooting
  ATM port failures, 552–558
  BPX
    line alarms, 701, 704–705
    trunk alarms, 691–700
  commands
    addextlp, 348
    addloclp, 346–347
    addrmtlp, 347–348
    clrlnalm, 344
    clrlog, 336
    clrtrkalm, 339
    cnflnalm, 342–343
    cnftrkalm, 338
    dellp, 349
    dspalms, 334–335
    dsplnalmcnf, 341–342
    dsplnerrs, 340–341
    dsplog, 335
    dsptrkerrs, 336–337
    resetcd, 345
    tstcon, 350–351
  slot alarms, 717
  with real-time statistics, 632
trunk card group (Cisco IGX switch), 21
trunk loading, expected versus actual, 286

trunks, 463, 464
  activating, 486–487
  adding, 474–475
  adding between nodes, 481
  alarms, 332, 690
    displaying, 314
    displaying configuration, 691–692
    reporting, 699
    statistical thresholds, 692
    status, displaying, 686
  as clock sources, 673
  bandwidth, displaying, 292–293
  bandwidth allocation, 650
  BPX, 362
  cell routing restriction, 34
  communication failures, 688
  configuring, 486–487
  deactivating, 487
  deleting, 81–82, 484–485
  detailed information, displaying, 483–484
  downing, 485
  errors, displaying, 689
  failures, 688
    line error counts, displaying, 696
    rerouting, 648
  fractional, 62
  framed
    cell transmission, 63
    FastPacket transmission, 63
  IGX
    adding, 67
    configurable parameters, 70–79
    configuring, 69–70
    displaying configuration, 68–69
    downing, 82
    framed versus unframed, 62
    notation, 63–64
    summary information, displaying, 65–66
  IGX switches, 24
  IMA, 63
  load model versus actual usage, 284
  MGX, displaying, 806
  NTM capacity, calculating, 64
  parameters, configuring, 477
  passing sync, 673
  physical versus virtual, 466
  physical errors, 690

resource partitions, 468
    card-level resource allocation, 470
    example, 471–473
    port-level resource allocation, 470
    resource allocation, 469
routing trunks, 59
    card groups, 60
    formats, 60
    technologies, 60
    transmission facilities, 60–61
T1/12, 62
unframed
    cell transmission, 63
    FastPacket transmission, 63
upping, 66, 474–476
usage statistics, displaying, 294–296
utilization, expected versus actual trunk
    loading, 653, 656
UXM capacity, calculating, 64
VI, 466–467
virtual, 465–467
TS (time-stamped) data FastPackets, 143–144
tstcon command, 350–354, 894–895, 958,
    1037, 1087
tstconseg command, 712–714, 1038
tstdelay command, 232, 895–896, 959, 1037, 1087
two-segment ATM interworking connections, 565

U

UAI (Universal ATM Interface) back card, 21–23
UBR (unspecified bit rate), 244, 363, 566
    characteristics
        modifying, 1032
    configurable parameters, 622
    connections, adding, 268
    traffic policing, 252–253, 581–582
UFI (Universal Frame Relay Interface)
    back card, 22
UFM (Universal Frame Relay Module) front card,
    22, 180
    creating logical Frame Relay ports, 189–190
    leaky bucket policing, 213–214
UFM-C card group (IGX), 84
    logical ports, removing, 203
UFM-U back card

active ports, displaying, 201
    mode, displaying, 200
uncongested networks, example, 940
unframed trunks, 62–63
UNI (User-Network Interface) cell headers,
    184–185, 366
unmultiplexed lines, 85
unstructured ports, card module support, 876
UPC (Usage Parameter Control), 400, 569
upcon command, 303, 665
Update Status messages, 537
upgrading modems to 64 kbps, 119
upln command, 58, 87–88, 490
Upper/lower RNR field (dspport command output),
    196
upping
    IGX lines, 87–88
    lines, 490
    trunks, 66, 474
upport command, 192–193, 238, 545
uptrk command, 58, 66, 474–476
user services, MGX switches, 731
user IDs
    BPX, adding to network, 425–426, 435
    IGX
        command syntax, 43
        login procedures, 40–42
        privilege levels, 43
    MGX, 773
    passwords, displaying, 49–50
users command, 774
utilization
    data channels, configuring, 162
    of voice channels, configuring, 117
    trunks, 653, 656
UVI (Universal Voice Interface) back card, 22
UVM (Universal Voice Module) front card, 22
UVM card group (IGX), 84
    Fax Relay, 109, 119–120
    line pass-through
        configuring, 109–110
        displaying, 111
    super-rate connections, 151
    transparent data connections, 152
    voice connections, adding, 106–108, 111–112
UXM (Universal Switching Module) card group,
    21–23, 60, 84, 101

ABR, 259
IMA trunks, 63
supported ATM connections, 244
trunk capacity, calculating, 64

V

V.35 data channels, 157
VAD (Voice Activity Detection), 30, 104, 116
VBR (Variable Bit Rate), 244, 566, 1003
    configurable parameters, 619
    connections, adding, 264–267
    example, 1008
    modifying characteristics, 1021–1022
    policing characteristics, modifying, 576–580, 1031
    traffic policing, 248–250
VC (virtual circuit) queues, 402, 532, 946–947, 977
    adjusting, 216
    characteristics, 1014
    congestion control, ABRFST rate adjustment, 261
    IBS, 947
    on ABR connections, 254
    on AUSM, 1012
        configuration example, 1014
        frame-based traffic control, 1012
    parameters, 212
    thresholds, 583
VC shaping parameter (IGX trunks), 79
VCs (virtual circuits)
    CoS, 1003
        CBR example, 1007
        VBR example, 1008
    PVCs, 851, 853
        circuit emulation connections, 879, 880
        example, 856–858
        on RPM, 1124
        provisioning, 852
    SPVCs, 853–854
        example, 858
        provisioning, 866–868
        status information, displaying, 872–875
    SVCs, 855–856
        example, 859
VD (virtual destination), 256

verifying
    APS operation, 518–520
    BPX card installation, 436–439
    BPX node names, 442
    BXM card statistics level, 635
        Level 1, 636–638
        Level 2, 639–640
        Level 3, 641–643
    continuity of connections, 1037
    Frame Relay line configuration, 188
versions of APS, 502–504
VIs (Virtual Interfaces), 466–467, 529, 532
virtual ports, 529–530
    creating, 538
    port queues, 532–533
    PVCs, signaling protocols, 535–537
    versus physical ports, 531
virtual trunk type parameter (IGX trunks), 78
virtual trunk VPI parameter (IGX trunks), 78
virtual trunks, 465, 466
    BPX support, 467
    displaying statistics, 482–483
    parameters, configuring, 477
    resource partitions, 468
        example, 471–473
        resource allocation, 469–470
    statistical alarms, clearing, 698
    versus physical trunks, 466
VISM (Voice Interworking Service Module), 750
    AAL2 coding schemes, 1063
    AAL2 trunking mode, 1064
    clocking options, 1070–1073
    connections, listing summary status information, 1082
    DSPs, 1070
    endpoints
        adding, 1079, 1080
        displaying detailed information, 1081
        listing, 1080
    historical connection statistics counters, listing, 1088–1089
    PCM, converting voice samples to ATM cells, 1061
    port status, displaying, 1076
    Release 1.5 features, 1056–1058
    Release 2.0 features, 1058
    Release 2.1 features, 1058

resource partitions, creating, 1077
VoATM services, creating, 1067–1070
voice connections, adding, 1082
voice mode, changing, 1076
voice mode configuration, displaying, 1074–1075
VoIP mode, 1065, 1067
VoAAL2 (Voice over AAL2) trunking mode, 1064
VoATM services, creating on VISM, 1067–1070
voice card group, Cisco IGX switches, 22
voice channels, 101, 115
    conditioning templates, 133
        configuring, 135–136
        displaying, 134
    configuring, 130–132
    connection state, displaying, 132–133
    echo, 122
    Fax Relay, configuring, 119–120
    gain, 120–121
    PCM voice sample processing, 116
    signaling, 126
        bit conversion, 136–140
        bit interpretation, 130
        bit timing, 126
        bit transport, 126
        timing parameters, displaying, 129–130
    summary configuration information, displaying, 140–141
    utilization, configuring, 116–117
    VAD, 116
voice compression schemes
    ADPCM, 103–104
    CS-ACELP, 104
    LD-CELP, 104
voice connections, 101, 1059
    AAL2 segmentation, 1062–1063
    adding, 106–108, 111–112
    CIDs, 1059
        adding, 1085–1086
        listing for specified LCN, 1086
    deleting, 115
    displaying, 112–113
    displaying detailed parameters, 114
    endpoints, 1059

voice channels
    connection state, displaying, 132–133
    echo, 122
    gain, 120–121
    level loss plan, 121
voice FastPackets, 102
voice lines, 101
VPC conns parameter (IGX trunks), 79
VPCs (Virtual Permanent Circuits), virtual trunks, 465–466
VPI address parameter (IGX trunks), 75
VPNs, MPLS, 1103–1105
    distribution of routing information, 1106
    label forwarding, 1106
    route-target communities, 1105
VS (virtual source), 256
VS/VD (Virtual Source/Virtual Destination), 571
VSI (Virtual Switch Interface) controllers, 395, 468–469
VSI-MPLS, resource partitioning, 491
VSI-PNNI, resource partitioning, 491
VT (virtual terminal), 25
vt command, 58, 80–81, 485

W—Z

window command, 453
working (W) line, APS, 502

X.21 data channels, 158
X.25 packets, encapsulation, 278
xcnfport command, 920–921
xcnfportq command, 987

Y-cable redundancy, 28
    BPX switches, 368
    versus APS, 509

ZCS (Zero Code Suppression) algorithm, 152

Hey, you've got enough worries.

Don't let IT training be one of them.

Get on the fast track to IT training at InformIT,
your total Information Technology training network.

 | **www.informit.com** |

■ Hundreds of timely articles on dozens of topics ■ Discounts on IT books from all our publishing partners, including Cisco Press ■ Free, unabridged books from the InformIT Free Library ■ "Expert Q&A"—our live, online chat with IT experts ■ Faster, easier certification and training from our Web- or classroom-based training programs ■ Current IT news ■ Software downloads ■ Career-enhancing resources

InformIT is a registered trademark of Pearson. Copyright ©2001 by Pearson.

Train with authorized Cisco Learning Partners.

Discover all that's possible on the Internet.

One of the biggest challenges facing networking professionals is how to stay current with today's ever-changing technologies in the global Internet economy. Nobody understands this better than Cisco Learning Partners, the only companies that deliver training developed by Cisco Systems.

Just go to **www.cisco.com/go/training_ad**. You'll find more than 120 Cisco Learning Partners in over 90 countries worldwide.* Only Cisco Learning Partners have instructors that are certified by Cisco to provide recommended training on Cisco networks and to prepare you for certifications.

To get ahead in this world, you first have to be able to keep up. Insist on training that is developed and authorized by Cisco, as indicated by the Cisco Learning Partner or Cisco Learning Solutions Partner logo.

Visit **www.cisco.com/go/training_ad** today.

CISCO SYSTEMS

EMPOWERING THE
INTERNET GENERATION™

Copyright © 2001 Cisco Systems, Inc. All rights reserved. Empowering the Internet Generation is a service mark, and Cisco, Cisco Systems, and the Cisco Systems logo are registered trademarks of Cisco Systems, Inc. or its affiliates in the U.S. and certain other countries. *Valid as of December 15, 2000.

Cisco Press

c i s c o p r e s s . c o m

Committed to being your long-term learning resource while you grow as a Cisco Networking Professional

Help Cisco Press **stay connected** to the issues and challenges you face on a daily basis by registering your product and filling out our brief survey. Complete and mail this form, or better yet ...

Register online and enter to win a FREE book!

Jump to **www.ciscopress.com/register** and register your product online. Each complete entry will be eligible for our monthly drawing to win a FREE book of the winner's choice from the Cisco Press library.

May we contact you via e-mail with information about **new releases, special promotions**, and **customer benefits**?

❏ Yes   ❏ No

E-mail address _____

Name _____

Address _____

City _____ State/Province _____

Country _____ Zip/Post code _____

Where did you buy this product?

❏ Bookstore
❏ Online retailer
❏ Mail order
❏ Other_____

❏ Computer store/Electronics store
❏ Direct from Cisco Press
❏ Class/Seminar

❏ Direct from Cisco Systems
❏ Office supply store
❏ Discount store

When did you buy this product? _____ **Month** _____ **Year**

What price did you pay for this product?

❏ Full retail price   ❏ Discounted price   ❏ Gift

Was this purchase reimbursed as a company expense?

❏ Yes   ❏ No

How did you learn about this product?

❏ Friend
❏ Cisco Press catalog
❏ Other catalog
❏ School
❏ Other_____

❏ Store personnel
❏ Postcard in the mail
❏ Magazine ad
❏ Professional organization

❏ In-store ad
❏ Saw it on the shelf
❏ Article or review
❏ Used other products

❏ cisco.com
❏ ciscopress.com

What will this product be used for?

❏ Business use
❏ Certification training
❏ Other_____

❏ School/Education
❏ Professional development/Career growth

How many years have you been employed in a computer-related industry?

❏ less than 2 years   ❏ 2–5 years   ❏ more than 5 years

Have you purchased a Cisco Press product before?

❏ Yes   ❏ No

How many computer technology books do you own?
❏ 1   ❏ 2–7   ❏ more than 7

Which best describes your job function? (check all that apply)
❏ Corporate Management   ❏ Systems Engineering   ❏ IS Management   ❏ Cisco Networking
❏ Network Design   ❏ Network Support   ❏ Webmaster   Academy Program
❏ Marketing/Sales   ❏ Consultant   ❏ Student   Instuctor
❏ Professor/Teacher   ❏ Other _____

Do you hold any computer certifications? (check all that apply)
❏ MCSE   ❏ CCNA   ❏ CCDA
❏ CCNP   ❏ CCDP   ❏ CCIE   ❏ Other _____

Are you currently pursuing a certification? (check all that apply)
❏ MCSE   ❏ CCNA   ❏ CCDA
❏ CCNP   ❏ CCDP   ❏ CCIE   ❏ Other _____

On what topics would you like to see more coverage?
_____
_____

Do you have any additional comments or suggestions?
_____
_____

Thank you for completing this survey and registration. Please fold here, seal, and mail to Cisco Press.

Cisco WAN Switching Professional Reference (1-58705-055-2)

Cisco Press
Customer Registration—CP050227
P.O. Box #781046
Indianapolis, IN 46278-8046

Place
Stamp
Here

Cisco Press
201 West 103rd Street
Indianapolis, IN 46290
ciscopress.com

CISCO SYSTEMS

IF YOU'RE USING

CISCO PRODUCTS,

YOU'RE QUALIFIED

TO RECEIVE A

FREE SUBSCRIPTION

TO CISCO'S

PREMIER PUBLICATION,

PACKET™ MAGAZINE.

Packet delivers complete coverage of cutting-edge networking trends and innovations, as well as current product updates. A magazine for technical, hands-on Cisco users, it delivers valuable information for enterprises, service providers, and small and midsized businesses.

Packet is a quarterly publication. To start your free subscription, click on the URL and follow the prompts:
www.cisco.com/go/packet/subscribe

CISCO SYSTEMS/PACKET MAGAZINE
ATTN: C. Glover
170 West Tasman, Mailstop SJ8-2
San Jose, CA 95134-1706

Place
Stamp
Here

☐ **YES!** I'm requesting a **free** subscription to *Packet*™ magazine.

☐ No. I'm not interested at this time.

☐ Mr.
☐ Ms.

First Name (Please Print)   Last Name

Title/Position (Required)

Company (Required)

Address

City   State/Province

Zip/Postal Code   Country

Telephone (Include country and area codes)   Fax

E-mail

Signature (Required)   Date

☐ I would like to receive additional information on Cisco's services and products by e-mail.

1. Do you or your company:
- A ☐ Use Cisco products
- B ☐ Resell Cisco products
- C ☐ Both
- D ☐ Neither

2. Your organization's relationship to Cisco Systems:
- A ☐ Customer/End User
- B ☐ Prospective Customer
- C ☐ Cisco Reseller
- D ☐ Cisco Distributor
- E ☐ Integrator
- F ☐ Non-Authorized Reseller
- G ☐ Cisco Training Partner
- I ☐ Cisco OEM
- J ☐ Consultant
- K ☐ Other (specify):

3. How many people does your entire company employ?
- A ☐ More than 10,000
- B ☐ 5,000 to 9,999
- C ☐ 1,000 to 4,999
- D ☐ 500 to 999
- E ☐ 250 to 499
- F ☐ 100 to 249
- G ☐ Fewer than 100

4. Is your company a Service Provider?
- A ☐ Yes
- B ☐ No

5. Your involvement in network equipment purchases:
- A ☐ Recommend
- B ☐ Approve
- C ☐ Neither

6. Your personal involvement in networking:
- A ☐ Entire enterprise at all sites
- B ☐ Departments or network segments at more than one site
- C ☐ Single department or network segment
- F ☐ Public network
- D ☐ No involvement
- E ☐ Other (specify):

7. Your Industry:
- A ☐ Aerospace
- B ☐ Agriculture/Mining/Construction
- C ☐ Banking/Finance
- D ☐ Chemical/Pharmaceutical
- E ☐ Consultant
- F ☐ Computer/Systems/Electronics
- G ☐ Education (K–12)
- U ☐ Education (College/Univ.)
- H ☐ Government—Federal
- I ☐ Government—State
- J ☐ Government—Local
- K ☐ Health Care
- L ☐ Telecommunications
- M ☐ Utilities/Transportation
- N ☐ Other (specify):

CPRESS

Packet magazine serves as the premier publication linking customers to Cisco Systems, Inc. Delivering complete coverage of cutting-edge networking trends and innovations, *Packet* is a magazine for technical, hands-on users. It delivers industry-specific information for enterprise, service provider, and small and midsized business market segments. A toolchest for planners and decision makers, *Packet* contains a vast array of practical information, boasting sample configurations, real-life customer examples, and tips on getting the most from your Cisco Systems' investments. Simply put, *Packet* magazine is straight talk straight from the worldwide leader in networking for the Internet, Cisco Systems, Inc.

We hope you'll take advantage of this useful resource. I look forward to hearing from you!

Cecelia Glover
Packet Circulation Manager
packet@external.cisco.com
www.cisco.com/go/packet

PACKET

PACKET